D1568650

Science
Experiments
Index for
Young People

Science Experiments Index for Young People

SECOND EDITION

Mary Anne Pilger

1996
LIBRARIES UNLIMITED, INC.
Englewood, Colorado

LIBRARIES UNLIMITED, INC.
P.O. Box 6633
Englewood, CO 80155-6633
1-800-237-6124

ELECTRONIC VERSION AVAILABLE
    For information on obtaining a license to use ASCII-formatted, tab-delimited files of this book (suitable for Mac/IBM-compatible word processors or databases), please contact Libraries Unlimited, Electronic Publishing: 1-800-237-6124.

Library of Congress Cataloging-in-Publication Data

Pilger, Mary Anne.
    Science experiments index for young people / Mary Anne Pilger. --
2nd ed.
        xxxii, 504 p. 22x28 cm.
        Includes bibliographical references.
        ISBN 1-56308-341-8
        1. Science--Experiments--Juvenile literature--Indexes.
    [1. Science--Experiments--Indexes.   2. Experiments--Indexes.]
    I. Title.
    Q182.3.P55   1996
    016.507'8--dc20   96-16815
                                                                CIP

CONTENTS

Introduction vii
List of Subject Headings ix
Key to Index xxxii

Alphabetical Index of Entries 1

Books Indexed by Number 479

INTRODUCTION

A child is surrounded by a living, moving, exciting world of happenings, and a child has many questions needing answers.

Ice crackles, snowflakes plop, smoke is blue, green, yellow; flames are blue, red, yellow, white; things go up in the air and down in the air; sparks fly from pavements; worms disappear like lightning down a hole; chipmunks pop up here and then over there; sticks float, rocks sink; an eye sees, an ear hears, a mouth tastes, skin feels.

Investigating science means finding answers to questions. The scientific investigation, the scientific process—what do they mean to children? The child has a question and needs an answer; he or she needs to know what to do to get the answer. Children may be unaware that the process of questioning, doing, and finding out will further their knowledge of the subject or that their knowing will lead to more complex questions. The scientific process is inherent in children and their curiosity. It is an ongoing process—finding answers to their problems, finding information and methods or ways to test their ideas. Science grows from observations and each child comes to the process from his or her own point of view. Children encouraged to follow an interest in science will arrive at the serious science fair project stage having already done scientific work. The research and preparation in the elementary grades are a necessary beginning to more intensive scientific investigation.

There is an abundance of science information available to children in many books, but at times it is difficult to locate this information. *Science Experiments Index for Young People,* Second Edition, was prepared to fulfill the need for easy access to information.

This guide, an index to experiments and activities found in elementary and intermediate-level science books, is intended for use by librarians, teachers, and children. Experiments range from the very simple to rather complex. Books indexed are both old and new; some are out-of-print, but most are still on library shelves. The nature and range of the projects and activities will assist children in the experience of science from the primary grades upward.

The purpose of the index is to guide children in finding information on science experiments for investigative projects, science projects for science fairs, and science projects for those children who want to find answers and are curious to develop methods to test their own ideas.

The index has both science experiments and science demonstrations; a demonstration is a method of showing what is known about the subject. The process of questioning and doing will move children from a lack of knowledge to thinking past the experiment to more complex questions, extension of their ideas, and the creation of new ideas and thoughts.

This index is a cumulation of the first edition of *Science Experiments Index for Young People* (Englewood, CO: Libraries Unlimited, 1988), *Science Experiments Index for Young People Update 91* (Englewood, CO: Libraries Unlimited, 1992), plus additional material to make it current as of 1994. The index includes the following types of information.

Models—Children need models for their experiments and for their related displays. Their efforts are hampered at times because they do not know how to build the things they need to express their ideas or to demonstrate scientific principles. For this reason several easy-to-build models are included here.

Math Books—Math is a tool in scientific study. Simple math books are indexed for use as ideas for math concepts, as ideas for further explorations, for creation of new math thoughts, or for application of math to other fields of science.

Social Science Experiments—Experiments in the social sciences have been indexed. Our children will face the challenge of meeting the various needs of humans as geographic, ecological, and economic systems change. The evolving structures and changing relationships of man and his environment provoke the need for new attitudes and new approaches in sciences. Solutions will have to be found to control both the needs of man and the needs of the environment.

Foods and Nutrition Resources—Recipes and food experiments are included for their value as science experiments in the testing of foods for the presence of starches, sugars, fat, proteins, etc. Also included are activities to promote an increased awareness of the benefits and importance of good nutrition.

New to this edition is the list of subject headings used in the index. It is included to provide an overview of the book's contents. The list begins on page ix.

SUBJECT HEADINGS

This listing contains all the subject headings used in the text. Consult the text for cross-references between headings.

3-D VIEWERS
ABACUS
ABERRATION OF LIGHT. *See* LENSES; LIGHT; STARS
ABIOTIC FACTORS
ABRASION. *See* EROSION
ABRASIVES. *See* SANDPAPER
ABSOLUTE DIFFERENCE
ABSORPTION
ABSORPTION OF MATERIALS
ACCELERATION
ACCELEROMETER
ACID BOGS. *See* BOGS
ACID RAIN
ACIDOPHILUS BACTERIA
ACIDS
ACIDS AND BASES
ACIDS AND BASES AND SALTS
ACIDS AND SALTS
ACORNS
ACOUSTICS
ACROBATS
ACTION AND REACTION
ADAPTATION. *See* ANIMAL BEHAVIOR; ECOSYSTEMS; ENVIRONMENT; GENETICS
ADDING MACHINES
ADDITION
ADDITIVES
ADHESION
ADHESIVES
ADOBE. *See* BRICKS
ADOBE HOUSE
ADSORBENT
ADSORPTION. *See* CHROMATOGRAPHY
AEOLIAN HARP
AEROBIC DECOMPOSITION. *See* DECOMPOSITION
AERODYNAMICS
AEROFOILS. *See* AERODYNAMICS
AERONAUTICS
AEROSPACE
AFTERIMAGES
AGE
AGING
AGRONOMY
AILERONS. *See* AERODYNAMICS; AERONAUTICS; AIRPLANES; FLIGHT; GLIDERS

AIR
AIR—COMPRESSED
AIR—CONVECTION
AIR—CONVECTION CURRENTS
AIR—PRESSURE. *See* AIR PRESSURE
AIR—PROPERTIES OF
AIR AND ITS GASES
AIR CONDITIONERS
AIR INVERSION
AIR MASS. *See* CLOUDS; WEATHER
AIR PLANTS
AIR POLLUTION
AIR PRESSURE
AIR PUMPS
AIR RESISTANCE
AIRCRAFT
AIRCRAFT—INSTRUMENTS
AIRCRAFT—JETS
AIRCRAFT CARRIER
AIRFLOW
AIRFOILS
AIRPLANES
AIRPORTS
AIRSHIPS
ALARM CLOCKS
ALARMS
ALBUMEN
ALCOHOL
ALCOHOL BURNER
ALCOHOL LAMP
ALGAE
ALGEBRA
ALHAZEN
ALIENS
ALKA SELTZER
ALKALIES
ALLELOPATHY. *See* PLANTS— GROWTH; SEEDS— GERMINATION
ALLOYS
ALMANACS
ALTERNATING CURRENT
ALTITUDE
ALUMINUM
ALUMINUM FOIL
AMATEUR RADIO. *See* RADIO
AMINO ACID. *See* PROTEIN
AMMETER
AMMONIA

AMOEBA
AMPERE, ANDRE
AMPERE. *See* ELECTROMAG- NETISM
AMPHIBIANS
AMPLIFIERS
AMUSEMENT PARKS
ANABANTIDS
ANAEROBIC DECOMPOSI- TION. *See* DECAY; DECOM- POSITION; ROT
ANALEMMA
ANAMORPHIC ART
ANATOMY—HUMAN BODY
ANEMOMETER
ANEMONE
ANEROBIC DECOMPOSITION. *See* DECAY; DECOMPOSI- TION; ROT
ANEROID BAROMETER. *See* BAROMETER
ANGLES
ANIMAL BABIES
ANIMAL BEHAVIOR
ANIMAL CAGES. *See* CAGES
ANIMAL CAMOUFLAGE
ANIMAL COMMUNICATION
ANIMAL COURTSHIP
ANIMAL GAMES
ANIMAL GROWTH
ANIMAL HABITATS
ANIMAL HOMES
ANIMAL INTELLIGENCE
ANIMAL KINGDOM
ANIMAL MIGRATION
ANIMAL POPULATIONS
ANIMAL SKIN
ANIMAL STRUCTURE AND ENVIRONMENT
ANIMAL SURVIVAL
ANIMAL TRACKS
ANIMALS
ANIMALS—ART ACTIVITIES
ANIMALS—EXTINCT OR ENDANGERED. *See* ENDAN- GERED ANIMALS
ANIMALS—PROTECTIVE COL- ORATION. *See* ANIMAL CAMOUFLAGE
ANIMALS—SOUND
ANIMALS—VISION

ANIMATION. *See* FLIP BOOKS;
   MOTION PICTURES;
   ZOETROPE
ANNUAL RINGS. *See* TREES
ANOLES
ANT LIONS
ANTACIDS
ANTHOCYANINS
ANTIBIOTICS
ANTIFREEZE
ANTS
ANTS—SOCIAL ORGANIZATION
APHIDS
APHIS LION
APPLE LEATHER
APPLES
APPLIANCES. *See* HOUSEHOLD
   APPLIANCES
AQUACULTURE SYSTEM
AQUAPLANING
AQUARIUM PROJECTION
AQUARIUMS
AQUATIC EXPLORING
AQUATIC INSECTS
AQUATIC PLANTS
AQUEDUCTS
AQUEDUCTS, ROMAN
AQUIFERS
ARABIC NUMBERS
ARABS
ARACHNIDA. *See* SPIDERS
ARAGO, DOMINIQUE
ARAGO, FRANCOIS
ARCHEOLOGY
ARCHES
ARCHIMEDES
ARCHIMEDES PRINCIPLE
ARCHITECTURE
ARCTIC WILDERNESS
AREA
AREA MEASUREMENT
ARISTARCHUS
ARISTOTLE
ARITHMETIC. *See* MATHEMAT-
   ICS; NUMBERS
ARRHENIUS, SVANTE
ARROWS
ART ACTIVITIES. *See* ANI-
   MALS—ART ACTIVITIES;
   NATURE—ART ACTIVITIES;
   PLANTS—ART ACTIVITIES
ARTICHOKES
ARTIFICIAL RIPENING
ASCORBIC ACID. *See* VITAMIN C
ASEXUAL REPRODUCTION
ASPIRATOR
ASPIRIN
ASTEROIDS

ASTROLABE
ASTROLOGY
ASTRONAUTS
ASTRONOMICAL PHOTOS
ASTRONOMICAL UNITS
ASTRONOMY
ATMOSPHERE
ATMOSPHERIC PRESSURE
ATOLLS
ATOMIC ENERGY
ATOMIC RADIATION
ATOMIC THEORY
ATOMIZERS
ATOMS
ATTRIBUTES
AUDIO-OSCILLATOR
AUGERS
AURORAS
AUTO KINETIC EFFECT
AUTOMOBILES
AUTUMN. *See* SEASONS—FALL
AUXINS
AVERAGES
AVIARY
AVOCADO
AXLES
AZIMUTH
BABYLONIAN COUNTING
BACTERIA
BAEKELAND, LEO HENDRIK
BAKING POWDER
BAKING SODA
BALANCE
BALL BEARINGS
BALL RISER
BALLOONS
BALLOONS—HELIUM
BALLOONS—HOT AIR
BALLS
BANANAS
BANK
BAR GRAPHS. *See* GRAPHS—
   BAR
BARGES
BARK RUBBINGS
BARNACLES
BAROMETER
BAROMETRIC PRESSURE
BAROSCOPE
BASE FIVE
BASEBALL
BASES
BASKETBALL
BATH FOAMING OIL
BATH SALTS
BATHYSPHERES. *See* DIVING—
   SUBMARINES
BATS

BATTERIES
BATTERIES—HOW TO MAKE
BATTERIES AND BULBS. *See*
   ELECTRICITY—BATTERIES;
   BULBS AND BATTERIES
BATTERIES AND CIRCUITS
BATTERY HOLDERS
BATTERY TESTER
BAYBERRY CANDLES
BEACH
BEACH FORMS
BEACH GLASS
BEACH MURAL
BEACH PLANTS
BEACH TERRARIUM
BEADS
BEAM BRIDGE. *See* BRIDGES
BEAMS
BEANS
BEARINGS. *See* BALL
   BEARINGS
BEAUFORT WIND SCALE
BEAUMONT, WILLIAM
BECQUEREL, ANTOINE
BEER
BEER—GINGER
BEES
BEES—POLLINATION
BEETLES
BEETLES—TRAPS
BEHAVIOR
BEHAVIOR—ANIMALS
BEHAVIOR—HUMAN
BEHAVIOR—INSECTS
BELL, ALEXANDER GRAHAM
BELLOWS AND TRIP HAMMER
BELLS
BELT—TWIG
BELT DRIVEN MACHINES
BELTS
BENHAM'S DISK
BENHAM'S TOP
BENHAM'S TOP AND OTHER
   SPIN OFFS
BERLESE FUNNEL
BERNOULLI, DANIEL
BERNOULLI BALANCE TRICK
BERNOULLI EFFECT
BERNOULLI'S LAW
BERNOULLI'S PRINCIPLE
BERTHOLLET, CLAUDE
BICARBONATE OF SODA
BICYCLES
BICYCLING
BIG BANG
BIMETALLIC STRIPS
BINOCULAR VISION
BINOCULARS

BIOASSAY
BIOCHEMICAL OXYGEN DE-
MAND. See POLLUTION—
WATER
BIOCIDES. See HERBICIDES;
PESTICIDES
BIOCONTROL AGENTS
BIODEGRADABILITY
BIODEGRADABLE
BIODEGRADATION
BIODIVERSITY
BIOELECTRONICS
BIOFEEDBACK
BIOGAS DIGESTER
BIOLOGICAL CLOCKS
BIOLOGICAL CONTROLS
BIOLOGICAL EXPERIMENTS
AND PROJECTS
BIOLUMINESCENCE
BIOMASS
BIOME
BIOREMEDIATION
BIORHYTHMS. See BIOLOGI-
CAL CLOCKS; TIME SENSE
BIOTIC COMMUNITIES. See
ECOLOGY; ECOSYSTEMS;
HABITATS
BIRD FEEDERS
BIRD MOBILES
BIRD SHELTERS
BIRD SPINNER
BIRD WATCHING
BIRDS
BIRDS—EGGS
BIRDS—FEATHERS
BIRDS—FOOTPRINTS
BIRDS—HOUSES
BIRDS—INJURED
BIRDS—MIGRATION
BIRDS—NESTS
BIRDS—ORPHANS
BIRDS—PELLETS
BIRDS—POLLUTION
BIRDS—SKULLS
BIRDS—SOCIAL ORGANIZATION
BIRDS—WATER
BIRDS OF PREY
BIRDSEED
BIREFRINGENCE
BIVALVES. See CLAMS
BLACK, JOSEPH
BLACK HOLES
BLADDERWORTS
BLEACH
BLIMPS
BLIND
BLIND SPOT
BLOCK AND TACKLE

BLOOD
BLOW HOLES—COASTLINE
BLUEPRINT PAPER
BLUEPRINTS
BOATING
BOATS
BOATS—SAILS
BOATS—TEST POND
BOATS—TYPES AND MODELS
BOBSLEDS
BODY CLOCKS
BODY LOTIONS
BOG TERRARIUM
BOGS
BOILING POINT
BONES
BONES—GAMES
BONES—HUMAN
BONSAI TREES
BOOKS
BOOMERANGS
BORAX BEAD TEST
BOTTLE
BOTTLE GARDENS
BOUNCE
BOUNCE HEIGHTS
BOUNCES AND SPRINGS
BOUNCING. See BALLS
BOXES
BOYLE, CHARLES
BOYLE, ROBERT
BOYLE'S LAW
BRAILLE ALPHABET
BRAKES
BREAD
BREATHING
BRICKS
BRIDGES
BRINE SHRIMP
BROMELIADS
BROODERS
BROOMS
BROWN, ROBERT
BROWNIAN MOVEMENT
BRYOZOA
BUBBLE BATH
BUBBLE GUM
BUBBLES
BUDS
BUFFER
BUG LIGHTS
BUGS. See INSECTS
BUILDING
BUILDING MATERIALS
BULB HOLDER
BULBS
BULBS—ELECTRIC
BULBS AND BATTERIES

BULL ROARER
BULLDOZERS
BUNSEN BURNER
BUOYANCY
BUOYS
BURGLAR ALARM
BURNERS
BURROWING ANIMALS
BURS
BUSES
BUTTER
BUTTERFLIES
BUTTERFLIES—COLLECTION
BUTTERWORTS
BUTTRESS
BUYS—BALLOTS LAW
BUZZERS
CABBAGE. See INDICATORS
CABLE CARS
CABLE STRUCTURES
CABOCHONS (GEMS FROM
ROCKS)
CACTUS
CADDIS FLY
CADDIS WORMS
CAFFEINE
CAGES
CALCIUM
CALCIUM—COOKERY
CALCULATORS
CALENDAR
CALORIC MASS
CALORIES
CALORIMETER
CAMELS
CAMERA OBSCURA
CAMERA LUCIDA
CAMERAS
CAMOUFLAGE
CAMP COOKER
CAN OPENERS
CANALS
CANCER
CANDLES
CANDY
CANNON
CANOES
CANOES—POLYNESIAN
CANS
CANTILEVERS
CANTILEVERS—BRIDGE
CAPACITORS
CAPILLARITY
CAPILLARY ACTION
CARBOHYDRATES
CARBON
CARBON BUTTON

CARBON CYCLE. See BREATH-
ING; PHOTOSYNTHESIS
CARBON DIOXIDE
CARBONATED DRINKS
CARBONATED WATER
CARBONATES
CARBONATES AND ACIDS
CARDIOVASCULAR SYSTEM.
See CIRCULATORY SYSTEM;
HEART
CARNIVOROUS PLANTS
CARNOT, NICOLAS
CAROUSEL
CARS
CART
CARTESIAN DIVER
CARTOONS
CARVER, GEORGE WASHINGTON
CASEIN
CASSINI, GIOVANNI
DOMENICO
CASTLE AND VILLAGE
CASTS
CATALYST
CATAMARAN—POLYNESIAN
CATAMARAN BOAT
CATAPULT LAUNCHER
CATAPULTS
CATENARY ARCH
CATERPILLARS
CATKINS
CATNIP PILLOW
CATS
CAUSTICS
CAVENDISH, HENRY
CAVERNS. See STALACTITES
AND STALAGMITES
CAVES
CAVES AND CAVEMEN
CEDAR APPLE GALLS
CELESTIAL NAVIGATION. See
NAVIGATION INSTRU-
MENTS; SOLAR STONE
CELLS
CELLS AND BATTERIES
CELLULOSE
CELSIUS, ANDERS
CEMENT
CENTER OF GRAVITY
CENTIPEDES
CENTRIFUGAL AND CENTRIPE-
TAL FORCES
CENTRIFUGAL EFFECT
CENTRIFUGAL FORCE
CENTRIPETAL FORCE
CEREAL PLANTS
CEREALS

CEREBELLUM. See HUMAN
BODY
CFCs. See CHLOROFLUORO-
CARBONS
CHAIN DRIVES
CHALK
CHALK—FORAMINIFERA
CHAMELEONS
CHANGE OF STATE
CHARCOAL
CHARCOAL BURNER
CHARLES, JACQUES
CHARLES' LAW
CHARTS
CHEESE
CHEMICAL CHANGES
CHEMICAL CYCLES IN
NATURE
CHEMICAL ELEMENTS. See
ELEMENTS
CHEMICAL GARDENS
CHEMICAL MAGIC
CHEMICAL PESTICIDES. See
HERBICIDES; PESTICIDES
CHEMICAL REACTIONS
CHEMICAL TEST
CHEMICALS
CHEMISTRY
CHEMISTRY—MAGIC TRICKS
CHEMORECEPTORS
CHEMOTROPISM
CHESTNUTS
CHEWING GUM
CHICKENS
CHIMES
CHIMNEYS
CHINESE
CHINESE WATER CLOCK
CHIRALITY
CHLADNI, ERNST F.
CHLADNI FIGURES
CHLADNI PATTERNS
CHLORINE
CHLOROFLUOROCARBONS.
See GREENHOUSE EFFECT
CHLOROPHYLL
CHLOROPLASTS. See
CHLOROPHYLL; PLANTS—
CHLOROPHYLL
CHOCOLATE
CHRISTMAS
CHROMATOGRAPHY
CHROMATROPE
CHROMOSOMES
CICHLIDS
CIDER
CIGARETTE SMOKE
CIGARETTES

CILIATES. See PARAMECIUM
CIPHERS
CIRCLES
CIRCULATORY SYSTEM
CIRCUMPOLAR STARS
CIRCUS
CITIES
CITRUS FRUITS
CITRUS PLANTS
CLAIRVOYANCE
CLAMS
CLAMSHELL SCRIMSHAW
CLASSIFICATION
CLAY
CLEANERS
CLICHE-VERRE. See
PHOTOGRAPHY
CLIMATE
CLIMATE AND PLANTS
CLIMATOLOGY. See WEATHER
CLIMAX COMMUNITY
CLINOMETER
CLOCKS
CLOCKWORK MOTOR
CLONING
CLOTH
CLOTHING
CLOUD CHAMBER
CLOUDS
CLOVER
COAGULATION
COAL
COAL FURNACE
COAL GARDEN
COAL PLANT
COASTS
COBALT CHLORIDE PAPER
COCKROACHES
COCOONS
CODES
COFFEE
COHESION
COINS
COLCHICINE
COLD
COLD—COMMON
COLD FRAMES
COLD FRONT
COLD LIGHT (LUMINESCENCE)
COLLECTING—EQUIPMENT
COLLISIONS
COLLOIDS
COLOR. See COLORS
COLOR BLINDNESS
COLOR WHEEL
COLORATION—PROTECTIVE
COLORED FILTERS
COLORED LIGHTS

COLORFASTNESS
COLORINGS
COLORS
COLORS—ABSORPTION
COLORS—INSECTS
COLUMNS
COMB JELLIES
COMBUSTION
COMETS
COMETS AND METEORS
COMICS
COMMUNICATIONS
COMMUNITIES
COMMUNITY LIFE
COMPASS
COMPASS PLANT
COMPOST
COMPOUND MACHINES
COMPOUNDS
COMPRESSED AIR. See AIR—
  COMPRESSED
COMPRESSIONAL STRENGTH
COMPRESSORS
COMPUTER EXPERIMENTS
COMPUTERS
COMPUTERS—PROJECTS
CONCERT HALLS
CONCRETE
CONDENSATION
CONDITIONED BEHAVIOR. See
  GOLDFISH
CONDITIONED REFLEX—
  ANIMALS
CONDITIONING. See BEHAV-
  IOR; LEARNING
CONDUCTION. See HEAT—
  CONDUCTION
CONDUCTORS
CONE
CONSERVATION
CONSERVATION OF ENERGY
CONSERVATION OF HEAT
CONSERVATION OF MASS—
  PIAGET
CONSERVATION OF
  MOMENTUM
CONSTANCY OF AXIS
CONSTELLARIUM
CONSTELLATIONS
CONSTRUCTION
CONSUMER
CONSUMER GOODS
CONTINENTS
CONTOUR LINES
CONTOURS
CONVECTION
CONVECTION CURRENTS
CONVEYORS

COOKERS—SOLAR
COOKERY
COOLING FAN
COORDINATION
COPERNICUS, NICHOLAS
COPPER
COPPER PLATING
COPYING FLUID
CORAL REEF
CORAL REEF ECOLOGY
CORBELS
CORIOLIS EFFECT
CORIOLIS FORCE
CORKS
CORN
CORN POLLINATION
CORNELL SOILLESS MIX
CORNHUSK DOLLS
CORNHUSKS AND CORNCOBS
CORNSWEET ILLUSION
CORONA. See ECLIPSES
CORROSION
CORROSION OF METALS
COSMETICS
COSMIC RAYS
COTTON
COTTON FIBERS
COUNT BUFFON
COUNTERWEIGHTS
COUNTING
COUNTING FRAME (ABACUS)
COUNTING STICKS
COVERED WAGON
COWS
CRABS
CRACK GARDEN
CRANES (ELECTRIC)
CRANES (MACHINES)
CRATERS
CRAYFISH
CRAYONS
CREAM
CREATIVITY
CREEPY CRAWLER
CRESTA RUN
CRICKETS
CRIMINAL INVESTIGATION.
  See DETECTIVES
CRITICAL MASS
CRITTERS
CROCODILES
CROSS STAFF
CROSSES
CROVA'S DISK
CRUSTACEANS
CRYOGENICS
CRYPTOBIOSIS
CRYSTAL SETS

CRYSTALLIZATION
CRYSTALS
CURIE POINT
CURRENTS—OCEAN
CURVES
CYCLOPS
CYLINDERS
CYTOKININS
D'ARSONVAL, ARSENE
DA VINCI, LEONARDO. See
  VINCI, LEONARDO DA
DAEDALEUM DEVICE
DAGUERRE, LOUIS J.
DAIRY PRODUCTS
DALTON, JOHN
DAMS
DANDELIONS
DANIELLE, JOHN F.
DAPHNIA
DARTS
DARWIN, CHARLES
DATA
DATA PROCESSING. See
  COMPUTERS
DATE PALM
DAVY, SIR HUMPHRY
DAY AND NIGHT
DAYLIGHT
DE VRIES, HUGO
DE WITT CLINTON STEAM
  ENGINE
DECAY
DECOMPOSERS
DECOMPOSITION
DECOMPRESSION. See
  DIVING—SUBMARINES
DEEP SEA DIVER. See
  CARTESIAN DIVER
DEFORESTATION. See ERO-
  SION; RAIN FOREST
DEGREE DAYS
DEHYDRATION
DELTAS
DEMAGNETIZATION
DENSITIES. See FLOATING
  AND SINKING; WATER
DENSITY
DENTIFRICES. See
  TOOTHPASTE
DEODORANTS
DEODORIZERS
DEPTH PERCEPTION
DERMATOGLYPHICS. See
  FINGERPRINTING
DESALINIZATION
DESCARTES, RENE
DESCARTES DIVER. See
  CARTESIAN DIVER.

DESERT ANIMALS
DESERT COMMUNITY
DESERT DISH GARDEN
DESERT GARDEN
DESERT PLANTS
DESERT TERRARIUM
DESERTIFICATION
DESERTS
DESMIDS
DETECTIVE WORK
DETECTIVES
DETECTOR RODS
DETERGENTS
DETERIORATION
DEW
DEW POINT
DIAPERS
DIATOMS
DIAZO PAPER PRINTS
DIESEL, RUDOLPH
DIESEL ENGINES
DIFFLUGIA AND ARCELLA
DIFFRACTION. *See* LIGHT
DIFFUSION
DIGESTION
DIGITAL DISPLAYS
DIMENSIONS
DINOSAUR BREAD
DINOSAURS
DIODES
DIORAMA
DIP NET
DIPPING NEEDLE
DIRECT CURRENT POWER
  SUPPLY
DIRECTION
DIRIGIBLES
DIRT. *See* SOILS
DISCO LIGHT SHOW MACHINE
DISCS
DISEASES
DISINFECTANTS
DISPLACEMENT
DISPLAY BOX
DISPLAY CASE
DISSECTION
DISSEMINATION. *See* SEEDS—
  DISPERSAL
DISTANCE
DISTILLATION
DISTURBED HABITATS. *See*
  ECOSYSTEMS; HABITATS
DIVING
DIVING—SUBMARINES
DIVING BELLS
DIVINING ROD FOR WATER
DIVISION
DNA MOLECULE

DODECAHEDRON 3-D DESK
  CALENDAR
DOGS
DOLLS
DOMES
DOMINANT TREE FOREST
DOORBELL—ELECTRIC
DOPPLER, CHRISTIAN
DOPPLER EFFECT
DOUBLE BLIND METHOD
DOUGHS
DRAFTS
DRAG
DRAGNETS
DRAGONFLIES
DRAGSTERS
DRAWBRIDGES
DRAWINGS
DREAMS
DREDGE
DREDGERS
DRIED FLOWERS
DRIFT BOTTLES
DRIFTWOOD
DRILLING
DRILLS
DRINKING STRAWS
DRINKING WATER—
  PURIFICATION
DROP HAMMER
DROPS
DROUGHT
DRUGS
DRY CELLS
DRY ICE (SOLID CARBON DI-
  OXIDE)
DRYING AND STERILIZING
  OVEN
DUCKS
DUCKS—WILD BABY
DUCKWEED
DUFAY, CHARLES
DULONG, PIERRE LOUIS
DUMP TRUCKS
DUNES
DUST
DUST EXPLOSION
DWELLINGS
DYES
EARDRUMS
EARPHONES
EARS
EARTH
EARTH—CRUST
EARTH—HORIZON
EARTH—ISLANDS
EARTH—ROTATION
EARTH—SPEED

EARTH'S MAGNETIC FIELD
EARTHQUAKES
EARTHWORMS
EARWIGS
EASTMAN, GEORGE
EATING. *See* DIGESTION; FOOD
ECHO
ECLIPSES
ECLIPSES—SOLAR
ECOLOGICAL PROJECTS AND
  EXPERIMENTS
ECOLOGY
ECOLOGY—LITTER
ECOLOGY—NATURE AND SO-
  CIETY
ECOLOGY—WATER TREAT-
  MENT
ECOSYSTEMS
EDDY CURRENTS
EDISON, THOMAS ALVA
EDISON EFFECT (RADIOTUBE)
EDISON'S EXPERIMENTS
EELGRASS
EGGS
EGYPTIAN COUNTING
EGYPTIAN WATER CLOCK
EGYPTIANS
EINSTEIN, ALBERT
ELASTICITY
ELECTRIC
ELECTRIC CELL
ELECTRIC MOTORS
ELECTRICITY
ELECTRICITY—BATTERIES
ELECTRICITY—CIRCUITS
ELECTRICITY—CONDUCTORS
ELECTRICITY—ELECTRIC
  CURRENT
ELECTRICITY—ELECTRICAL
  CHARGES
ELECTRICITY—INSULATORS
ELECTRICITY—RESISTANCE
ELECTRICITY—RESISTANCE
  TO
ELECTRICITY—STATIC
  ELECTRICITY
ELECTRICITY—SWITCHES
ELECTROCHEMISTRY
ELECTRODES
ELECTROLYSIS
ELECTROLYTES
ELECTROMAGNETIC CRANE
ELECTROMAGNETIC FIELDS
ELECTROMAGNETIC FORCE
ELECTROMAGNETIC INDUC-
  TION
ELECTROMAGNETIC
  RADIATION

ELECTROMAGNETIC WAVES
ELECTROMAGNETISM
ELECTROMAGNETS
ELECTROMOTIVE FORCE
ELECTRONIC CIRCUITS
ELECTRONIC GAMES
ELECTRONICS
ELECTRONICS—CALCULATORS
ELECTRONICS—CONDUCTORS
ELECTRONICS—OSCILLATORS
ELECTRONICS—RADIO
ELECTRONICS—TELEVISION
ELECTRONS
ELECTRO-OPTICAL RECOGNI-
    TION. *See* IMAGE RECOGNI-
    TION SYSTEM; SCANNERS
ELECTROPHORUS
ELECTROPLATING
ELECTROSCOPE
ELECTROSTATICS
ELECTROTYPING
ELEMENTS
ELEPHANTS
ELEVATION
ELEVATORS
ELF. *See* ELECTROMAGNETIC
    RADIATION
ELLIPSES
ELODEA
EMBRYOLOGY
EMBRYOS
EMF. *See* ELECTROMAGNETIC
    RADIATION
EMULSIFIERS
EMULSIONS
ENDANGERED ANIMALS
ENDANGERED SPECIES
ENERGY
ENERGY CONSERVATION
ENGINES
ENGRAVING
ENVIRONMENT
ENVIRONMENTAL PROTEC-
    TION. *See* ACID RAIN;
    BIODEGRADABILITY;
    BIODEGRADATION; LAND-
    FILLS; OIL SPILLS; OZONE
    LAYER
ENZYMES
EPIGENESIS
EPSOM SALT
EQUATOR
EQUINOXES
EQUIPMENT—HOW TO MAKE
EQUIPMENT AND CHEMICALS
ERASERS
ERATOSTHENES
EROSION

ESCHER, M. C.
ESKIMOS
ESP
ESSENTIAL OILS
ESTIMATION
ESTUARIES
ETHANOL
ETHERIC FORCE (WIRELESS)
ETHYLENE GAS
EUCALYPTUS
EUDOXUS
EUGLENA
EULER, LEONARD
EULER'S CIRCLES. *See* VENN
    DIAGRAMS
EUTROPHIC LAKES
EUTROPHICATION
EVAPORATION
EVOLUTION
EXPERIMENTS. *See* SCIENCE
    EXPERIMENTS
EXPLOSIONS
EXTENSIOMETER
EXTRATERRESTRIAL
    INTELLIGENCE
EYE
EYE TRICKS
EYEGLASSES
EYLAIS
FABRIC
FACES
FAHRENHEIT, GABRIEL
FAIRY RINGS
FAIRY SHRIMP
FAKIR, INDIAN
FALL
FALLING BODIES
FALLING OBJECTS
FALLING RATE
FAMILY TREE
FANS
FANTASY
FARADAY, MICHAEL
FARMING PROBLEMS
FARMS
FATS
FATS AND OILS
FAULTS
FEATHERS
FEELING. *See* SENSES—TOUCH
FELUCCA—EGYPTIAN
FERMENTATION
FERNS
FERTILIZERS
FETCHNER DISC
FIBER
FIBER OPTICS
FIBERS

FIBONACCI, LEONARDO
FIBONACCI SERIES
FIDDLER CRABS
FIELD OF FORCE. *See* MAG-
    NETIC FIELDS
FIELDS
FILM SHOW
FILM STRIP VIEWER
FILTERS
FILTERS AND FILTERING
FILTRATION
FINGER PAINT
FINGERNAILS
FINGERPRINTS
FINITE NUMBERS
FIRE
FIRE ALARMS
FIRE ENGINE
FIRE EXTINGUISHER
FIRE SAFETY
FIRE TRUCKS
FIREFLIES
FIREPROOFING
FIREWOOD
FIREWORKS
FISH
FISH SCALES
FISSION, NUCLEAR. *See*
    NUCLEAR BOMBS;
    NUCLEAR CHAIN REACTION
FLAG—AMERICAN
FLAG POLE
FLAGS—ELECTRIC
FLAME TESTS
FLAMES
FLARES—COLORED
FLASHLIGHT
FLATWORMS
FLAVORS
FLEAS
FLEMING, SIR ALEXANDER
FLEXURE. *See* PAPER
    ENGINEERING
FLIES
FLIES—FRUIT FLIES
FLIES—HOUSE FLIES
FLIGHT
FLIGHT—PRINCIPLES OF. *See*
    AERODYNAMICS; AERO-
    NAUTICS; AIRPLANES;
    GLIDERS
FLINT AND STEEL SPARKS
FLIP BOOKS
FLOATING—TOYS
FLOATING AND SINKING
FLOODS
FLOUR
FLOW

GILBERT, WILLIAM
GINGER
GINGER BEER
GIRAFFES
GIRDERS. See BEAMS;
    BRIDGES; STRUCTURES
GLACIERS
GLASS
GLASSES—3-D
GLASSES—DRINKING
GLASSES—WATER
GLIDE BAR
GLIDERS
GLOBAL WARMING
GLOBES
GLOBULES—FAT
GLOP
GLUCOSE
GLUES
GODDARD, ROBERT HUTCHINGS
GOGGLES
GOLD
GOLDFISH
GOLDFISH—THERMAL
    POLLUTION
GOOSE BUMPS
GRAFTING
GRAIN ELEVATORS
GRAMOPHONE
GRAND PRIX CAR RACES
GRANITE
GRAPES
GRAPHITE
GRAPHS
GRAPHS—BAR
GRAPHS—COMPUTER
GRAPHS—LINE
GRAPHS—PICTOGRAPH
GRAPHS—PIE
GRASS FLOWERS
GRASS HUT
GRASSES
GRASSHOPPERS
GRASSHOPPERS—MIGRATION
GRASSLANDS
GRAVITROPISM
GRAVITY
GRAVITY—CENTER OF
    GRAVITY
GRAVITY AND MOVEMENT
GRAVITY AND SLOPES
GRAVITY MACHINES
GRAYWATER. See WATER—
    CONSERVATION
GREEK
GREENHOUSE EFFECT
GREENHOUSES
GRIMALDI, FRANCESCO

GRIST MILLS
GROUNDHOG DAY
GROUNDWATER
GROWTH
GUERICKE, OTTO VON
GUINEA PIGS
GUITAR
GULLIVER EXPERIMENT
GUNS
GUPPIES
GYPSUM
GYROSCOPE
HABITATS
HABITATS—ANIMAL
HABITS
HAIL
HAILSTONES
HAIR
HAIR—HUMAN
HALES, STEPHEN
HALF-LIFE
HAMMER
HAMSTERS
HAND
HAND GLIDERS. See GLIDERS
HAND LOTIONS
HANDBALL
HANDEDNESS
HANDWRITING
HANG GLIDER
HARBORS
HARD WATER
HARDNESS OF MINERALS
HARDNESS SCALE. See MOHS'
    SCALE
HARMONICS
HARMONOGRAMS. See
    LISSAJOUS FIGURES
HARP, AEOLIAN
HARVEY, WILLIAM
HAT
HATCHING. See EGGS
HAUNTED HOUSES
HAY INFUSION
HAZARDOUS WASTES
HAZELNUTS
HEALTH
HEARING
HEARING AIDS
HEART
HEAT
HEAT—CONDUCTION
HEAT—CONDUCTORS
HEAT—CONVECTION
HEAT—CONVECTION
    CURRENTS
HEAT—EXPANSION
HEAT—INSULATORS

HEAT—RADIANT ENERGY
HEAT—RADIANT HEAT
HEAT—RADIATION
HEAT CONSERVATION. See
    ENERGY CONSERVATION;
    INSULATION; INSULATORS
HEAT LOSS. See ENERGY
    CONSERVATION
HEATERS—SOLAR. See SOLAR
    ENERGY; SOLAR HEAT;
    SOLAR WATER HEATERS
HEATING
HEATING SYSTEM
HEIGHT
HELICOPTERS
HELIOGRAPHY
HELIOTROPISM
HELIUM
HELIX
HELMONT, JOHANNES VAN
HENRY, JOSEPH
HENRY, WILLIAM
HERB GARDENS
HERBARIUM
HERBICIDES
HERBS
HEREDITY
HERMANN GRID ILLUSION
HERMIT CRABS
HERO'S AEROPILE
HERO'S ENGINE
HERSCHEL, WILLIAM
HIBERNATION
HIERONYMUS MACHINE
HILLS
HINDU CLIMBING BALLS
HINDU MAGIC TRICK
HINDUS
HOCKEY
HOLOGRAM
HOMES
HONEY
HONEYBEES
HOOKE, ROBERT
HOOKE'S LAW
HOOP ROLLING
HORIZON
HORMONES
HORNER, WILLIAM
HOROSCOPES
HORSE
HORSESHOE MAGNETS. See
    ELECTROMAGNETS
HORSEPOWER
HORSESHOE CRABS
HORSETAILS
HOT AIR BALLOON
HOT DOGS

HOT FRAMES
HOT SPRINGS. *See* GEYSERS
HOUSE FLIES
HOUSEHOLD APPLIANCES
HOUSEHOLD CHEMICALS
HOUSEHOLD CLEANERS
HOUSEHOLD PRODUCTS
HOUSEPLANTS
HOUSES
HOUSES—BEAMS
HOUSES—ELECTRICITY
HOUSES—FURNACES
HOUSES—HOUSE BUILDING
HOUSES—WATER SUPPLY
HOVERCRAFT
HUBBLE, EDWIN
HUBBLE TELESCOPE
HUMAN ANATOMY
HUMAN BEHAVIOR
HUMAN BODY
HUMAN ECOLOGY
HUMANS
HUMIDITY
HUMIDITY—RELATIVE
   HUMIDITY
HUMMINGBIRDS
HUMUS
HUNGER
HURRICANES
HYALLELA
HYDRA
HYDRAULIC MODELS
HYDRAULIC PRESSURE
HYDRAULICS
HYDROCARBONS
HYDRODYNAMICS
HYDROELECTRIC GENERATORS
HYDROELECTRIC POWER
HYDROGEN
HYDROGEN PEROXIDE
HYDROLOGIC CYCLE
HYDROMETER
HYDROPONICS
HYDROSTATICS
HYDROTROPISM
HYDROXIDES
HYGROMETERS
HYGROSCOPIC TOY
HYPERBOLIC PARABOLA
HYPOTHERMIA
HYPSOMETER
ICE
ICE CREAM
ICE CUBES
ICE CUBES—FREEZING POINT
ICE NUCLEATORS
ICE WATER—MELTING
ICEBERGS

ICICLES
IDIOPHONES
IGLOO
IGUANAS
ILLUSIONS
IMAGE RECOGNITION SYSTEM
IMAGES—REVERSE
IMPRINTING
IMPULSE—MAGNETIC
INCAS
INCHWORM
INCINERATION
INCINERATORS
INCLINED PLANE
INCUBATORS
INDIAN FAKIR TRICK
INDIAN PICTURE WRITING
INDIAN RICE TRICK
INDIAN ROPE TRICK
INDIANS
INDICATORS
INDOOR POLLUTION
INDUCTION
INDUSTRIAL WASTES
INERTIA
INERTIA—SPIN
INERTIA—TRICKS
INERTIA AND MOMENTUM
INFRARED RADIATION
INFUSIONS. *See* HAY INFU-
   SIONS; MICROORGANISMS—
   INFUSIONS
INFUSORIA
INK
INKBLOTS
INSECTICIDES
INSECTS
INSECTS—AIR POLLUTION
INSECTS—BEHAVIOR
INSECTS—BIOCONTROL
INSECTS—CAGES
INSECTS—COLLECTION AND
   PRESERVATION
INSECTS—GARDEN PESTS
INSECTS—NETS
INSECTS—POND
INSECTS—POPULATIONS
INSECTS—PROTECTIVE
   COLORATION
INSECTS—REPELLENTS
INSECTS—STICK INSECTS
INSECTS—TRAPS
INSECTS—WATER
INSTINCTIVE BEHAVIOR. *See*
   ANIMAL BEHAVIOR
INSTRUMENTS. *See* MUSICAL
   INSTRUMENTS
INSULATION

INSULATORS
INTEGERS—POSITIVE AND
   NEGATIVE
INTELLIGENCE
INTERLOCKING JOINTS
INTERMITTENT FUNNEL
INTERNATIONAL DATE LINE
INTESTINES
INVERTEBRATES
INVERTED TUMBLERS
INVESTIGATIONS—SCIENCE
   EXPERIMENTS
INVISIBLE INKS
INVISIBLE WRITING
IODINE
IONOSPHERE
IONS
IRON
IRON—RUST
IRON ACETATE
IRON ORE
IRON OXIDE
IRON SULFIDE
IRRIGATION
ISLANDS
ISOPODS
ISOTOPES
ISTHMUSES
JACOB'S LADDER
JAM
JELLYFISH
JET ENGINES
JET PLANES
JET PROPULSION
JET SKIS
JET STREAM
JET-PROPELLED TOYS
JETS
JOULE, JAMES PRESCOTT
JUMPING BEANS
JUNGLE TERRARIUM
JUNK MAIL
JUPITER
KALEIDOPHONE
KALEIDOSCOPES
KAYAKS
KAZOO
KELVIN, WILLIAM THOMSON
KELVIN SCALE. *See*
   THERMOMETERS
KETTLE HOLE LAKE
KEYNOTES
KIDNEYS
KINDLING POINT
KINETIC ENERGY
KING CRABS
KIRCHHOF, GOTTLIEB
KITCHEN UTENSILS

KITES
KITTY LITTER
KIWI
KNOTS
KON TIKI STAMP BOAT
LABELS
LABORATORY ANALYSIS
LABORATORY EQUIPMENT
LABYRINTH
LACTIC ACID. *See* MICROBES—
   BACTERIA; YOGURT
LADYBUGS
LAENNEC, RENE
LAKES
LAMPBLACK INK
LAMPS
LAND—ECOSYSTEM
LAND—EROSION
LAND CONTOURS
LAND POLLUTION
LAND ROVER
LAND USAGE
LAND USE
LAND YACHTS
LANDFILLS
LANDFORMS
LANE, TIMOTHY
LANTERN SLIDES
LANTERNS
LARVAE. *See* CATERPILLARS;
   INSECTS
LARYNX
LASERS
LATENT HEAT
LATEX
LATHE
LATITUDE
LATITUDE AND LONGITUDE
LAUNCHER
LAVA
LAVOISIER, ANTOINE
LAW OF DEFINITE PROPOR
   TIONS
LAW OF UNIFORM ACCELERA-
   TION. *See* GALILEO'S
   EXPERIMENTS
LAWNS
LE CHATELIER PRINCIPLE. *See*
   RUBBER BANDS
LE CLANCHE CELLS
LEAD
LEAD PENCIL
LEAD STORAGE CELL
LEAF LITTER
LEAF MINERS
LEAF PRINT
LEAF RUBBING
LEARNING

LEARNING MACHINES
LEAVENING AGENTS
LEAVES
LEAVES—COLLECTION AND
   PRESERVATION
LEAVES—PRESSED
LEECHES
LEFT-HANDED. *See* HANDEDNESS
LEGUMES
LEIDENFROST, JOHANN
LEMONS
LENS—EYE
LENSES
LENTILS
LENZ, H. F. E.
LEVEL
LEVERS
LEVITATION
LEYDEN JAR
LICHENS
LIFE SPAN OF ANIMALS
LIFEBELTS
LIFEBOATS
LIFESAVERS
LIFT
LIFTING
LIFTS
LIGHT
LIGHT—ABSORPTION
LIGHT—DIFFRACTION
LIGHT—POLLUTION
LIGHT—RADIANT ENERGY
LIGHT—RAYS
LIGHT—REFLECTED
LIGHT—REFLECTION
LIGHT—REFRACTION
LIGHT—RESPONSE TO LIGHT
LIGHT—VIBRATIONS
LIGHT—WAVES
LIGHT AND DARKNESS
LIGHT BULBS
LIGHT YEARS
LIGHTHOUSES
LIGHTNING
LIGHTNING AND THUNDER
LIGHTNING BUGS. *See* FIREFLIES
LIGHTNING CONDUCTOR
LIGHTS—COLORED
LILIENTHAL, OTTO
LIMESTONE
LIMEWATER
LIMPETS
LINDBERGH, CHARLES
LINES
LINES OF FORCE
LINT
LIPIDS. *See* FATS AND OILS
LIQUID SOAP DISPENSERS

LIQUIDS
LIQUIDS—SPECIFIC GRAVITY
LIQUIDS—SURFACE SKIN
LIQUIDS—SURFACE TENSION
LISSAJOUS, JULES ANTOINE
LISSAJOUS FIGURES
LISSAJOUS PATTERNS
LITHIUM
LITMUS PAPER. *See*
   INDICATORS
LITTER
LITTERBUG GAME
LIVERWORTS
LIVING THINGS
LIZARDS
LOBSTERS
LOCKS
LOCKS—WATERWAYS
LOCOMOTIVES
LOG CABIN
LOGIC
LOGIC—SYMBOLIC AND
   MATHEMATICAL
LOGS
LONGEVITY
LONGITUDE. *See* LATITUDE
   AND LONGITUDE
LUBRICANTS
LUBRICATION
LUMBER
LUMINOUS PAINTS
LUNAR CRATERS
LUNAR ECLIPSES. *See*
   ECLIPSES
LUNAR VEHICLE
LUNASCOPE
LUNGS
MACH, ERNST
MACHINES
MAGDEBURG SPHERE
MAGIC
MAGIC LANTERN
MAGIC SQUARES
MAGIC TRICKS
MAGIC TRICKS (CHEMISTRY)
MAGIC TRICKS—BALANCE
MAGLEV TRAIN
MAGNETIC COIL
MAGNETIC COMPASS
MAGNETIC FIELDS
MAGNETIC INDUCTION. *See*
   ELECTROMAGNETS
MAGNETIC LINES OF FORCE
MAGNETISM
MAGNETITE
MAGNETOMETER
MAGNETS
MAGNETS—GAMES

MAGNETS—NORTH POLE
MAGNETS—TRICKS
MAGNIFICATION
MAGNIFIERS
MAGNIFYING GLASS. *See*
  LENSES
MAIL
MALPIGHI, MARCELLO
MAMMALS
MANGO SEEDS
MANNED SPACE FLIGHT. *See*
  SPACE FLIGHT
MANOMETER
MAPLE SUGARING
MAPS
MARBLE
MARBLE GAMES
MARGARINE
MARINE ANIMALS
MARINE ECOSYSTEMS
MARINE LIFE
MARMALADE
MARS
MARSH PLANTS
MARSHLAND TERRARIUM
MARTIANS
MARTIN, ARCHER
MASS
MASS TRANSPORTATION
MATCHES
MATERIALS
MATH TRICKS
MATHEMATICS
MATHEMATICS—GAMES
MATHEMATICS—MAGIC WITH
  PAPER
MATTER
MAY FLY NYMPHS
MAYANS
MAYONNAISE
MAYOW, JOHN
MAZES
MEADOW TERRARIUM
MEADOWS
MEALWORMS
MEASUREMENT
MEASUREMENT—METRIC
MECHANICAL ADVANTAGE
MECHANICAL ENERGY
MECHANICAL FORCE—
  TRICKS USING
MECHANICS
MEDICINE WHEELS
MEDIEVAL CASTLE AND
  VILLAGE
MEGAPHONE
MELDE, F. E.
MELTING POINT

MELTS
MEMBRANES
MEMORY
MENDEL, GREGOR
MENDEL'S EXPERIMENTS
MENDELIAN GENETICS
MENISCUS MAGIC
MENSURATION
MERCURY
MERCURY
MERRY-GO-ROUND
METAL DETECTORS
METALS
METAMORPHOSIS
METEORITES
METEOROLOGICAL OPTICS.
  See RAINBOWS; RAIN-
  DROPS; STARS
METEOROLOGY. *See*
  WEATHER; WEATHER
  FORECASTING
METEORS
METERS
METHANE
METRIC SYSTEM
MEYER'S EXPERIMENT
  ILLUSION
MICE
MICROAQUARIUM
MICROBES
MICROBIOLOGY. *See*
  MICROBES; MOLDS; YEAST
MICROCLIMATE
MICROHABITAT
MICROMETER
MICROORGANISMS
MICROPARTICULATION
MICROPHONE
MICROPHOTOGRAPHY
MICROSCOPE
MICROSCOPE—HOUSE FLY
MICROSCOPE—MOSQUITO
MICROSCOPE—SLIDES
MICROTOME
MICROWAVE OVENS
MIGRATION
MILDEW
MILK
MILKWEEDS
MILKY WAY
MILLIPEDES AND CENTIPEDES
MILLS
MILLWORKS
MIND
MINERALS
MINERS
MINES
MINI CLIMATES

MINIBEASTS
MINING
MINNOWS
MINSKY—PAPER FIGURES
MIRAGES
MIRROR WRITING
MIRRORS
MIRRORS—FOCAL LENGTH
MIRRORS—REFLECTION
MISSILES. *See* ROCKETS
MISTLETOE
MITOSIS. *See* CELLULAR
  REPRODUCTION
MIXTURES
MOBILES
MOBIUS STRIPS
MODELS
MOEBIUS STRIPS. *See* MOBIUS
  STRIPS
MOHS, FRIEDRICH
MOHS' SCALE
MOIRE PATTERNS
MOIRES
MOISTURE
MOISTURE DETECTOR
MOLDS
MOLECULAR ACTION
MOLECULAR MODEL
MOLECULAR MOTION
MOLECULES
MOLLUSK STEW
MOLLUSKS
MOMENTUM
MOMENTUM—ANGULAR
MONEY
MONORAIL SYSTEM
MONORAILS
MONUMENTS
MOON
MOON BASE
MOON BUGGY
MOON MONTH
MOON PHASES
MOON VEHICLE
MORGAN, THOMAS
MORSE, SAMUEL
MORSE CODE
MORTAR
MOSQUITOES
MOSSES
MOTHBALLS
MOTHER OF VINEGAR
MOTHS
MOTHS—COCOONS
MOTHS—EGGS
MOTION
MOTION PICTURES
MOTOR VEHICLES

MOTORS
MOTORS—CLOCK MOTORS
MOTORS—ELECTRIC
MOUNTAINS
MOUSE. See MICE
MOUSETRAP
MOUTH—HUMAN
MOUTHWASH
MOVIES
MOVING PICTURES
MOVING SLIDES
MUD
MUD FLATS
MUD SNAILS
MUD WORMS
MULTIPLICATION
MUSCLES
MUSHROOMS
MUSIC
MUSIC—MAKING
MUSICAL INSTRUMENTS
MUSICAL SOUNDS
MUSSCHENBROEK, PIETER
MUSSELS
MUTATION
MUTOSCOPE
MYCELIUM. See MOLDS;
   SPORES
MYSTERY POWDERS
NADIR—ZENITH FINDER
NAILS
NAILS—HUMAN BODY
NATURAL SELECTION
NATURE
NATURE—ART ACTIVITIES
NATURE CENTER
NAVIGATION
NAVIGATION INSTRUMENTS
NEBULAE
NEGATIVE GEOTROPISM
NEGATIVE NUMBERS
NEMATODES
NEPHOSCOPE
NEPTUNE
NERVES
NESTING FISH. See CICHLIDS
NESTS
NETS
NETS—INSECTS
NETS—WATER INSECTS
NETTLES
NETWORKS
NEWSPAPER
NEWSPAPER LOGS
NEWTON, SIR ISAAC
NEWTON CAR
NEWTON'S ACTION
NEWTON'S COLOR WHEEL

NEWTON'S CRADLE
NEWTON'S FIRST LAW OF
   MOTION
NEWTON'S LAW OF MOTION
NEWTON'S RINGS
NEWTON'S SECOND LAW OF
   MOTION
NEWTON'S THIRD LAW OF
   MOTION
NEWTS
NICHOLSON, WILLIAM
NICOTINE
NIGHT
NIGHT AND DAY
NITRATES. See FERTILIZERS;
   WATER—POLLUTION
NITROGEN
NITROGEN FIXATION
NITROGEN OXIDE. See ACID
   RAIN
NOISE
NOISE—POLLUTION
NOISEMAKERS
NON-NEWTONIAN FLUID
NORMAN, ROBERT
NORTH POLE
NORTH STAR
NORTHERN LIGHTS
NOSE. See HUMAN BODY;
   SENSES—SMELL
NUCLEAR BOMBS
NUCLEAR CHAIN REACTION
NUCLEAR FUELS
NUCLEATION
NUMBER RECORDS
NUMBERS
NUTRITION
NUTS
NUTS AND BOLTS
NUTTY PUTTY
OAK APPLES
OBLIQUITY OF MOTION
OCEAN
OCEAN ANIMALS
OCEAN BOTTLES
OCEAN COLOR
OCEAN CURRENTS
OCEAN EVAPORATION
OCEAN FLOOR
OCEAN POLLUTION
OCEAN PRESERVATION
OCEAN SALINITY
OCEAN SEDIMENTS
OCEAN SHORELINES
OCEAN TIDES
OCEAN WAVES
OCEAN WINDS

OCEANOGRAPHY. See DIVING
   BELLS; SEAWATER
OCTOPUS
ODORS
OERSTED, HANS CHRISTIAN
OERSTED'S DISCOVERY
OERSTED'S EXPERIMENT
OHM, GEORG
OHM'S LAW
OIL
OIL FIELDS
OIL LAMP
OIL POLLUTION. See OIL
   SPILLS
OIL RIGS
OIL SLICKS
OIL SPILLS
OILS AND FATS. See FATS AND
   OILS
OLD GROWTH FOREST—
   NORTHWEST, PACIFIC
ONIONS
OPERANT CONDITIONING
OPTICAL BENCH
OPTICAL DENSITY
OPTICAL FIBERS
OPTICAL ILLUSIONS
OPTICAL ILLUSIONS—SHOW
OPTICAL ILLUSIONS—TRICKS
OPTICAL PROJECTIONS
OPTICAL ROTATION
OPTICAL TOYS—HOW TO
   MAKE
OPTICS
OPTICS—FIBER. See FIBER
   OPTICS; OPTICAL FIBERS
OPTICS—MIRRORS
ORANGES
ORBITER SPACE SCHUTTLE
ORBITS
ORES
ORGANIC COMPOUNDS
ORGANIC PRODUCE
ORGANIC WASTE
ORGANISMS—CONTROL
ORGANISMS—GAME
ORGANISMS AS MINERS
ORIENTEERING
ORIGIN OF THE SPECIES
   ACTIVITY
ORION
ORPHANS
ORRERY
ORTHO COPTER
OSCILLATOR
OSCILLOGRAPH
OSMOMETER
OSMOSIS

OSMOSIS—PLANTS
OSTRACODS
OUIJA BOARD
OUTDOORS
OUTER SPACE
OUTER SPACE—EXPLORA-
   TION. *See* SPACE SCIENCE;
   SPACE TRAVEL
OVALS
OVENS. *See* DRYING AND
   STERILIZING OVEN
OVERPOPULATION. *See*
   POPULATION
OWL HOUSE
OWL PELLETS
OWLS
OXIDATION
OXYGEN
OXYGEN—CARBON DIOXIDE
   CYCLE
OYSTERS
OZONE
OZONE LAYER
PACE. *See* DISTANCE
PACKAGING
PADDLE WHEEL BOAT
PAIN
PAINTING
PAINTS
PANTOGRAPH
PAPAYA SEEDS
PAPER
PAPER—ABSORPTION
PAPER—ENGINEERING
PAPER—HOT AND COLD
PAPER—MATH MAGIC
PAPER—TOPOLOGY
PAPER CHROMATOGRAPHY
PAPER CUTTING TRICKS
PAPER DOLLS
PAPER FOLDING GEOMETRY
PAPER MAKING
PAPER PUZZLERS
PAPER TOWELS
PAPER TRICKS
PAPIER MACHE
PARACHUTES
PARALLEL CIRCUITS. *See*
   ELECTRICITY—CIRCUITS
PARAMECIA
PARASITOIDS. *See* WASPS
PARTICLE DENSITY
PARTICLE MOVEMENT
PARTICLE SETTLING
PARTICLE SIZE AND SHAPE
PARTICLES
PASCAL, BLAISE
PASCAL'S LAW

PASSIVE SMOKE
PASTE
PASTEUR, LOUIS
PATTERNS
PEANUT BUTTER
PEANUTS
PEANUTS—GAME
PEBBLE SCULPTURES
PEBBLES
PECTIN
PELLETS—BIRD
PENCILS
PENDULUMS
PENICILLIN
PENS
PEPPER'S GHOST
PERCEPTION
PERCOLATION
PERCOLATOR
PEREGRINUS, PETRUS
PERFORMATION OR EPIGENESIS
PERFUMES
PERIPHERAL VISION
PERISCOPES
PERIWINKLES
PERMANENT WAVES
PERMEABILITY
PERPETUAL MOTION
PERSISTENCE OF VISION
PERSPIRATION
PESTICIDES
PETIT, ALEX THERESE
PETROLEUM
PETS
pH
PHANTASCOPE
PHAROAH'S SERPENT
PHASES OF MOON. *See* MOON—
   PHASES
PHENAKISTOSCOPE
PHENOLPHTHALEIN
PHENOLS
PHEROMONES
PHI PHENOMENON
PHONOGRAPH
PHOSPHATES
PHOSPHENES
PHOSPHORESCENCE
PHOTOCHEMISTRY
PHOTOCOPIERS
PHOTOELECTRICITY
PHOTOGRAMS
PHOTOGRAPHS
PHOTOGRAPHY
PHOTOMETER
PHOTOMICROGRAPHY
PHOTONS
PHOTOPERIODISM

PHOTOSYNTHESIS
PHOTOTROPISM
PHOTOVOLTAIC CELLS. *See*
   SOLAR CELLS
PHYSICAL CHANGES
PHYSICAL REACTIONS
PHYSICAL SCIENCES
PHYSICS
PHYSICS TRICKS
PIAGET. *See* CONSERVATION
   OF MASS
PIANO
PICKLES
PICTOGRAPHS. *See* GRAPHS—
   PICTOGRAPH
PICTURES
PIEZOELECTRICITY
PIGEONS
PIGMENTS
PIGPEN CIPHER
PIGS
PILGRIMS
PILL BUGS
PINBALL MACHINE
PINEAPPLES
PINECONES
PINHOLE CAMERA
PINHOLE OPTICS
PINWHEELS
PIPELINES
PIPETTE CAPILLARY
PITCH
PITCHER PLANTS
PITFALL TRAPS
PLANARIANS
PLANCK, MAX
PLANETARIUM
PLANETARY PROBES
PLANETS
PLANKTON
PLANKTON NET
PLANT LICE. *See* APHIDS
PLANTERS
PLANTS
PLANTS—ACID RAIN
PLANTS—ADAPTATIONS
PLANTS—AIR
PLANTS—AIR PLANTS
PLANTS—AIR POLLUTANTS
PLANTS—AQUATIC
PLANTS—ART ACTIVITIES
PLANTS—AUXINS
PLANTS—BACTERIA
PLANTS—BEACH
PLANTS—BIOLUMINESCENCE
PLANTS—BUDS
PLANTS—BULBS
PLANTS—CANCER

PLANTS—CAPILLARITY
PLANTS—CAPILLARY ACTION
PLANTS—CARBON DIOXIDE
PLANTS—CELLS
PLANTS—CELLULOSE
PLANTS—CHLOROPHYLL
PLANTS—CLONING
PLANTS—COLLECTION AND
    PRESERVATION
PLANTS—COLOR
PLANTS—COMMUNICATION
PLANTS—COMPUTER PROJECT
PLANTS—CRAFTS
PLANTS—DESERT
PLANTS—DYES
PLANTS—ENZYMES
PLANTS—EROSION
PLANTS—FEELINGS
PLANTS—FERNS
PLANTS—FERTILIZERS
PLANTS—FLOWERPOTS
PLANTS—FLOWERS
PLANTS—FOOD
PLANTS—FOOD STORAGE
    SYSTEMS
PLANTS—FRAMES
PLANTS—FREEZING
PLANTS—FRESH WATER
PLANTS—FRUITS AND SEEDS
PLANTS—FUEL
PLANTS—GENETICS
PLANTS—GEOTROPISM
PLANTS—GERMINATION
PLANTS—GRAFTS
PLANTS—GROWTH
PLANTS—HERBS
PLANTS—HORMONES
PLANTS—HOT BEDS
PLANTS—HUMIDITY
PLANTS—HYDROPONICS
PLANTS—IDENTIFICATION
PLANTS—INDOOR
PLANTS—INSECT EATING
PLANTS—INSECT PESTS
PLANTS—LEAF CUTTING
    PROPAGATION
PLANTS—LEAVES
PLANTS—LICE. See APHIDS
PLANTS—LICHENS
PLANTS—LIGHT
PLANTS—MOLDS
PLANTS—MOTION
PLANTS—MOVEMENT
PLANTS—MUSIC
PLANTS—NEMATODES
PLANTS—NUTRIENTS
PLANTS—OCEAN
PLANTS—OSMOSIS

PLANTS—OXYGEN
PLANTS—PAPER
PLANTS—PESTICIDES
PLANTS—PHOTOGRAPHY
PLANTS—PHOTOSYNTHESIS
PLANTS—PHOTOTROPISM
PLANTS—PIGMENTS
PLANTS—PLANT COMMUNITIES
PLANTS—POLLINATION
PLANTS—POLLUTION
PLANTS—POPULATIONS
PLANTS—POTATOES
PLANTS—PRESS
PLANTS—PRINTS
PLANTS—PROPAGATION
PLANTS—PUMPKINS
PLANTS—RESPIRATION. See
    PLANTS—OXYGEN
PLANTS—RIVERS
PLANTS—ROOTS
PLANTS—SEASIDE
PLANTS—SENSITIVITY
PLANTS—SHELTERS
PLANTS—SOIL
PLANTS—STARCH
PLANTS—STEMS
PLANTS—SWEET POTATO
PLANTS—TEMPERATURE
PLANTS—TOPIARY
PLANTS—TOUCH STIMULI
PLANTS—TRANSPIRATION
PLANTS—TRAVELING. See
    SEEDS—DISPERSAL
PLANTS—TROPISMS
PLANTS—VEGETATIVE
    PROPAGATION
PLANTS—VINES
PLANTS—WATER
PLANTS—WATER POLLUTANTS
PLANTS—WATERER
PLANTS—WEAVING
PLANTS—WEED KILLERS
PLANTS—WEEDS
PLANTS—WILD PLANTS
PLASTER CASTS
PLASTER OF PARIS
PLASTIC SCRAP
PLASTICS
PLATE TECTONICS
PLATELETS
PLATONIC SOLIDS
PLAY DOUGHS
PLAYING CARDS
PLIMSOLL LINE
PLUMB LINE
PLUMBING
PLUTO
PNEUMATIC MACHINES

PNEUMATIC ROOFS
POKERINO
POLARIMETER
POLARIS
POLARISCOPE
POLARITY
POLARIZATION OF LIGHT
POLARIZATION OF WORMS
POLARIZED GLASSES
POLARIZED LIGHT
POLE STAR. See POLARIS
POLLEN
POLLINATION
POLLS
POLLUTION
POLLUTION—AIR
POLLUTION—HEAVY METALS
POLLUTION—INDOOR
POLLUTION—INSECTICIDES
POLLUTION—LIGHT
POLLUTION—LITTER
POLLUTION—NOISE
POLLUTION—OIL
POLLUTION—PLANTS
POLLUTION—PLASTICS
POLLUTION—WATER
POLLUTION—WEED KILLERS
POLYGONS
POLYHEDRONS
POLYMER MOLECULES
POLYMERIZATION
POLYMERS
POLYNESIAN MAGIC CALABASH
POLYNESIANS
POLYUNSATURATES
POMANDERS
POMEGRANATE SEED
POND WATER TERRARIUM
PONDS
PONDS—ALGAE
PONDS—ANIMALS
PONDS—AQUARIUMS
PONDS—BIRDS
PONDS—COMMUNITY
PONDS—ECOSYSTEMS
PONDS—INSECTS
PONDS—PLANTS
PONDS—POLLUTION
POOTER—INSECTS
POPCORN
POPSICLES
POPULATION
POPULATION—ANIMAL. See
    ANIMAL POPULATIONS
POPULATION—BIRDS
POPULATION—HABITATS
POPULATION—INSECTS
POPULATION—PEOPLE

POPULATION—SNAILS
POROSITY
POSITIVE NUMBERS
POSTAL SCALE
POSTURE
POTATO POPGUN
POTATOES
POTATOES—SWEET
POTENTIAL ENERGY
POTPOURRI
POTTERY
POULTRY BROODER
POULTRY. See CHICKENS
POWDERS
POWER
POWER LINES
POWER OFF ALARM
POWER RESOURCES
PRAIRIES
PRAXINOSCOPE
PRAYING MANTIS
PRECESSION
PRECIPITATES
PRECIPITATION
PREDATORS
PREHISTORIC ANIMALS
PREHISTORIC MAN
PRESERVATION
PRESS—PLANTS
PRESSURE
PRETZELS
PRIESTLEY, JOSEPH
PRINTING
PRINTS
PRISMS
PROBABILITY
PROJECTILES
PROJECTORS
PROPAGATION. See PLANTS—
    PROPAGATION; PLANTS—
    VEGETATIVE PROPAGATION
PROPELLERS
PROPULSION
PROSPECTING
PROTECTIVE COLORATION
PROTEIN
PROTOPLASMIC STREAMING
PROTOZOA
PSYCHIC BOOK TEST
PSYCHIC MOTOR
PSYCHOLOGY
PSYCHROMETER
PUDDLES
PULFRICH, CARL
PULFRICH ILLUSIONS
PULL
PULLEYS
PULSE

PUMPKINS
PUMPS
PUNNETT SQUARE. See HEREDITY
PUPAS
PUPPETS
PURIFICATION WATER. See
    WATER PURIFICATION
PURKINJE SHIFT ILLUSION
PUTTY
PUZZLES
PYRAMIDS
PYROMETER
PYTHAGORAS
QUADRANT
QUADRATS
QUADRILATERALS
QUALITATIVE ANALYSIS
QUANTITATIVE ANALYSIS
QUASARS
QUICKSAND
QUILL PEN
QUIPU, INCA
QUIZ BOARD
QUIZ BOARD GAMES. See
    ELECTRONIC GAMES; QUIZ
    BOARD
QUIZ BOARD REAGENTS. See
    INDICATORS
QUIZ BOX GAME
RABBITS—WILD
RACCOONS
RACERS
RACING CARS
RADIANT ENERGY
RADIANT HEAT
RADIATION
RADIATION—ATMOSPHERE
RADIO
RADIO—AMPLIFIER
RADIO—ANTENNA
RADIO—RECEIVER
RADIO—SHORTWAVE
    RECEIVER
RADIO TRANSMITTERS
RADIO TUBE
RADIO WAVES
RADIOACTIVE ELEMENTS
RADIOACTIVE FALLOUT
RADIOACTIVE PARTICLES
RADIOACTIVITY
RADIOMETER
RADIUM WATCH DIAL
RADON GAS
RAFTS
RAILROAD TUNNELS
RAILROADS
RAIN
RAIN CYCLE

RAIN FOREST
RAIN GAUGE
RAINBOWS
RAINDROPS
RAISINS
RAMPS
RATS
RATTLE
RAYON
REACTION MOTOR
REACTION TIME
REACTIONS
REAGENTS. See INDICATORS
RECORD KEEPING
RECORDINGS
RECYCLING
RED BLOOD CELLS
REDI, FRANCISCO
REDUCING DIETS
REEFS
REFLECTION
REFLECTOSCOPE
REFLEX ACTION
REFLEXES
REFRACTION
REFRIGERATORS
REFUSE AND REFUSE
    DISPOSAL
REGELATION. See ICE CUBES
REGENERATION
RELAYS AND REMOTE CONTROL
REMOTE CONTROLS
RENEWABLE ENERGY
    SOURCE. See METHANE
REPELLENTS
REPLICAS
REPRODUCTION—LIVING
    THINGS
REPTILES
RERADIATION
RESINS—TREE
RESISTORS
RESONANCE
RESONATORS
RESOURCE USE
RESPIRATION
RESPIRATORY SYSTEM
RETINA
RETINA AND RODS AND
    CONES
RETINAL FATIGUE
RETTING
REVERSIBLE REACTIONS
REVOLVING PROJECTS
REY, JEAN
RHEOSTAT
RICCIOLI, JOHN BAPTIST
RICE

RIGHT ANGLE
RIGHT-HANDED. *See*
    HANDEDNESS
RING STAND
RING SUPPORT AND CLAMP
RIPPLE TANK. *See* WAVES
RITTER, JOHANN
RIVERS
RIVERS—ECOSYSTEMS
RIVETS
ROAD POLLUTION
ROADS
ROARING RULER
ROBOTS
ROBOTS—TOY
ROCK CANDY
ROCK CANDY SUGAR CRYSTALS
ROCK GARDENS
ROCKETS
ROCKETS—BALLOON
ROCKS
ROCKS—COLLECTION AND
    PRESERVATION
ROCKS—CRAFTS
ROCKS—IDENTIFICATION
ROCKS—SEDIMENTARY
ROCKS—WEATHERING
ROCKS AND MINERALS
RODENTS
ROLLER COASTER
ROLLERS
ROLLING CAN
ROMAN HOUSE WAGON AND
    CHARIOT
ROMAN NUMERALS
ROOFS
ROOTS
ROOTS—DIRECTION OF
    GROWTH
ROOTS—STORAGE
ROPE
ROT
ROTATIONAL MOTION
ROTIFERS
RUBBER
RUBBER—SYNTHETIC
RUBBER BALL
RUBBER BANDS
RUBBINGS
RUBBINGS—BARK
RUBE GOLDBERG MACHINES
RUBICS CUBE PAPER
RUDDERS
RUNNING
RUSHES
RUSHLIGHTS
RUST
SACHETS

SAFETY
SAFETY BELTS
SAFETY LAMP
SAILBOATS
SAILBOATS—MODELS
SAILING YACHT
SAILOR'S SOAP
SAILS
SALAMANDERS
SALINITY
SALINITY—OCEAN
SALIVA
SALT
SALT—POLLUTION
SALT MEADOW GRASS
SALT WATER SOAP
SALTMARSHES
SALTWATER
SALVAGE
SAND
SAND CASTING
SAND DUNES
SAND PAINTING
SAND PICTURES
SAND SCULPTURE
SANDPAPER
SANDSTONE
SANITARY LANDFILLS. *See*
    LANDFILLS
SATELLITES
SATELLITES—COMMUNICATION
SATELLITES—EARTH RE-
    SOURCES SATELLITES
SATELLITES—GEODETIC
SATELLITES—ORBIT
SATELLITES—PHYSICS AND
    ASTRONOMY SATELLITES
SATELLITES—WEATHER
SATURN
SAVART'S WHEEL
SAVONIOUS ROTOR
SAW MILL
SCALE INSECTS
SCALES. *See* FISH SCALES
SCALES—MEASUREMENT
SCALLOPS
SCANNERS
SCARECROWS
SCAVENGERS. *See* BIODE-
    GRADABILITY
SCHEMAGRAPH
SCHLIEREN PATTERN
SCHWEIGGER, JOHANN
SCIENCE EXPERIMENTS
SCIENCE FAIR PROJECTS
SCIENCE FAIRS
SCIENCE FICTION
SCIENCE KIT

SCIENCE PROJECTS
SCIENCE PROJECTS FAIR
SCINTILLATIONS
SCORCH
SCREEN PRINTING
SCREWS
SCUDS
SCULPTURE
SEA ANEMONE
SEA ANIMALS
SEA BREEZES
SEA LEVEL
SEA LIFE
SEA PLANTS AND ANIMALS
SEA STARS
SEA VEGETABLES
SEA WORMS
SEASCOPE
SEASHELLS
SEASHORE
SEASHORE BIOLOGY. *See*
    BARNACLES; LIMPETS;
    MUSSELS; PERIWINKLES;
    SEA STARS; SEAWEED
SEASHORE PLANTS
SEASONS
SEASONS—FALL
SEASONS—SPRING
SEASONS—SUMMER
SEASONS—WINTER
SEAT BELTS
SEAWATER
SEAWATER SALINITY. *See*
    OCEAN SALINITY
SEAWEED
SECCHI DISC
SECRET CODES
SECRET MESSAGES
SECRET WRITING
SEDIMENTARY ROCKS
SEDIMENTATION
SEDIMENTS. *See* EROSION;
    ROCKS
SEEBACKASCOPE
SEEBECK, THOMAS J.
SEED SHRIMP. *See* OSTRACODS
SEED WHISTLE
SEEDS
SEEDS (AKENES)
SEEDS—ANATOMY
SEEDS—AVOCADO
SEEDS—CRAFTS
SEEDS—DISPERSAL
SEEDS—FRUIT
SEEDS—GEOTROPISM
SEEDS—GERMINATION
SEEDS—GREENHOUSES
SEEDS—GROWTH

SEEDS—POTTING SOIL
SEEDS—PROPAGATION
SEEDS—SPROUTS
SEEDS—TREES
SEINE NET
SEISMOGRAPH
SEISMOMETER
SENSATIONS
SENSES
SENSES—HEARING
SENSES—SENSE RECEPTORS
SENSES—SIGHT
SENSES—SMELL
SENSES—TASTE
SENSES—TASTE AND SMELL
SENSES—TOUCH
SENSITIVITY—LIVING THINGS
SENSORS
SENSORY PERCEPTION—HOW
 DO HERBS AND SPICES
 FLAVOR OUR FOOD
SEPARATION
SEPTIC TANK
SEQUENCE
SEWAGE
SEWAGE SLUDGE
SEWAGE TREATMENT
SEXTANT
SHADOW CLOCKS (SUNDIALS)
SHADOWS
SHADUF
SHAMPOOS
SHAPES
SHELLS
SHELLS—COLLECTION AND
 PRESERVATION
SHELTERS
SHIPS
SHIPWRECKS
SHOCK WAVES
SHOES
SHORELINES
SHORT CIRCUITS
SHREWS
SHRIMP—BRINE
SHUTTLES
SIDEREAL DAY. See TIME
SIEVES
SIGNALS
SILK
SILK SCREENING
SILKWORMS
SILLY PUTTY
SILVER
SILVER CLEANER
SILVERPLATING
SIMPLE MACHINES

SIMPLE MACHINES—BALL-
 BEARINGS
SIMPLE MACHINES—BELTS
SIMPLE MACHINES—BLOCK
 AND TACKLE
SIMPLE MACHINES—CAMS
SIMPLE MACHINES—COM-
 POUND MACHINES
SIMPLE MACHINES—GEARS
SIMPLE MACHINES—
 INCLINED PLANE
SIMPLE MACHINES—LEVERS
SIMPLE MACHINES—LEVERS
 AND PULLEYS
SIMPLE MACHINES—PULLEY
SIMPLE MACHINES—RAMPS
SIMPLE MACHINES—SCREWS
SIMPLE MACHINES—WEDGES
SIMPLE MACHINES—WHEEL
 AND AXLE
SIMPLE MACHINES—WHEELS
SIMPLE MACHINES—WIND-
 LASS (WHEEL AND AXLE)
SIMPLE MACHINES—WORK
SIMPLESSE
SINGING
SIPHONS
SIREN DISK
SIZE
SIZE—RELATIVITY
SKATE SAIL
SKATERS
SKELETONS
SKIER
SKIING
SKIMMY
SKIN
SKIN—ANIMAL
SKIN—SENSE RECEPTORS
SKIN—SENSORS
SKIN CREAM
SKINKS
SKULLS
SKULLS—BIRDS
SKULLS—MAMMALS
SKUNKS
SKY
SKY—NIGHT
SKYSCRAPERS
SLEDGES
SLEEP
SLEIGH
SLIDE PROJECTORS
SLIDE RULE
SLIDES
SLIDES—MICROSCOPE
SLIDES—WATER
SLIME

SLIME MOLDS
SLOPES
SLOPES—NATURAL
SLUGS
SMOG
SMOKE
SMOKE RING CANNON
SMOKE RING MACHINE
SMOKING
SNAILS
SNAILS—COLLECTION AND
 PRESERVATION
SNAILS—WATER
SNAKES
SNAKES—CHEMICAL
SNAKES—COLLECTION AND
 PRESERVATION
SNELL, WILLEBRORD
SNOW
SNOW SNAKES
SNOWFLAKES
SNOWMOBILES
SNOWSHOES
SOAP
SOAP BOAT
SOAP BUBBLES
SOCCER
SOCIAL ORGANIZATION—
 ANIMALS
SOCIAL ORGANIZATION—
 ANTS
SOCIAL ORGANIZATION—
 BIRDS
SOCIAL SCIENCE
SOCIAL SCIENCE—CON-
 SUMER USE OF SOFT
 DRINKS. See SOFT DRINKS
SODIUM BICARBONATE. See
 BAKING SODA
SODIUM CHLORIDE. See SALT
SODIUM FLAME
SOFT DRINKS
SOIL CONSERVATION. See
 EROSION; SOILS—EROSION
SOIL POLLUTION
SOILS
SOILS—ECOLOGY. See EARTH-
 WORMS
SOILS—EROSION
SOILS—POTTING FOR PLANTS
SOLAR CELLS
SOLAR CLOCKS
SOLAR COLLECTORS
SOLAR COOKERS
SOLAR DISTILLATION. See
 SOLAR STILL
SOLAR ECLIPSES. See
 ECLIPSES—SOLAR

SOLAR ENERGY
SOLAR ENERGY—FURNACE
SOLAR ENGINE
SOLAR GREENHOUSE
SOLAR HEAT
SOLAR HEATERS
SOLAR HEATING
SOLAR STILL
SOLAR STONE
SOLAR SYSTEM
SOLAR WATER CLEANER
SOLAR WATER HEATER
SOLDER
SOLDERING
SOLENOID
SOLID WASTES
SOLID WASTES—RECYCLING
SOLIDS
SOLSTICE
SOLUBILITY
SOLUTIONS
SOLUTIONS—SUPERSATU-
  RATED. See CRYSTALS
SOLVENTS
SONIC BOOM
SONOMETER
SOOT
SOROBAN ANALOG COMPUTER
SOUND
SOUND—AMPLIFIERS
SOUND—ANIMALS
SOUND—DIFFRACTION
SOUND—DIRECTION
SOUND—DISTANCE
SOUND—DOPPLER EFFECT
SOUND—ECHOES
SOUND—EFFECTS. See SOUND
  EFFECTS
SOUND—FREQUENCY
SOUND—HUSHERS
SOUND—INSULATORS
SOUND—MUSICAL
  INSTRUMENTS
SOUND—PITCH
SOUND—REFLECTION
SOUND—REFRACTION
SOUND—RESONANCE
SOUND—SPEED
SOUND—TELEGRAPH
SOUND—TELEPHONE
SOUND—TONE
SOUND TOYS
SOUND—TRAVELS
SOUND—VIBRATIONS
SOUND—WAVELENGTH
SOUND—WAVES
SOUND EFFECTS
SOUNDING

SOW BUGS
SPACE
SPACE—MAN IN SPACE
SPACE BOX
SPACE CITY MODEL
SPACE COLONY
SPACE COMPUTERS
SPACE CREATURES
SPACE CREATURES—TOYS
SPACE CRUISER
SPACE EQUIPMENT
SPACE EXPLORATION
SPACE FACTORY
SPACE METEORS
SPACE MONSTER COSTUME
SPACE MONSTERS—TOYS
SPACE ORBIT MOBILE
SPACE PEOPLE
SPACE PEOPLE—TOYS
SPACE PLANTS
SPACE PROBES
SPACE PUPPETS
SPACE ROBOTS—TOYS
SPACE SCIENCE
SPACE SHUTTLE
SPACE STATION
SPACE SUITS
SPACE TOYS CONTAINER
SPACE TRAVEL
SPACE TRAVELER—TOYS
SPACE VEHICLES
SPACE WEAPONS—TOYS
SPACECRAFT
SPACECRAFT—FUTURISTIC
  MODELS
SPACECRAFT—TOYS
SPARKLERS
SPARKS
SPATTER PRINT BOX
SPEAKERS. See SOUND—
  AMPLIFIERS
SPEAKING TUBE
SPECIES DIVERSITY
SPECIES SURVIVAL
SPECIFIC GRAVITY
SPECIFIC HEAT
SPECIMENS
SPECIMENS—MARINE
  ANIMALS
SPECTOGRAPH
SPECTROSCOPE
SPECTRUM
SPEED
SPEED BOAT
SPICES
SPIDER WEBS. See SPIDERS—
  WEBS
SPIDERS

SPIDERS—COLLECTION AND
  PRESERVATION
SPIDERS—WEBS
SPIES
SPINNERS
SPINNING
SPINNING YARN
SPIRALS
SPIRIT LEVEL
SPIROGYRA
SPIROMETER
SPIROSTOMA
SPONGES
SPONTANEOUS GENERATION
SPOOL PEOPLE
SPOOLS
SPORE PRINTS
SPORES
SPORTS
SPRAY BOTTLES
SPRAYERS
SPRING
SPRING PEEPERS
SPRING SCALES
SPRINGS
SPRINGTAILS
SPRINKLERS
SPROUTS
SQUARES
SQUASH
SQUEEZE BOTTLE
SQUID
SQUIRRELS
STABILITY
STAGE PERFORMING BOX
STAGECOACH
STAIN REMOVERS
STAINED GLASS
STAINING
STAINS
STALACTITES
STALACTITES AND
  STALAGMITES
STAMENS
STAR MAPS
STAR WORLD
STARCH
STARFISH
STARS
STARS—CONSTELLATIONS
STATIC ELECTRICITY
STATISTICS
STATUES
STEADINESS TESTER
STEAM
STEAM ENGINES
STEAM LOCOMOTIVES
STEAM POWERED BOAT

STEAM TURBINE ENGINE
STEAMBOAT
STEAMROLLER
STEEL
STEEL WOOL
STEMS
STENTORS. See INFUSORIA;
    SPIROSTOMA
STEP DOWN TRANSFORMER
STEREOSCOPE
STETHOSCOPE
STICK—MAGNETIZED
STICKLEBACK FISH
STILTS
STIMULANTS
STOKES, GEORGE
STOKES' LAW
STOMATA
STONE AGE
STONE CIRCLES
STORAGE BATTERY
STORAGE CELL
STORMS
STOVES
STRAWS
STREAM TABLE
STREAMLINING
STREAMS
STREET LIGHTS
STRENGTH
STRENGTH—CYLINDER
STRESS
STRING
STRING INSTRUMENTS
STROBOSCOPE
STROBOSCOPIC EFFECTS
STRUCTURAL STRENGTH
STRUCTURES
STURGEON, WILLIAM
SUBLIMATION
SUBMARINES
SUBMARINES—MODELS
SUBMERSIBLES
SUCCESSION
SUCTION
SUGAR
SULFUR
SULFUR DIOXIDE
SUMMER
SUN
SUN—ECLIPSES
SUN ANIMALCULE
SUN CLOCK
SUN COMPASS
SUN PRINTS
SUN SCORCHER TRICKS
SUN SCREENS
SUN SPOTS

SUN TEA
SUN VIEWER
SUNBEAM ALARM CLOCK
SUNBURN CREAM
SUNDEW PLANTS
SUNDIALS
SUNFLOWERS
SUNGLASSES
SUNLIGHT
SUNLIGHT—REFLECTED
SUNSCREENS
SUNSETS
SUNSHINE RECORDER
SUNTAN LOTIONS. See
    SUNSCREENS
SUPER STRUCTURES
SUPERSTITIONS
SURFACE AREA
SURFACE TENSION
SURFACTANTS. See DETER-
    GENTS; SOAP; WATER
    SOFTENERS
SURFBOARD AND RIDER
SURVEYING
SURVEYING THEODOLITE
SURVIVAL
SUSPENSIONS
SUSPENSIONS—EMULSIONS
SWAMP BUGGY
SWAMPS
SWAN
SWEET POTATOES
SWEETENERS
SWEETNESS (TASTE)
SWIMMING POOL PHYSICS
SWINGS
SWITCHES
SYMBIOSIS
SYMBOLIC HIERONYMOUS
    MACHINE
SYMBOLIC MACHINES
SYMMETRY
SYNODIC TIME. See TIME
SYRUP
TADPOLES
TALBOT, WILLIAM HENRY
TALC
TALEIDOSCOPE
TALKING
TANGRAMS
TANK
TANKER
TAP DANCER
TAP ROOT
TARANTULAS
TARNISH
TASTE
TASTE AND SMELL

TAXIS BEHAVIOR
TEA
TECTONIC PLATES
TEEPEE
TEETH
TELEGRAPH
TELEKINESIS
TELEPATHY
TELEPHONE
TELESCOPE
TELEVISION
TEMPERATURE
TEMPERATURE—SPACECRAFT
TEMPERATURE INVERSION
TENDONS
TENNIS
TENSILE STRENGTH
TENTS
TERMITES
TERRARIUMS
TERRESTRIAL SUCCESSION
TERRITORIALITY
TESLA, NIKOLA
TESLA COILS
TESSELLATION
TEST TUBE
TESTS
TEXTILES
TEXTURE
THALES
THAUMATROPE
THEODOLITE
THEODORIC OF FREIBOURG
THERMAL INVERSION
THERMAL POLLUTION
THERMISTORS
THERMOCLINE
THERMOCOUPLES
THERMODYNAMICS
THERMOMETERS
THERMOSCOPE
THERMOSTAT
THIGMOTROPISM
THOMPSON, BENJAMIN
THREAD
THUMB. See HUMAN BODY
THUNDER AND LIGHTNING
THUNDERCLOUDS
THUNDERSTORMS
TIDE POOLS
TIDES
TIGHTROPE WALKERS
TILTMETER
TIME
TIME LINES
TIME TABLES
TIME ZONES
TIMERS

TIRES
TOADS
TOASTER
TOBACCO
TOBACCO HABIT. *See* SMOKING
TOILET PAPER
TOMATOES
TONGUE—HUMAN
TOOTHPASTE
TOOTHPASTE AND POWDER
TOOTHPICKS
TOPOGRAPHY
TOPS
TORNADOES
TORQUE
TORRICELLI, EVANGELISTA
TORTOISES
TOTEM POLES
TOUCH
TOURNIQUET
TOWERS
TOWERS AND BRIDGES
TOXIC CHEMICALS
TOYS
TRACING PAPER
TRACKS. *See* TRACKS AND TRACKING
TRACKS—BALL GAMES
TRACKS AND TRAILING
TRACTION ENGINE
TRAFFIC
TRAFFIC LIGHTS
TRAFFIC SAFETY
TRAFFIC SIGNS
TRAILBLAZING
TRAINS
TRANSECT
TRANSFORMER
TRANSISTORS
TRANSPIRATION
TRANSPORTATION
TRAPS
TRAPS—INSECTS
TRASH
TRAVEL
TRAVOIS (INDIAN)
TREASURE
TREES
TRIANGLES
TRIBOLUMINESCENCE
TRIPOD BURNER
TROLLEY
TROPICAL FISH
TROPISMS
TRUCKS
TRUSSES
TSUNAMIS

TUBERS. *See* PLANTS; ROOTS
TUBIFEX WORMS
TUGBOAT
TUNDRA ECOLOGY
TUNING FORKS
TUNNELS
TURBINES
TURBOJET ENGINE
TURBOPROP ENGINE
TURNER, C. J.
TURTLES
TWEEZERS
TWIGS
TWINING. *See* PLANTS— VINES; VINES
TYNDALL EFFECT
UFO
ULTRASONICS
ULTRAVIOLET RADIATION
UNDERGROUND HOMES. *See* HOUSES
UNDERGROUND WATER
UNDERWATER BINOCULARS
UNDERWATER DIVER
UNDERWATER FLASHLIGHT (TORCH)
UNDERWATER OBSERVATION
UNDERWATER VIEWER
UNIVERSE
URANUS
URCHINS
URINALYSIS
VACUUM
VACUUM PUMP
VALLEYS AND HILLS
VALSALVA'S EXPERIMENT
VAN GUERICKE, OTTO. *See* GUERICKE, OTTO VON
VAN MUSSCHENBROEK, PE-TER
VAPOR
VAPORIZATION. *See* SOLAR STILL
VARIATION
VEGETABLES
VEGETATIVE PROPAGATION. *See* PLANTS—VEGETATIVE PROPAGATION
VEHICLES
VELOCITY
VENN DIAGRAMS
VENTRAL SEGMENTS OF VIBRATION
VENTURI
VENTURI THROAT
VENTURI TUBE
VENUS
VENUS FLYTRAP

VERSORIUM
VERTEBRATES
VIBRATIONS
VIEWERS
VIEWERS—3-D
VIKING HELMET
VIKING LONG SHIP MODEL
VIKING SHIELDS
VIKING SHIP
VIKING SOLAR STONE
VINCI, LEONARDO DA
VINEGAR
VINES
VINES—LEAF CLIMBERS
VINES—ROOT CLIMBERS AND WEAVERS
VINES—TENDRIL CLIMBERS
VINES—TWINING
VIRUS
VISCOMETER
VISCOSITY
VISIBILITY
VISION
VITAMIN C
VITAMINS
VIVARIUMS
VOICE
VOLCANIC POLLUTION
VOLCANOES
VOLTA, COUNT ALESSANDRO
VOLTAGE
VOLTAIC CELL
VOLTAIC PILE
VOLTMETER
VOLUME
VOLVOX. *See* EUGLENA
VON GUERICKE, OTTO. *See* GUERICKE, OTTO VON
VORTEX RINGS
WAGONS
WALKIE TALKIE
WALL COVERINGS
WASPS
WASTE
WASTE—SPACECRAFT
WASTE TREATMENT
WASTEWATER TREATMENT
WATCHES
WATER
WATER—ABSORPTION
WATER—ADHESION
WATER—AQUIFER
WATER—BENDING
WATER—BUOYANCY
WATER—CAPILLARY ACTION
WATER—CLOCKS. *See* WATER CLOCKS
WATER—COHESION

WATER—CONDENSATION
WATER—CONVECTION
WATER—DENSITY
WATER—DESALINIZATION
WATER—DETECTOR RODS
WATER—DISPLACEMENT
WATER—DISTILLATION
WATER—DRINKING
WATER—ELECTROLYSIS
WATER—EROSION
WATER—EUTROPHICATION.
    See EUTROPHICATION
WATER—EVAPORATION
WATER—EXPANSION
WATER—FILTERS AND
    FILTERING
WATER—FILTERS AND
    FILTRATION
WATER—FLOATING AND
    SINKING
WATER—FOODS
WATER—FREEZING
WATER—FREEZING POINT
WATER—HARD AND SOFT
WATER—ICE
WATER—INSECTS
WATER—LEVEL
WATER—LIGHT
WATER—LIGHT REFRACTION
WATER—PLANTS
WATER—POLLUTION
WATER—PRESSURE
WATER—PURIFICATION
WATER—SALINITY
WATER—SALTWATER
WATER—SAMPLING
WATER—SECCHI DISC
WATER—SOFTENERS
WATER—SOLUTIONS
WATER—SPECIFIC GRAVITY
WATER—STEAM
WATER—STREAMS
WATER—SURFACE TENSION
WATER—TESTING
WATER—TOYS
WATER—TREATED
WATER—UNDERWATER
    OBSERVATION
WATER—USES
WATER—VAPOR
WATER—VIEWER
WATER—WASTE
WATER—WATER SPRAY
WATER—WEIGHT
WATER—WET AND DRY
WATER AND LIGHT
WATER ANIMALS
WATER BEDS

WATER CLOCKS
WATER CONSERVATION
WATER CYCLE
WATER DIVINING
WATER DROP MAGNIFIER
WATER DROPS
WATER DROPS—LENS
WATER FLEAS. See MICRO-
    SCOPE; DAPHNIA
WATER FOUNTAINS
WATER JET ENGINES
WATER LENS
WATER LILY
WATER MAGNIFIER
WATER OF HYDRATION
WATER POLLUTION. See
    WATER—POLLUTION
WATER POWER
WATER PRESSURE. See
    WATER—PRESSURE
WATER PURIFICATION. See
    WATER—PURIFICATION
WATER SCALE
WATER SCOPE
WATER SOFTENERS
WATER SUPPLY—HOUSES
WATER SUPPLY—ON
    SPACECRAFT
WATER TABLE
WATER TREATMENT PLANTS
WATER TRICK
WATER TURBINES
WATER VAPOR. See WATER—
    VAPOR
WATER WHEELS
WATER WRITING
WATERCLOCKS. See WATER
    CLOCKS
WATERFALL ILLUSION
WATERMARKS
WATERMELONS
WATERPROOFING
WATERSPOUT
WATERWAYS
WATERWHEELS
WATT, JAMES
WAVES
WAXES
WEATHER
WEATHER BALLOONS
WEATHER FORECASTING
WEATHER INSTRUMENTS
WEATHER PREDICTIONS
WEATHER STATION
WEATHER VANES
WEATHERING. See EROSION
WEAVING
WEAVING—PLANTS

WEBS
WEDGES
WEEDS
WEEDS—GERMINATION
WEEDS—WEED KILLERS
WEIGHING MACHINES
WEIGHT
WEIGHT LIFTING
WEIGHTLESSNESS
WEIGHTS AND BALANCES
WEIGHTS AND MEASURES—
    VOLUME
WELDING
WELLS
WET BULB. See HYGROMETER
WET CELL BATTERY
WETLANDS
WETLANDS—POLLUTION
WETTING AGENTS. See
    DETERGENTS; SOAP;
    SURFACTANTS
WHALES
WHEAT
WHEAT BERRIES
WHEATSTONE, CHARLES
WHEEL AND AXLE
WHEELS
WHEELS—AXLE
WHEELS—MEDICINE
WHIRLIGIGS INSECTS
WHIRLPOOLS
WHIRLWINDS
WHISTLES
WHITE BLOOD CELLS
WHIZZ BANG
WILD FLOWERS
WILDFLOWERS—COLLECTION
WILDLIFE MAP
WILDLIFE OBSERVATION
WILDLIFE ORPHANS
WILLIAM, THOMSON
WILSON CLOUD CHAMBER
WIND
WIND CAR
WIND CHIMES
WIND DARTS
WIND DETECTOR
WIND ENERGY
WIND POWER
WIND RESISTANCE
WIND SPEED
WIND TUNNELS
WIND TURBINES
WIND VANES
WINDLASS
WINDMILLS
WINE
WINE AND WATER TRICKS

KEY TO INDEX

The index is arranged in the following order:

Subject ⟍   Cross-reference

ABACUS. *See also* **ADDING MACHINES; COMPUTERS**

Experiment description ⟋   Abacus from old frame and beads, how to   Page number
            make 1248:22-25

            How to count with an abacus 509:36-40   Book number
            How to make 321:17; 507:1849-1850   (refer to "Books Indexed by
            How to make and use 625:10   Number" on page 479)
            Soroban Analog Computer—directions for
               making (advanced) 449:113-117
            Using an abacus, how to do 1349:14-17

ABERRATION OF LIGHT. *See* **LENSES; LIGHT; STARS**

ABIOTIC FACTORS
            Effect of light on aquatic ecosystem experiment
               978:120-121

ABRASION. *See* **EROSION**

ABRASIVES. *See* **SANDPAPER**

ABSOLUTE DIFFERENCE
            Absolute difference calculation example 1396:195

After finding an experiment of interest, check the book number in the back of the index to discover the author, title, and publication data for the book in which the experiment is printed.

ALPHABETICAL INDEX OF ENTRIES

A

3-D

3-D images, how to make using camera and stereoscope experiment 295:38-43:

Perception experiments; hole in hand and overlapping images; data tables 1004:2.006

3-D VIEWERS

3-D viewer, making 909:149

ABACUS. *See also* **ADDING MACHINES; COMPUTERS**

Abacus from old frame and beads, how to make 1248:22-25

How to count with an abacus 509:36-40

How to make 321:17; 507:1849-1850

How to make and use 625:10

Soroban Analog Computer—directions for making (advanced) 449:113-117

Using an abacus, how to do 1349:14-17

ABERRATION OF LIGHT. *See* **LENSES; LIGHT; STARS**

ABIOTIC FACTORS

Effect of light on aquatic ecosystem experiment 978:120-121

ABRASION. *See* **EROSION**

ABRASIVES. *See* **SANDPAPER**

ABSOLUTE DIFFERENCE

Absolute difference calculation example 1396:195

ABSORPTION. *See also* **FATS**

Absorbency of different materials experiment 1077:8-9

Absorption experiment—cooking dried lima beans 537:16-17

Absorption experiment—cooking dried lima beans recipe 537:62

Moisture detecting mermaid, how to make 1007:84-85

Paper towel; space between fibers and speed of water travel thru it experiment 984:59-61

Paper towels; which is the "quickest picker-upper" project 1210:41-42

Water race with two pieces of cloth—experiment 563:154

What happens when paper touches water [Primary] 69:37-39, 41

Which materials soak up water the fastest experiment 1509:8

ABSORPTION OF MATERIALS

Reverberation time; time it takes sound to become inaudible in room experiment 1155:78-81

ACCELERATION. *See also* **FORCE; GRAVITY; INERTIA**

Acceleration and amount of matter (weight of objects) being pulled experiment 1157:34-35

Acceleration experiment with adjustable slope and truck with drip timer 1179:65

Acceleration experiments with objects moving in a circle 1157:31-34

Acceleration of falling bodies due to gravity and air resistance experiment 1157:58-61

Crouched position gives sprinter an advantage experiment 1154:39-45

Cylinders roll down hill at different rates due to distribution of mass 1132:42-1-42-2

Diluting gravity reduces acceleration of falling object experiment 1502:40-42

Falling object accelerates experiment 1502:40-42

Force of gravity and acceleration experiment 1502:40-42

Galilei Galileo's falling objects have a constant acceleration rate experiment 1133:4.004

How fast do objects fall to Earth experiment 1004:5.008

Measure inward or centripetal acceleration experiment 763:84

Measure rate of acceleration and deceleration rate of car experiment 1136:34-35

Measure speed of toy car experiment 1521:18-19

Pendulum measures gravity's acceleration experiment data table given 1004:5.009

Projects with angular acceleration 1164:43-44

Robert Boyle's objects of different masses fall thru vacuum at same rate 1133:4.007

Two kinds of accelerometers 295:77-79

ACCELEROMETER

Accelerometer measures accelerations in the real world, how to make 1164:22-27

Accelerometer shows acceleration and direction of acceleration experiment 1502:37-39

Accelerometer to measure acceleration, how to make 1157:28-30

Accelerometer, make from paper clip, rubber band and fishing weight 1399:54-55

How to build 295:77-79

Projects with accelerometers 1164:28

Simple—how to make 763:83

ACID BOGS. *See* **BOGS**

ACID RAIN

Acid can dissolve a metal—experiment 594:48-49

Acid effect on statues experiment 1405:76

Acid fog effect on geranium plant experiment 1060:116

Acid lake; how to make mini acid lake and buffer it experiment 1328:63

Acid poured on rocks eats away at rocks experiment 1383:17

Acid rain acidity demonstrated using red cabbage indicator 1330:46-47

Acid rain affects growth of geranium plant cuttings experiment 1060:117

Acid rain affects leaf ratio in radish plants experiment 1060:116-117

Acid rain affects plants experiment using vinegar, lime and distilled water 1046:80-82

Acid rain effect on germination of seeds experiment 1150:76-77

Acid rain effect on growing plants experiment 1150:78; 1414:12-14

Acid rain effect on growth of geraniums experiment 1060:114-116

Acid rain effect on pH of water and soil experiment; chart given 1171:54-55

Acid rain effect on seed growth experiment 727:21

Acid rain effect on soils around your home experiment 1228:18-19

Acid rain effect on water plants and land plants experiment 1171:56-58

Acid rain effects on materials experiments 777:16
Acid rain effects on micro-organisms experiments 777:14
Acid rain effects on plants experiment 1324:60-64
Acid rain effects on seeds and plants experiment 978:177
Acid rain effects on water and land ecosystems experiment 978:178-179
Acid water test using litmus paper, how to make 1414:10-11
Acidity of rain at different times during storm experiment 1046:66-67
Acidity of rain collected in different areas project 1195:18-30
Acidity of rain that falls in your area project 1296:1972
Acidity of rainwater tested with red cabbage indicator experiment 1480:106
Airborne acid corrosion experiment with pieces of nylon stockings 1476:189
Algae; quantity and diversity of algae affected by acidified waters experiment 1450:128-134
Be an acid rain watcher 398:137-139
Buffering capacity of soils to buffer acid rain experiment 978:174-175
Building materials release materials that effect plant growth experiment 714:71-72
Buildings and statues damaged by acid rain experiment 1325:44-48
Buildings; effect of acid rain on building materials experiment 1233:85
Calcium carbonate (lime) effect on acid rain experiment 1046:74-76
Carbon dioxide causes water to become more acidic experiment 1325:39-43
Chemical properties of marble and why damaged by pollution experiment 871:3.026
Collect and test acidity of common household solutions experiment 864:131
Collecting acid rain experiment 950:169
Corrosion effects of acid rain on statues and buildings experiment 1134:6.006
Damage to stone & steel demo. With antacid tablet & vinegar 594:66-67
Determine if limestone can protect pine trees from acid rain experiment 997:93-94
Does acid rain affect the cell structure of Spirogyra experiment 997:99-101
Does acid rain hurt some buildings and statues 396:62-63
Does formic acid from ants contribute to acid rain problem investigation 864:98
Effect of acid on statues demonstration 1023:92-93
Effect of acid, alkaline and normal water on seedling growth—experiment 594:36-37
Effect of soil pH on plant growth experiment; data table given 871:2.009
Effect on plants and roots 398:133-137
Effects of acidity levels on freshwater animals chart 727:18
Effects of increased acidity on plankton experiment 864:130-132
Erosion of rocks by chemical experiment using rock, water and vinegar 1202:15
Experiment—to see if soil in your area can buffer acid rain 594:32-34
Experiment 371:24-26
Fish tank setup with pond and marsh plants demonstrates hydrologic cycle 1171:49-53

Household items tested for acid with red cabbage indicator experiment 1328:62
Household liquids and powders water solution effect on plant growth experiment 1465:109
How acid is your rain experiment 1232:67
How acid is your rainwater experiment 1013:91
Indicators; test variety of substances experiment 777:5-6
Lake water—demonstrate effect of acidity on aquatic life 594:23-25
Leaf responses to acid rain experiments 777:13
Lichens and pollution experiment 737:35
Lichens as indicator plants sensitive to acid rain experiment 933:29-30
Liming protects lakes from acid rain experiment 1325:49-53
Making acid rain experiment 727:9; 1171:36-39
Marble statues destroyed by acid rain; prove why experiment 1476:190-191
Measure acidity of rainwater experiment with red cabbage indicator 1465:108-109
Measuring amount of sulfur dioxide in air experiment 933:26-28
Monitoring rainfall experiment 777:9
Monitoring snowfall experiment 777:10
Neutralizing capacities of body of water experiment 1233:55
Nitrogen fixation affected by acid rain experiment 1450:72-76
pH concentrations experiments 777:8
pH experiments 777:7
pH level of rain, how to measure experiment; pH scale given 1063:363
pH of acid rain and snow experiment 1526:98
pH of acid rain in snow and rain experiment 978:175-177
pH of rain experiment 1150:75-76
pH of rainfall experiment; how to monitor; chart given 1171:39-42
pH of rainfall, how to measure 1233:22-23
pH of rainwater experiment to determine if acid rain is a problem 1427:68-69
pH of rainwater experiment 1060:114
pH tests for 594:9-15
Plant growth affected by acid rain experiment 1335:211
Plant growth stunted by air and water pollution experiment 1362:11
Plant seed responses to acid rain experiments 777:11
Plants affected by acid rain experiment 1063:364
Plants exposed to too much sulfur dioxide gas will be harmed experiment 1453:30-31
Plants; acid rain effect on growing plants experiment 1233:76-77
Plants; acid water affects plant growth experiment using vinegar 1362:17
Project evaluation, how to do 777:19
Rain sampling to test for acid rain experiment 1362:16
Rainfall; measure volume and quality of rainfall experiment 1134:2.004
Rusting; acid rain increases rate of rusting experiment 1396:162
Seedling responses to acid rain experiments 777:12
Soils and their ability to buffer acid rain experiment 727:15
Soils; pH of soil, how to measure 1233:69
Statues and buildings affected by acid rain experiment 1063:365

Stone wears away from vinegar acid experiment 1386:28

Subject areas to investigate for acid deposition 777:21-22

Sulfur dioxide gas, how to produce experiment 1171:35-37

Sulfur dioxide harms plants experiment 1324:65-68

Test for acid in rainwater experiment using red cabbage as indicator 1135:53

Test for acid rain in rainfall experiment 1003:123-124

Test for what acid rain can do to chicken bones, eggshells, paper experiment 1328:60-61

Test rain, snow, waters near your home for acid experiment using indicator 1228:14-17

Test rainfall for acidity experiment 1012:92-93

Test samples of rainwater for pH 586:62

Testing for acid rain experiment 741:17

Watering plants with vinegar water solution to show effects of acid rain 1331:86-87

Weaken acid rain using lemonade and distilled water experiment 1046:77-79

What can you do? Actions to take chart 777:17

What if? Consequences of acid rain 777:18

ACIDOPHILUS BACTERIA. *See also* **BACTERIA**

Yogurt—making your own 219:33-37

ACIDS

Remove shell from hard-boiled egg with vinegar 669:5

ACIDS AND BASES. *See also* **CHEMICAL REACTIONS; INDICATORS; SOLUTIONS**

A detective and his solutions—how to make indicator solutions 565:158-159

A simple indicator experiment 563:168

Acid base indicators from natural indicators 586:62-63

Acid base test; make the "indicator liquid" and test solution 600:14-15

Acid effect on baking; carbon dioxide produced experiment 905:202-203

Acid indicator from red cabbage leaves, how to make 1435:56-59

Acid or alkali test papers, how to make using turmeric/sodium carbonate 1244:8-9

Acid solution—a metal cleaner for coins 147:42

Acid test—what vinegar does to calcium substances—experiment 366:220-221

Acid test for carbonates experiment 1438:72-75

Acid test for different products experiment 748:118

Acid test sticks—making 676:29

Acid vinegar mixed with soluble salt, and baking powder makes a salt experiment 1435:16-17

Acid-base secret messages experiment, data tables given 1004:4.001

Acidity affects rusting rate of iron experiment 1526:101

Acidity of common household liquids; how to measure experiment 1013:92

Acidity of water experiment using red cabbage indicator 1325:12-17

Acids and bases neutralize one another experiment 1171:28-29

Ammonia produces color change on turmeric paper experiment 905:206-207

Antacids; strength of different brands of antacid tablets experiment 1396:77

Apples; acids effect on browning process of cut apples experiment 1526:96

Aspirin; strength of different brands of aspirin experiment 1396:76-77

Beet root indicator, how to make and test on different substances 790:30-31

Blow up balloon with gas experiment 827:53

Cabbage capers, colorful experiment 870:76-78

Cabbage indicator identifies lemonade as acid experiment 1405:64

Cabbage indicator paper test for acids and base experiment 905:194-197

Cabbage indicator test for citric acid in lemonade experiment 905:200-201

Cabbage indicator test for different acid concentrations experiment 905:198-199

Cabbage indicator used as test for acid and base experiment 1405:64

Cabbage juice indicator to test for acids and bases, making 935:26-27

Cabbage makes acid sauerkraut experiment 976:36

Cabbage water acid-base indicator, making 888:39-40

Cabbage water indicator experiment 884:80-83

Can acids and bases be identified with vegetable molecules 396:59-61

Carbonates and acids 84:39-42

Chalk; testing chalk with an acid experiment 1438:49-50

Chemical opposites—experiments to show 85:44-45

Chicken bone becomes soft in vinegar experiment 960:32

Clean pennies experiment 960:31

Colorful acids from fruit juices used to tie-dye fabric project 1210:56-57

Corrosion; testing aluminum for corrosion experiment using acids and alkalies 1438:90-93

Corrosiveness of acids experiment using black bathroom tile and vinegar 1171:29-30

Designing pH indicators to identify acids and bases 180:23

Dry solids must be wet to be tested with indicator paper experiment 905:208-209

Dyes; baking soda solution dribbled on fruit juice dyed fabric project 1210:56-57

Effect of acid (vinegar) on chicken bone experiment 1074:23

Effect of acids and bases on red cabbage indicator experiment 1396:67-72

Flower petal indicators for acid or base experiment; data table given 871:3.020

Flower petals used as indicators for acid or base experiment 1175:79

Foods are acid or alkali, test for 827:52

Gas bubbles cause coffee grounds to float experiment 884:84-86

Gases; test for acidic or basic nature of gases experiment with indicators 1396:70-72

Grouping chemicals according to their pH—experiment 180:10

Homemade indicators 30:37

Household cleaners; test for presence of base in powdered cleansers experiment 1479:65

Household items tested for acid or base experiment 976:38

Household items tested for acid using red cabbage indicator experiment 1328:62

Household liquids; test for acidity experiment 1046:63-65

How to detect acids in foods 122:106-107

How to detect an acid 122:104-106

Identifying acids and bases experiment using household materials/litmus paper 1171:26-27

Identifying acids and bases with litmus paper experiment 1526:87-90

Identifying unknown ingredients experiment using liquid indicator 1435:97-100

Indicator color change in the presence of acids and bases 87:15-23

Indicator from cabbage—making 122:120-121

Indicators—simple experiments with (Primary) 212:entire book

Indicators for magical liquid colors 146:58-59

Indicators plus Vitamin C pill in water identifies acids and bases experiment 1526:93-94

Indicators used to identify acids and bases—experiment 147:82-84

Indicators; test variety of substances experiment 777:5-6

Investigating acids and bases using litmus paper experiment 888:35-38

Jam experiments demonstrate 563:165-166

Juice sleuth experiment 829:35-36

Lemon and ammonia experiment to demonstrate 827:50-51

Lemon rocket, how to make 827:56

Lemon wet cell—make 608:45-46

Lemons—are lemons oily and does lemon oil burn 89:22-23

Lemons—cleaning with lemon juice 89:26-27

Lemons—color changes 89:10-11

Lemons—create rust problems 89:32-33

Lemons—effect of lemon juice on foaming action of detergents 89:52-53

Lemons—foaming action when mixed with baking soda and water 89:14-17

Lemons—hydrogen gas evolves when reacts with aluminum 89:28-29

Lemons—lemon batteries—how to make 89:40-41

Lemons—lemon oil and alcohol—what effect 89:38-39

Lemons—lemon power for a boat 89:24-25

Lemons—make a fire extinguisher 89:18-19

Lemons—secret writing with 89:34-35

Lemons—using to make 'foam' 89:20-21

Lemons as a silver cleaner 89:30-31

Lemons cause coagulation 89:36-37

Lemons contain acid experiment 860:55-57

Lemons separate water into hydrogen and oxygen 89:42-44

Lemons to show indicators and titrations 89:12-13

Lift that cube 16:58-61

Limestone; testing limestone with an acid experiment 1438:80-82

Litmus paper in solutions demonstrates acids, bases, neutrals exp. 882:14

Litmus paper test for acids and bases of common substances, how to do 1233:18-19

Litmus paper test for acids, bases and neutrals experiment; data sheet given 818:5

Litmus paper tests for solutions experiment 885:90-91

Litmus paper; why does litmus paper change colors experiment 1294:47-49

Litmus test for acids and alkalis, how to make litmus paper 1016:37

Magic potions 16:62-65

Magic trick; blood on your hand using ammonia and phenolphthalein experiment 1159:24

Make indicators to identify acids and alkalis 598:28-29

Make salt by mixing acid and base neutralization—experiment 6:29

Make your own lemon soda experiment 827:55

Mixing acids with alkalis 684:22-23

Neutralization of acids and bases by adding acids and bases experiment 1526:95-96

Neutralize a basic solution experiment 905:214-215

Neutralize a basic solution experiment with vinegar and limewater 1479:65

Neutralize an acid experiment using lemon juice and baking soda 1435:62-64

Neutralize an acid with a base—how to 319:72-73

Neutralizing acids with bases experiment 1233:52-53

Neutralizing an acid 122:117-120

Neutralizing stomach acid with a base experiment 1259:89-92

Neutralizing; how an acid is neutralized experiment 1396:73-78

Pennies get a green coating from vinegar experiment 905:92-93

pH concentrations experiments 777:8

pH effect on germination of radish and bean seeds experiment 1526:98

ph experiments 777:7

pH of lake water with added vinegar and limestone experiment 1526:98

pH of solution experiment using lemon, grape juice, milk, baking soda, water 1427:66-67

pH, the degree of acidity experiment 1526:97-98

Phenolphthalein; effect of acids and bases on phenolphthalein experiment 1479:64

Red cabbage indicator experiment to test for acids and bases 980:41-42

Red cabbage indicator experiment 1018:22-23

Red cabbage indicator for acids and bases experiment 814:52-54

Red cabbage indicator paper, how to make experiment 976:39-40

Red cabbage indicator strips test for acidity, how to make 1330:48-49

Red cabbage indicator tests for acids and bases experiment 1063:168

Red cabbage indicator tests substances for acid or base; chart given 960:28-30

Red cabbage indicator tests things found in kitchen for acid/alkaline 1016:34-37

Red cabbage indicator tests water/vinegar/baking soda/ for acids/bases 1229:46-47

Red cabbage indicator used as test for acids and alkalies experiment 1508:25

Red cabbage indicator used as test for acids and bases experiment 1286:20

Red cabbage indicator, how to make 1527:26-27

Red cabbage indicator, make to test for acid or base experiment 1179:37

Soap; why soap hurts your eyes experiment with cabbage juice acid/base indicator 1482:50-51

Soil; determine acidity or alkalinity of soil like material experiment 1323:31-35

Soils; test acidic basic nature of soil experiment 1396:71

Substances are acid or base experiment using cabbage leaves as indicator 1175:79

Tannic acid used to make leather—experiment 122:107-111

Tannin is a useful acid—demonstrate 122:111-112

Tea used as indicator for acids and alkalies experiment 1508:24

Tell acid from a base—how to 319:70-72

Telltale chemicals—indicators show acids and bases 30:35-36

Telltale chemicals—indicators show if substance is acid or base 72:56-57

Telltale colors test 676:26-28

Test chemicals around the house with base indicator 565:168

Test for acids and bases in fruit juices and common household items experiment 1159:22-24

Test for in foods 86:42

Test for limestone in rocks experiment 827:54

Test for phenolphthalein and turmeric 346:88-92

Test for presence of a base in common household cleaners experiment 905:210-211

Test for using aspirin 84:62-63

Test soaps and detergents to see if they are acidic or basic 441:19-21

Test substances with red cabbage indicator experiment 1028:54

Tester—make your own—for red cabbage, tea, flowers, berries, juices, etc. 381:18-22

Testing acids and alkalis with litmus paper 6:28

Testing for acids and bases 293:36

Testing for acids using red cabbage indicator experiment 1271:16

Testing soil for acid 122:116-117

Tests for acidity, alkalinity neutrality and bleaching with litmus paper 625:24

The bone in the pop—experiment 630:50

Turmeric indicator test experiment 980:43

Turmeric testing paper for presence of a base, how to make 905:204-205

Turmeric testing paper indicator identifies a base experiment 1405:65

Unsweetened grape juice indicator, how to make 1526:90-91

Vinegar and the vinegar eel; acetic acid production experiment 871:2.013

Volcano from red food coloring and baking soda experiment 1286:21

Water molecules form acidic or basic solution from dissolved materials 1403:60-63

Which is it 280:55-56

Why does litmus paper change colors experiment 860:53-55

Wood ash; make and test a basic solution experiment 905:212-213

Wood ashes change water to a base experiment with red cabbage juice indicator 1251:88-90

ACIDS AND BASES AND SALTS
Experiments to show 116:108-114

ACIDS AND SALTS
Indicator identifies salt solutions; acid, base, neutral, exp.data table 871:3.019

ACORNS
Activities with acorns 784:71-72

Make acorn snakes and acorn cap whistles and puppets 236:48

ACOUSTICS. *See also* **HEARING; SOUND; SOUND—PITCH; SOUND—VIBRATIONS**
Sound and architecture of concert halls experiment 1155:81-85

What materials are best for absorbing sound experiment 1209:84-85

ACROBATS
Windmill model turns acrobat figure attached to crank on blades experiment 1073:98-99

ACTION AND REACTION. *See also* **BERNOULLI'S PRINCIPLE**
Launching potato shows for every action there is equal but opposite react 1436:78-81

Sailboat motion with fan—demonstrate 95:12-13

Why gun and rocket kick back—demonstrate 95:10-11

ADAPTATION. *See* **ANIMAL BEHAVIOR; ECOSYSTEMS; ENVIRONMENT; GENETICS**

ADDING MACHINES
How to add with adding machine you made 389:14-23

How to subtract with adding machine you made 389:24-30

Roman numerals with adding machine you made 389:47-64

Some tricks with adding machine you made 389:31-37

Simple—how to make 389:9-13; 406:36-38

Other number bases to use with adding machine you made 389:38-46

ADDITION. *See also* **MATHEMATICS**
Fast addition 392:90-93

ADDITIVES. *See also* **FOOD—ADDITIVES**
Keep track of soft drink habits; determine amount of add. Being consumed 404:115

ADHESION. *See also* **COHESION; GLUES; WATER—SURFACE TENSION**
Cohesion and adhesion forces in operation experiment 1004:3.007

Force of adhesion demonstrated with oil and oil color paints 1289:30-31

Phewy putty made from cornstarch and glue, recipe, how to make 1289:22-23

Sand sculptures show adhesion between sand and water experiment 1396:156

ADHESIVES. *See also* **GLUES**
A formula for gum (gummed label glue) 336:60-62

Glues and how they work 544:25-30

Liquid—test for rate of set 336:68-69

Milk glue—a formula for milk glue 336:58-60

Paste—a formula for paste 336:57-58

Testing bond strength 336:64-67

Viscosity test experiment 336:62-64

White glues—the blush test for water resistance 336:67-68

ADOBE. *See* **BRICKS**

ADOBE HOUSE
Homemade adobe bricks—making 633:38

Model—how to make 415:42-43

ADSORBENT
Can charcoal remove molecules from water experiment 831:38-40

How air is cleaned by adsorbent chemicals experiment 1405:54

Test tube holder and stand for chromatography experiment, how to make 1476:129-130

Various materials which absorb and reflect light 549:8-10

ADSORPTION. *See* **CHROMATOGRAPHY**

AEOLIAN HARP. *See also* **MUSICAL INSTRUMENTS**
How to make 350:97-98; 358:62-63

5

AEROBIC DECOMPOSITION. *See*
 DECOMPOSITION
AERODYNAMICS. *See also* **AIRPLANES;**
 BERNOULLI'S PRINCIPLE; BOOMERANGS;
 GLIDERS; HELICOPTERS; HOT AIR BAL-
 LOONS; KITES; PARACHUTES; ROCKETS;
 STREAMLINING; WINDMILLS
A working aerofoil—how to make 419:30
Aerodynamics in a wind tunnel experiment 1476:88-90
Air friction, projects on 691:43-47
Air lift demonstration with piece of paper 1389:23
Air powered helicopter, making 981:23
Air speed affects flight demonstration 1404:103
Air streams—experiment 660:20-21
Airfoil—making 737:29
Airfoil cuts through air experiment 1332:22-23
Airfoil principle demonstrated with postcard, straws and
 blowing air 1073:19
Airspeed indicator, making 908:62-63
Airstreams and curved surfaces experiment 908:20-21
Airstreams and flat surfaces experiment 908:18-20
Balloon experiments demonstrate aerodynamic princi-
 ples 908:71-78
Bernoulli; ping pong balls demonstrate why planes can
 fly experiment 1372:38
Birds; why shape of bird's wing is important to flight ex-
 periment 904:134-135
Blow a sheet of paper to lift it high (Primary) 69:25
Boomerang, making 906:147
Build a wind tunnel 293:40-41
Cayley glider demonstrates forward thrust experiment
 1110:16-17
Curve ball thrown by pitcher demonstration 1404:98-99
Do gliders and kites fly the same way experiment
 783:14-16
Does angle of attack affect how a kite flies experiment
 783:21-22
Does shape of object affect how it flies experiment
 783:13
Does wind affect curved airfoil and flat plate differently
 experiment 783:19-20
Drag and streamlining experiment 908:27-29
Drag test for best flying design experiment 1110:18-19
Effect of speed on air pressure demonstration 1404:97
Experiments with ping pong balls demonstrate Bernoulli
 Effect 1179:128-129
Flat kite—making 112:44-45
Flying things are symmetrical experiment; make flying
 seagull 1110:14-15
Give it a lift—move paper without using your hands
 588:40
Helicopter—making 112:42
How airplanes stay up in the air demonstration 851:43-44
How does shape affect lift experiment 900:202
How planes fly 660:28-29
Indoor boomerang—making 112:40-41
Jet of air experiment 718:33-34
Land yacht shows importance of angle of attack of wind,
 how to make 1299:56
Lift; heavy airplanes supported by air from high and low
 air pressure 1208:18-19
Make and test movement of flat shape, round shape and
 tear drop shape in air 237:25-27
Moving air lifts wing model experiment 1028:12
Outdoor rotor—making 112:39

Paper airplane gliders, which design travels fastest ex-
 periment 1175:93-95
Paper Concorde—making 112:43
Paper glider demonstration, how to make 597:47
Paper glider demonstrations, how to make 588:41-43
Paper gyro, making 906:146
Paper tent demonstrates 780:24-25
Parachute—making 112:40-41
Parachute paper cones demonstrate aerodynamics, how
 to make 1175:92-93
Parachute, making 906:148
Perfume sprayer; how it works demonstration 1404:101
Pinwheel, making 906:145
Propeller produces forward thrust experiment 860:19-22
Shape and airflow experiments 908:29-31
Splat testing 162:123
Throw a piece of paper far—demonstrate (Primary)
 69:22-23
Use paper to show air moving—demonstrate, primary
 69:26-27
What does paper do as it falls thru the air (Primary)
 69:18-19
What effect do different measurements have on a kite ex-
 periment 783:23-24
Why do helium balloons rise experiment 860:1-2
Why do pilots wear parachutes experiment 860:2-4
Wind tunnel, how to build 1476:88-90
Wing shapes tested in wind tunnel experiment 860:27-30
AEROFOILS. *See* **AERODYNAMICS**
AERONAUTICS. *See also* **AIRPLANES;**
 BALLOONS; BERNOULLI'S PRINCIPLE;
 GLIDERS; HELICOPTERS; KITES;
 PARACHUTES; ROCKETS
Activities/strategies for teaching history and science of
 human flight 1475:1-191
Ailerons, elevators and rudders control flight of aircraft
 experiment 1201:15
Air lift and drag with air forks—demonstrate 225:18-
 23
Air lifts model wing experiment; how to build wing
 995:24-25
Airplane wing—fly 161:57-58
Bernoulli's principle—experiment 168:36-38
Bernoulli's principle—what holds an airplane up 55:153-
 159
Delta wing paper model glider demonstrates roll, pitch
 and yaw, make 1252:50-55
Flow of air effect on aircraft wing demonstration
 1161:13
Fly a 'slow roll' 161:55-56
Fly an air spinner (Primary) 64:unpaged
Gliders and helicopters—demonstrate 139:23
How airplane wings work—experiment 385:26-27
How an aircraft flies 142:16
How helicopter wings work—experiment 385:27-28
How hot air balloons work—demonstrate 139:27
How hovercraft works—demonstrate 139:26
How propellers work—demonstrate 139:24
How wings work and lift and spin—demonstrate 139:20-
 22
Jet propulsion—demonstrate 139:25
Lift; difference in air pressure creates lift experiment
 1201:11
Mach number and altitude in miles, how to figure
 1252:85

Paper airplane, helicopter and parachute—making 32:48-53

Paper darts, making 909:70-71

Paper helicopter—making 281:17

Primary experiments 105:14-17

Principles of flight—demonstration 291:102

Strange airplane—making (Primary) 64:unpaged

Streamlined shape helps air flow experiment 1201:17

The work of wings 72:18-19

Why plane does not flip over—demonstrate with paper plates 200:14-15

AEROSPACE. *See also* **FLIGHT**

Activities and experiment. To demonstrate advances in aerospace systems 564:34-50

AFTERIMAGES

Afterimage experiment; flash of light leaves image in your eye 1132:1-1-1-2

Afterimage experiments 1111:28-29

Afterimages using colors experiment 1158:142-143

Bird in the cage; stare at color and see it change experiment 1132:8-1-8-2

Brain judges how large something is according to how far away object is 1088:46

Colors that are not there 19:58

Human vision experiment, retinal afterimage, blind spot, dominant eye, depth 1004:2.007

Illusions 229:121-124

Pinwheel—making to demonstrate afterimage 736:22-24

See through grid experiment 736:29-30

Tests for several 258:49-55

Visions on the wall paper toy, making 999:37-38

AGE

Age you would be on other planets chart 816:16

AGING

Plants demonstrate aging process [Primary] 880:23

AGRONOMY. *See also* **SOILS**

Effect of different nutrients (foods) on plants 507:1851-1852

AILERONS. *See* **AERODYNAMICS; AERONAUTICS; AIRPLANES; FLIGHT; GLIDERS**

AIR. *See also* **ATMOSPHERE; CONVECTION; OXYGEN; SOUNDS; WINDS**

A bicycle pump and air compression 53:32-33

A paper helicopter—making 281:17

Air affects the way things move (Primary) 232:22

Air air everywhere (Primary) 232:23

Air and burning experiments 909:82-83

Air and inertia 55:115-121

Air and sound—experiments 660:38-39; 909:86-87

Air and space—experiment 605:7

Air and weight—experiment 605:8

Air around us—experiment to show 40:2

Air barometer—how to make 55:125-126

Air barometer—making 53:30-31

Air can be weighted experiment using yardstick balance and balloons 1251:11-13

Air can lift water—primary 143:32-35

Air can move objects (Primary) 232:25

Air carries things experiment [Primary] 742:10

Air compression produces heat 44:81

Air contracts when cooled and expands when heated experiments 1211:14-15

Air contracts when cooled experiment with water glasses and balloon 939:74-75

Air currents and wind demonstration with talc powder and lamp 1003:46

Air does work; 3 simple experiments 898:3-4

Air exerts pressure experiment with paper in glass of water 1005:26

Air expands and contracts experiment with balloon 1372:33

Air expands and contracts experiment 696:10-11

Air expands and contracts; balloon and bottle experiment 900:11-12; 900:47

Air expands and gets cooler experiment with bicycle pump 1219:9

Air expands and takes up more space as it gets hotter experiment 1201:7

Air expands when heated and makes coin tap—experiment 600:28-29

Air expands when heated 44:32-33

Air for life experiments 909:84-85

Air has body and weight (Primary) 232:24

Air has force balloon lifts book experiment (Primary) 695:17

Air has pressure 72:15

Air has weight—catching air in a paper bag 392:52-54

Air has weight—demonstrate 150:24-25; 253:53-54

Air has weight—experiment 128:77; 446:16-18; 651:10-11; 671:22

Air has weight—use 'air clamp' to break a slab of wood 179:21-22

Air has weight and takes up space experiments 1174:12-15

Air has weight experiment using balloons, straw and straight pins 1208:12-13

Air has weight experiment with balloons and yardstick 1084:15; 1252:3-6

Air has weight experiment with balloons on balanced yardstick 1404:9

Air has weight experiment with balloons 1373:29

Air has weight experiment with yardstick and balloons 1479:77

Air has weight experiment; balloons on balance stick demonstrates 1003:44

Air has weight experiment 1023:122-123; 1028:8-9; 1108:10; 1126:9

Air has weight; balloons on balance experiment 867:25

Air has weight; balloons on balance scale experiment 995:14-15

Air has weight 179:19-20; 44:7; 53:8-9; 96:6

Air hockey game using balloons and Ping-Pong balls 651:26-27

Air holds things up, jar of air, funnel of water and clay experiment 995:8-9

Air in human body 128:87

Air in lungs—experiment 40:4-7

Air in water experiment 741:19

Air is a gas that can dissolve in water experiment 1250:11-13

Air is all around us—experiments 597:8-9

Air is almost everywhere experiments 854:22-23

Air is cooler in the Winter demonstration 1023:136-137

Air is dissolved in water—experiment (Primary) 562:25-26

Air is everywhere—three bags full experiment 12:37-40

Air is everywhere balloon demonstrates (Primary) 695:15

Air is everywhere experiment 1126:8; 1373:29; 1441:179

Air is important when things burn—experiment 597:10-11

Air is real; container in water experiment 908:14-15

Air lifts model wing experiment; how to build wing 995:24-25

Air lifts things; balloon and books experiment 995:11

Air lifts things; straw and ping pong ball experiment 995:22-23

Air movement—using straw, balls, and paper to demonstrate 597:38-39

Air movement detector—making 694:92

Air movements in your home 53:22-23

Air moves—experiment 694:89-92

Air moves things balloon and water experiment (Primary) 695:16

Air moves things experiment [Primary] 742:9

Air moves; smoke bottle shows effect of hot/cold air on air movement 1211:10

Air moving—experiments 660:18-19

Air mystery—blow 'through' a bottle to put out candle 291:100-101

Air needed to make foods light—airy dessert 112:36-37

Air needs space experiment 909:53

Air occupies space 44:8-9; 53:3-5; 179:17-19

Air occupies space—filling an 'empty' bottle 53:6-7

Air occupies space—salt tougher than you think 16:23-25

Air power—matchbox sailboat demonstration, how to make 597:41

Air presses in all directions—experiment 446:20-21

Air pushes up against things; parachute experiment 995:16-17

Air seems to be magic—air pushes an egg into a bottle 96:22-23

Air seems to be magic—crushes a can 96:19-21

Air slows down moving things 96:16-17

Air streams—experiment 128:90-91; 660:20-21

Air streams follow a curved path 44:31

Air takes up room 30:10; 72:12; 96:8-11

Air takes up space (Primary) 232:26

Air takes up space—demonstrate 253:51-52

Air takes up space—does it 281:5-6

Air takes up space—dunk your roll but keep it dry 280:16

Air takes up space—experiment 597:12-13; 660:4-5; 671:9-11

Air takes up space—experiment (Primary) 562:8-17

Air takes up space—huff'n'puff trick 399:6

Air takes up space—no room, no room (Primary) 288:4-5

Air takes up space activity 759:34

Air takes up space and has weight experiment 1526:12-18

Air takes up space balloon experiment [Primary] 742:8

Air takes up space demonstration 1023:120-121; 1405:79-80

Air takes up space experiment with bottle and funnel 1003:42-43

Air takes up space experiment with plastic bag 905:14-15

Air takes up space experiment; paper towel in glass of water doesn't get wet 1372:18

Air takes up space experiment 705:3-5; 760:27; 829:13-14; 1231:2-5

Air takes up space; balloon in jar experiment 905:20-21

Air takes up space; blow balloon inside bottle experiment 937:28-29

Air takes up space; cloth in glass in bowl of water experiment [Primary] 897:50

Air takes up space; paper in glass in water stays dry experiment 905:22-23

Air takes up space 128:76-77

Air temperature and volume 53:10-11

Air temperature and weight 53:14-15

Air thermometer, how to make 53:18-19; 55:36-37

Air transport of water 363:153

Air's weight 243:10-11

Air-screw—making an air-screw to show warm air rises 360:4-5

Analyzing air for oxygen and nitrogen—experiment 625:24

Are there water molecules in the air 396:41-42

Atomizer shows push and pull of moving air experiment 705:91

Bag on stick demonstrates what happens when you pull a bag through the air 450:6-7

Balloon holds cups in air experiment 924:32

Balloon trick—experiments show air expands when heated 563:113

Balloon trick with hot air experiment 909:58

Balls floating on air—demonstrate 142:18

Barometer—an ink drop barometer 53:28-29

Barometer measures changes in atmospheric pressure 44:36-37

Be an air current detective (Primary) 70:42-44

Bernoulli effect—bet you can keep a ball in the air for an hour 228:74-75

Bernoulli's law—demonstrate the riddle of the hovering ping pong ball 186:15

Bernoulli's law—how does an airplane fly 186:16-17

Bernoulli's law using an airfoil 585:5-6

Bernoulli's principle—a dancing ball 114:99-101

Bernoulli's principle—making an airplane rise 53:48-50

Bernoulli's principle in action 53:46-47

Blow at object; candle behind it goes out experiment 846:3-9

Blow bubbles 32:54

Blow down a big book (Primary) 143:26-27

Blow out candle from behind obstacle experiment 937:30-31

Blow picture—making 32:55

Blowing a postcard (Primary) 70:24-30

Blowing air experiment 1108:7

Blowing bubbles (Primary) 232:21

Blowing bubbles 32:54-55

Burning air in jar with water and candle experiment 790:28

Burning candle, oxygen use and water levels in tubes experiment 1526:108-113

Can lift things; balloon and books experiment 940:32-33

Can salt remove water from the air experiment 831:41-42

Can you feel weight and pressure of air; plastic in jar experiment 900:36

Can you see air move; two glasses under water experiment 900:34

Candle burns oxygen in bottle and leaves nitrogen gas experiment 995:18-19

Candle needs air to burn 40:3-4

Candle that lifts water—oxygen is consumed when a fire burns 576:70-71

Carbon dioxide in the air 53:53-55

Carbon dioxide is heavier than air—experiment 291:69

Cards demonstrate how air slows things down 210:7

Cartesian divers—making 101:14-15
Chemical effects of air 128:87-89
Chinese rice bowl mystery 16:26-29
Circulation—paper cup makes hot air engine (Primary) 201:18-19
Coal burning furnace needs fresh air 26:29-30
Cold air and warm air balloon—experiment 585:2-3
Cold air takes up less space experiment using balloon in refrigerator 1208:62-63
Cold air takes up less space experiment 940:30-31
Cold air, how to pour from jar experiment 1439:29-31
Cold makes air molecules contract—balloon experiment 651:18-19
Compressed—use compressed air to push water thru a pipe—experiment 385:23-25
Compressed air—compressing air under water 360:78
Compressed air—experiments 660:24-27
Compressed air—how to compress air 281:15
Compressed air—plastic bottle experiment to show force of 379:6
Compressed air—the steel straw 16:45-47
Compressed air—tiny molecules can lift a heavy object—demonstrate 385:22-23
Compressed air can lift things 44:28-29
Compressed air demonstration (simple) 227:12
Compressed air exerts force 44:27
Compressed air experiments—turn a wheel, service station lift, vacuum etc. 12:110-111
Compressed air has energy; balloon and candle demonstrate 882:22
Compressed air heats up; pump heat—experiment 585:129-130
Compressed air in balloon raises book experiment 705:85
Compressed air is heavier experiment using yardstick and balloons 1439:26-28
Compressed air rocket—making 150:34-35
Compressed air weighs more than normal air experiment 940:28-29
Compression—a bicycle pump and air compression 53:32-33
Concorde dart like paper plane cuts thru air experiment 995:26-27
Condensation—build a cloud chamber 293:12
Condensation of air makes your breath visible experiment 1439:40-41
Convection—a convection box—making 128:97
Convection current—bet you can make ashes float up in the air 228:76-77
Convection currents—a heat motor experiment 563:124-126
Convection currents—candle at the door experiment 360:16
Convection currents—colorful whirligigs to make 392:82-86
Convection currents—how heat travels in water and air 281:62-63
Convection currents—make a draft—experiment how winds are formed 563:121-122
Convection currents—producing convections in air 175:68
Convection currents in air 53:20-21
Convection, hot air screw spiral demonstrates, making 981:19
Convection 243:24-25

Cooling causes a balloon to get smaller experiment 1250:24-25
Cooling down and keeping warm (Primary) 210:9
Current detector, how to make 908:60-61
Currents—thermals—make a snake windmill for the top of the radiator 186:17-18
Currents box—smoke—water and heat demonstration model—making 723:27-28
Dew point; determining dew point experiment 1447:31-35
Do air molecules move farther apart as air is warmed experiment 831:18-20
Does air have weight; balloon on balance experiment 900:35
Does air really exist experiment 834:75-76
Does air take up space 55:23-31
Does all air burn experiment using candle in dish of water 1073:86
Does cold air sink experiment 852:39-40
Egg in bottle trick demonstrates air expands and contracts 1247:26-27
Egg in the bottle trick 53:12-13
Elastic air—experiment 30:19
Evaporation tells us about humidity; wet-dry bulb hygrometer experiment 900:87-88
Exerts pressure down 44:10-11
Exerts pressure equally in all directions 44:16-17
Exerts pressure sideways 44:15
Exerts pressure up 44:12-13
Expanding air—what happens to air when it is heated 253:55-56
Expands when heated 44:32-33
Expands when heated experiment 836:11-12
Expands when heated—experiment with a balloon 597:22-23
Expands when heated experiment with balloon and jar of hot water 1519:7
Expands when heated in soda bottle experiment 882:20
Expands when heated; bottle, glass tube and colored water experiment 837:56-57
Expansion—effected by color using balloons 92:32-33
Expansion—how heat blows up a balloon 281:55
Expansion—popping penny into bottle 95:30
Expansion and contraction—putting an egg in a bottle 293:44
Expansion and contraction of air 585:3-4
Expansion from heat—dancing dime trick 202:102
Expansion from heat—heated air makes shadow picture 95:22
Expansion from heat makes toy twirl around experiment 1079:103-105
Expansion of warm air—moving a coin without touching it 150:28-29
Expansion shown with balloons 92:26-27, 30-31
Expansion; measuring air expansion experiment 836:9-11
Experiment with air using a balloon and books (Primary) 580:unpaged
Experimenting with air 175:70-71
Fill a glass with air experiment 909:53
Find out if air contains water—ice cube and jar experiment (Primary) 452:59
Fire needs air to burn experiment 1028:9; 1255:5
Fire needs oxygen to burn experiment with candle 1255:22

Fountains of colored water demonstrate hot air expands experiment 1211:15
Fungi spores from air experiment 737:23
Gases all around? Demonstrate 589:40
Getting water out of the air 30:28-29; 72:31-32
Hair hygrometer measures humidity demonstration 1023:146-147
Has weight experiment using two balanced balloons 1211:9
Has weight experiment with two balloons 1372:19
Has weight experiments 718:18-20
Has weight, balloons balanced experiment 898:3
Heat makes air expand demonstration with hot water in jug 939:71-73
Heated—fan mobile working on warm air—making 112:32-33
Heated—heated air versus cold air—experiment 128:96-97
Heated—hot air, cold air experiment 30:20
Heated—star mobile to show air currents 112:34-35
Heated air causes distortions in visual observation of atmosphere experiment 1062:10-11
Heated air expands demonstration with balloon on bottle of hot water 1229:36-37
Heated air expands experiment 829:7-8
Heated air expands make fountain spout experiment 696:8-9
Heated air expands; balloon and water in jar experiment 891:58-59
Heated air expands; cold air contracts experiment 1032:12-14; 1032:15
Heated air expands; jar and balloon experiment 814:25-27
Heated air rises experiment with paper spiral 1372:32-33
Heated air takes up more space experiment with balloons 1084:27
Helicopter—making 32:50-51
Hot air balloon—making 186:18-19
Hot air detector spiral, how to make 1007:83
Hot air expands and cold air contracts experiment using soda bottles/balloons 1208:66-67
Hot air expands balloon and bottle experiment 705:13-14
Hot air expands cold air contracts experiments 705:14-15
Hot air is lighter than cold air experiment shows why hot air balloon rises 1208:64-65
Hot air paper bag 53:16-17
Hot air rises 44:87
Hot air rises experiment demonstrated with hot air balloon, how to make 1179:51
Hot air rises experiment using hot-air balloon 1294:122-124
Hot air rises experiment with plastic bag 1032:10
Hot air rises experiment, how to make hot air balloon 1161:9
Hot air rises experiment; pinwheel on dowel demonstrates 1161:9
Hot air rises experiment 898:4; 989:9
Hot air rises, spiral paper snake demonstrates 1014:110
Hot air takes up more space than cold experiment with balloon and soda bottle 1288:4-5
Hot and cold—heated and cooled 55:33-39
Hot-air balloon, how to make 909:59
How airplanes fly 72:18-21
How do suction cups work 281:13

How does cold air behave; smoke in refrigerator experiment 900:48
How much does air weigh 96:14-15
How much does air weigh—experiments 597:14
How much of air is oxygen experiment 1159:26-27
How much oxygen does the air contain 186:21-22
How much oxygen is in the air—experiment 360:30
How much oxygen is there in air—experiment 586:58-59
How water goes into air 72:30-31
How water goes into the air 30:27-28
Humidity—hair hygrometer—how to set up and measure 364:101
Humidity—make a hygrometer 95:25
Humidity—measure moisture in air—simple experiment 14:47-49
Humidity—relative humidity of air 55:145-151
Humidity; measuring humidity of air experiment using wet and dry thermometers 1134:2.002
Interaction of warm and cold air masses—demonstrate 253:49-50
Invert a glass of water without spilling a drop 186:9
Investigating hot air experiment 909:58
Is everywhere experiments 718:15-17
Jet with a balloon—making 32:44-45
Keep boat dry under water experiment 888:29-31
Keep paper tissue dry experiment 909:55
Keeps fire burning (Primary) 322:22-23
Kite, making with towing line 450:8-11
Life giving plants make oxygen 112:8-9
Lighter than water—not so thin air trick 399:12
Looking for air experiment 909:52
Magic tricks with air 718:35-37
Make flying paper tails to demonstrate moving air 450:5
Making an airplane rise—Bernoulli's principle 53:48-50
Making sound with hot air 293:46
Mapping air flows around object experiment using blow dryer, jar and flags 1095:12
Measure flow rate of stream of air—make pitot tube and manometer 363:155-156
Measure moisture in the air experiment 900:85-86
Model hovercraft floats on cushion of air experiment 1332:18-19
Moisture—making psychrometer 9:92-93
Moisture content—measure relative humidity with dry and wet bulb thermometers 291:40-41
Moves experiments 718:11-14
Moving—what happens when objects move thru air 225:18
Moving air—cooling effect of moving air—experiment 532:109
Moving air experiments 909:66-67
Moving air follows a surface—demonstrate 385:25-26
Moving air has less pressure than still air experiment 1250:21-23
Moving air has less pressure 96:11-12
Moving air pushes less; colliding balls experiment 924:22-23
Oven—making 9:78-79
Oxygen—measure proportion of in air 319:30-31
Oxygen content—demonstrate how much of air consists of oxygen gas 472:2236
Oxygen content in the air experiment using steel wool 1003:47
Oxygen content of air measured by rusting steel wool experiment 1447:71-73

Oxygen in air burns; other gases in air do not burn experiment 1073:86

Oxygen in air demonstration using lit candle under glass 1179:119

Oxygen in air in proportion to other gases experiment with candle/water in jar 1244:21

Oxygen in the air 53:51-52

Oxygen in the air—using candle and bottle—demonstrate 55:17-22

Oxygen in the air experiment with candle and jar 1480:153

Oxygen needed for fire to burn experiment using candle and different snuffers 1073:86

Oxygen: what fraction of air is oxygen experiment with steel wool in water 1526:105-107

Oxygen; amount of oxygen in air experiment 1322:13-16

Oxygen; how much of air is oxygen; rusting steel wool experiment 1020:90-92

Oxygen; proportion of oxygen in air experiment with candle under jar 1474:18

Oxygen; what fraction of air is oxygen experiment with rusting steel wool 1516:22-25

Paper airplane—making 32:48-49

Paper and coin trick—experiment 563:115

Parachute—making 32:52-53

Parachute—why does a parachute come down slowly (Primary) 210:7

Parachute drop demonstrates air has weight and takes up space 1014:123

Parachute game—making (Primary) 232:49

Particles in the air 53:56-57

Pick up paper without touching it 143:30-31

Pinwheel—making 32:46-47

Pinwheel—making (Primary) 181:39

Pinwheel shows air can move things 322:6-7

Pinwheel uses the kinetic energy of air experiment 1030:10-11

Plants need air Vaseline on leaves experiment 705:38-39

Plastic bag—experiments (Primary) 99:16-32

Pour a glass of air 30:11

Pouring air experiment 1255:5

Primary experiments with air and water 982:1-69

Properties of air activities for classroom 1291:1-2

Properties of air and water experiment 1161:5

Push and pull of moving air experiments 705:89-91

Put paper under water and keep it dry (Primary) 143:28-29

Reaction of burning candle and air experiment with tubes in pan of water 1526:108-113

Relative humidity measured by psychrometer demonstration 1023:148-149

Salt used to measure humidity demonstration 1023:150-151

Saturated air has 100% humidity experiment 1405:80-83

Scintillations; experimenting with scintillations [twinkling] 958:26

Seeing air experiment 1108:6

Show how heavy air is 186:10

Show how moisture comes out of air 128:99-101

Show how moisture gets into air 128:98-99

Show that some materials hold air 101:6-7

Simple air experiments [Primary] 757:128-129

Smoke ring cannon—making 723:151-152

Sound with air experiment 718:38-39

Spinner—making 450:18-19

'Squeezing' water out of air and air out of water 179:22-24

Stopping air from pushing 96:13-14

Strength of air demonstration 1023:124-125

Super straw force 109:16-17

Takes up space cold and warm air experiment worksheet given 747:7-8

Takes up space experiment 718:5-10; 854:16-17

Takes up space, cup in water experiment 898:2

Takes up space; balloon in bottle experiment 940:26-27

Temperature affects air molecules experiment using balloon in refrigerator 1439:32-34

Temperature and its effect on air movement demonstration 1023:130-131

Temperature and weight 53:14-15

Temperature and weight—a hot air paper bag 53:16-17

Temperature effect on air experiment; make smoke bottle and hot-air balloon 1211:10-11

Temperature of air; measuring experiment 939:8-18

Temperature; coldest temperature of air experiment 1515:35-36

The "bottle imp" experiment 585:9-10

The airborne bag—warm air lighter than cold—air experiment 291:63

The Coanda effect 585:6

The insulating value of air—computer project 584:94-95

The prune paratrooper 280:13

Thermal expansion of gas (how heat affects air)—computer project 584:96-97

Toys—ball raiser 366:164

Toys—balloon rocket 366:167

Toys—diver 366:165

Toys—draft detector 366:166

Toys—parachute 366:163

Toys—warm air balloon 366:164

Transfer air into cup of water experiment 888:26-28

Turbine—paper plate—demonstrate (Primary) 200:16-17

Use bottle imp to demonstrate compressibility of water and air 179:39-41

Using a siphon 53:36-37

Using straws (Primary) 24:18-21

Vacuum—blowing out a candle trick 202:104

Vacuum—demonstrate the Magdeburg tumblers 202:103

Vibrations in air demonstrated with propeller made from pencil and tape 1289:42-43

Volume and pressure experiment—plastic bags 12:37-40

Volume of air and temperature of air experiment 1516:66-67

Volume of air of a gas affected by temperature experiment 1515:17-19

Warm air—what happens to warm air 281:9

Warm air—what happens to warm air (Primary) 210:8

Warm air convection currents—merry-go-round mobile 356:42-43

Warm air expands and rises experiments 767:57

Warm air expands; inflate balloon without blowing into it experiment 924:24-25

Warm air goes up—simple experiment 14:11-16

Warm air is less dense than cold air experiment 1516:66-67

Warm air is lighter than cold air 44:34-35

Warm air lighter than cold 382:68-70, 124

Warm air moves up 96:17-18

11

Warm air rises (Primary) 324:9

Warm air rises and expands; dancing coin on bottle experiment 924:26

Warm air rises experiment 660:8-9; 1108:11; 836:12-14; 909:56; 718:21-24

Warm air rises experiment with spiral snake; pattern given 1255:14-15

Warm air rises paper spiral experiment 705:15-16; 900:43

Warm air rises; paper spiral over lamp bulb demonstrates 1439:15-18

Warm air rises; smoke and milk carton chimney demonstrate 837:60-61

Warm air rises; spinning snake demonstrates 909:57

Warm air takes up more space—experiments 660:10-11

Warm air takes up more space than cold air experiment 1003:45

Warm air weighs less 96:7

Warm and cold—magic winter bubbles (Primary) 109:19

Water barometer—how to make 55:124-125

Water evaporates into air—simple experiment 14:17-21

Water gets into the air through evaporation experiment 1439:62-64

Water in air—hygroscopic shortbread 112:17

Water is always in the air—experiment 671:19

Water is in the air—experiments (Primary) 327:20-35

Water trick—air can push and has weight (Primary) 232:86

Water vapor—how does water get into the air 400:65

Water vapor—make fog in a bottle 95:26-27

Water vapor—moisture in the air 400:65

Weather vane—making (Primary) 73:21-22

Weighing air experiment 1516:57-59

Weighing air experiment 660:6; 909:54

Weighing air 30:11-13; 72:13-14

Weighing the air—how to calibrate your homemade barometer 565:180-183

Weighing the air—how to make barometer from household items 565:173-187

Weighing the air experiment 1086:14

Weighs less than water—experiment 660:7

Weight—does air weigh anything 281:7

Weight—how much does air weigh 295:37

Weight—measure weight of air (metric weight) 357:28-29

Weight—the invisible pusher 280:15

Weight—which is heavier—hot air or cold air 281:8

Weight of air—experiment 563:117-118

Weight of atmosphere pushes air up chimney experiment 1126:10

Weight: prove air has weight 585:3

Weight; does air have weight experiment 851:40-41

What can air move experiment [Primary] 744:12

What happens if paper and cork fall through air—test for parachutes 450:12-13

What happens if you push things through the air? 450:16-17

What happens when air gets warmer experiment 900:26-27

What happens when air gets warmer; glass over candle in water experiment 900:45

What happens when air is heated experiment 793:28

What happens when air is heated or cooled experiment 851:39-40

What happens when air is heated; paper bags on balance experiment 900:44

What happens when warm air and cold air mix; experiment with two jars 900:49

What is it 34:25-27

What is wind 281:10

What makes water go up a straw 72:16

What percent of air is oxygen experiment 706:72

Whistle-stick, how to make 1066:22-23

Why does electric fan cool us 101:19

You can not empty a box (Primary) 143:36-37

You can stretch air (Primary) 143:38-40

AIR—COMPRESSED. *See also* **CARTESIAN DIVER**

Air can be compressed and water cannot; deep-jar diver demonstrates 1212:21

Compressed air demonstrated with blowing up balloon in bottle 1208:40-41

Compressed air has power experiment using balloon lifting book 1208:30-31

Compressed air is powerful experiment using plastic bottle/clay plug 1198:18

Compressed air makes water sprinkler and pop-gun work experiment 1211:25

Helicopter, making 909:72

Lifting books with air 909:72

Parachute tests 909:74

Pneumatic man is fired by squeezing plastic bottle experiment 1446:30-31

Rocket, making 909:73

AIR—CONVECTION

Air movements due to convection experiment with balanced yardstick 1174:21-23

Aluminum pie plate over candles turns from heated air experiment 1519:10

Can you predict movement of air experiment 871:1.006

Convection box experiment, how to make 900:107-108

Convection currents demonstrated with candles and chimneys on box experiment 767:58

Convection currents demonstrated with twirling mobiles above heat experiment 1179:55

Convection cycle currents in air experiment, make spiral air current detector 1311:21

Convection cycle of heated and cooled air experiment 1447:27-30

Do heating and cooling affect air currents experiment 900:104-106

Hot air rises experiment using mobile, how to make 1332:10-11

Hot air rises experiment with hot-air balloon, how to make 1332:12-13

Revolving serpent toy demonstrates, how to make 861:145-150

Sea breeze convection currents experiment 767:59

Simulate how convection appears in atmosphere experiment 1465:28-29

Spinning snake from aluminum pie pan demonstrates 770:168

Temperature effect on air movement experiment with paper spiral 1479:78

Traveling heat—hot air rises—experiment 587:40

Warm and cool air cause convection currents; candle in box experiment 882:23

AIR—CONVECTION CURRENTS

Hot air balloons—making 737:15

AIR—PRESSURE. *See* **AIR PRESSURE**

AIR—PROPERTIES OF

How does air in bottle differ after bottle is held upside down over candle 168:43

AIR AND ITS GASES

Experiments to show 116:115-128

AIR CONDITIONERS

Water evaporation cools things experiment using clay pot/bottles of juice 1228:66-67

AIR INVERSION

Air inversion, what causes it experiment 1003:48-49

AIR MASS. *See* **CLOUDS; WEATHER**

AIR PLANTS

Exhibit of air plants 532:53

Plant that lives on air, how to grow 899:198-199

AIR POLLUTION. *See also* **LICHENS; POLLUTION— AIR; SMOG**

Acid rain effect on plants experiment 1063:364; 1324:60-64

Acid rain effect on statues and buildings experiment 1063:365

Acid rain effects on materials experiments 777:16

Air borne particles in air; paper and petroleum jelly experiment 1014:118

Air dirt collectors—making and using 400:13

Air filter—making 363:148

Air inversion, what causes it experiment 1003:48-49

Air particle collector experiment 1063:360

Air pollution and effect on plant growth experiment 874:217

Air pollution harms plants—experiments 10:21-25

Air Quality Index is higher on sunny day than rainy day experiment 1322:65-68

Air samples from indoor and outdoor air on Vaseline coated slides experiment 762:37-38

Airborne acid corrosion experiment with pieces of nylon stockings 1476:189

Airborne particulate matter or dust in household rooms project 969:88-89

Aluminum foil—corrosion test 363:141-142

Ammonia released from pea seeds experiment 933:49

Amount in air—measure 358:96-97

Analyzing dust from the air experiment 933:10

Auto emissions, convection, temp. Inversions, photo chemicals—smog experiment 371:45-50

Auto exhausts—Vaseline coated card test for pollutants—experiment 10:18

Automobile emissions and particulates in the air—experiment 371:38-45

Automobile exhaust particles experiment 705:118

Breath scrubber—limewater and candle measure carbon dioxide 363:144-146

Bucket of water collects traveling air pollution experiment 1328:36-37

Burning garbage creates smoke and ash experiment; chart for results given 1173:55-57

Burning rubbish, garbage, etc.—experiment for smell and combustion product 363:149

Capturing particles from the air experiment 1150:70-72

Car that is nonpolluting; build model car project 1458:34-35

Carbon dioxide from rotting vegetation experiment 933:47

Carbon dioxide gas made when marble and calcite dissolve in vinegar experiment 1295:98

Carbon dioxide; effects of industrial carbon dioxide on plant growth experiment 1174:49-50

Causes of—Vaseline coated cards to check visible sources of pollution 10:16-20

Chemical erosion of statues experiment using coins, salt and vinegar 1228:40-41

Chemicals travel through the air experiment using balloon and perfume 1228:24-25

Cigarette smoke effect on growing radish plants experiment 1328:38-39

Cigarette smoke pollutes your internal environment experiment 1427:56-58

Cigarette smoking machine experiment 933:41-42

Clothing affected by air pollution experiment 705:120-121

Coffee filter pollution tester, making 1017:50-51

Collecting acid rain experiment 950:169

Composition (makeup) and pollutants in the air 371:29-32

Cotton and felt air pollution testing device, how to make 834:140-142

Counting particles in the air experiment 705:116-118

Create smog in a jar experiment 1063:361

Detect amount of pollution in air with jar lids/bottle tops on cardboard 1414:11

Determine which section of town contains most airborne particles experiment 997:95-96

Dirt on evergreen trees affects photosynthesis experiment 1134:6.004

Dirty air check with coffee filters and petroleum jelly experiment 1240:45-46

Dust and debris collectors experiment 759:52

Dust particles in indoor and outdoor air experiment 1134:6.002

Dust particles in outside and inside air experiment 1322:75-79

Effects of air pollution on rubber bands experiment 1150:73-74

Effects of carbon dioxide and changing weather conditions on Earth—experiment 371:52

Effects of polluted air on stretched rubber bands on coat hangers experiment 1427:50-52

Erupting volcanoes produce sulfur dioxide experiment 1174:43-45

Estimate air pollution project 1070:30-31

Evidence of air pollution experiment 874:216-217

Exhaust fumes effect on germinating seeds experiment 933:43-45

Factory smoke stacks; taller the stacks farther the winds take pollution 1328:40-41

Forest fires and their role in naturally polluting the air—experiment 371:36-38

Forest fires produce carbon dioxide experiment 1174:40-41

Game; Drive from Home to School board game; get pollution points, make 1328:44-45

Grow algae collected on paper tissue from rain 597:49

Growth of plants affected by smoke experiment 1061:37-38

Harmful particulates in air from incomplete burning of fossil fuels experiment 1453:34-36

How clean is the air experiment with index cards and petroleum jelly 1476:188

Hydrocarbons in air pollution damage clothing experiment 1322:60-64

Hydrogen sulfide from rotting vegetation experiment 933:48

Identify components of atmospheric dust experiment 933:16-17

Increased carbon dioxide levels in atmosphere increase plant growth experiment 1174:49-50

Indoor pollution experiment using styrofoam cup 1324:69-72

Inversion model using aquarium and blue ink experiment 767:59

Killer smog—make smog in a jar or jug—experiment 10:34-38

Leaf fungi as indicator organisms for air pollution experiment 1134:6.005

Leaf washing experiment to determine amount of air pollution 1362:10

Lichen plants very sensitive to air pollution experiment 1145:30

Lichen test for amount of air pollution experiment 1362:22

Lichens and pollution experiment 737:35

Lichens response to smoke—air pollution experiment 714:118-119

Lichens show pollution 112:21

Light blocked by particulate matter and its effect on temperature experiment 969:100-101

Make your own smog experiment 906:30-31

Mass transportation saves fuel and reduces pollution experiment 969:111-112

Measure air pollution and keep records 508:17

Measure air pollution with sticky paper squares experiment 1379:34

Measure amount of pollutants using card and Vaseline experiment 760:53

Measure particulate matter sent into air from chimneys experiment 969:108-109

Measuring amount of sulfur dioxide in air experiment 933:26-28

Measuring oxygen content of air experiment 933:8-9

Measuring shade effect of soot on plant leaves experiment 933:21-23

Measuring soot content of atmosphere experiment 933:11-15

Methane gas from sewage [horse manure] experiment 933:50-51

Natural substances can be used as room deodorizers experiment 969:94-95

Nylon stocking squares collect pollutants 53:58-59

Nylon stockings sensitive to acid pollutants experiment 1322:64

Our polluted atmosphere—nylon stocking test for dirt and fumes 10:26-29

Ozone; make and smell ozone experiment 1322:69-72

Paper plate coated with Vaseline experiment 767:33

Paper towel measures air pollution in rain experiment 890:95

Particle trap—making 264:98

Particles in air measured experiment with index cards and petroleum jelly 1476:188

Particles in the air—Vaseline on cards—experiment to trap particles 10:13-15

Particles in the air 53:56-57

Particulate sampling panel—how to make 363:146-148

pH level of rain, how to measure experiment; pH scale given 1063:363

pH of rainfall, how to measure 1233:22-23

Plants—growth effected by air pollutants 398:56-60

Plants prove pollution; lichens absorb sulfuric acid 617:31

Pollution can harm clothing experiment 1322:60-64

Pollution collector—making 737:33

Rubber band test for polluted air 264:98

Simple experiment to collect dirt and dust in air with bowls of jelly 1105:23

Smog—making 112:21

Smog—making a climate experiment 737:19

Smog formation demonstration 1020:57-59

Smog formation; demonstrate how smog is formed experiment 978:171-172

Smoke density scale experiment 705:114-115

Smoke has tiny solid particles experiment 1322:84-88

Smoke in the air from many sources experiment 978:170-171

Smoking & air pollution—experiment—effect of cigarette. Smoke on living organ 10:32-33

Smoking & air pollution—Vaseline coated cards check smoking/nonsmoking on living organ 10:32-33

Smoky air 243:20-21

Snow pollution tester and chart, how to make 850:23

Static electricity charge removes dust particles from air experiment 1322:89-92

Sulfur dioxide harms plants experiment 1324:65-68

Sulfur dioxide gas effect on growth of seedlings experiment 1134:6.003

Tar, carbon dioxide, monoxide, hydrogen sulfide in coal smoke experiment 933:37-38

Temperature inversion experiment 1174:23-26; 769:23-28,36-37

Temperature inversion experiment; demonstrate what happens 978:173

Temperature inversion experiment; observe how warm air traps smoke particles 1447:68-70

Temperature inversion prevents convection and makes air stagnant experiment 1174:23-26

Test air for visible pollutants using jar and petroleum jelly experiment 1013:103

Test amount of air pollution around you experiment using petroleum jelly 1427:47-49

Test for air pollution in area using jar and petroleum jelly 1012:97-98

Test for air pollution in your home experiment 1161:30

Test for air pollution using white plate and petroleum jelly experiment 1371:34

Test for air pollution; sticky numbers on jar lids experiment 1362:11

Test for polluted air experiment using rubber bands 1371:32-33

Test pollution in your house with vacuum cleaner and cloth filters experiment 1328:34-35

Testing for 694:27-28

Thermal inversion effect on air pollution experiment 1322:55-59

Trapping fungal spores and pollen grains from the atmosphere experiment 933:31

Vaseline and cardboard collect particles in air experiment 950:156

Vaseline on cardboard demonstrates air pollution 854:24

Venturi tube—how to make 363:154-155

Volcanic action cools the Earth—experiment 371:50

Volcanic pollution of the air—experiment 371:32-36

Water scrubber to test for airborne materials—making 363:142-144

Watering plants with vinegar water solution to show effects of acid rain 1331:86-87

Ways to collect dust in air 1020:60-61

Weather affects air pollution experiment 1322:65-68

Weigh deposits of soot on plant leaves experiment 933:18-20

White cloth measures air pollution experiment 1388:26

White paper left outside to collect dust and debris experiment 1003:50

Wind and air pollution 243:54-55

AIR PRESSURE. *See also* **BAROMETER; PARACHUTES; SIPHONS**

A banana skins itself in a bottle 186:12

A bottle gun 114:38-39

A bottle trick experiment 563:116

A breath taking chance 222:53

A collapsing can 114:51-53

A colored geyser 114:53-56

A crushing experience 53:34-35

A mysterious pair of balloons 114:105-106

A radish vacuum 360:32-33

A trick bottle 281:12

Air and lift—demonstrate 225:19-21

Air boils water experiment; make water bubbles without heating it 1007:10-12

Air can hold a stick down 281:15

Air cannon shoots vortex of whirling air called a torus experiment 1330:82-85

Air crushes plastic bottle experiment 995:12

Air exerts pressure 128:77-79

Air exerts pressure down 44:10

Air exerts pressure equally in all directions 44:16

Air exerts pressure in all directions experiment 829:9-10

Air exerts pressure on glass filled with water experiment 1447:74-76

Air exerts pressure sideways 44:15

Air exerts pressure up 44:12

Air expands when heated experiment with balloons 1281:5

Air goes around can and blows out candle experiment 995:21

Air has pressure 30:14-15

Air has pressure—experiment 400:64; 718:24-32

Air has weight 44:7

Air has weight and exerts pressure experiment 1311:10-11

Air has weight experiment 706:74

Air holds up water in upside down glass experiment 1281:5

Air in balloon and large air bag demonstrates power of air pressure 1004:3.013

Air occupies space 44:8

Air power—move books with balloon 288:46-47

Air presses in all directions 281:10-11

Air presses in all directions—experiment 671:25-26

Air presses in all directions on balloon 360:68

Air presses in all directions water in glass experiment 705:9

Air pressure 72:17

Air pressure—experiment (Primary) 73:12-14; 73:6-9

Air pressure—experiments 693:52-53, 57-60

Air pressure affects water level experiment 939:109-111

Air pressure and falling objects 53:42-43

Air pressure and gravity using water experiment 696:30-31

Air pressure and suction cups 53:40-41

Air pressure atomizer—making 281:18

Air pressure can cause destruction 55:97-101

Air pressure decreases as its velocity increases 44:24-25

Air pressure demonstration construct simple barometer experiment 752:109-110

Air pressure demonstration with ruler and newspaper 1405:78

Air pressure demonstrations 577:project #12

Air pressure exists—2 experiments to show 399:36-37

Air pressure exists experiment with paper and glass in bowl of water 1465:37

Air pressure experiments 1079:108-126; 507:1896; 767:70

Air pressure greatest near the ground experiment with bottle of water 1465:39-40

Air pressure holds liquid in a tube experiment 837:19

Air pressure in tires 12:38-39, 108

Air pressure is all around us experiment 1126:26-27

Air pressure is needed to drink from a straw 44:18-19

Air pressure machine, squeeze bottle and string, making 1014:132

Air pressure makes spouting fountain experiment 1121:25

Air pressure makes squeeze bottle into shower experiment 1121:24

Air pressure pushes in which directions; crushed can experiment 900:37

Air pressure stronger than gravity experiment with rubber plunger 1251:29-30

Air pressure supports column of water experiments 1157:63-66

Air pressure weather tester—making 656:28-29

Air pressure; how measured demonstration 1023:142-143

Air pushes glass and straw demonstrate 759:34-35

Air pushes in all directions experiment 706:75-76

Airy surprises experiments 685:20-21

An ejector seat 146:37

Apples suspended on string move together when blown on experiment 971:13

Automatic water can—making 112:28

Balancing air pressure and water pressures in inverted containers 604:16-19

Ball stays on fountain of air from hair dryer experiment 1330:26-27

Balloon barometer—making 92:36-37

Balloon blown up, goes inside small bottle experiment 781:22-23

Balloon filled with air raises book experiment 1066:35

Balloon in a bottle—demonstration 360:72

Balloon in a glass (Primary) 73:18-19

Balloon in a jug experiment 563:114

Balloon sings different sounds experiment 1066:34

Balloons—show 92:54-55

Balloons as air-head persons experiment to demonstrate air pressure 1066:36-37

Balloons hanging on string move together when you blow on them experiment 999:120-121

Balloons move together when you blow on them experiment 995:20

Barometer—how to build (Primary) 327:42-43

Barometer—how to make 909:62; 293:11-12

Barometer—simple—making 236:163

Barometer and drinking fountain for birds in one—making 186:11

Barometer measures air pressure experiment 1042:32-33; 1332:8-9

Barometer measures air pressure experiment, how to make 1211:18

Barometer measures air pressure, how to make from glass jar and straw 1387:16

Barometer measures air pressure, how to make from glass, balloon/straws 1179:123

Barometer measures changes in atmospheric pressure 44:36-37

Barometer measures fluctuations in air pressure experiment, how to make 1447:38-41

Barometer measures pressure of air experiment, how to make 1063:442

Barometer measures pressure of air, how to make 1311:11

Barometer, straw and chart show changes in air pressure (Primary) 541:36-37

Bernoulli effect—air pressure draws electric bulb together—mystery 291:89

Bernoulli effect—blow paper square off a spool 291:92-93

Bernoulli effect—drop card into a bowl 291:98-99

Bernoulli effect—the dancing ball 291:90-91

Bernoulli's principle—blow ping pong ball out of funnel 291:96-97

Bernoulli's principle—demonstrate principles of flight 291:102

Bernoulli's principle—moving air and pressure 53:44-45

Bernoulli's principle—the aerobatic coin 16:53-55

Bernoulli's principle—what holds up an airplane 55:153-159

Bernoulli's principle—with spool and card—demonstrate 202:108-109

Blow in a bottle to blow a ball out (Primary) 64:unpaged

Blow out proof 222:57

Blowing a chance 222:52

Blowing out a candle through a funnel 150:16-17

Blowing straw at two ping pong balls demonstrates 846:22-23

Boat stays up in water glass magic trick 1216:34-36

Boiled egg in a bottle demonstrates 940:49-51

Bottle cannon, vinegar and baking soda experiment 1002:31

Bottle spouts like a fountain 186:12-13

Bottle trick with red string soap demonstrates air pressure 1066:38-39

Boyle's measuring the "spring" of the air experiment 1133:7.002

Breaking a stick with newspaper experiment 924:16-17

Breaking the newspaper (newspaper and ruler trick) 364:133

Can air hold up water 281:11

Can change in air pressure create a pulling force experiment 851:42-43

Can support a column of water—experiment 507:1896

Candle in bottle; banana is pulled into bottle experiment 1002:30-31

Card holds water in glass 670:74

Card over glass of water experiment 748:115

Card trick demonstrates 288:34-35

Cardboard keeps water in glass experiment [Primary] 1002:8

Carry glass of water upside down experiment 696:33

Cartesian diver—experiments—recover treasure from bottom of bottle 54:102-112

Cartesian diver—how to make 291:76; 363:156-157; 472:2213

Cartesian diver experiment, how to make 1007:17-19

Coin jumps up and down on plastic bottle experiment 1066:24-25

Collapsing bottle experiment demonstrates air pressure 1066:21

Collapsing can demonstrates 882:21

Collapsing can experiment demonstrates air pressure 1179:123

Collapsing can experiment 748:114

Collapsing jug experiment 906:26

Collapsing paper tent demonstrates air pressure 1066:31

Collapsing plastic bottle demonstrates air pressure 1028:7

Collapsing plastic bottle experiment 1255:6; 1480:157

Compressed air can lift things 44:28

Compressed air exerts force 44:27

Creating air pressure 12:107-112

Crumpled can experiment 27:96-97; 705:8; 767:69

Crush a metal can with air 291:86

Crush can with air pressure experiment 1211:17

Crush the can or jug experiment 700:55-56

Crushes a can 179:27-28

Crushing a can with air pressure 147:66-67

Cups stick to inflated balloon using water, not glue experiment 1208:14-15

Defy gravity; stop water from flowing out of bottle experiment 1031:28

Demo air pressure by blowing up balloon under book or can (Primary) 452:58

Demonstrate air pressure with yardstick and newspaper experiment 1084:20-21

Demonstrate low air pressure experiment 836:33-34

Demonstrating air pressure 150:20-21; 150:30-31

Demonstrations of 295:50-51

Difference in air pressure causes air to flow experiment using balloons 1208:22-23

Dipping water with a straw experiment 1230:16-17

Discovering air pressure 53:24-25

Diving bell—making 112:26-27

Does air exert pressure 55:91-95

Does air have weight experiment 831:15-17

Don't get wet 114:56-57

Dribble glass demonstrates 203:71

Drink milk with two straws 291:79

Drinking through a straw affected by gravity experiment 1399:62-63

Effect of air pressure demonstrated with glass of water and card 1387:15

Effects of air pressure—demonstrate 293:10-11

Effects of compressed air—experiment 128:85

Egg and bottle trick 660:17; 909:65

Egg comes out of bottle 179:25-27

Egg in a bottle trick 30:21-22; 202:101; 203:38-39

Egg in the bottle trick experiment 827:72

Egg is sucked into bottle with burning paper inside it experiment 1229:48-49

Egg jumps out of cup by blowing on it experiment 1007:23-24

Eggs sucked into narrow necked bottle experiment 1011:55

Empty water from glass without touching it experiment 1229:34-35

Expanding balloon experiment 906:24

Experiments to demonstrate air pressure 1063:339

Experiments to show 34:12-19

Experiments to show—simple 105:24-27

Experiments using air pressure I 597:16-17

Experiments using air pressure II 597:18-19

Experiments with amount of air balloons will hold 994:10-18

Experiments with balloon, newspaper and ruler, ping pong ball and funnel 1004:1.002

Experiments with cups—cup hums, roars, music maker, hear a heart beat 64:unpaged

Exploding egg—making 112:29

Feel air pressure with plunger (Primary) 541:34

File card folded won't blow over experiment 999:115-116

Filling a bottle by remote control 179:30-31

Floating ball demonstrates 202:105

Floating ping pong ball over straw demonstrates 999:122-123

Force exerted by pressure of air experiment 752:111-112

Fountain demonstrates—making 660:16

Fountain machine experiment 906:25

Fountain, how to make 909:64

From walking tumblers to hovercraft 161:51-52

Funnel and simple experiments demonstrate air pressure 846:14-19

Gas expansion bottle thermometer, making 906:22-23

Gathering waters—about vacuum cleaning 205:56-59

Genie in a bottle 114:32-34

Glass of water demonstrates 181:40-41

Glass of water turned upside down doesn't spill experiment 1007:12-13

Glass of water with cardboard demonstrates 721:12

Glasses brim to brim trick 202:114

Hanging apples demonstrate air pressure 1211:21

Heavy air yardstick and newspaper experiment 906:29

Heavy reading—the weight of air (break stick held by newspaper) 205:48-52

Hot air—cold air 72:22-24

Hovercraft—making 112:30-31; 142:23

Hovercraft experiment demonstrates air pressure 1108:12

Hovercrafts travel on cushion of air demonstration 1208:34-35

How air makes airplanes fly 576:73-74

How can air help us drink; straw in bottle experiment 900:42

How can air pressure make things stronger experiment 900:5

How does a straw work 281:12-13

How does air pressure affect water flow experiment 900:28

How hard can air push experiment 900:8

How hard can air push; balloon in bottle experiment 900:41

How pumps use air pressure 128:82-84

How straws work—experiment 660:16

How to measure air pressure 55:123-129

How your soda climbs the straw 280:14

Hydraulic lift, making 906:151

In eardrums; the elevator 55:103-107

In lungs 55:109-113

Index card holds water in upside down glass experiment 1009:16-17

Inside-out balloon experiments 563:118-119

Inverted glass experiment 906:21

Inverted tumbler—experiments with 54:69-100

Invisible bottle squasher 419:24

Juice experiment you can drink 671:27

Keep paper dry under water experiment 924:18

Keeping a card from falling by blowing down on it 150:6-7

Kitchen sink plungers demonstrate air pressure 1211:20

Leaky can trick and drinking straw trick demonstrate air pressure 1296:1997

Let air show its muscles—lift books with balloon 360:22

Lift 20 lbs of books with your breath 186:13-14

Lift a dime with soda straw 291:64-65

Lift a heavy object with balloon filled with air or water 156:28-29

Lift a heavy weight 585:7-8

Lift an upside down glass of water (Primary) 64:unpaged

Lift heavy container by blowing air experiment 1231:28-29

Lift pump—making 142:20

Lifting a glass with air pressure 150:22-23

Lifting action of water—make a piston and cylinder 385:17-18

Liquids rise in a tube experiment with straws 837:15-16

Loaded words—bet you can't flip a newspaper into the air with a ruler 222:48-49

Lung power experiments 563:114-115

Magdeburg Sphere principle experiment with glasses and candle 1007:14-16

Magic glass holds water 909:63

Magic jar #2 27:98-99

Make water in a bottle rise 291:209

Make water run uphill 385:14-15

Make your own smog experiment 906:30-31

Making a balloon almost impossible to blow up 150:18-19

Making a bottle rise and fall in water 150:10-11

Making a candle lift water 150:8-9

Making a dime dance 179:24-25

Making a fountain inside a bottle 150:38-39

Measure air pressure experiment; making a barometer 900.83-84

Measure air pressure with barometers 128:80-82

Milk bottle octopus experiments 563:112-113

Miniature fountain to show water and air pressure—making 142:21

Move a column of water 360:61-63

Moving two apples together without touching them 150:2-3

Mystery bottle experiment 563:120-121

Needed to drink from straw 44:18-19

Newspaper and ruler demonstrate 709:56-57

Newspaper sheet clings to table experiment 827:28

No windfall here 222:58

No-leak lunch bag trick experiment demonstrates air pressure 1288:22-23

Oil tin crushed by air pressure 186:9

Oxygen consumption helps reduce air pressure 44:20-21

Painting with air spray experiment 1373:30

Paper hearts come together when you blow between them experiment 1288:10-11

Paper in glass of water stays dry experiment 827:29

Paper napkin in glass of water stays dry experiment demonstrates air pressure 1064:34

Paper stays dry in under water glass demonstration 1230:22-23

Paper stays tight on mouth of bottle when submerged 722:28

Parachutes, how to make 1299:46

Pea spins over jet of air from straw experiment 1007:21-23

Pick up glass of water without touching glass experiment with blown up balloon 1208:38-39

Ping pong ball lifted from one glass to other demonstrates air pressure 1330:32-33

Ping-pong balls fly above stream of air experiment 1066:26-27

Pinwheel, paper, making 999:124-126

Plastic bottle demonstrates pressure in center of tornado experiment 1003:62-63

Plastic parachute, how to make to demonstrate air pressure 1066:32-33

Popping coin experiment 906:23

Popping ears due to change in air pressure experiment using balloons 1208:24-25

Potato puncture trick 202:99

Pouring air from one glass to another underwater 150:26-27

Pouring air into water 16:42-44

Power in air pressure—experiment 360:18-19

Power of air—experiments 660:14-15

Power of air pressure pushes water up straws experiment 1231:8-9

Power of air; ruler and paper trick 909:63

Predicting weather with air pressure experiment 767:72

Pressing air—air presses all ways on things 588:38

Pressure makes tin can crumple 472:2215

Pressure of air in a heated can 243:14-15

Pressure of fast air versus slow moving air experiment 829:11-12

Proving air pressure 617:4

Puffa-chute, making 669:32-33

Pump water out by blowing in tube 291:82-83

Puncture balloon without bursting it 291:66-67

Pushing paper underwater without getting it wet 150:4-5

Quarter sticks to wood from air pressure experiment 1007:24-25

Reducing air pressure with a funnel experiment 1436:6-8

Relationship between moving air and its pressure; ping pong balls experiment 900:13

Repeat Otto Van Guericke's air pressure experiment 448:37-38

Results of reducing air pressure—demonstrate 128:85-86

Reversible balloon experiment 906:27

Rising water candle experiment 906:28

Rubber sink plunger experiment 30:18

Ruler and newspaper demonstrate 419:24

Ruler and paper demonstrates 705:7

Ruler under newspaper demonstrates air pressure 1064:36

Ruler under newspaper on table breaks when hit experiment 1211:16

Ruler under sheet of paper demonstrates air pressure 1281:4

Satellite balloon demonstrates rapid cooling of air creates vacuum 669:44-45

Set up for investigating air pressure, how to make and use 891:19-22

Shrinking can experiment 924:27

Simple diving bell experiment 1007:16-17

Siphon—experiment (Primary) 73:15-17

Siphon—making 112:30

Siphon experiments; how to do and how to have siphon race 1157:68-70

Siphons—using 55:131-135

Siphons—using to show air pressure 53:36-37

Siphons use air pressure—show 128:84

Size of balloon affects air pressure inside balloon demonstration 1404:172-173

Soap bubble carries passenger man experiment, pattern given 1007:20-21

Soda straw atomizer experiment 563:111-112

Some surprises about air pressure 281:16

Sonic egg experiment 906:17

Speed of air affects its pressure 44:22-23

Speed of air flow affects air pressure experiment 1405:96-97

Spray gun, simple, making 981:15

Sprayers, principle of; when air goes faster its pressure falls 1211:22

Sprayers; how perfume sprayers work experiment 1405:97

Spraying fountain produced by using air pressure experiment 1405:79

Squeezing the air—ruler and newspaper experiment 360:21

Squirting bottle experiment 906:20

Stick two glasses together with air 186:13

Sticky cardboard and spool demonstrates force of air pressure 576:74

Straw picks up apple 288:26-27

Straw plunging through raw potato demonstrates air pressure experiment 1065:14

Straw; can straw work in sealed bottle experiment 1399:60-62

Straws and elephant trunks—experiment 30:16-17

Strength of air pressure demonstration with straw and potato 1405:80

Strong paper—paper holds down ruler 588:39

Suction cups stick like glue experiment to demonstrate air pressure 1208:32-33

Temperature affects air pressure demonstration 1479:78

Temperature affects air pressure experiment 1023:128-129

Temperature changes air pressure experiment 706:75

Test your strength with newspaper and ruler 399:2

The blow bottle experiment 563:126

The bouncing balloon—experiment 585:1-2

The chicken fountain experiment 563:116-117

The clinging cup—support by air pressure 205:52-55

The dancing balloon experiment (Bernoulli principle) 563:123-124

The direction of air pressure 53:26-27

The egg in the bottle trick 53:12-13

The elevator card experiment (Bernoulli principle) 563:127-128

The gypsy's brew 16:48-52

The hanging glass experiments 563:119-120

The leak proof hole 222:50-51

The magic bottle (Primary) 288:6-7
The mischievous ball—experiment (Bernoulli effect) 563:124
The obedient egg 72:24-25
The odds against blowing up 222:54-55
The rising paper experiment (Bernoulli principle) 563:122
The siphon 281:14
Tissue in glass of water experiment 900:7
Topsy turvy water (turn glass upside down) 112:29
Trick—soda bottle and straw race 392:33-35
Trick straw race demonstrates air pressure 1066:30
Tricks with air pressure 947:30-31
Tumbling dimes and sticky pennies—coins demonstrate air pressure 548:87-90
Two tests for air pressure 625:26
Two worse than one straw experiment 906:19
Up against the odds 222:59
Upside down magic with glass of water and postcard 419:24
Using air pressure to break a stick 53:38-39
Using air to stop a waterfall, water, glass, and paper experiment 888:32-34
Vacuum—boiling without heat trick 202:107
Vacuum causes metal can to collapse 605:9
Vooomm! Box blows out candle experiment 906:30
Wasted breath 222:56
Water and air pressure experiment with can and tubing 867:23-24
Water carried in a straw experiment 696:32
Water doesn't run out of glass experiment 926:56
Water enters upside down jar; candle and jar experiment 924:30-31
Water filled milk container with three holes demonstrates air pressure 1140:102-103
Water flows from can experiment to demonstrate air pressure 1003:60
Water flows uphill experiment using plastic bottle, tubing and balloon 1208:46-47
Water stays in a straw 73:10-11
Water stays in glass turned upside down demonstration 1388:13
Water stays in glass turned upside down; magic trick experiment 966:54-57
Water stays in overturned glass experiment 827:30
Water stays in upside down glass covered with cardboard experiment 1230:20-21
Water stays in upside down glass experiment 1216:46-48
Water stays in upturned glass demonstration 1028:7
Water stays inside upside down glass experiment 995:13
What can a card teach you about air experiment 900:6
What can air do to an egg experiment 900:3-4
What goes up may not come down 400:65
What is air pressure; glass of water and paper experiment 851:38-39
Why no blow up—experiment (Bernoulli principle) 563:123
Yardstick under paper on table experiment 940:46-48

AIR PUMPS
Boyle's and Charles's law 577:project #19

AIR RESISTANCE. *See also* **GLIDERS; PARACHUTES**
Air resistance as a life saver 161:55
Air slows things down 281:16
Blow a flame towards you 161:53-55
Blowing out a candle behind a bottle 150:14-15

Card trick demonstrates air resistance 966:49-53
Demonstrate with apple air streams 203:86
Drag race—aerodynamic action 205:59-62
Dropping a playing card onto a table 150:12-13
Experiment to show air resistance 106:29-34
Falling balls experiment 1159:46-47
Falling twirler demonstrates wind resistance 999:107-109
Falling; some objects fall slower than others experiment 1507:6
Free fall spinner demonstrates wind resistance, making 999:105-106
Parachute experiment 563:126
Parachute from handkerchief and metal washers experiment 1159:49-52
Parachute model demonstrates 472:2233
Parachute, simple, demonstrates [Primary] 1002:7
Parachutes; which material is best for a parachute experiment 1507:9
Parachutes; which shape makes the best parachute experiment 1507:8
Reducing air resistance experiment with book and sheet of paper 1159:47-49
Simple paper cup demonstration (Primary) 201:12-15

AIRCRAFT. *See also* **AERONAUTICS; AIRPLANES; GLIDERS; HELICOPTERS; JETS**
Make a wing section 379:11

AIRCRAFT—INSTRUMENTS
Make a model artificial horizon (gyroscope) 379:13

AIRCRAFT—JETS
How to make and flight test your own aircraft lift—how lift works 379:8-9
Jet noise decibels rating chart 379:21
Lift—how lift works 379:9
Sonic boom—small scale sound experiment 379:19
Thrust from compressed air—plastic bottle experiment—show force of 379:6
Why is Blackbird Spy Jet painted black—experiment 379:25

AIRCRAFT CARRIER
Model—how to make 431:26-27

AIRFLOW
Experiments to show 34:20-24

AIRFOILS
Airfoil principle demonstrated with postcard, straws and blowing air 1073:19
Airfoil principle demonstrated with water and spoon 1165:13
How to make and demonstrate 225:20-21
Make and demonstrate airfoils with fan experiment 940:133-134
Model airfoil demonstrates upward pushing force called lift experiment 1376:21
Testing pressure of moving air with paper airfoils and paper flags experiment 1110:21-23
What makes an airfoil experiment 1436:9-11
Which angle of attack generates the most lift experiment 997:151-155

AIRPLANES. *See also* **AERONAUTICS; HELICOPTERS; HOT AIR BALLOONS; JETS**
Acrobatic paper plane, how to make 1299:43
Air race board game, making 856:28-29
Air Scorpion paper airplane, how to make 1063:483
Air Scorpion, paper, making 856:12-13
Airfoils; what makes an airfoil experiment 1436:9-11
Airplane—solar powered 39:109-124

19

Amazing homemade airplanes—straw making plane and heli-paper 399:76-77

Balance plane tester, making 856:36-37

Balloon experiment to show how jet engine pushes airplane forward 450:26-27

Balsa wood plane, patterns given, how to make 1110:19-20

Barnaby paper airplane, how to make 1063:482

Bernoulli Effect; how airplanes fly experiment 1164:73-75

Biplane—making (Primary) 113:8-9

Blunt nose paper airplane, how to make 1063:481

Buffalo MK 1 and 2, paper, making 856:10-11

Catapult launcher for paper airplane, how to make 1419:21

Concorde dart like plane cuts thru air experiment 995:26-27

Dart paper airplane model, how to make 1063:477

Delta aircraft model—how to make 431:28

Delta wing paper plane, how to make 1299:42

Delta wing, how to make from paper and balsa wood 1392:29

Demonstrating how an airplane works project 833:286

Design and plane parts affect flying of plane experiments 1063:478-479

Direction in flight experiment using paper airplanes 1110:24-25

Elastic balsa wood flyer demonstrates energy stored in rubber band 1179:74-75

Electric propulsion airplane—making 176:78-79

Engine; how does airplane's jet engine work experiment 1293:11-12

Experiment to show power of a propeller 446:29-32

Experimental superplane, making 890:90-93

Fighter plane—making (Primary) 113:20-21

Flying saucer—making (Primary) 111:12-13

Folded paper plane—making (Primary) 113:12-13

Folded planes—making (Primary) 111:6-7

Free Flyer, paper, making 856:6-7

Fuselage strengthening demonstration 974:26

Glider—build and test fly your own glider 419:30-31

Glider—making 450:20-21

Glider—making (Primary) 111:8-11

Glider—will heavy glider fly as far as light one 450:23

Glider—will small glider fly as far as large one 450:22

Glider, drinking straw, making 856:18-19

Gravity screw spiral slide brings model planes toward ground experiment 1446:24-25

Hang gliders, straws and plastic, making 856:30-31

Hangar, paper and cardboard, making 856:20

Hawkeye Devastator, paper, pattern, making 856:22-25

How air makes airplane fly 576:73-74

How airplane wings work—experiment 385:26-27

How an airplane climbs—elevators experiment 446:51-53

How an airplane is lifted from the ground 446:22-26

How an airplane stays up 561:32

How planes fly 660:28-29; 909:76

How planes fly experiment 1063:473

Hurricane glider—how to make 450:24-25

Javelin Darts, paper, making 856:8-9

Jet airplane potato—how to make 113:16-17

Jet plane—making model 436:49

Jet version paper airplane, making 1014:138

Jungle fighter KH20, paper, pattern, making 856:20-21

KHO1 prototype, paper, making 856:4-5

Landing simulations; build runway and land flying planes, how to do 1252:77-82

Launcher, paper, making 856:38-40

Lift; heavy airplanes supported by air from high/low air pressure experiment 1208:18-19

Lindbergh, Charles; who was the first to fly the Atlantic Ocean project 1525:12-17

Matchstick plane—making 178:30-31

Missile launcher, paper, making 856:41

Model airplane—making 167:149-159

Model, paper, with tail flaps that work 561:44-45

Moon Bug, paper, pattern, making 856:16-17

National Aerospace plane model, how to build from balsa wood, patterns 1252:102-106

Paper—making 400:98

Paper—old-fashion paper plane—how to make 652:40-41

Paper—super-glider paper plane—how to make 652:42-43

Paper airplane—making 32:48-49

Paper airplane for distance flight, patterns given, make 1436:25-27

Paper airplane for duration, how to make; patterns given 1436:28-30

Paper airplane soars, making 900:205-206

Paper airplane, make to demonstrate flight path experiment 940:135-137

Paper airplane; designs for making 1159:51

Paper airplanes and paper clips demonstrate balance 241:43-45

Paper airplanes experiment; which type and material works best 1373:10

Paper airplanes, how to make 835:28-30

Paper Concorde—making 112:43

Paper glider demonstrates center of gravity 561:38-39

Paper glider demonstrates streamlining 561:35-36

Paper plane, how to make 1073:21; 1299:39

Plane paper pattern to build 561:40-41

Polarization and stress of airplane windows experiment 997:153-155

Propeller plane from balsa wood, how to make 1110:27-28

Propeller powered plane—making 178:28-29

Propeller produces forward thrust experiment 860:19-22

Propeller thrust pushes airplane through the air 446:27-28

Propeller; how does a propeller work experiment 1293:7-9

Range Moth, paper, pattern, making 856:14-15

Rubber band powered wooden airplane experiment, how to make 1446:38-39

Show how rudder turns an airplane 446:45-50

Simple experiments with paper airplanes 1412:71

Simple paper airplane, how to make 1419:27

Spinner—making (Primary) 111:14-15

Streamlining projects 691:43-44

Stunt flyer paper airplane, how to make 1063:480

Super paper plane, making 981:25

Super plane paper model demonstrates streamlining 561:46-48

Super Zoomer paper airplane, how to make 1063:484

'Tail fins' help plane fly in straight line—show 324:13Toothpaste box airplane—how to make 652:36-39

Toys—delta winged planes—how to make 365:23-25

Travel distance and weight in nose experiment 984:56-58

Tumbler paper toy demonstrates wing stabilizers 999:109-112

Two-ring paper airplane, how to make; patterns given 1436:31-33

What aircraft will you fly experiment 900:211-212

What keeps an airplane up 295:94-99

Why airplanes stay up activities 759:60-61

Why are paper airplanes so aerobatic experiments 1294:6-12

Wind tunnel—making 293:40-41

Wing and helicopter—paper—making 732:139-140

Wing and other control surfaces demonstration 974:27

Wings help airplanes fly experiment 860:6-11

Wings; how do airplane wings work experiment 1293:17-18

AIRPORTS

Baggage trucks—how to make 388:20-21

Bus or truck—how to make 388:22-23

Landing simulations; build runway and land flying planes, how to do 1252:77-82

Model for people 388:16-17

Passenger loader—how to make 388:18-19

Supply truck—how to make 388:24-25

Build your own 388:1-29

Airport buildings—how to make 388:8-9

Control tower—how to make 388:10-11

AIRSHIPS

Model airship, make from plastic bottle, glued paper strips 1448:14-15

ALARM CLOCKS

Using an alarm clock to turn on your radio—how to do 543:50-51

ALARMS. *See also* BURGLAR ALARMS; ELECTRIC; FIRE ALARMS

A power off alarm—how to build 563:30-31

Alarm for school bag, how to make 1020:30-32

Alarm system to wake you up 358:48-49

Alarm, antitheft magnetic reed switch, make from magnet/batteries/wire 1442:50-54

Burglar alarm—how to make 358:78-79; 391:75-80; 930:13; 1072:17; 1160:19

Burglar alarm—simple, making—how to install switch 23:59-62

Burglar alarm for under mat or rug experiment 1024:26-27

Burglar alarm for your door—how to make 543:22-23

Burglar alarm from battery, buzzer, wire and metal strip, how to make 1245:38-39

Burglar alarm model, how to make 961:9

Burglar alarm, electric, how to make 955:17

Burglar alarm, how to make from box, battery, bulb and buzzer 1382:19

Burglar alarm, portable, making 895:44-46

Clanging alarm for doors and windows, how to make 643:42-43

Fire alarm, simple, how to make 830:56-57

Make a rain alarm 538:103

Rain alarm—bell rings when it starts to rain 381:54-57

Room alarm, how to make 825:30-31

Temperature alarms 391:81-86

Wire a bell for your room—how to 278:48

ALBUMEN. *See also* EGGS

Separation experiment—making meringue shells 537:32-33

Separation experiment—meringue shells recipe 537:72

ALCOHOL

Demonstrate difference in pulling power of water and alcohol experiment 905:40-41

Effects of some make-believe drinking 400:38

ALCOHOL BURNER

Homemade burner to use for experiments 436:18

Making 57:53-54

Wire gauge pad for—how to make 319:16

ALCOHOL LAMP

Make your own alcohol lamp 563:20

Making 9:80-81

ALGAE. *See also* DIATOMS; MICROSCOPE

Adventure 11—beauty in unexpected places—algae under a microscope 403:36-42

Algae collection—how to dry and mount seaweed 530:54

Algae growing in saltwater environment experiment 1061:60-61

Are algae bacteria and do they photosynthesize experiment 864:35-36

Collecting and examining under microscope 82:40-42

Cookies made of algae—how to 564:105

Detrimental effect of phosphates in detergents on pond plants/animals experiment 1476:192

Diatoms—preparing a slide 505:39

Does acid rain affect cell structure of Spirogyra experiment 997:99-101

Effect of electromagnetic fields on Eremosphaena algae cells experiment 997:57-59

Effect of fertilizer on algae growth experiment 950:36

Feathery—how to mount 234:75

Grow algae experiment 904:74-75

Grow algae to demonstrate chlorophyll production experiment 1479:28

Grow some algae experiment 1181:15; 1183:23

How to press algae 646:110

Iodine stain shows starch in cells 294:21-22

Make microscopic algae jungle 279:34-36

Motile algae—attraction test using different wave lengths of light 500:140

Nutrient enriched waters and algae growth experiment 1450:135-142

Observe under microscope 889:36

Ocean plants grow only in sunny water—experiment (Primary) 470:2-5

Phosphate detergents overfeed algae and harm pond life experiment 1331:81

Quantity and diversity of algae affected by acidified waters experiment 1450:128-134

Soil from dried up marsh area contains life experiment 1074:66

Spirogyra and other algae under a microscope—observe 713:85-87

Test algae for sugar and starch experiment 714:116-117

Why is some pond water green experiment 1294:96-98

Why is some water green experiment 860:166-167

ALGEBRA. *See also* MATHEMATICS

Think of a number game—simple use of algebra 546:1-33

ALHAZEN

Looking at eclipses experiment 1133:6.002

ALIENS
How many aliens are there in the Galaxy experiment; make alien calculator 1478:146-147

ALKA-SELTZER. *See also* **CARBON DIOXIDE**
Alka-Seltzer and water reaction experiment 1526:65-67
Alka-Seltzer in water puts out candle flame experiment 1526:72-73
Carbon dioxide gas produced when Alka-Seltzer reacts with water experiment 1526:75
Changing speed of chemical reactions with Alka-Seltzer and water experiment 1526:68-70
Experiment #5—match test to see CO_2 gas produced by Alka-Seltzer 404:10
Gas volume from Alka-Seltzer and water reaction experiment 1526:71-74
Heat speeds up chemical reactions; time the fizz from Alka-Seltzer experiment 924:93
Kitchen products chemical reactions experiment with baking soda/Kool-aid 1526:63-64
Speedy Alka-Seltzer experiment—what factors affect rate of reactions 586:63
Tests for carbon dioxide from Alka-Seltzer experiment 888:41-43
Time release of carbon dioxide from Alka-Seltzer tablet experiment 905:78-79
Time release of carbon dioxide gas from Alka-Seltzer tablet experiment 1405:52

ALKALIES. *See also* **ACIDS AND BASES**
Test for 146:58

ALLELOPATHY. *See* **PLANTS—GROWTH; SEEDS—GERMINATION**

ALLOYS
Making an alloy 625:33

ALMANACS
Old Farmer's Almanac; testing the Almanac's accuracy experiment 1062:110-111
Phases of moon planting project using the Old Farmer's Almanac 1062:110-111

ALTERNATING CURRENT. *See also* **ELECTRICITY—ELECTRIC CURRENTS**
AC current demonstrated with magnet—wire and transformer 723:117-118
AC power supply—how to build 23:23

ALTITUDE
How to measure altitude 292:43
Measure altitude of stars and planets with instrument you build 834:124-125
Three dimensional elevation model to show altitude, how to make 874:205
Use your hands to give latitude and altitude 292:46

ALUMINUM. *See also* **MINERALS**
Aluminum pot shines when boiling water and lemons are used experiment 1435:65-66
Hardness test for aluminum experiment 1438:88-89
Oersted, Hans; who discovered and produced first aluminum project 1525:76-79
Testing aluminum for corrosion experiment using acids and alkalies 1438:90-93

ALUMINUM FOIL
Thickness of aluminum foil—experiment 586:63

AMATEUR RADIO. *See* **RADIO**

AMINO ACID. *See* **PROTEIN**

AMMETER
A hot wire ammeter—making 127:44-48
Jar ammeter, how to make 910:32-33

Moving iron ammeter—making 167:165-169

AMMONIA
Clear water turns red and then turns clear again experiment 781:42-43
The diaper mystery 366:219

AMOEBA. *See also* **MICROSCOPE; PROTOZOA**
Adventure 7—we seek the famous amoeba under a microscope 403:22-26
Amoeba's reactions to food, touch, chemicals and light under microscope 771:17-20
Catching and growing amoebae 400:1
Microscopic algae jungle—making 279:34-36
Observe operation of contractile vacuoles in amoebas and paramecia experiment 1425:21-22
Observe under microscope 889:35
Observing amoebas under microscope experiment 1425:12-13
Threatening an amoeba to show contraction—experiment 484:39

AMPERE, ANDRE
Coil of wire acts as bar magnet when carrying current experiment 1133:5.004
Magnetic properties of a spiral wire—experiment 63:46-47
Magnetic relationship in straight, coiled wires and current measuring device 209:43
Right hand grip rule of magnetic field experiment 1133:5.005
Wires carrying current attract and repel according to direction experiment 1133:5.006

AMPERE. *See* **ELECTROMAGNETISM**

AMPHIBIANS. *See also* **FROGS; SALAMANDERS; TOADS**
Activities with amphibians 236:69-70
Habitat for amphibians from gallon jar, how to make 1441:93
Terrarium for keeping amphibians and reptiles, how to make 1425:62-65

AMPLIFIERS. *See also* **SOUND—AMPLIFIERS**
Ear trumpet or megaphone amplifies sound experiment 1045:15

AMUSEMENT PARKS
Carousel ride demonstrates centripetal force experiment 1412:45-46
Experiments to demonstrate roller coaster science 1412:39-44
Fun house mirror experiment 1412:51
Physics experiment at an amusement park 1158:79-82
Projects at amusement parks 691:47-51
Rotating platform ride demonstrates centripetal force experiment 1412:5
Scrambler ride demonstrates centripetal force experiment 1412:46-47

ANABANTIDS
Fishes that make bubble nests 266:121-129

ANAEROBIC DECOMPOSITION. *See* **DECAY; DECOMPOSITION; ROT**

ANALEMMA
Analemma, recording (advanced) 658:14-15
Displaying the path of the analemma project 833:22

ANAMORPHIC ART
How real objects are reflected from curved surfaces experiment 1443:79-83

ANATOMY—HUMAN BODY. *See also* **HUMAN BODY**
Muscular system observations using grocery store meat 20:81-116
Skeletal system observations using grocery store meat 20:3-76

ANEMOMETER
Anemometer—making 117:95-100; 14:54-58; 175:75; 176:83-84; 264:97; 277:15-17; 293:10; 40:132-134; 624:31; 767:143
Anemometer—making (Primary) 327:40
Anemometer—making simple one 301:23
Anemometer from cardboard and straws, how to make 856:34-35
Anemometer from soda straws, how to make 837:14-15
Anemometer from tin can and plywood, how to make 1516:99-101
Anemometer measures speed of wind experiment 1211:13
Anemometer measures wind speed experiment, how to make 1063:436-437
Anemometer measures wind speed, how to make 1042:36-37
Anemometer tells how fast the wind is blowing, how to make 1281:15
Anemometer, how to make 830:61-62; 891:65-69; 947:39
Anemometer, wind speed gauge, how to make 1311:28
Build from skewers, ping pong balls, and coffee can 1465:10-12
Can wind speed be measured; making anemometer experiment 900:94-95
Cup anemometer, making 1003:106-107
How does anemometer work experiment 900:96
How fast can you blow experiment using anemometer, how to build 1279:23
How to make anemometer 588:48; 705:74-75; 737:21; 978:147
How to make anemometer from plastic cups, cardboard and dowel 1073:30-31
Make an anemometer 564:3
Make anemometer to record wind speed project 1070:22
Make from protractor, ping pong ball and fishing line, how to do 1012:14
Measure wind speed and direction experiment; make wind vane and anemometer 1134:2.003
Measure wind speed with anemometer; build using balsa wood, shoe box 1388:21
Meter to measure wind, making 981:11
Portable anemometer experiment, how to make 1521:31
Portable anemometer from ping pong ball and cardboard, how to make 1086:19
Protractor and ping pong ball measures speed of wind experiment 1372:36-37
Protractor anemometer—making 662:40-41
Speed of wind measured by anemometer experiment 1108:18
Speed of wind, measure with anemometer, how to make 834:142-143
Wind anemometer, how to make from cardboard, paper cups, dowel 1175:87-88
Wind speed indicator—making 694:100-102
Wind speed measurement demonstration 1023:134-135
Wind speed meter, wood and tin, how to make 918:31
Wooden anemometer, how to make 1086:18

ANEMONE
Feed a sea anemone 236:116-117
Food habits of anemones and crabs experiment 1503:31
How sea anemones secure themselves to rocks experiment 1405:33
How sea organisms attach themselves to rocks experiment 904:116-117

ANEROBIC DECOMPOSITION. *See* **DECAY; DECOMPOSITION; ROT**

ANEROID BAROMETER. *See* **BAROMETER**

ANGLES
Angles—what they are (Primary) 454:1-33
Angles, angles and more angles 444:62-63
How angles can be created, measured and used in various activities 1345:5-64
Right angle, Egyptian cord way to make 323:8-9
Right angles, paper folding geometry 504:1-33
Theodolite measures height of objects experiment, how to make 1521:28-29

ANIMAL BABIES
Matching to their parents (Primary) 232:31

ANIMAL BEHAVIOR
A butterflies taste response in the field and in the laboratory 266:28-29
Activity of mice and gerbils affected by light and darkness experiment 1158:136-137
Animal behavior and environment—experiment 268:107-111
Animal defense of a territory in the field and in the laboratory 266:153-156
Ants—response of ants to odors in the field and in the laboratory 266:18-20
Archer fish—expert marksman in the field and in the laboratory 266:79-82
Are some of commonly held beliefs about animals true 402:41-42
Astronomical influence on behavior in animals and humans experiment 1062:109
At the zoo—do more complex animals show almost human behavior 402:48-49
Bees—time sense in bees in the field and in the laboratory 266:33-37
Bird journeys in the field and in the laboratory 266:56-59
Building choice chambers to help small creatures answer questions experiment 1313:43-49
Butterflies—butterfly migration in the field and in the laboratory 266:59-62
Caterpillars—how they react to noises 266:23
Caterpillars—response of caterpillars to touch in the field and laboratory 266:26-27
Chickens—the 'pecking order' in chickens in the field and laboratory 266:150-153
Cockroach—build maze to test intelligence 279:29
Cockroaches—can follow maze home 264:70-72
Conditioned behavior experiment with goldfish 936:36-37
Daphnia—are they attracted to lights of different intensities—experiment 266:18
Designing animal behavior experiments 148:52-53
Dogs—can your dog locate sound in the field and in laboratory 266:21-22
Dogs—learning in dogs in the field and in the laboratory 266:115-118
Ducklings and the shape of a hawk in the field and in the laboratory 266:66-69

23

Ducks—becoming a mother to a duckling—imprinting 266:129-132

Earthworm—response of earthworms to light in the field and in laboratory 266:15-17

Earthworm learning—an earthworm maze in the field and in the laboratory 266:103-106

Earthworms prefer light or dark experiment 1158:138-140

Earthworms prefer which colored light experiment 1158:138-140

Fiddler crabs—daily changes in fiddler crabs in the field and laboratory 266:40-43

Fireflies—number of flashes and brightness affected by temperature 266:72

Fish—schools of fish in the field and in the laboratory 266:146-149

Frogs—frog hibernation in the field and in the laboratory 266:33-37

Goldfish—can goldfish hear 266:22

Goldfish—reactions to changes in temperature 266:69-72

Guppies—overcrowding guppies in the field and in the laboratory 266:76-78

Insects—insects find the way in the field and in the laboratory 266:52-56

Instinctive behavior of butterfly larvae experiment 936:27-28

Mammals as parents in the field and in the laboratory 266:132-136

Mammals use maze to examine learning in small mammals in field and laboratory 266:110-115

Mealworms response to humidity experiment 936:16-18

Minnows—animal camouflage in the field and in the laboratory 266:72-76

Paramecia—response to touch, light, chemicals in field and laboratory 266:23-26

Periodicity—can natural animal periods be changed 402:52-53

Planaria—learning in planaria in the field and in the laboratory 266:106-110

Reflex behavior in fruit flies experiment 936:14-16

Reflex behavior; fruit flies response to cold temperature experiment 936:15-16

Reflex behavior; fruit flies response to light experiment 936:14-15

Reflex behavior; mealworms response to light experiment 936:12-13

Snails—homing behavior in snails in the field and in the laboratory 266:49-52

Snails—snails pace affected by temperature 266:72

Sow bugs prefer dark and moist places experiment 1158:137-138

Sow bugs response to temperature experiment 936:18-19

Sow bugs response to touch experiment 936:20-21

Study of farm animal behavior 542:116-117

Termites—studying a social insect in the field and in the laboratory 266:142-146

Test animals response to high-pitched dog whistles and low-pitched sounds 266:22-23

Thinking—do animals think 402:52

ANIMAL CAGES. See **CAGES**

ANIMAL CAMOUFLAGE. See also **COLORATION—PROTECTIVE; PROTECTIVE COLORATION**

Camouflaging technique of animals experiment 1405:34

Colored toothpicks scattered area; collected and counted by color—demonstration 268:119-122

In the field and in the laboratory 266:72-76

Overlapping patterns in animals demonstration 1391:25

Spot the moth pattern experiment 1391:17

Zebra stripes experiment 1391:23

ANIMAL COMMUNICATION

Ants—what are some ways in which animals communicate 402:46

Bees—the language of bees in the field and in the laboratory 266:86-90

Birds—bird communication in the field and in the laboratory 266:96-100

Dogs—how dogs communicate in the field and in the laboratory 266:93-95

Minnows—communication by odor in minnows in the field and in the laboratory 266:90-93

Moths—caged female moth attracts males 266:92-93

ANIMAL COURTSHIP

Firefly courtship in the field and in the laboratory 266:136-138

Fishes that make nests in the field and in the laboratory 266:121-129

ANIMAL GAMES

Tortoise and hare relay game—predator and prey game 400:31-32

ANIMAL GROWTH

Can animal growth be intensified 402:85

ANIMAL HABITATS

Biotic and abiotic characteristics of three habitats experiment 978:84-86

Garden toad and lizard need different habitats/food (Primary) 559:1-31

ANIMAL HOMES

Insect cage, snake house—how to make 436:9

What kind of homes do animals have 402:47-48

ANIMAL INTELLIGENCE. See also **MAZES**

Pets—dogs—testing for attention span and curiosity 510:95-96

Pets—dogs—testing for learning 510:100-101

Pets—dogs and cats—testing common sense and good judgment 510:98

Pets—dogs and cats—testing for concentration 510:96-97

Pets—dogs and cats—testing for memory 510:101-102

Pets—dogs and cats—testing for reasoning and insight 510:98-100

Pets—hamster, mouse, gerbil or white rat—tests for special animals 510:102-103

Pets—testing for verbal comprehension 510:94-95

Pets—worms, turtles, rodents—mazes to test intelligence—how to make 510:103-109

ANIMAL KINGDOM

Chart of 236:54

ANIMAL MIGRATION

Grasshoppers—where do grasshoppers travel 402:47

ANIMAL POPULATIONS

Birds of certain kind are attracted to certain kind of food project 969:32-34

Counting animal populations using Lincoln Index experiment 1134:5.010

Factors that govern population change in animals experiment 1134:5.012

How a characteristic or gene spreads through a population experiment 1134:5.011

How are animal populations counted experiment 1293:115-116

Limitations of resources 263:24-27

Natural population controls 263:34-36
Overcrowding 263:53-55
Size; variations in population size experiment 1134:5.012
Snail population in your garden—experiment 625:61
Snails—estimating and calculating a snail population 507:1903
Territoriality—what's mine is mine 263:56-58
Why do animal populations change; rice and grid experiment 860:181-183

ANIMAL SKIN
Skinning and drying an animal skin—how to do 530:346

ANIMAL STRUCTURE AND ENVIRONMENT
Project 268:113-117

ANIMAL SURVIVAL
Keeping warm in winter experiment with four jars of water 1181:35
Keeping warm; how animals survive experiment 1183:43

ANIMAL TRACKS. *See also* **TRACKS AND TRAILING**
Animal track casts 236:139-140
Animal track casts, making 234:34-35; 436:10; 772:63-65
Casts of animal tracks, how to prepare using plaster of Paris 1425:74-77
Casts of animal tracks, plaster, how to make 918:24-25
Collect tracks from snow with plaster casts experiment 1372:78-79
Detective work around holes to identity tracks 633:23
How do animals' feet differ experiment 1293:99-100
How to collect 236:95
How to make casts 234:34-35
Plaster cast of animal footprints, how to do 1371:16-17
Plaster casts of animal tracks, how to make 1063:270; 1071:61
Plaster casts of mammal footprints, how to make 1147:31
Plaster paw prints, how to make 810:68
Sand casts, making 772:59-60
Sink factor of animal tracks, how to measure 864:107-110

ANIMALS. *See also* **MAMMALS; MARINE ANIMALS;** *names of individual animals*
Activities to identify and investigate animals [Primary] 758:27-36
Animal show—filmstrip viewer—how to make 312:34-39
Animal visitors to a vacant lot 233:43-48
Animals have homes (Primary) 232:36
Bioluminescence—do plants and animals emit light 402:18-19
Body heat; color of animals feathers affects its body temperature experiment 1397:51
Body heat; elephants use their ears to cool their bodies experiment 1397:40-42
Body heat; fat layer under skin keeps animals warm experiment 1397:48-50
Body heat; hair keeps animals warm experiment using thermometer/cotton balls 1397:44-46
Body heat; larger blood vessels allow blood to pass to body surface 1397:38-39
Body heat; water used to lower body temperature of warm blooded animals 1397:36-38
Breathing rate (breaths per minute) of animals at rest chart 1506:17
Burrowing animals—outdoor projects with 118:165-171
Cages—small animal—making 9:36-39

Carbon dioxide production balanced by plants and animals in environment 1427:42-43
Carbon dioxide; animals give off or take up carbon dioxide experiment 1427:38-39
Collection and preservation—specimen jars—how to do 293:22
Collection and preservation of, how to do 824:36-50
Conditioned reflex—is it possible to modify the normal responses of anima 402:42-43
Death feigning—can animals pretend to be dead 402:39
Defense mechanisms—is there a common pattern which animals defend themselves 402:39-40
Domestication—can animals be domesticated 402:82-83
Evolution; concept of evolution project using sheets of paper 1063:263
Fat or lard or blubber insulates against cold project 969:30-31
Food—is there any difference in the kind of food needed by plants and animals 402:35-36
Footprints—how to preserve 117:31-32
Frozen animals can survive experiment 1020:117-121
Geotropism—do plants and animals seek the Earth's center 402:34-35
Heart beats per minute of various animals chart 1506:13
Heat loss determined by surface area and volume experiment 820:27
How animals use their time project 1313:37-40
How many animals live in a pine cone experiment 924:83-84
Hypothermia—can animals be preserved by freezing, then revived by warmth 402:53-54
Insects and animals require care 232:32
Legs; how do animals stay upright experiment 1134:3.003
Life span—how long do animals live 402:84-85
Light response—how do plants and animals respond to light 402:17-18
Movement—what is characteristic of animal movements 402:37-38
Neighborhood—which animals live in the neighborhood 253:23
Observe and record a nature square project 901:75-82
Observing and recording what wild animals you see 590:41-42
Overeating—do animals overeat 402:50-51
Periodicity—can natural animal periods be changed 402:52-53
Record keeping of animal observations, how to do 1363:30
River banks—observe animals and birds on the river banks 290:30
Sensitivity—are animals more sensitive than plants 402:40
Skeletons—how to prepare 117:27-31
Skins for studying—how to make 117:24-27
Sleep habits and sleep cycles of humans and animals experiment 1506:98-99
Social organization groups—do animals benefit from living in groups 402:43-44
Sound—do animals make distinctive sounds 402:38-39
Stimuli—will animals respond to stimuli that appear to be real but are no 402:43
Succession of—experiments with 118:155-163
Sugar water attracts what animals and insects in daytime and night experiment 969:35

Survey—do animal survey of neighborhood and zoo 400:27

Survival—animals survive in different ways 268:119-122

Survival game; how animals survive the winter game, how to make 1180:38-39

Survival; how do animals survive experiment 1293:101-103

Temperature climate near ground for animals; temperature pole project 1313:80-81

Temperature regulation in animals using elephant ear models experiment 1134:3.004

Thinking—do animals think 402:52

Water—drag nets and water scopes to observe—making 234:44-45

Water—how is water used by plants and animals 402:14-15

Water—observe animals and fish in the river water 290:31

Weather and its effect on animal life experiment 978:138

Wild—trap to catch small animals—how to build 166:74-80

Winter—detecting animals in winter 277:20-43

Winter sleeping sites—test protection of outdoor sites with gelatin anima 277:42-43

ANIMALS—ART ACTIVITIES

Animal track discovery 582:72-74

Cutout nature shapes 582:59-61

Drawing from memory 582:40-42

Drawing patterns from nature 582:42-44

Drawing personality shield activity 582:50-52

Emotions drawing 582:52-55

Hand puppets from nature 582:67-69

Melted—texture drawing 582:58-59

Microscope drawing 582:44-48

Paper mash—masks making 582:55-57

Snow shelters—making 582:65-67

Tools from nature—making art with tools from nature 582:48-50

Twelve-inch hike 582:69-71

Weavings from nature 582:61-65

ANIMALS—EXTINCT OR ENDANGERED. *See* **ENDANGERED ANIMALS**

ANIMALS—PROTECTIVE COLORATION. *See* **ANIMAL CAMOUFLAGE**

ANIMALS—SOUND

Capturing animals on tape recording; recorder, microphone, large umbrella 1093:50-51

ANIMALS—VISION

Binocular vision produces three-dimensional view experiment 1397:22-23

Eyes of chameleons and what they see experiment 1397:22

Type of vision in animals whose eyes face forward experiment 1397:20-23

ANIMATION. *See* **FLIP BOOKS; MOTION PICTURES; ZOETROPE**

ANNUAL RINGS. *See* **TREES**

ANOLES

Animal structure and environment 268:113-117

How to care for 279:11-13

ANT LIONS

Collection, care and observation of 331:69-77

Outdoor experiments with 118:109-113

ANTACIDS

Antacids; commercial antacids compared as acid neutralizers experiment 1259:92-94

Neutralizing stomach acid with a base experiment 1259:89-92

Strength of different brands of antacid tablets experiment 1396:77

ANTHOCYANINS. *See also* **PIGMENTS**

Anthocyanin pigments in flower petals change in acid/alkaline soil experiment 1203:28-29

ANTIBIOTICS

Antibiotic-resistant bacteria present in or on fruits and vegetables experiment 1267:47-49

Soils contain molds and do these molds have antibiotic capabilities experiment 1267:71-75

ANTIFREEZE

Hydrometer—how to make 368:46-48

ANTS

Adventure 14—we see how ants keep clean—ants under a hand lens 29:74-77

Alarm pheromones experiment using ants and aphids 1096:110-117

Ant cages—eyedropper cage 395:50-51

Ant cages—how to build 234:58; 395:48-59

Ant cages—how to cage and care for 279:26-27

Ant cages—tunnel cage 395:52-59

Ant colonies and their function experiment 978:92-93

Ant colony—making 749:58-59

Ant colony in a jar, how to do 1063:429

Ant colony to watch ants work, how to make 1445:42-43

Ant experiments and ant farm, making 870:52-54

Ant farm from two jars, how to make 854:80

Ant farm made from old aquarium tank, fish bowl or jar 1274:43

Ant farm or formicarium, how to make 1363:19

Ant farm or formicarium, how to make from wood and Plexiglas 1182:32

Ant farm shows how ants live in colonies experiment 1293:113-114

Ant farm, how to build in glass jar 1189:24-25

Ant farm, how to construct and observe ants 1476:112-113

Ant farm, how to make 236:62; 264:59-60; 832:71

Ant farm, how to make (Primary) 616:32

Ant farm, make to demonstrate what ants do underground experiment 834:130-131

Ant farm, making to observe ant colony experiment 860:180-181

Ant farm, setting up, how to do 898:53-54

Ant house—how to make 62:50-51

Ant house—making 9:42-43

Ant house from large glass jar, how to make 1071:58-59

Ant house, build to study and observe ants 1176:24-25

Ant jar farm—making 732:28-29; 759:40

Ant maze—build your own 163:82-84

Ant maze—experiment 151:78-80

Ant nest—studying a social insect in an ant nest 266:145-146

Ant observation nest—making 128:57-58

Ant observations (Primary) 480:60-61

Ant trail—which substance do ants follow—experiment 174:42-43

Ant village—how to make 293:22-23

Ant village in a jar, how to make experiment 1464:79-81

Ant watching for communication and food trails 414:103-105

Ant-colony chamber or house for ants, how to build 1096:116

Ants and aphids under a microscope—adventure 54 403:209-212

Ants live in families (Primary) 232:33

Ants use chemicals to communicate with one another experiment 1096:124-129

Build an ant house 476:51-53

Care of as pets 354:13-22

Collect ants outside and put in jar to observe experiment 942:25

Collecting and studying ants 253:26-27

Collecting ants—how to 62:51-52

Collection and care of 390:25-28

Colony of ants, how to make using jars and soils 1433:24-30

Communication—what are some ways in which animals communicate 402:46

Does formic acid from ants contribute to acid rain problem investigation 864:98

Feeding experiment with blue food coloring in honey 414:109

Follow ants to observe behaviors and find their nest experiment 1189:22-23

Formicarium for ants, how to make 1183:80

Formicarium, how to build from wood and clear plastic to observe ants 1069:110-111

Game, make ant with throws of dice game, how to make 1182:8

Game; ant game, how to make and play 1183:56

Glass jar ant farm—making 414:105-107

Home for ants—how to make (Primary) 580:unpaged

House for ants from two jars, and sand, how to make 1114:70

House; ant palace to house ants, how to make 1188:60

How ants use pheromones experiment 1097:16-20

How to keep and observe 233:20-21

How to keep ants 821:53

Keeping ants and building a formicarium cage for ants 430:53

Living room zoo—how to make cages, feed and observe a colony (advanced) 565:31-42

Make home for ant colony 436:10-11

Outdoor projects with 118:99-107

Pheromones used by ants for communication system experiment 1476:114-115

Plants grow better in ant hill mound soil project 969:64-65

Plaster of Paris ant farm 414:107-108

Response of ants to odors in the field and in the laboratory 266:18-20

Sand jar ant ranch—how to make 494:35

Study of ants in an observation nest, how to do 1425:48-52

Taste test for ants using sugar and artificial sweetener experiment 1063:272

Terrarium for ant colony, how to collect ants, care for and observe experiment 1472:42-47

Trail tricks with ants 264:60-61

Watching ants perform using sugar, bacon and grass seed experiment 1464:78

Where are the ants going 333:87-89

ANTS—SOCIAL ORGANIZATION

Do ants living in groups have organization 402:45-46

APHIDS

Adventure 17—we spy on the aphids under a hand lens 29:85-88

Alarm pheromones experiment using ants and aphids 1096:110-117

Ants and aphids—adventure 54—ants and aphids under a microscope 403:209-212

Aphid colony, how to collect and observe 810:49

Aphids are eaten by predator insects experiment 1464:46-47

Aphids collected and studied experiment 1464:44-45

Aphids use pheromones as warning system experiment 1097:2-4

Ladybug predator eats aphids, how to observe 810:50

Population growth of aphids experiment 1096:39-44

Reproduction and growth of aphids experiment 1097:70-72

APHIS LION

Adventure 21—we hunt a lion under a hand lens 29:103-107

APPLE LEATHER. See also **FRUIT LEATHER**

How to make 629:143

APPLES

Acids effect on browning process of cut apples experiment 1526:96

Apple head dolls—making 236:48; 832:106

Apple heads—how to make 442:unpaged

Apple in cookie jar experiment 1238:69

Apple people puppets—making 231:95-96

Apple seeds must have dormancy and be chilled (stratified) to grow experiment 1060:60-61

Apples get mushy from cooking experiment 1238:68

Apples that you eat or bake experiment 1238:66-67

Browning of apples; what affects browning experiment 1020:105-108

Color and light effect on color of ripening apples 864:72

Dissecting apples (Primary) 535:14

Dried apple garland, how to make 1115:128

Dried apple granny doll, how to make 644:28-31

Effect of light on color experiment 875:75

Enzymatic browning of apples experiment 1396:47

Enzyme experiments with apples 875:73-75

Enzymes prevent apple from turning brown experiment 1238:75

Experiments with apples for moisture, sugar content and starch 875:68-73

How to dry 264:15

How to graft apple trees 231:94

Making vinegar from apple juice experiment 924:45

Oxidation apple and lemon juice demonstrate 759:50

Pale green lethal gene in apples experiment 875:78

Plant and grow apple seeds, how to do 1178:42

Preserve apples by drying 538:84

Red color of apple is from color pigment anthocyanin experiment 1395:110

Sliced apples kept from turning brown with different coatings experiment 1458:46

Sprouting and planting apple tree, how to do 1406:88-89

Sprouting apple seeds experiment 875:76-77

Why cut apples turn brown experiment 1484:55-56

Why do apples turn brown experiment 1508:17

Yeast cells in fermenting cider experiment 917:23

APPLIANCES. See **HOUSEHOLD APPLIANCES**

AQUACULTURE SYSTEM

How to develop an integrated aquaculture system 347:142-144

AQUAPLANING

Aquaplaning effect experiment with wooden block on water film in tray 1166:9

AQUARIUM PROJECTION

Tiny water cell filled with hydra and tiny animals made from glass slides 436:11

AQUARIUMS

A pond community aquarium 268:51-56

Amphibians—collection and care of 390:39-45

Ants—ant village—how to make 293:22-23

Ants—setting up ant aquarium 253:32-34

Aquarium habitat for frogs, how to make 810:75

Aquarium, how to set up 901:89-91

Aquarium, making 128:58-59; 820:21

Aquariums—how to make 442:unpaged

Aquariums for guppies and fishes 507:1872-1873

Aquariums for pond insects—how to set up and observe insect life 414:119-120

Aquariums for raising salamanders 436:69

Aquatic and terrestrial food webs in aquariums experiments 978:114-116

Balanced aquarium—demonstrate elements needed for a 'balanced' aquarium 294:72-73

Balanced aquarium—how long can an aquarium be balanced 381:122-124

Breeding native fishes experiment 1520:101-104

Cold-water aquarium for fish, how to make 810:76-77

Energy saving aquarium drainer—how to 399:56

Establishing a home aquarium 625:59

Explore link between land and water in terraqua column experiment 1527:61-63

Factors which limit growth of brine shrimp experiment 978:86-87

Feeding behavior of fishes observed experiment 1520:99-100

Fish—how to test a betta's fight response 163:41-45

Fish aquariums, set up and observe fish behavior 888:107-111

Fresh and saltwater aquariums—how to set up 234:46-47

Fresh water—how to set up 173:16

Fresh water—making 236:135-136

Fresh water—observing life in 118:179-186

Fresh water—set up to show pond and stream life 194:20-21

Freshwater aquarium, how to make 1069:76-77; 1146:31; 1246:26-27

Freshwater aquarium, how to set up and stock with animals 1524:14-15

Jar aquarium for observing water insects 277:97

Keeping an aquarium, how to do 930:6-7

Mammals—collection and care of 390:57-67

Marine—how to make 390:31-37

Marine—how to set up and maintain 359:54-56

Marine animals—barnacles—collection and care of 390:35-36

Marine animals—crabs—collection and care of 390:33-35

Marine animals—fish—killifish and pipefish—collection and care of 390:32-33

Marine animals—sea anemones—collection and care of 390:36-37

Marine animals—starfish—collection and care of 390:37

Marine life, saltwater aquarium—making 436:56

Marine reptiles—collection and care of 390:47-55

Micro-aquarium of organisms shown on slide projector experiment 1476:111

Mini pond animal aquarium—how to set up 279:19-20

Mini pond ecosystem—setting up and observing 285:39-41

Mini-aquarium for pond creatures, how to make 600:6-7

Observation cover to observe activities of fish in aquarium, how to make 1520:90-91

Oxygen gas from aquarium plants, how to collect 930:7

Pond—how to set up and experiments to do 163:12-17

Pond—set up and observe a pond aquarium 285:89

Pond life aquarium, how to set up 913:38

Predators and plant eaters natural cycle observed in fish aquarium 1520:100

Preparing and maintaining an aquarium, how to do 1425:58-59

Rocky shore aquarium, how to make 1069:89

Salt water—animals in a saltwater aquarium 93:60-61

Salt water—maintaining a saltwater aquarium 93:62-64

Salt water—observing life in 118:187-201

Salt water—setting up a saltwater aquarium 93:57-59

Saltwater aquarium, how to maintain 877:90-95

Saltwater aquarium, how to set up 1118:24-25; 877:79-83

Sea—how to make and keep 163:22-28

Sea animals for your aquarium, how to collect 877:84-89

Sea life aquarium, how to set up 1466:28

Soda bottle aquarium, how to make 1527:111

Swimming behavior of fish observations, how to do 1520:98-99

Wildlife—how to make 390:13

AQUATIC EXPLORING

How to make water scopes and drag nets 234:44-45

AQUATIC INSECTS. *See also* **INSECTS—WATER**

Adventure 31—inspect breathing apparatus of aquatic insects with lens 29:144-149

Insect populations are different in running and standing water experiment 1096:96-101

Respiration in water insects experiment 1097:98-100

AQUATIC PLANTS

Oxygen given off by plants during photosynthesis experiment 1214:14

Soil from dried up marsh area contains life experiment 1074:66

AQUEDUCTS

Arches support plastic canal in aqueduct model experiment, how to build 1518:28-29

Build an aqueduct 223:18-19

Model aqueduct, how to build from wood, cardboard, paints 1460:18-19

AQUEDUCTS, ROMAN

Model—how to make 415:48-51

AQUIFERS. *See also* **WATER—AQUIFERS**

Model aquifer, making 959:77

Water from aquifer fills well if surrounding sand is kept wet experiment 1331:60

Well that draws water from a small aquifer experiment 1331:60

ARABIC NUMBERS

Importance of zero 601:unpaged

ARABS

Experiments of their culture 601:entire book, unpaged

ARACHNIDA. *See* **SPIDERS**

ARAGO, DOMINIQUE

Magnet follows rotation of a copper disc experiment 1133:5.008

ARAGO, FRANCOIS

Checking up on Arago—experiment 627:30

ARCHEOLOGY. *See also* **FOSSILS**

Backyard dig of your own, how to do 1168:57-59

ARCHES. *See also* **BRIDGES; BUILDING**

Arch bridge from wooden crates or cardboard experiment; how to build 1518:26-27

Arch increases structural strength of cardboard bridge experiment 1436:101-102

Arch test of strength 566:43

Arch, cardboard, how to make 860:133-136

Arches and stacks—make model of 299:18

Arches support plastic canal in aqueduct model experiment, how to build 1518:28-29

Bridge built with beams and arches; which is strongest experiment 1094:15-16

Build a combined corbel and arch from sugar cubes and cardboard 557:24-25

Build a sugar cube arch 557:21

Build an arch center 557:20

Catenary arch—build a center for a catenary arch 557:26

Catenary 328:90

Domes and arches strength test 1011:43

Freestanding arch experiment, how to build 1476:97-98

Stone arch model from styrofoam or wood, how to build 1459:14-15

Suspension bridge model, how to build from wood and string 1459:18-19

Why arches don't fall down experiment 1294:22-24

ARCHIMEDES. *See also* **BUOYANCY; CARTESIAN DIVER; WATER**

Archimedean screw model lifts popcorn or cereal experiment 1446:26-27

Archimedes discovery; weight and volume measured by water displaced experiment 1156:18-19

Archimedes lever experiment 1156:18-24

Archimedes screw—how to make from wood 429:84-87

Archimedes screw draws water up a tube experiment 1198:30

Archimedes screw model moves water up plastic tube experiment 1523:28

Archimedes' principle or law of buoyancy experiment 1133:4.001

Buoyancy of water—experiment 368:50-54

Clothespin moving down wire to pop balloon demonstrates Archimedes screw 1523:29

Floating object displaces equal volume or weight of liquid experiment 1179:139

His experiments 42:6-11

Nails that float and sink—experiment 549:94-96

Principle—construct two model diving submarines 167:58-62

Principle—eggs floating midway in a jar 291:138

Principle—experiment on 128:110-111

Principle of levers experiment 1133:4.002

Repeat Archimedes experiment—weight/volume cause water to be displaced 448:16-18

Who discovered principles of specific gravity project 1525:89-91

Who invented the lever and the screw experiment 1525:24-26

Working model of Archimedes' screw—how to make 577:project 70

ARCHIMEDES PRINCIPLE

Add weight to water by touching it experiment 937:24-25

Archimedes Principle of buoyancy experiment with vinegar, baking soda, pasta 1290:9, 1.9

Demonstrate using jar, pie plate and small scale 642:6-7

Density of object related to water displacement experiment data tables 1004:3.002

How much does your hand weigh 577:project 65

How things float experiments 1164:62-65

Object immersed in liquid loses weight experiment 1456:32

One glass floats inside the other demonstration 722:22

Prove Archimedes Principle experiment using spring scale, water, block of wood 1243:30-31

Sink or float experiments 748:110-111

What makes a boat float experiments 835:16-18

ARCHITECTURE. *See also* **ARCHES; BRIDGES; BUILDINGS; HOUSES; STRUCTURES**

A masonry wall from sugar cubes—how to make 557:18

Appearance of building—how to change the appearance of a flat circle 557:77

Appearance of building—how to change the inside appearance of a cube 557:78

Appearance of building—how to change the outside appearance of a cube 557:79

Arch—build a sugar cube arch 557:21

Arch—build an arch center 557:20

Arch, cardboard, how to make 860:133-136

Balancing weight and distance project 557:12-13

Beam—build a simple device to find compression and tension in a beam 557:49-50

Beams—build a prestressed beam 557:67

Beams—build models to compare beam shapes 557:50-51

Beams—can you invent a beam 557:51-52

Build a combined corbel and arch from sugar cubes and cardboard 557:24-25

Build a curved shell with straight pieces of cardboard 557:69

Build a shell of thread to demonstrate hyperbolic, parabola form 557:68-69

Build a small, harmoniously proportioned building 557:45

Build a space frame from toothpicks 557:61-63

Buttress—build a flying buttress 557:28-29

Cable structures—build a hanging shell 557:72-73

Castle and village, medieval—how to make 415:54-60

Catenary arch—build a center for a catenary arch 557:26

Columns—invent a column shape 557:53

Columns—making paper columns 557:52

Columns—testing the difference between a pin and a rigid connection 557:54-55

Corbel from sugar cubes—how to make 557:19

Domes—build a ribbed dome 557:34-35

Folded plated—build a folded plate 557:71

Masonry column from sugar cubes—how to make 557:16-17

Measuring man 557:42-44

Modular game—make a 557:39-40

Sound and architecture of concert halls experiment 1155:81-85

Space—design a space 557:87

Textures—feeling material 557:80

29

Trusses—build a truss of rigid frames 557:65
Trusses—build a truss 557:61

ARCTIC WILDERNESS
Arctic mammal; invent one that might survive in the
Arctic project 1337:68-69
Calendar of Arctic wildlife activity through months of
year 1337:69-71
Food web to show interdependence of Arctic animals
1337:71-72
Hours of sunshine in one day using sundial experiment
1337:67-68
Oil spills effect on birds experiment 1337:72-73
Projects to understand why and how tundra ecology must
be saved 1337:64-75
Technology used by you in one day for your survival
1337:65
Time line showing history of people on Earth 1337:64

AREA
Area and volume introduced through problems and activities 1346:5-64
Small things have more surface area for their size experiment 1411:42-43
Surfaces and spaces in a room reconstructed in model
room, how to do 1521:24-25

AREA MEASUREMENT
Investigate properties of areas and ways of measuring
them (Primary) 524:1-33
Measuring area—big cities and small towns 304:28-
29

ARISTARCHUS
Who first tried to determine size of heavenly bodies
project 1525:50-52

ARISTOTLE
Aristotle's ancient idea of what caused earthquakes ex-
periment 1398:4-7
His experiments 42:1-5
Vehicle moves at constant speed when pulled with con-
stant force experiment 1157:25-26

ARITHMETIC. See MATHEMATICS; NUMBERS

ARRHENIUS, SVANTE
Separation of substances into electrically charged particles or ions experiment 1133:2.010

ARROWS
Fly straight with fins (Primary) 324:12-13

**ART ACTIVITIES. See ANIMALS—ART ACTIVI-
TIES; NATURE—ART ACTIVITIES; PLANTS—
ART ACTIVITIES**

ARTICHOKES
Artichoke makes water taste sweeter experiment 1083:29

ARTIFICIAL RIPENING
Can ethylene molecules cause fruits and vegetables to
ripen 396:72-73

ASCORBIC ACID. See VITAMIN C

ASEXUAL REPRODUCTION
Different kinds of plants undergo asexual reproduction
project 1296:1974
Plant experiment 507:1853-1854
Produce new plant by fragmentation experiment
1395:51-55

ASPIRATOR
Making 9:14

ASPIRIN
Effects of aspirin on brine shrimp experiment 950:21-22
Strength of different brands of aspirin experiment
1396:76-77

ASTEROIDS
Asteroids explained 292:92

ASTROLABE
Astrolabe—how to make 586:36; 657:89; 763:5
Astrolabe to show altitude of star, make from poster
board, straw, string 1434:42-44
Building an astrolabe 400:109
Compare distances between stars using astrolabe experi-
ment 1405:17
Distances between stars measured using astrolabe, how
to make 1394:176-177
How to build 710:68
How to make and set up 175:56-57
Make your own astrolabe 292:48-49
Making an astrolabe project 833:100-102
Measure altitude of stars and planets with instrument you
build 834:124-125
Measure altitude of stars and sun, how to make astrolabe
1115:134-137
Moon observe and chart movements—how to 748:157

ASTROLOGY
A galaxy of activities 400:103
Sun moves thru Zodiac as Earth moves experiment; work-
ing model demonstrates 1478:26-27

ASTRONAUTS
Activities and experiments to demonstrate training of
astronauts 564:81-85
Eating in space experiment 1502:74-75
Effect of gravity on height of Astronauts demonstration
1394:218-219
G-forces effect on (advanced) 668:30-32
How space suits affect an astronaut's blood demonstra-
tion 1394:214-215
Life support systems on space craft 564:73-80
Psychological aspects of travel (advanced) 668:58-
60
Space suit materials help regulate temperature demonstra-
tion 1394:212-213
Water inside space suit; what happens to it in space dem-
onstration 1394:216-217
Weightlessness effect on (advanced) 668:34-36

ASTRONOMICAL PHOTOS
With the Polaroid Instrument Camera 386:131-134

ASTRONOMICAL UNITS
Project 292:101-103

**ASTRONOMY. See also ASTROLABE; NAVIGATION
INSTRUMENTS; PLANETS; SOLAR SYSTEM;
STARS; TELESCOPES**
A galaxy of activities 400:103
A global view of Earth 586:37-39
A spiral nebula from ... tea leaves 161:93-94
Absorption nebulae, how to demonstrate 1394:152-153
Analemma, recording (advanced) 658:14-15
Ancient civilizations and their calendars project
1062:112-113
Archeoastronomy (advanced) 658:107
Astronomical influences on behavior in animals and hu-
mans experiment 1062:109
Astrophotography (advanced) 658:105-107
Auroras near Earth's poles; simulate charged particles ex-
periment 1405:11
Average person does poorly when asked simple astro-
nomical questions experiment 1062:76-77
Band of the Milky Way experiment; demonstrate with
flashlight and plastic 1478:132

Behavior of people regarding fad theories in astronomy project 1062:114-115

Big Dipper or Plow constellations, how to observe and record 1217:8

Blinking (advanced) 658:101-104

Cloud chamber—making (advanced) 658:87-88

Comets and meteors (advanced) 658:73-82

Compare distances between stars using astrolabe experiment 1405:17

Constellation projector, how to make 1293:57

Cosmic rays detection (advanced) 658:86-88

Counting stars 586:39-40

Diffusion of Sun's light keeps us from seeing stars in daytime experiment 1062:78

Distance in space measurements use common objects to show comparisons experiment 1062:12-13

Distances in space—demonstrate measuring distances by triangulation 175:54-55

Distances in space—how far away is it—ways to measure 253:196-198

Drawing star trails project 833:2-3

Earth's circumference, measuring (advanced) 658:67-71

Eratosthene's experiment (advanced) 658:67-71

Eyepiece filters for astronomy 386:151-152

Finding directions on Earth using Sun and Polaris experiment 1170:14

Finding true north—experiment 657:86-89

Handy Nadir-Zenith Finder 292:42

History of astronomy and calendars project 1062:112-113

Keeping track of the sun during the day project 833:5-7

Lunar eclipse (advanced) 658:46-47

Lunar surface (advanced) 658:47-48

Making a tennis sky dome project 833:3-4

Mapping the sun 586:33-35

Marking sunrise and sunset project 833:4-5

Mars, canals (advanced) 658:62

Martian "riverbeds" (advanced) 658:59-61

Measuring distances in the sky experiment 1170:15

Meteor showers (advanced) 658:79-82

Micrometeorites, collecting (advanced) 658:83-86

Milky Way model (advanced) 658:32-33

Model Milky Way experiment; make from poster board, paints, clay 1478:134

Moon—cratering (advanced) 658:48-51

Moon and planet study project, how to observe and record 1217:22-23

Moon illusion (advanced) 658:47

Moon mapping and watching with astrolabe 586:35-36

Moon observations (advanced) 658:44-51

Moons of Jupiter (advanced) 658:63-65

Nadir and zenith, how to find yours 1434:18-19

Observing the night sky project 833:1

Occulations used to detect astronomical bodies experiment; construct box/light 1062:14-15

Old Farmer's Almanac; testing the Almanac's accuracy experiment 1062:110-111

Optical telescope (advanced) 658:16-20

Orion constellation, how to observe and record 1217:9

Planetarium—building (advanced) 658:28-31

Planets, observing (advanced) 658:52-65

Potpourri projects (advanced) 658:107-111

Radio telescopes (advanced) 658:21-23

Sextant to measure altitude of stars, how to make 862:82-93

Size of the sun and moon 586:36-37

Sky observation linked to holiday activities on Earth project 1062:116-117

Space in the face of a clock 292:41-42

Spectroscope, construction and use (advanced) 658:24-27

Spiral galaxy movement demonstration 1394:154-155

Star chart, 3D—making (advanced) 658:33-34

Star clusters; explore stars around certain constellations experiment 1217:32-33

"Star gauging" the Milky Way (advanced) 658:98-100

Star stellar structure—model (advanced) 658:34-36

Starfinder (Edmund Scientific) 386:141-150

Stars; quadrant to determine stars altitude, how to make 862:45-56

Sun—observations (advanced) 658:37-41

Sun's radiation, measure (advanced) 658:42-43

Sun, photographing (advanced) 658:41

Sun, spectroscopic observation (advanced) 658:41-42

Sundials—making (advanced) 658:10-15

Telescope; learning how lenses in telescope work experiment 1170:19

Theodolite—building (advanced) 658:5-9

Theodolite, how to make from wooden post, straw, compass, protractor 1217:10-11

Timing of occultations (advanced) 658:94-97

Variable stars (advanced) 658:89-93

Watching the northern sky 586:31-33

Which way is north 586:30-31

Why aren't planets spherical (advanced) 658:71-72

Why outer space is dark experiment 906:78

ATMOSPHERE. *See also* **AIR; CLOUDS; WATER VAPOR; WEATHER**

Air has weight experiment 1023:122-123

Air pressure changes in Earth's sea of air experiment 1516:12-13

Air takes up space demonstration 1023:120-121

AM radio shows presence of ionosphere above Earth experiment 1322:23-27

Atmosphere affects falling objects demonstration 1394:64-65

Atmospheric gases and dust—activities to demonstrate 564:9

Atmospheric pressure—aneroid barometer—making 9:98-99

Atmospheric pressure—barometer—how to make 293:11-12

Atmospheric pressure—demonstrate 101:8-14

Atmospheric pressure—demonstrate pressure, relation to expansion/contract 293:11

Atmospheric pressure—experiment—show changes in pressure of atmosphere 385:20-22

Atmospheric pressure—what is atmospheric pressure 101:8-9

Chemicals travel through the air experiment using perfume and balloon 1228:24-25

Current of air in atmosphere returning from warm to cold experiment 1480:158

Demonstrate light bending effect on sunlight 231: unpaged

Density and pressure—activities to demonstrate 564:6-7

Diffusion of Sun's light keeps us from seeing stars in daytime experiment 1062:78

Distance from Sun affects atmospheric temperature experiment 1405:2

Distortions in visual observations of atmosphere caused by heated air experiment 1062:10-11
Five layers of the atmosphere illustration 1086:5
Heat in the atmosphere experiment 1447:18-22
Heat level of Earth remains constant demonstration 1023:126-127
Heated air causes distortions in visual observations of atmosphere experiment 1062:10-11
Jet stream—activities to demonstrate jet stream 564:7
Layers of 119:174-178
Magnetosphere—activities to demonstrate magnetosphere 564:10
Make water rise in inverted bottle 291:78
Masses of the atmosphere, hydrosphere and lithosphere differences experiment 1023:18-19
Oxygen; how much oxygen is in the air experiment 1322:13-16
Radiation—activities for demonstrating atmospheric radiation 564:8
Spacecraft—experiments to demonstrate atmosphere control in spacecraft 564:74-75
Strength of air demonstration 1023:124-125
Temperature—activities to demonstrate atmospheric temperature 564:5
Volcanic clouds lower atmospheric temperature and reduce sunlight experiment 1477:76-79
Weather—activities to demonstrate atmospheric weather 564:2-4
Weight of atmosphere on a compressible object experiment 1447:56-57
Weight of atmosphere pushes air up chimney experiment 1126:10

ATMOSPHERIC PRESSURE. *See also* **AIR PRESSURE; BAROMETER**
Balanced with air and water pressures in a self-filling drinking fountain 604:24-27
Barometer from plastic bottle and glass jar, how to make 1372:22-23
Barometer measures pressure of air experiment, how to make 1063:442
Collapsing can experiment demonstrates atmospheric pressure 1439:22-25
Crumpled can experiment 939:79-82
Demonstrate strength of atmospheric pressure 1479:77
Experiment 585:7
Glass of water and card demonstrate [Primary] 848:18-21
Goldfish [plastic] swims inside two glasses of water experiment 848:30-31
Otto Von Guericke's creating a vacuum demonstrates atmospheric pressure 1133:4.005
Plugged soda bottle and straws demonstrate [Primary] 848:13-17
Producing a partial vacuum in a jar 604:28-31
Siphoning system produces continuous running water experiment 884:77-78
Siphoning water, how to 884:73-76
Straws in glass of water demonstrate 848:3-12
Using atmospheric pressure to push a liquid up a tube 604:8-11
Using atmospheric pressure to speed flow of liquids from containers 604:20-23
Watching atmospheric pressure at work experiment 871:3.018
Water travels uphill experiment 884:68-71

ATOLLS
Illustration of 299:22
ATOMIC ENERGY
A chain reaction—how to demonstrate 489:148-149
ATOMIC RADIATION
Make a watch dial photograph itself 291:192-193
Test for uranium or thorium 291:190-191
ATOMIC THEORY
Dalton, John; who first proposed the atomic theory project 1525:70-72
ATOMIZERS
How perfume sprayers work experiment 1405:97
Making a 291:88
Straw atomizer, how to make 827:12-13
Two-straw magic experiment; blow in straw and water comes out of other straw 1230:56-57
ATOMS. *See also* **MOLECULES**
Atom and its parts; how to chart activity 976:8-9
Atom model, how to make using beads on cardboard 1179:26-27
'Atom smashing'—set up model to show 95:58-59
Atom sorter—make model of 95:56-57
Atomic element—make 3D model of 293:38
Atoms—breakdown—see atomic energy explosions on clock with luminous dial 381:28
Atoms and molecules—tests to show 85:6-7
Atoms have positive and negative parts experiment 1405:46
Build model atoms; table given 976:10-11
Cereals; can you see the iron in iron-fortified cereals experiment 1250:80-81
Chain reaction—experiment to show 106:62-64; 179:177-179
Chain reactions—controlled/uncontrolled chain reactions—experiment to s 179:179-180
Charged balloon moves toothpick inside glass experiment 905:10-11
Compound built from atoms—iron oxide from steel wool and water experiment 704:34-35
Construct model of lithium atom showing its electrical charges experiment 1501:4-7
Crystal models to see atoms arrangement 1266:61
Dalton, John; who first proposed the atomic theory project 1525:70-72
Different molecules made from play dough and small sticks experiment 1271:8
Do atoms in metal move farther apart when heated experiment 831:21-22
Do like charges attract or repel experiment 831:11-14
Domino model of a chain reaction experiment 895:114-115
Electric charge of object unbalanced—case of the jumping pellets—experiment 12:80-82
Electricity and copper pennies distinguish chloride and sulfate ions experiment 1250:91-94
Fluorescent bulb gives off light experiment 1250:63-64
Half lives of radioactive substances experiment 1004:3.010
Helium passes through a balloon faster than air experiment 1251:27-28
How to change the number of electrons 106:59-61
Indirect and direct measurement of pennies experiment; data table given 1004:3.011
Lithium model, how to make from clay and string 1403:4-7

Making a model of an atom 489:142
Methane physical structure, how to make 1403:40
Models of atoms 179:175-177
Molecules form atoms; demonstrate using paper circles and toothpicks 976:6-7
Oil drop model of a splitting atom experiment 895:113-114
Paper circles and balloon demonstrate positive and negative parts experiment 905:8-9
Radioactive fallout meter—constructing a 179:180-185
Space between atoms in a liquid observation 707:24
The magic motor 16:71-76
Watching atoms split 180:22
Water, alcohol and oil demonstrate splitting 781:10-11
"Working models" of atoms 577:project #16

ATTRIBUTES
How are pebbles we find alike and different 253:120

AUDIO-OSCILLATOR
How to make 43:145-163

AUGERS
Archimedes screw draws water up a tube experiment 1198:30

AURORAS
Auroras near Earth's poles; simulate charged particles experiment 1405:11
Watching for auroras 292:108-109

AUTO KINETIC EFFECT
Experiment 229:91-92

AUTOMOBILES
Aqua pod car, working model, how to build, patterns given 1022:38-43
Ball bearings in model car overcome friction experiment 1334:10-11
Balloon propelled car experiment 994:28-34
Braking experiment with toy car and rubber bands 762:96-98
Buggy bumpers, experiment with 806:49-50
Buggy elastic band motor, making 806:50-51
Buggy, how to make and experiment with wheels 806:46-49
Bumpers; demonstrate protection of with egg and toothpick experiment 860:129-130
Car going around curves; what happens is demonstrated by toy car experiment 945:26-29
Car lift for toy cars, how to make 945:36-37
Car squeaks from friction; toy car demonstrates 945:34-35
Car that is nonpolluting experiment; build model car 1458:34-35
Carton car model—how to make 431:6-7
Color most popular in cars project 1210:30-31
Dashboard model project, how to make 1470:26-27
Diesel, Rudolph; who invented the diesel engine project 1525:32-34
Drag on car and its effect on car's efficiency experiment 1152:114-117
Effects of road pollution on populations of insects and arthropods experiment 1096:69-74
Electric air car—working model 577:project #54
Exhaust fumes effect on germinating seeds experiment 933:43-45
Exhausts—Vaseline coated card for pollutants in exhaust—experiment 10:18
Flywheel in automobiles experiment using spinning tops 1334:16-17

Frictionless car demonstrates first law of motion experiment, how to build 1502:28-29
Gas mileage—how many miles on a gallon of gas 333:25-28
Gas mileage—projects on 691:51-53
Gears from cardboard demonstrate use of gearbox in autos experiment 1166:25
Gravity effects uphill and downhill movement of car; toy car experiment 945:30-32
How fast is your toy car; calculating speed experiment; data table 1004:5.003
Jet-propelled racing car—how to make 652:6
Kooky car—how to make 652:8-9
Measure rate of acceleration and deceleration rate of car experiment 1136:34-35
Miles per gallon experiment 1152:112-113
Model slope or ramp demonstrates effort needed to get car up slope experiment 1334:6-7
Model wheeled vehicle runs down slope experiment, how to make 1470:6-7
Motor car—making 96:44-46
Mousetrap car—build a 66:16-33
Mousetrap tractor—how to build from wood 429:75-77
Passenger movement in starts and stops of car safety experiment 945:16-17
Piston and crankshaft model; engine up down motion to rotary motion experiment 1166:21
Project 38—building better bumpers 654:84-85
Propeller car—making 178:53
Pulley for lifting cars, how to make 945:44-45
Ramp experiments with toy car 945:40-43
Roadster uses twisted rubber band to turn propeller for power experiment 1446:36-37
Sedan car model—how to make 652:30-31
Sliding wheels; toy car with its "brakes" on experiment 1159:41-42
Smooth tires on toy auto won't climb hill experiment 1073:13
Soap box derby car—wooden—plans—how to make 750:35-41
Steerable wheels demonstrated with model car made from cardboard experiment 1334:12-13
Stopping takes force; toy car demonstration 945:19
Streamlined shape in autos increases speed experiment with toy car 1166:29
Streamlining experiments 691:44-45
Suction pump action of auto fuel pump—demonstrate 217:46-50
Tiny racing car—how to make 652:4-5
Tire pressure and auto efficiency experiment 1152:113
Tires need friction to work on roads; toy car demonstrates 945:22-23
Toy car and doll demonstrate seat belt safety experiment 945:18
Toy car from carton and roller skate, how to make experiment 945:8-9
Weight of automobile and energy needed to move it experiment 1152:113-114
Which oil makes toy car go farthest; vegetable or automobile oil experiment 781:20-21

AUTUMN. *See* **SEASONS—FALL**

AUXINS
Apical dominance exhibited by terminal bud on white potato experiment 1395:57-61
Apical dominance; growth inhibitor experiment 1395:57-61
Auxin affects growth of oat seedlings experiment 1060:83-85
Auxin improves root formation in stem cuttings experiment 1060:99-100
Auxins and responses to stimulation experiment 878:48-49
Blossom-set products prevent fruit from falling off plant experiment 1395:60-61
Does direction of seed planting matter experiment 904:44-45
Effect of auxin on growth of lima bean plant experiment 1060:86-87
Effect of auxin on root formation in plant cuttings experiment 1060:86
Experiment with plants 398:128-129
Geotropism; effects of gravity on plant growth experiment 1405:27
Gravity and its effect on seed growth experiment 904:50-51
Gravity has effect on plant growth experiment 1399:48-51
Phototropism; plant winds its way toward light experiment 904:52-53
Phototropism; plants seek light experiment 904:54-55
Plants affected by 273:52-55

Projects with auxins 398:69

AVERAGES
Ideas for demonstrating (Primary) 525:1-33

AVIARY
Building an outdoor aviary (advanced) 625:57

AVOCADO
Avocado plant from seeds, how to grow 272:6-16; 376:12; 770:98; 810:30-31; 854:61; 879:167-168; 898:45; 991:29-30; 1078:22; 1178:38-40; 1335:107
Avocado plant, how to grow 1006:26; 1440:81-82; 1486:20-21
Grow an avocado tree, how to do 899:137; 1054:65; 1379:15
Pit grows into plant (Primary) 650:unpaged
Pit in water—how to grow 384:18-19
Plant grows from avocado stone experiment 1181:9
Sprouting and potting avocado seed, how to do 1406:56-59; 1491:19

AXLES. *See also* **SIMPLE MACHINES—WHEELS**
Wagon from wood with wooden wheels project, how to make 1423:14
Wagon with axles, simple project, how to make 1423:12-13
Wheels with axles project, how to make 1423:11

AZIMUTH
Theodolite to find altitude and azimuth of star, how to make 1434:45-49

B

BABYLONIAN COUNTING
How to count like a Babylonian 509:9-15
BACTERIA. *See also* **FOOD PRESERVATION; MICROBES; MICROSCOPE**
A coconut culture 585:150-151
Adventure 29—we go microbe hunting under a microscope 403:100-106
Amount of bacteria found on kitchen sponges/dishrags be reduced experiment 997:124-125
Analysis of bacteria/heavy metals in sewage before/after treatment experiment 997:128-129
Antibacterial agents; do they kill bacteria experiments 864:37-38
Antibiotic-resistant bacteria present in or on fruits and vegetables experiment 1267:47-49
Are algae bacteria and do they photosynthesize experiment 864:35-36
Are bacteria killed by boiling water or foods once experiment 864:32-33
Are your clams safe to eat experiment 997:130-131
Bacteria and factors that aid/hinder spread in apples experiment; data tables 1004:2.018
Bacteria cells under microscope, how to view 864:28-29
Bacteria from hay water under microscope—observe 713:97
Bacteria from yogurt under microscope—observe 713:97-98
Bacteria from your teeth under microscope—observe 713:95-97
Bacteria grow better in light or dark experiment 1395:123
Bacteria growing on potatoes 216:14-17
Bacteria have magnetite crystals that respond to magnetic force fields ex 1479:29
Bacteria in drinking water experiment using potato slices 1331:83
Bacteria of decay—growing one—celled microscopic organisms 294:20
Bacteria test for groundwater pollution experiment;, how to do 1173:41-42
Boiled juice doesn't grow bacteria experiment 723:62
Bury bone specimen in bacteria in bottle in the ground experiment 1169:12-13
Bury objects in soil to demonstrate growth of bacteria 216:24-27
Can antibacterial effects of garlic be increased experiment 997:141-144
Can trace amounts of heavy metals kill bacteria experiment 864:33-35
Carrot medium, how to make 864:26-28
Collection and observation of 11:118-127
Compare decomposition of aerobic and anaerobic bacteria project 969:60-61
Conditions affecting bacterial growth experiment 1395:121-126
Cultivation of bacteria—under what conditions can bacteria be developed 402:29-30
Decomposition bacteria, collect and observe 864:31-32
Deodorant soap kills bacteria or retards bacterial growth 441:21-24
Deodorant soap more able to kill bacteria than pure soap experiment 1395:123-124
Determine bacteria in P-traps and what products stop growth experiment 997:135-140

Determine optimal temperature for making yogurt exp.; Data table given 871:2.012
Dirt from fingernails grows molds on potato mush mixture experiment 1482:8-9
Do commercial septic tank products really contain bacteria experiment 864:33
Do disinfectants kill bacteria experiment 1395:124
Do popular cold remedies eliminate nasal culture bacteria experiment 997:102-103
Does brushing your teeth with toothpaste remove bacteria? 441:27-29
Effect of preservatives on bacterial growth experiment 904:86-87
Effect of temperature on growth of bacteria experiment 904:84-85
Examples of bacterial soft rot—bacterial colonies 216:35
Experiment to show sterilization effect of heat 182:56-57
Experiments to show growth of bacteria 128:49-51
Food bacteria, make and observe 864:31
Garlic; does it kill bacteria experiment 864:36-37
Gravy horror grows bacteria 112:25
Grow bacteria to study their plant characteristics 293:16
Growing bacteria on potatoes experiment 762:81-83
Growing bacterial cultures 148:10-11
Growth of bacteria experiment 878:34-35
Hot grass or manure experiments 563:58-59
How to culture bacterial growths experiment 1395:121-126
In polluted water 330:90-92
Lactobacilli—making cultures cream 152:23-27
Low-level EMR (electromagnetic radiation) affects bacterial growth experiment 1450:100-105
Magnetic bacteria experiment 1221:16-17
Magnetic bacteria; several experiments to test for 864:40-42
Make yogurt and experiment with bacteria growth 887:84-86
Mouth bacteria experiment with different mouthwashes 997:126-127
Mouthwash; how to make and test bacteria killing properties experiment 1259:61-62
Nitrogen-fixing bacteria change nitrogen so plants can use it experiment 1402:44-47
Nitrogen-fixing bacteria experiment with clover plant 864:38-39
Observing bacteria of decay 294:20-21
Pasteur's experiment with growth of bacteria from air 577:project 84
Plant materials changed into methane fuel experiment 1323:90-94
Preventing bacterial growth—how can bacteria be prevented from growing 402:30-31
Preventing growth of bacteria 148:14
Rotten apples demonstrate spread of infection experiment 1014:152
Rotting of food demonstration; bacteria causes decay 1073:89
Salt and vinegar used as preservatives to inhibit bacterial growth experiment 1395:130
Salt kills bacteria and prevents decay in food—experiment 26:87-88
Shapes of under a microscope 82:68
Soaps and deodorants kill underarm bacteria experiment 1221:21-22, 36-37

Soil bacteria necessary to plant growth experiment
1221:20
Soil bacteria, how to collect and observe 864:30-31
Stained slide of bacteria—how to make 500:51-53
Staining bacteria for microscope slides—how to do
11:128-135
Temperature affects bacterial growth experiment
1395:123
Temperature effect on growth of bacteria experiment
1405:31
Test for antibacterial activity on different seaweed prepa-
rations exp. 864:58-60
Testing for bacterial growth in milk experiment 924:43-
44
The invisible seeds—observe "gardens" for growth of
molds and bacteria (advanced) 565:43-53
Tiny but mighty 280:59-60
Transfer bacteria from rotten apple to good apple experi-
ment 723:78
Tyndall Effect experiments with bacteria 864:32-33
Using bacteria to clean up oil spills on beaches experi-
ment 1450:42-48
Water sewage and pollution experiment with bird ma-
nure 10:50-54
Which substance most effective to prevent bacteria in
water beds experiment 997:121-123
Which type of footwear grows the most bacteria experi-
ment 997:132-134
Why dead fish float belly side up experiment 1479:31
Why we wash our hands experiment with molds growing
on potato mush mixture 1482:8-9
Winogradsky column to observe growth of bacteria ex-
periment, how to make 1221:15-16

BAEKELAND, LEO HENDRIK
Who first discovered plastic project 1525:80-83

BAKING POWDER
Acid effect on baking; carbon dioxide produced experi-
ment 905:202-203
Baking powder added to acid experiment 1238:105
Baking powder gives off more carbon dioxide gas than
baking soda experiment 1208:87
Baking powder in water gives off gases experiment
1244:37
Baking powder is double-acting experiment 980:45
Baking powder; chemical reaction involved in baking ex-
periment 1159:20-22
Demonstrate why cake batter rises 780:48-49
How is baking powder different from baking soda experi-
ment 1238:104
Make baking powder biscuits 598:44-45
Muffins experiment with different methods of cooking
them 1238:107-108
Show how double-acting baking powder works experi-
ment 1484:73

BAKING SODA. See also **ACIDS AND BASES**
Acid effect on baking; carbon dioxide produced experi-
ment 905:202-203
Baking powder gives off more carbon dioxide gas than
baking soda experiment 1208:87
Baking soda puffs up bread and cake experiment
1238:103
How is baking powder different from baking soda experi-
ment 1238:104
Magic potions 16:62-65
Pancakes with baking soda experiment 1238:106

BALANCE. See also **MOBILES; SCALES**
A letter scale—how to make 241:2-3
A soda straw balance 295:19-21
A soda straw balance—building and using 400:91-92
Balance beam experiments with wooden balance beam,
how to build 1444:16-19
Balance beam toy experiment 1444:68-75
Balance beam, how to make 948:11
Balance blocks on a seesaw [Primary] 743:10
Balance board and fulcrum—making 631:57
Balance point is fulcrum 274:21
Balance scale—construct 436:12-13
Balance scale—simple—making 759:15
Balance scale from broom handle and board, how to
make 1014:188
Balance scale used to measure mass (amount of matter
present) experiment 1399:44-47
Balance scale, wooden, how to make 885:37-39
Balance skill spool, how to make 948:8-10
Balance to weigh letters experiment 1298:13
Balance; build to demonstrate lever used to weigh things
experiment 1157:109-116
Balances—how to make balance pans 631:55-56
Balances—use balance pans to weigh ingredients for
sugar cookies 631:56
Balancing—"impossible" balancing act with model tight-
rope walker 419:9
Balancing acrobat toy—making [Primary] 753:12-13
Balancing act 399:8
Balancing act contraption, making 779:6
Balancing act demonstrates center of gravity experiment
1031:18-19
Balancing activities for classroom 1291:27-29
Balancing acts—fooling around with forks 162:104-105
Balancing Bill and balancing Jill plastic bottles, patterns
given, make 1299:72-73
Balancing bird from cardboard and clay, making [Primary]
786:20
Balancing boat from tennis ball and knitting needle, how
to make 1299:75
Balancing boys from cardboard, balsa wood and wire,
how to make 1299:75
Balancing broom 95:3
Balancing butterfly, how to make (Primary) 1317:9
Balancing clown experiment demonstrates center of grav-
ity, how to make 1507:17
Balancing clown on wire demonstrates center of gravity
experiment 1031:20-21
Balancing dinner forks experiments 1079:32-35
Balancing doll from cardboard, clay, and eggshell, mak-
ing [Primary] 786:19
Balancing drinks on a tray experiment [Primary] 753:8-9
Balancing forks and toothpicks experiments 1330:80-81
Balancing guy—making 733:22
Balancing hammer tied to ruler on table experiment
1079:26-27
Balancing man toy, how to make 861:105-111
Balancing odd shaped objects experiments 1444:63-66
Balancing point—experiments 664:8-11
Balancing points of different objects experiments
1444:30-36
Balancing potato on the edge of a glass 150:76-77
Balancing rolling toy experiments; how to make tight-
rope walker 1444:50-52
Balancing ruler experiment [Primary] 753:6-7

Balancing symmetrical objects vertically experiments 1444:53-58

Balancing the impossible—three experiments—pencil, knife, hammer 360:24-25

Balancing tightrope acrobat toy—making [Primary] 753:16-17

Balancing toy experiments; how to make model toy 1444:42-49

Balancing trick with potato, forks, coin and cup 1522:29

Balancing tricks, how to do experiment 947:18-19

Balancing tricks, making 684:24-25

Balancing uneven weights experiments 1444:59-62

Balancing weights 253:170-171

Balancing witch tricks, how to do 1002:10-11

Balancing yardstick on your fingers experiment 1079:28-29

Ball and cardboard balance—making 733:18

Body model balanced vertically and horizontally experiment, how to build model 1444:20-29

Bridge made from cardboard demonstrates balance experiment 1444:88-89

Bucket balance activities 1128:24-25

Building a balance 295:22-27

Building better balance 586:68-71

Can with clay in bottom and top; which slides first experiment [Primary] 786:8-9

Can you walk in a straight line (Primary) 551:unpaged

Center of gravity—a balancing act 291:140

Center of gravity—experiments to show 106:3-7

Center of gravity affects a balance experiment with straw balance 1404:82-84

Center of gravity is balancing point of an object experiment 1404:79

Center of gravity point demonstrated with balancing forks 1404:90-91

Center of gravity; balance potato to demonstrate experiment 1507:16

Coin balances on rim of glass experiment 1007:68-69

Construct letter balance scale 167:73-77

Construct model of steel yard balance to demonstrate 167:67-72

Construct/experiment with simple balance from household items (Primary) 529:1-17

Constructing and using a balance 577:project 67

Cup with clay in bottom doesn't fall over [Primary] 786:6

Demonstrate balance with paper cup (Primary) 201:28-29

Demonstrate center of gravity 210:29; 295:12-13

Demonstrate the balance principle of a tightrope walker 545:38-41

Demonstrate the center of mass experiment 836:60-62

Demonstrate your center of gravity 295:14-15

Do you dare—person get out of chair, unglue one shoe, lift dollar, on toe 162:110-111

Does tilting effect center of gravity 274:25

Domino acrobatics demonstrates 1007:69-71

Easy to make balancing sculpture 241:18-21

Effects of darkness on balance and hearing experiment 1159:56-57

Experiment to show 128:122-123

Experiments with balance 107:17-26

Experiments with balance in animals and humans 1425:153-158

Fearsome Fred balancing face from thick cardboard, pattern given, make 1299:74

Find balance point of any flat cut out shape 419:9

Find center of an irregular shape 162:106-107

Find center of gravity of cardboard 274:23

Finding the balance point (center of gravity) 274:22

Finding the balancing point 596:14

Finding the center of gravity 241:16-17

Floating forks 16:32-34

Fork balancing act 203:77

Forks balance on cork experiment 940:85-86

Forks balance on glass, ruler stays on table, hammer and string experiment 1002:12

Gravity and building blocks 274:20

Great balancing tricks and how to make a balancing bird 600:8-9

High wire walker—how to make 410:24

Horizontal balancing points of different objects experiments 1444:30-36

How can one penny balance nine pennies experiment [Primary] 753:20

How can one penny lift nine pennies experiment 753:21

How good a gymnast are you 274:19

How to make a beam balance 57:66

How to make your own balance 126:167-170; 55:160-161

Human body balance; how steady are you experiment 1506:42-44

Human body balance; light effect on your balance experiment 1506:43-44

Ircus balancing act using unsymmetrical balancing device experiment 1444:84-87

Lowering the center of gravity—make a balancing doll 241:28-31

Machine mobiles demonstrate balance and first-class lever balance 1462:29-32

Magic balancing wand, making 669:26-27

Make a balance scale 293:42

Make a balancer toy (difficult) 172:89-92

Make a balancing horse 172:92-94

Make a balancing man (center of gravity) 142:61

Make a balancing needle 94:34

Make a balancing toy 274:26

Make a balancing toy (center of gravity) 142:60

Make a ball balance 32:60-61

Make a butterflier 162:112-113

Make a coat hanger balance 32:58-59

Make a comeback can 162:108-109

Make a cone creature for your nose 162:114

Make a noddy clown 94:30-31

Make a rocker clown 274:27

Make a swinging parrot 94:35

Make a tight rope walker 94:32-33

Make an equal arms balance 253:164-165

Make magic stair walkers toy to demonstrate 172:95

Make mobile that moves in a breeze 241:4-6

Make mobiles, equilibrium on a string 162:102-103

Making a seesaw balance 596:10-11

Making a sensitive balance 596:12

Making a straw balance 596:13

Milk carton balance—making 631:113

Mobile from cardboard shapes, making 786:21

Mobile from straws and cardboard demonstrates balance (Primary) 1317:28-29

Mobile that demonstrates balance—making 753:22-23

Mobile to demonstrate balance made from cardboard, straws, thread 1380:10-11

Mobile to demonstrate balance, how to make 1128:22-23
Mobile uses balanced forces—making 682:19
Objects center of gravity can be changed experiment 1399:36-39
Paper airplanes and paper clips demonstrate balance 241:43-45
Pendulum picture maker—how to make 241:40-42
Polynesian outrigger canoe—how to make 325:unpaged
Potato balances on forks experiment with center of gravity 1065:13
Racing hoops made out of paper demonstrate balance 1079:40-41
Raising the center of gravity 241:26-27
Salt shaker mystery trick—experiment 563:41
Scale from straws, making 827:19
Scale from strings, making 827:104-105
Scale, balancing, wooden, how to make 770:125
Scales from coat hanger and paper plates, how to make (Primary) 1317:25
Scales; simple scales, how to make 1248:8-9
Seesaw from wooden blocks experiment (Primary) 1317:13
Seesaw toy from cup and straw, making 786:14-15
Sensitive balance detects weight of the lightest objects experiment 1031:24-25
Shape of bottle affects stability 274:24
Simple balance for weighing 898:25-26
Simple balance, how to build and do experiments 1444:98-103
Simple balancing toys experiment, how to make 1446:28-29
Single-beam balance, how to make from cup, clay, string, wire hanger 1462:25-27
Skyhook, make to balance belt on your nose 887:44-45
Soda bottle balance, how to make 1527:115
Some strange balancing acts 295:16-18
Spring balance experiment (Primary) 1317:23
Spring balance, making 909:94
Stand up, do not fall down (Primary) 551:unpaged
Swinging monkey demonstrates—making 682:20
Symmetrical mobile experiments, how to build 1444:75-83
Test—how important is eyesight in keeping balance 335:108
Test—to demonstrate if person can remain motionless 335:106
Tightrope walker on string demonstrates balance, how to make 1136:11
Toothpick toy that balances—making [Primary] 753:28
Toppling toy that doesn't fall over, how to make 1128:17
Toys that balance, how to make tightrope walker, rocking snake 1128:18-19
Toys, balancing, how to make 868:69
Trick cyclist—how to make 410:25
Unsymmetrical mobile experiment, how to build 1444:90-97
Using a balance scale (Primary) 232:103
Vertical balance of tightrope walkers experiment 1444:37-41
Vertical balancing points of different objects experiments 1444:30-36
Wand balances on fingers trick 1216:22-24
Weights and balances—make your own 748:41
What a complication equilibrium 161:21
What three dolls can show us about balance 241:8-10

Why do things fall over experiment with box, string and washer 1399:32-35
You and balance—large diagram of ear 241:46-49
You can win this balance game with rulers (Primary) 551:unpaged
Your center of gravity 241:22-24

BALL BEARINGS. *See also* **FRICTION**
Ball bearing reduces friction, how to demonstrate 1033:21
Ball bearings in model car overcome friction experiment 1334:10-11
Ball bearings overcome friction experiment with marbles and tin cans 1436:72-74
Ball bearings reduce friction experiment with marbles and cans 940:82-84
Bearings reduce friction; marbles and jar lids experiment 837:34-35
Do ball bearings reduce friction experiment 834:62
Effect of ball bearings on motion demonstration 1479:100
Marble experiment 756:17
Metal cans and marbles—experiment 436:13
Model ballbearing using cans and marbles experiment 1523:22
Model bobsleds and run, how to make to demonstrate ball bearings 1446:14-15
Wheels can be made to rotate faster experiment 1400:60-63

BALL RISER. *See also* **BERNOULLI EFFECT**
Ping pong ball held in place by stream of air 366:164

BALLOONS
A balloon trick experiment 563:40-41
Air bag platform from balloons, making 994:75-78
Air from balloons makes jet planes and boats (Primary) 144:4-13
Air mattress from balloons, making 994:72-74
Air, helium, and carbon dioxide filled balloons behave differently exp. 888:130
As arches, beams and trusses 328:138-147
Balloon blows up; vinegar, baking soda mixed in bottle experiment 1014:34
Balloon blowup—bottle, vinegar and baking soda 558:52
Balloon in a jug—experiments to demonstrate air pressure 563:114
Balloon power demonstrated by letting blown up balloons go (Primary) 452:72
Balloon projectile experiment 994:64-68
Balloon propelled car experiment 994:28-34
Balloon rockets on string demonstrate propulsion experiment 994:19-27
Balloon spins like aeropile experiment 994:46-51
Balloon trick—experiments show air expands when heated 563:113
Balloons filled with water move in water experiment 994:43-45
Blow up by dry ice method 91:104-107
Blow up by heat method 91:104-107
Blow up by vacuum method 91:104-107
Blow up by water pressure method 91:104-107
Experiments with amount of air balloons will hold 994:10-18
Experiments with 107:84-89
Experiments with balloons 538:26-32
Inflatable furniture from balloons experiment 994:69-72

It's magic—trick experiment with polyethylene bag 563:35-36

Jet propelled boat experiment with balloons and test tank 994:35-45

Make a boat with balloon power 147:39

Make a soap bubble balloon with balloonist 172:71-73

Measuring force of air in balloons experiment using force measuring device 994:52-62

Skewer a balloon without popping it experiment 1083:55

The bashful balloon—static electricity experiments 563:105

The race is on—balloon race on water (Primary) 452:73

Warm air balloon 366:164-165

Why a balloon rises 382:68-72

Why does it rise 55:77-81

BALLOONS—HELIUM

How far did your helium balloon travel 333:30-32

Letter to enclose for finder 333:32

BALLOONS—HOT AIR. *See also* HOT AIR BALLOONS

Bottle with balloon in cold and hot water demonstrates principle 940:34-36

Hot air balloon—how to make 178:26; 605:30-33

Hot air balloon experiment 860:223-225

Hot air balloons—how to make 419:33; 419:37

How to make baggie type, paper tissue type 400:100

Make a hot air balloon 172:73-81; 186:18-19; 625:44

Making a hot air balloon and a helium filled balloon 225:11-12

Why hot air balloons rise 225:8-11

BALLS

Ball bounce affected by surface and temperature experiments 881:72-73

Bounce height of different balls experiment 1091:37-38

Bounce heights of ball as related to drop heights experiment data tables 1004:5.006

Bounce of rubber ball affected by temperature experiment 1404:210-211

Bounce; test how high ball bounces experiment using large paper ruler as scale 1380:32

Bouncing balls—experiment to test bounciness of balls 586:80

Experiments—show shape size across/around, bounce on different material 214:5-32

Falling balls experiment 1159:46-47

How high do balls bounce experiment 795:29

Investigate scientific principles behind toys experiments 1412:81-87

Make ball bounce by itself experiment 902:38

Projects with bouncing balls 1164:36-37

Rotating or spinning balls in sports experiments 1154:80-93

Temperature affects bounce of rubber ball experiment 1405:108

Which ball bounces the best experiment 754:21

Which surfaces are best for bouncing balls experiment 754:22-25

Why balls bounce, roll and push activities [Primary] 787:3-22

BANANAS

Banana tree, how to grow 1486:34-35

Ethylene gas promotes ripening in bananas experiment 1484:126-128

BANK

Thank you money bank—how to make 410:20-21

BAR GRAPHS. *See* GRAPHS—BAR

BARGES

Make a model barge 223:22-23

BARK RUBBINGS

Bark pattern rubbings, how to do 1142:15

Bark rubbing—how to 275:23

Bark rubbings—how to do 234:82; 236:20-22; 264:46; 918.39

Bark rubbings show textures of different trees experiment 1044:24-25

Crayon rubbing of tree bark, how to do 1368:94

Crayon rubbings from bark of tree, how to do 1183:99

How to do 1214:29; 442:unpaged

How to do bark rubbings 1379:33

How to make bark rubbings 1114:134-135; 1145:30

Making 480:79

Tree bark rubbings, how to do 932:22-23

BARNACLES

Adventure 44—we get to know the barnacle—barnacles under a hand lens 29:198-200

Barnacles feeding and influence of tide on feeding experiment 1225:17

Factors or stimuli that effect rate of barnacle feeding experiment 1225:18

Salinity of water and its effect on rate of barnacle feeding experiment 1225:18

Study of living barnacles 285:72-73

Succession in a barnacle community experiment; observation chart given 1225:18-19

Temperature of water and its effect on rate of barnacle feeding experiment 1225:17-18

What is a barnacle made of experiment; use acetic acid or vinegar 1225:19

BAROMETER. *See also* AIR PRESSURE

Air pressure changes in Earth's sea of air experiment 1516:12-13

Air pressure demonstration construct simple barometer experiment 752:109-110

Air pressure weather tester—making 656:28-29

Air pressure; how measured demonstration 1023:142-143

An air barometer (aneroid barometer) 53:30-31

Aneroid barometer—how to make 705:72-73; 978:148

Aneroid barometer, simple one from jar, straw and balloon, how to make 1104:9

Aneroid barometer, with activities, making 891:25-31

Balloon barometer, making 1003:102-103

Balloon, jar and straw barometer, making 1017:75

Barometer—aneroid 9:98-99

Barometer—how to make 605:64-65; 660:14; 732:50-51

Barometer from container, plastic wrap and straw, how to make 1086:14-15

Barometer from glass jar and bottle with food coloring, how to make 1135:31

Barometer from glass jar, balloon and ruler, how to make 1465:15

Barometer from glass jar, balloon, straw, graph paper, how to make 1476:154

Barometer from glass jar, balloon, straw, how to make 1114:18-19

Barometer from jar and balloon with rubber top, how to make 1430:19

Barometer from jar, balloon and straw, how to make 1115:64-65; 1149:7

Barometer from plastic bottle and glass jar, how to make 1372:22-23

Barometer made from bottle, glass and food coloring 1480:156
Barometer measures air pressure experiment, how to make 1211:18
Barometer measures air pressure experiment 1042:32-33; 1332:8-9
Barometer measures air pressure, how to make from glass jar and straw 1387:16
Barometer measures air pressure, how to make from glass, balloon/straws 1179:123
Barometer measures fluctuations in air pressure experiment, how to make 1447:38-41
Barometer measures pressure of air experiment, how to make 1063:442
Barometer measures pressure of air, how to make 1311:11
Barometer to measure atmospheric pressure experiment, how to make 1521:30-31
Barometer, how to make 947:42-43
Barometer, making 906:18; 909:62
Barometric pressure scale model—making 748:42
Bottle barometer, making 1003:100-101
Build a barometer 327:42-43
Can, balloon, and soda straw barometer, how to make 837:53-55
Cape Cod barometer—making 657:57-58; 959:94
Easy barometer, how to make 885:65
Experiments with 693:57-60
Homemade—how to make 234:98
Homemade barometer, how to make 940:40-42
How reliable is a milk bottle barometer 333:68-70
How to make 117:95-96; 178:32; 293:11-12; 629:57-58; 91:66-69
How to make a chemical barometer 172:127-128
How to make a homemade water barometer 172:122-123
How to make a mercury barometer 172:123-124
How to make an aneroid barometer 128:92-93
How to make mercury 128:80-82
How to make one 651:28-29
How to make to measure air pressure 588:46-47
How to make with glass, ruler and tubing 1237:41-42
Jar barometer, how to make 852:48-49
Make a balloon barometer 92:36-37
Make a simple barometer 179:28-30; 186:11; 236:163
Make an ink drop barometer 53:28-29
Make and assemble a barometer 175:72-73
Make two simple barometers 597:34-35
Make your own from baby food jar and straw 816:3
Make your own 679:14
Making a barometer 400:64
Making an air pressure measurer barometer project 833:144-145
Making barometer from jar, bowl and paper clips 1439:102-104
Measure air pressure experiment; making a barometer 900:83-84
Pascal's aneroid barometer testing the sea of air hypothesis experiment 1156:55-56
Plastic bottle barometer, making 1016:16
Simple barometer from can, straw and piece of balloon, how to make 1388:15
Simple barometer, how to make 860:189-190
Simple-how to make (Primary) 541:36-37
Soap bottle barometer—making 767:138
Thermos bottle and straw barometer, making 1012:21

Three homemade barometers to measure barometric pressure experiment 715:127-131
Tin can barometer—making 767:139
Torricelli's water barometer experiment 1156:54-55

BAROMETRIC PRESSURE
Expanding air 253:55-56
Three homemade barometers to measure barometric pressure experiment 715:127-131

BAROSCOPE
How to make 128:86

BASE FIVE
Activities to demonstrate 405:1-33

BASEBALL
Aluminum versus wooden bats experiment 1154:114-115
Baseball bat has sweet spot; how to find it experiment 1209:50-51
Pitchers throw different kinds of balls experiment 1154:93-100
Running the bases speed experiment 1154:45-49
"Sweet spot" on tennis racket or baseball bat experiment 1154:115-121

BASES. *See also* **ACIDS AND BASES; SOAP; SOLUTIONS**
How to detect a base 122:113-115
How to get magnesium hydroxide out of ocean 85:46-47

BASKETBALL
Home field playing gives winning advantage in sports experiment 1195:79-93

BATH FOAMING OIL
Recipe for 387:20-21

BATH SALTS
How to make bath salts experiment using washing soda, perfume and food colors 1435:45-48
Recipe for 387:17-18
Water softener experiment with bath salts made from washing soda/perfume 1179:38

BATHYSPHERES. *See* **DIVING—SUBMARINES**

BATS
Bat box, how to put up 963:42-43
Bat box, wooden, how to make 1147:30
Bat house, how to make from wood 1181:37
Make a bat box 740:27
Nesting box for bats, how to make from wood 1183:45

BATTERIES. *See also* **BULBS AND BATTERIES; DRY CELLS; ELECTRICITY—BATTERIES**
AC power supply unit, how to build 830:23-24
Batteries connected in reverse give no electric current 287:24
Batteries connected in series or parallel give different effects 287:23
Battery and bulb circuit used to demonstrate conductors 888:158-161
Battery and tinfoil make bulb light experiment 782:30-33
Battery attached to head phones makes sound experiment 1030:18-19
Battery from copper coins, zinc and salty water blotting paper experiment 955:13
Battery from salt, foil and copper coins experiment 1028:105
Battery from salty paper, coins and zinc experiment 1072:13
Battery from soap solution, aluminum, and penny makes electric currents 1482:54-55

Battery from strip of zinc and copper pipe in water, how to make 1179:150-151

Battery holder for D cells, how to make 830:17

Battery rejuvenator, how to make 830:24-25

Battery to produce electric current with salt, water, foil 1479:110

Battery wire—positive/negative test using a potato 563:94-95

Battery, bulb, and circuit experiment 888:154-157

Battery, simple, making 895:61-63

Battery-powered compass, making 627:28

Blinky the Blinker light—how to make 723:32-33

Build a better battery 586:100

Chemical reaction battery gives electricity Volta's way experiment 1063:164

Coins, foil and salt water battery, how to make 1382:6-7

Copper coin battery, making 929:9

Copper zinc plate battery, how to make experiment 1426:40-42

DC power supply unit, how to build 830:20-21

Demonstration storage cells 577:project #45

Door buzzer; Dr. Zed's Hum-Dinger-Door buzzer, making 890:23

Dry battery experiment, how to construct 1476:14

Dry cell—how can you bring a dead dry cell back to life 278:33-34

Dry cell; what is inside experiment 1426:42-44

Electric cell; make from two different metals and an electrolyte experiment 1159:108-110

Electric current produced by electrolytes in different liquids experiment 1004:4.008

Electricity from a lemon experiment 1072:13

Electricity from fruit and nails 586:99-100

Eleven cent battery—making 445:16

Experiments with 693:47-50

Find out how to make a battery 599:35-36

Find out what a battery is made from 599:33-34

First electric battery experiment 895:7-9

Flashlight, how it works experiment 906:104

Fruits and vegetables make batteries experiment 1296:1975

Hand battery experiment; your skin and 2 different metals create a battery 1132:57-1-57-2

How does dry-cell or flashlight battery work experiment 902:251-252

Insulated wire, how to make 888:160

Leclanche Cells—demonstration project 577:project #46

Lemon battery—how to make 507:1854-1855

Lemon battery demonstrates electrolyte 293:32

Lemon battery experiment 1396:94-96; 1411:36

Lemon battery experiment with copper nail, metal strip, wires and foil 1473:28

Lemon battery experiment, how to do 1501:40-43

Lemon battery, how to make 1244:32-33; 1271:28; 1382:6; 972:17

Lemon battery, how to make experiment 1514:111-113

Lemon battery lights bulb experiment 1139:68-69

Lemon battery, making 670.97; ; 929:9; 955:13; 1001:30

Lemon battery produces electricity experiment 895:6-7

Lemon battery you can eat experiment 1159:108-110

Lemon electric cell experiment; use lemon, and strips of copper and zinc 1218:39

Lemon juice and nails battery, making 998:228

Lemon juice, coins and aluminum foil battery, how to build 1076:30-31

Lemon power experiment using galvanometer, how to make 1476:15

Lemons produce electricity 599:36-37

Make simple electric circuit with battery and bulb 207:48-49

Making a battery experiment 1514:106-107

Money power experiment—coins produce electric current 563:98

Parallel or series battery circuit system; which makes bulb brightest ex 1012:59-60

Penny and dime battery, how to make 938:20-21

Poles of batteries can be identified experiment 1293:67-68

Positive battery terminal experiment with potato battery to demonstrate 1404:14-15

Potato battery experiment 1004:3.012

Potato battery, how to make 938:19

Potato indicates polarity of storage battery experiment 768:83

Produce electricity with a lemon experiment 902:253

Quiz board—how to make 293:47-49

Quiz game; Dr. Zed's Electrifying quiz game, making 890:26-27

Simple 'wet' cell experiment 22:9

Simple battery from jar of vinegar, zinc and copper metal, how to make 1160:30

Simple battery holder for D cells 23:16

Solar battery, how to wire and set up 830:25-26

Sources of electricity 23:15-23

Spacecraft—chemical batteries—activities/experiments to demonstrate 564:39-40

Storage battery—making 436:76

Storing electricity in a lead-acid cell experiment 972:39

Stunts with batteries 102:106-158

Use aluminum foil to light a bulb 144:22-31

Varying voltage and current in batteries experiment 23:17-20

Vinegar battery, how to make 1244:32-33

Wet battery experiment, how to construct 1476:13-14

Wet cell battery; make from dry-cell parts experiment 1426:44-47

Wet-cell battery from lemon experiment 1294:50-52

Which brand of battery lasts the longest experiment 888:162

Why do batteries have a positive and negative pole experiment 860:59-61

BATTERIES—HOW TO MAKE

A wet cell battery—how to make 341:31-32

IIow can you make a battery 278:32-33

How to make a simple storage battery 128:170-171

Lead storage cell—how you can make a lead storage cell 278:34-35

Make a dime and penny battery 185:16-18

Make a dry cell or battery 168:28-29

Make a lemon juice battery 287:15

Make your own battery 138:9

The electric lemon battery, making 627:25

Your own battery, how to make 627:24

BATTERIES AND BULBS. *See* **ELECTRICITY—BATTERIES; BULBS AND BATTERIES**

BATTERIES AND CIRCUITS

Colored lights 15:23

Game—light answer quiz game—how to make 15:20-21

Game—pinball game 15:30-31

Game—steady hand game 15:24-25

Game—stop—go traffic lights 15:28-29
Game—track the invisible wires 15:26-27
Game—traveling lights 15:22
Game—wriggly road game—how to make 15:18-19
How to make a bulb holder 15:10-11
Lemon battery circuits 677:8-9
Lemon juice and coins make wet cell experiment 827:57
Lemon makes electricity experiment 827:58-59
Making a know how bulb holder 15:12-13
Making a know how night light 15:16-17
Making a lantern 15:15
Making a light house 15:14
Morse code transmitters 15:32-35
Rollek the flashing robot 15:36-39

BATTERY HOLDERS
How to make a battery holder 400:89

BATTERY TESTER
How to make 366:243

BAYBERRY CANDLES
How to make 296:80-83

BEACH. *See also* **OCEAN; SEASHORE**
Action of water on coastlines experiment 1342:121-126
Adaptations of animals and insects to dune life experiment; record chart given 1225:194-195
Beach fleas, observation of, how to do 1225:176-177
Beach grass and sea oats observations, how to do 1225:187-188
Beach materials—collecting and labeling 299:10-11
Beach sand observations, how to do 1225:168-180
Calcium carbonates in beach sand determined; adding vinegar to sand experiment 1225:174
Collage—make collage of coral, driftwood, seaweeds, egg cases 296:53-61
Effect of wave height and length on coastlines experiment 1342:124-126
Erosion of beach sand by waves experiment 1290:54, 4.1
Exploring a sandy beach 285:68-69
Grains of sand compared and classified experiment 1290:57, 4.4
Greenhouse effect as cause of rise in sea levels project 1342:126
Heat and breeze at the beach experiment 939:62-64
Hourly weather conditions on foredune experiment; recording chart given 1225:192
Log of your beach observations, how to do 840:86-87
Make a beach sculpture with plaster of Paris 32:76-77
Model sand beach, how to make 1342:121
Objects found in strand line of beach; observe and record on chart experiment 1225:174-176
Organisms or living things found in beach zones; use transect line experiment 1225:175-176
Plant life samples on dunes using quadrat for sampling experiment 1225:190-192
Ripple patterns on beach sand experiment 1266:20
Sand dune observations, how to do 1225:182-196
Sand from different beaches compared experiment 1290:56, 4.3
Size of sand particles in relation to their location on beach experiment 1225:173
Stream table activities 400:56-57
Survival strategies of plants living in Atlantic Coast dune systems experiment 1225:189-192
Temperature variations above and below the sand experiment 1225:192-193

Temperature variations on foredune during twelve hour period experiment 1225:193
Tide observations, how to do 1225:198-207
Wave action and pebble distribution on beach experiment 1134:1.003
Wentworth Grain Size Scale for sand 1225:180

BEACH FORMS
Sand dunes and sand banks 299:15
Spits, bars and tombolos 299:16

BEACH GLASS
Make window ornament and hot plate 296:48-52

BEACH MURAL
Mural in 3-D to show physical construction, life forms, plant and animal life 359:28-33

BEACH PLANTS
How to collect and dry 296:83-85
Investigation of the plants of beach and dune 285:71-72

BEACH TERRARIUM
How to make 296:63-65

BEADS
Miniature bead garden—directions for making 449:95-99

BEAM BRIDGE. *See* **BRIDGES**

BEAMS. *See also* **BUILDING**
Beam structure—experiment 585:48
Bridge beams test for strength experiment 755:22-23
Bridge built with beams and arches; which is strongest experiment 1094:15-16
Build a prestressed beam 557:67
Build a simple device to find compression and tension in a beam 557:49-50
Build models to compare beam shapes 557:50-51
Can you invent a beam 557:51-52
Demonstrate tension and compression 328:19-22
Experiment to show steel reinforcement rods 328:28-29
I-Beam strength demonstration 1436:107-109
Laminated beam strength demonstration with yardsticks and clamps 1436:110-112
Making model paper beams for structural strength 550:68-69

BEANS. *See also* **SEEDS—GERMINATION**
Bean maze and light to demonstrate smart beans 366:98-99
Bean seeds, how to plant and grow indoors 1178:25
Mung—grow bean sprouts 376:4
Sprouts from beans, how to grow 1178:24

BEARINGS. *See* **BALL BEARINGS**

BEAUFORT WIND SCALE
Beaufort Scale chart 1108:17
Beaufort Scale for measuring wind in knots 1453:44
Beaufort Scale illustrated 1161:10; 1387:17
Beaufort Scale illustration 1042:37
Beaufort Scale 494:75; 935:59; 662:40
Beaufort Scale of wind speed chart 1516:100
Beaufort Wind Scale 1134:2.003; 1311:25
Beaufort Wind Scale chart 1063:437; 1474:57
Chart of 705:60; 767:63
Chart of Beaufort Scale 1003:108-109
Chart of Beaufort Wind Scale 1115:74
Chart of wind scale 1104:10; 1293:88; 879:24; 891:66
Explanation of Beaufort Scale 1355:51
How fast does wind move 660:31
How fast does the wind move scale 909:79
Illustrated scale of wind speeds 1180:5; 1183:133
Illustration of Beaufort Scale 1086:18-19

Illustration of Beaufort Wind Scale 1465:12
Wind force scale 737:21
Wind scale 860:195
Wind scale chart 1017:91
Wind scale given; record winds for 5 days 816:5

BEAUMONT, WILLIAM
Process of digestion experiment 1133:3.007

BECQUEREL, ANTOINE
His experiments 42:135-139

BEER
What puts the head on beer 366:77-78

BEER—GINGER
Recipe for 366:78

BEES. *See also* **HONEYBEES**
A method for showing that bees recognize patterns and
will return to them 414:89-90
Bees can detect water without touching it—experiment
414:92
Bees have a sense of time—experiment 414:92
Bumblebee nest box from flowerpot and wood, how to
make 1069:113
Can bees detect different concentrations of sugar experi-
ment 1096:48-50
Clover syrup, recipe, how to make 1464:73
Color vision—will bees come to red or blue sweet dishes
414:90-91
Color, fragrance and flavor attract bees; which is most
important experiment 997:43-45
Color; can honeybees see color experiment 1134:3.005
Feed honey bees 236:62
Game; bee game to show bees collecting nectar, how to
make 1445:38-41
Honeybee feeding habits experiment 1097:137-140
How honeybees find their way home experiment 1479:
31
How much sugar is in honey experiment 1096:144-148
Language of bees in the field and in the laboratory
266:86-90
Making your own nests to attract bees and wasps 414:96-
97
Observe and record bee dances and instructions to find
flowers and nectar 366:36-38
Observing bees at table with dishes of sugar experiment
1464:71-72
Record colors, smells and kinds of flowers a bee visits
414:39-40
Time sense in bees in the field and in the laboratory
266:37-39
Training bees to come to dish of honey or syrup 414:89-
90
Wasp model, how to make 1445:36-37
Wasp nest model, how to make 1445:44-45
Watch it feed 480:59
What colors attract honeybees to flowers experiment
1096:45-50
Will bees come to artificial sweeteners 414:91

BEES—POLLINATION
Honey bees and pollination 236:62
How the bees make colored flowers 366:90-91

BEETLES. *See also* **FIREFLIES; LADYBUGS;
INSECTS**
Adventure 52—operate on digestive tract of beetle under
microscope 403:202-205
Collecting and caring for beetles, how to do 915:10-19
Diving beetles 62:58

Footprints of beetles examined experiment using food
colors 1464:65
How to cage and care for 279:24-25

BEETLES—TRAPS
In ground trap for beetles, how to make 1464:64

BEHAVIOR
Brain and learning experiments 1267:54-56
How bright is your pet experiment 1425:113
How fast do you learn experiment 1425:113-119
Memory and learning; does high glucose liquid enhance
memory experiment 1267:56-57
Time limits on tests help or hinder performance experi-
ment 1267:58-59

BEHAVIOR—ANIMALS. *See also* **ANIMAL
BEHAVIOR**
Astronomical influences on behavior in animals and
humans experiment 1062:109
Building choice chambers to help small creatures answer
questions experiment 1313:43-49
Designing animal behavior experiments 148:52-53

BEHAVIOR—HUMAN
Astronomical influences on behavior in animals and
humans experiment 1062:109
Behavior of people regarding fad theories in astronomy
project 1062:114-115
Community life and human behavior projects 506:1-106;
542:1-141
Habit forming behavior experiment 936:31-32
Learning behavior experiment 936:38-40
Sky observations linked to holiday activities on Earth
project 1062:116-117

BEHAVIOR—INSECTS
Taste receptors in blow flies experiment 1096:105-
109
Which parts of fly's body sense taste experiment
1096:105-109

BELL, ALEXANDER GRAHAM
Bell's Photophone; modern day version, how to make
1249:17-24

BELLOWS AND TRIP HAMMER
Making from wood 429:105

BELLS
Can hand bells—make and play 363:129-131
How can you wire a bell for your room 278:48

BELT—TWIG
How to make 442:unpaged

BELT DRIVEN MACHINES
Belt driven machine—making 756:22-23
Build belt drive system 227:16-17
Demonstrating belt driven machines 180:42-43
Spool models 436:14

BELTS
Acrobats whirl around on belt drive experiment, how to
make 1446:16-17
Belts make spools turn, build using wood, spools and
belt 1033:14-15
Mobius strip as connecting belt for wheels experiment
1405:98

BENHAM'S DISK
Benham's Disk, rotating black and white disc produces
illusion of color 1132:5-1-5-2

BENHAM'S TOP
Benham disc experiment 827:40-41

BENHAM'S TOP AND OTHER SPIN OFFS
Project 229:78-81

BERLESE FUNNEL
Berlese funnel—how to make 585:159
How to make 175:30; 442:unpaged
How to make funnel to catch insects 832:67
How to make to catch insects 117:41-44
How to make to collect animals in leaf litter 285:85
Set up Berlese funnel to collect soil critters 864:95-96
Using Berlese funnel to collect animals in leaf litter and
      soil experiment 1505:24-25

BERNOULLI, DANIEL
A mist sprayer a la Bernoulli—how to make 600:32-33
His experiments 42:54-63
Ping pong balls demonstrate why planes can fly experi-
      ment 1372:38
Who discovered laws of gases or fluids in motion pro-
      ject 1525:92-94

BERNOULLI BALANCE TRICK
Wind from vacuum holds ball in air 364:135

BERNOULLI EFFECT
'Anti gravity' demonstrators with vacuum cleaner and
      balloons 392:36-46
Bernoulli effect on a water surface 585:19
Bet you can keep a ball in the air for an hour 228:74-75
Dancing ping pong ball on vertical jet of water 392:68-70
Experiments with ping pong balls demonstrate Bernoulli
      Effect 1179:128-129
How airplanes fly experiment 1164:73-75
How used to help airplanes fly—experiment 679:8-10
Moving air has less pressure than still air experiment
      1250:21-23
Puffed rice and glass chimney experiment 532:30
Straw and glass of water demonstrate 940:59-61
The dancing ball 291:90-91
The mischievous ball experiment 563:124
Using balloons 92:8-9, 16-17
Why airplanes fly experiment 1476:86-87

BERNOULLI'S LAW
Blow paper square off a spool 291:92-93
Demonstrate the 'two legged' card 291:94-95
Experiment to prove Bernoulli's law 385:42-43
How does an airplane fly 186:16-17
Tornado low air pressure experiment 1003:64-65
What keeps an airplane up 295:94-99

BERNOULLI'S PRINCIPLE
A dancing ball 114:99-101
Air on the move demonstrates Bernoulli's Principle
      1095:10
Balloon floats in air; magic trick demonstrates principle
      966:58-61
Balloon stays in air over hair blower experiment
      1208:20-21
Balloon that won't explode 114:98
Bernoulli Levitator experiment; suspend object in air by
      blowing down on it 1132:6-1-6-2
Bernoulli's principle in action—demonstrate 642:110-
      111,114-115
Blow-dryer and balls—demonstrate 670:12
Blowing through a bottle 114:49-51
Changes in air pressure may cause motion experiment
      837:37-38
Demonstrate principle 783:17-18
Demonstrate with paper bridge 176:87-88
Demonstrating Bernoulli's principle 180:43
Demonstration of with atomizer 291:88
Demonstrations—blow out proof 222:56-59

Demonstrations—no wind fall here 222:56-59
Demonstrations—up against the odds 222:56-59
Demonstrations—wasted breath 222:56-59
Experiment to demonstrate 168:36-38; 53:44-50
Experimenting with Bernoulli's Principle 1252:36
Feather flyer, making 669:12-13
Flying ping pong ball 27:82-83
Hiding from the wind 909:69
Hovering card trick 909:69
In not out experiment 906:35
Lift a paper strip 909:68
Lift; heavy airplanes supported by air from high/low air
      pressure experiment 1208:18-19
Paper and ruler demonstrate 722:90
Paper lift experiment 906:37
Shape of airplane's wing is important for flight demon-
      stration 1479:102
Simple demonstration with spool and card 202:108-109
Soda cans (empty) on row of straws demonstrates Ber-
      noulli's Principle 1229:10-11
Soda straws and cards demonstrate 532:31
Super breath experiment 906:37-38
The acrobatic coin 16:53-55
The dancing balloon experiment (Bernoulli principle)
      563:123-124
The rising paper experiment 563:122
The strange antics of a table tennis ball 161:72-73
What holds up an airplane 55:153-159
Why airplanes fly experiment 906:36
Why no blow up—experiment (Bernoulli principle)
      563:123
Wing, making 909:68

BERTHOLLET, CLAUDE
Bleaching powers of chlorine in solution experiment
      1133:2.007

BICARBONATE OF SODA. *See also* BAKING SODA
Baking powder gives off more carbon dioxide gas than
      baking soda experiment 1208:87

BICYCLES
Activities to explore and understand bicycles [Primary]
      758:93-95
Bicycles gear shift patterns experiment; data tables
      given 1004:5.005
Draft importance in bicycle racing experiment 881:86-
      87
Dynamo on bicycles, how to test for electricity experi-
      ment 1072:37
Experiments with a bicycle 1412:54-60
How far does bicycle wheel travel in different gears ex-
      periment 1507:21
Increase your pedal power 399:57
Is your bicycle efficient 586:83
Pedal power of bicycles demonstrated with working
      model cyclist on bike 1334:22-23
Precession experiments with bicycle wheel 1164:44-
      49
Project 3—how efficient is your bicycle 654:24-27
Speed experiment 691:15-16
Spinning wheels stay upright experiment 1035:24-25
Torque, force, axis of rotation experiment using bicycle
      wheel, spring scale 1164:40-43

BICYCLING
Use of helmets important in sports experiment 1154:69-
      72
Why do bicyclists wear helmets experiment 1294:18-19

BIG BANG

Big Bang to Big Crunch theory models experiment, how to make 1478:144-145

BIMETALLIC STRIPS

Fire alarm demonstrates 472:2218

BINOCULAR VISION

Binocular vision demonstration 1007:26-27

BINOCULARS

Cardboard tube binoculars, how to make 885:27-28

Paper rolls—making (Primary) 535:33

Paper tube binocular models—making [Primary] 742:50

Poncho for binoculars, making 778:17

BIOASSAY

Certain substances or solutions affect plant growth experiment 1527:93

BIOCHEMICAL OXYGEN DEMAND. *See* **POLLUTION—WATER**

BIOCIDES. *See* **HERBICIDES; PESTICIDES**

BIOCONTROL AGENTS

Biocontrol of insect pests by parasitoid wasps experiment 1097:134-136

Parasitoid wasps lay eggs in other insects experiment 1097:13-15

Parasitoid wasps' egg laying behavior experiment 1450:153-156

Praying mantis can eat how many insects experiment 1097:9-12

Using parasitoid wasps and praying mantis as biocontrol agents experiment 1450:144-152

BIODEGRADABILITY

Bury different kinds of garbage experiment to see what biodegrades 1063:378

Compare decomposition of different materials experiment 1323:85-89

Demonstrate weathering and decomposition of garbage in landfills experiment 1465:106

Do all buried things rot away experiment 1162:29

Evaluate household trash for recycling or biodegradability project 969:54-55

Garbage planted in soil experiment 1335:214-215

Landfill containment area with little biodegradation occurring experiment 1295:51-52

Materials buried underground; which ones decay experiment 1091:49-50

Microbes make things biodegradable experiment 1221:22

Miniature landfills experiment; biodegradability of materials in dry/wet soils 1295:51-52

Plant a garbage garden to see which things are biodegradable experiment 1371:62-63

Plastic bags/paper bags/newspapers compared for time to decompose experiment 997:97-98

Reverse garden—test materials that are or are not biodegradable 399:26

Twenty items; which will decompose in soil and which won't project 969:69-70

Types of plastic bags tested for biodegradability experiment using buried bags 1228:36-37

BIODEGRADABLE. *See also* **COMPOST**

Soil bacteria causes rot break down 216:24-27

BIODEGRADATION

Buried garbage items, how they decompose experiment; plastic/bones/sticks/peel 1328:78-79

Decomposers and release of carbon dioxide experiment 1057:33

Homemade plastic made from milk and vinegar decomposes experiment 1476:140-141

How biodegradable is garbage experiment with different materials in soil 1476:199

How different kinds of garbage pollute mountain soil experiment 1468:29

BIODIVERSITY

Biodiversity or species model of plants and animals experiment 1340:69-70

Concept of biodiversity demonstrated project 1338:66-67

Habitat destruction and the biodiversity of insects experiment 1096:77-82

Insect populations change in diversity and numbers when habitat changes 1096:77-82

BIOELECTRONICS. *See also* **PLANTS—GROWTH**

Electrical currents effect on plants experiment 1249:54-56

BIOFEEDBACK

How biofeedback works experiment 1425:90-95

BIOGAS DIGESTER

Biogas digester demonstration; yeast/sugar blow up balloon on bottle 1191:28-29

BIOLOGICAL CLOCKS

Human biological clocks 137:32

In plants and animal experiments 371:104-106

Rhythms 137:31

BIOLOGICAL CONTROLS. *See also* **INSECTICIDES**

Farmers alternatives to using toxic chemicals experiment using ladybugs/aphids 1427:88-89

Natural predator ladybugs control aphids on plant experiment 1176:17

Parasitoid wasps' egg laying behavior experiment 1450:153-156

Using parasitoid wasps and praying mantis as biocontrol agents experiment 1450:144-152

BIOLOGICAL EXPERIMENTS AND PROJECTS

Ideas for 51:127-132

BIOLUMINESCENCE. *See also* **FIREFLIES**

Do plants and animals emit light 402:18-19

Does light from fireflies give off heat experiment 1405:32

Experiment to show 182:46-47

Fireflies—determine relation between number of flashes and temperature 285:92

BIOMASS

Plant materials changed into methane fuel experiment 1323:90-94

BIOME

How does a balanced community function—experiment 371:92-104

Observation and study of biome, how to do 864:127-129

BIOREMEDIATION. *See also* **OIL SPILLS**

Using bacteria to clean up oil spills on beaches experiment 1450:42-48

BIORHYTHMS. *See* **BIOLOGICAL CLOCKS; TIME SENSE**

BIOTIC COMMUNITIES. *See* **ECOLOGY; ECOSYSTEMS; HABITATS**

BIRD FEEDERS

A suet feeder for insect eaters—how to make 277:55

Automatic feeder, how to make from plastic bottles 1175:122

Bird feeder bell on rope, how to make 1040:37

Bird feeder snow person—how to make 494:82

Bird feeder, making 779:9

Bird garden 236:81
Bird pudding—how to make 305:24-25
Bird pudding for feeder, recipe, how to make 1183:46
Bird pudding, recipe, how to make 1181:38
Bird table—build and observe birds 305:26-27
Bird table—wooden—making 724:56-57
Bird table feeder, how to make from wood 1181:38
Bird table for feeding birds, how to make from wood 1183:46
Birds at birdfeeders; observe and record kinds and behavior of birds 1189:10-11
Checklist for birds at your feeder, making 778:38
Coconut feeder, making 778:72
Coffee can and milk carton feeder—how to make 733:30
Directions for making three different kinds of food 629:107-109
Donut bird feeder—making 732:23-24
Drumlin farm bird pudding 236:80-81
Easy feeders for young children 236:81
Egg carton feeder—making 758:40
Eight simple feeders to make 850:58-59
Feed, feeders and waterer—making 480:70-71
Feeders you can make 476:28-30
Feeding preferences of birds investigation 1313:23-24, 28-30
Feeding station from pie tins and coffee can, how to make 810:62-63
Feeding; which birds prefer ground feeders or raised feeders project 1210:31-32
Food for seed eating birds and insect eating birds 277:50-58
Ground feeders, making 866:160-161
Growing bird seed experiment 888:51-54
How to make and set up 234:28-31
How to make 390:70-71
Hummingbird feeder, recipe for nectar, how to make 778:52-53
Hummingbirds—nectar (recipe given) feeder—how to make (Primary) 463:22-23
Making a bird feeder 253:35-36
Margarine tub feeder, how to make 1371:51
Milk carton—making 508:39
Milk carton and plastic jug feeders, making 835:32-34
Milk carton feeder—how to make 231:108; 376.18; 701:unp; 1013:127; 1175:120-121; 1371:50
Milk carton feeders and suet feeders—make, then observe birds (Primary) 462:unpaged
Milk carton, plastic jug and pine cone feeders, how to make 1071:54-55
Nut holder from plastic bottle, how to make 1183:47
Nut holder, how to make from plastic bottle 1181:39
Observe and record birds at feeder 760:15-16
Onion bag feeder, making 778:74
Peanut feeder, making 778:74
Pie tin feeder—how to 376:19
Pine cone feeder, making 778:74
Pinecone feeders, making [Primary] 880:7
Plastic bottle feeder—making (Primary) 535:17
Plastic bottle feeder, how to make 1127:34-35
Plastic jug feeder with suet chunks, popcorn strings and cranberries 1227:11
Plywood hanging feeder, how to make 1176:14-15
Seeds recipe for bird food, making 778:78
Seeds; which kinds of seeds birds prefer project 1210:31-32

Simple bird feeders, how to make 920:31-34; 932:18-21
Simple feeders from throwaways, how to make 1265:100
Simple ones—making 749:88-89
Simple ways to build 697:64
String feeders, making 866:162
Suet bell feeder, making 832:99
Suet cupcakes, recipe, how to make 1371:54
Suet dispensers, making 866:161-162
Suet hanging cake—make 661:43
Suet log feeder, making 778:73
Suet pine cones, how to make 810:60-61
Tin can feeder, making 778:75
Titmouse bell, flowerpot with suet and seeds, how to make 953:9
What do birds eat 402:50
Which fruits and seeds do birds like best experiment 799:28
Wooden bird feeder, making 901:83-84
Wooden feeding tray, how to make 1433:68-71
Wooden flat feeder, making 832:98
BIRD MOBILES
Bird mobiles and other art projects 236:87
Gull go round mobile, making 778:50-51
BIRD SHELTERS
Backyard sanctuary feeding shelter—how to do 442: unpaged
BIRD SPINNER
How to make 312:25-28
BIRD WATCHING
Basic blind, how to make from wood, rope and a covering 1192:23
Beak and feet adaptations 236:78-80
Bird behavior hunt 236:77-78
Bird walking 234:20-21
Bird watching and homemade feeder (Primary) 535:17
Blind for observing birds and animals, how to make 1063:419
Blind for observing birds, how to make from poles and netting 1069:141
Blind to watch birds and small animals, how to make 1115:12-14
Blinds for bird watching; umbrella blind and plant blind, making 778:62-63
How to 480:72
How to do 236:75-77
How to rough sketch birds you see 552:39
Keep a bird list 236:77
Mystery bird descriptions 236:77
Nesting mathematics 236:78
Observing birds (Primary) 535:32
Signs of birds 236:78
BIRDS
A dictionary of parts 231:109
Activities to identify and investigate birds [Primary] 758:37-46
Activities with bird houses, nests and eggs 236:81-84
Activities with bird songs 236:84
Activities with birds 236:75-80
Activities with feeding birds 236:80-81
Adaptations of bird you create project 1340:70-72
Bird bath, making 778:80-81
Bird blind—how to make 231:108; 234:22
Bird communications in the field and in the laboratory 266:96-100
Bird feeding stations—experiments with 118:49-50

Bird identification 62:35-38

Bird visitors to a vacant lot 233:37-42

Bird with flapping wings, how to make from wood 1419:22-23

Birdbath from sheet of plastic and stones, how to make 1040:35

Birds and people activities 236:85-87

Birds of certain kind are attracted to certain kinds of food project 969:32-34

Chart of bird parts 1063:267

Christmas for the birds 231:106-107

Crow call experiments 118:52-54

Determine effect that polluting detergents can have on birds experiment 904:138-139

Dummy owl pattern 118:52-53

Dust bath, making 778:81

Feed a bird from your hand 264:81

Feeding birds, observations at the feeder 820:17

Food preferences of birds activities for classroom 1291:39-41

Fright distance for wild birds project 1232:51

Fright distance of birds experiment 1063:276

Games; bird survival game, making 778:92-93

Getting birds close to you 234:23

How a bird flies 305:10

How birds fly 909:77

How do birds eat without teeth experiment using plastic bag, gravel, seeds 1397:32-35

Humming birds are attracted to color experiment 1020:123-124

Identifying birds from their footprints experiment 1134:3.002

In winter—guidelines for field and feeder observation 277:47-58

Interaction of stuffed owl with birds in tree 118:50-51

Observation chart to record birds at bird feeders 978:97-98

Observe birds on the river bank 290:30

Observe foods, nests and physical parts of bird 119:133-147

Oil spills effect on birds experiment 1337:72-73

Outdoor projects 118:29-47

Recognizing birds 234:18-21

Redwing blackbird territories investigation experiment 1313:14-17

Scare bottles to scare birds project; make from plastic soda bottles 969:44-45

Seeds with shells pass through bird's digestive system experiment 1397:34

Seeds; which kinds of seeds birds prefer project 1210:31-32

Songs; parabolic reflector with microphone for magnified recorded sound 1192:41

Spying on birds—observe and study birds in your area—project 586:132-134

What do birds like to eat; observe and record; data table given 871:2.004

Why shape of bird's wing is important to flight experiment 904:134-135

Windows; bird proof your windows, how to, hawk pattern given 778:86-87

Wings; model wings, how to make from frame and feathers 1448:6-7

BIRDS—BEAKS

Beak shape determines what kind of food birds eat experiment 1183:44

Game; beak shape determines food birds eat experiment 1181:36

Use of beaks 40:121-125

BIRDS—EGGS

Artificial birds eggs—how to make 476:25-27

Collect and identify broken shells 305:22-23

Experiments with eggs 236:82-83

Make from plaster of Paris 234:25

Oil spill damage to bird eggs experiment 1232:61

Testing eggshell strength experiment 1143:27

BIRDS—FEATHERS

Collect and display feathers, how to do 778:20-21

Collect and identify (Primary) 225:4

Collecting and displaying—how to 476:19-21

Difference in feathers 40:125-126

Effect of oil spills on bird feathers experiment 1295:70-71

Molting feathers—collection and identification 305:8

Wing shapes—collect and identify feathers 305:11

BIRDS—FOOTPRINTS

Bird prints in wax, how to collect 810:58

Plaster cast of—making 305:17

Plaster casting bird foot prints, how to do 1143:17

BIRDS—HOUSES

All around birdhouse—build 264:76-78

Barn swallow homes, how to make 1192:15

Bird house from wood, patterns given, how to make 1433:63-67

Bird house, how to make from wood, pattern given 1183:125

Bluebird house—how to build 236:81-82; 442:unpaged; 530:182-183

Building an outdoor aviary (advanced) 625:57

Dried gourd birdhouse, how to make 1491:70-71

Houses—how to make 390:72-73

How to build 436:14-15

How to make and set up 234:26-31

Milk carton birdhouse, making 778:32

Mrs. Wren's house, making 779:38-39

Observation bird house for your window—how to make 264:76-78

Owl house—of log—how to make 442:unpaged

Plastic bleach bottle house—how to build 376:19

Plastic container bird cottages, making 854:115

Plastic jugs and slab wood houses—how to make 476:31-33

Popsicle stick birdhouse, making 778:33

Simple bird houses, how to make 1192:15

Simple bird houses, making 901:87-88

Wooden birdhouse, patterns, how to build 899:144-145

Wooden box houses—making 749:90-91

BIRDS—INJURED

Caring for an injured bird 480:73

BIRDS—MIGRATION

Activities with bird migration 236:84-85

Bird journeys in the field and in the laboratory 266:56-59

Length of day is trigger that starts birds' migration experiment 1062:41

BIRDS—NESTS

Bird box, how to make, measurements given 1184:37

Bird nest bag—collect materials in mesh onion bags for birds (Primary) 535:33

Bird nest from clay dough—recipe given—making 748:81

47

Bird nest garden—making from old birds nest (Primary) 535:32

Clay or mud nest with and without straw—experiment 633:32-33

Collecting and displaying—how to do 476:22-23

Collecting nests and observing construction—use and kinds of birds 762:65-67

Design and make your own bird nest from bird type materials experiment 1094:50-51

Experiments with eggs 236:82-83

Identify materials used, note weight and size 305:21

Identifying bird nests 236:82

Make a ledge nest for pigeons and doves 264:78-79

Nest box—wooden—making 724:54-55

Nest box from wood, how to make 1069:139

Nest box, how to make 1143:25

Nest materials 40:126-127

Nesting box, how to build 810:65-66

Nesting materials—record use by birds 305:20

Nesting materials for the birds 236:82

Observe and gather feathers and pellets 234:25

BIRDS—ORPHANS

Baby bird formula, recipe 778:83

Caring for injured and orphan birds 390:73-77

BIRDS—PELLETS. *See also* **OWL PELLETS**

Dissecting owl pellets, how to do 778:47

Examine owl pellets—how to 749:50-51

Pellets—collect and identify materials 305:14-15

BIRDS—POLLUTION

Polluting detergents effect on bird feathers experiment 1479:33

BIRDS—SKULLS

Blackbird 375:12

Duck 375:13

Owl 375:12

Sparrow 375:13

BIRDS—SOCIAL ORGANIZATION

Do groups of birds have an organization 402:44-45

BIRDS—WATER

How long can water birds stay underwater; observe and chart 796:31

Observations of water birds 173:22

BIRDS OF PREY

Silhouette poster, paper, how to make 855:30-31

BIRDSEED

Grow-them-yourself birdseed plants 600:24-25

BIREFRINGENCE

Density and birefringence of plastics experiment data tables given 1004:4.006

Stress birefringence in gelatin experiment 1082:164-165

Stress birefringence in household plastic objects experiment 1082:165-166

BIVALVES. *See* **CLAMS**

BLACK, JOSEPH

Black's experiment with heat needed to melt ice 1156:86-88

Black's latent heat of boiling water experiment 1156:88

Black's mixing hot and cold liquids experiment 1156:88-89

Breathing out carbon dioxide experiment 1133:3.006

Discovery of carbon dioxide experiment 1133:2.003

Heat needed to melt ice—experiment 586:85-87

Latent heat experiment 1133:7.004

BLACK HOLES

Black hole formation demonstration 1394:132-133

Diagram of 292:116

Making a model of a black hole project 833:265-266

Model of black hole using box and T-shirt, how to make 1478:126

What happens to gas clouds and stars as they approach black hole experiment 1478:140

BLADDERWORTS

Adventure 46—we set some traps—bladderworts under a hand lens 29:204-207

BLEACH. *See also* **CHLORINE**

Activity of 146:25

Bleach colored cloth by the commercial process 319:90-91

Bleach effect on fabric samples experiment 1396:108-110

Bleach oxidizer acts on steel wool 203:45

Bleaching turns a flower white 157:29

Bleaching with oxygen 85:24-25

Dissolve hair in bleach experiment 905:216-217

Effect of dry bleach on color experiment 905:84-85

Observe magic disappearance of a color experiment 905:82-83

Tie bleach old T-shirt and jeans, how to do 887:48-50

Turning a red rose white 150:116-117

BLIMPS

Stop blimp from escaping experiment using string, balloon 1208:58-59

BLIND

Blind people use sound to get around experiment 1209:46-47

Read by feeling things experiment 1037:14-15

BLIND SPOT. *See also* **VISION**

Cat and mouse game on paper demonstrates blind spot in each eye experiment 1037:18

Test to locate blind spot on retina 258:15-16

What is a blind spot experiment 901:8

What is the blind spot and how can its size be mapped 402:65-66

BLOCK AND TACKLE

Demonstrations 281:50

How to make 543:48-49

Sticks and rope demonstrate 827:98

Strongman's secret 399:9

BLOOD. *See also* **HEART; HUMAN BODY**

Adventure 12—red blood under a microscope 403:42-46

Adventure 40—circulation of dragonfly larva blood under microscope 403:146-151

Amount people need—diagrams (Primary) 245:26-29

Blood cells under microscope, observe 889:54-57

Blood circulation in goldfish tail—observe 713:72-73

Blood circulation model—how to make 577:project #2

Circulation game demonstrating flow with players 436:23

Circulation in tail of goldfish 82:49-50

Clotting—how does blood clotting occur 402:63-64

Experiment 11:103-109

Flashlight shows where your blood is 245:4-9

Fresh blood smear to identify cells—how to do 148:72

How can blood flow in only one direction in blood vessels experiment 1397:78

How much blood moves with each heartbeat experiment 1397:78

Is blood a catalyst 291:210-211

Magic trick; blood on your hand using ammonia and phenolphthalein experiment 1159:24

Marcello Malpighi's discovery of capillaries experiment 1133:3.003

Oxygen carried by red blood cells (Primary) 245:12-19

Platelets—explanation of how stops bleeding 245:22-25

Typing blood 148:74-75

Vessels—see the blood vessels in your own eyes 366:126

White blood cells—diagram and explanation of (Primary) 245:20-21

William Harvey's circulation of blood experiment 1133:3.001

BLOW HOLES—COASTLINE

Illustration of 299:17

BLUEPRINT PAPER

Making 436:16

Recipe for blueprinting paper 436:16

BLUEPRINTS

Blueprints of garden plants, how to make 986:86

Blueprints of garden vegetables, how to make 1265:86

How to make 319:76-77

BOATING

Pleasure boating activities contribute to water pollution experiment 969:110

BOATS. See also SHIPS; SUBMARINES

A bathtub boat (Primary) 70:47-48

Air creates buoyancy needed to float salvage to surface of sea experiment 1167:29

Air propelled model boat 472:2219

Air-screw boat from balsa wood, how to make 1299:66

Aircraft carrier boat model, wooden, making 922:60-61

Balloon driven record breaker boat—how to make 410:31

Balloon powered boat—make a simple one 147:39

Balloon powered milk carton boat, making [Primary] 897:85

Balloon rig demonstrates water displacement 561:12-13

Balsa wood boats, how to make 1374:19; 1422:14

Balsa wood boats, patterns given, how to make 1299:65

Block boats and paddles—how to make 429:64

Boat that goes by soap power (Primary) 70:49-50

Boat that runs with soap 143:12-13

Boats built to enclose a lot of space float experiment 1159:29-30

Building boats that float experiment 1290:32,

Camphor boat—demonstrates surface tension 146:13

Camphor boat from balsa wood, how to make 1299:66

Carbon dioxide gas makes boat move experiment 851:53-54

Catamaran—making and sailing 561:18-19

Catamaran from wood and coffee cans—how to make 429:70

Cataraman from plastic bottle and wood pieces, how to make 1299:67

Center of gravity demonstrated with milk carton boat 561:14-16

Clay boats, how to make from modeling clay 1115:107-108

Currents and tides affect salvage of sunken ships from the sea experiment 1167:28

Elastic motor driven bottle boat experiment 806:21-22

Elastic motor driven paddle boat experiment 806:20-21

Electric motor in propeller-driven boat, how to make 1043:40-41

Ferryboat from milk carton—how to make 652:10-11

Find center of gravity of cardboard boat 274:23

Foil and clay boats float and sink experiment 1422:6-7

Glass bottom boat toy—how to make 467:32

H.M.S. Bounty model boat, wooden, making 922:64

Houseboat—make an elastic powered boat 223:24-25

Hovercraft toy boat sails above the water 561:26-27

How a boat floats and is propelled 344:10-15

Hull shape of boat and its effect on buoyancy demonstration 1165:9

Hull, hollow, how to make 922:48-51

Ice boat—wind car—how to make from wood 429:72-74

Identifying boats and parts of boats 344:16-21

Jet powered boat experiment with balloon and plastic tile 1389:31

Jet propelled boat—experiments with balloon 563:181-182

Jet propelled boat experiment with balloons and test tank 994:35-45

Keels and rudders, how to make 1422:15

Land yacht made from box, wheels, spools, axles and sail, how to do 1380:14-15

Leonardo's paddle boat—how to make 429:68

Lifeboat's ballast keeps boat upright; show with ping pong ball buoy 1165:37

Magnetic—how to make magnetic boats (Primary) 451:20-21

Magnetic boats, making 768:71-72

Make a soap boat 281:35

Making a variety of boats with common materials (Primary) 494:50-51

Milk carton boats—how to make 631:109

Milk carton sailboat—making 732:148-149

Model wooden steam boats powered by steam from candles experiment, how to make 1446:40-41

Motor boats trail of oil on water surfaces; effect on aquatic insects experiment 1097:45-47

Motorboat model toy—how to make (Primary) 467:8-9

Motorboat with balloon motor, how to make 1422:18

Motorboats powered by balloons, how to make and race 1208:48-49

Narrow canal boat, how to build from wood, cardboard, paints 1460:14-15

Newspaper boat, making 890:122-123

Newton's steamboat—how to make 429:69

Nutshell boat—how to make (Primary) 467:20-21

Outrigger boats built to test floating experiment 1422:11

Paddle boat from plastic bottle experiment 1024:16-17

Paddle boat, making 779:40

Paddle power moves boat through water experiment 1389:29

Paddle wheel boat—making a paddle wheel boat and experiments to try 606:106-111

Paddle wheel boat experiment, how to make 1230:54-55

Paddle wheel moves boat by pushing water backward experiment 1035:16-17

Paddle wheeler from a milk carton demonstrates paddles and propellers 561:20-23

Paddleboat from plastic bottle powered by water experiment 1035:16-17

Paddleboat, milk carton, making 947:26-27

Paddleboats from balsa wood, how to make 1422:17

Paddlewheel boat made from plastic bottle, sticks and clay, how to do 1310:28-29

Paper boat, diagrams given, how to make 1374:18

Paper boat, directions, how to make 1513:13

Paper boat, patterns given, how to make 1299:64

Plimsoll Line marks safe water level on boats demonstration 1310:15

Plimsoll lines, chart of 678:14

Plimsoll mark prevents ships from being overloaded 342:7

Powered model boats, how to make from wood 1115:104-106

Propeller driven boat, making 981:27

Propeller driven plastic bottle boat—how to make 410:30

Propeller plastic bottle boat, how to make 1422:23

Propelling toy boat with detergent 360:52

PT boat model, wooden, making 922:52-59

Riverboat model, how to build from wood, styrofoam, cardboard 1460:10-11

Rocket balloon boat demonstrates jet propulsion experiment 1024:4-5

Rocket boat from aluminum cigar tube and candles, how to make 1247:35

Rocket boat, metal cigar tube and candle, making 1001:17

Rubber band propeller milk carton boat, how to make 1288:21

Rudder changes direction of paddleboat, how to make 1310:30-31

Rudder determines direction boat goes demonstration 1165:14

Sailboat—how to make (Primary) 523:38-39

Sailboat—making 705:80; 909:81

Sailboat, plastic—how to make 652:7

Sailboat, super one, making 890:121

Sailboat, walnut shell, making [Primary] 897:86

Sailing boat model, wooden, making 922:24-31

Sailing yacht from ceiling tile—how to make 410:36-37

Santa Maria model boat, wooden, making 922:65-66

Self-righting boat experiment, how to make from wood 1471:18-19

Shape design—make, test movement of flat, round, tear drop shapes in water 237:13-24

Shape of boats keep them upright 342:10-11

Shape of hull affects a boat experiment 1290:34, 2.3

Shape of hulls determines what ship can do experiment 1471:6-7

Soap boat—how to make 364:113

Soap boat races across water experiment 1482:60

Soap powered boat, how to make 827:110

Soap-powered boat experiment 1161:26; 1230:52-53

Spray sailboat model, wooden, making 922:62-63

Steam boat—making 664:39

Steam powered jet boat—how to make with cigar tube and candle 419:35

Steamboat from balsa wood powered by candle, how to make 1179:48-49

Steamboat, candle powered—how to make 487:22-23

Steamboat, how to make 909:127

Stern wheeler boat model, wooden, making 922:32-37

Test some boat shapes for speed 342:8-9

Toy boat from milk carton (Primary) 561:8-10

Toy raft and boat from nutshells, how to make 644:20-21

Trimaran from plastic bottle and wood pieces, how to make 1299:67

Tug boat model toy—how to make 467:30-31

Tugboat from styrofoam—how to make 652:16-17

Tugboat model, wooden, making 922:16-23

Viking longboat model, how to make 1422:13

Viking Longship model—how to make 431:20-21

Viking style plastic bottle boat, how to make 1073:28-29

Visibility and salvage of sunken ships from the sea experiment 1167:28

Walnut boat, matchbox boat—how to make 431:10-11

Water powered boat, milk carton, making 999:81-84

Water pressure used to submerge and raise salvage at sea experiment 1167:29

Water-jet boat; demonstrate water jet power demonstration 1165:19

What makes a boat sink 561:11

Which boat designs are best at carrying cargo safely experiment 1161:24

Why do boats float experiment 1509:24

Wooden boat from oval piece of wood, how to make 1125:28

BOATS—SAILS. *See also* **SAILBOATS**

How to make 429:65-66

BOATS—TEST POND

Test pond for your boats—how to make 429:71

BOATS—TYPES AND MODELS

A milk carton boat 264:111

Barge—how to make 110:12-13

Camphor—how to make 77:30-31

Camphor boat—how to make 146:13

Carbon dioxide boat—how to make 293:37

Carved soap boat—make a 110:10-11

Catamaran, Polynesian—how to make 325:unpaged

Cruiser, model—how to make 344:49-53

Ferryboat, model—how to make 344:59-63

Folded paper boat—how to make (Primary) 110:18-20

Glass bottom boat—make a 110:17

Houseboat—make an elastic powered house boat 223:24-25

Hovercraft—how to make 342:22

Inca canoes—how to make (Primary) 326:27

Jet powered boats—how to make 342:23

Magnet boat—how to make 367:13-15

Milk carton boat—how to make 110:26-27

Motorboat, model—how to make 344:44-48

Navy boat—rubber band navy boat 401:73-76

Newspaper boat—make a 110:28-31

Nutshell—make a nutshell boat (Primary) 110:8-9

Ocean liner, model—how to make 344:64-68

Paddle boat—how to make (Primary) 110:21-23

Paddle boat—how to make 132:10; 342:18-19; 94:16-17

Paddle boat, matchbox boat, steam powered boat, catamaran—how to make 178:34-37

Paddle wheel boat—how to make 96:42-43

Paper boat propelled by glue 368:59-60

Paper speed boat—make a 98:25

Pirate ship—make a (Primary) 110:24-25

Powerboat—make a 110:14-16

Propeller driven boat—make a 132:11

Propeller driven boats—how to make 342:20

Raft—make a 110:32

Sailboat—how to make 342:15

Schooner, model—how to make 344:75-78

Sloop, model—how to make 344:69-74

Steam launch—make a steam launch to show jet propulsion 167:11-12

Steam powered—make a 342:16-17

Steam powered boat—make a 132:12

Steam turbine boats—how to demonstrate 342:21

Steamboat—make a simple steamboat 150:96-97
Submarines—how to make 342:25-27
The Nautilus, model—how to make 344:84-88
Tugboat and barge model—how to make 342:54-58
U.S. Coast Guard Cutter model—how to make 344:89-93
U.S.S. Forrestal model—how to make 344:79-83
Waterproof toy boat—how to make 320:12-13

BOBSLEDS
Model bobsleds and run, how to make to demonstrate
ball bearings 1446:14-15

BODY CLOCKS. *See also* **BIOLOGICAL CLOCKS**
I got rhythm—record your sleeping and waking 231:52

BODY LOTIONS
Determine if any difference among commercial hand and
body lotions experiment 997:106-107

BOG TERRARIUM
Making 465:155-158

BOGS
Bog soil compared to forest soil experiment 1061:58-59
A bog community terrarium 268:57-62
Insect-eating plants from bogs or swamps, how to grow
experiment 1074:24-25
Make a miniature bog 279:37
Observing insectivorous plants in an acid bog 285:79-80

BOILING POINT
Fahrenheit measurements versus Celsius measurements
experiment 1439:72-74

BONES. *See also* **HUMAN BODY—BONES**
Acid effect on bones experiment 1396:49-51
Backbone; how does your backbone move experiment
with straws and thread spools 1189:16-17
Baker's clay for making clay models of skeletons, recipe
1168:78-79
Bend a bone experiment; soak bone in vinegar 1370:38
Bone brush for painting, how to use 1168:13
Bone gets rubbery from soaking in vinegar experiment
1083:54
Bone in vinegar turns to rubber experiment 721:113
Bone soaked in vinegar gets rubbery experiment 792:13
Bone soaked in vinegar water bends, how to do
1239:101-102
Bones soaked in vinegar get soft experiment 1229:56-57
Bones, why are long bones hollow experiment 794:28
Brittle bone from baking it experiment 1168:15
Brittle bones—how to make 731:48
Bury bone specimen in bacteria in bottle in the ground ex-
periment 1169:12-13
Chicken bone becomes soft in vinegar experiment 960:32
Chicken bone calcium—experiment 585:99
Chicken bone turns to rubber experiment 1258:unp.
Chicken bones soaked in vinegar turn rubbery experi-
ment 1435:69-70
Cleaning bones experiment, how to do 1168:80-81
Create a new animal from bones 901:68-69
Determine how bones move experiment with chicken
foot 1479:41
Dinosaur built from chicken bones, how to do 811:8-9
Effect of acid (vinegar) on chicken bone experiment
1074:23
Experiments with 107:96-102
Glue chicken bones together to make a skeleton, how to
do 882:40
How much mineral matter is in bone 381:104

Make flexible bone by removing minerals experiment
904:184-185
Make rubber bone by taking calcium and phosphorous
out 83:35
Make rubbery chicken bone experiment 1506:80
Model of giraffe demonstrates need for skeleton 1168:11
Necklace from bones, how to make 1168:82
Produce flexible bone by removing minerals experiment
1405:4
Rubber bones—how to make 731:48
Rubber chicken bone experiment; vinegar removes miner-
als from chicken bone 1189:50-51
Rubber chicken bones magic trick using vinegar on
bones 1010:89-91
Rubbery chicken bone experiment; bone in jar of vine-
gar, how to do 1168:15
Shape a bone for using as a tool experiment, how to do
1168:82-83
Skeleton from turkey, how to make 917:42
Skeleton of human joints made with toothpicks, how to
do 898:67
Test strength of different hollow objects 623:28
Testing the structure of bones 148:58
What is bone like without the animal or mineral material
901:168

BONES—GAMES
Cup and pin game, how to make 1168:90
Spinning buzzer, how to make 1168:91

BONES—HUMAN
Photograph to show where bones are 366:134-135

BONSAI TREES
Instant bonsai tree, how to prepare tree and plant
1306:30-31

BOOKS
Bookmaking—how to do 631:70-72
Flick book makes pictures move; patterns for pictures
given 1299:22-23
Flipbook, how to make 770:145; 736:88-95
How to make flip books 400:78
Paperback sculpture—making 732:169-170
Phony book, how to make 643:34-35

BOOMERANGS
Cardboard boomerang, pattern given, how to make
1299:48
Cardboard version boomerang, making 854:116
How to make 112:40-41; 172:81-82
How to make mini-boomerangs 669:6-7
Make a boomerang (Primary) 111:16-17
Make a boomerang 186:19-20; 202:93; 360:42; 733:35;
861:53-57
Mini boomer—how to make 310:6-7
Square boomerang, making 823:105
Three wing boomerang, making 823:106-108
Two wing boomerang, making 823:105-106

BORAX BEAD TEST
To identify substances by color of inside and outside
flame 6:39

BOTTLE
Lifting with a straw 350:122-123
Make a trick bottle 585:82
Musical 350:94
Trombone bottle 45:96
Voice of a bottle 45:94
Whistles 45:95

51

BOTTLE GARDENS. *See also* **GARDENS—BOTTLE**
Garden in a bottle, how to make 1145:31
BOUNCE
Bounce height of different balls experiment 1091:37-38
How things bounce; the coefficient of restitution experiment 1164:33-36
Projects with bouncing balls 1164:36-37
Temperature affects bounce of rubber ball experiment 1405:108
Test how high ball bounces experiment using large paper ruler as scale 1380:32
Which ball bounces the most and highest experiment [Primary] 787:6-8
BOUNCE HEIGHTS
Bounce heights of ball as related to drop heights experiment, data tables 1004:5.006
Bounce of rubber ball affected by temperature experiment 1404:2
The way the ball bounces 295:70-72
Which ball bounces the best experiment 754:21
Which surfaces are best for bouncing balls experiment 754:22-25
BOUNCES AND SPRINGS
Testing for bounce (Primary) 210:30
BOUNCING. *See* **BALLS**
BOXES
Building boxes for strength experiment, how to build 1518:38-39
BOYLE, CHARLES
Boyle's orrery model experiment shows Earth, Moon, Sun revolving speeds 1476:162-165
BOYLE, ROBERT
Boyle's Law experiment on relationship between pressure and inverse of volume 1156:61-65
Measuring the "spring" of the air experiment 1133:7.002
Objects of different masses fall thru vacuum at same rate experiment 1133:4.007
Sound does not travel through a vacuum experiment 1133:6.006
Who first defined an element project 1525:63-64
BOYLE'S LAW
Boyle's and Charles's law 577:project #19
Boyle's Law and air pressure experiment 1158:69-72
Boyle's Law experiment 871:3.017
BRAILLE ALPHABET
Braille alphabet; make to test touch receptors in fingers 1246:34-36
BRAKES
Build frictionless car to demonstrate brakes 586:74-75
Make a simple hydraulic system 224:24-25
BREAD
Baking powder; chemical reaction involved in baking experiment 1159:20-22
Bread—how to make 400:2
Bread mold experiment 977:60
Bread mold growth and factors that produce growth experiment 1004:2.020
Bread mold; where does it grow the best experiment 1150:40-42
Damp bread grows molds experiment 1214:23
Determine why there are holes in bread slices experiment 1405:54
Experiment with yeast and making bread, recipe given 887:80-82
Experiments 26:104-105; 26:94-105

Food additive, calcium propionate, inhibits bread mold growth experiment 1395:127-132
From seeds to bread—grind seeds into flour and make bread 26:94-95
Grow bread mold experiment 1183:23; 904:80-81
Growth of bread mold experiment 978:52-53
High rise bread bake (recipe given) 452:66-67
How does bread dough rise experiment 1484:61-63
Mold formation on bread experiment 984:25-27
Mold growing on moist, dry and disinfected bread experiment 1038:28-29
Mold sample on bread, how to grow 860:154-156
Preservative chemicals keep bread from growing mold project 1210:54-55
Self rising flour bread, recipe, making 792:15
Seven grain bread, recipe for 832:93
Unleavened bread, recipe, demonstrates carbon dioxide from yeast experiment 790:11-12
What causes bread to toast brown experiment 1238:84
Why bread is full of holes—make bread with yeast and bread without yeast 26:101-102
Why bread molds experiment 1440:64-67
Why does bread get moldy experiment 834:83
Why does toast turn brown experiment 1484:30-31
Yeast bread, how to make 358:74-75
Yeast gives off carbon dioxide experiment 1214:24-25
Yeast works better with cold, warm or hot water project 1210:50-53
BREATHING. *See also* **HUMAN BODY; RESPIRATION**
Air-measuring device for how much air you blow out when breathing experiment 1279:10
Breath contains carbon dioxide experiment 1322:17-20
Breath in and out is different—exp. With candles (Primary) 683:17-21
Candle test for carbon dioxide in breath 679:16
Carbon dioxide turns limewater white experiment 905:72-73
Carbon dioxide turns limewater white—experiment (Primary) 683:26
Condensation trick 392:61-62
Detecting carbon dioxide in your breath experiment 1425:253
Exercise and the breathing rate 253:114
How much air can lungs hold 400:41
Joseph Black's breathing out carbon dioxide experiment 1133:3.006
Lung model—demonstrate 293:27-28
Show gas you exhale contains CO_2 319:31-32
BRICKS
Brick walls which is strongest overlapping or in piles experiment [Primary] 755:12
Brickmaker mold, making 779:12
Bricks and absorption of water experiment 1386:15
Homemade adobe bricks—making 633:38
How to make 326:21
How to see through a solid 350:136-137
Make your own 323:7
Make your own bricks from modeling clay, how to do 1300:28
Make your own bricks, how to do 1008:68-69
Mud bricks—how to make 358:106-107
Soil bricks, making 867:13
Strongest brick wall experiment 1518:8
Test different kinds of sand bricks for strength experiment 715:56-60

Test strength of two different brick walls experiment 802:12

Wet weather effect on bricks, how damp-proof course works experiment 802:28

What amount of straw, sand and clay makes the strongest brick experiment 1094:24-25

BRIDGES. *See also* **STRUCTURES**

Arch—build an arch bridge 348:16-18

Arch bridge from wooden crates or cardboard experiment, how to build 1518:26-27

Arch bridge model—how to build 328:116-121

Arch bridge; demonstrate with books and cardboard 1025:14

Arch bridges which supports the heaviest load experiment 755:20-21

Arch increases structural strength of cardboard bridge experiment 1436:101-102

Bascule moving—build a lifting bascule bridge 348:35-38

Beam bridge, test for strength experiment using books and cardboard 1025:13

Beam, cantilever and arch bridges, how to make from books experiment 1386:25

Bowstring bridge model in lattice patterns from bricks/plastic straws 1518:30-31

Box girder bridge model, how to build 1459:10-11

Bridge beams test for strength experiment 755:22-23

Bridge built with beams and arches; which is strongest experiment 1094:15-16

Bridge loads—test of stress—dead load and live load 566:39

Bridge made from cardboard demonstrates balance experiment 1444:88-89

Bridge models—how to exhibit 577:project 69

Bridge sag test 566:43

Bridge supports test different kinds experiment 755:18-19

Bridge that opens—how to build 755:28

Bridge types and experiments with 806:62-63

Bridgefinder's alphabet of different kinds of bridges 923:91-95

Building with drinking straws 3:42-58

Cantilever bridge demonstrated with books 827:32

Cantilever bridge, model from cardboard, making 802:23

Cantilever, testing a 691:26

Cantilevers, blocks demonstrate 532:16; 566:43

Cofferdam (temporary dam for bridge pier construction), how to build experiment 1025:22

Compare strength of beam bridge, arch bridge and box girder bridge experiment 1522:23

Compression and tension in bridges experiment 1119:17

Demonstrate how natural bridges stand 1479:76

Different ways of bridging the gap for maximum strength experiment 1119:14

Double bascule bridge; how to make from cereal boxes 1025:39

Drawbridge model, how to make 867:39

Experiments with 107:45-51

Floating bridge from plastic food containers, how to make 1025:40

Floating pontoon bridge; how much weight will it support experiment 1386:29

Knots and strength of boards project 691:24-25

Model aqueduct, how to build from wood, cardboard, paints 1460:18-19

Model arch bridge 550:74

Model beam bridge 550:72-73

Model footbridge; design and build using wood, dowels, cardboard tubes 1459:6-7

Model pier bridge 550:75-76

Model suspension bridge 326:31

Newspaper bridge—how to build 755:27

Operating drawbridge model experiment, how to build 1518:24-25

Paper bridge to test flexure 550:70-72

Paper bridges; which is the strongest experiment 1064:39

Projects with bridges 691:26-30

Ropes and cables—use of 328:76-85

Steel and concrete reinforced bridge—how to make 224:11-13

Stone arch model from styrofoam or wood, how to build 1459:14-15

Strength test for cardboard bridge experiment 1507:18

Stress test for bridges experiment 1476:99-100

Strong bridge shape, how to design it experiment 1162:26

Structural strength of corrugated cardboard bridge demonstration 1436:97-100

Suspension—build a suspension bridge 348:47-50

Suspension bridge model—making 755:24-25

Suspension bridge model, how to build from wood and string 1459:18-19

Suspension bridge model, how to make from bricks, wood strips, string 1518:32-33

Suspension bridge on towers experiment 1024:22-23

Suspension bridge, how to build with building blocks experiment 1025:33

Suspension bridge, how to make with chairs and rope 1119:8

Suspension bridge, model from cardboard, making 802:23

Suspension bridge; test for strength experiment 1025:37

Swing bridge—make a 223:12-13

Tensile strength of paper measured experiment 1157:76-78

The bridge experiment demonstrates stresses on bridges 563:194-195

Toothpick—how to build 66:78-92

Toothpick bridges, ideas for projects 858:1-28

Truss bridge, simple cardboard model, making 923:79-84

Truss triangle strength demonstration, how to make 923:85-86

Trusses, investigate strength of 691:26-27

Which bridge holds the largest force—experiment 682:28-29

Which bridge is best (Primary) 153:26-27

Wood position and strength of project 691:22-24

BRINE SHRIMP. *See also* **SHRIMP—BRINE**

Brine shrimp egg hatching experiment to see how many can survive 1069:23

Experiment with temperature, chemicals and salt effects on hatching eggs 864:91-92

Factors which limit growth experiment 978:86-87

Growing brine shrimp from fertilized eggs 400:19

Hatch brine shrimp, how to do and feed 1371:40-41

Hatching and studying brine shrimp in your home experiment 877:73-78

How to hatch and care for 500:108-110

How to raise shrimp 887:36-38

Oil spills effect on shrimp experiment 1058:94-95

53

Raise and do experiments with—how to 163:95-99
Raising brine shrimp 148:54
Stimulating weak brine shrimp—experiment 484:89-90
Test shrimp for reactions to light, color, cold, heat experiment 887:36-38

BROMELIADS
Tiny living things from water pockets in leaves—experiment 532:52

BROODERS. *See also* **CHICKENS; EGGS**
Brooder box, building, how to 866:156
Brooder, how to make and use for small chicks 810:72-74
Chicken brooder—made from orange crate 436:21
How to make 358:92-93

BROOMS
Garden broom from twigs, how to make 1183:124

BROWN, ROBERT
Brownian motion experiment 1156:108-109
Brownian motion of pollen grains experiment 1133:7.006

BROWNIAN MOVEMENT
Brownian motion of pollen grains experiment 1133:7.006

BRYOZOA
Adventure 33—we receive a pleasant surprise—bryozoa under microscope 403:115-119
Bryozoa, observe food canal and growth under hand lens 771:67-72

BUBBLE BATH
Bubble bath liquid, recipe, how to make 1228:83
Recipe for 387:18-20

BUBBLE GUM
Can oil be soaked up from oil spills experiment 1325:70-74

BUBBLES. *See also* **SOAP BUBBLES**
Basic bubble soap 162:24
Best bubble formula 162:30-31
Blow ice crystal balls 663:23
Blow the biggest bubble (Primary) 551:unpaged
Blowing bubbles (Primary) 558:50-51
Brew for blowing bubbles 508:19
Bubble gum science 676:41
Bubble recipe: blowing bubbles 663:23
Bubble solutions and bubble blowers—making (Primary) 535:36-37
Can you blow 100 bubbles (Primary) 551:unpaged
Floating bubbles 291:72-73
Fooling around with frames 162:27
How high can you float a bubble (Primary) 551:unpaged
Make a bubble blowing contraption 162:31
Make carbon dioxide bubbles sink and float 147:37-38
Make table-top bubbles 162:28-29
Make windows you don't have to wash 162:24-26
Soap bubbles—how to make big one 186:113
Surface tension of bubbles 210:17
Waterwheel bubble blowing device—how to make 606:86-91
Which lasts longer—egg white or soap 259:23

BUDS. *See also* **TREES**
How to identify 275:10-11
Spiral pattern of on potatoes 146:32
Winter tree identification 277:62-66

BUFFER
Acid lake; how to make mini acid lake and buffer it experiment 1328:63
Spinach—color changes in chlorophyll 74:93-95

BUG LIGHTS
Do bug lights differentiate between good and bad insects experiment 1450:20-25

BUGS. *See* **INSECTS**

BUILDING. *See also* **ARCHITECTURE; HOUSES—HOUSE BUILDING**
Beams—how to make 220:42-49
Bricks and absorption of water experiment 1386:15
Building blocks—making and putting together (Primary) 220:9-21
Buttresses add support to buildings experiment 1386:29
Chimneys—how to make (Primary) 220:27
Circles for modular construction—how to make 732:109-110
Columns—an experiment 220:28-33
Corbels and arches—how to build 220:52-61
Demonstrate what tornadoes, earthquakes and temperatures can do 328:58-65
Forces underneath roof support roof experiment 1386:20
Foundations support buildings experiment 1386:23
Glues and how they work 544:25-30
Gravity and air pressure holds things together 544:33-36
Height of building—how to measure 731:69
House built from rolled paper has strength experiment 1024:20-21
Houses, foundations (Primary) 220:38
Interlocking joints—how they work 544:46-48
Knocking down walls you build to test them for strength experiment 1386:28
Milk carton models 631:108
Nails—how they work 544:9-14
Nuts and bolts—how they work 544:15-18
Screws and rivets—how they work 544:19-24
Slotted card construction using milk cartons 631:112
Soldering experiment 544:44-45
Steel frame; the columns, the beams, the floor—build of paper 328:40-50
Stone wears away from vinegar acid experiment 1386:28
Swaying in the wind experiment using tower of building blocks 1386:29
The importance of shape in buildings—experiment 589:52
The shapes in building—making model paper beams for structural strength 550:68-69
Towers—how to make 220:22-26
Tying it together—experiment 544:37-39
Use of gypsum as building material experiment 1004:1.011
Welding it together 544:42-43

BUILDING MATERIALS. *See also* **BUILDING**
Effect of acid rain on building materials experiment 1233:85

BULB HOLDER
How to use a bulb holder 400:89

BULBS. *See also* **PLANTS**
Amaryllis bulb—how to plant and grow 712:38-40
Bulbs—forcing—how to 759:8-9
Bulbs grow in water experiment 1008:75
Can flowers be grown in winter in the home 402:31-32
Compare growth of onion seed and onion bulb 352:54-55
Effect of light on flowering bulbs 532:78
Flowering bulbs indoors, how to grow 899:200-201
Flowering bulbs; grow narcissus and hyacinths indoors experiment 1242:39

Force bulbs to bloom in a dish, how to do 810:28
Forcing for indoor bloom 465:102-105
Forcing and growing bulbs, how to 850:12-15
Forcing bulbs, how to 921:10-12
From a ball of roots to new green shoots—plant onion
    bulbs and observe 452:70-71
Grow plant from bulb [Primary] 757:21
Growing bulb in jar of water, how to do 1379:6
Growing bulbs in water 480:19
Growing bulbs inside—paperwhite, narcissus, crocus,
    hyacinth 376:8-9
Onion bulb grows in water 364:60
Planting bulbs in a pot 473:52
Planting bulbs indoors, how to do 931:10-11
Projects with vegetative propagation 398:64-66
Spring bulbs to grow indoors, how to plant 1306:14-15

BULBS—ELECTRIC. *See also* **ELECTRIC**
Bulb wired in simple circuit makes flashing light experi-
    ment 1307:16-17
Demonstrate air pressure 291:89
Electric light bulb—how to make 341:38-40
How can an unconnected fluorescent bulb glow 278:66
How many ways can you light a bulb experiment
    1426:40
How to make 400:89
Incandescent bulb—how to make 278:42
Lamp assembly (bulb socket), how to make 768:101-
    102
Light bulb, how to make experiment 1514:66-67
Making a light bulb experiment 871:4.017

BULBS AND BATTERIES
Experiments 538:99-101
Find out how to light a small torch (flashlight) bulb
    599:25-27
Make a penny pitching game 538:102

BULL ROARER
Bull roarer, making 732.134; 823:108-110
Cardboard bull roarer, patterns given, how to make
    1299:76
How to make 172:56-57; 629:149; 90:54-56
How to make and use 722:56
Making 861:199-203
Whirl a bull roarer, how to make from cardboard, tape
    and rubber bands 1209:86-87

BULLDOZERS
Model bulldozer, how to make 1420:15

BUNSEN BURNER
Construct your own 167:63-66

BUOYANCY. *See also* **ARCHIMEDES; FLOATING
    AND SINKING; WATER—BUOYANCY**
Archimedes principle of buoyancy experiment with vine-
    gar, baking soda, pasta 1290: 9, 1.9
Archimedes principle—up and down submarine 114:101-
    102
Archimedes' principle or law of buoyancy experiment
    1133:4.001
Balloons in hot and cold water demonstrate 722:23
Boat; shape of hull affects a boat experiment 1290:
    20
Bouncing raisins experiment 748:103
Build hot air balloon from tissue paper and wire, patterns
    given 1252:14-19
Buoyancy experiment with a balloon 563:189
Buoyancy force experiment with bubbles rising in
    liquids 1404:59

Buoyancy of ocean diving vessels changes demonstra-
    tion 1023:204-205
Buoyancy of substance can be changed experiment with
    clay and club soda 1404:62-64
Can it float 280:44-45
Carbon dioxide bubbles cause clay balls to float and sink
    experiment 1405:93
Cartesian diver experiment 906:12
Cartesian diver, how to make 1007:17-19
Checking the buoyancy of fluids 180:25
Clay boat demonstrates buoyancy 1476:78
Construct hydrometer to determine buoyancy of pure and
    salty water experiment 1396:126-127
Determine why objects float on water experiment
    1396:123-128
Diving baby—hydraulic pressure and buoyancy 205:77-
    81
Egg in fresh and salt water demonstrates 882:19
Experiment to make an object which neither floats or
    sinks 385:34-38
Experiment 368:49-55
Experiments to show 330:18-21
Float an egg 281:34
Float sinking things in a boat demonstration [Primary]
    935:48
Floating balloon—demonstrate 202:86
Floating egg in the middle of a glass of water 150:44-45
Floating eggs experiment 906:9-10
Floating object displaces equal volume or weight of liq-
    uid experiment 1179:139
Floating of heavy ships experiment; how heavy ships
    float 1404:60-63
Flying an airplane underwater 150:54-55
How buoyancy of ocean diving vessels changes demon-
    stration 1479:85
How do submarines go up and down experiment
    877:101-105
How things float experiments 1164:62-65
Hull shape of boat and its effect on buoyancy demonstra-
    tion 1165:9
Intelligent eggs! Buoyancy 205:70-74
Jumping rocks experiment 906:11
Lifting a heavy object with a weak thread 150:50-51
Making an underwater color fountain 150:56-57
Moving a glass of water without touching it 150:48-49
Objects in water have different weight than in air experi-
    ment 1405:93
Principle—experiment to show floating 168:38
Puffed cheese snack rises to top of rice grains in glass jar
    experiment 1083:38
Rising raisins! Buoyancy and surface tension 205:74-76
Salt affects buoyancy experiment with floating bottle in
    salt water 1404:54-55
Salt content of water measured experiment 1405:87
Salt water affects buoyancy experiment, 34,
Salt water has more buoyancy than fresh water experi-
    ment 884:44-47
Sink and float an egg experiment 937:42-43
Soap bubbles float on cushion of carbon dioxide gas ex-
    periment 1132:15-1-15-2
Stone, string and spring balance—experiment 657:106-
    107
Submarines lifted by using air experiment 1405:84
Telling bad from fresh eggs without breaking them
    150:42-43

Testing the buoyancy of water 687:45
Treasure divers experiment 906:14
Unbalancing a see saw without touching it 150:52-53
Uplifting force of water experiment 1481:180-183
Upthrust force of water and weight of object affect buoyancy experiment 1165:7
Weigh your hand experiment 906:13
Weight affects buoyancy demonstration 1023:206-207
Why do heavy metal ships float experiment 877:96-100
Why does a balloon rise 55:77-81
Why icebergs float—show 150:46-47
Why things float or sink experiment 884:40-43
You 'weigh' less in water 281:31

BUOYS
Lifeboat's ballast keeps boat upright; show with ping pong ball buoy 1165:37

BURGLAR ALARM. *See also* **ALARMS; ELECTRIC**
Burglar alarm for under mat or rug experiment 1024:26-27
Burglar alarm for your door—how to make 543:22-23
How to make 191:49-55; 358:78-79
Sensors that break a circuit and closed circuit burglar alarm 23:61-62
Simplest burglar alarm that can be built—how to make and install 23:59-61
Window burglar alarm—how to do 102:142-143

BURNERS
Homemade burner to use for experiments 436:18
Spirit burner—how to make 146:12-13
Spirit burner, how to make using glass jar, cotton lint, and wick 1179:10

BURROWING ANIMALS
Outdoor projects with 118:165-171

BURS
Bur baskets and other burry items 236:49

BUSES
Milk carton bus—how to make 431:8-9

BUTTER
Beat your own butter 630:77-78
Butter—margarine taste test 630:76
Can baking soda trap odor molecules experiment 831:70-71
Can cream be changed into butter experiment 831:65-67
Can you tell margarine from butter experiment 792:30
How to make (Primary) 322:24-25
How to make 122:98-99; 219:39-43; 280:52; 399:68; 77:24-25
Make with jar churn (Primary) 155:8-9
Making butter 585:99-100; 721:106
Turn cream into butter experiment 1231:36-37
What is butter experiment 885:89

BUTTERFLIES. *See also* **CATERPILLARS; MOTHS**
A butterfly's taste response in the field and in the laboratory 266:28-29
Adventure 24—we learn the use of perfume—butterflies under microscope 403:85-88
Attract butterflies with perennials, nectar bearing shrubs/flowers—list 480:56-57
Black swallowtail butterfly, how to raise 839:41-45
Butterfly behavior; observe and record; data table given 871:2.003
Butterfly dust under a microscope—observe 713:64-65
Butterfly migration in the field and in the laboratory 266:59-62
Butterfly tastes with its feet—experiment 414:43-44

Cage for, making and recipe for nectar to feed 480:54-55
Cage; net cage from cardboard box, how to make 1407:120-121
Care of as pets 354:23-35
Caterpillar in jar, keeping [Primary] 942:21
Caterpillar, how to keep until butterfly emerges 1320:43-45
Chrysalis changes into butterfly—observe 759:32
Collecting and housing butterflies, how to do 1407:102-103
Collecting butterflies—a killing jar, spreading board/net—how to make 476:44-47
Collecting eggs 279:22-23
Feeding and caring for butterflies 932:32-35
Flapping butterfly model, how to make from cardboard 1180:29
Flapping butterfly model, how to make from cardboard 1183:157
Game board for butterfly game, how to make and play 1182:12-13
Game; butterfly board game demonstrates growth of butterfly, how to make 1183:60-61
Habitat for butterflies from box, how to make 1441:93
House for caterpillars, plastic containers, making 932:32-35
How are butterflies and moths different experiment 904:98-99
How do butterflies develop; experiment with insect cages 901:116-118
How to keep butterflies 821:56-57
Incubator for raising butterflies, how to make 839:14-16
Instinctive behavior of butterfly larvae experiment 936:27-28
Keeping caterpillars, how to do 992:28
Life cycle of a butterfly experiment; build butterfly farm for caterpillars 1176:10-11
Life cycle of butterfly experiment using small aquarium tank 1504:31
Life cycle of butterfly on wheel disc from cardboard, how to make 1298:42-43
Life cycle of butterfly; observe caterpillar in jar experiment 810:52-53
Metamorphosis in butterfly experiment; observe larva in large glass jar 1187:26
Metamorphosis of butterflies and moths experiment 978:89-90
Metamorphosis; watch how butterflies metamorphose experiment 1144:15
Model butterfly, how to make 1445:30-31
Monarch—how to raise 442:unpaged
Monarch butterflies, how to raise 839:10-40
Monarch butterfly eggs, how to collect and hatch 1188:50-51
Observe effect of temperature on speed of wing flapping 174:14-15
Raising a monarch butterfly—how to 765:unp.
Raising butterflies in breeding cage, how to build 1069:103, 106
Raising butterflies, how to do 820:31; 854:81
Rearing cage for butterflies—how to make 430:56
Rearing cage for raising butterflies, how to make 839:20-23
Symmetrical butterfly wings, how to make with paint and paper 1182:14

Test a butterfly's ability to taste sugar against a person's ability 174:30-31
Test to see if butterfly can tell difference between sugar and salt solution 174:32-33
Test to show butterfly's reaction to food and other things 174:28-29
Watch caterpillars change into butterflies experiment 1524:13

BUTTERFLIES—COLLECTION
Butterfly collecting—how to 234:63-65
Butterfly net—how to make 293:24
Butterfly net—making 9:18-19
Collect and care for—how to 332:61-75
Get a close look at a butterfly 62:39

Riker mount—how to make 234:65
Spreading board—how to make 234:64
Tagging monarch butterflies 62:39-40
BUTTERWORTS
Butterworts, how to grow 1260:43
BUTTRESS
Build a flying buttress 557:28-29
BUYS—BALLOTS LAW
Centrifugal force 243:36-37
BUZZERS. *See also* **ELECTRIC**
Make a buzzer 267:48-49
Make a homemade buzzer 127:73-76

C

CABBAGE. *See* **INDICATORS**

CABLE CARS
Cable car—how to make 652:32-35
Make a water powered cable railway 269:24-25
Model cable car runs between towers experiment, how to build 1518:18-19

CABLE STRUCTURES
Build a hanging shell 557:72-73

CABOCHONS (GEMS FROM ROCKS)
Making 234:92-93

CACTUS
A desert community terrarium 268:30-33
Cactus garden in a dish, how to plant 1306:24-25
Cactus, how to grow 810:36-37
Cowboy's cactus garden—making 480:38-39
Desert garden for lazy gardeners 376:6-7
Flat-grafting cactus plants, how to do 1440:112-114
Grafting cactus, how to do 870:60-62
Grow your own cactus desert garden 416:36-37
How to graft 86:73-74
How to root cactus 879:177
Plant in pie tin (Primary) 650:unpaged
Rooting a cactus, how to do 1440:106-108
Watering effect on cactus plant growth experiment 1440:109-111

CADDIS FLY
Caddisfly and case model camouflaged, how to make 1183:71
Caddisfly for your aquarium, how to collect and observe experiment 913:40
Collecting and keeping, caddis larvae 414:134-138
Collection and care of 390:21-23
Net for catching caddis gnats, make from pillowcase and dowel 1476:118
Pond ecosystem in fishbowl shows relationship between plants and animals 1476:118-119

CADDIS WORMS
Adventure 24—caddis worms under a hand lens 29:119-122
Caddis worms, collect and observe, how to 771:158-164

CAFFEINE. *See also* **COFFEE**
Caffeine and pulse rate experiment 1267:101-102
Caffeine and the nervous system experiment 1267:102-104
Effect of caffeine on development and survival of mealworms experiment 997:113-115
Effect of regular and decaffeinated coffee on daphnia heart beat experiment 713:90
Heart beat increased by caffeine observe goldfish under microscope 713:73-74

CAGES. *See also* **ANTS; INSECTS—CAGES**
Ant house—observation—making 9:42-43
Ants—how to build 'ant farm' cage 279:26-27
Basic cage—how to make 313:6-8
Chart of maximum number of animals per cage 313:7
Critter carrier—how to make 313:4
Fly cage—making 9:40-41
Glass aquarium with wooden top for fish, insects, reptiles and small mammal 279:6
Insects—aquariums make nice cages—how to do 332:38-39
Insects—breeding cage—how to make 289:91-92
Insects—how to make 332:24-26; 442:unpaged

Insects—larval feeding cage—making 285:60
Insects—winter cage—making 277:84-88
Small animal breeding cage 285:91
Small animal observation cage 9:36-39
Snake cage—observation 9:46-47
Snakes—making 279:9
Wormery—observation cage—making 9:44-45

CALCIUM
Bone soaked in vinegar gets rubbery experiment 792:13
Bone soaked in vinegar water bends, how to do 1239:101-102
Chicken bone becomes soft in vinegar experiment 960:32
Chicken bone turns to rubber experiment 1258:unp.
Test for calcium in food 807:93

CALCIUM—COOKERY
Calcium cookies, recipe, how to make 1168:16
Molasses milkshake, recipe, how to make 1168:17
Salmon melt sandwich, recipe, how to make 1168:17

CALCULATORS. *See also* **ADDING MACHINES; COMPUTERS**
Binary calculator from paper, how to make 860:87-88
Handling a large calculation—experiment 591:72-73
How does the binary numbering system work experiment 1293:19-21
Pocket calculator simulation computer project 1021:91-92

CALENDAR
Ancient civilizations and their calendars project 1062:112-113
Cardboard circle calendar, how to make 1521:6
Designing your own calendar project 833:41-42
History of astronomy and calendars project 1062:112-113
Leap year prediction computer program experiment 1062:33-34
Making a Mayan calendar project 833:37-40
Making a perpetual calendar project 833:40-41
Moon as calendar (Primary) 324:30-31

CALORIC MASS
Caloric mass—experiment 586:86-87

CALORIES
Calculate gram calories and convert to food calories, how to do 1396:197
Calorie counter of daily foods eaten computer project 1021:134
Calories used during exercise—survey 400:43
Calorimeter to determine food energy in marshmallows experiment, how to make 1396:31-36
Does number of calories consumed on regular basis affect longevity experiment 1267:50
Food calories released by burning food experiment 1396:34-35
How many food calories do you need each day—experiment 628:74-75
Number of calories in food experiment 1259:22-24
Second Law of Thermodynamics experiment; some transferred energy is useless 1453:15-18
Snack survey 400:43

CALORIMETER
Calorimeter to determine food energy in marshmallows experiment, how to make 1396:31-36

CAMELS
Why camels can live for weeks without drinking water experiment 1405:35

58

CAMERA OBSCURA. *See also* **CAMERAS**
Alhazen's looking at eclipses experiment 1133:6.002
Camera obscura, how to make from tin can and card-board 1245:20-21
Camera obscura, how to make 906:66; 1138:24-25; 1296:1976
How to build using cardboard boxes, piece of glass, magnifying glass 1295:34-36

CAMERA LUCIDA
Enlarge or reduce drawings with lamp and glass 399:82

CAMERAS. *See also* **PHOTOGRAPHY; PIN HOLE CAMERA**
Box camera from box and magnifying lens, how to make 1019:24-25
Build your own camera kit 400:76
Camera obscura—how to make 172:20-26; 386:60-62; 399:72-73; 472:2238; 863:18-22; 1296:1976
Camera obscura—made from cereal box 203:10-11
Camera obscura kits—how to make 386:71-72
Camera obscura with back and shutter, patterns given, how to make 863:108-114
Camera obscura, how to make from tin can and card-board 1245:20-21
Camera obscura, make from milk cartons 837:61-62
Camera obscura, making 1001:18
Camera projects 400:78
Exploring the environment with a camera 400:77-78
Flash bulb tester, how to make 830:67-68
Homemade camera shows how a camera works 436:18-19
How camera sees; pinhole camera and candle demonstrate 902:6-7
How does box camera work experiment 834:116-117
How does camera lens focus light experiment 1283:21
How to make a camera 400:76
Magic room pinhole box camera experiment 911:22-23
Making a pinhole camera project 833:179-181
Measure shutter speed 333:44-47
Oatmeal box camera, making 887:88-90
Pinhole—making a 1:10-11; 291:181
Pinhole camera—how to make 507:1856-1857; 569:38; 595:22-23
Pinhole camera—how to make (Primary) 558:84-85
Pinhole camera—making 128:191; 135:13; 360:69-71
Pinhole camera—taking a picture with 128:200-201
Pinhole camera and projector—making 120:20-21
Pinhole camera demonstrates why cameras have lenses 1294:108-111
Pinhole camera from box, making 998:164
Pinhole camera from empty can, how to make 956:43
Pinhole camera from oatmeal box, how to make 860:206-209
Pinhole camera, how to build experiment 941:101-105
Pinhole camera, how to make from cardboard box 1179:90
Pinhole camera, making 1001:19
Processing and developing film from pinhole camera, how to do 1179:91
Remote flash construction, how to do 830:68-70
Simple camera model demonstrates how camera works experiment 1028:46
Telephoto attachment for pinhole camera, how to make 863:146-147
Telephoto lens—making 208:130-135

Wide angle attachment for pinhole camera, how to make 863:135-143

CAMOUFLAGE. *See also* **ANIMAL CAMOUFLAGE; ANIMALS—PROTECTIVE COLORATION; COLORATION—PROTECTIVE; PROTECTIVE COLORATION**
Camouflage figure remains still and then moves; compare ease of detection 1132:39-1-39-2
Camouflage outdoor hunt, how to do 1175:114-115
Camouflaging technique of animals experiment 904:126-127
Color of animals protects them from prey experiment 904:128-129
Colored paper activity to demonstrate camouflage 956:14-15
Game shows how worms and insects hide from birds, how to make 1063:262
Game; colors used by insects to hide or to warn they are poisonous 1182:26
Game; does camouflage work game 1183:71
Game; does camouflage work; use colored cards in yard, trees, grass experiment 1182:23
Scenery with camouflaged animals experiment 1417:10-13

CAMP COOKER. *See also* **SOLAR COOKERS**
Solar cooker—how to make with Fresnel lens 386:56-57

CAN OPENERS
Test your can opener for metal shavings 532:108

CANALS. *See also* **LOCKS—WATERWAYS**
Arches support plastic canal in aqueduct model experiment, how to build 1518:28-29
Make a model canal and tunnel 223:14-17
Model aqueduct, how to build from wood, cardboard, paints 1460:18-19
Model lock, how to build from wood, cardboard, paints 1460:22-23
Narrow canal boat, how to build from wood, cardboard, paints 1460:14-15
Waterway for boats model, how to build from cardboard boxes, paints 1460:6-7

CANCER
How effective is beta carotene in fighting cancer in plants experiment 997:54-56

CANDLES
A candle burning in water—experiment 563:45-46
Air is needed for candle to burn experiment 752:89
Automatic candle snuffer—how to make 487:26-27
Bayberry—how to make 296:80-83
Blowing out by sound 381:136-137
Blown out candle relights itself 228:38
Bright sparks show 146:50-51
Candle appears to be burning in water experiment 761:108-109
Candle carousel—how to make 487:28
Candle chemistry 84:47-48
Candle chemistry 85:16-17
Candle flame—chemistry of 146:48-49
Candle flame—demonstrate thru parts of burning candle flame 360:53
Candle flame—dissecting a candle flame 382:158-164
Candle flame—flame extinguished by 'nothing' 291:70-71
Candle flame—more with a candle flame 84:51
Candle gas—experiment 84:49-50

59

Candle powered steam turbine engine—how to make 487:24-25

Candle powered steamboat—how to make 487:22-23

Candle that lifts water—oxygen is consumed when a fire burns 576:70-71

Chemistry of candle flame and combustion experiment 752:90-91

Demonstrate area of greatest heat in candle flame experiment 752:88

Dipping candles—how to do 733:5

Faraday's investigating the properties of candle flames experiment 1133:7.007

How to make 322:10-11

How to make picture candles 186:112

Make a hollow candle 150:126-127

Make your own 888:20-22

Match flame jumps to relight candle trick 538:125

Physical properties of candle flame experiment 752:87

Prove smoke of candle will burn 364:91

Relight wick trick 360:94

Sand candle, how to make 1335:85

Snow candles—how to make 277:129-130

Solid substances in flame give off light experiment 752:92-93

Trick candle—burn candle at both ends—make it seesaw by itself 228:92

Vapor produced by burning candle burns experiment 752:85-86

CANDY
Make candy from garden violets 416:31

CANNON
Homemade cannon experiment using plastic bottle, vinegar and baking soda 1231:66-67

Naval cannon that shoots—how to make from wood 545:54-57

Make a carbide cannon 291:220-221

Make a safe 'pop' cannon 291:77

A spool cannon—how to make 543:6-7

CANOES
How to make model 415:9-10

Outrigger canoe model toy—how to make (Primary) 467:26-27

CANOES—POLYNESIAN
Toy outrigger canoe—how to make 325:unpaged

CANS
Can—crumpled—experiment 27:96-97

Can opener—how safe is your can opener—measure metal slivers 333:129-131

Crushing with air 291:86

CANTILEVERS
Cantilevers experiment; chart given for results 1462:52-54

CANTILEVERS—BRIDGE
Blocks demonstrate 532:16; 566:43

CAPACITORS
What are capacitors 278:71

CAPILLARITY
Water in the soil experiment 741:9

CAPILLARY ACTION. *See also* WATER— CAPILLARY ACTION
A capillary contest with paper 550:37-38

A cloth and sponge mystery experiments 563:78

Amount of water absorbed by different brands of paper towels experiment 1158:146-151

Capillarity again 161:66

Capillarity experiment with different liquids 563:84

Capillary action demonstrated with colored water and strips of paper 1331:29

Capillary action of water experiment 719:29-30

Capillary filtering of suspensions 360:87

Carnation flower drinks colored water and petals change color experiment 1379:20

Carnation flower in two glasses of colored water turns two colors experiment 1331:28

Celery—water and food coloring demonstrates 709:35

Celery and food coloring experiment with recording sheet 747:5-6

Celery and food coloring in water demonstrates capillary action 1004:1.006

Celery leaves, food coloring and water demonstrate capillary action 905:36-37

Celery stalk and food coloring—demonstrate 651:12-13; 899:183

Celery stalk blushes experiment 890:96

Celery stalk in jar of red colored water demonstrates capillary action 1393:22

Celery stalks—demonstrate 203:90

Clean muddy water by capillary action experiment 1405:47

Climbing water and capillary action experiments 959:35-37

Color a carnation using water and food coloring experiment 1054:86

Color a flower experiment 909:23

Colored flowers and celery experiment 684:10-11

Coloring celery stalks experiment 814:61-63

Fast cotton experiment with cotton cloth and polyester cloth 563:137-138

Filter dirty water with yarn demonstration 937:84-85

Flower power 77:10-11

Flowers and celery in colored water experiment 996:28-29

Great uphill water race 162:36

How plants drink 280:57

How sap rises 72:39-40

In candles 146:48-49

In plants 270:55-63

Ink travels up celery stalk experiment 1392:9

Lifting power of cardboard and water—demonstrate 176:97

Liquid moves up and down a glass experiment 937:48-49

Making water climb a hill—a water ladder of paper 550:35-37

Micro masterpieces 162:38-39

Moving matches trick—experiment 563:34-35

Observe circulation of water from roots to leaves 294:34

Open a flower experiment 909:23

Paper flower petals in bowl of water demonstrate capillary action 1310:20-21

Paper towels—water and colored markers experiment 760:36-37

Physical characteristics of osmosis and capillary action—demonstrate 293:19-20

Plant pipe patterns 162:42

Plants carry water from roots thru stems to leaves experiment 978:58-59

Salt and brick experiment with recording sheet 747:3-4

See red and blue veins in celery 508:13

Show with water experiments 142:28-29

Simple capillary siphon 202:115

Simple experiments 105:40-43
Sticky fingerprints 162:41
Striped celery 77:8-9
The hungry matches 350:102-103
The racing water drops 350:104-105
Towing floating objects by the attractive forces between them 604:56-59
Two-tone corsage—making 202:116
Two-tone flowers 364:103
Using blotting paper 146:10
Wacky wick experiments 563:74-75
Watch celery drink 264:15-16
Water—experiments to show 330:26-29
Water crawls the walls 162:40
Water crawls up celery stalk 364:102
Water flowing up—tree mystery experiment 399:35
Water moves in soil 253:130-131
Water moves thru a plant 273:12-13
Water pipe from wool or cotton threads—making 161:64-65
Water rises up paper towel demonstration 780:10-11
Water rises up plant stems—experiment 678:21
Water-soak clock experiment demonstrates soakability of materials 806:36-39
Wet and creepy—make dippy designs 162:34-35
What stems do for a plant 253:8-9

CARBOHYDRATES. *See also* **COMPOUNDS; STARCH; SUGAR**
Boiled winter squash—a study of cellulose 74:96-98
Gottlieb Kirchhof's starch is made up of sugar units experiment 1133:2.009
Identify sugar by flame test 83:32-33
Plant photosynthesis—determine what carbohydrates are produced 398:45-47
Sugar (carbohydrate) product of photosynthesis found in plant parts experiment 1061:26-27
Test for presence of monosaccharides (single sugars) in foods experiment 1396:61-66
Testing for carbohydrates 148:62
Testing for glucose in different foods experiment; data table given 871:2.019
What are they 261:31-35

CARBON. *See also* **CHARCOAL; COAL**
A lot of carbon—experiment 585:88
A test for carbon 30:34
Carbon—making 585:86
Carbon cycle—chart of 679:22
Heat test for 346:72
How to make charcoal 84:79-81
Properties of—make black nail turn silver 228:36
Role of carbon in life—experiment 402:5-6
Sugar used to make 146:45
Sulfur, carbon and their compounds—experiments with 116:156-169

CARBON BUTTON
Edison's experiments 230:33-38

CARBON CYCLE. *See* **BREATHING; PHOTOSYNTHESIS**

CARBON DIOXIDE. *See also* **ALKA-SELTZER; DRY ICE; MOLECULES**
A gas that puts out fire—experiment 72:58-60
A gas that puts out fires 30:38
Acid and baking soda reaction produces carbon dioxide experiment 1396:165-171
Acid test for carbonates experiment 1438:72-75

Air without carbon dioxide is cooler than air with carbon dioxide experiment 1174:31-33
Alka-Seltzer tablets produce how much carbon dioxide 538:83
Animals give off or take up carbon dioxide experiment 1427:38-39
Antacid tablet makes carbon dioxide experiment 781:2-3
Are some molecules heavier than others 396:18-19
Are there carbon dioxide molecules in your breath experiment 831:61-64
As temperature increases in soda amount of carbon dioxide increases experiment 984:41-44
Baking powder biscuits—making 219:19-21
Baking powder gives off more carbon dioxide gas than baking soda experiment 1208:87
Baking powder in water produces carbon dioxide demonstration 721:75
Baking soda and baking powder experiment using metric measure 702:87-88
Baking soda and vinegar together produce carbon dioxide experiments 782:12-14
Balloon and bottle—experiment 670:52
Balloon blowing experiment with club soda 960:15
Balloon inflates on bottle filled with water, yeast and sugar experiment 1229:20-21
Balloon on neck of bottle inflates from baking soda and vinegar gas experiment 1330:58-59
Blow up balloon on soda bottle with yeast, sugar, water and flour experiment 1208:90-91
Blow up balloon with gas experiment 827:53
Bouncing egg experiment 960:18
Bouncing raisins experiment 748:103
Breath contains carbon dioxide experiment 1322:17-20
Breath contains carbon dioxide experiment using limewater in jar 1435:95-96
Breath scrubber with limewater and candle to measure carbon dioxide in breath 363:144-146
Breathe into limewater; carbon dioxide experiment 959:76
Burning fossil fuels produce carbon dioxide experiment 1269:42-43
Burning wood produces carbon dioxide experiment 1269:46
Button in glass of soda rises and falls experiment 1079:87
Can expanding gas move an object through air experiment 851:55-56
Can popcorn float on bubbles experiment 780:6-7
Candle—baking powder and vinegar demonstrate gas 722:88
Candle test for carbon dioxide in breath 679:16
Candles and carbon dioxide 84:43-44
Carbon cycle in plant growth experiment using two plants in jars 1173:16-19
Carbon dioxide—making 146:27;146:45-46, 36-37; 85:36-37; 293:36
Carbon dioxide—making using moth balls 146:28
Carbon dioxide absorbed by plants in sunlight experiment 978:42-43
Carbon dioxide amount absorbed by trees and concrete building site experiment 1057:108
Carbon dioxide boat—making 293:37
Carbon dioxide bubbles cause clay balls to float and sink experiment 1405:93
Carbon dioxide by fermentation—experiment 563:170

Carbon dioxide causes water to become more acidic experiment 1325:39-43

Carbon dioxide extinguisher from baking soda and vinegar experiment 1073:87

Carbon dioxide extinguishes candle flame experiment 1396:169-170

Carbon dioxide extinguishes fire 122:133-134

Carbon dioxide flows down mountain because it is heavier than air experiment 1477:47

Carbon dioxide fog 291:54-55

Carbon dioxide from baking soda—making 122:132-133

Carbon dioxide from baking soda and vinegar puts out flame experiment 888:80-84

Carbon dioxide from lungs turns limewater cloudy—experiment 597:7

Carbon dioxide from vinegar and baking soda puts out flame 709:59

Carbon dioxide gas blows up balloon on bottle neck experiment 1208:86

Carbon dioxide gas blows up balloons experiment with baking soda and vinegar 1258:unp.

Carbon dioxide gas from baking soda and vinegar blows up soap bubble experiment 1482:38-39

Carbon dioxide gas from human breath detected by chemical indicator experiment 1427:36-37

Carbon dioxide gas from jar of water/baking soda/vinegar puts fire out 1229:44-45

Carbon dioxide gas from vinegar and baking soda experiment 1435:85-86

Carbon dioxide gas from vinegar and baking soda experiment 960:16-17

Carbon dioxide gas inflates balloon experiment 1028:10

Carbon dioxide gas made more rapidly when ginger added to yeast/sugar 1251:68-70

Carbon dioxide gas made when marble or calcite dissolves in vinegar experiment 1295:98

Carbon dioxide gas makes boat move experiment 851:53-54

Carbon dioxide gas makes raisins float in water experiment 1251:16-18

Carbon dioxide gas produced when Alka-Seltzer reacts with water experiment 1526:75

Carbon dioxide gas puts out candle flame experiment 1255:22

Carbon dioxide gas puts out fire—experiment 538:83

Carbon dioxide gas, make and use to smother fire experiment 895:11-12

Carbon dioxide given off or taken up by plants experiment 1427:40-41

Carbon dioxide in balloon puts out candle flame experiment 980:47

Carbon dioxide in batter; baking soda and baking powder experiment 885:91-93

Carbon dioxide in photosynthesis needed for plant growth experiment 1173:16-19

Carbon dioxide increase causes increase in plant growth experiment 1060:121

Carbon dioxide is common experiment 1057:18

Carbon dioxide is heavier than air experiment 752:116

Carbon dioxide is heavier than air experiment 836:14-15

Carbon dioxide is held in water experiment 1322:48-52

Carbon dioxide made from baking soda and vinegar in bottle experiment 1508:28

Carbon dioxide presence experiment; test for to predict volcanic eruption 1477:44-47

Carbon dioxide produces energy experiment 884:86-87

Carbon dioxide production balanced by plants and animals in environment 1427:42-43

Carbon dioxide puts out candle flame experiment; use baking soda/vinegar 1179:119

Carbon dioxide puts out fire experiment using vinegar and baking soda 1435:87-89

Carbon dioxide puts out flame—experiment 598:15

Carbon dioxide puts out flame experiment 705:27

Carbon dioxide release measured from germinating bean seeds experiment 1061:17-19

Carbon dioxide rocket—making 293:37-38

Carbon dioxide turns limewater white experiment 905:72-73

Carbon dioxide you add to the atmosphere experiment 1057:30

Carbon dioxide's heat-holding capabilities experiment 1174:31-33

Carbonated substances produce carbon dioxide when combined with acid experiment 1477:46-47

Carbonated water mixed with detergent/milk/toothpaste/ for best bubbles 1330:7

Carbonic acid gas—how to prepare 752:114-115

Carbonization in soda 50:62-63

Clouding things up—how your breath reacts with limewater 400:69

CO_2 in breath turns limewater white (Primary) 683:26

Dancing blueberries experiment 980:44

Dancing moth balls—experiment 83:52; 576:72-73

Dancing mothballs experiment with mothballs, vinegar and baking soda 1212:31

Dancing popcorn and carbon dioxide bubbles in water/vinegar/baking soda 1289:44-45

Dancing raisins experiment with Alka-Seltzer 814:34-36

Decomposers and release of carbon dioxide experiment 1057:33

Dry ice makes bubbles 122:140-141

Effects of carbon dioxide and changing weather conditions on Earth—experiment 371:52

Effects of industrial carbon dioxide on plant growth experiment 1174:49-50

Exhaled breath experiment; carbon dioxide in water produces acid 1396:70-72

Experiment #4—create carbon dioxide; 2 methods with baking soda & yeast 404:9

Experiment #5—match test to see CO_2 gas produced by Alka-Seltzer 404:10

Extract from soda pop 346:11-16

Feast for yeast experiment 735:28

Fermentation and its products experiment using yeast and sugar 1069:67

Fermentation of sugar and yeast produces carbon dioxide experiment 1396:168

Fermentation of yeast produces carbon dioxide experiment 1395:104

Fermentation of yeast produces carbon dioxide gas experiment 1221:18-19

Fiery model volcano; using vinegar and baking soda experiment 960:19

Fighting fire with carbon dioxide 122:141-143

Fire extinguisher made from vinegar and baking soda experiment 1212:10

Fire extinguisher 112:14-15

Fire extinguishers—make a model extinguisher 30:39

Fire extinguishing with carbon dioxide 186:108-109

Fizzing and foaming gas, making 685:6-7
Forest fires produce carbon dioxide experiment 1174:40-41
From plants and earth 97:28-29
Gas bubbles cause coffee grounds to float experiment 884:84-86
Gas bubbles pushed out of soda by salt experiment 1405:51
Gas cannon experiment with baking soda and vinegar in bottle 1136:21
Gas causes baby bottle nipple expansion 203:75
Gas from baking soda and vinegar blow up balloon experiment 782:16-17
Gas from bottle with vinegar and baking soda inflates balloon experiment 998:208-209
Gas in a soda 85:38-39
Gas pressure in a carbonated drink experiment 1250:14-17
Gas takes up more space than solids or liquids experiment with vinegar/b. Soda 1179:24-25
Gas that chokes fire 85:40-41
Ginger ale drink from yeast, recipe, how to make 1214:26-27
Green plants use and give off oxygen 273:18-23
Heat speeds up chemical reactions; time the fizz from Alka-Seltzer experiment 924:93
How carbon dioxide prevents flame experiment 939:114-116
How many substances in your kitchen produce carbon dioxide—exp. 598:10-11
How trees take in carbon dioxide experiment 1057:104
Humans and animals add carbon dioxide to the atmosphere experiment 1057:20
Increased carbon dioxide levels in atmosphere increase plant growth experiment 1174:49-50
Inflates a balloon 92:22-23
Invisible flame killer 249:9
Is a gas made by mixing vinegar and baking soda 396:16-17
Joseph Black's discovery of carbon dioxide experiment 1133:2.003
Leaf stops making chlorophyll due to lack of carbon dioxide experiment 1441:91
Lemon rocket, how to make 827:56
Lentils bounce up and down in water, vinegar and baking soda experiment 1393:29
Lime test to show carbon dioxide in your breath 291:208
Limestone; testing limestone with an acid experiment 1438:80-82
Limewater—making 122:135-136
Limewater test for carbon dioxide in household places experiment 1020:80-85
Limewater test for carbon dioxide produced by yeast experiment 905:74-75
Limewater test for 676:38
Limewater used as test for carbon dioxide experiment 752:113
Limewater used to test for presence of carbon dioxide experiment 1395:177-182
Make bubbles float 291:72-73
Make carbon dioxide—experiment using yeast 563:169-170
Make your own lemon soda experiment 827:55
Making from baking soda and vinegar; match test experiment 790:11

Mothballs dance a ballet for you 186:68
Moving mothballs 400:70
Obedient button trick 202:111
Observe gas bubbles being pushed out of soda by salt experiment 905:66-67
Organic fuels produce carbon dioxide when burned experiment 1396:168-169
Paper butterflies dance in air over carbon dioxide gas experiment 1216:37-39
Plants die from carbon dioxide deprivation experiment 1061:24-25
Plants exhale carbon dioxide experiment 904:36-37
Plants given more carbon dioxide grow better experiment 714:38-39
Plants need carbon dioxide gas to carry on photosynthesis experiment 1174:19-20
Plants need carbon dioxide to produce oxygen thru photosynthesis experiment 1173:46-47
Plants use carbon dioxide experiment 1324:48-53
Pop a cork experiment 735:27
Pop bottle cannon; make CO_2 from baking soda and water—experiment 576:71-72
"Pop" bottle experiment—water, vinegar and baking soda produce CO_2 563:168
Pour 'nothing' (CO_2) out of pitcher and extinguish candle flame 291:70-71
Presence of carbon dioxide in yeast bubbles experiment 998:207
Priestley, Joseph; who invented carbonated water project 1525:65-66
Producing carbon dioxide—experiment 180:16
Puts out flame 97:34-35
Raisins float and rise in water, vinegar and baking soda solution experiment 1229:14-15
Raisins rise and fall in jar of water with yeast experiment 1508:28
Raisins swim in carbonated soda experiment 900:17
Rate of photosynthesis affected by amount of carbon dioxide experiment 1060:23-25
Raw popcorn kernels in glass of soda water go up and down 560:38
Red cabbage extract used as test for carbon dioxide experiment 1395:177-182
Removal of gas from a solution inflates balloon experiment 1405:60
Removal of on space craft (advanced) 668:53-54
Respiration experiment; test for carbon dioxide in exhaled breath 1395:177-182
Respiration; does gender affect amount of carbon dioxide exhaled experiment 1395:177-182
Rising raisins experiment with vinegar and baking soda 960:17
Rising straw in carbonated drink demonstrates 721:24
Safe pop cannon—making 291:77
Salt added to carbonated drink causes gas to be released experiment 1251:23-24
Seeds; carbon dioxide released by germinating seeds experiment 1395:103-104
Show carbon dioxide in breath and atmosphere 122:136-139
Show carbon dioxide is heavier than air 186:108; 291:69
Show carbon dioxide is produce of exhalation 294:87
Show gas you exhale contains carbon dioxide 319:31-32
Show plants use carbon dioxide 282:25-33
Simple way to produce it 168:40

Smothers a fire 44:98-99
Snail shell dissolves in vinegar mixture experiment 1392:15
Soap bubbles float on cushion of carbon dioxide gas experiment 1132:15-1-15-2
Soda fountain from baking soda and vinegar 203:18
Soft drinks; carbon dioxide amount in popular soda pop drinks experiment 1208:89
Spaghetti—mothball substitute to demonstrate 203:14
Spaghetti worms rise and fall in mixture experiment 1066:50-51
Speedy Alka-Seltzer experiment—what factors affect rate of reaction 586:63
Sugar and yeast produce carbon dioxide experiment 1176:38-39
Test for carbon dioxide from burning wood experiment 1322:20
Test for carbon dioxide in air using limewater experiment 1322:20
Test for carbon dioxide in carbonated beverage experiment 1322:20
Test your breath in lime water 598:13
Testing chemicals in exhaled air 148:66
Testing for carbon dioxide experiment using vinegar, baking soda and limewater 1435:90-94
Testing solution for carbon dioxide; make limewater experiment 905:70-71
Tests for carbon dioxide from Alka-Seltzer experiment 888:41-43
The balloon blower upper 400:69
The flying flame—introducing a chemical reaction 205:110-115
The moving mothballs—experiment 598:12
The pop in soda pop—experiment 676:42-43
The rising raisins—buoyancy and surface tension 205:74-76
The spirited fire extinguisher—carbon dioxide in action 205:116-120
Time release of carbon dioxide from Alka-Seltzer tablet experiment 905:78-79
Time release of carbon dioxide gas from Alka-Seltzer tablet experiment 1405:52
Timothy Lane's carbon dioxide and the formation of rust experiment 1133:2.004
Trapping heat to demonstrate the greenhouse effect 1057:26
Unleavened bread, recipe, demonstrates carbon dioxide from yeast experiment 790:11-12
Use it to make chalk 97:24-25
Use yeast and sugar to fill a balloon 84:45-46
Using baking powder making biscuits 52:55-56
Vinegar and baking soda inflate balloon experiment 905:118-119
Vinegar and baking soda makes carbon dioxide experiment 924:110-111
Vinegar and baking soda mixed together make carbon dioxide gas experiment 1479:56
Vinegar and baking soda rocket—making 733:1
What happens when bubbles are blown into phenolphthalein solution 174:34-35
Why bubbles escape from a glass of soda, observe 905:64-65
Will air molecules float on carbon dioxide molecules 396:39-40

Yeast and limewater produce carbon dioxide experiment 723:80
Yeast and sugar mix makes carbon dioxide gas that inflates balloon experiment 1038:26
Yeast and sugar produce carbon dioxide gas experiment 1405:31
Yeast and sugar produce carbon dioxide gas that blows cork off bottle experiment 1479:53
Yeast gives off carbon dioxide experiment 1214:24-25
Yeast mixture in jar blows up balloon experiment 980:46
Yeast produces carbon dioxide experiment 1441:99

CARBONATED DRINKS. *See also* **SOFT DRINKS**
Are gas molecules farther apart than liquid molecules 396:14-15

CARBONATED WATER
Priestley, Joseph; who invented carbonated water project 1525:65-66

CARBONATES
Acid test for carbonates experiment 1438:72-75

CARBONATES AND ACIDS
Chemical properties of marble and why damaged by pollution experiment 871:3.026
Experiments 84:39-42

CARDIOVASCULAR SYSTEM. *See* **CIRCULATORY SYSTEM; HEART**

CARNIVOROUS PLANTS
Butterworts, how to grow 1260:43
Sundews, how to grow 1260:36
Venus flytraps, how to grow 1260:19-20

CARNOT, NICOLAS
Who discovered that heat is a form of energy project 1525:110-113

CAROUSEL
Candle carousel—how to make 487:28
Energy stored in twisted materials drives simple machines experiment 1073:16-17
Twisted rubber band energy demonstrated by model carousel, how to make 1073:17

CARS. *See also* **AUTOMOBILES**
Measure speed of toy car experiment 1521:18-19
Three models of cars to make that move freely 631:98-101

CART
Model—how to make 415:10-11

CARTESIAN DIVER
Adorable diving doll—how to make 392:54-58
Air can be compressed and water cannot; deep-jar diver demonstrates 1212:21
Air can be compressed; match in bottle experiment 900:51
Bottle submarine 281:33
Bubble diver goes up and down experiment 1161:21
Can air be compressed; medicine dropper in bottle experiment 900:50
Cartesian diver experiment, how to make 1007:17-19
Cartesian diver experiment 906:12
Cartesian diver lie detector game, how to make 1140:126-129
Cartesian pen top diver, making 909:36
Deep dive using medicine dropper in bottle of water experiment 748:109
Deep water diver experiment 996:18-19; 1066:76
Deep-sea diver experiment using plastic jar and eye dropper 1230:64-65

Diver from pen cap and clay in bottle of water experiment 1480:143

Diver goes up and down in plastic bottle filled with water experiment 1208:44-45

Diver in plastic bottle of water experiment 1298:16

Diver in the bottle, how to make 600:26-27

Diver made from eye dropper floats or sinks due to pressure changes experiment 1132:37-1

Diver made from pen top and clay rises and sinks in bottle of water experiment 1393:31

Diving baby—hydraulic pressure and buoyancy 205:77-81

Diving medicine dropper experiment 940:43-45

Experiments—recover treasure in bottle of water 54:102-112

Eye dropper in bottle of water demonstrates 780:42-43

Eye dropper sinks and rises experiment 905:28-29

Glass medicine dropper diver in bottle of water experiment 1465:39

How can air be compressed; dropper in bottle of water experiment 900:10

How can you control the mysterious diver—experiment 628:93-94

How to make 128:109; 172:162-163; 186:72-73; 363:156-157; 366:165; 642:101-104

Jellyfish dives and floats in water filled soda bottle experiment 1310:20-21

Make a Cartesian diver 142:22

Make a mystery diver 291:76

Make from plastic bottle 203:50-51

Make model to show law of flotation 167:13-15

Making a Cartesian diver 604:68-71

Medicine dropper diver in plastic bottle filled with water experiment 1509:25

Model diver in corked bottle experiment 1247:20-21

Model diver 472:2213

Octopus model floats up and down in bottle of water experiment 1024:32

Operation octopus—it dives up and down in bottle of water—experiment 573:35

Pen-top diver—making 663:28

Show using balloons 92:34-35

Sink and raise eyedropper by changing its density experiment 1479:49

Submarine model dives and surfaces in water filled bottle experiment 1256:13

Toy diver works in same way as a submarine experiment 1028:19

What makes a submarine rise and sink 126:45-49

CARTOONS

Cartoon movie, how to make from tin lid, stick and paper strips 1308:29

How to do animated cartoons experiment 1283:9

Strip cartoon show—how to make 410:29

CARVER, GEORGE WASHINGTON

His jelly from peach pits, how to make 879:104-105

His peanut milk, how to make 879:103-104

Investigate his discovery of peanut oil 602:unpaged

CASEIN. *See also* **GLUES; MILK**

Casein plastic from milk, how to make 827:69

Casein plastic—how to make 676:10-11

Casein from milk makes plastic 26:138-142

Extract from milk 122:99-102

CASSINI, GIOVANNI DOMENICO

Cassini's experiment using parallax to measure distance 1156:57-60

CASTLE AND VILLAGE

Medieval—how to make 415:54-60

CASTS. *See also* **PLASTER CASTS; TRACKS AND TRAILING**

Animal track casts—making 749:49; 772:63-65

Animal tracks; paraffin casts, how to make 921:33-34

Casts from tracks, how to make 850:25

Footprint casts, making 930:12

Footprint molds and casts of animal footprints—how to make 530:163

Footprints of animals, making 890:107

Plaster cast of animal track, how to make 1427:18-20

Plaster casts and molds of footprints, how to make 977:13

Plaster casts of animal tracks, how to make 932:44-45

Plaster casts of animal tracks, making 832:50

Plaster casts of footprints—how to make 507:1858-1859

Plaster casts of footprints—how to make 731:40

Plaster casts, making 870:64-66

Plaster of Paris casts of animal tracks, making 854:71

Plaster of Paris casts of tracks, how to do 1069:181

Plaster of Paris casts, how to make 824:48-49

Plaster of Paris casts, how to make 860:169-170

Plaster paw prints, how to make 810:68

Sand casts, making 772:59-60

CATALYST. *See also* **ENZYMES**

Burn sugar cube to demonstrate 202:19

Catalytic action—burning sugar 146:43

Catalytic reaction 84:83-88

Experiment—shows hydrogen peroxide splitting up into oxygen and water 6:24

Flaming sugar cube with ash as catalyst experiment 1244:18

How much of air is oxygen experiment 1159:26-27

Iron rusts faster using vinegar as a catalyst experiment 1159:26-27

Is blood a catalyst 291:210-211

Magic chemical reactions from catalysts 382:131-134

Magnesium dioxide is catalyst that speeds up rate of breakdown 346:53-54

Speed of chemical reaction directly related to strength of catalyst exp. 871:3.006

Speeding up chemical change 180:15

Yeast and hydrogen peroxide form oxygen 146:26-27

CATAMARAN—POLYNESIAN

How to make 325:unpaged

CATAMARAN BOAT

Catamaran from plastic bottle and wood pieces, how to make 1299:67

How to make from wood and coffee cans 429:70

Making and sailing 561:18-19

Trimaran from plastic bottle and wood pieces, how to make 1299:67

CATAPULT LAUNCHER

Catapult for paper airplane, how to make 1419:21

How to make 54:123

CATAPULTS

Catapult is example of third-class lever experiment 1462:59-61

Catapult powered by rubber band, how to make 1446:8-9

Small model catapult shows force needed to make object move 1507:15

Working catapult, how to make 1420:12-13

CATENARY ARCH
 Build a center for a catenary arch 557:26
CATERPILLARS. *See also* **BUTTERFLIES; MOTHS; SILKWORMS**
 Cage for caterpillars, simple wooden and wire cage to make 916:16-17
 Caterpillar cage—making 480:54
 Caterpillar in jar, keeping, how to do [Primary] 942:21
 Caterpillar life cycle—observation (Primary) 535:35
 Caterpillar, how to keep until butterfly emerges 1320:43-45
 Coffee can rearing cage for caterpillars 414:50-51
 Collect and care for 390:23-24
 Collect cocoons and caterpillars and care for 332:77-86
 Collect larvae and pupae to study 436:19
 Collect, keep and observe 233:18-19
 Collecting and caring for caterpillars, how to do 916:10-27
 Collecting and feeding caterpillars until they become butterflies experiment 1433:31-33
 Collecting caterpillars, cocoons and bagworms 62:47-49
 Crawling caterpillar toy—how to make (Primary) 466:6-7
 Directions for raising 478:30-34
 Do caterpillars eat more when it is cold or when it is warm 414:53
 Do caterpillars feed in the day or the night experiment; set up choice box 1313:45
 Feeding and caring for caterpillars 932:32-35
 Feeding tube made from material tied to tree, how to do 916:20
 House for caterpillars, plastic containers, making 932:32-35
 How much does a caterpillar eat—experiment 414:52
 How much lunch can caterpillar munch experiment 1464:58-59
 How they react to noises 266:23
 How to cage and care for 279:22-23
 How to cage and watch caterpillars 832:71
 How to care for 32:84-85
 How to care for (Primary) 256:entire book
 Keeping caterpillars experiment, how to do 1183:59
 Keeping caterpillars, how to do 1182:11
 Keeping caterpillars, how to do 992:28
 Life cycle of a butterfly experiment; build butterfly farm for caterpillars 1176:10-11
 Life cycle of butterfly; observe caterpillar in jar experiment 810:52-53
 Metamorphosis in butterfly experiment; observe larva in large glass jar 1187:26
 Metamorphosis; watch by keeping caterpillars in box, how to do 1445:32-33
 Metamorphosis; watch how butterflies metamorphose experiment 1144:15
 Plants caterpillars prefer for food experiment; set up choice box 1313:43-45
 Raising caterpillars, how to do 1116:16-17
 Response of caterpillars to touch in the field and in the laboratory 266:26-27
 Watch a caterpillar become a moth or butterfly 294:66-67
 Watch caterpillar turn into butterfly experiment, how to do 1488:13
 Watch caterpillars change into butterflies experiment 1524:13
 Woolly bear wanderings investigation experiment 1313:18-20
CATKINS
 Adventure 9—we learn the meaning of the word catkin—under hand lens 29:43-51
CATNIP PILLOW
 How to make 376:26
 Toys for your cat, making 879:186-187
CATS
 Cats' eyes glow in the dark experiment using coffee can and flashlight 1397:24-27
 Does size of pupil affect glow of cat's eye experiment 1397:26-27
 How tongue of cat can clean cats fur experiment 1405:36
 Is your cat right or left pawed (Primary) 551:unpaged
CAUSTICS
 Caustics; curved line patterns produced by curved mirrors and lights experiment 1443:84-91
CAVENDISH, HENRY
 Discovery of inflammable air experiment 1133:2.005
CAVERNS. *See* **STALACTITES AND STALAGMITES**
CAVES
 How are caves formed experiment 852:25-26
 How do stalactites form in caves experiment 852:27-28
 Model of how stalactites and stalagmites form in caves experiment 1046:88-90
 Stalactite formation demonstration 293:5
CAVES AND CAVEMEN
 Make a cave scene 415:32-34
CEDAR APPLE GALLS
 Adventure 50—we probe into complicated life history—under hand lens 29:217-220
CELESTIAL NAVIGATION. *See* **NAVIGATION INSTRUMENTS; SOLAR STONE**
CELLS. *See also* **PLANTS—CELLS**
 Algae—iodine stain shows starch in cells 294:21-22
 Blood cells and mouth lining cells—how to prepare microscope slides 729:28-29
 Blood cells under microscope—observe 713:74-76; 889:54-57
 Blood 82:45-49
 Cartilage cells under microscope—observe 713:69-70
 Cartilage cells 82:53-54
 Cell differentiation—what happens if you plant the leaf of coleus in soil 58:8-9
 Cell homeostasis experiment 1395:39-43
 Cell membranes—selectively permeable—membranes project—computer project. 584:32-33
 Cell models of frog embryos 436:20
 Cells dehydrate when placed into hypertonic solutions experiment 1395:42
 Cells of onion under a microscope, observe 794:13-14
 Cells placed in hypotonic and hypertonic solutions affect osmosis experiment 1395:39-43
 Cheek cells observed under microscope experiment 1425:14
 Cheek cells under microscope—observe 713:63-64
 Chromosome changes from water pollutants experiment using onions 1060:119-121
 Coconut milk stimulates growth in plant cell tissues experiment 1060:88-89
 Cork cells under microscope—examine 713:49-50
 Cork cells, how to prepare and observe under microscope 1295:76-77

Effect of water on turgor pressure on animal cell membrane experiment 1395:45-50

Egg in vinegar demonstrates semipermeability of cell membrane experiment 1479:35

Epithelial cheek cells under microscope, observe 889:52-54

Green plant cells under microscope—observe 713:52-54

Hooke's cork and cells experiment 1156:65

How the cell can be seen and explored 402:8-10

Human—observing cells of the human body 294:16-17

Is there a center of inheritance in the cell 402:101-102

Mitosis and meiosis—animal and plant mitosis (advanced) 372:4-29

Model; make model cross section of a cell experiment 1517:16-17

Muscle cells under microscope, observe 889:57-58

Muscle cells 82:50-53

Nerve cells; location of nerve cells on your body experiment using toothpicks 1189:18-19

Onion cells under microscope—observe as you stain them 713:50-52

Plant cell, diagram of 769:10-11

Plants—examining green plant cells—elodea 294:15-16

Plants—living plant cells from an onion skin 294:14-15

Plants; what happens to plant cells living in fresh water experiment 1395:42-43

Potato cells under microscope showing starch grains 713:54-55

Potatoes as models of cell membranes demonstrate osmosis experiment 1069:17

Red blood cells—explanation of (Primary) 245:12-19

Robert Hooke's discovery of cells in cork experiment 1133:3.004

Slide of cells—how to prepare 703:28-29

Slides of insect cells, how to make 990:28

Spirogyra and other algae under a microscope—observe 713:85-87

This is a cell 231:76

Turgor pressure; effect of water on plants experiment 1395:45-50

Typical cell structure 294:13-14

Use clay to see how cells split (Primary) 675:9

Water movement in and out of plant cells experiment 762:79-81

White blood cells—diagram and explanation of 245:20-21

Yeast cells under microscope—observe 713:90-92

CELLS AND BATTERIES. *See also* **BATTERIES**
Storage cell—how to make 381:60-61

CELLULOSE
Heat vs. Cellulose experiment—making a cooked vegetable platter 537:22-24

Heat vs. Cellulose experiment—making twice baked potatoes 537:24-25

How does heat affect cellulose—cooked vegetable platter recipe 537:66

How does heat affect cellulose—twice baked potatoes recipe 537:67

CELSIUS, ANDERS. *See also* **THERMOMETERS**
Comparison of Celsius thermometer to Fahrenheit thermometer (Primary) 648:28-32

Draw diagrams comparing Fahrenheit/Celsius/Kelvin thermometer scales experiment 1396:186-187

CEMENT. *See also* **CONCRETE; MINERALS**
Cement mixtures; which is strongest experiment 1094:27

Concrete pencil holder—making 26:36-39

Make different mixes of concrete to see which is best experiment 834:30-33

Making 26:35-42

Show characteristics of cement and concrete 128:62-63

Testing strength of concrete; make concrete bars experiment 795:30-31

CENTER OF GRAVITY. *See also* **GRAVITY—CENTER OF GRAVITY**
Acrobatic forks 161:20-21

Balance at center of gravity—demonstrate 295:12-13

Balance hammer and ruler together to demonstrate center of gravity 937:88-89

Balanced forks experiment 748:120

Balancing act experiment 748:121

Balancing blob experiment 906:109

Balancing match trick 670:98

Balancing point—experiments 664:8-11

Balancing point forks experiment 906:115

Balancing spoon and fork demonstrate 882:27

Big foot—body against the wall experiment 906:111

Bound to balance books 670:99

Building a balance 295:22-27

Butterfly magic experiment 906:114

Cane hangs on your hand magic demonstration 1010:25-27

Center of gravity affects a balance experiment with straw balance 1404:84-85

Center of gravity and sports experiment 1154:72-76

Center of gravity different in males and females experiment 904:204-205

Center of gravity is balancing point of an object experiment 1404:82-83

Center of gravity is balancing point of an object experiment 1405:95

Center of gravity point demonstrated with balancing forks 1404:92-93

Cork and needle—demonstrates 670:98

Demonstrate your center of gravity 295:14-15

Determine center of gravity point experiment 1405:95-104

Eggshell with iron filings in it doesn't fall over experiment 960:43

Find center of gravity in irregular shape experiment 940:90-98

Find center of gravity in long, thin object experiment 1132:18

Finding center of gravity using straws 827:20-21

Forks balance on cork experiment 940:85-86

Human body center of gravity, test for 881:16-17

Leaning cantilever paper toy demonstrates 999:31-32

Magic box experiment 906:113

Make a butterflier 162:112-113

Object's center of gravity effect on motion experiment 1405:94

Object's center of gravity; where is it experiment 1404:85

Objects center of gravity can be changed experiment 1399:36-39

Over the edge book experiment 906:110

Paper tube toy demonstrates 999:21-23

Parrot perching demonstrates center of gravity; make from cardboard/clay 1380:8-9

Plumb bob from paper demonstrates 999:25-27

Rack-a-baby paper toy demonstrates 999:32-34

Roll object uphill to demonstrate; paper cups and yardstick experiment 937:90-91

Rolling can experiment demonstrates 836:58-59

Rolling uphill 16:35-39

Ruler and hammer balance to demonstrate 940:87-89

Sky hook toy demonstrates, how to make 861:113-119

Some strange balancing acts 295:16-18

Spin a sea monster demonstration 827:90

Stand up when you're leaning against wall experiment 1083:18-19

Three straw toy demonstrates 999:28-30

Tightrope walker shows positioning center of gravity at certain point experiment 1399:38-39

What is center of gravity experiment 902:58

Where is your center of gravity experiment [Advanced] 871:4.003

Where is your center of gravity experiment 902:59

Who's stronger experiment 906:112

Wing walker paper toy demonstrates 999:23-24

CENTIPEDES

Centipede model—how to make (Primary) 466:22-23

CENTRIFUGAL AND CENTRIPETAL FORCES

Fishbowl and ball—experiment 585:43

CENTRIFUGAL EFFECT

Centrifugal puzzle 392:16-21

CENTRIFUGAL FORCE. *See also* **FORCE**

A sand and water mystery experiment 563:90-91

Against gravity—keeping sun, Earth and moon in place 274:16

Artificial gravity—making (advanced) 668:37-39

Ball goes up in rotating jar experiment 723:38-39

Can a button lift a stone demonstration 827:95

Centripetal force and satellites in orbit demonstration 1434:103-106

Coin balancing on coat hanger demonstrates centrifugal force 1079:42-43

Demonstrate circular motion (Primary) 169:10

Experiment to put opposing forces to work 385:54-56

Experiment to show 128:126-128

Flame in a jar—experiment 585:35

Fun with a clothes hanger and coin 392:12-15

Gravity and centrifugal force effect on plants grown on turntable experiment 1159:64-67

Lifting a marble without touching it 150:84-85

Lifting an apple without touching it 150:92-93

Loop-the-loop with rope, pail and ball demonstrates 827:94

Make a lifting spinner 142:10

Making mayonnaise 219:7-9

More sand and water mystery experiments 563:91-92

Ounce—lift up a pound 161:23-24

Pick up the marble experiment 909:122

Ping pong ball in cup demonstrates centrifugal force 1330:24-25

Relation of centrifugal force to velocity 577:project #37

Round and round—centrifugal lifter 260:24-25

Round and round—whirling water 260:24-25

Separate floating parts of a suspension by spinning experiment 905:162-163

Simple demonstrations of centrifugal force 898:24

Simple working model to demonstrate 577:project #30

Spin—experiments 664:34-35

Spin drier, making 909:123

Spin dryer tests principle of centrifuge and dries paper towels experiment 1136:32-33

Spinning and whirling experiments 685:10-11

Spinning water demonstrates 909:123

Spool, string and washer demonstrate centrifugal force experiment 947:16

Swing glass of water that won't spill experiment 1007:46-47

The Hindu climbing balls 350:108-111

The marvel of centrifugal force 161:22-23

The whirling bucket—demonstrates 291:144

The whirling coat hanger 350:106-107

Water flows uphill 142:11

Water in bucket whirled around demonstrates 699:27

Water in spinning bowl demonstrates centrifugal force in liquids 1079:44-45

Water stays in whirling container experiment 1389:13

What is centrifugal force experiment 902:60-61

Whirler balls in tube demonstrate, how to make 999:85-86

Whirling a glass of water upside down without spilling a drop 350:107-108

Why the vortex—experiments 563:92-93

CENTRIPETAL FORCE. *See also* **FORCE**

Acceleration experiments with objects moving in a circle 1157:31-34

Amusement park swing ride, construct to demonstrate centripetal force 1004:5.010

Anti-gravity ball 670:96

Apparatus to see how mass—radius and period relate to centripetal force 763:85-87

Carousel ride demonstrates centripetal force experiment 1412:45-46

Centripetal force and satellites in orbit demonstration 1434:103-106

Centripetal force measured by G meter, how to do experiment 1412:23-26

Cork moves in circle experiment 1028:112

Cork on string demonstrates centripetal force 1179:71

Ferris Wheel ride demonstrates centripetal force experiment 1412:28

Inuit Yo-Yo demonstrates centripetal force experiment 871:4.002

Marble and bowl demonstrate inertia and centripetal force experiment 836:68-69

Rotating platform ride demonstrates centripetal force experiment 1412:50-51

Satellites; centripetal force keeps satellites in orbit experiment 1479:9

Scrambler amusement park ride demonstrates centripetal force experiment 1412:46-47

The lariat 585:42

What is centripetal force—demonstrate 291:142-143

CEREAL PLANTS

Show growth of cereal plants versus other plants 119:63-67

CEREALS

Breakfast cereals have iron filings in them experiment 1083:59

Breakfast of Romans—how to make frumenty 231:84

Can you see the iron in iron-fortified cereals experiment 1250:80-81

Oatmeal cooked in cold or boiling water experiment 1238:85-86

Which cereal has more fiber experiment 1484:144

CEREBELLUM. *See* HUMAN BODY
CFCs. *See* CHLOROFLUOROCARBONS
CHAIN DRIVES
Chain drive on bicycle 227:18
CHALK
Acid test to show difference between white chalk and anti-dust chalk 336:45-46
Chalk, how to make 859:16
Hardness test for chalk experiment 1438:51-52
Make your own chalk 336:46-48
Test for chalk or limestone in rocks experiment 1277:31
Testing chalk with an acid experiment 1438:49-50
CHALK—FORAMINIFERA
Adventure 27—we find out what chalk is made of under a microscope 403:94-96
CHAMELEONS
Eyes of chameleons and what they see experiment 1397:22
How to care for 279:11-13
Why do chameleons change color experiment 1397:72-75
CHANGE OF STATE
Food changes when you heat or cool it experiments 1129:18-19
Make rags dirty and get them clean again experiments 1129:22-23
Things change if left in soil, in water, in warm place experiments 1129:24-25
Things change when they are stirred or shook experiments 1129:16-17
Things change when they are wet experiments 1129:20-21
Things change when water is added to them experiments 1129:12-13
CHARCOAL. *See also* **CARBON**
Distilled wood experiment 723:198-199
How to make 175:21; 84:79-81
How to make charcoal experiment 1075:77
Making from wood 26:25-27
CHARCOAL BURNER
Making 9:84-85
CHARLES, JACQUES. *See also* **CHARLES' LAW**
Charles' Law experiment of gas temperature and volume 1133:7.005
CHARLES' LAW
Charles' Law experiment of gas temperature and volume 1133:7.005
Charles' Law; boiling and freezing a balloon experiment 871:3.016
Charles' Law and gases experiment 1156.103-104
Fountain in a jug experiment 723:146-147
See Charles' Law in action with balloon—experiment 642:104-106
CHARTS. *See also* **GRAPHS**
Samples of charts and graphs 31:79-90
Window shades make good visual charts 436:20-21
CHEESE
Cheese from milk, making 870:20-22
Cottage cheese—making 732:65
Cottage cheese from whole and skim milk 152:27-33
Cottage cheese, how to make from sour milk experiment 1238:123-124
Curd—how to make 77:24-25
Curds and whey, how to make 827:68
Make your own cheese 607:80-81

Making hard ripened cheese 152:33-37
Making mold ripened cheese 152:37-43
Show how cottage cheese is made and how protein coagulates experiment 1484:102-103
Soft cheese—how to make 358:58-59
CHEMICAL CHANGES
Are chemical changes faster in hot or cold water experiment 831:50-52
Cabbage capers, colorful experiment 870:76-78
Can adding Epsom Salts to water make the water colder experiment 831:43-44
Chemical changes caused by heat; secret writing demonstrates 1219:42
Clean pennies with vinegar and salt 780:38-39
Epsom salts and ammonia produce precipitate experiment 723:197
Hydrogen peroxide changes into water and oxygen with help from potato 905:96-97
Ink eradicator experiment 723:198
Iron filings and powdered sulfur experiment to determine changes 976:18
Irreversible chemical change experiment with heated sugar 1219:42-43
Is dissolving solids a physical change or a chemical change experiment 902:22
Juice sleuth experiment 829:35-36
Light and chemistry produce outlines on paper—experiment 563:171
Make a magic landscape 172:136-137
Make milky, magnesia solution experiment 1479:54
Making new materials from old—experiment 180:20
Mystery message experiment 829:17-18
Pennies get a green coating from vinegar experiment 905:92-93
Physical and chemical changes experiment; chart given 960:13-14
Precipitate formation experiment using Epsom salts and ammonia 976:41
Prevention of rust experiment; coat steel wool with soap 905:88-89
Rusting iron gives off heat experiment 735:30
Silver tarnishes, what causes it experiment 976:50
Six experiments to observe chemical changes 400:71
Sugar—its elements change when heated 146:45
Sugar and yeast blow up balloons—experiment 589:50-51
Super paste, making experiment 960:34
Test clay you create experiment 871:3.004
Test for presence of iron in fruit juices experiment 905:112-113
To rust or not to rust—what makes things rust? Experiment 589:48-49
Vinegar and baking soda inflate balloon experiment 905:118-119
Vinegar and baking soda mix together experiment and produce carbon dioxide 1479:56
CHEMICAL CYCLES IN NATURE
Project 268:101-105
CHEMICAL ELEMENTS. *See* **ELEMENTS**
CHEMICAL GARDENS. *See also* **GARDENS—CHEMICAL**
A salt garden—experiment 585:22-23
Aluminum foil garden, making 883:49

Brick castle, making 883:53-54
Chemical garden, how to grow 866:159
Coal plant grows before your eyes 576:83
Crystal garden from coal, salt and water experiment 1435:82-84
Crystal garden in a pie plate, how to make 1229:70-71
Crystal garden, making 870:40-42
Garden of odds and ends, making 883:52
Grow a crystal garden 598:26-27
How to make 452:74-75; 87:81-82
Macrocrystal garden from water, salt, bluing, ammonia and dye, how to do 1295:94-95
Make a chemical garden 291:207
Mystery garden, making 883:54-57
Paper towel garden, making 883:48-50
Porous rock garden, making 883:49
Rock and charcoal garden, making 883:48-51
Salt and brick experiment with recording sheet 747:3-4
Salt garden experiment with salt in warm water poured over rocks 1331:22
Salt travels on glass of water experiment 721:77
Sponge garden, making 883:52
Super crystal garden, making 883:52-53
Surprise garden, making 883:53
What does your salt garden grow (Primary) 580:unpaged

CHEMICAL MAGIC. *See also* **LIQUIDS**
A flash of fire 350:68
Black hand 350:71
Changing two liquids into a solid 350:66
Dry water 350:67
How to make a chemical garden 87:77-87
How to make bouncing putty 87:77-87
How to make color changes in flowers 87:77-87
How to make magic coal garden 87:77-87
How to make mysterious mothballs 87:77-87
How to make smoke magic 87:77-87
The darting camphor 350:65-66
The ghostly faces 350:69
The indestructible card 350:64
The magic sand of Arabia 350:72-73
The magic wound 350:68-69
The red hand 350:70-71
The restless mothball 350:65
The tricky soap 350:66-67
With slates 87:53-55

CHEMICAL PESTICIDES. *See* **HERBICIDES;
PESTICIDES**

CHEMICAL REACTIONS. *See also* **CARBON
DIOXIDE; INDICATORS**
A big bad odor experiment using photographer's hypo 563:174
A detective and solutions—experiments with stock & indicator solutions 565:157-172
Acid or alkali test papers, how to make using turmeric/sodium carbonate 1244:8-9
Acid test—experiment—what vinegar does to calcium substances 366:220-221
Acid vinegar mixed with soluble salt and baking powder makes a salt experiment 1435:16-17
Alka-Seltzer and water reaction experiment 1526:65-67
Alka-Seltzer in water puts out candle flame experiment 1526:72-73
Alka-Seltzer tablets experiment shows small particles react faster than large 1251:55-57

Aluminum pot shines when boiling water and lemons are used experiment 1435:65-66
An 'eggsact' experiment 400:70
Apples; acids effect on browning process of cut apples experiment 1526:96
Are molecules on surface of eggshells necessary to dye eggs experiment 831:78-80
Aspirin and its effect on brine shrimp experiment 950:21-22
Baking powder in water gives off gases experiment 1244:37
Baking powder is double-acting experiment 980:45
Baking powder; chemical reaction involved in baking experiment 1159:20-22
Balloon blows up; vinegar, baking soda mixed in bottle experiment 1014:34
Balloon inflates from baking soda and vinegar trick 1010:83-85
Balloon inflates on bottle filled with water, yeast and sugar experiment 1229:20-21
Bathtub boats—experiment 656:22-23
Bleach flowers—experiments with ammonia 563:172-173
Bouncing mothballs 663:29
Bouncy egg experiment using vinegar 1005:4
Burn flour experiment 563:167-168
Can acid in lemon reduce fish odor experiment 831:72-74
Can baking soda trap odor molecules experiment 831:70-71
Can electricity make ions that change neutral water to a base experiment 831:58-60
Can molecules in air cause colors to fade experiment 831:53-54
Capturing smoke in a glass of water 350:58
Carbon dioxide—bottled anti force 114:39-41
Carbon dioxide—bouncing raisins 114:42
Carbon dioxide—dancing spheres—mothballs in vinegar 114:41-42
Carbon dioxide gas from baking soda and vinegar blows up soap bubble experiment 1482:38-39
Carbon dioxide gas inflates balloon experiment 1028:10
Carbon dioxide gas produced when Alka-Seltzer reacts with water experiment 1526:75
Catalysts experiment—hydrogen peroxide splitting into oxygen and water 6:24
Change color of ink with electricity from battery experiment 781:14-15
Changing speed of chemical reactions with Alka-Seltzer and water experiment 1526:68-70
Chemical heat from mixing water and plaster of Paris experiment 1519:21
Chemical reaction can produce heat; steel wool and vinegar experiment 905:182-183
Chemical reaction experiments 538:85-86
Chemical reaction powers rocket experiment 1162:11
Chicken bones soaked in vinegar turn rubbery experiment 1435:69-70
Clean a dirty penny with salt and vinegar (Primary) 64:unpaged
Clean copper or brass with ammonia—experiment 563:152-153
Clean copper pennies experiment 1231:56-57
Clean copper penny with salt and vinegar experiment 695:44

Clean the silver 366:220
Cleaning dirty coins experiment 790:29
Clever snuffer (copper coil) put out candle flame 366:223
Cobalt chloride clown changes as humidity changes experiment 1014:116
Coins—cleaning copper; corrosion of copper; corrosion of iron 548:35-38
Colored sands and water magic trick demonstrate 966:96-100
Conductivity of citrus fruit—computer project 584:140-142
Copper cleaner experiment 807:152
Copper penny shines when cleaned with vinegar and table salt experiment 1435:67-68
Corn starch and iodine used for secret messages 538:81
Dancing mothballs 366:219-220
Dancing popcorn and carbon dioxide bubbles in water/vinegar/baking soda 1289:44-45
Demonstrate color changes 346:58-59
Determine why there are holes in bread slices experiment 1405:54
Different substances burn with different colored flame experiment 1179:30-31
Displacement reaction (reduction)—iron nail in solution of copper sulfate 6:27
Dissolving substances in water—experiment 598:17
Dull pennies shine from salt and vinegar solution experiment 1005:8-9
Easy oxygen experiments produce oxygen 563:166
Effect of particle size on speed of chemical reaction experiment 871:3.005
Effect of temperature changes on speed of chemical reaction experiment 871:3.005
Effect of temperature on a chemical reaction 400:69
Egg rises in glass of salt water experiment 1005:4
Eggshell disappears experiment with raw egg and vinegar 1011:44
Electricity and copper pennies turn water blue experiment 1251:85-87
Electricity in salt water produces solids experiment using steel nails/battery 1251:82-84
Endothermic and exothermic reactions, make hot and cold packs experiment 1004:4.009
Enzyme activity—computer project 584:135-137
Enzyme effect on chemical reaction experiment with potato/hydrogen peroxide:1402
Etch your initials on an egg experiment 827:74
Experiments to show 116:86-96
Fast and slow chemical reaction with Seltzer pill in hot and cold water 1159:19-20
Fast and slow reactions experiment—speeding up and slowing down a reaction 6:22-23
Fire extinguisher uses baking soda on candle flame experiment 1435:118-119
Flame tests for metals 6:27
Flame tests for sugar and salt 30:35
Flaming sugar cube, invisible ink, message in an egg 472:2223
Flour and water paste chemical reaction experiment; recipe given 1271:14
Gas released from hydrogen peroxide and slice of raw potato experiment 1526:118-119
Gas volume from Alka-Seltzer and water reaction experiment 1526:71-74

Ghost in the glass magic trick demonstrates 966:93-95
Green blob from mixing iron acetate and vinegar experiment 905:102-103
Heat speeds up chemical reactions; time the fizz from Alka-Seltzer experiment 924:93
Household cleaners compared for hazards and disposal problems experiment 1361:50-51
How can a chemical change the speed of reaction—experiment 628:94-95
How to ripen a tomato 366:221
Hydrogen peroxide and potato release heat experiment 1087:13-14, 19-37
Identify chemical reactions in household items experiment; data tables 1004:4.010
Identifying acids and bases with litmus paper experiment 1526:87-90
Identifying elements by the flame test 180:9
Indicators plus Vitamin C pill in water identifies acids and bases experiment 1526:93-94
Indicators 146:58-59
Ink and food coloring are mixtures of other colors; chromatography experiment 1526:81-82
Insoluble gel forms from alum and ammonia experiment 905:98-99
Iodine stain—experiment 585:98
Is wine or is it water 350:56-57
Is vinegar necessary to dye eggs experiment 831:75-77
Jam experiments demonstrate indicators 563:165-166
Juice as a cleaner 585:90-91
Kitchen products and chemical reactions experiment with baking soda/Kool-aid 1526:63-64
Lemon acid removes oxide from penny experiment 827:46
Lemon juice keeps apple pieces from turning brown experiment 827:48
Lemon soda 400:71
Light stick emits less light at colder temperatures experiment 1251:58-61
"Live" rubber—experiment 585:103-104
Looking at compounds and how they are formed 6:18-20
Magic potions 16:62-65
Magic trick based on chemical clock reaction 1010:86-88
Magnesium milk from Epsom salt and ammonia experiment 905:100-101
Make a compound from iron filings and powdered sulfur 6:13
Make a molecular model of ethanol 6:32
Make a pharaoh's serpent from sugar 186:107
Make ink—experiment 563:178-179
Make oxygen experiment using flashlight battery and hydrogen peroxide 1435:104-106
Miracle with light—experiment 585:120-121
Molecule madness—experiment with baking soda and vinegar 651:34-35
Mothballs rise and fall in water, vinegar and baking soda 399:86
Mothballs swim up and down in water experiment 937:68-69
Mouth chewing chemical reactions experiment 905:108-109
Nail rusts faster in dry jar experiment 1244:12-13
Neutralization of acids and bases by adding acids and bases experiment 1526:95-96

Onions—molecules in onions are changed to sulfuric acid when peeling 366:221

Paper butterflies dance in air over carbon dioxide gas experiment 1216:37-39

Pennies change color experiment 829:37-38

Pennies get a green coating experiment 1405:55

Pennies shine like new 676:12-13

pH effect on germination of radish and bean seeds experiment 1526:98

pH of acid rain and snow experiment 1526:98

pH, the degree of acidity experiment 1526:97-98

Play dough sculptures chemical reaction experiment; recipe given 1271:14

"Pop" bottle experiment—water, vinegar & baking soda produce carbon dioxide 563:168

Precipitates testing for—fruit and tea punch—testing for iron 74:84-86

Precipitation—see precipitation of white magnesium hydroxide in a glass 508:18

Puzzling powders 400:72

Raisins float and rise in water, vinegar and baking soda solution experiment 1229:14-15

Reaction between Epsom Salt and ammonia experiment 1526:78-80

Reaction between iron, vinegar and ammonia experiment 1526:80

Reaction that makes solutions thicken demonstrated with pudding 1289:12-13

Reactions between pennies and vinegar experiment 1526:80-81

Reactions which produce heat—mixing vinegar with bicarbonate of soda 6:13

Red cabbage indicator tests for acids and bases experiment 1063:168

Red liquid trick 676:14

Releasing chemical energy from matches—experiment 489:85

Remove scorch—experiment 585:92

Reversible reactions 346:144-147

Rock pool using cobalt chloride and calcium chloride 146:54

Rubber chicken bones magic trick using vinegar on bones 1010:89-91

Rubber eggs, how to make using vinegar 1014:169

Rust forms quickly on nails experiment using battery, wire, and salty water 1435:110-112

Rusting experiment demonstrates electrical attraction 489:77

Rusting iron from steel wool in water produces oxygen gas experiment 1435:107-109

Rusting produces heat experiment 1405:62-63

Salt and vinegar on copper—experiment 563:164-165

Seltzer tablets in water in jars covered with balloons experiment 695:46

Shell removed from egg without cracking it vinegar experiment 1005:4

Shiny aluminum—experiment 585:87-88

Smoke from the fingertips—chemical reaction experiment 563:33

Snail shell dissolves in vinegar mixture experiment 1392:15

Spaghetti worms rise and fall in mixture experiment 1066:50-51

Speed of chemical reaction directly related to strength of catalyst exp. 871:3.006

Speeding up a chemical change—experiment 180:15

Spit in the bananas—turn starchy food into liquid 366:221

Steel wool and nails demonstrate 695:43

Steel wool ink, how to make using steel wool, tea bags and vinegar 1435:74-77

Sugar; chemical change in sugar when it is heated experiment 1435:18-20

Sunscreen molecules block sunlight that causes colors to fade experiment 1251:62-64

Technicolor cabbage experiments 563:165

Telltale chemicals—indicators show acids and bases 30:35-36

Temperature change during chemical reaction; bleach and water experiment 905:184-185

Tests to identify many powders experiment 1063:169

The age of aspirin—computer project 584:133-134

The amazing finger ring 350:61

The blue flashback—a reversible reaction 205:125-130

The color changing powder 350:63-64

The effect of chemicals on daphnia heart rate—computer project 584:138-139

The flying flame—introducing a chemical reaction 205:110-115

The magic flower seeds 350:62-63

The purple palette—a chemical indicator 205:130-133

The taste of electricity—experiment from coins in a lemon 489:88-89

Using ammonium chloride and litmus paper 146:55

Using white ammonium chloride and cobalt chloride—make green man 146:54-55

Valentine heart biscuits demonstrate chemical reaction, recipe given 1289:26-27

Vinegar and baking soda foam put out fire experiment 695:45

Vinegar and baking soda make bubbles experiment 1014:41

Vinegar and salt clean copper pennies experiment 1251:80-81

Vinegar and soda fire extinguisher experiment 489:83

Vinegar makes egg soft and rubbery experiment 937:64-65

Vinegar used as test for limestone in rocks 538:82

Wet or dry—experiment 400:71

What cleans pennies 381:26

What makes things rust—experiment 6:26

Wine and water trick 350:53-56

CHEMICAL TEST. *See also* **INDICATORS**

Testing for acids and bases 293:36

CHEMICALS

"Bad breath" experiment with jar, candle and breath from lungs 563:161-162

Common name and where available 319:17-19

Computer program for identifying an unknown substance 6:40-41

Identifying substances by flame tests and by borax bead test 6:38-39

Magic with 350:64-77

Parts per million (ppm); discover how small it is in chemicals experiment 1361:45

CHEMISTRY

A trick in volume—experiment with salt and water 563:161

Acids versus bases 72:56-58

Carbon dioxide—gas that puts out fire 72:58-60

Fire extinguisher 72:58-60
Laboratory—setting up laboratory how to 319:12-19
Laboratory techniques and safety rules—how to do
    319:20-28
Mysterious concoctions—essence of cabbage 346:7-11
Mysterious concoctions—extract of soda pop 346:11-16
Separate salt and sand—experiment 563:163-164
Shining your pennies (Primary) 70:54
Simple experiments 676:8-48
Test for starch 72:54-56

CHEMISTRY—MAGIC TRICKS. *See also* **MAGIC**
A clear shake 346:147-148
Blue again and again 346:144-147
Blush test on drawing on photo 346:142-144
Boron—magic green flame 27:48
Deep purple magic—iodine in oil 27:37
Magic flower—starch and iodine 27:34-36
Magic green flame 27:48-49
Magic ink 27:47
Magic ketchup 27:45-47
Magic wet fire—alcohol and water 27:43-44
More secret writing—magic candle 27:42-43
Red, white and blue 27:44-45
Secret writing 27:41
Thought waves for milk 346:148-150
Water to wine to water gambit 346:140-142

CHEMORECEPTORS
Mud snails' response to chemicals or dead snails
    chemoreception experiment 1225:136-137
Test to show butterfly's reaction to food and other things
    174:28-29

CHEMOTROPISM. *See also* **PLANTS—TROPISMS**
Insectivorous plants eat insects to get nitrates experi-
    ment 1061:90-91
Plant root response to odors in the air experiment
    1061:79-80

CHESTNUTS
Grow tree from chestnut, how to do 1486:28

CHEWING GUM
Can you remove chewing gum by freezing 333:131-132
Sugar content of chewing gum experiment; data tables
    given 1004:4.011

CHICKENS. *See also* **BROODERS; EGGS; INCUBATORS**
Bone gets rubbery from soaking in vinegar experiment
    1083:54
Bone; bend a bone experiment; soak bone in vinegar
    1370:38
Brooder—how to make 196:55-57; 358:92-93
Can heartbeat of chicken embryo be detected without
    breaking shell experiment 997:169-171
Chicken bone turns to rubber experiment 1258:unp.
Chicken bones soaked in vinegar turn rubbery experi-
    ment 1435:69-70
Chicken foot demonstrates action of tendons 577:project
    #5
Chicken fountain—experiment 563:116-117
Chicken pecks away in flip book—making 749:54-55
Chicken skeleton—making 749:28-29
Dissecting—how to 692:63-77
Egg incubator—making 436:45
Eggs—hatching chicken eggs 236:83-84
Eggs—incubation of chicken eggs 402:98-99
Glue chicken bones together to make a skeleton, how to
    do 882:40

Make a self filling drinking fountain 604:24-27
Make rubbery chicken bone experiment 1506:80
Observing four and eight day old embryos experiment
    1425:4-7
Rubber chicken bone experiment; vinegar removes miner-
    als from chicken bone 1189:50-51
Rubbery chicken bone experiment; bone in jar of vine-
    gar, how to do 1168:15
Studying the digestive organs of the chicken 294:77
Studying the structure of a chicken leg 294:78
The 'pecking order' in chickens in the field and in the
    laboratory 266:150-153
What are tendons and how do they work experiment
    901:167
Where do chickens come from—experiment 628:112-
    113

CHIMES
Electric chime 577:project #53
Experiment to hear chimes 381:137-138
Flower pot chimes—making 722:58
Wind chime—how to make from milk carton (Primary)
    523:20
Garden orchestra 356:56-59
Wind chimes—how to make 543:10-11

CHIMNEYS
Chimneys, box and candle demonstrate how chimneys
    work 939:137-139
How to make (Primary) 220:27
Measure particulate matter sent into air from chimneys
    experiment 969:108-109
Weight of atmosphere pushes air up chimney experiment
    1126:10

CHINESE
Chinese puzzle "chain reaction" trick 585:70
Experiments of their culture 321:entire book
How to count like the Chinese 509:30-35
Paper making 382:147-148
Rice bowl mystery 16:26-29
Toy—Jacob's ladder 27:109-111

CHINESE WATER CLOCK
Chinese water clock, how to make with experiments
    951:30-33

CHIRALITY
Optical activity and chirality; polarimeter identifies sub-
    stance experiment 1004:4.014

CHLADNI, ERNST F.
Chladni figures—experiment 585:13-15
Make Chladni's figures 172:65-66
Vibration of metal plates experiment 1133:6.010

CHLADNI FIGURES
Chladni patterns projects 691:78-81
Wave patterns—experiment 691:75-81

CHLADNI PATTERNS
Chladni plate interference patterns experiment 1155:70-71

CHLORINE. *See also* **BLEACH**
Chlorine breaks up water molecules and liberates oxy-
    gen 122:153-154
Claude Berthollet's bleaching powers of chlorine in solu-
    tion experiment 1133:2.007
How to bleach with chlorine 122:154-155
Produce chlorine, hydrogen and caustic soda experiment
    768:80-81
Release chlorine gas from household bleach 346:74-76
Release chlorine gas from salt water experiment 722:3

CHLOROFLUOROCARBONS. *See* **GREENHOUSE EFFECT**

CHLOROPHYLL. *See also* **PLANTS—CHLOROPHYLL**

Allows plants to use energy of light 273:34-35

Aluminum foil on leaves demonstrates effect of light on chlorophyll experiment 762:75-76

Chlorophyll absorbs red light photons—experiment with spinach and alcohol 366:204-205

Chlorophyll in leaf comes from light; tape a shape on leaf experiment 1184:20

Chlorophyll in plant leaves experiment 1294:68-71

Chlorophyll spectrum as seen through a spectroscope experiment 1060:27-28

Chloroplasts containing chlorophyll studied under microscope experiment 1060:21

Chromatogram of green plants, how to make and compare 864:77-80

Chromatograms of autumn maple tree leaves day by day experiment 1060:19-20

Chromatograms of chlorophyll compared in plants growing in shade and sun 1060:20

Color pigment in plant leaves affected by sunlight experiment 1395:107-112

Evergreen needles have more chlorophyll than deciduous tree leaves experiment 1061:35-36

Grass covered with board looses color experiment 919:38

Green plant life does not occur deep in the ocean experiment 904:56-57

Grow algae to demonstrate chlorophyll production experiment 1479:28

Isolating chlorophyll and testing for starch in a leaf 294:39

Lack of sunlight affects color of leaf experiment 1049:19

Leaf stops making chlorophyll due to lack of carbon dioxide experiment 1441:91

Leaves need light to stay green experiment using leaf and black board 1390:29

Martin Archer's separating components of chlorophyll pigments experiment 1133:2.011

Perishable quality of natural dyes experiment with flowers and ammonia experiment 1476:133

Plant pigments—what is cause of plant colors and can these colors be removed 402:27

Plant will die without sunlight to produce chlorophyll experiment 1479:26

Presence of green chlorophyll under flower colors experiment 1476:133

Separate chlorophyll pigments from plant leaves experiment 860:61-65

Separate plant pigments using paper chromatography, how to do 864:77-80

Separating colors using chromatography 864:75-77

Separating the chlorophyll pigments of plants experiment using chromatography 1060:18-20

Sunlight and its effect on plant growth experiment 904:58-59

Test proves chlorophyll in leaves makes food for plants 366:220

Testing for in leaves 146:52-53

Testing plant leaves for chlorophyll amount and density experiment 1061:32-34

What happens to grass when it doesn't receive sunlight experiment 1324:38-41

CHLOROPLASTS. *See* **CHLOROPHYLL; PLANTS—CHLOROPHYLL**

CHOCOLATE

Chocolate bar of your own—making 607:83

CHRISTMAS

Christmas for the birds 231:106-107

Festival of lights—how to build a kissing bough 231:104-105

CHROMATOGRAPHY

Absorbency of filter paper affects flow rate experiment 1396:101

Are colors what they seem to be experiment 696:18-19

Black ink on blotting paper separates into different colors experiment 1393:23

Calculate flow rate for yellow food dye experiment 1396:97-103

Can different molecules be separated from each other 396:31-33

Chromatogram of green plants, how to make and compare 864:77-80

Chromatograms of autumn maple tree leaves day by day experiment 1060:19-20

Chromatograms of chlorophyll compared in plants growing in shade and sun 1060:20

Chromatography test with inks, food colors, and plant pigments experiment 1476:129-131

Chromatography used to identify pen inks experiment 1151:74-77

Chromatography used to solve crime; analyze pen ink used by robber experiment 1004:4.002

Circle chromatography—experiment 550:46-48

Coffee filter butterfly demonstrates 733:15

Coffee filters and marking pens demonstrate 887:28-30

Color circle of blotting papers and inks experiment 1077:8-9

Colors are mixture of two or three primary colors experiment 871:3.002

Colors in pigment separate experiment 680:15

Colors move up strips of paper experiment using color markers and paper towels 1175:78-79

Crawling colors on absorbent paper demonstrates 882:15

Crazy colors experiments 685:24-25

Create separate colors experiment 960:35

Does red leaf produce food and contain chlorophyll experiment 871:2.022

Felt pens contain rainbow of other colors experiment 1063:180

Felt tip pens and absorbent paper experiment 1113:18

Finding hidden chemicals 676:24-25

Flower petal pigments, color test for pigments experiment 1068:23

Food colorings in candy and vegetables; chromatography test experiment 792:31

Hidden colors in felt tipped pens experiment 1018:20-21

How black is black experiment with black inks 1109:17

Ink and food coloring are mixtures of other colors; chromatography experiment 1526:81-82

Inks and dyes—experiment 659:32-33

Inks and food color in water travel at different rates thru paper experiment 1179:33

Inks are made up of several dyes experiment 1159:17-19

Inks, food coloring, and coffee filter experiment 1002:26-27

Investigating food coloring; separating colors experiment 780:2-3

Is chlorophyll the only color pigment in a leaf experiment 1395:110

Is wax applied to produce purchased from supermarkets experiment 1450:26-33

Leaf chromatography experiment; how to prepare 1396:101-103

M & M candy colors separate as they are absorbed experiment 781:34-35

Magic markers and blotting paper experiment 893:19

Making chromatograms 146:11

Martin Archer's separating components of chlorophyll pigments experiment 1133:2.011

Observe separation of colors in ink experiment 905:154-155

Orange spot on wet paper changes into other colors experiment [Primary] 788:8-9

Order of separating solutes is different if solvent flows down not up ex 1396:101

Paper—separate colored solutions 381:14-18

Paper chromatography analysis 336:31-33

Paper chromatography experiment 723:197

Paper chromatography 577:project #13

Paper coffee filters—demonstrate 203:26

Paper peacock and felt tip pens experiment 814:72-74

Paper rainbow pies, how to make 893:19

Pigment separation in leaves 273:36-37

Pigments in colors separated using chromatography experiment 1308:26-27

Pigments in leaves separated and identified experiment 904:38-39

Pigments in plants shown by chromatograms experiment 1069:40

Racing colors experiment with paper towels 770:129

Separate chemicals in inks with paper towels and water—experiment 6:11

Separate chlorophyll pigments from plant leaves experiment 860:61-65

Separate colored dyes in marking pens experiment data table given 1004:4.003

Separate colors from inks or food colorings experiment 1028:51

Separate colors using paper towels experiment 827:38

Separate different colors experiment, how to do 790:29-30

Separate pigments experiment 928:20

Separate pigments in felt tip pens and colored candies experiment 1016:28-29

Separate plant pigments using paper chromatography, how to do 864:77-80

Separating chlorophyll pigments of plants experiment using chromatography 1060:18-20

Separating colors experiment using blotting paper and felt tipped pens 1073:83

Separating colors from felt-tip pens experiment using blotting paper in water 1271:13

Separating colors in liquids—experiment 598:36

Separating colors on strips of paper experiment 924:10-11

Separating colors to make pictures experiment 924:12-13

Separating colors using chromatography 864:75-77

Separating colors using filter paper and glass of water experiment 1256:24-25

Separating colors 147:19-20

Separating dyes by chromatography experiment 1159:17-19

Separating the colors in inks 589:47

Separation of color experiment with coffee filter 1288:29

Separation of colors in ink experiment 1405:60-61

Simple chromatography experiment using porous paper strips and felt pens 1244:10-11

Simple experiment in 57:9-10

Streaking solutions experiment 748:106

Strip chromatography—experiment 550:43-44

Taking colors apart experiment 935:23

Techniques used by chromatographer 436:22

Test tube holder and stand for chromatography experiment, how to make 1476:129-130

Water chromatography—experiment 550:45-48

Water moves colors experiment with coffee filters and water markers 1124:28

What colored dyes are found in powder drink mix and colored markers experiment 997:73-75

Which colors from felt tip pens spread out the farthest experiment 1509:9

Write with color—experiment to demonstrate 346:124-128

CHROMATROPE

Chromatrope, how to make 861:69-76

CHROMOSOMES. *See also* **GENETICS; HEREDITY**

Chromosome changes from water pollutants experiment using onions 1060:119-121

Is there a center of inheritance in the cell 402:101-102

CICHLIDS

Fishes that make nests 266:121-129

CIDER

Make cider and wine 625:46-47

Yeast cells in fermenting cider experiment 917:23

CIGARETTE SMOKE

Cigarette smoke effect on growing radish plants experiment 1328:38-39

CIGARETTES. *See also* **SMOKING**

Cigarette smoke pollutes your internal environment experiment 1427:56-58

Second-hand smoke reduces lung capacity in children experiment 1195:69-77

CILIATES. *See* **PARAMECIUM**

CIPHERS. *See also* **CODES**

Indian picture writing 244:21-22

Number codes 244:6-9

Reverse and double letter code 244:12-14

Square box code 244:28-29

Symbol code 244:10-11

Tic-tac-toe codes 244:26-27

Transposition and substitution ciphers, how to do 808:78-82

Up-down code 244:24-25

Window code 244:30-31

CIRCLES

Circles and ovals, how to draw 1248:36-37

Circles or curves from straight lines, how to draw 1299:30-33

Finding the center of a circle 150:148-149

Giant compass arm to draw large circles, cardboard, making 999:51

Link strips of cloth experiment 842:7-8

Postcard cut forms circle experiment 842:3-5

Uses of circles through variety of problems, games and activities 1347:6-64

Working with a circle 444:64-68

CIRCULATORY SYSTEM. *See also* **BLOOD; GOLD-FISH; HEART**
Blood circulatory model—how to make 577:project #2
Circulation game—blood, demonstrating flow with players 436:23

CIRCUMPOLAR STARS
Constellation chart for circumpolar stars 231:116-118
Making a night clock nocturnal project 833:29-31

CIRCUS
Balancing rolling toy experiments; how to make tightrope walker 1444:50-52
Circus balancing act using unsymmetrical balancing device experiment 1444:84-87
Vertical balancing of tightrope walkers experiment 1444:37-41

CITIES
Design an ecological city for the future project 1067:115
Laying tunnels under a city, how to demonstrate 1327:35
Model city; how does design affect wind currents and shadows experiment 1094:38-39
Super structures for the future, how to make from clay and swizzle sticks 1094:40

CITRUS FRUITS *See also* **FRUITS; SEEDS—FRUITS**
Citrus seeds, how to grow indoors 1178:19-20
How to grow seeds 272:23-29
Orange peel contains a natural insecticide experiment 1250:89-90
Orange tree from seed, how to grow 899:138-139
What is characteristic of all citrus fruits 402:77-78

CITRUS PLANTS
Citrus tree, how to grow 899:139
How to grow 86:61

CLAIRVOYANCE
ESP experiment 400:114

CLAMS
Are your clams safe to eat experiment 997:130-131
Chart of inside 264:24
Dissecting—how to 692:23-30
Dissecting a clam experiment 1117:33

CLAMSHELL SCRIMSHAW
How to 359:1-3

CLASSIFICATION
Animal kingdom classification chart 1063:259
Classification computer project 584:83-85
Classifying collections (Primary) 232:99
Classifying pet and zoo animals activities for classroom 1291:24-25
Color circles project to demonstrate animals in habitat 817:15-16
Develop and make your own classification key 871:2.001
Fruit and vegetable classification demonstration with chart 901:51-52
Sort materials; floating, attracted by magnet, conduct electricity experiment 795:28

CLAY. *See also* **SOILS**
Baker's clay for making clay models of skeletons, recipe 1168:78-79
Clay recipe 811:30
Clay tiles from air-hardening clay, how to make 1244:28-29
Compare Silly Putty and clay experiment 782:18-21
Cooking with clay; hot dogs in clay molds, how to do 854:101

Flour and salt clay, recipe, how to make 1265:78
Goop clay—how to make 733:17
Kooky clay, how to make 644:12-13
Natural potter's clay, how to make 1012:105
Play clay—how to make 733:7; 960:33
Recipe for clay 854:92; 986:78
Salt clay—making 697:116-117
Sand clay—making 697:121
Sand clay is fun 236:105-106
What are clay and sand and how do they differ experiment 1323:22-25

CLEANERS
Clean copper or brass with ammonia—experiment 563:152-153
Juice as a cleaner 585:90-91
Metal 17:10-13, 16-17
Natural cleaners replace chemical cleaners experiment 1063:374
Silver—clean silverware the easy way 291:224-225
Test for presence of a base in common household cleaners experiment 905:210-211

CLICHE-VERRE. *See* **PHOTOGRAPHY**

CLIMATE
Climatic regions of the world 298:21-31
Color of clothes best for a hot climate experiment 1219:18
Effects of cube shaped Earth on climate/weather patterns/flora/fauna experiment 997:159-162
How mountain ranges affect climate experiment 1447:89-91
Moisture lifted up by model mountain experiment 1447:89-91

CLIMATE AND PLANTS
Compare garden plants that need hot versus cool climate 380:18-19

CLIMATOLOGY. *See* **WEATHER**

CLIMAX COMMUNITY
In water 268:97-99

CLINOMETER. *See also* **HEIGHT; SLOPES**
Clinometer from wood and protractor, how to make 1266:31
Clinometer, make to measure angle of elevation and depression experiment 978:19-20
Find height of any building with clinometer—how to make 472:2227
Height of tall building, how to measure using clinometer experiment 1345:59
How to make clinometer 1248:26
Make a clinometer from cardboard and protractor 1480:94

CLOCKS. *See also* **SUNDIALS; TIME**
A pattern for a night clock 292:65-66
A sand clock timer—making 304:18-19
Biological clocks in plants and animals—experiment 371:104-106
Calibrated candle, how to make 1355:13
Candle alarm clock from candle, metal nut and metal tray, how to make 1421:26
Candle alarm clock with electric light, how to make 1421:27
Candle clock—making 142:49
Candle clock from large candle, how to make 1421:19
Candle clock made from large candle 1421:19
Candle clock to measure time (Primary) 535:78
Candle clock, how to make 1446:44

76

Candle clock, making 803:14-16
Candle timer, making 887:24
Chinese water clock—making 132:14
Chinese water clock, how to make with experiments 951:30-33
Circular water clock, how to make with experiments 951:63-71
Clock can be used as compass experiment 1479:13
Clock from cardboard box and string, how to make 1103:27
Clock gears, how to make with experiments 951:86-95
Clocks, how they work 951:104-111
Custom sun clock—how to make 231:47
Demonstrate double suspension pendulums 137:19
Demonstrate regulating a pendulum clock 137:22
Do a watch survey 640:51
Dripping water clock from plastic jug—how to make 538:122
Egyptian style water clock, how to make from plastic cups 1421:16
Egyptian water clock, how to make with experiments 951:33-37
Escapement clock, swinging, how to make with experiments 951:80-86
Fire clock from incense stick, how to make 1115:126-127
Floating valve clock, how to make with experiments 951:45-53
Floral clock illustration of what time flowers open and close 1103:10
Flower clock—making 749:68-69
Flower clock garden to tell time—how to do 640:90
Flower garden clock—how to make 271:41-48
Homemade clock—making 142:48
Hourglass or 3 minute timer, making 887:26
Hours by flowers—time keeping flower garden 231:53
How vibrating and atomic clocks work 137:23
Making a night clock nocturnal project 833:29-31
Making water clocks project 833:27-29
Marble clock using marbles on ramp experiment, how to make 1521:16-17
Marble-operated clock made from wood, how to make 1446:42-43
Metric clock makes working with time easier experiment 1062:40
Nocturnal star clock, patterns, how to make 1063:298-299
Paper plate clock shows time zones (Primary) 303:26-27
Pendulum clock experiment, how to make 1521:14-15
Pendulum clock experiment 806:39-41
Pendulum clock, how to make 1446:45
Pendulum escapement clock, how to make 951:95-103
Pendulum from string and ball of clay tells time experiment 1103:28
Personal clock with daily activities (Primary) 535:78
Rolling ball clock—making 137:24
Rolling marble timed experiments 806:33-35
Salt timer experiment, how to make 1521:12-13
Sand clock measures time experiment; how to make from plastic bottles 1062:37-39
Sand clock, how to make 803:8-9; 868:25; 142:49; 1014:196; 1446:44
Sand timer, how to make 640:37; 885:43-44; 1103:25; 1355:14
Sand timer—making (Primary) 535:79

Sand timer, how to make from soda bottle, wood, jar lids and cardboard 1512:16-17
Sandglass clock, simple to make with experiments 951:72-76
Sandglass that runs for three (3) minutes experiment, how to make 1521:13
Shadow (sundial)—making (Primary) 297:22-29
Shadow clock—making 659:6
Shadow clock—making (Primary) 64:unpaged; 535:26
Shadow clock, how to make 588:50-51; 885:40-41; 909:134; 928:9
Show driving of pendulum clock 137:21
Show effect of weight on pendulum bob 137:16
Show how pendulum works 137:14-15
Show pendulum patterns 137:18
Show timing with a pendulum 137:17
Show working of joined pendulums 137:20
Sinking water clocks, how to make with experiments 951:37-40
Siphon clock working model, how to build, patterns given 1022:51-57
Siphon clock, how to make with experiments 951:41-45
Skittle game—making 137:13
Sky clock to tell time on clear nights—how to make 763:33-38
Solar clock, how to make from stones 1115:112-113
Star clock to tell time, patterns given, make from cardboard 1299:79
String timer, making 887:24
Sun alarm clock, how to make 947:10-11
Sun clock—how to make 312:11-14; 487:46-48
Sun clock from pencil and paper plate, how to make 1103:13
Sunbeam alarm clock—how to make 543:2-3
Water clock—how to make 178:22-23; 543:58-60; 663:16
Water clock experiment 1521:17
Water clock from plastic cups and wooden stand, how to make 1421:15
Water clock shows that gravity causes water to fall at regular rate experiment 1031:16-17
Water clocks, how to make 631:52-53; 640:34-35; 885:41-42; 909:24; 947:12-13; 1355:14; 1446:45
Water clock, tin can clock and hour bottle—making 231:48
Water clocks, making 803:10-13; 868:25,51
Water clocks, simple to make with experiments 951:22-29
Water powered clock—making 132:13
Water timer, making 887:24-25
Water-soak clock experiment 806:36-39
Water-wheel clock, how to make with experiments 951:53-63

CLOCKWORK MOTOR
How to make 260:16-17
CLONING. *See also* **PLANTS—PROPAGATION; PLANTS—VEGETATIVE REPRODUCTION**
Can plant cloning be used effectively by produce growers experiment 997:52-53
Cloning plants—experiment 586:124-126
Grow new plants from cuttings experiment 1063:406
Plant cells cloning techniques and projects 398:74-76
Propagate and clone plants by leaf and stem cuttings experiment 1176:36-37

Tissue culture of plants experiment 1060:103-106

CLOTH. *See also* **FABRIC; TEXTILES**
Bleach effect on fabric samples experiment 1396:108-110
Direct dyeing and indirect dyeing of cloth experiment 1396:107-108
Examine cloth under hand lens 29:13
Fading effect of sunlight on fabric samples experiment 1396:108-109
Flame test to show different kinds 83:27-28
Making cloth waterproof experiment 1162:23
Printing cloth with wooden blocks experiment 1485:17
Waterproofing—how to 321:29
Weave cloth from thread (Primary) 326:22-23
Weaving on cardboard hand loom 322:28-29

CLOTHING
Absorption and shrinkage of natural and synthetic fibers experiment 1259:80-81
Acids, bases and bleach effect on fibers experiment 1259:81-82
Appearance and strength of natural and synthetic fibers compared experiment 1259:77-80
Bacteria attacks fibers in fabrics and wears out clothing experiment 1259:83-84
Bedclothes as insulators, which is best experiment 868:65
Color and texture affect heat being absorbed experiment; T-shirts/thermometer 1275:20
Color of clothes best for a hot climate experiment 1219:18
Colors of clothing effect on human body experiment 1506:88
Combustibility of fibers; which will burn experiment 1259:82-83
Commercial fabric waterproofing agents tested for effect/durability experiment 1295:122-123
Does wool or cotton cloth hold more water project 1210:46-47
Dyeing fabric fibers by direct dyeing and by vat dyeing experiment 1259:86-88
Heat preserver experiment—compare wool and cotton to nylon, orlon, dacron 26:83
Heat retention of fibers in clothing experiment 1259:84-85
Hydrocarbons in air pollution damage clothing experiment 1322:60-64
Natural fiber clothes decompose faster than man made fibers project 969:57-58
Nylon stockings sensitive to acid pollutants experiment 1322:64
Pollution can harm clothing experiment 1322:60-64
Stain removers; duplicate advertising claims experiment using stained fabrics 1295:123
Weather wear—clothes are heat absorbing or heat reflecting 399:24

CLOUD CHAMBER
Cloud chamber—build to follow trails of particles experiment 704:61-64
Construct a "cloud chamber" 564:8
Detect cosmic rays in cloud chamber in jar experiment, how to make chamber 1476:184-185

CLOUDS. *See also* **NEPHOSCOPE**
Bagging a cloud—show condensation causes clouds 91:108-112
Build a cloud chamber 293:12

Cloud box—how to make 363:12-13
Cloud chamber from water cooler bottle and air pump—how to make 767:34
Cloud cover estimator, how to build from cardboard, thread, mirror 1480:163
Cloud experiment 363:11
Cloud formation—experiment 168:16-18
Cloud formation—making 293:13; 295:48-49
Cloud formations; how to observe and draw in notebook 1439:46-51
Cloud frame to check speed 805:15
Cloud in a bottle—making 128:100
Cloud in a bottle experiment 959:74-75
Cloud in bottle, how to make using candle experiment 1017:22-23
Cloud in plastic bottle experiment 1004:1.001
Cloudburst experiment using plastic soda bottle cloud and ice demonstration 1310:6-7
Clouds—making (Primary) 232:84
Clouds in a bottle experiment, how to make 1372:55-56
Clouds in a glass jar, how to make 1243:22
Clouds in a jar, making [Primary] 897:44
Clouds in the kitchen from teakettle experiment 1311:36
Clouds used to predict weather computer project 1021:146-148
Condensation of water vapor forms clouds 44:72-73
Demonstrate a cloud, how to 890:11
Demonstrate relationship of clouds to weather 119:158-163
Direction and speed—nephoscope shows 9:96-97
Direction and speed of clouds determined by using nephoscope experiment 1012:18
Experiment to demonstrate 382:128-130
Form cloud from boiling water experiment 1003:77
Forming clouds project 833:148-149
Four types of and chart 234:96-97
How cloud can be formed experiment with plastic bottle of water 1465:74-75
How tiny water droplets in clouds grow into raindrops experiment 1479:83
How to make a cloud 175:69
How to make a cloud (Primary) 242:18-23
How to make a simple one 14:42-46
How to make cloud in a glass jug experiment 1439:56-58
Identifying clouds experiment 1134:2.005
Investigation into cloud development 420:62-64
Light and dark clouds—experiment 585:115
Make a cloud in a bottle 694:71-73
Make a cloud in large glass jar experiment 1441:75
Make a cloud 507:1909; 759:14-15; 918:34
Make cloud using gallon jar and rubber balloon experiment 1012:24
Make miniature clouds in a glass jar 472:2239
Make water vapor from drops (Primary) 541:26
Making clouds experiment 1086:22
Making clouds, fog and smog experiment 947:36-37
Model; make model cloud in a bottle experiment 1516:32-33
Nephoscope measures direction of wind where clouds are experiment, how to make 1372:57-58
Nephoscope to check direction clouds are moving, how to make 1115:52-53
Nephoscope tracks cloud movement, how to make 1063:439

Observe clouds through cloud "windows", how to make 1465:81-82

Observe directions of clouds with homemade nephoscope 381:69-71

Set up a nephoscope to track directional movement of clouds 175:80

Simple cloud making experiments 767:33-34

Warm water in bottle and cold tray demonstrate clouds [Primary] 944:7

What causes clouds to form and break up experiment 1396:7-10

What holds up the clouds—experiment 563:79

Why clouds have different shapes experiment 1294:65-66

Why clouds look white experiment 1003:78

Why doesn't a cloud fall to the ground 243:52-53

Wilson cloud chamber—how to make 43:164-177

Wind direction determined by nephoscope demonstration 1023:144-145

CLOVER

Clover syrup, recipe, how to make 1464:73

COAGULATION

Coagulation experiment—making a cheese omelet, a cheese omelet recipe 537:21, 65

Coagulation experiment—making deviled eggs, deviled egg recipe 537:20-21, 64

Coagulation experiment—preparing hard boiled eggs, hard boiled egg recipe 537:18-20, 63

COAL

Coal deposit model—making 666:107

Converting coal to fuel gas experiment 895:105

Getting methane from coal experiment 895:104-105

How buried wood is changed into coal—make charcoal 26:25-27

Is soft coal softer than hard coal experiment 715:75-76

Make coke from coal 122:88-89

Plants exposed to too much sulfur dioxide gas will be harmed experiment 1453:30-31

Tar, carbon dioxide, monoxide, hydrogen sulfide, in coal smoke experiment 933:37-38

COAL FURNACE

How it works—candle experiment 26:29-30,34

COAL GARDEN

Magic coal garden—how to make 87:80-81

COAL PLANT

Chemical garden grows before your eyes 576:83

COASTS

Action of water on coastlines experiment 1342:121-126

Action of waves breaking changes the coastline demonstration 840:20

Arches and stacks—make model of headland with arches and stacks 299:18

Beach forms—sand dunes and sand banks 299:15

Beach forms—spits, bars and tombolos 299:16

Caves and blow holes—illustration 299:17

Chart of coastal offshore and onshore breezes 299:28-29

Cliffs with wave—cut platforms 299:19

Coastal wildlife—identify different species 299:30

Effect of wave height and length on coastlines experiment 1342:124-126

Greenhouse effect as cause of rise in sea levels project 1342:126

Model coastline; make to demonstrate gradual erosion of coastline experiment 1080:27

Model sand beach, how to make 1342:121

Pollution—map and chart areas of 299:31

COBALT CHLORIDE PAPER

How to make 55:163

COCKROACHES. *See also* **INSECTS**

Aggression in cockroaches experiment 809:56-57

Anatomy experiment 809:53

Arena for experiments, how to make 809:51

Catching, how to do 809:48-49

Cockroach pets in a jar home 264:70

Cockroaches favorite materials to live in experiment 1097:151-154

Escape behavior experiment 809:54-55

Feeding cockroaches, how to 809:49

Grooming experiment 809:52

Home for cockroaches, making 809:50

How do cockroaches live and change 253:28-29

How to cage and care for 279:28-29

How to make a cockroach maze 264:71-72

Is up the way out of jar 264:70

Odor response behavior experiment 809:56

Righting behavior experiment 809:53-54

Wall seeking behavior experiment 809:54

COCOONS. *See also* **BUTTERFLIES; CATERPILLARS; MOTHS**

Collect cocoons and hatch, how to do 917:31

Collecting cocoons to raise moths 476:48-50

Collecting cocoons with live young inside—how to 629:127

How to hatch 117:49-51

Moth can develop without a cocoon experiment 1020:121-122

Winter cocoons of moths, how to collect, cage and hatch 1188:18-19

CODES. *See also* **CIPHERS; SIGNALS**

Binary numeral code secret messages—how to do 536:1-33

Clock code, making 812:10-11

Code cylinders, cardboard, making 999:58-59

Code machines, making 812:16-17; 812:18-19

Code wheels, cardboard, making 999:54-57

Color dot codes, making 812:8-9

Color-bar code, how to make 643:7

Crack and create secret codes project 1070:28-29

Dot code messages, making 812:28-29

Indian picture writing 244:21-22

Keyword code and cracking a code—how to do 625:17

Knot messages, how to make 812:30

Morse code and semaphore—how to use 625:16-17

Morse code practice set, making 930:14

Morse code, how to do 812:44

Morse code 244:18-20; 930:14

Mystery codes, making 812:14-15

Number code 244:6-9

Picture messages, how to make 812:31

Pigpen cipher—how to write 629:23-24

Pocket code dialer, how to make 643:10-11

Quick codes, making 812:12-13

Quick signal code, how to do 812:45

Reverse and double letter code 244:12-14

Secret code machine—making 508:4-5

Secret code system, making 770:134

Secret telephone messages, making 812:38-39

Semaphore alphabet, how to do 812:43
Silent Morse signals, how to make 812:40
Space language, devise (advanced) 668:73-75
Square box code 244:28-29
Substitution codes, how to make 643:8-9
Symbol code 244:10-11
Tic-tac-toe codes 244:26-27
Up-down code 244:24-25
Window code 244:30-31

COFFEE. *See also* **CAFFEINE**
Adventure 25—we test our morning coffee under a microscope 403:88-90
Coffee under a hand lens 29:14
How much caffeine is there in coffee and tea 402:76

COHESION
Cohesive attractive forces among molecules of different liquids experiment 1004:3.008
Measure attractiveness (stickiness) between water molecules experiment 1396:153-158
Molecules stick together experiment 735:33-34
Sand sculptures show adhesion between sand and water experiment 1396:156
Simple experiments 105:36-39
Solutes affect the cohesiveness of water experiment 1396:156
Water has more cohesiveness than other liquids do experiment 1396:153-156
Watertight 222:61

COINS
Chemical reactions make a penny rusty—clean rusty penny, make others rusty 548:35-38
Clad coins—identifying by touch, sight and sound 548:41-42
Clean a penny 147:42
Clean copper penny with salt and vinegar experiment 695:44
Clean pennies experiment 960:31
Clean pennies using salt and vinegar, how to do 1175:78
Clean pennies with vinegar and salt 780:38-39
Cleaning dirty coins experiment 790:29
Coin recognizer reader, how to make 1249:26-30
Coins surface affected by routine handling experiment 1402:72-75
Copper penny shines when cleaned with vinegar and table salt experiment 1435:67-68
Dissolving coin trick 392:63-67
Dull pennies shine from salt and vinegar solution experiment 1005:8-9
Edison's ore separator, rejecting counterfeit coins experiment 895:39-40
Electricity and copper pennies distinguish chloride and sulfate ions experiment 1250:91-94
Electricity and copper pennies turn water blue experiment 1251:85-87
Magnetic coin trick 548:33-34
Make a scientific penny collection—each penny of different metal alloy 548:30-33
Metal composition of pennies/different dates determined by density experiment 1004:3.005
Pennies—will metal atoms combine with oxygen molecules 396:67-68
Pennies get a green coating experiment 1405:55
Slot machine uses magnetism to sort coins, how to make experiment 1309:26-27

Vinegar and salt clean copper pennies experiment 1251:80-81

COLCHICINE
Effects of colchicine on growth and development of seeds 402:90-91

COLD
Heated air expands; cold air contracts experiment 1032:12-14
Heated air expands; cold air contracts experiment 1032:15
Producing cold—instant ice cream 249:24
Producing cold—which way does the wind blow 249:25
Sense test 231:78
Thermometer measures temperature experiment using glass bottle, colored water 1032:16-17

COLD—COMMON
Do popular cold remedies eliminate nasal culture bacteria experiment 997:102-103
Germs spread by sneezes demonstrate 759:52-54
How is common cold economically important 402:86
What's in a sneeze experiment with bicycle pump and colored water 1270:11

COLD FRAMES
Cardboard cold frame, how to make 832:41
Cold frame effect on plants 380:44-45
Cold frame, constructing, how to 866:146-147
How to make 398:36-37

COLD FRONT
Cold front experiment; observe collision of cold and warm air 1447:61-64

COLD LIGHT (LUMINESCENCE). *See also* **FIREFLIES**
Experiment 87:33-37

COLLECTING—EQUIPMENT
Aspirator 9:14
Box trap 9:20-23
Conical tow net 9:32-34
Drop net for small fish 9:28-29
Field box and inclinator 9:24-25
Insect killing bottle 9:15
Insect net 9:12-13
Naturalists dredge 9:30-31
Simple butterfly net 9:18-19
Sweeping net 9:16-17
The collection connection—how to plan and organize your collection 452:36-38
Two handled seine 9:26-27

COLLISIONS
Experiments with collisions using bat and ball 1164:28-32
Force of collision experiment using toy truck 1507:14
Projects with collisions 1164:32-33
Tracks—ball game—experiment 373:65-67

COLLOIDS. *See also* **TYNDALL EFFECT**
Cloudy liquids using starch 85:32-33
Colloidal micelles can be separated from liquid by filtration experiment 1396:87-88
Colloidal particles can be made to coagulate experiment 1396:88-89
Cornstarch "quicksand" called colloidal suspension experiment 1258:unp.
Light used to distinguish colloidal suspension from pure solution experiment 1396:85-90
Liquid food and the Tyndall effect 74:31-33
Mayonnaise demonstrates emulsifying action of egg experiment; recipe given 1403:46-47

Milk separates into curds and whey experiment 905:114-115

Several experiments to demonstrate 382:143-146

Substance divided into colloidal size particles increases surface area 1396:89-90

Test to show colloidal mixture of milk and water experiment with flashlight 1476:128

Use of colloidal gel in absorbent diaper experiment, data table given 1004:4.012

COLOR. *See* COLORS

COLOR BLINDNESS

Are dogs color blind experiment 997:172-174

Painting triangle with red and green dots experiment 1109:9

COLOR WHEEL

Make to demonstrate principle of mixing colors 293:44-45

Making a 1:95-96

COLORATION—PROTECTIVE. *See also* CAMOUFLAGE

Colored toothpicks scattered; collected and counted by color—demonstration 268:119-122

COLORED FILTERS

Color combinations experiment using flashlights and colored cellophane 1092:46

COLORED LIGHTS. *See also* LIGHTS—COLORED

Afterimages using colors experiment 1158:142-143

Benham's Top; black and white design as it spins appears to be colored 1088:81

Clear glass that light can't get through experiment 1082:120-121

Color of light affects growth of seedlings experiment 1183:25

Color of light best for growth of plants experiment 1222:5-7, 22-26

Color wheel spinning experiment 1082:115-117

Colored cellophane and flashlight demonstrate changing colors experiment 1028:53

Colored light bulbs on different colored sheets of paper experiment 1253:30-31

Colored light effect on plant growth experiment 1395:86

Colored light effect on plant stem elongation experiment 1395:92

Colored light from color spinner experiment 1314:10-11

Colored lights affect seed germination experiment 1060:62

Colored lights and their properties 569:38

Colored lights experiment with recording sheet 747:13-14

Colored lights experiment; looking through colored filters 956:18

Colored lights experiment; making a color box 956:18-19

Colored lights experiment; mixing colored lights 956:19

Colored lights mixed and projected experiment using projectors/ colored filter 1153:43-45

Colored lights through water experiment 1082:100-102

Colored lights used to make additive color mixtures and colored shadows 1132:27-1-27-2

Colored lights wavelength affects photoperiodism in radish plants experiment 1060:73-74

Colored objects in colored lights experiment 1158:143-145

Colored shadows experiment 1159:90

Colors in different shades differ in effects on photosynthesis experiment 1060:27-28

Colors of light experiment with three flashlights and colored plastic 1049:14

Different wavelengths of colored lights affect phototropism experiment 1060:75

Disco light show machine—how to make 487:49-51

Earthworms prefer which colored light experiment 1158:138-140

Earthworms respond to different color light waves experiment 904:124-125

Experiment with different colored cellophane papers 911:27

Flashlights and colored filters experiment 1283:24

Flashlights and colored filters used in mixing colors with light experiment 1073:82

Green gumball turns black experiment 1082:110-112

Growth of plants in response to different colors of light experiment 1527:92

Light color and plant growth experiment 878:26-27

Light of different colors changes colors experiment 1018:14-15

Mix colored lights experiment using flashlight and colored filters 1283:25

Mix different colors of light experiment 1296:1978

Mixing colored lights experiment 1082:112-115

Mixing colored lights produces new colors experiment 1308:24-25

Mixing colors to make different colors experiment with flashlight/cellophane 1213:28-29

Photosynthesis affected by colors of the spectrum experiment 1060:27-28

Photosynthesis and respiration in plants affected by colors of light experiment 1395:103

Prism, slide projector and screen used to mix colored light experiment 1153:40-43

Seeds; color of light affects how seeds grow experiment 1181:17

Shadows under colored lights experiment 1158:140-142

Some colors easier to see from a distance than others experiment 1088:82

Three primary colors from flashlights produce white light experiment 1066:86-87

White light experiment, make white light from 3 filter lights; red, green, blue 1088:75

Why is light white experiment with different colored filters 1294:112-113

COLORFASTNESS

Bleach effect on fabric samples experiment 1396:108-110

Fading effect of sunlight on fabric samples experiment 1396:108-109

COLORINGS

Make your own vegetable coloring 319:88-89

COLORS

"After-image" color of colors of spectrum experiment 1369:55

3-D glasses—making 76:22-23

Activities mixing colors [Primary] 759:28-29

Activities to explore and understand colors [Primary] 758:96-98

All colors produce white 360:54-55

And lights—mixing colored lights 180:65-67

Are colors what they seem to be chromatography experiment 696:18-19

Automobiles; color most popular in cars project 1210:30-31

Background color affects the colors you see experiment 1109:10

Bees; can honeybees see color experiment 1134:3.005

Benham's Disk, rotating black and white disc produces illusion of color 1132:5-1-5-2

Bird in the cage; stare at color and see it change experiment 1132:8-1-8-2

Black and white on spinning disc produces colors experiment 736:41-44

Black colors absorb Sun's heat experiment with cans of water and thermometers 1213:30

Black hotter than white 289:33

Brain needs different amount of time to record color waves presence experiment 1405:38

Brightness mad and color crazed 229:70-82

Camouflage experiment with colored yarn pieces 680:16

Can molecules in air cause colors to fade experiment 831:53-54

Candy color circles—recipe given—how to make 732:164-165

Carousel of color on ceiling 356:32-35

Chromatograms—making 146:11

Color affects amount of radiation object absorbs experiment 1405:63

Color blend—plastic bottles/tubes, coloring & running water demo (Primary) 558:28-29

Color blind spot 1:8

Color blindness—demonstration to show 208:84-87

Color blindness—test your friends for color blindness 381:102

Color box experiment; tape pictures in box and use colored cellophane 1417:7

Color box shows rays bounce off to show color experiment 1018:13

Color carousel from posterboard and cellophane casts patterns on ceiling 558:32-33

Color change using blue and yellow cellophane experiment 885:50-51

Color changes—magic potions 16:62-65

Color changes when molecules in polarized glasses are stretched/twisted 1403:56-59

Color combinations experiment using flashlights and colored cellophane 1092:46

Color disc experiment 928:19

Color disc top to spin, how to make 1007:34-36

Color disk, making 941:48-51

Color experiment—food colorings (Primary) 535:74

Color filter turns the world red experiment 909:158

Color filters—experiment 659:30-31

Color filters change color of light experiment 860:214-216

Color flame tests 84:64-67

Color from spinning black and white lines experiment 761:46-47

Color in colored light 114:67-68

Color jars—how to make 732:153-154

Color mixer—disk spins to mix colors 288:44-45

Color on color background effects experiment 761:37-38

Color pyramid—colors of spectrum in a tetrahedon 76:20-21

Color scopes (Primary) 535:75

Color spinner—how to make 653:20-21

Color spinners, how to make 1115:124

Color turntable—make to view changing colors and shapes (Primary) 558:30-31

Color vision—red spots and green 280:25

Color wheel 535:75

Color wheel demonstrates how colors mix experiment with spinning color wheel 1213:26-27

Color wheel experiment; make with blotting paper, felt tip pen and water 1308:27

Color wheel spinners, making 898:29-30

Color wheel to demonstrate color changes during spinning 1016:20-21

Color wheel, making 906:81

Color wheels and experiments with color 835:84-86

Color; what color is light experiment 851:17-18

Colored cellophane and light projectors experiment show where colors come from 760:35-36

Color wheels from posterboard and cellophane (Primary) 558:26-27

Colored cellophane fun—see the world in different colors (Primary) 558:24-25

Colored filter transmits some colors and absorbs others experiment 1132:26-1-26-2

Colored filters absorptions measured by spectroscope experiment 860:215-216

Colored filters affect light experiment 1293:123-125

Colored filters change white light 428:39-40

Colored filters overlapped experiment 1283:23

Colored light on colors changes color experiment 928:23

Colored lights; mixing colored lights produces new colors experiment 1308:24-25

Colored sand, making 906:84

Colored shadows experiment 761:35-36

Colored spinners—making 142:34

Colored spinners experiment 1417:90

Colored spinning discs appear to be white experiment 1073:80-81

Coloring liquids red, violet or green with the same dye 150:122-123

Colors and scents of flowers that attract insects experiment 1183:76

Colors and scents that attract insects to flowers experiment 1182:28

Colors are mixture of two or three primary colors experiment 871:3.002

Colors at night; which show up best experiment 893:29

Colors from spinning black and white disc experiment 1063:178

Colors from the sun 657:83-84

Colors in colored light experiment 761:34

Colors in light 240:54-56

Colors in nature activities for classroom 1291:8-9

Colors in your flashlight (Primary) 206:unpaged

Colors mixed to form other colors; flashlight, colored cellophane experiment 818:20

Colors of light experiment with three flashlights and colored plastic 1049:14

Colors of night in the sky 292:123

Colors of thin films 4:78-79

Colors on spinning disc produces white experiment 736:45-46

Colors produced from black and white experiment; patterns for discs given 1020:19-22

Colors seem to change when placed against different backgrounds experiment 1132:25-1-25-2

Colors seen in different ways experiment 868:19

Colors spinners—making 659:27

Colors to wear on hot day, light or dark experiment using paper/water in sun 1017:15

Colors; light reflection—experiment 585:115-116

Creating colors (Primary) 232:98

Creeping colors 162:16-17

Dark cloth test—demonstrate darker colors warmer than light ones 291:48-49

Dark colored materials absorb and emit energy more than light colors experiment 1132:55-1-55-2

Demonstrate blending colors with light 208:59-61

Demonstrate disappearing colors (Primary) 210:24-25

Demonstrate pigment and color reflected to our eyes 208:62

Demonstrate sky colors 120:24

Demonstrate spectrum 208:50-51

Different colored dots look like one color experiment 1397:74-75

Different colors of light can be combined to make other colors exp. 836:51-53

Different lengths of time needed for brain to record color waves experiment 904:162-163

Diffraction grating spreads light into its component colors experiment 1132:90-1-90-2

Disappearing tricks with light and colors 684:18-19

Disc of colored dots; spinning makes rings of different colors experiment 1018:18-19

Discs spin and colors disappear experiment 696:20-21

Dispersion experiment; separation of light into colors using light and prism 1153:38-40

Does sunlight change the color of things experiment [Primary] 742:20

Effect of dry bleach on color experiment 905:84-85

Erupting color bubbles from oil and water experiment 1405:60

Experiment with 128:201-203

Exploding colors with milk, coloring and detergent in a pan (Primary) 558:16-17

Exploding colors 356:20-21

Eye color receptors—the illusion of color 366:202-205

Eye-color from parents' genes experiment 1048:26

Eyeglasses with frame to hold color cellophane pieces experiment 1417:8-11

Favorite colors and color preference charts and game 363:14-19

Fetchner disc—making 176:61-62

Filtering light with colored cellophane experiment 1109:13-14

Filtering light with colored plastic experiment 935:16-17

Focal length and color experiment 761:44-45

Growth of plants in response to different colors of light experiment 1527:92

Heat absorption and color 253:86

Heat absorption of dark and light colors—experiment 680:28

Heating by radiation depends on color experiment 1515:105-108

Hidden colors in felt tipped pens experiment 1018:20-21

How black is black 120:25

How do different colors absorb the sun's rays experiment 793:29

How far can you see colors experiment 1020:14-19

Human eyes equally sensitive to all colors of light experiment 1092:48

Humming birds are attracted to color experiment 1020:123-124

Identify colors in filtered light experiment 836:83-85

Illusions using color to see if eye or brain is doing it experiment 761:57-58

Insects; can insects see colors experiment 1097:73-74

Interference patterns of rainbow colors experiment using 2 sheets of Plexiglas 1132:13-1-13-2

Invisible colors of spectrum can be located experiment 715:112-114

Lack of sunlight affects color of leaf experiment 1049:19

Lateral inhibition experiment using shades of gray color 1132:56-1-56-2

Leaves; why do leaves change color explanation 1239:8-9

Light box—building to experiment with mixing colors 761:32-34

Light of different colors changes colors experiment 1018:14-15

Light reflected from colored surface will have that color experiment 836:48-50

Light with prisms, shadows and transparent materials experiments 1417:16-17

Light; mix different colors of light project 1296:1978

Luminous objects 91:34-41

Magic color change with cabbage leaves experiment 924:2-3

Magic color disc 281:86

Make a color experiment 906:82

Make a Newton's disk and prove that colors can add up to white 625:36

Make a pure light spectrum 625:36

Making a spectrum 180:64

Mercury street light viewed with compact disc shows separate colors experiment 1250:57-60

Meyer's experiment with colored shadows 761:37

Mix colors with spinning disc experiment 827:39

Mix primary colors recording results experiment 747:11-12

Mixing colored lights 76:22

Mixing colors—experiment 595:36

Mixing colors experiment with food dyes 1417:5.1

Mixing colors experiment with water and food coloring [Primary] 880:21

Mixing colors to get others activity [Primary] 897:41

Mixing colors to make different colors experiment with flashlight/cellophane 1213:28-29

Mixing colors to make white 150:132-133

Mixing colors with light experiment 928:18

Multicolored glasses—making 177:9-11

Mystery color wheel trick 585:81

Newton's color wheel—experiment 569:38

Newton's rings of color—making 186:100-101

Observe magic disappearance of a color experiment 905:82-83

Orange spot on wet paper changes into other colors experiment [Primary] 788:8-9

Painted circle cardboard whizzer turns white as it spins experiment [Primary] 788:14-15

Patterns—light show with paints 356:28-29

Peripheral vision and color experiment 762:55-56

Pigments in colors separated using chromatography experiment 1308:26-27

Polarized light reveals stress patterns in clear plastic experiment 1132:12-1-12-2

Polarized light stained glass window mosaic experiment 1132:78-1-78-3

Polarized light through sugar water gives beautiful colors experiment 1132:85-1-85-2

Polarized sunglasses experiment 1132:79-1-79-2

Primary color spinner, how to make 999:43-44

Rainbow pies—making 162:20-21

Rainbow spinner makes colors turn to white experiment 1050:7

Red cellophane eyeglasses, how to make [Primary] 788:10-11

Red cellophane filters and colored gum balls experiment 1083:108

Red spots and green 280:25

Secondary colors from primary colors activities for classroom 1291:41-42

Secret message color experiment 906:83

See colors that aren't there, spin circle experiment 807:149

Seeing the colors of an oil spill 180:66

Sensations of color 4:60-71

Separate colored dyes in marking pens experiment data tables given 1004:4.003

Separate colors using paper towels experiment 827:38

Separate different colors experiment, how to do 790:29-30

Separate light into colors experiment 1405:106

Separating colors experiment using blotting paper and felt tipped pens 1073:83

Separating colors in liquids—experiment 598:36

Separating the colors in inks 589:47

Separation of color experiment with coffee filter 1288:29

Sky; why is the sky blue; activities to demonstrate 1511:43-46

Snow melts faster with certain colors 277:11-12

Soap bubbles, colored, how to make 1179:94-95

Soap film painting creates array of colors experiment 1132:89-1-89-2

Source of color; activities to demonstrate where color comes from 1511:43-46

Spectroscope separates light into colors of rainbow experiment, how to make 1516:19-20

Spectrum—experiment to show 91:30-33

Spectrum colors in a rainbow 76:20

Spectrum colors on a whizzer wheel 76:18-19

Spectrum diffraction grating replica 386:63-66

Spin a disc 356:26-27

Spin some color, make a whizzer 868:21

Spinner demonstrates colors from three primary colors; data sheet given 818:19

Spinner of colors experiment 1109:11-12

Spinning colored discs make secondary colors experiment 1285:22-23

Spinning colors disc, making 935:18-19

Spinning colors 180:65

Spinning disc makes colors white, how to make 1179:97

Spinning disc with black and white colors shows other colors experiment 1369:56-57

Spinning disc with colors of spectrum experiment 1369:51-53

Spinning multicolored disks produce different colors 507:1860-1861

Spinning top changes colors experiment [Primary] 788:6-7

Stained glass window, making 909:159

Taking colors apart experiment 935:23

Test color vision and afterimages 258:49-55

Test for color changes in colored light 625:36

Testing the effect of colored lights on plant growth 180:66

The strange case of the creeping color dots—chromatography experiment 494:48

The world thru colored filters 114:69-70

Use filters to make new color or take it away 142:35

Vanishing colors in liquid experiment using bleach and food coloring 1175:78

Viewing box for colors, making 909:158

Viewing box to see colors, how to make from shoe box, cellophane papers 1179:96-97

Vision; do people see the same color at the same time project 1210:64-66

Warning colors experiment; test which colors reflect light best at night 1283:29

Warning colors experiment; test which colors work best on sign 1283:28

Water color bombs with jars, food coloring and flashlight (Primary) 558:18-19

Water separates light into different colors experiment 1250:55-56

Wave lengths—demonstrate blending colors with your eyes 208:54-58

Weather wear—clothes are heat absorbing or heat reflecting 399:24

Weaving colors with colored cellophane experiment 1109:15

Wet and wild colors—making 162:18-19

What color is at top of rainbow experiment 747:9

What color is white experiment 902:83-84

What is color; spinning disc experiment 902:100-101

Which colors absorb heat the best experiment 1519:14

Which colors of spectrum are hottest experiment 715:115

Whirling wonder discs 386:2-6

White light can be split into seven colors using glass prism experiment 1073:80-81

White light is made up of colors; make spinners to show 893:10

White light; how to see when spinning colored circle, how to do 1415:17

Why is light white; experiment with colored filters 860:217

Why is the sky blue 176:38

William Herschel's discovery of infrared rays experiment 1133:6.009

Yellow product labels attract consumer eyes experiment 1051:25

COLORS—ABSORPTION

Testing color absorption 180:67

COLORS—INSECTS

Investigation into the color preferences of insects 420:117-118

COLUMNS. *See also* **BUILDING; STRUCTURES**

Invent a column shape 557:53

Making paper columns 557:52

Testing the difference between a pin and a rigid connection 557:54-55

COMB JELLIES

Comb—jelly flashes—experiment 484:104

COMBUSTION. *See also* **FIRE**

Can a sugar lump burn 176:17-18

Can steel burn 176:16

Candle is a gas factory 122:75-78

Demonstrate with miniature fireworks 176:16

Different substances burn with different colored flame experiment 1179:30-31

Effect of oxygen on combustion experiment 752:117-118

Experiments to demonstrate 346:43-50

Faraday's investigating the properties of candle flames experiment 1133:7.007

Fires require oxygen 122:71-75

Flame consumes smoke when super heated in second flame experiment 752:96-97

Flame test to show kind of textiles present 176:18

How can a candle burn under water 176:18-19

Jean Rey's burning metals into ash experiment 1133:2.001

John Mayow's combustion to show air is a mixture experiment 1133:2.002

Make coke from coal 122:88-89

Make soot 176:19-20

Products of combustion experiment 871:3.007

Show carbon in a candle flame 122:78-79

Show water in a candle flame 122:79-80

The flaming spoon 291:228-229

Use candle to show products of combustion 176:14-15

Water is by-product of combustion experiment 752:97-98

Where does soot come from 176:17

COMETS

Astronomers compare photographs to find comets computer simulation project 1062:51-53

Comet computer database, how to set up 1062:56-57

Comet's orbit demonstrated with foamcore and marbles 1478:84

Discovering comets—system to use 710:51-52

How do comets travel experiment 1293:63-64

Making a model of a comet project 833:272

Model comet made from ping pong ball, cotton and feathers, how to do 1500:16

Reporting new comets—how to send your observations 710:52

Why comet's tail points away from Sun experiment 1479:21

COMETS AND METEORS

Observations and plotting of (advanced) 658:73-79

COMICS

Copy solution to make prints from comics 859:3

COMMUNICATIONS

Infrared communications system, how to make 860:119-125

Make a model communications system 226:27

Make a model communications tower 226:23

COMMUNITIES

A bog community terrarium 268:57-62

A desert community terrarium 268:29-33

A grassy field community terrarium 268:41-44

A pond community aquarium 268:51-56

A woodland community terrarium 268:17-21

Changing communities in a drop of water 268:95-99

Life in a rotting log 268:23-27

Life of a forest 268:11-15

Observe and study the structure of a pond community 285:32-41

Plant community—studying a plant community 268:67-71

The life of a grassy field 268:35-39

The life of a pond 268:45-50

COMMUNITY LIFE

Social science projects—examine aspects of community life & human behavior 542:1-141

Social science projects—examine aspects of community life & human behavior 506:1-106

COMPASS

A crafty compass—how to make 572:14-15

A needle with an eye for direction—making 280:29

Balancing compass, how to make 1043:33

Bar magnet compass—how to make 706:41-42

Card compass—making 128:161

Chinese hanging compass—making 302:13

Clay turtle compass, how to make 1076:17

Clock can be used as a compass demonstration 1394:86-87

Clock can be used as compass experiment 1479:13

Compass card—how to make 636:26-27

Compass cutups—experiment 563:101

Compass directional—experiment 436:24-25

Compass from magnetized needle, how to make 1218:21

Compass from needle and cork experiment 1072:32

Compass from needle and cork experiment 1160:11

Compass from needle and thread, how to make 1437:49-50

Compass from needle, magnet and cardboard disc, how to make 1073:40-41

Compass from slice of cork and needle, how to magnetize 1179:162

Compass from sticks and stones shows North-South, East-West line experiment 1365:17

Compass in a dish and bottle—making 293:40

Compass in jar swings freely, how to make 768:57-58

Compass made from magnet, needle and cork 1382:34

Compass made from magnet, needle and plastic tile 1480:38

Compass made from magnets experiment 973:23

Compass made from needle and cork, how to do 1381:19

Compass, how to make 947:14-15

Compass, making to find out how they work 870:28-30

Compass, making 627:6

Compass, simple one to make one from steel needle and cork 1224:29

Compasses to make 912:13

Construct a compass, how to do 1028:92

Construct a simple magnet compass 232:45

Construct simple compass, how to do 860:219-220

Current in a wire deflects magnetism experiment 895:21-22

Demonstrate relationship between a bar magnet and a compass 209:13

Dip circle—making 128:159

Discover deviation 302:51

Electric current affects compass experiment 1501:72-75

Experiments to discover principles involved in circles 519:4-33

Experiments with a compass 1309:19

Find out how to make a compass 599:14-15

Finding compass directions with a bar magnet 874:206

Finding north with magnetized blade 605:50-53

Floating compass from magnet experiment 973:25

Floating compass, how to make 768:55-57

Floating compass, making 136:16; 779:24; 826:13; 906:91

Giant compass rose—making 303:17-19

Hanging compass in glass jar, how to make 1401:35

Homemade compass—making 195:21-22; 341:4; 94:40-41

How does compass work experiment 1401:20-23

How it works 367:33-41

How to correct compass errors caused by nearby iron and steel 184:80-81

How to make a compass 827:61; 938:51-53

How to make your own compass card (Primary) 451:27

How to tell time with a compass experiment 938:54-55

Is compass like a magnet experiment 834:15-16

Jar compass, how to make 1043:33

Magnetic compass—making 142:40; 145:14-15; 191:5-8; 472:2240; 930:8

Magnetic compass, how to make with magnet, needle and cork slice 1201:35

Magnetic compass, how to make; compass design card given 1243:12-13

Magnetized steel needle—compass making 184:24-25

Magnets; experiments with a magnetic compass 1514:17-18

Make a compass experiment 902:204

Make a compass 1001:27; 955:32

Make compass using bar magnet experiment 961:17

Make your own 636:27-29; 682:22

Making a compass 587:50

Making a water compass project 833:112-115

Making 15:7; 179:150-152; 186:27; 278:20-22; 28:22-25; 291:158; 91:113-116

Margarine tub compass, making 1024:28-29

Mariner's compass—making 167:109-113; 360:34-35

Needle and cork compass—making 532:81

Needle compass—making 231:50; 320:17; 321:25; 670:53; 807:150-152; 1099:22

Needle compass that floats, how to make 1409:55

Needles—how to make simple one 128:157-158

Oersted's Discovery; electric current deflects compass needle experiment 1159:104-107

One foot compass—making 12:113-115

Phoenician floating compass—making 302:18-19

Shadow compass—making 207:29

Shadow stick compass, making 826:14

Simple compass from magnetized needle in a cork, how to make 1309:18-19

Simple compass from needle and cork, how to make 837:47-48

Small pocket sundial, cardboard, making 999:75-78

Solar stone to find North, how to make from cardboard, cork, dowel 1115:132-133

Sun compass—how to do 494:24

Sun compass, how to make from cardboard 1329:31

Supersensitive compass—making 532:80

Swinging compass, making 826:13-14

Swinging compass, making 906:90

Tell time with a compass 278:20-22

Tell time with compass experiment 768:65

The battery-powered compass, making 627:28

The clock as a compass trick 585:74

Trees as directional compasses using organism growth experiment 1134:5.008

Watch becomes a compass 202:15

Watch compass sundial, cardboard and watch, making 999:72-74

Watch dial compass, making 826:14

Watch used as compass 381:42-43

Water compass, how to make 1043:32

What is a compass experiment 902:203

Why does compass needle point North experiment 1294:114-116

COMPASS PLANT

To grow in your garden 271:64

COMPOST

Animal life in leaf litter experiment 1134:1.010

Breakdown of organic matter, how to demonstrate 986:77

Compost bins, how to make from wire and wood 1150:47

Compost effect on plant growth experiment 714:59-60

Compost heap reduces amount of garbage going to landfills experiment 1173:49-53

Compost heap, how to build 1013:112

Compost holder from plastic jug, how to make 1071:150

Compost made from kitchen or yard scraps project 1296:1987

Compost pile makes natural fertilizer from garbage experiment 1240:27

Compost pile; large, mixed compost pile, how to make 1150:46-48

Compost, how to make experiment 1328:80-81

Composter for your compost, how to make 1063:379

Composter, how to make from large packing crate 1328:81

Composting food wastes garbage experiment 1150:44-46

Composting reduces volume of materials sent to landfills experiments 1150:43-51

Earthworms composting garbage experiment 1150:48-49

Factors affecting breakdown of organic matter into humus experiment 762:46-47

Factors that affect composting experiment 1150:49-50

Garbage can composter, how to make 1371:61-62

Heap—make a compost heap 155:18-19

How to make a compost pile 436:25

How to make a compost pile experiment 1440:61-63

How to make compost 264:114; 1008:39

Humus and its effect on amount of water soil retains experiment data table 1004:1.008

Kitchen compost pile—making 607:29

Leaves—collect animals in leaf litter with a Berlese funnel (how to make) 285:85

Maximizing the efficiency of a compost heap experiment 1450:34-41

"Mini-compost" project recycles garbage 1265:77

Pile—food web of the compost pile 276:60

Pile for composting materials, how to do 1054:22

Polyethylene bag composting 363:107-108

Recipe for compost 1424:115-116

Soil from life—keep journal of decomposition time on indoor/outdoor pile 380:28-30

Super soil—how to make 376:39

Topsoil, examine for dominant species project 969:9-10

Topsoil, homemade, how to make science project 969:8

Vermi-composting; earthworms as recyclers, how to keep and feed 1206:8-13

What happens to pile of freshly cut grass clippings experiment 1323:79-84

Why a compost pile gets hot experiment 1440:58-60

Worm box to compost scraps and soil, how to make 1054:19

Worm composter, how to make using composter and live worms 1228:56-58

Worm system—set up worm composting system 276:1-90

COMPOUND MACHINES
Compound machine using gears, wheel and axle to lift a load experiment 1400:68-71
Compound machine, what is it experiment 1400:68-71
Examine complex machines 436:26
Pantograph is compound machine made up of levers; how does it work experiment 1400:76-79
Soap bubble machine; combining simple machines makes compound machine 1400:71

COMPOUNDS. *See also* **ORGANIC COMPOUNDS**
Breaking compound water into its elements experiment 976:26
Burning sugar to show elements of 85:20-21
Carbohydrates—caramel syrup—sugar decomposes 74:80-81
Carbohydrates—hygroscopic cookies 74:44-46
Carbohydrates starches 74:46-47
Carbohydrates starches—grape jelly—how pectin acts 74:49-50
Carbohydrates starches—tapioca 74:47-49
Carbohydrates syrups—solutions that don't crystallize 74:42-44
Combine iron and sulfur to make iron sulfide 157:12
Combining two elements to from compound experiment 976:27
Demonstrate iron and sulfur magic 146:17
Formation of new compounds having different colors 87:15-23
Investigating the solubility of compounds 180:28
Iron and oxygen make rust 157:13
Iron and water make rust experiment 707:30-32
Looking at compounds and how they are formed 6:18-19
Make a compound from iron filings and powdered sulfur 6:13
Make caramel to show elements of sugar 146:45
Make iron sulfide 97:14-15
Make toffee to show chemical reaction of compounds 157:28
Physical change of a compound 585:89-90
Separating compounds—experiment 180:27
Show chemical reactions change compounds into others 157:16-17
Show electricity breaks compounds apart—split salt; silver coins turn cop 157:20-21
Show how heat affects substances and reactions 157:18-19
Test clay you create experiment 871:3.004
Testing organic compounds—carbon dioxide turns limewater milky—experiment 6:30

COMPRESSED AIR. *See* **AIR—COMPRESSED**
COMPRESSIONAL STRENGTH
Simple experiments 105:52-55
COMPRESSORS
Compressed air is powerful experiment using plastic bottle/clay plug 1198:18
COMPUTER EXPERIMENTS
Experiments with sensors 665:24-31
Storing and correlating information 665:32-39
Travel time program 665:14-19
Speed, gravity, bounciness of ball experiment 665:8-9
Pulse rate—experiments 665:10-13
COMPUTERS
Analog computer, how to make 860:78-84
Architecture—center of mass 511:4-5

Architecture—length, surface area and volume 511:2-3
Astronomy and space—docking 511:8-9
Astronomy and space—Encke's Comet 511:10-11
Astronomy and space—inner planets 511:14-15
Astronomy and space—Mercury's orbit 511:12-13
Astronomy and space—satellite launch from Earth 511:18-19
Astronomy and space—satellite 511:16-17
Astronomy and space—three stage rocket 511:20-22
Biology—cone shell growth 511:34-35
Biology—cowry shell growth 511:36-37
Biology—grass stem growth 511:24-25
Biology—pond farming (aquaculture) 511:38-42
Biology—population forecast 511:28-29
Biology—sex probability 511:30-31
Biology—what to plant where 511:32-33
Biology—woody stem growth 511:26-27
Build a computer; how to make an abacus 625:10
Chemistry—diffusion 511:44-45
Chemistry—tevatron 511:46-47
Computer program to identify unknown substances (chemicals) 6:40-41
Creating images of sun with a computer project 833:185
Data management—alphabetic sort 511:60-61
Data management—bar graph 511:50-51
Data management—classification 511:56-57
Data management—label maker 511:58-59
Data management—minimum, maximum and mean 511:54-55
Data management—point plotter 511:52-53
Energy budgeting—food conversion 511:64-65
Energy budgeting—step saver 511:66-68
How to make your own analog computer 13:131-139
Hydraulics—river flow 511:70-71
Instrumentation—stroboscope 511:74-75
Measure ELF (extremely low frequency) radiation in personal computers 1450:106-112
Milk carton computer, making 770:132
Momentum—cannon 511:80-81
Momentum—car crash (inelastic collision) 511:84-85
Momentum—elastic collision 511:78-79
Momentum—explosion 511:82-83
Motion in a line—acceleration 511:90-91
Motion in a line—constant velocity 511:88-89
Motion in a line—deceleration 511:92-93
Motion in a line—drag strip 511:95-97
Motion in a line—gas-n-brake 511:94-95
Motion in a line—toss 511:98-99
Motion in a line—vertical lander 511:100-102
Motion in two dimensions—helicopter 511:110-111
Motion in two dimensions—horizontal throw 511:104-105
Motion in two dimensions—marble rolls off table 511:106-107
Motion in two dimensions—pendulum 511:114-115
Motion in two dimensions—river crossing 511:112-113
Motion in two dimensions—sailboat race 511:116-118
Motion in two dimensions—trajectory 511:108-109
Paper computer, advanced, how to make 860:86
Paper computer, simple, how to make 860:84-85
Position, mapping and design—hi resolution 3-D mapping 511:126-127
Position, mapping and design—radar 511:122-123

Position, mapping and design—radio direction finder 511:120-121

Position, mapping and design—sonar 511:124-125

Position, mapping and design—topographic map 511:128-130

Psychology—memory test 511:132-133

Psychology—reaction time 511:134-135

Soroban analog computer—directions for making (advanced) 449:113-117

Waves (sound, light, and water)—amplitude and wavelength 511:140-141

Waves (sound, light, and water)—lightning and thunder 511:138-139

Waves (sound, light, and water)—reflection 511:142-143

Why are computers good with math experiment with paper computer 1294:15-17

COMPUTERS—PROJECTS

Air—the insulating value of air project 584:94-95

Air—thermal expansion of gas (how heat affects air)—project 584:96-97

Alphabetical order project 853:130-134

Animal tree game—how to do 625:14-15

Astronomers compare photographs to find comets computer simulation project 1062:51-53

Base converter project 853:107-116

Biology matching quiz project 853:100-106

Build robot to draw shapes on paper with information from computer experiment 997:86-88

Calorie counter of daily foods eaten project 1021:134

Cell membranes—selectively permeable membranes—project 584:32-33

Chemical reactions—conductivity of citrus fruit—project 584:140-142

Chemical reactions—enzyme activity—project 584:135-137

Chemical reactions—the age of aspirin—project 584:133-134

Chemical reactions—the effect of chemicals on daphnia heart rate—project 584:138-139

Classification—project 584:83-85

Cloud identification project 853:54-60

Clouds used to predict weather project 1021:146-148

Coin toss probability project 1021:32-36

Comet computer database, how to set up 1062:56-57

Computer languages; some better suited to write programs than others 1021:110-111

Computer population model for population changes in tadpoles 864:119-120

Data and tracks on floppy diskette seen by iron filings on disc experiment 1021:11-13

Database file length shortened by removing unwanted records project 1021:79-82

Density project 584:103-105

Direction concept of N/S/E/W, using Etch-A-Sketch computer project 1021:131-133

Distance to the sun project 853:32-40

Electricity for home appliances not as expensive as people think project 1021:86-88

Escape velocity project 853:27-32

Family tree database program 1021:137-138

Force—Hooke's law constant—project 584:108-110

Force—mechanical advantage—project 584:106-107

Forces resultants and equilibrium—projects 584:111-113

Frequency and wave lengths project 853:139-145

Gasoline or fuel efficiency in expensive gasoline project 1021:54-55

Gene frequencies and population genetics—project 584:43-45

Genetics—natural selection—key to adaptation project 584:46-48

Genetics—pedigrees—project 584:86-88

Geological time clock project 853:41-46

Graphing concepts project 1021:50-53

Gravity—falling for "g" project 584:117-118

Gravity—projectile motion—project 584:121-122

Gravity—the path of a falling object—project 584:119-120

Height finder project 853:116-123

Height of distant object calculation project 1021:128-130

Heredity—introduction to heredity, Punnett squares project 584:37-39

Heredity—laws of chance and percent deviation project 584:40-42

Homeowners insurance not enough for replacement value of contents project. 1021:75-76

Landscaping with trees and shrubs in the best location database project 1021:63-68

Leap year prediction computer program experiment 1062:33-34

Life and death of yeast culture experiment 762:84-85

Light—depth of judgment—index of refraction project 584:125-126

Light—illumination—project 584:127-129

Lightning strike location on ground or on object project 1021:43-49

Logic function AND and OR truth table electric circuits project 1021:20-23

Loop to simulate a clock project 1021:112-116

Lottery numbers uniform distribution project 1021:41-42

Lung capacity project and survey 584:19-24

Magic squares program 625:12-13

Magnetic fields affect data stored on diskette project 1021:29-31

Measuring the Earth's circumference project 853:68-80

Metric conversion project 853:157-167

Metric system—working with linear units—project 584:67-69

Metric system—working with temperature scales project 584:72-74

Metric system—working with volume project 584:70-71

Minerals identified using database of characteristics project 1021:58-62

Muscular activity project 584:30-31

News publishing done effectively by computer project 1021:126-127

Numbers can be converted from one base to another project 1021:93-95

Pendulums project 853:151-157

Pepsi or Coke preferences, as to age groups/male/female computer project 1021:39-40

Photosynthesis—rates of photosynthesis—project 584:57-58

Planaria regeneration project 584:77-78

Planetary distances and diameters project 853:7-14

Plants—factors in plant growth project 584:53-54

Plants—magnetotropisms—project 584:61-63

Plants—paper chromatography (pigments in a leaf)—project 584:55-56

Pocket calculator simulation project 1021:91-92

Population stimulation project 853:94-100
Pretend data project 853:134-138
Prime numbers computer project 1021:135-136
Pulse rate time to recover project 584:27-29
Pulse rates project 584:25-26
Quantity buying is sometimes a marketing gimmick project 1021:89-90
Radio frequency energy near computer mapped to determine interference 1021:24-26
Rainfall; average daily amount of rainfall project 1021:37-38
Relative humidity computation project 1021:158-160
Rock identification project 853:46-54
Satellite orbital periods project 853:14-20
Science notation project 853:123-129
Song title index database project 1021:77-78
Species variation project 584:49-50
Speed of light project 853:145-151
Spelling vocabulary easily learned by elementary students tutor project 1021:139-140
Sports team analysis of players spread sheet program project 1021:72-74
Sports; home field playing gives winning advantage in sports experiment 1195:79-93
Stare glare project for human productivity while using computers experiment 1021:14-16
Supersonic bees project 853:81-89
Talk program simulating intelligent computer conversation project 1021:106-109
Television shows for children have more commercials per hour project 1021:84-85
Temperature scale conversions project 1021:156-157
Town database of names, phone numbers and business categories project 1021:69-71
Twelve hour forecast project 853:60-68
UV exposure experiment computer modeling software used to analyze 1450:49-57
Weather almanac—project 584:91-93
Weather history used to predict weather project 1021:152-155
Weather recording and reporting more efficient on a computer project 1021:161-164
Weather related heat and wind-chill warnings project 1021:99-101
Weeds—field studies: dandelion distribution project 584:59-60
Weight and mass—project 584:101-102
Weight of people on other planets project 1021:96-98
Weight on different planets project 853:21-27
Wind direction and pressure used to predict weather project 1021:149-151
Wind-chill factor computer program 1021:142-145
Work station; design efficient and comfortable work station project 1021:17-19
Yeast—population growth project 584:79-80
CONCERT HALLS
Sound and architecture of concert halls experiment 1155:81-85
CONCRETE. See also CEMENT
Artificial concrete rock from cement, sand and gravel, how to make 1202:6
Concrete mixes test for strength and hardness project 715:53-55
Concrete pencil holder—making 26:36-39
How to make 224:7; 733:8

How to make concrete 1438:68-71
Make different mixes of concrete to see which is best experiment 834:30-33
Mixtures of concrete that make the strongest bars experiment 1508:16
Steel rods strengthen concrete—experiment 26:41-42
Testing strength of concrete; make concrete bars experiment 795:30-31
CONDENSATION. See also MOISTURE; WATER
And evaporation 12:86-90
Boil water with ice 291:57
Condensation of air makes your breath visible experiment 1439:40-41
Condensation of water vapor 293:10-11
Experimenting with condensation 175:66
Jar and ice cube experiment 747:15
Soggy pancakes experiment 563:156
Water coming out of the air 281:20
Water from air 146:60
Water vapor condenses when cooled experiments 767:25-26
What is condensation demonstration 902:27
CONDITIONED BEHAVIOR. See GOLDFISH
CONDITIONED REFLEX—ANIMALS
Is it possible to modify the normal response of animals 402:42-43
CONDITIONING. See BEHAVIOR; LEARNING
CONDUCTION. See HEAT—CONDUCTION
CONDUCTORS. See also ELECTRONICS
Conductivity tester, how to build 768:106-107
Getting a charge out of a lime 180:47
How different materials conduct heat experiment 1179:53
Identifying solids that will conduct electricity 180:47
Materials that are the best conductors or best insulators of heat experiment 1090:38
Measure conductivity of solutions 363:85
Metal is good conductor of heat; wood and plastic are not experiment 1519:8
Metal wires conduct heat experiment 1090:36
Of heat 238:40-41
Test for conductors and insulators experiment with spoon, candy, hot water 1377:12
Testing for heat conductivity 180:75
Testing materials that might conduct electricity 180:46
Thermal conductivities of steel, glass and insulation experiment 1515:95-101
Using salt to conduct electricity 180:48
Which thermal wrappings have the best insulation experiment 1090:40
Why do some materials feel cold experiment 1519:9
Why not metal hangers 281:61-62
CONE
Cone birds—how to make 236:49
CONSERVATION
How to make soil 33:18
Model conservation farm, making 874:211-212
The re-pulping of paper 33:15
CONSERVATION OF ENERGY
Do you dare, victim waits for weighted can to swing back—experiment 563:44-45
Machines save energy experiment with block and ramp; data table given 1004:5.004

Swinging spool and weight on string demonstrate 940:117-119

What happens when moving object meets stationary object experiment 837:36-37

CONSERVATION OF HEAT

Conservation of heat when hot and cold water are mixed experiment 1515:62-65

CONSERVATION OF MASS—PIAGET

Simple experiments 105:48-51

CONSERVATION OF MOMENTUM

Conservation of Momentum experiment with marbles; data tables given 1004:5.001

Destructive changes to nature experiment using three patches of lawn 1328:26-27

Resources used by family in over three generations experiment 1328:24-25

CONSTANCY OF AXIS

Show how rotation and inertia work together 385:61-62

CONSTELLARIUM

How to make 128:68

CONSTELLATIONS. *See also* **STARS**

A system for seeing stars 231:16

Big Dipper or Plow constellations, how to observe and record 1217:8

Charting the constellations—how to do 710:64

Constellation finder, how to make 1063:461-464

Constellation gazer, shoe box and flashlight, making 998:160-161

Constellation projector, how to make 1293:57

Constellation viewers, how to make from tin cans, paper, glue 1114:133

Constellations in a shoe box experiment, how to make 1478:110-111

Constellations that turn around Polaris [North Star], how to find 1434:67-69

Construct a constellarium to show constellations 175:53

Create your own constellations based on modern object shapes experiment 1062:70

Drawing the signs of the zodiac 175:49

How can various constellations be located 253:186-187

How to chart 128:69

Learn the constellations 476:85-91

Learning the constellations project 833:52-57

Light box and slides with constellations experiment, how to build 1476:166-167

Make a constellation spotter 91:46-49

Make star shiner with can and flashlight 288:28-29

Model constellation made from poster board, clay, wooden skewers, paint 1478:110-111

Model of the zodiac—making 532:54-55

Model shows and explains changing pattern of stars in night sky experiment 1502:20-22

Orion constellation, how to observe and record 1217:9

Orion model from shoe box, straws and clay, how to make 1365:19

Orion, how to find in the sky 1434:77-78

Photographing the constellations—how to 762:17

Pictures of constellations with flashlight and coffee can (Primary) 426:28-31

Pinhole viewer—how to make 558:70-71

Planetarium from flashlight, how to build 967:22-23

Record position of Big Dipper and Polaris experiment 1479:20

Star maps—the night sky—make star maps to use with flashlight 588:52

Star patterns can be seen only from our particular position in space experiment 1062:74-75

Stellar pancakes, recipe given, help you see constellations 887:12-13

Tin can planetarium—how to make 292:18

Tube constellations Pringle can projector—making 748:152

Using a star chart project 833:57-58

CONSTRUCTION. *See also* **BUILDING**

Concrete mixes test for strength and hardness project 715:53-55

Nails—how they work 544:9-14

Nuts and bolts—how they work 544:15-18

Screws and rivets—how they work 544:19-24

Test different kinds of sand bricks for strength experiment 715:56-60

CONSUMER

Consumer's report on paper towel brands project—report chart given 748:95-96

Supermarket investigation project 630:69-71

Technology used by you in one day for your survival 1337:65

Yellow product labels attract consumer eyes experiment 1051:25

CONSUMER GOODS

Paper towels; which is the "quickest picker-upper" project 1210:41-42

Soaps; testing suds making ability of soaps experiment 1259:45-47

CONTINENTS

The big split—experiment 400:51

Continent drift puzzle (Primary) 153:6-7

Continent shapes; cut and try to fit together as in ancient times experiment 1383:9

Continental drift motion booklet shows how continents came to exist experiment 1063:232-235

Continental separation demonstration 1023:56-57

Continents a-go-go game 400:124

Expansion of Atlantic Ocean demonstration 1023:60-61

Land mass and continental drift, how to demonstrate 1437:93-97

Magnetism and plate tectonics investigations 1342:110-111

Matching of the continents by age of rocks 400:51

Ocean trenches formation demonstration 1023:62-63

Plate tectonic model used to show continental collision experiment 1342:106-110

Plate tectonic model, how to make 1342:106-110

World map tectonic jigsaw puzzle, how to make 1042:25

CONTOUR LINES

Demonstrating contour lines 874:207

CONTOURS

Land relief model—how to make 507:1862-1863

CONVECTION. *See also* **HEAT—CONVECTION**

Convection currents demonstrated with candle chimneys in box experiment 882:23

Convection currents demonstrated with candles and chimneys on box experiment 767:58

Convection in gas and liquid—experiment 681:13

Currents—make a spinning snake decoration 142:55

Demonstrate convection in liquids 291:42

Demonstrate with smoke and two jars experiment 722:116

Demonstrating convection in liquids 180:79
Drafts—ways of detecting drafts 142:54
Dust devil model—making 767:59
Experiments to show transfer of heat 128:147-148
Food coloring and water demonstrates 722:103
Heat travels in liquids and gases 238:42
In water using cobalt chloride 146:31
Sea breeze convection experiment 767:59
Shown with balloons 92:40-41
Test for convection experiment with hot water and food coloring 1377:15
Warm water rises experiment 741:11
Why does the wind blow 55:83-89

CONVECTION CURRENTS
Fresh water is lighter or less dense than salt water experiment 1331:32
Heat makes cardboard spiral turn experiment 1136:17
Simulate how convection appears in atmosphere experiment 1465:28-29
Temperature affects movement of water molecules experiment with food colors 1403:65
Temperature readings of room air at floor and ceiling levels project 1403:71
Warm water is lighter or less dense than cold water experiment 1331:31

CONVEYORS
Construct a conveyor from cardboard box and pens, how to do 1400:63
Gravity pulled conveyor machine experiment, how to make 1400:75
Make a belt conveyor 227:28-29

COOKERS—SOLAR. *See also* **SOLAR COOKERS**
How to build 289:40-41
Solar furnace cooker—how to make 289:43-45

COOKERY
Apples get mushy from cooking experiment 1238:68
Apples that you eat or bake experiment 1238:66-67
Baking soda makes cooked vegetables look good experiment 1238:51
Baking soda puffs up bread and cake experiment 1238:103
Beans cooked with acid and sugar experiment 1238:59-60
Beans soaked in water are less gassy to eat experiment 1238:57-58
Boiled potato cooks faster than baked potato experiment 1238:42-43
Carrots do not lose color when cooked experiment 1238:55
Cookies and the effect of weather on them experiment 1238:109-110
Gluten in action in popovers experiment 1238:93
Green vegetables cooked in cold and boiling water experiment 1238:52
Green vegetables cooked with and without pot lid experiment 1238:53
Green vegetables lose color in cooking experiment 1238:50
How do sauces thicken experiment 1484:50-51
Make toffee candy to show chemical reactions 157:28
Muffins experiment with different methods of cooking them 1238:107-108
Oatmeal cooked in cold or boiling water experiment 1238:85-86

Pancakes with baking soda experiment 1238:106
Size of pot effect on poached eggs experiment 1238:20-21
Taste and feel of different sugars in cookies experiment 1238:26-27
Why do some vegetables smell bad when cooking experiment 1238:48-49
Why not eat flour raw experiment 1238:87

COOLING FAN
Make a simple cooling fan 227:31

COORDINATION
Coordination tester—electrical circuit—how to make 366:236
Muscle coordination tester—how to make 543:34-35
Steadiness tester—how to make 487:32-33

COPERNICUS, NICHOLAS
Who first suggested that Earth revolves around Sun experiment 1525:43-46
Copying device lets you make copies of drawings experiment 1443:63-68
How are mirrors used in copiers experiment 1293:119-120
Sun is the center of our solar system, model to demonstrate 602:unpaged

COPPER
Copper penny shines when cleaned with vinegar and table salt experiment 1435:67-68
Corrosion of—experiment 382:167-168
Hardening and softening of copper—experiment 585:37
Strain hardening of copper wire—experiment 585:38

COPPER PLATING. *See also* **ELECTROPLATING**
Clean copper coins and copper plate a nail experiment 814:91-93
Copper plate a nail 291:216
Copper plate a paper clip with electrolysis experiment 1307:30-31
Copper plate an iron nail experiment 929:23
Copper plate steel nail using pennies and vinegar experiment 781:30-31
Copper plates nail using electricity experiment 1012:65
Copperplate key or nail experiment 790:31
Copperplating a key experiment 1476:16-17
Electroplating device 391:55-59
Experiment 146:35
Experiment 84:86-87
How can you copperplate a safety pin 278:50-51

COPYING FLUID
Copy newspaper print with turpentine copying fluid experiment 1020:93-96
Copy picture from newspaper with soap, water and mineral spirits experiment 1482:56-57
Copy pictures from newspaper 202:21

CORAL REEF
Coral reef—make your own—animal pictures given 730:30-31

CORAL REEF ECOLOGY
Coral polyp model made from paper bag and markers 1339:67-68
Coral reef species; invent one that is adapted to its environment experiment 1339:68-69
Oil spills can destroy coral reefs experiment 1339:71-72
Projects to understand how and why coral reefs must be saved 1339:64-73

CORBELS. *See also* **BUILDING**
 Build a combined corbel and arch from sugar cubes and
  cardboard 557:24-25
 Corbel from sugar cubes—how to make 557:19
CORIOLIS EFFECT
 Coriolis Effect experiment with paper on record player
  turntable 1012:13
 Earth's rotation effect on wind and water currents demon-
  stration 1405:86
 Winds are deflected by the effect of Earth's rotation ex-
  periment 1480:158-159
CORIOLIS FORCE
 Coriolis Effect and weather experiment 748:141
 Demonstrate Coriolis Force on spinning globe using
  chalk 1439:11-14
 Earth's rotation effect on wind and water currents demon-
  stration 1023:200-201
 Experiment 243:38-41
 Showing the effects of the Earth's spinning project
  833:155-156
CORKS
 Watch it float 480:78
CORN
 Cornhusk doll, how to make 1265:101
 Grow corn plants indoors, how to do 1486:27
 How to plant and grow indoors 1178:21-22
 Sprouting and potting popping corn, how to do 1406:70-
  74
CORN POLLINATION
 How to gather pollen to fertilize corn 366:106-108
CORNELL SOILLESS MIX
 Project 384:53-55
CORNHUSK DOLLS
 Cornhusk dolls, how to make 646:68-71
 How to make 231:69; 236:50
CORNHUSKS AND CORNCOBS
 Corn things to make 442:unpaged
CORNSWEET ILLUSION
 Experiment 229:76-77
CORONA. *See* **ECLIPSES**
CORROSION
 Airborne acid corrosion experiment with pieces of nylon
  stockings 1476:189
 Determine pH level that induces most corrosion in iron
  and copper experiment 997:62-63
 Iron atoms and oxygen atoms combine to form iron oxide
  experiment 1396:162
 Testing aluminum for corrosion experiment using acids
  and alkalies 1438:90-93
CORROSION OF METALS. *See also* **RUST**
 Corrosion—experiment 585:102-103
 Experiment 382:165-169
COSMETICS
 Bubble bath, recipe, how to make 1369:23
 Cold cream—make your own 441:40-44
 Cold cream, how to make experiment 1259:54-56
 Cream—emulsion stability test 441:44-45
 Face cream, how to make experiment 1259:56-57
 Face powder "wetting" test 441:94-96
 Face powder experiment to make different kinds 441:91-
  94
 Fragrances—perfumes—"triangle test" to see how well
  you smell 441:49-52
 Hand lotion, making 859:22

 Health and beauty products affect effectiveness of insect
  repellents experiment 1096:139-143
 Lipstick—make lip gloss out of a crayon 441:96-98
 Lipstick, how to make experiment 1259:57-58
 Lipstick, how to make 859:20
 Lotions and creams—how to make 387:11-15
 Lotions as a barrier to the evaporation of water from
  skin 441:33-36
 Oatmeal face mask, how to make 859:21
 Perfume and weaker scents—how to make 387:23-31
 pH of cosmetics and cleaning agents experiment
  1476:134-135
 Rosewater, recipe, how to make 1369:20-21
 Soaps, shampoos and bath oils—how to make 387:15-
  23
 Test various lotions and creams for different properties
  441:36-40
 Viscosity of body lubricants compared experiment
  1396:114-115
COSMIC RAYS
 Cloud chamber—build to follow trails of particles experi-
  ment 704:61-64
 Cloud chamber for observing (advanced) 658:86-88
 Detect cosmic rays in cloud chamber in jar experiment,
  how to make chamber 1476:184-185
 Detecting cosmic rays project 833:277-278
COTTON
 Cotton plant, how to grow 1486:14-15
 Does cotton cloth let heat escape experiment 1499:4
 Does heat change cotton cloth experiment 1499:6
 Does wool or cotton cloth hold more water project
  1210:46-47
 How are cotton threads made experiment 1508:10
 How strong is cotton thread experiment 1499:7
COTTON FIBERS
 Structure of cotton fibers 294:12
COUNT BUFFON
 Count Buffon's probability experiment with toothpicks
  (advanced) 565:81-83
COUNTERWEIGHTS
 Counterweight, test how it works experiment; make
  model crane for experiment 1198:25
 Counterweight, what is it and how does it make lifting
  load easier experiment 1400:64-67
 Elevator model demonstrates use of counterweights to
  raise weights experiment 1400:67
COUNTING
 How to count like a Babylonian 509:9-15
 How to count like a Chinese 509:30-35
 How to count like a computer 509:49-59
 How to count like a Greek 509:24-28
 How to count like a Hindu 509:42-47
 How to count like a Martian 509:60-66
 How to count like a Mayan 509:17-23
 How to count like an Egyptian 509:4-8
 How to count with an abacus 509:36-40
 Mysterious message from Mars 509:1-3
COUNTING FRAME (ABACUS)
 How to make 321:17
COUNTING STICKS
 Adding and subtracting with sticks 304:7-9
COVERED WAGON
 Model—how to make 415:11-12
COWS
 Cow skull—measurement and description 375:10

CRABS

Crab's shell soaked in vinegar demonstrates floppy chitin in shell 530:89

Food habits of crabs and anemones experiment 1503:31

CRACK GARDEN

How to plant 376:20-21

CRANES (ELECTRIC)

Electromagnetic crane experiment, how to make 1072:34-35

Magnetic crane, working model from cardboard, how to make 1073:67

Working model crane with electromagnetic coil, how to make 1043:36-37

CRANES (MACHINES)

Crane—making from wood 429:107

Crane, electromagnetic, how to make 955:34-35

Crane model lifts load experiment, how to make 1028:119

Counterweight, test how it works experiment; make model crane for experiment 1198:25

Electromagnetic crane experiment using boxes, iron bolts, battery 1476:29-30

Electromagnetic crane, how to make experiment 938:109-110; 961:25

Hook up tower crane, working model—how to make 410:32-33

How much can a crane lift experiment 802:30

How to make a crane (Primary) 466:12-13

How to make a junk yard crane 191:18-25

Magnetic crane—making 436:55

Magnetic pickup crane using electromagnet, how to build 1309:20-21

Make a bridge crane 227:24-25

Tower crane with swinging boom experiment, how to build 1518:22-23

Wooden model working crane, how to build 1179:72-73

Working crane from cardboard and wooden sticks experiment 1420:19

Working crane using an electromagnet experiment 1418:21

Wrecking crane uses pendulum effect experiment 1198:27

CRATERS

Comparing crater characteristics experiment 1062:98-99

Determining age of craters experiment 1062:96-97

How scientists create three-dimensional model of planet's surface experiment 1062:100-101

Meteorite crater model from plaster, how to make 1080:29

Meteors pulled by Earth's gravity—make craters 274:10

Surface and craters of Mars experiment 1062:98-99

CRAYFISH

Collecting and keeping crayfish, how to do 1117:45

Collecting crayfish 62:60-61

Crayfish trap—how to make 530:92-93

Crayfish, collect and observe behavioral responses in aquarium 771:164-169

Dissecting—how to 692:39-47

How crayfish breathe experiment 860:175-176

How do crayfish breathe experiment 1293:107-108

How to cage and care for 279:19-20

Observe and record a crayfish shedding shell 166:103-104

CRAYONS

Soap crayons—how to make 732:162

CREAM

How fat content affects whipping of cream from light and heavy cream experiment 1484:107-109

CREATIVITY

Fantasy trips for creativity 400:115

CREEPY CRAWLER

Creepy crawler toy—how to make (Primary) 466:32

CRESTA RUN

Experiment 356:50-55

CRICKETS

A cricket thermometer—experiment 563:57-58

Adventure 2—crickets under a hand lens to discover how cricket plays music 29:16-18

Cage for—how to make 515:14

Can cricket chirps give us the temperature 333:66-67

Can crickets sense temperature—experiment 515:36

Care of as pets 354:36-42

Collecting and keeping crickets, how to do 1117:51

Collecting crickets 62:49-50

Collection and care of 313:43-47

Collection, care and observation of 331:79-89

Cricket as a thermometer, how to use chirps to determine temperature 1464:37

Cricket cage—how to build 395:31-39

Cricket chirp thermometer, how to count chirps and determine temperature 1439:81-82

Cricket chirps as a thermometer—investigating "Dolbear's law" 515:39-40

Cricket chirps give temperature experiment 721:50

Cricket chirps used as gauge of air temperature, how to do 1209:59

Cricket thermometer experiment 1158:129-130

Cricket thermometer, how to count chirps and figure out temperature experiment 959:112

Cricket thermometer 236:63

Cricket trap—how to make from jar and screening 515:12-13

Crickets as pets—how to care for 563:58

Crickets respond to different colors—experiment 515:33-34

Crickets respond to light and darkness—experiment 515:31-33

Demonstrate how crickets react to changes in temperature 174:20-21

Determine temperature from a cricket's chirp experiment 904:104-105

Eggs need moist sand to hatch   how to prepare cage 515:30

Female cricket is attracted by calling song of male—demo with tape recorder 515:25

Food for caged crickets 515:14-16

How to cage and care for 279:28-29

How to care for 32:82-83

How to catch and keep crickets [Primary] 942:18

How to keep and study a cricket 117:47

Identify the territory of male crickets in cage—experiment 515:42-44

Model bush cricket, how to make 1445:14-15

Raising and observing crickets, how to do 1116:22-23

Raising crickets—how to 400:22

Raising crickets and grasshoppers, how to do 1505:35

Set up experiment to see how temperature affect a cricket 515:37-38

Sound behavior and cricket behavior experiment 1097:5-8

Tell temperature by number of chirps 414:36

Temperature of air measured by cricket chirps experiment 1372:91

What kind of odor or odors will attract crickets—experiment 515:34-35

CRIMINAL INVESTIGATION. *See* **DETECTIVES**

CRITICAL MASS

An undecided spring—experiment 586:82

CRITTERS

Critter carrier—how to make 313:4

CROCODILES

Crocodile model toy—how to make (Primary) 466:30-31

CROSS STAFF. *See also* **LATITUDE**

Cross staff used to measure altitude of stars, how to make 1115:140-142

Cross staff used to measure latitude, how to make 1115:140-142

Cross staff to find latitude, how to make using boards and nails 1434:38-41

Make a cross staff 292:46-48

Making a cross staff project 833:97-99

CROSSES

Cutting 392:109-110

CROVA'S DISK

Crova's disk demonstrates what happens to air when sound waves pass through 2:24-27

CRUSTACEANS. *See also* **BRINE SHRIMP; OSTRACODS; SOW BUGS**

Crab's shell soaked in vinegar demonstrates floppy chitin in the shell 530:89

Crayfish trap—how to make 530:92-93

Responses of terrestrial crustaceans 577:project #10

Sow bugs—are sow bugs afraid of the dark 264:37

CRYOGENICS

Frozen roses are preserved experiment 715:73-74

CRYPTOBIOSIS

Can fresh water animals survive a dry condition until water available? 500:143-144

CRYSTAL SETS

Crystal radio—how to make 472:2230

CRYSTALLIZATION

Crystals form from a solution 346:29-31

Seed crystal demonstrates heat of crystallization 346:40

CRYSTALS. *See also* **GARDENS—CHEMICAL; MELTS; ROCKS**

3D crystal shapes templates, making 998:76

A salt garden—experiment 563:163

Alum crystal, how to grow 1342:68-70

Alum crystals—making 83:48-49

Alum crystals formation 293:3-4

Aluminum foil garden, making 883:49

Bath time crystals—how to make 77:40

Blue crystals experiment, how to grow 1476:125

Blue giant from copper sulfate 77:42-43

Boric acid and Epsom salts—making 366:196

Brick castle, making 883:53-54

Can large crystals be made from small molecules experiment 831:35-37

Candy crystals from a sugar solution experiment 895:13

Case of the disappearing crystals—experiment 563:174-175

Chemical garden—how to make 452:74-75

Chemical garden, growing 866:159

Colored crystal trees—making 172:139-140

Creeping crystals, how to make 859:8

Crystal flower garden, how to make 1014:39

Crystal formations, making 807:147

Crystal garden—grow dishful of crystals using charcoal briquettes 565:55-58

Crystal garden—making 172:140-141; 231:79; 748:168; 86:31; 695:42; 854:91; 870:40-42; 870:40-42; 882:28; 898:13

Crystal garden from coal, salt and water experiment 1435:82-84

Crystal garden, how to grow 1063:223; 998:132

Crystal gardens—experiment 605:16-21

Crystal jewelry—making 172:140

Crystal light might benefit space travel demonstration using Life Savers 1394:200-201

Crystal models to see atoms arrangement 1266:61

Crystal pillars experiment 883:42-43

Crystal pillars that meet in the middle experiment 1136:14-15

Crystal pops from supersaturated sugar solutions 669:34-35

Crystal shapes 231:82; 77:44-45

Crystal solution—glue and food coloring spread on glass pane experiment 721:112

Crystal theory 231:80

Crystallization—make plaster of Paris 122:49-52

Crystallization—make rock candy 122:42-44

Crystallization—making alum crystals 122:40-41

Crystallization—making salt crystals 122:38-40

Crystallization—separate sand and salt 122:45-46

Crystals—making 281:26; 40:91-93

Crystals from more than one solution experiment 1342:65

Crystals from saturated solutions, how to make 1342:61-65

Crystals in hot and cold water 147:67-68

Crystals of sugar 85:8-9

Crystals on a pencil experiment 883:34-35

Crystals on charcoal experiment 781:8-9

Crystals on glass—Jack Frost like patterns 346:34-35

Crystals to eat—frozen suckers 364:104

Crystals, how to grow in jars of salt water experiment 1244:35

Demonstrate how crystals form 1405:70-71

Detecting efflorescence and deliquescence 319:57-58

Detecting water of hydration 319:56-57

Epsom salt crystals are long and needle shaped experiment 1479:58

Epsom salt crystals observed 1402:32-35

Epsom Salts crystals reflects arrangement of molecules in a solid experiment 1403:46-47

Experiments making 84:72-78

Experiments with growing crystals 175:24

Fast 'frozen' crystals—make using hypo 346:38-40

Floating crystals experiment 883:40

Formation of crystals—experiment 532:20-21

Formation of crystals demonstration 1023:26-27

Formation of 346:29-31

Formations of crystals, how to grow 1014:46

From household items 364:76

Frost from mothballs—making 203:57

Frosted glass 77:41

Frosty patterns, making 685:4-5

Fun with a microscope—watch crystals grow 538:123

Garden of odds and ends, making 883:52
Gems made from sugar and other household products 203:22
Good to eat crystals experiment 883:36
Grow a big crystal 176:25
Grow a crystal 157:9
Grow chemical crystals experiment 860:65-67
Grow crystals—experiment 563:162-163
Grow crystals—experiment 598:24-26
Grow crystals experiment 723:186-187
Grow crystals from a melted or dissolved substance 168:31-32
Grow crystals from soap powder experiment 1081:25
Grow crystals in salt water experiment with jar and string 1046:20-22
Grow crystals on string in glass of water and salt experiment 1403:50-51
Grow crystals 132:26; 253:132-133
Grow cubes of salt crystals experiment 905:142-143
Grow fluffy white crystals experiment 1405:59
Grow fluffy white crystals, how to do 905:134-135
Grow large crystals of salt project 1296:1979
Grow layer of lacy salt crystals experiment 905:140-141
Grow needle shaped crystals of Epsom salt experiment 905:138-139
Grow salt crystals on a string (Primary) 468:3-9
Grow string of crystals from sugar (rock candy) 565:63-64
Grow sugar crystals experiment 860:67-69
Grow your own—make a rock candy mountain 231:81
Grow your own crystals 689:46
Growing "gem" crystals—how to do (advanced) 565:60-63
Growing a crystal garden 319:58-59
Growing crystals (Primary) 232:101
Growing crystals—how to 733:2
Growing crystals experiment with alum, hot water, pencil and string 1212:25
Growing crystals experiment, how to do 1179:34
Growing crystals experiment 1042:29; 1266:62-63
Growing crystals in space experiment 1342:72-74
Growing crystals in supersaturated solution 374:36-39
Growing crystals on a string experiment 998:74
Growing crystals 147:69-71; 293:6; 472:2224
Growing crystals 589:38-39
Growing giant crystals 319:59-61
Growing large crystals, how to do experiment 790:24-25
Growing magnesium sulfate crystals to demonstrate stalactite and stalagmite 346:37 38
Growing sugar crystals and growing a crystal garden 577:project #26
Growing sugar crystals 374:59-62
Homemade crystals 317:26-27
How are sugar crystals shaped experiment 1293:73-74
How do crystals differ experiment 1293:69-71
How do crystals form experiment 852:18-19
How do crystals form experiment 900:145-146
How to grow 507:1864-1865; 1438:44-48
Hypo crystals experiment 723:192-193
Iron and lead crystal tree—making 172:137-138
Is there space between sugar crystals 396:12-13
Large crystals—how to grow 715:36-38
Large crystals, making experiment 960:38
Life Saver crystals broken by pressure give off light experiment 1405:19

Macrocrystals from salt solution, how to grow 1295:93-94
Magnesium sulfate crystals—making 85:10-11
Make large sugar crystal from tiny one experiment 902:42
Make sugar crystals 598:21
Making crystal columns (stalactites and stalagmites)—experiment 573:11
Mass of crystals experiment 883:39
Message written with shiny crystals, how to do 905:132-133
Message written with shiny salt crystals experiment 1405:58-59
Microcrystals on glass slides experiment, how to make from solutions 1295:95-96
Mysterious snow-capped mountains crystals experiment 814:65-67
Mystery garden, making 883:54-57
Mystical mothball tree crystal experiment 814:68-71
Other crystals to grow from salt, soda, cream of tartar 346:40-41
Paper towel garden, making 883:48-50
Poly-crystalline mass formation—experiment to show 374:28-30
Porous rock garden, making 883:49
Purple crystals experiment, how to grow 1476:124
Red and green crystals experiment, how to grow 1476:124-125
Rock and charcoal garden, making 883:48-51
Rock candy—making 116:172; 52:71-72; 709:18-20; 83:46-47
Rock candy and salt crystals experiments 1063:223
Rock candy crystals experiment with hot water, sugar and string 1331:22
Rock candy crystals, how to make experiment 976:47
Rock candy sugar crystals—how to grow 346:32-34; 1071:82
Rock candy, making experiment 960:37; 980:39
Rock salt crystal experiment 814:23-25
Salt and colored crystals, how to grow experiment 1476:122-125
Salt and water poured on rocks in pie pan make crystals experiment 1014:86
Salt crystals—how to grow 676:20; 866:158
Salt crystals—making 116:170-171; 146:14-15; 154:7-8; 364:77; 898:13
Salt crystals under a microscope 82:67
Salt crystals, how to grow using salt and water 1202:25
Salt crystals, how to grow 1277:43; 1509:14
Salt crystals, how to grow 797:13-14; 935:92-93; 1113:13-14; 1498:5
Salt, crystal garden, rock candy sugar crystals—how to make (Primary) 369:entire book
Salt; grow layer of lacy salt crystals experiment with water, salt, jar 1479:58
Saturated and supersaturated solutions experiment 883:33
Seven types of crystals 883:13
Size of crystals affected by temperature experiment 1046:23-25
Size of sand crystals experiment 1046:26-28
Soda crystals experiment 883:41
Special crystals experiment 883:37
Speed of evaporation affects shape of resulting crystals experiment 1403:49

Sponge garden, making 883:52
Sugar candy—making 77:44
Sugar candy trees—making 172:138-139
Sugar crystal formation—demonstration 293:8
Sugar crystals—making 399:69; 670:73; 676:18-19
Sugar crystals experiment; how to grow crystals 1175:81-83
Sugar crystals form on string left in sugar and water solution experiment 1229:62-63
Sugar crystals from sugar and water solution experiment 1392:5
Sugar crystals grow on string experiment 790:24
Sugar crystals, how to grow 1383:26-27; 1435:78-81
Sugar crystals, how to grow experiment 1124:23
Sugar or alum crystal, how to grow experiment 1480:90
Sugar, grow your own 666:71
Sugar; grow sucrose crystals in gelatin solution experiment 1396:117-122
Sugar; grow sugar crystals experiment 1484:137-138
Sulfur crystals experiment, how to do 1342:58-61
Super crystal garden, making 883:52-53
Super saturated solution—making 147:68-69
Supersaturation—experiment 585:95-96
Surprise garden, making 883:53
The meaning of "anhydrous"—experiment 585:101-102
To show common crystals and their formation 40:89-91
Variations in different types of crystals experiment; data tables given 1004:1.010
Walnut shaped crystals experiment 883:38
Water from crystals 85:12-13
We become crystal gazers under microscope 403:4-7
What kind of crystals can you grow 381:26-27
White needles from melting sodium thiosulfate 77:42

Wonderful crystals—making 146:14-15

CURIE POINT
Curie Point, piece of iron gets too hot and no longer attracted to magnet 1132:34-1-34-2

CURRENTS—OCEAN. *See also* **OCEAN**
Chart of warm and cold currents 299:14
Earth's rotation effect on wind and water currents demonstration 1405:86
Earth's rotation effect on wind and water currents demonstration 1023:200-201
Salinity currents; experiment to demonstrate 840:18
Temperature currents; experiment to demonstrate 840:19

CURVES
Circles or curves from straight lines, how to draw 1299:30-33
Curve stitching, how to do with darning needle and yarn 1299:34
Making a curve by drawing only straight lines 150:144-145
Transference of curves—clip joint 222:68

CYCLOPS
Cyclops, collect, care for and observe behaviors 771:195-198
Make a miniature algae jungle 279:34-36

CYLINDERS
Cylinder strength—sheet of paper holds up book 291:116
Graduated cylinders—glass—making 748:45
Simple primary experiment with cardboard tube 124:6-31
Test strength of different objects 623:28
Using straws (Primary) 24:10-13

CYTOKININS
Experiment with plants 398:130-131

D

D'ARSONVAL, ARSENE
Moving coil galvanometer 63:62-65
DA VINCI, LEONARDO. *See* **VINCI, LEONARDO DA**
DAEDALEUM DEVICE
Show motion pictures—how to build 507:1890-1891
DAGUERRE, LOUIS J.
Who is ancestor of today's photography project
1525:101-106
DAIRY PRODUCTS
Test for which dairy product has the most fat, how to do
1312:43
DALTON, JOHN
Who first proposed the atomic theory project 1525:70-72
DAMS
Build a dam 223:10-11
Cofferdam, how to make one from clay, plastic cup,
building blocks 1094:30
Damage from dam breaking experiment 1026:41
Dams have to be thicker at the bottom than at the top ex-
periment 1374:29
Dams to save soil from erosion—experiment 633:46
Embankment dam experiment, how to make 1026:16-17
Holding back water with different materials experiment
1026:37
How a dam breaks experiment 1120:26
Keeping dams from leaking experiment 1120:15
Milk carton dam—making 759:16-17
Pressure increases with depth experiment 802:26
Sandbox and garden hose demonstrate water holding
dam [Primary] 880:22
Strongest shape for a dam experiment, how to do
1518:14-15
Water dam from milk carton—making 631:110
Water exerts pushing pressure in dams experiment
1120:12
Water pressure experiment to demonstrate depth of water
and pressure on dam 382:92-96
DANDELIONS
Characteristics of dandelions experiment 1063:252
Dandelion activities 236:30-31
Dandelion fuzz grows plants indoors (Primary) 650:
unpaged
Dandelion fuzz has hundreds of fibers 257:12-13
Dandelion garland of flowers, how to make 953:30-31
Dandelion seed and parachute under microscope—
observe 713:60-61
Demonstrate why so hardy and undesirable in lawns
381:110-113
Environmental factors effect on dandelion seed germina-
tion; data tables 1004:2.017
Field studies: dandelion distribution computer project
584:59-60
Germination of dandelion seeds experiment 913:23
Make a dandy tasting salad activity 901:50
DANIELLE, JOHN F.
Project 26—Danielle cell—make and use (Advanced)
654:67-69
DAPHNIA. *See also* **MICROSCOPE; PROTOZOA;**
WATER FLEAS
Adventure 4—we learn the meaning of privacy—daphnia
under a microscope 403:12-14
Are daphnia attracted to lights of different intensities—
experiment 266:18

Creatures from a pond, how to collect and observe
810:54-56
Daphnia under a microscope—observe 713:88-90
Daphnia, how to keep and feed 771:174-175
Effect of regular and decaffeinated coffee on daphnia
heart beat experiment 713:90
Effect of temperature change on daphnia—experiment
10:65-69
Effects of nicotine on daphnia experiment 1267:97-101
Make a microscopic algae jungle 279:34-36
Observe heart beat under microscope experiment 913:40
The effect of chemicals on daphnia heart rate—computer
project 584:138-139
Toxicology test for pesticides on water fleas experiment
950:88-89
Water fleas (daphnia) collected and observed experiment
1402:72-75
Waterfleas, collect and observe behavior 771:169-175
DARTS
Paper dart, how to make and balance to fly well 1299:40-
41
DARWIN, CHARLES
Growth movement in plants toward light experiment
1133:3.008
His experiments with mud and the plants that grow from
it 879:97-98
Origin of the species activity 400:34
DATA
Skill in gathering scientific data 420:74-80
DATA PROCESSING. *See* **COMPUTERS**
DATE PALM
How to grow date palm tree 1486:30
DAVY, SIR HUMPHRY
'Davy safety lamp' for miners—experiment to show
106:42-43
Electrolysis of water 209:32-33
Principles of Davy or Miners Safety Lamp experiment
939:40-41
Who invented miner's safety lamp project 1525:98-100
DAY AND NIGHT. *See also* **NIGHT AND DAY**
Cardboard scene to demonstrate day and night 1111:8-9
Day and night cycle experiment with flashlight and mir-
ror 1023:14-15
Difference in color of the sky 40:242-243
Difference in length of day and night—cause of 128:74
Differences between night and day study, how to do
1063:218-219
Does the Earth rotate on an axis giving us day and night
project 1342:32-33
How night and day happen; demonstrate with flashlight
and tennis ball 1281:8-9
How we move from daylight to darkness (Primary)
614:20-23
Length of day and night changes with the seasons experi-
ment with globe/lamp 1478:26-27
Rotation of Earth on its axis causes day and night experi-
ment 1405:69
Sun can tell time of day 40:241-242
Time—what causes it 40:240-241
What makes day and night flashlight experiment [Pri-
mary] 742:21
DAYLIGHT
Length of day is trigger that starts birds' migration ex-
periment 1062:41

Length of sunlight shortens or lengthens equal amount each day experiment 1062:35-36

DE VRIES, HUGO
Plasmolysis in plant cells experiment 1133:3.010

DE WITT CLINTON STEAM ENGINE
Model—how to make 415:20-22

DECAY. *See also* **MOLDS; ROT**
Bacteria of decay—grow one-celled microscopic organisms 294:20
Decomposers break down leaves in soil experiment 1134:5.009
Effect of yeast on food decomposition experiment 904:92-93
Gas released by decay experiment 737:31
Leaf litter decay experiment 739:17
Observing bacteria of decay 294:20-21
Organic matter decay experiment 950:11
Rotting of food demonstration; bacteria causes decay 1073:89
Why a compost pile gets hot experiment 1440:58-60
Wood lying on ground decomposes faster than dead standing wood project 969:26-27

DECOMPOSERS
Decomposers and release of carbon dioxide experiment 1057:33
Insects role in recycling nutrients (dead animals and plants) experiment 1097:42-44

DECOMPOSITION. *See also* **COMPOST; MOLDS; ROT**
Above ground versus below ground decomposition project 969:73-74
Bacteria; compare decomposition of aerobic and anaerobic bacteria 969:60-61
Bread mold; where does it grow the best experiment 1150:40-42
Buried garbage items, how they decompose experiment; plastic/bones/sticks/peel 1328:78-79
Buried test for rotting; bury objects of different materials experiment 1414:20-21
Coating solutions stop rust on iron materials above and below soil experiment 969:75-76
Compare decomposition of different materials experiment 1323:85-89
Compost pile; large, mixed compost pile, how to make 1150:46-48
Composting food wastes garbage experiment 1150:44-46
Decompose leaves and soil in soda bottle column experiment 1527:15
Decompose leaves, scraps and newspapers in soda bottles columns experiment 1527:12-14
Decomposers break down leaves in soil experiment 1134:5.009
Demonstrate weathering and decomposition of garbage in landfills experiment 1465:106
Does recycled paper decompose faster than manufactured paper project 969:56
Factors that affect composting experiment 1150:49-50
Food leftovers in soil demonstrates decomposition experiment 1014:160
Game; forest recycling game to demonstrate food chains, how to play 1205:13
Homemade plastic made from milk and vinegar decomposes experiment 1476:140-141
Lawn clippings turn into detritus and humus experiment 1441:97

Maximizing the efficiency of a compost heap experiment 1450:34-41
Model landfill, small, demonstrates refuse decomposition 983:13-14
Natural fiber clothes decompose faster than man made fibers project 969:57-58
Natural material products decompose faster than man made project 969:59
Natural plastics decompose and synthetic petroleum plastics do not experiment 1476:140-141
Organisms of many types decompose trees project 969:62-63
Plastic bags/paper bags/newspapers compared for time to decompose experiment 997:97-98
Plastics; some plastics decompose in soil more readily than others experiment 969:71-72
Red pepper in plastic bag observed for days it takes to rot experiment 1414:180-181
Role insects play in decomposition experiment 1096:90-95
Soil and litter in flower pot experiment to determine what decomposes 1013:22-23
Toilet paper survey to determine which brand is best for the environment 1013:41
Twenty items; which will decompose in soil and which won't project 969:69-70
What happens to pile of freshly cut grass clippings experiment 1323:79-84
Which solution preserves wood the best project 969:77-78
Which substances will decompose and which won't experiment 1150:34-35

DECOMPRESSION. *See* **DIVING—SUBMARINES**
DEEP SEA DIVER. *See* **CARTESIAN DIVER**
DEFORESTATION. *See* **EROSION; RAIN FOREST**
Concept of biodiversity demonstrated project 1338:66-67

DEGREE DAYS
Annual conductive heat losses using degree days, how to measure experiment 1152:86-87
Number of degree days near your home experiment 1152:84-86

DEHYDRATION. *See also* **FOOD**
Evaporation experiment—drying apples worksheet 537:61
Evaporation experiment—drying apples 537:15-16
How foods are dried 52:81-82

DELTAS
Create a delta 175:34
Delta formation experiment 1074:32
Stream table activities 400:56-57

DEMAGNETIZATION
Bet you can erase a tape recording with a nickel 228:40

DENSITIES. *See* **FLOATING AND SINKING; WATER**
DENSITY. *See also* **LIQUIDS**
Are some liquids more dense than others 396:48-50
Ball floats and sinks in different solutions experiment 748:108
Boats float; measuring displaced water experiment 871:3.014
Can water float on top of water experiment 836:28-30
Carbon dioxide gas 146:36-37
Cartesian diver; eye dropper sinks and rises experiment 905:28-29
Colored liquid layers experiment 959:148-149

98

Colored liquids that sink or float experiment 959:146-147

Compare density of egg and water experiment 1526:25

Comparing densities of different substances experiment 1526:23-27

Comparing gas densities experiment 1526:28-31

Concentration and density in solutions of saltwater experiment data tables 1004:4.005

Demonstrate density of different materials 295:32

Density affects water movement demonstration 1405:86

Density and birefringence of plastics experiment data tables given 1004:4.006

Density computer project 594:103-105

Density differences cause water to move experiment 1405:84

Density investigations of gases 295:35-37

Density measured by hydrometer, how to make 935:49

Density of a box or sphere, how to measure 1396:217

Density of common household objects and liquids compared to water experiment 1004:4.004

Density of liquid measured by hydrometer, how to make 1179:141

Density of liquids and solids, floating of substances that don't mix experiment 1004:3.003

Density of liquids measured by hydrometer experiment, make from clay and straw 1310:13

Density of plants—experiment 402:27-28

Density of salt and fresh water experiment using eggs 1207:26

Density test of minerals experiment 1266:35

Determining the density of fluids 180:26

Do liquids have different densities experiment 884:48-50

Does salt water have greater density than water experiment 831:31-32

Effect of popping process on volume and density of corn experiment data tables 1004:3.004

Egg floats in salt water experiment 1216:28-30

Egg floats in salt water experiment 1244:16

Egg floats in salty water experiment 1393:25

Egg in salt water shows why it is easy to float in Great Salt Lakes experiment 1403:83

Eggs float up or down 114:47-49

Find the density of liquid experiment 909:38

Float different solids in layers of liquids experiment 937:40-41

Floating spheres of oil in glass of water and alcohol—experiment 532:42-43

Fluids of different densities; which ones are lighter experiment 1243:24-25

Fluids separate into distinct layers experiment 937:38-39

How dense is dense experiment with oil and water 748:107

Heat affects water density experiment 1290:10

How dense is dirt experiment 1527:40-41

How do you make an egg float experiment 827:71

Hydrometer measures density of liquid experiment 1028:21

Hydrometer measures density of liquids, how to make from straw and clay 1212:23

Hydrometer measures density of water and oil experiment, how to make 1521:26-27

Is cold water more dense than hot water experiment 831:28-30

Layers of colored salt water experiment prediction sheet given 748:104-105

Liquid parfait experiment 1007:66-68

Liquids float and sink experiment 1028:21

Liquids of different densities float on each other experiment 1179:140

Magic egg trick experiment 909:39

Making hydrometer to determine 436:44-45

Making snowman with moth crystals 146:29

Measuring the densities of some substances experiment 1526:19-20

Measuring the density of water, oil and clay experiment 1159:11-13

Metal composition of pennies/different dates determined by density experiment 1004:3.005

Molecules cause one liquid to float on another liquid experiment 1403:80-83

Object floats or sinks as air increases or decreases density experiment 1004:3.001

Objects and liquids sink or float according to their density experiment 1014:45

Oil, water, alcohol and food coloring experiment 814:44-46

Potato slice floats in salt water but sinks in fresh water experiment 1310:10-11

Relative densities of liquids and solids 577:project #22

Rock's specific gravity experiment to determine density of rock 1480:79

Rocks; calculating density of rocks experiment 1342:46-48

Solids; measuring density of different solids experiment 1179:19

Specific gravity of wood, how to measure experiment 1075:58

Submarine floats and sinks experiment 937:44-47

Temperature of water affects its density experiment 884:51-53

Water currents and effect of temperature and salinity on water density 871:1.003

Water is heavier than oil ice cube experiment 1289:34-35

What floats in water (Primary) 529:26-33

DENTIFRICES. *See* **TOOTHPASTE**

DEODORANTS
Soaps and deodorants kill underarm bacteria experiment 1221:21-22, 36-37

DEODORIZERS
Natural substances can be used as room deodorizers experiment 969:94-95

DEPTH PERCEPTION
Instrument to test perception—how to build 293:26

DERMATOGLYPHICS. *See* **FINGERPRINTING**

DESALINIZATION. *See also* **WATER—DESALINIZATION**
Collect salt and fresh water from sea water 687:45

Effect of solar energy on making fresh water from salt water experiment 978:124-125

Freezing desalts seawater experiment 1020:43-48

Fresh water—making 663:34

Fresh water from salt water experiment 947:22

Get fresh water from salty water 320:7

Make fresh water from salt water experiment 877:15-19

Of water—how to demonstrate 330:66-69

Removing the salt from water—experiment 180:22

Salt extracted from salty water by evaporation experiment 1081:23

Use sun's heat to make fresh water out of salt water—
experiment 634:12

DESCARTES, RENE. *See also* **CARTESIAN DIVER.**
Cartesian diver goes up and down in plastic bottle filled
with water 1208:44-45

DESCARTES DIVER. *See* **CARTESIAN DIVER.**

DESERT ANIMALS
Outdoor experiments with at night 118:203-213
Why camels can live for weeks without drinking water
experiment 1405:35
Why desert animals spend their day underground experi-
ment 904:132-133; 1479:32

DESERT COMMUNITY. *See also* **ECOSYSTEMS**
Model of desert scene, making 601:unpaged
Setting up and observing a desert community 285:89

DESERT DISH GARDEN
Desert dish garden, how to make 899:162-163
Making 465:161-163

DESERT GARDEN
Grow your own cactus desert garden 416:36-37

DESERT PLANTS
A study of desert plants and their distribution 285:78-79

DESERT TERRARIUM
Desert or woodland terrarium project, how to make
1296:1982
How to make 400:14; 465:145-146
Materials and animals for, how to set up and maintain
475:32-34

DESERTIFICATION. *See also* **DESERT; EROSION**
Growing plants in garden soil and desert soil experiment
1467:29

DESERTS
Evaporation of water experiment 1467:28
Growing plants in garden soil and desert soil experiment
1467:29
Gully to hold rainwater, making (Primary) 601:unpaged
Make a mini desert; plant box with desert plants 473:53
Mini-deserts in old aquarium, how to make 1068:59
Sand dunes formations and the different forms of dunes
experiment 1480:136-137
Water distillation experiment shows how desert plants
get moisture 1467:28
Wind erosion makes desert landscapes, how to demon-
strate 1080:23
Wind in the desert effect on landscape experiment
1480:136-137

DESMIDS. *See also* **MICROSCOPE**
Adventure 10—we make the acquaintance of the desmids
under a microscope 403:33-36

DETECTIVE WORK
Body signals, how to do 643:26-27
Casting footprints 625:43
Chromatography used to identify pen inks experiment
1151:74-77
Clanging alarm for doors and windows, how to make
643:42-43
Color-bar code, how to make 643:7
Daffy disguise 643:40-41
Density of glass and plastic; how to measure experiment
1151:46-47
Detective kit of tools, how to make 643:20-25
Developing fingerprint with superglue, how to do
1151:28-30
Disguise glasses, how to make 643:30-31
Drawing to identify a criminal, how to make 1151:59-60

Dusting for fingerprints, taking fingerprints, how to do
1016:26-27
Examining hair and fibers experiment 1151:64-65
Fingerprint notebook file, how to make 643:17
Fingerprinting kit, how to make 643:14-16
Fingerprints, making 930:12-13
Footprint casts, making 930:12
Hair analysis with microscope experiment 1253:26
Handwriting analysis experiment 1253:27
Identifying counterfeit money, how to do 1151:80-81
Identifying handwriting samples, how to do 1151:67-69
Identifying pen used to write a ransom note experiment
1151:74-77
Invisible inks, how to make 643:28-29
Lifting fingerprints and lip prints, how to do 1151:25-27
Make a photo-fit kit 625:43
Making and examining bite prints, how to do 1151:61-62
Making invisible ink 625:43
Match hairs and other evidence under your microscope
625:43
Microscope or magnifying projects to identify specimens
and fingerprints 1052:28-29
Mirror messages, how to read 643:4-5
Mirror writing, how to do 643:6
Phony book, how to make 643:34-35
Pocket code dialer, how to make 643:10-11
Reading blank sheets of paper and identifying types of
paper experiment 1151:70-72
Rearview drinking glass, how to make 643:22-23
Recording and classifying fingerprints by three methods
1151:14-21
Refractivity of glass experiment 1151:48-52
See and spy detective magazine, how to make 643:20-
21
Sending and breaking coded messages, how to do
1151:86-87
Substitution codes, how to make 643:8-9
Summing up a case chart, how to make 643:44-45
Taking fingerprints 625:42
Typewriter type compared and identified, how to do
1151:78-80
Use fingerprints to catch the criminal, how to do
1063:310
Using temperature to determine elapsed time experiment
1151:55
Visual memory test of criminal; make photofit kit
1253:24-25
Walkie-talkie, how to make 643:24-25
"Wanted" posters, how to make 643:36-39
Writing with invisible ink experiment 1151:73-74
Yarn wig, how to make 643:32-33

DETECTIVES
Carrying secret messages, how to do 812:4-5
Chromatography used to solve crime; analyze pen ink
used by robber experiment 1004:4.002
Disguises to make 812:34-35
Mustaches—making 732:82-83
Quick disguises, how to make 812:32-33

DETECTOR RODS
Experiments to demonstrate (Advanced) 393:10-19

DETERGENTS. *See also* **SOAP**
Biochemicals eat boiled egg experiment with regular and
"biological" detergent 1271:32
Carton boat and detergent demonstrate surface tension
780:28-29

Cleaning power in hard and soft water 83:39-43

Cleansing power of detergents on oil experiment 1403:71

Demonstrate why soap makes washing easier experiment 827:109

Detergent action—the invisible wave (Primary) 109:21

Detergent causes molecules to move experiment 1405:49

Detergent molecules help clean clothes experiment 1251:46-48

Detergent molecules, how they work experiment 1008:13

Detergents keep oil and water from separating experiment 1482:4-5

Detergents remove dirt, oil and grease experiment 1231:32-33

Determine effect that polluting detergents can have on birds experiment 904:138-139

Difference in effectiveness of different brands of dishwashing liquids 1403:79

Difference in effectiveness of different brands of shampoo experiment 1403:72-75

Dispersing oil experiment 741:31

Drops of soap needed to make suds in different water samples experiment 1396:131

Effect of detergents on aquatic life experiment 934:38-39

Effects of phosphate detergents on fish breathing rates experiment 950:58-60

Emulsifying and suspending "oily dirt" by the action of detergents 604:84-87

Enzyme detergent eats egg experiment using regular and enzyme detergent 1435:53-55

Enzymes in detergent effect on protein molecules experiment 1396:25-29

How detergent works experiment 914:14

How much soap is needed to soften water experiment 1396:132-133

Liquid detergent turns cloudy when it gets cold experiment 1250:50-51

Making water wetter 532:35

Milk fat globules—food coloring and detergent experiment 696:34-35

Phosphate amount in detergents; how phosphates affect sudsing experiment 1012:89-91

Phosphate detergents overfeed algae and harm pond life experiment 1331:81

Phosphates in detergents and their relationship to sudsing experiment 1013:88-89

Polluting detergents effect on bird feathers experiment 1479:33

Salty water doesn't make many soap bubbles experiment 1482:6-7

Secret messages written with laundry detergent experiment 1083:111

Soap bubbles; which detergents make the best bubbles project 1210:44-45

Soap doesn't dissolve easily in cold water but detergents do experiment 1482:14-15

Soap molecules spread more slowly on surface of water or oil experiment 1251:52-54

Soap or detergent acts as emulsifier experiment with oil/water/food colors 1476:128

Soap versus detergent—test different soaps and detergents 441:14-16

Soapless soap—how detergent works in hard water—experiment 26:117-118

Stains; laundry detergents effect on clothing stains experiment 1396:28

Stains; which laundry detergent or soap removes clothing stains project 1210:57-60

Synthetic detergent, how to make experiment 1259:44-45

Test for presence of enzymes in detergent experiment 1402:43

Test soaps and detergents to see if they are acidic or basic 441:19-21

Testing suds making ability of soaps experiment 1259:45-47

"Wet water" making water wetter 604:80-83

Wetter water experiment 914:15

Wetting ability of water increased by adding liquid laundry detergents 1403:31

Wetting effect of soap and detergent experiment 905:54-55

Wetting the water—experiment 585:25

What does detergent do to water experiment 1509:10

Which detergent makes the biggest bubble experiment 882:13

Which solution washes cleanest, soap or detergent experiment 804:28

"Whiter than white" soap experiment 1082:121-123

Why we use laundry detergent experiment 1509:11

DETERIORATION

Clay pot soaked in salt water deteriorates when buried in ground experiment 1169:16

DEW

Bottle, hot water and ice cube demonstrate formation of fog 882:24

Collect dew that forms on jar of ice experiment 1014:115

Dew formation experiment with paper placed outside 1012:23

Effect of overhead covering on dew formation experiment 1023:158-159

Finding dew 617:25

How dew and frost are made 291:35

How dew forms experiment 1126:11

How dew forms experiment 1231:40-41

Ice cubes in glass demonstrate vapor and dew experiment 996:24-25

Making dew experiment 767:26

Measure how much dew condenses in your yard experiment 1372:49

Surface temperature effect on dew formation experiment 1023:154-155

DEW POINT. *See also* **WATER**

Color effects on dew point experiment 1479:81

Determine dew point experiment 1003:117-118

Determine temperature at which dew forms experiment 1479:81

Determining dew point experiment 1447:31-35

Dew point used to determine relative humidity experiment; graph to use given 1063:446-447

How to measure dew point experiment 1396:10

Measure dew point temperature experiment 1465:64-65

Measure dew point with can of ice water experiment 1063:446

Measuring dew point experiment 940:55-56

Thermometer in tin can with ice cube, water and salt experiment shows dew point 1439:52-55

Color; how color affects dewpoint experiment 1023:156-157

Dew point—experiment 585:140

Dew-point temperature experiments 767:26-27

Finding the dew point 44:68-69

Observe and record dewpoint project 715:121-123
Show dew point—experiment 183:56-59
Temperature—experiment 128:100
Temperature at which dew forms experiment 1023:160-161
Water vapor condenses at what temperature experiment 852:42-43

DIAPERS
Amount of water that high absorbency disposable diaper will hold experiment 1396:147-152
Compare water absorbing ability of paper diapers and cloth diapers experiment 1479:59
Experiment with stay-dry diaper particles 1412:93
Suberabsorbent plastic from diapers experiment 1083:64-65
Test brands of disposable diapers experiment 1396:147-149
Use of colloidal gel in absorbent diaper experiment; data table given 1004:4.012

DIATOMS. *See also* **ALGAE; MICROSCOPE**
Adventure 9—dig for bones in ancient graveyard—diatoms under microscope 403:30-33
Collecting—how to 500:58-61
Collection for study 505:11-16
Make a microscopic algae jungle 279:34-36
Observe under microscope 889:37-38
Preparing a slide 505:39

DIAZO PAPER PRINTS
Making prints 436:27

DIESEL, RUDOLPH
Who invented the diesel engine project 1525:32-34

DIESEL ENGINES
Piston and crankshaft model; engine up down motion to rotary motion experiment 1166:21

DIFFLUGIA AND ARCELLA
Adventure 22—we meet some relatives of the amoeba under a microscope 403:78-80

DIFFRACTION. *See* **LIGHT**

DIFFUSION. *See also* **MOLECULES**
Apparatus for showing osmosis experiment 1425:19-20
Are water molecules in constant motion experiment with salt water/food colors 1403:24-27
Balloon and vanilla in box experiment 904:8-9
Demonstrate diffusion and osmosis with balloon and vanilla 1405:21
Diffusion in liquids experiment 884:92-93
Diffusion of molecules affected by heating water experiment 709:36-37
Diffusion of molecules through a gas experiment 1425:18-19
Diffusion of molecules through a gel experiment 1425:19
Diffusion of molecules through a liquid experiment 1425:19
Does temperature affect the speed of molecules experiment 902:29
Effect of molecular motion demonstrated by food coloring in water experiment 905:12-13
Experiment 146:58-59
Model for diffusion and active transport of molecules, how to make 1425:17-18
Observe diffusion 319:52-53
Perfume bottle demonstrates gas moving in room 709:49-50
Raw egg in vinegar experiment; data table given 871:2.018

Testing diffusion 148:29
Water molecules move experiment 1405:46-47
What is process of diffusion 402:17
You can see the motion of molecules in water 611:45-47

DIGESTION. *See also* **HUMAN BODY**
Saliva on meat—experiment 607:15
See how a watery substance passes through the walls of some materials 609:25
See how churning motions make food more watery 609:16
Simple experiments and diagrams (Primary) 394:1-33
Studying the digestive organs of the chicken 294:77
Test for starch, sugar, fat and protein in digestive processes experiment 1425:193-197
William Beaumont's process of digestion experiment 1133:3.007

DIGITAL DISPLAYS
How do digital displays work experiment 1293:31-34

DIMENSIONS
Simple experiments to demonstrate 408:1-33

DINOSAUR BREAD
Recipe 40:109-111

DINOSAURS
Activities and experiments about dinosaurs 1481:1-230
Activities to identify and investigate dinosaurs 758:47-56
Clay models, clay recipe given, how to make 854:92
Compare your stride to dinosaur stride—how to do 731:56-60
Demonstrate how a Sauropod's long tail counterbalanced its neck 1481:141-146
Determine if dinosaur eggs were laid in nests that exposed them to air 1481:163-165
Dinosaur built from chicken bones, how to do 811:8-9
Dinosaur diorama project, how to make 1296:1980
Dinosaur diorama 236:72
Dinosaur eggs—papier mache—how to make 731:96
Dinosaur footprints—potato printing—how to make 731:61
Dinosaur fossil from plaster of Paris, how to make 1175:141-143
Diorama—how to make 293:25
Diorama to build and some facts about common dinosaurs of the past 386:67-70
Draw, cut, glue paper shapes to make three dimensional dinosaurs 925:6-72
Flesh out a cardboard dinosaur skeleton with paper strips and paste experiment 1169:28-29
How were dinosaur tracks formed experiment using flour and cornmeal mud 1397:56-59
Make a model 40:102-109
Make reduced model of Compsognathus and determine its weight 1481:97-100
Pipe cleaner dinosaurs, how to make 1063:264
Weighing a dinosaur project 1364:42-43
Which dinosaurs were the fastest project 731:81-84

DIODES
The diode (1) experiment and the diode (2) experiment 563:24-26

DIORAMA
Cave and cavemen scene—how to make 415:32-35
Diorama models, how to make 874:219-220
Diorama, how to make 935:72-73
Dioramas to display insects, rocks, plants, how to make 824:95-99

Endangered animals habitat diorama, making 1013:130
How to make 172:45-47
Prehistoric animals—how to make 293:25
Shoe box diorama to show ways we are littering the Earth 1013:170
Dinosaur diorama project, how to make 1296:1980

DIP NET. *See also* **NETS**
How to make 359:48-51

DIPPING NEEDLE
How to make 382:21-22
Make a dipping needle 385:140-141

DIRECT CURRENT POWER SUPPLY
Drawing and circuit diagram and construction details of the DC power supply 23:20-21

DIRECTION
A solar stone—how to use it 292:22-23
Compass from sticks and stones shows North-South, East-West line experiment 1365:17
Direction concept of N/S/E/W, using Etch-A-Sketch computer project 1021:131-133
Finding directions from a shadow stick project 833:7
Finding directions on Earth using Sun and Polaris experiment 1170:14
Finding North by the Sun using stick in ground, how to do 1434:61-63
Finding North by using Sun and stick shadows on ground experiment 1437:9-11
Investigation into direction finding by radio 420:102-105
Investigation into maintaining direction 420:115-117
Mark direction in house using sun (Primary) 303:20-21
Shadow stick; make to determine East, West, North, South experiment 978:20-21
Solar stone—make your own 292:27
Star directions (Primary) 303:22
True north shadow stick trick 292:20
Which way is north 586:30-31
Working sun model to find true directions 532:68-69

DIRIGIBLES
Make a model dirigible 564:16

DIRT. *See* **SOILS**

DISCO LIGHT SHOW MACHINE
How to make 487:49-51

DISCS
Black and white on spinning disc produces colors experiment 736:41-44
Colors on spinning disc produces white experiment 736:45-46
Demonstrate momentum with a spinning disc 291:129
Spin-a-disc 356:26-27
Spinning disc—making 736:25-27

DISEASES
Environmental threats to health experiment 1267:77-80
How a disease is spread experiment 1267:66-67
Soils contain molds and do these molds have antibiotic capabilities experiment 1267:71-75
Virus transmission experiment 1267:68-69

DISINFECTANTS
Do disinfectants kill bacteria experiment 1395:124
Mold growing on moist, dry and disinfected bread experiment 1038:28-29

DISPLACEMENT
Demonstrations of 642:7-10

DISPLAY BOX
Displays for plants, insects and rocks, how to make 824:88-103

Plaster 9:118-119

DISPLAY CASE
Picture frame 9:120-121

DISSECTION
Beef ankle joint, dissecting—how to 692:57-61
Beef heart, dissecting—how to 692:79-86
Calf eye, dissecting—how to 692:87-92
Chicken leg and wing, dissecting—how to 692:63-70
Chicken, whole, dissecting—how to 692:71-77
Clam, dissecting—how to 692:23-30
Fish, dissecting—how to 692:49-55
Lobster or crayfish, dissecting—how to 692:39-47
Squid, dissecting—how to 692:31-37
Tools for dissection 335:26

DISSEMINATION. *See* **SEEDS—DISPERSAL**

DISTANCE. *See also* **MEASUREMENT**
Activities explain how time, distance and speed can be measured 1355:5-64
Cassini's experiment using parallax to measure distance 1156:57-60
Determine length of your pace experiment 826:15
Determine size and distance of object experiment 1132:87-1-87-2
Distances between stars measured using astrolabe, how to make 1394:176-177
How far away is the North Pole 333:108-110
How high above sea level are you 333:110-113
How high is the auditorium ceiling 333:113-115
How high is your school 333:115-116
How long is your pace for measuring—pace chart given 636:40-43
In space, measure (Advanced) 668:62-64
Measuring distance—how far is it 304:14-15
Measuring distances in the sky experiment 1170:15
Milepost you can make showing distances to any place on Earth 532:92-93
Mind is confused over size and distance of Moon horizon illusion experiment 1062:22-23
Wheel for measuring distance, how to make 1380:16
Wooden wheel measuring device—how to make 723:20-21

DISTILLATION. *See also* **WATER—DISTILLATION**
Destructive distillation of wood 122:82-84
Distillation of essential oils for perfumes 441:55-62
Distilling water 293:35
Fresh water from salt water project, how to do 1296:1981
Fresh water from salt water 577:project #24
Get pure water from salt water experiment 888:102-106
Model solar device for distilling salt water experiment 762:126-128
Purify salty water to make pure water 6:11
Salt evaporator—how to make 507:1865-1866
Separate salt from water experiment 1179:33
Separating substances from solutions by distillation 604:44-47
Simple salt water distiller—how to make 494:56
Solar distillation of water experiment using coffee can, plastic wrap, cup 1427:108-111
Solar water cleaner—how to make 399:25
Teakettle rain—demonstrate 364:103
Waste water on spacecraft can be purified by distillation—how to 564:105
Water—how to distill water 319:39-40

DISTURBED HABITATS. *See* **ECOSYSTEMS;**
    HABITATS

DIVING
Project to explain the great pressure beneath the sea
    877:25-29

DIVING—SUBMARINES
Buoyancy of ocean diving vessels changes demonstra-
    tion 1023:204-205
Diving bell investigation 613:10-12
How a ballast system works 613:42-43
How air keeps water out 613:75
How diving bells work 687:46
How nitrogen forms in the bloodstream 613:20
How water is blown from ballast tanks 613:54
How water pressure increases with depth 613:82
Making a jet-powered boat 613:89
Making a periscope 613:26-27
Ocean depth investigation 613:37
Turning a craft 613:51
Weight affects buoyancy demonstration 1023:206-207
Weight of water investigation 613:32
What pressures can do 613:87

DIVING BELLS. *See also* **DIVING—SUBMARINES**
How diving bells work 687:46
Miniature diving bell 360:88
Simple diving bell experiment 1007:16-17

DIVINING ROD FOR WATER
Dowsing for water with tree branch, how to do 879:40
How to do 358:108-109

DIVISION. *See also* **MATHEMATICS**
Demonstrate process of division with a guessing game
    comparison 457:1-33

DNA MOLECULE
Chart of 366:250-251

DODECAHEDRON 3-D DESK CALENDAR
How to make 1299 86:30

DOGS
Are dogs color blind experiment 997:172-174
Can your dog locate sound in the field and in the labora-
    tory 266:21-22
Dog skull, description and measurement 375:10
How dogs communicate in the field and in the laboratory
    266:93-95
Illustrations of dog's head to show fear and anger 366:
    44
Learning in dogs in the field and in the laboratory
    266:115-118

DOLLS
Apple head doll—how to make 236:48
Corn husk dolls—how to make 231:69; 236:50; 646:69-
    71; 986:101; 1265:101
Dried apple granny doll, how to make 644:28-31

DOMES
Books piled on eggshells demonstrate dome strength
    experiment 960:42
Build a dome on a squinch 221:31-34
Build a ribbed dome 557:34-35
Domes and arches strength test 1011:43
Egg power trick 399:13
Eggshell strength experiment with books and egg
    1011:42
Eggshell strength test to demonstrate strength of domes
    experiment 1386:28
Eggshells support books without breaking experiment
    1229:18-19

Geodesic (earth dividing) dome—how to make 221:51-55
House built from rolled paper has strength experiment
    1024:20-21
Large igloo from strong cardboard, how to make
    1518:42-43
Lattice dome; Stone Age tent experiment, how to build
    1518:36-37
Strength of domes with books on eggshells experiment
    1436:119-122

DOMINANT TREE FOREST
Project 268:70-71

DOORBELL—ELECTRIC. *See also* **ELECTRIC**
Doorbell chime, how to build 860:107-110
Mock-up of a doorbell circuit—making 532:106

DOPPLER, CHRISTIAN
Motion of sound source affects pitch of sound experi-
    ment 1133:6.012

DOPPLER EFFECT. *See also* **SOUND**
Alarm clock on cord swinging around you demonstrates
    721:9
Doppler Effect demonstration with alarm clock tied to
    strong string 1209:48-49
Doppler Effect experiment using tennis ball with battery
    and buzzer 1132:41-1-41-2
Doppler effect experiment using water waves in tank of
    water 1155:62-65
Doppler's motion of sound source affects pitch of sound
    experiment 1133:6.012
Repeat Doppler's motion sound and pitch experiment
    448:48-50
Sound of moving object demonstrates Doppler Effect
    1432:30-31
Wave machine to study wave motion 472:2221
What causes the doppler effect 161:46-47
Whistle and rubber tube demonstrate rise and fall in pitch
    as object moves 2:28-31
Whistle and the funnel experiment 360:76

DOUBLE BLIND METHOD
Use seeds to demonstrate medicine tested by double
    blind method 532:76-77

DOUGHS
Baker's clay play dough, recipe, making 1006:18
Edible play dough, peanut butter, recipe, making 1006:
    23
(Playdough), salt and flour, recipe, making 1014:35-
    36

DRAFTS
Draft catchers for door bottoms, how to make 1152:
    94
Draft detection in home experiment 1063:366
Draft detector—how to make 178:45; 366:166; 399:79
Draft dodger, how to make from fabric or old tights
    1071:151
How to make "official" draft finder 600:30-31

DRAG
Drag acting on different shapes experiment 1095:27
Drag and its effects experiment 881:78-79
Drag on car and its effect on efficiency experiment
    1152:114-117
Drag test with toy cars, making 981:12-13
In air and water—test drag from round shape, flat shape
    and teardrop shape 237:25-27

DRAGNETS
For water exploring—how to make 234:44-45

DRAGONFLIES
  Collection and care of 390:19-21
  Dragonfly model, how to make 1183:66
  Dragonfly nymph—food color shows breathing system used for movement 414:126-127
  Dragonfly nymph; collect and observe change to dragonfly experiment 913:41
  Dragonfly nymphs—behavior studied in aquarium—how to 414:126-130
  Dragonfly nymphs 62:58-59
  Dragonfly, how to make from balloon and pipe cleaners 1182:18
  Flying pattern and behavior of dragonflies and damselflies experiment 1097:116-117
  Model dragonfly, how to make 1445:18-19
  Raise damselfly nymph experiment, how to do 1492:80-81

DRAGSTERS
  Dragster from drink can demonstrates rubber band energy, how to make 1299:55

DRAWBRIDGES
  Operating drawbridge model experiment, how to build 1518:24-25

DRAWINGS
  3-D drawing 162:76-77
  Cardboard pantograph, making 999:63-66
  Drawing a perfect ellipse 150:142-143
  Easy copying with pane of glass 585:125-126
  Enlarge or reduce drawings with lamp and glass 399:82
  Make a curve by drawing only straight lines 150:144-145
  Make copies of with pantograph—how to make 472:1894
  Nature sketching—how to 234:12-13
  Trick drawing and writing with a pantograph—how to make 625:8-9

DREAMS
  Recall dreams by writing them down experiment 1272:17

DREDGE
  Dredge to collect water animals—how to make 9:30-31; 41:71

DREDGERS
  Working dredger, how to build from plastic bottles, wood, cardboard 1460:26-27

DRIED FLOWERS. See also **FLOWERS—COLLECTION AND PRESERVATION**
  How to dry 442:unpaged

DRIFT BOTTLES
  Drift bottle record charts 1000:46-48
  Drift bottle to launch, how to make 1000:41-43

DRIFTWOOD
  Candle holders, lamps and vases of driftwood 236:114
  Driftwood collages 236:114
  Driftwood mobiles 236:114
  Printing driftwood and driftwood sculptures, how to make 646:94-96

DRILLING
  Gas pressure can pump a liquid experiment 1081:15
  Pile driver and resistance of sand to it project 969:19-20

DRILLS
  Bow drill—directions for making 449:101-105
  The Indian drill—how to build 563:18-19

DRINKING STRAWS. See also **STRAWS**
  Building houses with 3:10-41
  Lift drinking glass with a soda straw 291:106-107
  Water rises in narrow tube 323:20-21

DRINKING WATER—PURIFICATION. See also **WATER—DRINKING; WATER—PURIFICATION**

DROP HAMMER
  Make a simple drop hammer 227:19

DROPS. See also **WATER DROPS**
  How big is a drop 381:85-86
  Liquid drop experiments 693:38-40
  Shape drops make when they hit water experiment 1393:27
  Size of water drops affected by cohesion and gravity experiment data tables 1004:3.009
  Why does water form drops experiment 851:46-47

DROUGHT
  During drought plants send roots deeper into soil for water experiment 1180:24
  Plants send roots deeper into soil for water experiment 1183:152

DRUGS
  Depressants effect on tetrahymena (single-celled organism) experiment 1267:92-93
  Stimulants effect on euglena microorganisms experiment 1267:93-97

DRY CELLS
  Bring a dead dry cell back to life 278:33-34
  How to make 179:126-128
  Revive dry cell 381:62

DRY ICE (SOLID CARBON DIOXIDE)
  Experiments with a chemical volcano 87:67-71
  Experiments with chemical color changes 87:67-71
  Experiments with the magic balloon 87:67-71
  Experiments with the magic ice box 87:67-71
  Magic with candles—putting out by magic 350:82-83
  Magic with dry ice 350:78-91
  Magic with fountain—making a 350:81
  Magic with rings, ghost 350:88-91
  Magic with snakes, rubber band 350:87
  Magic with soft drinks 350:88
  Magic with tricks 350:83-86
  Magic with vapor—jar of mysterious 350:86
  Magic with water—make boiling 350:83
  Magic with weighing 'nothing' 350:82
  Make a bushel of bubbles 122:140-141

DRYING AND STERILIZING OVEN
  How to make 57:56-57

DUCKS
  How ducks stay dry demonstrate [Primary] 759:59
  Mallard duck study; its environment and habits, how to do 796:14-15
  What makes ducks waterproof—experiment with feathers or brown bags (Primary) 488:unpaged

DUCKS—WILD BABY
  Care of 390:77

DUCKWEED
  Duckweed growth affected by water pollution experiment 1492:48-49
  Duckweed, how does it multiply experiment 796:30
  Experiments 236:137-138

DUFAY, CHARLES
  Studies in electrical conduction—experiment 627:17

DULONG, PIERRE LOUIS
  Law of Dulong and Petit experiment; specific heats/atomic weight of elements 1156:105-108

DUMP TRUCKS

Load in dump truck has to be raised to what height before it dumps experiment 1198:16

DUNES

Dune windbreak fences experiment to determine optimum spacing 715:89-91

Formation of sand dunes demonstration 1023:110-111

Investigation of the plants of beach and dune 285:71-72

Mini dune collage 359:7-10

Sand dunes erosion project—how to do 715:14-15

Water velocity can be slowed down to prevent erosion experiment 715:94-95

DUST

Analyzing dust from the air experiment 933:10

Collect dust—examine under microscope 364:78

Dust devil model—making 767:59

Dust particles in indoor and outdoor air experiment 1134:6.002

Dust particles in outside and inside air experiment 1322:75-79

Dust under a hand lens 29:15

Identify components of atmospheric dust experiment 933:16-17

Sky is blue and sunset is red; why? Experiment 1322:80-83

Static electricity charge removes dust particles from air experiment 1322:89-92

DUST EXPLOSION

Make an explosion in a can 291:80-81

DWELLINGS

Lattice dome; Stone age tent experiment, how to build 1518:36-37

DYES

All natural dyes—experiments 563:65-66

Baking soda solution dribbled on fruit juice dyed fabric project 1210:56-57

Color dyes from different plants, roots and leaves experiment 1044:44

Color intensity of egg dye affected by vinegar concentration experiment 1396:107

Colored dyes from parts of plants 436:70

Colorful acids from fruit juices used to tie-dye fabric project 1210:56-57

Direct dyeing and indirect dyeing of cloth experiment 1396:107-108

Dye test—filters used to separate dyes 157:23

Dyeing fabric fibers by direct dyeing and by vat dyeing experiment 1259:86-88

Dyeing with plant materials, how to do 784:15-17

Dyeing with plants 236:38

Dyeing wool yarn naturally using plant dyes experiment 1180:20

Dyeing wool yarn naturally using plant dyes experiment 1183:148

Dyes from green plants, making 870:30-34

Dyes from plants and their effect on different fabrics experiment 871:2.021

Dyes from plants, how to make 1020:86-90

Dyes, how to make your own 909:161

Dying T-shirts experiment 960:26-27

Extracting dyes from plants 148:18

Fabric dyed with beets or red cabbage, vinegar, and baking soda experiment 1295:122

Factors that affect how well different textiles absorb dyes project 1296:2003

Fading effect of sunlight on fabric samples experiment 1396:108-109

Goldenrod dye—how to make 530:350-351

How are fabrics dyed experiment 1508:11

How to dye material 442:unpaged

How to make dyes and how to dye cloth 598:32-33

Investigating inks and dyes experiment 909:160

Make your own plant dyes 574:40-41

Make your own vegetable colorings 319:88-89

Making plant dyes to dye wool 473:59

Natural colors from flowers, how to extract experiment 924:8-9

Natural dye colors—chart of 480:109

Natural dyes for eggs and clothing, how to make 924:6-7

Natural dyes from fall plants 442:unpaged

Natural dyes from parts of plants, how to make 1063:254

Natural dyes, how to make 1109:25

Natural vegetable and fruit dyes experiment, make and dye small cloth pieces 1476:132

Onion dye from onion skins; use to dye fabric experiment 1044:42

Onion dye, how to make 1390:27

Onion skin dye, how to make 859:38

Perishable quality of natural dyes experiment with flowers and ammonia experiment 1476:133

Plant dyes—making 659:33

Plant dyes experiment 680:24-25

Plant dyes for dyeing cloth, how to do 1368:24-25

Plant dyes; collect and use to dye yarn experiment 978:59-60

Presence of green chlorophyll under flower colors experiment 1476:133

Red cabbage blue dye, how to make 859:39

Red dye from beets demonstration 1440:79-80

Simple dye, how to make 790:26

Temperature of solution affects dyeing experiment 1396:107

Tie dyeing—how to 507:1867-1868; 909:161

Tie-dye a T-shirt experiment 1048:18

Tie-dye for different patterns experiment 1044:43

Tie-dye project, fabric and dyes, how to do 1417:13

Tie-dyeing a cotton pillowcase, how to do 1499:18

Tie-dyeing with natural dyes, how to do 1109:25-26

Use juice of berries and vegetables to dye cloth 324:18-19

Vegetable and fruit dyes, how to make 928:21

Vegetable dyes from onion skins, how to make 1018:28-29

Vinegar necessary for dyeing eggshells experiment 1396:105-110

Wax dyeing fabrics, how to do 1244:24-25

What colored dyes are found in powder drink mix and colored markers experiment 997:73-75

E

EARDRUMS
    Air pressure on in elevators 55:103-107
EARPHONES
    How you can build a microphone 278:53-54
EARS. *See also* **HUMAN BODY**
    Are two ears better than one 335:102
    Ear structure for hearing 134:23
    Ears as sound wave collectors—diagram 366:174-175
    Hearing and listening—test the difference 134:25
    Inner ear structure for balance 134:24
    Make a string telephone 134:21
    Semicircular canals help balance—large diagram given
        241:46-49
    Show sound travels through bone 134:22
    Show sound travels through things 134:20
    Soundscope lets you hear and see your voice 335:99
    Testing your ears 148:71
    The drums in your ears 686:16
    Tuning fork test for your own voice 335:103
    Two ears are better than one to hear sound 366:175
EARTH
    Air or wind movement experiment 706:76-77
    Assembling a global map project 833:90-91
    Axis tilt—charts to demonstrate seasons 246:10-14
    Axis tilt—demonstrate the Earth's tilted axis 189:27-34
    Balloons—exp. To see how mountains compare with size
        of the Earth 636:93
    Barycenter is center balancing point of Earth and Moon
        system experiment 1062:16-18
    Barycenter of Earth; position of demonstrated with string
        and clay 1394:62-63
    Barycenter; demonstrate position of Earth's barycenter
        experiment 1479:8
    Big time line of Earth 231:93
    Blue color of Earth's sky demonstrated with flashlights
        and milk 1394:28-29
    Bridges—project to show what bridge is best (Primary)
        153:26-27
    Canyons—make your own canyons (Primary) 153:16-
        17
    Center of gravity between Earth and Moon demonstra-
        tion 1394:24-25
    Chart of night and day 246:8-9
    Circumference—measuring (Advanced) 658:67-71
    Clay model of Earth's interior experiment, how to make
        1477:7
    Climates—hot and cold place—do an insulation experi-
        ment (Primary) 153:22-23
    Continent drift puzzle (Primary) 153:6-7
    Continent shapes; cut and try to fit together as in ancient
        times experiment 1383:9
    Continental separation demonstration 1023:56-57
    Convection cycle of heated and cooled air experiment
        1447:27-30
    Crust; balancing of continental crust and ocean crust ex-
        periment 1441:31
    Crust; how does volcanic movement change shape of
        Earth's crust experiment 1477:60-63
    Crust; tension force effect on Earth's crust experiment
        1479:72
    Crustal movement and folds; effect of compressional
        forces demonstration 1023:70-71
    Crustal movement; effect of heat produced by crustal
        movement demonstration 1023:54-55

Crustal movement; effect of heat produced by crustal
    movement experiment 1479:72
Demonstrate our rotating planet (Primary) 169:7
Demonstrate the spinning Earth 161:103-104
Demonstrating latitude and longitude project 833:89
Demonstrating the bulging of the Earth project 833:154-155
Determine why Earth is called the blue planet experi-
    ment 1405:2.1
Diagrams of four seasons on Earth 246:28-30
Does the Earth rotate on an axis giving us day and night
    project 1342:32-33
Drawing map projections project 833:92-94
Earth bulges at equator experiment 1405:68
Earth is a magnet experiment with magnet suspended in
    bowl of water 1507:26-27
Earth is protected from solar winds demonstration
    1394:98-99
Earth system with atmosphere, water, land, living organ-
    isms, how to make 1237:17-20
Earth's magnetic field—activities to demonstrate Earth's
    magnetic field 564:11
Earth's magnetic field—effect of the Earth's magnetic
    field—experiment 532:40
Earth's magnetic field—make with picture of Earth, mag-
    net and iron filings 572:13
Earth's magnetic field angle, dip indicator shows, how to
    make 938:80-82
Earth's magnetic field, how to trace 938:77-79
Earth's magnetic North Pole attracts North end of mag-
    net demonstration 1023:66-67
Earth's magnetism—angle of dip—how to measure
    567:15
Earth's magnetism, how to measure at different locations
    experiment 1401:52-55
Earth's rotation demonstrated with string and washer on
    record player 1394:26-27
Earth's rotation makes the seasons demonstration
    706:11-13
Earth's shadow extends into space and as umbra in-
    creases so does penumbra 1062:45-47
Earthshine on Moon from Earth experiment; make model
    to demonstrate 1478:46
Effects of cube shaped Earth on climate/weather pat-
    terns/flora/fauna experiment 997:159-162
Egg as model of 666:16-17
Eratosthenes measures the Earth experiment 1156:24-25
Evaporation rates of specific amounts of water from heat
    source experiment 1447:24-26
Faults; modeling fault types experiment; reverse, com-
    plex and normal faults 1480:70-71
Filing an extraterrestrial report on the planet Earth pro-
    ject 833:157-159
Folds; pressure required to fold the Earth's crust demon-
    stration 1023:72-73
Game; orbit of Earth demonstration game using flash-
    light and orange 1237:28-30
Geological time scale 400:28-29
Geysers and how they work demonstration 1023:58-59
Heat level of Earth remains constant demonstration
    1023:126-127
How are size and distance shown on a map 900:117
How can a flat map represent the Earth project 900:123
How do mountains affect yearly rainfall project 900:125
How does the nature of the Earth's surface affect tem-
    perature project 900:124

How high and low are the Earth's mountains and valleys project 900:122

How is the Earth like a jigsaw puzzle project 900:126

How is the Earth like your body project 900:127

Interior of Earth experiment; model shows sections/ temperature at each level 1477:4-7

Interpreting patterns of movement in water project 833:138

Intrusive volcanism changes shape of Earth's crust experiment 1477:60-63

Investigate curve of Earth (Primary) 601:unpaged

Isostasy; balancing movement of continental and ocean crust experiment 1441:31

Layers of Earth model, how to make 1042:22

Lithosphere of Earth demonstration using box and slips of paper 1398:21

Magma (liquid rock); what causes magma to move demonstration 1023:84-85

Magma explosive power demonstrated with plastic bottle of colored soda 1480:57

Magma or liquid rock moves around in Earth's mantle experiment 1383:7

Magma rise and sinking of crust at mid-ocean ridges experiment 1477:10-11

Magma; demonstrate what causes magma (liquid rock) to move 1479:73

Magma; gases in magma shown with antacid tablets in soda bottle experiment 1477:24-27

Magma; how does density affect movement of magma experiment 1477:12-15

Magma; how does pressure affect the gases dissolved in magma experiment 1477:24-27

Magma; how does temperature affect the movement of magma experiment 1477:16-19

Magnet; Earth as a magnet experiment 1478:18-19

Magnetic field; measurement of Earth's magnetic field experiment 1401:52-55

Magnetic force field around Earth protects it from solar winds experiment 1405:9

Magnetic lines of force span the Earth from pole to pole experiment 1309:16-17

Magnetic poles of Earth have moved to different places over time experiment 1401:56-59

Magnetism of the Earth experiments 706:41-44

Magnetize magnet with Earth's magnetic field experiment 938:83-84

Make a basketball Earth to show latitude and longitude 292:62

Make electromagnet to show how satellites utilize Earth's magnetic field 564:45

Making a model of Earth's changing surface [plate tectonics] project 833:136-137

Making a model of the expanding universe project 833:122-123

Making a model of the inside of the Earth project 833:133-136

Making a model of the magnetic Earth project 833:115-116

Making a moveable plan of the Earth centered universe project 833:72-75

Mantle; how does pressure affect rock in asthenosphere experiment 1477:8-11

Mantle; putty rock shows how rock in mantle behaves like liquid/solid ex 1477:8-11

Map of with grapefruit 382:114-120

Mapping elevations topographic map project 833:94

Maps—make a 3-D relief map 153:14-15

Mars and Earth have cold poles demonstration 1394:92-93

Mass of the Earth; how to find project 1342:30-32

Masses of the atmosphere, hydrosphere and lithosphere differences experiment 1023:18-19

Measure Earth's magnetic field 175:34-35

Measurements 292:86-87

Measuring the Earth experiment using broom handles, measuring tape, string 1480:30-31

Model of Earth showing position of magnetic and geographic poles experiment 1401:58-59

Model of three layers inside the Earth, how to make 1441:29

Models of fault and folded mountains, how to make 1042:24

Mountains—make a 3-D map (Primary) 153:14-15

Orbits—show by ball and bucket game 169:12

Orbits; what paths do Earth and similar objects follow experiment 900:236-238

Patchwork world of scraps—how to make 292:39-40

Plate tectonics map continents to form Pangaea project 715:10-11

Plate tectonics simulate collision of plates project 715:31-33

Plate tectonics; Earth's plates move in three different way experiment 1441:43

Precipitation records for Earth 1003:69

Proving that Earth is round experiment 1062:61

Proving that the Earth is not flat 150:150-151

Scale model of Earth and Moon experiment with posterboard 1478:40

Seasons due to Earth's axis tilt demonstration 1441:10

Seasons, why do we have seasons experiment 1003:34-36

Seasons; tilt of Earth causes changing seasons demonstration 1434:3-5

Shape of the Earth; how to find project 1342:21-26

Show your school grounds on a sheet of paper project 900:118

Showing the effect of the Earth's spinning project 833:155-156

Size of the Earth; how to measure project 1342:26-30

Spinning of Earth shown with Foucault's pendulum experiment 1480:16-17

Spinning planet Earth experiment; parts face Sun and parts turn away from Sun 1478:20-21

Sun does not come up or set in the East or West exactly same each day experiment 1062:48-50

Sun's angle affects seasons demonstration 1434:6-8

Sun's heat—affected by Earth's tilt 243:16-17

Sun's position at sunrise versus latitude and longitude experiment 1062:48-50

Sunrise not exactly in the East each day experiment 1062:48-50

Sunset not exactly in the West each day experiment 1062:48-50

Temperature and evaporation of water experiment 1447:24-26

Temperature records 1003:9

Tension force effect in rocks demonstration 1023:68-69

The world in your hands—demonstrate rotation of Earth 636:22

Water carves the Earth experiment 1441:69

What are the Earth's magnetic poles experiment 902:205-206

Why poles of Mars and Earth are cold experiment 1479:14

Winter chart of north and south poles 246:21

Winter tilt of axis diagram 246:19

World map tectonic jigsaw puzzle, how to make 1042:25

EARTH—CRUST

Layers of Earth model, how to make 1042:22

Sand bottle shows layers (Primary) 153:20-21

EARTH—HORIZON

How to measure the horizon experiment 958:20-21

What is your horizon 292:42-43

EARTH—ISLANDS

Islands in a tub (Primary) 153:12-13

EARTH—ROTATION

Composition of Earth affects its motion experiment 1405:68,

Copernicus; who first suggested that Earth revolves around Sun experiment 1525:43-46

Day and night cycle experiment with flashlight and mirror 1023:14-15

Demonstrate that Earth rotates experiment 1479:68

Does Sun rise in the morning experiment 1003:26-27

Earth orbits around the sun demonstration 860:31-33

Earth's rotation effect on wind and water currents demonstration 1405:86

Earth-moon rotation model 577:project #36

Foucault's Pendulum experiment to demonstrate Earth rotates 1003:28-29

How does the Earth move experiment 900:232-233

How does the Earth travel experiment 900:234-235

How to show spin or rotation of 91:42-45

How we move from daylight to darkness—experiment (Primary) 613:20-23

Know day and night by watching shadows of balls 292:37

Make Foucault pendulum to show 128:72-73

Measuring rotation of Earth experiment 1521:10-11

Movement of Earth's axis demonstration 1023:10-11

Movement of Earth's axis demonstration 1405:68

Orange and light demonstrate 697:14-15

Paper doll on globe and flashlight demonstrates rotation [Primary] 946:12-13

Prevailing winds experiment 1003:51-52

Proving the rotation of the Earth project 833:152-154

Rotation of Earth on its axis causes day and night experiment 1405:69

Rotation of the Earth 232:52

Sun in your room experiment to prove Earth changes position 1003:33

Why shadows form during the day experiment 1294:26-27

EARTH—SPEED

Clock Earth's speed with easy to make solar speedometer 399:20

EARTH'S MAGNETIC FIELD

Magnetic field that's stronger than the Earth's experiment how to make 1132:22-1-22-2

Norman Robert's angle of dip in Earth's magnetic field experiment 1133:5.002

EARTHQUAKES. See also **SEISMOGRAPH**

Aristotle's ancient idea of what caused earthquakes experiment 1398:4-7

Building materials suitable for earthquake areas project 715:16-17

Buildings on fault lines fall down during earthquake experiment 1383:11

Clay stacks pressed together to form folds demonstrates 816:8

Compression forces experiment; what happens when rock layers are squeezed 1398:8-11

Demonstrate and measure a little quake with seismograph 91:50-57

Demonstrate what they do to buildings 328:63-64, 73-75

Do different materials fault differently experiment 1342:93

Earth's surface distance from epicenter affects intensity of earthquake 1398:60-63

Earthquake proof buildings experiment 1342:94

Earthquakes in a box (Primary) 153:18-19

Effect of different materials on speed of p-waves experiment 1405:74-75

Fault display models from cardboard boxes, how to make 1398:26-27

How conditions affect speed and direction of earthquake waves experiment 706:36

How do buildings respond to lateral movements produced by earthquakes experiment 1398:76-79

How do earthquakes affect sea water experiment 1398:68-71

How do earthquakes affect unbraced frame structures experiment 1398:80-83

How do earthquakes crack the Earth's surface experiment 1398:64-67

How do faults produce earthquakes experiment 1398:12-15

How does rebounding of stretched rocks cause earthquakes experiment 1398:16-19

How does seismograph record magnitude of an earthquake experiment 1398:52-55

How is energy of seismic P-waves transmitted through the Earth experiment 1398:40-43

How mountains form and how earthquakes happen demonstration 1437:84-87

How much shaking energy does Richter scale measurement represent experiment 1398:56-59

Human seismograph demonstration with paper, pencil, toy car 1107:36

Lateral and vertical motion of earthquakes build seismograph to measure 715:24-28

Layers of rock made from clay demonstrate faults and rock sliding 1046:83-85

Lithosphere of Earth demonstration using box and slips of paper 1398:21

Lock fault model, how to make from clay and marbles 1398:15

Make earthquake in a box 153:18-19

Model artificial island, earthquake resistant, to house people experiment 1458:11

Model of a fault, how to make 1342:90-93

Model of earthquake made from blocks of wood and paper, how to build 1080:11

Plate spreading, plate subduction, plate sliding diagram display, make 1398:22-23

Plotting earthquakes—how to (Primary) 400:50

Primary waves and effect of different materials on P-waves 1023:78-79

Recording vibrations in the Earth 175:36

Resonant rings experiment; objects vibrate at different frequencies 1132:83-1-83-2

Resonator experiment; vibrate something at right frequency and get big reaction 1132:84-1-84-2

Richter scale demonstration using adding machine tape 1046:86-87

S-waves; what are they and how do they move in Earth's interior experiment 1398:36-39

Seismic waves and how different materials transmit them experiment 715:20-23

Seismic waves give clues to content of Earth's interior experiment 1405:75

Seismic waves give clues to Earth's interior demonstration 1023:80-81

Seismic waves move slowly through sand demonstration 1023:76-77

Seismic waves used to determine Earth's interior has different layers experiment 1398:48-51

Seismogram; demonstrate how seismogram is produced 1023:74-75

Seismograph—construct a simple seismograph 564:107

Seismograph to detect and record shock waves experiment build with adult help 1476:145-149

Seismograph, how to make and use in demonstration 1134:1.002

Shelter unit for earthquake survivors, how to make 1452:28

Shelter; lightweight houses for earthquake zones, how to make 1452:29

Slinky demonstrates earthquake vibrations 1063:236

Small seismograph—making 762:50-52

Temperature differences among Earth layers cause earthquake zones experiment 1398:28-31

Tsunami waves caused by ocean earthquake experiment 1441:45

Various materials liquefy when vibrated experiment 1342:94-95

What causes earthquakes experiment 900:130

What effect does duration of earthquake have on land surface experiment 1398:72-75

What happens to earthquake wave energy when it reaches surface experiment 1398:44-47

Where are earthquakes most likely to occur experiment 1398:20-23

Where on Earth's surface is strongest shaking of earthquake felt experiment 1398:24-27

Why seismic waves move slowly through sand experiment 1405:74

EARTHWORMS

Activities with earthworms 236:59

Adaptation and learning—an earthworm maze in the field and in the laboratory 266:103-106

Adventure 15—we find out how the earthworm moves under a hand lens 29:77-82

Animal behavior and environment experiment 268:107-111

Are earthworms complex; collect and observe behaviors experiment 1189:32-33

Are earthworms sensitive to water in the soil, experiment 516:40-41

Blood vessel beats per minute affected by cold and warm temperature experiment 1295:68

Box home for worms, make and observe worms 887:56-58

Building a wormery 253:30-31

Cage and care for—how to 279:32

Calling worms by rubbing board on stick makes them come out of ground experiment 1472:15

Can an earthworm learn to tell right from left 577:project #7

Can earthworms learn—T maze and electric shock experiment 516:42-44

Can organism population be controlled 402:91-92

Collecting and caring for 516:11-13

Collecting and observing earthworms, how to do 1433:40-42

Collecting 436:88

Construct a worm box 276:12-14

Cooking—how to 607:35

Cross section of an earthworm 231:54

Determine if one end of earthworm is more sensitive to odors experiment 904:118-119

Do earthworms prefer sweet or salty solutions 174:40-41

Do earthworms see "white light" experiment; worms in box with lid 1397:28-31

Earthworm activities for classroom 1291:50-51

Earthworm colony, how to start 899:38

Earthworm farm experiment 904:120-121

Earthworm farm in glass jar experiment, how to make 1328:21

Earthworm farm, how to set up for observing worms 1173:29-32

Earthworm mating and cocoon formation 276:25-28

Earthworm maze learning 151:47-48

Earthworm race, how to do 1014:171

Earthworm's responses to various stimuli experiments 1395:115-119

Earthworms can learn to make simple choices in maze experiment 1395:118

Earthworms can regrow body parts—experiment 516:20-22

Earthworms composting garbage experiment 1150:48-49

Earthworms decompose soil and leaves, observe in earthworm farm experiment 1328:21

Earthworms important to soil building experiment 978:86

Earthworms nervous system sensitive to different colors of light experiment 1397:30-31

Earthworms observation guide 593:11-12

Earthworms prefer light or dark experiment 1158:138-140

Earthworms prefer wet or dry surfaces experiment 1395:117

Earthworms prefer which colored light experiment 1158:138-140

Earthworms reaction to electricity experiment 768:84-85

Earthworms respond faster at higher or lower temperatures experiment 1395:117

Earthworms respond to different color light waves experiment 904:124-125

Earthworms, observe behaviors experiment 888:112-116

Effect of light rays—what are the effects of different rays on animal life 402:89-90

Effect of water on worms in soil 633:16-17

Experiment—earthworm regeneration 151:49

Experiment with 163:93-94

Exploring the earthworms world 163:86-94

Feeding your earthworms—how to 516:15-16

Flex action in earthworms being touched with end of string experiment 1397:10

110

Glass jar wormery to watch earthworm soil makers at work, how to do 1472:14-19

Heartbeats—investigation into the heartbeats of earthworms 420:48-49

Home for worms, making 789:10-11

How do different colors of light affect the earthworms—experiments 593:42-45

How do different parts of the earthworms react to light—experiments 593:42-45

How do earthworms change soil in which they live 516:45-46

How do earthworms develop 402:98

How do earthworms live experiment 901:97

How do earthworms react to damp and dry areas—experiments 593:39-42

How do earthworms react to light and darkness—experiments 593:32-38

How does soil treated in various ways affect animal life 402:88-89

How earthworms affect the soil experiment 1117:15

How quickly do earthworms learn direction experiment 834:132-133

How to catch, feed and house 231:56

How to make a home (vivarium) 163:88-89

How to make a wormery 128:55

How to test an earthworm's memory 117:54-56

Keeping earthworms in jar with soil, how to do 1433:43-45

Leaves earthworms prefer to eat—experiment 516:14-16

Leaves worms like to eat experiment 789:14-15

Listening to worms experiment 1182:35

Living things need different environments (Primary) 232:37

Make a worm farm 119:100-105

Making a wormery 625:58

Maze to show earthworms do learn experiment 1293:105-106

Maze to test intelligence of earthworm experiment 860:173-175

Mazes to test intelligence—T-shaped maze to test an earthworm—how to make 510:103-104

Measure heart rate of earthworms at different body temperatures experiment 1395:117-118

Movement through soil by worms in glass sided tank experiment 1187:11

Narrow wormery from Plexiglas, wood strips and soil, how to make 1292:18-19

Observation and care of 264:34-36

Observe and record activity in worm observation jars experiment 760:13-14

Observe effect of temperature on rate of breathing 174:16-17

One end of earthworm more sensitive to odors experiment 1405:33

Pesticides and fertilizers affect internal anatomy of earthworms experiment 1450:66-71

Polarity of worms—experiment 532:50

Race earthworms, how to do 888:115; 986:93; 1117:15; 1265:93; 1505:19

Reaction of worms to light experiment 797:30-31

Reaction of worms to music experiment 797:30-31

Reaction to electricity—how does an earthworm react to electricity 381:124-126

Reactions and movements of earthworms to light, touch, moisture experiment 978:95-96

Relationship between earthworms and humus in the soil experiment 1450:60-65

Reproduction—adventure 58—earthworm reproductive structure under micros 403:222-227

Response of earthworms to light in the field and in the lab 266:15-17

Responses to light and chemicals—experiment 532:51

Senses—are all parts of earthworms sensitive to light—experiment 516:33-35

Senses—blue light stimulates worm to move; red light does not—experiment 516:34-35

Senses—sound vibrations in the ground—experiment 516:32

Senses—touch, how earthworms respond to touch—experiment 516:35-36

Senses—use light with and without red filter to catch earthworms 516:31-32

Simple wormery, glass jar, making 897:95

Sound from sticks rubbing makes worm come out experiment [Primary] 942:23

Sounds; listening to worm sounds experiment 1183:83

Teach a worm to turn 163:90-93

Terrarium for, making 773:12-15

Test earthworm for its senses—feel, taste, light, surface, food 380:36-37

Vermi-compost; how to remove earthworms and harvest the compost 1206:20-21

Vermi-composting; earthworms as recyclers, how to keep and feed 1206:8-13

Watching an earthworm in an observation chamber you build 593:22-27

Watching worms in mapped area of lawn experiment 1182:35

What causes wavelike movement in earthworm's body experiment 1397:68-70

What kinds of food do worms like to eat experiment 797:30

Which end of earthworm is more sensitive to odor experiment 1395:117

Why earthworms surface during heavy rain experiment 904:122-123; 1405:34

Worm anatomy 231:54-55

Worm box to compost scraps and soil, how to make 1054:19

Worm compository system—how to set up 276:1-90

Worm composter in soda bottle experiment 1527:19-20

Worm composter, how to make using container and live worms 1228:56 58

Worm dance makes earthworms come to surface, how to do 1182:34

Worm farm in a jar, how to make 932:40-41; 1063:430-431

Worm farm; building Plexiglas and wood worm farm to observe earthworms 1134:3.001

Worm ranch observatory—making 759:35-36

Worm terrarium—making 738:25

Wormery—how to make and observe 507:1910-1911

Wormery—making 436:87; 480:64

Wormery for housing earthworms, how to make from gallon jug 1071:56-57

Wormery from jar, how to make 1014:165

Wormery from plastic and wood, how to make 1069:124-125

Wormery in a jar, how to make 913:10

Wormery in glass jar with soil and leaves to observe worms experiment 1476:116

Wormery to house earthworms, how to make from glass jar 1114:46-47

Wormery to house worms for observation, how to make 1371:18-19

Wormery to keep and observe worms, how to make 1183:82

Wormery to observe earthworms, make from wood and Plexiglas 1182:34

Wormery to observe the way earthworms crawl, how to make 1176:8

Wormery to observe worms working in soil experiment using glass jar and soil 1376:29

Wormery to observe worms, how to make from Plexiglas and wood 1115:22-23

Wormery, how to make 797:28-29; 832:51

Worms don't like light experiment 789:21

Worms in soil, how to count 789:4, 8-9

Worms like wet places best experiment 789:20

Worms prefer damp places experiment 1182:35; 1183:83

Worms respond to carbon dioxide in water in their burrows—experiment 516:39-40

EARWIGS

Rear earwigs in a glass jar 414:86

EASTMAN, GEORGE

Who is ancestor of today's photography project 1525:101-106

EATING. *See* **DIGESTION; FOOD**

ECHO. *See also* **SOUND—ECHOES**

Bet you can make an echo in a dish 228:50

Distance from wall to hear an echo 381:153

Echo produced with paper tubes experiment 1066:92-93

Echoing hose phone produces echo experiment 1476:64

Test different materials for best reflection of sound experiment 1163:15

ECLIPSES

Alhazen's looking at eclipses experiment 1133:6.002

Demonstrating eclipses 175:44

Earth's shadow extends into space and as umbra increases so does penumbra 1062:45-47

Eclipse of Sun or Moon demonstration with flashlight and two balls 1434:9-12

Eclipse of the moon—demonstrate 128:75

Eclipse of the sun—demonstrate 12:53-56

Experiment to demonstrate (Primary) 207:30-31

Flashlight, coin and white card demonstrate how eclipses occur 569:39

Lunar eclipse effect on studying Sun's corona demonstration 1394:82-83

Lunar eclipse model experiment, how to make 1478:44

Lunar eclipse, how to photograph experiment 958:70-72

Make model to show 128:71

Make your own eclipse of the sun and moon 161:94-95

Moon; why you can see eclipsed Moon experiment with illuminated Moon model 1478:45

Solar eclipse demonstrated with lamp, globe and ball 816:18

Solar eclipse demonstration 1023:20-21

Sun's eclipse and corona—build project to demonstrate 585:62-63

ECLIPSES—SOLAR

Eclipse viewer—how to make 436:28

Eclipse; what is it demonstration 900:249-250

Flashlight demonstrates solar eclipses 860:37-38

How to watch solar eclipse safely experiment 958:79-81

Make an eclipse with flashlight and tissue paper experiment 1500:21

Pinhole projector to watch eclipse (Primary) 421:22-27

Projector for observing eclipse made from shoe box, foil, black paint 1478:102

Solar eclipse demonstration using a sundial 1394:80-81

Solar eclipse demonstration 1023:20-21; 1138:22-24; 1394:78-79; 1479:12

Solar eclipse, how to demonstrate 1478:103

Solar eclipse, how to make 941:13-16

Sun projector—making to see picture of the sun [Primary] 716:27-29

Watching a solar eclipse, how to do 1170:32

Why a solar eclipse blocks out sun experiment 1294:36-38

Why Mercury does not cause an eclipse experiment 1479:3

ECOLOGICAL PROJECTS AND EXPERIMENTS

Ideas for 51:133-135

ECOLOGY. *See also* **ENVIRONMENT**

A bog community terrarium 268:57-62

A desert community terrarium 268:29-33

A grassy field community terrarium 268:41-44

A pond community aquarium 268:51-56

A weeds' way 268:77-81

A woodland community terrarium 268:17-21

Activities with ecology 236:162-172

Animal behavior and environment 268:107-111

Animal structure and environment 268:113-117

Animal track gives evidence animals interact with environment experiment 1427:18-20

Animals survive in different ways 268:119-122

Availability of needs affects populations project 1427:15-17

Basic needs of life affect how many animals can live in one place project 1427:22-25

Biodegradable materials—reverse garden—test materials for 399:26

Changing communities in a drop of water 268:95-99

Chemical cycles in nature 268:101-105

Clean water test (Primary) 154:26-27

Competition and population 263:28-30

Conservation—how to be a conservationist 40:197-200

Constructing a food web 268:63-66

Contribution of plants to human needs project 1427:30-31

Decisions about the basic needs of life, how do we make them project 1427:12-14

Ecology of a wall project 740:19

Ecosystems—desert—setting up and observing a desert community 285:89

Effects of overcrowding on people experiment; Asian food recipe given 978:161-162

Effects of overcrowding on people experiment 978:160

Food chain—meaning of 40:191-196

Food resources 263:62-66

Game—ecology tag—how to play 400:14

How humans interfere with the system 40:196-197

Human ecology; ideas for human ecology projects 1297:6

Ideas for environment or ecology projects 1297:5

Keep an ecology notebook, how to 625:60-61

Life in a rotting log 268:23-27

Life in the soil 268:89-93

Life of a forest 268:11-15

Life of a grassy field 268:35-39
Life of a pond 268:45-50
Make solar water cleaner (Primary) 154:28-29
Notebook to record observations on a ecosystem, how to do 1176:26-27
Owls interact with environment to obtain food to live; owl pellet experiment 1427:26-29
Plant growth and the environment 268:83-87
Plants compete for survival 268:73-76
Population—consuming resources—what it takes 263:44-46
Quadrat survey map of patch of ground experiment 1069:32-33
Rain forest destruction affects gases in atmosphere experiment 1427:42-43
Recyclers—make a fungus garden 264:31-33
Studying a plant community 268:67-71
Transect survey map; cross-section study of different types of ground experiment 1069:32-33
Vacant lot plants project; how to study using quadrat 1060:129-132
What is ecology 371:1-11

ECOLOGY—LITTER
Container survey—investigate the litter situation in your town 542:65-66
What is litter demonstration 900:186-187
Where can we begin with litter experiment 900:161

ECOLOGY—NATURE AND SOCIETY
Analyze impact of natural act on man and man-made act on nature and men 542:41-42

ECOLOGY—WATER TREATMENT
How does water treated in various ways affect animal life 402:87-88

ECOSYSTEMS. *See also* **BIODIVERSITY; HABITATS; LAND—ECOSYSTEM; TERRARIUMS**
Abandoned yard observation and study of an abandoned yard 285:45-46
Acid rain effects on water and land ecosystems experiment 978:178-179
Animal population and plant study of a specific ecosystem experiment 1395:145-150
Aquatic and terrestrial food webs in aquariums experiments 978:114-116
Aquatic ecosystem in a jar experiment 1063:210
Aquatic ecosystem, how to create using fish tank, plants, water animals 1172:29-34
Aquatic ecosystems; measure factors necessary to sustain life experiment 978:70-72
Bog terrarium—making 465:155-158; 748:79
Building a terrarium case 465:139-143
Closed ecosystem, how to make and do observations 864:124-127
Collage of ecosystem, how to make 1340:72-73
Cultivated dish garden—making 465:158-161
Cultivated garden terrarium—making 465:152-155
Desert dish garden—making 465:161-163
Desert terrarium—making 465:145-146; 748:77
Destructive changes to nature experiment using three patches of lawn 1328:26-27
Ecocolumn ecosystem experiment with soil, water, plants, fruit flies/snails 1527:76-78
Ecological succession; effects of on pond ecosystem experiment 978:117
Ecostrip—studying an ecostrip 148:41
Effect of pollution on aquatic ecosystems experiment 978:73

Effects of fertilizers and sewage in aquatic environments experiment 1450:121-127
Explore a meadow, field or vacant lot 285:43
Fallen log community—a micro habitat 285:80-81
Fallen tree log placed in terrarium allows you to study life in log experiment 1472:8-12
Field and meadow—survey/inventory animals supported by plants of field/me 285:52-53
Field habitat study, how to do 1063:216
Food web in a ecosystem; observe and record what is seen 1171:22-23
Forest ecosystem in large glass aquarium experiment 1063:211
Forest habitat study, how to do 1063:217
Forests—set up and observe forest floor community terrarium 285:88
Grasslands circle of life poster, how to make 1341:68
Grasslands; card game of grassland species, how to make 1341:68
Hardwood forest—a study of life in a hardwood forest 285:55-57
Heavy metal contamination in aquatic ecosystems experiment 1450:114-120
How do people fit into a personal ecosystem demonstration 900:173-175
How do you live at home demonstration 900:177-178
How do you live in your classroom demonstration 900:179
How does a balanced community function—experiment 371:92-104
How does school community function demonstration 900:180-181
How is energy transferred in an ecosystem demonstration 900:171-172
How is your school like an ecosystem demonstration 900:182-183
Interdependence of plants and animals in balanced ecosystem experiment 978:119-120
Lake—observing the life on the shore of a lake 285:77
Lawn ecosystem experiment; observe distribution of plants/animals; data tables 1004:2.010
Light and its effect on aquatic ecosystem experiment 978:120-121
Log or rock ecosystem; what kind of animals are found there experiment 1324:17-21
Meadow—exploring a meadow, a field or a vacant log 285:43
Micro-habitat study, how to do 1063:212
Niche of insect, animal and plant life experiment, how to make 1527:81-82
Notebook to record observations on a ecosystem, how to do 1176:26-27
Pine forest—investigate a softwood pine forest 285:61-62
Plankton in a pond community experiment using plankton net 1172:35-37
Plant ecosystem study, how to do 1063:253
Pond—observe and study the structures of a pond community 285:32-41
Pond—set up and observe a pond aquarium 285:89
Pond—setting up and observing a mini pond ecosystem 285:39-41
Pond community demonstration 900:165-167
Pond ecosystem in fishbowl shows relationship between plants and animals 1476:118-119

113

Pond terrarium—making 748:78
Quadrat study of area experiment; charts given 978:127-131
Reef; artificial reef in pond, how to make and observe wildlife/plants 1172:59-61
Rocky shores—zonation in rocky shores 285:69-70
Rotting log—set up and observe terrarium with a rotting log community 285:87-88
Sandy beach—exploring a sandy beach 285:68-69
School yard—a study of some food chains in a school yard 285:47
Seaweed—investigating marine animals associated with seaweeds 285:66-68
Simple ecosystem demonstration 900:168-170
Soil—observe the colonization of a small section of bare soil 285:48-50
Streams—the living community of a small brook or stream 285:76
Tide pool—exploring the micro community in a tide pool 285:68
Tree—study an individual oak, maple or other hardwood tree 285:57-61
Water habitat study, how to do 1063:213-215
What is a simple plant-animal community 900:164
Where do people fit into an ecosystem demonstration 900:173-175
Woodland terrarium—making 465:146-151; 748:76
Woodland terrestrial succession experiment; data tables given 1004:2.011
Woods—an introduction to a woods's ecosystem 285:41-43

EDDY CURRENTS
Eddy current motor, making 768:68-69
Eddy currents have magnetic field that opposes fall of magnet in tube experiment 1132:45-1-45-2
Eddy currents slow movement of pendulum experiment 1139:98-100
Eddy motion 243:48-49
Wind eddies experiments 767:60

EDISON, THOMAS ALVA
Battery, simple, making 895:61-63
Cigar box microphone, making 895:67-69
Code set telegraph, making
Edison's electric light experiment 895:42-44
Edison's experiment: phonograph pickup of sound experiment 895:39-40
Edison's ore separator, rejecting counterfeit coins experiment 895:39-40
Edison's reproducer experiment 1476:67-68
Electric pencil makes marks on metal, how to make 1442:85-89
Electric pencil, making 895:52-54
Investigate filament in electric lightbulb 602:unpaged
Motion picture experiment; persistence of vision effect 895:40-41
Reinvent Edison's phonograph experiment 1209:80-81
Relay in action on telegraph experiment 895:35-36
Simple phonograph, how to make 1007:63-64

EDISON EFFECT (RADIOTUBE). *See* **EDISON'S EXPERIMENTS**

EDISON'S EXPERIMENTS
Carbon button 230:33-38
Carbon transmitter principle experiment 895:16-17
Carbon transmitter, building 895:18
Carbon transmitter, testing experiment 895:18-19
Edison effect (radiotube) 230:85-91
Electric light 230:55-66

Electric pen 230:93-98
Etheric force (wireless) 230:77-83
Fuse 230:71-75
Insulation 230:48-52
Phonograph 230:103-109
Qudruplex 230:111-123
Speaking telegraph or telespecan 230:41-44
Telephone transmitter model, making 895:17
Variable conductivity of carbon experiment 895:16

EELGRASS
Food chains and food webs in eelgrass community survey project 1225:98-101

EGGS. *See also* **BIRDS—EGGS; CHICKENS; INCUBATORS**
Are molecules on surface of eggshells necessary to dye eggs experiment 831:78-80
Baffling bouncing egg experiment with vinegar 814:99
Bet you can squeeze a raw egg without breaking it 228:91
Boiling point of salt water cooks egg faster experiment 960:39
Bouncing egg experiment 960:18
Bouncy egg experiment using vinegar 1005:4
Brooder box, building, how to 866:156
Brooder, how to make and use for small chicks 810:72-74
Candling eggs—how to do 723:53-54
Compare density of egg and water experiment 1526:25
Density of salt and fresh water experiment using eggs 1207:26
Dome egg power trick 399:13
Egg albumin—slimy goo 259:18-22
Egg climbs waterfall experiment 1083:70
Egg drops—design container to protect egg when dropped from height 586:80
Egg expert—demonstrate inertia 260:21
Egg floats in middle of jar of salt water experiment 1229:16-17
Egg floats in salt water experiment 900:71; 1006:46; 1011:54; 1216:28-30; 1244:16; 1393:25
Egg floats to show why it is easy to float in Great Salt Lakes experiment 1403:81
Egg in a bottle stunt—put egg into milk bottle 291:74-75
Egg in a bottle trick 30:21-22
Egg in a bottle trick (Primary) 499:41
Egg in a jug—experiments demonstrate air pressure 563:114
Egg in bottle trick demonstrates air expands and contracts 1247:26-27
Egg in packing box dropped from height experiment 748:160-161
Egg in salt water experiment 900:226-227
Egg in the bottle trick experiment 827:72
Egg in vinegar solution loses shell and bounces experiment 781:6-7
Egg is fresh? Find out experiment with water and salt 1015:16-17
Egg is sucked into bottle experiment 814:101
Egg is sucked into bottle with burning paper inside it experiment 1229:48-49
Egg magic trick 27:103-104
Egg rises in glass of salt water experiment 1005:4
Egg shells under a hand lens 29:14
Egg stands alone on few grains of salt experiment 1288:12
Egg sucked into narrow necked bottle experiment 1011:55

Egg survives fall experiment 960:40
Egg white molecules linked together by heating experiment 1250:77-79
Egg whites; do chilled egg whites or warm egg whites whip faster experiment 1484:79
Egg-o-strength tester to demonstrate structural strength of an egg 487:60-61
Eggs contain air experiment 1066:40
Eggs-periment 231:24
Eggshell disappears experiment with raw egg and vinegar 1011:44
Eggshell plant pots, how to plant with seeds 1011:45
Eggshells support books without breaking experiment 1229:18-19
Enzyme detergent eats egg experiment using regular and enzyme detergent 1435:53-55
Etch your initials on an egg experiment 827:74
Experiments with 107:76
Float egg in 'magic' solution experiment 905:30-31
Floating egg (Primary) 109:6
Floating egg experiment 866:157; 906:9-10
Floating egg in water density experiment 829:47-48
Floating midway in a jar 291:138
Floating; make egg float in water experiment 1498:9
Foam made from egg whites experiment 1250:74-76
Fun with eggs 538:124
Hatching—how to watch the developing embryo 196:54-55
Hatching chicken eggs 236:83-84
Hatching eggs in a homemade incubator 196:42-53
Hatching eggs, how to do 901:109-110
Hatching eggs, how to incubate and care for 810:69-72
Hatching eggs; building incubator, how to 866:154-155
How are eggs graded (Primary) 213:24-25
How can you tell the difference between a hard boiled and a raw egg 213:26-29
How much space does egg take up (Primary) 213:9
How to blow out an egg 231:21
How to paint, scratch, carve eggs and make an English pace egg 231:21-22
Identifying hard-boiled eggs 392:59
Incubator—making an 293:21-22
Invent method to lift egg high above ground and drop it without breaking 487:54-56
Invent package so raw egg can be dropped from tall building without breaking 487:52-53
Is egg raw or cooked experiment 1231:62-63
Is vinegar necessary to dye eggs experiment 831:75-77
Lumpy custard experiment—heat hardens protein 563:156-157
Magic egg predictor, cooked or uncooked 607:88-89
Make egg stand on end experiment 1083:78
Make egg that bounces (Primary) 64:unpaged
Make fresh raw egg float in water (Primary) 213:11
Materials dissolved in water move through egg membrane experiment 1403:39
Molecular action of in water 146:33
Molecular structure of eggshell affects its strength experiment 1403:72-75
Mystery of the floating egg experiment 814:97
Obedient 350:120-121
Observe structure of a chicken egg 294:75-77
Observing four and eight day old embryos experiment 1425:4-7
Osmosis in 382:43-44
Parts of egg 231:23

Pickled eggs experiment 563:157-158
Protein; what happens when shape of protein molecule is changed experiment 1403:12-15
Pushing an egg into a bottle 150:138-139
Putting egg in a bottle 293:44
Raw egg comes out through hole in shell experiment 749:71
Raw egg in vinegar experiment 723:191
Remove egg's shell without breaking it experiment 1231:64-65
Remove shell from egg without cracking it vinegar experiment 1005:4
Remove shell from hard-boiled egg with vinegar 669:5
Rolling eggs (Primary) 213:12-15
Rubber egg experiment; vinegar dissolves limestone shell 1479:35
Rubber eggs, how to make using vinegar 1014:169
Secret message inside hard boiled egg experiment 1244:19
Shrinking egg in corn syrup experiment; egg changes in size and shape 1479:35
Size of pot effect on poached eggs experiment 1238:20-21
Spinning egg stops and then starts again experiment 1083:43
Standing and bouncing egg 109:14-15
Surface of egg yolks turns green during cooking experiment 1250:71-73
Tell raw egg from hard-boiled egg 669:4
Temperature of egg affects size of whipped egg whites experiment 1403:13-14
Test for fresh eggs experiment 960:41
Test structural strength of eggshells experiment 802:27
Testing egg shell strength experiment 1143:27
The obedient egg 72:24-25
The swollen egg—experiments with egg and vinegar 563:164
Uncooked or hard-boiled—determine by spinning 291:121
Viewing box to see inside of an egg, how to make 1069:136-137
Vinegar deepens shell color of hard boiled eggs experiment 1288:12
Vinegar makes egg soft and rubbery experiment 937:64-65
Vinegar removes shell from raw egg without breaking it experiment 905:94-95; 977:65
Watching changes in chick embryos 148:57
Water molecules can move through membrane of raw egg experiment 1403:36-39
What are parts of egg 213:22-23
What can air do to an egg experiment 900:3-4
What does beating do to liquid of egg (Primary) 213:21
What does heat do to egg 213:18-20
Whipped egg whites foam lasts longer with cream of tartar added experiment 1403:14-15
EGYPTIAN COUNTING
How to count like an Egyptian 509:4-8
EGYPTIAN WATER CLOCK
How to make with experiments 951:33-37
EGYPTIANS
Experiments of their culture 323:entire book
EINSTEIN, ALBERT
Photoelectric effect 209:50-53
ELASTICITY. *See also* **HOOKE'S LAW; RUBBER BANDS**
Bounce height of different balls experiment 1091:37-38
Creep experiment with wires 585:41-42

Creeping crawler, making 909:120

Creepy crawler insect demonstrates stored energy in rubber band experiment 1024:18-19

Dashing darts 909:120-121

Elastic balsa wood flyer demonstrates energy stored in rubber band 1179:74-75

Elasticity can be used in measurement; simple scale experiment 837:10-11

Elasticity experiment with a rubber balloon 563:189-190

Energy is used to stretch a rubber band; shooting rubber bands exp. 837:8-9

Energy stored in twisted materials drives simple machines experiment 1073:16-17

Force meter measures force of gravity pulling on object experiment 1073:15

Hooke's law—simple experiments 105:56-59

How far do rubber bands stretch experiment 754:8-9

How far will a rubber band stretch experiment 837:5-7

How strong is elastic experiment 754:7

Jumping frog model demonstrates elasticity 1077:12-13

Jumping monsters, making 909:118

Launch a model glider using rubber band and dowel launcher experiment 1073:16

Magic rolling can, making 909:119

Make obedient can to show elasticity 179:41-42

Make rubber ball do a delayed leap 228:28-29

Merry-go-round, making 909:121

More elasticity—experiment 563:190-191

Returning can experiment with coffee can, rubber bands and toothpicks 1436:93-96

Robert Hooke's science of stretching experiment 1133:4.008

Rocket and launch from stiff cardboard demonstrates elasticity experiment 1077:10-12

Rubber band molecules return to original position after stretching experiment 1091:39-40

Show with balloons 92:42-45

Shrinking rubber experiment 909:119

Soda bottle roller uses energy in rubber bands experiment 1377:28-29

Spring balance scale experiment 1521:20-21

Springy elastic toy—making 754:6

Stretch and twist—experiments 664:30-33

Test materials for their elasticity using washer as weight experiment 1380:28

The frisky handball 392:28-32

Thomas Young's measuring the strength and elasticity of materials experiment 1133:4.009

Twisted rubber band energy demonstrated by model carousel, how to make 1073:17

Which is more elastic—rubber or glass 291:105

Why are rubber bands available in different widths experiment 837:7-8

ELECTRIC. *See also* **BULBS—ELECTRIC; ELECTRICITY**

Alarm for school bag, how to make 1020:30-32

Alarm system in lunch box, making 998:230

Alarm; portable watchdog alarm, how to build experiment 1426:107-109

Bath water level alarm, how to make 910:18-19

Burglar alarm, electric, how to make 955:17

Burglar alarm, how to make from box, battery, bulb and buzzer 1382:19

Burglar alarm, how to make 1072:17; 1160:19

Buzzer—how to make 723:21-22

Buzzer and bell, how to make 910:34-35

Buzzer and relay, how to make 768:112-115

Buzzer from an electromagnet experiment 1028:94-95

Buzzer that makes noise, how to make from battery, wire, can, nail file 1076:40-41

Buzzer, electric, make from battery, electric leads, can and wire 1179:165

Buzzer; build electric buzzer experiment 1426:94-96

Circuit board quiz game, how to make 1043:24-25

Circuit puzzle game, how to make 1012:56

Circus nose that flashes, how to make 910:12-13

Corn pitching game, how to make 830:72-74

Dancing shadow machine from coffee can, magnets, batteries, wire, make 1442:55-60

Dimmers, variable resistors experiment to demonstrate switch dimmers 972:27

Door buzzer, Dr. Zed's Hum-Dinger-Door buzzer, making 890:23

Doorbell; magnetic suction experiment shows how doorbell works 1132:65-1-65-2

Dragon model; mouth snaps open experiment 1420:22-23

Edison's electric light experiment 895:42-44

Electric motor, how to demonstrate experiment 972:43

Electronic quiz game, how to make 955:21

Emergency lighting system—how to build 23:43-45

Fan with electric motor, how to build 1076:36-37

Flashing light from bulb wired in simple circuit experiment 1307:16-17

Flashlight; make your own flashlight experiment 1072:23

Fuse made from steel wool experiment 972:33

Fuse, how to make 768:85-86; 910:29

Fuse; making a fuse experiment 1514:68-70

Fuses; how fuses protect wires from overheating experiment 1501:64-67

Game board, making 885:79-81

Game; circuit board game with series and parallel circuits experiment 1307:22-25

Generator, how to build from battery, electric motors, wire, and bulbs 1073:56-57

Haunted house from box and three simple electric circuits, how to make 1076:20-23

Haunted house from cardboard, batteries and bulbs, how to make 1028:44-45

Hot wire cutter for making plastic animals 910:47

Lamp—building an electric lamp—experiment 23:40-42

Lamp assembly (bulb socket), how to make 768:101-102

Lamp puzzle, how to make 830:71-72

Lantern, electric, how to make from battery, bulb and wire 1382:22-23

Lie detector with sound buzzer experiment 1139:76-79

Light—production of light by means of an electrical current—experiment 23:38-39

Light bulb, how to make experiment 1514:66-67

Light; make an electric light experiment 1426:100-103

Lighthouse model, working model, how to make 1200:27

Lighthouse that lights up experiment 1072:19

Lighthouse that lights up experiment, how to build 955:19; 1199:14-15

Lighthouse, battery operated model, how to make 1043:12-13

Lock, electric, how to make experiment 938:117-118

Mathematic machine; bulb lights up for correct answer, how to make 1029:24-25

Merry-go-round electric model, how to make 1028:106-107

Merry-go-round moves from electric motor, how to build both 1076:34-37

Meter for home electricity use, how to read 972:15

Meter to detect current, how to make 1012:49

Meter, how to make using compass, wire, and dry cell battery 1164:88-90

Motor—how to make 23:53-58

Motor effect; magnet exerts force on current carrying wire experiment 1132:70-1-70-2

Motor with batteries, how to make 888:180-185

Motor, electric, demonstrates how motors use magnetism experiment 1034:27-29

Motor, electric, how to make 948:38-41; 1043:38-39

Motor, how does electricity make motor turn experiment 834:90-91

Motor: build complex electric motor experiment 1514:87-91

Motor: build small electric motor experiment 1514:83-86

Motor; basic working motor, how to make from diagrams given 1063:302-304

Motor; build electric motor, how to do 910:26-27

Motor; electric motor in propeller-driven boat, how to make 1043:40-41

Motor; electric motor made from board, battery, magnets and wire 1382:38-39

Motor; electric motor, make from magnets, battery, and cork 1218:34-35

Motor; simple electric motor, how to make 1426:96-98

Motor; stripped down simple motor experiment 1132:97-1-97-2

Motors; how motors and generators are related experiment 929:27

Nerve machine tests your nerves; make from battery, wire and bulb 1253:32-33

Pebble polisher, make from wood, batteries, electric motor 1480:90-91

Pencil radio trick plays radio 1139:79-82

Pencil; electric pencil makes marks on metal, how to make 1442:85-89

Puzzles using serial and parallel circuits made from wood/batteries/bulbs 1476:21-22

Quiz board game, making experiment 960:50-52

Quiz board truth detector, making 781:24-25

Quiz board, electric quiz board that lights up, how to make 1218:14-15

Quiz board, how to make from cardboard, wires, battery and bulb 1382:12-13

Quiz board; electrical quiz board experiment from batteries, bulb/cardboard 1514:49-51

Quiz game, electric, how to make 768:117; 910:16-17

Quiz game; Dr. Zed's Electrifying quiz game, making 890:26-27

Relationship between electric current and magnetism in electric motor 1136:36-37

Remote control electric powered vehicle, how to make 1418:24-27

Rheostat, how to make 910:46

Robot frog electric model with eyes that light experiment; patterns given 1493:30-31

Robot mask glows in the dark, make from batteries, wire, LED lights, foil 1076:32-33

Robot model with flashing eyes, how to make 1199:18-19

Robot, electric, make from box, foil, battery, bulbs and wire 1382:24-25

Signal lights when someone enters your room, how to make 870:88-90

Simple motor from battery, magnet and copper wire experiment 1139:94-95

Solenoid and electric meter, how to make 1020:25-30

Solenoid controlled signal, how to make 910:40-41

Spinning paint model machine makes colorful paint patterns, how to make 1043:44-45

Steadiness detector lights up if your hand trembles, how to make 1029:26-27

Steadiness hand tester, how to make 1418:16-17

Steadiness of hands tester, how to make 1218:16-17

Steadiness tester game experiment using batteries, wire and bulb 1043:18-19

Steadiness tester, how to make 910:14

Steadiness tester; how steady are you electric testers, making 768:115-116

Steady hand game experiment using battery, bulb and wire 1072:20

Steady hand game, how to make 955:20

Steady hand game, how to make using battery, bulb and wire 1016:44-45

Stock car with working headlights and turn signals, how to make and wire 1076:24-27

Switch, electric, how to make 768:105

Switch, how to make 828:33

Switches, 2 way and 3 way, how to make 910:8-11

Switches, several types to build, how to do 830:36

Switches; simple and double switch, how to make 1073:62

Table top penny pitching game, making 768:116

Toy robot eyes light up experiment using simple circuit 1418:13-14

Traffic lights, electric, how to make from box, battery, bulbs and wire 1382:26-27

Train; electric train working model, how to make 1043:42-43

Transformer, how to make 768:99-101

Trolley with electric motor moves things experiment 1299:57

Winch; electric winch from wood, string and small motor, how to make 1160:29

ELECTRIC CELL
Lemon electric cell experiment; use lemon and strips of copper and zinc 1218:39

ELECTRIC MOTORS. See also MOTORS—ELECTRIC
Faraday, Michael; who invented the electric motor project 1525:35-37

Rocking motor made from milk carton, ruler, batteries, wire 1442:90-96

Slow moving electric motor, how to make using milk carton/batteries/wire 1442:97-109

ELECTRICITY. See also BATTERIES AND CIRCUITS; ELECTRIC; GENERATORS
AC induction motor, making 627:61

Alternating current howler—how to make 577:project 62

Ammeter—make a hot wire ammeter 127:44-48

And water—make a saltwater switch 287:28

Bar magnet—wire and compass demonstrate electricity (Primary) 711:10-13

Bare wires produce a short circuit 65:50-51

Battery—make a dime and penny battery 185:16-18

Battery—voltaic cell and galvanometer—how to make 13:32-41

Battery—wet cell battery 391:50-54

Battery and tinfoil make bulb light experiment 782:30-33

Battery from strip of zinc and copper pipe in water, how to make 1179:150-151

Battery, bulb, and circuit experiment 888:154-157

Bell—dry cell, wires and doorbell—making 425:unpaged

Bell—construct to show power of electromagnet 167:114-119

Bell—demonstrate how a bell rings 185:47-49

Bell—how to make 391:101-108; 507:1869-1870; 677:25

Bell—how to make an electric bell 128:179-180

Bell—how to wire a bell for your room 278:48

Bending water with electricity 586:95-96

Bulb holder—how to use 400:89

Burglar alarm—how to make 13:106-110; 191:54-55

Buzzer—how to make 128:178-179; 191:49-55; 267:48-49

Buzzer—make a homemade buzzer 127:73-76

Buzzer, how to make 625:63

Can electricity make ions that change neutral water to a base experiment 831:58-60

Can ions carry electricity 396:64-66

Can mechanical energy produce electricity experiment 902:254-255

Can ocean waves be used to generate electricity experiment 997:76-77

Cell—how electric cell is made 381:57-58

Cell—lemon battery demonstrates property of electric cell 293:32

Cells—project 26—Danielle cell—make and use 654:67-69

Cells—project 27—Danielle cell experiment (Advanced) 654:69-70

Change water to gases with electricity 147:111-114

Charge some things by rubbing them 587:51

Chemical reaction battery gives electricity Volta's way experiment 1063:164

Compass can detect a current of electricity 65:62-63

Conductors and non conductors—experiment 693:33-35

DC power supply—drawing and circuit diagram and construction details 23:20-21

Demonstrate 'seeing' an alternating current 176:71

Detector—how to build simple one 23:3-5

Direct current motor—how to make 577:project 61

Direction of charge flow—design experiments to show 586:105

Does ice conduct electricity experiment 895:29-30

Dry cell—revive dry cell 381:62

Dynamo on bicycles, how to test for electricity experiment 1072:10

Earthworms reaction to electricity experiment 768:84-85

Eddy current brake—how to make 585:165

Electric air car—working model 577:project #54

Electric alarms—how to make 23:59

Electric arc lamps, making 627:54

Electric bell transformers, experiments with 532:97

Electric bulb—make a 'magic bulb' 127:35-39

Electric bulb—making a bulb 400:89

Electric cell—how to make simple one 128:170

Electric chime 577:project #53

Electric current detectors—how to make 445:14-15

Electric field—discover magnetic property of an electric field 293:34

Electric flag 391:140-145

Electric fuse—find out how to make a fuse 599:40; 610:65

Electric fuse—how a fuse works 96:80-81

Electric fuse—make a fuse 287:27

Electric fuse—make a fuse of metal foil 127:27-31

Electric fuse—show function of 185:42-46

Electric fuse—show purpose of fuse circuit breaker 179:137-139

Electric generator—how to make 507:1874-1875

Electric hammer 391:146-150

Electric lamp—make a lamp on twelve potatoes 176:69-70

Electric lamp—making an electric lamp 281:92-93

Electric light—Edison's experiment 230:55-56

Electric light bulb—how to make 341:38-40

Electric light bulb 391:65-69; 391:65-69

Electric light switch—how to make 610:62-63

Electric light under water—experiment 585:59-60

Electric lock—make a secret magnetic lock 127:82-87

Electric maxi motor, how to make and experiment with changes 647:85-118

Electric maxi motor, how to make 647:85-94

Electric maxi, midi, and mini motors—make them work for you 647:120-123

Electric meter—homemade meter detects small electric currents 381:47-50

Electric meter—how to read 391:87-90

Electric meter—making 693:46-47

Electric meter—reading the meter—how to 585:164-165

Electric meter—record watts used by electrical equipment in home 333:17-20

Electric midi motor, how to make and experiment with changes 647:53-84

Electric midi motor, how to make 647:18-24; 647:53-64

Electric mini motor, how to make and experiment with changes 647:18-52

Electric motor 391:131-139

Electric motor—an electric motor you can make 267:46-48

Electric motor—build an electric motor 253:157-159

Electric motor—build and measure speed of electric motor 209:34-36

Electric motor—construct an 167:124-130

Electric motor—how to make 23:53-58; 191:39-48; 278:57-59; 929:25

Electric motor—magnetic crane, making 647:121

Electric motor—make a hot shot motor 127:114-134

Electric motor—make a model electromagnetic crane 267:45

Electric motor—make a real electric motor 179:164-170

Electric motor—make a simple electric motor 227:10-11; 360:48-50; 385:148-150

Electric motor—make a tin can wonder motor 127:104-113

Electric motor—make an electric motor from nails 186:122-123

Electric motor—make an electric motor with an electromagnet 385:150-151

Electric motor—making a pin and cork electric motor 599:46-49

Electric motor—model 12:67-72

Electric motor, how to make 655:15-16; 948:38-41

Electric multiple choice questioner—how to make 577:project 60

Electric nerve machine—find out how to make a nerve machine 599:30-31

Electric night-light—how to make 585:61-62

Electric pen—Edison's experiments 230:93-98

Electric pendulum—how to make 532:90-91
Electric photometer—how to make a light meter 13:105-106
Electric projects—twelve keys to better projects 391:151-155
Electric questioner for matching tests—how to make 532:88-89
Electric quiz game—how to build 278:43-45
Electric quiz game—test skills and knowledge of friends 436:28-29
Electric sparks with a battery—make 176:77-78
Electric swing—making 608:19-20
Electric switch—how to make 487:30-31
Electric switch—make from a coffee can 436:30
Electric thermometer—how to make 13:102-105
Electric transformer from a C Clamp—making 532:96
Electrical color change—experiment 585:162-163
Electrical energy—electric motor 49:134-136
Electrical games using conductors and insulators—making 677:15-17
Electricity and magnetism are related experiment with battery/nail/wires 1404:48-49
Electricity can make a magnet 65:64-65; 96:82
Electricity can produce heat 281:94-95
Electricity causes heat 96:79-80
Electricity for home appliances not as expensive as people think project 1021:86-88
Electricity from a lemon—experiments 563:109-110
Electricity from a lemon experiment 895:6-7
Electricity from fruit and nails 586:99-100
Electricity is used to plate certain objects 65:72-73
Electricity produces heat and light experiment 768:79-80
Electricity produces heat 65:44-45
Electricity produces light 65:46-47
Electricity produces magnetism experiment 910:36-37
Electricity produces magnetism 281:91-92
Electrifying journey device tests hand steadiness 605:58-63
Electrodes—take salt apart—how to 127:54-59
Electrolyte current—detector (galvanometer) how to make 346:80-87
Electromagnets, making 910:36-39
Electrons—flow of conductors and insulators resisters—how to make 13:97-101
Electrons flow generates heat experiment with battery and foil 1404:10-11
Electrons move demonstration experiment with foil leaves in jar 1404:18-19
Electroplating—demonstrate 138:21
Electroscope device from tape and straws detects electrical charge experiment 1132:47-1-47-2
Energy and electric charge—experiment 586:103-105
Experiments with electric lights 127:11-18
Experiments with electric welding and cutting 127:32-34
Experiments with 186:81-93
Faraday's discovery; electricity from magnets experiment 1514:94-98
Faraday's experiment—electricity can be converted into magnetism 23:5-6
Faraday's experiment to make electricity experiment 973:43
Faraday's movement of current-carrying wire in a magnetic field experiment 1133:5.010
Faraday's way with magnetism producing electricity experiment 1063:165

Faraday, Michael—experiment—make electricity with magnet & coil of wire 445:17
Filaments and fuses—show 138:20
Find out how to light a small torch (flashlight) bulb 599:25-27
Flashing badge—how to make with batteries 76:26-27
Flashlight—how to build a flashlight 278:36
Flashlight, how it works experiment 906:104
Fluorescent tube, how it works experiment 1404:42
Force of attraction between charged particles demonstration experiment 1404:20-21
Franklin's experiment 12:50
From a battery 40:65-67
From light—photovoltaic cell or self generating cell—how to make 13:119-130
Fuse—how does it work—the short circuit 291:170
Fuse made from steel wool experiment 972:33
Fuse used to keep wires from getting too hot 65:56-57
Generate electricity with a magnet 253:156
Generate electricity with salt and lemons 253:152-153
Generating electricity with bar magnet generator 586:106-107
Generator 391:121-130
Generator—how to make a generator 278:54-56; 381:58-59
Generator—Van de Graaff generator—how to build 13:19-31
Generator, Faraday's electric generator, making 627:38
Generators; how motors and generators are related experiment 929:27
Get heat from electric power 138:19
Getting electricity from lemon experiment 768:78-79
Gilbert's versorium experiment 627:9
Halloween mask with lit up nose—how to make 127:51-53
Heater—demonstrate how electric heater works 291:166
Heater—experiment to show how it works 291:166
Heater for laboratory—how to make 57:55-56
How does electricity produce movement experiment 1501:8-11
How is electricity produced by chemical means experiment 902:249-250
How to make a simple cell 186:88
How to make hook up with batteries 127:5-10
How to measure 23:24-30
Identifying solids that will conduct electricity 180:47
Incandescent bulb—how to make 278:42
Investigating a dry cell 180:45
'Jacob's ladder'—make a 291:168-169
Lamp—how to wire 278:49-50
Law of attraction—experiment to show positive/negative charges 91:74-84
Lemon battery experiment (Primary) 567:7
Lemon wet cell battery—making 608:45-46
Lemons produce electricity 599:36-37
Light bulb—how to make 366:232
Light one bulb with two batteries experiment [Primary] 743:28
Lights can be wired in series 65:68-69
Liquids permit electricity to flow experiment 1426:55-57
Live wire is magnetic 65:60-61
Magnetic current—Faradays' discovery 23:5-6
Magnetism and electro magnets 23:46-52
Magnetism from electricity experiment 973:39
Magnetism produces electricity experiment 768:97-99

Magnets and electro magnets 72:50-53
Make an electricity detector 138:22
Make cylinder electrical machine to provide electric charge 172:158-161
Make electricity with wire wound around box and compass experiment 972:45
Make two light dimmers 127:22-26
Makes heat 238:30-31
Making a 'nervousness' tester 179:133-134
Materials that conduct electricity experiment with batteries, bulb, foil 1404:8-9
Materials that will conduct electricity experiment 1029:20-21
Measure speed of electric motor 209:34-36
Metal engraving tool—how to make an electric one 191:29-34
Metals are good conductors of electricity 65:76-77
Meter measures electricity used by house, how to read experiment 1426:38-39
Meters—how to read a watt hour ampere 278:63-64
Miniature lightning and thunder device 12:50-52
Mock-up of a doorbell circuit—making 532:106
Mock-up of a three-way electric lamp circuit—making 532:107
Model of circuit—how to make 91:85-88
Mouse in hole trick using coil, circuit and switch 127:77-81
Mystery light from friction tape 585:163-164
Ohm's Law experiment with current, voltage and resistance 1133:5.009
Ohm, Georg Simon; who discovered laws of flow of electricity project 1525:95-97
Oral electricity in your mouth 291:163
Photovoltaic cell produces electrical energy experiment 1502:69-70
Piezoelectricity; generate sound from piezoelectricity experiment 1426:31
Piezoelectricity; how can piezoelectricity be generated experiment 1426:26-29
Piezoelectricity; how does patio gas grill igniter work experiment 1426:30
Piezoelectricity; light a barbecue gas lighter experiment 1426:29-30
Piezoelectricity; make inexpensive surround sound experiment 1426:32-33
Plant growth affected by electrical stimulation experiment 1061:89
Pokerino game—how to make 23:63-70
Power station—make a potato power station 142:56
Produce electricity with a magnet and coil 128:181
Producing a charge with friction 180:44-45
Project 21—what voltmeter measures (Advanced) 654:58-60
Project 22—meters in home and school 654:60-61
Project 23—vacuum tube conducts electric charge 654:61-63
Project 31—generating electricity 654:72-73
Quiz board—make an electric quiz board 142:56-57
Repeat Michael Faraday's electricity from magnetism—experiment 448:44-45
Rheostat—making 585:178
Series use of—slow the fan down—experiment 585:179
Short circuit causes bell not to ring 65:54-55
Short circuit causes continuous ring 65:52-53
Show how it is made 40:68-70
Show why some wires heat up and give up light 179:130-132
Signaling by sound and light 127:88-92
Signaling light—how to make with batteries 76:24-25
Simple 'wet' cell experiment 23:11-12
Simple circuit—wire—battery and bulb experiment [Primary] 743:27
Simple electric motor that works—how to make 545:42-49
Solar cell experiment to make electricity 289:55
Solar cells—using 608:54-55
Solar electric system, how to make 1426:112-114
Solenoid and electric meter, how to make 1020:25-30
Sparkler—make a nail file sparkler 127:19-21
Split water into gases 146:34-35
Store electricity in a lead cell 138:18
Storing electricity in a lead-acid cell experiment 972:39
Switch—find out how to make a switch 599:27-28
Switch—how to make simple ones 128:173
Switch—making a 96:78-79; 655:32
Switch—making an electric switch 138:7
Switch—show how it works 185:32-36
Switch—switch lamp from series to parallel 291:167
Switch used to open and close a circuit 65:48-49
Switches—mercury switch—how to 391:31-34
Switches make lights/other appliances turn on/off from different places 391:27-30
Telegraph—how to make a telegraph set 185:53-59
Test for polarity using a potato 176:71-72
Testing materials that might conduct electricity 180:46
Thermo electricity—Seebeck effect—how to produce 13:111-113
Thermocouple—making 608:55-56
Thermocouple and thermopile—how to show 13:114-118
Thermocouples, electricity by—experiment 627:35
Toys—how to make electric boxes 172:143-145
Transformer—make your own transformer 291:165
Transformer—make your own 291:165
Turbine wheel—making 655:21
Ultra simple lemon battery demonstrates Volta's famous discovery 23:3-5
Use a potato to test current 127:98-100
Use of circuit 40:67-68
Using salt to conduct electricity 180:48
Variable resistor—how to make 176:69
Voltage drop—demonstrate 287:20
Voltaic pile—produce continuous current of electrons by means of 184:224-225
Voltaic pile—produce electric current with pairs of unlike metals 184:228-229
Water conducts electricity experiment with battery, light and salt water 972:35
Watts used in a house by each piece of equipment—test and record 333:17-20
Wave generator, making 647:122
Ways to save electricity 138:23
What does a voltmeter measure 586:105-106
What is resistance experiment 902:237
Which rocks conduct electricity experiment 900:141-142
Why does wire conduct electricity experiment 860:92-97
Wind turbine makes electricity experiment 1426:114-118
Windmill model to generate electricity—how to build 762:130-134
Wire a cardboard house for electricity experiment 1426:81-82

120

Wires give off light experiment 938:39-40
Working model of an electric lock 577:project #52
Yehudi's flashlight—make a 127:40-43

ELECTRICITY—BATTERIES. *See also* **BATTERIES; BATTERIES AND CIRCUITS**
Batteries 17:75-78
Battery 72:47-49
Battery—how to make 138:9; 278:32-33
Battery holder—how to make 400:89
Battery wire—positive/negative test using a potato 563:94-95
Connecting bulbs in parallel 102:32-35
Connecting bulbs in series 102:29-31
Connecting dry cells in parallel 102:25-28
Connecting dry cells in series E 102:21-24
Controlling a bulb from two different places 102:46-48
Demonstrate simple circuits 102:13-18
Demonstration panel of a dry cell 102:125-126
Edison's lamp 102:49-51
Electric fuses 102:36-39
Electrolysis of salt water 102:114-115
How does dry-cell or flashlight battery work experiment 902:251-252
Operating a bell from two different points 102:44-45
Produce electricity with a lemon experiment 902:253
Schematic diagrams 102:19-20
Simple conduction tester 102:40-43
Stunts—counterfeit coin detector 102:132-133
Stunts—dancing icicles 102:154-156
Stunts—electric maze 102:123-124
Stunts—electric writing 102:111-113
Stunts—electromagnetic launcher game 102:138-139
Stunts—light up the clown 102:106-107
Stunts—magic blinking tie clip 102:116-117
Stunts—magnetic brake 102:157-158
Stunts—magnetic liquid 102:150-151
Stunts—mysterious whirlpool 102:152-153
Stunts—steady nerve game 102:140-141
Window burglar alarm 102:142-143

ELECTRICITY—CIRCUITS
A light circuit and a short circuit—how to 366:231
A possible surprise experiment with water 586:103
Aluminum foil circuit—how to make 91:70-73
Ammeter tests current flowing in circuit, how to make 910:32-33
Automatic switches—how to make 138:17
Batteries connected in reverse give no current 287:24
Batteries connected in series or parallel 287:23
Battery and bulb circuit, making 882:12
Battery holder to demonstrate simple circuit, how to make 1442:23-30
Battery, wire and bulb make a circuit experiment 885:78-79
Bell rings in test for steady hand, how to make 938:27-28
Bug model demonstrates flow of electricity experiment 1028:104
Bulb and battery holders for circuits, how to make 1514:42-44
Bulb glows brightest in series or parallel circuits experiment 829:27-28
Bulb holder to demonstrate simple circuit, how to make experiment 1442:22-23
Bulb lights on simple circuit experiment using battery, wire and bulb 1367:11
Bulbs are brightest in series or parallel circuits experiment 1012:57-58
Bulbs connected in series or parallel 287:22
Bulbs in parallel, how to make 910:23
Bulbs in series, how to make 910:22
Buzzer on circuit, how to make 1476:19-20
Can CMOS logic, rather than potentiometer, regulate voltage experiment 997:83-85
Can electricity help us to communicate experiment 902:258-259
Can you make the bulb light up experiment 828:4-6
Cells and batteries in parallel, how to make 910:23
Cells and batteries in series, how to make 910:22
Choice card with printed circuit experiment 1418:23-26
Circuit board game using series and parallel circuits with switches experiment 1307:22-25
Circuit board quiz game, how to make 1043:24-25
Circuit board to send messages—how to make 138:8
Circuit board, how to make 828:24-25; 882:16
Circuit breaker, how to make 910:30-31
Circuit from battery, bulb and two wires, how to make 1382:10
Circuit from battery, bulb and wire, making experiment 960:48-49
Circuit game with bulb and batteries, how to make 910:20
Circuit made using switch, bulb and D-cell experiment 1426:51
Circuit resistance—demonstrate resistance in wires of different materials 209:44-47
Circuit resistance; what is it experiment 1426:74-76
Circuit tester, how to make 828:20
Circuit, how to make 929:10
Circuit; test for conductors and insulators experiment 938:29-31
Circuits 17:78-84
Circuits—less simple 400:89
Closed circuit—how to make 341:16
Complete circuit—experiment 22:6; 23:9; 830:9-10
Complete electric circuit experiment 829:25-26
Conductivity board—how to make 138:13
Conductivity board tests materials for conductors or insulators experiment 972:25
Conductors and insulators—simple conductivity tester for conductors and 23:10-11
Connect cells in series and parallel—how to 128:172
Construct a circuit experiment 1028:102-103
Coordination tester—how to build 366:236
Current through wire related to voltage experiment 1158:108-109
Demonstrate difference between series and parallel circuits 195:30-34
Demonstrating a short circuit 180:49
Demonstrating the function of a fuse 180:50-51
Discovering Ohm's law 577:project #44
Doorbell circuit, how it works experiment 895:2
Dry cells in series and parallel 341:29-31
Each light in parallel wiring is a complete circuit 65:70-71
Effects of connecting two D cells in parallel in a circuit experiment 1426:64-66
Effects of connecting two D cells in series in a circuit experiment 1426:61-62
Electric circuit demonstration using battery, wire and bulbs 1199:7-13

Electric circuit demonstration using battery, wires and bulb 1029:19

Electric circuit spins match box on motor experiment 910:4

Electric circuits 655:4

Electricity changes to heat in electric circuit experiment 1426:76-79

Electricity makes heat experiment with battery and bulb 1519:20

Experiment to show simple cells and circuits 128:168-175

Experiments with the complete electric circuit 610:60-61

Find out how to light two (flashlight) bulbs at the same time 599:28-30

Flashlight circuit diagram 22:5

Fuse; how does fuse work in a circuit experiment 1426:73-74

Fuses protect a circuit experiment 938:35-38

Game "who lives where" lights up when you match pictures experiment 1099:17

Ghostly light pictures demonstrate electric circuit experiment 1024:24-25

Glowing steel wool experiment 1072:15

Glowing steel wool trick demonstrates circuit 955:15

Homemade cell holder, bulb holder and switch, how to make experiment 1426:48-51

How do switches work 278:37

How is electricity changed to light experiment 1426:79-80

How to control a light with two switches 278:38

Instant electricity 655:5

Insulator/conductor tester tests conductivity of most materials 22:7

Light a bulb experiment 1514:37

Light circuit, make your own 825:7

Light or bell circuit, how to make 867:32

Make a parallel circuit 138:11

Make a question and answer board 138:13

Make a ring circuit 138:12

Make a series circuit 138:10

Make a tester for electrical circuits—experiment 563:108

Make a time switch 91:89-92

Make series and parallel circuits experiment 902:233-235

Make shaky hand detector switch 287:18

Make simple circuit with battery and bulb 587:52

Make simple electric circuit with switch experiment 1497:23

Make two-way switch circuit 287:19

Making circuit; simple experiment with battery, wires, bulb 1493:18-21

Mathematic machine; bulb lights up for correct answer, how to make 1029:24-25

Maze board wired with simple circuits shows insulators and conductors 1307:18-19

Open circuit—short circuit—experiment 585:166

Open circuits controlled by switch experiment; can use as telegraph 1307:12-13

Open, closed and short circuits 391:16-22

Oscillator; how do circuits cause lights to flash experiment 1293:27-29

Parallel and series circuits light two or more bulbs experiment 1073:60-61

Parallel and series circuits 391:23-26

Parallel circuit experiment with battery, wire and bulb 1418:60

Parallel circuit; how does it work experiment 1501:56-59

Parallel circuits—how to wire in parallel 278:40

Parallel circuits and properties of experiment; data table given 871:4.016

Parallel circuits, how to make 341:19; 972:23

Parallel or series battery circuit system; which makes bulb brightest ex 1012:59-60

Printed circuits experiment, how to make 1418:210-211

Project 19—ammeter in series and in parallel 654:54-55

Projects with electric circuits 1164:90-94

Quiz board game, making experiment 960:50-52

Quiz box game—how to make 366:234-235

Resistance coil on parallel circuit experiment 1073:61

Resistance in flashlight bulb circuit experiment 1158:117-121

Resistance in simple circuit experiment 1139:74-76

Resistance in wire reduces current as conductor gets longer/thinner experiment 1179:154

Resistance of flashlight bulb experiment 1158:110

Resistance of two resistors wired in parallel experiment 1158:115-117

Resistance of two resistors wired in series experiment 1158:113-114

Resistance of wire affected by temperature experiment 1158:109-110

Resistance of wire related to its area of cross section experiment 1158:110-111

Rheostat—make from lead pencil and battery 436:67

Rheostat regulates electricity in a circuit experiment 1426:66-71

Series—parallel circuit 577:project #48

Series and parallel circuit experiment, how to do 1160:23

Series and parallel circuit, how to make 955:15

Series and parallel circuits experiment to show difference in their use 1307:22-23

Series and parallel circuits experiment, how to make 768:107-109; 1043:14-15; 1072:15; 1514:45-50

Series and parallel circuits, demonstrate difference experiment 895:23-24

Series and parallel circuits, how to make and test for difference in use 1073:60-61

Series circuit and parallel circuit, how to make experiment 1179:155

Series circuit experiment with battery, wire and two bulbs 1418:6

Series circuit, how to make 341:18; 972:21

Series circuit; how does it work experiment 1501:52-55

Series circuits—how to wire in series 278:39

Series circuits and properties of experiment; data table given 871:4.015

Series or parallel—experiment 627:49

Short circuit—demonstrate 291:170

Short circuit—what is a short circuit 278:41

Short circuits—experiments to demonstrate 185:37-41

Short-circuit a electric circuit experiment 1514:38-39

Show series and parallel connections 291:164

Show water conducts electricity 138:16

Simple circuit experiment with battery, wire and bulb 1418:26-27

Simple circuit lights bulb experiment 1282:28

Simple circuit using single-cell battery experiment 1200:29-30

Simple circuit with battery, wires and bulb experiment 1139:70-71

Simple circuit with flashlight from soda can, how to make 1442:14-21

Simple circuit with switch experiment 1139:72-73

Simple circuit, battery, bulb and wire experiment 1016:42-43

Simple circuit, how to make from battery, bulb, and wire 1076:18-19

Simple circuit, how to make from wood, wire, bulb and screws 1179:152-153

Simple circuit, how to make using batteries, wire and bulb 1099:11

Simple circuit, how to make 445:42; 1072:14; 1160:16; 1476:18-19; 955:14; 972:19

Simple circuits 400:89

Simple electric circuit, making 895:1-2

Simple switch controls current 287:17

Single or double circuits, how to make from battery, bulb and wires 1382:14

Spoon and fork circuit, how to make 1382:17

Steadiness detector lights up if your hand trembles, how to make 1029:26-27

Steady hand tester experiment; simple circuit with battery, bulb and wire 1307:10-11

Streetlights wired in parallel circuit 436:77

Substances that electricity will or won't pass through—experiment 677:13

Switch for circuit, how to make using paper clips, fasteners, cardboard 1076:19

Switch lamp from series to parallel 291:167

Switch; how does two-way switch work in a circuit experiment 1426:71-73

Testing variable resistors 138:15

The impossible circuit trick 392:71-76

Thickness of wire affects flow of electric circuit experiment 1501:60-63

Two light bulbs in parallel light at same time experiment 1426:62-64

Two light bulbs in series experiment 1426:59-61

Two-way switch circuit experiment 1307:14-15

Variable resistors; make and compare amount of electricity passing thru 972:27

What is a circuit experiment 902:229

What is a short circuit experiment 902:230

Wiring a parallel circuit 180:51

Wiring a series circuit 180:50

Wiring in series and in parallel—how to 366:231-232

ELECTRICITY—CONDUCTORS

Battery and bulb circuit used to demonstrate 888:158-161

Battery and bulb test materials for conductors and insulators experiment 910:6-7

Circuit; test for conductors and insulators experiment 938:29-31

Conduction—what does electricity travel through 96:76-77

Conductivity board tests materials for conductors or insulators experiment 972:25

Conductivity tester, how to build 768:106-107

Conductor tester identifies conductors and insulators experiment; data sheet 818:10

Conductors and insulators—experiments to show what things carry electricity 185:23-28

Conductors and insulators 281:93-94

Conductors and insulators in electric circuit experiment 1282:29

Conductors and nonconductors 34:89-90

Conductors of electricity; test materials with bug tester, how to build 1076:28-29

Demonstrate electrical conductors and nonconductors 147:107-111

Experiment with conductors and insulators 955:16

Find out which materials conduct electricity 599:38-39

Find out which materials make good conductors experiment 898:41

How conductors determine what materials are conductors 278:28-29

Insulated wire, how to make 888:160

Is aluminum an electrical conductor experiment 1501:36-39

Liquid electrolytes tested for conductivity experiment 1476:11-12

Materials are conductors or insulators of electricity experiment; test for 1012:55

Materials that are conductors and insulators experiment 1200:30

Materials that do or do not conduct electricity experiment 1514:57-59

Materials that will or will not conduct electricity experiment 1493:12-13

Maze board wired with simple circuits shows insulators and conductors 1307:18-19

Solid substances tested for conductivity experiment 1476:10-11

Studies in electrical conduction—experiment 627:17

Test conductors and insulators experiment 1426:52-54

Test electrical conductivity of liquids experiment 959:149-150

Test for conductivity of materials experiment 895:3-4

Test materials for conductors and insulators experiment 1160:18

Test materials to see if they are conductors/insulators of electricity 1179:151

Test materials to see which allow electricity to flow through experiment 1382:16-17

Test to identify insulators and conductors of electricity experiment 1073:60

Testing conductors and non-conductors 586:96-98

Testing different materials to see if they conduct electricity experiment 1099:14

Testing for conductors experiment using simple circuit 1418:80

Use light bulb circuit to test materials as conductors experiment 830:10-11

What materials conduct electricity experiment 795:28

What materials will conduct electricity experiment 902:236

What objects conduct electricity experiment 1073:60

Which materials are conductors experiment 929:13

ELECTRICITY—ELECTRIC CURRENT. See also GALVANOMETER; TRANSFORMER

A lemon current 280:32

AC and DC—experiment 585:166-167

AC current demonstrated with magnet—wire and transformer 723:117-118

AC power supply unit, how to make 830:23-24

Alessandro Volta's Voltaic pile produces electric current experiment 1133:5.003

Amount of current—demonstrate with different materials/solutions 209:28-31

Amount of current in circuit with resistors—experiment 209:38-39

Arc lamp—how to make 128:186-187

Cause a momentary flow of electrons along a wire conductor 63:4-5

Checking Ohm's law—experiment 627:45

Chemical changes caused by 85:54-55

Chemical reactions generate current experiment with magnesium ribbon, bleach 1012:53

Compass affected by electric current experiment 1501:72-75

Conductivity of citrus fruit—computer project 584:140-142

Conductors and nonconductors of current electricity—experiment 179:128-130

Construction details of an experimenter's AC power supply 23:23

Control flow of current with lead pencil rheostat experiment 768:102-103

Controlling current with a pencil experiment 895:4-5

Current—detector—construction details of a compass-type current detector 23:3-5

Current and resistance—experiment 655:10-11

Current demonstration—control the current 95:42

Current detector—how to make 191:35-38; 195:28-30

Current detector, compass type, how to make 830:3-5

Current encounters resistance in wire 65:74-75

Current flowing through wire changes direction experiment 902:244

Current flows in a circuit 65:40-41

Current indicator, how to make experiment 961:21

Current measuring experiment 23:17-20; 830:16-20

Current produces a magnetic field 65:58-59

Detect electric currents 655:13

Detecting electric currents—how to make a galvanometer 253:150-151

Detecting small electric currents with a galvanoscope 127:93-97

Detector for electric currents, how to make 910:24

Detector to detect and measure electric current experiment 1514:78-79

Diode permits electric current to flow in one direction experiment 1426:80-81

Does electricity only flow through wires 210:37

Effect of electric current on plants experiment 830:74-76

Electric arc heater—how to make 128:185

Electric circuit, simple—how to make with battery, bulb, & switch (Primary) 434:22-25

Electric current affects magnet experiment 1404:12-13

Electric current can move through water and other solutions experiment 1501:44-47

Electric current detector or galvanometer 391:46-49

Electric current produced by electrolytes in different liquids experiment 1004:4.008

Electric current sets up magnetic field experiment with battery and compass 1456:45

Electric current traveling thru air creates sparks and invisible rays ex 1029:23

Electric sparks on file demonstrate current 722:6

Electric toaster—how to make 128:186

Electrically made magnet detects electric current experiment 1514:75-78

Electricity can produce heat 281:94-95

Electricity gives heat 280:33

Electricity produces heat and light—electric sparkler 287:25

Faraday experiment 195:50-51

Faraday, Michael; who invented alternating current project 1525:38-40

Galvanometer detects electric current experiment, how to make 1426:86-88

Galvanometer shows current and direction of current—how to build 293:30

Galvanometer, how to build 1476:31-33

Galvanometer, make to measure electrolytes in some common foods experiment 1004:4.007

Galvanometer, simple—how to make 63:60-61; 184:216-217

Galvanoscope (current detector), how to make 768:75-76

Generator experiment to demonstrate AC current 830:13-14

Generator experiment with coil of wire and bar magnet 23:12-13

Getting a charge out of a lime 180:47

Homemade meter registers electric current 291:156

Horseshoe electromagnet—how to make 184:212-213

How a fuse protects us 63:36-37; 184:192-193

How does electric current affect a compass experiment 902:238

How does electricity come to a light bulb experiment 834:52-53

How electricity works 656:4-5

How to connect batteries in series and parallel experiment 938:41-42

How to connect bulbs in parallel 63:28-29; 184:184-185

How to connect bulbs in series 63:20-21; 184:176-177

How to connect dry cells in parallel 63:16-17; 184:172-173

How to connect dry cells in series 63:12-13; 184:168-169

How to induce or stir up an electric current in a wire with magnet 63:76-77

How to keep electric current flowing 63:8-9

How to make a rheostat 278:60

How to make electric current flow along a wire 184:164-165

Induce electric current by moving wire through magnetic field experiment 1179:167

Induction—how it works 655:19

Instruments to show electric currents—how to make simple ones 128:169

Investigate the force on a current carrying wire in a magnetic field 63:56-57

Is electric current flowing through wire experiment 902:247-248

Lemon juice battery shows current 287:15

Lenz's law shows induced current opposes the motion producing it 63:80-81

Lines of force—experiment 489:132-133

Magnet can produce electric current experiment 1501:80-83

Magnet generates electric current experiment 1012:49-50

Magnet in coiled wire makes electric current experiment 1269:33

Magnet produces movement in current-carrying wire experiment 1501:76-79

Make a bar electromagnet 63:52-53; 184:208-209

Make a complete circuit 179:124-126

Make a current detector 17:72-75

Make a dry cell 179:126-128

Make a magnet out of a coil of wire 63:48-49; 184:204-205

Make a simple circuit 210:37

Make a simple electric circuit with battery and bulb (Primary) 207:48-49

Make electric current with a magnet 278:25

Making an electric current 340:16

Measure flow rate of electricity experiment 1501:33-35

Measuring electric charge experiments 1158:99-101

Meter that registers electric current—how to make 291:156

Meter to detect current, how to make 1012:49

More practice with fuses and circuits 63:40-41; 184:196-197

More practice with parallel circuits 63:32-33; 184:188-189

More practice with series circuits 184:180-181

Nerve machine 391:70-74

Oersted's Discovery; electric current deflects compass needle experiment 1159:104-107

Oersted's experiment—prove that electric current deflects compass needle 184:200-201

Oersted's experiment proving electric current deflects compass needle 63:44-45

Plant growth; effect of electrical current on plant growth experiment 1249:54-56

Produce a continuous current of electrons by means of a voltaic pile 63:68-69

Project 20—ammeters, clocks and charges 654:55-58

Prove that electric charges will flow along a conductor 184:160-161

Relationship between circuit and fuse—demonstrate 209:40-41

Relationship between electric current and magnetism—demonstrate 209:42-43

Repeat Volta's experiment with electric current 72:47-49

Resistance wire dimmer—how to make 128:184

Rheostat shows as resistance increases current decreases—how to make 293:32-33

Rheostat, simple—how to make 128:184

Self induction—produce a bright spark by stopping a current in a coil 63:72-73

Self induction—producing a bright spark by stopping a current in a coil 63:72-73

Send messages with a bulb battery and switch circuit 226:10

Series connected batteries—experiment 23:20

Show how AC differs from DC—experiment 532:86-87

Showing inductive current—experiment 627:37

Simple circuit—how to make 340:22

Simple lighting circuit—how to make 227.9

Testing electrical flow and resistance 625:31

Tongue test for electric current 287:14

Using a movable needle type galvanometer 184:220-221

Using pair of three way switches controls light from two different spots 63:24-25

Using the homemade galvanometer 63:64-65

Voltaic pile generates electric current experiment 752:103

Voltmeter—voltage/current indicator—how to build 23:25-30

Voltmeter; what does a voltmeter measure experiment 1158:102-106

Wet cell battery 391:50-54

What are the kinds of electricity we use 278:61-62

What happens when electric current flows through a wire experiment 902:239

What things conduct an electric current and what do not 287:16

ELECTRICITY—ELECTRICAL CHARGES

Balloons show attraction and repulsion 291:162

Charging plastic bags 13:9-11

Demonstrate electrical charge of different objects—make electroscope 293:31

Demonstration of attraction and repulsion of electrical charges 291:162

Electrical charge 12:80-82

Electrifying a bubble 360:36-37

Electrophorus—how to build 13:17-18; 278:31

Electroscope—how to build 13:13-17; 278:29-30

Electroscope—make a charge detector 17:69-72

Flying an airplane by electrostatics 13:12-13

How to get a charge of electricity 106:47-52

Magic wand and record negative and positive charge 287:13

Make a paper stick to the window (Primary) 69:31

Negative electrical charge—the Hindu thread trick 16:68-70

Test common objects for electric charges 293:31-32

ELECTRICITY—INSULATORS

Materials that do or do not conduct electricity experiment 1514:57-59

ELECTRICITY—RESISTANCE

Battery and resistance coil experiment 929:14

Dimmer switch, how to make 929:15

Making a light bulb experiment 871:4.017

Variable resistors, make and compare amount of electricity passing thru 972:27

ELECTRICITY—RESISTANCE TO

Circuit resistance; what is it experiment 1426:74-76

Electric resistance of different objects experiment 1136:30-31

Electricity changes to heat in electric circuit experiment 1426:76-79

Glowing light bulb experiment with battery, wire and bulbs 1476:25-26

How is electricity changed to light experiment 1426:79-80

Lead pencil demonstrates dimmer switch 287:21

Lead shows things can resist the flow of electricity 287:20

Make a resistance thermometer—flame dims light 95:43

Resisting electricity—measuring electrical resistance—experiment 586:100-103

Resistor in circuit used to make night-light with dimmer switch experiment 1307:20-21

Short circuit experiment to see what happens when fuse blows 1132:86-1-86-2

Strip of foil—too hot to handle 287:26

Thickness of wire affects flow of electric circuit experiment 1501:60-63

Wire length and resistance to electric charge flow experiment 1514:60-65

ELECTRICITY—STATIC ELECTRICITY. *See also* **ELECTROPHOROUS; LEYDEN JAR**

Attracting large objects to an electrified body 184:102-103

Attraction and repulsion prove there are two kinds of electrification 184:106-107

Attracts bits of paper 65:34-35

Balloon force field—negative and positive charge 287:10

Bend a stream of water without touching it 150:160-161
Bends a thin stream of water 65:38-39
Can static electricity do work experiment 851:13-15
Cereal acrobats 280:30
Charge objects with 195:14-15
Charge pith ball by contact 184:114-115
Charged balloon attracts water— bendy water 287:7
Charging balloons with static electricity 608:6-7
Clinging balloon 287:6
Dancing dolls—experiment 179:118-119
Dancing tissue paper dolls demonstrate static electricity 938:7-8
Demonstrate simple static electricity (Primary) 207:44-47
Demonstrate static electricity with balloons, puppets, puffed rice 576:67-70
Demonstrate static electricity 138:30-31
Detect static charges 138:32
Detector—how to make 195:16-19
Detector of electrical charges 287:8-9
Do electrically charged objects attract nonmetal objects experiment 851:11-13
Do electrified bodies attract all or only some light objects 184:98-99
Dolls dance by electricity 186:83-84
Effect of soap, shampoo and conditioners on hair—experiments 441:75-78
Electric antics with a record 287:12
Electric ghost—how to make 186:84-85
Electric pendulum—how to make 186:87
Electric roundabout—how to make 186:84
Electricity with a comb 655:6-7
Electrophorus—how an electrophorus 'works' 184:146-147
Electrophorus—how to charge and discharge an electrophorus 184:142-143
Electrophorus—make an electrophorus or simple electric generator 184:138-139
Electrophorus—prove metal plate of electrophorus is charged by induction 184:150-151
Electroscope—aluminum leaf electroscope to detect an electrical charge 184:122-123
Electroscope—charging a metallic object by induction 184:154-155
Electroscope—how to charge an electroscope by induction 184:130-131
Electroscope—how to charge an electroscope negatively 184:126-127
Electroscope—how to make 179:119-122; 186:87-88
Electroscope—make a metal leaf electroscope 184:118-119
Electroscope—make and use pith ball electroscope 184:86-91
Electroscope—use charged electroscope, identify charge on electrified object 184:134-135
Electrostatic airplane from aluminum foil demonstrates 938:9-10
Electrostatics—the wondrous wand 205:102-107
Exp.-static elec., Sticking newspaper to wall, bending water, fun with wool 599:17-19
Experiments to show static electricity 128:164-168
Fluorescent tube glows when rubbed demonstration 938:11-12
Flying cereal 95:40
Friction creates static electricity 232:47

Get electricity by rubbing 278:27-28
Getting a charge out of polyethylene and wool 627:4
Give yourself a charge 30:58-59
Is it charged 280:31
Leyden jar to store static electricity—how to make 209:20-21
Magic—separate salt and pepper 35:34
Magic comb trick (Primary) 210:36
Magic rabbits—demonstrate 656:7
"Magnetizing" amber—experiment 627:2
Make balloons hop about 179:115-118
Make lightning (Primary) 232:46
Make waltzing, swinging or walking figures to demonstrate 172:147-148
Making sparks (Primary) 210:36
Measure amount of static electricity—make an electrophorous 209:16-17
Paper caper—negative and positive charges 287:11
Pith ball electroscope—tests amount 184:94-95
Poof—magic trick 35:30
Produce static electricity 179:111-115
Produced by rubbing 65:32-33
Repels certain things 65:36-37
Rubbing fluorescent tube makes it glow 95:41
Rug power—experiment 563:104-105
Separate salt from pepper without touching them 150:158-159
Show electric charge by moving two balloons apart without touching them 150:156-157
Simple electroscope—how to make 563:103
Static electricity—experiments 34:86-90
Static electricity—simple experiments to show 185:8-11
Static electricity detector—how to make 436:74
Static electricity experiment with comb, paper and balloons 489:107-108
Sticky balloons experiment 30:59-60
Testing for static electricity 625:31
The "magic" comb—experiment (Primary) 567:6
The bashful balloon—experiments 563:105
The bent water trick 494:61
The comb and the ping pong ball 186:81
The dancing balloons 72:44-46
The ghost leg 16:77-79
The goofy ping pong ball—experiment 563:95-96
The obedient straw experiment 563:107-108
The wayward water—experiment 563:96
What is a spark 281:90
Why objects acquire an electric charge 184:110-111

ELECTRICITY—SWITCHES

Add lights and switches to doll house, how to do 955:18
Alarm, antitheft magnetic reed switch, make from magnet/batteries/wire 1442:50-54
Automatic switch machine experiment, how to make 1420:26-27
Circuit board game using series and parallel circuits with switches experiment 1307:22-25
Dim the lamps—experiment 563:100-101
Dimmer switch for night-light experiment using resistor 1307:20-21
Dimmer switch, how to make 929:15; 1043:21; 1382:20-21
Dollhouse lights and switches, how to make 1072:18
Double-throw switches, how to make 1476:20
Electric switch experiment with box, foil and battery 1418:7-16

Electric switch from block of wood and wires, how to make 1200:27

Find the switch trick, battery, wire and switches 1139:82-84

Homemade switch, making 867:30

Make a switch experiment 902:231-232

Make your own electric switch experiment 1072:17

Open circuit controlled by switch experiment; can use as telegraph 1307:12-13

Paper clip switch completes electric circuit experiment 955:17

Pressure switch, how to make 1043:20

Rotary switch traffic light, how to make from coffee can 1442:31-40

See-saw switch experiment, how to make 1420:25

Simple and double switch, how to make 1073:62

Simple switch on electric circuit experiment 1282:28-29

Simple switch to control circuit experiment 1160:17

Simple switch, how to make 929:11; 1043:20

Switch for circuit, how to make using paper clips, fasteners, cardboard 1076:19

Switch in electrical circuit in a shoe box room, how to make 1099:13

Switch turns electric current on and off experiment 1029:22

Switches, how to make from paper clip, clothes pin and cardboard experiment 1382:18

Tapper switch, how to make 1043:21

Tricky switches—experiment 563:99-100

Two way switch, how it works experiment 895:2-3

Two way switch, how to make 929:19; 1382:20-21

Two-way switch circuit experiment 1307:14-15

Two-way switch; build to show how switch works experiment 1012:61-62

ELECTROCHEMISTRY. *See also* **ELECTROLYSIS; ELECTROPLATING; ELECTROLYTES**

Batteries—a coin battery 102:94-96

Batteries—electrolysis of water 102:102-103

Batteries—electroplating 102:97-101

Batteries—make your own electric cell 102:88-93

Electric current produced by electrolytes in different liquids experiment 1004:4.008

Electricity and copper pennies distinguish chloride and sulfate ions experiment 1250:91-94

Produce chlorine, hydrogen and caustic soda experiment 768:80-81

ELECTRODES. *See also* **BATTERIES**

Nails for electrodes in electrolysis of water—experiment 532:17

ELECTROLYSIS. *See also* **WATER—ELECTROLYSIS**

Breaking up water into hydrogen and oxygen experiment 1514:114-119

Cathode protection experiment with nails 723:193-195

Chlorine formed during electrolysis removes color from ink experiment 1218:40

Copper—new clean penny (Primary) 109:12-13

Copper moves from copper coin to silver coin experiment 1081:21

Copper plate a nail experiment 827:47

Copper plate a paper clip with electrolysis experiment 1307:30-31

Decompose water by electrolysis 319:34-36

Decomposing water 13:50-51

Decomposition of water by electrolysis experiment 978:79-80

Electric current passed through water makes hydrogen and oxygen gases experiment 1172:17-20

Electric current splits water into hydrogen and oxygen 472:2235

Electric current splits water into hydrogen and oxygen gases experiment 1244:14-15

Electrical attack 287:29

Electricity breaks up some chemicals experiment 1218:40

Electricity changes a solution 127:101-103

Electricity passing thru water splits water into hydrogen and oxygen experiment 1473:32-33

Electrolysis and electroplating 43:109-124

Electrolysis of water 146:34-35

Electrolysis of water experiment 768:83-84; 1396:94

Experiment 112:10-12

Experiment with auto battery 363:86-87

Experiments to show 128:187-190

Faraday's first law of electrolysis experiment 1156:125-129

Galvanize a piece of iron—nails in zinc sulfate and copper sulfate solution 567:39

Gases from electrified saltwater experiment 895:9-10

How can you copperplate a safety pin 278:50-51

Lemon juice separates water into hydrogen and oxygen 89:42-44

Nails for electrodes—experiment 532:17

Project 24—electrolysis and charge per atom (Advanced) 654:64-66

Project 25—charge per atom for elements (Advanced) 654:66-67

Separate water into hydrogen and oxygen experiment using battery, wires, water 1435:101-103

Simple battery from lemon experiment 1396:94-96

Split water—electric gas 146:34-35

Split water into oxygen and hydrogen 176:25-26

Split water into oxygen and hydrogen experiment using salt water 1029:28-29

Splitting cooking salt by electrolysis 186:90-91

Splitting water—how to 346:60-67

Splitting water using battery and wire in salt water experiment 1271:29

Splitting water with electrolysis experiment 910:44-45

Taking salt apart 127:54-59

Water splits into hydrogen and oxygen when current is passed thru water 1179:157

William Nicholson's decomposition of water into hydrogen and oxygen experiment 1133:2.008

ELECTROLYTES

Aluminum silver—clean 203:61

Battery from lemon power experiment using galvanometer, how to make 1476:15

Detected by galvanometers 346:80-87

Detector (galvanometer)—how to make 346:80-87

Different solutions of water conduct current experiment 722:2

Electric cell; make from two different metals and an electrolyte experiment 1159:108-110

Electric current produced by electrolytes in different liquids experiment 1004:4.008

Electrical silver polish (electrolyte and aluminum) 346:95-96

Electricity from a lemon experiment 895:6-7

Electricity from fruit and nails 586:99-100
Electrolytes experiment with battery, salt, sugar and
    water 563:179-180
Galvanometer, make to measure electrolytes in some
    common foods experiment 1004:4.007
Lemon battery demonstrates need for current 293:32
Lemon battery you can eat experiment 1159:108-110
Liquid electrolytes tested for conductivity experiment
    1476:11-12
Liquids permit electricity to flow experiment 1426:55-57
Materials conduct electricity experiment; compare inten-
    sity of bulb glow 1396:93
Solutions—how to tell if solution is an electrolyte
    319:50-51
Svante Arrhenius's separation of substances into charged
    particles or ion 1133:2.010
Table salt is an electrolyte experiment 1396:91-96
Wet battery experiment, how to construct 1476:13-14
What is an electrolyte; test various household liquids ex-
    periment 895:5-6

ELECTROMAGNETIC CRANE
How to make 340:28-29

ELECTROMAGNETIC FIELDS
Effect of electromagnetic fields on Eremosphaena algae
    cells experiment 997:57-59
Wire coiled and battery make magnet 366:239

ELECTROMAGNETIC FORCE
Electromagnet, make to determine what makes it strong
    or weak experiment 1004:5.018
Experiment to measure strength of electric current
    385:146-147

ELECTROMAGNETIC INDUCTION. *See also* **FARA-
DAY, MICHAEL**
Faraday's Discovery that magnets create electricity ex-
    periment 1476:34-35
Faraday's electromagnetic induction experiment with bar
    magnet, compass, wire 1473:40
How to induce or stir up an electric current in wire with a
    magnet 184:232-233
More experiments with induced currents 184:236-237
Showing inductive current—experiment 627:37

ELECTROMAGNETIC RADIATION
Does extremely-low-frequency (ELF) affect fruit flies ex-
    periment 1096:53-57
Does low level electromagnetic radiation (EMF) affect
    fruit flies experiment 1096:53-57
Heating in microwave ovens requires water molecules ex-
    periment 1250:32-34
Low-level EMR (electromagnetic radiation) affects bacte-
    rial growth experiment 1450:100-105
Measure ELF (extremely low frequency) radiation in per-
    sonal computers 1450:106-112

ELECTROMAGNETIC WAVES
Secret broadcast 95:46
Transmit sound with a flashlight beam experiment
    1132:67-1-67-4

ELECTROMAGNETISM. *See also* **OERSTED'S DIS-
COVERY**
A simple relay—experiment 627:33
Ampere's wires carrying current attract/repel according
    to direction 1133:5.006
Andre Ampere's coil of wire acts as bar magnet when
    carrying current experiment 1133:5.004
Andre Ampere's right hand grip rule of magnetic field ex-
    periment 1133:5.005

Arago's magnet follows rotation of a copper disc experi-
    ment 1133:5.008
Batteries—circuit breaker 102:83-85
Batteries—electric current detector 102:67-68
Batteries—homemade buzzer 102:78-80
Batteries—horseshoe electromagnet 102:75-77
Batteries—how to make an electromagnet 102:58-61
Batteries—magnetic field around a coil 102:65-66
Batteries—magnetic field around a conductor 102:54-57
Batteries—making a permanent magnet 102:62-64
Batteries—transfer of current through space 102:69-74
Batteries—two way telegraph station 102:81-82
Checking the magnetic polarity of a solenoid experiment
    768:91-92
Checking up on Arago—experiment 627:30
Demonstrate magnetic field around current-carrying con-
    ductor experiment 768:88-90
Demonstrate with coils of different materials and number
    of wire turns 209:22-26
Effects of electromagnetism and how to wind electromag-
    netic coil experiment 1073:66-67
Electric current produces magnetic field experiment with
    battery/wire/compass 1218:30
Electricity and magnetism are related; how to show ex-
    periment 768:86-88
Electricity and magnets—experiment 677:21-22
Electricity can produce a magnet experiment 1501:68-71
Electricity from magnetism experiment 1133:5.011
Electricity makes magnetism experiment with battery,
    light and compass 972:41
Electromagnetic fields effect on seed germination experi-
    ment 1060:63-64
Faraday's electromagnetic induction experiment
    1133:5.012
Galvanometer detects electric current experiment, how to
    make 1426:86-88
Hans Oersted's electromagnetic field experiment
    1133:5.007
Induced current—experiment 585:171-172
Iron filings create abstract patterns 186:91
Loudspeaker; construct to demonstrate sound reproduc-
    tion experiment data table 1004:5.013
Magic diver goes up and down in water as current goes
    on and off experiment 768:103-104
Magnetic field experiments with battery, wire and com-
    pass 1139:86-89
Make Miss Paper Clip dance 186:92-93
Make model electromagnetic crane 267:45
Make mysterious portrait 186:91-92
Motor effect; magnet exerts force on current carrying
    wire experiment 1132:70-1-70-2
Oersted's Discovery; electric current passed thru wire
    produces magnetism 1473:34
Oersted's experiment—do it yourself 642:153-154
Oersted's famous experiment with electric current pro-
    ducing magnetism 1160:24
Plant growth affected by magnetism experiment 1061:87-
    88
Plant growth; electric currents affect plant growth experi-
    ment 1375:111-114
Proving Faraday's theory 627:40
Radio waves neutralized by aluminum foil experiment
    1216:43-45
Relationship between electric current and magnetism in
    electric motor 1136:36-37

Repeat Oersted's experiment 186:88-89
Show effect of electromagnetic field on permanent field experiment 768:96-97
Show electromagnetic field in three dimensions experiment 768:94
Show magnetic field of a conductor 186:90
Show magnetism and electricity 145:26-29
Slave magnet shows relationship between electric current and magnetism 1136:36-37
Solenoid; make solenoid and watch mouse hide in the cheese experiment 1309:22-23
Through the eye of a helix—experiment 627:29
Unfriendly paper clips demonstrate magnetic laws experiment 768:95-96
Which way is North experiment 1216:62-64
Wire with current flowing through it picks up iron filings experiment 768:91
X-ray vision magic trick experiment 1216:55-58

ELECTROMAGNETS
A simple electromagnet—making 585:168
Alarm; portable watchdog alarm, how to build experiment 1426:107-109
Amount of electric current affects strength of electromagnet experiment 1401:70
Bar electromagnet—how to make 184:208-209
Battery, wire and nail electromagnet, how to make 929:20-21
Bolt, battery and wire; make electromagnet experiment 885:79
Build electromagnet and measure its strength experiment 888:171-175
Buzzer from electromagnet experiment 1028:94-95
Buzzer that makes noise, how to make from battery, wire, can, nail file 1076:40-41
Buzzer, making 930:9
Buzzer; build electric buzzer experiment 1426:94-96
Can be made more powerful 65:66-67
Can electricity create magnetism experiment 834:89-90
Change the strength of electromagnet experiment 902:241
Change the strength of electromagnet experiment 902:242-243
Clown's nose held in place by electromagnet experiment, how to make 1307:26-27
Construction of solenoid type of electromagnet 23:51-52
Copper coils become electromagnetic pendulums experiment 1132:64-1-64-2
Crane, electromagnetic, how to make 955:34-35
Crane; electromagnetic crane experiment using boxes, iron bolts, battery 1476:29-30
Crane; working crane using electromagnet experiment 1418:21
Crane; working model with electromagnetic coil, how to make 1043:36-37
Dancing figure with paper clips and electromagnet experiment 938:106-108
Demonstrate with a dancing doll 179:156-157
Direction of current flow in electromagnet to show North and South poles 1034:26
Does direction of flow of current affect an electromagnet experiment 902:245-246
Does strength of electromagnet change with number of turns of wire 333:15-16
Doorbell, how to make 825:9

Edison's ore separator, rejecting counterfeit coins experiment 895:39-40
Electric bell 391:101-108
Electric current produces a magnetic field experiment 1405:92
Electric current produces magnetic field experiment with battery/nail/wire 1404:46-47
Electric flag 391:140-145
Electric motor experiment, how to make 912:38
Electric pencil makes marks on metal, how to make 1442:85-89
Electricity can produce a magnet experiment 1501:68-71
Electricity produces magnetism experiment 910:36-37
Electricity used to make a magnet experiment 1218:31
Electromagnet 391:91-94
Electromagnet—experiment with dry cell wire and nail 22:11-12
Electromagnet—how to make 610:63; 656:8-9; 670:75; 733:25
Electromagnet can be made stronger (Primary) 435:37
Electromagnet experiment with battery, bulb, nails 1418:190-191
Electromagnet from battery, switch, electric leads, wire, how to do 1179:164
Electromagnet from battery, wire and nail experiment 1072:33
Electromagnet from nail, wire, battery and switch experiment 1160:25
Electromagnet that works from wooden box, battery, switch, bolt, wire 1382:36-37
Electromagnet with two coils experiment 895:22-23
Electromagnet, how to make experiment 961:22-23
Electromagnet, how to make 625:28; 627:31; 768:93-94; 860:127-129; 906:104-105; 926:94-97; 930:9; 973:41; 1001:31
Electromagnet, make to determine what makes it strong or weak experiment 1004:5.018
Electromagnetic "gun" satellite launcher, how to make 1249:49-50
Electromagnetic crane experiment, how to make 1072:34-35
Electromagnetic crane, how to make experiment 938:109-110; 961:25
Electromagnetic games, how to make two games 910:42-43
Electromagnetic relay—how to make 23:49-50
Electromagnetic relay, how to make experiment 938:111-112
Electromagnetic telegraph sounder—how to make 23:46-47
Electromagnets, how to make experiment 938:103-105
Electromagnets, making 910:36-39
Experiments with an electromagnet 127:65-72; 179:153-156
Factors affecting strength—how to build 293:33-34
Find out how to make an electromagnet 599:45-46
Giant electromagnet—experiment 386:101-104
Horseshoe electromagnet 391:91-94
Horseshoe electromagnet—how to make 128:176
Horseshoe magnet—how to make 184:212-213
How does electromagnet work experiment 1200:29
How to make (Primary) 435:33-34
How to make an electromagnet and how to change poles of a hurricane 253:146-147

How to make and how to increase strength of electromagnet 72:51-53

How to make and test 677:21-23

How to make electromagnet stronger experiment 829:21-22

How to make electromagnet 984:22-24

How to make from a bolt 128:176

How to make from wire, tubing and battery 1164:98-100

How to make 123:61-66; 127:60-64; 138:24; 176:66-67; 178:50; 185:50-52; 186:89-90; 207:50-51; 278:17-18; 356:65; 385:144-145; 40:100-101; 400:87; 445:54; 94:42-43; 955:33

Induction motor; aluminum foil and spinning magnet experiment 912:29

Instant magnetizer—making 532:100

Iron bolt and wire electromagnet, making 867:31

Length of winding wire changes strength of electromagnet experiment data sheet 818:8

Light; make an electric light experiment 1426:100-103

Magnet makes electricity in coiled wire experiment 1367:23

Magnetic crane—making 436:55

Magnetic crane, working model from cardboard, how to make 1073:67

Magnetic field from electricity makes compass needle move experiment 1099:28

Magnetic patterns from electromagnet under cardboard experiment 1073:68

Magnetic pickup crane using electromagnet, how to build 1309:20-21

Magnetize nail experiment using battery and wire 1139:33-34

Magnetize screwdriver experiment using battery and wire 1139:32

Magtron the magnetic marvel electromagnetic device—how to make 487:34-35

Make a buzzer and send messages 176:67-68

Make a magnetic crane 179:158-159

Make a motor from an oatmeal box top 179:163-164

Make a real electric motor 179:164-170

Make a secret magnetic lock 127:82-87

Make a simple electric motor 138:27

Make a simple telegraph 179:159-162

Make an electromagnet experiment 1028:93; 1514:80-82

Make an electromagnet 30:68-69; 544:32; 567:39; 868:73

Make and test an electromagnet experiment with nail, wire and battery 1166:31

Make electromagnet from nail, battery and wire experiment 1136:18

Make electromagnet using 6 volt battery, wire and nail 1034:24-25

Make from horseshoe magnet 436:30-31

Make paper and paper clip doll to demonstrate electromagnets 487:36-38

Making 655:13

Making a transformer 138:29

Making an electromagnet experiment 895:21

Making electricity by 'induction' 138:28

Making electromagnet 898:40-41

Model railroad semaphore signal and simple track switch—how to make 23:47-48

Model railway signals, how to make using electromagnet experiment 961:22-23

Motor; slow moving electric motor made from milk carton, batteries, wire 1442:97-109

Motors, electric, how they work experiment 938:96-99

Nail size affects strength of electromagnet experiment 1401:70

Number of wire coils around nail affects strength of electromagnet experiment 1401:70

Playing with electromagnets 138:25

Poles of electromagnet can be reversed (Primary) 435:35-36

Power station model, simple, make to demonstrate electric current 912:37

Rocking motor made from milk carton, ruler, batteries, wire 1442:90-96

Screwdriver electromagnet, how to make 1076:38-39

Secret drawer lock, making 895:37-39

Show change in electromagnetic strength 168:45

Show effect of electricity on compass 385:142-143

Show effect of looped or coiled wire 385:143-144

Show magnetic field of a current carrying wire 385:143

Show use of electromagnetic power 138:26

Simple electromagnet—how to make 226:13; 340:14; 605:54-55; 1063:166; 1426:89-90

Simple electromagnet made from dry cell battery, bell wire and bolt 1249:48

Simple electromagnetic lock 23:51-52

Simple nail electromagnet, making 825:9

Single and double coil electromagnet experiment with battery/wire/iron bolts 1476:27-28

Solar electric system, how to make 1426:112-114

Sound making device to show electromagnetism experiment 1442:75-84

Stripped down simple motor experiment 1132:97-1-97-2

Strong electromagnet, how to make 1426:90-91

Swinging coil device to show electromagnetism experiment 1442:64-75

Telegraph set—making 436:78-79; 1426:91-93

The motor effect—experiment 585:177-178

Tiger cage door closes experiment using electromagnet 1307:28-29

Train; electromagnetic train model experiment 1249:50-52

Transformer, how to make experiment 973:45

What is an electromagnet experiment with wire, nail, battery, BBs 1401:68-71

What is an electromagnet experiment 902:240

Wind turbine makes electricity experiment 1426:114-118

Wire coiled around nail attached to battery attracts paper clips experiment 912:34

Working model of an electric lock 577:project #52

ELECTROMOTIVE FORCE

Induced electromotive force and resonance 577:project #47

ELECTRONIC CIRCUITS

Current affects bulb's brightness; resistors in series and parallel experiment 1179:176

ELECTRONIC GAMES

Black box game, how to make 860:92-97

Electronic quiz game, make with battery, bulb, wire and quiz questions 1072:21

Teaching machine 391:35-41

Tic-tac-toe game, how to make 860:92-97

ELECTRONICS

0-15 volt regulated power supply, how to build 1226:69-73

5-volt power supply, how to build 1226:69-70
555 integrated circuit, how to put together 1226:74-77
9-volt battery eliminator, how to build 1226:64-68
Audible tester, how to build 1226:77-79
Continuity tester, how to build 1226:54-55
Control center—making 667:8-9
Current flow—measurement 591:29-31
Digital timer, how to make 860:113-116
Electronic components—identify 667:6-7
Electronic dice pair, how to build 1226:101-105
Experiments—elementary 43:125-144
Flashing light, how to make 860:110-113
General purpose alarm, how to build 1226:79-82
How can unconnected fluorescent bulb glow 278:66
How can you make a simple radio 278:74-75
How does an electron tube work 278:67
How radio waves are used for broadcasting 278:73
Infrared communications system, how to make 860:119-125
Integrated circuits experiment 1226:88-96
Intercom, how to build 1226:88-90
Light dimmer, how to build 1226:97-100
Light sensor programs 667:34-35
Light sensors and circuits—making 667:28-33
Nand gate siren, how to build 1226:90-96
Ohm meter, high ohm meter, how to build 1226:110-113
Ohm meter, very low ohm meter, how to build 1226:106-108
Power controller—making 667:10-15
Power controller programs 667:16-17,36-38
Resistance—measurement of in a water hose—experiment 591:31-32
Resistors in series and parallel; how current affects bulb's brightness 1179:176
Solder components—how to 667:4-5
Solid-state capacitance meter, how to build 1226:108-110
Switch disguises—making 667:24-25
Switch programs 667:26-27
Switch sensor circuits—making 667:22-23
Switch sensors—making 667:18-21
Telegraph oscillator, how to build 1226:60-61
The speed of electricity and electron flow—experiment 591:16-17
Timer integrated circuit experiment 1226:74-87
Touch switch, how to build 1226:85-87
Transistor switch, make from transistor, resistors, elect. lead, battery 1179:177
Two-tone warbler, how to build 1226:82-85
What are capacitors 278:71
What are radio waves 278:71-72
What are resistors 278:70
What are some electronic symbols 278:68
What are transistors 278:69-70

ELECTRONICS—CALCULATORS
Handling a large calculation—experiment 591:72-73

ELECTRONICS—CONDUCTORS
Semiconductor diode—one-way flow in experiment 591:32-33

ELECTRONICS—OSCILLATORS
Oscillator circuit—building one experiment 591:43-45

ELECTRONICS—RADIO
AM radio—your own AM radio—experiment 591:61-63
FM radio—hearing quality of sound—the clean sound of FM—exp. 591:60-61

ELECTRONICS—TELEVISION
A close-up of a color TV picture—experiment 591:64
The scan lines in a TV picture—observation experiment 591:63-64

ELECTRONS. *See also* **MOLECULES; STATIC ELECTRICITY**
Balloon trick solution experiment 829:45-46
Construct model of lithium atom showing its electrical charges experiment 1501:4-7
Do like charges attract or repel experiment 831:11-14
How does matter become electrically charged experiment 1501:4-7
Negatively charged 16:72-76
Removal of tarnish from silver demonstrates electron flow between metals 871:3.024

ELECTRO-OPTICAL RECOGNITION. *See* **IMAGE RECOGNITION SYSTEM; SCANNERS**

ELECTROPHORUS
Building an electrophorus, how to 895:26
Electrophorus—making 608:11-13
Electrophorus, building, how to 768:16-17
Electrophorus, using, how to 768:17-18
How to make an electrophorus 385:151-153
How to make electrophorus from pie tin and ball point pen 1132:20-1-20-2
How to make 172:149-152; 278:31; 43:58-60
Learning how to use it—charging an electrophorus 5:58-61
Making an electrophorus or simple electric generator 5:54-57
Understanding how an electrophorus works 5:62-65
Your own charger: the electrophorus 627:20

ELECTROPLATING. *See also* **ELECTROLYSIS**
Copper coating nail experiment 976:49
Copper coats nail using electricity experiment 1012:65
Copper plate a paper clip with electrolysis experiment 1307:30-31
Coppering nails 176:24
Copperplate a paper clip experiment 1218:41
Copper plating a key experiment 1476:16-17
Copper plating key experiment using battery, wire leads, key and water 1179:156
Electroplate with copper experiment 752:104-105
Electroplating a key experiment 1426:57-59
Electroplating cell follows Ohm's Law experiment 1158:111-113
Electroplating device 391:55-59
Electroplating key experiment with battery, wire, and copper sulfate crystals 1244:26-27
Electroplating with copper experiment 972:37
Electroplating your house key experiment 895:30-31
Experiment to demonstrate 346:97-100
Experiment to show how electroplating is done 179:134-136
How can you copperplate a safety pin 278:50-51
How can you silver plate a key 278:52
How to 13:42-50
How to do copper and nickel plating 128:189
Nail and copper penny experiment 980:33
Plating a spoon with copper 180:48-49
Simple experiment to show 97:36-37

ELECTROSCOPE. *See also* **ELECTRICITY—STATIC ELECTRICITY; STATIC ELECTRICITY**
Building an electroscope, how to 895:27
Charging electroscope by induction 5:46-49
Cloud chamber, making 895:119-120
Construct an electroscope for use in detecting radiation 564:8
Discharging electroscope by radiation or ionization experiment 768:14-15
Electroscope—making 656:6
Electroscope detects static charge experiment, how to build 1476:8-9
Electroscope detects static charges experiment 1063:163
Electroscope detects static charges experiment, how to make 1426:20-22
Electroscope device from tape and straws detects electrical charge experiment 1132:47-1-47-2
Electroscope from paper detects static charges experiment 972:13
Electroscope in jar using aluminum strips measures static charge, make 1501:24-27
Electroscope measures strength of static charge, how to make 1179:149
Electroscope, making 895:119-120; 938:13-18
How to charge an electroscope negatively 5:42-45
How to make from newspaper 128:166
How to make metal foil ball electroscope 128:166
How to make metal leaf electroscope 128:167
How to make shadow electroscope 128:167
How to make 172:145-147; 179:119-122; 278:29-30; 293:31; 341:10-12; 43:64-71; 91:80-84
Make a charge detector 17:69-72
Make a paper electroscope to detect electric charge 253:148-149
Make a shadow electroscope 176:75-76
Make a static electric detector 195:16-19
Make an electroscope experiment 902:224-225
Make simple electroscope to test static charges 605:56-57
Make to measure electrostatic charge 143:53
Making an aluminum leaf electroscope 5:34-37
Making and using a pith ball electroscope 184:86-95
Metal foil leaves electroscope, how to make 768:11-14
Photoelectric effect experiment using electroscope, how to make 1153:119-123
Pith-ball electroscope—making and using 5:2-9
Pith-ball electroscope—more tests with 5:12-13
Proof plane brings small charge to electroscope, making 768:20-21
Shielding your electroscope, how to do 768:18-19
Simple electroscope—how to make 563:103
Simple one measures force of static electricity—making 682:24-25
Two ways to make an electroscope 436:31
Use to detect radiation 176:93-94
Using a charged electroscope to identify the charges on electrified objects 5:50-53

ELECTROSTATICS. *See also* **ELECTRICITY— STATIC ELECTRICITY**
Charge your friends to 10,000 volts experiment 768:36-37
Clean your records electrostatically experiment 768:35
Dancing soap bubbles experiment 768:33-34
Electric charge stored produces sparks experiment using electrophorus you make 1132:20-1-20-3
Electrify objects and test for static electricity experiment; data table 1004:5.017
Electrostatic charge detector, simple, how to make 768:26-27
Electrostatic jumping beans experiment 768:30
Electrostatic merry-go-round, how to make 768:27
Experiments 43:54-57
Free wheeling straw experiment 768:28-29
Hair raising experiment 768:31
Hindu thread trick, how to do 768:33
Homemade static machine 577:project #51
Magic fingers experiment; uncharged pencil follows your finger 768:29
Make electrostatic dancing men 142:53
Make fluorescent tube glow experiment 768:35-36
Nylon stocking fills out from charge demonstration 902:11
Picking up salt electrostatically experiment 768:32
Using balloons 92:10-15

ELECTROTYPING
Printing plates—how to do 97:38-39

ELEMENTS
Boyle, Robert; who first defined an element project 1525:63-64
Color test for 146:42-43
Colored fire from testing different elements experiment; chart given 960:36
Compound built from atoms—iron oxide from steel wool and water experiment 704:34-35
Flame test to show different elements 83:23-24
How to make hydrogen 157:14
Hydrogen and oxygen in water 83:17-18
Identifying elements by flame test 180:9
Match the element collection game, how to make and play 600:18-19
Models of common chemicals 436:32-33
Table of elements 278:81-83
Turn iron into copper 157:15
What is half-life of an element or isotope experiment 976:53

ELEPHANTS
Elephants use their ears to cool their bodies experiment 1397:40-42
Temperature regulation in animals using elephant ear models experiment 1134:3.004

ELEVATION
Measuring elevation using a transect 1117:41

ELEVATORS. *See also* **GLIDERS**
Air pressure on eardrums 55:103-107
Elevator model demonstrates use of counterweights to raise weights experiment 1400:67
How to make a model 128:119
Making a movable elevator 496:32-33
Model wooden crate elevator, making 867:40

ELF. *See* **ELECTROMAGNETIC RADIATION**

ELLIPSES
Curves from circles, how to draw patterns showing ellipses 1299:28-29
Drawing a perfect ellipse 150:142-143
Drawing planetary orbits [ellipses] project 833:161-162
Ellipse, how to make 1003:37
Elliptical orbits—demonstration 577:project #33
Experiments to show relationship between families of ellipses (Primary) 437:1-33
How to draw an ellipse 642:15-16; 1007:78-79

How to draw and color ellipses 1298:99

ELODEA

Determine effects of simulated oil spill on flora in aquatic environment 997:91-92

Examining green plant cells—elodea 294:15-16

Rate of photosynthesis measured by amount of oxygen given off experiment 871:2.024

EMBRYOLOGY. *See also* **CELLS**

Performation or epigenesis—decide difference between the two 402:95-96

Spontaneous generation—can life arise from lifeless material 402:94-95

EMBRYOS

Can heartbeat of chicken embryo be detected without breaking shell experiment 997:169-171

EMF. *See* **ELECTROMAGNETIC RADIATION**

EMULSIFIERS

Egg yolk as a natural emulsifier in mayonnaise experiment 1261:14

Mayonnaise, make to demonstrate action of emulsifier experiment 976:43

Soap or detergent acts as emulsifier experiment with oil/water/food colors 1476:128

EMULSIONS. *See also* **FOOD—SUSPENSIONS**

Casein glue—how to make 77:26-27

Cold cream—make your own 441:40-44

Curd cheese—how to make 77:24-25

Dressing a salad 77:23

Emulsifiying agent effect on fat demonstrated with dish washing liquid 1395:175

Emulsion in bottle of water and cooking oil experiment 1393:15

Emulsion stability—test of cosmetic creams 441:44-45

Emulsion you can eat mayonnaise—how to make 722:118

Erupting color bubbles from oil and water experiment 1405:60

Experiments 84:81-82

How do emulsions work experiment 1293:79-80

How does beating affect the ingredients—making mayonnaise, mayonnaise recipe 537:30-32, 71

How does emulsion-coated paper work experiment 1293:81-82

Liquid layers—make water float, sink and mix 98:18-19

Liquid sandwich of three liquids experiment 827:76

Make butter 77:24-25; 259:10-11

Make mayonnaise 219:7-9; 259:7-10

Make yogurt 77:27

Making an emulsion 180:20-21

Making mayonnaise to show how oil and vinegar can be mixed together experiment 1484:86-87

Making one 146:56

Marble of oil forms in water and alcohol solution experiment 1229:30-31

Mayonnaise demonstrates emulsifying action of egg experiment; recipe given 1403:46-47

Milky emulsion 77:22-23

Mix two liquids that do not mix experiment 882:11

Mixing oil and water experiment 1316:27

Observe the separation of an emulsion experiment 905:168-169

Oil and water do not mix experiment 827:75; 1066:74

Oil and water don't mix marbling paper experiment 696:36-37

Separation experiment—making whipped cream; whipped cream recipe 537:33-34; 73

Separation of an emulsion experiment 1405:62

Size of drops affects rate at which two liquids separate experiment 1403:44-47

Soap action—make an emulsion 585:93

Test various lotions and creams for different properties 441:36-40

Water and oil can mix with help of detergent experiment 1271:24-25

ENDANGERED ANIMALS

Diorama of endangered animals habitat, making 1013:130

Game; peregrine falcon in search of birds to eat 1232:28-29

Whooping crane egg from papier mache, how to make 1232:36-37

ENDANGERED SPECIES

Alien species in pet shop project; observe and research each species 1340:73-74

Biodiversity; concept of biodiversity demonstrated project 1338:66-67

What animals are extinct or endangered project 1427:32-35

ENERGY. *See also* **ATOMS; FORCE; GEYSERS; KINETIC ENERGY; RUBBER BANDS; SOLAR ENERGY**

Alcohol as fuel, recycling garbage into energy from ethyl alcohol experiment 997:80-82

Bet you can cut through an ice cube and it will seal itself behind you 228:46-47

Boomerang can demonstrates energy change—making 681:6

Bouncing energy from two balls demonstration 1330:28-29

Come back can experiment 1063:306

Conservation—energy activities 236:184-186

Conservation of energy—experiment 585:51-52

Conserve energy in your home project 1427:104-105

Creepy crawler insect demonstrates stored energy in rubber band experiment 1024:18-19

Determine direction of energy transfer of two materials experiment 1396:173-179

Dragster from drink can demonstrates rubber band energy, how to make 1299:55

Elastic and gravitational potential energy experiments 1158:64-68

Elastic motor driven bottle boat experiment 806: 20-21; 806:21-22

Elastic motor driven toy experiments 806:19-22

Elastic motor fan and blow meter experiment 806:17-19

Elastic powered roller designed to make it go further experiment 806:15-11

Elastic powered roller experiment 806:14; 806:15

Elastic powered roller, making 806:12-15

Energy—saving game 624:end sheets

Energy from burning foods and fuel experiment 739:15

Energy makes the world go—experiment 382:100-102

Energy patterns of moving objects when they stop experiment 1389:15

Energy race game 624:end sheets

Energy stored in twisted materials drives simple machines experiment 1073:16-17

Energy transfer—make your own Newton's cradle to demonstrate 575:16-17

Energy use chart to chart what kind of energy user you are project 1427:100-102

Energy values of machines chart 624:40

First Law of Thermodynamics experiment; light energy transferred/transformed 1453:14-15

Geothermal steam engine model, making 895:106-107

Gravity engine you can build 267:25

Heat causes coins in bottle to jump up and down experiment 1030:12

Heat energy moving in spoons—experiment 681:12

Height effect on energy of moving object demonstration 1404:154-155

Height effect on energy of moving object demonstration 1479:96

How energy can change its form demonstration 1479:97

Insulation conserves energy by keeping heat in experiment 1228:70-71

Kinetic—follow the bouncing ball point 222:88-89

Kinetic—the writhing snake!—kinetic and potential energy 205:84-87

Kinetic—what makes the Yo-Yo Yo-Yo 291:134

Kinetic and potential—roller coaster track and ball experiment 373:42-44

Kinetic energy— "rattlesnakes's teeth" trick 585:80-81

Kinetic energy—experiment—hammer and heat 585:130

Kinetic energy rolls round can back to you experiment 937:58-59

Light energy experiments 681:18-19

Machines save energy experiment with block and ramp; data table given 1004:5.004

Make things move 260:1-32

Measuring efficiency of energy 624:16

Meter measures electricity used by house, how to read experiment 1426:38-39

Miniature hydroelectric system, how to make 577:project 58

Newton and Planck; who discovered the quantum theory of energy project 1525:114-120

Newton's cradle toy experiment, how to make 1030:26-27

No-motor rotor; notched stick uses frictional energy to turn experiment 1063:167

Ocean thermal energy conversion demonstration 698:16-17

Pinwheel windmill demonstrates energy from wind, how to make 1380:37

Project 1—how powerful are you 654:22-24

Project 2—power and people 654:24

Project 3—how efficient is your bicycle 654:24-27

Project 32—the speed of a falling body 654:76-79

Project 33—kinetic energy of baseball (Advanced) 654:79-82

Project 34—kinetic energy of batted ball (Advanced) 654:82

Project 35—elastic potential energy 654:82-83

Project 36—elastic potential energy 654:83-84

Project 37—gravitational and elastic potential energy (Advanced) 654:84

Project 38—building better bumpers 654:84-85

Project 39—potential energy in molecules 654:85-87

Project 4—heat and temperature change 654:29-30

Project 40—heat of vaporization (Advanced) 654:87-88

Project 41—heat of melting 654:88

Project 42—heat of fusion (Advanced) 654:88-89

Project 5—heat and mass 654:30

Project 6—mass and temperature change 654:30-31

Project 7—a formula for heat 654:31-32

Project 8—specific heat 654:33-34

Putting energy to work with simple toy 587:38

Returning can experiment with can and rubber bands 940:108-111

Roll back can shows energy produced by unwinding rubber band experiment 1400:82-83

Rolling jar—E equals HW formula tested with jars on inclines (Advanced) 565:117-130

Rubber band changes from potential energy to kinetic energy experiment 1400:80-83

Second Law of Thermodynamics experiment; some transferred energy is useless 1453:15-18

Self propelled buggy, how to make experiment 937:60-61

Spool tank demonstrates rubber band energy, how to make 1299:54

Spring engines—rubber band model boat 267:29-30

Sprouts give energy for life, how to grow 1030:8-9

Steam engines—make a model steam turbine 267:40-41

Stop—go 260:18

Stored energy machine; roll back can with rubber band inside, making 1014:59

Thin or thick soup spins the fastest down ramp experiment 1330:40-41

Toast marshmallow with burning nut experiment 1083:90-91

Transfer of energy—make your own Newton's cradle 142:8-9

Transformation of energy experiment using your body as a speaker 1004:5.012

Transformation of energy from kinetic energy into mechanical energy experiment 1479:99

Turning trash into usable energy experiment 895:102-103

Twisted rubber band energy demonstrated by model carousel, how to make 1073:17

Upright matchbox 260:19

Water wheels—how to make 267:9-11

Wave power; model shows how waves can be used to produce electricity experiment 1134:7.002

Wheel—experiment to demonstrate (Advanced) 393:34-47

Wind generator model makes electricity experiment 698:12-13

Windmill—make a model 267:20-21

ENERGY CONSERVATION. *See also* **RECYCLING**

Annual conductive heat losses using degree days, how to measure experiment 1152:86-87

Building and weatherizing model house experiment 895:81-85

Can taking a shower help save electricity experiment 1012:71

Conserving energy by reducing conductive heat losses experiment 1152:93-95

Conserving energy by reducing convective heat losses experiment 1152:92-93

Conserving energy in your home experiments 1152:118-119

Convection (infiltration) heat losses in your home or school, calculate 1152:90-91

Converting model house to solar garden experiment 895:86-90

134

Draft catchers for door bottoms, how to make 1152:94

Draft detection in home experiment 1063:366

Draft detector, making 895:75

Energy saving experiment at home, how to do 895:80

Energy units converted to other units table 1152:32

Fuel costs for heating home experiment 1152:91-92

Heat and fuel needed to warm house or apartment experiment 1152:36

Heat losses due to conduction in homes, how to measure experiment 1152:82-84

Heat needed to change temperature of l gram of cooking oil by l degree 1152:32-35

Heat transferred and mass of water with temperature change constant experiment 1152:26-29

Heat transferred and temperature change of fixed amount of water experiment 1152:25-26

Home energy audit, how to do 895:74-77

How people can conserve energy resources experiment 1324:90-94

Insulating and building materials in your home or school experiment 1152:81-82

Insulation works to keep cold air out experiment 1371:81-82

Measuring heat from immersion heater in glass of water experiment 1152:23-25

Number of degree days near your home experiment 1152:84-86

Project 17—annual heating costs 654:49

Project 55—storm windows and doors 654:105-106

Project 58—electrical appliances 654:108-111

Project 59—saving heat 654:112

Project 60—do energy audit 654:112-119

R value for common insulating and building materials chart 1152:78

R value of cardboard, how to measure experiment 1152:77-81

Rate of heat flow is related to surface area experiments 1152:56-63

Rate of heat flow related to temperature difference experiment 1152:63-68

Rate of heat flow through different materials experiment 1152:68-72

Tire pressure and auto efficiency experiment 1152:113

Use electricity more wisely; chart of common household appliances use 895:78-79

Water as a heat storage material experiment 895:91

ENGINES. *See also* **TURBINES; WATER WHEELS; WINDMILLS**

Diesel, Rudolph; who invented the diesel engine project 1525:32-34

Electromagnetic crane—model—how to make 267:45

Gravity engine you can build 267:25

Light makes wheel turn engine—making 723:28

Piston and crankshaft model; engine up down motion to rotary motion experiment 1166:21

Rate of wear in engine metal reduced by oil lubricants experiment 1091:32-33

Solar engine experiment 289:48-54

Spring engines—rubber band model boat 267:29-30

Steam—make a model steam turbine 267:40-41

Steam turbine engine—candle powered steam turbine engine—how to build 487:24-25

Water wheels—how to make 267:9-11

Windmill—make a model windmill 267:20-21

ENGRAVING

Engraving, how to make using nail and copper foil experiment 1295:36-38

How to make a metal engraving tool 191:29-34

ENVIRONMENT. *See also* **ECOLOGY; ECOSYSTEMS; POLLUTION**

Adaptation—meaning of 40:178-179

Biology—field study—how to keep a journal 108:9-12

Blind walk and games 363:20-21

Desert terrarium—how to make 400:14

Environment projects; how to do your project scientifically 1297:12-44

Environmental system—how does a balanced community function 371:92-104

Ideas for environment or ecology projects 1297:5

Ideas for environment project exhibits, demonstrations and investigations 1297:9-12

Ideas for environmental management projects 1297:6

Living things affect their environment experiment 1324:23-27

Make a natural resources parade (Primary) 155:6-7

Natural resources scrapbook 155:4-5

Plants grow in different environments game, how to make 1044:16-19

Pollution—collect and chart kinds of litter 400:12

Records to keep on observations of the environment, how to do 1362:30

Sand table models of basic environments, how to make 874:219

Show plant and animal communities 40:176-177

Sounds of environment—where you are, what is it 363:22-24

Things to do—becoming aware of your environment 400:11-12

Woodland terrarium—how to make 400:14

ENVIRONMENTAL PROTECTION. *See* **ACID RAIN; BIODEGRADABILITY; BIODEGRADATION; LANDFILLS; OIL SPILLS; OZONE LAYER**

ENZYMES. *See also* **CATALYST; HUMAN BODY**

Acids and bases effect on catalase 273:50-51

Are enzymes found in all plant materials 273:44-45

Baked steak—acids, bases and enzyme action 74:119-126

Biochemicals eat boiled egg experiment with regular and "biological" detergent 1271:32

Browning of apples; what affects browning of apples experiment 1020:105-108

Can molecules in pineapple break large molecules into smaller ones experiment 831:84-87

Can molecules in yeast make a gas from hydrogen peroxide experiment 831:88-90

Catalase from piece of liver breaks down hydrogen peroxide experiment 1069:18

Catalase is an enzyme 346:54

Catalase removes hydrogen peroxide in plants 273:44-45

Detergent enzymes effect on protein molecules experiment 1396:25-29

Difference in effectiveness of manufactured processed food enzymes experiment 1395:171-176

Digestion of protein by enzymes in human body, experiment 482:34-37

Does concentration of food enzyme affect its activity experiment 1395:171-176

Effect of acids and bases on enzyme catalase 174:58-59

Effect of enzyme concentration 174:56-57

135

Enzyme action in potatoes under different conditions experiment 876:75-76

Enzyme activity—computer project 584:135-137

Enzyme acts as catalyst speeds up reaction of hydrogen peroxide 174:52-53

Enzyme detergent eats egg experiment using regular and enzyme detergent 1435:53-55

Enzyme effect on chemical reaction experiment with potato/hydrogen peroxide 1402:40-43

Enzyme effect on starch in digestive tract experiment 1395:171-176

Enzyme experiments with apples 875:73-75

Enzyme reaction rate controlled by temperature 273:46-47

Enzymes and salts—common chemicals act as enzyme inhabitants 273:48-49

Enzymes break things down experiment with hard boiled egg in detergent 1273:21

Enzymes from saliva experiment using soda crackers and baby food 1370:69

Enzymes improve dirt removing power of soap—experiment to test this 26:120

Enzymes prevent apple from turning brown experiment 1238:75

Experimenting with an enzyme 148:59

Flame from bubbling oxygen from hydrogen peroxide and meat experiment 1083:86

Function of digestive enzymes experiment 1395:165-170

Getting energy from food with enzymes 261:14-16

How does acid pH affect enzymatic activity on starch experiment 1395:174

Hydrogen peroxide changes into water and oxygen experiment 1405:56

Junket—a study of enzyme action 74:117-118

Laundry detergents effect on clothing stains experiment 1396:28

Liquids to gas yeast enzymes 77:36-37

Liver enzymes 77:36-37

Living things affect their environments experiment 1324:23-27

Proteins are changed by denaturing experiment 1396:55-59

Speed of chemical reaction directly related to strength of catalyst exp. 871:3.006

Test for enzymes in human saliva 482:32-34

Test for presence of enzymes in detergent experiment 1402:40-43

Watch an enzyme at work—experiment 6:25

What are enzymes and what do they do in the human body 402:70

Why cut apples turn brown experiment 1484:55-56

William Beaumont's process of digestion experiment 1133:3.007

Yeast—fresh bread—how to make 77:38-39

Yeast—gas from fruit 77:39

Yeast—sugar and water experiment 722:89

EPIGENESIS

Performation or epigenesis—decide difference between the two 402:95-96

EPSOM SALT

Reaction between Epsom Salt and ammonia experiment 1526:78-80

EQUATOR

Earth bulges at equator experiment 1405:68

Why is Equator hotter than North Pole experiment 1003:20-21

EQUINOXES. *See also* **SOLSTICE**

Length of sunlight shortens or lengthens equal amount each day experiment 1062:35-36

EQUIPMENT—HOW TO MAKE. *See also* **LABORATORY EQUIPMENT**

Air oven 9:78-79

Alcohol lamp 9:80-81

Burner tripod 9:86-87

Charcoal burner 9:84-85

Heavy spring scale 9:109

Laboratory tweezers 9:88-89

Making capillary pipette 11:72-74

Ring stand 9:76-77

Rubber band scale 9:108

Support bar 9:72-73

Test tube holder 9:72-73; 9:82-83; 146:12

Test tube rack 9:74-75

Tripod stand 146:12

EQUIPMENT AND CHEMICALS

Ideas for getting hold of chemicals & equipment needed for science experiment 6:44

ERASERS

Compare the reusability of different kinds of rubber 336:76-77

Erasers, how to make 859:13

ERATOSTHENES

Eratosthene's experiment repeat it (Advanced) 658:67-71

Eratosthenes measures the Earth experiment 1156:24-25

EROSION. *See also* **SOILS**

Abrasion shapes the land demonstration 1023:96-97

Binding force of roots prevents erosion 294:33

Can temperature changes cause erosion experiment 852:23-25

Coins surface affected by routine handling experiment 1402:76-79

Contour plowing and straight plowing effect on soil erosion experiment 1008:46-47

Contour plowing to save soil experiment 1371:73-74

Contours, making to demonstrate erosion 874:214-215

Create a dust bowl 666:59

Create or prevent erosion by trying to flush away mini mountain experiment 1328:77

Dams to save soil from erosion—experiment 633:46

Debris or moraine left at base of glacier experiment 1480:134

Demonstrate effects of erosion experiment 860:130-131

Demonstrate effects of water on soils experiment 760:49

Demonstrate erosion of rocks forms highlands and lowlands 301:8-9

Demonstrate wave erosion 175:32

Does rain erode soil experiment 852:22-23

Dune windbreak fences experiment to determine optimum spacing 715:89-91

Effect of acid on statues demonstration 1023:92-93

Effect of contour plowing on soil erosion experiment 978:31-32

Effect of grass on soil to protect against erosion experiment 978:29-30

Effect of mulch in preventing soil loss experiment 978:30-31

Effect of rain water on soil structure experiment 934:46
Effects of wind erosion experiment 978:140-141
Erosion by streams demonstration 934:43-45
Erosion cycle from water erosion experiment using stream table 1342:118-119
Erosion demonstrated with water hose 1437:107-109
Erosion difference in bare soil and in grass covered soil experiment 1379:29
Erosion of rocks by chemical experiment using rock, water and vinegar 1202:15
Erosion of soil experiments 563:73-74
Experiment to demonstrate 382:103-107
Experiment to show 330:79
Experiment with moving water wears away land 132:24
Flooding effect on towns and cities experiment using stream table 1342:119-120
Freezing water effect on rocks experiment 1046:32-34
Glacier ice collects rock that acts as sandpaper and erodes experiment 1480:133
Glaciers move by plastic deformation [creeping, thick liquid] experiment 1480:132
How ocean water rises to create storm surge experiment 1465:97
Humus and its effect on amount of water soil retains experiment data table 1004:1.008
Is ground cover effective, experiment 666:45-46
Loss of plants brings on soil erosion experiment 1060:43-44
Make your own canyon (Primary) 153:16-17
Measuring effect of dripping erosion experiment 715:82-83
Measuring erosion caused by rainwater runoff experiment 715:80-81
Measuring erosion caused by wind experiment 715:87-88
Measuring sand erosion of building materials experiment 715:85-86
Model of water erosion on a mountain experiment 1063:226-227
Models of methods to prevent soil erosion experiment; data tables given 1004:1.009
Moisture affects land erosion demonstration 1023:106-107
Moss works to protect soil from rain and prevent erosion experiment 1472:58
Motion and its effect on erosion experiment 1023:112-113
Mountains rise due to erosion demonstration 1023:116-117
Moving air causes erosion of uncovered soil experiment 1323:37-41
Moving water causes erosion of uncovered soil experiment 1323:42-46
Moving water effect on rocks experiment 1046:29-31
Natural bridges balance demonstration 1023:114-115
Of beach sand by waves experiment 1290:54, 4.1
Oxygen causes rocks to crumble demonstration 1023:90-91
Plant roots stop erosion experiment 1371:72-73
Plants affect erosion experiment 1046:55-57
Plants help prevent erosion experiment 1341:66
Plants prevent erosion of soil—experiment 633:45
Preventing soil erosion display ideas 1060:44
Project to demonstrate erosion of soil 864:123-124
Rain effect on hills with and without ground cover experiment 1405:76

Rain forest land erosion experiment 1240:21
Rain runoff and erosion effect on different mountain soils experiment 1465:93
Raindrops cause erosion experiment 1046:61-62
Rain splash erosion experiment; show layer of rock protects soil underneath 1480:119
Record water, air and plant erosion in your environment 380:34-35
River carves out path downhill demonstration with sand and gravel 1384:13
River erosion in action, how to demonstrate experiment 1281:32
"River soup" sediment sample—making 666:50
Rock erosion due to falling water demonstration 1023:100-101
Rocks change into sand and soil demonstration 1023:94-95
Roots hold the soil—experiment 585:149-150
Roots protect soil from erosion experiment 722:77
Runaway soil experiment demonstrates erosion 1424:80-81
Sand bottle—demonstrate 153:20-21
Sand dune erosion caused by wind experiment 978:113-114
Sand dune erosion project—how to do 715:14-15
Sediment flow and height experiment 666:46-47
Sheet erosion—demonstrate 723:89-90
Slope affects soil erosion experiment 1046:52-54
Slopes of sand eroded by water demonstration 1080:24
Soil aquarium—demonstration 293:4
Soils; some soils erode faster than other soils project 1195:10-17
Speed of running water affects erosion demonstration 1023:102-103
Stream table—how to build 400:56
Stream table activities 400:56-57
Stream table model of river; how to build and use 1342:114-118
Stream tables: a model for studying water flow and erosion 586:27-28
Venturi effect demonstrated with sand erosion project 715:12-13
Water carves the Earth experiment 1441:69
Water erosion of soil experiment 738:29
Water holding capacity of soils experiment 1424:108
Water velocity can be slowed down to prevent erosion experiment 715:94-95
Water wears away rock experiment using chalk sticks and jar of water 1202:12
What factors affect water erosion experiment 900:128-129
Why does soil erosion occur experiment 1294:20-21
Wind and water cause erosion experiments 1441:51
Wind causes soil erosion experiment 1046:58-60
Wind erosion demonstration 577:project #40
Wind erosion makes desert landscapes, how to demonstrate 1080:23
Wind erosion of land affected by moisture experiment 1405:77
Wind in the desert effect on landscape experiment 1480:136-137
Wind, dust and air pollution experiment to demonstrate erosion 874:217-218
Wind, ice and water erosion demonstrations with sand 816:7

ESCHER, M. C.
Escher picture patterns, how to make 1299:94-99
Picture patterns given; birds, ghosts, cyclops, plumber's nightmare 1299:94-99

ESKIMOS
Bull roarer—how to make 629:149
Eskimo buzzer spinning toy—making 629:147
Eskimo sculptures—how to make 629:148
Experiments of their culture 320:entire boo
Large igloo from strong cardboard, how to make 1518:42-43

ESP
An ESP test—or can you read minds? 625:40
ESP card tests for sixth sense 472:2214
ESP tester, circuit diagram given, how to make 1249:56-57
Experiments 114:15-21
Extra-sensory perception test, how to make 1248:39
Extrasensory perception—several experiments to test ESP 400:114
Extrasensory perception experiments in ESP with Zener Cards 532:24-25
Extrasensory perception tester, how to make 830:76-78
Performance tests for telepathy and clairvoyance 507:1871
The psychic ring pendulum 400:114
Thought message sending experiment with playing cards 1369:82-83
Thoughts as projects 400:114

ESSENTIAL OILS. *See also* **PERFUMES**
Extracting essential oils for perfumes 441:55-62

ESTIMATION
Art and science of estimating, how to do 1159:118-120
Estimate air pollution project 1070:30-31
Estimate snail population experiment 1070:26-27
Experiments and activities in estimating (Primary) 485:1-33

ESTUARIES
How does saltwater mix in an estuary experiment 997:67-69

ETHANOL
Make a molecular model of ethanol 6:32

ETHERIC FORCE (WIRELESS)
Edison's experiments 230:77-83

ETHYLENE GAS
A gas chamber for fruits 231:40
Can ethylene molecules cause fruits and vegetables to ripen 396:72-73
Ethylene gas effect on ripening fruits experiment 1060:56
Ethylene gas from banana causes tomato to ripen experiment 1440:77-78
Ethylene gas promotes germination of some seeds experiment 1375:86-88
Ethylene gas promotes ripening in bananas experiment 1484:126-128
Ripe fruit in a hurry experiment 827:65

EUCALYPTUS
Eucalyptus tree, how to grow 1486:36

EUDOXUS
Who was first to draw a map of the sky project 1525:53-55

EUGLENA. *See also* **PROTOZOA**
Adventure 8—we meet with a puzzle—euglena and volvox under a microscope 403:26-30
Collecting—how to 500:56-58
Observe under microscope 889:36
Stimulants effect on euglena microorganisms experiment 1267:93-97

EULER, LEONARD
His networks in Konigsberg 477:30-31

EULER'S CIRCLES. *See* **VENN DIAGRAMS**

EUTROPHIC LAKES
Acid lake; how to make mini acid lake and buffer it experiment 1328:63
Fertilizers in lakes cause overgrowth of plants experiment 1328:66-67

EUTROPHICATION. *See also* **ALGAE; LAKES; PONDS; WATER—POLLUTION**
Detrimental effect of phosphates in detergents on pond plants/animals experiment 1476:192
Fertilizers in lake water cause overgrowth of plants experiment 1328:66-67
How to measure in body of water 330:89-90
Nutrient enriched waters and algae growth experiment 1450:135-142
Nutrients added to lakes and ponds cause water pollution experiment 1325:55-59
Phosphate pollutant can be removed from water experiment 1325:60-64

EVAPORATION. *See also* **HEAT; WATER—EVAPORATION**
Activities to demonstrate [Primary] 759:43-44
Being wet increases cooling experiment 829:41-42
Can water evaporation be reduced 532:32
Case of the vanishing water 330:12-15
Causes and effects 55:137-143
Come back sugar (Primary) 288:12-13
Condensation 12:86-90
Cooling effect of evaporation experiment using two thermometers and fan 1397:43
Cooling is result of evaporation experiment 760:45
Demonstrations of 295:45-47
Does rate of evaporation affect cooling experiment 762:112-113
Evaporating water experiment with heat & air circulation; experiment worksheet 537:12-14, 59
Evaporation and vapor pressure experiment; data tables given 1004:3.014
Evaporation causes a liquid to cool down experiment 1090:30-31
Evaporation cools things—experiment (Primary) 601: unpaged
Evaporation experiment—drying apples; drying apples worksheet 537:15-16, 61
Evaporation experiment—making stewed tomatoes; stewed tomatoes recipe 537:14-15, 60
Evaporation in action—observe glass of water, rain puddle (Primary) 452:68-69
Evaporation of liquid dependent on surface exposed to air experiment 1090:28
Evaporation rates of specific amounts of water from heat source experiment 1447:24-26
Evaporation rates of water; how to measure experiment 978:139
Evaporation takes away heat experiment 1405:58
Experiments 693:18-19
How evaporation cools 281:58
Keeps things cool (Primary) 323:18-19
Leidenfrost's lifetime of droplets on very hot surfaces experiment 1133:7.003

Message written with shiny crystals, how to do 905:132-133

Message written with shiny salt crystals experiment 1405:59

Physical change of a compound 585:89-90

Temperature and evaporation of water experiment 1447:24-26

The paper towel soak up 295:31

Warm air speeds up evaporation activities [Primary] 759:44

Water going into the air 281:21

Water into vapor 146:61

Wet towel demonstrates 747:20

What does wind do to wet objects experiments [Primary] 744:14

What happens to wet objects left in the sun experiment [Primary] 744:11

What is left after water evaporates 232:89

EVOLUTION. *See also* **GENETICS; HEREDITY**

Concept of evolution project using sheets of paper 1063:263

Fossils—an evidence of evolution 402:103-105

Mutation—mechanism of evolution 402:105-106

EXPERIMENTS. *See* **SCIENCE EXPERIMENTS**

EXPLOSIONS

Making a miniature one in a can 291:80-81

EXTENSIOMETER

Extensiometer measures change in size of volcano experiment; how to make model 1477:52-55

EXTRATERRESTRIAL INTELLIGENCE

Decipher an alien message experiment 1478:146

How many aliens are there in the Galaxy experiment; make alien calculator 1478:146-147

EYE. *See also* **HUMAN BODY; VISION**

Abilities and inabilities of the human eye 402:67-69

Blind spot—locate 350:129-130

'Blind spot'—locate the 'blind spot' in your eye 291:204

Blind spot in eye—find your blind spot using coins 548:19-23

Calf eye, dissecting—how to 692:87-92

Correcting eye defects 135:31

Distance deception—coins used to test and demonstrate 548:26-28

Eye and light—demonstrate inverted image 208:10-15

Eye-color from parents' genes experiment 1048:26

Eye dissection (sheep or beef) 335:92

Eye dominance—right or left eyed 366:209

Eye from paper and straws—make (Primary) 673:23

Figuring out the job of the iris 148:73

Fovea of eye—experiment with coins to test size of fovea 548:13-16

Investigation into the resolving power of the eyes 420:49-53

Keeping the lids on 228:14

Locating your blind spot 148:77

Magnifying glasses 135:30

Make 'goggles'—protect from sunlight (Primary) 320:9

Making a model 595:12

Model eye—making 659:19

Persistence of vision—test for using coins 548:23-26

Retina, rods and cones—test for color vision and afterimages 258:49-55

Retinal fatigue—what is retinal fatigue 402:66-67

Test for dominant eye 258:44

Test to locate blind spot on the retina 258:15-16

The blink game—try not to blink (Primary) 551:unpaged

Two eyes—significance of—coins used as test 548:16-19

Why do we have two eyes experiment 794:31

EYE TRICKS. *See also* **OPTICAL ILLUSIONS; OPTICS**

Blind spot 27:106

Magic peephole 27:104-105

EYEGLASSES. *See also* **LENSES**

Detective disguise glasses, how to make 643:30-31

Eyeglass lenses rest on board—words or pictures show differences in types 558:82-83

How to clean eyeglasses 563:155-156

Identify types of eyeglasses 381:132-136

Peripheral vision is worse in people who wear glasses experiment 1195:63-69

Pinhole glasses, how to make 941:9-10

Rose-colored spectacles—how to make 358:100-101

Sungoggles—making 732:40-41

EYLAIS

Adventure 16—we make the acquaintance of eylais under a microscope 403:59-61

F

FABRIC. *See also* **CLOTH; TEXTILES**
Absorbency; which materials soak up water the fastest experiment 1509:8
Bleach effect on fabric samples experiment 1396:108-110
Commercial fabric waterproofing agents tested for effect/durability experiment 1295:122-123
Fabric dyed with beets or red cabbage, vinegar and baking soda experiment 1295:122
Fabric fibers, weaving and colors examined using magnifying glass experiment 1295:117-121
How are fabrics made; observe fibers under magnifying glass 1508:10
Stain removers; duplicate advertising claims experiment using stained fabrics 1295:123
Wax dyeing fabrics, how to do 1244:24-25

FACES
Your secret face—left and right sides 366:254-255

FAHRENHEIT, GABRIEL. *See also*
THERMOMETERS
Draw diagrams comparing Fahrenheit/Celsius/Kelvin thermometer scales experiment 1396:186-187
Fahrenheit scale to measure temperature—how he made it (Primary) 648:18-27

FAIRY RINGS
Investigate growth habits of fungi in fairy rings project 1313:69-71

FAIRY SHRIMP
Adventure 50—animal that swims on its back—fairy shrimp under microscope 403:191-193

FAKIR, INDIAN
Sit on an upside down bed of nails to investigate Fakir's trick 549:19-22

FALL. *See also* **SEASONS—FALL**
Animals—demonstrate how fur and feathers keep them warm 40:53-54
Color of leaves in fall explanation 1227:43
Fall activities 236:144-145

FALLING BODIES
Galileo; who discovered the laws of falling bodies project 1525:47-49

FALLING OBJECTS. *See also* **GRAVITY**
Acceleration of falling bodies due to gravity and air resistance experiment 1157:58-61
Catch the falling dollar bill experiment 960:47
Demonstrate bounce heights of balls 295:70-72
Different weight, different fall 295:54-55
Do objects of different sizes and weights fall at different speeds exp. 851:33-34
Egg survives fall experiment 960:40
Falling at constant speed 295:67-69
Falling objects—experiment 657:102-104
Falling sideways pendulums in motion 295:60-62
Falling sideways 295:73-75
Galileo and the Leaning Tower of Pisa 102:148-149
Galileo's methods for diluting gravity and measuring time experiment 1156:35-42
Law of falling bodies demonstration 940:120-121
Parachute canopy fabric and load carried affect rate of descent experiment 1004:5.007
Pendulums that dance and twist 295:63-64
Repeat Galileo's experiment 448:23-25
Robert Boyle's objects of different masses fall thru vacuum at same rate 1133:4.007

Speed of a falling ball 295:55-56
Submarine—up and down 295:69
What's your reaction time 295:59

FALLING RATE
Calculating falling rate, how to do 1395:207
Falling rate of objects changed by weight experiment 1399:12-15

FAMILY TREE
Family tree database computer program project 1021:137-138
Record how traits are inherited on family tree project 970:67-69

FANS
Fan with electric motor, how to build 1076:36-37

FANTASY
Fantasy trips for creativity 400:115

FARADAY, MICHAEL
Air is needed for candle to burn experiment 752:89
Air pressure demonstration construct simple barometer experiment 752:109-110
Carbon dioxide is heavier than air experiment 752:116
Carbonic acid gas—how to prepare 752:114-115
Chemistry of candle flame and combustion experiment 752:90-91
Construct gas generator to make hydrogen experiment 752:101-102
Decompose water using electricity experiment 752:106-107
Effect of oxygen on combustion experiment 752:117-118
Electroplate with copper experiment 752:104-105
Flame consumes smoke when super heated in second flame experiment 752:96-97
Force exerted by pressure of air experiment 752:111-112
Generate oxygen chemically experiment 752:108
Limewater used as test for carbon dioxide experiment 752:113
Oxidation of zinc experiment create Faraday's philosophic wool 752:94-95
Physical properties of candle flame experiment 752:87
Solid substances in flame give off light experiment 752:92-93
Vapor produced by burning candle burns experiment 752:85-86
Voltaic pile generates electric current experiment 752:103
Water expands upon turning to steam experiment 752:100
Water expands when freezing experiment 752:99
Water is by-product of combustion experiment 752:97-98
Electricity can be converted into magnetism—repeat famous experiment 23:5-6
His experiment—how to duplicate 23:5-6
Inventor of generator 209:37
Producing current by induction—experiment 63:74-77
Candle magic—experiment 146:48-49
Demonstration of Michael Faraday's famous experiment 830:6
Does ice conduct electricity experiment 895:29-30
Electricity Faraday's way with magnetism producing electricity experiment 1063:165
Electricity from magnetism experiment 1133:5.011
Electromagnetic induction experiment 1133:5.012
Electroplating your house key experiment 895:30-31
Faraday's discovery demonstrated by making an electric swing 608:19-20

140

Faraday's discovery experiment; generating electric current from magnets 1156:129-133

Faraday's discovery that magnets create electricity experiment 1476:34-35

Faraday's discovery; electricity from magnets experiment 1514:94-98

Faraday's electric generator, making 627:38

Faraday's electromagnetic induction experiment with bar magnet, compass, wire 1473:40

Faraday's experiment to make electricity experiment 973:43

Faraday's experiment with iron filings 1514:26-28

Faraday's experiment; how a magnet can induce electric current 1309:25

Faraday's ice pail experiment 5:74-77

Faraday's Ice-Pail experiments 895:27-29

His experiments 42:107-114

Investigating force on a current—carrying wire in a magnetic field 63:54-57

Investigating the properties of candle flames experiment 1133:7.007

Magnetism produces electricity experiment 768:97-99

Make a Faraday cage 176:76-77

Movement of current-carrying wire in a magnetic field experiment 1133:5.010

Project 31—generating electricity 654:72-73

Proving Faraday's theory—experiment 627:40

Regelation exp.—the melting and refreezing of ice in warm water 604:48-51

Repeat famous experiment—making electricity with a magnet and coil of wire 445:17

Repeat Faraday's magnetic field experiment 179:148-150

Repeat Michael Faraday's electricity from magnetism—experiment 448:44-45

Showing inductive current—experiment 627:37

Who invented alternating current project 1525:38-40

Who invented the electric motor project 1525:35-37

Demonstrate area of greatest heat in candle flame experiment 752:88

First law of electrolysis experiment 1156:125-129

FARMING PROBLEMS

The wheat game—making 607:55-57

FARMS

Compare local farmers markets with large food companies products 380:56-57

FATS

A test for fat 280:53

Brown paper bag fat test for fat in food 630:17

Butter—coalescing fat droplets from a suspension 74:54-55

Butter your bread 280:52

Chemical test for 335:79-80

Emulsifying agent effect on fat demonstrated with dish washing liquid 1395:175

Emulsifying fats 148:65

Fat in food 261:44-46

Fat in foods survey questions 1262:18-19

How fat content affects whipping of cream from light and heavy cream experiment 1484:107-109

Ice cream taste and texture compared with Simplesse fat substitute experiment 1484:132-133

Invisible fat in foods experiment 1262:7

Nut butter—pressing out oils 74:52-53

Shortening becomes clear when it melts experiment 1251:41-42

Test for fat in foods experiment 827:77

Test for fats in food 835:60-62

Test for which dairy product has the most fat, how to do 1312:43

Testing foods for fat activities for classroom 1291:29-30

Testing foods for fats experiment; chart given 792:29-30

Testing for fat in food—experiment 628:72-73

Testing for fat or grease in foods experiment 924:37

Testing for starch, fat and protein in food using chemicals experiment 1069:19

Tests for fat in food 253:115-116

Where's the fat—test for fats in foods you eat 607:53

Which foods contain fat experiment 901:216

FATS AND OILS

Do different oils become solid at different temperatures experiment 831:47-49

Fat test for fat in foods experiment 1214:13

Greasy goo (Primary) 259:5-6

Make mayonnaise (Primary) 259:7-10

Oil and grease molecules are slippery experiment 1251:43-45

Test for fats and oils in foods experiment 1259:27-30

FAULTS

Do different materials fault differently experiment 1342:93

How faults work demonstration 1080:17

Model of a fault, how to make 1342:90-93

FEATHERS

A feather mystery trick 585:76-78

Adventure 8—we examine a feather under a hand lens 29:41-43

Collect and display feathers, how to do 778:20-21

Collect and preserve feathers, how to do 1360:24

Compare feathers and observe their use 901:126-127

Different methods of cleaning oily feathers experiment 1134:6.012

Down feathers are good insulation 257:10

Effect of oil spills on bird feathers experiment 1295:70-71

Feather from paper, how to make 901:128

Feather writing 231:63

Gull feather pen—how to make 359:13-15

Parts of under microscope 82:69

FEELING. See **SENSES—TOUCH**

FELUCCA—EGYPTIAN

Sailboat—how to make 54:61

FERMENTATION. See also **FOOD; YEAST**

Ferment sauerkraut in soda bottle experiment 1527:24-25

Fermentation of yeast produces carbon dioxide experiment 1395:104

Making vinegar from apple juice experiment 924:45

Making wine—experiment 6:31

"Mother of vinegar"—experiment 585:157-158

Observing fermentation using yeast 52:46-48

Yeast produces more carbon dioxide gas when ginger added to sugar experiment 1251:68-70

Yogurt—making your own 219:33-37

FERNS

Adventure 27—we identify some ferns under a hand lens 29:129-133

Adventure 39—we trace the life history of ferns under a microscope 403:141-146

Cycles of a fern; how to grow ferns from spores experiment 1440:73-76

Fern cycle—growth observed 436:35

Fern life cycle experiment 1476:107

Fern spores, how to grow plants from 879:180

Ferns grown from spores experiment 1069:63

Grow your own ferns from spores—using brick, moss and water 483:42-44

Growing ferns indoors 294:28-29

Make collection of dried ferns 294:29-30

Propagating ferns from spores, how to do 784:38-39

Spore pod from fern opens to light and closes to water experiment 1214:21

Test tasting fiddleheads experiment 1061:118-119

When the weather's fine—collect fern seed to grow—experiment 574:20

FERTILIZERS

Compost pile makes natural fertilizers from garbage experiment 1240:27

Earthworms internal anatomy affected by pesticides and fertilizers experiment 1450:66-71

Effect of fertilizer on algae growth experiment 950:36

Effect of on plant growth experiment 829:59-60

Effect of phosphates and fertilizers on water quality for animals experiment 978:73-74

Effects of fertilizers and sewage in aquatic environments experiment 1450:121-127

Fertilizer and soil experiment 738:31

Fertilizers in lake water cause overgrowth of plants experiment 1328:66-67

Make plants grow (Primary) 326:16-17

Manure tea fertilizer, how to make 1265:90

Manure tea fertilizer, how to make 986:70

Mineral requirements of growing plants experiment 1060:68-72

Minerals from soil and hydroponic mineral solutions affect plant growth 1060:69-72

Minerals in soil determine growth of bean plants experiment 1060:68-69

Nitrogen and other nutrients are needed for plant growth experiment 1324:54-58

Nutrient enriched waters and algae growth experiment 1450:135-142

Nutrients added to lakes and ponds cause water pollution experiment 1325:55-59

Phosphate pollutant can be removed from water experiment 1325:60-64

Plant food makes plants grow better 324:24-25

Study of duckweed population and effect of fertilizers experiment 871:2.010

Toxicity test on invertebrates for effect of lawn fertilizers experiment 1267:81-83

FETCHNER DISC

How to make 176:61-62

FIBER

Amount of fiber in breakfasts we eat experiment 1193:26-28

Which cereal has more fiber experiment 1484:144

FIBER OPTICS. *See also* **OPTICAL FIBERS**

Bell's Photophone; modern day version, how to make 1249:17-24

Bend light and make it turn corners experiment 937:108-111

Bend light experiment using metal coffee can, flashlight and water 1411:64-65

Bend light with fiber optics experiment 860:213-214

Coin disappears in bowl of water experiment 1082:86-90

Color-sensing trick using fiber optic rod 1138:78-80

Fiber optics illuminator 386:7

Fiber optics kit 386:24-29

Glancing rays of light experiment using beam tank, how to build 1092:20

How are fiber optics used experiment 1293:121-122

How fiber optics work experiment 941:71-72

Light-beam receiver experiment 1249:20-21

Light-beam transmitter experiment 1249:18-19

Liquid light experiment to see how optical fibers work 1092:23

Pouring light experiment 1082:92-94

Send light through glass baking dish experiment 1082:80-86

Stream of light concentrated experiment using black plastic bottle/flashlight 1308:31

Total internal reflection experiment 762:32-35

Transmit sound with a flashlight beam experiment 1132:67-1-67-4

Transparent gelatin that light cannot get through experiment 1082:90-92

Why do doctors use fiber optics experiment 860:213-214

FIBERS. *See also* **MICROSCOPE; TEXTILES**

Absorption and shrinkage of natural and synthetic fibers experiment 1259:80-81

Acids, bases and bleach effect on fibers experiment 1259:81-82

Appearance and strength of natural and synthetic fibers compared experiment 1259:77-80

Bacteria attacks fibers in fabrics and wears out clothing experiment 1259:83-84

Combustibility of fibers; which will burn experiment 1259:82-83

Compare fibers of different fabrics experiment 795:15

Cotton—structure of cotton fibers under microscope 294:12

Cotton fuzz 257:14

Dandelion fuzz has hundreds of fibers 257:12-13

Dyeing fabric fibers by direct dyeing and by vat dyeing experiment 1259:86-88

Experiments 11:80-84

Fiber flame test 17:38-40

Flame tests and identification table for smell and ash 346:138

Heat retention of fibers in clothing experiment 1259:84-85

How are fibers dyed experiment 1508:11

How to get fibers from pineapple leaves 257:15-18

How to make rayon thread 319:85-87

Make paper from short lint fibers 257:30-32

Make thread by teasing and spinning 257:25-29

Natural or synthetic fibers absorbency experiment 1294:40-41

Natural rope 17:36-37

Silk—examine silk fibers and cocoons 257:20-22

Wool—how wool keeps a sheep warm 257:8-9

Wool fibers—pull and twist into yarn 26:77-78

FIBONACCI, LEONARDO

Fibonacci Rectangles investigation 1350:60

Fibonacci sequence of numbers investigation 1348:29-31

FIBONACCI SERIES

Fibonacci series of numbers information 1248:30-33

FIDDLER CRABS

Are fiddler crabs right handed or left handed experiment; survey chart given 1225:80-81

Daily changes in fiddler crabs in the field and in the laboratory 266:40-43

Eyes of fiddler crabs sensitive to movement experiment 1225:80

Observations of the world of fiddler crabs, how to do 1225:76-82

Reaction of fiddler crabs to vibrations experiment 1225:80

FIELD OF FORCE. *See* **MAGNETIC FIELDS**

FIELDS

A grassy field—community terrarium 268:41-44

Animals—looking for animals on your hands and knees (Primary) 108:51-57

Animals—observing animals in grassy places 60:49-57

The life of a grassy field 268:35-39

FILM SHOW

Making 356:12-13

FILM STRIP VIEWER

Cardboard tube viewer—how to make 558:73

FILTERS

Best filter for cleaning dirty water experiment 1509:16

Clean dirty water with activated charcoal experiment 1046:91-93

Clean dirty water with sand and coffee filter experiment 1344:21

Clean water from dirty water experiment in water filtration 1240:4

Cleaning dirty water experiment using filters 1134:6.008

Color filters change color of light experiment 860:214-216

Colored filter transmits some colors and absorbs others experiment 1132:26-1-26-2

Colored filters affect light experiment 1293:123-125

Device for filtering water through soil experiment 998:134

Evaluation of paper and cloth filters 363:77-78

Filter to filter water, make from plastic bottle, gravel, sand and cotton 1427:72-75

Filtering liquids—experiment 598:37

Filtering water experiment using flower pots 1362:17

Filtering water experiment 1234:81

Filtering water with model filtering plant 368:38-40

Funnel filters water through gravel and sand experiment 1243:18-19

How a filter works 360:79

How do filters help clean air experiment; examine new and used filters 1427:54-55

How to filter mixture 157:11

Make a filter 146:15-16

Materials that filter faster will not clean water experiment 969:105-107

Muddy water filtered through paper filter, sand and charcoal experiment 1371:38-39

Paper filter that filters best experiment 1509:17

Simple way to clean water with funnel filled with gravel 1105:14

Value of filters and strainers experiment 834:77-78

Water filter—making 741:27

Water filter for muddy water experiment 1161:31

Water filter from funnel, paper filter, gravel and sand, how to make 1331:77

Water filter using sand, gravel, and charcoal in flowerpot, how to make 1179:132-133

Water filter, how to make to filter dirty water 1414:16-17

Waterworks filter—making 678:26

Why is light white; experiment with colored filters 860:217

FILTERS AND FILTERING

Different methods of purifying water, how to demonstrate 978:80-81

FILTRATION. *See also* **WATER—PURIFICATION**

How can paper help clean muddy water (Primary) 69:42-43

Water, how to filter 663:35

FINGER PAINT

Make finger paint 563:160

FINGERNAILS

Different parts of a fingernail experiment 1402:68-71

Fingernails—how fast do they grow experiment 762:59-60

How fast do fingernails grow 381:102

How fast do human fingernails grow experiment 1506:93-94

How fast do your fingernails grow 538:117

FINGERPRINTS

Adventure 56—science of criminal detection—fingerprints under microscope 403:215-219

Be a fingerprint detective—how to do 538:118

Bloody fingerprint trick 966:104-106

Collect and lift fingerprints experiment 1506:95-97

Collect and observe patterns of finger prints experiment 1479:40

Collect and observe patterns of fingerprints experiment 904:176-177

Comparing fingerprints game, how to do 882:39

Dusting for fingerprints, taking fingerprints, how to do 1016:26-27

Experiments with 107:90-91

Fingerprint collection, how to discover and transfer fingerprints 508:63-65

Fingerprint notebook file, how to make 643:17

Fingerprint sleuth kit, how to make 600:58-59

Fingerprinting kit, how to make 643:14-16

Fingerprinting to show difference 293:29

Fingerprinting, how to do 870:12-14

Fingerprints with sticky tape—making 532:104

Fingerprints, making 930:12-13

How do fingerprints compare project 901:157

How fingerprints are transferred and analyzed experiment 1402:56-59

How is fingerprinting your body's signature—experiment 628:21-22

How to make fingerprints 399:48-49; 1246:38; 1370:24

Is there a positive way to identify every human being 402:73-74

Lipstick and Scotch tape fingerprints, how to make 1005:18

Make a study of fingerprints, how to 794:14

Making fingerprints 146:57

Making prints of your fingers 148:81

Observe similarities and differences in fingerprints 760:38

Pencil and paper prints 550:99-102

Pencil smudge method and ink pad method for fingerprinting experiment 1063:190

Taking fingerprints how to 625:42
Taking fingerprints 133:21
Ways to get fingerprints from different materials experiment 871:3.003
What is best way to take fingerprints 381:104

FINITE NUMBERS
Finite and ordinary numbers compared using a week—clock and old nursery rhyme 547:1-33

FIRE. *See also* **COMBUSTION; SMOKE**
Air keeps fire burning (Primary) 322:22-23
Alcohol water and fire—burn a handkerchief without hurting yourself 228:49
Burning candles need oxygen in air to keep burning experiment 1526:102-104
Burning consumes oxygen experiment 1396:19-21
Carbon dioxide extinguisher from baking soda and vinegar experiment 1073:87
Carbon dioxide from baking soda and vinegar puts out flame experiment 888:80-84
Carbon dioxide from vinegar and baking soda puts out flame experiment 709:59
Carbon dioxide gas puts out candle flame experiment 1255:22
Carbon dioxide smothers a fire 44:98-99
Carbon in flame deposited as soot if temperature of burning not high experiment 1435:115-117
Colored fire from testing different elements experiment; chart given 960:36
Does all air burn experiment with candle in dish of water 1073:86
Does all the air burn experiment 909:82
Does all the air burn 660:34
Experiment to show chemistry of 85:14-15
Fight fire with carbon dioxide 122:141-143
Fire bow, how to construct and make fire 1063:173
Fire bows to start a fire 66:106-124
Fire needs air to burn 660:34
Fire needs air to burn experiment with candle 1196:29
Fire needs air to burn experiment 1028:9; 1255:5
Fire needs air; three candle race experiment 909:82
Fire needs oxygen experiment with candle 902:35
Fire needs oxygen to burn—experiment with pumpkin and candle 452:61-63; 671:13
Fire needs oxygen to burn experiment using candle in covered jar 1435:113-114
Fire needs oxygen to burn experiment using candle, jar, and dish of water 1212:11
Fire needs oxygen to burn experiment with candle and jar 1219:43; 1322:15-16
Fire needs oxygen to burn experiment with candle, vinegar, and baking soda 1032:20-21
Fire needs oxygen to burn experiment 1162:7; 1332:6-7; 829:15-16
Fire needs oxygen to burn pumpkin and candle experiment 759:58
Fire needs oxygen to burn, candle under glass experiment 888:77-79
Fire proof paper—bet you can boil water in a paper cup 228:48
Fire-danger rating of your areas experiment 1063:288
Flame—discover what a flame is 319:63-64
Flame—what are different parts of a flame 319:64-65
Flame from bubbling oxygen from hydrogen peroxide and meat experiment 1083:86
Flammability of wood experiment 969:102-104

Flour flame 249:11
Golden sparkles; steel wool burns experiment 906:47
Identifying the gas necessary for fires 180:77
Invisible flame killer—CO_2 (carbon dioxide) 249:9
Lavoisier; who first discovered oxygen is necessary for fire project 1525:67-69
Magic—pyrophoric lead, smoke screen, writing with fire, pyrophoric iron 87:48-51
Make a fire on ice 291:218-219
Needs air to burn (Primary) 326:24-25
Needs oxygen to burn jar and candle experiment 743:22
Needs oxygen to burn; glass over candle experiment 898:3
Needs oxygen to burn 44:96-97
Oxygen fire—experiment 293:45
Oxygen in air burns; other gases in air do not burn experiment 1073:86
Oxygen in air keeps fire burning; lit candle under glass demonstrates 1415:22-23
Oxygen needed for fire to burn experiment with candle and different snuffers 1073:86
Oxygen needed for fire to burn; candle under glass experiment 976:34
Oxygen needed to keep fire burning experiment with candle and plant 978:121
Paper that won't burn experiment 906:48
Show fires need air 319:65-66
Stunt—make smoke come from your fingertips 228:34-35
Trick 27:43-44
Two flames from one 249:10
What is needed to cause a fire experiment 906:44-45
Why things burn—the disappearing flame 249:8

FIRE ALARMS
Fire alarm, how to make from battery and buzzer 1243:34-35
How to make 472:2218
Make from clothespins 203:54
System—making 12:103-106

FIRE ENGINE
Fire engine model—how to make 652:26-29

FIRE EXTINGUISHER
A gas that puts out fire—experiment 72:58-60
A paper extinguisher for a paper fire 550:110-111
Alka-Seltzer in water puts out candle flame experiment 1526:72-73
Carbon dioxide extinguisher from baking soda and vinegar experiment 1073:87; 1212:10
Carbon dioxide from baking soda and vinegar puts out candle flame experiment 1508:28
Carbon dioxide from vinegar and baking soda mixture puts out flame experiment 1415:9
Carbon dioxide gas from jar of water/baking soda/vinegar puts fire out 1229:44-45
Carbon dioxide gas from vinegar and baking soda experiment 960:16-17
Carbon dioxide gas puts out candle flame experiment 1255:22
Carbon dioxide gas puts out flame experiment with eggshell and vinegar 1271:22
Carbon dioxide gas, make and use to smother fire experiment 895:11-12
Carbon dioxide in balloon puts out candle flame experiment 980:47

Carbon dioxide puts out candle flame experiment; use baking soda/vinegar 1179:119

Carbon dioxide puts out fire experiment using vinegar and baking soda 1435:87-89

Demonstrate simple use 147:36-37

Fire extinguisher from baking soda, and vinegar in container experiment 1063:316

Fire extinguisher from tin can, baking soda, and vinegar, how to make 1244:22

Fire extinguisher gas—making 693:43-44

Fire extinguisher, making 909:83

Fire extinguisher uses baking soda on candle flame experiment 1435:118-119

Fire extinguisher, how to make 382:153-157; 605:34-37; 660:35

Fire extinguishing with carbon dioxide 186:108-109

Fire needs oxygen to burn experiment 1028:33

Foam type fire extinguisher—making 381:28-29

How to make 319:32-33

How to make using lemons and baking soda 89:18-19

Make a model extinguisher 30:39

Make fire extinguisher, how to 902:37

Make from detergent bottle, soda and vinegar 217:28-30

Make soda acid extinguisher 179:55-57

Make using balloon, siphon bottle and bicycle pump 217:21-27

Making 112:14-15; 150:124-125

Model from bottle and cork; baking soda and vinegar puts flame out 790:13

Put out fire with invisible extinguisher 291:212-213

Quench the fire—experiment with baking soda 563:152

Show carbon dioxide puts out flame 97:34-35

Soda fire fighter—how to make 203:19

The sensational CO_2 fire extinguisher, how to make 600:48-49

The spirited fire extinguisher—carbon dioxide in action 205:116-120

Tin can model—how to make 472:2220

Vinegar and baking soda foam put out fire experiment 695:45 Vinegar and soda fire extinguisher—experiment 489:83

FIRE SAFETY

Plan a fire escape route 508:16

FIRE TRUCKS

Fire fighting truck that squirts water—how to make 410:26-27

FIREFLIES

Can you communicate with fireflies experiment 904:96-97

Can you read by firefly light 333:83-85

Collection and care of 313:19-23

Collection, care and observation of 331:59-67

Communicate with fireflies experiment using flashlight 1479:30

Determine relation between frequency of flashes and temperature 285:92

Does carbon dioxide cause fireflies to flash more—experiment 174:54-55

Does light from fireflies give off heat experiment 1405:31

Does light from fireflies give off heat experiment 904:94-95

Effects of oxygen, temperature on brightness of light 414:32-34

Firefly courtship in the field and in the laboratory 266:136-138

Is rate of firefly reaction related to temperature of the environment 586:134

Lantern from fireflies using jar with lid, how to make 1188:63

Light production and behavior of fireflies experiment 1097:33-34

Number of flashes and brightness effected by temperature 266:72

Observation activities 759:39

Observe effect of temperature and light on number of flashes 174:12-13

Observe how firefly glows 294:67-68

Temperature affects flashing rate of fireflies experiment 1158:130-132

FIREPROOFING

Make clothing fire resistant 291:222

Make fireproof and weatherproof matches 291:223

FIREWOOD

Coloring firewood 180:81

Flammability of wood experiment 969:102-104

Measure moisture content of woods; softwood and hardwood experiment 969:102-104

Wood lying on ground decomposes faster than dead standing wood project 969:26-27

FIREWORKS

Fireworks and colored flames 87:39-47

Fireworks from a lemon—experiment 563:37

FISH. *See also* **GOLDFISH**

Activities with fish 236:68-69

Age of a fish, how to determine experiment 1405:32

Age of fish; how to determine age using fish scales 1295:63-64

Aggression in fish experiment 1520:104-105

Amount of air in swim bladder causes fish to move up/down in water experiment 1397:70-71

Anatomy of a fish, how to observe 1425:56-57

Aquarium for guppies and fishes 507:1872-1873

Archer fish—expert marksman in the field and in the laboratory 266:79-82

Aspirin and its effect on brine shrimp experiment 950:21-22

Behavior of schools of fish in the field and in the laboratory 266:146-149

Body shape of fish determines its behavior experiment 1520:92-93

Breathing rate of goldfish experiment 1395:133-137

Breeding native fishes experiment 1520:101-104

Can fish be conditioned 577:project #9

Colored water comes out fish's gill slits experiment 943:29

Colors of fish serve important purpose in fish's life experiment 1520:95-96

Compare breathing rate of fish and humans experiment 1395:136

Conditioned response experiment; training goldfish with sound 1069:82-83

Demonstrate how fish cells respond to fresh and salty water experiment 904:114-115

Determine age of fish from scales experiment 904:112-113

Dissecting—how to 692:49-55

Do fish exhale carbon dioxide when breathing experiment 1395:180-181

Does gulping rate of a fish change as water temperature changes 586:139-140

Does temperature affect movement of fish's operculum and mouth experiment 904:110-111

Effect of detergent on aquatic life experiment 934:38-39

Effect of industrial pollutants on behavior of convict Cichlid fish experiment 997:89-90

Effects of phosphate detergents on fish breathing rates experiment 950:58-60

Effects of water temperature on fish gill-cover beats experiment 1225:112-114

Experiment to show blood flow in tail of fish 174:44-45

Experiment to show how fish stay warm in winter 40:54-55

Eyes of fish determine how they live and find their food experiment 1520:97-98

Feeding behavior of fishes observed experiment 1520:99-100

Fish board—making a 11:107-109

Fish board for microscope 9:54-55

Fish breathe 232:91

Fish scales under microscope—observe 713:71-72

Fishes that make nests in the field and in the laboratory 266:121-129

Guppies; how to keep and raise guppies 1433:51-54

Habits and characteristics of a live fish 40:228

How a fish breathes experiment 1290:68, 5.1

How a fish breathes underwater 40:230-231

How fish bladder is used to change position and depth in water 40:229-230

How fish live in different temperature waters 40:231-232

How temperature affects cold-blooded animals 236:69

How to study fish and preserve them 117:33-37

Ideas for fish behavior experiments 864:113-115

Increased activity affects breathing rate of fish experiment 1395:136

Model—plaster model of fish—how to do 296:65-67

Nerve receptors in body of fish detect pressure and sound in water experiment 1397:18-19

Net—making 9:28-29

Observation cover to observe activities of fish in aquarium, how to make 1520:90-91

Observations of how they swim 173:20

Observe animals and fish in the river water 290:31

Observe circulation of blood in the tail of a goldfish 294:71-72

Observe how a fish breathes 294:70

Osmosis; how osmosis works in fish experiment 1492:62-63

Oxygen from green plants useful to fish experiment 1060:28-30

Parts of a fish 40:227-228

Population—recapture counting 263:47-49

Predators and plant eaters natural cycle observed in fish aquarium 1520:100

Print—art print of any fish—how to do 359:59-62

Printing fish, how to make prints 646:24-26

Printing; Japanese fish printing, Gyotaku, how to do 840:40-41

Prints—making fish casts and fish prints 234:49

Prints and casts—how to make 236:69

Prints of fish, how to make 1118:52-53

Reduce oxygen in fish tank so fish breathe more easily experiment 997:167-168

Respiration—test respiration and how much oxygen needed with goldfish 163:46-48

Respiration rate of fish affected by excitement and water temperature ex 1020:109-114

Saltwater fish can adapt to fresh water experiment 1020:114-117

Scales of a fish tells you about its lifestyle experiment 1520:93-94

Scales of fish; identify, draw and label project 1295:57-61

Stickleback, keep in aquarium, observe nest building and hatching eggs 771:76-83

Structure of fish scales 294:12-13

Studying the skeleton of a fish 294:70-71

Sunfish; how to collect and keep; observe nest building 771:129-132

Swim bladder helps fish to float demonstration 1186:14

Swimming behavior of fish observations, how to do 1520:98-99

Tails related to fish's method of swimming and how fast it moves experiment 1520:94-95

Temperature affects breathing rate of fish experiment 1395:135-136

Tropical fish—care of 390:79-84

Which animals in water are fish and which are not 40:229

Why dead fish float belly side up experiment 1479:31

FISH SCALES. *See also* **FISH**

Adventure 32—we do some fishing—fish scales under a hand lens 29:149-152

FISSION, NUCLEAR. *See* **NUCLEAR BOMBS; NUCLEAR CHAIN REACTION**

FLAG—AMERICAN

Grow an American red, white, and blue flag garden—how to do 416:40-41

FLAG POLE

How to make from wood 429:78-80

FLAGS—ELECTRIC

Making 391:140-145

FLAME TESTS

Borax bead flame tests for metals in minerals experiment 1266:37

Boric acid test experiment 723:199-200

Colored fire from testing different elements experiment; chart given 960:36

Colorful flames shows elements in salt, sugar, boric acid, copper sulfate 146:42-43

Different substances burn with different colored flame experiment 1179:30-31

Flame test for chemicals by color 360:82

Flame test for fibers and identification table for smell and ash 346:138

Flame test of unknown substances 72:55-56

Flame tests for fabrics 722:110

Flame tests for identification of metals 6:38

Flame tests for metals in minerals experiment 1266:36

Flame tests for metals 6:27

Flame tests for plastics 6:34

Flame tests for sugar and salt 30:35

For metals and their compounds 346:122-124

Identifying elements by the flame test 180:9

Test for metals experiment 723:200

To identify elements 85:34-35

To identify substances 157:22

FLAMES

Blown out candle relights itself 228:38

Chemical reactions of 346:43-50

Discover what a flame is 319:63-64

Faraday's investigating the properties of candle flames experiment 1133:7.007

Gases and 346:14-16, 53

Light a candle by using smoke 291:214

Make flame print 364:92

Not a burning question trick 222:86-87

Temperature of a flame experiment 1158:92-94

What are different parts of a flame 319:64-65

FLARES—COLORED

How to make 87:44-45

FLASHLIGHT

Build a flashlight, how to 888:163-164

Build a flashlight 278:36

Build your own flashlight 828:29

Dr. Zed's fantastic flashlight, making 890:22

Experiment to show how it works 128:171

Film can flashlight, how to make 1527:118

Find out how a flashlight works 180:45

Flashlight circuit experiment 23:8

Flashlight from liquid soap bottle, batteries, wires and bulb experiment 1030:20-22

Flashlight, how it works experiment 906:104

Flashlight, how to make 955:23; 998:229

How does a flashlight work experiment 1501:48-51

How does a flashlight work 253:154-155

How to make a flashlight experiment 938:24-26

Make your own flashlight experiment 1028:42-43; 1072:23

Mirror and flashlight experiments 885:54-56

Simple circuit from flashlight made from soda can experiment 1442:14-21

Simple flashlight—how to make 543:26-27

Underwater flashlight, making 821:54

FLATWORMS. *See also* **PLANARIANS**

Adventure 32—we meet some more worms—planarians under a microscope 403:112-115

Collect flatworms and observe under magnifying glass experiment 796:15

How to catch and preserve 117:37-38

FLAVORS. *See also* **FOOD—FLAVORINGS AND EXTRACTS**

Can the flavor of apples be isolated from apple cider vinegar 396:34-36

FLEAS

Adventure 42—we meet a champion—fleas under a microscope 403:154-155

Repellent to keep fleas off pets, recipe, how to make 1228:85-86

FLEMING, SIR ALEXANDER

Repeat Fleming's mold experiment 448:56-59

Who first discovered penicillin project 1525:73-75

FLEXURE. *See* **PAPER ENGINEERING**

FLIES

Adventure 42—we breed some flies—fruit flies under a hand lens 29:189-193

Blackfly larva under hand lens, observe 771:73-76

Effect of cigarette smoke on—experiment 174:48-49

Experiment to show what foods attract flies 174:26-27

Extreme changes in temperature affects behavior of flies and insects experiment 1014:167

Eye of fly under microscope—observe 713:65-67

Flight; fly's wings and thorax model, how to make 1445:16-17

Fly cage—making 9:40-41

Flying habits and patterns 414:23

Hover fly cage—making to watch its flight 414:41-42

How to mount 364:35

Observe life cycle of a fly experiment 904:108-109; 1405:32

Redi's famous experiment that decaying food doesn't produce living organisms 1397:6-7

Worms (maggots) grow from decaying bananas and other fruit experiment 1397:4-7

FLIES—FRUIT FLIES. *See also* **FRUIT FLIES**

Can fruit flies follow a scent—demonstration 174:22-33

Fruit fly—life cycle of the fruit fly 402:96

Fruit fly farms, fruit fly barn and fruit fly food—how to make 366:24-25

Fruit fly trap—how to make 276:64

Gestation periods—how long from formation of egg to emergence of fly 402:96-97

How to observe the life cycle of 128:59

Life cycle of the fruit fly 402:96

Natural population controls 263:34-36

Survival of a species—more than enough 263:31-33

FLIES—HOUSE FLIES. *See also* **HOUSE FLIES**

Experiment with flies 163:73

How to make cage 163:69-72

Investigations to do on life cycle 163:77

Make a breeding cage 163:74-77

Mutation—mechanism of evolution—experiment 402:105-106

FLIGHT

Activities and experiments to demonstrate flight in the atmosphere 564:13-25

Air speed affects flight experiment 1405:98

Bird with flapping wings, how to make from wood 1419:22-23

Drag—activities and experiments to demonstrate flight 564:21-22

Drag acting on different shapes experiment 1095:27

Feathers; looking at feathers to observe flight of birds 1095:18

Gravity—activities and experiments to demonstrate 564:19-20

Helicopter model with working rotors, how to make 1095:35

Hot air balloon, working model, how to make 1095:40

Lindbergh, Charles; who was the first to fly the Atlantic Ocean project 1525:12 17

Losing lift or upward force from paper wing experiment 1095:17

Principles of flight—activities and experiments to demonstrate 564:18; 564:22-25

Test flights of paper airplanes experiment using wind tunnel 1095:22-23

Thrust—activities and experiments to demonstrate 564:20-21

FLIGHT—PRINCIPLES OF. *See* **AERODYNAMICS; AERONAUTICS; AIRPLANES; GLIDERS**

FLINT AND STEEL SPARKS

Explanation of 322:20-21

FLIP BOOKS

Acrobatic pictures—making 696:26-27

Animated drawings move experiment 1369:42-44

Chicken pecks away in flip book—making 749:54-55

Flick book makes pictures move; patterns for pictures given 1299:22-23

Flip book, how to make 861:89-92

Flip books—how to make 1:108-110; 508:75; 558:116-117; 736:88-95; 861:89-92

Separate sequential images flash by in flip book experiment 1476:210

Stick person flip book, how to make 1417:26

FLOATING—TOYS

Glass bottom boat toy—how to make (Primary) 467:32

Jellyfish model toy—how to make (Primary) 467:18-19

Nutshell boat—how to make (Primary) 467:20-21

Outrigger canoe model toy—how to make (Primary) 467:26-27

Raft model toy—how to make (Primary) 467:28-29

Surfboard and rider model toy—how to make (Primary) 467:16-17

Swan model toy—how to make (Primary) 467:14-15

Three men in a tub model toy—how to make (Primary) 467:12-13

Tugboat model toy—how to make (Primary) 467:30-31

Water lily model toy—how to make (Primary) 467:10-11

FLOATING AND SINKING. *See also* ARCHIMEDES; BOATS; BUOYANCY; SHIPS; WATER—BUOYANCY

A floating object displaces its own weight 281:32

Afloat in a boat 98:14-15

Air filled object keeps heavy object floating experiment 791:14-15

Air keeps bottles afloat experiment [Primary] 791:10-11

Aluminum foil wads and water experiments [Primary] 849:16-17

Ball of clay doesn't sink when shaped like a boat experiment 1179:138

Balloon filled with water demonstrates 1256:17

Blow air into submerged bottle—experiment (Primary) 578:10-11

Boat; shape of hull affects a boat experiment 1290:5.2

Boats built to enclose a lot of space float experiment 1159:29-30

Boats; building boats that float experiment:35

Bottle diver—making 656:12-13

Bouncing mothballs experiment 909:37

Brick with rubber band in water experiment 868:57

Can depth of bathyscaph be controlled experiment 902:16

Can it float 280:44-45

Cargo ship of aluminum foil floats experiment 1316:13

Cartesian diver experiment 909:36

Clay ball and clay boat in water experiment [Primary] 849:18-19

Clay balls float at different levels experiments [Primary] 849:28-29

Clay boats and weights in dish of water demonstration 1310:14-15

Clay boat and marbles experiment 996:10-11

Coke Classic sinks and Diet Coke floats experiment 1063:144

Cup in water experiment [Primary] 849:20-21

Density of liquids and solids, floating of substances that don't mix experiment 1004:3.003

Density of object related to water displacement experiment data tables given 1004:3.002

Density of water determines amount of push it provides experiment 760:26

Determine why objects float on water experiment 1396:123-128

Different materials float or sink experiment 1161:23

Displaced water weighs the same as the floating object experiment 1028:18

Do cans with weight float in fresh and salt water experiment 804:30-31

Do objects float or sink in liquids other than water experiment 996:12-13

Do objects made from different materials float or sink 342:6-7

Do they float or sink (Primary) 678:8

Does it make a difference if boat is floating in fresh or salt water (Primary) 578:22-25

Does shape of object, way it is placed in water effect floating (Primary) 578:6-9

Egg float—experiment 670:33

Egg floats in middle of jar of salt water experiment 1229:16-17

Egg floats in water experiment 1498:9

Empty and full bottle experiment 780:16-17

Empty ship floats higher in water experiment 791:8-9

Experiment to demonstrate (Primary) 207:22-24

Experiment 98:12-13

Experimenting with floating using a brick and clay 1422:9

Floaters of clay and aluminum—how to make 400:57

Floating and sinking activities for classroom 1291:13-14

Floating and sinking experiments 663:24-31; 684:28-29

Floating needle on water experiment 766:unp.

Floating needles 98:23

Floating object displaces equal volume or weight of liquid experiment 1179:139

Floating objects (Primary) 232:87

Floating objects in fresh water and salt water experiment 1507:25

Floating without friction—styrofoam tray and cup Hovercraft—demonstrate 419:17

Foil and clay boats float and sink experiment 1422:6-7

Grape and soda water experiment [Primary] 849:14

How do submarines go up and down experiment 877:101-105

How do you make an egg float experiment 827:71

How objects float in differing densities 98:16-17

How to make your own sailboat to test floating (Primary) 578:26-27

How to play think or sink (Primary) 578:29

Hull shape of boat and its effect on buoyancy demonstration 1165:9

Hydrometer measures density of liquid experiment 1028:21

Jumping rocks experiment 906:11

Liquid layers—make water float, sink and mix 98:18-19

Liquids float and sink experiment 1028:21

Make a floating egg (Primary) 154:9

Make a needle float (Primary) 143:8-9

Make things float, then sink experiment 1028:17

Making a hydrometer to measure density of liquid 573:34

Matchbox with sail experiment [Primary] 791:20-21

Metric measure to find out why one object floats and one sinks 357:26-27

Needle floats on water experiment 1389:27

Object floats or sinks as air increases or decreases density experiment 1004:3.001

Object immersed in liquid loses weight experiment 1456:32

Objects and liquids sink or float according to their density experiment 1014:45

Oil spill effect demonstration using oil based paints, water and paper 1310:12-13

On water—place cork, stone and other things—record which floats (Primary) 578:3-5

Orange icebergs 280:18

Outrigger boats built to test floating experiment 1422:11

Plimsoll Line marks safe water level on boats demonstration 1310:15

Potato slice floats in salt water but sinks in fresh water experiment 1310:10-11

Primary experiments to test floating bodies 1100:4-29

Primary experiments with water 982:1-69

Rafts built to test floating experiment 1422:11

Raw egg and salt water experiments [Primary] 849:5-9

Raw egg and sugar water experiments [Primary] 849:10

Raw egg and vinegar water experiments 849:12-13

Salt water has more buoyancy than fresh water experiment 884:44-47

Separating things that sink and float experiment 1526:52-53

Shape affects how things float experiments 1230:4-7

Shape of hulls determines what ship can do experiment 1471:6-7

Shape of object affects floating experiment 1230:42-43

Shape of object determines whether it will float experiment 804:31

Shape of ship and load effect floating—experiment (Primary) 578:16-19

Ships of milk cartons (Primary) 321:27

Sink float game 32:72-73

Sink or float experiments 748:110-111

Size and shape affect floating experiment 909:34-35

Some things float and some sink experiment (Primary) 695:23

Some things float in water (Primary) 324:28-29

Steel ball and water—experiment 670:14

Submarine bottle floats and sinks—experiment 678:11

Submarine floats and sinks experiment 937:44-47

Submarine from plastic bottle rises and sinks experiment 1316:21

Teaching activities with floating and sinking 1056:12-14

Testing for floaters and sinkers 210:18-19

The sinking washer 92:50-51

The sunken treasure ship—how to raise experiment (Primary) 578:12-13

Things float at different levels in salt water and fresh water [Primary] 849:22-27

Things float better in salty water—experiment 678:13

Upthrust force of water and weight of object affect buoyancy experiment 1165:7

Volume of rock measured by amount of water displaced experiment 1507:24

Wad of foil and sheet of foil demonstrate 722:24

Water displacement—experiment (Primary) 578:20-21

Water pushes back up experiment 1509:23

What floats 281:31

What floats (Primary) 154:14-15

What floats and what sinks experiment 898:7; 1124:10-11

What floats and what sinks in water experiment 867:14-15

What floats or sinks, observe [Primary] 791:3-6

What makes a boat float experiments 835:16-18

What makes things float? 589:44-45

What sinks ? What floats ? Experiment with sponges and bottle [Primary] 880:20

Which things float in water experiment 1509:22

Why do boats float experiment 1509:24

Why do heavy metal ships float experiment 877:96-100

Why things float or sink experiment 884:40-43

Will clay sink in water experiment 766:unp.

Will it float in water experiment 909:32-33

Wood floats higher in salt water experiment 791:18-19

FLOODS

Flooding effect on towns and cities experiment using stream table 1342:119-120

House on stilts stays above water level of floods, how to make 1463:28

Rain runoff and erosion effect on different mountain soils experiment 1465:93

FLOUR. *See also* **WHEAT**

Create ornaments from flour experiment 1231:68-69

Flour flame 249:11

Gluten in flour dries hard experiment 1231:68-69

Wheat seed experiment to show white flour and brown flour 26:96-98

FLOW

Flow measurement of water 363:92-93

Flow of water from a gurgling jug 585:33

Flow of water from a jug—experiments number 1 and 2 585:31-32

Measuring flow of water and range of stream from a hose 604:64-67

FLOWER FACES

How to make 312:19-24

FLOWER PRESS

Botanist press, how to make from plywood 1169:15

Build a press for flowers and leaves 291:197

Flower press from plywood, bolts and paper, how to make 1127:57

Flower press from sheets of masonite, how to make 1214:17

Flower press from wood and cardboard, how to make 1044:34-35

Flower press, simple, how to make 1368:45-46

How to make 382:64-67

Plant press for pressing garden and weed flowers, how to make 1265.98

Plywood press for flowers, how to make 1236:21

Portable plant press, wooden, how to make 1335:120

Simple plywood press, how to make 854:55

FLOWERS. *See also* **PLANTS**

Adventure 12—we go botanizing—flowers under a hand lens 29:59-65

Adventure 47—flowers are not merely ornamental—flowers under microscope 403:179-185

Anthocyanin pigments in flower petals change in acid/alkaline soils experiment 1203:28-29

Artificially pollinate flower experiment 860:153

Bleach flowers—experiments with ammonia 563:172-173

Bloom calendar for local flowers project 1313:56-58

Candied violet or rose petals experiment 1368:13

Change colors with chemicals 87:82-83

Color carnation using water and food coloring experiment 1054:86

Color, fragrance and flavor attract bees; which is most important experiment 997:43-45

Color, scent and honey attract insects—experiment 158:12-13

Colors and scents that attract insects to flowers experiment 1182:28

Comparison of flower parts project 1060:50-51

Compound and composite flowers—demonstration 86:52

Cut flowers need water and food to survive experiment 760:7-8

Cut flowers; making cut flowers last project; chart given 1210:25-26

Different kinds of flowers—demonstrate 119:73-78

Dissect a flower, worksheet given 817:3

Dissecting a flower experiment 1069:46-47

Draw circular arrangement of 86:44

Drying and pressing 158:7

Find parts of flower (Primary) 540:23

Floral clock illustration of what time flowers open and close 1103:10

Floral diagrams—diagramming parts 436:36

Flower clock garden to tell time—how to do 640:90

Flower draws up colored water through stem experiment 1068:22

Flower model—making 532:64-65

Flower parts and pollination experiment 1063:247

Flower petal indicators for acid or base experiment; data table given 871:3.020

Flower sculpture—make to show parts of flower 483:45-48

Flower structures (parts) projects 1060:49-51

Flowers move 271:40-55

Flowers open quickly due to turgor pressure experiment 1405:3

Hours by flowers—time keeping flower garden 231:53

How seeds grow 158:18-19

How to pollinate flowers experiment 1491:42-43

Investigate flowers in a vacant lot 233:25-26

Keep cut flowers longer—how to 416:48-49

Keeping a record of preserved flowers 158:6-7

Lavender baskets, how to make 1180:28

Lavender baskets, how to make 1183:156

Light window pictures of flowers, how to make 646:58-60

Model flowers from colored papers, how to make 1044:32-33

Model of flower form paper and paint, how to make 1181:12; 1183:20

Natural colors from flowers, how to extract experiment 924:8-9

Parts of a flower 60:42-44

Parts of flower—demonstration 158:8-9

Parts of flower—experiments 128:46-47

Parts of flower—what are the main parts 253:18-19

Parts of flower and pollination—experiment 119:68-73

Parts of flower before and after pollination—demonstration 168:22-23

Parts of flower under microscope, observe water ducts 889:42-45

Parts that produce seeds 40:149-150

Perishable quality of natural dyes experiment with flowers and ammonia experiment 1476:133

pH of soil affects color of hydrangea flowers experiment 1060:114

Pigments in flower petals, how to do color test for pigments experiment 1068:23

Pollen quantity produced by flower experiment 860:152-153

Pollination—help pollinate the flowers 264:48

Pollination—how bees make colored flowers 366:90-91

Pollination and fertilization—experiment 158:12-15

Potpourri ingredients and how to make 552:41

Presence of green chlorophyll under flower colors experiment 1476:133

Preserving flowers 402:32-33

Press flowers and greens—how to 264:44

Pressing flowers and using dried flowers, how to 646:34-40

Respond to changes in moisture of air 271:50-51

Seed dispersal—observations 158:16-17

Stamen react to touch 271:52-55

Studying structure of a flower—the sweet pea 294:45-46

Tell time of day by blossoms opening and closing 271:41-48

The dandelion observation 585:160

Underwater garden of flowers, ferns/leaves in leak proof container—how to make 416:50-51

What are the parts of a flower demonstration 901:37-38

Why do flowers make pollen experiment 1294:83-85

FLOWERS—AMERICAN FLAG

Grow an American red, white and blue garden 416:40-41

FLOWERS—ARRANGING

Arrange flowers for fun and beauty 416:46-47

FLOWERS—CANDY

Make candy from garden violets 416:31

FLOWERS—COLLECTION AND PRESERVATION

Borax drying method for flowers, how to do 866:149

Dry and press flowers and make picture experiment 1524:16

Drying by air drying, sand drying, glycerin—how to 480:101

Drying flowers with weighted things 866:148

Flower preservation—drying flowers with borax 436:37

Flower press, how to make and use 932:36-39

How to dry flowers 473:55

How to press flowers 473:54; 480:99; 879:223-227; 1068:44

Keep favorite flowers by drying them 416:54-55

Make a pressed flower collection 476:55-57

Picture from pressed plants—how to make 473:54

Preserving flower by pressing experiment 1069:49

Press flowers and leaves and make scrap book—how to 416:52-53

Pressed flowers, how to press flowers 1491:66-67

Pressing and drying flowers, how to do 1181:13

Things to do—using flowers—pressing flowers and dried flower decorations 552:40

FLOWERS—DRIED

Bookmarks from pressed flowers, how to make 1071:91

Collect and dry flowers, how to do 1145:30

Dry flowers in sand, how to do 832:78

Dry flowers using silica gel experiment 1491:64-65

Drying flowers in borax and cornmeal, how to do 1014:149

Flower press from plywood, bolts and paper, how to make 1127:57

How to dry 442:unpaged; 1368:65-67
Preserve flowers by drying in borax and cornmeal mix, how to do 1071:90
Preserving flowers by drying with silica gel experiment 1069:49
Pressing flowers on newspaper, how to do 1071:89
Sand drying flowers, how to do 1335:121

FLOWERS—POLLINATION
Adventure 41—pollen structures of flowers under a hand lens 29:184-188
Artificial pollination of flowers experiment 860:153; 1060:52
Pollen quantity produced by flower experiment 860:152-153
Self-pollination and cross-pollination experiment 1060:52

FLOWERS—PRESSED
Pressed flowers for decorations, cards, pictures, how to do 1054:84-85

FLOWERS—WILD. *See also* **WILDFLOWERS**
Algae, feathery—how to mount 234:75
Collecting and preserving—how to 234:74-75
Identifying and recording 234:68
Protecting 234:69
Wild flower collection 532:61
Winter bouquets—how to make 234:75

FLUID DYNAMICS. *See also* **PASCAL'S LAW**
Make and test movement of flat shape, round and tear-drop shape in water 237:13-24

FLUIDS
Adhesion and capillary attraction experiment 940:16-17
Adhesion keeps water in glass experiment 940:8-10
Checking the buoyancy of fluids—experiment 180:25
Determining the density of fluids 180:26
Diffusion—how to observe diffusion 319:52-53
Drops—size of—how big is a drop 381:85-86
Fluid dynamics—making water threads experiment 669:16-17
Fluid dynamics; water stays in wire basket experiment 940:5-7
Fluid friction—measuring fluid flow—experiment 691:53-56
Fluid level changes in connected containers experiment 1515:45-50
Fluids takes shape of a sphere experiment 1084:29-30
George Stokes' effect of viscous drag on small spheres fall thru liquids 1133:4.010
Glob, creezy ooze, how to make to show "non-Newtonian" fluid 1396:139-140
Inks—scrambling ink colors (Primary) 70:55-56
Non-Newtonian fluid—making 670:74
Projectors on fluid frictions 691:56-58
Rules of fluid level change experiment 1515:51-55
Rules of temperature change experiment with fluid level changes 1515:45-55
Spherical objects falling in viscous fluid obey Stokes Law experiment 997:156-158
Sum is less than more 222:60
Transfer water by siphon experiment 940:18-20
Tricks using—bet you can 'boil' water without heat 228:66
Tricks using—bet you can keep a ball in the air for an hour 228:74-75
Tricks using—bet you can lift a dime with a straw 228:64
Tricks using—bet you can make a dry spot in two liquids 228:69
Tricks using—bet you can make ashes float up in the air 228:76-77
Tricks using—bet you can part a pepper sea 228:72
Tricks using—bet you can pour water sideways 228:73
Tricks using—bet you can push a plastic bag in jar so no one can pull it 228:65
Tricks using—bet you can put piece of paper underwater without getting it 228:68
Tricks using—bet you can sink a cork without touching it 228:67
Tricks using—water tower—bet you can lift water in an upside down glass 228:62-63
Turbulence patterns in flowing water experiment using Ivory detergent 1132:101-1-101-2
Vacuum pump—another bet for suckers—bet you can't suck water from a jar 222:47
Vacuum pump—make a sucker of suckers 222:46
Whirling water creates tornado in a bottle experiment 1132:104-1-104-2

FLUORESCENCE
Phosphorescence and fluorescence 577:project #23
Wintergreen life savers make mouth lightning experiment 814:94-95

FLUORESCENT BULB
How can an unconnected fluorescent bulb glow 278:66

FLUOROCARBONS. *See* **GREENHOUSE EFFECT**

FLYING. *See also* **AIRPLANES**
Make a bird kite (Primary) 111:28-31
Make a diamond kite (Primary) 111:24-27
Make a flying fish (Primary) 111:20-23

FLYING MACHINES—TOYS
Flying plates—how to make 365:27
Foam board flyer—how to make 365:26

FLYING SAUCER DETECTOR
How to build as science project 563:26-27

FLYING SAUCERS. *See also* **UFO**
Experiment with light reflection 585:105-106
Flying saucer—how to make 652:18-19
How to make (Primary) 113:6-7
Make a flying saucer 111:12-13
Paper plate flying saucer 494:64

FLYWHEEL
How can stored energy be released; button on string experiment 851:52-53
How to make 399:83

FOAM RUBBER
Making 26:63-65, 70

FOCAL LENGTH. *See also* **LENS—FOCAL LENGTH; MIRRORS**
Focal length of a lens, how to find experiment 941:115-116
Of lens—finding 291:187

FOG. *See also* **SMOG; WATER**
Bottle, hot water and ice cube demonstrate formation of fog experiment 882:24
Carbon dioxide fog 291:54-55
Dispersing fog with heat 577:project #38
Experiment to show 382:128-129
Fog chamber; portable cloud in a bottle experiment 1132:52-1-52-2
Fog demonstration with ice cube in bottle experiment 959:165-166
Fogs and mists—experiment 605:12-13

Fun with fog 291:34
How does fog form experiment 1293:85
How fog forms 44:70-71
How to make fog in a jar experiment 1439:59-61
How water becomes fog 295:41-42
Make fog—experiment 175:68; 291:34
Make fog in a bottle—experiment 95:26-27
Make fog to see why fog forms experiment 860:193-194
Pressure changes vapor to fog and fog to vapor—experiment 385:77-78
Problems caused by 298:14-15
Where does fog come from experiment 852:41-42

FOLDED PLATE
Build a folded plate 557:71

FOLDS
Compressional forces affect crustal movement of Earth experiment 1405:73
Pressure required to fold Earth's crust demonstration 1405:74

FOLIAGE. *See* **LEAVES**

FOOD. *See also* **FATS**
Acid effect on baking; carbon dioxide produced experiment 905:202-203
Acid effect on bones experiment 1396:49-51
Adventure 18—butter, flour, jams, cocoa, honey under a microscope 403:65
Amount of fiber in breakfasts we eat experiment 1193:26-28
Antibiotic-resistant bacteria present in or on fruits and vegetables experiment 1267:47-49
Baking powder—experimenting with 50:15-24
Baking powder—produces carbon dioxide—making biscuits 52:55-56
Baking soda in cakes—experimenting with 50:25-39
Calcium oxide restores firmness to blanched vegetables experiment 1396:51-52
Calculate gram calories and convert to food calories, how to do 1396:197
Calories in food released by burning food experiment 1396:34-35
Calories; number of calories in food experiment 1259:22-24
Calorimeter to determine food energy in marshmallows experiment, how to make 1396:31-36
Carbohydrates—cooking carbohydrates 261:38-42
Carbohydrates—what are they 261:31-35
Carbon dioxide—gas from yeast, baking powder and baking soda—experiment 50:55-62
Chart of four basic food groups you eat each day experiment 1264:27
Cheese—making cheese 52:24-25
Chemical tests for fat, starch and protein 335:79-80
Colloidal systems—gelatin—making a fruit-flavored gelatin 52:33
Cooking and preparation methods affect vitamin C content of foods experiment 1267:42-43
Cost of eating in poor countries compared to eating in U.S. project 1059:46
Crystals—making rock candy 52:71-72
Dehydration 52:81-82
Difference in effectiveness of manufactured processed food enzymes experiment 1395:171-176
Digestion—simple experiments and diagrams (Primary) 394:1-33

Does concentration of food enzyme affect its activity experiment 1395:171-176
Drying—dried foods do not spoil (Primary) 324:16-17
Egg white protein—applying heat to a protein 52:99
Emulsions—making a jar of mayonnaise 52:41
Enzymatic browning of apples experiment 1396:47
Enzymes get energy from food 261:14-16
Experimenting with cake recipes 50:8-14
Fat in food 261:44-46
Fat; testing foods for fat activities for classroom 1291:29-30
Fats and oils; test for fats and oils in foods experiment 1259:27-30
Fats; fat in foods survey questions 1262:18-19
Fats; invisible fat in foods experiment 1262:7
Fiber; compare water absorbency of various types of dietary fiber experiment 1267:50
Flavor enhancers—unlocking molecules of lemon oil 52:91
Food and eating—simple projects 621:28-29
Food book (Primary) 232:102
Food is mostly water 281:19
Food that's almost the real thing 229:48-51
Freezing is good way to preserve food experiment 1238:119-120
Fruit juices are a good source of vitamin C experiment 1267:42-43
Gelatin; magic of gelatin experiments 885:93-94
Growing food for people isn't easy experiment using plants 1059:38-39
How body keeps us from getting too much salt experiment 1238:14-15
How many food calories do you need each day—experiment 628:74-75
How much of the food you eat is water 295:35
Identify nutrients in a food test for sugar, starch, fat, protein 628:69-73
Iron; test for iron in foods experiment 1259:35-37
Is milk really the perfect food—experiment 628:75-76
Lunch meats; how much fat in lunch meats project 1210:28-29
Minerals in food 261:47-49
Minerals; chart of five most important minerals in food experiment 1264:22
Moisture—can it be water 280:19
No room on Earth to grow food experiment using beet seeds 1059:98
Nutritional value of artificial diet and natural diet of tomato hornworm 1096:34-38
Oil—making peanut butter 52:62-63
Oils; test for presence of unsaturated oil experiment 1396:37-42
Protein—what makes protein 261:26-30
Proteins are changed by denaturing experiment 1396:55-59
Proteins; test for proteins in foods experiment 1259:30-31
Rotting of food demonstration; bacteria causes decay 1073:89
Salt in food; effect of salt on vegetable experiment 1238:13
Salt; how much salt in various foods project 1210:27
Size of pot effect on poached eggs experiment 1238:20-21

Size of pot we cook in experiment 1238:19
Snacks survey 400:43
Starch—how to find starch 261:36-37
Starch; test for starch in various foods experiment 1259:26-27
Sugar; test for presence of monosaccharides (single sugar) in foods experiment 1396:61-66
Sugar; test for sugar in foods experiment 1259:24-26
Taste and feel of different sugars in cookies experiment 1238:26-27
Test foods for protein experiment 901:213
Test for acid in 86:42
Testing for fat or grease in foods experiment 924:37
Testing for microbes that grow on food experiment 924:41-42
Testing for starch in foods with iodine experiment 924:36
Testing for starch, fat and protein in food using chemicals experiment 1069:19
Testing your food for starch with iodine 571:35
Tests for fat or starch 253:115-116
Thermometer test for warmth of body from food energy 609:28
Transporting food to our homes project 1067:36-37
Vitamin C amount in various foods and vitamin tablets experiment 1396:43-48
Vitamin C content in food, how to calculate 1396:207
Vitamin C; analyzing foods for their vitamin C content experiment 1267:41-43
Vitamin C; effects of cooking and chemicals on vitamin C in foods experiment 1259:34-35
Vitamin C; starch iodine test for vitamin C in foods experiment 1259:33-34
Vitamin C; test for Vitamin C in foods experiment 1259:31-33
Vitamins in food 261:50-53
Vitamins; chart of vitamins found in common foods experiment 1264:11
Vitamins; which methods of food storage preserve vitamin C over time experiment 1267:42-43
Waste not, want not project with wasted school lunches 1059:48
Water in food 261:54-55
What colored dyes are found in powder drink mix and colored markers experiment 997:73-75
What makes food taste too salty experiment 1238:16-17
Where's the fat—test for fats in foods you eat 607:53
Which foods contain fat experiment 901:216
Which foods contain starch experiment 901:215
Which foods contain sugar experiment 901:214
Why does food go bad 261:56-62
Wonder food contest 630:80-81
Yeast—observing fermentation 52:46-48
Yeast bread—experimenting with yeast gas (carbon dioxide) 50:42-54
Yellow product labels attract consumer eyes experiment 1051:25

FOOD—ADDITIVES
Check food for vitamin C 152:64-69
Chromatography test with inks, food colors and plant pigments experiment 1476:129-131
Food additive, calcium propionate, inhibits bread mold growth experiment 1395:127-132
Food coloring—natural versus artificial 152:80-83

Food colorings destroy protozoa on microscope slide experiment 889:40
Foods' colorings in candy and vegetables; chromatography test experiment 792:31
How additives change the look, feel and taste of food cooking experiment 1261:8-9
MSG—a flavor enhancer 152:83-86
Taste of food connected with a particular color experiment 1261:17
Use chocolate pudding to show carrageenan stabilization 152:75-77
Vitamin C interferes with oxygen 152:69-72
Vitamin E as an antioxidant 152:72-74
Whipped topping—acid stabilized foam 152:77-80

FOOD—FLAVORINGS AND EXTRACTS
A 'tea' party—solubility of flavors 152:87-89
All kinds of extracts—distillation 152:97-100
Beef 'tea'—extraction of water soluble meat chemicals 152:94-97
Synthetic cola 152:100-102
Tea to a T—temperature for the 'perfect' infusion 152:90-93

FOOD—GAME
Fat game 400:122

FOOD—PRESERVATION
Canned fruits and vegetables—high acid versus low acid foods 152:56-61
Dried foods—banana chips—making 607:74-75
Ferment sauerkraut in soda bottle experiment 1527:24-25
Food additive, calcium propionate, inhibits bread mold growth experiment 1395:127-132
Food dryer using solar energy, how to build 986:89
Making beef jerky—drying and curing 152:44-50
Preserve apples by drying 538:84
Preserving food by drying experiment 1395:129
Salt and vinegar used as preservative to inhibit bacterial growth experiment 1395:130
Sauteed mushrooms—dehydration and reconstitution 152:50-52
Sugar used as preservative for fruit experiment 1395:130
Which solution preserves fruit the best experiment 1343:17
Zucchini—freezing and thawing 152:52-56

FOOD—SPACECRAFT
Experiments to demonstrate food supply on a spacecraft 564:75-76

FOOD—SPOILAGE
Can certain molecules in the air cause food to spoil 396:74-75
Salt kills bacteria and prevents spoilage in food 26:87-88

FOOD—SUPPLY
Population explosions—eat until we burst 263:71-73

FOOD CHAINS. *See also* **FOOD WEBS**
A study of some food chains in a school yard 285:47
Amount of lost energy in the food chain in the production of beef experiment 1074:59
Aquatic and terrestrial food webs in aquariums experiments 978:114-116
Aquatic food chain in fish tank experiment, how to make 1453:25-27
Construct food chain project; watch different animals and food they eat 1296:1984
Constructing a food web 268:63-66
Food chain demonstration with paper chains, how to make 1335:34

153

Food chain game, making 772:86-91
Food chain mobile, how to make 1181:32; 1183:40; 1335:32-33; 1422:27
Food chain pictures, how to arrange in order 796:13
Food chain pyramid model, how to make 1335:30-31
Food resources 263:62-66
Game; forest recycling game to demonstrate food chains, how to play 1205:13
How do insects fit into a food chain experiment 1097:65-67
In ponds 194:26-27
Mobile; making a food chain mobile experiment 1134:5.001
Mobile of food chain, how to make 1371:46-47
Mobile to illustrate food chain; who's eating what and whom, how to make 1063:205
Mobile to show sequence of food chain 822:17-18
Mobiles—making 436:59
Observations of in fresh water 173:23
Pesticides; accumulating pesticides in food chains experiment 1134:6.013
Predator and prey game, making 898:57-58
Pyramid food chains of land, sea and fresh water 1185:10-11
Setting up a food chain 148:55
Simple explanation 312:14
Survey and inventory types of animals supported by plants of fields 285:52-53

FOOD WEBS. *See also* **FOOD CHAINS**
Constructing a food web 268:63-66
Construction of based on observations 532:48-49
Food web of the compost pile 276:60
Food web in a ecosystem; observe and record what is seen 1171:22-23
Food web to show interdependence of Arctic animals 1337:71-72
Game; food web game, how to make and play 1181:32-33; 1183:41
Make your own "food web" game 556:28-29
Predator-prey soda bottle column experiment with soil, plants, and insects 1527:51-54

FOOTPRINTS
Casting footprints 625:43
How to make casts and molds of animal footprints 530:163
Plaster casts of—how to do 507:1858-1859
Plaster casts of animal footprints—how to make 472:2232
Sand cast a footprint—how to 494:33

FOOTWEAR
Which type of footwear grows the most bacteria experiment 997:132-134

FORAMINIFERA
Adventure 27—we find out what chalk is made of under a microscope 403:94-96

FORCE. *See also* **CENTRIFUGAL FORCE; CENTRIPETAL FORCE; NEWTON'S LAW; STRENGTH**
A piercing moment—bet you can't pop a balloon with a pin 222:40
A pressing problem—bet you can't keep your fists together 222:28-29
A raw deal—bet you can't fool me with a hard-boiled egg 222:41
A sure rip off—bet you can't tear a piece of paper into three inches 222:36-37
Acceleration and amount of matter (weight of objects) being pulled experiment 1157:34-35
Acceleration experiments with objects moving in a circle 1157:31-34
Action and reaction balloon demonstrates 699:11
Action and reaction toy car experiment [Primary] 945:12-13
Action and reaction 260:14-15
An untearable situation—bet you can't rip a tissue 222:34-35
Area affects pressure experiment with balloon and bed of nails 1140:97-101
Attraction—magnetic 350:3-4
Balance of forces 253:168-169
Balloon toy provides power to move something experiment 924:28-29
Centrifugal 350:106-111
Centripetal force—an inward force 295:82-83
Collision—what accounts for the force of a collision 333:33-35
Collision force—super tough tissue paper—a nonelastic collision 205:32-36
Crack the walnut 585:39-40
Demonstrating recoil action with a potato 150:94-95
Equal but opposite forces demonstration with skateboards 1434:100-102
Force (pull) measuring device—how to make 419:5
Force meter measures force needed to get things moving experiment 1028:110
Force of gravity—the obedient can 360:80
Forces resultants and equilibrium—print—computer project 584:111-113
Fulcrum—a match that's no contest—bet you can't break a match 222:30
Hooke's Law Constant—computer project 584:108-110
How much energy is stored in a bow experiment 902:46
Karate payoff—what force is about 205:29-32
Knife wrapped with paper slices through apple; not the paper experiment 1083:35
Lower the broom 222:31
Make things move 260:1-32
Make your own mousetrap using ramps, levers and forces 554:28-29
Making a cord impossible to pull straight 150:90-91
Measuring the force needed to pull a toy truck 419:12
Mechanical advantage—computer project 584:106-107
Mousetrap car, making 906:150
No pushover—bet you can't push me backward 222:32-33
No shattering experience—bet you can't break a light bulb on a floor 222:42
Pick up apple with straw 288:26-27
Plug in pop toy 260:6-7
Projects on force and motion 691:58-60
Push and pull—accelerometer measures big pulls, little pulls 295:79-80
Reasonance—it happens on the dot 161:14-15
Repulsion—magnetic 350:3-4
Rocker can from can and rubber bands demonstrates force 882:9
Roller can experiment 906:149
Shoving objects of different sizes and materials experiment 1334:8-9
Standing on a bed of nails 114:103-105

154

Stopping car takes force; toy car demonstration 945:19

Straw through potato trick 203:67

Super strength with string and bare hands 202:98

Three spout pressure gauge experiment using milk carton 999:98-100

Transfer of force experiment with paper cups, string and weights 999:95-98

Turning forces experiment using ruler and coins 1456:16

Turtle racing game demonstrates how simple machines transmit forces experiment 1523:16

Unbreakable match—demonstration 202:94

Vehicle moves at constant speed when pulled with constant force experiment 1157:25-26

What happens when two objects push or pull one another experiment 1157:38-44

Wind power and winch lifts bucket in model well experiment 1334:18-19

FORCE—RECOIL

Experiments with recoil—model catapult gun and balloon jet—demonstrate 419:34-35

FORCE AND ACCELERATION

Experiments to demonstrate 295:77-89

FORCE AND ENERGY

Balance potato to demonstrate center of gravity experiment 1507:16

Balancing clown demonstrates center of gravity experiment, how to make 1507:17

Catapults; small model catapult shows force needed to move object 1507:15

Collision; force of collision experiment using toy truck 1507:14

Do heavy objects fall faster than light ones experiment 1507:5

Force meter measures force of gravity pulling on object experiment 1073:15

Heat causes coins in bottle to jump up and down experiment 1030:12

Newton's cradle toy experiment, how to make 1030:26-27

Pinwheel uses the kinetic energy of air experiment 1030:10-11

Roll back toy rolls back to you experiment 1030:16-17

Simple primary experiments with forces of energy that cause movement 1130:8-29

Surface skimmer skims over table on a cushion of air experiment 1030:28-29

Two fruits suspended on strings demonstrate kinetic energy experiment 1030:24-25

Water wheel from plastic bottle, clay, tubing, blades, how to make 1030:13-15

Weight; downward force of gravity on objects experiment 1507:4

FORCE AND MOTION

Ball hanging with tassels on string demonstrates stored energy experiment 1496:26-27

Cardboard spinner on string demonstrates stored energy experiment 1496:18-19

Coins on smooth surface demonstrate 844:27-31

Experiment to show 128:129-130

Force needed to overcome friction on different surfaces experiment 1378:12

Force, amount needed to move big and small things (Primary) 539:10-11

Marbles demonstrate force and motion 844:3-26

Science and athletics—experiment 382:97-99

Toy demonstrates energy from twisted rubber band experiment 1496:16-17

FORCES OF ATTRACTION

Stringing water (water runs along string from one container to another) 114:57-59

FORECAST. *See* WEATHER FORECASTING

FORENSIC SCIENCE. *See* DETECTIVES

FOREST. *See also* WOODS

Air introduction to a woods ecosystem 285:41-43

Ancient forest structure layers, how to draw project 1336:64

Animals—pitfall traps for collecting small animals from forest floor 285:83-84

Climax community 268:70

Conifers in your neighborhood or park, how to identify project 1336:63

Fallen tree log placed in terrarium lets you study life in log experiment 1472:8-12

Fires and their roles in naturally polluting the air—experiment 371:36-38

Floor community—setting up/observing terrarium with forest floor community 285:88

Floor terrarium—forest plants in glass-enclosed terrarium—how to make 294:25-26

Food web in ancient forests project, how to do 1336:64

Forest floor terrarium, how to make 1075:32-33

Forest terrarium in large soda bottle, how to make 1071:76-77

Game; forest recycling game to demonstrate food chain, how to play 1205:13

Ideas to help save the ancient forests 1336:62-63

Investigate a softwood pine forest 285:61-62

Life of a forest 268:11-15

Log investigation; identify insects, animals and soil project 1336:64

Magic forest of trees—how to make 312:29-33

Mini forest habitat in aquarium, how to plant and care for experiment 1472:48-53

Quadrat used to study composition of a forest experiment 1075:102-103

Study of life in a hardwood forest 285:55-57

Succession; turn pond into forest experiment with one habitat replacing another 1472:60-63

FOREST FIRES

Forest fires produce carbon dioxide experiment 1174:40-41

FORKLIFTS

Make a simple hydraulic lifting system 227:26-27

FORMICARIUM. *See* ANTS

FORTUNE COOKIES

How to make 358:46-47

FOSSIL FUELS

Burning fossil fuels produce carbon dioxide experiment 1269:42-43

Burning wood produces carbon dioxide experiment 1269:46

Harmful particulates in air from incomplete burning of fossil fuels experiment 1453:34-36

Nuclear fuel produces more energy than fossil fuels experiment 1453:54-56

Plants exposed to too much sulfur dioxide gas are harmed experiment 1453:30-31

Soot ash and smoke experiment 1269:10

Sulfur dioxide harms plants experiment 1324:65-68

FOSSILS

An evidence for evolution 402:103-105
Artificial fossils from plaster of Paris 532:74-75
Caring for and protecting your fossils, how to do 1364:30-31
Cast fossil from a mold project 1364:33-35
Cast of fossil, how to make 1089:79-80
Casts of fossil leaves, bones or footprints project 1296:1977
Chiseling a fossil out of rock project 1364:29
Collecting and classifying fossils project 1413:170-171
Collecting and observing fossils, how to do 1364:26-27
Collecting fossils, how to do 1126:24-25
Collection and care of—how to 507:1892-1893
Demonstrate how fossils are preserved 293:7
Demonstrate how fossils were made 175:25
Dinosaur fossil, how to make from plaster of Paris 1175:141-143
Diorama showing fossil's original habitat project 1413:106
Excavation area built in shoe box for simulated dig project 715:69
Field project—how to find 507:1892-1893
Finding fossils—how to do 731:123-126
Finding tiny fossils in clay project 1364:23
Finding tiny fossils in sand project 1364:22
Footprint fossil, plaster of Paris, how to make 1008:37
Fossil bones, how to make from dough, and plaster gauze 1175:143-144
Fossil cast from fossil mold, how to make from plaster of Paris 1480:88
Fossil cast, how to make from plaster of Paris 1169:23
Fossil casts, how to make your own 1063:230
Fossil casts, how to make 1266:53
Fossil imprints from today's materials project 715:71-72
Fossil pictures, plaster, how to make 947:20-21
Fossil plaster casts, how to make 1044:40-41
Fossil preserved in amber experiment 1364:21
Fossil rocks—how to make 666:88-89
Fossil time line 816:12
Good places for finding and collecting fossils 625:20-21
How fossils became embedded in ice demonstration 1023:50-51
How fossils were formed 128:66
How fossils were preserved demonstration 1023:48-49; 1479:71
How to collect and clean fossils 1438:114-118
How were dinosaur tracks formed experiment using flour and cornmeal mud 1397:56-59
Leaf casts, how to make 1266:53
Make a permanent shell imprint experiment 900:152-153
Make mock fossils with beach materials 359:84-87
Make plaster of Paris fossil from clay mold of shell experiment 1481:12-14
Make your own fossil cast, how to do 1075:21
Make your own fossils with plaster of Paris and modeling clay 1383:19
Making fossils 400:32
Models of fossils, making 898:14-15
Mold and cast a fossil, how to do 1441:39
Mold and cast fossils experiment to show how fossils are formed 1134:1.004
Mold of fossil from plaster of Paris project 1364:33-35
Organizing your collection of fossils, how to do 1089:73-75

Petrified paper towel—making to show mineral replacement project 715:70
Plaster fossil cast, how to make 860:162-163
Plaster of Paris fossils—making 748:176
Plaster of Paris fossils, how to make 970:97
Plaster of Paris models, making 797:14-15
Preparing your fossil specimens, how to do 1089:59-60
Removing fossils from ironstone—how to do 625:21
Weighing a dinosaur project 1364:42-43
Why are fossils found in rock experiment 1294:92-95

FOUCAULT, JEAN

Pendulum experiment shows spinning of Earth 1480:16-17
Who invented the gyroscope project 1525:107-109

FOUCAULT PENDULUM. *See also* **PENDULUMS**

Foucault pendulum—how to make 763:80-81

FOUCAULT PENDULUM PRINCIPLE. *See also* **GYRO-SCOPES; PENDULUMS**

Foucault pendulum model experiment 1502:33-34
Foucault's Pendulum experiment to demonstrate Earth rotates 1003:28-29
How to demonstrate 577:project #29
Prove Earth turns experiments 723:214-215

FOUNTAIN—DRINKING

Make a self filling drinking fountain 604:24-27

FOUNTAINS

Bottle fountain experiment with plastic bottle and food coloring 1377:29
Flowing fountain experiment 1066:46-47
Fountain demonstrates water pressure increases with depth experiment 1310:24-25
Fountain in a jar experiment with jars, straws and modeling clay 1436:46-48
Fountain, making 909:64
Fountains of colored water demonstrate hot air expands experiment 1211:15
How do fountains work experiment 1509:19
Pressure fountain moves water upwards experiment 1179:136
Siphon fountain in plastic bottle with straws and cork experiment 1243:26-27
Spraying fountain produced by using air pressure experiment 1405:79
Water flows uphill experiment 996:16-17

FOUNTAINS AND PUMPS

Kits 386:81-84

FRACTIONS

Activities and puzzles demonstrate concept of one half, thirds, and fourths 443:1-33

FRAGRANCES. *See* **COSMETICS; PERFUMES**

FRANKLIN, BENJAMIN

His experiments 42:64-75
Make static electricity to see "small" lightning 602:unpaged

FRAUNHOFER, JOSEPH VON

Fraunhofer's dark lines in spectrum experiment; how to make simple spectroscope 1478:97

FREEMASON'S CIPHER

Freemason's cipher secret code—how to write 629:23-24

FREEZING. *See also* **HEAT; ICE; WATER—FREEZING**

Effects of low temperature on different household liquids experiment 836:6-7
Fahrenheit measurements versus Celsius measurements experiment 1439:72-74

Freezing and melting experiments 538:37-42

Freezing experiment with olive oil 563:134-135

Freezing is good way to preserve food experiment 1238:119-120

Freezing of tissue in vegetables—experiment 563:60-61

Freezing point—lift that cube 16:58-61

Freezing point and boiling point of water experiment 1219:31

Freezing point of water changes when you add salt experiment 1004:3.006

Ice and fork trick 249:27

Ice and salt make things very cold; make ice cream experiment 1032:28-29

Lower the freezing point—fun with ice and salt 281:59

Orange juice will not freeze like water experiment 1405:58

Put pressure on ice 249:26-27

Temperature of freezing mixtures—experiment 183:48-51

Thermometer in tin can with ice cubes, water, salt experiment shows dew point 1439:52-55

Water expands on freezing 281:22

Water expands when it freezes—experiment 672:19

What happens when water freezes 253:43-44

FREEZING POINT

Lowering freezing point; make ice cream experiment 871:3.010

FREQUENCY. *See* **SOUND—FREQUENCY**

FRESHWATER. *See also* **LAKES; PONDS; STREAMS**

Areas—activities with diverse fresh water areas 236:140-142

Biology—collecting pond life—equipment needed for 62:56

Exploration of a pond, marsh, swamp for frog, toad or salamander eggs 285:77

Insects—a study of insects in a pond 285:75-76

Life—activities with fresh water life 236:132-140

Measure pH, temperature and light penetration 285:26-28

Streams—the living community of a small brook or stream 285:76

FRESHWATER ANIMALS

Effects of acidity levels on freshwater animals chart 727:18

FRESHWATER AQUARIUMS

Description and building 236:136

FRICTION. *See also* **HEAT; SLIDING TOYS; STATIC ELECTRICITY**

A shove—half penny game 247:28

A streamlined shape moves faster in water 247:31

Affect on winds 243:42-43

Air car demonstrates motion is affected by friction 1404:158-159

Air cars reduce friction experiment 1476:85

Air friction, projects on 691:43-47

Air reduces friction between surfaces 247:32

Areas of friction—3 different blocks—how many coins moves each—experiment 247:19-20

Balancing trick demonstrates friction 1035:20

Ball bearing reduces friction, how to demonstrate 1033:21

Ball bearings in model car overcome friction experiment 1334:10-11

Ball bearings overcome friction experiment with marbles and tin cans 1436:72-74

Ball bearings reduce friction experiment with marbles and cans 940:82-84

Bearings reduce friction; marbles and jar lids experiment 837:34-35

Bicycle tires—increase your pedal power 399:57

Block sliding on smooth and rough surfaces experiment 1159:34-40

Board and weights moving on sandpaper—experiment 587:46

Brakes—nail, reel and piece of wood—demonstrate brake action 247:21

Can friction be controlled with lubricants experiment 851:22-23

Cane hangs on your hand magic demonstration 1010:25-27

Card trick demonstrates friction 966:42-45

Climbing toy demonstrates friction, how to make 1523:25

Coefficient of friction equals tangent of the angle experiment 1164:19-22

Compare rolling friction with sliding friction experiment 902:144

Compare starting and sliding friction experiment 902:142-143

Counterweight, what is it and how does it make lifting load easier experiment 1400:64-67

Demonstrate rollers and wheels reduce friction 247:30

Different surface textures affect friction experiment 836:63-65

Different surfaces on adjustable slope used to investigate friction 1179:61

Discovering friction at work—experiment 651:20-21

Does water reduce friction—reducing friction on wet surfaces 247:27

Experiment with friction forces 419:17

Experiments and tricks to demonstrate friction 1137:80-91

Experiments to demonstrate 186:40-47

Fighting friction—demonstration with marbles 575:14

Fluid friction—projects on 691:53-58

Force demonstrated by dragging block over different surfaces 247:16

Force needed to overcome friction on different surfaces experiment 1378:12

Friction affects motion demonstration with turning wooden spool 1404:16

Friction affects motion demonstration 1479:95

Friction and what it does activities for classroom 1291:43-44

Friction between objects generates heat experiment 1219:8

Friction causes heat experiment 851:21-22

Friction causes heat, bending wire experiment 860:228-229

Friction creates heat experiment with dowel and block of wood 1462:120-121

Friction fraction or coefficient of friction tables and data 1157:92-97

Friction in water experiment 909:104

Friction makes heat experiment with bow, dowel and block of wood 1519:22

Friction produces heat experiment 836:57-58

Friction tester 295:87-89

Frictionless air car; make two cars to investigate motion experiment 1157:12-13

"Frictionless" air-car experiment 1159:39-40

George Stokes' effect of viscous drag on small spheres fall thru liquids 1133:4.010

Glass of water pulled by rubber band demonstrates 699:21

Hovercraft demonstrates friction; make from balloon, food tray 1380:24-25

Hovercraft demonstrates how cushion of air reduces friction experiment 1179:60

Hovercraft reduces friction experiment 1523:23

How ball bearings work—experiment 585:50-51

How different surfaces affect friction demonstration 1479:96

How does the force of friction change 253:179-180

How friction affects inertia experiment 1405:101

How hot can you make it (Primary) 551:unpaged

How to make heat by friction 281:54

Inclines affect forces needed to overcome gravity and friction experiment 1157:98-101

Indian rice trick with ruler in jar of rice grains demonstration 1523:25

Investigate friction—experiments 664:16-19

Lift jar with balloon experiment 722:33

Liquids and lubricants reduce friction experiments 1136:13

Load in dump truck has to be raised to what height before it dumps experiment 1198:16

Magic broomstick 27:92-93

Magic trick; rope appears to stay in bottle experiment 1010:32-36

Materials with different surfaces experiment to test friction 1462:116-119

Measuring friction when surfaces rub together—measuring apparatus 586:72-74

Measuring friction with ramp and protractor measuring device experiment 1476:83-84

Measuring frictional forces experiment; four ways to measure friction 1157:80-84

Measuring the amount of friction 180:38

Move something over smooth or rough surface 125:4-6

Move something rough or smooth in water 125:7-9

Move something rough or smooth thru air 125:10-11

Moving objects on inclined plane experiment; data table given 871:4.006

Objects move more easily over smooth surfaces experiment 760:30

Oil reduces friction (Primary) 323:12-13

Overcome—prove smooth slides easier than rough (Primary) 320:11

Paper cup—experiment to show (Primary) 201:16-17

Perceptual motion—demonstrate with marbles and cardboard tubes 472:2239

Plastic bottles, one with water, on sloping boards demonstrate friction 1079:38-39

Produces heat—sandpaper experiment [Primary] 743:23

Produces heat 44:78-79

Producing an electrical charge with friction 180:44-45

Projects with friction 1164:22

Pull away tricks to demonstrate 205:22-28

Pulleys can reduce friction experiment with spool, pencil, string, cups 1400:61-62

Reducing friction experiment 867:36-37

Reducing friction with oil and grease experiment 909:107

Reducing friction with rollers experiment 1523:23

Reducing friction with water experiment 909:106

Ridges on fingertips affect ability to pick up objects experiment 1397:60-63

Rig to build to test friction forces, how to make 1243:14-15

Roll ball down slope—measure distance ball rolls on smooth/coarse material 247:15

Rollers overcome friction experiment 1423:5

Rollers reduce friction experiment 1035:22-23

Rolling along 280:49

Rolling along experiment 909:109

Rolling and sliding wheels-build frictionless air car to demo. Brakes 586:74-75

Rolling right along—experiment with cans of sand 563:192

Rolling wheels reduce friction experiment 1159:40-41

Rope and tree experiment 747:21-22

Rope friction—experiment 585:43-44

Rough surfaces and weight experiment 247:17

Rubber bands and shoe box demonstrate static and moving friction experiment 940:79-81

Science friction ruler 399:16

Shown by running marble 162:124

Simple scales for experimenting with friction 926:122-125

Skiing—make model skis—test in sand or salt 247:26

Skimmer reduces friction experiment 1028:111

Sliding mat—of 3 materials which is fastest 247:13

Sliding wheels; toy car with its "brakes" on experiment 1159:41-42

Smooth surfaces produce less friction—experiment 682:13

Smooth tires on toy auto won't climb hill experiment 1073:13

Smoothing reduces friction 125:12-13

Starting/moving—drag wood block over different surfaces—measure friction 247:18

Static friction is greater than moving friction experiment with box/rubber band 1436:75-77

Static versus moving friction—experiment 585:46-47

Surface area affects friction demonstration 1404:156-157

Surface friction experiment with wooden block and cup of marbles 1380:22-23

Surfaces that slow down rolling toy car experiment 1507:13

Test for friction experiment 1028:111

Test for friction on different surfaces experiment using toy truck and ramp 1004:5.002

Texture of surface affects motion experiment 1404:152-153

The brake—experiment 563:192-193

The end of the line 16:20-22

The force of friction 260:11-13

Things slide easiest on what surfaces experiment 834:24-26

Thread and spool tank model overcomes friction and climbs slope experiment 1334:14-15

Tires need friction to work on roads; toy car demonstrates 945:22-23

Use of friction and overcoming friction—experiment 128:120-121

Useless matches 249:7

Water, soap, and oil reduce friction 125:13-15

Wear—test different materials—wool, cotton and nylon 247:23
Weight and friction effect on energy of moving object demonstration 1404:164-167
Weight and surface area effects on force of friction experiment 1157:85-88
What is friction demonstration with wooden blocks, sandpaper and soap 1436:66-71
What is friction 281:44
Wheels and rollers effect on friction experiment 1157:88-92
Wheels and rollers experiment 867:37
Wheels reduce friction experiment with toy cars 1166:6
Which slides first—use objects on 7 different materials 247:14
Why use wheels 281:43
Wooden pieces with and without detergent demonstrates 699:23
Wooden slide test for friction experiment 1035:21
Yo-Yo will climb string no one is holding experiment 1083:46-47

FRISBEES
Experiments 66:37-49
Skimmy—how to make 310:14-16

FROG BOARD
How to make 11:107-109

FROGS. *See also* **TADPOLES**
Aquarium habitat for frogs, how to make 810:75
Aquarium preparation and how to care for eggs 400:23
Aquaterrarium to raise frogs experiment, how to make 1492:68-69
Collect eggs and hatch, how to keep and feed 796:25-26
Collecting and keeping frogs 517:11-16
Collecting and raising tadpoles of frogs 475:38-42
Collection and care of 313:33-37; 390:39-41
Demonstrate breathing rate of frog with and without carbon dioxide 174:36-37
Do frogs prefer one kind of light or color over the other—experiment 517:30-32
Experiment to show what they do when cold weather comes 40:55-56
Exploration of pond, marsh or swamp for frog, toad or salamander eggs 285:77
Follow the life cycle of a frog 148:56-57
Frog development from eggs kept under several different conditions—experiment 500:145-148
Frog hibernation in the field and in the laboratory 266:33-37
Frog watcher—how to be 517:7-10
Frog with red and black markings warns of poison experiment 1391:19
Frogs in aquarium, how to keep 913:39
From a tadpole to a frog 232:38
Get a frog to hibernate experiment 913:41
Hatching frog eggs experiment 1063:417
Hibernating frogs—experiment 693:14-15
Hibernating frogs in aquarium, how to care for 1433:37-39
Hibernation experiment—what happens when frog goes into hibernation 517:40-42
Hibernation experiment with frog hibernating in aquarium, how to do 1476:117
Hibernation of frogs 436:44
How do tadpoles turn into frogs experiment 1293:109-111

How frogs grow experiment with frog spawn 1181:29
How frogs grow experiment 1183:37
How temperature affects hatching time 517:26
How to catch and care for 234:40-41; 279:17
Indoor puddles for tadpoles 264:106
Learning—can frogs learn—experiments 517:35-38
Learning—frog jumps around obstacle to get food—experiment 517:37-38
Learning—frogs learn to avoid unpleasant food 517:35-37
Learning—test with sounds and frog recordings 517:34
Life cycle of frogs experiment; hatch frog eggs 1504:31
Make a frog hibernate 381:105-107
Make a frog hibernate 532:66-67
Metamorphosis or change of tadpoles into frogs experiment 978:90-91
Observations while rearing frogs 173:21
Observe and record a tadpole changing into a frog 166:101-103
Observe the metamorphosis of a frog 294:73-74
Raise frogs in a mini-aquarium—how to do 476:42-43
Record frog choruses 236:70
Senses—learn about frog's senses through simple experiments 517:29-34
Simulate formation of African tree frog's nest experiment 1479:33
Tadpole growth, observation experiment 860:176-180
Tadpoles—collection and care of 313:24-28
Tadpoles in aquarium turn into frogs, how to do 1433:34-36
Tadpoles 62:61-63
Tree—catch, observe and record behavior of spring peepers 166:107-110
Tree—collection and care of 313:38-42
Vision—size and movement of food—response experiment 517:32

FROGS—COLLECTION AND PRESERVATION
Collecting frog eggs, how to do 774:10-11
Diet for a frog 774:20-21
Handling frogs, how to 774:12-13
Housing frogs, how to 774:14-15
Pond for, simple, making 774:16

FROST. *See also* **ICE**
Demonstrate frost formation experiment 1396:10-11
Demonstrate how frost forms 1479:82
Experiment to show 40:58-60
Frost—how to make [Primary] 744:22
Frost formation experiment 715:132-133
Frost prints on blueprint paper, how to make 921:50-52
Frosty patterns, making 685:4-5
How are dew and frost made 291:35
How frost forms experiment 1023:162-163; 1231:40-41
Make from mothballs 203:57
Making frost (Primary) 232:90
Pattern of frost on plate placed in freezer experiment 1281:23

FRUIT. *See* **FRUITS**

FRUIT FLIES. *See also* **FLIES—FRUIT FLIES**
Basic needs of life affect how many flies can live in one place project 1427:22-25
Does extremely-low-frequency (ELF) affect fruit flies experiment 1096:53-57
Does low level electromagnetic radiation (EMF) affect fruit flies experiment 1096:53-57

159

Effect of food supply on fruit fly density experiment 871:2.011

Fruit flies offspring affected by parent's exposure to radiation experiment 1267:89-90

Fruit fly trap experiment with soda bottle trap 1527:48-50

Habitat for fruit flies, how to make 835:56-58

Heredity in fruit flies experiment 1425:23-28

Jar for trapping and raising fruit flies 414:81-82

Life cycle of fruit flies observed experiment 1395:139-144

Metamorphosis of fruit flies observed experiment 1395:139-144

Observe life cycle of a fly experiment 1405:32

Observe life cycle of a fly experiment 904:108-109

Percentage of fly population that is male or female experiment 1395:143

Praying mantis can eat how many insects experiment 1097:9-12

Raise and observe fruit flies, how to 835:56-58

Reflex behavior; response to cold temperature experiment 936:15-16

Reflex behavior; response to light experiment 936:14-15

Reproduction and development of fruit flies experiment 978:91-92

Thomas Morgan's sex linkage in fruit flies experiment 1133:3.011

FRUIT LEATHER

Making 697:60

Sun power—sun dried fruit leather 494:11

FRUITS. *See also* **CITRUS FRUITS; SEEDS—FRUIT**

A gas chamber for fruits 231:40

Apple chips dried, how to do 1406:98-99

Avocado pit—how to plant and grow 712:12-13

Avocado plant, starting and growing, how to 898:45

Banana in refrigerator experiment 1238:76

Cherries—chart of cherry development from flower to fruit 366:88-89

Citrus seed plants—how to grow 1406:12-15

Citrus tree, how to grow 899:139

Citrus tricks and fruit skin sculpture 231:110-111

Compare vitamin C content of fruit juices experiment; data table given 871:2.020

Demonstrate ripening process of fruit 152:19-23

Does heat effect vitamin C content of fruit juices experiment 871:2.020

Dried fruits do not swell in salty water experiment 723:100-101

Drying fruits—how to 697:59-60

Drying raisins experiment 1238:114-115

Effect of oxygen on darkening of fruit experiment 905:80-81

Ethylene gas effect on ripening fruits experiment 1060:56

Ethylene gas from banana causes tomato to ripen experiment 1440:77-78

Fruit dish, armored orange (pomander) and marmalade (how to make) 231:112-113

Fruit dryer solar collector, making 870:16-18

Fruit is mature ovary of flower seed experiment 1060:55

Fruit prints, how to make 1368:75-76

Fruit; one end is sweeter experiment 1238:70

Fruits and seeds move 271:56-63

Grow apple in a bottle 176:32-33

Grow plants from vegetable and fruit tops; grapefruit, pineapple, beets 1071:74-75

Growing a tree from pits or seeds, how to do 590:52

How to make fruit leather 231:38

Is water important to life experiment with apples 1324:28-31

Is wax applied to produce purchased from supermarkets experiment 1450:26-33

Keep fruits from turning brown project 1210:62-63

Making jam to show effect of pectin on crushed fruit experiment 1484:145-146

Mango and papaya seeds—how to sprout and grow 1406:63

Orange seed—how to plant and grow 712:9

Orange tree from seeds, how to grow 1054:65

Oxygen effect on darkening of fruit experiment 1405:52-53

Peach skin under microscope—observe 713:59-60

Pear grows inside bottle experiment; demonstrates greenhouse effect 1524:27

Pineapple and gelatin experiment 1238:77-78

Plants from orange and lemon seeds, how to grow 1486:22-23

Preservation; which solution preserves fruit the best experiment 1343:17

Preserving pears as jam or jelly experiment 1238:121-122

Prints of fruit on paper, how to make 1142:31

Prints of fruits and vegetables; how to make and display 1044:30-31

Protective covering on fruit keeps water inside fruit experiment 1324:28-31

Raisins; heat causes raisins to change experiment 888:88-90

Ripen a fruit experiment 1238:71

Ripening—can ethylene molecules cause fruits and vegetables to ripen 396:72-73

Ripening fruit using ethylene gas, how to do 784:74

Seeds—avocado seeds—how to grow 272:6-16

Seeds—collect different tree fruits 275:21

Seeds—discover and chart numbers of seeds different fruits contain 400:21

Seeds—grow a tree seed 275:18-19

Seeds—kiwi seed—how to grow 272:42-47

Seeds—mango—how to grow 272:30-35

Seeds—papaya—how to grow 272:17-22

Seeds—pomegranate seed—how to grow 272:36-41

Seeds from fruit, how to grow 888:55

Seeds of orange grow tree, how to do 899:138-139

Seeds; citrus seeds, how to plant and grow 1440:55-57

Seeds; grow apple or orange plants from their seeds experiment 1490:23

Seeds; grow plants from fruit seeds, how to do 1306:10-11

Seeds; lemons, how to grow 827:63

Sugar used as preservative for fruit experiment 1395:130

Sun jam—making 697:60-61

Test for presence of iron in fruit juices experiment 1479:53

Test for presence of iron in fruit juices experiment 905:112-113

Vitamin C; detect Vitamin C in fruits and vegetables experiment 1476:136-137

Vitamin C; heat destroys Vitamin C in fruit juices experiment 1476:137

Water amount; how much water do fresh grapes lose when dried project 1210:33-34

Water quantity in vegetables and fruits experiment 1189:46-47

Water; amount of water in fruits experiment 1509:26

What stops oxidation in fruits and vegetables experiment 885:88

FRUITS—DRIED

Dried apple garland, how to make 1115:128

Dried apple slices, making 899:123

Raisins, making 784:72-73

FRUITS—SEEDS. *See also* SEEDS—FRUIT

Citrus—how to grow 272:23-29

Citrus seeds, how to grow 1006:27

Orange tree, how to grow from seeds (Primary) 985:31

Pineapple; grow plant from top 879:170-171

FUEL

Alcohol as fuel, recycling garbage into energy from ethyl alcohol experiment 997:80-82

Fuel cell—making 698:30-32

How you can make fuel 319:66-68

Litter from trees dried and compressed for fuel use project 969:79-80

Plant materials changed into methane fuel experiment 1323:90-94

FUEL CELL

Fuel cell for energy, making 895:108-109

FULLER, BUCKMINSTER

Dymaxion tent—how to make a wooden model 429:81-83

FUNCTIONS

Game to demonstrate basic principles of functions and graphs 456:1-33

FUNGI. *See also* SLIME MOLDS; SPORES; YEAST

Bracket or shelf fungi grow on trees at the same height experiment 1061:114-115

Bread mold experiment 977:60

Collecting fungi 148:12-13

Effect of yeast on a sugar solution experiment 904:82-83

Effect of yeast on food decomposition experiment 904:92-93

Examining edible mushrooms 294:24-25

Experiments to test for fungi in compost pile 864:47-48

Fairy rings; investigate growth habits of fungi in fairy rings project 1313:69-71

Food spoilers, experiments with fungi 864:49

Fungal spore guide 864:47

Fungi spores from air experiment 737:23

Fungi that spoil food, identification key given 1295:50

Grow a fungus garden—experiment 563:53-54

Grow bread mold experiment 1183:23

Grow molds and observe under a microscope 889:49-50

Grow some fungi on bread experiment 1181:15

Key; visual guide to identify type of fungi 864:49-50

Lichens; which part is fungus or protist experiment 864:51-53

Make a fungus garden 264:31-33

Make a spore print 480:91

Mold garden in plastic bags experiment 1063:413

Mold growing on moist, dry and disinfected bread experiment 1038:28-29

Mushroom spore prints on paper, how to make 1038:27

Mushroom spores grow into mushrooms to eat, how to plant experiment 1306:18-19

Pilobolus, the shotgun fungus, experiments with 864:50-51

Reproduction of spores experiment; make spore prints, how to do 978:54

Spore print from mushroom cap, how to make 1214:22

Spore prints from toadstool caps, how to make 1069:69

Spore prints from wetland mushrooms experiment 1492:50-51

Spores from nature; collect and observe 864:45-46

Spores identify different types of fungi experiment 1134:4.002

Testing mushrooms for sugar or starch experiment 1061:112-113

Trapping fungi spores and pollen grains from atmosphere experiment 933:31

Why a puffball smokes demonstration 1440:71-72

Yeast and sugar mix makes carbon dioxide gas that inflates balloon experiment 1038:26

FUNNELS, BERLESE. *See* BERLESE FUNNEL

FURNACES—SOLAR. *See* HEATING SYSTEM; SOLAR FURNACES

FURNACES. *See* HOUSES—FURNACES

FUSES. *See also* ELECTRIC; ELECTRICITY—ELECTRIC CURRENT

Demonstrate how fuse works experiment 895:24-25

Demonstrating the function of a fuse 180:50-51

Edison's experiment 230:71-75

Find out how to make a fuse 599:40

Fuse from battery, bulb, and paper clip, how to make 1243:36-37

Fuse made from steel wool experiment 972:33

Fuse, how to make 768:85-86

Fuses protect a circuit experiment 938:35-38

Fuses, how to make 910:29

How does electrical fuse work 291:170

How fuses protect wires from overheating experiment 1501:64-67

How is fuse like a switch experiment 834:50

Let's make a fuse 610:65

Make a fuse—see how it works 287:27; 445:39

Make a fuse of metal foil 127:27-31

Make a tester for fuses—experiment 563:108

Making a fuse experiment 1514:68-70

Model working fuse, how to make 828:30-33

Short circuit experiment to see what happens when fuse blows 1132:86-1-86-2

Show purpose of fuse circuit breaker—experiment 179:137-139

Simple fuse made from battery, wires and bulbs 1476:23-24

FUSION, NUCLEAR *See* NUCLEAR FUELS

G

G-FORCES

How to experience G-Forces demonstration 1434:97-99

Shape of soap bubble where gravity force is greater than on Earth experiment 1399:74

What causes feeling of weightlessness experiment 1399:52-55

GAGARIN, YURI A.

Who was the first man in space project 1525:18-23

GALAXIES

Band of the Milky Way experiment; demonstrate with flashlight and plastic 1478:132

Cannibal galaxies demonstration with magnet, cork, pins and water 1478:139

Classification and sequence cards 400:109

Demonstrate movement of a spiral galaxy 1405:15

Detecting cosmic rays project 833:277-278

Determine how galaxies may be moving experiment 1479:8

Drawing the shape of the galaxy project 833:279-280

Galaxies; how galaxies may be moving demonstration with balloon 1394:58-59

How many aliens are there in the Galaxy experiment; make alien calculator 1478:146-147

Hubble discovery; measuring red shifts of galaxies shows speed of objects 1478:142-143

Making a model of a comet project 833:272

Model Milky Way experiment; make from poster board, paints, clay 1478:134

Star clusters; explore stars around certain constellations experiment 1217:32-33

The Local Group galaxies; make model to show galaxies and distances experiment 1478:138-139

Tracking and photographing a meteor shower project 833:274-275

Viewing galaxies, nebulae, and clusters with a telescope project 833:278-279

GALILEO, GALILEI

Construct model of Galileo's gas thermometer experiment 1396:181-187

Falling objects have a constant acceleration rate experiment 1133:4.004

Galileo's drop experiment with marble and ball 1014:62

Galileo thermometer—making 385:118-120

Galileo's drop in a vacuum experiment 1132:50-1-50-2

Galileo's thought experiment; effect of gravity on pendulum 1157:16-18

Hammer and nail fall at same speed 549:93-94

His experiments 42:24-33

How hot is hot experiment 1133:7.001

Making a Galileo type telescope 400:105

Pendulum—experiments that Galileo did—how to do 642:22-24

Periodic time of a pendulum is constant experiment 1133:4.003

Repeat Galileo's experiment 448:23-25

Water drop lens demonstrates his experiments with lenses 602:unpaged

Who first discovered the laws of falling bodies project 1525:47-49

GALILEO'S EXPERIMENT

Body in motion maintains its motion experiment 1502:30-31

Different weight, different fall? In a vacuum? 295:54-55

Dilute force of gravity 295:56-58

Falling sideways—pendulums in motion 295:60-62

Falling sideways 295:73-75

Frictionless car demonstrates first law of motion experiment, how to build 1502:28-29

Galileo's drop experiment with marble and ball 1014:62

Galileo's experiment; predicting the path of a projectile 1156:42-47

Galileo's methods for diluting gravity and measuring time experiment 1156:35-42

Galileo's pendulum experiments 1156:28-30

Object remains at rest until force is applied to it experiment 1502:30-31

Objects at rest remain at rest 295:64-65

Pendulum experiment; moving object moves unless force changes its motion 1502:26-28

Speed of a falling ball 295:55-56

Swing time string experiment 827:100-101

Weight and falling of steel ball and marble 274:11

GALLS

Adventure 37—we invade the privacy of gall makers—galls under hand lens 29:169-174

Cedar apple galls—adventure 50—cedar apples under a hand lens 29:217-220

Collecting and observation 277:106-114

Collection of galls—making 414:62-69

Find out about galls 236:36

Gall cage—how to build 234:59

Galls of insects; collect and observe 1295:84-86

How to demonstrate different kinds 117:82-84

Insect galls, how to collect and hatch 1188:21

Make ink from oak apples 146:7

Making a mounted gall collection 277:107

Observation chamber—how to make 277:106-108

GALVANOMETER

Battery from lemon power experiment using galvanometer, how to make 1476:15

Construct a galvanometer to measure electric current 167:19-28

Electric current affects magnet experiment 1404:14-15

Electric current detector or galvanometer 391:46-49

Galvanometer detects electric current experiment, how to make 1426:86-88

Galvanometer detects electric current experiment, how to make 1479:109

Galvanometer to test electric cell, how to make 1159:109

Galvanometer, how to make 938:87-88

Galvanometer, make from pocket compass, battery, wire and wood 1247:32-33

Galvanometer, make to measure electrolytes in some common foods experiment 1004:4.007

Galvanometer, making 930:8

How to build galvanometer 293:30; 1476:31-33

How to make 127:93-97; 176:72-73; 253:150-151; 341:28-29; 346:81-87; 382:30-31; 436:38; 472:2226; 57:75-76

Make a simple galvanometer 63:60-61; 291:160-161

Making galvanometer using a lemon 827:60

Simple current detector, making a galvanometer 837:45-46

Using the homemade galvanometer 63:64-65

GALVANOSCOPE

How to make 123:56-61

How to make 127:93-97

GAMES. *See also* **BATTERIES AND CIRCUITS**
Ball bearing and magnet game—how to make 543:12-15
Boat game in water with cork and balsa wood boats, how to make 1043:30-31
Build an electric quiz game 278:43-45
Circuit board quiz game, how to make 1043:24-25
Continents a-go-go 400:124
Electric game board, making 885:79-81
Electric quiz game, making 768:117
Electronic quiz game, make with battery, bulb, wire and quiz questions 1072:21
Fat game 400:122
Game of chance—what's the chance of success 472:2222
Games of chance; what's the chance; dice and checkers demonstrate 1248:28-29
Litterbug game 400:120-121
Living things game 400:123
Marble games—how to make a marble maze and "jumping" board 543:20-21
Marble zig zag ramp game, making 779:30-31
Quiz game, Dr. Zed's Electrifying quiz game, making 890:26-27
Snow games 277:127-129
Soccer board game with magnets, how to make 1043:28-29
Table top penny pitching game, making 768:116
The challenge game 400:125
Wet and wild game—trip down a river 400:126-129

GARBAGE
Biodegradable and non biodegradable garbage experiment 978:162-163
Buried garbage items; how they decompose experiment; plastic/bones/sticks/peel 1328:78-79
Burning garbage creates smoke and ash experiment; chart for results given 1173:55-57
Bury different kinds of garbage experiment to see what biodegrades 1063:378
Compost pile makes natural fertilizer from garbage experiment 1240:27
Compost pile; large, mixed compost pile, how to make 1150:46-48
Composting food wastes garbage experiment 1150:44-46
Demonstrate weathering and decomposition of garbage in landfills experiment 1465:106
Different kinds of garbage pollute mountain soil experiment 1468:29
Effects of waste on environment and ways to reduce it experiment 978:163-165
Estimate amount of garbage family and members make in one week experiment 1012:83
Evaluate household trash for recycling or biodegradability project 969:54-55
Fast-food restaurant food wrappers; which can be recycled project 1427:96-97
Food leftovers in soil demonstrates decomposition of garbage experiment 1014:160
Garbage planted in soil experiment 1335:214-215
Graph containers and packaging used by family for one week 1013:29
How biodegradable is garbage experiment with different materials in soil 1476:199
How much waste do you generate experiment 1150:59-60

Incineration reduces volume and weight of garbage experiment 1012:88
Landfill; make miniature landfill to test what decomposes 807:180
Measure amount of different kinds of garbage used by your family experiment 1228:43-44
One week project to analyze garbage in the home 1134:8.002
Sculpture from paper trash, making 1013:26
Set up worm compost system 276:1-90

GARDENING. *See also* **HYDROPONICS; SOIL**
A country garden—how to 376:38
Climate and plants—compare garden plants that need hot versus cool climate 380:18-19
Cold frame effect on plants 380:44-45
Community gardens—research 380:55
Companion planting—chart 380:48-50
Compare local farmers' markets with large food companies products 380:56-57
Drawing gardening plan 380:50-51
Experiments 380:1-84
Grow a garden on your window sill—how to do (Primary) 580:unpaged
Grow a salad—radishes, lettuce, tomato, cucumbers 376:40-43
Keep monthly record of environmental changes in garden 380:9
Nutrition from plants—design garden containing important vitamins/mineral 380:5-15
Pest control—natural recipe for 380:72-73
Planting the garden—seeds and seedlings 380:52-53
Plants maturity—prepare planting dates and harvesting dates for 10 vegetables 380:16-17
Roots—waterworks of plants—build root viewing box to see how roots work 380:58-59
Soil—collect different types and analyze 380:24
Sunlight—determine hours of sunlight garden has for sun/shade loving plan 380:20-21
Tools for gardening—invent 3 new ones from natural materials 380:46-47
Vegetable garden—making 436:84
Vegetable tops—grow into a garden—carrots, turnips, beets, parsnips 376:13
Vegetables for city gardens 376:32-33
Water cycle and watering 380:62-63
Weeds—make weed collection and make weed cookbook 380:70-71

GARDENS
Bottle cap gardens for world's tiniest plants, how to plant and grow 1527:103
Film can garden, how to plant and grow 1527:104
Journal of your garden activities, how to keep 1054:14-15
Miniature garden, how to plant and care for 1292:12-13
Miniature garden, make and grow 868:17
No soil mini garden, how to make from sand and plastic container 1289:14-15
Wildlife garden in window box, how to plant 1414:28-31
Window sill garden, how to make 1175:108-109
Crystal garden—making 748:168

GARDENS—BOTTLE. *See also* **TERRARIUMS**
Bottle garden—how to make 574:10-11
Bottle garden—making 480:40
Bottle garden demonstrates water transpiration in plants experiment 1181:21

163

Bottle garden with plants, how to make 1379:22-23
Bottle garden, how to plant and care for 1246:12-15
Bottle garden, how to plant and grow 1214:31; 1368:56-57; 1486:18
Create a garden in a bottle experiment 1028:64-65
Garden in a bottle, how to make 1145:31
Grow cucumbers in a bottle—how to do 723:56
How to plant and grow bottle garden 810:38-39
Jar garden , how to make using jar, soil, and plants 1054:32-33
Miniature garden of plants in bottle, how to plant 1306:22-23
Moss garden—making 480:41
Mossy fern garden in bottle, how to make 932:28-31
Plants in a bottle garden, how to make 1371:24-26
Pumpkin or squash grow in bottle, how to plant and care for 1127:10

GARDENS—CHEMICAL. *See also* **CHEMICAL GARDENS**
Aluminum foil garden, making 883:49
Brick castle garden, making 883:53-54
Chemical garden, how to grow 866:159
Chemical garden, making [Primary] 897:45
Chemical magic—how to make 87:81-82
Crystal garden—how to make 695:42
Crystal garden from coal, salt, and laundry bluing, how to make 1127:39
Crystal garden in a pie plate, how to make 1229:70-71
Crystal garden, how to grow 1063:223
Crystal garden, how to make 854:91
Crystal garden—making 748:168; 870:40-42; 882:28; 898:13
Crystal gardens—experiment 605:16-21
Garden of odds and ends, making 883:52
Grow a 'seaweed' garden 97:43
Grow a crystal garden 598:26-27
Grow white or colored crystal garden from charcoal briquettes 577:project #26
How to make 452:74-75
Make a chemical garden 291:207
Mystery garden, making 883:54-57
Paper towel garden, making 883:48-50
Porous rock garden, making 883:49
Rock and charcoal garden, making 883:48-51
Sponge garden, making 883:52
Super crystal garden, making 883:52-53
Surprise garden, making 883:53

GARDENS—INDOOR
Cress garden—how to grow 712:52
Dish garden of small plants, how to plant experiment 1306:20-21
How can a garden be kept indoors 402:32
Mini farms—how to prepare, plant and care for 465:61-71
Mini-garden—how to make and grow 712:42-43

GARDENS—PESTS
Do marigolds really repel pests 398:39-40

GARDENS—SOILESS
Air plants grow without soil in dish garden, how to plant 1306:28-29
Hydroponics—how to do 382:46-50

GARDENS—WATER
Floating garden—how to make and plant water lilies 483:58-60
Water garden of aquatic plants, how to plant 1306:26-27

GARDENS—WINDOW BOX
Making 480:43

GARDENS WITHOUT SOILS. *See* **HYDROPONICS**

GARLIC
Can antibacterial effects of garlic be increased experiment 997:141-144
How to plant and grow indoors 1178:13-14

GAS GENERATOR
Construct gas generator to make hydrogen experiment 752:101-102
Experiment 391:60-64
Make with baking soda 50:34-39

GAS STATION
Model—how to make 431:18-19

GAS STOVE PILOT LIGHTS
Meter helps determine cost per month 381:144-147

GAS TURBINE ENGINES
Turbine spinner, cardboard and wire, making 1001:15

GASES. *See also* **CARBON DIOXIDE; HELIUM; HYDROGEN; OXYGEN**
A burning candle—candles and air—oxygen and a burning candle 147:88-98
A gas chamber for fruits 231:40
A jumping flame to show flammable vapor 114:45
Acidic or basic nature of gases tested with paper indicators experiment 1396:70-72
Air, helium, and carbon dioxide filled balloons behave differently exp. 888:130
Alka-Seltzer and water reaction experiment 1526:65-67
Alka-Seltzer in water puts out candle flame experiment 1526:72-73
Ammonia gas fountain demonstrates air pressure 203:52
Ammonia gas released by decay experiment 737:31
Balloon blowup—bottle, vinegar and baking soda 558:52
Balloon's volume will decrease when balloon is frozen experiment 1140:22
Bernoulli; who discovered laws of gases or fluids in motion project 1525:92-94
Boat with power 147:39-40
Bouncing mothballs 147:84-86
Bouncing raisins experiment 748:103
Boyle's Law experiment 871:3.017
Burning consumes oxygen experiment 1396:19-21
Burning wood; gas and other substances produced from burning wood experiment 1244:20
Can expanding gas move an object through air experiment 851:55-56
Can molecules in yeast make a gas from hydrogen peroxide experiment 831:88-90
Candle burns oxygen in bottle and leaves nitrogen gas experiment 995:18-19
Candle magic—experiment 146:48-49
Carbon dioxide—bubble power 112:14
Carbon dioxide—carbon dioxide and baking experiment 147:72
Carbon dioxide—cupcakes—how cakes rise 74:74-79
Carbon dioxide—dancing raisins (Primary) 109:10-11
Carbon dioxide—dancing raisins 147:86
Carbon dioxide—fire extinguisher gas—making 147:36-37
Carbon dioxide—make an ejector seat 146:37
Carbon dioxide—make invisible fizz gas 146:36-37
Carbon dioxide—make sherbet with a fizz 146:45
Carbon dioxide—making sinking balloons, floating balloons 147:38-39

Carbon dioxide—mothballs rise and fall in a glass—experiment 150:120-121

Carbon dioxide—speedy and not so speedy Alka Seltzer 147:120-121

Carbon dioxide—what puts the fizz in Alka Seltzer 147:120

Carbon dioxide bubbles—make sinking and floating carbon dioxide bubbles 147:37-38

Carbon dioxide gas inflates balloon experiment 1028:10

Carbon dioxide is heavier than air experiment 836:14-15

Carbon dioxide made from baking soda and vinegar in bottle experiment 1508:28

Carbon dioxide produced when vinegar and baking soda are mixed together 1479:56

Change water to gases with electricity 147:111-114

Changing a gas to a solid—experiment 180:12

Changing a liquid to a gas—experiment 180:12

Changing a solid to a gas 180:14

Changing speed of chemical reactions with Alka-Seltzer and water experiment 1526:68-70

Charles' Law experiment of gas temperature and volume 1133:7.005

Charles' Law and gases experiment 1156:103-104

Charles' Law; boiling and freezing a balloon experiment 871:3.016

Claude Berthollet's bleaching powers of chlorine in solution experiment 1133:2.007

Comparing gas densities experiment 1526:28-31

Comparing gases—which is heavier 180:11

Construct gas generator to make hydrogen experiment 752:101-102

Cooling a gas—experiment 147:43-44

Dancing raisins experiment with Alka-Seltzer 814:34-36

Density—density investigation of gases 295:35-37

Do balloons leak 147:106-107

Do gases dissolve in liquids 147:32

Do gases dissolve in other gases 147:32-33

Electric current splits water into hydrogen and oxygen gases experiment 1244:14-15

Electric gas—split water into gases 146:34-35

Electricity passing thru water splits water into hydrogen and oxygen experiment 1473:32-33

Expanding gas causes coin to rise and fall on top of bottle experiment 1435:24-26

Expanding gas effects on coin on top of soda bottle experiment 1405:62

Falling balloons show speed of different gases 147:104-106

Fast and slow chemical reaction with Seltzer pill in hot and cold water 1159:19-20

Gas and candle under glass experiment 748:112

Gas contracts when cooled experiment 836:85-86

Gas expands; clicking coin on soda bottle demonstrates 905:180-181

Gas expansion bottle thermometer, making 906:22-23

Gas flame produces water and carbon dioxide 585:88-89

Gas generator 391:60-64

Gas pressure in carbonated drink experiment 1250:14-17

Gas released from hydrogen peroxide and slice of raw potato experiment 1526:118-119

Gas takes on shape of its container experiment 1140:23-24

Gas takes up more space than solids or liquids experiment with vinegar/b. Soda 1179:24-25

Gas takes up space glass in water experiment 709:50-51

Gas volume from Alka-Seltzer and water reaction experiment 1526:71-74

Gases dissolved in gases experiment 1526:48-49

Gases dissolved in liquids experiment 1526:48

Gases expand when heated experiment with balloons 1219:35

Gases move fast—experiment 676:32

Gases take up space experiment with glass and towel placed under water 1479:47

Gases that form when a candle burns 55:49-57

Heat and cold, effect on gases 676:31

Heat effect on gas molecules model experiment using wire cage and foam balls 1132:53-1-53-2

Henry Cavendish's discovery of inflammable air experiment 1133:2.005

Hot air rises experiment demonstrated with hot air balloon, how to make 1179:51

Hot gas and cold gas—volume experiment 147:65

Hydrogen—making 146:34-35

IIydrogcn—popping gas making 146:44

Identifying the gas necessary for fires 180:77

In soda pop 346:11-16

Is gas made by mixing vinegar and baking soda? 396:16-17

John Mayow's combustion to show air is a mixture experiment 1133:2.002

Joseph Black's discovery of carbon dioxide experiment 1133:2.003

Lemon fizz—a reaction forms a gas 74:73-74

Lighting a candle without touching it 150:112-113

Make a displacement pan to collect gases 57:65-66

Make a fountain in a glass jar 161:50

Make your own gasworks 161:56-57

Mist forms above liquid of carbonated drink when it is opened experiment 1250:18-20

Mix a glass of bubbles with baking soda and vinegar (Primary) 64:unpaged

Molecular motion in a gas 577:project #15

Molecules in a gas move faster when gas is heated up experiment 1090:11

Mothball bounces 146:28

Observe gas bubbles being pushed out of soda by salt experiment 905:66-67

Oxygen—making 146:25; 146:26-27; 146:34-35

Oxygen and a burning candle 147:94-98

Partial vacuum in cooled can experiment 709:53-54

Perfume bottle demonstrates gas moving in room 709:49-50

Pressure of gas in closed container experiment with water/vinegar/baking soda 1479:52

Raisins rise and fall in jar of water with yeast experiment 1508:28

Seltzer tablets in water in jars covered with balloons experiment 695:46

Show expansion of gases when heated 183:24-27

Show gas is product of chemical reaction in a solution 346:51-54

Show if gases expand on heating 179:50-52

Simple observations to make and test 198:48-61

Solubility in water 55:41-47

Solubility of gases in liquids—demonstrate 126:149-157

Sonic egg experiment 906:17

Temperature readings of room air at floor and ceiling levels project 1403:69

Temperature's effect on liquids, solids and gases experiment 1435:21-23

The balloon and the bottle—experiment 161:51

The bubble machine (Primary) 109:18

Volume of air of a gas affected by temperature experiment 1515:17-19

Water drops are skaters 161:52-53

Weighing gases—experiment 586:59-60

What happens to gases as they are heated and cooled experiment 902:53

What happens when a gas becomes hotter experiment 851:24-25

Why bubbles escape from a glass of soda; observe 905:64-65

GASES—COMPRESSED

Boyle's and Charles' law 577:project #19

Create pressure to compress air with can and balloon experiment 709:51-53

GASES—EXPANSION

Hot air balloons—how to make 419:33

GASES—HEATED

Boyle's and Charles' law 577:project #19

GASES—MOLECULES

Are gas molecules farther apart than liquid molecules 396:14-15

GASES—PLANTS

Gas plants vapor will flash and burn 271:64-66

GASOLINE

Gasoline or fuel efficiency in expensive gasoline project 1021:54-55

How many miles on a gallon of gas 333:25-28

Storage tank—experiment to demonstrate 382:87-91

GASOLINE ENGINES

Piston and crankshaft model; engine up down motion to rotary motion experiment 1166:21

GASTROPODS *See* **SLUGS; SNAILS**

GAUSS, KARL FRIEDRICH

Gauss law and Gaussian curve (Advanced) 565:83-87

GAY-LUSSAC'S LAW

Use electrolysis to separate water into hydrogen and oxygen—experiment 642:122-124

GEARS. *See also* **SIMPLE MACHINES—GEARS**

Bicycle gear shift patterns experiment; data tables given 1004:5.005

Bottle top gears 281:48

Build simple gear system 227:14-15

Changing direction with gears experiment 909:111

Clock gears, how to make with experiments 951:86-95

Demonstrating with egg beater (Primary) 539:43-45

Gear ratio experiment using jar lids and thread spools 1179:72

Gear wheel experiment 756:20-21

Gears from cardboard demonstrate use of gearbox in autos experiment 1166:25

How far does bicycle wheel travel in different gears experiment 1507:21

Make gear wheels 224:21-22

Model helicopter's working blade demonstrates gears experiment; patterns given 1494:30-31

Simple demonstrations of how gears work 1494:2-27

Wheels with strong teeth 280:48

Working with gears 180:42

GECKOS

How to care for 279:11-13

GEIGER COUNTERS

Build a Geiger counter [class project] 895:123-127

Build a Geiger counter 278:78-79

Test for radioactive fallout in your neighborhood 278:79-80

GELATIN

Pineapple and gelatin experiment 1238:77-78

GEMS

Cabochons—making from rocks 234:92-93

Making gemstones 400:52

GENDER

Effect of gender identity on short term memory experiment 997:46-48

GENERATORS

Building a simple generator, how to do 1164:95

Double acting high voltage generator—how to make 43:78-92

Electric—electric generator 391:121-130

Electric—gas generator 391:60-64

Electric motors; how motors and generators are related experiment 929:27

Electricity from a hand generator 128:181-182

Faraday's electric generator—making 627:38

Faraday's electromagnetic induction experiment with bar magnet, compass, wire 1473:40

Generator experiment to demonstrate AC current 830:13-14

Generator experiment with bar magnet and coil 22:9-10

Generator experiment with coil wire and bar magnet 23:12-13

Generator; how to build with battery, two electric motors, wire and bulbs 1073:56-57

Hand powered generator, how to make 910:25

How generator works experiment 1164:92-94

How to make a generator 278:54-56; 507:1874-1875

Hydroelectric generator with paddle wheel experiment 1126:28-29

Magnetic generator—making 608:19-20

Making an electrophorus or simple electric generator 5:54-57

Wind generator—building 608:38-40

GENES. *See also* **HUMAN BODY—GENES**

Eye color—chart of blue and brown eye colors in relatives 366:149

Funny genes—photographs of 366:150-151

Generation game to see vast number of possible genetic variations experiment 1517:42-43

Hair color and eye color are inherited together or separately project 1210:69-70

Identical genes produce identical organisms experiment with potatoes 970:102-103

Observe traits in your class; earlobes, tongue rolling; data sheet given 817:21

Record how traits are inherited on family tree project 970:67-69

GENETICS. *See also* **EMBRYOLOGY; HEREDITY**

Albinism in corn experiment 1060:96

"Alike as two peas in a pod" experiment 1060:96-97

Chromosomes and genes—is there a center of inheritance? In the cell 402:101-102

Counting the probability of incomplete dominance 148:17

Cross pollination of dwarf and tall pea plants experiment 1060:93-94

Cross-pollination effect on next generation of plants experiment 1458:31

Environment influences action of genes experiment using lima beans 1060:97-98

Eye-color from parents' genes experiment 1048:26

Gene frequencies and population genetics—computer project 584:43-45

Generation game to see vast number of possible genetic variations experiment 1517:42-43

Genetics and organic evolution (Advanced) 372:93-100

Hair color and eye color are inherited together or separately project 1210:70-72

Heredity grid for straight and curly hair project 1070:20-21

Heredity in fruit flies experiment 1425:23-28

How a characteristic or gene spreads through a population experiment 1134:5.011

Human genetics (Advanced) 372:81-92

Hybridize morning glory plants experiment 1060:95-96

Identical genes produce identical organisms experiment with potatoes 970:102-103

Inheritance of acquired characteristics 402:101

Investigate codominance in snapdragon flowers experiment 1060:95

Is it a boy or a girl—experiment 628:114-115

Medicine and modern genetics (Advanced) 372:101-103

Mendel's experiments—genetic experiment with peas 398:91-96

Mendel's pea experiments, how to do 1060:92-95

Mendel's Principle of Independent Assortment experiment using peas 1060:95

Mendel's Principle of Segregation experiment 1060:92-93

Mutation—mechanism of evolution 402:105-106

Natural selection: key to adaptation computer project 584:46-48

Overcrowding affects action of genes experiment using sunflowers 1060:98

Pale green lethal gene in apples experiment 875:78

Pedigrees—computer project 584:86-88

Projects on the physical basis of heredity (Advanced) 372:47-80

Record how traits are inherited on family tree project 970:67-69

Rules of inheritance found by Gregor Mendel 402:100-101

Selective breeding produces lima beans that are either large or small experiment 1060:97

Single-gene inheritance experiments 1267:106-112

Species variation computer project 584:49-50

Species variation in people 400:33

Sweet potato; will sweet potato change seed's genes experiment 1375:58-60

Thomas Morgan's sex linkage in fruit flies experiment 1133:3.011

Tissue culture of plants experiment 1060:103-106

Trace and chart your tree of life 400:35

Traits from parents experiment 1063:191

Variation in lima beans experiment 1060:97

Variation in tree leaves experiment 1060:97

What is genetics (Advanced) 372:2-3

GEOLOGICAL TIME LINE

Geological clock shows events in Earth's geological history, how to make 1480:93

GEOLOGICAL TIME SCALE

Chart of geologic time scale 1004:1.012

Construct model of Earth's geologic eras, how to do 1481:46-49

Construct paper version of geological time scale project 1413:142-143

Geological time line walk, how to do 1063:231

Geological time scale chart 871:1.007

Measure geological time experiment 706:107-108

Project 400:28-29

GEOLOGY

Mass of the Earth; how to find project 1342:30-32

Newspapers used to stimulate reconstruction of geologic history project 1342:80-81

Shape of the Earth; how to find project 1342:21-26

Size of the Earth; how to measure project 1342:26-30

GEOMETRIC DESIGNS

Adding color to pencil designs 444:84-92

Make with pencil, ruler and protractor 444:9-92

GEOMETRIC FIGURES. *See* **FRACTIONS; MATHEMATICS**

GEOMETRY. *See also* **ANGLES; CURVES; TOPOLOGY**

Angles—what they are (Primary) 454:1-33

Angles, angles and more angles 444:62-63

Circles—working with a circle 444:64-68

Curved line designs 444:69-83

Designs from squares and curves 444:38-52

Experiments to show relationship between families of ellipses (Primary) 437:1-33

Five-pointed stars—making 444:28-31

Hyperbolic paraboloid model, how to make 808:48-49

Hyperboloid model, how to make 808:47-48

Konigsberg bridge problem experiment 808:60

Lines of different lengths produce different curves 444:53-61

Make a curved line by using straight lines 444:32-37

Math curves from angles, how to draw experiment 1253:38-39

Mathematical hieroglyphics experiment 808:61-63

Non-round rollers experiment 1132:71-1-71-5

Octahedron mobiles project, how to make 1353:49

Polygons—making hexagon, octagon, pentagon 444:21-27

Puzzling geometry puzzle 1248:38

Right angles, paper folding geometry 504:1-33

Schlegel diagrams, a way of drawing solids 1353:57

Shadows—projects with light, shapes, cut outs and many objects (Primary) 534:1-33

Shapes; how they can be drawn, measured and used in various activities 1352:1-64

Simple concepts of volume in spaces and shapes 527:1-33

Solid shapes; how to create, measure and use in activities and projects 1353:1-64

Triangles—experiments—paper folding, basic concepts of triangles (Primary) 503:1-33

Triangles; theory, problems and puzzles 1356:1-64

Twenty-one sided polygon, how to make 808:56-58

Working with a circle 444:64-68

GEOMETRY—TRICKS USING

Make 65 squares out of 64 228:98-99

Make a rubber band jump from one finger to another 228:107

Math maneuver called 'sectioning' 228:100-101

Mobius strip in typewriter 228:104
Pass a quarter thru a hole the size of a dime 228:105
Pass your body thru a 3x5 card 228:102-103

GEOTHERMAL ENERGY. *See* **GEYSERS**

GEOTROPISM. *See also* **PLANTS—TROPISMS; ROOTS**

Bean plant in jar demonstrates geotropism experiment 1457:19

Bean plants reaction to geotropism experiment 1294:78-79

Bean seed roots grow down and leaves grow up experiment 1379:16

Bean seeds grown upside down in jar show effect of gravity on growth 1038:16

Bean shoot roots in jar grow downward experiment 913:27

Centrifugal motion effects seedlings root and stem growth experiment 1060:77-78

Direction that seed is planted affects growth of stems and roots experiment 1395:79

Do plants and animals seek the Earth's center 402:34-35

Do tree roots always grow down 264:51

Effect of gravity on growth of seedlings experiment 1060:76-77

Effects of gravity on plant growth experiment 1405:27

Force of gravity affects way roots grow experiment 986:80

Geotropism demonstrated with sprouting seeds between glass panes experiment 986:80

Geotropism effect on plant seeds experiment 978:43

Geotropism in germinating bean seeds experiment; data tables given 1004:2.016

Gravity affect on seeds, roots and shoots experiment 1181:16

Gravity affects plant growth experiment 1395:75-81

Gravity affects seeds, roots and shoots experiment 1183:24

Gravity affects the way roots grow experiment 1265:80

Gravity effect on mature plants experiment 1395:79

Gravity effect on plant growth experiment 904:48-49

Gravity has effect on plant growth experiment 1399:48-51

Growing seeds in rotating container of soil experiment 1061:81-82

Hydrotropism and geotropism compared as to which affects plant the most 1061:94-95

Plant roots grow downward experiment 1078:5

Plant roots respond to gravity and grow downward experiment 1014:158

Plants change direction in which they grow experiment 878:46-47

Root of plant responds to gravity and grows downward experiment 1069:45

Root of potato grows downward experiment 876:77

Roots—direction of growth—what goes up, won't go down—experiment 574:27

Roots always grow downward experiment 819:46

Roots always point down experiment 1368:39

Roots from bean seeds grow downward experiment 1063:407

Roots grow downward and shoots grow upward experiment 1181:16

Seed sense—does it matter which way you plant a seed 399:21

GERBILS

Activity of mice and gerbils affected by light and darkness experiment 1158:136-137

Behavior observations to make 370:23-26

Cage—how to make 370:12-13

Care and observation of 163:101-104

Care for 32:80-81; 390:86-89

Foods and feeding 370:17-22

Gerbil babies—care and observation of 370:27-32

Learning—investigate how long it takes to handle new situation 370:39-41

Learning—maze experiment 370:41-42

Mazes—T maze variations to test intelligence—how to make 510:106-109

Population turnover—a circular track 263:12-15

Senses—color vision experiment 370:34-37

Senses—hearing—noise experiment 370:37-38

Senses—smell experiment—can a gerbil smell its food 370:38

Senses—temperature—can gerbils tell differences in temperature 370:38

GERMINATION. *See also* **SEEDS—GERMINATION**

Do cotyledons help seed growth 236:46

Force of germinating seeds 236:44

Germination and growth experiments 236:45

Growing seeds indoors 236:44

Make a jar germinator 203:33

Planting seeds outdoors 236:45

Planting wild seeds 236:45

Watching seeds germinate 236:44

GERMS

Germs spread by sneezes demonstrate [Primary] 759:52-54

Rotten apples demonstrate spread of infection experiment 1014:152

GESTATION PERIOD

How long from formation of egg to emergence of the organism 402:96-97

Of some animals 231:32-33

Species with long gestation periods, have long life spans project 969:24-25

GEYSERS

Geyser in the kitchen—experiment 382:121-123

Geysers and how they work demonstration 1023:58-59

Hot water rises—experiment 641:26

Make a spring—experiment 641:23

Make a turbine—experiment 641:43

Make your own geyser 1383:29

Water has pressure—experiment 641:20

What happens to metal in salt water—experiment 641:59

What spinning does to remove pieces of rocks 641:46

Working model of a geyser—how to make 532:103

Working model of a geyser 577:project #41

GIBBERELLIC ACID

Effect on plant growth 273:56-57

Plant growth and chemicals experiment 878:52-53

Solutions—serial solutions—how to make 398:12-18

GIBBERELLINS

Experiments with plants 398:131-132

Gibberellins affect growth of dwarf pea plants experiment 1060:86-88

Gibberellins influence size and flowering in geranium plants experiment 1060:88

GIBSON, JAMES
How we perceive the world around us experiment 1133:3.012

GILBERT, WILLIAM
Wire clips stand up on magnet experiment 723:131-132
Explanation—magnetic compass 209:15
Gilbert's Versorium—experiment 627:9
Substances that conduct static electricity experiment 1133:5.001

GINGER
Ginger pot gives fresh ginger roots 366:101

GINGER BEER
Recipe for 231:60

GIRAFFES
Does your heart pump as hard as does a giraffe's; make heart pump experiment 1399:83

GIRDERS. *See* **BEAMS; BRIDGES; STRUCTURES**

GLACIERS. *See also* **EROSION; ICE**
Debris or moraine left by glacier demonstration 1480:134
Glaciers move by plastic deformation [creeping, thick liquid] experiment 1480:132
Glaciers; melting mini-glaciers to get water experiment 959:166-167
How is snow compacted into ice to form glaciers experiment 900:133
Ice cube demonstrations 666:59-60
Kettle hole lake 577:project #42
Mini-glacier moves down dirt slope experiment 1441:73
Movement of glaciers demonstration 1023:82-83
Pieces of rock carried by glacier slow glacier down experiment 1384:11
Rock collected in glaciers acts like sandpaper and erodes experiment 1480:133
Ways that glaciers might move demonstration 1479:73

GLASS
Bending glass experiment 26:46-47
Blowing glass 26:48
Contraction of insulator from internal stresses 585:40-41
Hardness test of metals and glass experiment 1438:97-99
Make glass 709:20-21
Sealing glass 26:47
Shape and thickness affect music from glass experiment 1357:28
Sheet of glass from sugar—how to make 374:19
Stained glass window, how to make 1357:29
Trick—cutting glass with scissors 27:94-95

GLASSES—3-D
3D glasses, how to make 935:74-75
How to make 162:75
How to make 76:22-23

GLASSES—DRINKING
Expansion and contraction 291:24
Lifting with a straw 291:106-107
Magical humming 350:98-99
Music from glasses 45:92-93
Musical 350:94-96

GLASSES—WATER
Make music from water glass 291:150-151
Whirling water without spilling 350:107-108

GLIDE BAR
How to make 358:50-51

GLIDERS. *See also* **AIRPLANES**
Balsa wood glider, how to make 1299:44
Build a simple glider 900:203-204

Build and test fly your own glider 419:30-31
Cayley's 1804 glider, how to build using styrofoam or balsa wood 1252:30
Centriglide model glider climbs to land on high platform, how to make 1190:25-31
Delta wing paper model glider demonstrates roll, pitch and yaw, make 1252:50-55
Distance glider—how to make 310:11-13
Do gliders and kites fly the same way experiment 783:14-16
Easy glider from wood and roller skate wheels and a sail—how to make 429:56-59
Energy stored in twisted materials drives simple machines experiment 1073:16-17
Glider—making 450:20-21
Glider demonstrates principles of flight experiment 1332:26-27
Glider to use for test flights, how to make from cardboard 1073:20-21
How can gliders be turned experiment 900:207
How to build/demonstrate rudders, ailerons, elevators with paper/balsa wood 225:13-17
How to make 178:27; 400:99
How to make egg carton foam gliders 54:124-125
Hurricane glider—how to make 450:24-25
Launch a model glider using rubber band and dowel launcher experiment 1073:16
Leonardo da Vinci style mini glider, how to make 1419:19
Lilienthal, Otto; who invented the hang glider experiment 1525:7-11
Make a paper glider 625:45
Make gliders go up and down experiment 900:208
Making a glider from cardboard, patterns given 1252:28-30
Making and testing gliders from cardboard, straws, tissue paper 1448:18-19
Model glider from plastic, how to make 1197:28
Paper airplane gliders, which design travels fastest experiment 1175:93-95
Paper glider—how to make 597:47
Paper glider experiment, how to make 1507:11
Paper glider, making 868:70; 1389:25
Paper glider, pattern given, how to make 1126:16-17
Paper glider, patterns, making 1014:134-135
Paper gliders—how to make to demonstrate flight principles 588:41-43
Paper gliders, how to make, patterns given 1376:29
Paraglider, making 908:56-58
Propeller-powered glider model, how to make 1448:22-23
Simple glider, making 908:56
Simple paper glider—how to make 494:69
Straw and paper rings glider, how to make 1288:8-9
Styrofoam glides in air, pattern, making 1014:136-137
Super-glider paper plane—how to make 652:42-43
Superglider, paper, pattern, making 1016:30-32
What aircraft will you fly experiment 900:211-212
Will heavy glider fly as far as light one 450:23
Will small glider fly as far as large one? 450:22
Wooden balsa glider; how to make and fly 1419:9-10
Wooden glider, pattern, making 998:221
Wright Brothers glider, how to build from styrofoam/balsa wood, patterns 1252:40-42

GLOBAL WARMING. *See also* **GREENHOUSE EFFECT**
  Carbon dioxide amount absorbed by trees and concrete building site experiment 1057:108
  Carbon dioxide is common experiment 1057:18
  Carbon dioxide you add to the atmosphere experiment 1057:30
  Cool water takes up more room if it is warmed experiment 1057:56
  Decomposers and release of carbon dioxide experiment 1057:33
  Global warming effects on the human village project; how to set up 1174:52-59
  Global warming will melt the polar ice cap experiment 1174:52-59
  Global warming; what's causing it experiment with shoe box/plastic/thermometer 1240:37
  How trees take in carbon dioxide experiment 1057:104
  Humans and animals add carbon dioxide to the atmosphere experiment 1057:20
  Level of oceans affected by greenhouse warming experiment 1322:44-47
  Thermal expansion of sea water experiment 1057:56
  Trapping heat to demonstrate the greenhouse effect 1057:26
  Volcanic clouds lower atmospheric temperature and reduce sunlight experiment 1477:76-79
GLOBES
  Balloon globe—how to make (Primary) 303:8-9
  Be it yourself gyroscope 292:40-41
  Globe clock, how to make 947:6-7
  Make a patchwork world of scraps 292:39-40
  Make globe with globe gores from paper, ball, wood base, paints 1480:26-27
  Papier mache globe, how to make 1042:8-9
  Stretching the globe 303:14-15
GLOBULES—FAT. *See also* **FATS**
  Making butter 219:39-43
GLOP
  Gooey Green Glop, recipe, how to make 1526:35
GLUCOSE
  Function of digestive enzymes experiment 1395:165-170
  Saliva effect on a starch experiment 1395:168-169
GLUES. *See also* **ADHESIVES**
  A formula for gum (gummed label glue) 336:60-62
  Casein glue—how to make 176:22; 77:26-27
  Casein plastic—how to make 676:10-11
  Experiments 17:40-44
  Formula for milk glue 336:58-60
  Glue from flower and water 259:15-16
  Glue from milk—how to make 565:67-70
  Glue from milk—making 733:6
  Glues and how they work 544:25-30
  Gluten from flour makes glue 203:20
  Make casein glue from milk 203:36
  Make glue 585:94-95
  Milk glue, recipe, how to make 1312:19
  White—blush test for water resistance 336:67-68
GODDARD, ROBERT HUTCHINGS
  Test his rocket discovery with a balloon 602:unpaged
GOGGLES
  Anti-glare goggles, how to make 850:22
GOLD
  Panning for gold experiment 1081:19
  Panning for gold, how to do 1266:48

GOLDFISH
  Aquarium for—how to set up 235:13-16
  Attracting fish with weak current of electricity—experiment 484:94
  Blood circulation in a goldfish experiment 1425:232-235
  Blood circulation in goldfish tail—observe 713:72-73
  Breathing rate of goldfish experiment 1395:133-137
  Can goldfish hear 266:22
  Colored water comes out fish's gill slits experiment 943:29
  Compare breathing rate of fish and humans experiment 1395:136
  Conditioned behavior experiment 936:36-37
  Conditioned response experiment; training goldfish with sound 1069:82-83
  Do certain foods affect growth of babies 235:28
  Do dissimilar organisms benefit from each other 402:92-93
  Do fish exhale carbon dioxide when breathing experiment 1395:180-181
  Do fish locate food by using color experiment 864:114-115
  Effect of different temperatures on goldfish—experiment 607:65
  Estimate speed of goldfish alone and in group 235:35-36
  Fish aquariums, set up and observe fish behavior 888:107-111
  Goldfish effected by direction of light—experiment 607:65
  Goldfish kept in groups eat more than goldfish kept singly—experiment 235:37-38
  Goldfish learn to swim thru a hoop 235:40-42
  Heart beat increased by caffeine observe under microscope 713:73-74
  How do different temperatures affect animal life 402:89-90
  How does water treated in various ways affect animal life 402:87-88
  How fast does a goldfish breathe experiment 924:85
  How temperature affects cold-blooded animals 236:69
  How to keep goldfish 964:28-29
  Increased activity affects breathing rate of fish experiment 1395:136
  Keeping and feeding goldfish—how to do 725:54-55
  Marcello Malpighi's discovery of capillaries experiment 1133:3.003
  Observe circulation of blood in fish's tail 235:19-21
  Observe circulation of blood in tail 294:71-72
  Reactions to changes in temperature 266:69-72
  Reduce oxygen in fish tank so fish breathe more easily experiment 997:167-168
  Respiration rate of fish affected by excitement and water temperature ex 1020:109-114
  Seeing blood circulation in goldfish—experiment 484:91
  Temperature affects breathing rate of fish experiment 1395:135-136
  Temperature or crowding affects the hatching time—experiment 235:23-27
  Test effect of water temperatures on goldfish 235:32-33
  Test goldfish responses to light and colored lights 235:30-32
  Test if goldfish hear things 235:29-30
  What happens when not enough oxygen in the water 235:17-19

GOLDFISH—THERMAL POLLUTION
Effect of temperature change on goldfish—experiment 10:65-69
GOOSE BUMPS
What are they 366:136
GRAFTING. *See also* **PLANTS—VEGETATIVE REPRODUCTION**
Burbank's grafting experiments 879:100-102
Flat-crafting cactus plants, how to do 1440:112-114
Graft a plant, how to do 1440:103-105
Graft potato and tomato plants to get a pomato experiment 1476:108
Graft tomato plant and potato plant experiment 1060:101-102
Grafting plants 436:38-39
How to make a graft 398:70-74
Potato-tomato graft 532:63
Stem graft apple tree experiment 1060:102
Tomato plants grafted to potato plant experiment 834:148-149
GRAIN ELEVATORS
Auger lifting machine demonstrates lifting power of auger, how to make 1033:10-11
GRAMOPHONE
How to make simple one 128:137-140
GRAND PRIX CAR RACES
How to make track and race toy cars 410:46-47
GRANITE
Testing granite for hardness experiment 1438:100-102
Testing granite with an acid experiment 1438:103-104
GRAPES
How much water do fresh grapes lose when dried to make raisins project 1210:33-34
GRAPHITE
Hardness test for graphite, the lead in pencils experiment 1438:83-84
GRAPHS
Basic explanation of graph theory and networks 477:1-33
Curves—be a curve watcher for misleading graphs 351:51-56
Game to demonstrate basic principles of functions and graphs 456:1-33
Graphing Fruit Loops activities for classroom 1291:6-7
Graphing your data 31:46-65
Samples of charts and graphs 31:79-90
GRAPHS—BAR
Composite 351:30
Experiment to obtain data 351:29
Frequency histograms 351:30-34
Horizontal 351:30
Truncated 351:52-55
Whale catch 351:26-29
GRAPHS—COMPUTER
Drawing with a mouse 351:61
Graphing concepts computer project 1021:50-53
Hardware 351:58-59
Menu driven 351:59-60
Microcomputers 351:57-58
Programs 351:59
Special equipment 351:60-61
GRAPHS—LINE
Comparison 351:19-20
Experiment to try 351:18-19
Floating baseline 351:20-22
Misleading 351:51-52
Table of data 351:14-18
Using a decimal ruler 351:22-25
GRAPHS—PICTOGRAPH
Data experiment 351:46-48
Design for 351:44-46
Distorted 351:55-56
Ideas 351:48-50
GRAPHS—PIE
Chemical composition of air 351:35-37
Data for 351:41
How to make 351:36-40
Irregular 351:55
GRASS FLOWERS
Adventure 20—we investigate the structure of grass flowers under hand lens 29:99-103
GRASS HUT
Model—how to make 415:44-45
GRASSES
Cereals and fibers 231:84
Collect by making photographic print of them 231:85
Grass covered with board loses color experiment 919:38
Grass haired people—how to make 236:50
Grass seed grows in potato and in eggshells experiment 1071:78-79
Grass seed grows on Big Foot sponge, how to do 918:14
Grass seed starters—making (Primary) 535:44
Grass weaving 236:38; 749:82-83
Grow grass on a sponge 416:6-7
Grow windowsill grass 155:10-11
Growth of grass plants versus other plants 119:58-63
Liquid fertilizer effect on rhizome formation on lawn grass experiment 1295:81-83
Make pulp for paper from grasses 231:87
Paper made from grass clippings, how to do 887:76-78
Spelling name with sprouting grass seed, how to do 898:46
Sponge grows grass 1006:27
Sprout grass seeds on sponge experiment 942:11
Stem of grass observation [Primary] 942:4-5
Weaving grasses—how to do 646:46-50
What happens to pile of freshly cut grass clippings experiment 1323:79-84
Where there's life there's grass 231:83
GRASSHOPPERS
Adventure 59—nervous system of grasshopper under a microscope 403:228-232
Collecting grasshoppers to watch nymphs grow and molt 414:54-55
How to catch and keep grasshoppers [Primary] 942:14-16
Raising grasshoppers and crickets, how to do 1505:35
Studying a grasshopper—a typical insect 294:64-66
What is distinctive about the growth of grasshoppers 402:97
GRASSHOPPERS—MIGRATION
Where do grasshoppers travel 402:47
GRASSLANDS
Game; card game of grassland species, how to make 1341:68
Grasslands circle of life poster, how to make 1341:68
GRAVITROPISM. *See also* **PLANTS—TROPISMS**
Gravitropic response of two different kinds of seeds experiment 1375:81-84
Gravity affects bean seed roots experiment 1047:15

Plant grows in response to force of gravity experiment 1527:91

GRAVITY. *See also* **FALLING OBJECTS**

A gravity engine you can build 267:25

Acceleration effect of gravity calculated experiment, how to do 1478:52

Acceleration of falling bodies due to gravity and air resistance experiment 1157:58-61

Against the law of gravity—experiment 400:87

Air and static electricity overcome gravity experiment 888:127-129

Air pressure holds things together 544:33-36

Air pressure stronger than gravity experiment with rubber plunger 1251:29-30

Air reduces the pull of gravity (Primary) 207:15-17

Anti gravity—rolling uphill 16:35-39

Anti-gravity cardboard cones roll uphill experiment, how to make 1380:36

'Anti-gravity' demonstrations with vacuum cleaner and balloons 392:36-46

Anti-gravity force at work—experiment 651:14-15

Anti-gravity magic; water flows upward experiment 1066:114-115

Antigravity machine demonstration using funnels on yardsticks 1229:22-23

Artificial gravity can be produced demonstration 1394:198-199

Artificial gravity model experiment 1502:75-76

Astronauts; effect of gravity on height of Astronauts demonstration 1394:218-219

Balancing forks demonstrate gravity 1294:119-121

Balloon rocket overcomes pull of gravity (Primary) 207:18-19

Balls of different sizes land in different places experiment 1031:10-11

Bean planter model machine, how to make 1190:32-38

Blood flow; coin in hand trick demonstrates gravity of blood flow experiment 1216:16-18

Bobbing toy 'tom tumbler' demonstrates 207:14

Calculate trajectory of ball launch experiment [Advanced] 871:4.005

Catch a falling buck 114:93-94

Catch the falling dollar bill experiment 960:47

Centrifugal force pull—keeps sun and Earth and moon in place 274:16

Centriglide model glider climbs to land on high platform, how to make 1190:25-31

Centripetal force measured with G meter, how to do experiment 1412:16-17

Clipper model collects and deposits paper clips from space station, make 1190:39-47

Coin balances on rim of glass experiment 1007:68-69

Curved space; gravity and curved space experiment with cellophane drum and bbs 1476:186

Deck of cards; magic trick demonstrates gravity 966:46-48

Defy gravity—how to experiment with celery and food coloring 651:12-13

Defy gravity fork trick 860:221-222

Defy gravity; stop water from flowing out of bottle experiment 1031:28

Defy laws of gravity—amazing spin dry experiment 231:121

Defying gravity—experiment 563:184-185

Demonstrate craters formed by meteors 274:10

Demonstrate overcoming the forces of gravity experiment 905:44-45

Dilute the force of gravity 295:56-58

Diluting gravity reduces acceleration of falling object experiment 1502:40-42

Direction and rate of fall of coins 274:12

Does gravity pull harder on bigger objects experiment 851:32-33

Domino acrobatics demonstrates 1007:69-71

Drinking through a straw affected by gravity experiment 1399:62-63

Drop and catch pebble from measured height 274:7

Earth's force of gravity related to mass on which it pulls experiment 1157:56-57

Egg—obedient 350:120-121

Eggs away 16:13-16

Egyptian engineering demonstrated with shoe box, string and lump of clay 1073:12

Experiment with gravity 175:42

Experiment 243:26-27

Experiments—simple 46:13-55; 105:28-31

Experiments to show 128:123-126

Falling—experiment 664:4-5

Falling bodies demonstration 587:48

Falling coins experiment 909:93

Falling for "g"—computer project 584:117-118

Falling object accelerates experiment 1502:40-42

Falling object affected by gravity experiment using drops of ink 1380:35

Falling objects hit ground at the same time experiment [Primary] 1002:6

Falling rate of objects changed by weight experiment 1399:12-15

Falling together 114:91-93

Flight time of a bullet 114:95-97

Floating forks 16:32-34

Follow that ball—experiment (Primary) 651:6-7

Force meter measures force of gravity pulling on object experiment 1073:15

Force of—the obedient can 360:80

Force of gravity—bet you can't out pull a book 222:24

Force of gravity and acceleration experiment 1502:40-42

Force of gravity is proportional to mass of object experiment 1502:43-45

Force of gravity on falling balls demonstration 1434:107-109

Force of magnet against force of gravity experiment 888:131-133

Force of water works against force of gravity experiment 1031:26-27

Free-falling objects pulled straight down toward Earth's center by gravity 1399:8-11

Galileo's drop in a vacuum experiment 1132:50-1-50-2

Galileo's experiment—different weight different fall in a vacuum 295:54-55

Galileo's experiment—speed of a falling ball 295:55-56

Galileo's methods for diluting gravity and measuring time experiment 1156:35-42

Galileo; who discovered the laws of falling bodies project 1525:47-49

Gravity affects formation of stalactites experiment 1399:64-67

Gravity affects playing paddle ball experiment 1399:76-79

Gravity affects siphoning process experiment 1399:68-71

Gravity and centrifugal force effect on plants grown on turntable experiment 1159:64-67

Gravity and falling bodies demonstration with coins 1434:110-111

Gravity and its effect on seed growth experiment 904:50-51

Gravity and its grip 260:8-10

'Gravity defying' funnels roll uphill 203:60

Gravity effect on plant growth experiment 904:48-49

Gravity fighter to demonstrate low center of gravity—making 288:32-33

Gravity has little effect on oil drops submerged in liquid experiment 905:58-59

Gravity machine made from candles 202:82

Gravity power demonstrated by simple model merry-go-round 419:6

Gravity pulls all things down at same speed experiment 1404:70-71

Gravity pulls more on heavier objects experiment [Primary] 742:13

Gravity pulls on you experiment [Primary] 742:12

Gravity pulls the taffy 280:43

Gravity screw spiral slide brings model planes toward ground experiment 1446:24-25

Hanging objects always point in the same direction experiment 1399:4-7

Heavy object falls faster than light object? Experiment 1031:8-9

Height; gravity affects human height experiment 1399:80-83

Hitting the ground; measure the dent experiment 909:93

Horse—prancing 350:117-118

How are satellites launched into orbit around the Earth experiment 1399:24-27

How do you pitch a ball 281:38-39

How does gravity affect heavy and light objects experiment 902:57

How does gravity affect objects experiment 900:223

How fast do objects fall to Earth experiment, data tables 1004:5.008

How gravity affects inertia experiment 1405:20

How gravity affects plant growth 294:42-43

How hard does gravity pull (Primary) 539:18-19

In the playground 274:18-19

Inertia; gravity affects inertia demonstration 1394:208-209

Investigating falling speed of objects 909:92

Is water really heavy 126:13-16

Length of pendulum affects time of each swing experiment 1404:74-76

Light and heavy objects fall at same speed demonstration 1436:1-2

Love that chair—without center of balance; can't fight gravity 288:20-21

Machines; gravity pulled conveyor machine experiment, how to make 1400:75

Magic trick defying gravity 35:23-24

Magnetic attraction can overcome pull of gravity experiment 1401:28-31

Magnetic hill, how to make from cone and cardboard 1289:10-11

Magnetism exceeds gravity experiment 768:49-50

Mass of falling water affects energy it produces as it falls experiment 1399:56-59

Materials separate because of gravity experiment 1502:67-68

Measure falling in air and water 274:17

Mines; pit head model of winding gear at top of mine shaft, how to make 1190:48-55

Model gas station demonstrates making gravity in space 419:19

Monorail working model, how to make 1190:56-62

Moon; gravity on Moon; how much can you lift on Moon experiment 1478:54

Object rolls uphill experiment 1007:66

Objects dropped from same height experiment 1441:17

Objects with different horizontal speeds fall at same rate experiment 1399:16-19

Oil; gravity has little effect on drops of oil submerged in liquid experiment 1479:51

Overcoming gravity 12:116-123

Paper plate parachute to demonstrate 200:12-13

Paper clip horse—simple 12:28-30

Parachute from plastic bag, string and small toy demonstrates gravity experiment 1073:9

Parachute to test gravity—making 225:6

Parachutes of different shapes and sizes test gravity 225:7

Path of object dropped from a moving body experiment 1399:20-23

Pendulum measures gravity's acceleration experiment; data table given 1004:5.009

Pendulum; what makes a pendulum swing experiment 1399:28-31

Pendulums; each swing of pendulum takes same amount of time experiment 1031:14-15

Pin floats in air experiment 781:26-27

Pipe—magic 350:116-117

Plant growth; gravity has effect on plant growth experiment 1399:48-51

Plants; geotropism experiment; roots grow downward and shoots grow upward 1181:16

Plants; gravity affect on seeds, roots and shoots experiment 1181:16

Plants; how would plants grow in a rotating space station experiment 1399:50-51

Plumb bob determines if structure is vertical, how to make 1399:6-7

Plumb line—making 274:8

Precarious balancing 350:118-120

Projectile motion—computer project 584:121-122

Properties of gravity (Primary) 232:55

Pulse rate; how gravity affects pulse rate experiment 1399:83

Racing car on ramp demonstrates gravity controls speed experiment 1031:12-13

Record height of ball bounce 274:9

Repeat Galileo's experiment 448:23-25

Rolling uphill 16:35-39

Roly poly toy—making (Primary) 73:32-35

Sand machine to demonstrate—making 172:96-103

Scan can model satellite; axles turn by falling weight power, make 1190:16-20

Sensitive balance detects weight of the lightest objects experiment 1031:24-25

Shape affects speed of rolling objects experiment 1404:76-79

Shape of soap bubbles affected by gravity experiment 1399:72-75

Shape of trajectory depends on how object is thrown experiment 1389:9

Size affects speed of falling parachute experiment 1404:68-71

Size of water drops affected by cohesion and gravity experiment data tables 1004:3.009

Skater model speeds up spin at end, how to make 1190:21-24

Snow using building blocks 274:20

Speed and falling bodies demonstration with ruler and marble 1434:112-115

Spinal cord; gravity effect on spinal cord experiment 1399:80-82

Spring scale, how does it work experiment with paper cup, Slinky and string 1399:40-43

Straw; can straw work in sealed bottle experiment 1399:60-62

Testing "gripability" of different objects experiment 1073:12

The falling ball trick 585:65-66

The magic pipe 350:116-117

The path of a falling object—computer project 584:119-120

The prancing horse 350:117-118

The precarious forks 202:81

The siphon 281:14

Tides and gravity 274:15

Toy parachute slows down force of gravity—how to make 651:22-23

Toy seems to defy gravity 202:87

Tricks and experiments with gravity 596:16-17

Up or down—objects are pulled to Earth 274:13

Wacky wheel model; machine driven by its own weight goes uphill, make 1190:11-15

Water clock shows that gravity causes water to fall at regular rate experiment 1031:16-17

Water flows upward experiment with soda bottles, food coloring, water 1229:32-33

Weight and falling of steel ball and marble 274:11

Weight and gravity—experiment 664:6

Weight effects speed of pendulum's swing experiment 1404:72-75

Weight of various masses when weighed on Moon's surface experiment 1502:44-45

Weight; do heavy objects fall faster than light ones experiment 1507:5

Weight; downward force of gravity on weight of objects experiment 1507:4

Weightless falling objects—weightless clothes pins—demonstrate 203:55

What is gravity (Primary) 210:28

Which box or ball will hit ground first experiment 699:8-9

Whirler toy to demonstrate—making 172:87-89

Whirling gravity ball—demonstration 651:8-9

Why do things fall down 281:37

Why do things fall over experiment with box, string and washer 1399:32-35

GRAVITY—CENTER OF GRAVITY. *See also* **BALANCE; CENTER OF GRAVITY**

Balance potato on point of toothpick experiment 1231:60-61

Balance potato to demonstrate center of gravity experiment 1507:16

Balance the books trick 585:70-72

Balancing act 399:8

Balancing act and crazy ball show center of gravity 156:20-21

Balancing act demonstrates center of gravity experiment 1031:18-19

Balancing clown experiment demonstrates center of gravity, how to make 1507:17

Balancing clown on wire demonstrates center of gravity experiment 1031:20-21

Balancing experiments 210:29

Balancing point of cardboard shows center of gravity 202:85

Bet you can't pick up a chair unless you are female 222:16-17

Candle seesaw, make 909:97

Center of gravity demonstrated with milk carton boat 561:14-16

Center of gravity with ball 281:41

Chair bound to show center of gravity 156:17

Demonstrate with the chair problem (lifting chair) 291:110-111

Do people have a center of gravity experiment 851:36-37

Does tilting effect center of gravity 274:25

Easy to make balancing sculpture 241:18-21

Experiment shows how Earth-moon system rotates around common center of gravity 385:60

Experiment to find another center of gravity 385:57-59

Experiment to locate center of gravity 385:56-57

Experiments and tricks to demonstrate center of gravity 1137:20-44

Find center of gravity in irregular shape experiment 940:90-91

Find center of gravity of cardboard boat 274:23

Find the balancing point experiment 909:96

Find the center of gravity—experiment 585:47-48

Finding the balance point 274:22

Finding the center of gravity 241:16-17; 360:12-13

Floating forks 16:32-34

Forks balance on cork experiment 940:85-86

Glued to your chair 222:19

Gymnast, making 909:98-99

Inertia—an unbeatable fast ball 222:22-23

Lowering the center of gravity—make a balancing doll 241:28-31

Magic balance box demonstrates 909:97

Magic forks demonstrates center of gravity 576:65-66

Magic matchbox to show center of gravity 156:18-19

Making a balancing toy 274:26

Making a rocker clown 274:27

Mountaineer model on pen demonstrates center of gravity experiment 1024:30-31

Moving the center of gravity from side to side 241:38-39

Nose dive—bet you can't pick up a handkerchief with your teeth 222:20

Objects center of gravity effect on motion experiment 1404:64-67

On your toes 222:21

Person floats up with friends lifting with fingertips experiment 1216:31-33

Potato balances on forks experiment with center of gravity 1065:13

Potato wobbler wobbles and doesn't fall over experiment with center of gravity 1065:12

Raising the center of gravity 241:26-27

Ruler and hammer balance to demonstrate 940:87-8

Seesaws, making 909:99
Stand up when you're leaning against wall experiment 1083:18-19
Table top toy—experiment 656:16-17
The strange straw—a shift in the center of gravity 205:43-45
Tight rope walker, making 909:98-99
Toe hold—bet you can't jump forward on your toes 222:18
Up against the wall—show center of gravity 222:14-15
Wand balances on fingers trick 1216:22-24
What is center of gravity experiment 851:35-36
What is center of gravity 402:62-63
Wheel rolls uphill to demonstrate center of gravity 1031:22
Wheel that rolls uphill demonstrates center of gravity 576:66-67
Will it tip 253:166-167
Your center of gravity 241:22-24

GRAVITY AND MOVEMENT
Lifting a stone 274:28
Potential energy of machines that use gravity 274:29

GRAVITY AND SLOPES
Demonstrate overcoming gravity with toy car and rubber band 274:31
Measure traveling speed and distance of marble from different heights 274:30

GRAVITY MACHINES
Gravity used to power a compound machine experiment 1400:72-75

GRAYWATER. *See* **WATER—CONSERVATION**

GREEK
How to count like a Greek 509:24-28

GREENHOUSE EFFECT
Absorption and reflection experiment 737:11
Air without carbon dioxide is cooler than air with carbon dioxide experiment 1174:31-33
Carbon dioxide increase causes increase in plant growth experiment 1060:121
Carbon dioxide is held in water experiment 1322:48-52
Carbon dioxide you add to the atmosphere experiment 1057:30
Carbon dioxide's heat-holding capabilities experiment 1174:31-33
Decompose and release of carbon dioxide experiment 1057:33
Demonstrate greenhouse effect with glass jars and thermometer 1322:35-39
Demonstrating the greenhouse effect project 833:227
Diffusion of gases experiment 813:57-58
Erupting volcanoes produce sulfur dioxide experiment 1174:43-45
Experiment 183:84-87; 253:89-90; 289:38-39
Forest fires produce carbon dioxide experiment 1174:40-41
Forest; mini forest habitat in aquarium, how to plant and care for experiment 1472:48-53
Gases can travel experiment 813:57-58
Global warming effects on the human village project; how to set up 1174:52-59
Global warming will melt the polar ice cap experiment 1174:52-59
Global warming; what's causing it experiment with shoe box/plastic/thermometer 1240:37

Greenhouse effect—experiment 585:144-145
Greenhouse effect and rising water level in oceans experiment 1150:22-23
Greenhouse effect as cause of rise in sea levels project 1342:126
Greenhouse effect demonstrated with glasses of water and thermometer 1281:38
Greenhouse, how to build 813:60
Heat absorption of air compared to Carbon Dioxide experiment; data table given 1004:1.003
How Earth is warming up experiment with glass jars and thermometers 1063:359
How greenhouse effect works experiment 1134:2.001
How greenhouse effect works experiment with thermometers 1387:29
Humans and animals add carbon dioxide to the atmosphere experiment 1057:20
Investigate basic idea of greenhouse effect using two thermometers 1388:29
Level of oceans affected by greenhouse warming experiment 1322:44-47
Light blocked by particulate matter and its effect on temperature experiment 969:100-101
Observe greenhouse effect on trays of seedlings experiment 1176:9
Pear grows inside bottle experiment; demonstrates greenhouse effect 1524:27
Planet surface warmed more by greenhouse effect than by Sun's rays experiment 1062:64-66
Plastic bags and thermometers experiment demonstrates Greenhouse Effect 1003:38-39
Rainfall measuring experiment 813:58
Sea level rise experiment 813:58-60
Snow and ice reflect sunlight; dirt and dark ground absorb it experiment 1322:40-43
Thermometer in car parked in sunlight demonstrates greenhouse effect 1170:37
Trapping heat to demonstrate greenhouse effect 1057:26
Venus; Sun's heat is trapped by gases in Venus's atmosphere experiment 1478:67
Volcanic clouds lower atmospheric temperature and reduce sunlight experiment 1477:76-79
What is the greenhouse effect experiment using glass jars and thermometers 1427:60-61
Why will the oceans rise experiment 813:58-60

GREENHOUSES
Box greenhouse, how to make 810:41
Coldframe, constructing, how to 866:146-147
Greenhouse from plastic pots, how to make 1243:16
Greenhouse in a bag, how to make 810:40
Greenhouse, how to build 813:60
Growth from heat experiment with jar over patch of grass 1377:29
How does a greenhouse work experiment 793:29
Indoor greenhouse experiments 563:57
Make your own indoor greenhouse 416:44
Making from storm windows 436:39
Mini-greenhouse from plastic bottle, how to make and grow plants 1127:33
Mini-greenhouse, how to make from plastic box experiment 1486:16
Miniature greenhouse, how to make 1440:90-92
Plant teepee, how to make from wooden molding and clear plastic 1115:122-123

Planting seeds in miniature greenhouse, how to do 810:43-44

Plastic cup greenhouse, making 1014:146

Solar greenhouse collector, how to make 870:16-18

Temperature inside greenhouse compared to outside temperature experiment 1228:46-47

GRIMALDI, FRANCESCO

Diffraction of light experiment 1133:6.005

GRIST MILLS

Grist mill—making from wood 429:103

Model grist mill works, how to make 1115:93-96

GROUNDHOG DAY

Project 231:120

GROUNDWATER

Bacteria test for groundwater pollution experiment; how to do 1173:41-42

Demonstrate formation of caliche (calcium carbonate) deposits experiment 1479:69

Groundwater system model to demonstrate contamination of groundwater 1342:127-130

Groundwater system model to demonstrate groundwater movement 1342:127-130

pH test for groundwater pollution, how to do 1173:40

Testing permeability of materials to groundwater erosion experiment 1480:120

Water pollution from landfills experiment fish tank with pond/landfill area 1173:36-42

GROWTH

Habitat size and number of organisms living there project 969:22-23

Measuring height with growth chart 304:10-11

GUERICKE, OTTO VON

Creating a vacuum to demonstrate atmospheric pressure experiment 1133:4.005

His experiments 42:34-37

"Magdeburg hemispheres"—experiment 507:1896

Magdeburg Sphere principle experiment with glasses and candle 1007:14-16

Produced first electrostatic generators 209:19

Repeat his air pressure experiment 448:37-38

GUINEA PIGS

Care of 390:86

Mazes—T maze variations to test intelligence—how to make 510:106-109

Nutrition experiments with guinea pigs 577:project #6

Raising 436:40

GUITAR. *See also* **MUSICAL INSTRUMENTS**

Cigar box guitar—how to make 543:46-47

GULLIVER EXPERIMENT

Life on planets, detect (Advanced) 668:67-69

Life on planets; detect; repeat Gulliver Experiment 887:72-74

GUNS

Potato pop gun—how to make 563:29-30

Velocity of water "bullet" experiment 1158:72-79

GUPPIES

Breeding guppies 402:99-100

Care of 163:33-36

Fish aquariums, set up and observe fish behavior 888:107-111

How to keep and raise guppies 1433:51-54

Overcrowding effect on populations of guppies experiment 1476:200-201

Overcrowding guppies in the field or in the laboratory 266:76-78

Raising guppies—how to 400:22

Raising guppies 148:56

Raising 436:40-41

Rules of inheritance found by Gregor Mendel—experiment 402:100-101

GYPSUM

Hardness test for gypsum experiment 1438:57-58

How to make gypsum experiment 1438:53-56

Testing chalk with an acid experiment 1438:49-50

Use of gypsum as building material experiment 1004:1.011

GYROSCOPE

Phonograph record becomes gyroscope experiment 940:112-114

Balancing act 260:28

Be-it-yourself gyroscope 292:40-41

Bicycle wheel gyroscope experiment 1132:7-1-7-2

Foucault, Jean; who invented the gyroscope project 1525:107-109

Gyro spinner, cardboard, making 999:87-88

Gyroscope from old phonograph record shows gyroscope use in space travel 1434:116-119

How a gyroscope works—experiment 385:62-64

Investigate scientific principles behind toys experiments 1412:81-87

Make a figured gyroscope 177:39-41

Make a model artificial horizon 379:13

Make gyro Yo-Yo 177:36-38

Model—making 12:73-75

Mystery force 260:29

Stabilizing a space craft (Advanced) 668:22-23

The coin on edge trick 585:69-70

The disc gyrotrick 585:67-68

H

HABITATS. *See also* **ECOSYSTEMS; TERRARIUMS**
Activities with habitats 236:167-172
Aquatic ecosystem in a jar experiment 1063:210
Biodiversity; concept of biodiversity demonstrated project 1338:66-67
Biotic and abiotic characteristics of three habitats experiment 978:84-86
Chart of types of habitats—animals, food, plants and temperature for habitat 475:47
Comparing pond and stream microhabitats experiment 1134:5.014
Destructive changes to nature experiment using three patches of lawn 1328:26-27
Exploring micro-habitats project 1313:79-83
Field study of habitats, how to do 1063:216
Forest ecosystem in large glass aquarium experiment 1063:211
Forest habitat study, how to do 1063:217
Forest; mini forest habitat in aquarium, how to plant and care for experiment 1472:48-53
Habitat destruction and the biodiversity of insects experiment 1096:77-82
Habitat size and number of organisms living there project 969:22-23
Habitat study recording sheets 236:167-170
Insect populations change in diversity and numbers when habitat changes 1096:77-82
Mapping habitats and vegetation project 1313:87-89
Meadow habitat wall frieze, how to make 1182:38
Micro-habitat study, how to do 1063:212
Microclimate study of small areas experiment 1063:287
Minibeast yard habitat, how to make 1182:37
Niche of insect, animal and plant life experiment, how to make 1527:81-82
Quadrat study of habitat conditions project 1313:89-92
Quadrat survey map of patch of ground experiment 1069:32-33
Rain gauges for measuring habitat rainfall project 1313:81-83
Soil profiles in habitats project 1313:83-87
Succession; turn pond into forest experiment with one habitat replacing another 1472:60-63
Temperature climate near ground for animals; temperature pole project 1313:80-81
Transect survey; cross-section study of different types of ground experiment 1069:32-33
Water habitat, how to study 1063:213-215
Woodland habitat terrarium, how to make 1188:22-23

HABITATS—ANIMAL
Find out which habitat some animals like best 590:39

HABITS
Demonstrate the strength of habit 294:92
Force of habit 335:119
Habit formation—demonstrate 294:92
Habit forming behavior experiment 936:31-32

HAIL
What causes hail experiment 1003:84-85

HAILSTONES
Hailstones, how to make 1017:65

HAIR
Adventure 16—discover that there are different kinds of hairs under hand 29:82-85
Hair color and eye color are inherited together or separately project 1210:70-72
Hair types and hair roots of animals and humans, identify and label 1295:64-67
How strong is your hair experiment 1280:25
Microscope—observe single human hair 294:11-12
Standing on end—the Hindu thread trick 16:68-70
Strength of human hair 133:30
What can hair tell you experiment 901:5-6
What makes hair curly experiment 1397:52-55

HAIR—HUMAN
Bleaching hair—experiment 441:81-85
Curl—experiments—kinds of curl you get in differently treated hair samples 441:79-80
Dissolve hair in bleach experiment 905:216-217
Effect of soap, shampoo and conditioners on hair—experiments 441:75-78
Experiments to explore properties of hair 441:70-73
Hair stretches—experiment to demonstrate (Primary) 469:unpaged
Hair, how strong is a hair; how to measure experiment 794:29
How many hairs on different peoples heads experiment 1506:91-92
Permanent waves—experiment 441:80-81
Shampoo containing no chemicals, recipe, how to make 1228:88
Strength of hair—testing experiment (Primary) 469: unpaged
Test strength of human hair strand with weights experiment 1370:26-27
What does hair look like under microscope 901:158

HALES, STEPHEN
Movement of sap in plants experiment 1133:3.005

HALF-LIFE
Half lives of radioactive substances experiment 1004:3.010

HAMMER
How much force can a hammer apply to a nail 549:22-25

HAMSTERS
Care of 390:86
Mazes—T maze variations to test intelligence—how to make 510:106-109
Overeating—do animals overeat 402:50-51
Periodicity—can natural animal periods be changed 402:52-53

HAND. *See also* **HUMAN BODY**
How to cast your entire hand in plaster to make hand mold sculpture 543:52-57

HAND GLIDERS. *See* **GLIDERS**

HAND LOTIONS
Determine if any difference among commercial hand and body lotions experiment 997:106-107

HANDBALL
The frisky handball 392:28-32

HANDEDNESS
Are fiddler crabs right handed or left handed experiment; survey chart given 1225:80-81
Cats are right pawed or left pawed—experiment 532:46
Percentage of people who are left-handed or right-handed project 1210:69-70

HANDWRITING
Handwriting analysis, how to do 1063:320-321

HANG GLIDER
Rogallo hang glider 54:113-126

HARBORS
Harbor activities 236:107-108

HARD WATER. *See also* **WATER—HARD AND SOFT**
Compare hardness of different water samples experiment 1396:131
Does hard water clean as well as soft water 396:51-53
Drops of soap needed to make suds in different water samples experiment 1396:131
Effect of hard water on soap experiment 441:12-14
Faucet water tested for hardness, how to do 1179:39
Hard water made soft experiment using tap water and washing soda 1435:39-41
How much soap is needed to soften water experiment 1396:132-133
How soft is rain water experiment 1396:131
Make hard water soft 26:120-121
'Soapless soap' detergent—how it works in hard water 26:117-119
Test for hardness of water experiment 1396:129-133
Test for water hardness experiment 762:40-41
Testing for hard water experiment using tap water, distilled water and soap 1435:35-38
Water-softening chemicals added to hard water make more suds experiment 1396:131
What hard water does to soap 26:115-117
Where do bathtub rings come from experiment with hard water and soap 1482:58-59
HARDNESS OF MINERALS
Hardness test standards 336:44-45
HARDNESS SCALE. *See* **MOHS' SCALE**
HARMONICS
How to find on piano 187:29
Resonance; air columns, resonance and standing waves experiments 1155:48-52
HARMONOGRAMS. *See* **LISSAJOUS FIGURES**
HARP, AEOLIAN. *See also* **MUSICAL INSTRUMENTS**
Making 350:97-98; 358:62-63
HARVEY, WILLIAM
Circulation of blood experiment 1133:3.001
Take your pulse on pressure points see discovery of blood circulation 602:unpaged
HAT
Pinwheel parade hat—how to make 310:24-27
HATCHING. *See* **EGGS**
HAUNTED HOUSES
Haunted house from box and three simple electric circuits, how to make 1076:20-23
Haunted house from cardboard, batteries and bulbs, how to make 1028:44-45
HAY INFUSION. *See also* **MICROORGANISMS**
Hay infusion, how to make 889:31-32
Hay infusion, make to study protozoa experiment 978:88-89
How to make 403:105
How to make to observe one celled organisms 86:13
Microbes from hay infusion under microscope, observe 889:32-34
Protozoa under microscope, observe four groups 889:33-35
HAZARDOUS WASTES
Community hazardous waste problems, how to investigate 1361:25
Neutralization of hazardous wastes by changing pH experiment 1361:86
Types of hazardous wastes in your home experiment 1361:58-59

HAZELNUTS
Grow hazelnut bush from hazelnut, how to do 1486:29
HEALTH
Depressants effect on tetrahymena (single-celled organism) experiment 1267:92-93
Environmental threats to health experiment 1267:77-80
Fruit flies offspring affected by parent's exposure to radiation experiment 1267:89-90
Nicotine; effects of nicotine on daphnia experiment 1267:97-101
Stimulants effect on euglena microorganisms experiment 1267:93-97
Test for radiation with film badges experiment 1267:89
Toxicity test on invertebrates for effect of lawn fertilizers experiment 1267:81-83
HEARING
Binaural hearing experiment; locating objects with sound 1155:77-78
Brain tricked by reversing signals coming from your ears experiment 1069:173
Direction of sound experiments 1141:42-44
Do ear trumpets work experiment 1284:16
Ear protectors experiment; which materials work best 1284:28
Ear to the table experiment 400:45
Ear trumpet—paper—how to make 734:10
Effects of darkness on balance and hearing experiment 1159:56-57
Game to check friends hearing, how to make 1209:20-21
Hearing and where sound is coming from experiment 1411:43
Hearing sensitivity and frequency of sound experiment 1155:75-76
Hearing through water experiment 1284:22
How accurately can people hear under noisy conditions experiment 1020:125-129
How do speaking tubes work experiment 1284:17
How good is your hearing experiment 734:9
Identify objects by sounds they make 253:100
Locate direction of sounds we hear 253:101-102
Play a music game 32:24-25
Testing your ears 148:71
Two ears are better than one 134:7
HEARING AIDS
Hearing aid and how it works experiment with shoe box and rubber bands 1209:14-15
HEART. *See also* **BLOOD; HUMAN BODY**
Beef heart, dissecting—how to 692:79-86
Blood circulation diagram (Primary) 245:12-13
Circulatory system 349:18-25
Demonstrate suction pump action 217:46-50
Effect of regular and decaffeinated coffee on daphnia heart beat experiment 713:90
Experiment shows effect of coffee and alcohol on daphnids heartbeat 174:46-47
Feel the beat—experiment with match and lump of clay 571:27
Heart, animal's blood circulation 436:41
How your heart pumps (Primary) 349:5-17
Make your pulse visible with a matchstick 150:78-79
Nail pulse detector 202:25
Observe effect of temperature on heartbeat rate of daphnia (water flea) 174:18-19
Observe the human heart and pulse 294:85
Observing a beef heart 294:83-84

178

Pulse—how to find, feel and show your pulse 349:26-35
Pulse—observe the beating pulse 293:28
Stethoscope—make to hear heartbeats 293:28
Stethoscope—making to hear heart beats 436:75
Testing the strength of cardiac muscle 148:69

HEAT. *See also* COMBUSTION; FIRE; INSULATION; TEMPERATURE; THERMOMETERS

Absorption—experiment to show melting ice absorbs heat 385:68
Absorption—prove that evaporating liquid absorbs heat—experiment 385:70-71
Absorption—the warm sleeve experiment with dark and light sleeve 563:136
Absorption and material—do all materials absorb heat equally 253:87-88
Absorption of colors—papers on the snow 550:102-105
Absorption of colors—so there's no snow 550:105-106
Absorption of heat experiment with recording sheet 747:1-2
Affects color of object 12:83-84
Air compression produces heat 44:80-81
Air contracts when cooled experiment with water glasses and balloon 939:74-75
Air expansion and contraction 34:54-58
And cold—ball and ring experiment; heat expands, cold contracts (Primary) 73:44-45
And cold—experiments to show 116:97-107
Bending wire creates heat experiment 939:44-45
Bimetallic strip in a thermostat—experiment 183:20-23
Bioluminescence experiment 182:46-47
Black's latent heat of boiling water experiment 1156:88
Black's mixing hot and cold liquids experiment 1156:88-89
Boil water in paper cup 179:52-53
Boil water in paper cup experiment 906:46
Boil water with ice experiment 906:51-53
Boil water without heat experiment 937:54-55
Boiling point and effect of pressure—experiment 183:60-63
Boiling water in a paper basin 186:64
Boiling water in a paper cup 44:100
Boiling water with water experiment 939:83-86
Burning iron [heat against mass] experiment 939:42-43
Calibration of heat—experiment 182:24-25
Caloric mass—experiment 586:86-87
Can ice cubes make water boil faster 179:54-55
Can you tell hot from cold 281:53
Carbon dioxide smothers a fire 44:98-99
Carnot and Joule; who discovered that heat is form of energy project 1525:110-113
Catch ice cube on string experiment 906:49-50
Change energy in your muscles into heat 249:6
Change ice to liquid water using heat energy experiment 1519:26
Changing electrical energy into heat energy 180:80
Chemical changes caused by heat; secret writing demonstrates 1219:42
Chemical heat from mixing water and plaster of Paris experiment 1519:21
Chimneys, box and candle demonstrate how chimneys work 939:137-139
Circulation—a sawdust roundabout 161:76
Clean dirty water by heating and cooling it experiment 1032:18-19
Cloth test of temperature with dry and wet cloth on thermometer in sun 568:40

Cold metal and warm wood may be the same temperature experiment 1132:24-1-24-2
Cold water is heavier than hot water 186:65
Cold water is heavier than hot water—experiment 651:16-17
Colder with soda and hypo 161:78-79
Color and texture affect heat being absorbed experiment; T-shirts/thermometer 1275:20
Color of clothes best for a hot climate experiment 1219:18
Colors to wear on a hot day, light or dark experiment with paper/water in sun 1017:15
Compare materials to find the best insulators experiment 1073:92
Condensation—demonstrate 182:30-31
Conservation of heat when hot and cold water are mixed experiment 1515:62-65
Conservation; measuring heat from immersion heater in glass of water experiment 1152:23-25
Contraction— balloon gets smaller when cold (Primary) 499:42
Contraction—contraction of air sucks egg into bottle (Primary) 499:41
Contraction and expansion—heated rubber band moves mysterious arrow 202:118-119
Cool under fire 222:96
Cooling by evaporation 161:77-78
Cooling curves of ice and water experiment 1515:88-91
Cooling effect of evaporation experiment using two thermometers and fan 1397:43
Cooling effects of evaporation—experiment 183:52-55
Copper wire expands and contracts experiment 939:22-24
Crazy water experiment with hot and cold water faucets 563:135-136
Creating heat by shaking experiment 1515:110-115
Dark colored materials absorb and emit energy more than light colors experiment 1132:55-1-55-2
Degree and calorie 281:60-61
Demonstrate kindling temperature of different materials 179:48-50
Density of liquids—experiment 182:32-33
Dew point—experiment 182:28-29; 183:56-59
Difference between heat and temperature experiment 1158:85-92
Difference between temperature and heat—demonstrate 126:129-136
Distortions in visual observations of atmosphere caused by heated air experiment 1062:10-11
Do gases and liquids expand on heating 179:50-52
Do materials conduct heat at the same rate 179:60-61
Do solids expand on heating and contract on cooling 179:46-48
Does insulation trap heat experiment 829:39-40
Effect of insulation—experiment 182:54-55
Effect of stretching of rubber—experiment 183:12-15
Effect on yeast—experiment 182:58-59
Effects of insulation on amount of heat retained 253:93-94
Electricity makes heat experiment with battery and bulb 1519:20
Electricity makes heat 238:30-31
Energy—experiment to show 400:84-85
Energy—make a heat "engine" with pinwheel and candle 549:30-32

Energy—no straining allowed 222:90
Energy—the greenhouse effect 253:89-90
Energy units converted to other units table 1152:32
Engines—how they work—experiment 128:153-155
Escapes faster from black object—simple experiment to show 379:25
Evaporating water keeps milk cool experiment 1519:18
Expands metal 280:36
Expands solids—why sidewalks have spaces 281:56
Expansion—boiling teakettle experiment (Primary) 499:40
Expansion—demonstrate peculiar expansion of water 385:123-124
Expansion—expansion indicator 249:12
Expansion—jumping lid 249:13
Expansion—show expansion by heat 176:85
Expansion—show how materials change in size 95:28-29
Expansion—the expanding rod experiment—how to do 419:32
Expansion and contraction—jar lid opens under hot water, not cold (Primary) 499:43
Expansion and contraction; objects change size when heated or cooled experiment 1132:30-1-30-2
Expansion effect—experiment 128:141-143
Expansion of bimetallic strip—experiment 183:16-19
Expansion of gases when heated—experiment 183:24-27
Expansion of liquids—experiment 182:50-53
Expansion of solids—experiment 385:125-126
Expansion of solids when heated—experiment 183:8-11
Expansion of water on freezing—experiment 183:40-43
Experiment with heat and distance and graph it 182:18-19
Experimenting with contraction and expansion 180:78-79
Experiments to demonstrate 186:64-67
Explosions on the kitchen stove—experiment (popcorn) 563:129
Fat or lard or blubber insulates against cold project 969:30-31
Finding the kindling temperature of materials 180:74-75
Fire needs oxygen to burn 44:96-97
Fluid theory of heat experiment 1515:95-101
Freezing point—experiment 182:16-17
Freezing rates of hot and cold water and how to chart 182:20-21
Friction and heat 34:59
Friction between objects generates heat experiment 1219:8
Friction causes heat experiment 851:21-22
Friction causes heat, bending wire experiment 860:228-229
Friction creates heat—scout bow and drill experiment (Primary) 499:17
Friction makes heat experiment with bow, dowel and block of wood 1519:22
Friction produces heat experiment 836:57-58
Friction produces heat 44:78-79
From refrigeration 382:83-86
Gases expand when heated experiment with balloons 1219:35
Get a howl from dry ice and metal 291:45
Greenhouse effect—experiment 183:84-87
Hammer and heat—experiment 585:130
Hammering produces heat 44:82-83
Heat absorption 243:18-19
Heat absorption and color 253:86

Heat and breeze at the beach experiment 939:62-64
Heat and fuel needed to warm house or apartment experiment 1152:36
Heat convection in liquids experiment 1515:102-104
Heat energy changes to movement experiment balsa wood steamboat, how to do 1179:48-49
Heat exchange experiment to measure movement of heat between metal nut/water 1179:47
Heat experiment and demonstrations with nails 549:30-51
Heat flow—experiment 656:24-25
Heat flow from different materials experiment 1164:56-59
Heat from Sun burns hole in paper experiment 1519:12
Heat in the atmosphere experiment 1447:18-22
Heat loss and surface area—experiment 586:89-90
Heat loss and surface area relationship in melting ice experiment 959:167-169
Heat loss and temperature difference—experiment 586:90-91
Heat makes air expand demonstration with hot water in jug 939:71-73
Heat motion by radiation experiment 1515:105-108
Heat needed to change temperature of 1 gram of cooking oil by 1 degree 1152:32-35
Heat needed to melt ice—experiment 586:85-86
Heat of vaporization experiment 1158:94-96
Heat or temperature?—experiment 585:135-136
Heat rises; colored water in jar demonstrates 924:92
Heat tolerance and sensitivity—demonstrate 182:8-9
Heat transferred and mass of water with temperature change constant experiment 1152:26-29
Heat transferred and temperature change of fixed amount of water experiment 1152:25-26
Heat transferred through conduction, convection and radiation experiments 1073:94-95
Heat trap takes heat from sun and warms water experiment 1032:8-9
Heat used to produce steam experiment with metal cigar tube 1219:39
Heat without fire—experiment with hands 489:58
Heated air causes distortions in visual observations in atmosphere experiment 1062:10-11
Heated air expands; cold air contracts experiment 1032:12-14
Heated air expands; cold air contracts experiment 1032:15
Heated wire expands experiment 939:25-26
Heating by radiation depends on color experiment 1515:105-108
Heating with colored solar energy 586:93
Hidden heat of melting ice experiment 1515:81-84
Hidden heat; melting, boiling, freezing and condensation experiment 1515:76-84
Hilsch tube mystery experiment 723:33-34
Hot air rises 44:86-87
Hot and cold hands—experiment 585:156
'Hot dog' cooker 391:42-45
Hot grass or manure—experiments 563:58-59
Hot water is lighter than cold water; colored water explosion experiment 1136:20
Hot water is lighter than cold water; ink bottle in bowl of water experiment 937:98-99
Hot weight—experiment 563:133

How a percolator works experiment 939:94-96

How a thermometer works 281:56-57

How do things lose heat and get cold—instant ice cream 249:24

How evaporation cools 281:58

How heat acts—experiment 106:41-46

How heat blows up a balloon 281:55

How heat changes liquid to gas 281:58

How heat changes solid to liquid 281:57

How heat travels in water and air 281:62-63

How hot is a flame—experiment 586:87-88

How ice behaves at its melting point 183:36-39

How to make an electric arc heater 128:185

How to make heat by friction 281:54

How to make heat from electricity 281:55

Hydrogen peroxide and potato release heat experiment 1087:13-14, 19-37

Ice on a wire experiment 906:50-51

Identifying the gas necessary for fires 180:77

In a geyser 382:121-123

Infrared radiation—experiment 183:80-83

Insulated bottle stores heat experiment 1028:32

Insulated container keeps water warm experiment 1032:22-23

Insulation and R values—experiment 586:91-93

Insulation increase causes loss of heat to decrease experiment 984:44-46

Insulator experiment using different materials 837:50-51

Irreversible chemical change experiment with heated sugar 1219:42-43

Joseph Black's latent heat experiment 1133:7.004

Keeping warm—what is a good insulator—experiment 587:42

Kindling temperature—experiment 182:12-13

Laboratory thermometer measurement of several objects experiment 1515:32-34

Latent heat—make a paper pot to boil water 142:47

Latent heat experiment with glass of water and thermometer 939:87-88

Latent heat of melting ice experiment 1515:81-84

Latent heat of vaporization of water experiment 1515:85-88

Liquid crystal experiment 386:73-78

Magnetism and heat—experiment 350:5-6

Make a hollow candle 150:126-127

Make pair of scales for weighing hot and cold air 186:67

Mass and temperature change are involved in measuring heat experiment 1515:56-62

Match versus charcoal—experiment 585:139

Materials which carry or conduct heat the best demonstration 1358:27

Measure heat absorption 175:69

Measuring temperatures 34:45-50

Melting and boiling—experiment to show 128:150-153

Metal expands when heated—demonstration 605:38-39

Metal expands when heated; twisting trick with foil demonstrates 1219:38

Metal rods expand when heated and shrink when cold experiment 1090:12-14

Metals are good conductors of heat 44:92-93

Metals expand and contract experiment; how they do it 939:18-21

Mind reading trick with coins (Primary) 109:29

Model of matter to demonstrate heat processes experiment 1515:116-123

Molecular movement and heat 12:83-85

Molecules in a gas move faster when gas is heated up experiment 1090:11

Molecules in collision in hot and cold water experiment 1090:10

Nail hit by hammer gets hot experiment 939:46-49

Newton's Law of Cooling experiment 1090:20-21

Objects expand when heated 44:84-85

One will, one won't; hot water rises in bottle experiment 906:43

Outdoor temperature experiment—make a graph of heat 568:40

Paper dolls—dancing 350:112-113

Parabolic shapes concentrate energy experiment 1132:58-1-58-2

Pick the right coin every time 161:85-86

Pressure causes ice to melt—experiment 183:44-47

Pressure produces heat 44:76-77

Project 10—flame temperatures 654:34

Project 11—conductive heat losses and surface area (Advanced) 654:39-41

Project 12—heat loss and temperature differences (Advanced) 654:41-42

Project 13—determine heat loss relationship (Advanced) 654:42-43

Project 14—R value 654:44-45

Project 15—determine heat loss from buildings 654:47

Project 16—heat loss from infiltration in buildings 654:49

Project 4—heat and temperature change 654:29-30

Project 40—heat of vaporization (Advanced) 654:87-88

Project 42—heat of fusion (Advanced) 654:88-89

Project 44—heat of melting 654:88

Project 5—heat and mass 654:30

Project 6—mass and temperature change 654:30-31

Project 7—a formula for heat 654:31-32

Project 8—specific heat 654:33-34

Pump heat—experiment 585:129-130

Rate of heat flow is related to surface area experiments 1152:56-63

Rate of heat flow related to temperature difference experiment 1152:63-68

Rates of melting—experiment 182:36-37

Rays—heat can travel in rays—black hot tin can 249:18

Rays—penetrating heat 249:19

Refrigerator from clay flowerpot keeps drinks cold experiment 1032:24

Rub hands together to generate heat (Primary) 499:9

Rules of temperature change experiment with fluid level changes 1515:45-55

Rules of temperature change experiment, how to graph 1515:38-44

Should radiators be painted black 381:75-76

Show how heat affects substances and reactions 157:18-19

Show if color affects melting rates 182:48-49

Show quantity of heat 182:40-41

Show solubility at different temperatures—experiment 182:38-39

Simple experiments describing changes of hot and cold (Primary) 417:1-33

Smoking chimney experiment 906:41

Snow and ice reflect sunlight; dirt and dark ground absorb it experiment 1322:40-43

Solubility of sugar cube in water—experiment 182:26-27

Some metals conduct heat better than others 44:94-95
Specific heat—experiment 182:22-23; 183:32-35
Specific heat of materials calculated experiment
    1396:177-178
Specific heat; compare specific heat of metals experi-
    ment 1515:72-75
Speed of cooling experiment 1090:20-21
Spinning spiral experiment 906:42
Squeeze bottle experiment—heated air expands (Char-
    les's law) 563:132
Starchy bubbles experiment—pressing pot on heating ele-
    ment increases boiling 563:136-137
Steam, vapor, gas—experiment 585:127
Sterilization of bacteria—experiment 182:56-57
Stop heat moving—keep things hot or cold 249:22
Sun warms different substances by different amounts ex-
    periment 1281:7
Temperature—water heats up and rises (Primary) 499:37
Temperature and heat content of different materials—
    experiment 183:28-31
Temperature by touch experiment 1515:8-10
Temperature changes in water and cooking oil experi-
    ment 1515:65-69
Temperature effect on the length of wires experiment
    1515:12-14
Temperature of a flame experiment 1158:92-94
Temperature of freezing mixtures—experiment 183:48-
    51
Testing for heat conductivity 180:75
Testing temperatures of water—experiment with hands
    489:55-56
The dancing paper dolls 350:112-113
The obliging balloon—experiment 563:129-130
The revolving snake 350:113-114
The sticking ice tray 585:137
Thermometer measures temperature experiment using
    glass bottle, colored water 1032:16-17
Tin can—thermometer and light demonstrate black
    absorbs heat experiment 722:114
Tire pump generates heat experiment 939:118-119
Transfer of heat—experiment 128:145-150
Transmitted by convection 44:88-89
Transmitted by radiation 44:90-91
Travels (Primary) 322:16-17
Two frictions—experiments with wire coat hanger
    563:131
Volume of air of a gas affected by temperature experi-
    ment 1515:17-19
Volume of liquids affected by temperature experiment
    1515:15-16
Warming up to show latent heat—experiment 182:10-11
Water heats up in paper pan experiment 939:50-52
Waves—motions of waves produce sound; making sound
    with hot air 293:46
Which coffee cools faster—experiment 585:143-144
Which colors absorb heat the best experiment 1519:14
Which metals holds the most air 147:73-75
Why is this candle hollow 161:77
You can't measure temperature of water with your fin-
    gers 238:50-52

HEAT—CONDUCTION

Boiling water in a paper cup 291:52-53
Conduction—experiment 12:85
Conduction—show how it works 238:40-41
Conduction of heat along metal experiment 939:27-30
Conduction of heat in a coin experiment 939:31-32
Conduction test—simple experiment 568:36
Conserving energy by reducing conductive heat losses ex-
    periment 1152:93-95
Copper tube and paper demonstrate kindling point
    939:33-34
Copper wire—paper clips—and candle demonstrate
    760:28
Do all materials conduct heat equally 253:73-74
Do large things cool more quickly than small ones experi-
    ment 793:30
Experiment to show conduction of heat 183:64-67
Experiment to show conduction 182:34-35
Fast cotton experiment with cotton cloth and polyester
    cloth 563:137-138
Find the best heat conductor 249:16
Fire put out by 291:60
Fork and spoon demonstration of heat conduction
    939:53-55
Heat conduction—experiment 585:133-134; 585:74-75
Heat conduction of different metals experiment 939:35-
    36
Heat conduction race experiment 1515:97-99
Heat loss from water in wrapped vs. Unwrapped tin cans
    489:60-61
Heat losses due to conduction in homes, how to measure
    experiment 1152:82-84
Heat moves through metal experiment 882:4
Heat strainer with candle 249:17
House insulation keeps heat in and out experiment; data
    tables given 1004:1.004
How fast does heat travel along metal knitting needle ex-
    periment 793:28
In metals—experiment to make a compound bar
    385:126-129
Insulated bottles demonstrate recording sheet given
    747:16-17
Mass versus heat 291:217
Measuring expansion of copper tube experiment 939:37-
    39
Metal is good conductor of heat; wood and plastic are not
    experiment 1519:8
Metal spoon and plastic spoon in hot water—experiment
    (Primary) 499:25
Nails—board and ice demonstrate 721:41
Rate of heat flow through different materials experiment
    1152:68-72
Show heat conductivity 183:68-71
Some materials conduct heat better than others experi-
    ment 1396:192
The devil's handkerchief—heat conduction 205:87-90
The fireproof handkerchief—experiment 563:132
Thermal conductivities of steel, glass and insulation ex-
    periment 1515:95-101
Water is used to lower body temperature of warm-
    blooded animals experiment 1397:36-38
Why not metal handles 281:61-62
Windows; how much heat energy is lost through win-
    dows experiment 1396:191

HEAT—CONDUCTORS

Boil water in a glass test tube while holding it 95:24
Candle, metal and wax balls show good conductor
    629:26-27
Cloth trick of heat 360:17
Experiment on wood and metal 360:15

Heat conducted along long nail experiment using candle wax and nail 1073:94

Heat conductors 146:51; 280:37

Heat conducts through some materials experiment 836:87-90

Materials that are the best conductors or best insulators of heat experiment 1090:38

Metal wires conduct heat experiment 1090:36

Paper saucepan that will not burn 360:56-57

Red hot trick 399:7

Some materials conduct heat experiment 1028:30

Test for conductors of heat experiment using rods of different materials 1219:14

Test objects for conduction of heat experiment 1032:11

What things does heat go through experiment 793:27

Which materials absorb heat the best experiment 1519:15

Which materials does heat go through experiment 795:31

Which thermal wrappings have the best insulation experiment 1090:40

Why do some materials feel cold experiment 1519:9

Wool sock insulator keeps heat from being lost experiment 1219:20

HEAT—CONVECTION. *See also* **CONVECTION**

Air rises when it gets hot; make hot-air balloon to demonstrate 1028:31

Aluminum pie plate over candles turns from heated air experiment 1519:10

Bubble balloons 249:20

Christmas tree angel spiral revolves from heat, how to make 1299:81

Convection currents—experiment 585:136-137

Convection currents experiment using hot colored water 1073:94

Convection currents experiment with ink volcano in bowl of water 939:126-129

Convection currents in liquids experiment 939:89-91

Convection currents in water in aquarium; project shadows onto screen 1132:28-1-28-2

Convection currents of heated air demonstrated with paper spiral snake 1219:19

Convection heat losses in your home or school; how to calculate experiment 1152:90-91

Demonstrating convection in liquids 180:79

Experiment to show convection 182:42-45

Experiment to show convection 183:72-75

Flashlight throws shadow of glass of hot water on wall—experiment 568:38

Heat can be transmitted by convection 44:88-89

Heat convection in liquids experiment 1515:102-104

Heat makes cardboard spiral turn experiment 1136:17

Heat moves around in a liquid experiment 1028:30

Heat travels in liquids and gases 238:42

Hot air rises and moves spiral snake experiment 1073:95

Hot air rises experiment with plastic bag 1032:10

Hot air rises; spiral snake demonstrates 1014:110

Hot water rises and cold water falls experiment with colored water 1519:11

How a room warms experiment 1090:44

How can convection currents be detected 253:75

Make a spinning snake to demonstrate convection 172:105-106

Make a windmill figure to demonstrate (difficult) 172:106-109

Make small windmill from stiff cardboard to demonstrate 568:38

Paper teakettle boils water 95:23

Revolving snake demonstrates air currents, how to make from thick paper 1299:80

Rising rice in hot water demonstrates convection 1090:43

Seeing convection currents—experiment 489:62-63

Simple experiments with colored water in glasses 568:38

Spiral paper snake dances experiment 827:34

Spiral turns in warm air demonstration 939:65-70

Test for convection experiment with hot water and food coloring 1377:15

Too hot to handle 249:23

Underwater chimney 249:21

HEAT—CONVECTION CURRENTS. *See also* **HEAT—CONVECTION**

Build Christmas tree angel to demonstrate rotation 167:8-10

Construct a hot air balloon 167:99-105

Convection cycle shown with colored liquid and glass pot (Primary) 499:30

Experiment to show convection currents in air 385:130-131

Make tree snake to demonstrate rotation 167:5-7

HEAT—EXPANSION

Heat and expansion experiment—with bottle and balloon 587:39

HEAT—INSULATORS

Do big things stay warm longer than small things experiment 1519:17

Materials that are the best conductors or best insulators of heat experiment 1090:38

Testing wool, foil and fabric for insulation qualities experiment 1519:16

Which thermal wrappings have the best insulation experiment 1090:40

HEAT—RADIANT ENERGY

How to make heat by radiant energy 281:54

HEAT—RADIANT HEAT

Feel bulb gives radiant and convection heat (Primary) 499:7

Heat radiation experiments 577:project #25

Heating by radiation 281:63

Radiated heat reflected away experiment; glass jars, water, black/silver paper 1073:95

Sunlight warms black pan first; object in sun warmer than in shade (Primary) 499:33

The tin can test measures radiant heat 568:40

Transferring heat by radiation 180:76

HEAT—RADIATION. *See also* **SOLAR COLLECTORS; SOLAR ENERGY**

Absorption of radiant heat by water and soil experiment 1516:47-48

Black affects radiation experiment with black can and shiny can 939:122-124

Dark cloth test 291:48-49

Greenhouses trap sunlight and warmth speeds growth of plants experiment 1090:49

Heat can be transmitted by radiation 44:90-91

How can effects of heat radiation be observed 253:76

How well do materials and colors absorb heat radiation experiment 1090:48

Radiant heat from Sun makes energy in space experiment with cans of water 1434:120-123

Radiation and absorption of heat experiment using clear and black covered jars 1179:55

Radiation experiment 183:76-79

Radiation of the sun bath 291:50
Some colors soak up heat easily 238:44-45
What bleach does 291:51
HEAT CONSERVATION. *See* **ENERGY CONSERVA-TION; INSULATION; INSULATORS**
HEAT LOSS. *See* **ENERGY CONSERVATION**
HEATERS—SOLAR. *See* **SOLAR ENERGY; SOLAR HEAT; SOLAR WATER HEATERS**
HEATING
Electric heaters—experiment to show how it works 291:166
Fuel costs for heating home experiment 1152:91-92
Heating by refrigeration—experiment 382:83-86
How to make model hot water heating system 128:147-148
Make a water heater model—experiment 385:129-130
HEATING SYSTEM. *See also* **HOUSES—FURNACES**
HEIGHT
Clinometer to measure height of tall building, how to make 1345:56-58
Estimating the height of a tree, how to do 784:103-104
Height calculations and surface mapping of planets experiment 1062:100-101
Height of building—how to measure 731:69
Height of distant object calculation project 1021:128-130
Height of tree measured by using Sun's shadows experiment 1294:31
Height, diameter, circumference of tree measurement experiment 978:50-51
How tall is that tree?; How to measure using shadows 1073:72
Hypsometer measures height of things, how to make 1115:41-43
Hypsometer, making to measure how tall something is 999:59-62
Measure heights and weights of kids in your class; graph results experiment 794:27-28
Measuring height—make a growth chart (Primary) 304:10-11
Shadow meter from nail—how to make to measure height of object 549:103-104
Shadow used to measure height of objects experiment 941:23-24
Simple measuring device to measure height of tall things, how to make 834:137-138
Theodolite measures height of objects experiment, how to make 1521:28-29
Trees; measuring height of trees, how to do 1145:31
Using a nail and its shadow determine height of objects 549:100-104
HELICOPTERS
Air powered helicopter, making 981:23
Balsa wood helicopter with model pilot, how to make 1419:14-15
Demonstrate helicopters have wings 860:11, 17-19
Factors affecting flight of helicopter experiment 1063:475
Gyrocopter model, how to make 1507:10
Helicopter—making 660:24-25
Helicopter experiments to demonstrate flight of helicopters 564:24-25
Helicopter model with working rotors, how to make 1095:35
Helicopter paper pattern—making 561:42-43
Helicopter parachute, how to make 861:169-174
Helicopter rotor—how to make 419:36
Helicopter rotor model, how to make and fly 1201:23
Helicopter rotor, plastic, how to make 1161:15
Helicopter spinner, how to make from cardboard, straws, and clay 1073:23
Helicopter, how to make 909:72
Helicopters and how they fly 382:73-77
How does a helicopter fly experiment 1293:3-5
How to make 112:42
How to make a paper helicopter (Primary) 69:24
How to make paper helicopter Make a helicopter 32:50-51
Make paper helicopter to show air reduces pull of gravity (Primary) 207:17
Make your own toy helicopter (Primary) 153:28-29
Matteson's flying helicopter, how to make 861:163-168
Mini helicopter demonstrates Newton's Third Law of Motion 1289:28-29
Model—how to make 388:12-13
Model helicopter's working blade demonstrates gears experiment; patterns given 1494:30-31
Model rotors demonstrate lift experiment 1332:30-31
Paper helicopter flies, how to make 1436:3-5
Paper helicopter that spins, how to make 1376:15
Paper helicopter, how to make 27:57-58; 281:17; 597: inside front cover; 733:35; 1016:32; 1108:28-29; 1115:70-71; 1373:11; 1419:13
Paper model helicopter experiments 1412:76
Paper spinner, how to make 1389:25
Plastic helicopter, how to make 1299:51
Potato—how to make 113:24-25
Simple paper helicopter, how to make 940:126-127
Spinner helicopters, paper, pattern, making 1014:124-125
Tin helicopter, how to make 1299:50
Weather whirlybird—how to make 652:20-23
Weight affects rotation speed of paper helicopter demonstration 1404:148-149
Weight affects rotation speed of paper helicopter experiment 1405:103
Whirly copter—how to make 310:8-10
Wing position affects direction of helicopters rotation experiment 1405:104
Wing position affects direction of paper helicopters rotation experiment 1404:15
HELIOGRAPHY
Heliograph—how to build 507:1878-1879
HELIOTROPISM. *See also* **PLANTS—TROPISMS**
Bean plant grows through box maze toward light experiment 1063:410
HELIUM
Change voice by breathing helium 291:68
Helium bubbles from helium balloon experiment 1482:46-47
Helium filled balloon experiment 1208:60-61
Helium passes through a balloon faster than air experiment 1251:27-28
Why do helium balloons rise experiment 860:1-2
HELIX. *See also* **ELECTRICITY—ELECTRIC CURRENT**
Let's make a bar electromagnet 63:52-53
Making a magnet out of a coil of wire 63:48-49
HELMONT, JOHANNES VAN
Growth of plants experiment 1133:3.002

HENRY, JOSEPH
His experiments 42:115-125
About self induction 63:70-73
Bar-shaped magnet 63:50-53
Discoverer of electromagnet telegraph 209:48-49
Make your own electromagnet to test his discovery 602:unpaged
HENRY, WILLIAM
His experiments 42:93-96
HERB GARDENS
Outdoor projects with 118:233-241
HERBARIUM. *See also* **SEAWEED**
Pressing and collecting seaweed to start a herbarium, how to do 1118:36-37
HERBICIDES
Black walnut trees release chemicals that prevent plant growth project 969:50-51
Natural weed control for lawns project 969:46-47
HERBS
Aromatic oils—adventure 47—aromatic oils under a hand lens 29:207-209
Basil; grow your own basil plant experiment 1484:98
Drying herbs, how to do 879:188-189
Freezing herbs experiment 1238:116-117
Growing pot herbs from seeds, how to do 784:60
Herb drying tips 376:31
Herb garden 436:42
Herb tea, how to make 879:188
Herbal bug repellent, recipe, how to make 1335:116
Herbal moth bags, recipe, how to make 1335:116
Herbal shampoo, recipe, how to make 1335:116
Herbal talcum—how to make 480:115
Indoor herb garden, how to grow 899:190
Microwave herb drying project 980:77
Pot of herbs, how to grow 810:34-35
Uses for 480:115-117
Window herb garden—how to 376:30-31
Windowsill herb garden project 980:75-76
HEREDITY. *See also* **GENETICS**
Albinism in corn experiment 1060:96
"Alike as two peas in a pod" experiment 1060:96-97
Environment influences action of genes experiment using lima beans 1060:97-98
Family traits 436:42-43
Generation game to see vast number of possible genetic variations experiment 1517:42-43
Heredity grid for straight and curly hair project 1070:20-21
Heredity in fruit flies experiment 1425:23-28
Hybridize morning glory plants experiment 1060:95-96
Inheritance of acquired characteristics 402:101
Introduction to heredity: Punnett squares—computer project 584:37-39
Investigate codominance in snapdragon flowers experiment 1060:95
Investigation into the relationship of heredity and environment 420:131-133
Laws of chance and percent deviation computer project 584:40-42
Mendel's pea experiments, how to do 1060:92-95
Mendel's Principle of Independent Assortment experiment using peas 1060:95
Mendel's Principle of Segregation experiment 1060:92-93

Mendelian genetics and laws of heredity (Advanced) 372:30-46
Overcrowding affects action of genes experiment using sunflowers 1060:98
Projects on the physical basis of heredity (Advanced) 372:47-80
Rules of inheritance found by Gregor Mendel 402:100-101
Selective breeding produces lima beans that are either large or small experiment 1060:97
Single-gene inheritance experiments 1267:106-112
Traits from parents experiment 1063:191
Variation in lima beans experiment 1060:97
Variation in tree leaves experiment 1060:97
HERMANN GRID ILLUSION
Project 229:74-76
HERMIT CRABS
Hermit crab observation 1290:69,
How to care for 475:27-31
HERO'S AEROPILE
Balloon spins like aeropile experiment 994:46-51
HERO'S ENGINE
Building a steam motor project 833:283
Construct to show jet propulsion 167:29-32
Hero's wheel demonstration with milk carton, string and water 837:62-63
HERSCHEL, WILLIAM
Discovery of infrared rays experiment 1133:6.009
HIBERNATION
Get a frog to hibernate experiment 913:41
Hibernation of frogs 436:44
Make a frog hibernate 381:105-107; 532:66-67
Winter sleeping sites—test protection of outdoor sleeping sites 277:42-43
HIERONYMUS MACHINE
Experiment to demonstrate (Advanced) 393:60-71
HILLS. *See also* **SLOPES**
Height—measure height of hill 381:147-148
How to measure the slope of a hill 175:18-19
Making contour maps 303:24-25
HINDU CLIMBING BALLS
Project 350:108-111
HINDU MAGIC TRICK
Jar and rice trick 1010:37-39
With jar and rice 563:37
HINDUS
How to count like a Hindu 509:42-47
HOCKEY
Air hockey game using balloons and Ping-Pong balls 651:26-27
HOLOGRAM
Making a hologram 681:23
HOMES
Earth shelters to determine temperatures above and below ground experiment 1094:43
HONEY
How much sugar is in honey experiment 1096:144-148
Sugar in honey experiment; how much sugar is there in honey 1097:141-143
HONEYBEES. *See also* **BEES**
Adventure 14—learn what it means to be stung under a microscope 403:50-53
Adventure 13—we go marketing with a honey bee—bees under a microscope 403:46-50

Color; can honeybees see color experiment 1134:3.005
Feed honey bees 236:62
Honey and honeybee activities [Primary] 759:56
Honey bees and pollination 236:62
Honeybee feeding habits experiment 1097:137-140
How honeybees find their way home experiment 1479:31

HOOKE, ROBERT
Cork cells, how to prepare and observe under microscope 1295:76-77
Discovery of cells in cork experiment 1133:3.004
His experiments 42:38-42
Hooke's cork and cells experiment 1156:65
The science of stretching experiment 1133:4.008

HOOKE'S LAW. *See also* **ELASTICITY**
Experiment—the elastic nature of rubber 336:78-81
Hooke's Law experiments with screen door spring 1158:60-64
Law of stretch 39:36-43
Relationship between force applied to spring and amount spring stretches 1156:65-67

HOOP ROLLING
Gravity 12:61-66
Low pressure 12:61-66
Magnetic 12:61-66
Weighted 12:61-66

HORIZON
How to measure the horizon experiment 958:20-21
What is your horizon 292:42-43

HORMONES. *See also* **AUXINS; GIBBERELLINS; PLANTS—HORMONES**
"Feed back loop"; amount of hormone in your blood demonstration 1272:22
Fly larvae; hormone flow through the larvae's body experiment 1096:29-33

HORNER, WILLIAM
Daedaleum motion picture device—how to make 507:1890-1891

HOROSCOPES
Accuracy of horoscope predictions experiment 1062:107-108

HORSE
Prancing 350:117-118

HORSESHOE MAGNETS. *See* **ELECTROMAGNETS**

HORSEPOWER
Horsepower of human body measured experiment 1020:130-132
How much horsepower do you have experiment 902:64
How much power can you develop experiment 1152:18-19
Measure your own horsepower experiment 1157:107-108
You and a horse—experiment 563:184

HORSESHOE CRABS
Observation of life of horseshoe crab, how to do 1225:84-90
Rate of speed of old crabs versus young crabs experiment 1225:89

HORSETAILS
Adventure 38—horsetails under a hand lens 29:174-176

HOT AIR BALLOON. *See also* **BALLOONS—HOT AIR**
3D hot air balloon model, pattern, making 998:215
Air expands and takes up more space as it gets hotter experiment 1201:7
Air rises when it gets hot; make hot-air balloon to demonstrate 1028:31

Bottle with balloon in cold and hot water demonstrates principle 940:34-36
Build hot air balloon from tissue paper and wire, patterns given 1252:14-19
Construct a 167:99-105
Construct and fly your own hot air balloon experiment 1126:32-33
Garbage bag balloon and candle—demonstrate 363:161
Hot air balloon—how to make 419:33; 419:37; 737:15; 909:59
Hot air balloon experiment 860:223-225
Hot air balloon from tissue paper, how to make 1115:54-56; 1255:19
Hot air balloon made from papier mache, how to do 1110:12-13
Hot air balloon, working model, how to make 1095:40
Hot air is lighter than cold air experiment shows why hot air balloons rise 1208:64-65
Hot air rises and cold air sinks experiment; make hot-air balloon to show 1211:11
Hot air rises experiment demonstrated with hot air balloon, how to make 1179:51
Hot air rises experiment using hot-air balloon 1294:122-124
Hot air rises experiment with hot air balloon, how to make 1332:12-13
Hot air rises experiment with plastic bag 1032:10
Hot air rises experiment; how to build hot air balloon 1476:92-94
Hot air rises experiment; how to make hot air balloon 1161:9
Hot-air balloon, patterns given, how to make from tissue paper 1299:53
Make a hot air balloon 564:16; 660:11
Making a hot air balloon project 833:284-285
Model hot-air balloon, make from papier mache 1416:9
What happens when air is heated; paper bags on balance experiment 900:44
Working model hot air balloon, how to make 1448:11

HOT DOGS
'Hot dog' cooker 391:42-45

HOT FRAMES. *See also* **GREENHOUSES.**
How to make 398:38

HOT SPRINGS. *See* **GEYSERS**

HOUSE FLIES. *See also* **FLIES—HOUSE FLIES**
Adventure 6—we learn how a fly walks upside down under a microscope 403:18-22
Mutation—mechanism of evolution—experiment 402:105-106

HOUSEHOLD APPLIANCES. *See also* **ENERGY CONSERVATION**
Conserving energy in your home experiments 1152:118-119
Spin dryer tests principle of centrifuge and dries paper towels experiment 1136:32-33

HOUSEHOLD CHEMICALS
Household chemicals effect on germination and height of seedlings experiment 1004:2.012
Household cleaners compared for hazards and disposal problems experiment 1361:50-51
Household items tested for acid using red cabbage indicator experiment 1328:62
Household liquids; test for acidity experiment 1046:63-65

Natural cleaners replace chemical cleaners experiment 1063:374

HOUSEHOLD CLEANERS

Labels on cleaning products experiment 1361:56

pH of cosmetics and cleaning agents experiment 1476:134-135

Test for presence of base in common powdered cleansers experiment 1479:65

HOUSEHOLD PRODUCTS

Absorbency; which materials soak up water the fastest experiment 1509:8

Paper towels; which is the "quickest picker-upper" project 1210:41-42

Toilet paper; how fast do brands of toilet paper break up in water experiment 1371:64

HOUSEPLANTS

New plants from old, how to do 991:20-23

HOUSES. *See also* **BUILDING**

Adobe houses—making bricks for 633:38

Building a mud house 633:34-35

Building with drinking straws 3:10-41

House boat—make an elastic powered house boat 223:24-25

House built from rolled paper has strength experiment 1024:20-21

House on stilts stays above water level of floods, how to make 1463:28

Humidity; which areas of home are most humid project 969:84-85

Insulation works to keep cold air out of houses experiment 1371:81-82

Polynesian 'village' of toy huts—how to make 325: unpaged

Room—model of—how to make (Primary) 303:10-11

Super structures—how to make 399:71

Treehouse—making 749:78-79

HOUSES—BEAMS

Building a house 399:70

HOUSES—ELECTRICITY

Electromagnet—how to make 610:63

Experiments with the complete electric circuit 610:60-61

How to make a light switch 610:62-63

Let's make a fuse 610:65

HOUSES—FURNACES

Air circulation and expansion of heated water—experiment 610:52-54

Heat conductivity of metal and wood—experiment 610:54

HOUSES—HOUSE BUILDING

Bricks—shape of—how made to bond together 337:10

Demonstrate damp rising in bricks 337:13

Demonstrate heat loss from materials in cavity of walls 337:14

Demonstrate water tanks and flow of water 337:20-21

Electrical supply—demonstrate electrical circuits, switches and fuses 337:27-31

Foundations—make a model of 337:9

How doors and hinges work 337:15

Plumb lines and spirit levels—how to make 337:12

Plumbing—demonstrate drainage in sinks 337:24

Roof—build triangle trusses for roofs 337:18

Toilet tanks—demonstrate water flow 337:22-23

Water pipes freezing—demonstrate 337:25

Windows—demonstrate effect of heat loss glass and double glazed windows 337:17

HOUSES—WATER SUPPLY

Standpipe—need for demonstration 610:44

Water supply in houses—experiment to demonstrate 610:42-43

HOVERCRAFT

Cushion of air reduces friction experiment with balloon hovercraft 1179:60

Demonstration of how hovercraft works 1378:15

Electric motor in propeller-driven boat, how to make 1043:40-41

Hoverboat, how to make 908:67-69

Hovercraft demonstrates friction; make from balloon and food tray 1380:24-25

Hovercraft experiment demonstrates air pressure 1108:12

Hovercraft from cardboard and balloon, how to make 1115:68-69

Hovercraft toy boat sails above the water 561:26-27

Hovercraft type propeller boat, how to make 1247:36-37

Hovercrafts travel on cushion of air demonstration 1208:34-35

How a hovercraft works demonstration 1165:24

How hovercraft reduces friction experiment 1523:23

How to make hovercraft 679:11; 908:65-70

Land hovercraft, how to make using plastic record, thread spool, balloon 1208:54-55

Make a model hovercraft 260:13

Make a simple hovercraft 225:29

Make to show air pressure 112:30-31

Model hovercraft floats on cushion of air experiment 1332:18-19

Model hovercraft, how to make from shoe box lid 1073:23

Simple hovercraft experiment using paper plate and balloon 1318:21

Simple hovercraft from styrofoam tile, how to make 1416:24-25

Surface skimmer skims over tabletop on cushion of air experiment 1030:28-29

The hovering Hovercraft—model demonstrates moving force of air 575:37

Water hovercraft, how to build from plastic lid, straw and balloon 1208:52-53

HUBBLE, EDWIN

Hubble discovery; measuring red shifts of galaxies shows speed of objects 1478:142-143

HUBBLE TELESCOPE

Resolution of a lens demonstration 1394:190-191

HUMAN ANATOMY

Chest cavity—make working model of the chest cavity 294:85-86

The human mouth 294:80-81

HUMAN BEHAVIOR

Astronomical influences on behavior in animals and humans experiment 1062:109

Sky observations linked to holiday activities on Earth project 1062:116-117

HUMAN BODY. *See also* **BLOOD; EARS; EYES; FINGERPRINTS; HAIR; HEART; INTESTINES; KIDNEYS; LUNGS; NAILS; SENSES; SKIN; TEETH**

Air in human body 128:87

Anatomy—experiments to show parts of 128:206-210
Are you as long as your arms (Primary) 551:unpaged
Are you in shape—experiment 586:112-114
Arm—working model of an arm—how to make 577:project #4
Arm and finger; bone and muscle model of arm and finger, how to make 1063:183
Arm, make a working model arm of cardboard 794:15
Arm; model arm from cardboard, how to make 1287:9
Arm; model moving arm from cardboard experiment 1420:9
Arms; length of your body compares to length of your forearm project 1210:66-67
Arms; your arms rise by themselves after being pressed against door frame 1083:26-27
Balance—how good is your sense of balance 482:84-86
Balance; how steady are you experiment 1506:42-44
Balance; light effect on your balance experiment 1506:43-44
Blood cells and mouth lining cells—how to prepare microscope slides 729:28-29
Blood cells under microscope 713:74-76
Blood circulation—blood circulation model—how to make 577:project #2
Blood circulation; blood flows in one direction in blood vessels experiment 1397:78
Blood flow; watching your blood flow experiment 1506:14-15
Blood pressure has daily pattern experiment 1220:16
Blood pressure; experiments with blood pressure 1425:216-225
Blood vessels—model to illustrate 334:83-84
Blood; blood sample model demonstrates blood flow 1270:15
Blood; coin in hand trick demonstrates gravity of blood flow experiment 1216:16-18
Blood; how space suits affect an astronaut's blood demonstration 1394:214-215
Blood; make model that shows what blood is made of experiment 1517:20-21
Blood; William Harvey's circulation of blood experiment 1133:3.001
Body systems—experiment about 628:13-14
Body temperature—computer experiment 665:28
Body temperature; curling up to keep warm experiment with foil and thermometer 1275:28
Body temperature; world chart shows places hotter than body temperature 1275:28
Bones—bony project activities [Primary] 759:57
Bones—can you change your height overnight—experiment 628:32
Bones—dissect a long bone (beef) 335:27
Bones—how true is the expression "dry as a bone"—experiment 628:28
Bones—knot a bone (chicken) 335:23
Bones—landmarks 335:25
Bones—shrink test for backbone 335:29
Bones—what happens when minerals are removed from bones—experiment 628:29-30
Bones and muscles—how to make model of arm, foot, heart and neck 128:206
Bones, why are long bones hollow experiment 794:28
Bones; how does your backbone move experiment with straws and thread spools 1189:16-17
Brain—brain dissection (beef) 335:115
Brain—dominance tests 335:121
Brain and learning experiments 1267:54-56
Brain can measure speed of sound experiment 1432:130-132
Brain tricked by reversing signals coming from your ears experiment 1069:173
Brain; experiments to test brain use 1063:193-195
Brain; hemisphere dominance experiment 1267:60-64
Brain; how big is your brain demonstration 1276:13
Brain; logical thoughts to solve puzzles; find way through maze experiment 1276:17
Brain; make skull cap model to show brain control of body actions experiment 1517:32-33
Brain; memory test; how good is your memory experiment 1276:19
Brain; the more you use your brain the better you use it experiment 1063:194
Brain; trick to make brain remember things better experiment 1063:195
Breath contains carbon dioxide experiment 1322:17-20
Breathing—see how much air you exhale—experiment 637:27-29
Breathing rate (breaths per minute) of various people experiment 1506:16-17
Breathing rates while resting and running (Primary) 637:24
Breathing; air-measuring device for how much air you blow out experiment 1279:10
Breathing; are carbon dioxide molecules in your breath experiment 831:61-64
Breathing; how much air do you breathe experiments 1506:18-21
Cartilage cells under microscope—observe 713:69-70
Cell; make model cross section of a cell experiment 1517:16-17
Cells—demonstrate controlled burning that happens in your cells 335:74
Cells—observing cells of the human body—cheek—lining cells 294:16-17
Cells of onion under a microscope, observe 794:13-14
Cells; demonstrate semi-permeability of cell membrane experiment 904:146-149
Cells; movement of particles through a membrane experiment 904:144-145
Center of gravity different in males and females experiment 904:204-205
Center of gravity test for human body 881:16-17
Center of gravity; where is your center of gravity experiment [Advanced] 871:4.003
Cheek cells observed under microscope experiment 1425:14
Cheek cells under microscope—observe 713:63-64
Chemicals in the human body; diagram shows proportions of main chemicals 1271:33
Circulatory system—how does blood flow in blood vessels—experiment 628:49-50
Circulatory system—how does the circulatory system work—experiment 628:48-49
Collect and lift fingerprints experiment 1506:95-97
Colors of clothing effect on body experiment 1506:88
Cooling the body on hot summer day experiment 1506:86-87

Detecting carbon dioxide in your breath experiment 1425:253

Digestion—acid test to see what happens in your stomach 630:32

Digestion—charting the food tube 335:77

Digestion—digestion of protein by enzymes in human body—experiment 482:34-37

Digestion—digestive system—experiment to demonstrate 40:7-13

Digestion—how does digested food get into the body—experiment 628:77-78

Digestion—how does food move through the digestive tract—experiment 628:67

Digestion—how does saliva work—experiment 628:68

Digestion—starch and spit test 335:78

Digestion; chewing aids digestion experiment 1004:2.002

Digestion; does concentration of food enzyme affect its activity experiment 1395:171-176

Digestion; does shape of intestine increase absorbency experiment 1395:170

Digestion; does some digestion occur in the mouth experiment 904:202-203

Digestion; effects of saliva on a starch experiment 1395:168-169

Digestion; enzyme effect on starch in digestive tract experiment 1395:171-176

Digestion; enzymes break things down experiment 1273:21

Digestion; enzymes from saliva experiment using soda crackers and baby food 1370:69

Digestion; function of digestive enzymes experiment 1395:165-170

Digestion; how does acid pH affect enzymatic activity on starch experiment 1395:174

Digestive system—what happens to the food in your body 482:28-37

Digestive system in cardboard robot, making 792:26

Digestive system; make life-size model digestive system project 1517:28-29

Disease; how a disease is spread experiment 1267:66-67

Ear model demonstrates how you hear sounds experiment 1037:8-9

Ear; direction of sound we hear; construct game to test experiment 1045:10-11

Ear; ear model from cardboard tube, and paper cone, how to make 1037:8-9

Ear; hearing test; ability to hear based on age experiment 1093:26

Ear; model of human ear; working model demonstrates how we hear experiment 1045:8-9

Ears—ears as sound wave collectors—diagram 366:174-175

Ears—why people get dizzy 563:49-50

Ears; change sound coming to your ears experiment 1028:71

Ears; do we really need both ears experiment 1209:12-13

Ears; do you need both ears to hear experiment 1189:38-39

Ears; eardrum model demonstrates how we hear 1333:10-11

Ears; ears are sound receivers and direction finders experiment 1253:22

Ears; ears help find position of sound; blindfold test experiment 1276:7

Ears; experiments with hearing 1425:148-152

Ears; hearing aid and how it works experiment with shoe box and rubber band 1209:14-15

Ears; how sound is heard experiment 1405:39

Ears; how we hear experiment using spoons and cardboard tube 1433:113-115

Ears; how your ears work experiment with piece of balloon over juice can 1209:10-11

Ears; locating source of sound experiment 1132:94-1-94-2

Ears; model ear demonstrates how ear works, how to build 1028:67

Ears; model ear from paper and aluminum foil, how to make 1284:6-7

Ears; popping ears due to change in air pressure experiment using balloons 1208:24-25

Ears; shape of ear that is best for collecting sound experiment 1209:18-19

Ears; why we get dizzy explanation 1433:132-133

Ears; why we have two ears for hearing experiment 1037:10-11

Endurance; flexibility, agility and coordination experiment 1267:37

Endurance; testing endurance by measuring VO_2 max experiment 1267:26-34

Endurance; training effects on muscle strength and endurance experiment 1267:34-37

Endurance; VO_2 max highest amount of oxygen body uses during hard work 1267:26-34

Epidermis cells are rubbed off demonstration with soap and sandpaper 904:194-195

Esophagus; peristalsis pushing action in esophagus walls demonstration 1273:19

Evaporation of water and other liquids from body experiment 1506:87-88

Exercise and the breathing rate 253:114

Experiments and projects about construction and function of body 1220:4-48

Eye—the sensitive pupil 585:108

Eye lens; demonstrate how eye lens works experiment 904:152-153

Eye model shows how light enters eye and forms images experiment 1037:16-17

Eye model, how to make 993:16-17

Eye sees things for short time after they are out of sight experiment 1037:20-21

Eye, why do we have two eyes experiment 794:31

Eye; cat and mouse game on paper demonstrates blind spot in each eye experiment 1037:18

Eye; effect of light on size of eye pupil experiment 904:156-157

Eye; effect of tiring the rods and cones in the eye experiment 904:158-159

Eye; hole in the hand experiment 1063:345

Eye; how the eye works demonstration with lamp and sheet 1063:344

Eye; human eyes equally sensitive to all colors of light experiment 1092:48

Eye; monocle makes words clearer experiment 904:154-155

Eye; pupil of eye controls how much light enters eye experiment 1132:80-1-80-2

Eye; touch the dot experiment 1063:345

Eye; tricks your eyes play; 9 experiments to try 870:48-50

Eye; two eyes are better than one experiment; target practice game demonstrates 1037:19

Eyes—catch ball with two and then one eye 335:88

Eyes—comparing the eye with a camera chart 482:76

Eyes—how to dissect an eye 128:209

Eyes—stereo vision—experiment to show what eyes see separately and together 335:89

Eyes—what is your best reading distance—experiment 482:78-80

Eyes; blind spot experiment 1506:51-52

Eyes; blind spot in eye and how to find it experiment 1390:7

Eyes; blind spot in your eyes experiment 1132:10-1-10-2

Eyes; blind spot; testing your blind spot experiment 1088:27; 1276:10

Eyes; brain sometimes makes you see things that aren't there experiment 1037:22

Eyes; contrast and brightness and their effects on vision experiments 1088:64-71

Eyes; do eyes help you keep your balance experiment 1020:132-134

Eyes; dominant eye experiment 1506:55-56

Eyes; eye-color from parents' genes experiment 1048:26

Eyes; eyeball model that sees; make from papier mache covered balloon 1088:17-19

Eyes; focusing near and far experiment 1506:52-54

Eyes; fovea and periphery of eye see differently experiment 1088:24

Eyes; fovea of eye sees color but periphery of eye is color blind experiment 1088:25

Eyes; hair and eye color are inherited together or separately project 1210:70-72

Eyes; hand steadiness tester, make to test two eyes working together 1069:166

Eyes; how do images of large objects fit on retina of eye experiment 1402:28-31

Eyes; how eye lens works experiment 1405:36-37

Eyes; how your eyes work experiments 1088:22-31

Eyes; illusion of depth from motion experiment using lamp, clay, pipe cleaner 1088:61

Eyes; images like those on the retina experiment 1506:49-51

Eyes; irradiation or spillover effect on vision experiment 1476:217-218

Eyes; jerky motion of your eyes experiment 1088:30

Eyes; judging distance with one eye and both eyes experiment 1506:56-57

Eyes; light and color and their effect on vision experiments 1088:72-82

Eyes; make model eye to show how eyes work experiment 1517:36-37

Eyes; making sense of what you see experiments 1088:42-51

Eyes; model eye demonstrates how eyes work experiment 1028:68

Eyes; model eye or pinhole camera, how to make 1092:38

Eyes; model eye, how to make 909:147

Eyes; motion makes something look 3-D experiment 1088:62-63

Eyes; movement; how you see movement experiments 1088:52-63

Eyes; peripheral vision test for how much peripheral vision people have 1506:64-65

Eyes; persistence of vision experiment with cards 1506:61-63

Eyes; pinhole camera demonstrates how lens in eye works 1308:12-13

Eyes; pupil's reaction to bright and dim light experiment 1506:48-49

Eyes; right-eyed or left-eyed test using pencil 1433:111-112

Eyes; rod cells and cone cells experiment 1506:58-59

Eyes; see blood vessels in your eyes experiment 1020:134-136

Eyes; stereo vision; seeing depth with your eyes experiment 1088:34

Eyes; two eyes are better than one for 3-D vision experiment 1088:40

Eyes; two eyes working together let you judge distance experiment 1069:166

Eyes; why do we need two eyes experiment 1283:10

Eyes; why it is hard to see when you walk into a dark theater experiment 1088:70

Eyes; wobble detector demonstrates need for two eyes to judge distances 1028:70

Eyes; your eyes as cameras experiment 1506:59-60

Feet—are both your feet the same size 381:103

Feet—plaster of Paris mold of feet—how to make 364:73

Feet, how hard can you push with one foot experiment 794:28-29

Feet; plaster of Paris cast of your feet, how to make 1370:34-35

Finger power demonstrations 1005:22

Fingernails—how fast do they grow experiment 762:59-60

Fingernails; different parts of a fingernail experiment 1402:64-67

Fingernails; how fast do they grow experiment 1506:93-94

Fingers—finger hangs loose 228:20

Fingers; ridges on fingertips affect ability to pick up objects experiment 1397:60-63

Forearm cardboard model to demonstrate third-class lever experiment 1400:19

Forearm is like third-class lever experiment 1400:16-19

Genes—taking stock of your variations 335:125-127

Goo from you 259:30-36

Growth—activities and demonstrations of (Primary) 675:6-28

Growth—how cells split (Primary) 675:9

Growth chart—wildflower growing chart—how to make 651:46-47

Growth; how fast do you grow experiment 1506:89-90

Hair—under a magnifying glass (Primary) 675:21

Hair acts as insulator to help maintain body temperatures project 969:28-29

Hair under microscope—compare to other kinds 713:40-41

Hair, how strong is a hair; how to measure experiment 794:29

Hair; how many hairs on different peoples heads experiment 1506:91-92

Hair; test strength of human hair strand with weights experiment 1370:26-27

Hair; what does hair look like under microscope 901:158

Hands; iodine and cornstarch test for sweat glands in hands experiment 1370:28

Hands; thumb's importance to human hand for grasping things experiment 1168:31

Hearing—play a music game 32:24-25

Hearing; do ear trumpets work experiment 1284:16

Hearing; ear protectors experiment; which materials work best 1284:28

Hearing; game to check friends hearing experiment 1209:20-21

Hearing; hearing test; ability to hear based on age experiment 1093:26

Hearing; hearing through water experiment 1284:22

Hearing; how accurately can people hear under noisy conditions experiment 1020:125-129

Hearing; how do speaking tubes work experiment 1284:17

Heart—hear heartbeats through loudspeaker experiment 723:10-11

Heart—age chart to show age and heart rate 334:85

Heart—arterial blood pressure 334:23-24

Heart—blood—chart of blood flow 335:52

Heart—blood flow—tourniquet to demonstrate blood flow 335:54

Heart—blood flow in the heart 334:15

Heart—blood pressure—design to show high blood pressure 334:81

Heart—blood vessels in the heart 334:15

Heart—can you see your pulse—experiment 628:46-47

Heart—chemicals—effect of chemicals on the heart 334:42-44

Heart—display to show how astronauts can be protected in space 334:85

Heart—feel the beat—experiment with match and lumps of clay 571:27

Heart—heart's role in oxygen/carbon dioxide exchange 334:37-38

Heart—high blood pressure—heart's response to standing still 334:51-55

Heart—how can you hear your heart—experiment with heart beat and pulse 482:56-62

Heart—how can you hear your own heart—experiment 628:44

Heart—how hard does the heart work—experiment 628:47-48

Heart—lifestyle and blood pressure 334:22-23

Heart—listen to your heart beat—tube of colored water demonstrates beat 577:project #1

Heart—muscles in the heart 334:15

Heart—pollution and oxygen consumption of small animals 334:39-42

Heart—pulse—match stick pulse meter 335:55

Heart—pulse—stress test to measure against athletes 335:56-58

Heart—respiration and heart rate 334:56-57

Heart—simple things to do to check pumping action 620:28-29

Heart—smoking and the heart 334:32-33

Heart—tennis ball squeeze 335:50

Heart—Valsalva's experiment—influence of respiration on blood circulation 334:38-39

Heart—what makes your heart work harder—experiment 628:45-46

Heart beat—display to show how the heart beats 334:84

Heart beat increased by caffeine observe goldfish under microscope 713:73-74

Heart beats heard through stethoscope, how to make 1036:18

Heart beats of people of different types and ages during activities experiment 1506:12-13

Heart beats per minute of various animals chart 1506:13

Heart circulatory system—experiment to demonstrate 40:13-18

Heart dissection (lamb heart)—how to 335:53

Heart drugs—effect of drugs on the heart 334:44-50

Heart electrocardiograph—using and analyzing the electrocardiograph 334:25-32

Heart emotions—controlling responses to emotional stress 334:68-71

Heart emotions—effect of emotional stress on the heart 334:66-68

Heart environment—reacting to the environment 334:24

Heart exercise—display to show effect of exercise on the heart 334:82

Heart exercise—effect of exercise on heart muscles 334:74-76

Heart exercise—recovering from exercise 334:23; 334:55-56

Heart function—design to show how the human heart functions 334:81

Heart model—how to build—diagram given 748:65

Heart sounds 334:23

Heart sounds—make stethoscope to hear heart 335:51

Heart stimulants—effect of stimulants and depressants on heart rate 334:72-73

Heart structure—demonstrate the structure of the mammalian heart 334:84

Heart structure—different heart structures 334:35-37

Heart—arteries and veins demonstration 759:12-13

Heart—pumping action demonstration 759:11-12

Heart; does your heart pump as hard as does giraffe's; make heart pump 1399:83

Heart; experiments with heartbeats and pulses 1425:207-215

Heart; heart beats have daily pattern experiment 1220:15-16

Heart; heartbeat sounds and what they mean experiment; make stethoscope 1209:44-45

Heart; how much blood moves with each heartbeat experiment 1397:78

Heart; make pumping model to show four chambers of heart working experiment 1517:22-23

Heart; simple stethoscope to hear heart sounds, how to make 1370:54-55

Heart; stethoscope from tubing and funnel lets you hear heart beats, make 1433:105-107

Heart; why does heartbeat of mammals make a sound experiment 1397:76-79

Heartbeat; observe vibration of match on wrist experiment 904:188-189

Heartbeats; hear, see and calculate heartbeats, how to do 881:10-11

Height; gravity affects human height experiment 1399:80-83

Hormones; "feed back loop" amount of hormone in your blood demonstration 1272:22

Horsepower of human body measured experiment 1020:130-132

How fast do fingernails grow—measure length and weight—experiment 482:81-83

How much air do your lungs hold experiment 794:30-31

Human body like a machine—experiment 628:12-13

"Internal clock"—does your body have a clock in it—experiment 482:89-91

Intestines—demonstrating absorption in the small intestine 148:68

Intestines; demonstrate how shape of intestine increases absorbency experiment 904:198-199

Intestines; movement of soluble materials thru small intestine lining 904:200-201

Jaw cardboard model to demonstrate third-class lever experiment 1400:15

Joints; make styrofoam block joints experiment 1517:10-11

Joints; wooden model joints, how to make 1069:158-159

Kidneys—how does filtration work in the kidneys—experiment 628:84-85

Kidneys—kidney dissection (lamb) 335:86

Kidneys—measure flow of liquid thru 335:84

Kidneys; how kidneys work as filtering system experiment 1517:31

Larynx—how your larynx works—demonstrate with balloon (Primary) 513:16-21

Ligaments; flexibility test for 881:12-15

Limbs—limb levitation 335:117

Lips; upper lip as temperature detector experiment 1083:21

Liver; bile from liver lets oils and fats mix with water demonstration 1185:25

Lung capacity—how to measure with homemade spirometer 335:64

Lung capacity—who has the largest lung capacity 333:54-56

Lung capacity computer project and survey 584:19-24

Lung capacity experiment; data table given 1004:2.005

Lung capacity experiment 901:154-155

Lung capacity test 881:36-37

Lung capacity tester, how to make 1069:164

Lung model and capacity tester—how to make 366:126-127

Lung model from plastic bottle and balloon, how to make 1069:165

Lung model, how to make 993:32-33

Lungs—lung capacity experiment 721:90

Lungs—model shows how air is taken into lungs 737:25

Lungs—"bad breath" experiment with jar, candle and breath from lungs 563:161-162

Lungs—breathing model of lungs—how to make 482:63-69

Lungs—can you simulate breathing by building a model—experiment 628:55-56

Lungs—carbon dioxide from lungs turns limewater cloudy 597:7

Lungs—changes in rate and depth of breathing 334:57-64

Lungs—charting oxygen intake 335:63

Lungs—experiment to show air in 40:4-7

Lungs—experiment to show how lungs work 128:210

Lungs—hear the way sounds change in your lungs 637:7

Lungs—how do lungs work—experiment 628:54

Lungs—how much air do your lungs hold in one breath—experiment 628:56-57

Lungs—how much air is in your lungs—experiment to test lung capacity 482:71-73

Lungs—how much carbon dioxide do you produce in your breath—experiment 628:59-61

Lungs—is cigarette smoking really harmful—experiment 628:62-63

Lungs—limewater test for carbon dioxide 676:38

Lungs—lung power—experiments 563:114-115

Lungs—measure air you can blow out in one breath 618:28

Lungs—measure how breathing changes when you exercise 618:29

Lungs—measuring lung capacity 253:112-113

Lungs—measuring respiratory minute volume 334:65-66

Lungs—model—demonstrate how lungs work 293:27-28

Lungs—model lung—how to make 335:62

Lungs—model to demonstrate breathing 334:83

Lungs—models—two bottles demonstrate two methods of breathing 532:105

Lungs—nose and throat connection 335:67

Lungs—percussing—how to 335:60

Lungs—respiratory model—making 436:66

Lungs—spirometer—how to make to measure lung capacity 577:project #3

Lungs—test lung exhaust air over candle 335:65

Lungs—the breathing machine—make your own lung model 571:26

Lungs—the oxygen-carbon dioxide exchange 334:64-65

Lungs—tidal, vital and total capacities of lungs—how to measure 507:1899

Lungs—what is in breath—experiment 628:58

Lungs how much air do you breathe experiment 762:60-62

Lungs; air in your lungs experiment; measure amount with plastic bottle 1376:28

Lungs; amount of air in your lungs experiment 1230:58-59

Lungs; balloon and straw in glass demonstrate breathing air into lungs 1330:12-13

Lungs; balloon model of lungs shows how you breathe, how to make 1189:20-21

Lungs; breath contains carbon dioxide experiment using limewater in jar 1435:95-96

Lungs; breathe into limewater; carbon dioxide experiment 959:76

Lungs; carbon dioxide in breath detected by chemical indicator experiment 1427:36-37

Lungs; how big are your breaths experiment plastic cup, straw/bowl of water 1278:17

Lungs; how far can you blow experiment 1279:23

Lungs; how fast can you blow experiment using anemometer, how to build 1279:23

Lungs; how much air can lungs hold experiment 993:33

Lungs; how much air can your lungs hold experiment with gallon jug and tubing 1189:26-27

Lungs; how much air can your lungs hold experiment 1517:24-25

Lungs; how much air do lungs hold experiment using rubber tubing and jar 1433:92-94

Lungs; how much air do lungs hold experiment 909:84

Lungs; how much air do you breathe in experiment 1489:19

Lungs; how much air your lungs hold experiment 1161:6

Lungs; how we breathe experiment with model showing how lung works 1506:22-23

Lungs; how your lungs work model using plastic bottle and balloons 1279:9

Lungs; Joseph Black's breathing out carbon dioxide experiment 1133:3.006

Lungs; measure amount of air that can be forced out of lungs experiment 904:186-187

Lungs; measure amount of air that can be forced out of lungs experiment 1479:41

Lungs; measure amount of air you can exhale experiment 1397:82-83

Lungs; measure breath you take in and blow out experiment 1370:64-65

Lungs; measure how much air comes out of your lungs experiment with soap bubble 1482:42-43

Lungs; measure how much air your lungs hold experiment 1255:5

Lungs; measure lung air capacity using lung model experiment 1395:153-158

Lungs; measure your lung capacity experiment 1063:185

Lungs; measuring air volume of lungs experiment 1425:245-247

Lungs; model of moving lungs experiment, use plastic bottle, balloons, straw 1208:16-17

Lungs; model of the diaphragm and lungs made with jar, tubing, balloons 1425:241-243

Lungs; model of working lung using jar, tube and balloon, how to make 1433:88-91

Lungs; model to show how your lungs breathe experiment 1370:62-63

Lungs; second-hand smoke reduces lung capacity in children experiment 1195:69-77

Lungs; spirometer measures amount of air in lungs experiment 1220:18

Lymph nodes; lymph nodes swell and feel hard during infection experiment 1270:13

Memory—association of ideas helps your memory 381:94-98

Memory and learning; does high glucose liquid enhance memory experiment 1267:56-57

Memory; game to test your short-term memory, how to make 1517:35

Memory; optical illusions show how brain can be fooled experiment 1517:34

Mind—a trick of the mind—experiment 563:52

Mouth bacteria experiment with different mouthwashes 997:126-127

Mouth chewing chemical reactions experiment 905:108-109

Movement—test how bones and muscles work together 623:28-29

Movements; teach your body some new movements experiment 1276:25

Muscle—"body feedback"—experiment—mystery motion 585:146-147

Muscle—muscle, tendon, joint dissection 335:46

Muscle fatigue—experiment to test 586:118

Muscle fibers; which are fast-twitch fibers 881:18-19

Muscle learning 335:119

Muscle pairs—measure strength of experiments 586:116-118

Muscle strength affected by sugar—experiment 630:43

Muscle tissue under microscope—observe 713:68-69

Muscles—arm, make a model arm 335:39

Muscles—can you build a model showing how an arm muscle works—experiment 628:36-37

Muscles—can you hold a pencil—experiment 563:47

Muscles—dissecting and magnifying muscles (beef) 335:40

Muscles—experiment to demonstrate 40:25-30

Muscles—flexibility test 335:48

Muscles—hairpin dance to observe contractions 335:43

Muscles—heart muscle explanation (Primary) 645:26-27

Muscles—how do cooking methods make meat tender or tough—experiment 628:38-39

Muscles—how do muscles work in pairs—experiment 628:35-36

Muscles—investigating muscle pain 253:108-109

Muscles—lever lifters 335:44-45

Muscles—measure strength of finger muscles—experiment 538:112

Muscles—moving madness—test of your muscles 571:40

Muscles—muscle fatigue experiment 400:37

Muscles—muscle habit—demonstration 563:49

Muscles—muscle landmarks 335:41

Muscles—muscles need exercise demonstration (Primary) 645:28-33

Muscles—skeletal muscles—demonstration (Primary) 645:14-21

Muscles—smooth muscles—demonstration (Primary) 645:20-25

Muscles—the rising arms—experiment 563:51-52

Muscles—what happens when muscles become tired—experiment 628:40-41

Muscles—working model to demonstrate how muscles move and control bones 436:16-17

Muscles control movement of bones experiment using wooden models, how to make 1433:81-84

Muscles in arm (biceps and triceps)—demonstration (Primary) 645:4-13

Muscles in face, arms and leg help you move (Primary) 645:1-3

Muscles—make a popgun to demonstrate force of muscles 699:7

Muscles; arm model to show how muscle works; made from cardboard tubes 1278:13-14

Muscles; contraction of muscles experiment 1425:175-179

Muscles; effects of temperature and fatigue on muscle action experiment tables 1004:2.003

Muscles; experiments with anatomy and actions of muscles 1425:168-174

Muscles; how arm muscles work experiment using chicken wing; data tables given 1004:2.004

Muscles; make working muscle model experiment 1517:12-13

Muscles; why your muscles get tired experiment 1189:8-9

Muscles; wooden model of arm demonstrates movement of muscles experiment 1069:161

Muscular computer activity project 584:30-31

Muscular control testing device—how to make 577:project 57

Nails; how fast do your nails grow experiment 901:156

Nerve cells; location of nerve cells on your body experiment using toothpicks 1189:18-19

Nerves—exploring nerve reflexes 253:110-111

Nerves—making a 'nervousness' tester 179:133-134

Nerves; nerve machine tests your nerves; make from battery/wire/bulb 1253:32-33

Nervous system—can trial and error improve your learning—experiment 628:106-107

Nervous system—what are reflex actions—experiment 628:101-103

Nervous system—what is your reaction time—experiment 628:99-101

Nervous system; make model of nervous system experiment 1517:18-19

Nose trick—hang spoon on end of your nose 228:18-19

Organs of the human body—experiment to demonstrate 128:209-210

Overweight; overweight people and reducing diets experiment 1267:51

Pain—a pinch for pain—experiment 563:61-63

Power—how powerful are you—experiment 586:115-116

Pulse—count your pulse [Primary] 757:81

Pulse—does pulse always remain the same experiment recording sheet given 747:33-34

Pulse—experiment to demonstrate pulse 128:210

Pulse—see the pulse beat—experiment 563:64-65

Pulse—see your pulse move 381:101

Pulse—show pulse with match stick 94:27

Pulse—what is pulse and how can it be measured 402:56-57

Pulse counter from match and tack, making 794:16

Pulse increases with exercise experiment 760:18-19

Pulse rate activity 748:63

Pulse rate, how to measure 1246:32-33

Pulse rate; how does gravity affect pulse rate experiment 1399:83

Pulse rate; measure how long pulse rate gets back to normal after race 1278:23

Pulse, how does exercise affect your pulse experiment 794:31

Pulse; find your pulse points; make a pulse meter experiment 1063:184

Pulse; ice makes your heart beast faster experiment 1083:14

Pulse; pulse meter to count your pulse experiment 1370:52-53

Pulse; pulse rate, how to observe using ball of clay and toothpick experiment 1189:44-45

Pulse; see pulse in wrist with straw in clay ball experiment 1506:10-11

Pulse; test your fitness during exercise by recording pulse rates 1287:29

Pulse; watching your pulse with wooden match on wrist, how to do 1433:98-100

Purification system; make model of kidneys and bladder experiment 1517:30-31

Reaction time—how quickly can you react 400:44

Reaction time—measure someone's reaction time—experiment 586:114-115

Reaction time—method to test reaction time 381:90-93

Reaction time experiment 1389:11

Reaction time experiments 993:24-25

Reflexes—dollar drop 335:117

Reflexes—tests for 762:57-58

Reflexes and reaction time experiments 1425:105-111

Reflexes; compare person's reaction time with apparatus experiment 930:4

Respiration—measuring effect of CO_2 in blood on breathing rate 148:70

Respiration experiment; test for carbon dioxide in exhaled breath 1395:177-182

Respiration; breathe into limewater; carbon dioxide experiment 959:76

Respiration; compare breathing rate of fish and humans experiment 1395:136

Respiration; does gender affect amount of carbon dioxide exhaled experiment 1395:177-182

Respiration; exercise increases breathing/heart rate/temperature experiment 1441:95

Respiration; exhaled breath experiment; carbon dioxide produces acid in water 1396:70-72

Respiration; limewater used to test for presence of carbon dioxide experiment 1395:177-182

Respiration; red cabbage extract used as test for carbon dioxide experiment 1395:177-182

Respiration; test for carbon dioxide in your breath experiment 1396:170

Rhythms of temperature of pulse of your body—experiment 640:99-101

Running experiment; how to measure your stride 1389:19

Saliva—test for enzymes in human saliva 482:32-34

Saliva; effects of saliva on a starch experiment 1395:168-169

Saliva; enzymes from saliva experiment using soda crackers and baby food 1370:69

Senses—experiments to demonstrate senses 128:207-209

Senses—how good are your senses of taste and smell—experiment 628:103-105

Senses—smell, what your nose knows—experiment 571:16

Senses—taste—the taste test experiment 571:17

Simple observations and experiments about the human body and how it works 1131:8-29

Size—how large is your body—what is volume in pints—bath tub experiment 538:117

Size; how big is the average person your age; chart and compare project 901:151-152

Skeleton—experiment to demonstrate 40:18-25

Skeleton of human joints made with toothpicks, how to do 898:67

Skin—blood flow—write a secret message on your arm 228:22

Skin—chart the sensitive spots on skin 335:17

Skin—do sunscreens prevent sunburn—experiment 628:24

Skin—evaporation—test for evaporation 335:12

Skin—experiment to demonstrate 40:30-34

Skin—how does sweating keep you cool—experiment 628:82-83

Skin—sensors—map the sensors on the back of your hand 335:16

Skin—sweat glands—test to locate in palms of hands 335:13

Skin—under a magnifying glass (Primary) 675:18

Skin—what are your senses of temperature—experiment 628:17-18

Skin—what skins can taste 366:214

Skin—where are the wear areas of your skin—experiment 628:25

Skin—where can you find the sweat pores of your skin—experiment 628:22-23

Skin epidermis; demonstrate how epidermal cells are rubbed off experiment 1479:42

Skin protection needed from rays of sun experiment using newspapers/cellophane 1228:22-23

Skin receptors project, data sheet given 817:18

Skin touch receptors experiment 1220:17-18

Skin; effect of light on skin color experiment 1405:40-41

Skin; how does our skin protect us project 901:159

Skin; make model of skin that shows what goes on beneath skin experiment 1517:14-15

Skin; pain receptors in skin experiment 1506:26-28

Skin; sense receptors in your skin, how to find experiment 1369:10-11

Skin; temperature receptors in skin experiment 1506:28-30

Skin; test for sensitivity of different parts of skin experiment 904:196-197

Skin; touch receptors in skin experiment 1506:24-26

Skin; where is skin most sensitive experiment 1369:12-13

Skull; make cardboard skull with hinged jawbone experiment 1517:8-9

Sleep habits and sleep cycles of humans and animals experiment 1506:98-99

Smell—play a smell game 32:22-23

Smell important to recognizing and tasting food experiment 1506:33-34

Smell; can the acid in lemon reduce fish odor experiment 831:72-74

Smoking—display to illustrate dangers of smoking 334:82

Snoring; what makes a person snore experiment 1405:42-43

Sound and the ear—experiment to demonstrate 40:39-44

Sound and the voice—experiment to demonstrate 40:34-39

Spinal cord; gravity effect on spinal cord experiment 1399:80-82

Spinal cord; model of spinal cord from cardboard tube and straw 1276:13

Spine model from thread spools and sponge show cartilage function making 754:16-17

Stereo vision experiments 1088:32-41

Stomach—things that go growl in the stomach observations 607:16

Stomach; borborygmus, stomach rumbling, how to demonstrate 1330:66-67

Surgical procedure; light travels through tube in dark box experiment 1019:16-17

Sweat affected by clothes you wear experiment 881:20-21

Sweat glands; iodine and cornstarch test for sweat glands in hands experiment 1370:28

Sweat glands; locating the active sweat glands in the body experiment 1425:94

Taste—play a taste game 32:20-21

Teeth—acid—demonstrate acid attack (use eggshell) 335:35

Teeth—cast—make a cast of your teeth 335:32

Teeth—dissection—tooth dissection—how to 335:34

Teeth—green teeth—food coloring on plaque 607:21

Teeth—how can you reduce plaque on your teeth—experiment 628:30-31

Teeth—make chart to show which foods have sugar and which do not 619:29

Teeth—nippers, rippers, grinders—test 335:33

Teeth—plaque—red alert—demonstrate 335:36

Teeth—test for plaque 619:28

Teeth—the acid test on eggshells 607:21

Teeth; make model molar tooth experiment 1517:26-27

Teeth; sound vibrations through our teeth experiment 1432:58-59

Temperature—graph body temperature during day 333:56-58

Temperature—how good a heat producer are you—experiment 629:30-31

Temperature—what is normal temperature of human body 402:55-56

Temperature—what regulates temperature of body—experiment 628:91-92

Temperature magic—cellophane fish experiment 697:32

Temperature; body temperature has daily pattern experiment 1220:15

Tendons—action of tendons demonstrated with chicken foot 577:project #5

Tendons—how can you pull a toe by the "string"—experiment 628:37-38

Tendons; how tendons work experiment with chicken foot or chicken wing 1168:29

Tendons; what are tendons and how do they work experiment 901:167

Test for starch, sugar, fat and protein in digestive processes experiment 1425:193-197

Thumb; how important is your thumb experiment; data tables given 1004:2.001

Thumbs—great thumbless survival test 335:30

Tongue—experiment to find the four taste bud areas on human tongue 482:44-47

Tongue—tongue map 366:215

Tongue, mapping taste areas of your tongue, how to do 835:44-46

Tongue, where can you taste certain things test 792:25

Tongue; make gigantic styrofoam model tongue experiment 1517:39

Tongue; map your tongue experiment 1028:71

Tongue; map your tongue's taste buds experiment 1369:32

Tongue; mapping your tongue for taste experiment 1238:8-9

Tongue; taste receptors on tongue experiment 1506:31-32

Tongue; wet or dry tongue affects tasting time experiment 1506:35

Tongue; which part of the tongue is most sensitive to taste experiment 901:181-182

Tooth soaked in Cola has decay experiment 1069:163

Touch—experiment to test how close or far apart skin touch receptors are 482:87-88

Touch mystery touch box—how to make 32:18-19

Touch—sense of touch 32:16-17

Urine—how can you test urine for glucose (sugar)—experiment 628:85-87

Using urinalysis techniques 148:81

Virus; virus transmission experiment 1267:68-69

Vision; binocular vision test 881:39

Vocal cords, stretched rubber band—demonstrates 637:13

Vocal cords; demonstrate how vocal cords change pitch of sound experiment 1479:40

Vocal cords; female singers have higher voices than male singers experiment 1209:58-59

Vocal cords; vocal cord sound vibrations compared to balloon sounds 1189:6-7

Voice; seeing sound experiment; see picture of your voice 1385:9

195

Voice; why your voice doesn't sound like you on a tape recording experiment 1209:16-17

Watts of power your body can generate experiment 1063:182

Weight—how much do you eat in relation to your weight 607:27

Weight; chart of weight of 100 pound person on the Moon and planets 1157:36

What are we made of; water and food demonstration 901:14-15

What holds you up—investigating the bones and muscles in your body 482:10-27

What is a blood pressure cuff demonstration 901:17-18

HUMAN ECOLOGY

Ideas for human ecology projects 1297:6

HUMANS

How are humans similar and different 253:98-99

HUMIDITY. *See also* **HYGROMETERS; MOISTURE; PLANTS**

Cobalt chloride clown changes as humidity changes experiment 1014:116

Cobalt chloride humidity block, how to make 882:25

Cobalt chloride indicator reacts to moisture in air experiment 814:49-50

Coil hygrometer from cardboard strip, how to make 1104:14

Compare wet-dry bulb and hair hygrometer experiment 900:89-90

Demonstrate absolute humidity 295:43-44

Evaporation tells us about humidity; wet-dry bulb hygrometer experiment 900:87-88

Hair hygrometer—how to build 507:1880

Hair hygrometer and milk carton hygrometer—making 767:24-25

Hair hygrometer measures humidity in air experiment 1211:30; 1372:46-48; 834:125-126; 1405:82

Hair hygrometer measures moisture in air experiment, how to make 1063:443

Hair hygrometer, how to make and use experiment 1396:13-18

Hair hygrometer, how to make using wood, cardboard and hair 1439:95-97

Hair; which hair works best in hygrometers; build hair hygrometer 1020:61-65

High humidity makes body sticky and uncomfortable experiment 1439:38-39

How does water get into the air experiment 1003:70

How to make hygrometers 128:94-95

Humidity and comfort—experiment 585:127-129

Humidity indicator experiment using cobalt chloride, paper and paint 1244:34

Humidity indicator, how to make 1439:69-71

Humidity indicator, making 885:66-67

Hygrometer from coffee filter paper soaked in cobalt chloride experiment 1396:18

In air—hair hygrometer measures—how to set up 364:101

Is cobalt chloride moisture indicator reliable 381:66-68

Make a hygrometer to measure 91:62-65

Make hygrometers to measure humidity experiment 834:54-55

Measure humidity in air with wet and dry bulb hygrometer experiment 1474:32

Measure moisture in the air experiment 900:85-86

Measure using Stevenson screen and wet and dry bulb thermometers experiment 1311:43

Measuring humidity of air experiment using wet and dry thermometers 1134:2.002

Measuring humidity with a hair 617:40

Measuring humidity with a hygrometer, how to make 1516:107-111

Moisture detecting mermaid, how to make 1007:84-85

Relative humidity computation computer project 1021:158-160

Relative humidity measured by psychrometer demonstration 1023:148-149

Relative humidity table 1003:113

Salt used to measure humidity demonstration 1023:150-151

Salt used to measure humidity in air demonstration 1479:80

Saturated air has 100 % humidity experiment 1405:81

Static electricity demonstrates humidity levels 1023:152-153

Static electricity used to indicate humidity levels experiment 1405:82-83

Temperature humidity index 1003:115-116

Warm air holds more water than cool air experiment 767:24

Water dissolves in air—experiment 693:42

Water dissolves in air; measure humidity experiment 959:191-193

Water dissolves in air 295:42-43

Water in the air-find absolute & relative humidity of air inside—experiment 586:23-25

Water vapor in air measured by psychrometer experiment, how to make 1281:17

Weather house predicts weather experiment; make from cardboard, wood, hair 1480:161

Weather indicator—make to measure humidity 472:2231

Wet and dry bulb thermometers measure humidity in air experiment 1359:14

Which areas of home are most humid project 969:84-85

Whirling weather wheel—how to make a hygrometer 573:28-29

HUMIDITY—RELATIVE HUMIDITY

Calculate the relative humidity experiment 1070:23

Dew point used to determine relative humidity experiment; graph to use given 1063:446-447

How to calculate indoor relative humidity experiment 1465:113

Hygrometer measures humidity, make with two thermometers/wood/dowels 1476:150-151

Hygrometer measures relative humidity; how to make project 1296:1986

Indicator to measure relative humidity experiment, how to make 1447:46-49

Making a hygrometer 253:59-61

Measure amount of moisture in the air 291:40-41

Measure relative humidity in room chart given 715:124-126

Measuring relative humidity with a hygrometer, how to make 1516:107-111

Psychrometer measures relative humidity of air experiment, how to make 1479:80

Psychrometer, constructing to calculate relative humidity experiment 860:187-189

196

Relative humidity determines our comfort experiment 1294:62-64

Relative humidity measured by psychrometer experiment; psychrometer graph given 1063:444-445

Relative humidity measured by psychrometer, how to make 1439:98-101

Relative humidity of air 55:145-151

Relative humidity; how to find using dry and wet bulb thermometers experiment 959:113-114

Wet and dry bulb thermometers measure relative humidity of air experiment 1480:160

HUMMINGBIRDS
Feeding bottle with nectar, how to make 810:59

Hummingbird feeder, recipe for nectar, how to make 778:52-53

Nectar feeder (recipe given) for hummingbirds—how to make (Primary) 463:22-33

Sugar water feeder—recipe—making 697:68

HUMUS
How much humus is there in soil experiment 1134:1.006

Lawn clippings turn into detritus and humus experiment 1441:97

Relationship between earthworms and humus in the soil experiment 1450:60-65

Relationship between humus and diversity and number of insects experiment 1096:83-89

Which soils contain most humus project 969:15-16

HUNGER
Cost of eating in poor countries compared to eating in U.S. project 1059:46

Growing food for people isn't easy experiment using plants 1059:38-39

No room on Earth to grow food experiment using beet seeds 1059:98

Waste not, want not project with wasted school lunches 1059:48

HURRICANES
Eye of hurricane yo-yo experiment 1003:66-67

How ocean water rises to create storm surge experiment 1465:97

Satellite pictures from newspaper of cloud/weather patterns experiment 1447:99-101

Wind and pressure systems 243:44-45

HYALLELA
Adventure 11—we watch some acrobats perform—hyallela under hand lens 29:57-59

HYDRA. *See also* MICROSCOPE; PROTOZOA
Adventure 5—we follow in the footsteps of Hercules—hydra under microscope 403:14-18

Encouraging sexual reproduction—experiment 484:52-53

Experiments with hydras 500:142-143

How well can a hydra stick (stay attached)—experiment 484:52

Hydra's response to temperature, chemicals and foods experiment 864:90-91

Hydras and light—experiment 484:53

Make a miniature algae jungle 279:34-36

Nematocyst explosion—experiment 484:53

Observation of hydra experiment 1425:31-33

Reproduction and regeneration of hydra experiment 978:93-94

Self repair of hydras—experiment 484:52

Water animals and plants killed by heat pollution from industry experiment 1074:84-85

HYDRAULIC MODELS
Working dredger, how to build from plastic bottles, wood, cardboard 1460:26-27

HYDRAULIC PRESSURE
A hot water bag lifts books 281:30

Air pressure can lift things; balloon and books experiment 940:32-33

Diving baby—hydraulic pressure and buoyancy 205:77-81

"Hydraulic" machine uses water to lift weight, how to make 1033:24-25

Lift a load with water experiment 1028:118

Liquid under pressure pushes with a force experiment 1198:11

Plastic tubing and syringes demonstrate how hydraulic systems work 1179:135

HYDRAULICS
Hydraulic lift demonstration using two water filled plastic bottles 1310:22-23

HYDROCARBONS. *See also* AIR POLLUTION
Methane physical structure, how to make 1403:8-11

HYDRODYNAMICS
Evangelista Torricelli's velocity of jets of liquid escaping receptacle 1133:4.006

HYDROELECTRIC GENERATORS
Hydroelectric generator with paddle wheel experiment 1126:28-29

HYDROELECTRIC POWER. *See also* TURBINES; WATERWHEELS; WIND TURBINES
Construct a working model of a hydro-electric power plant 167:160-164

Miniature hydroelectric system, how to make 577: project 58

Water powered wheel produces energy experiment 1269:56

Water turbine, simple, how to make from knitting needle, cork, container 1212:17

HYDROGEN. *See also* ELECTROLYSIS; WATER—ELECTROLYSIS
Collecting hydrogen gas 346:65-67

Experiments to show 84:88-89

Henry Cavendish's discovery of inflammable air experiment 1133:2.005

How to make hydrogen 146:34-35; 157:14

How to prepare hydrogen 128:102-103

Popping gas 146:44

Produce chlorine, hydrogen and caustic soda experiment 768:80-81

HYDROGEN PEROXIDE
Enzyme reaction rate of potato catalase 273:46-47

Enzymes catalase removes it from plants 273:44-45

Hydrogen peroxide changes into water and oxygen experiment 1405:55

Hydrogen peroxide changes into water and oxygen with help from potato 905:96-97

HYDROLOGIC CYCLE. *See also* WATER CYCLE
Fish tank setup with pond and marsh plants demonstrates hydrologic cycle 1171:49-53

HYDROMETER
Construct hydrometer to determine buoyancy of pure and salty water experiment 1396:126-127

Demonstration hydrometer—how to make 577:project #14

Density measured by hydrometer, how to make 935:49
Density of liquid measured by hydrometer, how to make 1179:141
Density of liquids measured by hydrometer experiment, make from clay and straw 1310:13
How to make 41:156; 77:18-19; 106:22-23; 368:46-48; 381:87-88
Hydrometer from plastic cup and straw, how to make 1248:10-11
Hydrometer measures density of liquid experiment 1028:21
Hydrometer measures density of liquids, how to make from straw and clay 1212:23
Hydrometer measures density of water and oil experiment, how to make 1521:26-27
Hydrometer to measure density of a liquid—how to make 573:34
Investigations with 41:162-164
Liquids float and sink experiment 1028:21
Make a hydrometer 71:17-20; 98:16; 436:44-45
Salt content of water measured experiment 1023:210-211; 1405:87
How does hydrometer work experiment 900:72-73; 902:40-41

HYDROPONICS
Algae grown in saltwater environment experiment 1061:60-61
Bean plants grown hydroponically experiment 1241:33
Bulbs grow in water experiment 1008:75
Can plants be grown without soil 402:80
Construct a hydroponicum for growing tomato plants experiment 1395:33-38
Containers for growing plants—box garden 384:56-61
Containers for growing plants—bushel basket vegetables 384:62-65
Containers for growing plants—plastic bag 'pillow' planter 384:68-69
Containers for growing plants—plastic pail planter 384:66-67
Cornell soilless mix—how to make 384:53-55
Culture medium—water culture and sand culture—how to 398:80-84
Cuttings—how to grow 398:85-86
Do hydroponic plants require less root systems experiment 714:63-64
Do plants grown with hydroponics have dormancy periods experiments 714:65-66
Experiments and projects in hydroponics 398:89-90
Feeding plants—nutrient solutions from fertilizers—how to make 384:47-52
Gardens without soil—how to do 382:46-50
General purpose nutrient solution formula 1061:44
Gravel garden—gravel, nutrient solution and seedlings project 483:56-57
Grocery store nutrient solution formula 1061:44
Growing plants in solutions of ground up materials of same plants experiment 1061:64-65
Growing plants without soil experiment 878:40-41
Home grown tomatoes 384:30-33
How to grow vegetables hydroponically 1061:39-50
How to start seed 398:84-85
Hydroponic unit—how to make 398:86-88
Light needed for photosynthesis process in hydroponic grown plants experiment 1061:66-67
Make your own hydroponic garden 607:62-63

Minerals from soil and hydroponic mineral solutions affect plant growth 1060:69-72
Nitrogen-fixing bacteria replace nitrogen compounds in hydroponic solution 1060:112
Nutrient solution formula—general purpose formula—making 714:45
Nutrient solution formula—grocery store solution—making 714:46
Nutrient solution formula—poor man's formula—making 714:46
Nutrient solution formula—U.S. Dept. Agriculture—making 714:45
Nutrient solutions—how to make 398:79-80
Nutrient solutions, recipes and how to make 1061:44
Nutrient solutions, recipes for 1061:44
Organisms and bacteria in soils not completely destroyed by heating experiment 1061:51-53
pH of solution best for growing radishes experiment 1061:70-72
pH ranges that are best for growing common vegetables 1061:42
pH scale test for water used to grow plants hydroponically 1061:40-42
Plant food—how to mix your own 384:49-50
Plant grows in hydroponic solution experiment 1060:71
Plants grow in water solution experiments 1014:151
Plants grow without soil experiment 1063:412; 1176:22-23
Plants grown hydroponically require more light than plants in soil experiment 714:67-68
Plants in water—how to grow 384:22-29
Poorman's nutrient solution formula 1061:44
Potting plant in soilless media—how to 384:34-37
Potting plant in soilless media by double pot method 384:38-41
Seedlings growth compared when grown in liquid fertilizers and soil experiment 1395:15-19
Subirrigation systems for flooding method to feed and water plants—how to 384:42-46
Training roots to hang onto artificial support experiment 1061:68-69
U.S. Deptartment of Agriculture nutrient solution formula 1061:44
Water types evaluated for effect on plant growth experiment; tap, distilled, et 1061:56-57
Which growing medium produces best plant growth experiment 714:51-52

HYDROSTATICS
Make a siphon 161:66-67

HYDROTROPISM. See also **PLANTS—TROPISMS**
Growing seeds in tilted planter experiment 1061:83-84
Hydrotropism and geotropism compared as to which affects plant the most 1061:94-95
Plants grow toward water experiment 978:55-56; 1368:40
Roots of pea seeds grow toward water experiment 913:33
Roots react to source of moisture experiment 1060:75-76

HYDROXIDES
How to precipitate aluminum hydroxide 122:124-126
How to precipitate milk of magnesia 122:122-124
Purify water with aluminum hydroxide 122:128
Settle muddy water with alum 122:126-127

HYGROMETERS
Coil hygrometer from cardboard strip, how to make 1104:14

Compare wet-dry bulb hygrometer and hair hygrometer experiment 900:89-90

Decorative simple hygrometer, making 891:54

Evaporation tells us about humidity; wet-dry bulb hygrometer experiment 900:87-88

Hair hygrometer—how to build 507:1880

Hair hygrometer—how to set up 364:101

Hair hygrometer—making 585:58-59; 705:73-74

Hair hygrometer and milk carton hygrometer—making 767:24-25

Hair hygrometer measures humidity demonstration 1023:146-147

Hair hygrometer measures humidity in air experiment 834:125-126; 1211:30; 1372:46-48; 1405:82

Hair hygrometer measures moisture in air experiment, how to make 1063:443

Hair hygrometer, how to make using wood, cardboard and hair 1439:95-97

Hair; which hair works best in hygrometers, build hair hygrometer experiment 1020:61-65

How to construct wet and dry bulb hygrometers to calculate relative humidity 175:64-65

How to make from wood, plastic and hair 1237:84-85

How to make wet and dry bulb and hair hygrometer 128:94-95

How to make 55:147-148; 95:25; 112:18; 176:96; 234:98; 629:56-57

How to use hygrometer; relative humidity chart given 1012:27

Human hair hygrometer, making 891:54

Humidity in air measured with wet and dry bulb thermometers experiment 1474:32

Hygrometer from cardboard, tape and hair, how to make 1248:14-15

Hygrometer from thermometers and tissue paper, how to make experiment 1519:19

Hygrometer measures humidity, make with two thermometers/wood/dowels 1476:150-151

Hygrometer measures relative humidity; how to make project 1296:1986

Hygrometers from hair and coffee filter experiment 1396:13-18

Make a huge one 381:74-75

Make hygrometers to measure humidity experiment 834:54-55

Making a hygrometer 253:59-61

Measure air moisture with simple type hygrometer—how to make 563:21

Measure moisture in the air experiment 900:85-86

Measuring humidity and relative humidity with a hygrometer, how to make 1516:107-111

Milk carton hygrometer, making 767:140; 1003:111-112

Oatmeal box, rubber bands and thermometer hygrometer, making 1012:26

The whirling weather wheel—how to make a hygrometer 573:28-29

HYGROSCOPIC TOY
Make a fortune-telling fish 550:54-57

HYPERBOLIC PARABOLA
Build a shell of thread 557:68-69

HYPOTHERMIA
Can animals be preserved by freezing and then revived by warmth 402:53-54

HYPSOMETER
Hypsometer, making to measure how tall something is 999:59-62

Hypsometer measures height of things, how to make 1115:41-43

I

ICE. *See also* **FREEZING; SNOW; WATER—
FREEZING**

A cold fact 222:92-93
An ice puzzle—experiment with water contraction 585:141
Arctic antics 142:46
Black's experiment with heat needed to melt ice 1156:86-88
Breaks rocks 382:106-107
Burning ice—how to demonstrate 87:84
Change ice to liquid water using heat energy experiment 1519:26
Cool under fire 222:96
Cooling curves of ice and water experiment 1515:88-91
Cut ice with a string experiment 663:10; 909:18
Cutting ice with wire and forks experiment 1415:32
Determine most effective of seven substances used to melt ice experiment 997:60-61
Does ice melt in boiling water 161:83-84
Does ice sublimate experiment [Advanced] 762:113-114
Expands when frozen experiment using plastic bottle 996:27
Experiments 117:102-115
Experiments with ice (Primary) 580:unpaged
Freezing experiments 538:38-39
Freezing point—fun with ice and salt 281:59
Freezing point—fun with ice cubes 281:59-60
Fresh water freezes faster than salt water—experiment 492:38
Frozen water takes up more space 288:14-15
Fun experiments with ice 75:89
Heat energy to melt ice experiment 1441:71
Heat loss and surface area relationship in melting ice experiment 959:167-169
Heat of fusion of ice experiment 871:3.009
Heat of fusion of ice: energy to melt ice—experiment 585:139-140
Heat to melt ice—heat flow and surface area 586:22-23
Hidden heat of melting ice experiment 1515:81-84
Hidden heat; melting, boiling, freezing and condensation experiment 1515:76-84
Hot water freezes first—experiment 670:72
How long does it take ice to melt experiment 1519:25
How to make from wood 429:72-74
Ice afloat—miniature icebergs 249:29
Ice afloat expanding ice 249:28
Ice and fork trick 249:27
Ice and salt make things very cold; make ice cream experiment 1032:28-29
Ice castles, how to make 850:113
Ice cube castle—how to make 494:94
Ice expands and floats experiment 867:17-18
Ice floats in water experiment 1066:54
Ice is lighter than water 281:23
Ice keeping: the art of insulating ice with mini-icehouses 586:20-21
Ice melting raises water level experiment (Primary) 989:20
Ice melts under pressure—experiment 492:38
Ice needs space experiment 663:9; 909:17
Ice on a string 360:60
Ice on a wire experiment 906:50-51

Ice takes up more space than water experiment 1073:93
Ice test to show water expands when it freezes 492:38
Ice tree—how to make 75:94-95
Ice under pressure experiment 762:114-116
Investigating the clarity of ice 604:36-39
Latent heat of melting ice experiment 1515:81-84
Lift ice with a match experiment 663:11; 909:19
Lift that cube—salt causes ice to melt 202:20
Make ice colder experiment using ice cubes, salt and thermometer 1393:11
Make ice melt and instantly freeze again 249:26-27
Making a column of ice 150:36-37
Melted ice takes up less space than frozen 611:49-50
Melting—does melting ice raise water level 381:87
Melting experiments 538:40-42
Melting ice—finding ways to make ice melt faster 586:22
Melting ice from solid to liquid experiment 1090:26
Melting ice in air and in water experiment 959:39
Melting point—show that pressure can lower melting point of ice 385:75-76
Melting under pressure—experiment 563:75
More than you started with 280:17
Mystery ice experiments with soft drinks 563:131
Orange icebergs 280:18
Polar ice caps; why don't they melt away experiment 852:52-53
Power of ice as it expands experiment 1281:33
Power of ice to weather and shatter rocks experiment 1480:106
Pressure causes ice to change to liquid experiment with ice cubes 1251:36-38
Pressure melting—bet you can cut through an ice cube 228:46-47
Pressure melting—experiment 656:27
Pressure melts ice experiment 1378:17
Properties of ice; six experiments [Primary] 880:16-18
Racer, ice imp, how to make 948:16-18
Racer, super slider for ice, how to make 948:12-15
Regelation—experiment 585:132-133
Right through ice but the ice stays whole 161:82-83
Salt affects the grouping of water molecules into ice crystals experiment 1403:52-55
Salt lowers freezing point of ice experiment 1435:10-12
Salt lowers the melting point of ice experiment 867:22
Salt makes ice melt faster 26:91-92
Salt melts ice experiment 884:56-59; 1498:11
Salt put on icy sidewalks for a reason experiment 1020:148-150
Salt test to see ice melt rapidly 492:41
Show how ice behaves at its melting point 183:36-39
Show how pressure causes ice to melt 183:44-47
Show that melting ice absorbs heat 385:68
Soap bubbles make an ice crystal ball 161:81
Storing ice; ice cube keeper contest experiment 959:39
Strength of ice experiment 1126:14
Surface area of ice affects rate of melting experiment 1159:113-114
Temperatures of ice, ice water, and ice brine vary experiment 884:60-63
The great ice experiment 573:22
Thompson's caloric theory experiment; there is no mass change when ice freezes 1156:94

200

Water and ice (Primary) 232:85
Water expands during freezing experiment 1484:121
Water expands when it freezes 360:44
Water vapor from air changes to solid ice experiment 1325:29-32
What can ice do to glass experiment 766:unp.
What happens when you put salt on ice experiment 1519:24
Wire meets ice—experiment 670:91
Wire pressure melts ice demonstration 882:6
Wire through ice illusion experiment 881:85

ICE CREAM. *See also* **SIMPLESSE**
Baked ice cream 607:89
Homemade ice cream—making 607:72-73
How ice cream freezes experiment 1289:36-37
How to make 358:82-83; 629:144-145
Ice and salt makes things very cold; make ice cream experiment 1032:28-29
Ice cream machine, how to make, recipe given for ice cream 835:72-74
Instant ice cream 249:24
Lowering freezing point; make ice cream experiment 871:3.010
Make your own ice cream experiment 1028:35
Make your own ice cream 161:79-80
Making homemade 219:45-48
Making ice cream 600:20-21; 697:43-44
Old recipe for ice cream (1861),—how to make 630:83-84

ICE CUBES
Bet you can cut through an ice cube and it will seal itself behind you 228:46-47
Boiling water with 291:57
Catch a cube on a string experiment 996:26-27
Catch ice cube on string experiment 906:49-50
Crushed ice cubes melt faster experiment 721:33
Cut an ice cube with thin wire experiment 1079:101-103
Experiments with 107:1-10
Freeze with fingers 585:131-132
Ice cube experiments 884:64-66
Ice cube lift with string experiment 814:27-29
Ice cube necklaces for hot day, making 1014:105
Ice cube on a string experiment 827:87
Ice cubes on threads stick together experiment 721:31
Ice on a string—experiment 629:146
Insulation used to keep ice cube from melting experiment 1159:110-113
Lift cubes with string and salt experiment 766:unp.
Lift ice cube by thread 228:37
Lift ice cube with string experiment 1244:17
Lift ice cube with string experiment 937:50-51
Magic ice cube—cut through ice cube without halving it 291:59
Melt ice cube by applying pressure experiment 937:52-53
Melting ice cubes experiments 793:31
Melting point of ice experiment 939:99-100
Pick up ice with string experiment 924:65
Pick up one ice cube with another ice cube experiment 1231:38-39
Regelation exp.—the melting and refreezing of ice in warm water 604:48-51
Storing ice; ice cube keeper contest experiment 959:39
String trick with ice cubes experiment 829:3-4

Surface area of ice affects rate of melting experiment 1159:113-114
Water gets bigger when it freezes experiment 1230:38-39
Water is heavier than oil ice cube experiment 1289:34-35
What will melt ice cube experiment [Primary] 744:24-25
Wire cuts through ice cube experiment 939:101-106; 1028:34; 1032:26-27; 1229:50-51

ICE CUBES—FREEZING POINT
Lift ice cube out of glass of water with string 399:4

ICE NUCLEATORS
Particulate matter affects ice-nucleating protein freezing water experiment 1450:157-162

ICE WATER—MELTING
Can water containing ice get warm 381:81-84

ICEBERGS. *See also* **BUOYANCY**
Floating iceberg demonstration with balloon and water 1384:23
Heat loss and surface area relationship in melting ice experiment 959:167-169
How much of the iceberg floats experiment 877:106-109
Ice cubes demonstrate 636:104-106
Ice floats demonstration with ice cubes 1429:7
Iceberg floats and melts in soda bottle experiment 1310:8-9
Iceberg floats in water experiment 1316:23
Miniature iceberg, how to make 360:59
The danger of icebergs 93:70-71
Why an iceberg floats 399:46
Why do icebergs float experiment 852:35-36

ICICLES
Make it yourself icicles 236:148
Measuring snow and icicles experiment 885:46
Study icicles and make your own experiment 1063:286

IDIOPHONES
Wine glasses and water idiophone make music experiment 1209:66-67

IGLOO
How to do 277:130
Model—how to make 415:45-46
Large igloo from strong cardboard, how to make 1518:42-43

IGUANAS
How to care for 279:11-13

ILLUSIONS. *See also* **MAGIC; OPTICAL ILLUSIONS**
Ames window illusion 229:66-69
Aristotle's illusion 229:10-11
Benham's top—a color illusion 205:142-147
Bizarre boomerangs—a size illusion 205:151-154
Black art magic show 350:140-150
Book has several illusions for you to try and demonstrate 229:1-142
Decapitated princess illusion 350:137-140
Illusion circles 732:43-44
In advertising 1:32-33
In clothing design 1:33-36
In interior decorating 1:36
Magic illusion wheels, how to make 600:22-23
Magical illusions; create using transparent plastic sheets 1443:69
Make paper plate illusion 203:69
Matter through matter—a motion illusion 205:139-142
Optical illusions 293:27
Possessed pendulum—a depth illusion 205:147-150
Quick money—reaction time 205:136-139

Simple experiments to show 202:28-41
Staircase illusion 27:80

IMAGE RECOGNITION SYSTEM
Coin recognizer reader, how to make 1249:26-30

IMAGES—REVERSE. *See also* **MIRRORS**
Magic mirror 27:93-94

IMPRINTING
Becoming a mother to a duckling in the field and in the
laboratory 266:129-132

IMPULSE—MAGNETIC
Experiment 350:24-25

INCAS
Experiments of their culture 326:entire book

INCHWORM
Inchworm model toy—how to make (Primary) 466:18-19

INCINERATION
Incineration reduces volume and weight of garbage experiment 1012:88

INCINERATORS
Burning garbage creates smoke and ash experiment chart
for results given 1173:55-57

INCLINED PLANE. *See also* **SIMPLE MACHINES—
INCLINED PLANE; PYRAMIDS**
How does an inclined plane make work easier—
experiment 586:71-72
Measuring the effect of an inclined plane 180:31
Rolling uphill 16:35-39
Show function of 128:118
Show long way is easier 125:24-27
Use of a small force to lift a greater weight 253:177-178
What is an inclined plane experiment 902:179-182

INCUBATORS
Box incubator for hatching eggs, how to make 810:69-70
Chicken egg—making 436:45
Construct a chicken incubator 167:170-184
For reptile eggs—making 532:47
Hatching eggs; building incubator, how to 9:64-65;
57:71; 128:59; 196:42-53; 293:21-22; 866:154-155

INDIAN FAKIR TRICK
Bet you can lift a jar of rice with a knife 228:90

INDIAN PICTURE WRITING
Project 244:21-22

INDIAN RICE TRICK
Indian rice trick with ruler in jar of rice grains demonstration 1523:25

INDIAN ROPE TRICK
Experiment 16:68-70

INDIANS
Experiments of their culture 324:entire book

INDICATORS. *See also* **CHEMICAL REACTIONS**
A clear shake 346:147-148
A detective and his solution—how to make several indi-
cator solutions 565:158-159
A simple indicator experiment 563:168
Acid—base indicators from natural materials—how to
prepare 586:62-63
Acid indicator from red cabbage leaves, how to make
1435:56-59
Acid test sticks—making 676:29
Acid-base secret messages experiment; data tables given
1004:4.001
Acidity of water experiment using red cabbage indicator
1325:12-17
Acids and bases effect on red cabbage indicator experi-
ment 1396:67-72

Apples drawn on paper turn red with indicator experi-
ment 814:50-52
Beet root indicator, how to make and test on different
substances 790:30-31
Bloody fingerprint trick 966:104-106
Blue again and again 346:144-147
Blue to red with ammonium chloride 146:55
Blush test on drawing on photo 346:142-144
Brom thymol blue solution, how to make 1395:197
Brom thymol blue testing solution, how to make
1396:203
Cabbage capers, colorful experiment 870:76-78
Cabbage indicator identifies lemonade as acid experi-
ment 1405:64
Cabbage indicator used as test for acid and base experi-
ment 1405:64
Cabbage indicator, how to make 905:190-191
Cabbage juice indicator to test for acids and bases, mak-
ing 935:26-27
Cabbage makes acid sauerkraut experiment 976:36
Cabbage paper indicator, how to make 905:192-193
Cabbage water acid-base indicator, making 888:39-40
Cabbage water indicator experiment 884:80-83
Clear water turns red and then clear again experiment
781:42-43
Cobalt chloride indicator reacts to moisture in air experi-
ment 814:49-50
Color magic—experiment 605:14-15
Designing pH indicators to identify acids and bases
180:23
Dracula's favorite soap makes your hands turn red experi-
ment 827:108
Dyes extracted from plants can be used as indicators for
acids/bases experiment 1403:63
Experiments to show 400:70
Experiments 83:26-27; 84:31-33
Experiments with cobalt chloride—moisture from flies in
bottle 174:38-39
Flower petal indicators for acid or base experiment; data
table given 871:3.020
Flower petals used as indicators for acid or base experi-
ment 1175:79
Homemade indicators 30:37
Household items tested for acid or base experiment
976:38
Identifying acids and bases with litmus paper experiment
1526:87-90
Identifying unknown ingredients experiment using liquid
indicator 1435:97-100
Indicator identifies salt solutions; acid, base, neutral exp.
Data table 871:3.019
Indicator sticks and papers, how to make 1526:93
Indicator sticks from cabbage solution, how to make us-
ing cotton swabs 1175:80
Indicator, making to see if soap is acid or base experi-
ment 781:40-41
Iodine as a test for starch 84:52-53
Iodine indicator 400:71
Iodine to show starch 85:29
Is cobalt chloride moisture indicator reliable 381:66-68
Jam experiments demonstrate indicators 563:165-166
Limewater solution, how to make 1395:197-198
Limewater testing solution, how to make 1396:203
Litmus paper—how to make using red cabbage and blot-
ting paper 1414:12-13

Litmus paper indicator experiment 400:70
Litmus paper test for acids, bases and neutrals experiment; data sheet given 818:5
Litmus paper tests for solutions experiment 885:90-91
Magic color change with cabbage leaves experiment 924:2-3
Magical liquid color 146:58-59
Make a green man 146:54-55
Make a rock pool using calcium chloride 146:54
Make a shipwrecked sailor and a life jacket in a jar 146:31
Make a snowman in a jar 146:29
Make a snowman 146:29
Make a weather man 146:30-31
Make a weather picture 186:23
Make your own from materials in your home 381:18-22
Make your own indicator 553:28-29
Making indicators to identify acids and alkalies 598:28-29
Monosaccharide testing solution, how to make 1396:204
Of acid and alkaline 77:34-35
Paper indicators, how to make using paper towels or paper coffee filters 1435:60-61
Phenolphthalein indicator, how to make 1479:64
Phenolphthalein indicator, how to make 1526:91-92
Phenolphthalein test solution 84:28-30
Phenolphthalein testing solution, how to make 1396:204
Purple cabbage indicator, how to make 904:36
Purple palette—a chemical indicator 205:130-133
Purple potion experiment 684:22-23
Red cabbage extract testing solution, how to make 1396:205
Red cabbage extract, how to make 1395:198
Red cabbage indicator—making with experiments 749:30
Red cabbage indicator experiment 1018:22-23
Red cabbage indicator experiment to test for acids and bases 980:41-42
Red cabbage indicator for acids and bases experiment 814:52-54
Red cabbage indicator identifies pH of common household products exp. 871:3.021
Red cabbage indicator paper, how to make experiment 976:39-40
Red cabbage indicator strips test for acidity, how to make 1330:48-49
Red cabbage indicator tests for acids and bases experiment 1063:168
Red cabbage indicator tests substances for acid or base; chart given 960:28-30
Red cabbage indicator tests things found in kitchen for acid/alkaline 1016:34-37
Red cabbage indicator used as test for acids and alkalies experiment 1508:25
Red cabbage indicator used as test for acids and bases experiment 1286:20
Red cabbage indicator, how to make 1115:86; 1228:17; 1271:16; 1362:16; 1480:100; 1527:26-27
Red cabbage indicator, make to test for acid or base experiment 1179:37
Red cabbage juice shows presence of hydroxyl and hydrogen ions experiment 1403:60-63
Red cabbage litmus paper, how to make 827:49
Sodium chloride testing solution, how to make 1396:205
Starch and iodine trick 538:81

Substances are acid or base experiment using cabbage leaves as indicator 1175:79
Tea used as indicator for acids and alkalies experiment 1508:24
Telltale chemicals—indicators show if substance is acid or base 72:56-57
Telltale colors test 676:26-28
Test for acids and bases with phenolphthalein and turmeric 346:88-92
Test for acids of base—make your own indicators and pH scale 594:10-12
Test for vitamin C 585:100-101
Test substances with red cabbage indicator experiment 1028:54
Thought waves for milk 346:148-150
Turmeric indicator test experiment 980:43
Turmeric indicator, how to make 1526:91
Turmeric testing paper for presence of a base, how to make 905:204-205
Turmeric testing paper indicator identifies a base experiment 1405:64
Turmeric testing paper indicator works with wet materials experiment 1405:65
Unsweetened grape juice indicator, how to make 1526:90-91
Use of universal indicator paper 157:24
Use red cabbage to test reactions of acids and bases 203:87
Water to wine to water magic tricks 346:140-142
Weather indicator for humidity 472:2231
What happens when bubbles are blown into phenolphthalein solution 174:34-35
White paper turns blue; test for starch experiment 781:44-45
Wood ashes change water to a base experiment with red cabbage juice indicator 1251:88-90

INDOOR POLLUTION. *See also* **POLLUTION— INDOOR**
Bucket of water collects traveling air pollution experiment 1328:36-37
Test pollution in your home with vacuum cleaner and cloth filters experiment 1328:34-35

INDUCTION. *See also* **ELECTROMAGNETIC INDUCTION; FARADAY, MICHAEL**
How to induce an electric current in a wire by means of a magnet 63:76-77

INDUSTRIAL WASTES
Effect of industrial pollutants on behavior of convict Cichlid fish experiment 997:89-90

INERTIA. *See also* **NEWTON'S FIRST LAW OF MOTION**
Bar of soap flies up and into glass experiment 1079:15-16
Bet you can remove only the bottom checker of a stack without touching it 228:82-83
Block of wood and string to demonstrate 360:91
Blocks and coins in stack demonstrate inertia 847:3-8
Break a stick with air 291:123
Break piece of thread with hammer attached experiment 1079:13-14
Broom trick demonstrates 203:53
Button on card demonstrates inertia 1035:14
Card and coin trick 291:119
Card, coin and glass demonstrate 905:2-3

Coin dropped into glass without touching it experiment 1009:25-26

Coin remains after card is pulled from under it demonstration 1007:53-54

Coins and piece of paper on top of bottle experiment 1063:338

Coins from under 114:97-98

Coins, card and glass of water demonstrate 847:13-14

Compare gravity and inertia; rocks on string experiment 900:21

Cut string without using sharp instrument experiment 847:20-24

Demolish the checker tower 909:103

Demonstrate inertia with card and corn 1405:44-45

Demonstrate inertia with rock and string 291:120

Demonstrate with "snap the checker" trick 202:124-125

Detecting the hard-boiled egg experiment 827:70

Drop coin into glass without touching it experiment 1005:29

Eggs away 16:13-16

Eggs-periment 670:97

Elevated napkin ring trick demonstrates inertia 1007:50-51

End of the line 16:20-22

Experiments to demonstrate 128:128-129; 186:37-39

Experiments to demonstrate inertia using paper, ping pong balls, marbles 1380:20-21

Experiments with finger and newspaper 291:124-125

Flick card and coin falls into glass experiment 1063:145

Flywheel from a button 161:19

Force affects inertia demonstration with clothespin on paper 1404:138-139

Force applied to string to break it experiment 937:36-37

Frictionless car demonstrates first law of motion experiment, how to build 1502:28-29

Fun with a clothes hanger and coin 392:12-15

Getting things moving experiment 909:100

Glass of water stays on table experiment 827:31

Gravity affects inertia demonstration 1394:208-209

Gravity pulls the taffy 280:43

Hard to start bricks moving forward 95:5

How does inertia affect objects experiment 900:224

How forces affect inertia experiment 1405:100-101

How friction affects inertia experiment 1405:101

How gravity affects inertia experiment 1405:20

How inertia works—coin in a bottle 291:122

Immovable tower 161:15-16

Inert coins 360:90

Inertia—experiment 585:45-46

Inertia demonstration 656:21

Inertia demonstrations using checkers on table and paper under wood 1243:10-11

Inertia keeps peas in spinning cup experiment 1035:28-29

Inertia tricks 399:3; 585:68-69; 600:36-37

Law of inertia demonstration with glass of water, coins, paper 1436:90-92

Lazy coin experiment 909:102

Lazy coins 95:4

Lazy newspaper won't move on table when ruler is hit 288:30-31

Magic checkers demonstrate law of inertia 1289:24-25

Magic tricks with coins demonstrates 1007:48-50

Marble and bowl demonstrate inertia and centripetal force experiment 836:68-69

Marble climbs up and down inside soda bottle experiment 1007:54-55

Marble drops into bottle without marble being touched experiment 1079:18-19

Marble in glass demonstrates inertia experiment 1009:31-32

Moments of inertia experiment 722:96-97

More about inertia 281:43

Moving objects have inertia demonstration with small toy car 1404:1290, 6, 1.6

Moving objects have inertia demonstration 1479:99

Mysterious breaking string trick 399:5

Oatmeal boxes with weights inside demonstrate 999:93-95

Object continues to move due to inertia demonstration 1479:98

Object remains at rest until force is applied to it experiment 1502:30-31

Object remains stationary due to inertia demonstration 1479:98

Object remains stationary due to inertia experiment 1405:100

Objects at rest experiments 1157:21-23

Objects at rest remain at rest 295:64-65

Odd one out 16:17-20

Overcoming inertia experiment using scale, pencils and toy car 1179:58-59

Paper removed from under bottle without tipping bottle over experiment 1079:20-21

Pendulum experiment; moving object moves unless force changes its motion 1502:26-28

Penny snap experiment 906:122

Primary experiments with inertia 100:28-32

Pull tablecloth from under plates without moving them experiment 937:34-35

Put coin in glass without touching it experiment 900:20

Reluctant movers the immobile coin—egg experiment 260:20-21

Remove bottom checker in stack of checkers experiment 1079:10-11

Sand design double pendulum experiment 906:124-125

Show with coin and glass and book 106:8-10

Simple experiments 105:32-35

Snap! Dime in jar experiment 906:120

Spinning egg demonstrates inertia 1035:15

Spinning egg puzzle experiment 909:101

Spinning eggs experiment 906:119; 1002:18-19

Stack of checkers demonstrates inertia 1007:52

Start and stop—experiments 664:12-15

Stop and go; chairs and swinging weight experiment 906:125

String around brick; lift easy and hard to demonstrate inertia 940:102-104

Swing glass of water that won't spill experiment 1007:46-47

Swings; how swings work activity 1230:10-11

Tablecloth trick experiment 909:102

Talking string demonstrates; button spins on string 827:96-97

Tell raw egg from hard-boiled egg 669:4

Testing for inertia—experiment 625:26

The rolling cans—experiment 585:44-45

Thump-marbles on ruler experiment 906:123

Toy car and passenger demonstrate inertia experiment 945:16-17

Toy car demonstrates inertia experiment 945:14-15

Toy truck with weight on string demonstrates 699:17

Understanding inertia 180:41

Uphill roller experiment 906:126

Weight effect on inertia demonstration with cola bottle 1404:132-133

What is inertia experiment 902:62

Wizard stick propeller experiment 906:127

Zip! Paper under bottle experiment 906:121

INERTIA—SPIN

Flip flop match book keeps moving 95:15

Lazy Susan keeps moving 95:14

Spinning egg stands up 95:16

INERTIA—TRICKS. *See also* MAGIC

Coin on a card 27:51-52

Energetic coins 27:50

Lazy jar 27:51

Spearing a potato 27:51

Tower of discs 27:50-51

Wandering sixpence 161:18

Where does the coin fall 161:17

Which will you break—the hairs or the stick 161:16-17

INERTIA AND MOMENTUM

A dollar bill puzzle with empty bottles—experiments 563:2-3

Balance a hatchet 563:3-4

Center of gravity experiments with pencils 563:3

Flip the penny trick 563:38

Fool your friends with inertia tricks 419:8

The elastic coins—experiment 563:1-2

INFRARED RADIATION

William Herschel's discovery of infrared rays experiment 1133:6.009

INFUSIONS. *See* HAY INFUSIONS; MICROORGANISMS—INFUSIONS

INFUSORIA

Adventure 23—paramecium, stentor, vorticella and carchesium under microscope 403:80-85

INK. *See also* CHROMATOGRAPHY; INVISIBLE INKS; SECRET WRITING

Artificially aging ink—how to make 336:28-29

Bark ink, recipe, how to make 1064:11

Berry ink, how to make 1064:11; 1368:22-23

Black ink formula, how to make 814:19-21

Change color of ink with electricity from battery experiment 781:14-15

Chromatography test with inks, food colors and plant pigments experiment 1476:129-131

Copy picture from newspaper with soap, water and mineral spirits experiment 1482:56-57

Criminal writing—test to catch forgers 162:20-21

Demonstrate color changes in chemical reactions 346:58-59

Disappearing ink 114:31-32; 114:34-35; 146:57

Green grass ink, making 935:24

Inks and pens; observe and test markings on different kinds of paper experiment 1295:113

Inks fade differently; clue in the counterfeit check experiment 814:31-33

Invisible 77:33; 87:25-31

Invisible ink, making 859:29

Invisible writing 85:22-23

Iron ink—how to make 336:24-28; 346:54-57

Iron ink, making 859:27

Lampblack ink—how to make 321:21

Lampblack ink, making 859:28

Light fastness—compare different inks with bleach 336:29-31

Liquid ink eradicator 146:57

Make fingerprints 146:57

Make ink—experiment 563:178-179

Make ink from oak apples 146:7

Making real ink disappear 147:78-79

Marbling on paper 77:21

Message written with shiny crystals, how to do 905:132-133

Nut ink, recipe, how to make 1064:11

Observe separation of colors in ink experiment 905:154-155

Oxidation—secret messages 112:12

Paper chromatography analysis 336:31-33

Permanent ink—make your own honey soot ink 336:21-24

Red ink from poppies—making 749:35

Salt writing, how to do 859:30

Spreading and rising inks 77:12-13

Steel wool ink, how to make experiment using steel wool, tea bags and vinegar 1435:74-77

Test tube holder and stand for chromatography experiment, how to make 1476:129-130

Vanishing ink—how to make 87:92

Watermarking, how to do 859:31

Write your name with hypo 176:23-24

INKBLOTS

What do you see—experiment 653:28-33

INSECTICIDES

Citrus seed and skin repellents 398:119-120

Flea and insect killer made from orange gratings 530:214

Homemade insect spray from garlic, hot pepper and onion, how to make 1265:92

Orange peel contains a natural insecticide experiment 1250:89-90

Organic insecticides—home-brewed insecticides 398:113-116

Plants produce chemicals to repel insects experiment 1324:32-36

INSECTS

Activities to identify and investigate insects [Primary] 758:57-66

Activities with insects 236:60-64

Activities with spiders 236:64

Adventure 10—we study the wings of insects under a hand lens 29:51-57

Adventure 18—become familiar with eating habits of insects under hand lens 29:89-92

Alarm pheromones experiment using ants and aphids 1096:110-117

Ant lion diggings, how to investigate experiment 1313:20-23

Antennae—adventure 13—we compare insect antennae under a hand lens 29:65-73

Antennae; make antennae to demonstrate how insects feel way around 1445:12-13

Antlions—collection, care and observation 331:69-77

Ants—care of as pets 354:13-22

Ants—collecting and studying ants 253:26-27

Ants—collection and care of 390:25-28

Ants—where are the ants going 333:87-89

Ants use chemicals to communicate with one another experiment 1096:124-129

Aphids—how to care for and observe 395:45-47

Aphids are eaten by predator insects experiment 1464:46-47

Aphids collected and studied experiment 1464:44-45

Aphids; reproduction and growth of aphids experiment 1097:70-72

Attract summer insects to white cloth taped to porch light experiment 1227:28

Backswimmers—collection and care of 390:23

Beetles; model beetle, how to make 1445:26-27

Berlese funnel—how to make to catch insects 117:41-44

Biocontrol of insect pests by parasitoid wasps experiment 1097:134-136

Body structures of an insect experiment 1097:118-119

Breathing; how insects breathe experiment 1097:107-109

Bug keeper—making (Primary) 535:35

Butterflies—collect and care for 332:61-75

Butterflies and moths—care as pets 354:23-25

Caddis fly larvae—collection and care for 390:21-23

Camouflage game; does camouflage word; use colored cards in yard/trees 1182:23

Case making insects under hand lens—adventure 25 29:122-125

Caterpillars—collection and care of 390:23-24

Caterpillars—study appetite of insect larvae 234:61

Chart of insect parts 1063:266

Clay insects—how to make 236:64

Cockroaches—catching, caring and experimenting with 163:78-81

Cockroaches—how do cockroaches live and change 253:28-29

Cockroaches favorite materials to live in experiment 1097:151-154

Collecting and observing bugs in nature, how to do 962:42-43

Color—investigation into the color preference of insects 420:117-118

Colors and scents of flowers that attract insects experiment 1183:76

Colors and scents that attract insects to flowers experiment 1182:28

Colors used by insects to hide or to warn they are poisonous game 1182:26

Colors; can insects see colors experiment 1097:73-74

Cricket as a thermometer, how to use chirps to determine temperature 1464:37

Cricket cage—how to build 395:31-39

Cricket; model bush cricket, how to make 1445:14-15

Crickets—care of as pets 354:36-42

Damage from insects when produce is grown organically or with pesticides 1096:133-138

Demonstrate night movements 94:26

Digestive system of insects experiment 1097:113-115

Disease carrying insects experiment 1097:148-150

Dissection—how to 414:25-26

Diversity and number of insects affected by amount of topsoil humus experiment 1096:83-89

Do bug lights differentiate between good and bad insects experiment 1450:20-25

Dragonflies and damselflies—collection and care of 390:19-21

Dragonflies; flying pattern and behavior of dragonflies experiment 1097:116-117

Dragonfly, how to make from balloon and pipe cleaners 1182:18

Drawing insects 430:58

Eggs—adventure 39—insect eggs under a hand lens 29:177-184

Extreme changes in temperature affects behavior of flies and insects experiment 1014:167

Fireflies—can you read by firefly light 333:83-85

Fireflies—collection, care and observation of 331:59-67

Fireflies—observe how it glows 294:67-68

Flight; fly's wings and thorax model, how to make 1445:16-17

Fly larvae; hormone flow through the larvae's body experiment 1096:29-33

Food for antlions 331:70-72

Food for crickets 331:80-82

Food for ladybirds 331:52-54

Food for praying mantises 331:43-46

Food for water striders 331:32, 35-36

Food for whirligigs 331:27-30

Footprints of beetles examined experiment using food colors 1464:65

Gall observation and collection 277:106-114

Galls from insects, how to collect and hatch 1188:21

Game; ladybugs survive the winter if summer aphid supply is plentiful 1182:27

Grasshopper—studying a typical insect 294:64-66

Habitat destruction and the biodiversity of insects experiment 1096:77-82

Hatching cocoons 117:49-51

Honeybee feeding habits experiment 1097:137-140

How does an insect walk—experiment with food coloring 414:20-21

How far can an insect jump 333:85-87

How fast do insects and small animals move 333:89-91

How to cage house flies and do investigations 163:68-77

How to make a cockroach maze 264:71-72

How to tell from other animals 40:205

Insect antennae under microscope, observe 889:60-62

Insect eating plants—insectivorous plants 279:37-38

Insect eyes under microscope, observe 889:62

Insect legs under microscope, observe 889:60

Insect mouths under microscope, observe 889:62-64

Insect parts—adventure 51—insect parts under a microscope 403:194-202

Insect pets 159:28-29

Insect populations are different in running and standing bodies of water 1096:96-101

Insect wings under microscope, observe 889:62

Insects and animals require care (Primary) 232:32

Insects attracted at night by heat or light of bulb project 969:40-41

Insects find the way in the field and in the laboratory 266:52-56

Insects in the dark—weather factors and insect populations 586:137

Insects role in pollination experiment 1097:40-41

Insects role in recycling nutrients (dead plants and animals) experiment 1097:42-44

Investigate insects in a vacant lot 233:15-22

Investigation into variations in living things 420:59-61

Is up the way out of a jar 264:70

Jumping; how far can insects jump experiment 1097:110-112

Keeping ants and building a formicarium cage for ants 430:53

Keeping water insects 159:25

Killing bottle for insects 382:62

Ladybird beetles—collection, care and observation of 331:51-57

Larvas, temperature and moisture experiment 117:47-48

Leg structures in insects experiment 1097:120-123

Looking at parts under microscope 82:55-64

Make a singing chorus of insects 332:45-53

Mealworm experiments 163:64-67

Mealworms—collection and care of 390:28-29

Mealworms; life cycle of mealworms experiment 1464:23-24

Metamorphosis of insect, show 168:21-22

Milkweed bugs, how to raise and observe 1116:28-29

Model insect, how to make 1445:6-7

Moths—collection and care of 332:61-75

Moths—light box to collect—how to make 332:64

Mouth part types of different insects experiment 1097:104-106

Movement and homes of insects activities for classroom 1291:5-6

Night insects; how insects find their way at night experiment 1097:75-77

Night-flying insects; what kind and how many of them experiment 1097:54-56

Nutritional value of artificial diet and natural diet of tomato hornworm 1096:34-38

Observe live insect habits 40:206-209

Outdoor projects with 118:81-98

Parts and structures of insects; identify, draw and label project 1295:54-57

Praying mantis—care of as pets 354:52-60

Praying mantis—collection and care of 390:24-25

Praying mantis—collection, care and observation of 331:39-49

Praying mantis—how to care for 332:55-57

Predators; ladybugs control aphids on plant experiment 1176:17

Proboscis; make to demonstrate insect feeding 1445:20-21

Protective coloration in insects; how common is it experiment 1097:30-32

Protective coloration of insects experiment 1097:27-29

Protective coloration; does it really work in insect habitats experiment 1096:118-123

Relationship between humus and diversity and number of insects experiment 1096:83-89

Relaxing jar—making 436:47

Repellents—bugs away—salt water objectionable to insects 563:154

Role insects play in decomposition experiment 1096:90-95

Scales of insects; identify, draw and label project 1295:57-61

Shape of insects brooches, how to make 1373:24-25

Silk of silkworm differs from silk of other insects experiment 1097:131-133

Slides of insect cells, how to make 990:28

Slides of insect cells, how to prepare and keep 896:28-29

Smells and taste that attract different insects test experiment 1274:25

Soil insects in three different kinds of soil experiment using Berlese funnel 1097:51-53

Soil insects; observe insects caught in funnel/bottle under light 1188:38-39

Sounds—amplifier to magnify insect sounds—how to make 364:37

Sounds; amplifying insect sounds experiment 1464:36

Sow bugs—are sow bugs afraid of the dark? 264:37

Spiders—care of as pets 354:43-51

Strip-mache insect—how to make model 646:54-56

Studying insects 234:54-55

Sugar in honey experiment; how much sugar is there in honey 1097:141-143

Sugar water attracts what animals and insects in daytime and night experiment 969:35

Survey of insects living in buildings experiment 1097:144-147

Sweeping for insects—how to 586:138-139

Taxis—behavior in daphnids—reaction to strong light 174:50-51

Testing strength of insects 118:115-118

Toy insect with wheels, how to make 1423:17

Treehoppers and leafhoppers—how to care for 332:58-60

Vision; insect eyeglasses from cardboard demonstrate how insects see 1445:11

Watch change to moth or butterfly 294:66-67

Watching insects and recording information 430:52

Water loss in insects experiment 1097:124-126

What insects live in your home and what are their living preferences experiment 1096:149-157

Whirligigs—observe movement and eating 331:28-30

Wing development on insects experiment with mealworms 1097:92-94

Wings; model to demonstrate insect defense, how to make 1445:22-23

Winter—observation and collection of 277:77-90

Winter—some common pond and stream insects 277:96-103

Winter water insects—observation and collection of 277:91-106

Winter; surviving the cold winter; how do insects do it experiment 1097:95-96

Wood lice and insects prefer dry or damp, light or dark places experiment 1182:7

INSECTS—AIR POLLUTION

Pests—growth affected by air pollution 398:60

INSECTS—BEHAVIOR

Food; what plants do insects like to eat experiment 1097:81-83

Homes; insects that make their homes in plants experiment 1097:84-86

How ants use pheromones experiment 1097:16-20

How far do insects travel experiment 1097:101-103

How insects react to a stimulus experiment 1097:24-26

Parasitoid wasps lay eggs in other insects experiment 1097:13-15

Praying mantis can eat how many insects experiment 1097:9-12

Taste receptors in blow flies experiment 1096:105-109

Taste; how insects sense taste experiment 1097:78-80

What kind of food do insects eat experiment 1097:21-23

Which parts of fly's body sense taste experiment 1096:105-109

INSECTS—BIOCONTROL. *See also* **BIOLOGICAL CONTROLS**

Parasitoid wasps' egg laying behavior experiment 1450:153-156

Using parasitoid wasps and praying mantis as biocontrol agents experiment 1450:144-152

INSECTS—CAGES

Ant cage—how to build 234:58

Aquariums—make nice cages—how to do 332:38-39

Breeding and rearing cages to observe stages of development 285:90-92

Breeding cage for rearing insects, how to make from plywood 1069:102-103

Bug cage, how to make from milk carton and panty hose 1335:123-124

Bug hotel, milk carton, making 897:101

Bug house, how to make 919:15

Bug keeper—making (Primary) 535:35

Butterfly and moth cages—how to make 395:8-14

Cake pan insect cage 236:61-62

Cans and screen cage, how to build for keeping insects 899:146-147

Cardboard box cage 395:15-17

Construct insect cage from screen wire 832:70

Creature cage—making 732:67-68

Critter cages; ideas for making (Primary) 580:unpaged

Gall cage—how to build 234:59

Homemade insect cages, making 901:117

Homes for insects from glass jars, screening and boxes, how to make 1063:427-428

How to make 57:72; 277:84-88; 332:24-26; 436:9; 442:unpaged

How to make an insect cage 40:206

Jam jar vivarium for flies 128:56

Keeping insects 159:26-27

Lady beetle cage—how to build 395:40-44

Magnifying insect cage, how to make 1464:13-14

Making insect traps and cages 118:82-98

Milk carton cage 395:18-19

Milk carton insect cage 236:61

Portable insect cage, how to make 1464:15

Praying mantis cage, how to make 1265:74

Pupa cages—how to make 234:61

Wire screen cage 395:20-21

Wire screen cage—making 697:79-80

INSECTS—COLLECTION AND PRESERVATION. *See also* **BERLESE FUNNEL**

Aquarium to study pond or stream insects, how to make 1274:15

Aspirator for catching insects, how to make 1445:9

Attracting male moths by "assembling" 414:35-36

Beater tray to collect small insects; how to make from wood and fabric 1069:34

Berlese funnel used to collect animals in leaf litter and soil experiment 1505:24-25

Bug box to house bugs; make from plywood and screening 1114:72

Bug catcher, how to make from jar and straws 1188:31

Bug house from milk carton , how to make 1071:63

Bug jar for catching insects—how to make 40:208

Butterflies and moths 395:22-30

Butterfly collections—how to 234:63-65

Collect insects and display in box, how to do 919:20-21

Collecting and studying insects 253:24-25

Collecting bottle—how to make 530:212

Collecting insects, how to do 1116:44-45

Collecting insects 62:39-55; 657:1-15

Collecting with a beating tray 430:57

Collecting with net 436:46-47

Collecting, mounting and labeling insects, how to do 1425:38-43

Collecting, preserving and displaying insects, how to do 1320:107-114

Collection and care of 390:17-29

Crawling insects, how to collect using jar in ground 1433:11-13

Displaying collection, how to do 824:88-95

Dragonflies' cage—how to make 234:61

Finding and capturing insects—how to 234:56-57

House insects, how to collect and mount 1464:16-17

How to capture insects without hurting them 1464:11-12

How to collect, house and observe 119:111-122

Hunting for insects—how to 234:62-63

Insect display blocks 9:116-117

Insect display box 9:112-113

Insect homes—how to make 234:58-59

Insect killing bottle 9:15

Insect killing jar—how to make 57:73; 62:43-44; 234:63; 436:47; 657:9; 723:81

Insect mounting—how to 62:44-45

Insect mounts—making 436:48

Insect pitfall trap—how to make 590:44

Insect setting board to dry and 'set' 9:114-115

Insect spreading board—how to make 57:73-74; 62:45-46; 234:64; 436:48

Insect terrarium for observing and keeping insects, how to make 1320:38

Insect watching and collecting, how to do 1144:9, 30

Killing jar for killing insects, how to make 824:52-53; 1433:8-10

Larval feeding cage—how to make 285:60

Larvas from water—how to collect 117:44-45

Light and old sheet used to catch insects at night, how to do 1169:34-35

Light trap for collecting night insects 414:29-31

Mounting insects, how to do 1433:21-23

Net from wire and fabric, how to build 986:97

Night insects attracted to white sheet and light experiment 1464:38

Observe insects in a jar, how to do 810:51

Pooter device to collect small insects; make from plastic tubing and jar 1114:71

Pooter for collecting small insects—how to make 285:51

Pooter picks up tiny animals without harming them; how to make 1069:35

Raising insects 234:60-61

Relaxing jar for insects you are collecting, how to make 1433:14-17

Riker mount—how to make 234:65

Setting board—how to make 530:217

Small creature strainer—how to make 277:88-90

Spreading board for insects, how to make 1433:18-20

Sugaring to collect night insects 414:34-35

Trapping wild insects—three different ways 538:123

Vacuum jar for catching ground insects—making 749:74-75

What color light attracts most insects—experiment 414:31-32

Winter zoo of insects—making 629:126

INSECTS—GARDEN PESTS

Collect, observe—experiments using different types of safe pest controls 380:72-75

Do marigolds really repel pests 398:39-40

INSECTS—NETS

Butterfly net—how to make 293:24

Collection net from coat hanger and netting, how to make 1063:427

How to make an insect net 442:unpaged; 452:39; 530:206-207

Insect collecting net—how to make 9:12-13; 60:58-63; 62:41-43; 313:5; 332:20-22; 824:52-53; 832:70; 1265:97

Insect net from wire, broom handle and cheese cloth, how to make 1433:4-7

Insect net, coat hanger and cheesecloth, how to make 919:18

Making and using an insect net (Primary) 108:58-63

Net for catching caddis gnats, make from pillowcase and dowel 1476:118

Net for pond dipping to collect water insects, how to make 1182:16

Net from wire and fabric, how to build 986:97

Net from wire coat hanger, dowel and netting, how to make 1320:33-35

Skimmer net, how to make from wire and pantyhose 1115:98-99

Sweep net to catch insects, how to make 1188:46-47

Sweeping net how to make 234:62

Sweep net—making 657:2-4

INSECTS—POND

A study of insects in a pond 285:75-76

INSECTS—POPULATIONS

Insect populations change in diversity and numbers when habitat changes 1096:77-82

Population growth in insects experiment 1097:87-89

INSECTS—PROTECTIVE COLORATION

Colored toothpicks in grass demonstrate insect camouflage 1464:29-30

INSECTS—REPELLENTS

Bug hat to keep insects off you, how to make 1188:31

Citrus seed and skin repellents 398:119-120

Do some insect repellents work better than others experiment 1096:139-143

Experiment in folklore: mint leaves and ants 585:152-153

Health and beauty products affect effectiveness of insect repellents experiment 1096:139-143

Herbal bug repellent, recipe, how to make 1335:116

Insect repellents experiment 1097:128-130

Insect spray, homemade, recipe, how to make 986:92

Natural recipe for pest control 380:72-73

Plants produce chemicals to repel insects experiment 1324:32-36

Repellent to keep clothes moths away, recipe, how to make 1228:87

Repellent to keep fleas off pets, recipe, how to make 1228:85-86

Scent of marigolds in window box repels gnats project 969:42-43

INSECTS—STICK INSECTS

Keeping stick insects, how to do 1183:38

Stick insects; how to keep and observe 1181:30

INSECTS—TRAPS

Bait to trap insects; which solution works best project 969:38-39

Beetle trap—how to make 332:22

Beetle trap for rainy season, how to make 1320:76-77

Beetle traps, how to make and set traps 1320:31-33

Berlese funnel captures small insects that are in soil, how to make 1096:85-88; 1097:51-53

Bug catcher, how to make from jar and straws 1188:31

Catch insects in jar with funnel and fruit lure, how to do 1188:73

Fruit fly traps—how to make 276:64

Ground trap, how to make from can and jam or jelly 1188:33

In ground trap for beetles, how to make 1464:64

Insect traps—how to make 331:16-17; 382:60-63

Japanese beetle trap, how to make 986:84; 1265:84

Light trap—making 657:5-6

Moth trap with light bulb, how to build using plywood 1069:109

Pit trap for insects, making 932:26-27

Pitfall trap in ground to collect insects, how to make 1274:51

Pitfall trap to catch insects, how to make 740:21; 915:12-13; 1445:8

Pooter device to collect small insects; make from plastic tubing, jar 1114:71

Pooter for catching minibeasts, how to make 1182:4

Pooter to catch insects, how to make from plastic sheet, clay, straws 1274:9

Pooter trap; making and using a pooter to sample small animals experiment 1134:5.002

Screen trap—how to make 332:36-37

Survey of insects living in buildings experiment 1097:144-147

Trap in ground for night crawling insects experiment, how to make 1371:10-11

Traps to catch insects, simple, how to make 919:22

Vacuum trap to catch small insects, how to make 1183:52

INSECTS—WATER

Collecting screen—how to make 277:95-96

Collecting water insects and how to make collecting net and underwater torch 430:54-55

Effect of detergent on aquatic life experiment 934:38-39

How to care for 279:21

How to collect and keep 821:54-55

How to feed and care for back swimmers 332:44

How to feed and care for diving beetle 332:41

How to feed and care for water boatmen 332:44

How to feed and care for water scavenger 332:43

How to feed and care for water strider 332:42

How to feed and care for whirligig beetle 332:40

Increased temperature of water effect on insect growth experiment 1097:48-50

Insect populations are different in running and standing bodies of water 1096:96-101

Instant water insect aquarium—how to make 494:52-53

Jar aquarium—how to collect, set up and observe 277:97

Key to identifying winter water insects 277:147-149

Larvae and insects—how to collect 332:34-37

Measuring water pollution by recording plants and animals experiment 934:40-41

209

Motor boats trail of oil on water surfaces; effect on aquatic insects experiment 1097:45-47

Net for pond dipping to collect water insects, how to make 1182:16

Ponds; observe pond insects in aquarium experiment, how to do 1472:30-35

Respiration in water insects experiment 1097:98-100

Skimmer net, how to make from wire and pantyhose 1115:98-99

Water fleas (daphnia) collected and observed experiment 1402:72-75

Water strider model, how to make 1445:28-29

Water striders—observation of movement and eating 331:33-37

Water striders and whirligigs—how to collect and care for 331:21-38

Water top insects affected by oil and soap reducing surface tension experiment 1097:61-62

INSTINCTIVE BEHAVIOR. *See* **ANIMAL BEHAVIOR**

INSTRUMENTS. *See* **MUSICAL INSTRUMENTS**

INSULATION. *See also* **INSULATORS; WOOL**

Blanket warmth—experiment 585:134-135

Cloth insulation experiment 153:22-23

Cooling down jars experiment 909:61

Demonstrate heat loss from materials in cavity of walls 337:14

Does insulation trap heat experiment 829:39-40

Down feathers trap air 257:10

Edison's experiments 230:48-52

Effects of insulation on amount of heat retained 253:93-94

Experiment—to show effects of insulation 597:25

Find the best insulation—experiment 660:12-13

Heat flow from different materials experiment 1164:56-59

Heat preserver—compare wool and cotton with nylon, orlon, dacron, etc. 26:83

Heat preserver—do woolens keep us warmer? 26:72-74

Hot potato test for (Primary) 320:23

Ice cube in cloth demonstration 780:40-41

Ice cubes wrapped in different materials (Primary) 535:19

Insulated container retains heat longer than uninsulated one experiment 1453:59-60

Insulating materials keep hot things hot and cold things cold experiment 1377:27

Insulation and R values—experiment 586:91-93

Insulation conserves energy by keeping heat in experiment 1228:70-71

Insulation increase causes heat loss to decrease experiment 984:44-46

Insulation used to keep ice cube from melting experiment 1159:110-113

Insulation works to keep cold air out experiment 1371:81-82

Jars with cotton layers—experiment 681:16

Keeping cool; insulation experiment 587:41

Keeping warm—what is a good insulator—experiment 587:42

Model houses test effectiveness of home insulation methods experiment 1134:7.005

Project 14—R value 654:44-45

Project 18—ice cubes keeping 654:49

Protection of payload on spacecraft—activities and experiments 564:48-50

Stop drafts with a dragon 236:185

Store some heat 249:22

Test for insulation with thermometer in refrigerator experiment 1086:11

What makes good insulation 236:150

Which form of insulation is most effective experiment 997:78-79

Wool keeps sheep warm 257:8-9

INSULATORS

Are some solids better insulators than others experiment 831:23-25

Candy test for which materials are good insulators experiment (Primary) 1315:21

Compare materials to find the best insulators experiment 1073:92

Comparing insulators experiment 820:25

Do big things stay warm longer than small things experiment 1519:17

Electricity conductors and insulators 281:93-94

Fat or lard or blubber insulates against cold project 969:30-31

Hair acts as insulator to help maintain human body temperatures project 969:28-29

Heat conduction race experiment 1515:97-99

Heat losses due to conduction in homes, how to measure experiment 1152:82-84

House insulation keeps heat in and out experiment; data tables given 1004:1.004

How can we stay warm on cold days experiment [Primary] 744:23

How much heat energy is lost through windows experiment 1396:191

Insulated bottle stores heat experiment 1028:32

Insulated container keeps water warm experiment 1032:22-23

Insulating against loud sounds experiment 1155:81

Insulating and building materials in your home or school experiment 1152:81-82

Insulator experiment with different materials 837:50-51

Jars wrapped in different materials experiment 1014:69

Materials are conductors or insulators of electricity; experiment to test for 1012:55

Materials that are the best conductors or best insulators of heat experiment 1090:38

Measuring insulation effects experiment using jars, insulation, thermometer 1179:52

Plastics are better insulators than natural materials experiment 1483:22-23

R value of cardboard, how to measure experiment 1152:77-81

R values for common insulating and building materials chart 1152:78

Sand has insulating properties determination experiment 1396:189-193

Space suit materials help regulate temperature demonstration 1394:212-213

Styrofoam cups are insulators experiment 836:73-74

Test for conductors and insulators experiment with spoon, candy and hot water 1377:12

Testing insulated containers experiment; graph given 924:89-90

Testing wool, foil and fabric for insulation qualities experiment 1519:16

The insulating value of air computer project 584:94-95

Thermal conductivities of steel, glass and insulation experiment 1515:95-101

Thermos bottle, make to demonstrate insulation 807:152

Which material holds heat best 629:34

Wool sock insulator keeps heat from being lost experiment 1219:20

INTEGERS—POSITIVE AND NEGATIVE

Meaning of integers, games and uses 406:1-47

INTELLIGENCE. *See also* **ANIMAL INTELLIGENCE**

Build maze to test intelligence of cockroaches 279:29

INTERLOCKING JOINTS

How they work 544:46-48

INTERMITTENT FUNNEL

Demonstration 532:29

INTERNATIONAL DATE LINE

Time and dates around the Earth 577:project #39

INTESTINES. *See also* **HUMAN BODY**

Demonstrating absorption in the small intestine 148:68

INVERTEBRATES. *See also* **BRINE SHRIMP;**
EARTHWORMS

Activities with 236:58

Activities with earthworms 236:59

Activities with land snails and slugs 236:59-60

Activities with sow bugs 236:60

Ants—experiment ant maze 151:78-80

Brine shrimp—raising brine shrimp 148:54

Collecting invertebrates, how to do 824:51-66

Collecting, examining and feeding planarians experiment 1425:34-37

Experiment—earthworm maze learning 151:47-48

Experiment—earthworm regeneration 151:49

Experiment—habituation in protozoa 151:39-40

Experiment—planarian regeneration 151:57-58

Experiment—snail maze 151:66-68

Feeding a stinging hydra 148:46

Finding animals in a drop of water 148:47

Finding invertebrates 236:58-59

Finding out how snails behave 148:51

Hydra's response to temperature, chemicals and foods experiment 864:90-91

Hydra; observation of hydra experiment 1425:31-33

Microinvertebrates in pond water, how to collect and study 1117:54-55

Raising generations of fruit flies 148:48-49

Regenerating animals 148:50

Soil-animal survey to see what animals live underground experiment 1117:13

Toxicity test on invertebrates for effect of lawn fertilizers experiment 1267:81-83

Watching 'worms' grow into beetles 148:48

INVERTED TUMBLERS

Experiments with 54:69-100

INVESTIGATIONS—SCIENCE EXPERIMENTS. *See*
also **SCIENCE EXPERIMENTS**

Choosing your equipment and test procedures 31:33-39

Drawing your conclusions 31:66-69

Graphing your data 31:46-65

How to select one 31:9-25

Planning your investigation 31:26-32

Recording your data 31:40-45

Reporting your results 31:70-78

INVISIBLE INKS

A secret until you heat it 280:38

Ammonia and phenolphthalein invisible ink experiment 1159:25

Cornstarch invisible ink, recipe, how to make 1064:75

Create and reveal hidden messages with lemon juice 814:16-18

Grape juice and baking powder ink, making 935:25

How are secret invisible messages written 381:25-26

How to make 288:42-43; 360:92; 399:75; 643:28-29930:15

How to make and write with 244:15-17

Invisible fruit inks 203:88

Invisible ink from lemon juice, how to make 1435:71-73

Invisible writing 550:99

Invisible writing trick 585:72-73

Invisible writing with lemons 89:34-35

Invisible writing, how to do 1006:43; 812:26-27

Lemon and iodine invisible ink experiment 1018:24-25

Lemon and milk ink—making 733:3

Lemon ink secret message 1002:20

Lemon ink, making 827:44-45

Lemon juice ink and salt make secret message experiment 1005:10-11

Lemon juice ink for secret messages experiment 895:10-11

Lemon juice ink makes invisible message, how to do 1406:20-23

Lemon juice invisible ink message experiment 1028:55; 1124:20-21; 1258:unp.

Lemon juice invisible ink, how to make and write with it 1271:19

Lemon juice message disappears and appears, how to do 790:10-11

Make and send invisible messages 770:135

Make invisible ink 146:22-23; 147:75-78; 281:25; 291:227; 400:71; 625:43; 939:56-57

Make invisible writing and bring out with heat 179:57-58

Make with cobalt chloride 97:42

Making real ink disappear 147:76-78

Making the visible invisible 147:76-78

Message magically appears experiment using iodine and lemon 1405:56-57

Milk ink 146:22-23

Milk ink to help you write invisible messages, how to do 1312:11

Mystery message experiment 829:17-18

Onion ink 146:22-23

Photographic invisible ink 87:61

Recipe for 116:175-177

Secret message inside hard boiled egg experiment 1244:19

Secret message note using milk or lemon juice experiment 1244:19

Secret messages 146:23

Secret messages—how to 364:90

Secret messages made with lemon juice experiment 860:57-59

Secret writing—fun with milk 579:44

Secret writing trick 84:34-36; 585:73-74

Send secret messages 146:23

Watermark writing 202:74

Why is invisible ink invisible experiment 1294:53-55

Write a message that magically appears experiment 905:110-111

Write secret message experiment 902:24; 980:55-56

Write with invisible ink, how to make experiment 186:110-111; 937:66-67

INVISIBLE WRITING. *See also* **INVISIBLE INKS;**
  SECRET WRITING
  Wax writing for invisible message, how to do 1236:11
IODINE. *See also* **STARCH**
  How to remove stains 122:95-97
  Iodine and starch 85:29
  Iodine is more soluble in mineral oil than in water experiment 1435:13-15
  Iodine is violet not brown experiment 1083:81
  Iodine stain—how to remove 585:98
  Starch iodine test for vitamin C in foods experiment
    1259:33-34
  To test for starch 84:52
  White paper turns blue; test for starch experiment
    781:44-45
IONOSPHERE
  AM radio shows presence of ionosphere above Earth experiment 1322:23-27
IONS
  Estimating the maximum volume of an ion—experiment
    586:65-66
IRON. *See also* **MINERALS; RUST**
  Burning steel 85:28
  'Burning' steel experiment—shows formation of iron
    oxide (rust) 346:67-71
  Bright sparks to demonstrate iron oxide 146:50-51
  Can you see the iron in iron-fortified cereals experiment
    1250:80-81
  Experiments with using steel wool 84:53-60
  Iron and sulfur, iron and oxygen, combine to make iron
    sulfide and rust 157:12-13
  Iron sulfate solution—how to prepare 346:17-22
  Iron test 346:55-57
  Magnetic separation of iron ore 102:121-122
  Make iron sulfide 97:14-15
  Oxygen added to iron makes rust 97:22-23
  Rusting of iron 85:26-27
  Rusting 26:11-23

Show rust is compound of iron, oxygen and water
    146:24-25
  Test for iron in foods experiment 1259:35-37
  Test for presence of iron in fruit juices experiment
    905:112-113; 1479:53
  Turn iron into copper 157:15
IRON—RUST
  Experiments—simple 26:22-23
  Prevent rusting of iron 26:19-21
IRON ACETATE
  How to make ink 146:7
IRON ORE
  Making 26:14
IRON OXIDE
  How to make 146:50-51
IRON SULFIDE
  How to make 146:17
IRRIGATION
  Clay ditches—demonstrate 323:15-16
  Irrigation canals and ditches experiment 1026:9
  Irrigation water leaves salts in soil experiment 1323:51-
    55
ISLANDS
  Island and isthmus demonstrated with rocks, sand and
    water 1437:103-106
  Islands in a tub (Primary) 153:12-13
  Model artificial island, earthquake resistant, to house
    people experiment 1458:11
ISOPODS
  Isopod race, how to set up and do 1189:14-15
ISOTOPES
  What is half-life of an element or isotope experiment
    976:53
ISTHMUSES
  Island and isthmus demonstrated with rocks, sand and
    water 1437:103-106

J

JACOB'S LADDER
Balsa wood blocks ladder, making 770:157
Make a Jacob's ladder 291:168-169; 861:213-218

JAM
Beach plum 296:78-79
Making jam to show effect of pectin on crushed fruit experiment 1484:145-146

JELLYFISH
Jellyfish dives and floats in water filled soda bottle experiment 1310:20-21
Jellyfish model toy—how to make (Primary) 467:18-19

JET ENGINES
How jet engines work; make balloon rocket to demonstrate 1376:22

JET PLANES
Jet of air experiment 718:33-34

JET PROPULSION. *See also* **NEWTON'S THIRD LAW OF MOTION; ROCKETS**
Air-power balloon demonstrates 651:24-25
Balloon filled with air demonstrates jet propulsion 1201:24
Balloon jet—how to make 260:15
Balloon jet demonstrates thrust experiment 860:21-24
Balloon jet flier experiment 1110:26
Balloon on string between chairs demonstrates jet propulsion experiment 940:37-39
Balloon on string experiment 999:89-90
Balloon rocket blasts along string experiment 1208:36-37
Balloon rockets demonstrate how rocket launches 1241:11
Balloon rockets on string demonstrate propulsion experiment 994:19-27
Balloon taped to string flies at high speed experiment 995:28-29
Balloon traveling on string demonstrates jet propulsion 1028:13
Balsa wood boat and balloon—demonstrate 507:1881
Boat, wooden, with balloon, demonstrates jet propulsion project 1296:1988
Bottle with vinegar and baking powder on scale demonstrates 1001:14
Building a model jet turbine project 833:291-292
Buzzy bee balloon experiments 685:18-19
Construct Hero's engine to show 167:29-32
Demonstrate with balloon and straws 225:30
Demonstrate with steam launch boat 167:11-12
Demonstrating how a jet works project 833:289-291
Flying boat—experiment 605:42-43
How jet plane gets the power to fly; heated air experiment 781:16-17
Jet balloon, making 868:71
Jet powered boat experiment with balloon and plastic tile 1389:31
Jet propelled boat experiment with balloons and test tank 994:35-45
Jet propulsion demonstrated with balloon in waterproof container 1411:8-9
Jet-powered boats—how to make 342:23
Jet-propelled racing car—how to make 652:6
Rocket balloon boat demonstrates jet propulsion experiment 1024:4-5
Rocket balloon on string demonstrates jet propulsion experiment 1126:18-19
Rocket power—model rocket demonstrates jet propulsion 575:36
Rocket thrust demonstrated with balloon and thread 1478:33
Thrust activities and experiments to demonstrate jet propulsion 564:20-21
What makes jet plane move forward experiment 747:23-24
Your jet engine runs on water 161:20

JET SKIS
Water-jet boat; demonstrate water jet power experiment 1165:19

JET STREAM
Activities to demonstrate jet stream 564:7

JET-PROPELLED TOYS
Make a rocket, lorry and boat 142:51

JETS. *See also* **AERONAUTICS; AIRCRAFT—JETS; HERO'S ENGINE; TURBOJET ENGINE**
Balloon on string between chairs demonstrates jet propulsion experiment 940:37-39
Balloon jet demonstrates thrust experiment 860:21-24
Balloon experiment to show how jet engine pushes airplane forward 450:26-27
Balloon jet experiment 908:38-42
Balloon powered jets, how to make from balloons, nylon cord and tape 1448:26-27
Balloon taped to string flies at high speed experiment 995:28-29
Business jet model—how to make 388:26-27
Delta wing jet—how to make 410:14-15
How can hot gases make a plane go forward 446:36-37
How does airplane's jet engine work experiment 1293:11-12
How does jet engine work; experiment with balloon 834:97-98
How jet plane gets the power to fly; heated air experiment 781:16-17
How jet works with toy balloon—experiments 72:21
Jet engine compressor demonstration 974:25
Jet plane—making model 436:49
Jumbo jet model—how to make 388:14-15
Make a model turbo jet engine and a model turbo prop engine 564:21
Potato jet airplane—how to make 113:16-17
Rocket jet kite, how to make 1115:57-58
Steam powered jet boat—how to make with cigar tube and candle 419:35

JOULE, JAMES PRESCOTT
Who discovered that heat is a form of energy project 1525:110-113

JUMPING BEANS
Experiment 563:37

JUNGLE TERRARIUM
Materials and animals for, how to set up and maintain 475:20-26

JUNK MAIL
How much junk mail comes to your home project 1210:35-37

JUPITER. *See also* **PLANETS**
Centrifugal forces affecting Jupiter and its bulging waistline experiment 1478:72-73
Charting the movement of Jupiter's moons project 833:240-241

K

KALEIDOPHONE
Kaleidophone—how to make 2:76-79

KALEIDOSCOPES
Cardboard and mirrors kaleidoscope, how to make 1019:13-15
Cardboard kaleidoscope, how to make 885:56-57
Construct a kaleidoscope 167:78-80
Corner reflector shows multiple images of an object experiment 1132:31-1-31-2
Crayon shavings, wax paper, paper tubes, how to make 897:74
Hall of mirrors, making 669:20-21
Homemade kaleidoscope—how to make 577:project 78
How to build a kaleidoscope experiment 941:89-91
How to make (Advanced) 208:95-100
How to make (Primary) 210:23
How to make kaleidoscope and how it works experiment 911:6-7
How to make using mirrors, cardboard, and cellophane 1039:27
How to make 8:118-127; 128:195; 172:29-31; 265:42-43; 356:30-31; 385:103-105; 410:19; 472:2225; 507:1882-1883; 558:88-89; 563:22; 653:36-37; 656:15; 659:9; 696:22-23; 835:48-50; 861:45-51; 868:77; 892:28; 909:137; 1417:14-15
Kaleidoscope from cardboard and mirrors, how to make 1213:15; 1245:12-13
Kaleidoscope from oak tag, how to make 1308:15
Mailing tube and sheet of clear acetate kaleidoscope, how to make 1114:58-60
Make a projecting kaleidoscope 177:31-32
Make kaleidoscope from mirrors and colored beads 1073:76
Make kaleidoscope from three mirrors experiment 1299:11
Milk carton kaleidoscope, how to make 935:40-41
Miniature kaleidoscope room—make 670:28
Multiple images of yourself from large mirrored kaleidoscope experiment 1132:44-1-44-2
Projection kaleidoscopes 386:11-13
Simple kaleidoscope, how to make 595:40-41; 860:209-211; 1283:15
Taleidoscope—making 732:34-35
Tennis ball can kaleidoscope, making 885:57-58
Tin can kaleidoscope, how to make 770:138
Tiny kaleidoscope from slides and tape, how to make 1476:53-54

KAYAKS
Waterproof toy—how to make 320:12-13

KAZOO. *See also* **MUSICAL INSTRUMENTS**
Make a kazoo 32:28-29

KELVIN, WILLIAM THOMSON
Draw diagrams comparing Fahrenheit/Celsius/Kelvin thermometer scales experiment 1396:186-187

KELVIN SCALE. *See* **THERMOMETERS**

KETTLE HOLE LAKE
Project 577:project #42

KEYNOTES
A singing pan 280:42

KIDNEYS. *See also* **HUMAN BODY**
Studying a lamb kidney 294:91

KINDLING POINT
A paper pot to boil water 550:106-109
Burning sugar 291:215
Candle flame and strainer demonstrate kindling point 937:100-101
Copper tube and paper demonstrate kindling point 939:33-34
Demonstrate kindling temperature of different materials 179:48-50
Finding the kindling temperature of materials 180:74-75
Light a candle through its smoke experiment 939:112-113
Mystery of the wick 291:214
Nothing to get burned up about 222:91

KINETIC ENERGY. *See also* **ENERGY**
Boltzmann Distribution kinetic energy experiment 871:3.012
Book of things to make 356:1-68
Compare potential energy and kinetic energy experiment 902:63
Cotton thread spool (reel) tank—demonstrates 624:11
Cylinders roll down hill at different rates due to distribution of mass 1132:42-1-42-2
Effect that mass has on kinetic energy demonstration 1404:146-147
Falling dominoes 162:116-117
Finger pool game with checkers demonstrates kinetic energy 1035:18-19
Kinetic energy rolls round can back to you experiment 937:58-59
Pinwheel uses the kinetic energy of air experiment 1030:10-11
Self inflating balloon trick demonstrates 1010:40-42
Self propelled buggy, how to make experiment 937:60-61
Surface skimmer skims over a tabletop on cushion of air experiment 1030:28-29
Swinging spoons demonstrate potential and kinetic energy experiment 1377:28
The writhing snake—kinetic and potential energy 205:84-87
Two fruits suspended on strings demonstrate kinetic energy experiment 1030:24-25
Waterwheel demonstrates kinetic energy experiment, how to make 1377:25

KING CRABS
King crabs' water—crab's reaction to change from salt to fresh water 484:102-103

KIRCHHOF, GOTTLIEB
Starch is made up of sugar units experiment 1133:2.009

KITCHEN UTENSILS
Amount of bacteria found on kitchen sponges/dishrags be reduced experiment 997:124-125

KITES
Animal kite, how to make from paper and string 1289:16-17
Basic kite, making 823:121-122
Ben's kite—how to build 400:95
Bird kite, make using sticks, paper, plastic, string; patterns given 1436:18-22
Bow top kite, making 823:123
Box kite from fabric or plastic sheeting, and dowels, how to make 1042:34-35
Box kites, making 823:126-128
Building a better kite project 762:105-107
Ceiling tile kite, making 868:71
Centipede kite, how to make 1115:61-62
City kite—making 732:125-126

Do gliders and kites fly the same way experiment 783:14-16

Does a dihedral stabilize a kite experiment 783:25-26

Does angle of attack affect how a kite flies experiment 783:21-22

Easy kite, patterns, making 1014:130-131

Eddy kite—how to build 400:96

Effect of kite's tail on flight of kite experiment 1404:92-94

Experimental plastic kite, how to make 908:49-50

Ferry kite, how to make 861:21-25

Fighting kites, making 823:126

Flat kite—how to make 764:unp.

Flying frog kite, paper, making 823:102-103

Flying saucer kite, paper, making 823:96-99

Heights flown—computer experiment 665:39

Hexagonal kite, making 823:123

High flying kites, making 870:72-74

How high, on a set line length, does a kite fly experiment 783:33-34

How to fly kites 1063:486-487

How to make 321:7; 493:43; 660:27; 823:111-121; 909:75

How to make a kite 597:inside front cover

How to make and demonstrate air lift and drag 225:24-25

How to make flat kites 112:44-45

Is aspect ratio related to how kite flies experiment 783:40

Is weight to area a factor for kite design experiment 783:41

Kite construction (Primary) 535:53

Kite—making with towing line 450:8-11

Kite flying—kite tail gives low center of gravity 241:36-37

Malay-Eddy kite, making 823:124-126

Measuring the wind—a butterfly kite 304:25-27

Message kite, how to make 1126:30-31

Mini box kite—how to make 494:72

Mini kite from plastic and straws, how to make 1063:485

Miniature kites to test flight experiment 1110:10-11

Mini-kite from paper and plastic straws, how to make 1416:14-15

Newspaper kites, making 854:110

Oaktag kite—making [PRIMARY] 742:44

Paper kite, how to make 832:39; 1001:12-13

Parachute kite, making 823:95

Plastic bag kite, how to make 897:88; 1073:22; 1161:11

Plastic garbage bag and dowel kite, how to make 1372:24-27

Plastic garbage bag kite, how to make and fly 1419:24-26

Plastic trash bag kite, pattern, making 1024:6-7

Polystyrene sheet kite, how to make and decorate 1376:28

Rocket jet kite, how to make 1115:57-58

Simple kite from wood frame and paper, how to make 1373:14-15

Simple kite to make 679:6-7

Sled kite, how to make 935:56-57; 983:94-95

Snake kite—how to build 400:96

Snake kite, how to make 953:28

Square kite, making 823:122

Strawberry kite—how to make 310:22-23

Tail of kite affects movement of kite experiment 1405:96

Tile kite, making 856:32-33

Traditional diamond shaped kite from fabric and sticks, how to make 1168:42-43

Trash bag sled kite—how to make 494:73

Trash can liner, dowel rods and string kite, how to make 1299:52

Two stick kite, how to make 879:23

Two-stick bow kite, make from sticks, plastic bag, string; patterns given 1436:12-17

Two-stick kite, how to make 1063:488-489

Valentine kite—how to make 310:17-21

What effect do different materials have on kite's performance experiment 783:29-30

What effect do different measurements have on a kite experiment 783:23-24

What effect does tail have on how kite flies experiment 783:27-28

What is force exerted on kite at any one speed experiment 783:44

What weather makes it possible to fly kites; wind project experiment 783:38-39

What wind speed is required to fly a kite experiment 783:42-43

Will different configurations have effect on box kite flight experiment 783:31-32

Wind dragon 356:36-39

Wind-sled kite—making 733:34

KITTY LITTER

How to make from crushed peanut shells and baking soda 560:34

KIWI

How to grow 272:42-47

KNOTS

How to make 399:50

KON TIKI STAMP BOAT

How to make 54:65

L

LABELS

Labels on cleaning products experiment 1361:56

LABORATORY ANALYSIS

Laboratory analysis tests on milk; data tables given 1004:4.013

LABORATORY EQUIPMENT. *See also* **EQUIPMENT—HOW TO MAKE**

Alcohol burner—how to make 57:53-54

Beam balance—how to make 57:66

Displacement pan to collect gases—how to make 57:65-66

Drying and sterilizing oven—how to make 57:56-57

Electric heater—how to make 57:55-56

How to build a home laboratory 57:7-118

Incubator—how to make 57:71

Insect cage—how to make 57:72

Insect killing jar—how to make 57:73

Insect spreading board—how to make 57:73-74

LABYRINTH

Marble maze, making 861:39-44

LACTIC ACID. *See* **MICROBES—BACTERIA; YOGURT**

LADYBUGS. *See also* **INSECTS—CAGES**

Game; game to demonstrate survival of ladybugs, how to play 1183:75

Game; ladybugs survive winter if summer supply of aphids is plentiful 1182:27

How many aphids can a ladybug eat 414:82-83

Ladybird beetles—collection, care and observation of 331:51-57

Ladybugs—how to care for 279:25

Model of ladybug, how to make 1183:74

LAENNEC, RENE. *See also* **STETHOSCOPE**

His experiments 42:97-106

LAKES. *See also* **FRESHWATER; PONDS; STREAMS**

Acid lake; how to make mini acid lake and buffer it experiment 1328:63

Algae; quantity and diversity of algae affected by acidified waters experiment 1450:128-134

Convection in water to show how lake 'turns over'—experiment 175:32

Demonstrate evaporation process of 197:22-23

Demonstrate how deposited sediments form layers in bottom of lake 1481:56-58

Eutrophication or oxygen depletion of water in lakes and ponds experiment 978:75

Fertilizers in lake water cause overgrowth of plants experiment 1328:66-67

How bottom sediment in lakes is mixed with water at upper levels experiment 1479:87

Kettle hole lake 577:project #42

Landfills and leachates experiment 1234:68

Liming protects lakes from acid rain experiment 1325:49-53

Nutrients added to lakes and ponds cause water pollution experiment 1325:55-59

Observing the life on the shore of a lake 285:77

pH of lake water with added vinegar and limestone experiment 1526:98

Phosphate pollutant can be removed from water experiment 1325:60-64

Stream table activities 400:56-57

Succession—how does succession occur in a lake 371:58-65

Temperature changes density of water experiment 1325:18-21

Temperature of soil at bottom of lake when top is frozen project 969:17-18

Water travels faster thru soil in lake with bottom vegetation project 969:12-14

What is thermal water pollution experiment 1325:65-69

Why lakes don't freeze solid experiment 1439:42-43

Why lakes dry up experiment 1023:172-173

LAMPBLACK INK

How to make 321:21

LAMPS

Arc lamp—making 128:186-187; 627:54

Electric lamp—making 281:92-93

Lamp assembly (bulb socket), how to make 768:101-102

Lamps, how to make 543:28-31

Make your own alcohol lamp 563:20

Mock-up of a three-way lamp circuit—making 532:107

Oil burning lamp—how to make 320:25; 325:unpaged

Substage for microscope 11:4-5

Wiring—how can you wire a lamp 278:49-50

LAND—ECOSYSTEM. *See also* **ECOSYSTEMS**

Field meadow—survey in the spring and early summer for its plant population 285:50-52

Field meadow—survey/inventory animals supported by field and meadow plant 285:52-53

Hardwood forest—a study of life in a hardwood forest 285:55-57

Hardwood forest—study individual oak, maple or other mature hardwood tree 285:57-61

School yard—study of some food chains in a school yard 285:47

Softwood forest—investigate a softwood pine forest 285:61-62

Soil, bare—observe the colonization of a small section of bare soil 285:48-50

Yard—observation and study of an abandoned yard 285:45-46

LAND—EROSION. *See also* **EROSION**

Abrasion by wind 243:56-57

LAND CONTOURS

Clay models of land features and land usage, making 874:220

Relief model—how to make 507:1862-1863

LAND POLLUTION

Kind of litter most common in your area project 1296:1996

LAND ROVER

Electric air car—working model 577:project #54

LAND USAGE

Design and build a model city based on land use and community plans project 978:167-168

LAND USE

Factors that aid in soil formation experiment 1424:33

Life existing in soils experiment 1424:35

Measuring a slope of land experiment 1424:47

Plant growth in different soils experiment 1424:16

Runaway soil experiment demonstrates erosion 1424:80-81

Soil layers examined experiment 1424:36-37

Testing the soil for nutrients experiment 1424:62-63

Water holding capacity of soils experiment 1424:108

LAND YACHTS

Land yacht from balsa wood and spools, how to make 1416:24-25

Land yacht shows importance of angle of attack of wind, how to make 1299:56

LANDFILLS. *See also* **BIODEGRADABILITY; GARBAGE; POLLUTION**

Above ground versus below ground decomposition project 969:73-74

Bacteria test for groundwater pollution experiment; how to do 1173:41-42

Bury different kinds of garbage experiment to see what biodegrades 1063:378

Chemical waste landfill experiment 950:132-133

Composting reduces volume of materials sent to landfills experiments 1150:43-51

Demonstrate weathering and decomposition of garbage in landfills experiment 1465:106

Incineration reduces volume and weight of garbage experiment 1012:88

Landfill containment area with little biodegradation occurring experiment 1295:51-52

Landfills and leachates experiment 1234:68

Miniature landfill investigation to see how landfill works experiment 1012:85-86

Miniature landfills experiment; biodegradability of materials in dry/wet soils 1295:51-52

Model landfill in glass jar experiment 1366:24

Model landfill, small, demonstrates refuse decomposition 983:13-14

Model of landfill to see what materials break down experiment 1240:25-26

Packaging costs and size of consumer goods experiment 1150:62-64

Packaging scavenger hunt; chart given to record numbers of product wraps 1013:27

Packaging; ways to reduce packaging of consumer goods experiment 1150:64-65

pH test for groundwater pollution, how to do 1173:40

Plastics; some plastics decompose in soil more readily than others experiment 969:71-72

Product container size relation to waste products and consumer use 969:81-82

Separating trash experiment using magnets and static electricity 1150:37-38

Soil and litter in flower pot experiment to determine what decomposes 1013:22-23

Some substances in landfills are toxic to living things experiment 1427:85-87

Twenty items; which will decompose in soil and which won't project 969:69-70

Water pollution from landfills experiment use fish tank with pond/landfill area 1173:36-42

What is a landfill experiment; miniature landfill shows pollution problems 1427:82-83

Which items will decompose in a landfill experiment; chart for results given 1173:32-35

LANDFORMS

Heating and cooling of different type model landforms experiment 1447:78-83

Heating and cooling rates of soil, grass, saltwater, water and sand experiment 1447:84-88

Show the formation of eskers, kames and moraines 175:16-17

LANE, TIMOTHY

Carbon dioxide and the formation of rust experiment 1133:2.004

LANTERN SLIDES

For projecting—making 436:50

LANTERNS

Electric lantern, how to make from battery, bulb and wire 1382:22-23

Sand bag lanterns—how to make 494:44

Sand lanterns—how to make 296:10-11

Tin can lanterns—how to make 558:68-69

LARVAE. *See* **CATERPILLARS; INSECTS**

LARYNX. *See also* **HUMAN BODY; VOICE**

How your larynx works—demonstrate with balloon (Primary) 513:16-21

LASERS

Coin recognizer reader, how to make 1249:26-30

Hologram—making 681:23

Simulated laser, how to build 1249:40-46

Stream of light concentrated experiment using black plastic bottle/flashlight 1308:31

Transmit sound with a flashlight beam experiment 1132:67-1-67-4

LATENT HEAT

Joseph Black's latent heat experiment 1133:7.004

LATEX. *See also* **RUBBER**

Making rubber ball 26:63-65

Making rubber things from latex 26:65-66

LATHE

Make a simple lathe 227:21

LATITUDE. *See also* **CROSS STAFF**

Cross staff—make a cross staff to find your latitude 292:46-48

Find your latitude using Polaris experiment 1478:18

Finding your latitude 400:109

Hands—use your hands to give latitude and altitude 292:46

How to tell latitude by altitude 292:44

Investigation into finding latitude 420:93-97

Magic calabash—make a magic calabash to show your home latitude 292:28-29

LATITUDE AND LONGITUDE

Calculate your longitude, how to do 1437:12-15

Cross staff used to measure latitude, how to make 1115:140-142

Cross staff to find latitude, how to make from boards, and nails 1434:38-41

Demonstrating latitude and longitude project 833:89

Explanation of time zones and lines of longitude 1434:15-17

Finding your latitude using the North Star, how to do 1437:23-26

Finding your location 382:108-113

Height of Sun and relationship to latitude experiment 1480:18-19

Make a basketball model Earth to show 292:62

Make a model of globe to demonstrate 175:58-59

Stick shadows on ground in sunlight demonstrate longitude 1437:4-8

Sun does not come up or set in the East or West exactly the same each day 1062:48-50

Sun's position at sunrise versus latitude and longitude experiment 1062:48-50

Sunrise not exactly in the East each day experiment 1062:48-50

Sunrise position versus latitude and longitude experiment 1062:48-50

Sunset not exactly in the West each day experiment 1062:48-50

Your latitude on Earth, how to find it using astrolabe, how to make 1115:134-137

LAUNCHER. *See also* **ROCKETS**

Electromagnetic "gun" satellite launcher, how to make 1249:49-50

Make a balloon launcher 92:46-47

LAVA

Lava flow demonstration 1266:17

LAVOISIER, ANTOINE

Lavoisier's experiment looking for mass changes 1156:96-97

Lavoisier's oxidation experiments 1156:97-103

Who first discovered that oxygen is necessary for fire project 1525:67-69

LAW OF DEFINITE PROPORTIONS

Description 346:65

LAW OF UNIFORM ACCELERATION. *See* **GALILEO'S EXPERIMENTS**

LAWNS

Liquid fertilizer effect on rhizome formation on lawn grass experiment 1295:81-83

LE CHATELIER PRINCIPLE. *See* **RUBBER BANDS**

LE CLANCHE CELLS

Le Clanche cells demonstration 577:project #46

LEAD

Lead in household water; how to test for project 969:92

LEAD PENCIL. *See also* **PENCILS**

Why does a pencil write on paper (Primary) 69:16-17

LEAD STORAGE CELL

Make a lead storage cell 278:34-35

LEAF LITTER

Animal life in leaf litter experiment 1134:1.010

Animal life in soil and leaf litter experiment 1134:1.012

LEAF MINERS

Adventure 34—we trace some tunnels—leaf miners under a hand lens 29:158-162

LEAF PRINT. *See also* **LEAVES**

Leaf print—how to make 563:42

LEAF RUBBING

How to do 473:59

Leaf rubbing, how to do 917:13

LEARNING. *See also* **GERBILS; MAZES**

Brain and learning experiments 1267:54-56

Can an earthworm learn to tell right from left 577: project #7

Can fish be conditioned 577:project #9

Demonstrate a simple lesson in 'learning' 294:94-95

Determine time it takes person to trace mirror image of pattern experiment 1395:183-188

How bright is your pet experiment 1425:113

How fast do you learn experiment 1425:113-119

Learning by trial and error 294:93-94

Learning experiments for rodents 577:project #8

Memory and learning; does high glucose liquid enhance memory experiment 1267:56-57

Time limits on tests help or hinder performance experiment 1267:58-59

LEARNING MACHINES

Investigation into machine that learns 420:118-123

LEAVENING AGENTS. *See also* **BAKING POWDER; BAKING SODA; YEAST**

Leavening experiment—growing wheat sprouts 537:38-39; 537:76

Leavening experiment—making apple puffs; apple puffs recipe 537:35-37,74

Leavening experiment—making wheat germ pancakes with baking powder 537:39-40; 537:77

Leavening experiment—making wheat germ pancakes with yeast 537:40-41

Leavening experiment—watching yeast and baking soda in action 537:37-38

Sodium bicarbonate—making baking powder biscuits 219:19-21

Unleavened bread—making 219:23-25

Yeast and baking soda recipe 537:75

LEAVES. *See also* **STOMATA**

Adventure 46—leaves under a microscope 403:173-179

Animal life in leaf litter experiment 1134:1.010

Anthocyanin pigments in flower petals change in acid/alkaline soils experiment 1203:28-29

Area; measuring area of leaves experiment 1148:6

Autumn crown of leaves, making 953:48

Bleach prints from leaves, making 819:54

Book of leaves, how to make 917:14-15

Chlorophyll in leaf comes from light; tape a shape on leaf experiment 1184:20

Chlorophyll removal 146:52-53

Chromatograms of autumn maple tree leaves day by day experiment 1060:19-20

Chromatography of leaf experiment; how to prepare 1396:101-103

Color—how to dissolve out leaf colors 117:67-68

Color—why leaves change color—experiment 40:51-53

Color change—why leaves turn color in the fall 294:44

Color in leaves—experiment 30:49-50

Color; why do leaves change color explanation 1239:8-9

Colors in autumn leaves—experiment 72:40-41

Colors in leaves—experiment 693:15-16

Decomposition rate of different leaves experiment 1184:21

Does red leaf produce food and contain chlorophyll experiment 871:2.022

Edges of leaves, classify leaves by using 817:6

Evergreen leaves don't lose water or dehydrate like deciduous leaves experiment 1184:19

Food factories—photosynthesis explained 380:66-68

Growth and properties of—experiments to show 128:44-46

Insect traps—leaves catch insects—sun dew and Venus's flytrap plants 271:30-39

Isolating chlorophyll and testing for starch in a leaf 294:39

Lack of sunlight affects color of leaf experiment 1049:19

Leaf cuttings—how to make a cutting 398:67-68

Leaf litter decay experiment 739:17

Leaf patterns—make leaf patterns with foil and iodine 146:53

Leaf pictures—how to make 264:44-45

Leaf print—carbon—how to make 731:55

Leaf prints—carbon paper, spatter, photo and printing ink prints 234:80-81

Leaf prints—how to make ink pad prints 62:21-22

Leaf prints—leaf printing—how to make stamp pad prints and spatter prints 476:62-65

Leaf prints—making 128:43-44; 784:88-89

Leaf prints—making by xerography 59:24-31

Leaf prints—making with ink 59:12-23

Leaf prints—nature printing with leaves, weeds 293:18

Leaf prints—printing leaves 32:13
Leaf prints—spatter print box 9:122-123
Leaf prints from poster paints, how to make 1114:56-57
Leaf skeleton—making 117:79-80; 146:52; 62:22-23;
    854:46-47; 1169:14-15
Leaf skeleton art—how to make 483:35-37
Leaf skeletons, how to make experiment 1069:58
Leaf's anatomy—how to see by separating leaf's layers
    483:38-39
Leaf's anatomy—see by separating leaf's layers 563:48-
    49
Leaves breathe experiment with plastic bag over leaves
    1142:17
Leaves changing color activities [Primary] 759:54-55
Light needed to make chlorophyll in leaves experiment
    1183:108
Litter—collect animals in leaf litter with a Berlese fun-
    nel—how to make 285:85
Lively leaf litter 236:155
Make a leaf skeleton 625:48
Model; construct model of internal structure of leaf pro-
    ject 1296:1989
Movement—leaves move—show night and day changes
    271:11-29
No two leaves alike experiment 563:48-49
Painting leaf shadows, how to do 1183:102
Paintings; leaf paintings, how to make 1184:14
Paintings; leaf shadow paintings, how to make 1184:14
Photosynthesis—how a green leaf produces food 294:37-
    38
Pictures of leaves, how to make 1184:21
Pigment—autumn colors from pigments 273:36-37
Pigment—pigment separation from leaves 273:36-37
Pigment—what effects pigment production 273:38-39
Pigments in leaves separated and identified experiment
    904:38-39
Plants breathe through leaves experiment 1368:55
Plaster of Paris leaf cast, how to make 1368:48-49
Predicting what color leaf will turn in the fall 413:46-48
Preserve image of leaf with soot, ink pad or spray paint
    project 1313:66-68
Preserving leaves in water and glycerin, how to do
    1184:15
Preserving leaves, how to do 693:17; 1183:103
Pressed leaves, making 508:67; 819:55
Prints of leaves, how to 646:16-19; 733:28; 1505:14-15
Prints of leaves; how to make and display 1044:28-29
Prints; shadow prints of leaves experiment with light sen-
    sitive paper 1476:102
Reproduction—plants grow from leaves 270:19-22
Rub a leaf for record of vein patterns, how to do 1142:19
Rubbings from leaves, how to do 275:15; 832:101;
    898:49; 1071:95; 1183:102; 1184:14
Shape of leaves; why leaves are the shape they are experi-
    ment 1184:16
Skeleton of leaf, how to make 1176:19; 1183:108
Skeleton of leaf, how to make 1184:20; 1368:47;
    1524:23; 879:212-213
Spatter prints, making 819:56-57
Stained glass leaf collage, how to make 854:49
Starch test on leaves 146:52-53
Starch test proves leaves make food for plants 366:220
Stencils from leaves, how to make 832:101
Stomata holes in leaves give off water from tree experi-
    ment 1184:18

Stomata impressions, make using Duco cement, observe
    under microscope 1295:76-81
Stomata in leaf structure and transpiration of water and
    plant gases experiment 1004:2.013
Stomata under a microscope, how to do 886:28-29
Stomata; how many stomata on leaf surfaces experiment
    1134:4.005
Stomate density (number per area)—on leaves experi-
    ment 762:78-79
Stomates—the undersurface of a leaf—stomates 294:39-
    40
Stomates of leaves affected by moisture experiment
    1060:35
Stomates of leaves close or open during day and night ex-
    periment 1060:35
Stomates of leaves give off water vapor into air experi-
    ment 1060:35
Stomates of leaves observed under microscope experi-
    ments 1060:33-36
Stomates of leaves when blocked affect the leaves
    experiment 1060:35
Sunshine needed for leaf growth experiment 1368:54
Trees lose water through leaves experiment 1183:106
Trees lose water through stomata on bottom of leaves ex-
    periment 1183:106
Vein pattern rubbings—how to do 530:106
Vein skeleton of leaves, how to make 784:84-85
Vein structure—study vein structure of various leaves
    294:34-35
Water loss from tree leaves experiment 1184:18
Water loss through a leaf on a twig experiment; how to
    measure 1069:59
Water moves through leaf experiment with colored
    water 1183:152-153
Water moves thru leaf experiment with colored water
    1180:24-25
What makes leaves change color—experiment 413:44-46
Why are leaves important experiment 901:35-36
Why leaves are the shape they are experiment 1183:104
Why leaves fall observation 1440:24-27
Winter's effect on tree leaves; how to imitate experiment
    1184:19

LEAVES—COLLECTION AND PRESERVATION

Collect and preserve leaves found in a vacant lot 233:30
Collecting leaves—press leaves 32:12
Collecting leaves—print leaves 32:13
Collection of tree leaves—making 294:35-37
Identify shapes of broad leaves and conifers 275:12-
    13
Leaf collecting/records by rubbing, make silhouette,
    printing and pressing 480:85
Leaf collection—pressing leaves 32:12
Leaf collection—to identify different trees—making
    275:14
Leaf collection—ways to preserve 436:51
Leaf collections—how to mount 234:81
Leaf identification cards, how to make 1321:58-59
Leaf press—how to make 436:52; 1321:58
Leaf prints, how to make 1321:60-61
Leaves ironed between sheets of waxed paper, how to do
    913:36
Mounting leaves 62:20
Plaster casts—making 413:40
Preserve leaves and make leaf prints, how to do
    1145:15; 1440:28-30

Preserving and printing leaves 657:32-35
Preserving autumn leaves 413:48
Preserving leaves—carbon leaf print, spatter print—making 413:37-39
Preserving leaves—leaf prints, leaf rubbings, sorting and matching 236:18-20
Press for flowers and leaves—building a 291:197
Pressing leaves, how to do 899:166
Waxed paper leaves, how to make 1321:104-105

LEAVES—PRESSED

How to press leaves [Primary] 880:26

LEECHES

A leech's grip—experiment 484:65
Adventure 26—ascertain how the leech sucks blood using a hand lens 29:125-129
Collect and observe, how to 796:27; 500:100-102; 1117:17
Leech senses—experiment 484:65
Observe leeches behavior in jar of water with plants experiment 1492:70-71

LEFT-HANDED. *See* **HANDEDNESS**

LEGUMES

Acid rain effect on nitrogen fixation experiment 1450:72-76

LEIDENFROST, JOHANN

Lifetime of droplets on very hot surfaces experiment 1133:7.003

LEMONS. *See also* **ACIDS; INVISIBLE INKS; SECRET WRITING**

Battery from lemon power experiment using galvanometer, how to make 1476:15
Battery you can eat experiment 1159:108-110
Electricity from a lemon experiment 1072:13
Fireworks from lemon slice put near candle flame experiment 1083:52
Juice from a lemon experiment 1238:72
Lemon battery experiment with copper nail, metal strip, wires and foil 1473:28
Lemon battery experiment 1411:77
Lemon battery experiment, how to do 1501:40-43
Lemon battery lights bulb experiment 1139:68-69
Lemon battery, how to make experiment 1514:111-113
Lemon battery, how to make 972:17; 1001:30; 1244:32-33; 1382:6
Lemon electric cell experiment; use lemon and strips of copper and zinc 1218:39
Lemon up for lemonade—examine lemon and its characteristics 452:79
Lemons contain acid experiment 860.55-57
Secret messages made with lemon juice experiment 860:57-59
Simple battery from lemon experiment 1396:94-96
Wet-cell battery from lemon experiment 1294:50-52

LENS—EYE. *See also* **EYE; HUMAN BODY**

Comparison of pinhole camera to lens of eye—diagram 555:23
Giant gelatin lens from gelatin and water—how to make 558:46
Lens sampler—words or pictures show differences in types—eyeglass lenses 558:82-83

LENSES. *See also* **MICROSCOPE; OPTICAL PROJECTORS; TELESCOPES**

3-D snapshot viewer—making 8:103-105
Aberrations—defects in simple lens 4:34-35

Activities to demonstrate how lenses magnify 1511:37-40
Activities to demonstrate how lenses work 1511:32-35
Bend light rays 240:42-47
Bending light with a lens 295:112-113
Build your own lenses 691:94-98
Calculating the magnitude of lenses 180:70
Can dense materials form lenses experiment 1402:8-11
Concave lens demonstration with number on paper behind glass of water 999:45-46
Converging Fresnel lenses make solar furnace 289:43-45
Converging lenses experiment 1138:83-85
Converging lenses focus suns rays to focal point 289:36-37
Convex lens—make fire with ice disks 179:104-106
Convex or converging lens 4:30-31
Cylindrical lenses and triangular prisms experiments 586:51
Cylindrical lenses focal length affected by light experiment 762:29-30
Diverging lens—how to make 691:100-101
Does water affect light travel experiment 902:77
Drop of water magnifying lens—making 26:54-56, 58
Droplet lenses experiment 1257:43-44
Eye lens; demonstrate how eye lens works experiment 904:152-153
Eye; effect of light on size of pupil experiment 904:156-157
Eye; effect of tiring the rods and cones in the eye experiment 904:158-159
Eye; monocle makes words clearer experiment 904:154-155
Field of vision decreases as lens magnification increases experiment 1062:24-25
Film can hand lens, how to make 1527:109
Find focal length—experiment 691:95-98
Find out how much a lens magnifies 333:47-50
Focal length—find focal length of a lens 291:187
Focal length of a convex lens, how to find experiment 1257:33-35
Focal length of a lens, how to find experiment 941:115-116
Focal length of convex lens experiment 1053:33-35
Focal length of magnifying lens, how to measure 1088:16
Focal point experiment with converging light rays 1082:48-51
Focus and focal lengths—demonstrate (Advanced) 208:110-115
Focus light rays with a magnifying glass 291:184
How a lens works experiment 898:33
How are convex and concave lenses different experiment 902:79
How does lens affect light travel experiment 902:81-82
How lenses shape light experiment 860:199-200
How lenses work 8:59-71; 909:144-145
How lenses work—experiments 659:14-17
How polarized sunglasses reduce glare experiment 941:11-12
Ice lens magnifies things experiment 1053:29-31
Image viewing box from cardboard and lens experiment 1053:12-14
Increasing magnification can compound or increase distortion experiment 1062:26-27

Jell-O lenses experiment 1257:27-28
Jell-O lenses magnify things experiment 1053:27-28
Lens from drop of water, making 902:78
Lens making techniques experiments with ice lens
     1082:57-61
Lens power of convex lens and concave lens experiment
     1092:34
Lens refraction—experiment to show 291:185
Lens refraction of a magnifying glass experiment
     941:119-120
Lens refraction, how to determine experiment 837:58-60
Lenses as magnifiers 8:73-77
Lenses bend or refract light experiment 1073:78
Light bends; experiments with prisms demonstrates
     956:34-35
Light-ray box demonstrates that light rays are bent by
     lenses experiment 1073:78
Liquid lenses—concave and convex liquid lens—
     experiment 532:82
Living picture [outdoor objects appear on paper indoors]
     experiment 906:67
Looking with lenses to demonstrate convex, concave and
     cylindrical lens 142:38-39
Magnification of objects, hair, etc. 366:194-195
Magnifying glass or reading glass—making 208:116-119
Magnifying lens from jar of water, how to use 1390:21
Magnifying lens to focus light rays 291:184
Magnifying power of a lens—how to determine 532:39
Meaning of 2X magnification experiment 1402:16-19
Measure magnifying power of a lens experiment 902:80
Opaque projector, making 906:70
Optical bench 9:62-63
Optics bench—how to make 691:96-97
Pinhole camera demonstrates why cameras have lenses
     1294:108-111
Pinhole glasses experiment 906:64-65
Projects with lenses 691:98-101
Rear-projection projector using TV picture experiment
     1082:54-56
Resolution of a lens demonstration 1394:190-191
Resolution of a lens demonstration 1479:21
Shape of lens affects its magnification experiment
     1402:12-15
Soap bubble lens experiment 1257:41-42
Submerged lens underwater experiment 1257:45-46
Sun torch—making 142:58
Tasty magnifying lens; syrup experiment 906:63-64
Telephoto lens—making 208:130-135
Telescope, making 909:145
The concave mirror—experiments 1 and 2 585:118-120
Topsy turvy words; baby food jar experiment 906:61
TV picture viewed upside down on paper experiment
     1082:51-54
Underwater lens experiment 1053:45-46
Upside down images 656:11
Using lenses 19:32-34
Water drop lens made from plastic tray and plastic wrap
     1331:91
Water drop lens, how to make 909:142; 1073:78
Water drop magnifier, how to make 862:102-104
Water drop magnifier, simple experiment 1163:26
Water drop microscope, making 906:62-63
Water droplet lenses experiment 1053:43-44
Water lens from plastic wrap and oatmeal box, how to
     make 1115:103

What a lens does 19:30
What a lens is 19:28
What is a lens and how does it work experiment with
     flashlight and eyeglasses 1411:33-34
Working with concave and convex lenses 180:69

LENTILS
Lentil seeds, how to plant and grow indoors 1178:27-28
Sprouts from lentils, how to grow 1178:27-28

LENZ, H. F. E.
Lenz's law 63:78-81

LEVEL
Carpenter's level model tells if surface is flat or tilted ex-
     periment 1230:46-47
How to make simple accurate level 167:16-18
Level for road building, how to make 1326:17

LEVERS. See also SIMPLE MACHINES—LEVERS
Calculating mechanical advantage of levers 180:37
Classifying lever action 180:36
Crowbars and seesaws—experiment 125:20-23
Experiment—with weighted match box 596:8
Experiments with second and third class levers 902:155-
     164
Function of—experiments to show 128:115-118
How can we lift objects with levers 253:173-174
How levers work—simple demonstrations (Primary)
     419:11
Lifting a giant 280:46-47
Lifting power—showing 156:25
Multiplied muscle power experiment with hammer
     563:185
Predict effort required to lift load with first class lever ex-
     periment 902:149-151
Principle of the lever demonstrated 293:42-43
Seesaw lifting power—demonstrate (Primary) 204:12-13
Seesaws and scales are levers 281:46-47
The haunted hanky—levitation with a lever 205:36-42
Tumbler's seesaw 156:22-23
Two pieces of wood demonstrate lifting power of lever
     204:10-11, 16-17
Using a lever 180:35
What is advantage of first class lever experiment
     902:145-146
What is lost as force is gained with a lever experiment
     902:152-154

LEVITATION
Levitate lady model in magic show using magnets experi-
     ment 1309:28-29

**LEYDEN JAR. See also ELECTRICITY—STATIC
ELECTRICITY**
Constructing a Leyden jar 627:19
How to make 43:72-77; 172:152-155; 768:19-20;
     209:20-21

LICHENS. See also ACID RAIN; AIR POLLUTION
Adventure 21—we come upon a strange partnership—
     lichens under microscope 403:75-78
Adventure 7—we visit fairy land—lichens under a hand
     lens 29:34-41
Collecting 436:53
How polluted is the air 660:37
Indicator plants sensitive to acid rain experiment 933:29-
     30
Lichen plants very sensitive to air pollution experiment
     1145:30
Lichen test for amount of air pollution experiment
     1362:22

Lichens and pollution experiment 737:35
Lichens response to smoke—air pollution experiment 714:118-119
Lichens show how polluted the air is 909:85
Lichens; which part is fungus or protist experiment 864:51-53
Plants prove pollution; lichens absorb sulfuric acid 617:31
Project 60:40-44
Rocks are broken down by plants experiment 1323:47-50
Show polluted air 112:21
Water absorbing ability of lichens experiment 904:72-73; 1479:28

LIFE SPAN OF ANIMALS
How long do animals live 402:84-85
Species with long gestation periods have long life spans project 969:24-25

LIFEBELTS
Model lifebelt, how to make from styrofoam, corks and chicken wire 1471:22-23

LIFEBOATS
Lifeboat's ballast keeps boat upright; show with ping pong ball buoy 1165:37

LIFESAVERS. *See also* **TRIBOLUMINESCENCE**
Sparks in your mouth from Lifesavers experiment 1083:89

LIFT
Model airfoil demonstrates upward pushing force called lift experiment 1376:21

LIFTING
Lift a person with your fingertips 291:112-113

LIFTS
Hydraulic lift demonstration using two water filled plastic bottles 1310:22-23

LIGHT. *See also* **COLOR; MICROSCOPE; PLANTS—LIGHT; SHADOWS; SPECTRUM**
A feather mystery trick 585:76-78
Accommodation 4:42-43
After image experiment—let's make ghosts 176:48
Alhazen's looking at eclipses experiment 1133:6.002
Apparent size of objects 4:42-43
Beam of light made visible experiment using talcum powder 1390:15
Beam tank with particles of milk in water makes light beams more visible 1092:18
Bend light and make it turn corners experiment 937:108-111
Bending light—experiment 693:66-68
Bending light experiment with coin in dish 1283:18
Bending light experiment with TV picture shows on cardboard screen 1257:10-11
Bending light experiment with TV set and lens 1053:10-11
Bending light experiment; make image box to capture picture 1257:12-14
Bending light experiments; water makes coin disappear 1257:20-22
Bending light rays 72:64; 120:16-17
Bending light with a lens 295:112-113
Bending light with a magnet experiment 1158:13-14
Bending light; does light always move in a straight line experiment 851:16-17
Bending light 71:41-45; 135:29; 295:111-112
Bending of visibility and bet you can make a glass disappear in a glass 228:56

Benham's Top; black and white design as it spins appears to be colored 1088:81
Benham's top 4:66-67
Bilateral symmetry experiment 956:22-23
Blacker than black 19:37
Bouncing light experiment; make a periscope to demonstrate 956:28-29
Camera obscura—making 186:97-98
Cameras 34:108-110
Can light be bent with magnets 586:57
Can light be made by breaking sugar crystals 396:69-71
Can sugar molecules rotate light experiment 831:91-94
Can you 'pipe' light thru plastic tube 381:138-139
Can you pour light experiment 900:67
Can you see light (Primary) 206:unpaged
Caustic curve 4:38-39
Chlorophyll increases or decreases in leaves with amount of light experiment 714:31-32
Clear glass that light can't get through experiment 1082:120-121
Color affects amount of light that object absorbs experiment 1479:63
Color affects energy absorbed from light experiment 902:71-72
Color blindness—demonstration 208:84-87
Color complements demonstrate 'Meyer's' experiment 202:79
Color filters 4:74-75
Color filters change color of light experiment 860:214-216
Color from spinning black and white lines experiment 761:46-47
Color in colored light 114:67-68
Color on color background effects experiment 761:37-38
Color sensations 4:70-71
Color wheel spinning experiment 1082:115-117
Color; green gumball turns black experiment 1082:110-112
Color; what color is light experiment 851:17-18
Colored filters affect light experiment 1293:123-125
Colored filters change white light 428:39-40
Colored light effects growth of plants experiment 714:29-30
Colored light experiments—rainbow, disappearing colors 210:24-25
Colored light from color spinner experiment 1314:10-11
Colored lights and their properties 569:38
Colored lights; mixing colored lights experiment 1082:112-115
Colored lights; mixing colored lights produces new colors experiment 1308:24-25
Colored lights; mixing light using flashlights with colored filters experiment 1073:82
Colored lights; why is light white experiment with different colored filters 1294:112-113
Colored paper filtering of white light stained glass window experiment 1308:8-9
Colored shadows—diffraction of light 19:54
Colored shadows experiment 761:35-36
Colored spinning discs appear to be white experiment 1073:80-81
Colors from spinning black and white disc experiment 1063:178
Colors in colored light experiment 761:34

Colors in filtered light that can be identified experiment 836:83-85

Colors in light 240:54-56

Colors in your flashlight (Primary) 206:unpaged

Colors of light can be combined to make other colors experiment 836:51-53

Colors of light experiment with three flashlights and colored plastic 1049:14

Colors of light mixed together—experiment 680:6-8

Colors of spectrum experiment 696:16-17

Colors of thin films 4:78-79

Colors; light shining through water splits into colors experiment 1365:13

Colors; mix different colors of light experiment 1296:1978

Concentrated light experiment demonstrates lasers using black plastic bottle 1308:31

Convex or converging lens 4:30-31

Dark box for light experiments—making 240:48-53

Dark colored materials absorb and emit energy more than light colors experiment 1132:55-1-55-2

Demonstrate light trapped in a water jet 176:39-40

Demonstrate principle of motion pictures 179:103-104

Depth of judgment—index of refraction computer project 584:125-126

Determining how light travels 180:70

Diffraction—show with a hankie 120:28

Diffraction grating (how we see) 8:19-28

Diffraction grating replica—use to see spectrum 386:63-66

Diffraction grating 4:82-83

Diffraction of light experiment 941:27-30

Disappearing tricks with light and colors 684:18-19

Disc sets—flow painting, moving montage, color wheels, polarizing color 386:8-9

Dispersion of light 4:54-58

Do we need light to see—shoe box experiment [Primary] 742:14

Does heavy layer of canopy trees effect plant growth experiment 714:36-37

Dust helps us to see 281:81

Effect of light on flowering bulbs 532:78

Effects of light on many things in your environment—observe 761:90-95

Effects of light on plants 8:97-101

Electric light from your arm with fluorescent bulb 186:102

Energy—light energy changes into heat energy—experiment 428:16-17

Energy from light in plants 76:8-9

Excited molecules give off extra energy as light experiment 1250:61-62

Experimenting with prisms and light project 833:187-188

Experiments with color 128:201-203

Fiber optics illuminator 386:7

Fiber optics kit 386:24-29

Filter—Pulfrich illusion—the funny pendulum 16:92-95

Filtering light with colored plastic experiment 935:16-17

Fire with ice discs (double convex lens)—making 179:104-106

First Law of Thermodynamics experiment; light energy transferred/transformed 1453:14-15

Focal length and color experiment 761:44-45

Focus a beam of light without a lens 179:96-97

Focusing lines of light and the inverted image experiment 941:96-100

Fog lights does yellow light pass thru fog better than white light experiment 762:35-36

From transparent to opaque 240:30-31

Fruit flies response to light experiment 936:14-15

Ghost colors experiment—see "ghost" image of what you stare at 570:12

Gratings and what they do (diffraction grating) 19:56

How bright is light 19:36

How light travels experiment 906:139

How light travels 240:18-19

Human eyes equally sensitive to all colors of light experiment 1092:48

Illuminated fountain—making 385:111-113

Illumination—computer project 584:127-129

Illusions using color to see if eye or brain is doing it experiment 761:57-58

Image in a mirror—experiment to locate 385:102

Image viewing box from cardboard and lens experiment 1053:12-14

Images formed by plane mirrors 4:14-15

Images from a pinhole 295:110-111

Images in a plane mirror 295:104-108

Images in a plane mirror 4:14-15

Intensity—experiment to measure the brightness of light 385:100-101

Intensity—make photometer to measure 436:62-63

Interference lines (1) and interference lines (2)—experiment 585:112-114

Internal reflection—experiment 385:111

Internal reflection 4:26-27

Inverse square law experiment; light looks dimmer the farther away we get 1132:59-1-59-2

Inverted ghosts—determining focal length of a convex lens 114:74

Inverted image in mirror—experiment 385:107-108

Investigating shadows—experiment 586:54

Johann Ritter's discovery of ultraviolet rays experiment 1133:6.011

Kaleidoscope—making 186:98-99

Lambert's method 4:70-71

Lateral inhibition experiment using shades of gray color 1132:56-1-56-2

Lens power of convex lens and concave lens experiment 1092:34

Lenses 34:105-107

Lenses—aberration (defects) 4:34-35

Light and colloids—experiment 382:143-146

Light and color—mixing colored lights 114:65-67

Light and sight—experiments 659:18-23

Light box—building to experiment with mixing colors 761:32-34

Light breaks into different colors 428:28-30

Light by friction with fluorescent bulb 585:121

Light can be absorbed and changed into heat energy 428:16-17

Light catcher, dodecahedron, how to make from heavy paper and shiny paper 1115:129-131

Light changes when it passes through substances experiment 1250:52-54

Light from candy experiment 906:141

Light goes thru transparent and translucent things but not opaque things 956:10-11

Light is affected by the depth of water experiment 877:30-34

Light meter, how to make 830:66

Light scattered by large molecules experiment with water, gelatin and sugar 1251:71-74

Light sensor and program—making—computer project 665:30-31

Light shines through some things experiment [Primary] 742:16

Light show from oatmeal box and flashlight (Primary) 558:48-49

Light sources appear to wiggle and flash when you give them Bronx cheer 1132:14-1-14-2

Light travels in a straight line 40:77-78; 253:77-78; 555:8

Light travels in a straight line—experiment 892:5; 128:191-192; 208:26-27

Light travels in a straight line experiment with a candle 1073:74

Light travels in straight line magic trick 1010:55-60

Light travels in straight line shown with flashlight and cards 1404:18

Light travels in straight line; demonstrate with pinhole camera 1394:174-175

Light travels in the dark 8:1-9

Light turns a corner—making a periscope 240:24-26

Light waves can stop each other 19:50

Light with prisms, shadows and transparent materials experiments 1417:5

Lingering shadows—using color to produce colored shadows 114:70-72

Liquid light experiment to see how optical fibers work 1092:23

Magic box 8:111-117

Magic with light—experiment 385:108-109

Magnetic field exerts a force on a light beam experiment 1158:13-14

Magnification—reading glass 281:84

Magnifying glass 72:65

Magnifying power of convex lens 4:50-51

Magnifying things 34:102-104

Make a glass disappear experiment 902:99

Make names on apples 176:32-33

Making a spectrum 180:64

Making halves and coronas 8:134-136

Making light rays bounce 72:63

Making rainbows 586:55-56

Maxwell's disks 4:62-63

Mealworm response to light experiment 936:11-13

Measure the brightness of light with photometer experiment 1405:18

Measuring light—making a light meter or photometer 8:10-18

Measuring wave length of light 8:39-47

Mercury street light viewed with compact disc shows separate colors experiment 1250:57-60

Meter—making 8:11-18

Meyer's experiment with colored shadows 761:37

Mirror images—curved images show two flames 120:15

Mirror images—curved surface gives strange images 120:14

Mirror images—make a periscope to show mirror images 120:12-13

Mirrors 34:98-99

Mirrors—experiments with 295:103-117

Mirrors—what mirrors do 291:175

Mirrors that bulge out 19:18

Mirrors to show reflection of light 135:26-28

Mixing colored light—experiment 586:52-54

Mixing colored lights 180:65

Mixing colors to make different colors experiment with flashlight/cellophane 1213:28-29

Model eye or pinhole camera, how to make 1092:38

Movement of light through transparent and opaque materials demonstration 1479:93

Moves in a straight line 19:2

Moving colors—make a mini movie 76:30

Newton's color disk 4:67

Newton's rings experiment 1133:6.008

Newton's rings of color—making 186:100-101

Newton's white light through a prism experiment 1156:73-76

Newton's white light's constituent colors experiment 1133:6.007

Opaque, transparent and translucent materials experiment 1111:15-17

Optical illusions 76:29

Optical projection—how to make projectors 128:204-205

Periscope—making 96:64-65; 186:99-100

Photoelectric cell experiment 1153:127

Photoelectric effect—effect distance/color on intensity 209:50-53

Photoelectric effect experiment using an electroscope, how to make 1153:119-123

Pictures made of light (Primary) 206:unpaged

Pinhole camera shows that light travels in a straight line 240:20-23

Pinhole ghosts—inverted images 114:63-65

Pinhole image 19:4

Pinhole images—experiment 586:55

Pinhole viewer—build to show light travels in straight lines 595:20-21

Plants—show which colors in sunlight plants bend to most 270:58-60

Polariscope—how to make 43:44-53

Polarized—crystals of magnesium sulfate act like Polaroid lenses 346:37-38

Polarized light—experiments with 532:38

Polarized light stained glass window mosaic experiment 1132:78-1-78-3

Polarized light through sugar water gives beautiful colors experiment 1132:85-1-85-2

Polarized light 4:86-87; 8:78-94

Polarized sunglasses experiment 1132:79-1-79-2

Polarizing color disc set and spinner wheel 386:14-16

Polarizing spinner 6' and stand 386:32

Primary experiments with light and mirrors 1451:4-29

Primary experiments with light 100:6-13

Projection kaleidoscopes 386:11-13

Projectors—500 W 35 mm visual effects projectors 386:20-23

Pulfrich's illusions experiment 1133:6.013

Pupil of eye controls how much light enters eye experiment 1132:80-1-80-2

Radiates and travels in straight lines 428:10-11

Radiating light from candle dims as you move from light source experiment 1390:13

Rainbow making 32:36-37; 35:32; 253:84-85; 281:85

Rays—light travels in a straight line 96:58-59

Reflections in a spoon experiment using spoon mirrors and beam tank 1092:25
Rippling color accessory 386:30
Rotating plane of polarized light experiment 1153:114-116
Rotating polarized light with Karo syrup experiment 1153:116-117
Scattered and unscattered light experiment 1153:112-113
Scattered light 19:48
See nonluminous things with reflected light 240:11-13
Seeing green after you see red—experiment 179:99-100
Seeing things in colored light 19:46
Sensation of color 4:62-63, 66-67
Shadow—a disappearing shadow 114:76-77
Shadow—experiment 659:4-7
Shadow picture shows how light breaks down molecules 85:58-59
Shadows—how shadows are formed 72:62
Shadows and shadow theater experiment 135:25
Shadows 240:32-35
Show light travels in a straight line 179:85-87
Show plants need light for proper growth 179:101-102
Show polarized light with sunglasses 120:29
Show why a pencil appears broken when in water—refraction 179:93-95
Signaling light—how to make 76:24-25
Simple magnifying glass 4:46-47
Smooth surfaces reflect light better than rough surfaces 240:12-13
Sodium light—making 186:96-97
Some colors easier to see from a distance than others experiment 1088:82
Some light is absorbed by all things—opaque and translucent objects 428:41-43
Sparkling bicycle wheels—making 177:25-27
Spectroscope—making 8:49-53
Spectroscope separates light into colors of rainbow experiment, how to make 1516:19-20
Spectrum—demonstrate a simple one 120:22-23
Spectrum—dispersion 4:54-55, 58-59
Spectrum—make white light by spinning wheel of different colors 555:16
Spectrum—making prism 436:64
Spectrum—seeing the spectrum—experiment 570:8-9
Spectrum; how to make using mirror, cardboard, container of water 1073:81
Speed of light in different media experiment 762:30-33
Spin a color top 19:44
Spinning colors 180:65
Spinning colors disc, making 935:18-19
Stained glass window experiment 1111:18
Straight line path of light demonstration 837:20-21
Stroboscope—how to make 202:73
Sun powered light show 494:19
Taking white light apart (prism)—experiment 179:98-99
Temperature—sunlight has heat 96:62
Test light going thru transparent versus opaque (Primary) 320:21
Testing the effect of colored lights on plant growth 180:66
The colors in light—make your own rainbow 587:45
The double prism makes a rainbow 291:182-183
Things that reflect light 240:27-29
Transparency—investigation into transparency 420:105-107

Travels—how light travels 8:21-23
Travels—how light travels—wave theory 8:26-28
Travels in a straight line demonstration 1479:93
Travels in a straight line experiment 898:30; 941:3-5; 956:7
Trick light box—how to make 723:29
Tricks; stamp under glass of water disappears experiment 898:32
Twenty-one primary experiments with household items (Primary) 409:unpaged
Tyndall effect or why the sky is blue 102:127-129
Useful bands of color (light interference) 19:52
Versatile spotlight and adjustable aperture 386:10
Visual effects—projector set 386:33-36
Water separates light into different colors experiment 1250:55-56
Wave lengths—make spectrum of light on ceiling 202:76
Waves—diffraction—light can be bent 95:50
Waves—easy diffraction interference patterns—experiment 585:106-107
Waves—make an image thru lens—hollow mirror demonstration 95:48-49
What color of light attracts most insects—experiment 414:31-32
What does prism do to light experiment 902:85
What happens when light is blocked experiment [Primary] 742:17
What makes shadows experiment 906:140
What path does light follow experiment 902:70
Whirling wonder discs 386:2-6
White light can be split into seven colors using glass prism experiment 1073:80-81
White light experiment; make white light from 3 filter lights, red, green, blue 1088:75
White light is made up of colors; make spinner to show 893:10
White light; how to see when spinning colored circle, how to do 1415:28-29
"Whiter than white" soap experiment 1082:121-123
Why is light white; experiment with colored filters 860:217
Why light is white experiment 941:45-47
Why night is dark 72:62

LIGHT—ABSORPTION
Testing light absorption 180:71
LIGHT—DIFFRACTION
Grimaldi's diffraction of light experiment 1133:6.005
LIGHT—POLLUTION
Different lights tested in simulated starry night sky diorama experiment 1476:202-206
Light pollution diorama to show shielded and unshielded lighting effects 1476:202-206
Light pollution survey of your local area project, how to do 1478:31
Streetlight pollution experiment; design better light polluting streetlight 1478:30-31
Streetlight pollution of night sky viewing experiment; which pollutes most 1478:30-31
LIGHT—RADIANT ENERGY
3-D snapshot viewer—illusions 8:103-105
Corona—producing 8:134-136
Diffraction grating 8:21-26
Focal point of lens 8:63-68
Grating effect 8:26-28

Halos and coronas 8:134-136
Kaleidoscope 8:118-127
Kaleidoscope—open 8:118-119
Kaleidoscope—permanent 8:121-126
Kaleidoscope—projector 8:126-127
Lens—convex and concave 8:75-77
Lens image—how produced 8:64-68, 76
Light filters—working of 8:53-56
Light meters 8:11-18
Light travels in dark 8:1-9
Measuring—light meter making 8:16-18
Measuring—light meter making—principles of Robert
    Bunsen 8:14-16
Measuring—making light meter or photometer 8:10-14
Microscope water drop 8:108-110
Optical bench—how to make 9:62-63
Plants—effect of color on 8:100-101
Plants—light effect on 8:97-101
Polarization of light waves 8:79-80, 82-83, 84-87
Polarized light 8:79-82; 8:92-93
Prism and color of light 8:48-51
Reflecting or transmitting light 'magic box' 8:112-116
Refraction—lens 8:60-62
Spectroscope—making 8:49-51
Stroboscope 8:130-132
Wave length of light—measuring 8:42-43
Wave length of sodium light 8:41-44
White light from colored light 8:55-56

LIGHT—RAYS
Bending light experiment—how to make incident and re-
    flected rays 586:49-50
Bending light rays 281:83
Bending light rays—experiment 30:54
Bending of light rays—a coin you can't see 548:81-84
Bent—why do light rays bend in water 291:180
Bouncing rays 280:24
Display of rays in bowl of water 120:16
Flashlight and comb demonstrate light rays shine straight
    experiment 843:12-15
Game "mirror monsters" demonstrates how light rays
    travel experiment 1443:26-33
Glancing rays of light experiment using beam tank, how
    to build 1092:20
How light rays fool us—experiment 385:109-110
Lenses bend light rays 240:42-47
Light bends in water experiment 902:10
Light mobile demonstrates—making 697:19
Light rays bend in water—the archer fish test 607:31
Light rays can be observed experiment 836:53-54
Light rays obstructed by opaque object shown by shadow
    puppets experiment 1308:6-7
Light rays visible—experiment 176:40-42
Light rays 34:100-102
Light travels in a straight line flashlight and cards experi-
    ment 742:15
Light travels through tube in dark box experiment
    1019:16-17
Magnifying lens focus light rays 291:184
Make a glass disappear experiment 902:12
Making a light box-what happens-light rays strike reflect-
    ing surfaces 586:45-49
Making light rays bounce—experiments 30:53
Periscope making 291:178
Pinhole camera to demonstrate—making 281:80
Primary color spinner, how to make 999:43-44

Ray tracing board to measure angle of incoming and out-
    going ray of light 1092:19
Show light rays trapped 120:11
Size of mirror needed for full image 291:173
Smoke box to study light rays—making 128:191-192
The burning glass 291:179
The inverted image 291:176
Water makes light bend 96:59-60
What are the effects of different rays on animal life
    402:89-90
What causes a shadow 281:84-85
Why do light rays 'bend' in water 291:180

LIGHT—REFLECTED
An underwater flame 114:79-80
Can you pour light experiment 902:97-98
Comparing colors; reflecting power in dark experiment
    898:33
Create an optical illusion 291:177
Demonstrate reflected light with mirror and flashlight ex-
    periment 892:8-9
Dissolved light 114:77-78
Experiments with light 693:60-68
Experiments with reflected light 532:22-23
Flashlight on stream of water demonstrates 892:19
How light bounces 281:81
How many images can you see experiment 902:92-93
Light is reflected by objects 428:19-22
Make 'light bird' with mirror, foil, coins, paper [Pri-
    mary] 329:16-21
Mirror cards from aluminum foil 558:62-63
Mirror magic experiment 570:28
Mirrors—the boundless menagerie 350:132
More experiments with reflected light 532:26
Night vision—can we see in the dark 281:78-79
Periscope—how to make 293:43; 281:82-83
Reflected images—the magic mirror—see yourself up-
    side down 114:81-83
Reflected light (Primary) 206:unpaged
Reflected light with plane mirror 295:103-104
Reflected waves—experiment to show 106:53-58
Seeing round corners—make a periscope 570:29
The broken peppermint stick 280:23
What is difference between reflected light and source
    light experiment 902:88
What is reflected light experiment 902:89

LIGHT—REFLECTION. See also KALEIDOSCOPES;
    MIRRORS; PERISCOPES
A light mystery—silvery egg—experiment 585:111-112
A 'magic candle' experiment 385:103
A skin diver's mystery—pencil in jar of water demonstra-
    tion 563:139-140
Activities to demonstrate regular reflection and diffuse re-
    flection 1511:6-13
Angle of reflection, measuring experiment 941:86-88
Angles of an incoming and reflected light beam with mir-
    ror experiment 1159:73-76
Anti-gravity mirrors make you appear to be flying experi-
    ment 1132:2-1-2-2
Backward writing in mirror experiment 960:46
Bouncing light off mirrors experiment 898:30-31
Brain expects image it sees in mirror is your other hand
    experiment 1132:66
Can you control reflection of light experiment 902:94-95
Candle appears to burn underwater experiment with jar
    of water, sheet of glass 1153:23-24

Candle seems to burn in glass of water experiment 843:3-6

Caustics; curved line patterns produced by curved mirrors and lights experiment 1443:84-91

Christmas tree balls give spherical reflections experiment 1132:91-1-91-2

Coin in bowl of water demonstrates light reflection experiment 1073:77

Collage of things that shine—making [Primary] 742:48

Color disc experiment 928:19

Colored light on colors changes color experiment 928:23

Colors mixed to form other colors; flashlight, colored cellophane experiment 818:20

Colors: light reflection—experiment 585:115-116

Corner reflector shows multiple images of an object experiment 1132:31-1-31-2

Cylindrical mirror lets you see yourself as others see you experiment 1132:35-1-35-3

Demonstrate the law of reflection 253:81-83

Demonstrate with a disappearing coin 179:95-96

Demonstrate with mirrors 179:87-92

Demonstrate with optical illusion 208:79

Dot on piece of paper in cup of water demonstrates 999:46-47

Double image from glass experiment 941:83

Enlarge or reduce drawings 399:82

Experiment to show 128:192-196

Experimenting with reflection 180:72

Find the focal length of a curved mirror—experiment 385:106-112

Fire under water experiment 906:73-74

Flashing solar mobile—how to make 651:40-41

Flour and water suspension experiment; show reflection with flashlight 905:166-167

Flying saucers—experiment 585:105-106

Game "finding location of object" shows light reflected off flat surface 1443:37-43

Game "finding person around barrier" controls path of reflected light experiment 1443:33-37

Glass and light; compare window and plate glass experiment 956:21

Glass object disappears when reflection is eliminated experiment 1132:40-1-40-2

How a mirror works experiment 941:73-75

How do you really look 281:82

How does mirror invert an image 291:176

How is light reflection like the bounce of a ball experiment 902:90-91

How mirror can produce distorted images experiment 941:78-79

How mirror reflection can be reversed experiment 941:76-77

Images formed by plane mirrors experiment [Advanced] 871:4.012

Images of images can repeat forever experiment 1132:61-1-61-2

Investigate reflections 909:136-137

Kaleidoscope—how to make 385:103-105; 909:137

Kaleidoscope made from mirrors and colored beads, how to do 1073:76

Law of reflection—experiment to demonstrate 642:66-67

Law of reflection experiment using glass slides or pane of glass 1153:14-18

Light and dark clouds—experiment 585:115

Light flows inside water experiment 941:67-70

Light meter experiment 906:75-76

Light mill spins in sunlight experiment, how to make 1213:30-31

Light reflected from colored surface will have that color experiment 836:48-50

Light reflected in water experiment; make model to explain 1158:14-19

Light reflects through transparent materials such as glass or water experiment 1132:33-1-33-2

Light-ray box, how to make using shoe box, flashlight and mirror 1073:74

Magic color disc 281:86

Make simple picture copier 202:78

Making and reflecting narrow beam of light experiment 1159:73-76

Mirror affects reflected image shown by copying writing from mirror 1404:194-195

Mirror experiment to demonstrate (Primary) 210:22-23

Mirror image; where is mirror image experiment using mirror, pins 1153:19-21

Mirror images 76:12-17

Mirror images demonstration 555:12

Mirror reflects rays from comb experiment 911:10

Mirror writing experiment 937:112-113

Mirrors at an angle, multiple images experiment 1153:23-27

Mirrors can be used to change the path of a light beam experiment 836:46-47

Mirrors change the direction of light 96:60-61

Mirrors reflect light—experiment 659:8-11; 1063:176

Mirrors used to multiply reflections experiment 941:80-82

Mirrors; images in a mirror experiment 956:25

Mixing colors with light experiment 928:18

Multiple images of your face moving past each other experiment 1443:57-63

Objects reflect light so we see them; shoe box with door/object inside 1014:60

Parabolas experiment with mirrors 1132:73-1-73-2

Parabolic shapes concentrate energy experiment 1132:58-1-58-2

Particle model and reflection of light experiment 1153:62-63

Penny reappears in dish of water experiment 1066:84

Pepper's ghost, making 911:8

Peppers Ghost—making 142:37

Periscope—making 179:92-93

Periscope demonstrates reflection of light rays, how to make 1308:14-15

Periscope from cardboard carton and mirrors, how to make 1163:23

Periscope, making 906:76-77; 909:138

Periscope, milk carton, build to demonstrate reflection 851:19-20

Polarized light—experiment 563:149-150

Preventing reflection of light 180:71

Produce infinite images of object using mirrors experiment 937:106-107

Rainbows in a bubble—experiment 585:123-124

Reflecting beams of light experiment 941:84-85

Reflecting power of dark and light surfaces demonstrated with flashlight 1179:82-83

Reflection inside water experiments 911:18-19

Reflection of by mirrors—bet you can see to infinity 228:54-55

Reflection of by water—bet you can pour light 228:52-53
Reflection of light 4:10-11
Reflections in a plane mirror experiment 956:26
Rock reflector demonstrates diffused reflection 563:146
Shiny paper collage demonstrates reflected light 1111:20
Some surfaces reflect light better than others 40:78-79
Specular reflection experiment; x-ray eyes see through book 1253:34-35
Star race experiment 906:74-75
The light pipe—experiment 585:122
The Tyndall effect demonstrated with a light, coffee cans and milk 563:147-148
The window reflection 585:117-118
Theodoric of Freibourg's how rainbows are formed experiment 1133:6.003
Thermometer shows lower temperature under white or dark cloth—exp. 601:unpaged
Touch the spring experiment 1132:100-1-100-2
Transparent mirrors; how light travels through them experiments 1443:47-56
Transverse vibrations in a string; transverse wave motion of light experiment 1132:96-1-96-2
Tricky reflections 684:26-27
Two mirror tricks with pencil and human face 563:144
Two-way mirrors experiment so you become composite person of your partner 1132:48-1-48-2
Use mirrors to demonstrate 208:72-78
What affects the quality of reflection experiment 902:87
What colors are in sunlight 96:63-64
Where is your image—experiment 586:41-45
Why outer space is dark experiment 906:78
Words in a mirror experiment 747:29-30

LIGHT—REFRACTION

A stamped out stamp—light refraction 205:90-93
Activities to demonstrate how light bends 1511:26-31
Angle of refraction and angle of incidence experiment 1158:10-29
Astigmatism in a curved mirror experiment 1082:72-76
Bend light experiment using metal coffee can, flashlight and water 1411:33
Bend straw without touching it 827:16
Bending light and the reappearing coin experiment 1159:77-80
Bending light demonstration using straws in glass of water 1016:48
Bending light experiment with flashlight and cardboard 1213:21
Bending light experiments 595:24-25; 659:12-13; 909:140-141
Bending wire in glass of water experiment 1138:68-69
Bottle bender experiment—bottle of water, flashlight and cardboard—demo 570:27
Broken pencil experiment 906:58
Broken pencil in water experiment 941:57
Button, straw in glass of water demonstrate bending light rays 1019:18-19
Can water make a coin appear experiment 902:9
Coin appears in glass of water experiment 1082:28-29
Coin disappears in glass of water experiment 1005:21
Coin in cup of water demonstrates refraction of light 1415:17
Coin in cup of water experiment 843:22-27
Coin in cup trick demonstrates 892:29
Coin in glass disappears experiment 736:31
Coin in water experiment 941:59-61

Coin vanishes in glass of water trick 1010:46-50
Colors of sunlight experiment 1391:7
Compare round and square glass containers experiment 941:62-64
Convex lens produces picture 681:20
Cylindrical lenses and triangular prisms—experiment 586:51
Demonstrate with flashlight, water and milk 208:67
Demonstrate with water, coins and pan 208:66
Dispersion experiment; separation of light into colors using light and prism 1153:38-40
Experimenting with refraction 180:72
Experiments to show 128:196-201
Experiments with magnifying glass 291:185
False pencils in water experiment 1082:33-36
Find the coin experiment 902:74
Flashlight beam in fish tank filled with milky water demonstrates 722:122
Focal point experiment with converging light rays 1082:48-51
Fresnel lens creates image that hangs in mid-air experiment 1132:54-1-54-3
Glass object disappears when you eliminate reflection experiment 1132:40-1-40-2
Glass of water magnifies print experiment 1066:81
Glasses that magnify—pencil in glasses of water 563:141
Hide the pennies trick 585:68
How rays of light bend experiment with flashlight and glass of water 1049:10
Index of refraction and density experiment 762:25-28
Index of refraction and density of materials experiment 1158:30-31
Index of refraction experiment 1082:38-41
Index of refraction measured in liquids other than water experiment 1153:33-34
Jell-O lenses magnify things experiment 1053:27-28
Light bends demonstration with flashlight and milky water 1179:84
Light bends in tubes in water experiment 911:15
Light bends; experiments with prisms demonstrates 956:34-35
Light box—making 762:26
Light box model to demonstrate refracting or bending light experiment 1476:42-43
Light can be bent 240:36-41; 253:79-80
Light changes direction by refraction 428:23-25
Light does not travel at same speed through air, water and glass 428:26-27
Light from flashlight bends in warm air and produces distorted image 555:15
Light on jar of water in box demonstrates bending light experiment 1019:20-21
Light ray bends as it goes through water; demonstrate 892:20
Light reflects through transparent materials such as glass or water experiment 1132:33-1-33-2
Light refraction demonstrated with glass of water and straw 1288:6-7
Light travels slowly through glass experiment 956:33
Light-ray box demonstrates that light rays are bent by lenses experiment 1073:78
Light-ray house demonstrates how light is refracted and reflected, make 1179:86-87
Liquids magnify objects project 1296:1998

Magic trick demonstrates; blank card prediction 1010:51-54

Make a burning glass 291:179

Make a silvery egg 76:28-29

Make a water drop lens 95:47

Make big screen TV with curved mirror experiment 1082:71-72

Make jar disappear into thin air experiment 937:114-115

Making a coin appear in dish 569:24

Measuring angles of incidence and refraction of water experiment 1153:30-33

Mirror and bowl of water create spectrum from sunlight project 967:14-15

Nail is bent by magic trick 1010:43-45

Odds that are out of sight 222:94-95

Off-the-wall TV control experiment 1082:67-69

Particle model and refraction of light experiment 1153:64-66

Pencil in water demonstrates 719:33-34

Penny in a bowl trick 360:74

Postage stamp hides under clear glass experiment 902:75

Prism, slide projector and screen used to mix colored light experiment 1153:40-43

Rainbow in the dark experiment using water, mirror and flashlight 1331:94

Rear-projection projector using TV picture experiment 1082:54-56

Refraction and total internal reflection experiment 871:4.013

Refraction circus experiments; four to try 911:16-17

Refraction in action in beam tank experiment, how to build 1092:30

Refraction of light 4:18-19

Refraction of light—experiment 585:108-109

Refraction of light in liquids experiment; data tables given 1004:5.015

Refraction thru rectangular glass plate 4:22-23

Repeat Isaac Newton's experiment that light is composed of many colors 448:29-32

Spectrum colors spinning wheel experiment 1111:26-27

Spoon in glass of water demonstrates refraction of light 555:14

Stretched penny shape in water demonstrates light refraction 1053:22

Test refraction with coin in glass of water experiment 1163:25

Testing light refraction 625:34

The double image from black paper and piece of glass—demonstration 563:145-146

The fat reflection in a car door 563:143-144

Theodoric of Freibourg's how rainbows are formed experiment 1133:6.003

Total internal reflection in a prism experiment 1153:36-39

TV picture viewed upside down on paper experiment 1082:51-54

Use water loop lens to demonstrate 208:69

Vanishing postage stamp 202:75

Watch TV with curved magnifying mirror experiment 1082:69-70

Water bends light and makes penny reappear experiment 1053:20-21

Water bends light so object can't be seen experiment 1231:18-19

Water bends light; spoon in glass of water demonstrates 898:10

Water drop microscope demonstrates refraction of light 1308:18-19

Water makes a coin appear experiment 900:69

Water sphere lens experiment 1132:105-1-105-2

Water stars demonstration with light and water drops in darkness 563:150-151

Water used to separate light into its separate colors demonstration 1404:188-189

What happened to the pencil experiment 902:73

What makes a rainbow 291:174

What makes light bend experiment 902:76

Where's the penny experiment 906:57

Why the dark spots—demonstration 563:142-143

Willebrord Snell's law of refraction of light experiment 1133:6.004

Wineglass raindrop experiment 958:10-11

LIGHT—RESPONSE TO LIGHT

How do plants and animals respond to light 402:17-18

LIGHT—VIBRATIONS

Rainbow of colors experiment 906:68-69

LIGHT—WAVES

Build a spectrometer 586:56

Colors in clear acetate wave interference experiment 1082:141-142

Different lengths of time needed for brain to record color waves experiment 904:162-163

Diffraction experiment; light can bend around edges 1132:38-1-38-2

Diffraction grating experiment with feather 1082:144-145

Diffraction of light waves experiment 1153:85-86

False pencils in water experiment 1082:33-36

Interference patterns of light waves experiment 1153:97-102

Interference patterns of rainbow colors experiment using 2 sheets of Plexiglas 1132:13-1-13-2

Interference patterns using a diffraction grating experiment 1153:102-103

Interference; constructive and destructive, see thru model demonstrates 1132:19-1-19-3

Light consists of waves experiment with pinhole in paper and flashlight 911:25

Light transmitted thru different types of transparent substances experiment 1004:5.014

Light travels in straight lines experiment with flashlight and cardboard 1163:19

Light waves bend; spoon in water demonstrates 872:41

Light waves blend to produce white light shown with color wheel 1404:19

Light waves interference experiment using bubble films 1082:138-141

Moire pattern interference experiment with pocket comb 1082:142-144

Periodic waves experiments in ripple tank 1153:76-79

Poisson's spot experiment; diffraction of light around small disk 1153:103-106

Polarization of sky light experiment 1153:110-112

Polarized waves, how to make 1153:108-109

Reflection of water waves similar to reflection of light experiment 1153:73-74

Refraction waves using ripple tank experiment 1153:74-76

Scattering of blue light waves experiment using water, milk, flashlight 1397:75

Slinky demonstrates how light waves travel 1479:94

Wave model for light using a Slinky experiment 1153:67-69

Wavelength of light experiment 1158:34-43

LIGHT AND DARKNESS

Differences between night and day study, how to do 1063:218-219

How shadows form 30:51-52

Shadows move as sun moves experiment 956:8-9

Why night is dark 30:52

LIGHT BULBS. *See also* **BULBS—ELECTRIC**

Brightness of light bulb measured by photometer experiment, how to make 1501:23

Fat light meter to determine which bulb is brighter experiment 827:78-79

Filament wire resistance makes brighter glow 287:26

Find out how to make a light bulb 599:43

Fluorescent tube lights up from static electricity on balloon experiment 1208:78-79

Fluorescent tube, how it works experiment 1404:8-9

How to make 366:232

Inside the light bulb trick 585:76-77

Light bulb—making 436:54

Light bulb, how to make using wire, nails, battery and jar 1243:38-39

Light bulb, how to make 1012:63-64

LIGHT YEARS

How far is a light year—chart to measure 292:120

LIGHTHOUSES

Lighthouse model, working model, how to make 1200:27

Lighthouse that lights up experiment, how to build 955:19; 1199:14-15

Lighthouse that lights up experiment 1072:19

Lighthouse, battery operated model, how to make 1043:12-13

Model lighthouse—making 342:32; 543:32-33

Model lighthouse with light, how to make 868:72

Model lighthouse with turning, warning light, how to make 1307:16-17

LIGHTNING

Demonstration 12:50-52

Life Saver lightning in your mouth experiment 1017:24

Lightning produces radio waves demonstration 1023:180-181

Lightning strike location on ground or on object computer project 1021:43-49

Make your own lightning 694:47-48

Make your own lightning experiment 1281:24

Making lightning (Primary) 232:46

Photographing lightning, how to 586:57

Positive and negative charges experiments with balloons 972:11

Why does it lightning—balloons in dark room—experiment (Primary) 452:54

LIGHTNING AND THUNDER

How far away is the storm, how to figure 1003:91

Make lightning experiment 1028:97

Measuring distance to a storm, how to do 1439:105-109

What causes thunder experiment 1003:90-91

What is lightning demonstration with comb 1003:86-87

LIGHTNING BUGS. *See* **FIREFLIES**

LIGHTNING CONDUCTOR

Demonstrate with magic wand and record 287:13

LIGHTS—COLORED

Colored lights experiment; looking through colored filters 956:18

Colored lights experiment; making a color box 956:18-19

Colored lights experiment; mixing colored light 956:19

Colored lights experiments with recording sheet 747:13-14

Disco light show machine—how to make 487:49-51

LILIENTHAL, OTTO

Who invented the hang glider experiment 1525:7-11

LIMESTONE

Acid effect on statues experiment 1405:76

Chemical properties of marble and why damaged by pollution experiment 871:3.026

Collect limestone and then chemically remove it experiment 1479:55

Determine if limestone can protect pine trees from acid rain experiment 997:93-94

How do rocks react to vinegar experiment 900:139

Scratch test to tell limestone from quartzite [sandstone] experiment 1438:78-79

Scratch testing limestone experiment 1438:76-77

Stalactites and stalagmites, how to make experiment 1042:28-29

Test for chalk or limestone in rocks experiment 1277:31

Test for limestone experiment 1023:32-33; 1405:71

Test local rocks for limestone experiment 715:65-66

Testing limestone with an acid experiment 1438:80-82

Vinegar test for limestone in rocks experiment 1014:89

Vinegar used as test for limestone in rocks 538:82

Which rocks can be dissolved in water experiment 900:143-144

LIMEWATER

Breath contains carbon dioxide experiment 1322:17-20

Breathe into limewater; carbon dioxide experiment 959:76

How to make 55:163; 122:135-136; 128:214

Limewater test for carbon dioxide produced by yeast experiment 905:74-75

Limewater testing solution, how to make 1396:203

Limewater used as test for carbon dioxide experiment 752:113

Test for carbon dioxide 676:38

Test for carbon dioxide in soda pop 676:42

Testing solution for carbon dioxide; make limewater experiment 905:70-71

LIMPETS

Slipper limpet community; who lives with them experiment; survey chart given 1225:36

Slipper limpets growth rate effected by particulate pollution in water 1225:36-37

Slipper limpets; do they move about on the rocks experiment 1225:36

Slipper limpets; finding and identifying experiment 1225:35-36

LINDBERGH, CHARLES

Who was the first to fly the Atlantic Ocean project 1525:12-17

LINES

Demonstrate principles of straight, parallel and perpendicular lines 440:1-33

LINES OF FORCE. *See also* **MAGNETIC LINES OF FORCE**

Cutting magnetic lines of force 532:37

Dipping the needle—experiment 532:41

Investigating lines of force with magnet 532:36

LINT

Make paper from short lint fibers 257:30-32

Paper—how to make 336:12-13

LIPIDS. *See* **FATS AND OILS**

LIQUID SOAP DISPENSERS

Water flows uphill experiment using plastic bottle, tubing and balloon 1208:46-47

LIQUIDS. *See also* **FLUIDS; WATER**

A sea change—bleach turns blue water white 161:72

Absorption—which paper towel is best, fastest, strongest 147:20-21

Acid—fizzy lemonade 77:32-33

Acid—invisible ink 77:33

Acid and alkaline—dancing mothballs 77:34

Acid and alkaline—indicators 77:34-35

Are some liquids runnier than others experiment 1508:22

Bending water 147:40-41

Bernoulli; who discovered laws of gases or fluids in motion project 1525:92-94

Boiling point of liquids experiment using test tubes and spirit burners 1179:23

Brownian motion of pollen grains experiment 1133:7.006

Capillary action 77:10-11

Capillary action—striped celery 77:8-9

Capillary attraction 71:27-29; 350:102-105

Centrifugal force in liquids demonstrated with water in spinning bowl 1079:44-45

Chameleon liquids—how to show 87:86-87

Change of state activities for classroom 1291:45-47

Changing a liquid to a solid—experiment 180:13

Chemical magic colors change solution to green to red to purple 87:78-79

Chromatography—separating colors—experiment 147:19-20

Climbing water and liquids 147:12-14, 18

Cohesion and adhesion forces in operation experiment 1004:3.007

Cohesive attractive forces among molecules of different liquids experiment 1004:3.008

Cohesiveness 71:23-26

Colored liquid layers experiment 959:148-149

Colored liquid layers 147:101-104

Colored liquids that sink or float experiment 959:146-147

Colored liquids that sink or float 147:99-101

Colors in inks 71:35-37

Concentration and density in solutions of saltwater experiment data tables 1004:4.005

Contraction and expansion—ice lollies—how to make 77:15

Contraction and expansion—water thermometer 77:14

Convection—demonstrate convection in liquids 291:42

Density 280:21

Density—are some liquids more dense than others 396:48-50

Density—drop test to compare densities of liquids 295:33-34

Density—hydrometer—how to make 77:18-19

Density—liquid layers 77:16-17

Density—liquid layers—experiment 663:30

Density—liquid sandwich—colored liquids in a bottle 360:83

Density—magic egg trick 663:31

Density—marbling 77:21

Density—riding the waves 77:18-19

Density—swimming egg 77:19

Density—wax sculptures 77:20

Density experiment; molecules cause one liquid to float on another liquid 1403:80-83

Density experiments 685:22-23

Density measured by hydrometer, how to make 935:49

Density of liquid measured by hydrometer, how to make 1179:141

Density of liquids and solids, floating substances that don't mix experiment 1004:3.003

Density of liquids measured by hydrometer experiment, make from clay and straw 1310:13

Density of liquids tested by floating things experiment 1016:10-11

Density; find the density of liquid experiment 909:38

Density; magic egg trick experiment 909:39

Detergents keep oil and water from separating experiment 1482:4-5

Different liquids have different viscosities experiment 836:69-70

Different liquids have different viscosities experiment 836:71-73

Diffusion in liquids experiment 884:92-93

Dissolving time; Life Savers experiment 782:8-11

Do all liquids mix experiment with water drops 1124:8-9

Do gases dissolve in liquids 147:32

Do gases dissolve in other gases 147:32-33

Do liquids have different densities experiment 884:48-50

Do liquids mix experiment 1028:22

Do objects float or sink in liquids other than water experiment 996:12-13

Does hot water rise 147:33-36

Evangelista Torricelli's velocity of jets of liquid escaping receptacle 1133:4.006

Evaporation—drying wet towels 147:14

Evaporation and vapor pressure experiment; data tables given 1004:3.014

Evaporation causes a liquid to cool down experiment 1090:30-31

Evaporation of liquid dependent on surface exposed to air experiment 1090:28

Expansion and contraction from temperature changes experiments 1164:66-71

Expansion race of three fluids 360:81

Experiments to show with egg 106:22-23

Eyedropper 71:21-22

Falling water 147:23-25

Filtering 147:29

Find the density of liquid experiment 909:38

Float different solids in layers of liquids experiment 937:40-41

Flow of liquids experiment 1028:22

Flow of liquids in a group of siphons 604:12-15

Fluids of different densities; which ones are lighter experiment 1243:24-25

Fluids separate into distinct layers experiment 937:38-39

Forces in space affect shape of drops of liquid demonstration 1394:206-207

Freezing—do all liquids freeze at same amount of time at same temp. 277:13

Freezing—ice cream—making homemade 219:45-48

Freezing point—discover factors that affect freezing point of liquids 175:62-63

Gases dissolved in liquids experiment 1526:48
Genie in a bottle—using ink, hot and cold water 147:33-34
Green blob from mixing iron acetate and vinegar experiment 905:102-103
Heaping liquids 147:9-10
Heat convection in liquids experiment 1515:102-104
Heat needed to boil water 147:63-65
Heating liquids to see which gets hottest (reaches highest temp.) Experiment 1179:46
Higher weights of motor oil indicate more viscosity experiment 1396:114
How do sauces thicken experiment 1484:50-51
How heat changes liquid to gas 281:58
How strong is a liquid's skin experiment 1091:23-24
Hydrometer measures density of liquid experiment 1028:21
Hydrometer measures density of liquids, how to make from straw and clay 1212:23
Immiscible liquids—all wet sandwich 162:59
Immiscible liquids—breakers in a bottle 162:56
Immiscible liquids—make a bead in a bottle 162:57-58
Immiscible liquids—make puddle paper 162:54-55
Immiscible liquids behavior experiment 1402:36-39
Immiscible liquids do not mix together experiment with oil/water/food colors 1476:128
Indicators—cider to ink—grape to mint to grape 114:35-38
Inks—spreading and rising inks 77:12-13
Liquid drop experiments 693:38-40
Liquid layers demonstrate specific gravity 723:95-96
Liquid moves up and down a glass experiment 937:48-49
Liquid parfait experiment 1007:66-68
Liquids combined take up less space than original liquids experiment 1091:20
Liquids expand and contract when heated and cooled experiment 902:52
Liquids expand as they grow hot—experiment 605:40-41
Liquids float and sink experiment 1028:21
Liquids have different densities—experiment 179:38-39
Liquids in liquids—miscible and emulsion 147:31-32
Liquids mix together in liquids or don't mix experiment 1162:9
Liquids of different densities float on each other experiment 1179:140
Liquids rise in a tube experiment with straws 837:15-16
Liquids seek their own level demonstration 837:19-20
Liquids that dissolve "miscible" and don't dissolve "immiscible" experiment 1179:35
Liquids that dissolve in other liquids experiment 1526:46-47
Magic color changes—indicator color change when acids and bases present 87:15-23
Make a liquid tri-color 161:69-70
Materials separate because of gravity experiment 1502:67-68
Measuring liquids—water glass chimes 304:22-23
Melting ice—what affects it—several experiments 147:45-61
Melting point of different substances experiment 1179:20
Meniscus magic (curved upper surface) bulge at top 364:111
Mix two liquids that do not mix experiment 882:11

Mixtures—use food colors, sugar, salt, oil to demonstrate mixtures 144:14-21
Molecules; do water molecules in liquid water fit tightly together experiment 1403:16-19
Molecules; space between molecules in liquids experiment with sugar and water 1179:22
Non-Newtonian fluid; how it behaves experiment 1405:54-55
Objects and liquids sink or float according to their density experiment 1014:45
Oil and vinegar from the same bottle 161:68-69
Oil and water do not mix; salad dressing activity 1014:37
Osmosis—bouncing peas 77:11
Refraction of light in liquids experiment; data table given 1004:5.015
Relative densities of liquids and solids 577:project #22
Shape and volume of drops show which liquid will form biggest drops 147:11-12
Shape assumed by a free liquid exp.—suspend drops of oil in a liquid 604:52-55
Show how liquids hold together 179:33-35
Show how liquids mix 179:32-33
Show if liquids expand on heating 179:50-52
Simple observations to make and test (Primary) 198:32-47
Size of drops affects rate at which two liquids separate experiment 1403:44-47
Solids—disappearing into solutions—experiment 147:26-29
Solids changing to liquids—experiment 280:20
Solids dissolve in liquids experiment 1162:9
Solids take up less space than liquids experiment 1179:21
Solvents—two solutes in one solvent, other solvents 147:31
Solvents; liquids other than water as solvents experiment 1526:45
Sound can travel through a liquid 281:67
Stickiness—measure the stickiness of different liquids 295:29-31
Surface affects shape 147:12
Surface tension—test surface tension—experiment 179:35-37
Surface tension experiments 719:23-27
Temperature affects viscosity of liquids experiment test with marbles in liquid 1477:19
Temperature affects viscosity of oil experiment 1396:114
Temperature of liquid affects its viscosity experiment with viscometer, make 1477:64 67
Temperature of liquid affects its viscosity experiment 1396:112
Temperature of water affects its density experiment 884:51-53
Temperature's effect on liquids, solids and gases experiment 1435:21-23
Test conductivity of 147:110-111
Test electrical conductivity of liquids experiment 959:149-150
Thick liquids—thin liquids 147:122-123
Time controlled reactions with chemicals—think wine, it appears 87:64
Time controlled reactions with chemicals by command—ink 87:63
Time controlled reactions with chemicals, a chemical clock 87:65

Time controlled reactions with chemicals, chemical changes in solutions 87:65

Time controlled reactions with chemicals: think gold, it appears 87:64

Time controlled reactions with chemicals: think milk, it appears 87:65

Titrating household liquids 586:61-62

Toothpaste is both plastic liquid and visco elastic experiment 1091:33-34

Tricks from surface tension of liquids project 1296:2002

Tricks using—bet you can hold water in a sieve 228:70-71

Turbulence patterns in flowing water experiment using Ivory detergent 1132:101-1-101-2

Use bottle imp to demonstrate compressibility of water and air 179:39-41

Using atmospheric pressure to push a liquid up a tube 604:8-11

Using atmospheric pressure to speed flow of liquids from containers 604:20-23

Viscometer measures flow rate of fluid experiment, how to make 1477:64-67

Viscometer measures flow rate of liquids experiment 1396:111-116

Viscosity of body lubricants compared experiment 1396:114-115

Viscosity of liquids compared by dropping marble in liquid samples experiment 1396:114

Viscosity of liquids experiment 1091:31

Viscosity of liquids experiment using test liquids 1179:22-23

Viscosity of other liquids compared to viscosity of water experiment 1396:112-113

Viscosity of other liquids compared to water experiment with viscometer, make 1477:64-67

Volume of liquids affected by temperature experiment 1515:15-16

Water drops leap together—oil drops don't 147:11-12

Water on the level, demonstrate 589:41

Water rises and defies gravity—experiments 147:13-14, 15-18

Water's skin 147:25

Weighing solids in liquids 295:39

Weight; are some liquids heavier than others experiment 1508:23

What dissolves in a liquid experiment recording sheet given 747:18-19

What is viscosity experiment 902:33

Whirling water creates tornado in a bottle experiment 1132:104-1-104-2

Will liquids mix together experiment; chart given 960:20-21

LIQUIDS—SPECIFIC GRAVITY

Demonstration hydrometer—how to make 577:project #14

Determining specific gravity 436:44-45

LIQUIDS—SURFACE SKIN

Looking at the surface skin of liquids 573:39

LIQUIDS—SURFACE TENSION. *See also* **WATER— SURFACE TENSION**

Shimmering liquids—experiment 563:80

LISSAJOUS, JULES ANTOINE

Lissajous Patterns from swinging cup funnels of fine sugar experiment 1330:92-94

LISSAJOUS FIGURES

Pendulum moving in two directions creates beautiful designs experiment 1132:43-1-43-2

See these figures in vibrations of rods and wires—experiment 2:76-79

LISSAJOUS PATTERNS

Lissajous Patterns from swinging cup funnels of fine sugar experiment 1330:92-94

LITHIUM

Lithium model, how to make from clay and string 1403:90-91

LITMUS PAPER. *See* **INDICATORS**

How to make using red cabbage and blotting paper 1414:12-13

LITTER. *See also* **ECOLOGY—LITTER POLLUTION**

Beachcombing for litter experiment 1150:56-57

Biodegradable and non biodegradable garbage experiment 978:162-163

Collect and chart different kinds of litter 740:37

Collect and chart kinds of litter 400:12

Count litter in your environment project; data chart given 1012:84

Food leftovers in soil demonstrates decomposition experiment 1014:160

How much waste do you generate experiment 1150:59-60

Kind of litter most common in your area project 1296:1996

Litter chart to record types of litter found in your environment 1013:20

Litter in your neighborhood or school yard experiment 1150:57-59

Litter survey of your neighborhood, charts for different kinds given 795:27

Shoe box diorama to show ways we are littering the Earth, making 1013:170

Soil and litter in flower pot experiment to determine what decomposes 1013:22-23

What litter is biodegradable 236:183

Which kinds of litter take the longest to rot experiment 795:31

LITTERBUG GAME

The game 400:120-121

LIVERWORTS

Adventure 45—we seek the liverwort—liverworts under a hand lens 29:200-203

LIVING THINGS

Diffusion—what is process of diffusion 402:17

Game—the living game 400:123

Growth—what kind of growth is characteristic of living things 402:10-11

Investigation into shapes of living things 420:64-67

Investigation into variations in living things 420:59-61

Living things contain water experiment; chart given for recording results 1172:40-41

Osmosis—what is process of osmosis 402:16-17

Oxidation—how is oxygen involved with life 402:15-16

Protoplasmic streaming 402:13-14

Reproduction—ways in which living things reproduce 402:11-12

Sensitivity—are living things more sensitive than non-living things 402:7-8

LIZARDS

Anole lizard—how to care for 475:23

Chameleon lizard—how to care for 475:23-24

Collection and care of 390:54-55
Horned lizard—how to care for 475:33-34
How to care for 279:11-13
How to catch and make a lizard cage 234:36-37
Iguana lizard—how to care for 475:24-26
Lizard vivarium, how to make 810:78-79
Outdoor projects with 118:65-72
Vivarium—how to make 720:54-55

LOBSTERS
Dissecting—how to 692:39-47
Lobster shell chitin effect in filtering wastewater metallic
    ions experiment 997:64-66

LOCKS
Combination lock; make from wood strips, dowels, card-
    board, and nails 1512:20-21
Electric lock, how to make 938:117-118
Model canal lock experiment, how to make 1518:16-17
Secret drawer lock, making 895:37-39
Working model of an electric lock 577:project #52

LOCKS—WATERWAYS. *See also* **CANALS**
How to build 223:20-21
Model canal lock experiment, how to make 1518:16-17

LOCOMOTIVES
How to make an old-fashioned steam locomotive 545:20-
    23
Make a small electric motor 269:18-19

LOG CABIN
Make a toothpick log cabin (Primary) 155:14-15
Model—how to make 415:40
Popsicle stick log cabin, making 860:131-133
Log cabin from sticks of wood, how to make 1125:29

LOGIC
How to be generous without losing a cent 548:85-87

LOGIC—SYMBOLIC AND MATHEMATICAL
Introduction to switching patterns in mathematical logic
    464:1-33

LOGS
Rotting—set up/observe terrarium with a rotting log com-
    munity 285:87-88

LONGEVITY
Does number of calories consumed on regular basis
    affect longevity experiment 1267:50

LONGITUDE. *See* **LATITUDE AND LONGITUDE**

LUBRICANTS
Can friction be controlled with lubricants experiment
    851:22-23
Rate of wear in engine metal reduced by oil lubricants ex-
    periment 1091:32-33
Which oil makes toy car go farthest; vegetable or automo-
    bile oil experiment 781:20-21
Why do we oil machines 281:45

LUBRICATION
Liquids and lubricants reduce friction experiments
    1136:13

LUMBER
What is difference between hard wood and soft wood
    402:79-80

LUMINOUS PAINTS
How to make 87:72-75

LUNAR CRATERS. *See also* **MOON**
Demonstrate formation of lunar craters on the moon—
    experiments 564:65

LUNAR ECLIPSES. *See* **ECLIPSES**

LUNAR VEHICLE
Make from spool 203:84

LUNASCOPE
Moon phases 12:91-94

LUNGS. *See also* **BREATHING; HUMAN BODY;
    RESPIRATION**
Air pressure in lungs 55:109-113
Calculating your lung capacity 148:66-67
Functioning of 12:40
How much air can your lungs hold 400:41
How much air do lungs hold 660:36
How much air do your lungs hold experiment 794:30-
    31
How we breathe air in and out of our lungs—demon-
    strate 385:12-13
Lime test to show carbon dioxide in your breath 291:208
Lung capacity experiment 901:154-155
Lung capacity experiment; data table given 1004:2.005
Lung model—make working model of chest cavity
    294:85-86
Lung model—making 293:27-28
Lung model—working model of the chest, lungs and
    diaphragm—making 385:13-14
Lung model and capacity tester, how to make 366:126-
    127
Lung power experiments 563:114-115
Lungs how much air do you breathe experiment 762:60-
    62
Lungs; measure amount of air that can be forced out of
    lungs experiment 904:186-187
Measuring lung capacity 253:112-113
Model—two bottles demonstrate two methods of breath-
    ing 532:105
Respiratory model—making 436:66
Show breath power 112:22
Show CO_2 is product of exhalation 294:87
Test capacity of 112:24
Testing chemicals in exhaled air 148:66
The breathing machine—make your own model lung
    571:26
Tissue—examine lung tissue from a beef or calf 294:
    88
Water vapor is present in exhaled air—experiment
    294:87-88

M

MACH, ERNST
Mach bands—demonstration 563:149
MACHINES. *See also* **FORCE; SIMPLE MACHINES**
Automatic machine sorts marbles experiment 1028:113
Balancing weights 34:63-65
Bean planter model machine, how to make 1190:32-38
Belt driven spool models 436:14
Compound machines examine complex machines and tools 436:26
Demonstrating belt driven machines 180:42-43
Hand-grinding process versus blender method—demonstrate 759:33
Machines save energy experiment with block and ramp; data table given 1004:5.004
Nuts and bolts 34:68-73
Simple—use a grinder to make peanut butter 32:64-65
Slopes, ramps and wedges 34:66-67
The pendulum 34:74-77
MAGDEBURG SPHERE. *See also* **GUERICKE, OTTO VON**
Magdeburg Sphere principle experiment with glasses and candle 1007:14-16
MAGIC. *See also* **CHEMISTRY TRICKS; INERTIA—TRICKS; MAGNET TRICKS; MATH TRICKS; PAPER CUTTING TRICKS; PAPER TRICKS**
Anti gravity magic 577:project #28
Arithmetic illusion experiment 761:116-117
Balancing fun 35:82-83
Black art magic show 350:140-150
Blind spot 27:106
Box—reflecting light 8:112-116
Card trick—coin through a card 35:88
Card tricks 35:79-80
Card tricks—illusions 35:65
Chemistry 350:51-77
Color test 35:84
Creative tricks 35:93-109
Dancing egg 35:39
Defying gravity 35:23-24
Dry ice 350:78-91
Floating lady illusion experiment 761:109-110
Floating needle 35:29
Galloping dice 35:81
Genie in a bottle 35:25-26
Houdini escape trick—tied hands 35:19-20
How to make a rainbow 35:32
Jumping rubber band 35:86
Magic from foods in your kitchen 607:88-89
Magic pencil trick—make pencil move without touching it 563:38
Magic pennies 35:71
Magic rolling crayon 35:21-22
Magic squares game—how to make 472:2217
Magnetism 350:1-29
Math tricks 35:53-62
Memory illusion experiment 761:115-116
Memory tricks 35:45-50
Mental telepathy experiment 761:112-115
Mind reading illusion experiment 761:110-112
Numbers 350:30-50
Of science—catalysts make magic reactions—sugar, chlorophyll and salt 382:131-134
Optical illusion 35:66-67; 35:74-75
Paper trick—to the loop 35:89

Peephole—hole in hand 27:104-105
Physics 350:92-150
Poof—static electricity 35:30
Producing a rabbit 35:87
Rising and falling button 35:42
Rolling up a hill 35:40-41
Salt and pepper—how to separate 35:34
Sawing someone in half optical illusion 761:105-109
Solar energy trick 35:94-95
Spooks alive 35:85
Water expanding machine—how to make 487:14-15
MAGIC LANTERN
Magic lantern, how to make 861:129-135
MAGIC SQUARES
Magic square from cardboard and counters, how to make 1248:34-35
Magic squares, how to make 1299:82-83
MAGIC TRICKS
Egg magic 27:103-104
Jacob's ladder 27:109-111
Magic counting block 27:101-103
Magic dollar bill 27:107-108
Paper stretcher 27:100-101
Pin in a balloon 27:107
MAGIC TRICKS (CHEMISTRY)
A clear shake 346:147-148
Blue again and again 346:144-147
Blush test on drawing or photo 346:142-144
Thought waves for milk 346:148-150
Water to wine to water magic trick 346:140-142
MAGIC TRICKS—BALANCE
Assorted tricks—a snip in the air 495:56
Assorted tricks—an apple a day 495:44
Assorted tricks—balancing water in a sieve 495:53
Assorted tricks—drop in the hat 495:49
Assorted tricks—Herculean fingers 495:45
Assorted tricks—magic dice 495:55
Assorted tricks—magically separating matches 495:50
Assorted tricks—the balancing deck of cards 495:48
Assorted tricks—the bouncing handkerchief 495:55
Assorted tricks—the candle seesaw 495:51
Assorted tricks—the spinning handkerchief 495:50
Assorted tricks—tossing a knot into a handkerchief 495:54
Balancing tricks—balancing a handkerchief on your nose 495:13
Balancing tricks—balancing forks 495:15
Balancing tricks—balancing matches 495:17
Balancing tricks—the balancing cane 495:19
Balancing tricks—the balancing magic wand 495:14
Balancing tricks—the balancing pipe and belt 495:16
Ball tricks—sticky ball and yardstick 495:23
Ball tricks—the balancing balls 495:22
Ball tricks—the floating ball 495:24
Ball tricks—the rolling ball 495:25
Coin tricks—balancing a coin on a handkerchief 495:27
Coin tricks—the acrobatic dime 495:34
Coin tricks—the balancing coins 495:26
Coin tricks—the falling dime 495:28
Coin tricks—the precarious quarter 495:29
Coin tricks—the spinning penny 495:32
Coin tricks—the zip away quarter 495:31
Conjuring tricks—a magic rabbit 495:57
Conjuring tricks—faster than the eye 495:64
Conjuring tricks—four tissues in a box 495:75

Conjuring tricks—newspaper Samson 495:58
Conjuring tricks—the amazing paper bands 495:67
Conjuring tricks—the cut and restored paper strip 495:79
Conjuring tricks—the jumping rubber band 495:60
Conjuring tricks—the magic snowstorm 495:81
Conjuring tricks—the patriotic paper balls 495:70
Conjuring tricks—the penetrating rings 495:62
Conjuring tricks—the transpositioned balls 495:73
Conjuring tricks—tricky rope 495:68
Egg tricks—the balancing egg 495:36
Egg tricks—the flying egg 495:37
Egg tricks—the spinning egg 495:35
Tricks with glasses—balancing a glass on a table 495:40
Tricks with glasses—balancing a glass on the edge of a
    card 495:38
Tricks with glasses—balancing a glass on the edge of a
    plate 495:39
Tricks with glasses—breaking a stick between two
    glasses 495:43
Tricks with glasses—picking up six glasses in one hand
    495:41
Tricks with glasses—the old napkin trick 495:42
Try your hand at juggling and balancing 495:84

MAGLEV TRAIN
How Maglev train works demonstration with magnets ex-
    periment 1309:28-29
Levitate lady model in magic show using magnets experi-
    ment 1309:28-29

MAGNETIC COIL
How to make 128:162-163

MAGNETIC COMPASS. *See also* **COMPASS**
Construction of 12:113-115

MAGNETIC FIELDS
Automatic mapping of magnetic fields 577:project #50
Bacteria have magnetite crystals that respond to magnetic
    force fields ex 1479:29
Ball bearings become magnetic when in magnetic field
    experiment 1034:20
Bearded face on paper plate using iron filings and mag-
    net, how to make 1309:30
Buzzing bee suspended in air over flower experiment
    1309:31
Compass cut ups—experiment 563:101
Cutting magnetic lines of force 532:37
Demonstrate magnetic field around current-carrying con-
    ductor experiment 768:88-90
Demonstrate magnetic fields using magnet and iron fil-
    ings experiment 1247:14-15
Direction of magnetic fields experiment 723:121
Do magnetic and electromagnetic fields have an effect on
    plant growth 398:123-124
Earth's magnetic field angle, dip indicator shows, how to
    make 938:80-82
Earth's magnetic field model to test Earth's magnetic
    field experiment 912:30-31
Earth's magnetic field, how to trace experiment 938:77-
    79
Earth's magnetism, how to measure at different locations
    experiment 1401:52-55
Effect of the Earth's magnetic field 532:40
Electric current sets up magnetic field experiment with
    battery and compass 1456:45
Field around bar magnet demonstrates 930:8
Find out about magnetic fields 599:8-9

Force field box, make to demonstrate fields of attraction
    and repulsion 912:24-25
Fun with filings experiment 1001:29
Funny faces from iron filings 677:22
How to shield from a magnetic field experiment 938:73-
    75
Induce electric current by moving wire through magnetic
    field experiment 1179:167
Investigating lines of force 532:36
Iron filings and magnet demonstrate [Primary] 880:25
Iron filings demonstrate magnetic fields experiment
    1028:90-91
Iron filings in clear honey form magnetic patterns very
    slowly experiment 1076:14-15
Iron filings on cardboard over bar magnets demonstrates
    magnetic fields 1296:1990
Iron filings on glass demonstrate 723:124; 768:43-44
Iron filings on plastic lid demonstrate magnetic fields
    1034:16-17
Iron filings show magnetic fields experiment 1309:8-9
Iron filings sprinkled on paper with magnet underneath
    show fields experiment 1218:23
Lines of force, plotting on paper experiment 973:34-35
Magic diver goes up and down in water as current goes
    on and off experiment 768:103-104
Magnetic field around a magnet, how to find 1164:94-97
Magnetic field around bar magnet experiment 938:64-65
Magnetic field around bar magnet experiment with iron
    filings 1480:39
Magnetic field around horseshoe magnet experiment
    938:66-67
Magnetic field exerts a force on a light beam experiment
    1158:13-14
Magnetic fields demonstration with cardboard on top of
    magnet 1139:30-31
Magnetic fields, how to see experiment using bar mag-
    nets, iron filings 1401:36-39
Magnetic forces act through paper experiment 1401:12-
    15
Magnetic forces in liquids experiment 1401:15
Magnetic lines of force—dipping needle experiment
    532:41
Magnetic poles of Earth have moved to different places
    over time experiment 1401:56-59
Magnetism acts in three dimensions experiment with iron
    filings and oil in jar 912:24-25
Magnetize magnet with Earth's magnetic field experi-
    ment 938:83-84
Making magnetic fields experiment; data sheet given
    818:6
Measurement of Earth's magnetic field experiment
    1401:52-55
Metals affect a magnetic field experiment 1405:92
Model of Earth showing position of magnetic and geo-
    graphic poles experiment 1401:58-59
Monsters magnet game in water 1001:29
Norman Robert's angle of dip in Earth's magnetic field
    experiment 1133:5.002
Paper cup and aluminum foil ball magic trick demon-
    strates magnetic field 966:67-71
Patterns of magnetic fields shown with iron filings ex-
    periment 1063:160
Permanent pictures of magnetic fields—how to do
    723:127-128

Pictures with iron filings experiment 1043:34-35

Plant growth affected by magnetism experiment 1061:87-88

Preserve magnetic field patterns on paper, how to do 912:26-27

Sculpture of paper clips experiment 1309:30

See a magnetic field experiment 706:43-44

See magnetic field experiment 902:201

Show effect of electromagnetic field on permanent magnet field experiment 768:96-97

Show electromagnetic field in three dimensions experiment 768:94

Show magnetic field in three dimensions experiment 768:46-47

Strength of magnetic field demonstration 1479:106

The pinch effect—experiment 585:170-171

Three dimensional magnetic fields, how to make experiment 973:32-33

Three-dimensional nature of magnetic field experiment with iron filings in oil 1309:10-11

Trace magnetic field with floating magnet experiment 938:68-70

Tricks with magnetic fields, how to do 912:32-33

Unfriendly paper clips demonstrate magnetic laws experiment 768:95-96

Volcanoes; strength of magnetic field used to predict volcanic eruption 1477:40-43

What is a magnetic field shaped like experiment 851:7-8

Wire with current flowing through it picks up iron experiment 768:91

MAGNETIC INDUCTION. *See* **ELECTROMAGNETS**

MAGNETIC LINES OF FORCE. *See also* **LINES OF FORCE**

Bar magnet and iron filings demonstrate magnetic force field 1507:27

Can magnetism be shielded by nonmagnetic materials experiment 768:69-70

Compass and magnet demonstrate experiment 768:44-46

Create and make permanent records of by tracing or photographing 381:50-54

Dipping needle follows lines of force around magnet experiment 1401:48-51

Direction of magnetic lines of force around magnets experiment 1401:40-43

Faraday's experiment with iron filings 1514:26-28

Faraday's filings experiment, how to repeat 912:23

Follow direction of magnetic lines of force around a magnet experiment 1401:48-51

Fun with filings experiment 1001:29

Investigating magnetic forces project 833:111-112

Invisible force around magnets demonstrated with iron filings 1160:7

Iron filings experiment to demonstrate 961:14-15

Iron filings form pattern on cardboard over magnet experiment 1473:16

Iron filings on paper demonstrate 912:22-23

Iron filings show patterns of magnetic lines of force experiment 1309:8-9

Iron filings trace lines of magnetic field in three dimensions experiment 1132:63-1-63-2

Magnetic lines of force span the Earth from pole to pole experiment 1309:16-17

Magnetic patterns from electromagnet under cardboard experiment 1073:68

Magnetic shielding experiment 768:70-71

Meter magnet demonstrates 748:130

Pattern of magnetic force fields demonstrated with iron filings 1404:42-43

Patterns of magnetic force fields around different shape magnets experiment 1405:91

Permeable/nonpermeable materials effect on magnetic lines of force experiment 1401:46-47

"Seeing" the lines of force—experiment 627:7

Shield magnetic materials from magnetic force field experiment 1401:44-47

Three-dimensional lines of force in a magnetic field—experiment 585:169-170

MAGNETISM. *See also* **COMPASS**

A needle with an eye for direction 280:29

Can magnetism create electricity experiment 834:51

Can magnetism do work experiment 902:56

Can some things block out magnetism experiment 851:2-3

Can you feel magnetism 278:11

Can you see magnetism 278:12

Compass 12:113-115

Compass, floating one, how to make 768:55-57

Compass, magnetized needle or nail can be used as a compass 65:26-29

Conducting magnetism through materials 180:56

Curie Point, piece of iron gets too hot and is not attracted to magnet 1132:34-1-34-2

Current in a wire deflects magnetism experiment 895:21-22

Dancing clown's paper clip arms and legs demonstrate magnetism 1076:12-13

Demagnetize a magnet 291:159

Demagnetize a needle 291:159

Demonstrate change in magnetic effect with different materials 209:10-12

Demonstrate magnetizing and demagnetizing a steel needle 184:16-17

Demonstrate relationship between a bar magnet and a compass 209:13

Demonstrate relationship between magnet and your location on Earth 209:14

Demonstrate what happens when 2 bar magnets are brought near each other 209:8-9

Demonstrating a magnetic field 13:60-64

Discovering laws of magnetism—experiment 489:112-114

Does radiator have north and south poles 333:12-13

Earth's magnetism, how to measure at different locations experiment 1401:52-55

Eddy currents have magnetic field that opposes fall of magnet in tube experiment 1132:45-1-45-2

Electricity and magnetism are related experiment with battery/nail/wires 1404:50-51

Electricity produces magnetism 281:91-92

Electromagnet—electric buzzer—how to make 13:70-75

Electromagnetism—electric motor—how to make 13:82-90

Electromagnetism—electro magnetic cannon—how to make 13:90-92

Electromagnetism—generator—how to make 13:94-96

Electromagnetism—solenoid coil—how to make 13:65-67

Electromagnetism—telegraph—how to make 13:76-80

Experiment to demonstrate Faraday's magnetic lines of force 179:148-150

238

Experiment to illustrate the law of magnetism 179:147-148

Experiment to show 128:156-163

Experiment to show magnetic effect of electric current 128:175-183

Experiment with magnets—plotting magnetic fields 507:1886-1887

Faraday's movement of current-carrying wire in a magnetic field experiment 1133:5.010

Fields of magnetic force—experiment 489:114-115

Float a magnet in space 13:55-60

Game; hockey game proves magnetism travels thru nonmagnetic material experiment 1309:14-15

Heat can demagnetize a magnet 65:24-25

Heat destroys magnetism experiment 768:54-55

How do materials become magnetized experiment 902:207-208

How to magnetize a screwdriver 291:155

Illustrate magnetism with iron filings, salt and magnet 768:65

In a transformer 382:31-32

Induced and residual magnetism experiment 768:52-53

Induced magnetism demonstration; suspend paper clip under magnet 1401:62-63

Induced magnetism experiment with bar magnet, bbs, cardboard 1401:60-63

Induction—can magnetize certain things 65:20-21, 22-2

Induction and polarity demonstration 938:56

Inductive magnetism—experiment 585:175

Iron filings test demonstrates how iron bar becomes magnetized 567:17

Iron rod hit with hammer becomes magnet experiment 860:220-221

Like poles of a magnet repel each other 65:14-15

Like poles repel and unlike poles attract experiment 768:48-49

Lines of force—experiment 489:132-133

Magic merry-go-round 280:28

Magic with magnetism—a complete magical magnetism act 350:19-29

Magic with magnetism—the 'animal magnetism motor' 350:13-15

Magic with magnetism—the dancing doll 350:7-9

Magic with magnetism—the human magnet 350:16-17

Magic with magnetism—the levitated needle 350:4

Magic with magnetism—the magic arrow 350:11-13

Magic with magnetism—the magnet brush 350:1-2

Magic with magnetism—the magnetic motor 350:5-6

Magic with magnetism—the magnetized crane 350:17-18

Magic with magnetism—the magnetized poker 350:2

Magic with magnetism—the revolving pencil 350:9-10

Magic with magnetism—the swinging magnets 350:3-4

Magnet holds tacks in jar demonstration 722:7

Magnet on turntable moves tacks demonstration 722:8

Magnet produces a magnetic field 65:10-11

Magnetic attraction 13:52-55

Magnetic compass, making 930:8

Magnetic field of two parallel, current carrying wires exert forces experiment 1132:23-1-23-2

Magnetic field that's stronger than the Earth's experiment, how to make 1132:22-1-22-2

Magnetic fields displaying and plotting 507:1886-1887

Magnetism—what kind of materials will magnetisms pass thru 253:143-144

Magnetism by induction—experiments 563:104

Magnetism by induction—paper clip experiment 722:11

Magnetism can pull thru things 65:8-9

Magnetism exceeds gravity experiment 768:49-50

Magnetism from electricity experiment 973:39

Magnetism produces electricity experiment 768:97-99

Magnetism through paper—experiment 567:38

Magnetism works through plastic jar of water experiment 1309:15

Magnetize a needle 291:157

Magnetize a screwdriver 722:4

Magnetize a screwdriver experiment 938:85-86

Magnetize the scissors—experiments 563:105-106

Magnetize your screwdriver experiment 768:95

Magnetizers to build—how to 723:23-27

Magnets—making magnets from iron by three different methods 179:144-146

Magnets can produce electricity 65:30-31

Magnets used to make other magnets 65:16-17

Make a magnetic fishing game—magic spinner and magnetic boat 128:161-162

Make an electromagnet 278:17-18

Materials magnetism will pass through experiment 1200:28-29

Metal detector experiment using a magnet 1309:6-7

Michael Faraday's experiment—electricity can be converted to magnetism 23:5-6

Nails repel when current flows through them 722:9

Of the earth 382:20-22

Permanent magnet—how to make 13:68-69

Project 30—magnetism from electricity 654:71-72

Proving that magnetism goes through air 180:55

Proving the theory of magnetism experiment 768:53-54

Repeating Oersted's discovery—experiment 489:119-120

Repulsion can suspend a magnet 65:18-19

Seeds; magnetism effect on seed germination experiment 1375:107-110

Show what happens when a magnet is broken in half 184:12-13

Showing the magnetic effect of electricity 180:56

Showing the strength of magnetism 180:57

Slot machine uses magnetism to sort coins, how to make experiment 1309:26-27

Testing for magnetism 625:28

The Curie point—experiment 563:108-109

The dip needle experiment 563:98-99

The dipping wire—experiment 585:176-177

Toy car moves without touching it experiment using bar magnets 1034:22-23

Try to stop magnetism (Primary) 435:29-31

Unlike poles of a magnet attract each other 65:12-13

Using salt and iron fillings 146:16

What conducts magnetism experiment with wire—compass and tube 723:117

What is special property of magnetism experiment 902:200

What will a magnet attract 278:7

What will magnet attract experiment 768:42

What will magnetism pass through experiment 902:197-198

Will magnetism pass through materials 278:8-10

MAGNETITE. *See also* **MAGNETS**

Magic dancing beach sand 359:4-6

MAGNETOMETER

Model of magnetometer to measure magnetic strength of materials experiment 1477:40-43

Model shows strength of magnetic field used to predict volcanic eruption 1477:40-43

Simple magnetometer—how to make 577:project #56

MAGNETS. *See also* **ELECTROMAGNETS**

A magnet will pull thru your finger (Primary) 143:60-61

A magnetic mystery trick 563:40

A magnetic swing—experiment 585:168-169

Activities to explore and understand magnets [Primary] 758:99-101

Adjustable gap magnets experiments 386:98-100

And nonmagnets 34:81-84

Are there magnetic forces in the space around a magnet 184:36-37

Attraction and repulsion of magnets activity 973:27

Attraction and repulsion of magnets experiment with suspended needle in air 1309:13

Balancing matchboxes with magnets 150:162-163

Bar magnet experiments with poles of magnets 638:50-55

Bashful needle—experiment demonstrates like poles repel; unlike poles attract 563:102

Battery powered magnet, making 779:7

Behavior of a magnet in a uniform magnetic field 28:44-45

Bending light with a magnet experiment 1158:13-14

Bet you can 'kill' a magnet 228:39

Block a magnet's power experiment 961:11

Boating game, how to make 955:27

Boats, magnetic, making 768:71-72

Break a magnet in two 28:12-13

Breakfast cereals have iron filings in them experiment 1083:59

Breaking magnets—what happens when magnets are broken or cut 253:142

Butterfly magnet moves around on different materials experiment 1099:25

Can magnetic attraction overcome pull of gravity experiment 1401:28-31

Can magnets attract through substances 281:88-89

Can magnets work thru other materials experiment (Primary) 695:36-37

Can you feel a magnet's force experiment [Primary] 743:16

Can you find the poles of a lodestone experiment 902:209

Ceramic magnets—experiments 386:92-93

Chaotic motion experiment with magnets 1132:95-1-95-2

Compare the strength of magnets 136:19

Compass—how it works 367:33-41

Compass from needle and cork experiment 1072:32

Compass made from magnet, needle and cork 1382:34

Compass made from magnets experiment 973:23

Compass magnets experiments 885:73

Compass, making to find out how they work 870:28-30

Compass; experiments with magnetic compass 1514:17-18

Copper coils become electro-magnetic pendulum experiment 1132:64-1-64-2

Counterfeit coin detector machine, simple, how to make 912:42

Curie Point; piece of iron gets too hot and is not attracted to magnet 1132:34-1-34-2

Dancing figures, making 885:72-73

Demonstrate fields of force 145:12-13

Demonstrate magnetic attraction and power experiment [Primary] 880:25

Demonstrate strong and weak areas of a magnet 837:22-23

Discover magnetic poles 145:10-11

Diver in jar works with magnet experiment 912:16

Dividing a magnet experiment 938:62-63

Does it or doesn't it 280:26

Dollar bill attracted to magnet experiment 1083:58

Dolls dance as magnet attracts them through cardboard 827:35

Doorbell; magnetic suction experiment shows how doorbell works 1132:65-1-65-2

Driving skills game with magnetic cars, how to make 955:28-29

Earth magnet—making a model of the Earth 136:32

Earth magnet—show Earth's magnetic field 136:31

Earth magnet—using a magnetic compass 136:30

Earth's magnetic North Pole attracts North end of magnet demonstration 1023:66-67

Easy magnet experiments 318:entire

Eddy Current motor, making 768:68-69

Effect of magnets on recording tapes experiment 973:37

Effects of magnets on space around them 400:88

Electric current affects magnet experiment 1404:14-15

Electric current detector to detect and measure electric current experiment 1514:78-79

Electric motor demonstrates how motors use magnetism experiment 1034:27-29

Electric motors—simple experiments to show how they work 195:62-65

Electrically made magnet detects electric current experiment 1514:75-78

Electricity made with a magnet experiment 912:36

Electromagnet—how to make 733:25

Electromagnet—making a motor—experiment with electromagnet and bar magnet 489:121

Electromagnet—making an electromagnet—experiment 489:120-121

Electromagnets 34:85-86

Electromagnets—bombing game 15:44-45

Electromagnets—build an electromagnet 145:26-27

Electromagnets—electromagnet game—putting the shot 15:41

Electromagnets—experiment to show 168:35

Electromagnets—forfeit and fortune-telling games 15:46

Electromagnets—how to make and use 367:47-56

Electromagnets—how to make from a bolt 128:176

Electromagnets—how to make 195:61-62; 72:51-53

Electromagnets—magnet power from electricity 136:24

Electromagnets—make a transformer 136:28

Electromagnets—making an electromagnet 136:25

Electromagnets—making electricity from a magnet 136:27

Electromagnets—making stronger electromagnets 136:26

Electromagnets—mighty magnet pickup truck 15:42-43

Electromagnets—the telegraph—how to make 22:11-21

Experiment to make a dipping needle 385:140-141

Experiment to show shielding a space from a magnetic fields 184:68-69

Experiment to test the attractive power of your magnets 184:20-21

Experiment with magnets—plotting magnetic fields 507:1886-1887

Experiment-magnetic lines by placing different materials in path of lines of force 184:52-53
Experiments to show magnet power 136:4-9
Experiments with magnets 693:44-45
Experiments with magnets 867:27-29
Find out how to make a compass 599:14-15
Find out how to make a magnet 599:13
Find out through which different materials magnets will work 599:9-11
Find out what happens when two magnets are brought together 599:7
Find out which is the strongest magnet in your collection 599:11-12
Find out which substances a magnet will pick up 599:6-7
Find the polarity of your magnets 647:10-11
Finding north with a magnet 96:73-74
Fish and chip puzzle—making (Primary) 451:19
Fishing game, how to make 955:27; 960:45
Fishing game, how to make using magnets 1016:40-41; 1072:27
Fishing with a magnetic fishing rod 186:29
Floating compass experiment 906:91-92
Floating compass from magnet experiment 973:25
Floating magnet 102:130-131
Floating magnet—magnets make things float in air 367:42-46
Floating magnet demonstrates repelling force between magnetic poles experiment 1073:44-45
Floating magnets experiment 906:89
Floating magnets, making 768:66-67
Floating paper clips under magnet experiment 1073:45
Flying frog experiment 906:93
Follow the master 280:27
Force between poles of magnets experiment 1160:8
Force of attraction or repulsion between charged bodies experiment data table 1004:5.019
Force of magnet against force of gravity experiment 888:131-133
Force of magnet fields—round magnets and iron filings show (Primary) 435:16-17
Force of magnet; how to stop magnetic force experiment 955:26
Force of magnetic field—opposite magnetic poles attract each other (Primary) 435:14-15
Fun with magnets—cat and dog game 288:38-39
Fun with magnets 30:64-65; 72:50-51
Funny faces from iron filings experiment 1200:13
Game; boat game in water with cork and balsa wood boats, how to make 1043:30-31
Game; boat racing game using pins, cork and magnets, how to make 1034:12-13
Game; boating game using boats and magnets, how to make 1072:27
Game; cars and road game using magnets 1072:29
Game; fishing game using paper clips and magnets, how to make 1034:8-9
Game; fishing game with magnetic fish, how to make 1043:26-27
Game; fishing game with magnets experiment 1200:13
Game; fishing game with magnets, how to make 1160:13
Game; fishing game, how to make with magnets 1218:24-25
Game; fishing game; magnets, sticks, string, fish, and bowl of water 1073:46-47

Game; Jack walks up beanstalk game; magnet, paper clip and cardboard 1073:43
Game; magnetic boat game from balsa wood, dowels and magnets, how to do 1179:163
Game; magnetic dolphins game made from cardboard shapes and bar magnets 1382:32
Game; magnetic hockey; magnets, sticks, plastic cups, cork puck 1073:48-49
Game; magnetic maze game from paper plate and magnet 1382:30
Game; magnetic pinball game experiment shows moving object changing direction 1035:10-11
Game; racetrack game experiment using magnets 1136:19
Game; sailing boats game, how to make with magnets 1218:25
Game; sheep roundup game with magnets, how to make 1160:13
Game; soccer board game with magnets, how to make 1043:28-29
Game; toy car pushed and pulled on game board experiment 1309:12-13
Games with magnets 912:46
Going fishing 15:8
Grab bag of objects magnet will or will not attract (Primary) 435:27-28
Heat and hitting destroy magnets experiment 973:20-21
Hitting magnet weakens its magnetic strength experiment 1401:72-75
How a magnet works experiment 938:46-48
How can you make a compass 278:20-22
How can you make a permanent magnet 278:19-20
How can you make a temporary magnet 278:15-16
How can you make electric current with a magnet 278:25
How do the poles of a magnet act 278:13-15
How magnets work (Primary) 695:34-35
How strong are magnets experiment 955:25
How strong is a magnet [Primary] 435:25-26
How strong is a magnet experiment [Primary] 924:108
How they work—how to make a magnet from another magnet [Primary] 424:unpaged
How to destroy a magnet experiment 938:59-60
How to identify the north pole and south pole of a horseshoe magnet 28:28-29
How to identify the north pole and south pole of a horseshoe magnet 184:28-29
How to make a horseshoe electromagnet 128:176
How to make a magnet 253:140-141
How to make a magnet experiment 938:49-50
How to make a repulsion meter 128:177
How to make a straight or bar magnet 184:4-5
How to make a straight or bar magnet 28:2-5
How to make an attraction meter 128:177
How to make bar magnets 128:156
How to make magnetic boats (Primary) 451:20-21
How to make your own compass card (Primary) 451:27
How to make your own magnet (Primary) 451:16-17
Identify poles of a magnet experiment 938:61
Indian rope trick with magnet 912:16
Indian rope trick with magnets experiment 1200:12-13
Induced current from a magnet experiment 938:89-91
Induced current in a closed loop experiment 938:92-95
Investigating patterns formed by iron filings in a magnetic field 28:48-49

Investigating patterns formed by iron filings in a magnetic field 184:48-49
Investigation into the strength of magnets 420:99-102
Invisible force of magnets experiment 829:23-24
Iron filings for magnetic experiment—how to make 549:54-55
Iron filings show magnetic field 366:240-242
Is compass like a magnet experiment 834:15-16
Junkyard crane—how to make 191:18-25
Kissing toy magnet, making 912:6
Levitate lady model in magic show using magnets experiment 1309:28-29
Lifting power of magnet 28:20-21
Lifting power of magnets shown in holding frame (Primary) 435:18-19
Like poles repel and unlike poles attract experiment 1139:24-25
Lodestones made from iron bearing rocks experiment 715:29-30
Loop magnet—how to make 723:121-122
Magic butterfly trick using a magnet 1072:26
Magic butterfly trick; magnet pulls butterfly around on board 955:26
Magical magnets experiments 684:16-17
Maglev train, how it works experiment 961:13
Magnet activities for classroom 1291:32-33
Magnet can produce electric current experiment 1501:80-83
Magnet finds direction North experiment 747:25-26
Magnet floats in air experiment 1200:12
Magnet from needle, how to make 1016:39
Magnet generates electric current experiment 1012:49-50
Magnet made by induction experiment with bar magnet, box of bbs, cardboard 1401:60-63
Magnet magic—simple experiments with magnets (Primary) 452:76-78
Magnet maze game 210:34
Magnet myth—experiments with screwdrivers 563:106
Magnet power—make a simple magnet motor 253:145
Magnet produces movement in current-carrying wire experiment 1501:76-79
Magnet racers, making 851:9-10
Magnetic and nonmagnetic matter experiment; what attracts and what doesn't 1514:22-25
Magnetic attraction—how to make a magnetic dunking machine 191:26-29
Magnetic attraction; charm a snake, fly a kite experiments 1028:87
Magnetic attraction; which materials are attracted to a magnet experiment 955:24
Magnetic boat—how to make 367:13-15
Magnetic brake 102:157-158
Magnetic compass—how to make 191:5-8
Magnetic detector, find magnetic or nonmagnetic materials experiment 973:29
Magnetic dunking machine—how to make 191:26-28
Magnetic field of bar and horseshoe magnet (Primary) 435:12-13
Magnetic fields—demonstrate magnetic fields 293:33
Magnetic fields—demonstrate magnetic property of electrical field 293:34
Magnetic fields—experiment to see and preserve forms of fields 385:137-139
Magnetic fields have strange effects 145:22-25
Magnetic fishing game—making [Primary] 743:32

Magnetic fishing pole experiment 906:94
Magnetic floor sweeper 386:96-97
Magnetic force—pull of magnet goes thru some things 96:69-70
Magnetic force—seeing the strength of a magnet 96:68-69
Magnetic force activities [Primary] 759:55-56
Magnetic force field strength demonstrated experiment 1404:40-41
Magnetic force moves floating object; needle on water experiment 1404:36-37
Magnetic force suspends paper airplane experiment 1404:38-39
Magnetic force used to suspend paper airplane experiment 1405:90-91
Magnetic forces in space around a magnet 28:36-37
Magnetic images—pictures from fillings 399:80-81
Magnetic induction experiment with paper clips 912:19
Magnetic induction trick with paper clips in cup 1139:29-30
Magnetic induction trick with pennies 1139:27-28
Magnetic induction 28:32-33; 184:32-33
Magnetic keepers, how they work experiment 912:9
Magnetic maze 356:18-19
Magnetic motor; magnets can be used to cause motion experiment 837:25-26
Magnetic nails—experiments 549:52-73
Magnetic or not—experiment with different objects 563:96-97
Magnetic poles—like and unlike poles (Primary) 539:30-31
Magnetic poles—where are the poles of a magnet 253:137-138
Magnetic poles north and south—bar magnets demonstrate (Primary) 539:28-29
Magnetic poles of magnet experiment 1139:22-24
Magnetic poles; are both magnetic poles the same experiment 851:5-6
Magnetic poles; which parts of the magnet work best experiment 851:4
Magnetic power—poles of magnets, push, pull, finding north 210:34-35
Magnetic puppet show, how to make 851:8-9
Magnetic puppets 143:62-64
Magnetic puzzle—experiment with a permanent magnet and one that is not 532:101
Magnetic separation of iron ore 102:121-122
Magnetic shield, test for materials that control magnetism experiment 973:15
Magnetic snail toy—how to make (Primary) 466:14-15
Magnetic theater, making 779:28-29
Magnetism rubs off—experiment to show 367:25-28
Magnetize iron experiment 706:43
Magnetized boats experiment 906:92
Magnetizer—make a magnetizer 585:175-176
Magnetizing a steel rod by utilizing the Earth's magnetism 184:60-65
Magnetizing a steel rod by utilizing the Earth's magnetism 28:60-61
Magnetizing a steel rod 28:64-65
Magnetometer, making to test strength of magnets experiments 973:31
Magnets act through things experiment 973:13
Magnets and compasses—experiment 382:18-22
Magnets and their properties—demonstrations 567:16-17

Magnets attract steel and iron 367:5-10
Magnets attract through different materials experiment 782:34-38
Magnets attract through paper, glass and wood 367:11-20
Magnets can push 145:18-19
Magnets distort the TV picture 585:172-173
Magnets have different strengths experiment; data sheet given 818:7
Magnets have poles 96:71
Magnets have strongest attraction at ends experiment 782:39
Magnets placed together have increased combined magnetic attraction experiment 1401:76-79
Magnets push—experiment to show 367:21-24
Magnets will pick up only certain materials (Primary) 232:100
Magnets with more than two poles 577:project #49
Magnets work through glass to pick up paper clips experiment 1218:22
Make a fishing game 155:12-13
Make a homemade compass 195:21-22
Make a magnet (Primary) 143:56-57
Make a magnet 885:71
Make a magnetic boat 145:9
Make a magnetic car 94:44-45
Make a magnetic compass 145:14-15
Make a magnetic drag 95:44-45
Make a magnetic sculpture 94:37
Make a razor blade climb 360:73
Make a sun torch 142:58
Make a swinging magnet 94:39
Make a temporary and permanent magnet 136:12-13
Make and demonstrate magnetic compass 142:40
Make dancing metal 94:37
Make little magnetic boats 186:28
Make magnet from nail experiment 961:19
Make magnet using needle, paper clip and cork 1034:18-19
Make magnetic sailing ships 142:41
Make needle stand in the air 143:59
Make patterns with magnets 136:20-21
Make your own magnet (Primary) 695:39
Make your own magnet 288:40-41
Make your own magnets 1160:9
Making a compass 15:7
Making a dipping needle 28:76-77; 184:76-77
Making a floating compass 136:16
Making a horseshoe magnet out of a bar magnet 184:56-57
Making a horseshoe magnet out of a long thin magnet 28:56-57
Making a magnet float over another magnet 28:68-69
Making a magnet from a needle 587:49
Making a magnet with four poles 28:72-73
Making a magnet 96:72; 567:17
Making a magnetic compass 136:15
Making a magnetic racetrack 136:10
Making a miniature magnetic chick 28:80-81
Making a nail magnetic experiment 829:19-20
Making an electromagnet 15:40
Making and identifying the poles of magnets experiment 895:20-21
Making magnetic word games 136:11
Making magnets by stroking experiment 912:10
Making magnets, how to 768:47-48

Making magnets 180:52-53
Making pictures of magnetic fields 136:22-23
Making your own compass 28:22-25
Many magnets from one 143:58
Mapping a magnetic field by means of a floating magnet 28:40-41; 184:40-41
Mapping a magnetic field with a compass needle 184:44-45
Mayer's floating needles experiment 1007:45
Metals affect magnetic field experiment with magnet, foil, paper clips 1404:52-55
Meter to detect electric current, how to make 1012:49
More tests for your homemade bar magnet 184:8-9
Motor—make with magnets 748:131
Motor, simple, make using magnet experiment 768:67-68
Mystery pendulum—experiment 585:173-174
Nail becomes magnet experiment 1063:159
Needle magnet—how to make 367:29-32
North end of magnet always points to Earth's magnetic North Pole experiment 1404:30-32
North pole of magnet always points to Earth's magnetic North Pole demonstration 1479:107
Observe magnets and what they attract 770:128
Paper boats with magnet move on table experiment 721:7
Paper clip magic trick demonstrates magnetism 966:64-66
Paper clip magnet, making 926:91-92
Paper clip trick 6—with magnet 15:6-7
Paper clips show where bar magnet is strongest 638:46-49
Part of magnet that has strongest attracting ability experiment 1401:8-11
Patterns with a magnet experiment 1200:13
Pencil magnet—how to make 723:119-120
Permanent magnet, how to make experiment 973:19
Permanent magnets; how they are made experiment 1401:64-67
Pin floats in air experiment 781:26-27
Placing different materials in the path of lines of force 28:52-53
Play a magnet fishing game 32:68-69
Play a magnet sorting game 32:66-67
Play a magnet sorting game and fishing game 32:66-69
Poles attract and repel; clay lion and clay clown magnet toys demonstrate 1076:16-17
Poles of—show that like poles repel and unlike poles attract 385:135-137
Poles of a magnet experiment with pin 888:165-167
Poles of a magnet 367:18-20, 21-2
Poles of magnet; how to find experiment 1034:14-15
Poles of magnets attract and repel each other experiment 1401:16-19
Poles of unmarked magnet, how to identify experiment 1401:32-35
Poles; identifying a magnet's poles experiment 1514:15-18
Poles; which parts of the magnet work best experiment 851:4
Power of magnet destroyed experiment 912:19
Power of magnet reaches out and pulls object toward it experiment 1034:11
Produce electricity with magnet and coil 128:181
Pulling power of magnets experiment with ruler, magnets and paper clips 1382:29

Pushing and pulling action of magnets experiment 1072:30

Race cork boats with magnets experiment 1028:88

Racing cork boats 15:9

Recording tapes affected by magnets experiment 1401:80-83

Refrigerator magnets, how to make from clay, paint, flat magnets 1076:10-11

Rob magnet of its power using nail experiment 1034:21

Rust makes magnet weaker experiment 1020:33-36

Sand—magic dancing beach sand 359:4-6

Screwdriver magnet, how to make experiment 1507:28

Search out the magnet—make record of all magnets in your environment 452:43

See how magnets can attract objects and produce magnets 145:16-17

Seed growth affected by magnets experiments 912:39

Separate filings from salt 146:16

Shaking effect on magnet experiment 1404:44-47

Shape of magnet affects its area of strength experiment 1401:10-11

Shields from magnetic power demonstration 912:28-29

Show—and will Earth's magnetic field pulls end of magnetized needle down 184:72-73

Show effect of electromagnetic field on permanent magnet field experiment 768:96-97

Show heat destroys magnetism 186:30-31

Show magnetic attraction and repulsion 136:18

Show magnetic field patterns 136:21

Show magnetism and electricity 145:26-29

Show marvels with magnets using paper and record player 176:100

Show racing magnets 94:38

Simple experiments with magnets 1200:10-13

Static electricity 34:86-90

Stopping the force of a magnet experiment 1072:26

Strange attractor experiment with magnets 1132:95-1-95-2

Strength of bar magnet test activity 973:11

Strength of magnet experiment 1507:29

Strength of magnet experiment with paper clips 1160:7

Strength of magnet, measure using paper clips experiment 888:168-170

Strength of magnets compared experiment 1401:24-27

Strength of magnets experiment; how strong are magnets? 1072:25

Strength of magnets test activity 973:7

Strength test for magnets experiment 1073:42

Strength; which magnet is the strongest experiment using paper clip chain 1218:24

Stronger magnets—how to make one 638:40-45

Strongest magnet tests with paper clips experiment 912:15

Suspended magnet always points to Earth's magnetic North experiment 1073:40

Swinging compass experiment 906:90

Temporary magnet made with iron nail (Primary) 435:22-24

Temporary magnet, making 743:19

Temporary magnet, how to make experiment 973:17

Test for different materials for magnetic attraction experiment 1160:6

Test your magnet 143:54-55

Testing materials that magnets will attract 180:53

Testing the poles of a magnet 180:54

The floating magnet; bar magnet experiment to find direction (Primary) 451:24-26

The jiggling filament in a light bulb 585:174

The swinging magnet—bar magnet experiment to find direction (Primary) 451:22-23

Theater; magnetic theater with actors from cardboard, paint, magnets 1382:31

To explore pulling power of a magnet 40:94-96, 98-9

To make an electromagnet 40:100-101

To show a magnetic field 40:96

To show North and South Poles 40:97-98

Toy car moves by magnets, how to make 1028:89

Trick to get tacks out of glass of water 723:37-38

Trick; get paper clip out of glass of water with magnet 1073:43

Tricks with magnets 912:43-45

Use a magnet to generate electricity 253:156

Use magnets and record player to show bewitched tacks 176:100-102

Using homemade bar magnet 28:8-9

Vanishing magnetism 145:20-21

Ways to magnetize and demagnetize steel 28:14-17

What can a magnet do experiment 885:71-72

What do magnets attract experiment 851:1-2

What does a magnet do 281:87-88

What happens when magnet can turn freely experiment 902:202

What happens when you cut a magnet into pieces 278:23

What happens when you put two magnets together (Primary) 451:18

What is attracted to a magnet experiment 1404:50-51

What is inside a magnet 30:66-67

What is strongest part of magnet experiment [Primary] 743:17

What kind of materials are attracted to magnets experiment 760:32-33

What materials are attracted to a magnet experiment 1401:4-7

What objects around us are magnets 253:139

What part of magnet has the strongest pull experiment 902:199

What part of magnet is the strongest experiment (Primary) 695:38

What things will a magnet attract (Primary) 451:3-9

What will magnets pick up experiment [Primary] 902:193

What will magnets pick up 96:67

Where is a magnet the strongest 281:89

Where is magnet the strongest experiment 768:51

Which magnet is strongest experiment 768:50-51

Which objects stick to magnets experiment [Primary] 743:15

Which part of the magnet is best for attracting things (Primary) 451:10-15

Which rocks are attracted by a magnet experiment 900:140

Why do magnets attract experiment 1294:117-118

Will magnet's force go through glass and water experiment [Primary] 743:18

Work of magnets 367:47-49, 52-5

MAGNETS—GAMES

A ball bearing and magnet game—how to make 543:12-15

Magnetic pick up sticks, making 768:72

MAGNETS—NORTH POLE

Magnetic dip or inclination experiment 768:60-61

Magnetic poles can be anywhere experiment 768:58-59

Make giant compass rose 303:17

Produce magnet with only one pole experiment 768:62-63

MAGNETS—TRICKS. *See also* **MAGIC**

How steady are you; trick with magnet, nail and needle 768:65

Magic boat 27:65-66

Magic jar #1 27:70-71

Magic rings 27:67-69

Rescue paper clip from glass of water, how to 768:64

MAGNIFICATION

A water drop magnifier 253:46

Blowing up things—make a grid 162:84-85

Field of vision decreases as lens magnification increases experiment 1062:24-25

Find out how much a lens magnifies 333:47-50

From drop of water 26:54-56, 58

How to make 208:116-119

How to make simple magnifying glass 4:46-47

How to make water drop magnifying glass 178:54

Increasing magnification can compound or increase distortion experiment 1062:26-27

Lens refraction of a magnifying glass experiment 941:119-120

Magnifying bucket—making 656:10

Magnifying glass from milk bottle and water drop magnifier—make 595:28-29

Magnifying glasses—experiment 30:54-56

Magnifying power of a convex lens 4:50-51

Magnifying power of a lens—how to determine 532:39

Make a magnifier (Primary) 70:40-41

Make a magnifying glass without glass 176:51-52

Make a magnifying lens 162:86

Make a miniature microscope 120:18

Make a simple telescope 120:19

Make a water drop lens 95:47

Make a water drop magnifier 203:32

Make drop lenses from syrup 203:23

Make it big—in an expansion chamber 162:80-81

Make your own version of a microscope 399:78

Meaning of 2X magnification experiment 1402:16-19

Measure the magnifying ability of your lens 162:83

Microscopes—how to make simple, water drop and compound microscope 128:198-199

Optical bench 9:62-63

Paper and pin magnifier—how can you see very tiny objects 381:139

Photographs through a magnifying glass 9:60-61

Simple experiments with water drop and magnifying glass 885:19-23

Water drop magnifier—experiment—how to do 653:14-15

Water drop magnifier—how to make 363:5-7; 364:46; 494:58

Water lens, how to make 600:56-57

Water magnifying lens from pail and plastic 558:78-79

Water scope from plastic bucket, making 885:23-24

MAGNIFIERS

Activities with a magnifying glass [Primary] 880:15

Focal length of magnifying lens, how to measure 1088:16

Homemade magnifier from container of water, how to make 1063:308

Ice lens magnifier, how to make experiment 941:111-114

Magnifying glass from water and plastic wrap experiment 1231:42-43

Pin hole magnifier, paper, making 999:41-42

Pinhole magnifier experiment 1132:76-1-76-2

Soda bottle bottom for collecting and observing small things, how make 1527:118

Water drop lens, how to make 1073:78

Water drop magnifier, making 770:127

Water drop magnifier, simple experiment 1163:26

Water drop magnifies print experiment 1285:16

Water drop makes things larger experiment 902:8

Water drop microscope, making 890:108; 906:62-63

Water lens from plastic wrap and oatmeal box, how to make 1115:103

Water lens, how to make 827:80-81

Water lens—making 732:31-32

Water magnifies print experiment 1283:19

Water magnifying lens, how to make experiment 941:109-110

Water microscope—how to make 631:54

Water pail microscope—making 759:27

Waterscope—making 732:58-59

MAGNIFYING GLASS. *See* **LENSES**

MAIL

How much junk mail comes to your home project 1210:35-37

MALPIGHI, MARCELLO

Discovery of capillaries experiment 1133:3.003

MAMMALS

Activities with mammals 236:93-98

Keeping and observing mammals 253:37-38

Small—how to cage for 163:107

Why does heartbeat of mammals make a sound experiment 1397:76-79

MANGO SEEDS

How to grow 272:30-35

MANNED SPACE FLIGHT. *See* **SPACE FLIGHT**

MANOMETER

Depth changes water pressure; measure with manometer experiment 1020:41-42

Homemade manometer measures osmotic pressure in plant root experiment 1061:104-105

Make a simple one 281:29

Manometer; making to measure air and water pressure experiment 1020:37-40

MAPLE SUGARING

Collecting and making maple syrup experiment 1060:127-128

How to 442:unpaged

MAPS

3-D map, how to make 1042:14-17

Assembling a global map project 833:90-91

Bearing board to measure an angle, how to make 1381:20-21

Conic projection lighted globe map, how to make 808:64-67

Contour—making hills and valleys 303:24-25

Contour lines and maps demonstration 978:26-28

Contour lines on sand or soil, how to make 1381:15

Contour lines show shape of mountain; show with clay mountain and water 1437:29-32

Depression contours on maps, how to demonstrate 1437:33-35

Distance on a road map, how to read 1437:38-40

Drawing map projections project 833:92-94

Earth—round Earth; flat orange peel—experiment 303:12-13

Flat map of Earth, how to make 1381:24-25

Grapefruit map (polar projection map) 382:114-120

Grid lines map, how to make 1381:17

Grid patterns to show density of populations, how to do 1437:60-63

How are maps constructed experiment 1293:49-51

How are size and distance shown on a map 900:117

How can a flat map represent the Earth project 900:123

How can a flat map show three dimensions project 900:119

How can we make a map 253:122-123

How high and low are the Earth's mountains and valleys project 900:122

Isolines on map show density of populations, how to do 1437:64-66

Land use on maps, how to do 1437:74-76

Map distortion experiment 1253:28-29

Map from grapefruit—making 636:68-71

Map of your neighborhood—how to make 636:29-31

Map of your room, how to make an accurate map 1381:7

Map projections, cylindrical, planar, conical, how to demonstrate 1480:28-29

Mapping an area experiment, how to do 978:21-23

Mapping elevations topographic map project 833:94

Measuring area—big cities and small towns on graph paper 304:28-29

Measuring distance on a map, how to do 1437:41-44

Mercator projection lighted globe map, how to make 808:64-67

Mountain from molding clay, how to make to demonstrate contour map 1235:21

North and magnetic North variations demonstration 1437:53-59

Optical transformer map trick project, how to make 808:68-72

Pacing distances and reading compass experiment 978:25

Pizza U.S. geography map, make and eat 870:56-58

Scale and contour lines map, how to make 1042:18-19

Scale map of book, how to make 1381:10

Show your school grounds on a sheet of paper project 900:118

Slope patterns, how to plot on map 1437:36-37

Symbols—map keys unlock map secrets (Primary) 303:16

Symbols for maps, how to make 1381:11

Three dimensional pattern maps, making 874:208

Treasure Island game, how to make 1042:10-13

Treasure Island map, how to make 1381:23

Treasure map—how to make 303:28-29; 1235:17

What are contour lines project 900:120

What is a contour map project 900:121

Your own map, how to make 1409:16

MARBLE

Marble statues destroyed by acid rain; prove why experiment 1476:190-191

Testing marble for hardness experiment 1438:105-107

Testing marble with an acid experiment 1438:108-109

MARBLE GAMES

How to make a marble maze and a "jumping board" marble game 543:20-21

Marble maze, making 861:39-44

MARGARINE

Butter—margarine taste test 630:76

Can you tell margarine from butter experiment 792:30

MARINE ANIMALS. *See also* **TIDE POOLS; WATER ANIMALS**

Collect and observe small marine life in rock crevices 285:82-83

Collecting and preserving, how to 772:77-79

Hermit crab observation 68-69

How a fish breathes experiment 1290:50

How to preserve specimens 530:76

Investigating marine animals associated with seaweeds 285:66-68

MARINE ECOSYSTEMS

Coral reef species; invent one that is adapted to its environment experiment 1339:68-69

Oil spills can destroy coral reefs experiment 1339:71-72

Projects to understand how and why coral reefs must be saved 1339:64-73

MARINE LIFE

Aquarium—making 436:56

MARMALADE

How to make 231:113

MARS. *See also* **PLANETS**

Canals on Mars demonstrated with red paper and black paint experiment 1478:69

Craters on Moon different from those on Mars demonstration 1394:124-125

Create Martian landscape project 967:6-7

Mars and Earth have cold poles demonstration 1394:92-93

Mars backward motion demonstration 1394:30-31

Martian "riverbeds," create model of (Advanced) 658:60

Measurements 292:90-91

Models compare largest volcanoes on Mars and on Earth experiment 1478:68

Reproduce Martian surface channels (river beds) experiment, how to make 1476:161

Showing how Mars goes backwards project 833:231-233

Surface and craters of Mars experiment 1062:98-99

Testing for life on Mars experiment with sand, yeast, salt, sugar, b. Powder 1478:70-71

Why Mars is red experiment with sand, steel wool and water 1478:69

Why poles of Mars and Earth are cold experiment 1479:14

MARSH PLANTS

Observation of salt marsh plants project 1225:118-130

Ecological survey of marsh; observe and record animal, plant life exp. 871:2.007

Estuary 3-D board, make to show healthy marsh versus man's invasion of 840:73-75

Grow your own marsh experiment 1146:30

Marsh plants investigation project 1074:78

Observations of life in marshes 173:29

Plankton; grow some plankton experiment 1492:28

Salt run off from highways destroys plants in wetlands experiment 1074:83

Soil from dried up marsh area contains life experiment 1074:66

Testing water for oxygen, carbon dioxide and pH in marshes experiment 1074:22

MARSHLAND TERRARIUM

Materials and animals for—how to set up and maintain 475:36-46

MARTIANS

How to count like a Martian 509:60-66

MARTIN, ARCHER

Separating components of chlorophyll pigments experiment 1133:2.011

MASS

Balancing acts to demonstrate center of mass experiment 1157:74-75

Center of mass on flat object experiment; use pencil, string, washer 1157:71-74

Compare mass of different materials using balance scale experiment 1521:22-23

Demonstrate the center of mass experiment 836:60-62

Experimenting with mass and momentum 180:40

Force of gravity is proportional to mass of object experiment 1502:43-45

Force of gravity on falling balls demonstration 1434:107-109

Gravity and falling bodies demonstration with coins 1434:110-111

How mass can be measured in space experiment 1405:16

Lavoisier's experiment looking for mass changes 1156:96-97

Mass can be measured in space demonstration 1394:170-171

Measuring mass in space experiment 763:101-102

Speed and falling bodies demonstration with ruler and marble 1434:112-115

Weight of various masses when weighed on Moon's surface experiment 1502:44-45

MASS TRANSPORTATION

Mass transportation saves fuel and reduces pollution experiment 969:111-112

MATCHES

Break the match trick 585:66-67

Diabolical matches—how to make 87:90

Hungry 350:102-103

Lifting 350:121-122

Make fireproof and weatherproof matches 291:223

Safety matches—how to make 87:89

'Snakes' and matches—how to make 87:90

Sparkling matches—how to make 87:91

Sputtering matches how to make 87:89-90

Useless matches 249:7

MATERIALS

Floating wood experiment; which kind of wood floats best experiment 1508:5

Particleboard; make particleboard experiment 1508:4

Wood; testing kind of wood best to use for flooring experiment 1508:5

MATH TRICKS

Calendar trick 27:15-17

Magic addition boxes 27:17-19

Magic numbers 27:21-24

Magic squares 27:13-15

Math tricks 35:53-62

Subtraction trick 27:19-20

Take a number 27:20-21

MATHEMATICS. *See also* **DIMENSIONS; GEOMETRY; MEASUREMENT; STATISTICS; TOPOLOGY; VOLUME**

A perplexing mathematical stunt 392:96-99

Add multi-digit numbers by matrix addition 1010:69-71

Algebra—think of a number game—simple use of algebra 546:1-33

Angles—what they are (Primary) 454:1-33

Area measurement—examine properties of areas/ways of measuring them (primary 524:1-33

Averages—ideas for demonstrating averages (Primary) 525:1-33

Binary numbers—principles of; writing in sequence and in secret binary codes 536:1-33

Card prediction trick 1010:66-68

Circles—experiments to discover principles involved in circles 519:1-33

Coded punched cards system for data retrieval, how to make 808:25-29

Conic projection lighted globe map, how to make 808:64-67

Division—demonstrate process of division with a guessing game comparison 457:1-33

Ellipse—experiments to show relationship between ellipse families (Primary) 437:1-33

Estimation—experiments and activities in estimating (Primary) 485:1-33

Finite and ordinary numbers compared using a week clock and old nursery rhyme 547:1-33

Flexatube flexagon, how to make 808:73-77

Fractions—activities/puzzles demonstrate concept of one half, thirds, fourth 443:1-33

Graphs—basic explanation of graph theory and networks 477:1-33

Graphs—concept of sets, kinds of relations (Primary) 453:1-33

Hyperbolic paraboloid model, how to make 808:48-49

Hyperboloid model, how to make 808:47-48

Konigsberg bridge problem experiment 808:60

Line vanishes from sheet of paper magic trick 1010:63-65

Lines—straight, parallel, perpendicular; experiments demonstrating principle 440:1-33

Logic, symbolic introduction to switching patterns in mathematical logic 464:1-33

Magic squares puzzle—how to do 625:12

Magic tricks based on mathematics, how to do 966:75-89

Math magic tricks with coins 548:60-79

Math magic with nails 549:74-89

Mathematical hieroglyphics experiment 808:61-63

Mercator projection lighted globe map, how to make 808:64-67

Metric system—simple experiments with principles of metric system 423:1-33

Multiplication—games to demonstrate structure and principles 533:1-33

Nothing grinder, how to make 808:102-107

Number families—explains numbers of families and their functions 526:1-33

Numbers—concepts of odd, even, squares, triangular numbers through pictures 439:1-33

Numbers—history of numbers 520:1-33

Numbers—odds and evens; games, puzzles and questions 498:1-33

Numbers base five—activities to demonstrate 405:1-33
Optical transformer map trick project, how to make 808:68-72
Positive and negative numbers—activities and game to explain concept 458:1-33
Predict line from book magic trick 1010:72-75
Probability—Count Buffon's toothpick experiment how to repeat (Advanced) 565:81-83
Probability—experiments in probability and using data to make predictions 486:1-33
Probability—Gauss's law and Gauss's curve (Advanced) 565:83-87
Probability—times marble falls into slot 1 of board you build (Advanced) 565:77-96
Probability curve experiment with marbles 808:16-19
Roman numerals—Roman numeral system explained; with activities 407:1-33
Seesaw mobile, how to make 808:51-55
Size—relativity of size—big, bigger, small, smaller (Primary) 455:1-33
Soap film highways experiment to figure shortest route 808:93-96
Symmetry—test for line and point symmetry (Primary) 521:1-33
Symmetry designs and experiment (Primary) 521:8-15
Telephone book predictions trick 392:94-95
Tower of Hanoi puzzle, how to make 808:30-34
Twenty-one sided polygon, how to make 808:56-58
Venn diagrams—tools of logic that can be used to sort objects or ideas 461:1-33
Yarn and computing board problem solver, how to make 808:108-112
Zero—zero and its many uses 522:1-33

MATHEMATICS—GAMES
First pyramid game 438:2-6
First, second and third checker games 438:17-20
Game for magicians 438:29-33
Game to demonstrate basic principles of functions and graphs 456:1-33
Magic squares—how to make 472:2217
Nim—a game for two players 438:25-28
Second pyramid game 438:7-9
Second shifting game 438:12-15
Shifting games for one player 438:10-11
Take away games for two players 438:21-24

MATHEMATICS—MAGIC WITH PAPER
How to mail ten letters in nine envelopes 550:78-80
Mathematical progression—double trouble—you can't cut this paper in half 550:83
The wonderful vanishing line 550:80-82
Trick—two fishermen and five fish 550:85-91
Trick—why I can't go to school 550:94-96
Trick—your friend's age 550:91-94

MATTER
Balloon's volume will decrease when balloon is frozen experiment 1140:22
Bounce height of different balls experiment 1091:37-38
Breaking the surface tension of water experiments 1091:27-28
Brittleness of substances, how to test 1179:17
Can matter be destroyed 55:59-65
Changing matter from one state to another experiment 1441:22
Changing matter of materials in cups of water experiment; data sheet 818:2

Construct model of lithium atom showing its electrical charges experiment 1501:4-7
First and second laws of thermodynamics experiment; data tables given 1004:3.015
Floating objects and their density experiment 1091:15
Four tests to determine whether something is metal experiment 1162:17
Gas takes on shape of its container experiment 1140:23-24
Goo is neither liquid or solid experiment 1063:157
How does matter become electrically charged experiment 1501:4-7
How does temperature effect movement of molecules experiment 834:73-74
How strong is a liquid's skin experiment 1091:23-24
Liquid molecules are attracted to one another experiment 1091:25-26
Liquids combined take up less space than original liquids experiment 1091:20
Materials buried underground; which ones decay experiment 1091:49-50
Matter has physical properties experiment; data sheet given 818:4
Matter is made up of molecules experiment 834:72-73
Metal fatigue; breaking point of bent metal paper clips experiment 1091:42-43
Model of matter to demonstrate heat processes experiment 1515:116-123
Molecules change of state from solid to liquid experiment with peas 1090:23
Pieces of matter can't occupy same space experiment 1405:47
Pieces of matter cannot occupy same space at same time experiment 905:16-25,66-67
Preparing iron sulfate solution 346:17-22
Properties—cotton—stuff two handfuls of cotton into full glass of water 228:41
Properties—hang a pop top on ashes 228:31
Properties—lift ice cube by thread 228:37
Properties—magnet—bet you can 'kill' a magnet 228:39
Properties—make black nail turn silver 228:36
Properties—make smoke come from your fingertips 228:34-35
Properties—make sugar cube float 228:32
Properties—recording tape—erase a tape recording with nickel 228:40
Properties—stab pencil thru water bomb without 'exploding' it 228:33
Rubber band molecules return to original position after stretching experiment 1091:39-40
Silly Putty experiments 1091:47-48
Solubility of salt and sugar in hot and cold water experiment 1091:18
Sorting materials according to their properties experiment 1091:13-14
Three basic states of matter experiment using an egg 1441:21
Toothpaste is both plastic liquid and visco elastic experiment 1091:33-34
Two forms of matter can't occupy the same space experiment 1066:45
Vinegar and baking soda inflate balloon experiment 905:118-119
Viscosity of liquids experiment 1091:31

Water and sugar cannot occupy the same space at the same time experiment 1479:48

Water drops attraction to liquids and solids experiment 1091:25-26

What is matter experiment; chart of materials to test given 960:10-12

MAY FLY NYMPHS

Collection and observation of 414:117-119

MAYANS

How to count like a Mayan 509:17-23

Making a Mayan calendar project 833:37-40

MAYONNAISE

Making mayonnaise to show how oil and vinegar can be mixed together experiment 1484:86-87

MAYOW, JOHN

Combustion to show air is a mixture experiment 1133:2.002

MAZES. See also EARTHWORMS; HAMSTERS; MICE; PHOTOTROPISM; RATS; TURTLES

Bean seed grows through box maze toward light experiment 1063:410

Bean seeds planted in box maze grow toward light experiment 1189:48-49

Build maze to test intelligence of cockroaches 279:29

Can an earthworm learn to tell right from left 577:project #7

Earthworms can learn to make simple choices in maze experiment 1395:118

How quickly do earthworms learn direction experiment 834:132-133

Learning experiments for rodents 577:project #8

Light beam from flashlight finds way through maze using mirrors experiment 1330:78-79

Make a maze for rats 264:63-64

Marble maze on thick cardboard, how to make 1298:10

Marble maze, making 861:39-44

Maze to show earthworms do learn experiment 1293:105-106

Maze to show plant's growth toward light, how to make 986:85

Maze to test intelligence of earthworm experiment 860:173-175

Phototropism; plants grow toward light in maze experiment 1476:104

Phototropism; potato shoot grows in maze toward light source experiment 1236:6-7

Plant grows toward light in maze experiment 1028:61

Plant maze demonstrates plants grow toward light experiment 1038:14-15

Plant maze with bean plant growing toward light experiment 1368:41

Plant maze, making 901:39

Potato grows through maze in box to find light experiment 1379:25

Potato shoots grow toward light in cardboard box maze experiment 1524:26

Simple T-shaped maze to test an earthworm—how to make 510:103-104

T maze variations to test rodents—how to make 510:106-109

T-shaped and stilted turtle mazes to test turtle's intelligence—how to make 510:104-105

Using a maze to investigate learning in small mammals in the field and lab 266:110-115

MEADOW TERRARIUM

Materials and animals for—how to set up and maintain 475:14-20

MEADOWS

Meadow habitat wall frieze, how to make 1182:38

MEALWORMS

Breathing; how insects breathe experiment with mealworms 1097:107-109

Care, feeding and study of mealworms 586:134-135

Collection and care of 390:28-29

Compare mealworms to earthworms experiment 901:119-120

Different surfaces affect distance mealworms travel experiment 997:165-166

Do mealworms prefer light or dark experiment 1159:68-70

Effect of caffeine on development of mealworms experiment 997:113-115

Effects of ultrasonic humidifier on mealworms experiment 997:163-164

Experiment with 163:64-67

Experimenting with mealworms 888:117-121

How insects react to a stimulus experiment 1097:24-26

How mealworms react to various conditions experiment 760:16-17

How to raise mealworms 832:70

Life cycle of mealworms experiment 1464:23-24

Meal worm farms and meal worm food—how to make 366:24-25

Mealworms response to ammonia and vinegar experiment 1159:69

Propagate mealworms to feed terrarium animals—how to 465:165-166

Reflex behavior; mealworms response to humidity experiment 936:16-18

Reflex behavior; mealworms response to light experiment 936:12-13

Sample observation sheet for recording metamorphosis 769:5

What kind of food do insects eat experiment 1097:21-23

Wing development on insects experiment using mealworms 1097:92-94

Winter; surviving the cold winter, how do insects do it experiment 1097:95-96

MEASUREMENT. See also DISTANCE; HEIGHT

Accuracy demonstration 12:57-60

Area measuring area—big cities and small towns 304:28-29

Counting sticks—adding and subtracting 304:7-9

Different ways of measuring 141:6-69

Direction investigation into direction finding by radio 420:102-105

Distance—make a distance measuring flashlight—(complicated) 177:16-20

Distance—measuring distance—how far is it 304:14-15

Foot feat—measurements of your body 228:13

Height—measuring height—make a growth chart 304:10-11

Hill height—how to measure 381:147-148

How high is a tree 585:106-107

How long is your pace—pace chart given 636:40-43

How to measure with the sun and shadows 494:15

Hypsometer, making to measure how tall something is 999:59-62

249

Indirect and direct measurement of pennies experiment data tables given 1004:3.011
Latitude—investigation into finding latitude 420:93-97
Liquids—measuring—water glass chimes 304:22-23
Magnets—investigation into the strength of magnets 420:99-102
Measuring activities—measurement in ancient times and today (Primary) 447:1-33
Measuring speed—how fast can you go 304:16-17
Measuring temperature—how cold is it 304:24-25
Measuring time—a sand clock timer 304:18-19
Measuring time—an anytime calendar 304:20-21
Measuring wheel, cardboard, making 999:52-54
Measuring with yarn, ribbons (Primary) 535:69
Metals—investigation into creeping metals 420:90-92
Metric system—simple experiments with principles of metric system 423:1-33
Moon—investigation into measuring craters on the Moon 420:87-90
Optical micrometer—making 762:22-23
Screw clamp measures one thousandth of an inch 381:141-144
Surfaces and spaces in a room reconstructed in model room, how to do 1521:24-25
Time—investigation into rolling liquids 420:85-87
Time—investigation into the measurement of time 420:82-85
Transparency—light investigation into transparency 420:105-107
Use paper clips for measurement 253:163
Water—soils—investigation into the water—holding capacity of soils 420:110-113
Weighing machine made from wood, cardboard, wire and paper, how to do 1512:8-9
Weight—measuring weight—a weight guessing game 304:12-13
Width of river, how to approximate the width experiment 978:66
Wind—measuring the wind—a butterfly kite 304:26-27
Wooden wheel measuring device—how to make 723:20-21

MEASUREMENT—METRIC
Air—measure weight of air 357:28-29
Calculate a constant—investigating pi 357:20-21
Decimal measurements and units 357:10-11
Graph—make a prediction 357:12-13
Measuring speed 357:18-19
Measuring time—seconds pendulum 357:9
Measuring weight—coat hanger balance 357:6
Measuring weight—simple spring scales 357:7-8
Pressure—measuring pressure of foot on floor 357:22-23
Tree—find height of tree 357:16-17
Volume—find the volume 357:24-25

MECHANICAL ADVANTAGE
Calculating mechanical advantage formulas 1462:127-129

MECHANICAL ENERGY
Can you make a ball roll uphill experiment 743:8
Falling weight does work 281:39
Which objects roll the farthest experiment 743:9

MECHANICAL FORCE—TRICKS USING
Bet you can hold off ten people 228:84-85
Bet you can keep a friend in a chair with one finger 228:86-87
Bet you can lift a jar of rice with a knife 228:90

Bet you can make a ball defy gravity 228:93
Bet you can make a candle seesaw by itself 228:92
Bet you can out tug-of-war 228:88-89
Bet you can remove only the bottom checker of a stack without touching 228:82-83
Bet you can squeeze a raw egg without breaking it 228:91

MECHANICS
Gravity 350:115-121
Idea for a useless invention—how to make 577:project 63
Lift glass bottle with straw experiment 1007:80-81
Mechanics of the bicycle—experiment 585:52-53
Suspension 350:121-124
The rubber eraser—experiment 563:181
Working model of a solar engine—how to make 577:project 64

MEDICINE WHEELS
Make your own 292:70-71

MEDIEVAL CASTLE AND VILLAGE
How to make 415:54-60

MEGAPHONE
Cardboard and tape megaphone, how to make 1102:20
Ear trumpet or megaphone amplifies sound experiment 1045:15
How to make a simple one 569:43
How to make megaphone from oak tag 1279:27
Megaphone from large paper cone, how to make 1385:15
Megaphone from paper, how to make (Primary) 1319:9
Megaphone from plastic jug demonstrates sound waves experiment 1066:106-107

MELDE, F. E.
Melde's experiment—how to repeat 2:60-63

MELTING POINT
Melting point of different substances experiment 1179:20

MELTS
Experiment to show complex melt 197:14-15
Experiment to show density of melts 197:16-17

MEMBRANES. *See also* **OSMOSIS**
Another way of observing osmosis 319:54-55
How you can observe osmosis 319:53-54

MEMORY
Association of ideas helps your memory 381:94-98
Blindfold test for memory experiment 930:4-5
Visual memory of shapes to draw experiment 1253:10-11

MENDEL, GREGOR
Albinism in corn experiment 1060:96
Cross pollination of dwarf and tall pea plants experiment 1060:93-94
Hybridize morning glory plants experiment 1060:95-96
Investigate codominance in snapdragon flowers experiment 1060:95
Mendel's pea experiments, how to do 1060:92-95
Mendel's Principle of Independent Assortment experiment using peas 1060:95
Mendel's Principle of Segregation experiment 1060:92-93
Mendelian inheritance—rules of inheritance found by Mendel 402:100-101
Single-gene inheritance experiments 1267:106-112

MENDEL'S EXPERIMENTS
Genetic experiment with peas 398:91-96

MENDELIAN GENETICS. *See also* **GENETICS**
And laws of heredity (Advanced) 372:30-46

MENISCUS MAGIC

Demonstrate 364:111

MENSURATION

Simple experiment to demonstrate dimensions 408:1-33

MERCURY. *See also* **PLANETS**

Brightness of Sun from Mercury experiment 1478:64

Making craters on Mercury project 833:221-223

Mercury doesn't cause eclipse of Sun demonstration 1394:18-19

Mercury's position to the Sun affects observation of its surface experiment 1394:16-17

Why Mercury does not cause an eclipse experiment 1479:3

Why Mercury's day is longer than its year experiment 1478:65

MERCURY

Measurements 292:81-83

MERRY-GO-ROUND

Merry-go-round electric model, how to make 1028:106-107

Merry-go-round moves from electric motor, how to build both 1076:34-37

Merry-go-round turns from static electricity on balloon experiment 1208:82-83

Simple model merry-go-round demonstrates gravity power 419:6

Working model merry-go-round, patterns given, how to make 1496:30-31

METAL DETECTORS

Metal detector experiment using magnet 1309:6-7

METALS

Alloy, making 625:33

Anodizing with aluminum 97:18-19

Are good conductors of heat 44:92-93

Can metals burn experiment 976:48

Corrosion of—experiment 382:165-169

Do atoms in a metal move farther apart when heated experiment 831:21-22

Expands when heated—never fail lid remover—experiments 399:54

Expansion caused by heat—experiment to see how solids expand 385:125-126

Expansion meter to test expansion in a thick wire experiment 1179:50

Experiments with metal compound 116:140-155

Flame test for metals and their compounds 346:122-124

Flame tests for identification of metals 6:38

Four tests to determine whether something is metal experiment 1162:17

Hardening and softening of copper—experiment 585:37

Hardness test for aluminum experiment 1438:88-89

Hardness test for metals experiment 1438:85-87

Hardness test of metals and glass experiment 1438:97-99

Hardness; are all metals very hard experiment 1508:14

Heat expands metals 280:36

Identifying metals 586:60-61

Investigation into creeping metals 420:90-92

Jean Rey's burning metals into ash experiment 1133:2.001

Magnetic; are all metals magnetic experiment 1508:14

Make a simple drop hammer to shape metals 227:19

Make metals melt in hot water 87:82

Memory metal used by orthodontists for braces experiment 1083:62-63

Metal composition of pennies/different dates determined by density experiment 1004:3.005

Metal expands when heated—experiment 605:38-39

Metal expands when heated; twisting trick with foil demonstrates 1219:38

Metal fatigue investigation using paper clips experiment 1295:99-100

Metal fatigue; breaking point of bent metal paper clips experiment 1091:42-43

Metal rods expand when heated and shrink when cold experiment 1090:12-14

Metals affect a magnetic field experiment 1405:92

Metals expand and contract experiment; how they do it 939:18-21

Project 9—identifying metals 654:34

Proving that metal expands when heated 150:98-99

Removal of tarnish from silver demonstrates electron flow between metals 871:3.024

Rusting; do all metals rust experiment 1508:15

Some metals conduct heat better than others 44:94-95

Specific heat; compare specific heat of metals experiment 1515:72-75

Strain hardening of copper wire—experiment 585:38

Temperature effect on the length of wires experiment 1515:12-14

Testing aluminum for corrosion experiment using acids and alkalies 1438:90-93

Thickness of aluminum foil—experiment 586:63

Which metal holds the most heat 147:73-75

Why does metal rust experiment 1294:45-46

METAMORPHOSIS. *See also* **BUTTERFLIES; MOTHS**

Life cycle of butterfly experiment using small aquarium tank 1504:31

Metamorphosis in minibeasts experiments 1183:58-59

Metamorphosis of fruit flies observed experiment 1395:139-144

Observe the metamorphosis of a frog 294:73-74

METEORITES

Angle of meteorite's entry to Earth's atmosphere experiment 1062:93-95

Collecting micrometeorites (Advanced) 658:83-86

Comparing crater characteristics experiment 1062:98-99

Determining age of craters experiment 1062:96-97

Meteorite crater—how to make your own 649:18-19

Meteorite fragment dispersal experiment 1062:91-92

Micrometeors, how to collect, examine and display experiment 1476:182-183

Size of meteor on impact experiment 1062:91-92

Size of meteorite determined by sampling pieces found in an area experiment 1062:89-90

Specific gravity of rocks and meteorites, how to measure experiment 1062:86-87, 93-94

Testing rocks for meteorite characteristics experiment 1062:84-88

METEOROLOGICAL OPTICS. *See* **RAINBOWS; RAINDROPS; STARS**

METEOROLOGY. *See* **WEATHER; WEATHER FORECASTING**

METEORS

Gravity affects speed of meteor travel experiment 1062:93-95

Making meteor observations—how to do 710:59-60

Meteor showers annual pattern experiment; some good and some bad years to view 1062:102-104

Meteor showers observations of (Advanced) 658:79-82

Meteorite crater model from plaster, how to make 1080:29

Meteorites and micrometeorites, how to collect 1170:58

Observing meteor showers, how to do 1170:55

Observing meteors using observing log chart 1329:46-47

Pulled by Earth's gravity—make craters 274:10

Reporting meteor observations—how to send your observations 710:60

Time table for watching 231:42

Tracking and photographing a meteor shower project 833:274-275

Watching for meteors 292:107-108

METERS

Current meter to measure current in electric motors, how to make 1179:170

Electric meter, how to make using compass, wire and dry cell battery 1164:88-90

Homemade meter—how to make 291:156

How can you read a watt-hour ampere 278:63-64

Light meter, how to make 830:66

Make meter that registers electric currents 291:156

Meter for home electricity, how to read 972:15

Optical micrometer—making 762:22-23

METHANE

Converting coal to fuel gas experiment 895:105

Getting methane from coal experiment 895:104-105

How to make a tabletop methane digester 347:132-134

Methane gas from sewage [horse manure] experiment 933:50-51

Methane physical structure, how to make 1403:8-11

Plant materials changed into methane fuel experiment 1323:90-94

METRIC SYSTEM. *See also* **MEASUREMENT— METRIC**

Baking soda and baking powder experiment using metric measure 702:87-88

Metric clock makes working with time easier experiment 1062:40

Simple experiments with principles of metric system 423:1-33

Working with linear units—computer project 584:67-69

Working with temperature scales computer project 584:72-74

Working with volume—computer project 584:70-71

MEYER'S EXPERIMENT ILLUSION

Experiment 229:77-78

MICE

Activity of mice and gerbils affected by light and darkness experiment 1158:136-137

Description and measurement 375:11

Experiment to show learning in a puzzle box 163:113-119

How to make a cage for 163:107

How to make a can trap for mice 264:67

How to train a mouse 163:105-108

Keeping a mouse 264:66

Make a maze for mice 264:63-64

Mazes—T maze variations to test intelligence—how to make 510:106-109

Mouse climbing experiments 264:65

Raising in cage 436:56-57

Train a mouse to ring a bell 163:109-112

Wild—collection and care of 390:57-59

MICROAQUARIUM

Grow your own mini beasts in a micro aquarium 400:3

MICROBES. *See also* **BACTERIA; MOLDS; YEAST**

Bacteria—yogurt—how bacteria produce lactic acid 74:113-115

Bacteria and factors that aid/hinder spread in apples experiment; data tables 1004:2.018

Explanations of activities of microbes 81:11-95

Grow your own microbes 412:8 pages of unpaged book

Hand washing—demonstrate the presence of microorganisms on hand 80:70-71

Hay infusion, how to make 889:31-32

How living microbes make things change—curds and whey experiment 412:4 pages of unpaged book

How living microbes make things change—yeast and dough experiment 412:2 pages of unpaged book

Ideas for doing your microbe project and safety and record keeping 1221:31-34

Ideas for microbe exhibits, demonstrations and investigations 1221:12-22

Ideas for microbe projects 1221:9-22

Ideas for planning your microbe project and gathering information 1221:23-30

Ideas for presenting microbe project using graphs, displays, reports 1221:35-43

Invisible seeds—prepare/observe gardens for mold/bacteria growth (Advanced) 565:43-53

Lemon disease—to show the transfer of disease by contact 80:64-65

Lemon penicillin, how to observe 827:64-65

Louis Pasteur's do microbes arise spontaneously experiment 1133:3.009

Micro gardens—demonstrate growth of molds, yeast, and bacteria 80:68-70

Microbes cause decay—experiment with grass 412:2 pages of unpaged book

Microbes from hay infusion under microscope, observe 889:32-34

Microbes grow in milk jars experiment 1063:192

Microbes make things biodegradable experiment 1221:22

Protozoa under microscope, observe four groups 889:33-35

Show effect of moisture on growth of bacteria 80:67-68

Soaps and deodorants kill underarm bacteria experiment 1221:21-22, 36-37

Some types of wood rot faster than others do experiment 1221:5-7, 28

Souring of milk in glass bottles—microbial activity and influence of temp 80:62-63

Testing for microbes that grow on food experiment 924:41-42

Things you can't see can affect your body experiment 1063:192

Yeast—Sally Lunn bread—a study of yeast activity 74:106-110

Yeast balloons—to show fermentation by yeasts 80:65-67

Yeast pretzels—inhibiting yeast action 74:110-112

MICROBIOLOGY. *See* **MICROBES; MOLDS; YEAST**

MICROCLIMATE

How to map 364:136-137

Microclimate study of small areas experiment 1063:287

MICROHABITAT. *See also* **HABITATS**
Investing a fallen log community—a microhabitat 285:80-81
Observe and collect small marine life in rock crevices 285:82-83

MICROMETER
Micrometer from wood, bolt and nut, how to make 1248:12-13

MICROORGANISMS. *See also* **ALGAE; BACTERIA; BRINE SHRIMP; DIATOMS; EUGLENA; HYDRA; LEECHES; OSTRACODS; PARAMECIA; MICROBES; PLANARIANS; SLIME MOLD**
Acid rain effects on micro-organisms experiments 777:14
Collecting at the pond—how to 500:36-39
Collecting in the city 500:39-40
Grow your own mini beasts in a microaquarium 400:3
Infusion—hay infusion—how to make 500:42
Infusion—make infusions to get microorganisms to study 500:40-43
Micro-aquarium of organisms shown on slide projector experiment 1476:111
Specimens—care of—ascellus 500:117
Specimens—care of—brine shrimp 500:108-110
Specimens—care of—gastrotrichs 500:124
Specimens—care of—hydra 500:121
Specimens—care of—leeches 500:100-101
Specimens—care of—ostracods 500:111
Specimens—care of—water mites 500:127-128
Why does food go bad 261:56-62

MICROPARTICULATION. *See also* **SIMPLESSE**
Ice cream taste and texture compared with Simplesse fat substitute experiment 1484:132-133

MICROPHONE
Cigar box microphone, making 895:67-69
How can you build a microphone 278:53-54

MICROPHOTOGRAPHY
Tiny creatures photographing 436:57

MICROSCOPE
Activities to explore and understand microscope [Primary] 758:102-104
Adventure 1—examine common objects—human hair, air bubble, fish scales 403:1-4
Algae 61:56-59
Algae—adventure 11—we find beauty in unexpected places 403:36-42
Algae zoo 61:121
Algae; observe under microscope 889:36
Amoeba—adventure 7—we seek the famous amoeba 403:22-26
Amoeba; observe under microscope 889:35
Ants and aphids—adventure 54—intrigued by a delightful relationship 403:209-212
Bacteria 11:118-127
Bacteria—adventure 29—we go microbe hunting 403:100-106
Bacteria from hay water under microscope—observe 713:97
Bacteria from yogurt under microscope—observe 713:97-98
Bacteria from your teeth under microscope—observe 713:95-97
Bead-lens microscope, how to make (advanced project) 1295:24-28

Beetles—adventure 52—digestive tract of beetle under microscope 403:202-205
Blood 11:103-109

Blood—adventure 40—observe circulation of blood of dragonfly larva 403:146-151
Blood cells and mouth lining cells—how to prepare microscope slides 729:28-29
Blood cells under microscope—observe and compare 713:74-76
Blood cells under microscope, observe 889:54-57
Blood circulation in goldfish tail—observe 713:72-73
Bread mold—grow and observe under microscope 713:92-94
Bryozoa—adventure 33—we receive a pleasant surprise 403:115-119
Build a simple microscope 168:25-27
Build a simple microscope 860:202-204
Butterflies—adventure 24—we learn the use of perfume 403:85-88
Butterfly dust under a microscope—observe 713:64-65
Cartilage cells under microscope—observe 713:69-70
Cells—examining green plant cells—elodea 294:15-16
Cells—human—observing cheek lining cells 294:16-17
Cells—plant—living plant cells from an onion skin 294:14-15
Cells—typical cell structure—'empty' cork cells 294:13-14
Cheek cells observed under microscope experiment 1425:14
Cheek cells under microscope—observe 713:63-64
Coffee—adventure 25—we test our morning coffee 403:88-90
Construct a microscope 167:51-57
Cork cells under microscope—examine 713:49-50
Crystals—adventure 2—we become crystal gazers 403:4-7
Crystals of salt—sugar and sand—compare 713:39-40
Culturing protozoa 11:68-77
Dandelion seed and parachute under microscope—observe 713:60-61
Daphnia—adventure 4—we learn the meaning of privacy 403:12-14
Daphnia under a microscope—observe 713:88-90
Desmids—adventure 10—we make the acquaintance of the desmids 403:33-36
Desmids 61:59
Detecting paper materials 61:85-88
Detecting pollution 61:123-128
Diatoms—adventure 9—we dig from bones in an ancient graveyard 403:30-33
Diatoms; observe under microscope 889:37-38
Diatoms 61:59-60
Difflugia—adventure 22—we meet some relatives of the amoeba 403:78-80
Earthworm reproduction—adventure 58—observe a provision of nature 403:222-227
Epithelial cheek cells under microscope, observe 889:52-54
Euglena—adventure 8—a puzzle of natural history—euglena and volvox 403:26-30
Euglena; observe under microscope 889:36
Eye of fly under microscope—observe 713:65-67
Eylais—adventure 16—we make the acquaintance of eylais 403:59-61

253

Fairy shrimp (phyllopods)—adventure 50—an animal that swims on its back 403:191-193

Ferns—adventure 39—we trace the life history of ferns 403:141-146

Fibers 61:74-76

Fibers textiles 11:80-84

Film can microscope, how to make 1527:114

Fingerprints 61:82-84

Fingerprints—adventure 56—approach the science of criminal detection 403:215-219

Fish board 9:54-55; 11:107-109

Fish scales under microscope—observe 713:71-72

Flagellates 61:62

Flatworms—adventure 32—meet some more worms—planarians 403:112-115

Flea glass microscope, how to build your own 864:14-19

Fleas—adventure 42—we meet a champion 403:154-155

Flower animals 61:63-65

Flowers—adventure 47—flowers are not merely ornamental 403:179-185

Food—adventure 18—butter, flour, cocoa, jam, honey under microscope 403:65-68

Foraminifera—adventure 27—we find out what chalk is made of 403:94-96

Frog board 11:107-109

Fruit fly zoo 61:120-121

Green plant cells under microscope—observe 713:52-54

Grow molds and observe under a microscope 889:49-50

Hair—human—observe different kinds and compare 713:40-41

Hairs—identifying 61:76

Hay infusion, how to make 889:31-32

Hints for examining specimens 500:26-29

Homemade microscope to view water animals experiment 943:10-11

Honey bees—adventure 13—we go marketing with a honey bee 403:46-50

Honey bees—adventure 14—we learn what it means to be strong 403:50-53

Hooke's cork and cells experiment 1156:65

How to grow bacteria 61:122

How to make and use a well slide 61:42-47

How to make your own 163:55-58

How to measure with a microscope 163:59-62

How to mount specimens on slides 163:52-54

Hydra 61:65-67

Hydra—adventure 5—we follow in the footsteps of Hercules—hydra 403:14-18

Hydra, amoeba, paramecia, algae, other invisibles 79:44-45

Identifying bloodstains 61:91-92

Identifying foods 61:76-81

Identifying pollen 61:81-82

Images in compound microscope appear upside down and backwards experiment 1402:24-27

Infusoria—adventure 23—paramecium, stentor, vorticella and carchesium 403:80-85

Insect antennae under microscope, observe 889:60-62

Insect eye 61:13-15

Insect eyes under microscope, observe 889:62

Insect legs 61:17-21

Insect legs under microscope, observe 889:60

Insect mouths 61:22-28

Insect mouths under microscope, observe 889:62-64

Insect parts—adventure 51—we receive a lesson in evolution 403:194-202

Insect wings under microscope, observe 889:62

Leaf stomata under a microscope, how to do 886:28-29

Leaves—adventure 46—we tour through one of nature's factories 403:173-179

Lichens—adventure 21—we come upon a strange partnership 403:75-78

Life in a drop of pond water, observe 882:37

Look at newsprint under a microscope 294:10-11

Looking at cells 61:93-98

Magnifying glass microscope, make from dowels, velcro, pocket magnifier 1295:22-24

Make a microscope; list of materials given (Advanced) 565:109-116

Make a microscope 176:52-53; 570:38-39

Make a water drop microscope 142:59

Make microscopic algae jungle 279:34-36

Make your own from water drop, box, night light and thread spool 1510:40-44

Make your own version of a microscope 399:78

Making a microscope from two lenses experiment 1257:36-37

Making a simple water drop microscope 57:10-11

Making microscope using two lenses experiment 1053:36-37

Making permanent slides 79:28-30

Making specimens 11:38-43

Making water drop microscope 8:108-110

Microbes from hay infusion under microscope, observe 889:32-34

Microscope from plastic milk jug, making 779:36-37

Microtome 11:36-38

Microtome—make to prepare specimens for viewing 436:58

Millipedes and centipedes—adventure 49—train lens on these two creature 403:189-191

Molds—adventure 36—we become farmers 403:130-133

Molds 11:85-92

Mosses—adventure 34—we examine a moss plant 403:119-124

Muscle cells under microscope, observe 889:57-58

Muscle tissue under microscope—observe 713:68-69

Mushrooms—adventure 35—we make a study of toadstools 403:124-130

Nervous system of a grasshopper—adventure 59—what makes an animal go 403:228-232

Objects looked at through compound microscope experiment 1402:20-23

Observe single hair 294:11-12

Onion cells under microscope—observe as you stain them 713:50-52

Paper—adventure 48—we investigate the structure of paper 403:185-189

Paramecia; observe under microscope 889:35

Paramecium and blepharisma 61:99-102

Paramecium culture—how to make and observe 713:82-85

Parts of flower under microscope, observe water ducts 889:42-45

Peach skin under microscope—observe 713:59-60

Penicillin mold—grow and observe under microscope 713:95

Photomicrography with a pen microscope 386:45

Photomicrography 11:136-140

Planaria zoo 61:118-119
Plant cells under a microscope, how to do 886:28-29
Pollen grains under a microscope, observe 889:45-46
Pollen grains under microscope—observe sprouting 713:56-58
Pond water under a microscope experiment 1176:32-33
Pond water under microscope observe life 713:77-81
Potato cells under microscope showing starch grains 713:54-55
Powdery mildews—adventure 57—we solve a mystery 403:219-221
Preparing cultures 61:114-122
Protists from mud, puddles and other ooze observed under microscope exp. 864:60-62
Protists under the microscope; experiments to perform 864:55-58
Protozoa under microscope, observe four groups 889:33-35
Radioactive particles 11:115-116
Red blood—adventure 12—we stab ourselves for love of science 403:42-46
Rhizopods 61:60-62
Roots—adventure 44—we acquire insight into the structure of roots 403:160-167
Rotifers—adventure 15—we meet with an optical illusion 403:54-59
Rotifers or wheel bearers 61:67-69
Seeds under a microscope, observe 889:47
Simple microscope, how to make 861:158-162
Simple microscope, how to make 892:29
Simple things to try 79:7-57
Slide box—how to make 500:32-33; 713:32
Slide of cells—how to prepare 703:28-29
Slide storage box 9:58-59
Slides—how to prepare a slide 400:3
Slides—making—how to do 436:58; 713:28-31
Slides—preparing 436:58
Slides—staining and making permanent slides 500:31-33
Slides of insect cells, how to make 990:28
Slides of insect cells, how to prepare and keep 896:28-29
Slime molds—adventure 53—we prove that appearances can be deceptive 403:205-209
Snail radula (teeth)—adventure 41—surgery on a snail's teeth 403:151-153
Snowflakes—observe and draw 713:45-47
Soda bottle microscope, how to make 1527:112-113
Spices—adventure 30—mustard and pepper under a microscope 403:107-109
Spiders—adventure 43—we inspect a spinning machine 403:156-160
Spirogyra and other algae under a microscope—observe 713:85-87
Sponges—adventure 26—we learn something about sponges 403:91-94
Spores under a microscope, observe 889:47-48
Spring tails—adventure 37—we view the most primitive insects 403:133-136
Staining 11:128-133
Starch—adventure 17—take a lesson in food analysis—starch in food 403:61-65
Stems—adventure 45—we examine an extraordinary pipe line 403:167-173
Stomata experiment plants 11:51-57
Stomate density (number per area) on leaves experiment 762:78-79
Structure of cotton fibers 294:12

Structure of fish scales 294:12-13
Studying bacteria 61:106-109
Studying blood 61:103-105
Substage lamp making 11:4-5
Substage light for 9:52-53
Sun animalcule—adventure 55—we look at the sun animalcule 403:212-215
Textile fibers—adventure 38—learn to distinguish textile fibers 403:136-141
The invisible world of the onion 400:6
Tools, methods and cultures for examining water animals 484:5-20
Tubifex worms—adventure 31—we dig for worms 403:109-111
Urine analysis 61:89-90
Water bears—adventure 19—we go bear hunting 403:68-70
Water drop lens 11:12-15
Water drop microscope—how to make 532:83
Water drop microscope demonstrates refraction of light 1308:18-19
Water drop microscope, making 906:62-63
Water fleas—adventure 3—we hunt a one-eyed monster—water fleas 403:7-12
Water fleas, water bear and polyzoa 61:70-73
Water microscope—how to make 631:54
Water microscope, how to make 1291:22-23
Water plants 61:50-55
Why does microscope enlarge objects experiment 1294:103-105
World through a drop of water—make a water drop lens 565:107-108
Yeast—adventure 28—we inquire into the nature of yeast 403:97-100
Yeast and molds 61:110-113
Yeast cells under microscope—observe 713:90-92
Yeast cells under microscope, observe 889:50-51
Yeast 11:95-100
MICROSCOPE—HOUSE FLY
Adventure 6—learn how a fly walks upside down 403:18-22
MICROSCOPE—MOSQUITO
Adventure 20—discover a zoological radio station 403:70-75
MICROSCOPE—SLIDES
Mounting a slide, how to 889:20-22
Permanent slide mounts, making 889:22-24
Preparing microscope slides, how to do 1395:195
Wet mount slide specimen, how to prepare 1402:80-83
Wet mount with bubbles, making 889:28
MICROTOME
Make to prepare specimens for microscope viewing 436:58
Making—to cut thin sections of plants & other materials 9:56-57; 11:36-38
MICROWAVE OVENS
Heating in microwave ovens requires water molecules experiment 1250:32-34
MIGRATION. *See also* **BIRDS—MIGRATION**
Activities with bird migration 236:84-85
Butterfly migration in the field and in the laboratory 266:59-62
MILDEW
Effect of light on molds and mildews—experiment 532:110

Powdery mildews—adventure 57—powdery mildews under a microscope 403:219-221

Rotten cotton—dirty sock experiment to show growth of mildew 216:18-23

MILK. *See also* **BUTTER; CASEIN; CHEESE; ICE CREAM**

Can acid molecules curdle milk experiment 831:68-69

Cottage cheese from whole and skim milk 152:27-33

Curdling milk experiment 400:71

Demonstrate bacteria in making cultured cream 152:23-27

Extract casein from milk 122:99-102

Fat globules in milk—food coloring and detergent experiment 696:34-35

Glue from milk—making 733:6

Is milk really the perfect food—experiment 628:75-76

Laboratory analysis tests on milk experiment; data tables given 1004:4.013

Making hard—ripened cheese 152:33-37

Making mold—ripened cheese 152:37-43

Milk separates into curds and whey experiment 905:114-115; 1405:57

Milk turns into plastic experiment using milk and vinegar 1271:31

Protein in milk can be denatured by addition of vinegar experiment 1403:15

Secret writing—fun with milk 579:44

Test for which dairy product has the most fat, how to do 1312:43

Testing for bacterial growth in milk experiment 924:43-44

Watching changes in milk—souring 579:46-47

What happens to milk left in the sun experiment [Primary] 744:10

MILKWEEDS

Identify community of organisms with red cellophane flashlight exp. 864:133

Milkweed bugs, how to raise and observe 1116:28-29

Milkweed pod boat—how to make 236:50-51

MILKY WAY

Band of the Milky Way experiment; show with plastic and flashlight 1478:132

Creating a picture of the Milky Way project 833:68-70

Making a moveable plan of the Earth centered universe project 833:72-75

Making models of the platonic solids project 833:71-72

Milky Way appears to be a hazy cloud demonstration 1394:146-147

Model—making (Advanced) 658:32-34

Model Milky Way experiment; make from poster board, paints and clay 1478:134

Why Milky Way appears to be hazy cloud experiment 1479:18

MILLIPEDES AND CENTIPEDES

Adventure 49—we train our lens on two familiar creatures under a microscope 403:189-191

Millipede model from old stocking, how to make 1183:57

Millipede, how to make stuffed stocking millipede 1182:9

MILLS

Straw mill demonstrates wind energy 1523:26

Wind energy raises toy or model windmill 1523:27

MILLWORKS

Bellows and trip hammer—making from wood 429:105

Crane, making from wood 429:107

Grist mill—making from wood 429:103

Hammer mill to grind grains—how to make from wood 429:91-93

How to make from wood 429:98-102

Model grist mill works, how to make 1115:93-96

Pump—making from wood 429:106

Sawmill—making from wood 429:104

MIND

Mind over matter—demonstrate power of suggestion 291:202-203

MINERALS. *See also* **ROCKS AND MINERALS**

Acid effect on bones experiment 1396:49-51

Acid test 37:13-14

Adventure 29—study of minerals in crystal form under a hand lens 29:137-139

Adventure 35—continue study of minerals—rocks under a hand lens 29:162-166

Aluminum experiments 37:43-44

Borax bead flame tests for metals in minerals experiment 1266:37

Calcium oxide restores firmness to blanched vegetables experiment 1396:51-52

Caliche deposits formation demonstration 1023:28-29

Carbon dioxide gas made when marble and calcite dissolve in vinegar experiment 1295:98

Chart of five most important minerals in food experiment 1264:22

Chemical weathering experiments 666:40-41

Cleavage line in minerals demonstration 1023:40-41

Cleavage test for mineral identification experiment 1046:15-17

Color properties of minerals; identification test experiment 1046:9-11

Demonstrate some minerals have definite cleavage line 1405:72-73

Density test of minerals experiment 1266:35

Differences between rocks and minerals experiment 1438:39-41

Do diets of adolescents supply them with their mineral requirements experiment 1267:44-47

Effect of water on 37:46-48

Flame test to identify 666:74

Flame tests for metals in minerals experiment 1266:36

Froth flotation to concentrate valuable minerals experiment 1266:49

Granite experiment 37:22-25

Gypsum experiments 37:29-31

Hardness of minerals identification test experiment; hardness scale given 1046:12-14

Hardness test 37:10-12; 234:90

Hardness test for chalk experiment 1438:51-52

Hardness test for graphite, the lead in pencils experiment 1438:83-84

Hardness test for various minerals 860:163-164

Hardness test standards 336:44-45

Hardness test to identify 666:72-73

Hydraulic mining demonstration 1023:46-47

In food 261:47-49

Iron experiments 37:36-39

Leaching minerals from rocks experiment 1266:49

Limestone experiment 37:15-18

Marble experiment 37:19-21

Mineral hunting; collecting and classifying minerals project 1413:83-95

Mineral identification chart 400:49

Minerals from the earth—experiment with plants 563:63

Minerals identified using database of characteristics computer project 1021:58-62

Mohs' scale—testing minerals for hardness 625:19

Observe and collect minerals around you 300:8-9

Panning for gold—how to 666:76-77

Phosphorescence and fluorescence 577:project #23

Placer ore deposits; how they are formed experiment 1479:71

Portland cement experiments 37:40-42

Rubber chicken bone experiment; vinegar removes minerals from chicken bone 1189:50-51

Salt experiments 37:32-35

Sandstone experiment 37:26-28

Shiny aluminum—experiment 585:87-88

Specific gravity of rocks and meteorites, how to measure experiment 1062:86-87

Specific gravity of rocks and minerals, how to measure experiment 1062:93-94

Streak test for minerals demonstration 1023:34-35

Streak test for minerals 1266:32

Streak test of a mineral experiment 1438:42-43

Test for limestone experiment 1023:32-33

Testing water for minerals experiment 1438:23-25

Tests to examine rocks and minerals experiment; identification guide given 1063:396-399

Tests to identify minerals using vinegar (acid) experiment 1046:18-19

Tumble polish your minerals—how to 625:18

Use of gypsum as building material experiment 1004:1.011

Water isn't pure 281:23

MINERS

Davy, Sir Humphry; who invented miner's safety lamp project 1525:98-100

MINES

Pit head model of winding gear at top of mine shaft, how to make 1190:48-55

MINI CLIMATES. See also ECOSYSTEMS

Finding out about winds in different places (Primary) 108:20-23

Finding temperature in little climates (Primary) 108:16-20

Temperature, light, wind 108:14-27

MINIBEASTS

Collect minibeasts and decide which are insects experiment 1183:57

Habitat survey of minibeasts, how to do 1183:54

Living conditions that minibeasts like best experiment 1183:55

Metamorphosis in minibeasts experiments 1183:58-59

Minibeast meadow frieze, how to make 1183:86

MINING

Panning for gold experiment 1081:19

MINNOWS

Communication by odor in minnows in the field and in the laboratory 266:90-93

MINSKY—PAPER FIGURES

Illusions 229:119-120

MIRAGES

And other visual oddities—illusions 229:108-127

How to observe mirages 761:86-89

Light from flashlight bends in warm air and produces distorted image 555:15

MIRROR WRITING

Friend reads your message by holding paper up to mirror 360:84

Write wrong 228:16

MIRRORS. See also KALEIDOSCOPES; PERISCOPES

Angles of an incoming and reflected light beam with mirror experiment 1159:73-76

Backward writing in mirror experiment 960:46

Bilateral symmetry experiment 956:22-23

Boundless menagerie 350:132

Brain expects image it sees in mirror is your other hand experiment 1132:66

Camera used to check distance of your reflection behind the mirrors experiment 1245:18-19

Candle appears to be burning in water experiment 761:108-109

Car mirrors (Primary) 345:9

Caustics; curved line patterns produced by curved mirrors and lights 1443:84-91

Convex and concave mirrors in places and things around you (Primary) 345:28-29

Convex and concave mirrors, what you can see experiment 1283:16-17

Corner cube mirror reflects straight back 265:24-25

Corner reflector shows multiple images of an object experiment 1132:31-1-31-2

Curved mirrors—making real images with a concave mirror 586:45-49

Curved mirrors experiment; concave versus convex mirrors 956:31

Cylindrical mirror lets you see yourself as others see you experiment 1132:35-1-35-3

Demonstrate mirror images (Primary) 207:42

Device to see through solid objects—how to make 507:1888-1889

Experiment to locate image in a mirror 385:102

Experiment to see the inverted image 385:107-108

Experiment with multi mirrors 295:108-109

Experiments with mirror reflections 1138:51-60

Experiments with mirrors 532:18-19; 693:60-66

"Finding person around barrier" controls path of reflected light experiment 1443:33-37

Flexible mirrors bend to concave or convex experiment 1111:23-24

Game "finding location of object" shows light reflected off flat surface 1443:37-43

Game "mirror monsters" demonstrates how light rays travel experiment 1443:26-33

Hinged mirrors give correct image 265:20-21

Hinged mirrors give several images 265:22-23

How a mirror works experiment 941:73-75

How can a mirror help you see around corners—experiment (Primary) 345:10

How can you see what is behind you without turning your head (Primary) 345:8

How can you use mirrors to see the back of your head (Primary) 345:12-13

How do mirrors work experiment 1283:12

How mirror can produce distorted images experiment 941:78-79

How mirror reflection can be reversed experiment 941:76-77

How real objects are reflected from curved surfaces experiment 1443:79-83

How to do trick writing 208:88-91

How to play hunt the hobbit—experiment (Primary) 345:11

How to see thru a solid brick 350:136-137

Idiot test—make idiot box and follow path with pencil while looking in mirror 538:120-121

Images in a plane mirror 295:104-108

Images in three different types of mirrors experiment 1004:5.016

Images of images can repeat forever experiment 1132:61-1-61-2

Kaleidoscope—make simple one 595:40-41

Light travels in straight line magic trick 1010:55-60

Magical illusions; create using transparent plastic sheets 1443:69

Make a kaleidoscope 265:42-43

Make a mystery box 208:92-93

Make a periscope 265:36-37

Make a transparent mirror 208:106-109

Make crazy mirrors 142:33

Make periscope from milk carton (Primary) 207:38-40

Making and reflecting narrow beam of light experiment 1159:73-76

Mirror activities [Primary] 759:22-23

Mirror affects reflected image experiment 1405:106

Mirror affects reflected image shown by copying writing from mirror 1404:194-195

Mirror and flashlight experiments 885:54-56

Mirror box trick 1138:58-59

Mirror box used in magic shows, how to make 1296:1991

Mirror glass trick 1138:56-58

Mirror image; where is mirror image experiment using mirror and pins 1153:19-21

Mirror images demonstrate light reflection 555:12

Mirror images with two small mirrors 558:96-97

Mirror trick 585:124

Mirror writing, how to do 643:6

Mirror writing 295:109-110

Mirrors and penny demonstrate reflection 721:60

Mirrors at an angle, multiple images experiment 1153:23-27

Mirrors reflect light—experiments 659:8-11; 1063:176

Mirrors used to multiply reflections experiment 941:80-82

Multiple images in a mirror 265:26-27

Multiple images of your face moving past each other experiment 1443:57-63

Mysterious x-ray machine allows you to see through book or brick—how to make 487:18-20

Mystery mirror writing with mirror viewer, how to do 600:12-13

Parabolas experiment with mirrors 1132:73-1-73-2

Parabolic shapes concentrate energy experiment 1132:58-1-58-2

Periscope—how to make 350:135

Periscope from two mirrors—making 26:58

Playing with mirrors 180:68

Polar grid experiment, how to do 1111:25

Printing your name while you look in a mirror (Primary) 551:unpaged

Reflected design experiment 1111:22

Reflected images experiment 1111:21

Reflections in a spoon experiment using spoon mirrors and beam tank 1092:25

Reflections in four plane mirrors game, finding the other person 1443:18-19

Reflections in four plane mirrors game, lining up the stickers 1443:22-25

Reflections in four plane mirrors game, making a face 1443:20-21

Reflections in mirrors experiment 1283:14

Reflections in two plane mirrors experiment 1443:11-17

Secret message written in front of mirror, how to do 1415:24

See images of images (photons) with two large mirrors 366:196-197

See through solid objects—experiment 507:1888-1889

Simple experiments with mirrors, letters and pictures 1299:7-10

Size of mirror needed to reflect full—length image 291:173

Spoon mirrors demonstrate concave and convex mirrors 1073:77

Spoon mirrors reflect light rays in opposite ways demonstration 1415:32-35

Steam on mirror in bathroom; how long does it take to disappear project 1210:38-41

The 'seebackascope' 350:134-135

The concave mirror—experiment 1 and 2 585:118-120

The decapitated princess illusion 350:137-140

The magic mirror 350:133-134

The mirror monster game (Primary) 345:7

Through the looking glass—mirror writing—experiment 585:116-117

Topsy-turvy world of mirrors experiment 1092:17

Trace drawings from images in a mirror 265:15-19

Transparent mirrors; how light travels through them experiments 1443:47-56

Two-way mirrors experiment so you become composite person of your partner 1132:48-1-48-2

What happens when you look into a mirror (Primary) 345:4-6

What mirrors do 291:175

Why mirrors are used in photocopiers experiment 860:211-212

Writing—what happens to writing when you look at it in a mirror (Primary) 345:18-19

MIRRORS—FOCAL LENGTH

Experiment to find the focal length of a curved mirror 385:106-112

MIRRORS—REFLECTION

Make a kaleidoscope (Primary) 345:25

Shapes, half shapes and pictures reflected—experiments (Primary) 345:14-17

The corner reflector demonstration of geometrical optics 563:145

Two mirror tricks with pencil and human face 563:144

What happens if you use two mirrors side by side (Primary) 345:20-24

Where else can you see your reflection (Primary) 345:26-27

MISSILES. *See* **ROCKETS**

MISTLETOE

Grow mistletoe, how to do 1524:22

MITOSIS. *See* **CELLULAR REPRODUCTION**

MIXTURES. *See also* **EMULSIONS; SOLUTIONS**

Color sculpture in jar shows water and oil don't mix 890:97

Colored soap bubbles from baking soda, vinegar and food coloring experiment 919:31
Corn starch mixture is soft, hard and liquid experiment 781:4-5
Dissolving tests experiment 909:40
Experiments to show 116:71-76
Glop from cornstarch and water, how to make 919:30
How to separate a mixture 157:10-11
How to separate mixtures experiment 180:26; 586:61; 1508:19
Mixing oil and water experiment 909:40
Ooblik mixture from corn starch and water does strange things experiment 1330:54-57
Play clay, making 960:33
Salt in water trick 909:40
Separating salt and sand experiment 790:29
Separating things out of mixtures—methods to use 6:10-11
Separating things that sink and float experiment 1526:52-53
Separating three chemicals, sand, salt and iron filings experiment 1271:13
Test clay you create experiment 871:3.004
Water mixtures—experiment 663:32-33
What are mixtures and solutions demonstrations 902:21
Which are mixtures and which are solutions—experiment 598:19
Will liquids mix together experiment; chart given 960:20-21

MOBILES
Flashing solar mobile—how to make 651:40-41
Food chain—making 436:59
Gull go round mobile, making 778:50-51
How to make a mobile from driftwood 646:97-99
Make models that move in a breeze 241:4-6
Merry-go-round mobile 356:42-43
Mobile demonstrates balance—making [Primary] 753:22-23
Mobile merry-go-round—how to make 410:13
Nature mobiles—how to make 312:15-18
Pinwheel mobile—how to make 494:78
Planets—make a planet mobile 293:39
Seesaw mobile, how to make 808:51-55
Simple mobile, making 935:64-65
Space orbit mobile 356:40-41
Symmetrical mobile experiments, how to build 1444:75-83
Three mobiles, how to make 1299:91
Unsymmetrical mobile experiment, how to build 1444:90-97

MOBIUS STRIPS
Colored Mobius strip experiment 1352:57
Cut a loop of paper in half (Primary) 69:35-36
Cut paper in half and still get one piece experiment 937:16-17
Experiment 550:111-115
Figure eight Mobius strip, how to make 1083:118
How to make 399:34
Magic trick with paper belts 1010:77-80
Mobius bands, how to make 1247:8-9; 291:234-236
Mobius strip as connecting belt for wheels experiment 1405:98
Nature cycles explored with Mobius strip experiment 1063:207
No loophole here 222:72-74

Paper Mobius strip, how to make 827:36; 1298:23
Siamese Mobius strip, how to make 1083:119
The will that wouldn't 222:78-79
Trick in typewriter 228:104

MODELS
Airplane fighter—cardboard—how to make 113:20-21
Biplane—cardboard—how to make 113:8-9
Earth—make basketball Earth to show latitude and longitude 292:62
Fish—make plaster model of fish 296:65-67
Helicopter—potato—how to make 113:24-25
Jet airplane—potato—how to make 113:16-17
Make a model of atomic element 293:38
Moon buggy—egg carton—how to make 113:26-27
Moon phases—faces of the Moon model 292:67
Paper plane—folded—how to make 113:12-13
Robot—carton—how to make 113:22-23
Rockets—cardboard tube—how to make 113:14-15
Room model—how to make (Primary) 303:10-11
Satellites—Explorer XVIII interplanetary monitoring platform (IMP)—how 315:60-72
Satellites—Explorer XXIX geodetic explorer satellite—how to make 315:87-98
Satellites—Lunar Orbiter V—how to make 315:124-137
Satellites—Mariner 5 Venus Spacecraft—how to make 315:111-123
Satellites—OAO orbiting astronomical observatory—how to make 315:99-110
Satellites—OGO—orbiting geophysical observatory—how to make 315:138-153
Satellites—ORS octahedral research satellite—how to make 315:81-86
Satellites—OSO-1—satellite model—how to make 315:22-31
Satellites—relay communications satellite model—how to make 315:40-48
Satellites—Secor—how to make 315:73-80
Satellites—Syncom—synchronous communications satellite—how to make 315:49-59
Satellites—TRS—tetrahedral research satellite—how to make 315:32-36
Satellites—yogurt container—how to make 113:10-11
Shuttle soda bottle 113:28-29
Solar system 292:102-103
Space Shuttle Orbiter—paper model—making and flying 314:77-82
Space station—plastic container how to make 113:18-19
Spaceships that fly from paper plates, straws, styrofoam cups 311:9-40
Tent model—how to make 328:13-14

MOEBIUS STRIPS. See MOBIUS STRIPS
MOHS, FRIEDRICH
Mohs' scratch test for hardness of rocks and minerals 572:19
MOHS' SCALE
For rock hardness 364:74
Mohs' hardness scale 689:45; 1342:50; 1413:99
Mohs' scale of hardness test for rocks and minerals 1480:77
Mohs' scale of hardness 1266:33
Mohs' scale to compare hardness of minerals 1295:97
Rock chart with Mohs' scale for identification 748:172
MOIRE PATTERNS
Making 532:28

Moire pattern interference experiment with pocket comb 1082:142-144

Overlap materials with repetitive lines to create moire patterns experiment 1132:68-1-68-3

MOIRES

Flowering spiral—prison bars 356:7-11

How to make 176:54-55

MOISTURE. *See also* **EVAPORATION; HUMIDITY**

Gradient box—how to build 371:56-57

Moisture detecting fish—making 150:110-111

Moisture detecting mermaid, how to make 1007:84-85

MOISTURE DETECTOR

Make a fortune telling fish 550:54-57

MOLDS. *See also* **FUNGI; SLIME MOLDS**

A coconut culture 585:150-151

Adventure 36—we become farmers—molds under a microscope 403:130-133

Adventure 48—we assume the role of farmers—molds under a hand lens 29:209-212

Best conditions for growing molds experiment 1048:23

Black bread mold—growing and viewing under microscope 82:38-40

Bread mold—experiment 563:53

Bread mold—grow and observe under microscope 713:92-94

Bread mold experiment 977:60

Bread mold growth and factors that produce or prevent growth experiment 1004:2.020

Bread mold growth experiment 1014:157

Bread mold; where does it grow the best experiment 1150:40-42

Bread molds grow in dark, damp place experiment 882:36

Catch a case of mold—experiment for catching molds in the air 216:10-13

Collect spores from molds and grow on bread experiment 714:114-115

Culture media, how to make 860:156

Culture medium for growing molds experiment 1294:87-88

Damp bread grows molds experiment 1214:23

Dirt from fingernails grows molds on potato mush mixture experiment 1482:8-9

Effect of light on molds and mildews—experiment 532:110

Examples of blue & gray mold rot, rhizopus soft rot, black and green mold rot 216:33-34

Experiment to determine best way to grow penicillin 904:90-91

Experiment to determine where molds grow best 904:88-89

Experiments to show growth & structure of 128:51

Experiments with 107:107-110

Food additive, calcium propionate, inhibits bread mold growth experiment 1395:127-132

Formation of mold comparison 293:16

Fungi that spoil food, identification key given 1295:50

Grow a fungus garden—experiment 563:53-54

Grow a mold garden (Primary) 64:unpaged

Grow a mold garden 364:45

Grow bread mold (Primary) 540:13

Grow bread mold experiment 1183:23; 1405:30; 904:80-81

Grow different kinds of molds; observe differences in growth project 1296:1992

Grow mold mycelium on a piece of bread 459:10-14, 24-25

Grow mold on bread 607:33

Grow molds and observe under a microscope 889:49-50

Grow some fungi on bread experiment 1181:15

Growing a garden of molds 148:14-15

Growing mold and observing experiment 792:30-31

Growth needs—grow one type of mold 293:15

Growth of bread mold experiment 878:32-33

Growth of bread mold experiment 978:52-53

Growth; determine best environment for mold growth experiment with coconut 1479:29

How does penicillium mold grow and what does it look like experiment 1402:52-55

How mold grows on bread and fruit experiment 781:38-39

How to grow molds on food experiment 1231:46-47

Investigations into bread mold 420:40-43

Invisible seeds—prepare/observe gardens for mold/bacteria growth (Advanced) 565:43-53

Invite a mold to dinner (meal for molds) and watch it grow 366:79

Micro soup—how to make to demonstrate mold activity 364:47

Miniature landfill investigation to see how landfill works experiment 1012:85-86

Mold culture medium—experiments 563:53

Mold formation on bread experiment 984:25-27

Mold garden grows in glass jar experiment using cheese, bread, fruit peels 1441:98

Mold garden in plastic bags experiment 1063:413

Mold garden, assorted foods in aluminum tray filled with soil experiment 1115:19-20

Mold garden, how to grow 899:182

Mold gardens 236:35

Mold growing on moist, dry and disinfected bread experiment 1038:28-29

Mold grows on bread and apple experiment 1176:20

Mold growth experiment 901:41

Mold sample on bread, how to grow 860:154-156

Molds need moisture and food to grow experiment 760:12-13

Moldy food—experiment 598:47-48

Moldy fruit—experiment to see how mold grows 216:6-9

Moldy tomato soup demonstrates spores 203:17

Penicillin mold—grow and observe under microscope 713:95

Pin mold, how to grow experiment 1069:66

Plants—do microscopic plants have special characteristics 402:28-29

Preservative chemicals keep bread from growing mold projects 1210:54-55

Produce spores from bread mold 294:23-24

Repeat Fleming's mold experiment 448:56-59

Rotten cotton—experiment to show mildew growth on cotton 216:18-23

Soils contain molds and do these molds have antibiotic capabilities experiment 1267:71-75

Testing for microbes that grow on food experiment 924:41-42

Tiny but mighty 280:59-60

What does mold grow on activity 901:43

What is this strange plant activity 901:42

Where do molds grow experiment 834:84-85

Where do spores come from experiment 852:3-5

Why bread molds experiment 1440:64-67
Why does bread get moldy experiment 834:83
Why does mold grow experiment 1294:86-88
Why we wash our hands experiment with molds growing on potato mush mixture 1482:8-9
Will bread mold grow on other materials experiment 714:112-113

MOLECULAR ACTION
Eggs in water 146:33
Molecules move from one kind of liquid to another experiment 747:27-28
Using cobalt chloride in hot and cold water 146:31
Water currents and effect of temperature and salinity on water density 871:1.003

MOLECULAR MODEL
Make a molecular model of ethanol 6:32

MOLECULAR MOTION
Effect of molecular motion demonstrated by food coloring in water experiment 905:12-13

MOLECULES. *See also* MATTER—PROPERTIES; POLYMER MOLECULES
Air and water toys shows molecules in motion 366:163-167
Air is a gas that can dissolve in water experiment 1250:11-13
Air needed for paint to harden experiment 1251:65-67
Alcohol and water take up less space than just water experiment 1435:6-9
Alka-Seltzer tablets experiment shows small particles react faster than large 1251:55-57
Apparatus for showing osmosis experiment 1425:19-20
Are gas molecules farther apart than liquid molecules 396:14-15
Are molecules attracted by charges 396:20-22
Are molecules on surface of eggshells necessary to dye eggs experiment 831:78-80
Are molecules small 396:8-9
Are rubber molecules less bouncy when cold 396:37-38
Are soap bubbles attracted by a negative charge 396:56-58
Are some liquids more dense than others 396:48-50
Are some molecules heavier than others 396:18-19
Are some solids better insulators than others experiment 831:23-25
Are there water molecules in the air 396:41-42
Are water molecules in constant motion experiment with salt water/food colors 1403:24-27
Boiled egg pot—experiment 399:58
Breaking the surface tension of water experiments 1091:27-28
Brownian motion of pollen grains experiment 1133:7.006
Can acid in lemon reduce fish odor experiment 831:72-74
Can acid molecules curdle milk experiment 831:68-69
Can acids and bases be identified with vegetable molecules 396:59-61
Can baking soda trap odor molecules experiment 831:70-71
Can certain molecules in the air cause food to spoil 396:74-75
Can charcoal remove molecules from water experiment 831:38-40
Can cream be changed into butter experiment 831:65-67
Can different molecules be separated from each other 396:31-33

Can electricity make ions that change neutral water to a base experiment 831:58-60
Can ethylene molecules cause fruits and vegetables to ripen 396:72-73
Can ions carry electricity 396:64-66
Can iron combine with oxygen and water to from rust experiment 831:55-57
Can large crystals be made from small molecules experiment 831:35-37
Can light be made by breaking sugar crystals 396:69-71
Can molecules be broken into smaller molecules 396:28-30
Can molecules in air cause colors to fade experiment 831:53-54
Can molecules in pineapple break large molecules into smaller ones experiment 831:84-87
Can molecules in yeast make a gas from hydrogen peroxide experiment 831:88-90
Can molecules move through a membrane experiment 831:81-83
Can molecules of water hold grains of sand together experiment 1250:46-47
Can oil be soaked up from oil spills experiment 1325:70-74
Can oil help you see through paper experiment 1250:48-49
Can perfume get into a sealed balloon experiment 902:31
Can salt keep water from freezing 396:54-55
Can stretching molecules make them give off heat 396:26-27
Can sugar be changed to carbon 396:76-77
Can sugar molecules rotate light experiment 831:91-94
Can the flavor of apples be isolated from apple cider vinegar 396:34-36
Can water act like glue experiment 831:26-27
Can you freeze water with ice experiment 1250:38-40
Capillary action demonstrated with colored water and strips of paper 1331:29
Capillary action; why does water rise in paper towel experiment 1403:28-31
Carbonated water mixed with detergent/milk/toothpaste for best bubbles 1330:7
Chemical change in silver molecules—clean silver experiment 704:47-48
Chewing gum is less flexible when cold experiment 1250:65-67
Chewing gum is less sticky when cold experiment 1250:68-70
Cleansing power of detergents on oil experiment 1403:72-75
Clouding things up—how your breath reacts with limewater 400:69
Cohesive attractive forces among molecules of different liquids experiment 1004:3.008
Combine molecules of two substances salt in water experiment 704:46
Cooling causes a balloon to get smaller experiment 1250:24-25
Demonstrate diffusion and osmosis with balloon and vanilla 1405:24
Demonstrate molecular theory 382:139-142
Demonstrate space exists between molecules experiment 834:74-75
Demonstrate spaces between molecules 360:14

261

Density experiment; molecules cause one liquid to float on another liquid 1403:73

Detergent causes molecules to move experiment 1405:48-49

Detergent molecules help clean clothes experiment 1251:46-48

Detergent molecules, how they work experiment 1008:13

Detergents keep oil and water from separating experiment 1482:4-5

Difference in effectiveness of different brands of dish-washing liquids 1403:72-75

Difference in effectiveness of different brands of shampoo experiment 1403:72-75

Difference in pulling power of water and alcohol molecules experiment 1479:49

Different kinds of paper products affect capillary action of water experiment 1403:31

Different molecules made from play dough and small sticks experiment 1271:8

Diffusion in liquid 146:58-59

Diffusion of molecules affected by heating water experiment 709:36-37

Diffusion of molecules through a gas experiment 1425:18-19

Diffusion of molecules through a gel experiment 1425:19

Diffusion of molecules through a liquid experiment 1425:19

Display models to explain spacing between molecules, how to do 1403:15

Dissolution of sugar by heating activities for classroom 1291:9-10

Do air molecules move farther apart as air is warmed experiment 831:18-20

Do all materials that dissolve in water make hydroxyl or hydrogen ions 1403:60-63

Do different oils become solid at different temperatures experiment 831:47-49

Do hot molecules move faster than cold molecules 396:10-11

Do molecules move 396:6-7

Do plastic bags tear when they are punctured experiment 831:45-46

Do similar molecules attract each other 396:23-25

Do soap molecules spread out on the surface of water 396:43-44

Do water molecules and oil molecules mix 396:45-47

Do water molecules in liquid water fit tightly together experiment 1403:12-21

Does 1 plus 1 always equal 2 experiment with solids and liquids 1526:36-38

Does acid rain hurt some buildings and statues 396:62-63

Does hard water clean as well as soft water 396:51-53

Does lemon juice reduce fishy smell of fish experiment 1396:135-140

Does popcorn dissolve in water experiment 1250:41-42

Does temperature affect solubility experiment 902:30

Does temperature affect speed of molecules experiment 900:74

Does temperature affect the speed of molecules experiment 902:29

Effect of heat on 12:83-85

Egg white molecules linked together by heating experiment 1250:77-79

Epsom salts crystals reflects arrangement of molecules in a solid experiment 1403:48-51

Evaporation causes a liquid to cool down experiment 1090:30-31

Evaporation of liquid dependent on surface exposed to air experiment 1090:28

Evaporation of water molecules causes cooling experiment 1250:29-31

Excited molecules give off extra energy as light experiment 1250:61-62

Expansion meter to test expansion in a thick wire experiment 1179:50

Foam made from egg whites experiment 1250:74-76

Fog chamber; portable cloud in a bottle experiment 1132:52-1-52-2

Forward movement of wave energy demonstration 1405:85

Gelatin used to dye plastic spoons experiment 1250:82-85

Hard, flexible and slippery 366:160

Heat affects movement of molecules in rubber bands experiment 1403:63

Heat breaks starch into smaller molecules experiment using cornstarch 1251:77-79

Heat effect on gas molecules model experiment with wire cage and foam balls 1132:53-1-53-2

Heat makes molecules move wire—candle and wax experiment 704:44-45

Heating in microwave ovens requires water molecules experiment 1250:32-34

Helium passes through a balloon faster than air experiment 1251:27-28

Holes in water experiment 1028:23

Hot water is lighter than cold water; colored water explosion experiment 1136:20

How big is a molecule—experiment 586:63-65

How does temperature affect movement of molecules experiment 834:73-74

How molecules behave—salt in water experiment 704:41-42

Hydrophobic molecules demonstrated with exploding colors 1289:18-19

Incredible shrinking molecules of air in balloons—exp. 651:18-19

In motion—holes in water experiment—vegetable coloring in glass of water 366:159

In motion 83:19-20

Inflated balloon can be seen through experiment 1251:25-26

Is a gas made by mixing vinegar and baking soda 396:16-17

Is there space between sugar crystals 396:12-13

Is vinegar necessary to dye eggs experiment 831:75-77

Light changes when it passes through substances experiment 1250:52-54

Light scattered by large molecules experiment with water, gelatin and sugar 1251:71-74

Light stick emits less light at colder temperatures experiment 1251:58-61

Liquid detergent turns cloudy when it becomes cold experiment 1250:50-51

Liquid molecules are attracted to one another experiment 1091:25-26

Liquids combined take up less space than original liquids experiment 1091:20

Lithium model, how to make from clay and string 1403:4-7

262

Materials dissolved in water move through egg membrane experiment 1403:34

Matter is made up of molecules experiment 834:72-73

Mayonnaise demonstrates emulsifying action of egg experiment; recipe given 1403:46

Measure attractiveness (stickiness) between water molecules experiment 1396:153-158

Measuring size of molecule experiment using oil 1179:29

Melting ice from solid to liquid experiment 1090:26

Mercury street light viewed with compact disc shows separate colors experiment 1250:57-60

Methane physical structure, how to make 1403:8-11

Mist forms above liquid of carbonated drink when it is opened experiment 1250:18-20

Model for diffusion and active transport of molecules, how to make 1425:17-18

Molecular motion in a gas 577:project #15

Molecular structure of eggshell affects its strength experiment 1403:76-79

Molecules are always moving activity 976:5

Molecules change of state from solid to liquid experiment with peas 1090:23

Molecules from atoms; demonstrate using paper circles and toothpicks 976:6-7

Molecules in a gas move faster when gas is heated up experiment 1090:11

Molecules in collision in hot and cold water experiment 1090:10

Molecules move faster in hot things experiment with hot water and food colors 1377:10

Molecules of vanilla extract, soya sauce, and lemon juice experiment 1208:26-27

Molecules of water cling tightly together experiment 1331:25

Molecules of water contract when cold experiment 1066:61

Molecules of water pull together experiment 1405:50

Molecules of water take up less space as a liquid or a gas experiment 1251:33-35

Molecules stick together experiment 735:33-34

More molecules in air will dissolve in cold water than in hot water experiment 1250:11-13

Movement of water molecules in waves demonstration 1405:85

Moving air has less pressure than still air experiment 1250:21-23

Oil and grease molecules are slippery experiment 1251:43-45

Orange peel contains a natural insecticide experiment 1250:89-90

Paper and glue demonstrate attraction between molecules experiment 905:56-57

Perfume bottle demonstrates gas moving in room 709:49-50

Pick can of regular cola from can of diet soda blindfolded experiment 1083:76-77

Pressure causes ice to change to liquid experiment with ice cubes 1251:36-38

Properties of materials depend on organization of polymeric chains experiment 1396:141-146

Protein in milk can be denatured by addition of vinegar experiment 1403:14-15

Protein; what happens when shape of protein molecule is changed experiment 1403:12-15

Proving molecular motion 180:24

Pull of gravity and 12:123

Raindrop sizes compared experiment 1405:83

Reaction that makes solutions thicken demonstrated with pudding 1289:12-13

Recipe for Nutty Putty, how to make 1083:60-61

Rubber band molecules return to original position after stretching experiment 1091:39-40

Salt added to glass of water experiment in volume 1435:3-5

Salt affects the grouping of water molecules into ice crystals experiment 1403:54-55

Salt dissolves more in water than in rubbing alcohol experiment 1250:43-45

Salt in water demonstrates space around molecules 709:30-31

Salty water doesn't make many soap bubbles experiment 1482:6-7

Sand sculptures show adhesion between sand and water experiment 1396:156

Saturated solution of sugar and water affected by water temperature experiment 1403:42

Seeing molecules in a liquid 735:40

Shortening becomes clear when it melts experiment 1251:41-42

Show how tiny molecules can lift a heavy object 385:22-23

Simple experiments to test the molecular action of water 308:entire book

Simple molecule experiment 735:40-43

Size of drops affects rate at which two liquids separate experiment 1403:42

Smelling molecules in a gas experiment 735:39

Soap molecules spread more slowly on surface of water or oil experiment 1251:52-54

Solutes affect the cohesiveness of water experiment 1396:156

Space between molecules in liquids experiment with sugar and water 1179:22

Space between water molecules experiment with alcohol/water/food colors 1479:48

Space problem with water and alcohol mixture 563:167

Spaces exist between molecules where other molecules can fit experiment 1164:52-54

Speed of evaporation affects shape of resulting crystals experiment 1403:50-51

Starch molecules larger than sugar molecules experiment 1251:75-76

Strength of materials affected by molecule arrangement experiment 1403:79

Sugar added to water forms homogenous mixture experiment 1403:37

Sugar molecules and water—experiment 676:15-16

Sugar molecules make soap bubbles last longer experiment 1251:49-51

Sugar water evaporates slower than pure water experiment 1250:26-28

Sun and air cause vanilla to lose its odor experiment 1250:86-88

Sunscreen molecules block sunlight that causes colors to fade experiment 1251:62-64

Surface of egg yolks turns green during cooking experiment 1250:71-73

Temperature affects air molecules experiment using balloon in refrigerator 1439:32-34

Temperature affects molecular motion of water molecules experiment 1396:138

Temperature affects movement of water molecules experiment with food colors 1403:68-71

Temperature of egg affects size of whipped egg whites experiment 1403:83

Temperature of water affects amount of sugar that will dissolve experiment 1403:41

Tire pump generates heat experiment 939:118-119

Visibility of food coloring molecules in concentrated to diluted water 1251:91-94

Warm water holds more sugar—experiment 676:17

Water and alcohol added together give less than total volume experiment 937:12-13

Water appears to boil experiment 1405:49

Water drops attraction to liquids and solids experiment 1091:25-26

Water freezes fastest when it is warm or cold experiment 1403:51

Water goes from a liquid to a gas when popcorn is heated experiment 1250:35-37

Water has more cohesiveness than other liquids do experiment 1396:153-156

Water molecules are in constant motion experiment 1396:137-138

Water molecules can move through membrane of raw egg experiment 1403:33

Water molecules form acidic or basic solution from dissolved materials 1403:57

Water molecules move experiment 1405:47

Water molecules movement experiment with warm and cold water and food colors 1479:63

Water molecules pull on each other and stick together experiment 1479:50

Water separates light into different colors experiment 1250:55-56

Water; how close do molecules of water have to be to attract experiment 1403:23

Wetting ability of water increased by adding liquid laundry detergents 1403:33-34

Wetting action of water; why do some materials get wetter than others ex 1403:29

What makes a spring springy 366:162

What molecules are made of—burned sugar experiment 704:32-34

Whipped egg whites foam lasts longer with cream of tartar added experiment 1403:130-131

Why do onions make you cry experiment 1484:28

Will air molecules float on carbon dioxide molecules 396:39-40

Will metal atoms combine with oxygen molecules 396:67-68

You can see the motion of molecules in water 611:45-47

MOLLUSK STEW
How to make 530:69

MOLLUSKS
Experiment 236:117-119

MOMENTUM
Bicycle wheel gyroscope experiment 1132:7-1-7-2

Billiards, tracks and ball game 373:62-67

Bumping bottles demonstrate momentum experiment 723:2-3

Circular raceway—track and ball experiment 373:49-53

Coin's momentum keeps it going experiment 1136:16

Coins on smooth surface demonstrate 844:27-31

Conservation of Momentum experiment with marbles; data tables given 1004:5.001

Conservation of momentum, wave transmission—experiment 585:38-39

Conservation of momentum; ball and box experiment 871:4.007

Demonstrate loop return 291:128

Demonstrate momentum with a spinning disk 291:129

Experimenting with mass and momentum 180:40

Jump the gap tracks and balls experiment 373:54-58

Loop the loop tracks and ball experiment 373:45-48

Marbles demonstrate force and motion 844:3-26

Newton's Law of Conservation of Momentum experiment 1132:69-1-69-2

Newton's Third Law of Motion; balloon rocket experiments demonstrate 1157:48-52

Roll back oatmeal box and rubber bands experiment 999:91-92

Spool—string and strip of paper demonstrate 723:5-6

What is angular momentum 291:132-133

MOMENTUM—ANGULAR
What makes the Yo-Yo yo-yo 291:134

MONEY
Experiment to make money disappear 176:42

MONORAIL SYSTEM
For transporting small articles or messages between two places 543:8-9

MONORAILS
Monorail working model, how to make 1190:56-62

MONUMENTS
Chemical erosion of statues experiment using coins, salt and vinegar 1228:40-41

Marble statues destroyed by acid rain; prove why experiment 1476:190-191

MOON. See also ECLIPSES
Appearance of the surface of the Moon demonstration 900:245-246

Astronomical influences on behavior in animals and humans experiment 1062:109

Atmosphere—ball in bottle—experiment to test sound on Moon 564:64

Atmosphere—demonstrate lack of atmosphere on the Moon—experiment 564:65

Barycenter is center balancing point of Earth and Moon system experiment 1062:16-18

Button measures size of Moon experiment [Primary] 946:27

Center of gravity between Earth and Moon demonstration 1394:24-25

Craters are formed by falling meteorites demonstration 1394:116-117

Craters making (Advanced) 658:48-51

Craters on Moon different from those on Mars demonstration 1394:124-125

Craters on Moon experiment; make craters from plaster of Paris 1478:50

Craters; what might have produced craters on Moon demonstration 1479:15

Craterscape of Moon experiment, how to make 1476:160-161

Daytime temperature of Moon demonstration 1394:126-127

Demonstrate craters on the Moon (Primary) 169:17

Diameter of Sun and Moon, how to measure experiment 1158:43-46

Diameter of the Moon—how to measure 763:16
Diameter of the Moon, how to measure 1434:25-28
Distance to Moon from Earth, how to measure with retroreflector 1394:172-173
Dough model of Moon—recipe given—making [Primary] 742:52
Earth—Moon rotation model 577:project #36
Earthshine on Moon from Earth experiment; make model to demonstrate 1478:46
Eclipse; why you can see eclipsed Moon experiment with illuminated Moon model 1478:45
Eclipses of Moon model using light, tennis ball, how to do 1329:20-21
Eclipses; demonstrate umbral and penumbral eclipses of the Moon 1170:26
Effect of Moon's weight on gravity demonstration 1394:120-121
Effect on tides—how Moon pulls water upward 40:223-224
Experiment to show motion of the Moon 168:10-11
Experiment to show phases and causes of 128:75
Finding position of the Moon experiments 951:16-21
Gravitational pull of Moon affects the tides on Earth experiment 1062:43-44
Gravity on Moon; how much can you lift on Moon experiment 1478:54
Height of Moon mountains measured by shadows they cast experiment 1478:50-51
How bright is the Moon experiment 762:21-22
How does Moon give light; globe and flashlight experiment 900:24
How does the Moon travel around the Earth demonstration 900:244
How the Moon shines experiment 1479:16
How to measure the distance to the Moon experiment 1405:16
Investigation into measuring craters on the Moon 420:87-90
Landscape study and Moon calendar activity 400:108
Landscape study of Moon's location 400:108
Light from the Moon and time it takes to reach the Earth demonstration 1394:108-109
Lunar crater model, how to make 1170:24
Lunar eclipse effect on studying Sun's corona demonstration 1405:8
Lunar eclipse model—making (Advanced) 658:46-47
Lunar eclipse model experiment, how to make 1478:44
Lunar eclipse, how to photograph experiment 958:70-72
Lunar surface model—making (Advanced) 658:48-51
Make large drawing of what you see on the Moon (Primary) 169:14
Man in the Moon image; demonstrate the cause of it 1394:122-123
Man in the Moon image; determine cause experiment 1405:12-13
Mapping the Moon experiment, how to make Moon map 1478:48-49
Measure the size of the Moon 175:38
Measurements 292:88-89
Mind is confused over size and distance of Moon horizon illusion experiment 1062:22-23
Mobile of the Moon—how to make 40:254
Model of Moon made from papier mache, how to do 1365:43

Model of Moon's path—how to make 763:16-19
Moon and planet study project, how to observe and record 1217:22-23
Moon illusion (Advanced) 658:47
Moon illusion experiment 761:95-98
Moon illusion why does the full Moon look larger when it first rises 585:109-110
Moon mapping and watching with astrolabe 586:35-36
Moon observe and chart movements—how to 748:157
Moon orbits around Earth demonstration with flashlight 860:34-36
Moon phases—charting 748:163
Moon rotates on its axis demonstration 1394:118-119
Moon rotates on its axis demonstration 1405:12
Moon studies project 400:108-109
Moon town space base from papier mache, how to make 1449:14-15
Moon tracker—making 760:41-42
Moon watch 231:70-72
Moondial tells you where the Moon is experiment, how to make 1478:47
Moonlight and color; can you see color by Moonlight experiment 1390:11
Observation of projects (Advanced) 658:44-51
Phases of Moon demonstration with flashlight 816:17
Phases of Moon experiment with flashlight and ball 1063:295
Phases of the Moon—demonstration 649:8-9
Phases of the Moon demonstration 900:247-248; 1170:23; 1441:15
Phases of the Moon experiment 871:1.012
Phases of the Moon over a month observe and record [Primary] 742:23
Phases; why does the Moon have phases experiment 852:50-51
Photographing the Moon—how to 381:44; 762:16
Planting by phases of the Moon project using the Old Farmer's Almanac 1062:110-111
Project to check month's phases of the Moon 640:67
Record movements of the Moon daily (Primary) 169:15
Record phases of the Moon daily (Primary) 169:16
Reflected sunlight from Moon onto the Earth demonstration 1441:14
Reflecting "telescope" to look at the Moon, how to make 1308:16-17
Rilles or valleys on Moon surface from lava flow demonstration 1477:83
Rocks; Moon rocks color compared to color of Earth rocks experiment 1478:54-55
Scale model of Earth and Moon experiment with poster-board 1478:40
Show phases of the Moon 175:39
Showing how the Moon's phases occur project 833:207-212
Showing how the tides occur project 833:212-213
Side of Moon facing us changes position experiment 1062:54-55
Size—gravity, atmosphere, surface, revolution of Moon surface—experiments 564:63-67
Size of—is full Moon really larger 381:46
Sketching the Moon project 833:218
Surface—demonstrate formation of lunar craters on the Moon—experiments 564:65
Surface—measure (Advanced) 668:65-66
The Moon illusion 585:110-111

Tide dial gives tide progression as Moon orbits Earth experiment 1478:53

Timed photograph of Moon's track across the sky experiment 1126:38-39

To show phases of Moon 40:252-253

Weight of various masses when weighed on Moon's surface experiment 1502:44-45

What time is the tide due experiment, make tide dial to demonstrate 1478:53

Why it would be useful to place large optical telescope on Moon experiment 1479:20

Why Moon appears and disappears experiment 1479:16

Why Moon appears to change shape 40:253-254

Why Moon appears to change shape experiment 1294:32-35

Why Moon stays in orbit demonstration 1405:110-111

Why sun and Moon look the same size experiment 706:14-15

Why the Moon appears and disappears demonstration 1394:114-115

Why the Moon shines demonstration 1394:110-111

Why the Moon stays in orbit demonstration 1394:112-113

MOON BASE

Model—how to make 415:65-78

MOON BUGGY

Make an egg carton Moon buggy (Primary) 113:26-27

MOON MONTH

Indians use Moon as a calendar 324:30-31

MOON PHASES

Create Moon phases with model 967:10-11

Faces of the Moon model 292:67

Lunascope demonstration 12:91-94

Model of Moon phases; why Moon waxes and wanes project 1296:1993

Moon bone—do it yourself Moon bone 292:68

Phases and features of Moon observation; Moon phase recording chart 1329:11-13

Phases of Moon 253:188-189

Phases of Moon effect on plant growth experiment 1375:43-45

Phases of Moon model, how to make using light and tennis ball 1329:17-20

Phases of Moon, how to create with flashlight and round objects 1365:41

Recording phases of Moon on calendar experiment with foil/black paper/cardboard 1478:42-43

MOON VEHICLE. *See also* **SPACE VEHICLES**

Creeping Moon bug—how to make 410:4-5

MORGAN, THOMAS

Sex linkage in fruit flies experiment 1133:3.011

MORSE, SAMUEL

Telegraph from wood, wire, tacks and battery, how to make 1209:90-93

MORSE CODE. *See also* **TELEGRAPH**

Code chart 825:28

Code tapper telegraph, how to make 1418:16-19

How to do 244:18-20

Make bulb, battery and switch circuit to send 226:10-11

Morse Code chart 1209:93

Morse Code sender, how to make; Code given 1248:20-21

Morse Code symbols 1043:22

Morse code transmitter, how to make 955:21

Project 391:100

Telegraph using Morse Code, how to make 1072:22

Telegraph with Morse Code experiment 1160:20

Transmitters 15:32-35

MORTAR

A clothespin mortar—how to make 543:44-45

MOSQUITOES

Adventure 20—mosquitoes under a microscope 403:70-75

Collect eggs, hatch and observe with magnifying glass 796:27

Collect larvae and pupae and observe life cycle 771:119-124

How do insects fit into a food chain experiment with mosquitoes 1097:65-67

Mosquito wrigglers—collection and observation of 414:114-116

Wrigglers die in water and oil experiment 943:6-7

MOSSES. *See also* **SPORES**

Adventure 34—we examine a moss plant under the microscope 403:119-124

Collect and grow to demonstrate moss cycle 436:60

Environment needs mosses; observe mosses in jar moss garden experiment 1472:54-59

Grow mosses in glass-enclosed terrarium 294:27

Hairy cap moss—adventure 36—moss spores under a hand lens 29:166-169

Moss garden—making 739:19

Moss garden terrarium—how to make 483:68-70

Moss magic experiment; mosses dry up but don't die 1472:57

Moss milk—how to make to grow moss from moss spores 530:104-105

Moss works to protect soil from rain and prevent erosion experiment 1472:58

Plants grow in sphagnum moss experiment 904:76-77

Testing moss for water retention experiment 1061:116-117

MOTHBALLS

Bouncing mothballs experiment 909:37

Bouncing mothballs 147:84-86

Bouncing mothballs 663:29

Chemical magic—dancing mothballs 87:78

Dancing moth balls demonstrate formation of carbon dioxide 576:72-73

Dancing mothballs 77:34; 366:219-220; 382:135-138

Dancing mothballs experiment with mothballs, vinegar and baking soda 1212:31

Give off molecules 382:141-142

Make a snowman in a jar of water 146:29

Make dancing mothballs 291:230

Making mothballs rise and fall in a glass 150:120-121

Mothball bouncers 146:28

Mothballs swim up and down in water experiment 937:68-69

Moving mothballs 400:70

Rising and falling mothballs in water 399:86

The moving mothballs—experiment 598:12

MOTHER OF VINEGAR

"Mother of vinegar"—experiment 585:157-158

MOTHS. *See also* **BUTTERFLIES; CATERPILLARS**

Attract moths with sweet mixture, how to do 1063:432

Attracting moths 442:unpaged

Attracting moths at night, how to do 1144:31

Attracting moths by "sugaring" a tree, how to do 430:57; 1188:54

Cage; net cage from cardboard box, how to make 1407:16-17

Camouflage; spot the moth pattern experiment 1391:17

Catching moths at night with sugar solution, how to do 1182:15

Catching moths using light and sugary food experiment 1183:63

Cocoons; winter cocoons of moths, how to collect, cage and hatch 1188:18-19

Collect and care for—how to 332:61-75

Collecting—attracting male moths by "assembling" 414:35-36

Collecting and housing moths, how to do 1407:100

Collecting cocoons and watching moths emerge, how to do 1425:44-47

Collecting cocoons of moths and hatching them experiment 1464:54-56

Frozen animals can survive experiment 1020:117-121

How are moths and butterflies different experiment 904:98-99

How to keep moths 821:56-57

Light and old sheet used to catch insects at night, how to do 1169:34-35

Light box to collect—how to make 332:64

Light on sheet attracts moths at night, how to do 1188:55

Mating in captivity 478:25-26

Metamorphosis of butterflies and moths experiment 978:89-90

Moth can develop without a cocoon experiment 1020:121-122

Moth trap with light bulb, how to build using plywood 1069:109

Pupa—care of 478:34

Raising caterpillars—food, moisture, air and caging needs 478:30-34

Raising caterpillars for cocoons 478:28-34

Raising moths from cocoons—how to do 476:48-50

Repellent to keep clothes moths away, recipe, how to make 1228:87

Sugaring to attract moths, how to do 1320:31

Trap to catch moths, how to do 1445:34-35

MOTHS—COCOONS

Cocoon collection—care of 478:35-36

Collecting cocoons—how to 478:12-17

How cocoons are made 478:6-9

Identifying various cocoons 478:37-68

Moth alarm clock; moth emerging completes circuit; causes alarm to ring—make 478:21-22

Raising adults from cocoons—cage and where to keep 478:18-23

MOTHS—EGGS

Care of eggs 478:27

MOTION. *See also* **FORCE; GRAVITY; KINETICS; NEWTON'S FIRST LAW OF MOTION; NEWTON'S SECOND LAW OF MOTION; NEWTON'S THIRD LAW OF MOTION; PENDULUMS**

Acceleration and amount of matter (weight of objects) being pulled experiment 1157:34-35

Accelerometer to measure acceleration, how to make 1157:28-30

Acting and reacting—Newton's third law of motion—demonstrations 180:39

Action experiment; get better start by pushing against something solid 1389:5

Air car demonstrates motion is affected by friction 1404:158-159

Amplitude of motion demonstration 1405:78-79

And force—athletics and science 382:97-99

As energy—perpetual motion 49:130

As energy—power 49:125-128

As energy—work 49:122-124

Back and forth motion can be changed to rotary motion—experiment 168:39-40

Balancing trick demonstrates friction 1035:20

Black pepper and detergent demonstration of motion 1404:17

Button on card demonstrates inertia 1035:14

CO_2 rocket demonstrates Newton's third law of motion 338:52-53

Coins demonstrate laws of motion 548:43-59

Crawling experiment with rubber band and spool crawler 1389:17

Demonstration of motion of air, sound, light, earth, molecules, electrons 306:entire book

Effect of air on motion demonstration 1479:97

Energy patterns of moving objects when they stop experiment 1389:15

Every action has equal opposite reaction—sprinklers and rockets 281:40

Experiments—acceleration—accelerometers 49:64-74

Experiments—air car 49:60-61

Experiments—centrifugal force—bicycle centrifuge 49:74-75

Experiments—falling objects—Galileo's laws 49:83-91

Experiments—inertia 49:62-63

Experiments—marble down a hill—up a hill 49:56

Experiments—pendulum 49:57-58

Experiments—push force experiments 49:75-83

Experiments—spin your wheels 49:59

Experiments—spinning eggs 49:63-64

Experiments to demonstrate 295:77-89

Experiments with pendulums 1157:16-21

Faster and farther motion of wagon with different loads experiment 1035:12-13

Find speed you travel over a distance experiment 1389:7

Finger pool game with checkers demonstrates kinetic energy 1035:18-19

Force meter measures force needed to get things moving experiment 1028:110

Force of flowing water causes can to rotate experiment 940:105-107

Friction affects motion demonstration with turning wooden spool 1404:162-163

Friction tester 295:87-89

Frictionless air car; make two cars to investigate motion experiment 1157:12-13

Galileo's thought experiment; effect of gravity on pendulum 1157:16-18

Game; magnetic pinball game experiment shows moving object changing direction 1035:10-11

Hand motion—try to stop piece of wire from 'walking' 291:108-109

Height effect on energy of moving object demonstration 1404:154-155

How can we use action-reaction experiment 900:218-219

How fast is your toy car; calculating speed experiment; data table 1004:5.003

267

Illusions—phantom moves 229:83-107

Inertia keeps peas in spinning cup experiment 1035:28-29

Jumping experiment; frog jumps from twisted rubber band 1389:21

Laws of motion—experiments to show 106:11-18

Lift off force makes cup rocket fly upward experiment 1035:8-9

Marble game demonstration of motion 900:217

Merry-go-round and wheels 49:100-106

Mobile demonstrates circular motion 1112:11-12

Motion experiments—up & down, round & round, shadow, sand & wave pendulum 49:107-110

Moving wagon model demonstrates motion experiment 1112:7-8

Newton car—demonstrates Newton's second law of motion 338:57-59

Newton's First Law of Motion—coin/hanger demonstrate straight line motion 548:58-59

Newton's First Law of Motion; experiments to demonstrate 1156:76-78

Newton's law—things in motion continue in motion 295:65-67

Newton's Second Law of Motion; experiments to demonstrate 1156:79-82

Newton's Third Law of Motion; balloon rocket experiments demonstrate 1157:48-52

Newton's Third Law of Motion; experiments to demonstrate 1156:82-84

Object's center of gravity effect on motion experiment 1405:94

Of animals—demonstrate burrowing worms 94:22-23

Of plants—sensitive plants 94:24-25

Paddle power moves boat through water experiment 1389:29

Paddle wheel boat—demonstrates 94:16-17

Paddle wheel moves boat by pushing water backwards experiment 1035:16-17

Paddleboat from plastic bottle powered by water experiment 1035:16-17

Pascal's law—mysterious match heads float up and down 202:113

Pendulum swinging in elliptical path experiment 1157:19-21

Perpetual motion machine using a marble, how to make 1243:8

Playground swings used to investigate motion experiments 1159:30-33

Projects on force and motion 691:58-60

Push-push back law 295:84-86

Put opposing forces to work—experiment 385:54-56

Rate of acceleration making things go round and round 295:81-82

Returning can experiment with can and rubber bands 940:108-111

Rockets—demonstrate motion of rocket driven vehicles 295:91-102

Rollers reduce friction experiment 1035:22-23

Rolling test of objects rolling down a slope experiment 1112:24

Running experiment; how to measure your strides 1389:19

Shape of trajectory depends on how object is thrown experiment 1389:9

Shoving objects of different sizes and materials experiment 1334:8-9

Show how rotation and inertia work together—experiment 385:61-62

Simple pendulum 49:92-100

Sound created by motion experiment with spinning disc 1035:26-27

Speed of rotating object affected by distance from center experiment 1404:168-169

Spinning—make a spinning egg 94:18

Spinning egg demonstrates inertia 1035:15

Spinning motion—make a lunar buggy 94:14-15

Spinning motion—make a mini Yo-Yo 94:18-19

Spinning motion—make a spinning pin acrobat 94:20-21

Spinning wheels stay upright experiment 1035:24-25

Stop and go 281:42

Straight-line movement experiment using card-pull picture 1112:6-7

Surface area affects friction demonstration 1404:156-157

Swaying antennae 356:48-49

Texture of surface affects motion experiment 1404:152-153

The science of swinging—experiment 577:project 66

Thread and spool tank model overcomes friction and climbs slope experiment 1334:14-15

Time, distance, speed experiment with toy cars; data table given 871:4.001

Unbalanced forces produce motion experiment 1405:102

Unbalanced forces produce motion shown with balloon rocket on string 1404:14

Vehicle moves at constant speed when pulled with constant force experiment 1157:25-26

Vinegar cannon demonstrates law of motion 203:29

Wagon with jointed wheels demonstrates motion 1112:24

Water rocket demonstrates action and reaction principle 1179:63

Water rocket demonstrates Newton's second law of motion 338:54-56

Water stays in whirling container experiment 1389:13

Weight and friction effect on energy of moving object demonstration 1404:162-163

What happens when two objects push or pull one another experiment 1157:38-44

What is friction 281:44

Why do things fall down 281:37

Why do we oil machines 281:45

Why use wheels 281:43

Wooden slide test for friction experiment 1035:21

MOTION PICTURES. *See also* **MOVIES; ZOETROPE**

Caging a rabbit and pecking duck—how to make 410:28

Daedaleum—a motion picture device—how to make 507:1890-1891

Demonstrate principle of motion pictures 179:103-104

Fish in a bowl moving picture 595:inside front cover

Flick book makes pictures move; patterns for pictures given 1299:22-23

Flip book,—making 659:25

Flip-flop "magic" moving pictures, how to make 600:4-5

How do movies move—mini movie experiment 399:47

How to make flip books 400:78

How to make pictures move 909:152-153

Make magic movies 142:32

Make pictures move 659:24-25

Make your own movie 653:22-23

Making motion pictures with a phenakestoscope 558:120-121

Motion picture experiment; persistence of vision effect 895:40-41

Movie wheel—making 732:46-48

Movie wheel with pictures from photocopy of movie wheels, how to make 1088:56

Movie, make your own 176:48-49; 909:153

Moving pictures, how to make from record turntable, strips of pictures 1245:24-25

Panorama toy from box, making 861:225-231

Parrot praxinoscope, how to make 1308:28-29

Persistence of vision experiment with cards 1506:61-63

Phantascope, how to make 861:27-32

Phenakistoscope to make pictures move; make with picture patterns given 1299:18-21

Phenakistoscope, how to make to show mini moving pictures experiment 935:80-81

Separate sequential images flash by in flip book experiment 1476:210

Stick person flip book, how to make 1417:26

Strip cartoon show—how to make 410:29

Thaumatrope, make to show how movies work experiment 1216:40-42

Zoetrope toy to see moving pictures, patterns given, how to make 1299:24-27

Zoetrope, how to make from cardboard and dowel 1179:92-93

MOTOR VEHICLES. See also AUTOMOBILES

Make a model vehicle 224:16-19

MOTORS

Attraction motor—making 128:182-183

Build complex electric motor experiment 1514:87-91

Build small electric motor experiment 1514:83-86

Clockwork motor—making 260:16-17

Control panel for your motors—how to make 164:64-72

Current meter to measure current in electric motors, how to make 1179:170

Direct current motor—how to make 577:project 61

Display cases for your motors 164:73-77

Eddy Current motor, how to make 768:68-69

Electric motor—how to make 23:53-58

Electric motor demonstrates how motors use magnetism experiment 1034:27-29

Electric motor from magnets, battery and cork, how to make 1218:34-35

Electric motor in action, how to make 929:25

Electric motor in propeller-driven boat, how to make 1043:40-41

Electric motor made from board, battery, magnets and wire 1382:38-39

Electric motor with batteries, how to make 888:180-185

Electric motor, build, how to do 910:26-27

Electric motor, how to demonstrate experiment 972:43

Electric motor, how to make from wood, wires, battery and switch 1179:171

Electric motor, how to make 948:38-41; 1043:38-39

Electric motor, simple one, how to make 1426:96-98

Electric motor; basic working motor, how to make from diagrams given 1063:302-304

Electric motors; how motors and generators are related experiment 929:27

Electric train working model, how to make 1043:42-43

Generator, how to build with battery, two electric motors, wire and bulbs 1073:56-57

Hot shot motor—making 127:114-134

Magnet motor—make a simple one 253:145

Magnet, motor, simple, how to make 768:67-68

Make a tin can wonder motor using batteries 127:104-113

Models to turn with your motor—windmill, crane, color wheel 164:78-88

Motor—make with magnets 748:131

Motor, how to make experiment 938:122-125

Motors, electric, how they work experiment 938:96-99

Pin and cork motor—making 128:182

Rubber band racer, how to make 1033:22-23

Simple motor—making 128:183

'Skinny' the skeleton motor—how to make 164:32-41

Spinning paint model machine makes colorful paint patterns, how to make 1043:44-45

Stripped down simple motor experiment 1132:97-1-97-2

The "psychic" motor—how to build 563:28-29

Tin can motor—how to make 164:16-31

Trolley with electric motor move things experiment 1299:57

Water motor—how to make 260:17

'What's it' motor—how to make 164:52-58

Wood motor—how to make 164:42-51

Zoetrope motor, deluxe, how to make 1215:105-109

Zoetrope motor, simple, how to make 1215:102-104

MOTORS—CLOCK MOTORS

Old clock motors used for revolving projects 543:36-39

MOTORS—ELECTRIC. See also ELECTRIC; ELECTRIC MOTORS

Build a real motor 532:99

Build an electric motor 253:157-159

Electric motor you can make 267:46-48; 278:57-59

Electric motor, making 895:46-49

Magic motor—making 532:98

Make an electric motor with an electromagnet 385:150-151

Simple electric motor—making 360:48-50

Simple electric motor experiment—making 385:148-150

MOUNTAINS

Anticline; layers of rock folded to make mountain experiment 1277:35

Contour lines show shape of mountain; show with clay mountain and water 1437:29-32

Contour model of mountains, making 826:66-68

Cooling formation of mountains demonstration 1441:49

Demonstrate faulted highlands 301:12-13

Demonstrate fold mountains 301:10-11

Erosion of grassy soil compared to plain soil experiment 1468:28

Fold mountains demonstrated with clay 1266:24

Fold mountains model, make from clay and paper 1383:14

Fold mountains project, how to make from clay experiment 1134:1.001

Folding mountains demonstration 1441:49

Folding mountains demonstrations with foam rubber and clay 1480:66-67

How different kinds of garbage pollute mountain soil experiment 1468:29

How faults work demonstration 1080:17

How mountain ranges affect climate experiment 1447:89-91

How mountains are formed experiment 706:65-66

How mountains form and how earthquakes happen demonstration 1437:84-87

Humps or mountains demonstrated with modeling clay 1277:19

Make a 3-D map 153:14-15

Models of fault and folded mountains, how to make 1042:24

Moisture lifted up by model mountain experiment 1447:89-91

Mountain on poster board framework, how to make 1042:20-21

Mountain ranges and peaks, making to demonstrate mountains 874:216

Mountains rise due to erosion demonstration 1023:116-117

Mountains rise due to erosion demonstration 1023:116-117

Rain runoff and erosion effect on different mountain soils experiment 1465:93

Rocks can be squeezed and folded demonstration using layers of clay 1438:4-7

Wind currents over mountains shown with pile of books, tissue paper, fan 1439:86-88

MOUSE. *See* **MICE**

MOUSETRAP

Make your own mousetrap using ramps, levers and forces 554:28-29

MOUTH—HUMAN. *See also* **HUMAN BODY; SENSES—TASTE**

The human mouth 294:80-81

MOUTHWASH

How to make mouthwash and test bacteria killing properties experiment 1259:61-62

Mouth bacteria experiment with different mouthwashes 997:126-127

MOVIES. *See also* **MOTION PICTURES**

Create your own movie 870:36-38

MOVING PICTURES

Acrobatic pictures—making 696:26-27

Cartoon movie, how to make from tin lid, stick and paper strips 1308:29

How to make pictures move 909:152-153

Movie, make your own 909:153

MOVING SLIDES

Moving slides toy, how to make 861:137-143

MUD. *See also* **SOILS**

Magic mud, making 669:8-9

MUD FLATS

Measuring speed of mud snail's pace experiment 1225:136

Mud snail trails in mud observations project 1225:135

Mud snails reaction to touch experiment 1225:136

MUD SNAILS

Estimating populations of mud snails experiment; chart given 1225:137-138

How deep do mud snails burrow vertically into mud for winter migration 1225:138

Measuring speed of mud snail's pace experiment 1225:136

Mud snail trails in mud observations project 1225:135

Mud snail's reaction to touch experiment 1225:136

Mud snail's response to chemicals/other dead snails chemoreception experiment 1225:136-137

MUD WORMS

Observations of world of mud worms, how to do 1225:156-164

Pulse of mud worm under normal, warm and cold water temperatures experiment 1225:164

MULTIPLICATION. *See also* **MATHEMATICS**

Games to demonstrate structure and principles 533:1-33

MUSCLES. *See also* **HUMAN BODY—MUSCLES**

Experiment to show involuntary versus voluntary type using frogs 174:36-37

Investigating muscle pairs 253:108-109

Moving madness test of your muscles 571:40

Muscle coordination tester—how to make 543:34-35

Muscle tissue under microscope—observe 713:68-69

Muscles and leverage—experiment 563:182-183

MUSHROOMS. *See also* **FUNGI; SPORES**

Adventure 35—we make a study of toadstools under a microscope 403:124-130

Examining edible mushrooms 294:24-25

Fairy rings; investigate growth habits of fungi in fairy rings project 1313:69-71

How to grow 358:98-99

Mushroom spore prints, how to make 784:39-40

Mushroom spores grow into mushrooms to eat, how to plant experiment 1306:18-19

Spore patterns from mushroom caps, how to make 1379:13

Spore prints, how to make 166:58-60; 382:56-59; 1063:256; 1114:62-63; 1145:29; 1298:53

Spore print from a mushroom, how to make 1440:68-70

Spore print from mushroom cap, how to make 1214:22; 1457:35; 1490:43

Spore prints from mushrooms, how to make 1071:86; 1313:126-127

Spores—collecting to see growth patterns 459:28-32

Spores—how to see 264:33

Spores identify different types of fungi experiment 1134:4.002

Testing mushrooms for sugar or starch experiment 1061:112-113

MUSIC

Concordant and discordant sounds from vibrating strings experiment 1155:90-91

Drum overtones, make column of tin can drums to demonstrate 1209:71

Effect of sound and music on plants 398:124-127

Harmonious and discordant notes experiment 1155:94-96

Major diatomic scale experiments 2:72-75

Music and its effect on plant growth experiment 714:89-90

Music effect on plant growth experiment 1375:100-104

Music stimulates plants to grow better experiment 1209:42-43

Music vision sets—audible vibrations into light patterns 386:17-19

Musical intervals experiments 2:68-71

Musical magic with everyday objects 684:20-21

Piano overtones, how to investigate 1209:70

Pythagoras's relationship among sound pitch, string length and tension 1133:6.001

Send music over a beam of light 291:242-243

Shape and thickness affect music from glass experiment 1357:28

Song title database computer project 1021:77-78
Stringed instrument makes different tones—demonstrate 293:45-46
Tuning forks—experiment with 400:83
Vibrating strings experiment with rubber band banjo, how to make 1155:87-90
Waterwheel mechanical music maker—how to make 606:80-85

MUSIC—MAKING

Does tension of string affect the note 134:12
Experiment to show wind instruments 134:15
Experiment with tuning forks 134:19
Length of string and sound it makes 134:11
Made from water glass 291:150-151
Making and playing straw whistles 134:16-17
Making different sounds 134:10
Making drums 134:18
Music from glasses 45:92-93
Playing a bottle organ 134:14
Thickness affects sound 134:9
Use light to make music 291:244-245

MUSICAL INSTRUMENTS. *See also* SOUNDS— MUSICAL INSTRUMENTS

Banjo—ham-can rubber band-banjo—how to make 363:131-132
Banjo—making 178:40
Banjo—one-string—making 734:36
Banjo from ice cream tub, making 1028:84-85
Banjo from wood, string and plastic tub, how to make 1045:42
Bass—packing case—making 734:26
Bass fiddle—how to make 585:54-55
Bass fiddle from juice can and string demonstrates how to vary pitch 1209:60-61
Bass from pail and pole, how to make 1298:14
Bass from wooden box and broom handle, how to make 1045:40
Bass viol from string, box and broom demonstrates sound vibrations/pitch 1432:66-69
Bells—can hand bells—make and play 363:129-131
Bells—tubular pipe—making 734:34
Bells—water bells—how to make 400:80
Bells—water bells from drinking glasses 494:54
Bells from copper pipe, how to make 1333:21
Bells, clay pot, making 903:32
Bells; tubular bells experiment 1045:29
Body band—one person plays many instruments 358:8-9
Bongos—coffee can bongos—make and play 363:132-134
Bottle band from glass bottles, how to make 1073:36
Bottle band using pop bottles and water, how to do 1331:99
Bottle music—making 734:28
Bottle organ demonstrates musical notes of octave scale, how to make 1045:26-27
Bottle organ from glass bottles, how to make 1385:24
Bottle organ, making 957:25
Bottle pipes filled with water produce different musical notes experiment 1036:26-27
Bottle string instrument—how to make 358:60-61
Bottles—musical bottles (Primary) 288:16-17
Bottles, singing, making 909:87
Cardboard tubes—making 186:59
Castanets—making (Primary) 696:43
Castanets—walnuts—making 708:57-59
Chimes—water glass chimes—how to make 251:8-10; 304:22-23
Chimes—wooden chimes—how to make 400:81
Chimes from different objects, how to make 1385:21
Chimes, bottle and jar, making 903:33
Chimes, coat hanger, making 903:34
Clackers from garden labels, making 903:35
Clappers, coconut, making 903:33
Claves—broomstick—making 708:61
Claves, how to make 957:20-21
Combs—the musical comb 291:152
Cymbals—can lid cymbals—make and play 363:136-137
Designing and building musical instruments—experiment 691:68-75
Double bass instrument from cardboard box and broom handle, how to make 1333:22-23
Drum—an empty coffee can makes a good drum 251:11-13
Drum—making 436:68-69; 686:8-9;
Drum—making (Primary) 696:42
Drum—plastic bowl—making 734:33
Drum—simple—tin can—making 708:50-51
Drum box—making 732:37-38
Drum coffee can drum—making 723:12-14
Drum from plastic bowl and clear plastic sheet, how to make 1385:16
Drum from plastic bowl and plastic sheet, how to make 1036:22
Drum; bongo drum from tin can, how to make 1045:34
Drum; tuneable drums from cardboard tubes, how to make 1045:35
Drums from containers covered with plastic, how to make 1073:36
Fiddle; bucket base fiddle, making 779:14
Flute—bottle flute—how to make 366:183
Flute from cardboard tube, straw and paper, how to make 1036:28-29
Flute from drinking straws, how to make 1369:74-75
Flute from straw, making 779:58
Flute from tubing, bamboo cane and cork, how to make 1245:34-36
Flute, magic drinking straw flute, how to make 600:46-47
Flutes—make flutes from bottles 251:21-23
Garden hose recorder—how to make 400:82
Garden orchestra 356:56-59
Glass bottles or glasses filled with water make music experiment 1255:27
Glass harmonica—how to make 472:2224; 1007:60-61
Glass harmonica from drinking glasses—how to make 723:21
Glass harmonica from glasses filled with water 1245:37
Glasses—how to set up musical glasses 172:62-64
Glockenspiel, how to make 957:19
Gong experiments 686:21-22
Gong; great gong, making 779:25
Gongs—make music outdoors with garden gongs 251:29-31
Guitar—cigar box guitar—how to make 543:46-47
Guitar—elastic band—making 734:27
Guitar—make a flat iron guitar 186:60
Guitar—making 142:45
Guitar—making (Primary) 696:42
Guitar—one string stick guitar—making 400:80

Guitar—rock with a cigar box guitar 251:26-28
Guitar—tune guitar without using your ears 350:96
Guitar from baking pan and rubber bands, how to make 1036:24-25
Guitar from cardboard box and rubber bands, how to make 1255:28
Guitar from cigar box experiment 1066:98-99
Guitar from plastic box and rubber bands, how to make 1385:31
Guitar from plywood and cardboard demonstrates sound waves 1333:14-15
Guitar from shoe box and rubber bands, how to make 1045:43
Guitar from shoe box, how to make 1102:15; 1179:112
Guitar, how to make and demonstrate how notes change on guitar experiment 1432:123-126
Harmonica from wine glasses—making 186:58
Harmonica—turn a comb into a harmonica 251:6-7
Harp—Aeolian harp—how to make 172:57-62; 350:97-98
Harp—ear harp—how to make 400:80
Harp from baking tin and rubber bands, making 1016:23
Harp from tissue box and rubber bands demonstrates amplification 1209:56-57
Harp, making 909:86
Horn from hose and funnel, making 1028:83
Horn, how to make from funnel and hose 1179:113
Hosepipe horn—making 187:28
How do we get high and low sounds from musical instruments—exp. 587:43
How whistles work 686:30-33
Jingle Bells—why do they jingle? 686:23
Jingle stick, making 903:35
Kazoo—make a paper tube Kazoo 203:74
Kazoo—make a simple kazoo 251:24-25
Kazoo—making 32:28-29; 732:26
Kazoo hummers, cardboard tubes, making 1014:55
Kazoo, how to make from cardboard tube 1289:4-5
Kazoo, paper tube, making 897:79
Maraca from papier mache covered balloon and dried beans, how to make 1333:18-19
Maracas—make maracas from electric light bulbs 251:14-17
Maracas—milk containers—making 708:60
Maracas—paper mache maracas (rattles)—how to make 363:134-135
Maracas from paper cups, cardboard tube and dried beans, how to make 1385:23
Maracas, how to make from yogurt containers and seeds 1179:113
Melody instruments—how to make 631:46-47
Monochord—making 45:118-121
Music from bottles filled with water experiment 1207:26
Musical glasses experiment 686:25-28
Musical instrument—making 65:100-101
Musical instruments—make several simple ones to demonstrate sound 128:134-136
Oboe—make a straw oboe 203:66
Oboe, straw, making 827:14
Organ—from empty bottles—making 186:56-57; 187:26
Pan pipes demonstrate sound wavelengths experiment 1333:26-27
Pan pipes from straws and corrugated cardboard, how to make 1385:26
Pan pipes from straws, making 1016:23

Pandean pipes, how to make 861:99-103
Panpipes experiment, how to make 1045:28
Panpipes from garden hose, how to make 1255:28
Panpipes from plastic pipes, making 1028:82-83
Panpipes, how to make from straws 1179:113
Piano—make a nail piano 186:55
Piano—make a pin piano 203:82
Piano—thumb—how to make 178:41
Piano—thumb—making (Primary) 696:43
Piano—tongue depressor finger piano—how to make 400:82-83
Pin piano, how to make 1432:119-122
Pinging strings from nails, rubber band, wood, how to make 1385:30
Pipes—reed pipes—making 187:25
Pipes cut at different lengths play scales and tunes 436:72
Pipes from plastic straws, how to make 1163:12
Pipes of Pan—making 90:66-67; 734:29
Polynesian instrument—how to make 325:unpaged
Pot and pan band, how to make 1102:10
Projects with musical instruments 691:74-75
Rain stick musical instrument, how to make from plastic pipe 1115:76
Rattle from stick and bottle caps, how to make 1045:33
Rattle; whirling rattle from wood, how to make 1045:36-37
Rattles from cookie tins, how to make 1102:9
Recorder from thick cardboard tube, how to make 1045:30-31
Reeds from cardboard tubes, how to make 1333:28-29
Rhythm band—making 436:68-69
Rhythm instruments, how to make drums, nail scraper, flower pots, etc. 631:48-51
Sand blocks—how to make 400:81
Sandpaper blocks, making 903:34
Sandpaper or wooden rasp, how to make 1045:33
Scraper from wood and sandpaper—making 734:35
Scrapers from plastic bottle, how to make 1385:20
Shaker—making 734:32
Shakers from bottles, cartons or small boxes, how to make 1385:22
Shakers from cups or plastic bottles, how to make 1045:32-33
Shakers from small plastic bottles, how to make 1073:36
Shakers, simple, how to make 1036:23
Singing bottles from glass bottles, how to make 1385:25
Spinner from poster board hums, how to make 1045:39
Spoons—how to play 734:34
Stereo metal hanger instrument, making 888:151-153
Stick scraper, making 903:34
Sticks—music sticks—making 45:113-114
Straw horn—making 732:53
Straw reed—making 734:30
Straws, musical straws, how to make 1385:28
String bass from a box and a piece of string—making 161:35-36
String bass from large box and wooden pole, how to make 1163:11
String instrument from wood, string and wire, how to make 1245:32-33
Stringed instruments have sounding board experiment; make guitar and piano 1155:98-104
Stringed things—making 32:30-31
Strings—stretched strings—making 187:24

Tambourine—paper plates make good shakers 251:18-20
Tambourine—pie tin—making 708:52-53
Tambourine—wood block tambourine—how to make 400:82
Tambourine, how to make from stick and bottle caps 1179:113
Tambourine, making 436:68-69; 903:35
Thunder stick musical instrument, how to make from plastic pipe 1115:76
Timpani—toy timpani—making 187:27
Tin drum from cookie tin, making 1028:80-81
Tom-tom drum from plastic flowerpots, making 1028:80-81
Tom-toms, making 686:12
Toy musical instrument—how to make 321:13
Trombone—water trombone—making 186:55
Trombone from plastic piping and pail of water, how to make 1385:29
Trombone, cardboard, making 957:25
Trombone, straw, making 827:15
Trumpet from hose and funnel, how to make 1163:11
Trumpet from large paper cone, how to make 1385:15
Twanging rulers, how to make 957:19
Violin—making 436:68-69
Wails from a ruler—making 186:57
Water glass music, how to make using glasses of water 1331:98
Water glasses, how to set up [Primary] 897:81
Weather cock—make a musical weather cock 172:64-65
Whip cracker from rulers—making 734:35
Whirrer from poster board hums, how to make 1045:39
Whistle—how to make a Swanee whistle 161:34-35
Whistle—make a whistle pipe 142:45
Whistle—straw—making 90:62-63
Whistle and flute, how to make 887:20-22
Whistle from straw, how to make 1102:12
Whistle; slide whistle from copper pipe, how to make 1045:31
Whistles—making (Primary) 696:42
Whistling wine glasses 494:55
Why a horn honks 686:36-40
Why does a bell ring? 686:17-21
Wind chimes—how to make 400:80-81
Wind instruments experiment with reed made from straw 1155:104-107
Woodwind (panpipe) from plastic tubing experiment 1155:107-109
Xylophone—bottle or can xylophone—make and play 363:135-136
Xylophone—glass—making 734:25
Xylophone—making 142:44; 161:32-34; 178:39; 385:93-94; 436:89; 708:64-66; 90:63-66
Xylophone—making (Primary) 696:43

Xylophone—simple xylophone—making 45:116-117
Xylophone from bottles and water, how to make 1333:20-21
Xylophone from bottles filled with water, making 1016:23
Xylophone from cardboard and pencils, making 1028:82
Xylophone from nails on block of wood, how to make 1385:20
Xylophone from steel pipes, how to make 1115:48-49
Zither—make a zither with elastic bands 186:54-55
Zither from strings and bottles, how to make 1045:41

MUSICAL SOUNDS
Making with straws 12:20-23
Using sticks and strings 12:24-27

MUSSCHENBROEK, PIETER
Constructing a Leyden jar 627:19
Inventor of Leyden jar (device for storing electricity) 209:20-21

MUSSELS
Age and size of blue mussels dependent on their location experiment 1225:45-46
Blue mussel's shape is an advantage in its habitat experiment 1225:43-44
Blue mussels and how they attach themselves observations 1225:42-43
Blue mussels siphons observed using food coloring in small tank experiment 1225:45-46
Blue mussels; where and how they live observations 1225:42-47
Byssal threads of blue mussels measured for strength using spring scale 1225:46-47
How do starfish open shells of mussels experiment 1397:64-67
Mussels, collect and observe young mussels under hand lens 771:60-64
Position in the intertidal zone and growth rate of blue mussels experiment 1225:45-46
Relationship between byssal anchor threads and size of mussel experiment 1225:43
What is a filter feeder 236:119-120

MUTATION
Mutation—mechanism of evolution 402:105-106
Mutation experiment with plants 398:97-100

MUTOSCOPE
Separate sequential images flash by in flip book experiment 1476:210

MYCELIUM. *See* **MOLDS; SPORES**

MYSTERY POWDERS
Experiments with 107:114-115

N

NADIR—ZENITH FINDER
Project 292:42
NAILS
Experiments and demonstrations with 549:7-106
How much force can a hammer apply to a nail 549:22-25
How they work 544:9-14
Why is point of a nail sharp, why is point of nail dull 549:26-29
NAILS—HUMAN BODY
Experiment to investigate nail polish 441:101-103
How fast do your nails grow experiment 901:156
NATURAL SELECTION
Brine shrimp egg hatching experiment to see how many can survive 1069:23
NATURE
Cycles in nature explored with Mobius strip experiment 1063:207
Garden nature study—how to do 662:38
Nature mobiles—how to make 312:15-18
Nature photography—how to do 234:14-17
Nature sketching—how to do 234:12-13
NATURE—ART ACTIVITIES. *See also* **ANIMALS—ART ACTIVITIES; PLANTS—ART ACTIVITIES**
Bamboo wind chimes—making 582:89-91
Box relief miniature landscape—making 582:135-137
Broken glass mosaic—making 582:91-93
Charcoal drawing 582:108-110
Circle drawing 582:114-116
Clay impressions—making 582:125-127
Color awareness drawing 582:105-108
Fabric wall hanging 582:84-86
Floating objects from nature—making 582:118-120
Grab bag drawings 582:110-112
Group mural drawing 582:78-80
Hand building with clay 582:127-129
Imaginative sand dwellings—making 582:93-95
Jewelry form nature 582:82-84
Litter sculpture—making 582:95-97
Mobiles from nature—making 582:129-132
Nature collage—making 582:112-114
Preparing natural clay 582:123-125
Sand candles—making 582:120-123
Sand painting—making 582:132-135
Sculptures from nature 582:116-118
Sketchbook—journal—making 582:87-88
Stencil drawing 582:80-82
Story illustration—making 582:99-102
Trace-hand environment—making 582:97-99
NATURE CENTER
Making 436:61
NAVIGATION
Altitude—how to measure 292:43
Latitude—how to tell latitude by altitude 292:44
Latitude—use your hands to give latitude and altitude 292:46
Navigation tricks 231:50
Solar stone—how to use it 292:22-23
Solar stone—make your own 292:27
NAVIGATION INSTRUMENTS
Astrolabe—make your own 292:48-49
Astrolabe to show altitude of star, make from poster board, straw, string 1434:42-44
Cross staff—making 292:46-48

Cross-staff to find latitude, how to make from boards and nails 1434:38-41
Gyroscope from old phonograph record shows gyroscope use in space travel 1434:116-119
Making a cross staff project 833:97-99
Making a quadrant and azimuth measuring instrument project 833:96-97
Making a sextant project 833:103-109
Making an astrolabe project 833:100-102
Measure altitude of stars and sun, how to make astrolabe 1115:134-137
Solar stone to find North, how to make from cardboard, cork, dowel 1115:132-133
NEBULAE
Star clusters; explore stars around certain constellations experiment 1217:32-33
NEGATIVE GEOTROPISM. *See also* **GEOTROPISM; PLANTS—TROPISMS**
How gravity affects plant growth 294:42-43
NEGATIVE NUMBERS
Activities and game to explain concept of positive and negative numbers 458:1-33
NEMATODES
Animal life in soil and leaf litter experiment 1134:1.012
How to catch a nematode 364:55
Microscopic life in soil experiment 1134:1.009
Nematodes and other soil animals; collect with Berlese funnel experiment 1063:416
NEPHOSCOPE
Direction and speed of clouds determined by using nephoscope experiment 1012:18
Direction of wind determined by use of nephoscope experiment, how to make 1405:82
How to make nephoscope 9:96-97; 381:69-71; 852:49; 978:151
Nephoscope measures direction of wind where clouds are experiment, how to make 1372:57-58
Nephoscope to check direction clouds are moving, how to make 1115:52-53
Nephoscope tracks cloud movement, how to make 1063:439
Track directional movement of clouds 175:80
Wind direction determined by nephoscope demonstration 1023:144-145
NEPTUNE. *See also* **PLANETS**
Making a model of the orbits of Uranus, Neptune, and Pluto project 833:249-251
Measurements 292:96
Neptune's Scooter and the Great Dark Spot experiment with models 1478:78
Pinpointing Neptune experiment 1478:79
NERVES. *See also* **HUMAN BODY**
Exploring nerve reflexes 253:110-111
Nerve machine 391:70-74
NESTING FISH. *See* **CICHLIDS**
NESTS. *See also* **BIRDS—NESTS**
Nest box for squirrels—making 264:92
NETS
Butterfly—how to make 293:24
Conical tow—net making 9:32-34
Dip net—how to make 41:66
Drag nets for water exploring—making 234:44-45
Hand dip net for collecting water animals, how to make 1331:66

Insect net—how to make 313:5; 332:20-22; 382:61-62; 824:52-53

Insect net, coat hanger and cheese cloth, how to make 919:18

Net for catching caddis gnats, make from pillowcase and dowel 1476:118

Plankton net—how to make 285:35-37

Plankton net—tiny net for plankton—making 400:59

Plankton net, dip net and scoop—how to make 359:48-51

Plankton net, how to make from nylon stocking and wire 1172:36-37

Plankton net, making and using 625:55

Plankton net, making from coat hanger and stocking 864:131-132

Pond dipping net, how to make 1146:30

Seine net—how to construct and use 359:43-47

Sweep net for spiders—making 286:18-19

Sweep net from food strainer or old pair of tights, making 796:11-12

Sweeping net—making 9:16-17

NETS—INSECTS. *See also* INSECTS—NETS

Butterfly net—an easy to make net 476:45-46

How to make 442:unpaged

Water insect net, making 821:54

NETS—WATER INSECTS

Net for collecting water insects—how to make 430:54

NETTLES

Making nettle paper 598:35-36

NETWORKS

Basic explanation of graph theory and networks 477:1-33

NEWSPAPER

Copy newspaper print with turpentine copying fluid experiment 1020:93-96

Copy picture from newspaper with soap, water and mineral spirits experiment 1482:56-57

New paper from old newspaper, how to make 983:15

Newspaper clothing, making [Primary] 854:107

Newspaper hats, making [Primary] 854:108

Newspaper kites, making 854:110

Observe rapid aging of a newspaper experiment 905:86-87

Rapid aging of a newspaper experiment 1405:53

Reuse newspaper; making paper project 900:191

NEWSPAPER LOGS

How to make 508:34-35

How to make fireplace logs 347:120-121

Logs for burning from old newspapers, how to make 1228:90-91

NEWTON, SIR ISAAC. *See also* GRAVITY; MOTION

Acting and reacting Newton's third law of motion—demonstrations 180:39

His experiments 42:43-53

His experiment; curved mirrors used to concentrate or spread light 1511:24

Flying boat demonstration—force produces reaction in the opposite direction 605:42-43

Make your own Newton's cradle 142:8-9

Newton's cradle experiment using rulers and coins 1247:16-17

Newton's cradle toy experiment, how to make 1030:26-27

Newton's Law of Conservation of Momentum experiment 1132:69-1-69-2

Newton's Law of Cooling experiment 1090:20-21

Newton's Law of Cooling experiment with coffee and cream 871:3.011

Newton's law of gravitation—experiment with a bag of marbles 602:unpaged

Newton's Law of Motion experiments and tricks to demonstrate 1137:52-72

Newton's rings experiment 1133:6.008

Newton's steamboat—how to make 429:69

Newton's white light through a prism experiment 1156:73-76

Non-Newtonian fluid—how it behaves experiment 1405:55

Repeat Isaac Newton's experiment that light is composed of many colors 448:29-32

Speed of cooling experiment 1090:20-21

White light's constituent colors experiment 1133:6.007

Who discovered the quantum theory of energy project 1525:114-120

NEWTON CAR

Demonstrates Newton's action-reaction principle and his second law of motion 338:57-59

NEWTON'S ACTION

Reaction principle Newton car—demonstrates 338:57-59

NEWTON'S COLOR WHEEL

Experiment 569:38

NEWTON'S CRADLE

Make your own Newton's cradle 575:16-17

NEWTON'S FIRST LAW OF MOTION

A frictionless air car 114:108-110

Card and cloth 114:106-108

Coins and piece of paper on top of bottle demonstrate inertia 1063:338

Experiments to demonstrate First Law of Motion 1156:76-78

Experiments to demonstrate 186:32-47; 295:77-89

Flick card and coin falls into glass experiment 1063:145

Frictionless air car demonstrates—how to make 763:60-61

How friction affects inertia experiment 1405:101

Inertia trick with coin 642:35

Magic checkers demonstrate law of inertia 1289:24-25

Measuring force and acceleration experiment 763:62-64

Reaction motor built from coffee can—demonstrates 392:47-51

Things in motion continue in motion 295:65-67

NEWTON'S LAW OF MOTION

Hockey puck and Newton's Laws of Motion experiment 1154:30-37

Unbalanced forces produce motion experiment 1405.103

NEWTON'S RINGS

Demonstrate Newton's Rings with soap bubbles experiment 1007:36-37

NEWTON'S SECOND LAW OF MOTION

Accelerometer shows acceleration and direction of acceleration experiment 1502:37-39

Experiments to demonstrate Second Law of Motion 1156:79-82

Force effect on motion experiment with block of wood, washers and thread 1502:35-37

Force of gravity is proportional to mass of object experiment 1502:43-45

Launch a simple rocket 68:4-5

Newton car—demonstrates 338:57-59

Principle of rockets illustrated by simple model 532:44

Water rocket—demonstrates 338:54-56
Weight of various masses when weighed on Moon's surface experiment 1502:44-45

NEWTON'S THIRD LAW OF MOTION
Activities and experiments to demonstrate rocket propulsion 564:28-29
Balloon rocket experiments demonstrate Third Law of Motion 1157:48-52
Balloons and string—experiment 670:96
Boards and pendulum demonstrate 723:212
Can expanding gas move an object through air experiment 851:55-56
Carbon dioxide rocket 338:52-53
Experimenting with Newton's Third Law using balloon 1252:90-91
Experiments to demonstrate 1156:82-84
Ice skates or roller skates demonstrate Third Law of Motion 1154:37-39
Illustrating Newton's third law—experiment 585:56-57
Law demonstrated with plastic bottle filled with vinegar/baking soda 1456:11
Make a simple match rocket 68:6-9
Marble cannon demonstrates Newton's law experiment 836:65-68
Measuring rocket power 68:9-11
Mini helicopter demonstrates Newton's Third Law of Motion 1289:28-29
Motion and momentum experiment with board on dowels 763:68-69
Paddle boat on water demonstrates 1404:164-167
Paddleboat demonstrates Newton's Law of action and reaction 1405:104
Paper rockets with straws demonstrate Newton's Third Law of Motion experiment 1014:126
'Penny' rocket demonstrates propulsion 291:87
Push-push back experiment with toy trucks 1502:46-49
Rocket boat, how to build 600:42-43
Simple demonstration of 642:42
Simple experiments to demonstrate 763:67-68
Toy locomotive on section of track demonstrates 722:111

NEWTS
Collect and observe newts in terrarium, how to do 771:143-150
How do newts and salamanders hear without external ears experiment 1397:16-19
How to cage and care for 279:18
Newts in aquarium, how to keep 913:39

NICHOLSON, WILLIAM
Decomposition of water into hydrogen and oxygen using electricity experiment 1133:2.008

NICOTINE
Effects of nicotine on daphnia experiment 1267:97-101

NIGHT
Colors of night sky 292:123
Making a night clock nocturnal project 833:29-31
Why night is dark 30:52

NIGHT AND DAY. *See also* **DAY AND NIGHT**
Differences in night and day (Primary) 232:50
How we move from daylight to darkness—experiment (Primary) 614:20-23

NITRATES. *See* **FERTILIZERS; WATER—POLLUTION**

NITROGEN
Candle burns oxygen in bottle and leaves nitrogen gas experiment 995:18-19

Nitrogen-fixing bacteria change nitrogen so plants can use it experiment 1402:48-51
Nitrogen-fixing bacteria help clover plants to grow experiment 1060:111-112
Nitrogen-fixing bacteria on clover plant nodules experiment 1060:110
Nitrogen-fixing bacteria on roots of legume plants experiment 1060:110
Nitrogen-fixing bacteria replace nitrogen compounds in hydroponic solution 1060:112
Produce pure sample of nitrogen 346:72-74

NITROGEN FIXATION
Effect of acid rain on nitrogen fixation experiment 1450:72-76

NITROGEN OXIDE. *See* **ACID RAIN**

NOISE
Blow on paper sheets to make noise experiment 1079:54-55
Decibel survey chart of house noises 364:142
Filtering out noises—what do we hear tape recorder experiment 734:16
Hearing; how accurately can people hear under noisy conditions experiment 1020:125-129
Make a hose trombone 538:69
Megaphone from large paper cone, how to make 1385:15
Molecules as sound 366:173-175
Noisemaker; buzz saw from cardboard makes noise, pattern given, make 1299:77
Noisemaker, from paper, how to make 1036:14-15
Noisemakers—how to make pig grunter, twanger and bottle flute 366:182-183
Observe and chart kinds of noises in your environment 740:39
Paper pistol—making 734:17
Paper snapper, how to make 1385:11
Piece of cellophane makes horrible noise when blown on 1079:55-56

NOISE—POLLUTION. *See also* **POLLUTION—NOISE**
Ability to concentrate affected by background noise experiment 1093:30-31
Intensity of sound; how to measure experiment 1155:75
Shrubs tested as natural sound barriers for homes project 969:90-91

NOISEMAKERS
Bullroarer—making 732:134

NON-NEWTONIAN FLUID
Discover how non-Newtonian fluid behaves experiment 1479:54
Glob, creezy ooze, how to make to show "non-Newtonian" fluid 1396:139-140

NORMAN, ROBERT
Angle of dip in Earth's magnetic field experiment 1133:5.002

NORTH POLE
How far away is the North Pole 333:108-110
Magnetic deviation is increasing or decreasing but not fluctuating experiment 1062:67-68
Why is equator hotter than North Pole experiment 1003:20-21

NORTH STAR
A solar stone—how to use it 292:22-23
Constellations that turn around Polaris [North Star], how to find 1434:67-69

Finding Polaris [North Star] in the sky, how to do 1434:64-66

Finding your latitude 400:109

Finding your latitude using the North Star how to do 1437:23-26

How to tell latitude by altitude 292:44

Latitude from 382:110-111

Magnetic deviation is increasing or decreasing but not fluctuating experiment 1062:67-68

Make a magic calabash to show your home latitude 292:28-29

North circumpolar map 292:25

Path of stars near North Star seems longer than stars farther away experiment 1062:71-73

Photographing North Star—how to 762:15-16

Polaris used as reference point for finding stars in night sky experiment 1062:79-80

Solar stone—make your own solar stone 292:27

Solar stone to find North, how to make from cardboard, cork, dowel 1115:132-133

NORTHERN LIGHTS

Attraction of charged particles near Earth's poles demonstration 1394:104-105

Flashlights and cellophane paper demonstrate 759:6-7

NOSE. *See* **HUMAN BODY; SENSES—SMELL**

NUCLEAR BOMBS

Chain reaction that occurs in nuclear fission project 1361:34-35

NUCLEAR CHAIN REACTION

Illustrate how chain reaction works experiment 976:55

NUCLEAR FUELS

Nuclear fuel produces more energy than fossil fuels experiment 1453:54-56

NUCLEATION

Salt added to carbonated drink causes gas to be released experiment 1251:23-24

NUMBER RECORDS

Quipu, Inca—how to make 326:10-11

NUMBERS. *See also* **EULER, LEONARD; MATHE-MATICS**

Arabic, Egyptian, Babylonian, Roman, Greek and Mayan symbols for numbers 1349:9

Base five—activities to demonstrate 405:1-33

Concepts of odd, even, squares, triangular numbers demonstrated thru pictures 439:1-33

Experiments with 107:103-106

Fibonacci sequence of numbers investigation 1348:29-31

Finite and ordinary numbers compared using a week clock and old nursery rhyme 547:1-33

Fun with numbers 538:87-90

History of numbers 520:1-33

Importance of zero 601:unpaged

Magic squares to copy and complete and make your own magic square 1348:9-15

Magic tricks with numbers 350:30-50

Magic with age and loose change trick 350:32-33

Magic with erased number—guessing the 350:36-37

Magic with five odd figures 350:37-38

Magic with funnies 350:46-48

Magic with funny arithmetic 350:35-36

Magic with guessing 350:44-45

Magic with human calculator 350:41-44

Magic with psychic book test 350:38-40

Magic with tricky numbers 350:30-31

Math concepts introduced through variety of problems, games, activities 1349:7-64

Negative numbers game, how to make and play 1349:54-55

Number patterns introduced through problems and games 1348:5-64

Odds and evens—games, puzzles and questions 498:1-33

Pascal's triangle of numbers investigation 1348:41-47

Person's name has magic number, how to figure 1348:7

Positive and negative numbers—activities and game to explain concept 458:1-33

Zero—zero and its many uses 522:1-33

Zero and its uses 949:3-32

NUTRITION. *See also* **FOOD**

Activities to identify and understand four food groups [Primary] 758:85-92

Analyze school lunch menu for a week to determine nutrition experiment 1267:49-50

Chocolate milk & white milk-what is the difference between 402:70-71

Do diets of adolescents supply them with their mineral requirements experiment 1267:44-47

Does number of calories consumed on regular basis affect longevity experiment 1267:50

Effect of different nutrients (foods) on plants 507:1851-1852

Fiber; compare water absorbency of various types of dietary fiber experiment 1267:50

Game—the fat game 400:122

How healthy are fast-food meals experiment 1267:50

Nutrition experiments with guinea pigs 577:project #6

Nutrition from plants-design a garden that contains most important vitamins & minerals 380:5-15

Nutritional value of artificial diet and natural diet of tomato hornworm 1096:34-38

Proper weight—what is proper weight for a grown person 402:71-72

Snack food guide 380:15

NUTS

Prove nuts have oil in them 322:14-15

Toast marshmallow with burning nut experiment 1083:90-91

NUTS AND BOLTS

How they work 544:15-18

NUTTY PUTTY

Recipe for Nutty Putty, how to make 1083:60-61

O

OAK APPLES
    Make ink from oak apples 146:7

OBLIQUITY OF MOTION
    Revolving snake—experiment 350:113-114

OCEAN
    Action of waves breaking changes coastline demonstration 840:20
    Aquarium and seaside activities 840:1-113
    Artificial sea water, making 860:164-166
    Beachcombing for litter experiment 1150:56-57
    Beware! Undertow! 41:103-109
    Carbon dioxide is held in water experiment 1322:48-52
    Collecting and examining sediments on the ocean floor experiment 877:120-125
    Expansion of Atlantic Ocean demonstration 1023:60-61
    Green plant life does not occur deep in ocean experiment 1405:28
    Green plant life does not occur deep in the ocean experiment 904:56-57
    Greenhouse effect and rising water level in oceans experiment 1150:22-23
    Greenhouse effect as cause of rise in sea levels project 1342:126
    How ocean gets its salt demonstration 1023:208-209
    Level of oceans affected by greenhouse warming experiment 1322:44-47
    Light is affected by the depth of water experiment 877:30-34
    Make an ocean in a jar—experiment 538:119
    Make and stock a mini-ocean 657:47-51
    Making a profile of the ocean floor, how to do 877:115-119
    Making waves in the bathtub experiment 877:40-43
    Midocean ridges, how to demonstrate 1437:88-92
    Ocean breezes on lands near ocean shown with thermometer, water, and fan 1437:114-117
    Ocean salt compared to table salt experiment 1290:7, 1.7
    Ocean thermal energy conversion demonstration 698:16-17
    Ocean thermal energy conversion experiment 895:100-101
    Ocean trenches formation demonstration 1023:62-63
    Plants—ocean plants grow only in sunny water—experiment (Primary) 470:2-3
    Project to explain the great pressure beneath the sea 877:25-29
    Salt content of water measured experiment 1023:210-211
    Salty ocean water, how to make 1438:30-32
    Sand castles & water tables 41:140-144
    Seawater mixture used by marine aquariums, how to make 1294:76-77
    Shape of shorelines affects height of tides demonstration 1023:218-219
    Show osmosis in salt water experiment 741:33
    Solar energy affects ocean salinity demonstration 1023:212-213
    Teaching activities about the ocean; art, music and science 1056:38-79
    Temperatures affect ocean currents experiment 706:88
    Tide observations, how to do 1225:198-207
    Time and tides; connection between Moon and ocean experiment 877:67-72
    Water and air affect land temperatures near oceans experiment 1003:17
    Water pressure affected by volume experiment 1023:202-203
    Water temperature changes with depth experiment 877:35-39
    Water waves—projects with 691:104-107
    Water; is deep ocean water warmer or colder than surface water exp. 852:33-34
    Why doesn't water from ocean fall as salty rain experiment 852:31-32
    Why is the ocean salty experiment 860:164-166; 1294:76-77
    Why ocean is not frozen at the Poles demonstration 1023:216-217

OCEAN ANIMALS
    Teaching activities about coral, crabs, fish, and jelly fish 1056:54-61
    Teaching activities about octopuses, sea horses, sea stars 1056:62-67
    Teaching activities about sharks, and whales 1056:68-71

OCEAN BOTTLES
    Drift bottle record charts 1000:46-48
    Drift bottle to launch, how to make 1000:41-43

OCEAN COLOR
    How color of water changes with amount of light 40:220-221
    How color of water changes with color of underwater surface 40:221
    How depth of water affects color 40:219-220
    Water color according to what is in it 40:218-219

OCEAN CURRENTS
    Chart of warm & cold currents 299:14
    Cold water is heavier than warm water experiment with colored water 1281:11
    Currents & salinity 93:37-38
    Currents & temperatures 93:34-36
    Currents & the Earth's rotation 93:39-40
    Earth's rotation effect on wind and water currents demonstration 1405:86
    How salinity affects ocean currents experiment 877:57-60
    How to send a message by sea experiment 877:110-114
    How water temperature affects ocean currents experiment 877:53-56
    Investigating longshore currents 41:93-94
    Investigating tides 41:109-123
    Salinity currents; experiment to demonstrate 840:18
    Send a message in a bottle 93:72-73
    Temperature currents; experiment to demonstrate 840:19
    What causes ocean currents experiment 877:61-66

OCEAN EVAPORATION
    Demonstrate evaporation process of 197:22-23

OCEAN FLOOR
    Make a profile of the ocean floor 93:74-75
    Model of ocean floor to map hills and valleys experiment 1290:54-55

OCEAN POLLUTION
    Teaching activities about ocean pollution in art, music and science 1056:74-79

OCEAN PRESERVATION
    Teaching activities about ocean preservation in art, music and science 1056:74-79

OCEAN SALINITY
    How salt gets from land into the ocean 40:217-218

How salty is the sea 41:153-162
Why is the ocean salty—experiment 672:22

OCEAN SEDIMENTS
Collecting sediments on the ocean floor 93:78-79

OCEAN SHORELINES. *See also* **SEASHORE; SHORE-LINES**
How sea changes sandy shore that has a steep slope experiment 1480:144
Longshore current or zigzag movement experiment with stream table demonstration 1480:147
Mapping the beach's profile 41:123-129
Model coastline; make to demonstrate gradual erosion of coastline experiment 1080:27
Shape of shorelines affects height of tides demonstration 1405:87
Studying the beach 41:130-152
Wave action and pebble distribution on beach experiment 1134:1.003

OCEAN TIDES. *See also* **TIDES**
How the Moon pulls water upward 40:223-224
Investigating tides 41:109-123

OCEAN WAVES. *See also* **WAVES**
Can ocean waves be used to generate electricity experiment 997:76-77
How ocean water rises to create storm surge experiment 1465:97
How to make waves 40:222
How wind produces water waves out at sea demonstration 1479:86
Investigating waves in the surf 41:95-103
Model shows how waves can be used to produce electricity experiment 1134:7.002
Motion of water waves demonstration 1479:87
Studying waves 41:83-93
Tsunami waves caused by ocean earthquake experiment 1441:45
Wave action and pebble distribution on beach experiment 1134:1.003
Wave refraction or curved shape of wave experiment 1480:145
Wave shapes demonstration 1290:4, 1.3

OCEAN WINDS
Breezes; cause of land and sea breezes demonstration 1023:132-133
Convection cycle of wind experiment 1447:58-60
Sea and land breezes caused by land or water heating up experiment 1020:53-57
Why winds always blow 41:144-152

OCEANOGRAPHY. *See* **DIVING BELLS; SEAWATER**

OCTOPUS
Felt toy, pattern, making 894:55-56
Octopus model toy—how to make (Primary) 467:22-23

ODORS. *See also* **SENSES—SMELL**
How air is cleaned by adsorbent chemicals experiment 1405:54
How fast do odors travel experiment 901:177
Identify objects by their odor 253:104-105
Identify odors activity 822:10-11
Molecules move to cause odors 382:139-140
Sun and air cause vanilla to lose its odor experiment 1250:86-88

OERSTED, HANS CHRISTIAN. *See also* **ELECTROMAGNETISM**
Electromagnetic field experiment 1133:5.007
His battery-powered compass—experiment 627:28-29

Oersted's discovery experiment; the link between electricity and magnetism 1514:72-74
Project 30—magnetism from electricity 654:71-72
Repeating Oersted's discovery—experiment 489:119-120
Who discovered and produced first aluminum project 1525:76-79

OERSTED'S DISCOVERY
Compass needle is deflected by magnetic field from electric current experiment 1309:24-25
Current in a wire deflects magnetism experiment 895:21-22
Do Oersted's experiment yourself 642:153-154
Electric current deflects compass needle experiment 1159:104-107
Electric current passing thru wire produces magnetism experiment 1473:34
Electricity and magnetism are related; how to show experiment 768:86-88
Electricity produces magnetism 281:91-92
How to make a simple galvonometer 63:58-61
Oersted discovered electric current can deflect a compass needle 209:20-27
Oersted's experiment 63:42-45
Oersted's famous experiment with electric current producing magnetism 1160:24
Spin the compass experiment 1309:24-25

OERSTED'S EXPERIMENT
Do Oersted's experiment using compass 599:44-45

OHM, GEORG
Checking Ohm's law experiment 627:45
Discovered resistance in electrical currents 209:47
Ohm's law 23:24-30
Ohm's Law experiment with current, voltage and resistance 1133:5.009
Who discovered laws of flow of electricity project 1525:95-97

OHM'S LAW
Discovering Ohm's law 577:project #44
Electroplating cell follows Ohm's Law experiment 1158:111-113
Ohm's Law experiment with current, voltage and resistance 1133:5.009
Variable resistors; make and compare amount of electricity passing thru 972:27

OIL
Build a pipeline to move oil or gas experiment 1027:39
Can oil help you see through paper experiment 1250:48-49
Dispersing oil experiment 741:31
How oil fields are formed experiment 1302:28
Hydrometer measures density of water and oil experiment, how to make 1521:26-27
Motor oils; higher weights of motor oil indicate more viscosity experiment 1396:114
Oil as lubricant experiment 1302:29
Oily pictures, how to make 1316:25
Temperature affects viscosity of oil experiment 1396:114
Temperature changes in water and cooking oil experiment 1515:65-69
Test for presence of unsaturated oil experiment 1396:37-42

OIL FIELDS
How oil fields are formed experiment 1302:28

OIL LAMP
How to make 320:25; 325:unpaged

279

Making a candle without wax 150:128-129

OIL POLLUTION. *See* **OIL SPILLS**

OIL RIGS
How to make 342:28-29
Tapping oil from beneath the sea, how it is done experiment 1027:33

OIL SLICKS
Effect of oil slicks on insects and ecosystems experiment 1096:64-68

OIL SPILLS. *See also* **POLLUTION—WATER**
Animal life harmed by oil spills experiment; remove oil from fur/cloth/feathers 1476:197-198
Breaking up oil spill using emulsifier experiment 1058:107
Can oil and water be easily mixed experiment recording sheet given 747:31-32
Can oil be soaked up from oil spills experiment 1325:70-74
Cleaning up an oil spill experiment 950:114-115; 1058:99
Containing oil spill and cleanup experiment; use fish tank and floating boom 1172:53-57
Determine effects of simulated oil spill on flora in aquatic environment 997:91-92
Different methods of cleaning oily feathers experiment 1134:6.012
Effect of oil spill on eggs experiment 1427:76-77
Effect of oil spill on feathers experiment 1427:78-79
Effect of oil spills on aquatic ecosystems experiment 978:76-77
Effect of oil spills on bird feathers experiment 1295:70-71
Effectiveness of techniques to get rid of oil floating on seawater experiment 1134:6.011
Effects of oil spills on zooplankton experiment 1058:92
How oil spills harm animals experiment 1324:73-77
Impact of oil spills on environment experiment using popcorn in stream or lake 1228:32-33
Oil and water won't mix experiment 1058:38
Oil damage to bird eggs experiment 1232:61
Oil slick prevents aquatic plants from process of photosynthesis experiment 1172:52
Oil slick, how to make and clean up experiment 1328:64-65
Oil spill clean up; find the best method experiment 840:98-99
Oil spill effect demonstration using oil based paints, water and paper 1310:12-13
Oil spill, how to keep from spreading experiment 1027:37
Oil spills affect marine life experiment 1290:5-6, 1.5
Oil spills are difficult to clean up experiment 1063:375
Oil spills are harmful to aquatic environments experiment 1453:32-34
Oil spills can destroy coral reefs experiment 1339:71-72
Oil spills effect on birds experiment 1337:72-73
Oil spills effect on shrimp experiment 1058:94-95
Plants damaged by oil spills experiment 1058:78-79
Pleasure boating activities contribute to water pollution experiment 969:110
Removing oil from water experiment 1290:4-5, 1.4
Seeing the colors of an oil spill 180:66
Shoreline damage from oil spill demonstration 1058:55
Simple experiment with cleaning an oily feather 1105:18
Surface tension or "clinginess" of oil experiment 1058:20
Temperature of water best for containing oil spill experiment 1058:53
Using bacteria to clean up oil spills on beaches experiment 1450:42-48
Why spilled oil is difficult to remove from water experiment 1013:97

OILS AND FATS. *See* **FATS AND OILS**

OLD GROWTH FOREST—NORTHWEST, PACIFIC
Ancient forest structure layers, how to draw project 1336:64
Food web in ancient forests project, how to do 1336:64
Ideas to help save the ancient forests 1336:62-63
Log investigation; identify insects, animals and soil project 1336:64
What soil is made of and what animals live in soil experiment 1336:65

ONIONS
The invisible world of the onion under a microscope 400:6
Why do onions make you cry experiment 1484:28
Why onion juice causes tears 721:117
Why onions make your eye water experiment 980:67

OPERANT CONDITIONING
Determine time it takes person to trace mirror image of pattern experiment 1395:183-188

OPTICAL BENCH
Optical bench 9:62-63

OPTICAL DENSITY
Shown using balloons 92:48-49

OPTICAL FIBERS. *See also* **FIBER OPTICS**
Communicate with person who is on opposite side of house project 1458:39
Glancing rays of light experiment using beam tank, how to build 1092:20
Liquid light experiment to see how optical fibers work 1092:23

OPTICAL ILLUSIONS. *See also* **ILLUSIONS; MAGIC**
3-D illusions experiment 761:65-81
3-D reversal illusions experiment 761:75
A hole in the hand—experiment 563:33-34
A sausage from the fingers 563:140-141
Afterimages experiment 761:42-44
Ames window, make to show much of what we see happens in our mind experiment 1088:48-49
An illusion with mirrors 625:38
An illusion with weight on a string 563:146-147
Bent stick illusion 1253:9
Binocular vision illusions experiment 761:70-71
Bird in a cage illusion 941:42-44
Blind spots 736:13
Book of illusions for you to try & to demonstrate 229:1-142
Bouncing ring 736:11
Brain can be tricked—pictures 622:28-29
Brain judges how large something is according to how far away object is 1088:46
Brain sometimes makes you see things that aren't there experiment 1037:22
Brightness illusion; see gray where there is no gray experiment 1083:24-25
Broken pencil 736:19
Can you save the fish 901:7
Can you see with your eyes closed 653:12-13
Canary in a cage—demonstration 595:inside front cover
Candle burning under water illusion 941:35-40

Candle seems to burn in glass of water, how to do 1283:13
Circle illusions 736:75-76
Circles and angles 736:67-69
Coin in glass disappears 736:31
Color illusion 736:39-40
Colored bars 736:65
Come and go 736:96-98
Create an optical illusion 291:177
Curved illusion 736:60
Dancing spots 736:48-51
Dark and light 736:66
Demonstrate an optical illusion with lines on paper 1479:36
Demonstrate one pin & double pin 176:54
Disco illusion, making 911:39
Don't believe your own eyes 176:43-45
Drawing demonstrates persistence of vision 563:55-56
Drawing in front of mirror 845:3-6
Drawings to show 208:16-17
Exhibit of optical illusions project 532:84-85
Experiments to demonstrate 128:207-208
Experiments 366:205-209; 386:87-90
Eye speed 366:206-208
Eye tricks 684:6-7
Face appears on pumpkin 293:27
False images & brain teasers 76:32-33
Familiar illusions 1005:16-17
Famous line illusions 761:52-56
Fish in a bowl illusion, how to make 1417:19
Flip books—making 736:88-95
Floating finger illusion 941:31-32
Floating finger 736:8-9
Floating sausage illusion 1253:9
Focal length and color experiment 761:44-45
Fool your eyes illusions 1287:23
Fool your eyes 95:54-55; 659:22-23; 909:150-151
Gray ring of paper on black and white paper illusion 1159:54-55
Growing new fingers 736:12
Hidden colors illusion 653:10-11
Hole in your hand 366:208; 736:14-15
Hole in your hand (Primary) 558:100-101
Hole in your hand and finger sausage illusions 1369:40-41
Hole in your hand illusion 941:33-34; 1005:24
How big is small illusion 653:42-43
How many boxes illusion 653:18
How many do you see illusion 653:45
Ideas for and activities with optical illusions 927:11-86
Illusion circles—how to make 558:112-113
Illusion pictures to use for demonstrations 1299:14-15
Illusions in the natural world experiments 761:82-103
Illusions of color and contrast experiments 761:21-47
Illusions with lines experiments 761:48-64
Illusions with pencils 558:114-115
Inexplicable arches 16:85-88
Inside of outside the box illusion 653:19
Investigation into optical illusions 420:71-73
Is seeing believing 280:63
Jumping finger 736:10
Kanizsa triangle illusion experiment 761:59-63
Lines and lines 736:17
Lines on chalkboard demonstrate optical illusion 882:34
Look through tube, hole appears in other hand 845:15-16

Looks can be deceiving—experiment 586:109-111
Mach bands demonstration 563:149
Mach bands illusions 761:29
Magic candles—light one, both seem to be burning 558:111
Magic tricks 35:74-75
Make a full Moon shrink 228:21
Make Mr. Wink 176:47
Make simple optical illusions in geometrical figures 291:233
Make your own optical illusions 595:44-45
Making moving pictures to demonstrate illusions 956:41
Mason disk for record players creates colors—how to make 558:108-109
Mind is confused over size and distance of Moon horizon illusion experiment 1062:22-23
Mirages and where to look for them 761:86-89
Moon illusion experiment 761:95-99
Moon mirage 366:206
Motion and illusions experiment 761:75-81
Move cardboard just by staring at it experiment 1083:23
Movie wheel with pictures from photocopy of movie wheels, how to make 1088:56
Moving line illusions experiment 761:58-59
Moving spirals experiment 1112:29
Moving wagon wheel illusion, how to make 1479:37
Muller-Lyer's mystery arrows experiment 911:30-31
Narrow slit gives full view 736:28
Necker cube illusions experiment 761:49-51
Optical illusion—experiment 563:43
Optical illusion letters, how to make 1245:14-15
Optical illusions to test yourself 1283:8
Optical illusions 114:22-30
Optical illusions 35:66-67; 114:22-30; ; 399:60
Opticklers 400:45
Pendulum movement illusion viewed through darkened glasses experiment 1020:22-24
Pendulum of magic using cellophane, frame and picture 558:102-103
Pepper's ghost made from cardboard box, lamp, and small figurines 1245:16-17
Persistence of vision illusions experiment 761:71-73
Perspective and illusions experiment 761:67-70
Picture cards twirled on rubber bands 845:20-21
Ping! Or solid through solid 16:89-91
Pinwheel afterimages—making 736:22-24
Pulfrich illusions 16:92-95
Pulfrich pendulum experiment 761:78-81
Pulfrich's illusions experiment 1133:6.013
'Rubber pencil' 16:82-94
Sausage between fingers 845:17
Schroder staircase illusion—experiment 563:56
Science and magician illusions experiment 761:104-117
See—all cat's eyes making 669:36-37
See through grid 736:29-30
Seeing spots at intersections and irradiation experiment 761:41-42
Several experiments & explanations 258:1-78
Shadow technique for writing words 472:2237
Simple optical illusions 1002:21-25
Size of objects and illusions experiment 1062:22-23
Spinner picture illusions 736:79-85
Spinner scope, making 779:56
Spinning cardboard shapes 845:22-24
Spinning circle illusion experiment 1405:43

Spinning colors 736:41-44
Spinning disc making 736:25-27
Spinning discs experiment 1112:28-29
Spinning wheels illusion 653:38-39
Spokes that aren't there 736:72-74
Square and not square 736:61
Stopping motion experiment make stroboscope 761:73-75
Stopping motion experiment make stroboscope 761:73-75
Straight lines appear to be circles on spinner—how to make 721:4
Strange motion with disc 736:33-34
Taste illusions experiments 761:101-103
Temperature illusions experiment 761:100
Tenpenny ghost illusion, making 911:39
Thaumatrope—how to make 558:118-119
The phantom floating sausage 625:34
The secret word illusion 653:46-47
Three arrows 736:18
Touch and temperature illusions experiment 761:101
Traveling rectangle 736:16
Tricky illusions 736:120-127
Tricky mirror 736:52-53
Turntable illusions, how to make 1289:20-21
TV turned into stroboscope, how to do 1289:40-41
Two faced 736:20
Upside-downer viewer—how to make 653:16-17
Vertical distances and horizontal distances; which is longer experiment 1159:53-54
Watch the birdie illusion 653:24-25
Waterfall effect illusion experiment 1132:93-1-93-2
Weight illusions experiment 761:99-100
Well known optical illusions to try 872:54-55
Where are all the illusions experiment in the eye or in the brain 761:57-58
Which is bigger—experiment 653:4-7
Which is the picture 653:8-9
Which pup is bigger illusion 653:44
Which way—right or left illusion 653:40-41
Young girl or old woman—duck or rabbit illusion 653:34-35

OPTICAL ILLUSIONS—SHOW
It's an illusion! 142:30-31
OPTICAL ILLUSIONS—TRICKS
Corinth Canal 27:78
Impossible fork 27:79
Long and short of it 27:73
Magic boomerang 27:74-76
Magic box 27:76-78
Magic hexagon 27:76
Magic pile of boxes 27:81
Magic staircase 27:80
Tunnel flip flop 27:72-73
OPTICAL PROJECTIONS
How to make a projector for colored pictures 128:204-205
How to make a projector for film slides & strips 128:204
How to make a simple microprojector 128:205
OPTICAL ROTATION
Optical activity and chirality; polarimeter identifies substance experiment 1004:4.014
OPTICAL TOYS—HOW TO MAKE
Camera obscurer 172:20-26
Diorama 172:45-47

Kaleidoscope 172:29-31
Pepper's ghost 172:26-29
Periscope 172:17-20
Phenakistoscope 172:38-41
Praxinoscope 172:44-45
Stereoscope 172:31-36
Thaumatrope 172:36-38
Zoetrope 172:41-44
OPTICS. *See also* **OPTICAL ILLUSIONS**
Anatomy of a shadow experiment 1082:10-14
Binocular vision demonstration 1007:26-27
Blind spot 350:129-130
Brick, how to see through 350:136-137
Color disc 350:127-128
Color illusions/discs—how to make 577:project 72
Decapitated princess illusion 350:137-140
Double shadows experiment 1082:16
Increasing magnification can compound or increase distortion experiment 1062:26-27
Inverse square law—how to demonstrate 577:project 74
Invisible coin trick 350:124-125
Light reflects through transparent materials such as glass or water experiment 1132:33-1-33-2
Magic box gives different images—how to make 577:project 75
Magic mirror 350:133-134
Magnifying mirror system—how to make 577:project 79
Newton's rings experiment 1133:6.008
Optical micrometer—making 762:22-23
Periscope 350:135
Pinhole images, how to make using box, lighted bulb, black paper experiment 1153:50-52
Prism rainbow 350:126
Projecting wave images in a ripple tank—how to do 577:project 77
Pulfrich's illusions experiment 1133:6.013
Ripple tank demonstrates wave patterns 577:project 76
Seebackascope 350:134-135
Simulated laser, how to build 1249:40-46
Stroboscopic motion-how to make stroboscope to demonstrate 577:project 73
Thaumatrope 350:128-129
Translucency of piece of paper changes experiment 1082:20-22
Water mirror 350:131
OPTICS—FIBER. *See* **FIBER OPTICS; OPTICAL FIBERS**
OPTICS—MIRRORS
Corner reflector demonstration of geometrical optics 563:145
ORANGES. *See also* **SEEDS—FRUIT**
Christmas orange, fruit dish, marmalade, how to make 231:112-113
Citrus tricks 231:110-111
Orange tree, how to grow 899:138-139
ORBITER SPACE SCHUTTLE. *See also* **SPACE SHUTTLE**
Orbiter paper model, making and flying 314:77-82
ORBITS
Elliptical orbits—demonstration 577:project #33
ORES
Froth flotation to concentrate valuable minerals experiment 1266:49
Leaching minerals from rocks experiment 1266:49

ORGANIC COMPOUNDS
Make a molecular model of ethanol 6:32
Make your own plastic 6:34
Testing organic compounds—carbon dioxide turns lime-
water milky—experiment 6:30
ORGANIC PRODUCE
Insect damage differs when produce grown organically
or with pesticides 1096:133-138
ORGANIC WASTE. *See also* **COMPOST;**
EARTHWORMS
Organic matter decay experiment 950:11
Plant materials changed into methane fuel experiment
1323:90-94
Set up worm compost system 276:1-90
What happens to pile of freshly cut grass clippings ex-
periment 1323:79-84
ORGANISMS—CONTROL
Can organism population be controlled 402:91-92
ORGANISMS—GAME
Living game 400:123
ORGANISMS AS MINERS
Can plants and animals concentrate certain chemical ele-
ments 402:80-81
ORIENTEERING
Game to understand maps, how to do 890:114-117
Orienteering route and science activities on route, how to
set up 1063:152-153
ORIGIN OF THE SPECIES ACTIVITY
Project 400:34
ORION. *See also* **CONSTELLATIONS**
How to find Orion in the sky 1434:77-78
ORPHANS
Baby bird formula, recipe 778:83
Orphaned wildlife—how to feed 442:unpaged
ORRERY. *See also* **PLANETARIUM**
Boyle's orrery model experiment, shows speed of Earth,
Moon, Sun orbits 1476:162-165
Make your own orrery—shows how planets move in
their orbits—how to make 502:28-29
Orrery demonstrates movement of Earth, Sun and Moon,
how to make 1480:14-15
ORTHO COPTER
How to make 172:69-71
OSCILLATOR
Morse code oscillator, how to make 860:101-105
Operate with your tongue 291:240-241
Oscillator—building one experiment 591:43-45
Oscillator; how do circuits cause lights to flash experi-
ment 1293:27-29
OSCILLOGRAPH
How to make 356:60-61; 558:86-87
OSMOMETER
How to make 128:41-42; 577:project #27
OSMOSIS
Apparatus for showing osmosis experiment 1425:19-20
Balloon and vanilla in box experiment 904:8-9
Bouncing peas 77:11
Can molecules move through a membrane experiment
831:81-83
Carrot and straw demonstrate osmosis in plants experi-
ment 784:94-95
Celery stalk and food coloring in water demonstrate
913:26
Celery stalk in red food coloring experiment 1238:31-32

Cell homeostasis experiment 1395:39-43
Cells dehydrate when placed into hypertonic solutions ex-
periment 1395:42
Cells placed in hypotonic and hypertonic solutions affect
osmosis experiment 1395:39-43
Cells; movement of particles through a membrane experi-
ment 904:144-145
Demonstrate diffusion and osmosis with balloon and va-
nilla 1405:24
Demonstrate how water rises in plants 293:19
Demonstrate marvel of osmosis 176:97-98
Demonstrate with beans 291:200
Demonstrate with eggs 146:33
Demonstrate with potatoes 146:32-33
Effect of osmosis on a raisin experiment 1405:24
Effect of osmosis on potato using salt and sugar solutions
experiment data tab 1004:2.015
Effect of osmosis on raisins experiment 904:12-13
Egg; vinegar in water passes through cell membrane of
egg experiment 1479:35
Eggs; shrinking egg in corn syrup experiment as egg
changes in size and shape 1479:35
Experiment using salt and sugar 129:30-32
How osmosis works in fish experiment 1492:62-63
How plants get water 72:38-39
Hugo de Vries's plasmolysis in plant cells experiment
1133:3.010
Make a crystal garden 86:31
Materials dissolved in water move through egg mem-
brane experiment 1403:39
Membrane—another way of observing osmosis 319:54-
55
Membranes—how you can observe osmosis 319:53-54
Osmometer—how to make 577:project #27
Osmosis—experiment 585:24
Osmosis experiment with potatoes 1238:44-45
Osmosis experiment with vegetables 585:152
Osmosis in potatoes and imbibition of water in lima bean
seeds experiment 1004:2.014
Osmosis with a carrot or egg experiment 382:41-45
Pickles—making to demonstrate osmosis 563:153-154
Plants drink too—osmosis and transpiration—experi-
ment 573:16
Potato slices in fresh and salt water demonstrate osmosis
904:10-11
Potatoes as models of cell membranes demonstrate osmo-
sis experiment 1069:17
Raw and cooked potato demonstrate osmosis 721:102
Raw egg in vinegar experiment; data table given
871:2.018
Root pressure transports water in plant experiment; ma-
nometer measures 1061:104-105
Show osmosis in salt water experiment 741:33
Sodium ions increase effect on extracellular fluids experi-
ment 1396:52
Splitting stalks of rhubarb—experiment 585:153-154
The egg trick to show 291:201
The swollen egg—experiments with egg and vinegar
563:164
Water enters plant thru roots by osmosis experiment
978:56-58
Water molecules can move through membrane of raw
egg experiment 1403:36-39
Water passes thru walls of potato by osmosis experiment
1214:9

OSMOSIS—PLANTS. *See also* **PLANTS—OSMOSIS**
Raw and cooked potato experiment 360:46
Raw vegetable salad—how plants take in water 74:89-92
Striped celery snack—how water moves up stems 74:92-93
Using potatoes 146:33
What is process of osmosis 402:16-17

OSTRACODS
Ostracods, the seed shrimp, collect and observe 771:198-201
Seed shrimp, how to collect and care for 500:110-111

OUIJA BOARD
Ouija board—experiment 563:42-43

OUTDOORS
Investigations of life in fields, ponds and forests 166:entire book

OUTER SPACE
Create your own star world 632:1-71

OUTER SPACE—EXPLORATION. *See* **SPACE SCIENCE; SPACE TRAVEL**

OVALS
Circles and ovals, how to draw 1248:36-37

OVENS. *See* **DRYING AND STERILIZING OVEN**

OVERPOPULATION. *See* **POPULATION**

OWL HOUSE
Log sided owl house—how to make 442:unpaged

OWL PELLETS
Dissecting owl pellet experiment 1505:21
Dissecting owl pellets, how to do 778:47; 1069:134-135
How to examine owl pellets 1168:59
Identify bones in 375:46
Owls interact with environment to obtain food to live; owl pellet experiment 1427:26-29

OWLS
Game; hungry owls survival game, how to make 1180:11; 1183:139

OXIDATION. *See also* **COMBUSTION; RUST**
A secret until you hear it 280:38
Acidity affects rusting rate of iron experiment 1526:101
Apple and lemon demonstrate [Primary] 759:50
Apple does a slow burn 400:71
Bleach on steel wool pads shows release of oxygen 203:45
Browning of apples; what affects browning of apples experiment 1020:105-108
Coating solutions stop rust on iron materials above and below ground experiment 969:75-76
Experimenting with oxidation 180:18
Fading effect of sunlight on fabric samples experiment 1396:108-109
Fruity oxidation 112:13
How does oxygen in the air affect foods 537:9-11
How to prevent rust—experiment 598:38-39
Iron atoms and oxygen atoms combine to form iron oxide experiment 1396:162
Iron rusts faster when wet experiment 1396:162
Lavoisier's oxidation experiments 1156:97-103
Making slim-slice potato cake; worksheet and recipe 537:56
Oxidation and the corrosion of iron—experiment 586:66-67
Oxidation of zinc experiment create Faraday's philosophic wool 752:94-95

Oxidize iron experiment with steel wool and candle 563:177-178
Produces heat 55:67-72
Replacing metals—experiment 180:19
Rusting metals—experiment 180:19
Rusting of iron in steel wool pad experiment 1396:21-22
Rusting uses oxygen experiment 1212:13
Staples in three solutions show rusting experiment 721:121
Steel wool rusts faster when bleach is added to water and vinegar experiment 814:55-57
Using candles 146:48-49
Using steel wool and water 146:24
Vitamin C fruit salad—oxidation of fruit 74:81-83
Watching air discolor fresh fruit—recipe 537:57
What stops oxidation in fruits and vegetables experiment 885:88
Why do apples turn brown experiment 1508:17
Why does metal rust experiment 1294:45-46
Write with invisible ink, how to make experiment 937:66-67

OXYGEN. *See also* **ELECTROLYSIS; WATER—ELECTROLYSIS**
Air; what fraction of air is oxygen experiment with rusting steel wool 1516:22-25
Amount of oxygen in air; how to determine experiment 978:169-170
An oxygen fire experiment 293:45
"Bad breath" experiment with jar, candle and breath from lungs 563:161-162
Bleach and baking soda make oxygen experiment 723:197
Bleaching with oxygen 85:24-25
Burning candle, oxygen use and water levels in tubes experiment 1526:108-113
Burning candles need oxygen in air to keep burning experiment 1526:102-104
Burning consumes oxygen experiment 1396:19-21
Burning takes oxygen from the air experiment 705:20
Candle test for amount in air 679:26
Candle that lifts water—oxygen is consumed when a fire burns 576:70-71
Carbon dioxide extinguisher from baking soda and vinegar experiment 1073:87
Collecting from electrolysis 346:61-67
Collecting oxygen gas from 'burning' steel 346:70-71
Demonstrate proportion of oxygen to other gases in air 472:2236
Dissolved oxygen content of body of water; how to measure experiment 978:69-70
Do plants really make oxygen 283:11-26
Does all air burn experiment using candle in dish of water 1073:86
Easy oxygen experiments produce oxygen 563:166
Effect of oxygen on combustion experiment 752:117-118
Effect of oxygen on darkening of fruit experiment 905:80-81
Fire needs oxygen to burn 44:96-97
Fire needs air to burn (Primary) 326:24-25
Fire needs air to burn experiment with candle 1196:29
Fire needs oxygen—the disappearing flame 249:8
Fire needs oxygen to burn experiment 671:13; 1028:9; 1028:33; 1162:7; 1332:6-7
Fire needs oxygen to burn experiment using candle in covered jar 1435:113-114

Fire needs oxygen to burn experiment using candle, jar and dish of water 1212:11

Fire needs oxygen to burn experiment with candle 1255:22

Fire needs oxygen to burn experiment with candle and jar 1219:43; 1322:15-16

Fire needs oxygen to burn experiment with candle, vinegar and baking soda 1032:20-21

Flame from bubbling oxygen from hydrogen peroxide and meat experiment 1083:86

From plants and earth 97:28-29

Frothy fun test for oxygen 146:25

Gas collected from underwater plants is oxygen experiment 1069:40-41

Generate oxygen chemically experiment 752:108

Getting oxygen out of compounds 85:18-19

Green plants give off oxygen 273:18-23

Green plants make oxygen gas experiment 1324:42-47

Green plants make oxygen; pond plant in jar experiment 790:12-13

Green plants produce oxygen experiment 1174:16-19

How is oxygen involved with life 402:15-16

How much of air is oxygen experiment 1159:26-27

How much of air is oxygen; rusting steel wool experiment 1020:90-92

How much oxygen in the air 360:30

How much oxygen is in the air experiment 1322:13-16

How much oxygen is there in air—experiment 586:58-59

How to make 97:20-21

Hydrogen peroxide changes into water and oxygen experiment 1405:56

In candle 382:158-164

Joseph Priestley's dephlogisticated air oxygen experiment 1133:2.006

Lavoisier; who first discovered oxygen is necessary for fire project 1525:67-69

Leaves carrying out photosynthesis give off oxygen gas experiment 1069:40-41

Leaves give off oxygen experiment 1183:28

Leaves of plants give off oxygen experiment 1181:20

Make oxygen experiment using flashlight battery and hydrogen peroxide 1435:104-106

Makes fire burn 382:161-164

Making 146:34-35

Making and burning 146:25

Making and testing oxygen experiment 1526:116-120

Making, using yeast and hydrogen peroxide 146:26-27

Measure, proportion of in air 319:30-31

Measuring oxygen content of air experiment 933:8-9

Measuring oxygen released by plant leaves during photosynthesis experiment 1061:28-29

Needed to burn steel 360:6

Oxygen and air—using a candle 84:61

Oxygen as by-product of photosynthesis experiment 1060:28-30

Oxygen combines with iron and forms rust experiment 705:21

Oxygen content in the air experiment using steel wool 1003:47

Oxygen content of air measured by rusting steel wool experiment 1447:71-73

Oxygen effect on darkening of fruit experiment 1405:53

Oxygen experiment using candles, glass and jar 563:176-177

Oxygen from green plants useful to fish experiment 1060:28-30

Oxygen from plants 30:41

Oxygen from rusty nails experiment 735:29

Oxygen gas bubbles collect in jar over plant in water experiment 1271:23

Oxygen gas from aquarium plants, how to collect 930:7

Oxygen gas from green water plants 472:2220

Oxygen given off by plants during photosynthesis experiment 1214:14

Oxygen in air burns; other gases in air do not burn experiment 1073:86

Oxygen in air demonstration using lit candle under glass 1179:119

Oxygen in air in proportion to other gases experiment with candle/water in jar 1244:21

Oxygen magic—ink color removed by bleach 146:25

Oxygen needed for fire to burn experiment using candle and different snuffers 1073:86

Oxygen needed for fire to burn; candle under glass experiment 976:34

Oxygen needed to keep fire burning experiment with candle and plant 978:121

Oxygen production affected by amount of light during photosynthesis experiment 1060:28-30

Oxygen released when plants start to photosynthesize experiment 1146:9

Photosynthesis—measure photosynthesis rate by measuring production 398:47-49

Photosynthesis—show oxygen is a by product of photosynthesis 294:40-41

Photosynthesis and oxygen production experiment 878:30-31

Plant bubbles oxygen experiment 1028:62

Plants breathe oxygen out through their leaves experiment 1371:71

Plants produce oxygen during photosynthesis experiment 978:52

Plants produce oxygen experiment 1396:161-163

Pollution and oxygen consumption of small animals 334:39-42

Prepare oxygen—experiment 585:85-86

Produce oxygen and test for presence of oxygen gas experiment 1396:159-164

Producing oxygen—experiment 180:17

Production rate of oxygen from plants during photosynthesis; how to measure 1060:28-30

Proportion of oxygen in air experiment with candle under jar 1474:18

Rate of photosynthesis affected by amount of carbon dioxide experiment 1060:23-25

Reaction of burning candle and air experiment with tubes in pan of water 1526:108-113

Replacing in a space craft (Advanced) 668:50-52

Rust uses up oxygen 360:66

Rusting iron from steel wool in water produces oxygen gas experiment 1435:107-109

Show rust is compound of iron, oxygen and water 146:24-25

Show that fires need air 319:65-66

Steel wool and water—experiment 676:35

Takes up space—putting an egg in a bottle 293:44

Testing for oxygen manufactured by plants 574:34

Testing for oxygen production in plants project 833:123-125

Water plants give off oxygen experiment 796:14

Water plants make oxygen; collect gas in test tube experiment 1246:16

What fraction of air is oxygen experiment with steel wool in water 1526:105-107

Where does oxygen come from experiment 909:85

Working with oxygen—make oxygen and test for it 30:40

OXYGEN—CARBON DIOXIDE CYCLE

Cycle; demonstrate using sealed aquarium and fish experiment 978:88

Do plants breathe 273:18-23

Experiment 268:101-105

Fish benefit from green plants in water experiment 1060:108

Plants benefit from fish in water experiment 1060:108

Plants need carbon dioxide to produce oxygen thru photosynthesis experiment 1173:46-47

OYSTERS

Oyster and pearl—examining 294:63

OZONE

Make and smell ozone experiment 1322:69-72

Thermal inversion effect on air pollution experiment 1322:55-59

OZONE LAYER. *See also* **GREENHOUSE EFFECT**

Chemicals travel through the air experiment using perfume and balloon 1228:24-25

Skin protection needed from rays of sun experiment using newspapers/cellophane 1228:22-23

Using computer modeling software to analyze UV exposure experiment 1450:49-57

P

PACE. *See* DISTANCE

PACKAGING

Graph containers and packaging used by family for one week 1013:29

Packaging costs and size of consumer goods experiment 1150:62-64

Packaging scavenger hunt; chart given to record numbers of product wraps 1013:27

Ways to reduce packaging of consumer goods experiment 1150:64-65

PADDLE WHEEL BOAT

How to make 54:67

Paddlewheel boat made from plastic bottle, sticks and clay, how to do 1310:28-29

Rudder changes direction of paddleboat, how to make 1310:30-31

PAIN

A pinch for pain—experiment 563:61-63

What is pain 402:63

PAINTING

Action painting 356:24-25

PAINTS

Air needed for paint to harden experiment 1251:65-67

Different paints are equally as good on a piece of wood project 1210:60-61

Drying oils—are they drying, semi-drying or non-drying experiment 17:25-27

Lampblack from a lot of carbon—make flat black paint 585:88

Making pigments and oil paints 116:172-174

Mix your own paints from homemade paint binders and pigments—how to do 17:28-30

Paint films—experiment to explore different kinds of paint films 17:22-25

Pigments—grind your own pigments 17:27-28

PANTOGRAPH

Cardboard pantograph, making 999:63-66

Copy drawings—how to make 472:1894; 507:1894

How to make pantograph from yardstick 808:97-101

Pantograph drawing machine with linked levers, how to make 1446:10-11

Pantograph drawing machine, making 870:68-70

Pantograph is compound machine made up of levers; how does it work experiment 1400:76-79

Trick drawing and writing with a pantograph—how to make 625:8-9

PAPAYA SEEDS

How to grow 272:17-22

PAPER

A paper extinguisher for a paper fire 550:110-111

A paper pot to boil water 550:106-109

Absorbency; which materials soak up water the fastest experiment 1509:8

Aging paper, how to do 1295:108

Annual tree growth needed to make one ton of paper 363:124-125

Antiaging formula to preserve paper experiment 1083:53

Blender paper, how to make 859:15

Boil water in a paper pot 142:47

Boiling water in a paper cup 291:52-53

Broccoli paper, how to make pulp and screened frames 1330:50-51

Different types and structures of paper examined under microscope experiment 1295:105-108

Does recycled paper decompose faster than manufactured paper project 969:56

How strong can paper get experiment 827:27

How strong is wet paper compared to dry paper (Primary) 69:40

How to make paper from shredded paper project 1296:1994

Investigating papers; test paper samples experiment 1268:26-27

Light and chemistry produce outlines in sunlight—experiment 563:171

Make paper—how to 748:94

Make paper from old newspapers, how to do 1183:123

Make paper from recycled paper experiment 1148:28-29

Make your own from colored toilet paper 795:13-14

Make your own paper, how to do 1064:26-27; 1368:19-21

Making nettle paper 598:35-36

Making paper 550:12-33

Making paper—steps 550:19-33

Making paper from newspapers, how to do 1142:45; 1184:35

Making paper from scrap paper, how to do 854:118-119

Making pulp by recycling paper, how to do 1268:12-13

Making your own paper, how to do 1295:109-112

Marbelized paper—how to make 558:138-139; 733:14; 835:68-70; 1115:88-89

Marbled paper made using paints on water 1247:10-11

New paper from old newspaper, how to make 983:15; 1063:380-381; 1105:6; 1323:67-71; 1371:75-77; 1427:92-93

New paper from waste paper, how to make 1134:7.006

Newspaper dowels for construction—how to make 631:67

Paper bridge—making (Primary) 70:20-21

Paper experiments 105:10-59

Paper from cabbage leaves, how to make 1244:30-31

Paper impossibilities—what you can't do with paper 550:8-11

Paper logs for construction—how to make 631:66

Paper made from grass clippings, how to do 887:76-78

Paper recycled to make new paper experiment 1150:32-33

Paper under a hand lens 29:12-13

Paper worm absorbs water, moves and wiggles 288:22-23

Paper, recycle your own, how to do 1012:102-103

Papermaking; how to make paper 1268:10-17

Papermaking; making a mold from wood, how to do 1268:10-11

Papermaking; making colored and textured papers, how to do 1268:20-21

Papermaking; making paper from plants, how to do 1268:18-19

Powerful paper holds your weight 95:7

Primary science tricks with paper 69:14-45

Puzzles—quarter through the hole 550:115-116

Puzzles—your head through a hole 550:116-118

Rapid aging of a newspaper experiment 1405:53

Recycle your own paper project 1223:29

Recycled paper, making 866:150-151

Recycling paper—how to do 363:123-124; 371:88-91

Recycling paper, how to do using old newspapers experiment 1508:7

Reuse newspaper; making paper project 900:191

Scratch-and-sniff paper, how to make 1228:62-63

Show paper is stored sunshine, a spring, a trap, a pump, a support 91:93-103

Squeeze your body through a piece of paper experiment 937:14-15

Strength test of different kinds of paper experiment 1508:8

Strong paper holds your weight experiment 721:78

Structural strength of paper bridges experiment 829:29-30

Tensile strength of paper measured experiment 1157:76-78

Test different types of paper for tearing, writing and absorbency experiment 1063:318

Test for starch in paper experiment using iodine as indicator 1435:33-34

Test water absorption rate of different papers 336:18

Tissue paper strength test experiment 1508:9

Towels—which brand of paper towels is most absorbent or the strongest—test 538:126

Towels; space between fibers and speed of water travel thru it experiment 984:59-61

Tracing paper—make 563:159-160

Trick—paper card cut so person can step through it 563:36

Trick—pepper trick—experiment 563:32-33

Wall coverings; is plastic or paper best for wall covering experiment 1508:13

Waste paper can be recycled experiment; how to make pulp and new paper 1173:60-61

What makes corrugated box strong experiment 827:26

Yellowing process of paper, how to slow it down experiment 1295:107

PAPER—ABSORPTION
Capillary action—a capillary contest with paper 550:37-38

Capillary action—making water climb a hill—a water ladder of paper 550:35-37

Chromatography—strip chromatography—experiment 550:43-44

Chromatography—water chromatography—experiment 550:45-48

Circle chromatography—experiment 550:46-48

Water through paper—filter papers—experiment to test 550:48-53

PAPER—ENGINEERING
Balance a paper 550:60-62

Destructive testing of folded sheets of paper 550:62-65

Model arch bridge 550:74

Model beam bridge 550:72-73

Model pier bridge 550:75-76

Paper bridge to test flexure 550:70-72

Table with paper legs 550:66-68

The shapes in building—making model beams for structural strength 550:68-69

PAPER—HOT AND COLD
Papers on the snow 550:102-105

So there's no snow 550:105-106

PAPER—MATH MAGIC. *See also* **MAGIC**
How to mail ten letters in nine envelopes 550:78-80

Mathematical progression—double trouble—you can't cut this project in half 550:83-85

The wonderful vanishing line 550:80-82

Trick—two fishermen and five fish 550:85-91

Trick—why I can't go to school 550:94-96

Trick—your friend's age 550:91-94

PAPER—TOPOLOGY
Famous Mobius strip 550:111-115

PAPER CHROMATOGRAPHY. *See also* **CHROMATOGRAPHY**
Separate colored dyes in marking pens experiment data tables given 1004:4.003

PAPER CUTTING TRICKS. *See also* **MAGIC**
Hex and double hex 27:61-64

Magic paper doorway 27:55-57

Magic star 27:53-55

Monster doll 27:58-60

Paper cutting tricks 392:106-112

Paper helicopter 27:57-58

PAPER DOLLS
Paper dolls—dancing 350:112-113

PAPER FOLDING GEOMETRY
Basic concepts of triangles (Primary) 503:1-33

Right angles, paper folding geometry 504:1-33

PAPER MAKING
Dip hand mold—making 316:96-101

Hand mold—how to build mold, deckle and sieve 316:32-39

Homemade paper, how to make 924:112-113

Make a mold, make pulp, make a sheet of paper 231:88

Making paper on cloth 316:63-65

Oiled paper—how to make 322:30-31

Paper—how to make 316:5-11, 21-23; 382:147-152; 733:10

Paper from rags—making 26:125-129

Paper from short knit fibers—making 257:30-32

Paper press—how to make 316:91-95

Plant paper—how to make 264:46

Rag paper—how to make 336:11-12

Rag paper—making 321:19

Recycled paper—how to make 336:6-9

Recycling—make new paper from old 316:56-62

Sheet—dipping a sheet 316:101-105

Sheet—double couching Japanese paper—how to make 316:72-75

Sheet—drying by board, press 316:87-95

Sheet—ferns, leaves, etc. Or words inside the sheet—double couching 316:68-72

Sheet—make colorful pretty sheet with threads 316:65-66

Sheet—make surface transplant with favorite comic strip 316:66-68

Sheet—sizing with aerosol spray, gelatin, liquid starch 316:81-85

Sheet—watermarks—how to make 316:75-77

Sheet dyeing—with food colors, acrylics and fabric dyes 316:78-81

Sheet of paper—making 316:40-55

PAPER PUZZLERS
Rubic's Cube and tangram puzzle—answer 399:52

Rubic's Cube and tangram puzzle 399:44-45

PAPER TOWELS
Amount of water absorbed by different brands of paper towels experiment 1158:146-151

Paper towels; which is the "quickest picker-upper" project 1210:41-42

Water absorption of paper towels experiment 829:43-44

Which brand of paper towel is the most absorbent experiment 1064:73

PAPER TRICKS
Paper stretcher 27:100-101
Very tight squeeze—pass your body thru hole in paper 399:17

PAPIER MACHE
How to make 795:13

PARACHUTES
Air pushes up against things; parachute experiment 995:16-17

Better parachute using plastic bag—making 721:110

Canopies of parachutes in different shapes experiment 1110:7-9

Canopy fabric and load carried affect rate of descent experiment data table 1004:5.007

Experiments with toy parachutes 806:28-30

How a parachute works activities [Primary] 759:60

How a parachute works demonstration 1479:105

Make and fly parachute experiment 940:122-125

Make parachute and experiment with its characteristics 1063:472

Making and trying to improve efficiency experiment 760:54-55

Materials; which material is best for a parachute experiment 1507:9

Model parachute demonstrates air resistance 472:2233

Model parachute, how to build 888:135-137

Model parachutes, how to make from paper, thread and clothes pin 1095:46

Paper doll parachutist, making 779:41

Paper parachutes experiment; which shape and weight works best 1373:11

Papier mache paratrooper, how to make 835:76-78

Parachute—making 32:52-53; 111:18-19; 112:40-41; 172:79; 366:163; 400:98; 450:14-15; 625:45; 733:33; 861:187-192; 1299:46

Parachute—theory of demonstrated with paper and corks 450:12-13

Parachute drop demonstrates air has weight and takes up space 1014:123

Parachute experiment 563:126

Parachute from nylon scarf and string, how to make 1247:24

Parachute from plastic bag, string and small toy demonstrates gravity experiment 1073:9

Parachute from tissue paper, how to make 1255:11

Parachute game—making 232:49

Parachute helps overcome force of gravity experiment 1073:9

Parachute made from paper, cloth or plastic, how to do 1376:14

Parachute tests 660:26; 909:74

Parachutist to go with hot air balloon—making 172:78-80

Pint sized parachutes—how to make 494:77

Plastic garbage bag parachute, how to make 1127:16

Plastic parachute, how to make 1161:14

Plastic parachute, how to make to demonstrate air pressure 1066:32-33

Pocket parachute—making 732:128-129

Shape; which shape makes the best parachute experiment 1507:8

Simple napkin parachute, making 897:106

Simple paper parachute, how to make 1416:19

Simple parachute, how to make 868:71; 908:60; 917:11; 981:17

Test gravity with different size and shape parachutes 225:6-7

The prune paratrooper 280:13

Toy parachute slows down force of gravity—how to make 651:22-23

Which fabric makes the best parachute; cotton, burlap or silk experiment 1485:9

Why do pilots wear parachutes experiment 860:2-4

Why does a parachute come down slowly 210:7

PARALLEL CIRCUITS. *See* ELECTRICITY— CIRCUITS

PARAMECIA. *See also* INFUSORIA; MICROSCOPE; PROTOZOA
Attracting paramecia to weak acid—experiment 484:41

Collecting and preparing stained slides 500:75-78

Effect of water pollution on 330:97

Hot and cold paramecia—show temperature they are comfortable with—experiment 484:40-41

Observe operation of contractile vacuoles in amoebas and paramecia experiment 1425:21-22

Observe under microscope 889:35

Observing paramecia under microscope experiment 1425:13-14

Paramecia response to light, touch, chemicals under microscope 771:24-26

Paramecia, digestion observed using yeast cells and red food dye experiment 771:21-22

Paramecia, digestion observed using yeast cells and red food dye experiment 771:21-22

Paramecium culture—how to make and observe 713:82-85

Polarity of parameciums 577:project #11

Response of paramecia to touch, light & chemicals in the field & laboratory 266:23-26

PARASITOIDS. *See* WASPS

PARTICLE DENSITY
Demonstrate particle density 197:44-45

PARTICLE MOVEMENT
Use homemade wind tunnel to demonstrate 197:48-49

PARTICLE SETTLING
Demograded bedding in rivers (layers of different size particles) 197:54-55

PARTICLE SIZE AND SHAPE
Demonstrate how movement is affected by size and shape 197:46-47

Objects of greater size will settle faster than lesser size experiment 871:1.005

Sugar and soap in water demonstrate 722:99

PARTICLES
Cloud chamber—build to follow trails of particles experiment 704:61-64

Particle size and speed of dissolving experiment 984:53-55

Space between particles determine loudness of sounds 45:36-39

PASCAL, BLAISE
Pascal's aneroid barometer testing the sea of air hypothesis experiment 1156:55-56

Pascal's triangle of numbers investigation 1348:41-47

PASCAL'S LAW. *See also* AIR PRESSURE; WATER— PRESSURE
Experiment 385:39-41

Lift a heavy weight 585:7-8

Water pressure increases with depth of water—demonstrate 642:87-89

Water pressure pushes in all directions equally—demonstrate 642:90-91

PASSIVE SMOKE

Does passive smoke harm mosquito larvae experiment 1096:58-63

PASTE

A formula for paste 336:57-58

Super paste, making experiment 960:34

PASTEUR, LOUIS

Do microbes arise spontaneously experiment 1133:3.009

Pasteur's experiment with growth of bacteria from air 577:project 84

Repeat his experiment that microbes can make things change 602:unpaged

PATTERNS

Branching patterns experiment with ruler and toothpicks 1391:27

Spiral patterns experiment; draw a spiral 1391:29

PEANUT BUTTER

How to make peanut butter project 980:87

Make your own peanut butter 508:56; 560:35

Peanut butter poll survey 630:75

Use a grinder to make peanut butter 32:64-65

PEANUTS

Effect of cotyledon removal on peanut embryos experiment 871:2.008

George Washington Carver's peanut milk, how to make 879:103-104

Growing peanuts from seeds, how to do 784:62-63

How to plant peanuts 264:13

Measuring peanuts, data sheet given 817:4

Peanut mulch and peanut kitty litter—how to make 560:34

Peanut patch—how to plant 560:31

Plant and grow in pot 376:15

Potted peanut plant, how to plant and grow 1406:47

PEANUTS—GAME

Pin the peanut on the plant 560:46-47

PEBBLE SCULPTURES

Make from beach pebbles and seaweeds 296:19-21

PEBBLES

How are pebbles we find alike and different 253:120

Pebble polisher, make from wood, batteries, electric motor 1480:90-91

PECTIN

Making jam to show effect of pectin on crushed fruit experiment 1484:145-146

PELLETS—BIRD. *See also* **BIRDS—PELLETS**

Collect and identify materials in bird pellets 305:14-15

PENCILS. *See also* **LEAD PENCILS; WRITING INSTRUMENTS**

Electric pencil, making 895:52-54

Hardness test for graphite, the lead in pencils experiment 1438:83-84

Kind of pencil used on paper determined by magnifying glass experiment 1295:114

Test to compare pencils of different hardness 336:51-52

PENDULUMS. *See also* **FOUCAULT PENDULUM PRINCIPLE**

Behavior of simple pendulum; length, mass, amplitude exp. Data table 871:4.008

Bicycle wheel pendulum—how to make 558:60-61

Brick on string demonstrates resonant frequency experiment 722:101

Build and find out how period of a pendulum is related to bob mass 586:80-82

Can you split seconds accurately 333:119-121

Carnival game with pendulum, how to make 1063:311

Changing weight and string length effect on pendulum experiment 898:23

Chaotic motion experiment with magnets 1132:95-1-95-2

Copper coils become electromagnetic pendulums experiment 1132:64-1-64-2

Demonstrate our rotating planet (Primary) 169:7

Double suspension pendulums—demonstrate 137:19

Each swing of pendulum takes same amount of time experiment 1031:14-15

Easy, odd, circle swinger, couples—experiment 400:90

Eddy current slows movement of pendulum experiment 1139:98-100

Effect of weight on pendulum bob—demonstrate 137:16

Electric pendulum from static electricity—cans and balloon experiment 723:128-129

Electrified pendulum—how to make 532:90-91

Experiment to demonstrate (Advanced) 393:48-59

Experiment with 693:19

Experimenting with pendulums for swing time 1421:22

Experiments that Galileo did—how to do 642:22-24

Experiments with a pendulum 1412:78

Experiments with pendulums 1157:16-21

Falling sideways—pendulums in motion 295:60-62

Foucault model pendulum experiment 1502:33-34

Foucault pendulum—how to make 763:80-81

Foucault pendulum principle—demonstration 577: project #29

Foucault's pendulum—making 161:102-103

Foucault's pendulum experiment shows spinning of Earth 1480:16-17

Frequency of pendulum swings is determined by its length experiment 836:26-28

Galilei Galileo's periodic time of a pendulum is constant experiment 1133:4.003

Galileo and the pendulum—experiment 114:84-87

Galileo's pendulum experiments 1156:28-30

Galileo's thought experiment; effect of gravity on pendulum 1157:16-18

How can we measure time? 253:192-193

How pendulum works—demonstrate 137:14-15

How to make a pendulum 596:41

Investigating pendulums—experiments 664:28-29

Investigating pendulums 909:116

Joined pendulums—show working of joined pendulums 137:20

Length and weight of pendulums experiments 806:39-41

Length of pendulum affects number of swings experiment 760:30-31

Length of pendulum affects time of each swing experiment 1404:76-77

Length of pendulum affects time of each swing experiment 1405:95

Lissajous Patterns from swinging cup funnels of fine sugar experiment 1330:92-94

Magic pendulum 356:14-15

Measure time with a string experiment 827:102-103

Painted picture using pendulum experiment 1112:17-18

Patterns from a pendulum 142:7

Pendulum artwork 400:90
Pendulum bowl game with plastic containers, how to make 1014:73
Pendulum clock—Galileo 385:64-65
Pendulum clock experiment, how to make 1521:14-15
Pendulum clock, how to make 1446:45
Pendulum escapement clock, how to make 951:95-103
Pendulums experiment, double and triple (simple) 1507:22
Pendulum experiment; moving object moves unless force changes its motion 1502:26-28
Pendulum experiments 34:74-77; 538:107
Pendulum experiments that Galileo did—how to do 640:40-41
Pendulum from string and ball of clay tells time experiment 1103:28
Pendulum games 400:91
Pendulum, making 803:18-19
Pendulum, making (simple) 128:123-124
Pendulum measures gravity's acceleration experiment, data table given 1004:5.009
Pendulum movement illusion viewed through darkened glasses experiment 1020:22-24
Pendulum moving in two directions creates beautiful designs experiment 1132:43-1-43-2
Pendulum patterns experiments 1247:28-29
Pendulum patterns from sand, salt or sugar experiment 1063:311
Pendulum pattern maker—how to make 241:40-42
Pendulum person, making 779:42
Pendulum picture—show 137:18
Pendulum skittles game, making 909:117
Pendulum swinging in elliptical path experiment 1157:19-21
Pendulum using different string lengths and widths experiment 748:123
Pendulum with funnel on string makes patterns from sand experiment 898:23
Pendulums that dance and twist 295:63-64
Pendulums trade swings back and forth experiment 1132:32-1-32-2
Pendulums transferring energy from one to another experiment 940:97-99
Period of a pendulum, how to test experiment 1198:27
Period of motion of pendulum depend on weight, amplitude or length experiment 997:145-147
Prove Earth turns experiments 723:214-215
Pulfrich illusion 16:92-95
Pulfrich pendulum illusion of motion experiment 761:78-81
Regulating a pendulum clock—demonstrate 137:22
Relationship between length of pendulum swing and number of periods experiment 1412:70
Resonance and non resonance in pendulums experiment; pendulum pushing pendulum 1155:44-46
Resonance of sound demonstrated by swinging pendulums 1179:109
Resonant pendulum experiment; big swings from little pulls grow 1132:82-1-82-2
Resonating pendulums experiment 722:95
Rigid-arm pendulum experiment 1112:17
Salt designs from pendulum experiment 723:208
Salt patterns from swinging pendulum experiment 999:100-102
Salt pendulum experiment, making 935:66-67

Salt pendulum makes patterns on paper experiment 1298:83
Sand painting with pendulums experiment 1066:123-125
Seconds pendulum—making 161:13-14
Shifting pendulums experiment 909:117
Show driving of pendulum clock 137:21
Spring—nails and string pendulum experiment 723:17
Strange attractor experiment with magnets 1132:95-1-95-2
String, sinker and broomstick demonstrate pendulum experiment 940:94-96
Swing pendulum experiment 1112:16
Swing-gauge pendulum experiment 1136:28-29
Swing time—to and fro 260:23
The crazy pendulum—experiment 585:49
The switch and the twist—experiment 114:87-89
The sympathetic pendulums—experiment 585:49-50
Time it takes pendulum to swing from side to side experiment 1456:50
Timing with a pendulum—show 137:17
Transfer of energy between connecting pendulums experiment 1405:102
Undecided pendulum—experiment 114:89-91
Weight affects speed of pendulum's swing experiment 1404:74-75
What determines timing in a pendulum 291:130
What makes a pendulum swing experiment 1399:28-31
Wrecking crane uses pendulum effect experiment 1198:27

PENICILLIN
Bread mold produces spores 294:23-24
Experiment to determine best way to grow penicillin 904:90-91
Fleming, Sir Alexander; who discovered penicillin project 1525:73-75
How does penicillium mold grow and what does it look like experiment 1402:48-51
Repeat Fleming's mold experiment 448:56-59

PENS. *See also* **WRITING INSTRUMENTS**
Ball-point pen, how to make one experiment 1063:319
Gull feather pen—how to make 359:13-15
Quill pen, how to make from feather 857:30-31; 1143:6; 1246:28-29

PEPPER'S GHOST
Making 142:37; 172:26-29; 229:124-125
Pepper's ghost, making 911:8

PERCEPTION. *See also* **3-D; ILLUSIONS; VISION**
Afterimage experiment; flash of light leaves image in your eye 1132:1-1-1-2
Anti-gravity mirrors make you appear to be flying experiment 1132:2-1-2-2
Benham's Disk, rotating black and white disc produces illusion of color 1132:5-1-5-2
Bird in the cage; stare at color and see it change experiment 1132:8-1-8-2
Blind spot in your eyes experiment 1132:10-1-10-2
Book of illusions for you to try and to demonstrate 229:1-142
Boxes seen and moving where there are none experiment with black box and light 1132:51-1-51-2
Colored light bulbs on different colored sheets of paper experiment 1253:30-31
Colors seem to change when placed against different backgrounds experiment 1132:25-1-25-2

Depth perception—build instrument to test depth perception 293:26

Dot fades from your view experiment 1132:49

Dot picture experiment; Jaques Cousteau in seashells; pattern given 1132:60-1-60-3

Experiment to demonstrate 222:100-112

Eyes receive different images experiment; friend disappears but smile remains 1132:21-1-21-2

James Gibson's how we perceive the world around us experiment 1133:3.012

Lateral inhibition experiment using shades of gray color 1132:56-1-56-2

Light sources appear to wiggle and flash when you give them Bronx cheer 1132:14-1-14-2

Loopy puzzle brain teaser 1253:10-11

Nerve machine tests your nerves; make from battery, wire and light bulb 1253:32-33

Persistence of vision experiment with horse and rider pictures 1138:36-38

Persistence of vision experiment; see pictures in thin air 1132:62-1-62-2

Rotating spiral makes things seem to move toward or away from you experiment 1132:36-1-36-2

Seeing with one eye 253:103

Sound vibrations demonstration with sugar on top of drum experiment 1253:20

Stereoscope simulates depth perception using homemade drawings experiment 1476:219-221

Stroop Effect experiment with color words written on different colored cards 1476:215-216

Visual—demonstrate principle of mixing colors—make color wheel 293:44-45

Visual cues to your eyes determine what you see 1132:17-1-17-3

Visual memory of shapes to draw experiment 1253:10-11

Waterfall effect illusion experiment 1132:93-1-93-2

PERCOLATION. *See also* **SOILS**

Water moves in soil 253:130-131

PERCOLATOR

What makes the percolator perk 291:56

PEREGRINUS, PETRUS

His experiments 42:12-15

PERFORMATION OR EPIGENESIS

Decide difference between the two 402:95-96

PERFUMES. *See also* **COSMETICS**

Extracting essential oils for perfumes 441:55-62

How perfume changes over time—experiment 441:62-64

Make a bottle of spicy perfume experiment 905:172-173

Make bottle of spicy perfume experiment with cloves and alcohol 1479:62

Making perfume experiment 1259:62-64

Making perfume from flowers experiment 1242:37

Perfume staying power 441:64-65

Perfume, how to make 859:23

Recipe for 387:23-27

Recipe for "pure joy" perfume 441:105

Scratch-and-sniff paper, how to make 1228:62-63

"Triangle test" to see how well you smell 441:49-52

PERIPHERAL VISION. *See also* **VISION**

Peripheral vision is worse in people who wear glasses experiment 1195:63-69

PERISCOPES

Activities to explore and understand periscope [Primary] 758:108-110

Bouncing light experiment; make a periscope to demonstrate 956:28-29

Box and mirror periscope, making 887:52-54

Build simple periscope from milk carton, mirrors and tape 1511:20-21

Camouflaged periscope, how to make from cardboard box and mirror 1115:16-17

Cardboard box periscope, making 770:139

Directions for construction 167:1-4

From two mirrors—making 26:58

How does a periscope work experiment 902:96

How to build using mirrors, paper tube, and cardboard 1039:26

How to make a periscope 861:241-248

How to make a periscope experiment 941:92-95

How to make simple periscope 595:38-39

How to make using cardboard and mirrors 1179:82-83

How to make 410:18; 472:2236; 558:90-91; 605:24-27; 733:13

Make a model periscope 128:194

Make a simple periscope 892:28

Make periscope from cardboard box and mirrors experiment 1345:53-54

Make your own periscope experiment 928:10-11

Make your own periscope from cardboard and mirrors 1073:75

Making a periscope 96:64-65; 142:36; 172:17-20; 178:48; 179:92-93; 240:24-26; 265:36-37; 281:82-83; 291:178; 293:43; 350:135; 360:27-29; 399:74; 436:62; 452:22-23; 555:28-29; 696:24-25; 860:204-206; 1417:17-21

Making—(Advanced) 208:101-105

Making—(simple) 76:12-13

Making from milk carton 781:36-37

Milk carton periscope, how to make 851:19-20; 935:42-43; 1019:10-12; 1229:68-69

Model of periscope made from two mirrors experiment 1159:81-84

Peeking periscope from poster board, and mirrors experiment 1476:49-50

Periscope demonstrates reflection of light rays, how to make 1308:14-15

Periscope from cardboard and mirrors, how to make 1213:17

Periscope from cardboard carton and mirrors, how to make 1163:23

Periscope from cardboard tube and mirrors, how to make 1245:26

Periscope from milk carton—making 207:38-40

Periscope hat making 177:12-15

Periscope, how to make 625:34; 906:76-77; 909:138

Periscope, how to make and use 659:10; 736:54-57

Periscope, making from wood 868:77

Periscope; build to look around corners experiment 1028:38-39

Pop-up periscope, making 779:44

Seeing round corners—make a periscope 570:29

Shoe box and mirrors periscope, how to make 885:58-60

Shoe box periscope, making to see around corners experiment 924:99-100

Simple periscope from milk carton and mirrors experiment 1369:93-94

Super snooper, making 684:26-27

Up periscope—how to make a periscope 587:44

Weird periscope making 400:75
Why do submarines use periscopes experiment
1294:106-107
PERIWINKLES
Effects of periwinkle grazing on seaweed growth experiment 1225:67-68
Mini-aquarium for observing grazing habits of periwinkles experiment 1225:67
Observations of world of periwinkles, how to do 1225:62-68
Tidal memory of rough periwinkle observed in mini-aquarium experiment 1225:68
PERMANENT WAVES
Hair experiment 441:80-81
PERMEABILITY
More particles—less permeability—experiment 92:52-53
Show particle permeability—using balloons 92:24-25
PERPETUAL MOTION
Marbles and cardboard tube machine demonstrates 472:2239
Perpetual motion machine using a marble, how to make 1243:8
Will it work 126:91-95
PERSISTENCE OF VISION. *See also* **ZOETROPE**
Eye on face on paper appears to blink experiment 1479:37
Eye sees things for short time after they are out of sight experiment 1037:20-21
Persistence of vision experiment with horse and rider pictures 1138:36-38
Persistence of vision experiment; Chinese ring trick 1138:41-42
Persistence of vision experiment; ghost tube trick 1138:42-44
Persistence of vision experiment; square circle trick 1138:44-46
Turntable illusions, how to make 1289:20-21
PERSPIRATION
What is perspiration 402:69
PESTICIDES
Accumulating pesticides in food chains experiment 1134:6.013
Earthworms internal anatomy affected by pesticides and fertilizers experiment 1450:66-71
Farmers alternatives to using toxic chemicals experiment using ladybugs/aphids 1427:88-89
Insect damage to produce differs when grown organically or with pesticide 1096:133-138
Natural predator ladybugs control aphids on plant experiment 1176:17
Pollution of our waters 371:77-80
Toxicology test for pesticides on water fleas experiment 950:88-89
PETIT, ALEX THERESE
Law of Dulong and Petit experiment; specific heats/atomic weight of elements 1156:105-108
PETROLEUM
Build a pipeline to move oil or gas experiment 1027:39
Geologist search for magnetic rocks experiment 1027:13
Petroleum deposit—water and sand model 666:103
Tapping oil from beneath the sea, how it is done experiment 1027:33
PETS
How many pets can you find survey project 901:60-62

pH
Acid rain effect on growth of geraniums experiment 1060:114-116
Determine pH level that induces most corrosion in iron and copper experiment 997:62-63
Effect of soil pH on plant growth experiment; data table given 871:2.009
Floating seeds—does pH of streams affect dispersal distance experiment 714:133-135
Grouping chemicals according to their pH—experiment 180:10
How does pH scale work experiment 1046:68-70
Measure pH of soils 285:21-23
pH effect on germination of radish and bean seeds experiment 1526:98
pH of acid rain and snow experiment 1526:98
pH of cosmetics and cleaning agents experiment 1476:134-135
pH of lake water with added vinegar and limestone experiment 1526:98
pH of ocean water experiment 1290:8
pH of rainwater experiment 1060:114
pH of rainwater experiment to determine if acid rain is a problem 1427:68-69
pH of soil affects color of hydrangea flowers experiment 1060:114
pH of soil affects growth of different plants experiment 1060:113
pH of soil experiment 1046:71-73; 1134:1.008
pH of water; how to determine experiment 978:75-76
pH ranges that are best for growing common vegetables 1061:42
pH scale 1003:122
pH scale test for water used to grow plants hydroponically 1061:40-42
pH values of some common substances 285:22
pH, the degree of acidity experiment 1526:97-98
Red cabbage indicator identifies pH of common household products exp. 871:3.021
Red cabbage indicator, how to make to test pH 1527:26-27
PHANTASCOPE
Phantascope, how to build 861:27-32
Phantascope, how to make, pattern given 1007:30-32
PHAROAH'S SERPENT
Make one from sugar and chemicals 186:107
PHASES OF MOON. *See* **MOON—PHASES**
PHENAKISTOSCOPE
Phenakistoscope, how to make 911:44; 172:38-41
Phenakistoscope, how to make to show mini moving pictures experiment 935:80-81
Persistence of vision experiment using phenakistoscope, how to make 1405:42
Phenakistoscope to make pictures move; make with picture patterns given 1299:18-21
Wooden phenakistoscope with mirror experiment, pattern given, how to make 1476:211-212
PHENOLPHTHALEIN. *See also* **INDICATORS**
Apples drawn on paper turn red with indicator experiment 814:50-52
As indicator in invisible ink 146:23
Clear water turns red and then turns clear again experiment 781:42-43
Effect that acids and bases have on phenolphthalein experiment 1479:64

Indicator, making to see if soap is acid or base experiment 781:40-41
Test solution 84:28-30

PHENOLS
Plants that repel insects—experiment 398:117-118

PHEROMONES. *See also* **ANTS**
Alarm pheromones experiment using ants and aphids 1096:110-117
Ants; pheromones used by ants for communication system experiment 1476:114-115
Aphids use pheromones as warning system experiment 1097:2-4
Caged female moth attracts males 266:92-93
Communication by odor in minnows in the field and in the laboratory 266:90-93
How ants use pheromones experiment 1097:16-20
Plant communication experiments 398:127-128
The response of ants to odors in the field and in the laboratory 266:18-20

PHI PHENOMENON
Phi phenomenon 229:94-95

PHONOGRAPH
Edison's experiment; phonograph pick up of sound experiment 895:34-35
Edison's experiments 230:103-109
How phonograph record makes sounds experiment 1432:133-135
Reinvent Edison's phonograph experiment 1209:80-81
Simple phonograph, how to make 1007:63-64

PHOSPHATES. *See also* **WATER—POLLUTION**
Detrimental effect of phosphates in detergents on pond plants/animals experiment 1476:192
Phosphate amount in detergents; how phosphates affect sudsing experiment 1012:89-91
Phosphate detergents overfeed algae and harm pond life experiment 1331:81
Phosphates in detergents and their relationship to sudsing experiment 1013:88-89

PHOSPHENES
Prisoner's cinema illusions 229:111-113

PHOSPHORESCENCE
Phosphorescence and fluorescence 577:project #23
The Phantom memory—phosphorescence 205:94-97

PHOTOCHEMISTRY
Experiment to show photochemical reaction—wet plate 346:135-136
Experiment with certain silver polishes and light 17:13-16

PHOTOCOPIERS
How are mirrors used in copiers experiment 1293:119-120

PHOTOELECTRICITY
Photoelectric cell experiment 1153:127
Photoelectric effect experiment using electroscope, how to make 1153:119-123

PHOTOGRAMS. *See also* **PHOTOGRAPHY**
How to make 472:2228-2229
Photogram from Polaroid film experiment 860:69-71

PHOTOGRAPHS
Easy way to print photographs 538:127
How to copy 176:95
Thru a magnifying glass 9:60-61
Viewer for a 3-D look—making 176:57-58

PHOTOGRAPHY. *See also* **CAMERAS; PINHOLE CAMERA**
3-D photography—how to do 472:2242
Black photo negative gives picture print experiment 1020:96-97
Blueprint—how to make 319:76-77
Camera obscura, making 906:66
Changing bag for film, how to make 863:120-122
Cliche-Verre (drawing with light) project—how to do 25:56-61
Color slides without a camera—how to make 47:22-26
Contact points—how to make 76:40-41
Create photos with light on photographic paper experiment 1028:47
Darkroom—how to set up 76:38-39; 863:104-105
Darkroom instructions for developing pictures from pinhole camera 887:91-92
Developing photos, how to do 863:123
Emulsions, how to make 860:72-75
Exploring the environment with a camera 400:77-78
Flash bulb tester, how to make 830:67-68
Fresnel lens image brightener for ground glass camera 386:54-55
Homemade reflector—making 291:188-189
How does emulsion-coated paper work experiment 1293:81-82
How does film make negatives experiment 1293:75-78
How to print from a negative or making a positive 319:83-84
Kirlian electrophotography kit with piezoelectric power supply 386:38-44
Light meter, how to make 830:66
Light sensitive paper—how to make 319:77-79
Magic—spirit pictures 87:57-61
Magic lantern, how to make 861:129-135
Microphotography—photograph tiny creatures 436:57
Mystery photos—experiments with 107:27-38
Nature photography—how to 234:14-17
Negative—how to make 319:81-83
Oatmeal box camera, making 887:88-90
Paper negatives—printing paper negatives 25:87-94
Permanent negative prints, making and fixing, how to do 863:65
Photo of objects on photographic paper, how to do 1019:26-27
Photogram from Polaroid film experiment 860:69-71
Photogram greeting cards—how to make 25:52-56
Photograms—design a photogram calendar 25:36-38
Photograms—making 25:17-29; 76:44-45
Photograms—multiple exposure photograms—making 25:29-31
Photograms—photo-mobile—how to make 25:38-44
Photograms—photogram mural—making 25:44-47
Photograms—using three dimensional objects to cast shadows 25:32-35
Photographic plates—how to make 319:79-81
Photographing lightning, how to do 959:111
Photographing stars and planets project 833:181-182
Pinhole box camera—how to make and use 25:62-86
Pinhole camera—construct with quarter plates 167:81-88
Pinhole camera—making 47:27-34; 76:36-37
Pinhole camera—making a people-size camera from a large box 25:95-98

Pinhole camera—making and using a pocket-size camera 25:98-109

Pinhole photography 76:42-43

Positive prints, how to make 863:124

Printing and developing negatives, how to do 863:116-119

Reflector for photography, how to make experiment 941:106-108

Remote flash construction, how to do 830:68-70

See effect of sunlight on hydrogen peroxide 319:74-75

Special effects and trick photography kit 386:46-52

Stereoscope to view 3-D photographs, how to build 1253:36-37

Sun pictures—how to make 47:13-21

Sun print greeting cards—how to make 25:47-52

Sun prints—how to make 359:24-47; 494:22-23

Sun prints—non permanent—making 25:7-12

Sun prints—permanent—making 25:12-16

Sun prints of natural materials, how to make 1071:94

Sunlight pictures—making 400:77

Taking pictures—some tips 400:79

Three-dimensional photographs experiment 1253:36-37

Watch dial photographs itself—how to do 291:192-193

Who is ancestor of today's photography project 1525:101-106

PHOTOMETER

Brightness of light bulb measured by photometer experiment, how to make 1501:23

Making 436:62-63

Measure the brightness of light with photometer experiment 1405:17

Simple photometer, how to make 1138:32-34

Use fat spot on paper to compare negative brightness of two lights 203:43

PHOTOMICROGRAPHY

How to do with ordinary camera of homemade device 11:136-140

With a pen microscope 386:45

With twin lens reflex camera 9:48-51

PHOTONS

Diagram of photon paths from mirror 366:196-197

PHOTOPERIODISM. *See also* **PLANTS—PHOTOSYNTHESIS**

Christmas cactus produces flowers when amount of light is reduced experiment 1060:74

Colored lights wavelength affects photoperiodism in radish plants experiment 1060:73-74

Length of daylight experiment with flower seeds 878:18-21

Photoperiodism response of radish plants experiment 1060:73

What effect does amount of light have on plant growth 402:24-25

PHOTOSYNTHESIS. *See also* **PLANTS—PHOTOSYNTHESIS**

Amount of light affects amount of oxygen produced during photosynthesis 1060:25-26

Amount of light affects photosynthesis experiment 1060:25-26

Aquarium plants give off oxygen gas-coll. In test tube & light 146:18-19

Are algae bacteria and do they photosynthesize experiment 864:35-36

Bean sprout experiment demonstrates photosynthesis 928:24

Carbohydrate formation in plants during photosynthesis; test for starch 1060:21-23

Carbon cycle in plant growth experiment using two plants in jars 1173:16-19

Carbon dioxide amount absorbed by trees and concrete building site experiment 1057:108

Carbon dioxide deprivation causes plants to die experiment 1061:24-25

Chlorophyll extracted from plant leaves demonstrates starch in plants 978:41-42

Chlorophyll spectrum as seen through a spectroscope experiment 1060:27-28

Chlorophyll; testing plant leaves for amount and density of chlorophyll 1061:32-34

Color effect on chlorophyll production in plant leaves experiment 1082:187-191

Colors in different shades differ in effects on photosynthesis experiment 1060:27-28

Colors of the spectrum affect photosynthesis experiment 1060:27-28

Demonstrate marvel of photosynthesis 176:32

Demonstrate plants need for sunshine 293:15

Determine what carbohydrates are produced by plants 398:45-47

Do all plants use photosynthesis to make food experiment 852:14-15

Do plants make sugar and starch 283:27-38

Do plants really make oxygen 283:11-26

Do plants really need light, water and carbon dioxide to make food 282:9-24

Does color of light effect rate of growth 273:28-29

Effect of light on growth of plants experiment 1061:30-31

Effect of temperature on 273:30-31

Evergreen needles have more chlorophyll than deciduous tree leaves experiment 1061:35-36

Experiments and projects with plants 398:44-49

Experiments to show 346:136-137

Explanation of 380:66-68

Fat test for food storage in plants experiment 1214:12-13

Gas collected from underwater plants is oxygen experiment 1069:40-41

Gas released by plants experiment 737:9

Grass turns yellow; what causes it experiment 1020:146-147

Green plants make oxygen gas experiment 1324:42-47

Green plants need light, water or carbon dioxide for photosynthesis experiment 1453:20-24

How a green leaf produces food 294:37-38

How trees take in carbon dioxide experiment 1057:104

Illustration of 236:14

Initials placed over growing seedlings shows photosynthesis experiment 1308:10-11

Isolating chlorophyll and testing for starch in a leaf 294:39

Leaves carrying out photosynthesis give off oxygen gas experiment 1069:40-41

Leaves in sunlight give off oxygen gas 97:28-31

Light important to photosynthesis exp.; Leaves make photographs 871:2.023

Light is needed for photosynthesis experiment 1324:42-47

Light needed for photosynthesis process in hydroponic grown plants experiment 1061:66-67

Light needed for 273:26-27
Light provides energy for photosynthesis experiment 1060:25-26
Measure photosynthesis rate by measuring oxygen production 398:47-49
Measure rate of photosynthesis in leaves contaminated with soot experiment 933:24-25
Measure rate or speed of 273:24-25
Measuring oxygen released by plant leaves during photosynthesis experiment 1061:28-29
Mini-investigations to explore photosynthesis experiment 1063:244
Oil slick prevents aquatic plants from process of photosynthesis experiment 1172:52
Oxygen as by-product of photosynthesis experiment 1060:28-30
Oxygen collected from plants during photosynthesis experiment 1060:23-24
Oxygen from green plants useful to fish experiment 1060:28-30
Oxygen gas bubbles collect in jar placed over plant in water experiment 1271:23
Oxygen gas bubbles from green plant under water experiment; candle burns 1457:15
Oxygen gas collection experiment from green water plants 472:2220
Oxygen given off by plants during photosynthesis experiment 1214:14
Oxygen production affected by amount of light during photosynthesis experiment 1060:28-30
Oxygen production rate from plants during photosynthesis; how to measure 1060:28-30
Photos from photosynthesis experiment show starch produced in plant leaf 1476:105-106
Photosynthesis and oxygen production experiment 878:30-31
Photosynthesis and respiration in plant tissue experiment 1395:101-105
Photosynthesis and respiration in plants affected by colors of light experiment 1395:103
Photosynthesis in green plants experiment 878:28-29
Photosynthesis needed for plant growth experiment; carbon dioxide needed 1173:16-19
Photosynthesis process demonstrated by bubbling plants in water 1038:23
Plant leaves breathe in carbon dioxide and breathe out oxygen 146:46
Plants breathe oxygen out through their leaves experiment 1371:71
Plants make starch experiment 737:13
Plants need carbon dioxide gas to carry on photosynthesis experiment 1174:19-20
Plants need carbon dioxide to produce oxygen thru photosynthesis experiment 1173:46-47
Plants produce oxygen during photosynthesis experiment 978:52
Plants produce oxygen experiment 1396:161-163
Preventing photosynthesis experiment 878:38-39
Preventing photosynthesis 402:22-23
Rain forests; photosynthesis absorbs carbon dioxide/ makes water vapor 1174:38-39
Rate of photosynthesis affected by amount of carbon dioxide experiment 1060:23-25
Rate of photosynthesis measured by amount of oxygen given off experiment 871:2.024

Rates of photosynthesis computer project 584:57-58
Show plants use carbon dioxide 282:25-33
Show that oxygen is by product of photosynthesis 294:40-41
Smoke affects growth of plants experiment 1061:37-38
Starch in leaves experiment 1060:21-23
Starch in plants demonstration 978:40
Starch is produced in plant leaves during photosynthesis experiment 1479:25
Starch is produced in plant leaves experiment 904:28-29
Starch is produced when leaves photosynthesize experiment 1308:11
Starch test for food storage in plants experiment 1214:12-13
Starch test for leaves of plant kept in sunlight and in darkness experiment 1069:43
Sugar (carbohydrate) product of photosynthesis found in plant parts experiment 1061:26-27
Sunlight needed by plant to produce food experiment 1440:15-17
Volcanic clouds lower atmospheric temperature and reduce sunlight experiment 1477:76-79
Water plants make oxygen; collect gas in test tube experiment 1246:16
What happens to grass when it doesn't receive sunlight experiment 1324:38-41
What is photosynthesis 402:21-22

PHOTOTROPISM. See also **PLANTS—TROPISMS**
Bean plant grows through box maze toward light experiment 1288:24-25
Bean plant grows toward light in shoe box maze experiment 1068:41
Bean seedlings grow toward light experiment 1078:5
Bean seeds planted in box maze grow toward light experiment 1189:48-49
Charles Darwin's growth movement in plants toward light experiment 1133:3.008
Cress seedlings grow toward light through hole in cup experiment 913:32
Different wavelengths of colored lights affect phototropism experiment 1060:75
Do plants grow towards the light 402:23-24
Do potato plants grow toward light experiment 876:77-78
Effect of light on plant growth experiment; box maze demonstrates 978:54-55
Geranium plant project 1060:75
Grow plants in a maze experiment 1265:85
Growth of plants in response to light experiment 1527:92
Light can bend plant experiment 860:149-150
Light needed for plants to grow experiment using box with cover 1019:28-29
Maze demonstrates plants need sunlight to grow experiment 1014:156
Maze to show plant's growth toward light, how to make 986:85
Phototropism demonstrated as plant grows toward light experiment 1069:45
Plant bends toward light experiment 924:76-77
Plant in box grows toward light experiment 882:33; 1328:15
Plant maze demonstrates plants grow toward light experiment 1038:14-15

Plant maze with bean plant growing toward light experiment 1368:41

Plant turns toward light experiment 1246:10-11

Plant winds its way toward light experiment 904:52-53

Plants grow toward light experiment 1047:17

Plants grow toward light experiment 749:44-45; 878:42-43; 898:49-50

Plants grow towards light in box maze experiment 913:27

Plants in a maze experiment 878:44-45

Plants seek light experiment 904:54-55

Potato grows through maze in box to find light experiment 1379:25

Potato grows toward light through maze in box experiment 1145:11

Potato plant grows toward light in box maze experiment 810:29

Potato plant in box maze grows toward light experiment 1214:11

Potato shoot grows toward light source in maze experiment 1236:6-7

Potato shoots grow toward light in cardboard box maze experiment 1524:26

Response of oat seedlings to light experiment 1395:83-88

Responses to light in growing plants experiment 784:114-115

Why house plants should be rotated experiment 1294:78-79

PHOTOVOLTAIC CELLS. *See* **SOLAR CELLS**

PHYSICAL CHANGES

Cutting card changes it into large super chain experiment 905:6-7

Iron filings and powdered sulfur experiment to determine changes 976:18

Is dissolving solids a physical change or a chemical change experiment 902:22

Mixture of iron filings and powdered sulfur—how to separate them 6:10

Physical and chemical changes experiment; chart given 960:13-14

Plaster of Paris and tempera paint demonstrate [Primary] 759:46-47

Test clay you create experiment 871:3.004

PHYSICAL REACTIONS

Identify physical reactions in household items experiment, data tables 1004:4.010

PHYSICAL SCIENCES

Ideas for projects and experiments 51:136-140

PHYSICS

Magic with 350:92-150

Some science puzzles to solve 625:6-7

PHYSICS TRICKS

Crumpled can 27:96-97

Cutting glass with a scissors 27:94-95

Flying ping pong ball 27:82-83

Magic broom stick 27:92-93

Magic comb 27:90-92

Magic glass rod 27:88-90

Magic harbor 27:98

Magic jar #2 27:98-99

Magic lung power 27:87

Magic mirror 27:93-94

Magic peg board 27:84-86

PIAGET. *See* **CONSERVATION OF MASS**

PIANO

Bottle listens to piano 45:104-105

Find the keynote 45:108-109

How to find harmonics 187:29

Piano listens to you 45:101-103

Piano patter and hear octaves 45:82-85

PICKLES

Pickles—making to demonstrate osmosis 563:153-154

PICTOGRAPHS. *See* **GRAPHS—PICTOGRAPH**

PICTURES

Accordion folded pictures, how to make 1299:92-93

Lines of black & white spots form a television picture 12:76-79

Making pictures with leaves 264:45

Pantograph to copy pictures—how to make 507:1894

Transfer comics with solution—how to do 723:43-44

PIEZOELECTRICITY

Generate sound from piezoelectricity experiment 1426:31

How can piezoelectricity be generated experiment 1426:26-29

How does patio gas grill igniter work experiment 1426:30

Light a barbecue gas lighter experiment 1426:29-30

Make inexpensive surround sound experiment 1426:32-33

PIGEONS

Homing pigeons—how to care for 358:114-115

Make a ledge nest 264:78-79

PIGMENTS. *See also* **CHROMATOGRAPHY; LEAVES; PAINTS**

Anthocyanin pigments in flower petals change in acid/alkaline soils experiment 1203:28-29

Calculate flow rate for yellow food dye experiment 1396:97-103

Chromatography test with inks, food colors and plant pigments experiment 1476:129-131

Leaf chromatography experiment; how to prepare 1396:101-103

Leaves; why do leaves change color explanation 1239:8-9

Mixing colored pigments 180:29

Pigments in colors separated using chromatography experiment 1308:26-27

Pigments in leaves separated and identified experiment 904:38-39

Pigments in plants shown by chromatograms experiment 1069:40

Red color of apple is from color pigment anthocyanin experiment 1395:110

Test tube holder and stand for chromatography experiment, how to make 1476.129-130

Which colors from felt tip pens spread out the farthest experiment 1509:9

PIGPEN CIPHER. *See also* **SECRET WRITING**

Secret code—how to write 629:23-24

PIGS

Products made from pigs survey 607:84-85

PILGRIMS

Experiments of their culture 322:entire book

PILL BUGS. *See also* **SOW BUGS**

Collect and observe sow bugs, how to do 913:12-13

Home for sowbugs, how to make 1289:32-33

Isopod race, how to set up and do 1189:14-15

PINBALL MACHINE

How to make 429:52-55

PINEAPPLES

Grow plant from pineapple top 879:170-171

Pineapple crown, how to plant and grow indoors 1178:15-16

Pineapple leaf fibers used for cloth and nets 257:15-18

Pineapple plant, how to grow 899:180

Pineapple planted with apple wedges so fruit buds are produced experiment 1406:40-43

Pineapple top grows into plant, how to do 1440:85-86

Pineapple top, how to grow 770:100-101

Sprouting and planting a pineapple, how to do 1406:48-51

Top grows into plant 376:14

Top grows plant (Primary) 650:unpaged

PINECONES

Pinecone rain meter; observe dry and wet for seed dispersal mechanism 784:72

PINHOLE CAMERA. *See also* **CAMERAS; PHOTOGRAPHY**

Camera—making 733:12

Camera obscura, make from milk cartons 837:61-62

Coffee can camera, making 895:41-42

Comparison of pinhole camera to lens of eye—diagram 555:23

Darkroom instructions for developing pictures from pinhole camera 887:91-92

Experiment with pinhole images 693:22-23

How does box camera work experiment 834:116-117

How to make 507:1856-1857; 595:22-23

How to make (Primary) 558:84-85

How to make and use 240:20-23; 507:1856-1857; 595:22-23; 691:89-93

How to make using shoe box, flat black paint and film 1153:55-56

Light travels in straight line; demonstrate with pinhole camera 1394:174-175

Make a pinhole camera or camera obscura 625:35

Make a pinhole camera, how to do 1283:20

Make pinhole camera from oatmeal box, foil and paint 1525:101-103

Making (Advanced) 208:38-47

Making a pinhole camera project 833:179-181

Model eye or pinhole camera, how to make 1092:38

Oatmeal box camera, how to make 1476:51-52

Oatmeal box camera, making 887:88-90

Paper cup makes a pinhole camera (Primary) 201:26-27

Pinhole 'camera'—making 291:181

Pinhole camera demonstrates how lens in eye works 1308:12-13

Pinhole camera demonstrates why cameras have lenses 1294:108-111

Pinhole camera from empty can, how to make 956:43

Pinhole camera from oatmeal box, how to make 860:206-209

Pinhole camera to observe sunspots—making 231:19

Pinhole camera, how to build experiment 941:101-105

Pinhole camera, how to make, pattern given 863:27-45

Pringle can camera—making 748:122

Projects with a pinhole camera 691:94

Shoe box camera—how to make 569:38

Shoe box pinhole camera, how to make 1454:24

Telephoto attachment for pinhole camera, how to make 863:146-147

Wide angle attachment for pinhole camera, how to make 863:135-143

PINHOLE OPTICS

Pinhole images, how to make using box, lighted bulb, black paper experiment 1153:50-52

PINWHEELS

Pinwheel, how to make 1416:10-11

Pinwheel, paper, making 999:124-126

Windmill in shape of pinwheel, how to make from paper 1299:49

PIPELINES

Build a pipeline to move oil or gas experiment 1027:39

PIPETTE CAPILLARY

Making capillary pipette to snare small organisms 11:72-74

PITCH. *See also* **SOUND—PITCH**

Experimenting with pitch 180:62-63

PITCHER PLANTS

Insectivorous plants, how to grow 279:37-38

PITFALL TRAPS

Insect pitfall trap—how to make 590:44

Pitfall trap captures night animals experiment 1180:27

Pitfall trap captures night animals experiment 1183:155

Pitfall trap for collecting small animals or invertebrates 864:97

Pitfall trap, how to make 1182:4; 1183:52

PLANARIANS

Adventure 32—we meet some more worms—planarians under a microscope 403:112-115

Collecting and experimenting with 500:93-94

Collecting planarias 436:88

Collecting, examining and feeding planarians experiment 1425:34-37

Compare movement of with other small pond animals 173:18

Contraction in planarias 484:64-65

Finding planaria experiment 1117:24

Learning in planaria—in the field and in the laboratory 266:106-110

Make a microscopic algae jungle 279:34-36

Planarian regeneration experiment 151:57-58

Planarians, collect and observe feeding, response to light, regeneration 771:99-108

Planarias and light—experiment 484:63

Planarias and water currents—experiment 484:63-64

Polarity of worms—experiment 532:50

Raising planaria experiment 1117:26

Regenerating animals 148:50

Regenerating planarias 484:64

Regeneration computer project 584:77-78

Regeneration of planaria experiment 1117:27

PLANCK, MAX

Who discovered the quantum theory of energy project 1525:114-120

PLANETARIUM. *See also* **ORRERY**

Box planetarium produces images of the night sky, how to make 1394:144-145

Canetarium from juice cans and flashlight—how to make 476:92-94

Cereal box planetarium, how to make 1063:300

Crystal planetarium from round bottom chemist's flask, star maps, make 1476:168-170

Flashlight planetarium—how to make 710:75-76

How planetariums produce images of the night sky experiment 1405:15

Make from cereal box 203:12

Making to project night sky 436:63

Oatmeal box planetarium, making 879:231

Oatmeal box, flashlight, cellophane; make your own terrarium 887:12-14

Planetarium—making (Advanced) 658:28-31
Planetarium from flashlight, how to build 967:22-23
Planetarium you can make from tinker toys 532:94-95
Star theater planetarium experiment made from battery,
    wires, bulb, posterboard 1478:108-109
Tin can planetarium, how to make 292:18; 1434:71-74
Umbrella planetarium—making 128:68; 532:56-57;
    1063:300
Umbrella planetarium with star patterns mounted on um-
    brella, make 1476:171-172

PLANETARY PROBES

Galileo probe model of probe NASA sent to Jupiter, how
    to make 1478:82-83

PLANETS

Activities and experiments to demonstrate space probe in-
    formation 564:68-71
Age you would be on other planets chart 816:16
Aliens survive on planet you invent experiment
    871:1.010
Blink comparator helps to discover planets, how to make
    1478:80-81
Boyle's orrery model experiment shows Earth, Moon,
    Sun revolving speeds 1476:162-165
Chart of planets' places in space 231:100-101
Chart of the weight of 100 pound person on the Moon
    and planets 1157:36
Charting the movement of Jupiter's Moons project
    833:240-241
Color affects planet's surface temperature experiment
    with tin cans 1394:6-7
Color affects planet's surface temperature experiment
    1479:2
Comparing the distance and size of planets 898:17
Comparing the sizes of the planets 898:16-17
Create Martian landscape project 967:6-7
Demonstrate motion of planets and satellites using batter-
    ies 102:134-137
Demonstrating planetary orbits project 833:165-167
Distance affects planet's period of revolution experiment
    1405:2
Distance from Sun affects atmosphere temperature of
    planets experiment 1394:12-13
Distance from Sun affects planet's period of revolution
    demonstration 1394:14-15
Distances between the planets—demonstrate 169:22;
    292:101-102
Distances of planets from the Sun for wall model, how to
    do 1365:35
Drawing planetary orbits [ellipses] project 833:161-162
Earth measurements 292:86-87
Earth; barycenter of Earth; position of demonstrated with
    string/clay 1394:62-63
Effect of distance on orbiting speed of planets experi-
    ment 1479:7
Elliptical orbit of planets around Sun experiment 1478:64
Elliptical orbits—demonstration 577:project #33
Finding Venus morning, noon and night project 833:224-
    226
Force that keeps satellites in orbit around the Earth dem-
    onstration 1405:7
Forces effect orbital movement of planets experiment
    1405:6
Galaxies; how galaxies may be moving demonstration
    with balloon 1394:58-59

Gravity affects movement of celestial bodies demonstra-
    tion 1394:66-67
Gravity affects movement of celestial bodies experiment
    1405:6
Gravity on—computer experiment 665:9
Group game to know the planets, how to do 1063:290
Height calculations and surface mapping of planets ex-
    periment 1062:100-101
How big are the planets—demonstrate 169:23
How do positions of planets change 253:194-195
How scientists create three-dimensional model of
    planet's surface experiment 1062:100-101
Hunting the sky at night for planets, how to do 1329:44-
    45
Information chart on planets 1063:291
Jupiter measurements 292:93-94
Jupiter's colored clouds; possible cause demonstration
    1394:32-33
Jupiter's magnetic field demonstrated experiment
    1478:73
Jupiter's red spot movement demonstration 1394:34-35
Jupiter's ring shines; demonstrate with flashlight and
    baby powder 1394:36-37
Jupiter's storms demonstrated with food colors experi-
    ment 1478:73
Jupiter; centrifugal forces affecting Jupiter and its bulg-
    ing waistline 1478:72-73
Jupiter; demonstrate movement in Jupiter's red spot ex-
    periment 1405:3-D
Jupiter; determine what might cause Jupiter's colored
    clouds experiment 1479:4
Jupiter; determine why Jupiter's ring shines experiment
    1405:4
Jupiter; determine why lightning flashes continually on
    Jupiter experiment 1479:5
Jupiter; Galilean Moons of Jupiter, how to observe
    1170:47
Jupiter; lightning continuously flashing on Jupiter demon-
    stration 1394:42-43
Life on planets, detect (Advanced) 668:67-69
Life on planets; detect; repeat Gulliver Experiment
    887:72-74
Magnetic fields of planets demonstration 1394:88-89
Magnetic force around planets demonstration with iron
    filings 1365:49
Make your own orrery—show how planets move in their
    orbits—how to make 502:28-29
Making a model of Saturn project 833:243-245
Making a model of the orbits of Uranus, Neptune, and
    Pluto project 833:249-251
Making craters on Mercury project 833:221-223
Making models of conic sections project 833:162-164
Mars and Earth have cold poles demonstration 1394:92-
    93
Mars backward motion demonstration 1394:30-31
Mars measurements 292:90-91
Mars; canals on Mars demonstrated with red paper and
    black paint experiment 1478:69
Mars; crater landscape of Mars experiment with asteroids
    crashing into flour 1365:37
Mars; demonstrate apparent backward motion of Mars ex-
    periment 1405:3
Mars; material that causes surface of Mars to have its red
    color experiment 1405:5

Mars; models compare largest volcanoes on Mars and on Earth experiment 1478:68
Mars; observe and plot movements, how to do 1170:42
Mars; reproduce Martian surface channels (river beds) experiment, how to make 1476:161
Mars; testing for life on Mars experiment with sand/yeast/salt/b. Powder/sugar 1478:70-71
Mars; why Mars is red experiment with sand, steel wool and water 1478:69
Mars; why poles of Mars and Earth are cold experiment 1479:14
Measure altitude of stars and planets with instrument you build 834:124-125
Measure how far apart the planets are in space experiment 1500:13
Mercury doesn't cause eclipse of Sun demonstration 1394:18-19
Mercury measurements 292:81-83
Mercury's position to the Sun affects observation of its surface experiment 1394:16-17
Mercury; brightness of Sun from Mercury experiment 1478:64
Mercury; show how Mercury's position affects observation of its surface 1405:4-7
Mercury; why Mercury does not cause an eclipse experiment 1479:3
Mercury; why Mercury's day is longer than its year experiment 1478:65
Meteorite craters formation project, how to do 967:8-9
Mobile of Solar System with sizes of planets done to scale experiment 1478:60-61
Model of nine planets & differences in their distance from the sun-making 130:30-31, 34
Model of Solar System to scale, how to make 1441:5-6
Models of planets made from cardboard, how to do 1365:35
Moon and planet study project, how to observe and record 1217:22-23
Moon measurements 292:88-89
Motion and speed of planets as they travel around the Sun experiment 1478:62-63
Movement of planets around the Sun demonstration with cardboard spinner 1394:56-57
Movement of planets demonstration with marble in pan 1394:54-55
Movement; determine why planets continue to move experiment 1479:7
Movement; determine why planets move smoothly around the Sun experiment 1479:6
Neptune becomes the outermost planet experiment with elliptical orbits 1394:60-61
Neptune measurements 292:96
Neptune's Scooter and the Great Dark Spot experiment with models 1478:78
Orbital movement; effect of forces on shown with swinging cup of sand 1394:50-51
Orbiting speed; effect of distance on orbiting speed demonstration 1394:52-53
Photographing stars and planets project 833:181-182
Planet mobile—making 293:39
Planet models—how to build 175:40-41
Planet surface warmed more by greenhouse effect than by Sun's rays experiment 1062:64-66
Planet's surface temperature can vary demonstration with thermometers 1394:8-9

Plants can't grow on Mars and Pluto experiment 1441:9
Pluto discovered by using blink comparator, how to make 1478:80-81
Pluto measurements 292:96-97
Project solar system—study of planets size, distance and life 400:106-107
Radius of orbits—time to orbit Earth—diameter—mass and density table 763:30
Satellites appear to be stationary demonstration 1394:72-73
Satellites stay in orbit demonstration 1394:68-69
Satellites stay in orbit due to centripetal force demonstration 1394:70-71
Saturn and its rings, how to observe 1170:50
Saturn measurements 292:94-95
Saturn seen through its rings demonstration 1394:44-45
Saturn's changing shape experiment with foamcore, and orange 1478:74
Saturn's Moons affect the planet's rings demonstration 1394:46-47
Saturn's rings and ringlets experiment with rotating cake stand 1478:75
Saturn; determine how Saturn can be seen through its rings experiment 1479:6
Showing how Mars goes backwards project 833:231-233
Size and distance of planets experiment using two scale models 1062:58-60
Size of planets and their distances from each other model, how to make 1441:5-6
Soil with least reflectivity has highest temperature due to absorption ex 1062:62-63
Space acts as heat shield for planets demonstration 1394:40-41
Surface mapping and height of objects experiment 1062:100-101
Temperature of planet's surface can vary experiment 1479:2
Thickness of planet's atmosphere affects bending of light demonstration 1394:10-11
Twinkling; why stars twinkle and planets do not experiment 1478:114-115
Uranus measurements 292:95-96
Uranus model revolves around Sun to show its topsy turvy traveling experiment 1478:76
Uranus; discovery of Uranus's rings experiment with foamcore/paint/flashlight 1478:77
Venus measurements 292:84-85
Venus' atmosphere hard to see through demonstration 1394:20-21
Venus' atmosphere traps infrared waves making it very hot demonstration 1394:22-23
Venus; how to find Venus in the sky 1434:75-76
Venus; phases of Venus experiment with foamcore, battery and wires 1478:67
Venus; phases of Venus, how to observe and draw 1170:38
Venus; plumb line experiment to demonstrate radar mapping of Venus 1478:66
Venus; Sun's heat is trapped by gases in Venus's atmosphere experiment 1478:67
Venus; why Venus is so hot experiment 1479:4
Venus; why Venus' atmosphere is so hard to see through experiment 1479:3
Weight and mass—computer project 584:101-102

Weight of people on other planets computer project 1021:96-98

When Mercury is most visible from Earth experiment 1405:5

Why aren't planets spherical (Advanced) 658:71-72

Why planets are not spherical 577:project #32

Why satellite stays in orbit demonstration 1405:7

PLANKTON

Activities with plankton 236:109

Collect and examine plankton experiment 1118:40-41

Collecting and studying plankton 400:59

Effects of increased acidity on plankton experiment 864:130-132

Effects of oil spills on zooplankton experiment 1058:92

Grow some plankton experiment 1492:28

How to collect 41:62-65

Plankton dip net—making 175:22-23

Plankton in a pond community experiment using plankton net 1172:35-37

Plankton net to catch and observe plankton, how to make 1176:30-31

Plankton net, how to make from nylon stocking and wire 1172:36-37

PLANKTON NET

How to make 285:35-37; 359:48-51; 530:52-53

Make a tiny net for plankton 400:59

Making and using a plankton net 625:55

PLANT LICE. *See* **APHIDS**

PLANTERS

Coconut shell planter—making 264:123

Eggshell planters—making 508:47

Milk carton planter—making 631:112

PLANTS. *See also* **ALGAE; FLOWERS; FUNGI; MOSSES; ROOTS; SEAWEEDS; SEEDS; SPORES;** *and names of plants*

Activities to identify and investigate plants [Primary] 758:67-76

Air needed for plant growth experiment 760:9-10

Air; do plants need air experiment 852:5-6

Altitude—demonstrate effects of altitude on plants and animals 301:27-28

Amusing plant uses—grass whistles, popping leaves, crowns, necklaces 236:40-41

Annual life history of your favorite plant species project 1313:54-56

Asexual reproduction—experiment 507:1853-1854

Avocado—grow an avocado plant 416:15

Avocado tree—how to grow indoors 497:22-26

Bean bomb—demonstrates force of germinating seeds 146:40

Bean sprouts—six stages of a bean sprouting 497:33

Beet tops—how to grow 497:14-16

Blueprints of garden vegetables, how to make 1265:86

Bottle garden—how to make 158:28-29; 574:10-11

Bulbs and bulb like plants—how to grow indoors 497:65-74

Cacti and other succulents—grow indoors—ice plant and Indian corncob 497:95-99

Carbon dioxide given off or taken up by plants experiment 1427:40-41

Carbon dioxide production balanced by plants and animals in environment 1427:42-43

Carrot ferns—how to grow 497:12-13

Carrot top garden (Primary) 535:42

Cells; what happens to plant cells living in fresh water experiment 1395:42-43

Cereal—show growth of cereal plants versus other plants 119:63-67

Citrus orchards—how to grow plants from citrus seeds indoors 497:31-32

Citrus plants—how to grow 86:61

Color and light effect on color of ripening apples experiment 864:72

Compass plant to grow in your garden 271:64

Contribution of plants to human needs project 1427:30-31

Controlled plant experiments for science projects—how to do 398:5-18

Culture solution for plants—how to make 128:214

Dandelion activities 236:30-31

Density—is there a large range of densities in plants 402:27-28

Dish gardens—plants and mosses for 497:50-61

Do leaves use water experiment 804:29-30

Do plants need sunlight for growth—experiment 489:15-16

Edible parts of plants, chart given 817:7

Elements used by plants and functions they perform 1061:45-46

Energy from burning foods and fuel experiment 739:15

Feelings; do plants have feelings experiment 980:81

Flowering house plants—how to plant and grow indoors 497:75-82

Foliage plants—how to grow indoors—piggyback plant, Chinese evergreen 497:83-93

Force of growing plants experiments 706:23-24

Freezing related to dissolved nutrients in plants experiment 904:26-27

Galls—demonstrating growth of galls 117:82-84

Garden in a bottle—how to make 473:53

Good luck ti plant—grow "good luck" from long Hawaiian ti plant—indoors 416:19

Grass seeds grow in a window sill garden 155:10-11

Grass weaving—how to 236:38

Green plants make oxygen; pond plant in jar experiment 790:12-13

Greenhouse effect with solar collectors 289:38-39

Grocery farm—grow plants from grocery vegetables and fruits 565:97-106

Grow a little forest of carrots and beets from tops indoors 416:16-17

Grow plants from seed seedlings dropped by birds 530:194

Grow plants under an electric lamp 416:45

Grow your own special place to hide with peas and stakes (Primary) 580:unpaged

Growing flowers from vegetables 148:19

Growing fruit seeds and pits 473:53

Growing plants from the kitchen—carrots, potato, onion, corn 32:8-11

Growing plants without using seeds 232:60

Heat is product of plant respiration experiment, data sheet given 817:8

How plants get water 30:42-43

How sap rises 30:44-45

Ideas for doing your plant project, and safety and record keeping 1222:30-33

Ideas for planning your plant project and gathering information 1222:19-29

301

Ideas for plant project exhibits, demonstrations and investigations 1222:10-18
Ideas for plant projects 1222:8-18
Ideas for presenting your plant project with graphs, displays, reports 1222:34-43
Investigation into the effect of table salt on plant life 420:133-134
Is soil best? What do plants need to grow in—experiment 590:40
Keep your plants growing experiment 901:32-33
Key for classifying plants; game and key 1063:242-243
Leaf responses to acid rain experiments 777:13
Magnet and electromagnetic fields effect on plants—experiment 398:123-124
Make a V.I.P. cube (box) for plant-print information (Primary) 580:unpaged
Moon phases—effect on plants 398:132-133
Moon phases planting project using Old Farmer's Almanac 1062:110-111
Movement of water and food in plants experiment 829:57-58
Nitrogen nodules 112:12
Observing and recording wild plants—what you see 590:42
One-celled plants from hay infusion—view under microscope 86:13
Overpopulations of plants experiment 978:168-169
Oxygen from plants 30:41
Oxygen needed to keep fire burning experiment with candle and plant 978:121
Parts of plants—demonstrate 108:37-40
Parts of some common plants demonstration 901:34
Parts we eat (Primary) 535:13
Pet plant to grow from lamb's ear, sea pink, and Irish moss, how to do 1054:91
Pigments in plants shown by chromatograms experiment 1069:40
Pineapple—grow a pineapple plant indoors 416:18
Pits—grow into plants—how to do 158:28
Plant detective game 264:84
Plant hospital—a small greenhouse made from sticks, glue and plastic 483:52-53
Plant hospital for ailing indoor plants 497:121-122
Plant movement-maze shows plants grow or move in certain directions 590:46-47
Plant needs to breathe experiment 784:92-93
Plant observation activities 236:32-33
Plant pigment—what parts of plants produce pigments 273:40-41
Plant pigments—magic potions using red cabbage 16:62-65
Plant seed responses to acid rain experiments 777:11
Plant trail—how to make 248:12-13
Planting box, how to make 830:75-76
Planting dates and harvesting dates for 10 vegetables—show 380:16-17
Planting food—a children's garden (Primary) 232:65
Plants absorb water through veins experiment 759:18-19
Plants and people—activities 236:38
Plants around the world 248:15-31
Plants around you—how to make a map of an area 248:10-11
Plants break up rocks experiment using bean seeds planted in plaster 1438:14-17
Plants breathe—experiment to show 85:56-57; 273:18-23

Plants breathe—finding out how 148:26
Plants exhale carbon dioxide experiment 904:36-37
Plants grow in different environments game, how to make 1044:16-19
Plants have seeds and flowers, primary activities to demonstrate 854:51-52
Plants in containers—make a coconut shell planter 264:123
Plants keep soil from being washed away (Primary) 262:unpaged
Plants need air Vaseline on leaves experiment 705:38-39
Plants produce water vapor—simple experiment to show 597:36-37
Plants with animals in mind 264:124-125
Pollen—a study of 148:16
Pollen grains grow experiment 819:58
Pollution effect on plants experiment 739:39
Potting plants, how to do 1440:97-99
Printing with plant leaves, stems, and roots, how to do 1054:48-49
Reactions of plants—discovering how plants react 148:32-33
Repotting plants—how to do 398:31-32
Rush lights from rushes—making 236:39
Seedling responses to acid rain experiments 777:12
Seeds; number of seeds that survive to adulthood project 1313:63-65
Sound and music experiments 398:124-127
Sprayer for plants, how to make 909:67
Starch test experiment 739:13
Starch; experiments in finding starch in plants 784:78-79
Stomata—regulators of water loss—make and compare slides in light/dark 500:135-136
Succession of plants—experiments 118:155-163
Succession of plants experiment 739:25
Sunflowers—giant sunflower race with friends 376:16-17
Sunlight—determine hours of sunlight your garden has for plants 380:20-21
Sunlight—how plants need—leaf kept out of sunlight—experiment (Primary) 540:29
Sweet potato vine—grow a sweet potato vine 416:12-13
Sweet potato vines—how to grow 497:19-21
Symbiotic relationship between some species of plants experiment 978:95
Test for glucose sugar in leaves 86:41
Testing for oxygen manufactured by plants 574:34
Testing for starch—prove that starch is produced in a leaf 574:35
Testing how plants work 473:56-57
Turgor pressure experiment with rhubarb stalks 904:16-17
Turgor pressure experiment with wilted celery 904:14-15
Turgor pressure; effect of water on plants experiment 1395:45-50
Vacant lot plants project; how to study using quadrat 1060:129-132
Vegetation zones—cold lands 248:30
Vegetation zones—cool forests 248:18-19
Vegetation zones—cool grasslands 248:20-21
Vegetation zones—desert areas 248:26
Vegetation zones—Mediterranean lands 248:22-23
Vegetation zones—mountain areas 248:24-25
Vegetation zones—swamplands 248:31
Vegetation zones—tropical forests 248:28-29

Vegetation zones—tropical grasslands 248:27
Warp plants protect themselves 233:27-29
Water and sun needed for healthy plants—experiment
    (Primary) 535:39
Water garden indoors—how to set up 497:118-119
Water; where does water enter plants experiment 852:7-8
Waterer for plants—making 722:73
Weather and its effect on plant life experiment 978:138
What are plants 248:4-5
What parts of plants do we eat 236:38
What plant is this; plant identification experiment 901:13
Window box garden—how to make 473:52
Window boxes for plants—vegetables and flowers to
    grow indoors 497:34-49

PLANTS—ACID RAIN
Effects on plants 398:133-137

PLANTS—ADAPTATIONS
How do different types of plants adapt to varying water
    conditions 371:53-58
How plants survive 380:69

PLANTS—AIR
Plant that lives on air, how to grow 899:198-199

PLANTS—AIR PLANTS
Air plants—how to grow 483:54-55
Exhibit of air plants 532:53
How plants need it—Vaseline keeps air from leaf—
    experiment (Primary) 540:30

PLANTS—AIR POLLUTANTS
Acid fog effect on geranium plant experiment 1060:116
Acid rain affects growth of geranium plant cuttings ex-
    periment 1060:117
Acid rain affects leaf ratio in radish plants experiment
    1060:116-117
Acid rain effects on plants experiment 1324:60-64
Building materials release materials that effect plant
    growth experiment 714:71-72
Carbon dioxide increase causes increase in plant growth
    experiment 1060:121
Measuring shade effect of soot on plant leaves experi-
    ment 933:21-23
Nitrogen dioxide—experiments 398:59-60
Plants contain less chlorophyll if leaf stomata are
    blocked experiment 714:33-35
Smoke affects growth of plants experiment 1061:37-38
Sulfur dioxide—experiments 398:56-59
Sulfur dioxide harms plants experiment 1324:65-68
Sulfur dioxide gas effect on growth of seedlings experi-
    ment 1134:6.003
Weigh deposits of soot on plant leaves experiment
    933:18-20

PLANTS—AQUATIC
Soil from dried up marsh area contains life experiment
    1074:66

PLANTS—ART ACTIVITIES
Apple dolls—making 582:21-23
Back-to-back drawing from verbal description 582:4-5
Cornhusk dolls—making 582:25-28
Drawing from a still life 582:8-10
Drawing moss and lichens 582:17-19
Dyeing from vegetable matter 582:30-33
Hand lens drawing of mosses, lichens and leaf structures
    582:10-12
Linear drawing of motion in nature 582:12-14
Nature rubbings 582:6-8
Photo paper designs 582:19-21

Plant pressing 582:28-30
Printmaking from nature 582:15-17
Sawdust modeling dough 582:33-35
Wood carving 582:23-25

PLANTS—AUXINS. *See also* **PLANTS—HORMONES**
Apical dominance exhibited on terminal bud of white
    potato experiment 1395:57-61
Apical dominance; growth inhibitor experiment 1395:57-
    61
Blossom-set products prevent fruit from falling off plant
    experiment 1395:60-61
Geotropism; gravity affects plant growth experiment
    1395:75-81
Response of oat seedlings to light experiment 1395:83-88

PLANTS—BACTERIA
Cultivation of bacteria—experiment 402:29-30
Grow bacteria to study their plant characteristics 293:16
Nitrogen-fixing bacteria change nitrogen so plants can
    use it experiment 1402:48-51
Nitrogen-fixing bacteria help clover plants to grow ex-
    periment 1060:111-112
Nitrogen-fixing bacteria on clover plant nodules experi-
    ment 1060:110
Nitrogen-fixing bacteria on roots of legume plants experi-
    ment 1060:110
Nitrogen-fixing bacteria replace nitrogen compounds in
    hydroponic solution 1060:112

PLANTS—BEACH
Investigation of the plants of the beach and dune 285:71-
    72

PLANTS—BIOLUMINESCENCE
Do plants and animals emit light 402:18-19

PLANTS—BUDS
How terminal buds affect lateral buds 603:38-39, 65-66
Opening buds—experiment 603:37, 65
Parts of a bud—experiment 603:33-36

PLANTS—BULBS
Experiment—start bulbs in light and dark—chart results
    333:97-99

PLANTS—CANCER
How effective is beta carotene in fighting cancer in
    plants experiment 997:54-56

PLANTS—CAPILLARITY
Capillarity experiment 577:project 95
See red and blue veins in celery 508:13
Testing how stems work with celery and flower 473:56

PLANTS—CAPILLARY ACTION
Blue carnations experiment 882:32
Capillarity and water cohesion of plants—experimenting
    with 148:28
Capillary action in plants 270:46-54
Capillary action stops at what size diameter string and
    tube experiment 714:109-110
Carnation flower colored with two different dyes experi-
    ment 1060:39-41
Carnation flower drinks colored water and petals change
    color experiment 1379:20
Carnations and green food coloring demonstrate 722:83
Carnations in colored demonstrate how flowers drink and
    where water goes 1016:12-13
Celery—water and food coloring demonstrates 709:35
Celery and carnations in colored water demonstrate
    854:44
Celery experiment 780:4-5
Celery in colored water experiment 832:52

Celery stalk and food coloring demonstrate 899:183
Celery stalk in food coloring demonstrates capillary
  action 971:28
Celery stalk in red food coloring experiment 1238:31-32
Celery stalk turns different colors experiment 1231:20-21
Celery turns blue experiment 1258:unp.
Colored inks show movement of water in plants 146:9
Colored water is drawn up into leaf experiment 1243:19-
  20
Colored water moves up stalk of celery experiment
  879:89-90
Colored water traveling through flower and celery stem
  experiment 1236:7
Colored water travels up celery stalk experiment
  1063:249
Colored water travels up stems of carnations experiment
  1044:14-15
Coloring celery stalks experiment 814:61-63
Coloring celery stalks experiment 898:47
Demonstrate how water rises in plants 293:19
Dirty water test for pollutants getting into plants experi-
  ment, how to do 1414:16-17
Does water move in stems and leaves 60:32-33
Flower in colored water experiment 1335:118
Flowers and celery in colored water experiment 996:28-
  29
Flowers change color experiment 1028:27
Food and water—how they travel in plants experiment
  733:26
Food colorings—salt—sugar and celery stalk experiment
  714:96-98
Green flowers from dyes experiment 1246:18
How much water does a plant absorb over time experi-
  ment 1044:15
How plants drink 280:57
How plants get water 72:38-41
How water moves in plant experiment 1183:26
Identify xylem tubes in plants using colored water experi-
  ment 714:104-105
Ink travels up celery stalk experiment 1392:9
Patriotic colored celery stalks in colored water experi-
  ment 1078:21
Plant pipe patterns 162:42
Plants absorb nutrients thru roots—celery and colored
  water exp. 384:3-4
Plants carry water from roots thru stems to leaves experi-
  ment 978:58-59
Plants drink contaminated water; celery stalk and colored
  water experiment 1127:37
Polluted water can get into food experiment using celery,
  water, food coloring 1228:28-29
Primary experiments to show 104:30-33
Red ink rises up in celery stalks under different condi-
  tions experiment 1060:39
Red ink water rises through plant experiment 1060:39
Roots and stems pull water into celery stalk and carrot ex-
  periment 1368:32-33
Rose in clear and colored water experiment 712:54-55
Stems of carnations take up blue water to show capillary
  action experiment 1038:22
Tubes carry water to leaves experiment with celery and
  colored water 1440:5-7
Turning white flowers to red—green and blue flowers ex-
  periment 762:74-75
Two-tone carnation flower experiment 1258:unp.

Watch stalk of celery drink colored water 264:16
Water circulation through plants—experiment 585:147-
  148
Water is transported through plants experiment with cel-
  ery in food coloring 1402:43
Water moves in plants experiment using celery stalk and
  red food coloring 1181:18
Water travels in plant experiment using celery stalk in
  red colored water 1207:7
White rose turns red and blue 150:114-115
Wicks used to demonstrate capillary action in plants ex-
  periment 1061:102-103

PLANTS—CARBON DIOXIDE
Carbon dioxide produced by plants in the dark—
  experiment 97:29
Germinating seeds give off carbon dioxide experiment
  722:70-71
Plant grows faster in soda water, which provides extra
  CO_2 86:30
Plant in plastic bag demonstrates carbon cycle 950:11-
  12
Plants use carbon dioxide experiment 1324:48-53
Plants use carbon dioxide 282:25-33

PLANTS—CELLS
Cells of an onion 82:43-44
Cellulose cell wall—experiment 402:20-21
Examine green plant cells—elodea—under microscope
  294:15-16
Examine living plant cells from an onion skin under
  microscope 294:14-15
Hugo de Vries's plasmolysis in plant cells experiment
  1133:3.010
Leaf stomata under a microscope, how to do 886:28-29
Movement in living cells—observe 148:34
Plant cells under a microscope, how to do 886:28-29
Show what plant cells and tissues look like 284:9-13
Water movement in and out of plant cells experiment
  762:79-81

PLANTS—CELLULOSE
Boiled winter squash—a study of cellulose 74:96-98

PLANTS—CHLOROPHYLL. *See also* **CHLOROPHYLL**
Aluminum foil on leaves demonstrates effect of light on
  chlorophyll experiment 762:75-76
Chlorophyll allows plants to use light energy 273:34-35
Chloroplasts containing chlorophyll studied under micro-
  scope experiment 1060:21
Chromatograms of autumn maple tree leaves day by day
  experiment 1060:19-20
Chromatograms of chlorophyll compared in plants grow-
  ing in shade and sun 1060:20
Color pigment in plant leaves affected by sunlight experi-
  ment 1395:107-112
Determining the role of chlorophyll in plants 148:24-
  25
Grass grown in dark experiment 1159:63-64
How do leaves that are not green make their food 86:63
Is chlorophyll the only color pigment in a leaf experi-
  ment 1395:110
Leaf covered with black paper experiment 1159:64
Leaves need light to stay green experiment using leaf and
  black board 1390:29
Light necessary to produce chlorophyll experiment
  1440:8-11
Plant cells filled with chlorophyll—see under micro-
  scope 86:47

Separate chlorophyll pigments from plant leaves experiment 860:61-65

Separating the chlorophyll pigments of plants experiment using chromatography 1060:18-20

Spinach—color changes in chlorophyll—experiment 74:93-95

Sunburned vegetables—experiment 585:151-152

What happens to grass when it doesn't receive sunlight experiment 1324:38-41

PLANTS—CLONING

Can plant cloning be used effectively by produce growers experiment 997:52-53

Cloning plants—experiment 586:124-126

Jumping strawberries—build box, plant and watch for runners 483:40-41

PLANTS—COLLECTION AND PRESERVATION

Collecting—plants that are already dry 59:32-40

Collecting a whole plant and mounting botanical specimens 62:28-30

Collecting and photographing plants 59:75-83

Collecting and planting live plants 59:65-74

Collecting and preserving plants, how to do 117:58-59; 824:24-35

Collecting and pressing fresh plants 59:54-64

Collecting and pressing plants, how to do 1505:30-31

Drying plants—how to—recipe for inexpensive drying agents 59:41-53

How to dry flowers 473:55

How to press flowers 473:54

Picture from pressed plants—how to make 473:54

Plant press for preserving plants, making 864:66-69

Pressing leaves and plants, how to do 1395:203-205

PLANTS—COLOR

Color effect on chlorophyll production in plant leaves experiment 1082:187-191

pH of soil affects color of hydrangea flowers experiment 1060:114

PLANTS—COMMUNICATION

Can we communicate with plants experiment 901:3-4

Communication in plants—experiments 398:127-128

PLANTS—COMPUTER PROJECT

Factors in plant growth project 584:53-54

Paper chromatography (pigments in a leaf)—project 584:55-56

Rates of photosynthesis—project 584:57-58

PLANTS—CRAFTS

Plant craft activities 236:37-38

PLANTS—DESERT

A study of desert plants and their distribution 285:78-79

PLANTS—DYES. See also **DYES**

Dyeing with plant materials, how to do 784:15-17

Dyes from plants and their effect on different fabrics experiment 871:2.021

Dyes from plants, how to make 1020:86-90

Extracting dyes from plants 148:18

Make your own plant dyes 574:40-41

Making plant dyes to dye wool 473:59

Natural dyes from parts of plants, how to make 1063:254

Plant dyes; collect and use to dye yarn experiment 978:59-60

PLANTS—ENZYMES

Acids and bases effect on catalase enzyme in plants 273:50-51

Enzyme catalase removes hydrogen peroxide in plants 273:44-45

Enzyme in plant materials—experiment 273:44-45

PLANTS—EROSION. See also **EROSION**

Plants help prevent erosion experiment 1341:66

PLANTS—FEELINGS

Feelings, do plants have feelings experiment 980:81

PLANTS—FERNS. See also **FERNS**

Fern insect repellent—making 236:39

Ferns and spores—primary experiments to show growth from spores 104:40-46

Grow your own ferns from spores using brick, moss and water 483:42-44

PLANTS—FERTILIZERS

Effect of fertilizers on plant growth experiment 784:122-123

Experiment with plant food 416:10

Fertilize your plants—how to 398:33

Fertilizer makes your plants grow (Primary) 326:16-17

Grow your initials in the lawn with plant food 416:10-11

Growing plants with chemicals 148:31

Minerals from the earth—experiment with plants 563:63

Nitrogen and other nutrients are needed for plant growth experiment 1324:54-58

Plant food makes plants grow better (Primary) 324:24-25

PLANTS—FLOWERPOTS

Flowerpot experiments 398:40-41

PLANTS—FLOWERS. See also **FLOWERS**

Parts of a flower 60:42-44

Parts of a typical flowering plant 294:30-31

PLANTS—FOOD

Starch test for starch in plant leaves experiment 1028:63

PLANTS—FOOD STORAGE SYSTEMS

Bulbs store food for growth—grow hyacinth bulbs in water 384:19-20

Plants store food experiment with onion 1181:24

Plants store food experiments 1183:32-33

Roots store food for growth—hanging carrot experiment 384:11-15

Tubers store food for growth—grow potato or sweet potato in H_2O 384:16-19

PLANTS—FRAMES

Hot and cold frames—how to make 398:36-38

PLANTS—FREEZING

Nutrients dissolved in leaves affect freezing rate of plants experiment 1479:24

Water protects plants from freezing temperatures experiment 1405:29

PLANTS—FRESH WATER

Algae—iodine stain shows starch in cells 294:21-22

PLANTS—FRUITS AND SEEDS. See also **SEEDS—FRUIT**

Observe flowers as they turn to fruits and seeds 380:80-84

PLANTS—FUEL

Plant materials changed into methane fuel experiment 1323:90-94

PLANTS—GENETICS

Genetic engineering process—experiment 398:101-107

Mendel's experiment with peas 398:91-96

Mendel's work with peas—incomplete dominance experiment 148:17

Mutation experiment 398:97-100

Project with hybrids 398:96

Will sweet potato change seed's genes experiment 1375:58-60

305

PLANTS—GEOTROPISM. *See also* **PLANTS—TROPISMS**

Demonstrate bean stems grow up; roots grow down 288:18-19

Do plants and animals seek the Earth's center 402:34-35

Down they go—roots always turn downward—experiment 560:23-24

Effect of centrifugal force on geotropism 577:project 82

Spiral roots experiment—seeds send roots down 576:81

Upside down roots—experiment 600:52-53

PLANTS—GERMINATION. *See also* **SEEDS—GERMINATION**

Development of plants from seeds (Primary) 232:63

From seed to seedling 7:68-82

Growing a plant from seed 60:11-13

Growing beans (Primary) 232:62

Household chemicals effect on germination and height of seedlings experiment 1004:2.012

How seeds grow 72:36-37

Observe seeds sown in different types of soil 294:52

Plant embryo—observe parts of a seed 400:21

Planters and seed starters from cans 264:112

Planting beans (Primary) 232:61

Pollution from metals—effect of copper salts on germination 33:22-23

Seedling—observe growth of cotyledons, embryos and stem 86:67

Seeds from flowers—how to grow 400:20

Seeds grow without soil 293:14

Seeds need water to sprout 154:18-19

Seeds need water, air and warmth to germinate—experiment 146:41

Seeing the plant embryo in seeds 60:9-10

Showing the strength of growing seeds 148:24

Sowing seeds—compare germination and growth 146:41

Testing effect of heat and light on germination 148:36

The flying monster plant—sponge and bird seed 376:10

What happens if seeds are crowded 60:47

PLANTS—GRAFTS

Burbank's grafting experiments 879:100-102

Flat-grafting cactus plants, how to do 1440:112-114

Graft a plant, how to do 1440:103-105

Graft potato and tomato plants to get a pomato experiment 1476:108

Grafting plants 436:38-39

How to make a graft 398:70-74

Potato—tomato graft 532:63

Tomato plant grafted to potato plant experiment 834:148-149

PLANTS—GROWTH

Acid fog effect on geranium plant experiment 1060:116

Acid rain affects growth of geranium plant cuttings experiment 1060:117

Acid rain affects leaf ratio in radish plants experiment 1060:116-117

Acid rain affects plants experiment using vinegar, lime and distilled water 1046:80-82

Acid rain effect on growing plants experiment 1150:78; 1233:76-77; 1324:60-64; 1335:211

Acid rain effect on growth of geraniums experiment 1060:114-116

Acid rain effect on seed growth experiment 727:21

Acid rain effects on seeds and plants experiment 978:177

Acid water affects plant growth experiment using vinegar 1362:17

Adaptations by plants to water supply experiment using moisture-gradient box 1172:42-45

Air—water and light effect on plant growth experiment [Primary] 758:74

Air pollution and effect on plant growth experiment 874:217

Allelopathy experiment; chemicals from plants inhibit growth of other plants 1060:133

Auxins—effect on growth of plants 273:52-55

Auxins and responses to stimulation experiment 878:48-49

Batch plants together observe growth at center and perimeters experiment 714:91-92

Bean plant grows through box maze toward light experiment 1288:24-25

Bean plant grows toward light in shoe box experiment 1068:41

Bean plants, how to grow 1486:6-7

Bean seed grows in glass experiment 1028:60

Bean seeds grown upside down in jar show effect of gravity on growth 1038:16

Bean seeds show how plants grow experiment 931:2

Better growth curve—experiment 603:14-15, 58-59

Black walnut trees release chemicals that prevent plant growth project 969:50-51

Boiled water makes plants grow better experiment 722:78

Borage plants stimulate growth of strawberry plants experiment 1060:132-133

Bottle base water reservoir to keep plants watered, how to make 1527:101

Building materials release materials that effect plant growth experiment 714:71-72

Calendar time needed for growing different experimental seedlings 1222:25

Can a plant amaze you experiment 901:39-40

Can parts of a plant be poisoned 577:project 83

Carbon dioxide increase causes increase in plant growth experiment 1060:121

Carbon dioxide; effects of industrial carbon dioxide on plant growth experiment 1174:49-50

Certain substances or solutions affect plant growth experiment 1527:93

Change plants into dwarfs or giants with chemicals 86:17-18

Chemotropism—black walnut tree effect on plant growth experiment 714:78-79

Chemotropism—plants grow toward nutrients they need experiment 714:80-81

Chemotropism; plant root response to odors in the air experiment 1061:79-80

Chlorophyll increases or decreases in leaves with amount light experiment 714:31-32

Chromosome changes from water pollutants experiment using onions 1060:119-121

Coconut milk stimulates growth in plant cell tissue experiment 1060:88-89

Color of light affects growth of seedlings experiment 1183:25

Color of light best for growth of plants experiment 1222:5-7, 22-26

Colored light effect on plant growth experiment 1395:86

Colored light effect on plant stem elongation experiment 1395:92

Colored light effects growth of plants experiment 714:29-30

Compacted soil and effect on plant growth experiment 714:53-55

Composition of soil; what makes up soil experiment 1134:1.005

Compost effect on plant growth experiment 714:59-60

Conditions necessary for plant life experiment 706:99-100

Cotyledons—experiment to test the importance of cotyledons 86:66

Crowding affects growth of plant seeds project 1296:1995

Cucumber grows in bottle experiment 879:136-137

Different plants need different amounts of water experiment 1172:42-45

Direction of growth of roots, stems and leaves experiment 1395:69-74

Do plants grow only from seeds experiment 852:2-3

Do plants have feelings 745:65-74

Do plants need air and sunlight to live 233:29

Do plants need air 236:36

Do plants need light to grow 60:16-17

Do plants need water to grow 60:14-15

Do young plants use the food in the endosperm 60:20

Does covering leaves effect plant growth experiment 714:24-26

Does heavy layer of canopy trees effect plant growth experiment 714:36-37

Does popcorn seed grow better in subsoil, topsoil, or drained soil exp. 835:36-38

Does salt runoff from roads affect plant growth experiment 1527:67-68

Drought; plants send roots deeper into soil for water experiment 1180:24

Droughts; plants send roots deeper into soil for water experiment 1183:152

Effect of a deficiency and additional carbon dioxide on plant growth 577:project 88

Effect of cotyledon removal on peanut embryos experiment 871:2.008

Effect of different soils on plant growth experiment 797:31

Effect of electric current on plants experiment 830:74-76

Effect of light on plant growth—projects 398:49-53

Effect of salt on plant growth experiment 921:41

Effect of soil pH on plant growth experiment; data table given 871:2.009

Electric currents affect plant growth experiment 1375:111-114

Electrical currents effect on plants experiment 1249:54-56

Electrical stimulation effect on plant growth experiment 1061:89

Elongation of dicot plant stem experiment 1395:69-74

Experimenting with types of soil and effect on plant growth 898:52

Fertilizer effect on growth experiment 829:59-60

Find out what plants need—experiment 480:18

Force of growing plants 146:40

Force of plants pushes weights aside experiment 723:74

Freezing temperatures effect on plants experiment 1180:8

Freezing temperatures effect on plants experiment 1183:136

From roots—root of sweet potato grows vine (Primary) 540:38

From seeds—avocado seed grows in water (Primary) 540:37

From stems—stem from geranium grows in water (Primary) 540:39

Fruit smell affects plant growth experiment 749:38

Game; build a plant game to demonstrate plant growth 1335:103

Game; growth game board shows how plants grow and change, how to make 1181:26-27

Game; growth of plants game, how to make 1183:34-35

Garlic bulbs—planting for indoor growth 712:34

Geotropism—effect of gravity on germination of seeds experiment 714:82-84

Gibberellic acid—solutions for plants 398:12-18

Gibberellic acid effects growth of plants 273:56-57

Gibberellins affect growth of dwarf pea plants experiment 1060:86-88

Gibberellins influence size and flowering in geranium plants experiment 1060:88

Gravity affects seeds, roots and shoots experiment 1183:24

Gravity and centrifugal force effect on plants grown on turntable experiment 1159:64-67

Gravity and its effect on seed growth experiment 904:50-51

Gravity and way it affects growth movement 480:25

Gravity—demonstrate effect of gravity on plants 291:199

Gravity has effect on plant growth experiment 1399:48-51

Green peanuts—can the plant grow without seed leaves—experiment 560:18-20

Green plant life does not occur deep in the ocean experiment 904:56-57

Greenhouses trap sunlight and warmth speeds growth of plants experiment 1090:49

Grow bucket from 5 gallon plastic bucket, circular fluorescent bulb experiment 1527:105-106

Grow plants from tops, fruit seeds and bird seed 231:26-27

Growing a root system experiment 738:21

Growing food for people isn't easy experiment using plants 1059:38-39

Growing plants from seeds 603:21-22, 60-61

Growing plants in garden soil and desert soil experiment 1467:29

Growing plants in space experiments 763:98-99

Growing plants without soil experiment 878:40-41

Growth checkup—measure popcorn and peanut seedling roots 560:21

Growth curve—experiment 603:10-13, 57-58

Growth from stored food—demonstrate 158:22-23

Growth of bean seed demonstration 1440:41-45

Growth of grass plants versus other plants 119:58-63

Growth point of plants demonstrated by growing and trimming grass seeds 1069:52-53

Growth regulators—projects with auxins 398:69

Habitat and niche experiment 739:27

Habitat plant community experiment 739:29

Heat pollution from industry kills plants experiment 1074:84-85

307

Heat, light and water needed for plants to grow experiment 1358:20
Household liquids and powders water solution effect on plant growth experiment 1465:109
How do flowering plants reproduce?—experiment 628:110-111
How fast do plants grow 236:34
How fast do some plants grow 333:102-104
How gravity affects plant growth 294:42-43
Increased carbon dioxide levels in atmosphere increase plant growth experiment 1174:49-50
Investigation into the growth of a plant 420:78-80
Is different food needed by plants and animals 402:35-36
Johannes Van Helmont's growth of plants experiment 1133:3.002
Keeping track of plant growth 364:51
Kitchen garden project 236:34
Light effect on plant stem elongation experiment 1395:89-93
Light needed by plants for growth experiment 1181:16
Light needed for plant growth experiment 1183:24
Light needed for plants to grow experiment using box with cover 1019:28-29
Light, heat and water; effect on plant growth experiment 867:7-8
Limiting factors affecting plant growth experiment 978:118-119
Magnetism effect on plant growth experiment 1061:87-88
Malnourished children using plants project 1059:35
Maze demonstrates plants grow toward light experiment 1038:14-15
Measure growth rate of plant stem grown in shade experiment 904:68-69
Measuring root and stem growth experiment 1044:12-13
Mineral requirements of growing plants experiment 1060:68-72
Minerals from soil and hydroponic mineral solutions affect plant growth 1060:69-72
Minerals in soil determine growth of bean plants experiment 1060:68-69
Mini-houses with grass lawns; make from burger boxes and seeds 854:56
Mold gardens projects 236:35
Moon; phases of Moon effect on plant growth experiment 1375:43-45
Music and its effect on plant growth experiment 714:89-90; 878:54-55; 879:97
Music effect on plant growth 745:129-140
Music effect on plant growth experiment 1375:100-104
Music stimulates plants to grow better experiment 1209:42-43
Music to stimulate plant growth 745:129-133
Needs of growing plants; make green sheep experiment 669:18-19
Nitrates and phosphates in different soils experiment 1395:25
Nitrogen and other nutrients are needed for plant growth experiment 1324:54-58
No room on Earth to grow food experiment using beet seeds 1059:98
Nutrient differences in soils experiment 1395:21-25
Nutrients leached from soil are sufficient for plant growth experiment 1395:21-25
Observe seed growth experiment [Primary] 822:4

Oil spills effect on plant growth experiment 714:69-70
One more growth curve experiment 603:16-17, 59-60
Parsley or grass seed planted in pumpkin grows green hair experiment 1246:17
People talk to plants 745:31-36
pH of soil affects growth of different plants experiment 1060:113
Photoperiodism—light effect on plant growth 402:24-25
Phototropism—do plants grow towards the light 402:23-24
Phototropism—plant in box follows sun experiment 714:75-77
Phototropism; plant in box grows toward light experiment 1328:15
Plant competition for water and nutrients experiment 878:36-37
Plant grows in hydroponic solution experiment 1060:70
Plant growth activities 236:34-36
Plant growth and the environment—experiment 268:83-87
Plant growth chemicals experiment 878:52-53
Plant growth in different soils experiment 1424:16
Plant growth record—chart given 748:87
Plants compete for survival 268:73-76
Plants from tubers and bulbs 40:161-163
Plants given more carbon dioxide grow better experiment 714:38-39
Plants grow better in ant hill mound soil project 969:64-65
Plants grow from seeds—lentil, grapefruit, orange, lemon, avocado, pear 270:23-31
Plants grow from stems—potatoes, onions, narcissus, pussy willows, flower 270:12-18
Plants grow in sphagnum moss experiment 904:76-77
Plants grow on air experiment 1008:71
Plants grow toward light experiments 898:49-50
Plants grow without soil experiment 1176:22-23
Plants growing in the light and the dark—experiment 146:40-41
Plants grown in different soils experiment with compost, sandy and clay soil 1292:29
Plants need air, water, soil, and light to grow experiment; use 5 plants 1171:17-19
Plants need sun 236:35
Plants need water and sunlight; good care and neglect of plant experiment 897:43
Pollutants; test for dirty water getting into plants experiment 1414:16-17
Pollution effect on plant growth experiment using bleach and detergents 1073:88
Pollution from air and water stunts plant growth experiment 1362:11
Pollution; leaf washing experiment to determine amount of air pollution 1362:10
Potato; growing potato shoots in water and planting in soil experiment 1379:7
Power of growing plants demonstrated with paper towel covers 1330:44-45
Pressure of growing plants 60:36
Region of most rapid growth in plant's root experiment 1060:42
Root, stem and leaf growth experiment 959:58
Roots; how do plant roots respond to different soils experiment 1527:42

Salt on roads and sidewalks and its effect on plant growth experiment 1061:76-78

Salt run off from highways destroys plants in wetlands experiment 1074:83

Salt water and its effect on plant growth experiment 714:61-62

Salt water effect on growing plants experiment 1509:15

Saltwater and its effect on growing plants experiment 888:97-101

Seedlings growth compared when grown in liquid fertilizers and soil experiment 1395:15-19

Show leaf development on stem—cotyledons & true leaves 86:52

Smoke affects growth of plants experiment 1061:37-38

Soil bacteria necessary to plant growth experiment 1221:20

Soil contains what plants need for growth experiment 714:56-58

Soil with nutrients needed for plant growth experiment 1328:17

Soil; effect of soil composition on plant growth experiment 1134:1.011

Soil; topsoil is good for growing plants; spoiled soil is not good experiment 1476:196

Soils; do all soils provide necessary nutrients for plant growth experiment 1395:19

Space weightlessness effect on plant growth experiment 1434:124-127

Space; how would plants grow in a rotating space station experiment 1399:50-51

Stimulation deprivation experiment—do plants need stimuli to grow 714:93-94

Streambed plant growth affected by water flow experiment 1061:92-93

Sulfur dioxide harms plants experiment 1324:65-68

Sun helps things grow experiment [Primary] 717:20-25

Sun, water and food needed for growth activities [Primary] 854:54

Sunlight amount affects tomato plant growth experiment 1395:36-37

Sunlight and its effect on plant growth experiment 904:58-59

Sunlight; effect on growth experiment 829:51-52

Terrarium project demonstrates plant growth 236:35

Testing the effect of colored lights on plant growth 180:66

Testing the soil for nutrients experiment 1424:62-63

Thermotropism—plant's response to heat experiment 714:85-86

Thigmotropism—plants grow better if touched experiment 714:87-88

Touch; water, wind and touch stimuli affect plant growth experiment 1450:77-84

Toward water—will plants try to find water—experiment 590:48

Toxic chemicals hurt plants experiment using two plants, one watered with salt 1427:85-87

Transplant peanut and popcorn plants—how to 560:29-30

Transplanting seedlings—how to 560:27

Turgor or stiffness in plant cells affected by saltwater experiment 1061:109-110

Value of hotbed for growth—demonstration 86:38

Vegetable and fruit seed window garden experiment 1020:137-142

Vegetable tops grow plants—how to do 732:61-63

Water drainage effect on plant growth project 1195:37-41

Water needed for plant growth experiment; cress seeds in dry/moist/wet soil 1271:33

Water needed for plant growth experiment; seedlings soaked, wet, moist, dry 1328:16

Water types evaluated for effect on plant growth experiment, tap, distilled, et 1061:56-57

Waterlogged seeds and plants don't grow experiment 1063:411

Weeds affect growth of plants experiment 1254:29

What a plant needs to grow experiment 695:62

What are some factors in growth and development of plants 402:25-27

What do plants need to grow experiment 898:49

What green plants need to live and grow 253:14-15

What makes plants grow 248:6-9

What plants need to grow 40:163-165

PLANTS—HERBS

Grow a circle of herbs or flowers outdoors 416:26-27

Grow herbs on the window sill indoors 416:24-25

Herbs to eat—how to grow indoors 497:62-64

Indoor herb garden, how to grow 899:190

Make tasty gifts of herbs 416:28-29

Window herb garden—how to make 376:30-31

PLANTS—HORMONES. *See also* **AUXINS**

Apical dominance exhibited by white potato terminal bud experiment 1395:57-61

Apical dominance; growth inhibitor experiment 1395:57-61

Auxin affects growth of oat seedlings experiment 1060:83-85

Auxin experiments 398:128-129

Auxin improves root formation in stem cuttings experiment 1060:99-100

Blossom-set products prevent fruit from falling off plant experiment 1395:60-61

Coconut milk stimulates growth in plant cell tissues experiment 1060:88-89

Cytokinins experiments 398:130-131

Effect of auxin on growth of lima bean plant experiment 1060:86-87

Effect of auxin on root formation in plant cuttings experiment 1060:86

Gibberellin's experiments with plants 398:131-132

Gibberellins affect growth of dwarf pea plants experiment 1060:86-88

Gibberellins influence size and flowering in geranium plants experiment 1060:88

Sprouting potato eye produces hormones experiment 876:78-80

PLANTS—HOT BEDS

Hot beds—how to make 86:20-22

PLANTS—HUMIDITY

Relative humidity experiments 398:55-56

Temperature and humidity—amount needed 398:30-31

PLANTS—HYDROPONICS. *See also* **HYDROPONICS**

Apparatus for water culture experiments 577:project 85

Do hydroponic plants require less root systems experiment 714:63-64

Do plants grown with hydroponics have dormancy periods experiment 714:65-66

Grow bean plants hydroponically experiment 1241:33

Nitrogen-fixing bacteria replace nitrogen compounds in hydroponic solution 1060:112

Nutrient solution—how to make 398:79-80

Nutrient solution formula—general purpose formula—making 714:45

Nutrient solution formula—grocery store solution—making 714:46

Nutrient solution formula—poor man's formula—making 714:46

Nutrient solution formula—U.S. Dept. Agriculture—making 714:45

Plants grown hydroponically require more light than plants in soil experiment 714:67-68

Which growing medium produces best plant growth experiment 714:51-52

PLANTS—IDENTIFICATION

Identifying plants in grassy places (Primary) 108:30-36

Plants—how to identify 108:28-47

PLANTS—INDOOR

Make a plastic bag "plant sitter" 416:57

Water plants with a wick 416:56

PLANTS—INSECT EATING

Catch insects in jar with funnel and fruit lure, how to do 1188:73

Grow Venus flytrap plant from bulb 416:34-35

Insect and meat eating plants—demonstrate 294:55-56

Insect and meat plants—demonstrations with insectivorous plants—experiment 279:37-38

Insect-eating plants from bogs or swamps, how to grow experiment 1074:24-25

Insectivorous plants eat insects to get nitrates experiment 1061:90-91

Investigate insect eating plants 166:111-116

Leaves of sundew and Venus's flytrap plants 271:30-39

Observing the insectivorous plants in an acid bog 285:79-80

Plants that eat animals experiment 878:56-57

PLANTS—INSECT PESTS. *See also* **INSECTS—GARDEN PESTS**

Growth of insect pests effected by air pollution 398:60

Plant growth experiments—do marigolds really repel pests 398:39-40

Plant pest experiments—project with insect predators 398:110-116

Plants produce chemicals to repel insects experiment 1324:32-36

Plants that repel insects 398:116-120

PLANTS—LEAF CUTTING PROPAGATION

Bits that grow big 465:126-132

Starting leaf cuttings in soil and water 465:122-126

PLANTS—LEAVES

Acid rain affects leaf ratio in radish plants experiment 1060:116-117

Chlorophyll in plant leaves experiment 1294:68-71

Color pigment in plant leaves affected by sunlight experiment 1395:107-112

Gas comes out of plant leaves experiment 784:86-87

Getting raw material into a plant—importance of stoma experiment 148:26-27

How plants breathe—experiment 585:155-156

Leaf structures of plant affects rate of freezing experiment 904:24-25

Leaves give off moisture experiment with leaf in jar 1440:20-23

Light necessary to produce chlorophyll experiment 1440:8-11

Number of stomates on leaves experiment 1158:125-127

Rate of evaporation from different leaf structures experiment 1479:25

Rate of evaporation from different leaf structures experiment 904:34-35

Restricting petiole movement affects amount of starch/sugar in leaf experiment 1061:100-101

Stomata—examination under a microscope experiments 11:51-57

Stomata—examine stomata in slice of leaf under microscope 86:75

Stomata allow gases to move in and out of leaves experiment 1405:25

Stomata on bottom surface of plant leaves allow plant to breathe experiment 1440:12-14

Stomata; gas exchange regulators in plant leaves experiment 1395:95-99

Stomata; how leaves pull water through plants experiment 784:85-86

Stomata; plant leaves have openings through which gas can enter experiment 1395:95-99

Stomates of leaves affected by moisture experiment 1060:35

Stomates of leaves close or open during day and night experiment 1060:35

Stomates of leaves give off water vapor into the air experiment 1060:35

Stomates of leaves observed under microscope experiments 1060:33-36

Stomates of leaves when blocked affect the leaves experiment 1060:35

Technique for the study of stomates 577:project 97

Testing leaves for food (starch) 473:57

Transpiration in plant leaves experiment using two plants; one plant covered 1061:98-99

Transpiration, loss of water from leaves experiment 904:32-33

Type of leaves 60:21-23

Water moves in plant through stomata holes and xylem tubes experiment 1405:25

Which side of leaf transpires more rapidly experiment 1060:35-36

Which side of plant leaf takes in gases experiment 904:30-31

Why leaves fall observation 1440:24-27

PLANTS—LICE. *See* **APHIDS**

PLANTS—LICHENS. *See also* **LICHENS**

Plants that don't grow in soil (Primary) 108:40-44

PLANTS—LIGHT

Amount needed for growth 398:29-30

Amount of light affects amount of oxygen produced during photosynthesis 1060:25-26

Artificial light and plant growth experiment 878:24-25

Bean plant grows toward light in shoe box maze experiment 1068:41

Color of light affects how seeds grow experiment 1181:17

Color of light best for growth of plants experiment 1222:5-7, 22-26

Colored light effect on plant growth experiment 1395:86

Colored light effect on plant stem elongation experiment 1395:92

310

Colored lights affect seed germination experiment 1060:62

Demonstrate that plants need sunlight using two house plants 1481:210-212

Do plants need light experiment 852:11-12

Do plants need light to grow 60:16-17

Do plants transpire at same rate under different sources of light experiment 997:49-51

Do stems bend to all colors of light 60:39-40

Does amount of sunlight plant receives effect blooming experiment 762:77-78

Effect of direct sunlight—mark initials on tomatoes with foil 86:19

Effect of light on growth of plants experiment 1061:30-31

Effect of light on plant 8:95-101

Effect of light on plants 76:8-11

Grass grown in dark experiment 1159:63-64

Grow plants under colored transparent films experiment 784:115

How do plants and animals respond to light 402:17-18

How light affects stems and leaves 60:37-41

How various amounts of sunlight affect plants (Primary) 108:24-27

Leaf covered with black paper experiment 1159:64

Leaves need sunlight experiment 819:53

Light color and plant growth experiment 878:26-27

Light cylinder shows how light helps plants grow 483:27-29

Light effect on plant stem elongation experiment 1395:89-93

Light important to photosynthesis experiment 871:2.023

Light is needed for healthy plant growth 86:68-69

Light needed by plants for growth experiment 1181:16

Light provides energy for photosynthesis experiment 1060:25-26

Make plants bend and contort with light sources 86:14-16

Maze demonstrates plants grow toward light experiment 1038:14-15

Night work for leaves—plants given light during day and night grow bigger 560:28-29

No grow—plants need light to grow—experiment 570:17

Oxygen collected from plants during photosynthesis experiment 1060:23-24

Photomorphogenesis; plant responses to light experiment 1395:89-93

Photosynthesis and respiration in plants affected by colors of light experiment 1395:103

Phototropism demonstrated as plant grows toward light experiment 1069:45

Phototropism; potato plant in box maze grows toward light experiment 1214:11

Plant grows toward light in maze experiment 1028:61

Plant in box grows toward light experiment 760:8-9

Plant in box maze grows toward light experiment 882:33

Plant maze shows effect of light on plants 86:78-79

Plants grow into the light—test with cardboard box 473:57

Plants grow toward light experiment 749:44-45

Plants in the dark experiment with brick on grass 1181:22

Plants in the dark turn yellow experiment 1183:30

Plants need for sunshine—demonstrate 293:15

Plants need light 270:55-63

Plants need light for proper growth 179:101-102

Poinsettia leaves turn red when kept in dark experiment 1242:9

Potato plant in shoe box grows toward light from hole in box 565:104-106

Responses to light in growing plants experiment 784:114-115

Roots grow toward water not light experiment 749:44-45

Show what colors in sunlight plants bend to most 270:58-60

Stems grow toward light experiment 819:48; 1047:17

Sun seekers—compare seedlings grown in the dark and in the light 146:40-41

Sunlight and plant growth experiment 878:22-23

Sunlight effect on survival of plant experiment 1479:26

Tattoo on plant leaf tests absence of light 364:49

What happens to a leaf if part of it is shaded 60:41

What light does to seedlings 595:9

Which plants like the light experiment 1183:31

PLANTS—MOLDS

Do microscopic plants have special characteristics 402:28-29

PLANTS—MOTION

Effect of motion on plants—experiments 398:133

Sensitive plants show motion of plants 94:24-25

PLANTS—MOVEMENT. *See also* **PLANTS—VINES**

Grow the surprising sensitive plant 416:32-33

Night and day leaf changes; observe clover, oxalis, kidney beans, locust 271:11-29

Plant movements—demonstrate 158:24-25

PLANTS—MUSIC

Music effect on plant growth experiment 1375:100-104

Music stimulates plants to grow better experiment 1209:42-43

PLANTS—NEMATODES

How to catch a nematode 364:55

PLANTS—NUTRIENTS. *See also* **FERTILIZERS; PLANTS—FERTILIZERS**

Effect of different nutrients (food) on plants 507:1851-1852

PLANTS—OCEAN

Green plant life does not occur deep in ocean experiment 1405:28

Ocean plants grow only in sunny water—experiment (Primary) 470:2-3

PLANTS—OSMOSIS. *See also* **OSMOSIS**

Carrot and straw demonstrate osmosis in plants experiment 784:94-95

Celery stalk and food coloring in water demonstrate 913:26

Effect of osmosis on potato using salt and sugar solutions experiment data tab 1004:2.015

Flower draws up colored water through stem experiment 1068:22

Observing in a carrot or beet 148:30

Osmosis in potatoes and imbibition of water in lima bean seeds experiment 1004:2.014

Plants drink too—osmosis and transpiration experiment 573:16

Raw vegetable salad—how plants take in water 74:89-92

Striped celery snack—how water moves up stems 74:92-93

Water enters plant thru roots by osmosis experiment 978:56-58

Water passes thru walls of potato by osmosis experiment 1214:9

PLANTS—OXYGEN

Green leaves breathe experiment 819:51

Green plants make oxygen gas experiment 1324:42-47

Green plants produce oxygen experiment 1174:16-19

How oxygen gas leaves the plant—demonstrate 86:54

Leaves give off oxygen experiment 1183:28

Leaves of plants give off oxygen experiment 1181:20

Leaves of plants produce oxygen in sunlight, demonstrate 186:24

Life giving plants make oxygen 112:8-9

Oxygen released when plants start to photosynthesize experiment 1146:9

Oxygen use in plants, demonstrate 146:18-19

Plant bubbles oxygen experiment 1028:62

Plant's gas vapor will flash & burn 271:64-66

Plants breathe oxygen out through their leaves experiment 1371:71

Testing gases plants give off 148:23

PLANTS—PAPER

Plant papers—how to make 264:46

PLANTS—PESTICIDES

Natural predator ladybugs control aphids on plant experiment 1176:17

PLANTS—PHOTOGRAPHY

Photographing plants 59:75-83

PLANTS—PHOTOSYNTHESIS. *See also*
    PHOTOSYNTHESIS

Amount of light affects amount of oxygen produced during photosynthesis 1060:25-26

Bean sprout experiment demonstrates photosynthesis 928:24

Candle burns longer in jar with plants experiment 879:90

Carbohydrate formation in plants during photosynthesis; test for starch 1060:21-23

Carbon cycle in plant growth experiment using two plants in jars 1173:16-19

Carbon dioxide absorbed by plants in sunlight experiment 978:42-43

Carbon dioxide deprivation causes plants to die experiment 1061:24-25

Carbon dioxide in photosynthesis needed for plant growth experiment 1173:16-19

Cardboard circles on leaves experiment 860:145-146

Chlorophyll extracted from plant leaves demonstrates starch in plants 978:41-42

Chlorophyll in plant leaves experiment 1294:68-71

Chlorophyll increases or decreases in leaves with amount of light experiment 714:31-32

Chlorophyll spectrum as seen through a spectroscope experiment 1060:27-28

Chlorophyll; testing plant leaves for amount and density of chlorophyll 1061:32-34

Color effect on chlorophyll production in plant leaves experiment 1082:187-191

Colored light effects growth of plants experiment 714:29-30

Colors in different shades differ in effects on photosynthesis experiment 1060:27-28

Colors of the spectrum affect photosynthesis experiment 1060:27-28

Demonstrate breathing leaves 146:46

Diagram of and experiments 769:13,29,41-45

Do all plants use photosynthesis to make food experiment 852:14-15

Do plants make sugar and starch 283:27-38

Do plants really make oxygen 283:11-26

Do plants really need light, water and carbon dioxide to make food 282:9-24

Does color or light effect rate of photosynthesis 273:28-29

Does covering leaves effect plant growth experiment 714:24-26

Does heavy layer of canopy trees effect plant growth experiment 714:36-37

Effect of filtered light on photosynthesis 577:project 94

Effect of filtered light on photosynthesis 86:70

Effect of light on growth of plants experiment 1061:30-31

Effect of temperature on photosynthesis 273:30-31

Experiment and projects 398:44-49

Experiment to show 346:136-137

Fat test for food storage in plants experiment 1214:12-13

Game; air cycle relay game demonstrates plants are air filters of world 1335:117

Gas collected from underwater plants is oxygen experiment 1069:40-41

Gas released by plants experiment 737:9

Grass turns yellow; what causes it experiment 1020:146-147

Green leaves make food experiment 819:52

Green plants make oxygen gas experiment 1324:42-47

Green plants need light, water or carbon dioxide for photosynthesis experiment 1453:20-24

Green plants produce oxygen experiment 1174:16-19

How plants make their food 625:49

Illustration of 236:14

Initials placed over growing seedlings shows photosynthesis experiment 1308:10-11

Is starch found in leaf—stem or root of plant experiment 714:27-28

Leaf stops making chlorophyll due to lack of carbon dioxide experiment 1441:91

Leaves carrying out photosynthesis give off oxygen gas experiment 1069:40-41

Leaves give off oxygen experiment 1183:28

Leaves important for plants getting carbon dioxide for photosynthesis 1189:40-41

Leaves of plants give off oxygen experiment 1181:20

Light and its effect on plants experiment 860:146-147

Light important to photosynthesis experiment 871:2.023

Light is essential for food in green plants—test leaves for starch—experiment 586:130-131

Light is needed for photosynthesis experiment 1324:42-47

Light necessary to produce chlorophyll experiment 1440:8-11

Light needed for photosynthesis process in hydroponic grown plants experiment 1061:66-67

Light needed for 273:26-27

Light provides energy for photosynthesis experiment 1060:25-26

Measure rate of photosynthesis in leaves contaminated with soot experiment 933:24-25

Measure rate of speed of photosynthesis 273:24-25

Measuring oxygen released by plant leaves during photosynthesis experiment 1061:28-29

Mini-investigations to explore photosynthesis experiment 1063:244

Oil slick prevents aquatic plants from process of photosynthesis experiment 1172:52

Oxygen as by-product of photosynthesis experiment 1060:28-30

Oxygen collected from plants during photosynthesis experiment 1060:23-24

Oxygen from green plants useful to fish experiment 1060:28-30

Oxygen gas bubbles collect in jar placed over plant in water experiment 1271:23

Oxygen given off by plants during photosynthesis experiment 1214:14

Oxygen production affected by amount of light during photosynthesis experiment 1060:28-30

Oxygen production rate from plants during photosynthesis; how to measure 1060:28-30

Oxygen released when plants start to photosynthesize experiment 1146:9

Photos from photosynthesis experiment show starch produced in plant leaf 1476:105-106

Photosynthesis and oxygen production experiment 878:30-31

Photosynthesis and respiration in plant tissue experiment 1395:101-105

Photosynthesis and respiration in plants affected by colors of light experiment 1395:103

Photosynthesis in green plants experiment 878:28-29

Photosynthesis process demonstrated by bubbling plants in water 1038:23

Plants contain less chlorophyll if leaf stomata are blocked experiment 714:33-35

Plants given more carbon dioxide grow better experiment 714:38-39

Plants grown hydroponically require more light than plants in soil experiment 714:67-68

Plants make starch experiment 737:13

Plants make sugar from sunlight energy; measure that stored energy experiment 1134:7.004

Plants make their own food experiment 1405:27

Plants need carbon dioxide gas to carry on photosynthesis experiment 1174:19-20

Plants need carbon dioxide to produce oxygen thru photosynthesis experiment 1173:46-47

Plants need light experiment 1294:72-73

Plants produce oxygen during photosynthesis experiment 978:52

Plants produce oxygen experiment 1396:161-163

Plants use carbon dioxide experiment 1324:48-53

Potato tuber made up of starch from photosynthesis in leaves experiment 1069:42

Preventing photosynthesis experiment 878:38-39

Preventing photosynthesis 402:22-23

Providing raw material for photosynthesis 148:22

Rate of photosynthesis affected by amount of carbon dioxide experiment 1060:23-25

Respiration reaction and photosynthesis reaction in plants experiment 1405:26

Show how roots and plants together make food 284:33-38

Show photosynthesis 158:21

Show that oxygen is a by product of photosynthesis 294:40-41

Smoke affects growth of plants experiment 1061:37-38

Starch in leaves experiment 1060:21-23

Starch in plants demonstration 978:40

Starch is produced in plant leaves during photosynthesis experiment 1479:25

Starch is produced in plant leaves experiment 904:28-29

Starch is produced when leaves photosynthesize experiment 1308:11

Starch test for food storage in plants experiment 1214:12-13

Starch test for photosynthesis during different times of plant growth 864:65-66

Starch test for photosynthesis experiment 864:65

Starch test on leaves of plant kept in sunlight and in darkness experiment 1069:43

Sugar (carbohydrate) product of photosynthesis found in plant parts experiment 1061:26-27

Sunlight needed by plant to produce food experiment 1440:15-17

Testing for oxygen production in plants project 833:123-125

The world's largest manufacturer—experiment 563:59-60

Volcanic clouds lower atmospheric temperature and reduce sunlight experiment 1477:76-79

Water plants make oxygen; collect gas in test tube experiment 1246:16

What happens to grass when it doesn't receive sunlight experiment 1324:38-41

What is photosynthesis 402:21-22

PLANTS—PHOTOTROPISM. *See also* **PLANTS—TROPISMS**

Lively stems and leaves—popcorn seedlings grow and bend toward light 560:25-26

Maze demonstrates plants grow toward light experiment 1038:14-15

Plant in box grows toward light experiment 760:8-9

Plants grow toward light experiment 878:42-43

Plants in a maze experiment 878:44-45

Seedlings grow towards light 480:24

Stems grow toward light experiment 1047:17

PLANTS—PIGMENTS

Chromatogram of green plants, how to make and compare 864:77-80

Chromatography experiment 436:22

Chromatography test with inks, food colors and plant pigments experiment 1476:129-131

Color pigment in plant leaves affected by sunlight experiment 1395:107-112

Is chlorophyll the only color pigment in a leaf experiment 1395:110

Red color of apple is from color pigment anthocyanin experiment 1395:110

Separate chlorophyll pigments from plant leaves experiment 860:61-65

Separate plant pigments using chromatography, how to do 864:77-80

Separating colors using chromatography experiment 864:75-77

Separating plant pigments—experiment 586:120-122

Test tube holder and stand for chromatography experiment, how to make 1476:129-130

What causes plant colors—can these colors be removed 402:27

PLANTS—PLANT COMMUNITIES

Plant community—observe types of plants on hills and lowlands 301:27

Plant community—studying a 268:67-71

Plants in the neighborhood—what kind can be found 253:3-4

PLANTS—POLLINATION

Artificial pollination of flowers experiment 1060:52
Flowering plants experiment 739:21
Insects role in pollination experiment 1097:40-41
Self-pollination and cross-pollination experiment
1060:52
Try to create new varieties of plants by pollinating plants
yourself 530:208-209

PLANTS—POLLUTION

Acid rain effect on plants experiment 1063:364
Cigarette smoke effect on growing radish plants experiment 1328:38-39
Does salt runoff from roads affect plant growth experiment 1527:67-68
Duckweed growth affected by water pollution experiment 1492:48-49
Oil spills are harmful to aquatic environments experiment 1453:32-34
Plants damaged by oil spills experiment 1058:78-79
Polluted water can get into food experiment using celery,
water, food coloring 1228:28-29
Pollution in water carried into plants experiment 1067:60
Watering plants with vinegar water solution to show effects of acid rain 1331:86-87

PLANTS—POPULATIONS

Limitations of resources for growth 263:24-27
Observe growth in small section of bare soil 285:48-49
Overcrowding and its effect on plants 263:53-55
Survey a field or meadow for its plant populations
285:50-52

PLANTS—POTATOES. *See also* **POTATOES**

A sprout in the dark and the brown bag monster 231:29
How can a plant grow from a potato 253:12-13

PLANTS—PRESS

Collecting and pressing plants, how to do 1505:30-31
How to build a plant press 530:196-197; 749:21
Make a plant press, how to 832:58
Plant press for pressing garden and weed flowers, how to
make 1265:98
Plant press from heavy cardboard, how to make 1441:89
Plant press, how to make and use 824:30-34; 986:98

PLANTS—PRINTS

Fruit and vegetable prints—how to make 473:58-59
Making leaf prints by xerography 59:24-31
Making leaf prints with ink 59:12-23
Nature printing with leaves, weeds 293:18
Print with plants 264:45
Printing leaves, how to 646:16-19
Printing seaside flowering plants, how to do 646:114-115
Spatter printing of small leaves and plants 293:18-19

PLANTS—PROPAGATION. *See also* **PLANTS—
VEGETATIVE PROPAGATION**

Acid rain affects growth of geranium plant cuttings experiment 1060:117
Another way to grow plants experiment 901:31
Cuttings from African violet plant root in soil, how to do
1236:8
Cuttings from geranium plant root in soil, how to do
1236:9
Cuttings from impatiens, geranium, spider plants grow
into plants experiment 1306:12-13
Cuttings from plants give new growth, how to do 1379:8-
11
Grow new plant from cuttings experiment 1063:406

New plants from stem cuttings, how to grow 1054:60-61
Plant propagation from stems, leaves, roots, tubers, runners, bulbs experiment 1014:154-155
Plants from cuttings; how to cut off shoots and plant experiment 1038:18
Propagate and clone plants by leaf and stem cuttings experiment 1176:36-37
Propagating plants from leaves experiment 577:project
81
Strawberry plants grow from plant runners experiment
1038:19
Tissue culture of plants experiment 1060:103-106

PLANTS—PUMPKINS

Plant and grow a perfect pumpkin 376:22-23
Pumpkin race—who grows the largest pumpkin 376:
24

PLANTS—RESPIRATION. *See* **PLANTS—OXYGEN**

PLANTS—RIVERS

Observe and collect river plants 290:29

PLANTS—ROOTS

Beans; grow bean in glass jar to observe roots experiment 1214:6-7
Carrot and potato plant grow from roots experiment
1063:405
Check growth of seedling roots each day and chart
growth project 854:50
Cuttings from plants demonstrate root growth in water experiment 1490:17
Demonstrate the value of root system experiment
860:147-149
Do potato roots pick up dye experiment 876:77
Erosion; plant roots stop erosion experiment 1371:72-73
Experiment shows roots will grow to source of water
86:55
Gravity effect on plant roots; radish seeds experiment
784:96-97
If leaves are big—are roots big also experiment 714:100-
101
Learning about roots—what roots do 146:19
Loss of plants brings on soil erosion experiment
1060:43-44
Nitrogen-fixing bacteria on roots of legume plants experiment 1060:110
Onion root cells examined under microscope experiment
1060:44-47
Plants absorb water through their roots—experiment
86:12
Power of growing roots demonstration using eggshells
and marigold plants 1038:20-21
Preventing soil erosion display ideas 1060:44
Region of most rapid growth in plant's root experiment
1060:42
Root cage for orchid bulb to show growth from root
483:32-34
Root development of bean seed experiment; region of
most rapid growth 1060:42
Root hairs and water experiment 959:57
Root hairs on roots—experiment 603:44-46
Root hairs—show what root hairs look like 284:20-25
Root pressure transports water experiment; manometer
measures osmotic pressure 1061:104-105
Root strength demonstrated by beans planted in Plaster
of Paris experiment 784:95-96
Root system collects and transports water experiment
760:5-6

Root viewer to view growing roots, how to make 1115:26-27

Root window shows how roots grow 483:30-31

Rooting—primary experiments to show 104:36-39

Roots—show strength of growing roots 86:77

Roots find way around obstacle—experiment 86:32-33

Roots hold soil together experiment 1368:31

Roots protect soil from erosion experiment 722:77

Show what roots look like 284:14-19

Size, depth and width of fibrous root system of common weeds experiment 1060:40

Strength of growing roots experiment 1368:38

Testing acidity of growing roots 148:37

Testing how roots take up water from the soil 473:56

Tubes carry water to leaves experiment with celery and colored water 1440:5-7

Types of roots—experiment 60:27-29

What does inside of root look like 284:26-32

What part of a popcorn seedling root grows 560:22

What part of a root grows in length 60:30-31

When does root stop storing food experiment 714:102-103

Which part of the root binds to the soil experiment 1060:43

Why plants have roots experiment 1294:74-75

PLANTS—SEASIDE

Activities with seaside plants 236:111-114

PLANTS—SENSITIVITY

Are animals more sensitive than plants 402:40

PLANTS—SHELTERS

House of sticks—how to make 483:64-65

PLANTS—SOIL

Determining how much soil plants use 148:25

Soil and water experiments 398:43-44

Soil pH—how to adjust 398:34

PLANTS—STARCH

Do plants produce starch 273:32-33

Food (starch) in plants—iodine test for 60:18-19

Starch—we can't make it but plants can 280:54

Starch digestion by enzymes 273:42-43

Starch in plants—a test for 86:39-40

PLANTS—STEMS. *See also* STEMS

Carnation flower colored with two different dyes experiment 1060:39-41

Demonstrate physical characteristics of osmosis and capillary action 293:19-20

Discovering areas of mitosis in stems and roots 148:35

Fun with potatoes to demonstrate stems 146:32-33

How they carry water—carnation and colored water experiment (Primary) 540:19

Parts of a stem or twig experiment 60:24-25

Power of stems—experiment to see stem's transport tubes 380:60-61

Red ink water rises through plant experiment 1060:39

Red ink water rises up in celery stalks under different conditions experiment 1060:39

Stems absorb water experiment 819:49

Stems carry water experiment 802:27

Stems carry water upward in plant experiment 760:6-7

Stems grow straight up 270:60-63

Stems sensitive to light—potato obstacle race—experiment 480:26

Testing how stems work 473:56

Turgor pressure change causes plant stems to wilt experiment 1405:24

Water moves in plant through stomata holes and xylem tubes experiment 1405:25

What do stems do for a plant 253:8-9

What part of a stem grows in length 60:26

Xylem investigations with celery and carnations experiment 864:70

PLANTS—SWEET POTATO

Sweet potato plants grow in water 270:7-10

Sweet potato vines—how to grow 231:44-45

Vine grows from potato rooted in water experiment 722:72

PLANTS—TEMPERATURE

Stay warm but don't lose your cool 398:35-36

Temperature and humidity—amount needed 398:30-31

What happens to leaves of rhododendron as temp goes below 32 degrees 58:10-11

PLANTS—TOPIARY

Green animals—grow/trim plants on wire mesh/coat hanger to look like animals 483:61-63

PLANTS—TOUCH STIMULI. *See also* PLANTS—TROPISM; THIGMOTROPISM

Water, wind and touch stimuli affect plant growth experiment 1450:77-84

PLANTS—TRANSPIRATION

Bottle garden demonstrates water transpiration in plants experiment 1181:21

Bottle garden with plants demonstrates transpiration experiment 1183:29

Cobalt chloride test for 769:12-14

Comparative transpiration 398:55

Do plants give off water vapor 236:35

Do plants lose water through their leaves experiment 714:98-99

Do plants transpire at same rate under different sources of light experiment 997:49-51

Flower in colored water shows how water travels up a plant experiment 1490:19

Food dye drawn up stem of flower colors petals experiment 1069:48

Green plants give off water from their leaves 294:41-42

How does water leave a plant experiment 852:10-11

How much water evaporates from leaves experiment 1063:245

How to demonstrate transpiration 117:61-64

How water is moved thru plant stems experiment with carnation and food colors 1479:24

Humidity affects rate of transpiration in plants experiment 1395:66-67

Leaves give off moisture experiment with leaf in jar 1440:20-23

Leaves give off water vapor experiment 819:50

Measure rate of transpiration in plant 86:62

Measuring water levels in two bottles—one with plant, one without to demo 146:61

Observing transpiration 148:27

Plant in air tight plastic bag demonstrates 898:48

Plant in plastic bag demonstrates 780:36-37

Plant leaves give off water into the air 233:30

Plants give off water—experiments 382:37-40

Plants lose water 282:34-41

Plants release water experiment 959:58-59

Plants take up water through roots and pass water out thru plant leaves 1379:20

Plants transpire experiment 978:45-46

Plants transpire more at night or during the day experiment 1395:67

Rate of evaporation from different leaf structures experiment 904:34-35

Rate of transpiration—experiment 577:project 93

Stephen Hales's movement of sap in plants experiment 1133:3.005

Stomata in leaf structure and transpiration of water and plant gases experiment 1004:2.013

Stomata on leaves let out water and take in carbon dioxide experiment 1075:48

Stomates of leaves give off water vapor into the air experiment 1060:35

Testing how plants lose water 473:56

Transpiration—experiment 585:149

Transpiration and humidity experiments 398:53-56

Transpiration experiment 739:11

Transpiration in plant leaves experiment using two plants; one plant covered 1061:98-99

Transpiration, loss of water from leaves experiment 1405:26

Transpiration, loss of water from leaves experiment 904:32-33

Transportation of liquid through plants vascular system experiment 1395:63-67

Transportation of liquids in plants activities for classroom 1291:18-19

Turgor or stiffness in plant cells affected by saltwater experiment 1061:109-110

Vascular tubes differ with age of plant experiment 1061:106

Water from leaves—experiment 563:49

Water given off by plants as water vapor experiment 1214:15

Water is formed when plants breathe—experiment 146:47

Water loss amount and plant location—experiment 398:54

Water loss from leaves experiment 1134:4.006

Water lost by plants thru transpiration experiment; construct potometer 978:46-47

Water movement in plants demonstration with plastic bag over plant 1254:8

Water moves out of a plant 273:14-15

Water travels all the way thru plants experiment; dye flowers in colored water 1214:15

Watery plants 112:19

Where does water go in plant experiment 1183:27

Where does water go in plants experiment with plastic bag over leaf 1181:19

Which part of plant draws up water experiment 1509:29

Which side of leaf transpires more rapidly experiment 1060:35-36

PLANTS—TRAVELING. *See* **SEEDS—DISPERSAL**
PLANTS—TROPISMS. *See also* **CHEMOTROPISM; GEOTROPISM; GRAVITROPISM; HELIOTROPISM; HYDROTROPISM; PLANTS—GROWTH; PHOTOTROPISM; THIGMOTROPISM**

Bean plant grows through box maze toward light experiment 1288:24-25

Bean plant grows toward light in shoe box maze experiment 1068:41

Bean seeds grown upside down in jar show effect of gravity on growth 1038:16

Bending; making plants bend experiments 1158:127-129

Charles Darwin's growth movement in plants toward light experiment 1133:3.008

Chemotropism—black walnut tree effect on plant growth experiment 714:78-79

Chemotropism—plants grow toward nutrients they need experiment 714:80-81

Chemotropism; plant root response to odors in the air experiment 1061:79-80

Crooked plants—grow a crooked plant 107:80-83

Darwin's theory of tropism—shown by experiments 86:84-88

Do roots always grow down and shoots grow up experiment 799:30-31

Effect of different light colors on phototropisms 577:project 96

Geotropism—effect of gravity on germinating seeds experiment 714:82-84

Geotropism demonstrated with sprouting seeds between glass panes experiment 986:80

Geotropism effect on plant seeds experiment 978:43

Geotropism experiment with seeds 879:80-81

Geotropism in germinating bean seeds experiment; data tables given 1004:2.016

Geotropism roots grow downward experiment 723:73-74

Geotropism, force of gravity affects way roots grow experiment 986:80

Geotropism; bean plant in jar demonstrates geotropism experiment 1457:19

Geotropism; bean plants reaction to geotropism experiment 1294:78-79

Geotropism; bean seed roots grow down and leaves grow up experiment 1379:16

Geotropism; bean shoot roots grow downward experiment 913:27

Geotropism; centrifugal motion affects seedlings root and stem growth experiment 1060:77-78

Geotropism; direction seed is planted affects growth of stems/roots experiment 1395:79

Geotropism; effect of gravity on growth of seedlings experiment 1060:76-77

Geotropism; effects of gravity on plant growth experiment 1405:27

Geotropism; gravity affect on seeds, roots and shoots experiment 1181:16

Geotropism; gravity affects plant growth experiment 1395:75-81

Geotropism; gravity affects seeds, roots and shoots experiment 1183:24

Geotropism; gravity affects the way roots grow experiment 1265:80

Geotropism; gravity effect on mature plants experiment 1395:79

Geotropism; gravity has effect on plant growth experiment 1399:48-51

Geotropism; growing seeds in rotating container of soil experiment 1061:81-82

Geotropism; plant roots respond to gravity and grow downward experiment 1014:158

Geotropism; plants change direction in which they grow experiment 878:46-47

Geotropism; plants growth in response to gravity experiment 1476:103-104

Geotropism; root of plant responds to gravity and grows downward experiment 1069:45

316

Geotropism; root of potato grows downward experiment 876:77

Geotropism; roots always grow downwards experiment 819:46

Geotropism; roots always point down experiment 1368:39

Geotropism; roots from bean seeds grow downward experiment 1063:407

Geotropism; roots grow downward and shoots grow upward experiment 1181:16

Geotropism; roots grow downward experiment 1078:5

Geotropism; simple experiment demonstrates 860:150

Graviotropism; gravitropic response of two different kinds of seeds experiment 1375:81-84

Graviotropism; gravity affects bean seed roots experiment 1047:15

Gravitropism experiment with corn seeds 864:81-83

Gravitropism; plant grows in response to force of gravity experiment 1527:91

Gravity effect on plant growth experiment 904:48-49

Gravity effect on plant roots; radish seeds experiment 784:96-97

Heliotropism experiment with radish seeds 879:78-79

Heliotropism roots grow toward water not light experiment 749:44-45

Heliotropism; bean plant grows through box maze toward light experiment 1063:410

Hydrotropism and geotropism compared as to which affects plant the most 1061:94-95

Hydrotropism experiment with melon seeds 879:81-82

Hydrotropism in plants; root observation box experiment 864:83-84

Hydrotropism roots grow toward water experiment 723:72

Hydrotropism; growing seeds in tilted planter experiment 1061:83-84

Hydrotropism; plants grow toward water experiment 878:50-51

Hydrotropism; plants grow towards water experiment 1476:103

Hydrotropism; roots grow toward water experiment 1368:40

Hydrotropism; roots of pea seeds grow toward water experiment 913:33

Hydrotropism; roots react to source of moisture experiment 1060:75-76

Insectivorous plants eat insects to get nitrates experiment 1061:90-91

Leaf movement in lima bean seedling experiment 1060:79-81

Leaves turn to face sun—heliotropism—experiment 86:35

Magnetotropisms project 584:61-63

Maze to show plant's growth toward light, how to make 986:85

Phototropism—light cylinder shows how plants grow toward light 483:27-29

Phototropism—plant in box follows sun experiment 714:75-77

Phototropism—the sun seeking sweet potato in the shoe box experiment 494:17

Phototropism demonstrated as plant grows toward light experiment 1069:45

Phototropism experiment with a sweet potato maze 879:79-80

Phototropism experiment with bean seeds 879:79

Phototropism plant in box grows toward light experiment 760:8-9

Phototropism plants grow toward light experiment 723:74

Phototropism plants grow toward light experiment 749:44-45

Phototropism; bean seedlings grow toward light experiment 1078:5

Phototropism; bean seeds planted in box maze grow toward light experiment 1189:48-49

Phototropism; cress seedlings grow toward light thru hole in cup experiment 913:32

Phototropism; different wavelengths of colored lights affect on experiment 1060:75

Phototropism; do plants always grow toward the light experiment 852:12-14

Phototropism; do potato plants grow toward light experiment 876:77-78

Phototropism; effect of light on plant growth; box maze demonstrates 978:54-55

Phototropism; flowers turn toward sunlight experiment 1524:17

Phototropism; geranium plant project 1060:75

Phototropism; grow plants in a maze experiment 1265:85

Phototropism; growth of plants in response to different colors of light 1527:92

Phototropism; growth of plants in response to light experiment 1527:92

Phototropism; light can bend plant experiment 860:149-150

Phototropism; maze demonstrates plants need sunlight to grow experiment 1014:156

Phototropism; plant bends toward light experiment 924:76-77

Phototropism; plant in box grows toward light experiment 1328:15

Phototropism; plant in box grows toward light experiment 882:33

Phototropism; plant maze with bean plant growing toward light experiment 1368:41

Phototropism; plant moves toward light experiment 1405:27

Phototropism; plant turns toward light experiment 1246:10-11

Phototropism; plant winds its way toward light experiment 904:52-53

Phototropism; plants bow to the light experiment 909:162

Phototropism; plants grow toward light experiment 878:42-43

Phototropism; plants grow toward light experiments 898:49-50

Phototropism; plants grow toward light in maze experiment 1476:104

Phototropism; plants grow towards light in box maze experiment 913:27

Phototropism; plants in a maze experiment 878:44-45

Phototropism; plants seek light experiment 904:54-55

Phototropism; potato grows through maze in box to find light experiment 1379:25

Phototropism; potato plant in box maze grows toward light experiment 1214:11

Phototropism; potato shoot grows toward light source in maze experiment 1236:6-7

Phototropism; potato shoots grow through box to reach light source experiment 1390:31

Phototropism; potato shoots grow toward light in cardboard box maze experiment 1524:26

Phototropism; response of oat seedlings to light experiment 1395:83-88

Phototropism; vine from sweet potato experiment 1375:60-62

Phototropism; why houseplants should be rotated experiment 1294:78-79

Phototropisms—plants are drawn to light 236:35

Plant stems bend up experiment 924:75

Plants grow toward light in maze experiment 1028:61

Plants grow toward water experiment 978:55-56

Plants grow upright even if seeds are planted upside down experiment 722:81

Plants need light experiment 909:162

Potato grows toward light through maze in box experiment 1145:11

Potato plant grows toward light in box maze experiment 810:29

Responses to light in growing plants experiment 784:114-115

Root growth showing geotropism and heliotropism—experiment 146:19

Root growth viewing box, how to build 986:76

Sleep movements in lima bean seedling experiment 1060:79-81

Thermotropism—plant's response to heat experiment 714:85-86

Thigmomorphogenesis; effect of rubbing leaves on plant's growth experiment 1060:78

Thigmotropism—plants grow better if touched experiment 714:87-88

Thigmotropism experiment with bean or cucumber seeds 879:82-83

Thigmotropism; leaf triggering mechanism on mimosa leaves experiment 1061:85-86

Thigmotropism; response of sensitive plant to touch experiment 1060:79

Thigmotropism; water, wind and touch stimuli affect plant growth experiment 1450:77-84

Traumatropism—Darwin's theory—plant turns from injury 86:89

Tropism—test plants' response to magnetism, gravity and light 86:49-51

PLANTS—VEGETATIVE PROPAGATION. *See also* **PLANTS—PROPAGATION**

African violets from leaf cuttings, how to do 879:70-72

Asexual reproduction of different plant cuttings experiment 1061:22

Auxin improves root formation in stem cuttings experiment 1060:99-100

Bulbs—forcing 465:102-105

Bulbs—projects with vegetative propagation 398:64-66

Can plants grow without seeds experiment 901:30

Carrot hanging basket, how to grow 1078:22

Carrot plant grows from piece of carrot root experiment 1038:17

Carrot top grows into plant (Primary) 650:unpaged

Carrot top grows into plant experiment 1440:52-54

Cloning—basic cloning techniques and projects 398:74-76

Cutting from plant roots and grows experiment 722:67-68

Cutting from plants grow—experiment 352:56-57

Cuttings from plant—how to plant and grow 712:20-23

Cuttings grow roots experiment 1145:24

Cuttings grow to show a variety of foliage 86:80

Different kinds of plants undergo asexual reproduction project 1296:1974

Display of examples of vegetative propagation project 1060:102-103

Graft tomato plant and potato plant experiment 1060:101-102

Grafting cacti 86:73-74

Grafting coleus 86:71-72

Grafting experiment with coleus 117:65-66

Grow an African violet "child" indoors from African violet leaf 416:21

Grow new plant from cutting experiment 1479:27

Grow plant from leaf experiment 860:151-152

Grow plants without seeds experiment 834:42-43

Growing plants from bulbs 603:30, 63-64

Growing plants from leaves 603:28-29, 63

Growing plants from parts other than seeds 294:52-54

Growing plants from roots 603:26-27, 62-63

Growing plants from stems 603:23-24, 61-62

Growing plants without seeds 532:62

Growing roots on a tree branch—experiment 86:59

Hanging carrot basket, how to make 644:10-11

How do leaves affect the development of new roots? 603:25, 62

How plants can be grown from cuttings 253:10-11

Ivy plant roots in water (Primary) 650:unpaged

Layering to get a new plant, how to do 879:72-74

Leaf cuttings—how to plant and grow 398:67-68

Leaf from plant grows roots experiment 1294:80-82

Leaf garden from vegetables, how to grow 646:63-64

Making baby plants, how to do 931:22-23

New plants from branches, how to grow 810:45-46

New plants from cuttings, how to do 832:41

New plants from leaves—experiment 563:64

New plants from old plants, how to do 1242:30-31

New plants propagated by layering experiment 1060:100

Onion bulb—how to grow in water 465:100-102

Parts of plants grow new plants experiment 899:180-181

Pineapple top grows into plant (Primary) 650:unpaged

Plant grows from cutting experiment 904:62-63

Plants from cuttings—how to plant and grow 384:21-22

Plants from cuttings 480:23

Plants grow from leaves—begonia, African violets, snake plants 270:19-22

Plants grow from parts of original plant 400:24-25

Plants grow from roots—sweet potato, carrots, beets, turnips, parsnips 270:7-11

Plants grow from stems experiment 1014:153

Plants grow from vegetable roots and tops 264:20-21

Potato (tubers)—how to grow 465:99-100

Potatoes can propagate experiment 1479:27

Potatoes can propagate experiment 904:64-65

Propagate plants from leaf cuttings experiment 1060:99

Propagate plants from stem cuttings experiment 1060:99

Propagate your plants 625:50-51

Reproduce plants from cuttings 40:160-161

Reproduction of plants from cuttings of stem or root 86:56-58

Rhizome rearing (underground stems)—how to grow 465:96-97

Rooting plants from cuttings, how to do 866:153

Rooting softwood and hardwood cuttings experiment 1078:24-25
Runners or stolons root from their runners—how to make 465:94-96
Stem cutting grows plant experiment 1440:95-96
Stem graft apple tree experiment 1060:102
Stem tip cuttings—how to grow 465:89-93
Sweet potato plant, how to grow 1078:22
Taking cuttings from houseplants to grow new plants 590:51
Tops of vegetables grow into hanging garden experiment 1440:49-51
Vegetative propagation of potatoes experiment 1061:20-21

PLANTS—VINES. *See also* **VINES**
Climbing plants will climb on frame of wire 483:49-51
Darwin's Exp.—light effect on twining plant motion 86:86
Darwin's experiment shows plant movement can be affected by weather 86:88
Darwin's experiment to demo revolving action of the tip of a twining plant 86:86-87
Darwin's experiment to show revolving action of a twining plant 86:85
Determine direction of winding plants experiment 904:46-47
Do all vines turn in the same direction 333:100-101
Leaf climbing vines—rub petioles to make leaves bend 271:91-96
Root climbing vines—observe growth 271:120-127
Tendril climber vines—observe and record growth of tendrils 271:97-119
Twining vines—observe and record circling action 271:74-90

PLANTS—WATER
Absorption of water by seeds 60:34-35
Amount of water seeds need to germinate experiment 1509:28
Can a plant have too much water? 603:50-51, 69-70
Circulation of water from roots to leaves—experiment 294:34
Do plants ever lose water? 603:47-48, 67-69
Do plants use water 236:35
Factors that affect water loss in plants 273:16-17
How do plants keep from losing too much water 603:49, 69
How does water get from roots to the leaves in plants experiments 852:8-10
How does water travel in a plant experiment 901:27-28
How is water used by plants and animals 402:14-15
How much water does a large plant use experiment 1509:28
How much water does a plant contain experiment 1183:26
How much water in plants experiment; how to measure 1181:18
How much water is in an apple 333:95-97
How much water is there in plants 603:42-43, 66-67
How rapidly does water enter a plant 273:12-13
How water moves in plant experiment 1183:26
Leaves and stems of plants act like a straw experiment 904:22-23
Nutrients are transported through plant stems experiment 904:20-21
Parts of plants that take in water 40:165-168

Patriotic celery demonstrates water absorption 576:81
Plants absorb water through their roots—experiment 86:12
Plants need water 270:43-54
Power of plants as they absorb water 60:35
Recycled water used to water plants experiment 1323:72-76
See route of water through a plant—make a flower bush 480:17
Turgidity of plants depends on amount of water 273:11
Water enters plant thru roots by osmosis experiment 978:56-58
Water in plants experiment 1183:26
Water is transported through plant stems experiment 904:18-19
Water levels in plants—measuring 146:60-61
Water movement in plants 273:10-11
Water movement through plant veins experiment with celery and colored water 784:83-84
Water moves in plants experiment using celery stalk and red food coloring 1181:18
Water needed by plants experiment; build moisture-gradient box 978:44-45
Water plants in your absence—how to do 381:118-119
Water protects plants from freezing temperatures experiment 1405:29
Water travels in stems and leaves experiment 878:16-17
Water usage by plants on daily basis experiment 978:44
Watering needs for outdoor seeds and plants 398:34-35
Watering rules 398:27-29
What do plants need—no water makes plant die—experiment (Primary) 540:32
What effect does salt have on plants 603:52-55, 70-71
Where does water go in plants experiment with plastic bag over leaf 1181:19
Where does water go in plants experiment 1183:27
Where water enters a plant experiment 878:14-15

PLANTS—WATER POLLUTANTS. *See also* **WATER—POLLUTION**
Chromosome changes from water pollutants experiment using onions 1060:119-121

PLANTS—WATERER
Make an automatic plant waterer using shoelace 494:49

PLANTS—WEAVING
Weed weaving—how to do 483:66-67

PLANTS—WEED KILLERS
Over growth induced by chemicals 577:project 92

PLANTS—WEEDS
How to plant a weed 264:85

PLANTS—WILD PLANTS
Growing plants from wild seeds 60:45-46
Viability of wild plant seeds—experiment 289:92-93
Wild gardens—outdoor projects with 118:223-232

PLASTER CASTS. *See also* **CASTS; TRACKS AND TRAILING**
Animal footprints cast in plaster, how to do 1363:17
Animal footprints made in plaster casts, how to do 1371:16-17
Animal track casts—making 749:49
Bird foot prints in plaster casts, how to do 1143:17
Casts from tracks, how to make 850:25
Casts of animal prints using plaster of Paris, how to make 1180:13
Casts of animal prints using plaster of Paris, how to make 1183:141

Casts of animal tracks, plaster, how to make 918:24-25
Casts of tracks from plaster of Paris project 1313:115-120
Collect tracks from snow with plaster casts experiment 1372:78-79
Footprint casts, making 930:12
Footprints of animals, making 890:107
Fossil plaster casts, how to make 1044:40-41
Hand—how to cast your entire hand in plaster to make hand mold sculpture 543:52-57
How to make 472:2232
How to make plaster casts 1246:20-21
Make a permanent shell imprint experiment 900:152-153
Mammal footprints in plaster casts, how to make 1147:30
Plaster—how to make 697:119
Plaster casting in sand—how to do 733:9
Plaster casts and molds of footprints, how to make 977:13
Plaster casts of animal tracks—how to make 726:58-59; 921:33; 932:44-45
Plaster casts of footprints—how to make 731:40
Plaster casts, making 870:64-66
Plaster of Paris casts, how to make 824:48-49
Plaster of Paris prints—making 697:120

PLASTER OF PARIS
Feet molds—how to make 364:73
How to make 122:49-52
Observe change due to addition of water experiment 905:144-145

PLASTIC SCRAP
Effect of plastic garbage pollution on sea animals experiment 1479:34

PLASTICS
Above ground versus below ground decomposition project 969:73-74
Baekeland, Leo Hendrik; who first discovered plastic project 1525:80-83
Casein plastic—how to make 676:10-11
Casein plastic from milk, how to make 827:69
Density and birefringence of plastics experiment data tables given 1004:4.006
Embedding delicate plants and animals in 436:34
Experiment to make 85:48-49
Experiments with 26:150-152
Fake plastic, how to make 859:11
Holes poked in plastic bag don't leak experiment 1231:58-59
Homemade plastic made from milk and vinegar decomposes experiment 1476:140-141
Hot wire cutter for making plastic animals 910:47
Identify different types of plastics for recycling experiment; code given 1323:62-66
Identifying plastics chart—flame test given 6:34
Is paper as strong as plastic experiment 1508:12
Make plastic sulfur 157:27
Make your own plastic 6:34
Making from casein in milk 26:138-142
Making plastic from milk and vinegar experiment 1179:40
Milk turns into plastic experiment using milk and vinegar 1271:31
Model glider from plastic, how to make 1197:28
Natural plastics decompose and synthetic petroleum plastics do not experiment 1476:140-141

Plastic bags/paper bags/newspapers compared for decomposing time experiment 997:97-98
Plastic waste used in one week by family project 1013:47
Plastics are better insulators than natural materials experiment 1483:22-23
Plastics of different chemical compositions separated by their density 1396:144-145
Polyethylene plastic—making a warm goo plastic 259:29
Produce plastic from milk and vinegar 157:26
Rubbery plastic from milk and vinegar experiment 1162:19
Self stick plastic, how to make 859:12
Silly Putty experiments 1091:47-48
Some plastics decompose in soil more readily than others project 969:71-72
Superabsorbent plastic from diapers experiment 1083:64-65
Test the strength of plastics experiment 1197:29
Thermoplastic or thermosetting—how are they different 26:143-148
Types of plastic bags tested for biodegradability experiment using buried bags 1228:36-37
Wall covering; is plastic or paper best for wall covering experiment 1508:13
What is polyethylene experiment 902:39

PLATE TECTONICS
Magnetism and plate tectonics investigations 1342:110-111
Plate tectonic model used to show continental collision experiment 1342:106-110
Plate tectonic model, how to make 1342:106-110

PLATELETS. *See also* **BLOOD**
Explanation of how platelets stop bleeding (Primary) 245:22-25

PLATONIC SOLIDS
Dodecahedron 3-D desk calendar, how to make 1299:86
Models of regular solids; cube, tetrahedron, octahedron, icosahedrone 1299:87

PLAY DOUGHS
Glue and oobleck play substances made from household chemicals, how to 1115:101

PLAYING CARDS
House of cards, how to make 1299:71
Tower of cards, how to make 1299:71

PLIMSOLL LINE
Plimsoll Line marks safe water level on boats demonstration 1310:15
Chart of 678:14

PLUMB LINE
How to make plumb line to check true vertical of things experiment 1247:18
Making a plumb line to show gravity 274:8

PLUMBING
Determine bacteria in P-traps and what products stop growth experiment 997:135-140

PLUTO. *See also* **PLANETS**
Blink comparator helps to discover planets, how to make 1478:80-81
Making a model of the orbits of Uranus, Neptune, and Pluto project 833:249-251
Measurements of 292:96-97
Pluto discovered by using blink comparator, how to make 1478:80-81

PNEUMATIC MACHINES
Pneumatic man is fired by squeezing plastic bottle experiment 1446:30-31

PNEUMATIC ROOFS
Making a model of 328:142-147

POKERINO
Pokerino game—how to make 23:63-70

POLARIMETER
Optical activity and chirality; polarimeter identifies substance experiment 1004:4.014

POLARIS. *See also* **NORTH STAR**
A pattern for a night clock 292:65-66
Constellations that turn around Polaris [North Star], how to find 1434:67-69
Finding directions on Earth using Sun and Polaris experiment 1170:14
Finding Polaris [North Star] in the sky, how to do 1434:64-66
Magnetic deviation is increasing or decreasing but not fluctuating experiment 1062:67-68
Path of stars near North Star seems longer than stars farther away experiment 1062:71-73
Polaris and Earth's latitude—ideas for experiment 762:19
Polaris used as reference point for viewing stars in night sky experiment 1062:79-80

POLARISCOPE
Construct polariscope, how to do 997:153-154
How to make 43:44-53

POLARITY
Checking the magnetic polarity of a solenoid experiment 768:91-92
Polarity of parameciums 577:project #11
Potato indicates polarity of storage battery experiment 768:83

POLARIZATION OF LIGHT
Transverse vibrations in a string; transverse wave motion of light experiment 1132:96-1-96-2

POLARIZATION OF WORMS
Polarity of worms—experiment 532:50

POLARIZED GLASSES
Color changes when molecules in polarized glasses are stretched/twisted 1403:53

POLARIZED LIGHT
Corn syrup rotates polarized light experiment 1083:110
Depolarizing light experiment 1082:167
Experiments with polarized light 532:38
Haidinger's brush experiment to detect polarized light 1153:113-114
How polarized light moves experiment 1405:105
How Polaroid sunglasses reduce glare experiment 941:11-12
How sunglasses reduce glare experiment 1293:127-128
Magnesium sulfate crystals act like Polaroid lenses 346:37-38
Polarization of sky light experiment 1153:110-112
Polarized light box, how to make 1476:55-57
Polarized light experiment using Polaroid sheets 1153:109-110
Polarized light experiment 563:149-150
Polarized light reveals stress patterns in clear plastic experiment 1132:12-1-12-2
Polarized light stained glass window mosaic experiment 1132:78-1-78-3
Polarized light through sugar water gives beautiful colors experiment 1132:85-1-85-2

Polarized sunglasses experiment 1132:79-1-79-2
Polarized sunglasses stop time on LCD wristwatch experiment 1082:162-164
Rotating plane of polarized light experiment 1153:114-116
Rotating polarized light with Karo syrup experiment 1153:116-117
Scattered and unscattered light experiment 1153:112-113
Stress birefringence in gelatin experiment 1082:164-165
Stress birefringence in household plastic objects experiment 1082:165-166

POLE STAR. *See* **POLARIS**

POLLEN
Artificially pollinate flower experiment 860:153
Brownian motion of pollen grains experiment 1133:7.006
Grow pollen tubes of flowers experiment 1060:53
Help pollinate the flowers 264:48
Investigate pollen in the air experiment 1060:53-55
Pollen grains grow experiment 819:58
Pollen grains under a microscope, observe 889:45-46
Pollen grains under microscope—observe sprouting 713:56-58
Pollen quantity produced by flower experiment 860:152-153
Study of pollen under microscope experiment 1060:52-53
Studying pollen 148:16
Trapping fungal spores and pollen grains from the atmosphere experiment 933:31
Why do flowers make pollen experiment 1294:83-85

POLLINATION. *See also* **BEES—POLLINATION; PLANTS—POLLINATION**
Artificially pollinate flower experiment 860:153
Bag or stocking over buds experiment 414:45-46
Cross-pollination effect on next generation of plants experiment 1458:31
Experiment 236:36
Flowers; how to pollinate flowers experiment 1491:42-43
How the bees make colored flowers 366:90-91
How to gather pollen to fertilize corn 366:106-108
Insects role in pollination experiment 1097:40-41
Pollen quantity produced by flower experiment 860:152-153

POLLS
Statistic gathering projects for home and school 528:1-33

POLLUTION
A comparison of returnable and nonreturnable bottles 33:35
A survey of land use associated with housing 33:31
Activities with pollution 236:183-184
Air pollution, ideas for projects 841:64
Chemical waste landfill experiment 950:132-133
Cost of nonreturnables used in the home 33:34
Design environmentally sound town project 1059:116-117
Domestic refuse—the analysis of household refuse 33:12-14
Effect of herbicides on plants experiments 950:101-102
Effect of pollution on plants experiment 739:39
Garbage—trash and treasure 10:81-85
Garbage pollution, ideas for projects 841:67-69
Insecticides—friend or foe 10:101-105
Land pollution, ideas for projects 841:64
Making accurate land—use maps of the area around the school 33:29

Organic matter pollution in soil and water experiment 950:75-76

Overpopulation and the environment 10:106-110

Pesticides pollution, ideas for projects 841:66

Problem of litter 10:86-90

Road pollution effects on populations of insects experiment 1096:69-74

Smog—make your own smog 236:183-184

Solid waste pollution—causes 40:184-186

Toxic substances, ideas for projects 841:66-67

Using the line transect to measure litter pollution 33:10-11

Using the quadrat frame to measure litter disposition 33:8-9

Water protection, ideas for projects 841:63-64

What litter is biodegradable 236:183

What things are biodegradable 10:91-95

Where has all the soil gone 10:96-100

POLLUTION—AIR. *See also* **AIR—POLLUTION**

Air pollution—causes of 40:182-183

Air pollution—test for pollutants 236:184

Airborne particulate matter or dust in household rooms project 969:88-89

Chemical properties of marble and why damaged by pollution experiment 871:3.026

Collecting acid rain experiment 950:169

Collecting air pollutants 175:79

Effect of soil pH on plant growth experiment; data table given 871:2.009

How clean is town air experiment 740:9

Lichens show polluted air 660:37

Making and using air dust collectors 400:13

Measure amount in air 358:96-97

Measure with bottle caps on cardboard experiment 749:93

Sulfur dioxide and nitrogen dioxide effect on plant growth 398:56-60

Vaseline and cardboard collect particles in air experiment 950:156

POLLUTION—HEAVY METALS

The effect of copper salts on the germination of grass seeds 33:22-23

POLLUTION—INDOOR

Bucket of water collects traveling air pollution experiment 1328:36-37

Cigarette smoke effect on growing radish plants experiment 1328:38-39

Indoor pollution experiment using styrofoam cup 1324:69-72

Test pollution in your home with vacuum cleaner and cloth filters experiment 1328:34-35

POLLUTION—INSECTICIDES

A second experiment with insecticides 33:49

Lime sulfur and copper sulfate as examples of fungicides 33:44

Testing the effectiveness of pyrethrum as a cockroach killer 33:43

Toxicology test for pesticides on water fleas experiment 950:88-89

POLLUTION—LIGHT

Different lights tested in simulated starry night sky diorama experiment 1476:202-206

Light pollution diorama to show shielded and unshielded lighting effects 1476:202-206

POLLUTION—LITTER

Collect and chart kinds of litter 740:37

Container survey—investigate the litter situation in your town 542:65-66

Kind of litter most common in your area project 1296:1996

POLLUTION—NOISE. *See also* **NOISE—POLLUTION**

Can we improve our noise environment experiment 900:185

Noise pollution and its causes 40:186-187

Observe and chart kinds of noises in your environment 740:39

Shrubs tested as natural sound barriers for homes project 969:90-91

POLLUTION—OIL. *See also* **OIL SPILLS**

Cleaning up an oil spill experiment 950:114-115

Emulsifying oil with detergent 33:39

Removal of oil from feathers and clothes 33:38

POLLUTION—PLANTS

Growing plants in solutions of various pH values 33:19

The growth of plants in industrial wastes 33:26-27

POLLUTION—PLASTICS

Identifying plastics 33:52-58

POLLUTION—WATER. *See also* **WATER—POLLUTION**

Bacteria in polluted water 330:90-92

Cleaning up an oil spill experiment 950:114-115

Collect and check water samples—how to 358:102-103

Collect samples of water—record results 330:85-88

Determine effect that polluting detergents can have on birds experiment 904:138-139

Effect of fertilizer on algae growth experiment 950:36

Effects of phosphate detergents on fish breathing rates experiment 950:58-60

Experiments in cleaning up pollution 330:94-97

Filtering muddy water with model filtering plant 368:36-40

How clean is town water experiment 740:13

Measuring clarity of body of water—how to 330:89-90

Measuring water pollution by observing organisms called pollution indicators 507:1895

Observations of pollution in a pond 173:31

Organic matter pollution in soil and water experiment 950:75-76

Outreaching effect of small amount of pollution on stream and wildlife 904:140-141

Test for BOD 'biochemical oxygen demand' 330:93-94

Toxicology test for pesticides on water fleas experiment 950:88-89

Water pollution—cause of 40:183-184

POLLUTION—WEED KILLERS

An experiment with a herbicide 33:46-48

Effect of herbicides on plants experiment 950:101-102

POLYGONS

Making hexagon, octagon, pentagon 444:21-27

POLYHEDRONS

Nets or flat sheet fold into polyhedrons experiment, how to build 1518:40-41

POLYMER MOLECULES

Are rubber molecules less bouncy when cold 396:37-38

POLYMERIZATION

Air needed for paint to harden experiment 1251:65-67

POLYMERS

Amount of water that high absorbency disposable diaper will hold experiment 1396:147-152

Can oil be soaked up from oil spills experiment 1325:70-74

Chewing gum is less flexible when cold experiment 1250:65-67

Chewing gum is less sticky when cold experiment 1250:68-70

Density and birefringence of plastics experiment data tables given 1004:4.006

Do plastic bags tear when they are punctured experiment 831:45-46

Effect of temperature on vulcanized rubber experiment 1396:145

Experiment with stay-dry diaper particles 1412:98-99

Is rubber in rubber cement natural or vulcanized experiment 1396:145

Plastics of different chemical compositions separated by their density 1396:144-145

Properties of materials depend on organization of polymeric chains experiment 1396:141-146

Recipe for Nutty Putty, how to make 1083:60-61

Test brands of disposable diapers experiment 1396:147-149

POLYNESIAN MAGIC CALABASH
Make a magic calabash to show your home latitude 292:28-29

POLYNESIANS
Experiments of their culture 325:entire book

POLYUNSATURATES
What are polyunsaturates—iodine test for saturated/unsaturated molecules 6:35

POMANDERS
How to make 231:112; 832:107
Recipe for and how to make 387:30-31
Orange-clove pomander ball, how to make 1369:22

POMEGRANATE SEED
How to grow 272:36-41

POND WATER TERRARIUM
Materials and animals for—how to set up and maintain 475:35-38

PONDS. See also FRESHWATER; LAKES; STREAMS
Activities with pond water 236:127-130
Algae; why is some pond water green experiment 1294:96-98
Aquatic ecosystem, how to create using fish tank, plants, water animals 1172:29-34
'Backflushing' to observe pond creatures 236:134
Build a pond (Advanced) 625:52
Build a pond in your yard, how to 796:28
Comparing pond and stream microhabitats experiment 1134:5.014
Demonstrate oxygen in fresh water 173:26
Demonstrating pond zones 173:28
Ecological succession; effects of on pond ecosystem experiment 978:117
Eutrophication or oxygen depletion of water in lakes and ponds experiment 978:75
Food chain pictures, how to arrange in order 796:13
Food chains—demonstrate how water is colonized by plants and animals 194:27
Food chains—observations of food chains in freshwater 173:23
How to build with plastic sheets and rocks 430:55
How to make a pond 194:14-15
How to make with plastic 740:31

Keeping temperature records of a pond experiment 934:54-57
Life in a drop of pond water, observe under microscope 882:37
Light penetration in water with Secchi disc 285:27-28
Make a backyard pond 264:89-90
Make a pond using plastic sheet, stones, sand and plants, how to do 1183:67
Make a pond with plastic sheet, rocks and plants 1182:19
Make a pond 832:65
Make and stock a pond 657:43-47
Mapping your pond or stream 173:5
Measure pH of pond water 285:26
Mini backyard pond from garbage can, how to make 1115:91
Mini-aquarium for pond creatures, how to make 600:6-7
Mini-pond, how to make experiment 943:25
Net; pond dipping net, how to make 1146:30
Observation of moving water 173:25
Observations of mud and sand 173:14
Observing life in 118:173-179
Phosphate detergents overfeed algae and harm pond life experiment 1331:81
Plankton in a pond community experiment using plankton net 1172:35-37
Pond bottle garden, with plants and animals, making 796:26-27
Pond dipping experiment 741:25
Pond environment aquarium, how to stock with plants and animals project 1363:10-11
Pond kit—what to collect to catch pond creatures 194:8-10
Pond viewer—how to make to observe pond life 194:6-7
Pond water under a microscope experiment 1176:32-33
Pond water under microscope observe life 713:77-81
Pond; making from wading pool, how to do 918:17
Populations of pond, observe and record, data sheet given 817:9
Record the seasons 173:24
Recording plants and animal life 173:6-7
Succession; turn pond into forest experiment with one habitat replacing another 1472:60-63
Temperature of fresh waters 285:26-27
Test pond for your boats—how to make 429:71
The life of a pond 268:45-50
Thermocline to check water temperature—making 741:23
Underwater viewer, how to make 1146:31
Why is some water green experiment 860:166-167

PONDS—ALGAE
Make microscopic algae jungle 279:34-36

PONDS—ANIMALS
Amphibians—frogs—record daily changes in frog spawn of eggs 194:16-17
Clams—use dish of sand and water to observe 'foot' and siphons 194:11
Collect eggs and hatch, how to keep and feed 796:25-26
Do pond animals prefer dim light or bright light experiment 796:28-29
Examining life found in a pond experiment 1134:5.005
Flatworms, collect and observe under magnifying glass experiment 796:15
How much food does water snail eat in a day experiment 796:29-30

How to catch and preserve 117:37-38
Leeches, collect and observe, how to 796:27
Looking for small animals 173:15
Make mini pond aquarium 279:19-20
Microinvertebrates in pond water, how to collect and study 1117:54-55
Observations of animals in the water 173:11
Observations of animals on stones and in the mud 173:13
Observations of animals on the water's surface 173:9
Observing with waterscope 285:37-39
Snails, collect eggs, hatch and observe 796:26
Sticklebacks, frogs and newts in aquarium, how to keep 913:39
Studying protozoa experiment 1293:95-97
Vertebrates and invertebrates in ponds; make chart of them 796:27-28

PONDS—AQUARIUMS
A pond community aquarium 268:51-56
Aquarium set up to show pond creatures 194:20-21
Pond life aquarium, how to set up 913:38
Set up and observe a pond aquarium 285:89
Setting up a freshwater aquarium 173:16
Setting up and observing a mini pond ecosystem 285:39-41

PONDS—BIRDS
Bird life—make plan to record area of pond used by certain birds 194:22-23
How long can water birds stay underwater; observe and chart 796:31
Observations of water birds 173:22

PONDS—COMMUNITY
Observe and study the structure of a pond community 285:32-41

PONDS—ECOSYSTEMS
Pond ecosystem in fishbowl shows relationship between plants and animals 1476:118-119

PONDS—INSECTS. *See also* WATER INSECTS
A study of insects in a pond 285:75-76
Collect eggs, hatch and observe with magnifying glass 796:27
Examining life found in a pond experiment 1134:5.005
How to hunt and catch pond insects 166:95-100
Insect aquarium to study pond or stream insects, how to make 1274:15
Net for pond dipping to collect water insects, how to make 1182:16
Observations of water insects 173:19
Observe pond insects in aquarium experiment, how to do 1472:30-35
Water insects—how to care for 279:21

PONDS—PLANTS
Duckweed, how does it multiply experiment 796:30
Green plants make oxygen; pond plant in jar experiment 790:12-13
Observations of water plants 173:12
Plants, aquatic—demonstrate substances needed for growth 194:12-13
Pondweed, how small a piece is needed to make new plant experiment 796:31
Water plants give off oxygen experiment 796:14

PONDS—POLLUTION
Detrimental effect of phosphates in detergents on pond plants/animals experiment 1476:192
Effect of detergents and phosphates on living things—experiment 10:60-64

Nutrients added to lakes and ponds cause water pollution experiment 1325:55-59
Observations of water pollution in 173:31
Phosphate pollutant can be removed from water experiment 1325:60-64
Study of duckweed population and effect of fertilizers experiment 871:2.010

POOTER—INSECTS
Make a pooter for collecting small insects 285:51

POPCORN
Can popcorn float on bubbles experiment 780:6-7
Carbon dioxide produces energy experiment 884:86-87
Dancing popcorn and carbon dioxide bubbles in water/vinegar/baking soda 1289:44-45
Demonstrate how popcorn pops 759:61-62
Does popcorn dissolve in water experiment 1250:41-42
Effect of popping process on volume and density of corn experiment data tables 1004:3.004
Experiments with popcorn 1412:82
Grow kernel of popcorn in plastic container—how to 701:unp
Growing popcorn 366:104-108
Heat causes corn seeds to pop experiment 888:85-87
How to get all popcorn kernels to pop experiment 924:39
How to make 560:36-37
How to pop to eat and make jewelry 629:141-143
Is weight of popcorn same after popping 538:107
Pop off with popcorn investigation 748:89
Popcorn plant grows in plastic cup; observe growing parts 1189:42-43
Popcorn recipes for different flavors of popcorn 1484:19-26
Popcorn soaked in water or heated in oven doesn't pop experiment 1229:60-61
Popping popcorn experiment 1238:88-89
Room-temperature popcorn or frozen popcorn; which pops better project 1195:31-43
Senses used when popping corn activities for classroom 1291:19-20
Sprouting and potting popping corn, how to do 1406:74-76
Water goes from liquid to a gas when popcorn is heated experiment 1250:35-37
What makes popcorn pop experiment 980:66
Why does wet or dry popcorn pop better experiment 1484:17-18
Why popcorn pops experiment 939:78; 1405:107

POPSICLES
How to make 32:74-75; 793:25

POPULATION
Animal population and plant study of a specific ecosystem experiment 1395:145-150
Availability of needs affects populations project 1427:15-17
Basic needs of life affect how many animals can live in one place project 1427:22-25
Brine shrimp egg hatching experiment to see how many can survive 1069:23
Counting animal populations using Lincoln Index experiment 1134:5.010
Even distribution of population experiment; data tables given 1004:2.009
Factors that govern population change in animals experiment 1134:5.012

Genetics; how a characteristic or gene spreads through a population experiment 1134:5.011

Lawn ecosystems experiment; observe distribution of plants/animals; data table 1004:2.010

Overcrowding effect on populations of guppies experiment 1476:200-201

Overgrowth of population effect on yeast colony experiment 1476:201

Overpopulations of plants experiment 978:168-169

Population growth of aphids experiment 1096:39-44

Sampling of population distribution experiment; data tables given 1004:2.009

Uneven distribution [herding] of population experiment; data tables 1004:2.009

POPULATION—ANIMAL. *See* **ANIMAL POPULATIONS**

POPULATION—BIRDS

Birds of certain kind are attracted to certain kind of food project 969:32-34

POPULATION—HABITATS

Habitat size and number of organisms living there project 969:22-23

POPULATION—INSECTS

Population growth in insects experiment 1097:87-89

POPULATION—PEOPLE

Age profiles of people—how young, how many 263:20-23

Aggregation—together we stand 263:37-39

Competition and population 263:28-30

Consuming resources—what it takes 263:44-46

Cost of eating in poor countries compared to eating in U.S. project 1059:46

Design environmentally sound town project 1059:116-117

Earth's population growth over the next two centuries project 1150:18-19

Effects of overcrowding on people experiment; Asian food recipe given 978:161-162

Effects of overcrowding on people experiment 978:160

Food resources 263:62-66

Growing food for people isn't easy experiment using plants 1059:38-39

How does population change the food supply experiment using yeast 1324:85-89

Human population—growth and effect on Earth—experiment 371:107-111

Infant mortality 263:59-61

Investigation into population growth 420:135-136

Limitations of resources 263:24-27

Malnourished children using plants project 1059:35

Model artificial island, earthquake resistant, to house people experiment 1458:11

Model the population growth of the world experiment 1324:80-84

Natural population controls 263:34-36

No room on Earth to grow food experiment using beet seeds 1059:98

Number of people and size of their country playground project 1059:28-29

Overcrowded land project 1059:31

Overpopulation—a tight squeeze 263:9-11

Photo censusing 263:51-52

Population density—how many, how close 263:6-8

Population explosions—eat until we burst 263:71-73

Population growth patterns 263:67-70

Population turnover—a circular track 263:12-15

Predicting populations 263:40-43

Recapture counting—a fish story 263:47-49

Resources used by family in over three generations experiment 1328:24-25

Sex ratio—sir or madam 263:16-19

Survival of a species 263:31-33

Territoriality—what's mine is mine 263:56-58

Waste not, want not project with wasted school lunches 1059:48

World's population will double in thirty years project 1150:20-21

POPULATION—SNAILS

Estimate the snail population experiment 1070:26-27

Estimating and calculating a snail population 507:1903

POROSITY

Bricks soak up water 253:45

How porous are sand, clay and rock experiment 1027:11

POSITIVE NUMBERS

Activities and game to explain concept of positive and negative numbers 458:1-33

POSTAL SCALE

Make an accurate postal scale 381:151-152

POSTURE

Posture checkup 400:39

POTATO POPGUN

How to make 563:29-30

POTATOES. *See also* **PLANTS—POTATOES**

Boiled potato cooks faster than baked potato experiment 1238:42-43

Do potato roots pick up dye experiment 876:77

Does green color [chloroplasts] in potatoes disappear in dark closet exp 876:76

Enzyme action in potatoes under different conditions experiment 876:75-76

Food stains removed from clothing using potatoes experiment 1065:14

Grow a real live monster in the dark (Primary) 580:unpaged

Grow a sprout in the dark and a brown bag monster 231:29

Grow in a bucket 376:11

Grow your own potato plant experiment 1484:40

Growing bacteria on potatoes experiment 762:81-83

Growing indoors 480:48

Growing potato shoots in water and then planting in soil experiment 1379:7

Hairy potato head from grass seeds—making 508:10

Hand heater from potatoes, how to make 1065:34

How can a plant grow from a potato 253:12-13

How to grow 264:11; 358:110-111

How to plant and grow potatoes 1065:57

How to sprout a potato 1440:87-89

Indoor potato garden from potato eyes, how to make 1330:52-53

Iodine test to show starch in potato 876:72-74

Irish potato bread, recipe, making 792:27

Is potato eye needed for growth of potato experiment 722:79

Is potato eye needed for growth of potato experiment 722:79

Osmosis experiment with potatoes 1238:44-45

Phototropism; potato plant in box maze grows toward light experiment 1214:11

Phototropism; potato shoot grows toward light source in maze experiment 1236:6-7

Positive battery terminal demonstrated with potato battery 1404:16-17

Potato balances on forks experiment with center of gravity 1065:13

Potato battery experiment 1004:3.012

Potato grows through maze in box to find light experiment 1379:25

Potato print 231:30

Potato prints of repeating patterns experiment 1391:13

Potato shoots grow through box to reach light source experiment 1390:31

Potato shoots grow toward light in cardboard box maze experiment 1524:26

Potato tuber made up of starch from photosynthesis in its leaves experiment 1069:42

Potato wobbler wobbles and doesn't fall over experiment with center of gravity 1065:12

Potatoes as models of cell membranes demonstrate osmosis experiment 1069:17

Potatoes can propagate experiment 1479:27

Potatoes can propagate experiment 904:64-65

Potatoes have starch experiment 1238:40-41

Raw potato absorbs what substances experiment 876:74

Root of potato grows downward experiment 876:77

Showing it is a stem with buds 146:32

Specific gravity is higher in high starch potatoes than in low starch experiment 1065:41

Sprouting potato eye produces hormones experiment 876:78-80

Straw plunging through raw potato demonstrates air pressure experiment 1065:14

Test for starch in potatoes experiment 1065:41

White potato plant, how to grow indoors 1178:16-18

White potato potted plant, how to plant and grow 1406:38-39

POTATOES—SWEET. *See also* **SWEET POTATOES**

Dried sweet potatoes 231:45

Sweet potato sprouting—observe 352:49

Vine devine—how to grow 231:44-45

POTENTIAL ENERGY

Compare potential energy and kinetic energy experiment 902:63

How is work measured experiment 902:45

Potential energy of machines that use gravity 274:29

Swinging spoons demonstrate potential and kinetic energy experiment 1377:28

Thin or thick soup spins the fastest down ramp experiment 1330:40-41

POTPOURRI

Create blend of different scents experiment 1037:28-29

Easy potpourri—making 480:118

Flower potpourri, how to make 1068:45

How to make 416:30

Ingredients for potpourri and how to make 552:41

Make potpourri from dried flower petals and spices, how to do 1368:68-69

Recipe for potpourri and how to make sachets 1071:92-93

Recipe for potpourri 387:29-30; 832:104

Rose leaves potpourri, how to make 1181:10

POTTERY

How to make 321:11

Paper roll pottery—how to make 732:172-173

Prehistoric pottery pots from clay, how to make 1168:53

POULTRY BROODER. *See also* **BROODERS**

How to make 358:92-93

POULTRY. *See* **CHICKENS**

POWDERS

Identifying unknown ingredients experiment using liquid indicator 1435:97-100

Puzzling powders 400:72

Testing some common powders for different properties experiment 790:27-28

Tests to identify many powders experiment 1063:169

POWER

How powerful are you—experiment 586:115-116

POWER LINES

Plant growth affected by magnetism experiment 1061:87-88

POWER OFF ALARM

How to build 563:30-31

POWER RESOURCES

Paddleboat race; use twisted rubber band energy to push boats thru water 1497:8-9

PRAIRIES

Prairie grasses garden, how to grow 1232:53

PRAXINOSCOPE

How to make 172:44-45

Parrot praxinoscope, how to make 1308:28-29

PRAYING MANTIS

Care of as pets 354:52-60

Collection and care of 390:24-25

How many insects can praying mantis eat experiment 1097:9-12

How to cage and care for 279:28-29

How to care for 332:55-57

How to hatch 117:51-52

How to keep and observe 233:20

How to raise praying mantis from an egg case experiment 1527:55-56

Keep as pet—how to 414:80-82

Observation of movement and eating 331:39-49

PRECESSION

Crazy wheel 260:27

Gyroscope mystery force 260:29

Movement of Earth's axis demonstration 1023:10-11

Precession experiments with bicycle wheel 1164:44-49

Spinning bicycle wheel demonstrates 699:29

Spinning wheel demonstrates 472:2231

PRECIPITATES. *See also* **SOLUTIONS**

Alum and ammonia mixed produce white precipitate experiment 721:119

Iron test to show formation of precipitate 346:54-57

Making a precipitate 180:21

Precipitate formation experiment using Epsom salts and ammonia 976:41

See precipitation of white magnesium hydroxide in a glass 508:18

Think milk! Precipitation demonstration 205:121-124

PRECIPITATION

Earth's precipitation records 1003:69

How to measure snowfall as precipitation experiment 1439:92-94

PREDATORS

Parasitoid wasps lay eggs in other insects experiment 1097:13-15

Praying mantis can eat how many insects experiment 1097:9-12

Predator competition experiment with normal color/monochromatic vision; tables 1004:2.008

Predator-prey soda bottle column experiment with soil, plants and insects 1527:51-54

PREHISTORIC ANIMALS

Diorama—how to make 293:25

PREHISTORIC MAN

Lattice dome; Stone Age tent experiment, how to build 1518:36-37

Prehistoric pottery pots from clay, how to make 1168:53

PRESERVATION

Making raisins and other dried fruits 219:27-32

PRESS—PLANTS. *See also* **PLANTS—PRESS**

Build a press for flowers and leaves 291:197

Flower press, how to make and use 932:36-39

Make a plant press, how to do 832:58

Plant press, how to make and use 291:197; 824:30-34; 986:98

PRESSURE. *See also* **AIR PRESSURE; BAROMETER; WATER—PRESSURE**

Measure pressure of foot on floor (metric) 357:22-23

PRETZELS

Make from yeast—breath experiment 231:59

PRIESTLEY, JOSEPH

His experiments 42:76-80

Candle burns longer in jar with plants experiment 879:90

Dephlogisticated air oxygen experiment 1133:2.006

Who invented carbonated water project 1525:65-66

PRINTING

Block printing—how to 321:23

Block printing—how to do and how to make rollers 631:77

Copying a newspaper picture 150:136-137

Corrugated cardboard printing—how to do 631:78

Electro-typing printing plates—how to do 97:38-39

Fish prints of any fish—how to do 359:59-62

Fish prints, how to make 1118:52-53

Make your own secret printing press 146:56

Making potato prints 507:1897

Making your own watermarks on paper 150:130-131

Nature printing with leaves, weeds 293:18

Oil, water and paint printing on paper, how to do 1018:26-27

Potato print paper—how to do it 376:27

Potatoes cut in shapes make simple prints 472:2215

Printing with plant leaves, stems, and roots, how to do 1054:48-49

Roller and stamp printing—how to do 732:159-160

Roller printing using tin can and knitting needle, how to make 1247:22-23

Skinny printing—how to do 392:87-89

Spatter printing of small leaves and plants 293:18-19

Spatter printing, how to do 644:36-37

Stamp pad and stamps—how to make 631:73-76

PRINTS

Fish printing, how to 646:24-26

Fruit and vegetable prints—how to make 473:58-59

Fruit prints, how to make 1368:75-76

Fruits and vegetable prints, how to make 644:22-23

Grass and leaf prints, making 772:83-85

Instant prints 356:22-23

Leaf prints, how to make 784:88-89

Mushroom spore prints, how to make 784:39-40

Of mushroom spores 382:57-59

Potato prints of repeating patterns experiment 1391:13

Printing driftwood, how to do 646:94-95

Printing flowers, how to 646:40

Printing, rubbing, taking an imprint—how to 480:102-103

Seaweed prints, how to make 784:37

Spore—how to do 442:unpaged

Stamp printing with vegetables 646:65-66

Sun pictures of weeds, how to make 646:8-10

PRISMS. *See also* **SPECTRUM**

A water prism 19:40

Colored filters absorption measured by spectroscope experiment 860:215-216

Experiment with different colored cellophane papers 911:27

Colored lights through water experiment 1082:100-102

Colored spinning discs appear to be white experiment 1073:80-81

Colors in different shades differ in effects on photosynthesis experiment 1060:27-28

Diffraction grating spreads light into its component colors experiment 1132:90-1-90-2

Experimenting with prisms and light project 833:187-188

Experiments 350:126-128

Filters change the color of light experiment 941:56

Ghost of sunlight 19:38

Homemade prism using gelatin experiment 924:96-97

How prism works demonstration 1390:18

Invisible colors of spectrum can be located experiment 715:112-114

Light bends; experiments with prisms demonstrates 956:34-35

Light with prisms, shadows and transparent materials experiments 1417:5

Long flat rainbow, how to make using mirror in bowl of water experiment 1281:27

Make a prism experiment 902:86

Making a rainbow 253:84-85

Making a spectrum analyzing instrument project 833:189-192

Making colors of the spectrum experiment 956:12-13

Measuring the temperature of infrared rays project 833:188-189

Model of periscope made from two mirrors experiment 1159:81-84

Newton's white light through a prism experiment 1156:73-76

Photosynthesis affected by colors of the spectrum experiment 1060:27-28

Prism—making 436:64

Prism splits white light into a rainbow experiment 1283:22

Prism, how to make experiment 941:54-55

Prism, make your own experiment with a pail of water and mirror 1088:74

Source of color; activities to demonstrate where color comes from 1511:43-46

Spectra and splitting light—experiment 569:39

Sunset in glass of water experiment 1082:103-107

Use prism to break light into mini-rainbow experiment 1063:177

Use water prism to make rainbow 893:9

Water prism experiment 1082:98-100

What does prism do to light experiment 902:85

Which colors of spectrum are hottest experiment 715:115

White light can be split into seven colors using glass prism experiment 1073:80-81

Why is light white; experiment with colored filters 860:217

PROBABILITY

Basketball "insurance" project 1070:32-33

Betcha game demonstrates Pascal's theory of probability 966:87-89

Calculate probability in three projects; coins, dice, and deck of cards 1070:8-9

Cards and your math skills show you are a genius experiment 1070:16-17

Do you have ESP? 669:38-39

Experiments in probability and using data to make predictions 486:1-33

Game of chance, Forgotten Planet, how to play 1070:10-11

Likely or unlikely—computer experiment 665:40-41

Probability curve experiment with marbles 808:16-19

Roll a coin game of chance; calculate your chances of winning 1070:12-13

PROJECTILES

A baseball projectile—experiment 586:78-79

Angle of launch determines travel distance experiment; data tables given 871:4.004

Balloon projectile experiment 994:64-68

Calculate trajectory of ball launch experiment [Advanced] 871:4.005

Catapult experiment 748:142

Galileo's experiment; predicting the path of a projectile 1156:42-47

Launching and mapping projectiles—experiment 586:75-78

Projectile launcher, how to make 1063:307

Projectile motion experiment with vertical and horizontal motion 1158:50-60

Ramp shows speed affects path of ball launched horizontally—making 763:70-72

PROJECTORS

Flashlight slide projector and slide show, how to make 1257:15-18

Flashlight slide projector, how to make 1053:15-16

How an opaque projector works experiment 1405:104-105

How to make projectors; filmstrips, strips 128:204-205

Milk carton filmstrip projector—making 631:110

Movie projector from gallon jug, making 870:36-38

Opaque projector, making 906:70

Overhead projectors—how to make 386:58-59

Rear-projection projector using TV picture experiment 1082:54-56

Simple projector, how to make 1417:21

Slide projector—how to make 472:2241

Slide projector in a shoe box—how to make 631:60-62

Slide projector, how to make from cardboard boxes and flashlight 1245:22-23

Visual effects projectors—500W 35mm 386:20-23

PROPAGATION. See PLANTS—PROPAGATION; PLANTS—VEGETATIVE PROPAGATION

PROPELLERS

Air propelled model boat 472:2219

Air vibrations demonstrated with propeller made from pencil and tape 1289:42-43

Autogyro propeller, how to make 908:34-38

Experiment to demonstrate propeller—powered machines 225:26-28

Experiment to show power of a propeller 446:29-32

Experiment with fan on small wagon 72:20-21

Feather propeller, how to make 908:43

Hovercraft type propeller boat, how to make 1247:36-37

How a propeller works 561:24-25

How does a propeller work experiment 1293:7-9

Magic propeller—how to build 563:19-20

Make a propeller—powered machine 225:26

Power of plane propeller shown with spool device experiment 1063:474

Propeller driven balsa wood car—demonstrate 507:1897-1898

Propeller driven boat, making 981:27

Propeller produces forward thrust experiment 860:19-22

Propeller pulls balsa wood aircraft along nylon line experiment 1201:20

Propeller stick—making 732:145-146

Propeller test stand, making 940:128-132

The obedient propeller 392:24-27

PROPULSION

Candle boat—experiment 656:20

Demonstration of the 'penny' rocket 291:87

Using balloon 92:18-19

PROSPECTING

Magnetometer, simple—how to make 577:project #56

PROTECTIVE COLORATION

Camouflaging technique of animals experiment 1405:35

Camouflaging technique of animals experiment 904:126-127

Color of animals protects them from predators experiment 1479:32

Color of animals protects them from prey experiment 904:128-129

Colored paper activity to demonstrate camouflage 956:14-15

Does protective coloration really work in insect habitats experiment 1096:118-123

Experiment 268:119-122

Find scraps of colored paper from area outdoors to demonstrate 817:13

Frog with red and black markings warns of poison experiment 1391:19

Game shows how worms and insects hide from birds, how to make 1063:262

Game; colors used by insects to hide or to warn they are poisonous 1182:26

Game; does camouflage work; use colored cards in yard, trees, grass experiment 1182:23

Overlapping patterns in animals demonstration 1391:25

Protective coloration in insects; how common is it experiment 1097:30-32

Protective coloration of insects experiment 1097:27-29

Spot the moth pattern experiment 1391:17

Zebra stripes experiment 1391:23

PROTEIN. See also ALBUMEN

Chemical test for 335:79-80

Coagulation experiments 684:12-13

Custard—coagulating protein 74:61-63

Detergent enzymes effect on protein molecules experiment 1396:25-29

Digestion of protein by enzymes in human body—experiment 482:34-37

Egg white molecules linked together by heating experiment 1250:77-79

Foam made from egg whites experiment 1250:74-76

Gelatin—sol-gel transformation 74:64-67

Gelatin gumdrops experiment 814:39

Gelatin used to dye plastic spoons experiment 1250:82-85

Gluten—how to isolate gluten in wheat flour 86:43

Gluten from flour experiment 1238:90-91

Gluten in action in popovers experiment 1238:93

How much of your weight is protein 1194:7

Jelly pops—protein reaction to hot and cold, making 669:14-15

Lumpy custard experiment—heat hardens protein 563:156-157

Meringues—the properties of egg white 74:57-61

Muffins—a study of gluten—the wheat protein 74:67-70

Protein in milk can be denatured by addition of vinegar experiment 1403:15

Protein molecules—applying heat to a protein—white of a egg 52:99

Protein reaction to mixing and heating experiment 669:40-41

Protein; what happens when shape of protein molecule is changed experiment 1403:8-11

Proteins are changed by denaturing experiment 1396:55-59

Show how cottage cheese is made and how protein coagulates experiment 1484:102-103

Sour milk proteins—protein denatured by acid 74:63

Surface of egg yolks turns green during cooking experiment 1250:71-73

Temperature of egg affects size of whipped egg whites experiment 1403:13-14

Test foods for protein experiment 901:213

Test for proteins in foods experiment 1259:30-31

Testing for protein in eggs—experiment 628:70

Testing for proteins 148:63

Testing for starch, fat and protein in food using chemicals experiment 1069:19

What is a test for protein 402:78-79

What makes protein 261:26-30

Whipped egg whites foam lasts longer with cream of tartar added experiment 1403:14-15

PROTOPLASMIC STREAMING

Is there material common to all life 402:13-14

PROTOZOA. *See also* **AMOEBA; DAPHNIA; PARAMECIA; ROTIFERS; SPIROSTOMA; WATER ANIMALS**

Culturing 11:68-77

Dirt from fingernails grows molds on potato mush mixture experiment 1482:8-9

Food colorings destroy protozoa experiment 889:40

Four protozoa groups under microscope, observe 889:33-35

Grow a protozoa culture experiment 860:167-169

Hay infusion, make to study protozoa experiment 978:88-89

Making a hay infusion to study protozoa 294:59-61

Making cultures to test which one protozoas like 484:43

Observe operation of contractile vacuoles in amoebas and paramecia experiment 1425:21-22

Observing amoebas under microscope experiment 1425:12-13

Observing paramecia under microscope experiment 1425:13-14

Observing protozoa and other small organisms under microscope experiment 1425:9-12

Seeing under a microscope 82:21-34

Staining protozoa—how to 484:43

Studying protozoa experiment 1293:95-97

Why we wash our hands experiment with molds growing on potato mush mixture 1482:8-9

PSYCHIC BOOK TEST

Experiment 350:38-40

PSYCHIC MOTOR

The "psychic" motor—how to build 563:28-29

PSYCHOLOGY

Habits—formation of 294:92

Inkblots—what do you see—experiment 653:28-33

PSYCHROMETER

Making 9:92-93

Psychrometer measures relative humidity of air experiment, how to make 1479:80

Psychrometer, constructing to calculate relative humidity experiment 860:187-189

Relative humidity measured by psychrometer demonstration 1023:148-149

Relative humidity measured by psychrometer experiment; psychrometer graph given 1063:444-445

Relative humidity measured by psychrometer, how to make 1439:98-101

Sling psychrometer, how to make 978:148-150

Water vapor in air measured by psychrometer experiment, how to make 1281:17

Wet bulb thermometer, how to make 865:86

PUDDLES

How to make your own puddle—outdoor & indoor, instant 264:105-107

Life in a puddle 264:105-107

PULFRICH, CARL

Pulfrich's illusions experiment 1133:6.013

PULFRICH ILLUSIONS

Experiment 16:92-95

PULL

Travois makes pulling easy 324:14-15

PULLEYS. *See also* **SIMPLE MACHINES—PULLEYS**

A simple pulley 156:26-27

Block and tackle 281:50

Demonstrate ease of effort by movable pulley 204:34-35

Demonstrate ease of lifting using fixed pulley and movable one 204:36-44

Demonstrate increase in work efficiency 293:43-44

Demonstrate pulleys; how to make 32:62-63

Egyptian tubes; magic trick demonstrates pulleys 966:33-38

Experimenting with pulleys 596:26-27

Experiments to show function of 128:115-118

Experiments with fixed and movable pulleys 902:169-178

Fixed pulley from spool and wire—how to make and use 204:30-33

How a pulley works 281:49

How can we use pulleys to move objects 253:175-176

How much can a crane lift experiment 802:30

How pulleys work experiment 802:29

Make a spool pulley 203:85

Match box moves under its own power; magic trick demonstrates pulleys 966:25-29

Milk carton pulley, how to make 945:44-45

Pulley can be used to lift a load experiment 836:36-39

Pulley wheel—making 756:18

Rising ring on pencil; magic trick demonstrates pulleys 966:30-32

Working with fixed and movable pulleys 180:32-33

PULSE. *See also* **HEART; HUMAN BODY**

Does pulse always remain the same experiment recording sheet given 747:33-34

Heartbeat; observe vibration of match on wrist experiment 904:188-189

How can you see your pulse experiment 901:16

How does exercise affect your pulse experiment 794:31

Match stick lets you watch your pulse 360:95

Observe the beating pulse 293:28

Observe the human heart and pulse 294:85

Pulse counter from match and tack, making 794:16

Pulse increases with exercise experiment 760:18-19

Pulse rate—computer experiments 665:10-13

Pulse rate—exercise and the breathing rate 253:114

Pulse rate activity 748:63

Pulse rate time to recover computer project 584:27-29

Pulse rates computer project 584:25-26

See the pulse beat—experiment 563:64-65

See your pulse move 381:101

What is pulse and how can it be measured 402:56-57

PUMPKINS

Parsley or grass seed planted in pumpkin grows green hair experiment 1246:17

Plant a perfect pumpkin 376:22-23

Pumpkin race—who grows the largest pumpkin 376:24

Pumpkin seed activities 662:43

Roasted pumpkin seeds—how to 376:25

PUMPS

Cooking baster makes a force pump 217:54-56

Cooking baster makes simple pump 217:51-53

Gas pressure can pump a liquid experiment 1081:15

How pumps use air pressure-syringe, lift, lamp chimney, test tube pumps 128:82-84

Lift pump—making 436:54

Pump—making from wood 429:106

Pump for water, wooden, really works, how to make 948:36-37

Pumping station from throwaways, making 779:45

Pumps and fountains kits 386:81-84

Suction pumps—demonstrate pulling water uphill 217:46-50

Waterwheel pumps—how to make 363:89-91

Wheel can be used as a pump demonstration 1404:116-117

PUNNETT SQUARE. *See* **HEREDITY**

PUPAS

Pupa cages—how to make 234:61

PUPPETS

Apple people puppets 231:95-96

PURIFICATION WATER. *See* **WATER PURIFICATION**

PURKINJE SHIFT ILLUSION

Experiment 229:81-82

PUTTY

Bouncing putty—how to make 87:79-80

Phewy putty made from cornstarch and glue, recipe, how to make 1289:22-23

PUZZLES

Hexaflexagon puzzle—making 732:90-91

Making puzzling peg 392:113-117

Paper puzzlers—Rubic's cube and tangram 399:44-45

'River-crossing' electrical game—how to build 23:67-68

Turn three nails so all heads face away from you 549:12-15

PYRAMIDS

Experiment to demonstrate (Advanced) 393:20-33

Show inclined plane was used to get stone blocks up sides of pyramids 448:7-10

The great pyramid experiment 386:85-86

PYROMETER

Optical pyrometer measures temperature of hot lava flow from volcano experiment 1477:42-43

PYTHAGORAS

His experiments with sounds of different vibrating strings 602:unpaged

Relationship among sound pitch, string length and tension experiment 1133:6.001

Q

QUADRANT

Quadrant to determine stars altitude, how to make 862:45-56

QUADRATS

Edison's experiments 230:111-123

Make 4 x 4 wire quadrat 285:57

Make to use for sampling areas 285:48-49

Quadrat study of area experiment; charts given 978:127-131

Quadrat study of composition of forest experiment 1075:102-103

Vacant lot plants project; how to study using quadrat 1060:129-132

QUADRILATERALS

Fibonacci Rectangles investigation 1350:60

Quadrilateral jigsaw puzzle, how to make 1350:17

Quadrilaterals; closed shapes made up of four straight lines; problems 1350:7-64

Tricky squares with match sticks 1350:21

QUALITATIVE ANALYSIS

Laboratory analysis tests on milk experiment, data tables given 1004:4.013

QUANTITATIVE ANALYSIS

Laboratory analysis tests on milk experiment data tables given 1004:4.013

QUASARS

How small is a quasar experiment 1478:141

What happens to gas clouds and stars as they approach black hole experiment 1478:140

QUICKSAND

How to make 615:unpaged; 666:101

What is quicksand 291:38-39

QUILL PEN

Gull feather pen—how to make 359:13-15

Quill pen, how to make from feather 1143:6

QUIPU, INCA

How to make 326:10-11

QUIZ BOARD

Electric quiz game, making 768:117

Electrical quiz board experiment from batteries, bulb and cardboard 1514:49-51

Electronic quiz game, how to make 955:21

Electronic quiz game, make with battery, bulb, wire and quiz questions 1072:21

How to make 293:47-49

Quiz board game, making experiment 960:50-52

Quiz board truth detector, making 781:24-25

Electric quiz board that lights up, how to make 1218:14-15

Quiz board made from cardboard, wires, battery and bulb, how to do 1382:12-13

QUIZ BOARD GAMES. *See* **ELECTRONIC GAMES; QUIZ BOARD**

QUIZ BOARD REAGENTS. *See* **INDICATORS**

QUIZ BOX GAME

Electric—how to make 366:234-235

R

RABBITS—WILD
Collection and care of 390:61

RACCOONS
Collection and care of 390:62-66

RACERS
Balloon powered wooden racer, how to make 1416:21
Land yacht from balsa wood and spools, how to make 1416:23

RACING CARS. *See also* **AUTOMOBILES**
Formula XF Bullet Car—how to make 410:40-41
Grand Prix car races—how to make track and race toy cars 410:46-47
Land racer with sails experiment 1108:25-27
Racing car on ramp demonstrates gravity controls speed experiment 1031:12-13
Rubber band racer, how to make 1033:22-23
Soap box derby car—wooden—plans—how to make 750:35-41
Stock car with working headlights and turn signals, how to make and wire 1076:24-27
Which oil makes toy car go farthest; vegetable or automobile oil experiment 781:20-21

RADIANT ENERGY. *See also* **HEAT RADIATION**
Can Sun produce heat—magnifying glass and paper experiment 743:21
Darker colors warmer than lighter ones 291:48-49
Heat radiation experiment 577:project #25
Materials that absorb radiant energy experiment using tin cans and thermometers 1439:5-7
Pie pans sand in the sun and shade experiment [Primary] 743:20
Project to use radiated energy 681:14
Radiated heat reflected away experiment; glass jars, water, silver/black paper 1073:95
The sun bath 291:50
What black does 291:51
Why is spring sometimes late experiment with soils and light bulb 1003:13

RADIANT HEAT
Absorption of radiant heat by water and soil experiment 1516:47-48
Heat motion by radiation experiment 1515:105-108
Heating by radiation depends on color experiment 1515:105-108

RADIATION
Color affects amount of radiation object absorbs experiment 905:186-187; 1405:63
Detecting radiation with an electroscope 176:93-94
Fruit flies offspring affected by parent's exposure to radiation experiment 1267:89-90
Make your own display model to show how some types of radiation are absorbed 67:28-29
Protection from infrared radiation experiment with foil and water glasses 928:26
Radiation of heat using candle and colors 238:44-45
Test for radiation with film badges experiment 1267:89
Transfer of heat—experiment 128:148-150

RADIATION—ATMOSPHERE
Activities for demo of atmospheric radiation—make electroscope/cloud chamber 564:8

RADIO
AM radio—make your own AM radio—experiment 591:61-63

Amplified crystal radio, how to build 1226:56-59
Basic radio, making 895:64-66
Construct a one transistor radio receiver 167:41-50
Crystal radio—how to make 22:50-61; 472:2230; 835:88-91; 1226:56-59; 1247:38-39
Crystal receiving sets, making 930:10-11
FM radio—hearing quality of sound—the clean sound of FM—exp. 591:60-61
Homemade crystal radio set 436:64-65
Magnet makes electricity in coiled wire experiment 1367:23
Make a radio, difficult project but directions and illustrations given 1076:42-47
Make a simple radio 278:74-75
Make radio using transistors, resistors, capacitors and battery, how to 1179:178-179
Pencil radio trick plays radio 1139:79-82
Radio alarm clock—using an alarm clock to turn on your radio—how to do 543:50-51
Radio beacons in space (Advanced) 668:42-43
Radio waves demonstrated with homemade radio experiment 1045:24-25
Radio waves you can hear experiment using D cell and wire 1367:16
Receiving radio signals project 833:194-195
Regenerative receiver—circuit layout and construction details 22:58-61
Shortwave—how to build 22:62-67
Simple radio, how to make 860:105-107
Solar powered—how to make 39:91-108
Transmitters—how to build 22:68-73
Vibrations from radio speaker demonstrated by inflated balloon experiment 1367:22
Wireless transmission experiment 22:50-52

RADIO—AMPLIFIER
How to build, connect amplifier to basic receiver 22:58-61

RADIO—ANTENNA
Construction and parts of an antenna—how to build 22:52-54

RADIO—RECEIVER
Elementary receiver you can build 22:54-57

RADIO—SHORTWAVE RECEIVER
How to build 22:62-67

RADIO TRANSMITTERS
Addition of simple switch to enable antenna to be used for transmitting or 22:72-73
Increase sensitivity of small portable radio 22:72
Simple oscillator circuit—how to build 22:69-70
Where to add a carbon microphone to the oscillator for voice transmissions 22:71
Where to hook a key for telegraph transmissions 22:71

RADIO TUBE
Edison effect—Edison's experiments 230:85-91

RADIO WAVES
Communication satellites; how they work demonstration 1394:188-189
How radio waves are used for broadcasting 278:73
Metal and its effect on energy waves from stars demonstration 1394:182-183
Radio wave receivers are curved demonstration 1394:186-187

Satellite's position affects direction of its signal demonstration 1394:184-185
Simple demonstration of 102:108-110
What are radio waves 278:71-72
What materials stop radio waves experiment 781:18-19

RADIOACTIVE ELEMENTS
Half lives of radioactive substances experiment 1004:3.010
Model of radioactive decay experiment 1132:81-1-81-2

RADIOACTIVE FALLOUT
Test for radioactive fallout in your neighborhood 278:79-80

RADIOACTIVE PARTICLES
Project 11:115-116

RADIOACTIVITY
Demonstration of how radioactivity can be shielded experiment 895:121-122
Observing radioactivity by radiography experiment 895:117-118
Observing radioactivity with a cloud chamber experiment 895:118-120
Observing radioactivity with an electroscope experiment 895:115-117
Observing radioactivity with radium dial clock and magnifying glass 489:146

RADIOMETER
Black objects absorb colors of light; white colors reflect colors of 1213:30-31
How to make 172:109-115

RADIUM WATCH DIAL
Experiments with 291:192-193

RADON GAS
Radon poisoning risk, how can we reduce it demonstration 1427:62-63

RAFTS
How to make model 415:8
Raft model toy—how to make (Primary) 467:28-29
Rafts built to test floating experiment 1422:11

RAILROAD TUNNELS
Piston relief tunnel demonstration 968:28
Tunnel boring machine (TBM) demonstration 968:29
Tunnel shapes, compare strength of flat and curved shape experiment 968:28

RAILROADS
Bogie wheels and train model project, how to build 1470:22-23
Bridge—make a model bridge 269:14
Cable—make a water powered cable railway 269:24-25
Cable railways, making 690:44-45
Hovertrain—make a hovertrain 269:22
Make a magnetic lever train 269:23
Model railroad semaphore signal and simple track switch—how to make 23:47-48
Model railroad signal, how to make experiment 938:119-121
Model railway signals from electromagnet, how to make experiment 961:22-23
Old fashioned railroad signal experiment, how to make 1420:7
Planning a railroad schedule project 690:46
Rack railroad, making 690:45
Signals—model railroad signal—how to make 278:59
Signals—simple and electric signals—making 269:29-31

RAIN. *See also* **WEATHER**
Acid rain effect on growth of geraniums experiment 1060:114-116
Air speed and direction effect on falling rain experiment 1023:168-169
Cloudburst experiment using soda bottle cloud and ice demonstration 1310:6-7
Clouds in the kitchen from teakettle experiment 1311:36
Demonstrate rain process with double boiler 203:63
Diary of how much rain falls in one week, how to do using chart given 1359:29
Do mountains affect yearly rainfall experiment 900:125
Evaporation experiment 805:10-11
Falling drops splash pattern—making 657:104-105
Graph rainfall experiment 767:46-53
Gully to hold desert rain water, making (Primary) 601:unpaged
Homemade rain 399:32
Homemade rainstorm 30:30
Homemade rainstorm—experiment 72:33
How does rain form experiment 852:44-45; 1293:89
How much did it rain 236:162
How much rain falls—experiment 694:10-14
How rain is formed 40:143-144
How rain is made—experiment (Primary) 535:55
How soft is rainwater experiment 1396:131
How to make for simple demonstrations 14:31-37
How to make rain using jar, water and ice cubes experiment 1439:65-68
Indoor rainmaking 400:66
Make a rain alarm 538:103
Make it rain in jar experiment 1441:59
Make rain in the kitchen with double boiler experiment 1003:79
Make rain; hot water and ice cubes experiment 900:53,59
Make your own rain 360:67
Making rain 694:15; 874:210
Making rain [Primary] 744:20
Making rain demonstration 767:43
Measure rainfall with jar and ruler experiment 1054:37
Measure rainfall with jar and ruler experiment [Primary] 944:12
Measuring slant of to determine wind speed 381:73
Motion booklet shows meeting of cold front and warm front produces rain 1063:280-283
Nutrients in topsoil affected by rain experiment 1405:76-77
pH of rain experiment 1150:75-76
pH of rainfall experiment; how to monitor; chart given 1171:39-42
pH of rainfall, how to measure 1233:22-23
pH of rainwater experiment 1060:114
pH of rainwater experiment to determine if acid rain is a problem 1427:68-69
Rain affects topsoil demonstration 1023:98-99
Rain and steam experiment using tin can and ice 1017:30-31
Rain detector alarm, how to make 1387:23
Rain drops, seeing the size of 694:8-9
Rain gauge—how to build 9:94-95; 128:94; 166:63-64; 175:60; 234:98; 253:62-63; 293:9; 400:66; 617:17; 694:11-13
Rain gauge—how to make a simple one 14:38-41
Rain gauge—make a (Primary) 154:18-19; 327:22-23
Rain gauge from soft drink bottle, how to make 1135:21

Rain stick musical instrument, how to make from plastic
    pipe 1115:76
Raindrops, collect and measure size 657:71-72
Rainfall; average daily amount of rainfall project
    1021:37-38
Rainfall; measure volume and quality of rainfall experi-
    ment 1134:2.004
Rainmaking experiment 1126:12
Rainstorm in a saucepan 382:128-130
Recording rainfall, how to do 1086:27
Simple projects; measure rain in cup, colored chalk rain
    pictures, make 1227:21
Speed and direction of air affect falling rain demonstra-
    tion 1479:83
Test for acid in rainwater experiment using red cabbage
    as indicator 1135:53
Testing for acid rain experiment 741:17
Testing tap water and rain water for hardness experiment
    1438:26-29
What is the rain cycle experiment 852:45-46
What makes rain experiment 900:109-110
Where does rainwater go experiments 834:114
Why does it rain—boiling water in saucepan—experi-
    ment 452:53
Why does it rain experiment 860:195-196
Why doesn't water from ocean fall as salty rain experi-
    ment 852:31-32

RAIN CYCLE. *See also* **WATER CYCLE**
Experiment to show 128:100
How water vapor behaves in air 319:33
Teakettle rain—demonstrate 364:103

RAIN FOREST
Biodiversity; concept of biodiversity demonstrated pro-
    ject 1338:66-67
Build a rain forest with fish tank, gravel, soil, exotic
    plants 1338:65-66
Create tropical rain forest in glass container terrarium ex-
    periment 1469:28
Rain forest destruction affects gases in atmosphere ex-
    periment 1427:42-43
Rain forest in a soda bottle terrarium experiment
    1335:150
Rain forest plants—how to grow 728:15
Rain forest projects to understand how/why rain forests
    must be saved 1338:65-69, 76-79
Erosion of land in rain forests that have been stripped of
    trees experiment 1240:21
Photosynthesis absorbs carbon dioxide and makes water
    vapor experiment 1174:38-39
Self-sustaining nature of rain forests experiment
    1174:38-39

RAIN GAUGE
Bottle and funnel gauge measures rainfall experiment
    1372:66-67
Coffee can gauge, how to make 885:44-45
Coffee can rain gauge—making 767:46
Funnel and bottle rain gauge, how to make 1136:27
Funnel and bottle rain gauge, how to make 1430:19
Gauge to measure rainfall made from plastic bottle and
    funnel 1387:23
How to make (Primary) 541:28
How to make rain gauge 588:47; 832:48; 909:15;
    978:151-152
Jar and funnel rain gauge, making 1012:28
Jar and long thin glass rain gauge, how to make 1463:29

Jar and ruler rain gauge, how to make 1175:88-89
Jar, funnel and tape rain gauge, how to make 959:75
Large can or jar rain gauge, how to make 1516:102-103
Make rain gauge from plastic bottle, marking pen
    1480:170-171
Make rain gauge using coffee can, jar, and ruler, how to
    do 1439:89-91
Make to measure amounts of rainfall experiment
    1003:119
Rain gauge—making 657:58-59; 662:41; 663:7; 705:76;
    759:25-26; 805:8-9; 830:62-63; 947:40-41; 965:7
Making (Primary) 508:12
Making from plastic bottle 868:47
Making simple one 749:11; 1359:16
Measure how much rain falls, making gauge to show
    834:18
Measure rainfall with calibrated gauge, how to make
    1063:448
Measure rainfall with rain gauge, how to make 1281:20
Measure rainfall; making rain gauge experiment 900:97
Measuring rainfall with plastic bottle rain gauge, how to
    make 1042:40-41
Measuring rainfall with plastic funnel and glass jar ex-
    periment 1393:9
Plastic bottle and ruler rain gauge, how to make 1465:17
Plastic bottle rain gauge, how to make 1086:26-27
Plastic bottle rain gauge, how to make 1362:25
Plastic bottle rain gauge, making 1016:16
Rain collector—how to make 651:30-31
Rain gauge from detergent bottle, making 804:15
Rain gauge from glass jar and ruler, how to make
    1441:83
Rain gauge from plastic soda bottle, how to make
    1311:37
Rain gauge holder for buildings—wooden—making
    721:92
Rain gauge to measure rainfall, how to make 1028:24
Rain gauge, making with activities 891:52-54
Rain gauges for measuring habitat rainfall project
    1313:81-83
Rainfall measured with rain gauge experiment 1149:15
Ruler and tin can gauge, how to use 983:103-104;
    1265:91
Tin can gauge, how to make 986:91; 865:89-90
Wide mouthed jar gauge, how to make 918:29

RAINBOWS. *See also* **PRISMS**
Activities with colors of rainbows 759:28-29
Artificial rainbow—making 656:14
Color spinners, making 909:155
Colors of rainbow on wall experiment using mirror and
    pan of water 1017:37
Colors of rainbow wreath, paper, how to make 832:49
Colors of the rainbows experiment using mirror, water
    and oaktag 1308:22-23
Crayons, wax paper, and heat; make a rainbow 885:54
Demonstrate rainbow with mirror in pan of water
    1079:92-93
Demonstrate scattering of light into separate colors
    126:111-117
Different ways of making rainbows experiment 1163:30-
    31
Filters change the color of light experiment 941:56
Floating rainbows, oil, water and food coloring experi-
    ment [Primary] 1014:31
Glass of water makes rainbow experiment 1135:51

Glass, mirror and cardboard; make rainbow experiment 885:52-53

Homemade rainbow with mirror and water 935:14-15

Homemade rainbows—making 670:54

How to make 605:22-23

How to make rainbows; water prism with mirror experiment 911:4-5

How to make rainbows with mirror and water 600:40-41

Inside and outside rainbow—how to make 363:8-10

Investigation into rainbows 420:58-59

Long flat rainbow, how to make using mirror in bowl of water experiment 1281:27

Make a rainbow experiment 1028:49

Make a rainbow in the room 295:113-114

Make a rainbow with a glass of water experiment 1050:7; 1051:8

Make a rainbow with mirror and water (Primary) 452:56-57

Make a rainbow 32:36-37; 35:32:40; 40:144-145; 142:30-31; 175:62; 176:59-60; 281:85; 291:182-183; 595:32-33; 696:16-17; 909:154

Make rainbow with pan of water and mirror experiment 928:6-7

Make rainbow with garden hose 617:26; 767:47; 860:196-197

Make your own rainbow experiment 782:22-25; 1003:92-93; 1149:27

Making rainbows 586:55-56; 659:26

Making rainbows to show colors of spectrum experiment 956:12-13

Mirror in pan of water experiment [Primary] 944:20-21

Order of colors 40:145-147

"Paint" rainbow, how to make 1050:14

Prism makes a rainbow—how to do 680:5

Prism splits white light into a rainbow experiment 1283:22

Prism, how to make experiment 941:54-55

Puddle rainbow 291:186

Rainbow catcher from straws and colored cellophane, making 1014:198

Rainbow color wheel—how to make (Primary) 181:18-19

Rainbow cookies—recipe for 40:146-147

Rainbow from water hose experiment 958:13

Rainbow in the dark experiment using water, mirror and flashlight 1331:94

Rainbow lenses from cellophane, making [Primary] 880:9

Rainbow magic in dish; dry milk, detergent, food coloring, water exp. 854:33

Rainbow reflector—how to make indoors 494:18

Rainbow waters 350:75-77

Rainbows in a bubble—experiment 585:123-124

Spectroscope separates light into colors of rainbow experiment, how to make 1516:19-20

Spinner mixes rainbow colors, how to make 944:22-23

Sunlight makes spectrum or rainbow experiment 1213:27

The double prism—make a rainbow 291:182-183

Theodoric of Freibourg's how rainbows are formed experiment 1133:6.003

Use water prism to make rainbow 893:9

Water in dish and mirror give you a rainbow [Primary] 788:13

Water separates light into different colors experiment 1250:55-56

Water, mirror and flashlight rainbow experiment 1018:8-9

What makes a rainbow 291:174

What makes a rainbow experiment [Primary] 744:21

Wineglass raindrop experiment 958:10-11

RAINDROPS

Calculate the size of a raindrop experiment 1447:42-45

Capture raindrops and preserve them experiment 1465:62-63

Catch, preserve and measure raindrop using flour and sieve experiment 1017:32-33

Cloud droplets grow into raindrops experiment 1023:166-167

Collect and compare raindrop sizes experiment 1405:83

Condensation nuclei from salt particles on spider webs experiment 959:92-93

How big are raindrops 586:16-18

How big are raindrops experiment; capture drops and observe 1516:38

How raindrops form experiment 1479:82

How tiny water droplets in clouds grow into raindrops experiment 1479:83

Making raindrops experiment 1480:171

Measure size of raindrops using flour in pie plate experiment 767:43

Measuring size of raindrop experiment 1003:80

Raindrops; collect and compare sizes experiment 1023:170-171

Raindrops; how raindrops form experiment 1023:164-165

See size of raindrops using flour experiment 944:11

Shape of raindrops experiment 959:92

Size of raindrops experiment 959:91-92

Splash pattern of raindrops experiment 959:193-195

The shape of raindrops 586:18

Water jets experiment 959:93-94

What does a raindrop look like after it lands 586:18-19

Wineglass raindrop experiment 958:10-11

RAISINS

How much water do fresh grapes lose when dried to make raisins project 1210:33-34

Raisins, making 784:72-73

RAMPS. *See also* **INCLINED PLANES**

Dumper truck, making 779:18-19

Investigate slopes experiment 909:108

Ramp experiments with toy car 945:40-43

Ramps help lift things (Primary) 326:12-13

Ramps magic experiment—rock and rubber band 399:55

Something about ramps 281:51

RATS

Maze for rats—making 264:63-64

Maze used to investigate learning 266:110-115

Mazes—T maze variations to test intelligence—how to make 510:106-109

Raise a rat with a high IQ in stimulating cage 366:30-31

Rat climbing experiment 264:65

Report. and population. Growth for one year—incredible rat statistics 366:31-33

RATTLE

Make a rattle 32:26-27

RAYON

How to make from chemicals 97:40-41

REACTION MOTOR

Build from coffee can 392:47-51

REACTION TIME
Auditory stimuli effect on reaction time experiment 1395:191
Blinking is a reflex action experiment 1397:8-11
Compare person's reaction time with apparatus experiment 930:4
Experiments to test how fast your reactions are 400:44; 640:56; 586:114-115; 628:99-101; 881:42-43; 901:223; 993:24-25; 1028:73; 1037:23; 1389:11; 1425:105-111
Falling object—what's your reaction time 295:59
Message passing—measuring reaction time experiment 748:53
Visual stimuli effect on reaction time experiment 1395:189-193
Yardstick experiment how fast can you catch it 721:72

REACTIONS
Reaction tester—how to build 23:67-70

REAGENTS. *See* **INDICATORS**

RECORD KEEPING
Project 11:58-63

RECORDINGS
Recording tapes affected by magnets experiment 1401:80-83

RECYCLING. *See also* **SOLID WASTES**
Alcohol as fuel, recycling garbage into energy from ethyl alcohol experiment 997:80-82
Bacteria; compare decomposition of aerobic and anaerobic bacteria 969:60-61
Compost heap reduces amount of garbage going to landfills experiment 1173:49-53
De-inker solvent lifts ink off magazine or newspaper experiment 1064:68
Do you conserve resources wisely game 900:190
Does recycled paper decompose faster than manufactured paper project 969:56
Evaluate household trash for recycling or biodegradability project 969:54-55
Fast-food restaurant food wrappers; which can be recycled project 1427:96-97
Garbage poster (Primary) 535:61
Garbage; one week project to analyze garbage in the home 1134:8.002
Household waste can be recycled experiment 1323:57-61
Identify different types of plastics for recycling experiment; code given 1323:62-66
Kitchen compost pile—making 607:29
Make a fungus garden 264:31-33
Make models from plastic bottles 795:26
Model of egg carton caterpillar covered with throw away things 1105:29
Natural fiber clothes decompose faster than man made fibers project 969:57-58
Natural material products decompose faster than man made project 969:59
New paper from old newspaper, how to make 1371:75-77
New paper from waste paper, how to make 1134:7.006
Newspaper clothing, how to make [Primary] 854:107
Newspaper hats, making [Primary] 854:108
Newspaper kites, making 854:110
Paper from newspapers, how to make 1063:380-381; 1323:67-71; 1427:92-93
Paper, recycled, how to do 371:88-91; 866:150-151; 1012:102-103
Paper recycled to make new paper experiment 1150:32-33
Paper; how to make from shredded paper project 1296:1994
Paper; make paper from recycled paper experiment 1148:28-29
Paper; new paper from old newspaper, how to do 1105:6
Paper; recycle your own paper project 1223:29
Paper; recycling paper, how to do using old newspapers experiment 1508:7
Reusable grocery bags from fabric, how to make experiment 1336:66-67
Scare bottles to scare birds project; make from plastic soda bottles 969:44-45
Set up worm composting system 276:1-90
Solid waste generated by people project 1173:22-24
Things to make from scrap paper 854:107-111
Things to make with cardboard 854:116
Things to make with plastic 854:114-115
Things to make with yarn and fabric scraps 854:112
Waste paper can be recycled experiment; how to make pulp and new paper 1173:60-61

RED BLOOD CELLS. *See also* **BLOOD**
Explanation of (Primary) 245:12-19

REDI, FRANCISCO
Does life arise by spontaneous generation experiment 1156:50-51
Duplicating his experiment of spontaneous generation 402:94-95
Great Redi experiment with maggots 723:76
Great Redi experiment with putrefaction 585:148
Redi's famous experiment that decaying food-does not produce living. organisms. 1397:6-7

REDUCING DIETS
Overweight people and reducing diets experiment 1267:51

REEFS
Artificial reef in pond, how to make and observe wildlife and plants 1172:59-61

REFLECTION. *See also* **LIGHT—REFLECTION**
Experiment with light 19:6-20
Internal reflection 4:26-27
Make crazy mirrors 142:33
Of light experiments 181:14-17
Reflection of light 4:10-11

REFLECTOSCOPE
Making of 1:81-82

REFLEX ACTION. *See also* **REACTION TIME**
Blinking is a reflex action experiment 1397:8-11
How long does it take to catch falling object experiment 1397:12-15
Reflex action in earthworms being touched with end of a string experiment 1397:10

REFLEXES
Blinking experiment to see if blinking can be controlled 1189:2-3
Investigating common reflexes experiment 1189:28-29
Nerve machine tests your nerves; make from battery, wire and bulb 1253:32-33
Reflexes—tests for 762:57-58

REFRACTION. *See also* **LIGHT—REFRACTION**
Air can bend light 19:26
Glass can bend light 19:22
Of light experiments 4:18-23
Water can bend light 19:24

REFRIGERATORS
Water evaporation cools things experiment using clay pot/bottle of juice 1228:66-67

REFUSE AND REFUSE DISPOSAL. *See also* **LANDFILLS**
Model landfill in glass jar experiment 1366:24

REGELATION. *See* **ICE CUBES**

REGENERATION. *See also* **PLANARIANS**
Learning in planaria in the field and in the laboratory 266:106-110
Regeneration computer project 584:77-78

RELAYS AND REMOTE CONTROL
How to make 43:178-193

REMOTE CONTROLS
Remote control electric powered vehicle, how to make 1418:26-27
How do remote controls work experiment 1293:39-42

RENEWABLE ENERGY SOURCE. *See* **METHANE**

REPELLENTS. *See also* **INSECTS—REPELLENTS**
Do some insect repellents work better than others experiment 1096:139-143
Experiment in folklore: mint leaves and ants 585:152-153
Fern insect repellent 236:39
Health and beauty products affect effectiveness of insect repellents experiment 1096:139-143
Insect repellents experiment 1097:128-130

REPLICAS
Plaster—how to make 9:124-125

REPRODUCTION—LIVING THINGS
Ways in which living things reproduce 402:11-12

REPTILES
Activities with reptiles 236:70-73
Habitat for reptiles from gallon jar, how to make 1441:93
Raising reptiles 436:65
Reptile eggs—incubation of reptile eggs (lizards, snakes, turtles) 532:47
Reptile house—making 436:65
Scales of reptiles; identify, draw and label project 1295:57-61
Terrarium for keeping amphibians and reptiles, how to make 1425:62-65

RERADIATION
Measuring the Sun's energy 289:31-32

RESINS—TREE
Collecting and smelling 480:78

RESISTORS
What are resistors 278:70

RESONANCE. *See also* **SOUND—RESONANCE**
Resonant pendulum experiment; big swings from little pulls grow 1132:82-1-82-2
Resonant rings experiment; objects vibrate at different frequencies 1132:83-1-83-2
Resonator experiment; vibrate something at right frequency and get big reaction 1132:84-1-84-2

RESONATORS
Xylophones use columns of air to amplify the musical sounds experiment 1209:68-69

RESOURCE USE
Recycling paper experiment 371:88-91

RESPIRATION. *See also* **BREATHING; HUMAN BODY; LUNGS**
Do fish exhale carbon dioxide when breathing experiment 1395:180-181
Joseph Black's breathing out carbon dioxide experiment 1133:3.006
Measuring the effect of carbon dioxide in blood on breathing rate 148:70
Respiration rate before and after exercise 58:12-13
Respiratory model of lungs—making 436:66
What is respiration 402:64-65

RESPIRATORY SYSTEM. *See also* **RESPIRATION**
Tidal, vital and total capacities of lungs—how to measure—experiment 507:1899

RETINA. *See also* **BLIND SPOT; EYE; VISION**
Test to locate blind spot 258:15-16

RETINA AND RODS AND CONES
Test for color vision and after images 258:49-55

RETINAL FATIGUE
What is retinal fatigue 402:66-67

RETTING. *See also* **ROT**
Retting is rotting by wetting 257:15-18

REVERSIBLE REACTIONS
Experiment 346:144-147

REVOLVING PROJECTS
Old clock motors used for—how to do 543:36-39

REY, JEAN
Burning metals into ash experiment 1133:2.001
Construct model of Rey's liquid thermometer experiment 1396:184-187

RHEOSTAT. *See also* **ELECTRICITY—ELECTRIC CURRENT**
Build one to show—as resistance increases, current decreases 293:32-33
Control flow of current with lead pencil rheostat experiment 768:102-103
Make from lead pencil and battery 436:67
Rheostat, how to make 910:46; 938:32-34
Two rheostats to make—how to 723:35-36

RICCIOLI, JOHN BAPTIST
Double star; who was first to detect a double star project 1525:59-60

RICE
Compare cooking times of white and brown rice experiment 1484:152

RIGHT ANGLE
Make like Egyptians did with cord 323:8-9

RIGHT-HANDED. *See* **HANDEDNESS**

RING STAND
How to make 9:76-77

RING SUPPORT AND CLAMP
On upright stand—how to make 319:16-17

RIPPLE TANK. *See* **WAVES**

RITTER, JOHANN
Discovery of ultraviolet rays experiment 1133:6.011

RIVERS. *See also* **EROSION**
Amount of water flowing per second in river; how to measure experiment 978:68-69
Animals and birds on the river bank—observe 290:30
Animals and fish in the water—observe 290:31
Delta formation experiment 1074:32
Deltas form when river's soil load sinks faster in salty water experiment 1384:18
Depth of river, how to measure experiment 978:67-68
Erosion cycle from water erosion experiment using stream table 1342:118-119
Erosion from river, how to demonstrate experiment 1281:32

Flooding effect on towns and cities experiment using stream table 1342:119-120

Floods and flood controls—demonstrate 223:28-29

Flow in rivers is not smooth but turbulent demonstration 1480:126

Games—wet and wild games—trip down a river 400:126--129

Graded bedding (layers of different size particles as they settle)—demon. 197:54-55

Gradient (tilt) and velocity (speed) of river—demonstrate 197:38-39

How does saltwater mix in an estuary experiment 997:67-69

Make a river outside, how to do 919:12

Mapping a river and its drainage net project 1413:96

Meandering of rivers and how meanders develop experiment 1480:128-129

Measuring discharge 290:16

Measuring river gradient 290:12-13

Measuring river speed 290:14

Measuring river width and depth 290:15

Model river—make 223:6

Observe river and make a river scrap book 290:5-11

Ripples or dunes in stream bed formation demonstration 1480:124

River carves out path downhill demonstration with sand and gravel 1384:13

River plants—collection and observation 290:29

River's soil load sinks faster in salty water than in fresh water experiment 1384:18

Rivers change land through which they flow project 1296:1999

Speed of flow or how fast stream flows demonstration 1480:127

Storm effect on river's catchment area experiment 1480:127

Stream table model of river; how to build and use 1342:114-118

Stream tray shows how rivers form and change over time experiment 1480:122-123

Temperature changes density of water experiment 1325:18-21

Velocity of river, how to measure experiment 978:67

Volcanic explosion effect on rivers and streams experiment 1477:72-75

Water flows faster on outside curve of river experiment 1384:17

Water volume and flooding—demonstrate 197:40-41

What is thermal water pollution experiment 1325:65-69

Where does river water come from 290:4

Width of river; how to approximate the width experiment 978:66

RIVERS—ECOSYSTEMS. *See also* **ECOSYSTEMS**

Depict the different food webs in slow and fast moving streams 371:58-65

RIVETS

How they work—experiment 544:22-24

ROAD POLLUTION

Effects of road pollution on populations of insects and arthropods experiment 1096:69-74

ROADS

Cat's eyes (reflector buttons)—make 224:29

Concrete road—how to make 224:6-10

Crash barriers—making 224:32

Level for road building, how to make 1326:17

Model road in shoe box, build using modeling clay, how to do 1326:25

Potholes in roads caused by freezing water project 715:98-99

Roadway, model, making 802:24

Roman road model—how to build 1326:9

Town street play mat; design model buildings and street layout project 1470:14-15

Traffic count of vehicles using road, how to do 1326:14

Traffic lights—make traffic lights 224:30-31

Traffic survey of traffic speeds at various times project 1070:34-35

Tunnels—how to make 224:14-15

ROARING RULER

Experiment 360:86

ROBOTS

Build robot to draw shapes on paper with information from computer experiment 997:86-88

Digestive system in cardboard robot, making 792:26

Electric robot, how to make from box, foil, battery, bulbs, and wire 1382:24-25

Electromagnet robot arm—making simple one 227:22-23

Making 18:1-117

Model carton robot—how to make 113:22-23

Robot frog electric model with eyes that light experiment; patterns given 1493:30-31

Robot mask glows in the dark, make from batteries, wire, LED lights, foil 1076:32-33

Robot model with flashing eyes, how to make 1199:18-19

Rollek the flashing robot 15:36-39

Sandbox robot model, making 779:50-51

Servo-mechanisms of robots; heat control unit/light source seeker experiment 1249:31-39

Toy robot eyes light up experiment using simple circuit 1418:14-15

ROBOTS—TOY

Directions for making toy robots 250:4-32

Robots—how to make 365:34-35

ROCK CANDY

Recipe for rock candy 832:89

Rock candy and salt crystals experiments 1063:223

Rock candy crystals experiment with hot water, sugar and string 1331:22

Rock candy sugar crystals, how to grow 1071:82

Rock candy, making experiment 960:37

ROCK CANDY SUGAR CRYSTALS

How to grow 346:32-34

ROCK GARDENS

Rock garden indoors—how to prepare 497:113-114

ROCKETS

Activities and experiments to demonstrate rockets 564:27-33

Air-powered rocket balloon, how to make 1073:28-29

Altitude and mass ratio, compute (Advanced) 668:14-16

Angle of launch determines travel distance experiment; data tables given 871:4.004

Balloon propelled car experiment 994:28-34

Balloon rocket and multistage balloon rocket experiment 1502:55-57

Balloon rocket blasts along string experiment 1208:36-37

Balloon rocket—making 981:29

Balloon rockets demonstrate how rocket launches 1241:11

Build a model of a launch vehicle 564:31

Carbon dioxide rocket—making 293:37-38
Carbon dioxide rocket demonstrates Newton's third law of motion 338:52-53
Cardboard tube rocket—making (Primary) 113:14-15
Chemical reaction powers rocket experiment 1162:11
Control panel for model rockets 338:77-80
Demonstrate motion of rocket-driven vehicles 295:91-102
Demonstrating how a solid fuel rocket works project 833:285-286
Develop more thrust; carbon dioxide capsule experiment 900:220-221
Escape velocity—experiment (Advanced) 668:19-21
Escape velocity of space rockets demonstration 1394:204-205
Experiments with rockets you make 835:64-66
Forces that affect rocket's performance experiment 900:222
Friction—going down in flames 68:24-46
Fuel—how to make 68:15-17
Heat shields 68:27-29
How can we use action-reaction experiment 900:218-219
How does a rocket work 253:190-191
How rockets move in space demonstration 1394:194-195
How they work balloon and string demonstrate 759:42
How to escape from Earth 68:18-20
Jet engines; how jet engines work; make balloon rocket to demonstrate 1376:22
Jet rocket from balloon and nylon fishing line, how to make 1299:45
Launch—how to make a simple launch 68:4-5
Launch pads—how to build 338:72-77
Launcher for rockets, how to make from paper cone and straws 1289:8-9
Launching two stage rockets 12:13-15
Make a rocket model—how to 652:44-47
Making simple rocket 12:13-15
Match rocket—making 68:6-9
Measuring rocket power 68:9-11
Measuring thrust 92:20-21
Model rockets—how to build 338:60-84
Models from oatmeal boxes, making 898:19-20
Multistaging—balloons and cup model—demonstrate 564:32
Paper match rocket—experiment (Advanced) 668:9-11
Paper rockets simulate flight 338:46-47
Paper rockets with straws demonstrate Newton's Third Law of Motion experiment 1014:126
'Penny' rocket demonstrates propulsion 291:87
'Pop' bottle demonstrate action—reaction 338:50-51
Pop bottle rockets demonstrate internal fuel supply of rockets exp. 860:24-27
Principle of rockets illustrated by simple model 532:44
Projects with rockets 691:35-36
Rocket—making 660:25; 909:73
Rocket and launch from stiff cardboard demonstrates elasticity experiment 1077:10-12
Rocket balloon on string demonstrates jet propulsion experiment 1126:18-19
Rocket boat from aluminum cigar tube and candles, how to make 1247:35
Rocket boat, how to build 600:42-43
Rocket boat, metal cigar tube and candle, making 1001:17
Rocket jet kite—how to make 1115:57-58

Rocket power—model rocket demonstrates jet propulsion 575:36
Rocket propulsion—Newton's third law—experiment to demonstrate 564:28-29
Rocket propulsion experiment 908:82-84
Rocket staging—demonstrate 338:48-49
Rocket staging demonstration 1394:196-197; 1405:18-19
Rocket's thrust, measure (Advanced) 668:12-13
Simple balloon rocket—making 763:73
Single stage rocket, multiple stage rocket models—how to make 415:62-64
Space rockets; how do space rockets work experiment 1293:13-15
Spacecraft rocket model, how to make from plastic soda bottle, paper 1449:6-7
Spinning can shows rotational thrust 338:44-45
Testing for pure fuels (Advanced) 668:17-18
Thrust of rocket demonstrated with balloon and thread 1478:33
Two stage Saturn rocket—how to make 410:22-23
Use gyroscope to steady rocket 68:21-23
Vinegar and baking soda rocket—making 733:1
Vinegar rocket launcher 203:28
Water powered rocket—make a 68:12-14; 132:18
Water powered rocket—make a (Primary) 169:6
Water powered rocket experiment, how to make 1446:32-33
Water rocket blasts off from launch pad experiment 1126:22
Water rocket demonstrates action and reaction principle 1179:63
Water rocket demonstrates Newton's second law of motion 338:54-56
Water rocket, how mass and pressure affect flight 691:32-35

ROCKETS—BALLOON
Balloon jet 260:15
Balloon rocket—how to make 295:92; 366:167; 400:100
Balloon rocket—making (Primary) 169:5
Experimenting with balloon rockets 175:56
Flight testing homemade rocket balloons 333:28-30
Launch a balloon rocket (Primary) 207:18-19

ROCKS. *See also* **CRYSTALS; MELTS**
Abrasion in rocks—demonstrate 197:28-29
Acid poured on rocks eats away at rocks experiment 1383:17
Acid test for carbonates in minerals and rocks experiment 1480:78
Activities to identify and investigate rocks [Primary] 758:9-18
Activities with rocks and soil 236:164-167
Adventure 35—continue study of minerals—rocks under a hand lens 29:162-166
Analysis of different rocks record sheet given [Primary] 758:13
Artificial concrete rock from cement, sand and gravel, how to make 1202:6
Calculating density of rocks experiment 1342:46-48
Calculating specific gravity of rocks experiment 1342:44-46
Can people identify rocks by feel alone experiment 715:61-62
Carbonates—test for 364:73
Chemical weathering experiments 666:40-41

Chemical weathering of rocks experiment with water, vinegar and nail 1438:94-96

Classify by carbonate content 40:86-87

Classify of group by metallic content 40:85-86

Classify or group by hardness of the mineral content 40:83-85

Classifying rocks—demonstration 175:20-21

Cleavage test for mineral identification experiment 1046:15-17

Collect and identify rock samples 301:5-7

Collect and start a rock collection 155:16-17

Collect examine rocks [Primary] 759:42-43

Collecting—how to keep your collections (Primary) 639:26-27

Collecting and displaying 300:22-23

Collecting and identifying characteristics project 715:43-44

Collecting rocks [Primary] 757:123

Collecting 62:11-17; 234:88-89

Collection—how to set up 234:90-91

Collection—how to start 666:109-110

Color properties of minerals; identification test experiment 1046:9-11

Comparing rocks experiment 738:9

Concretion rock—how to make 666:87

Conductivity of heat in rocks experiment 1342:52-53

Conglomerate rock—how to make 666:85-86

Coquina rock—how to make 666:86-87

Cross bedding or sediments laid down in sloping beds demonstration experiment 1480:87

Crystals—how to make 317:26-27

Density of rock measured with specific gravity experiment 1480:79

Density test of minerals experiment 1266:35

Describe and record samples 300:26-27

Desiccation (drying) in rocks—demonstrate process of 197:26-27

Differences between rocks and minerals experiment 1438:39-41

Do all rocks and minerals contain carbonates experiment 852:28-29

Erosion—dissolving rocks to show 293:7-8

Erosion—erosion forms highlands and lowlands—demonstrate 301:8-9

Erosion—rocks break down into soil 262:unpaged

Erosion of rocks by chemical experiment using rock, water and vinegar 1202:15

Faulted highlands—demonstrate 301:12-13

Fold mountains—demonstrate 301:10-11

Fold mountains project, how to make from clay experiment 1134:1.001

Folding (bending) of rocks in layers—demonstrate 197:62-63

Formation—show how rocks are made 119:31-39

Formation of metamorphic rocks experiment 1405:72

Formation of two types of igneous rocks experiment 706:28

Fossil casts, how to make your own 1063:230

Fossil rocks—how to make 666:88-89

Fracturing of—demonstrate 197:24-25

Freezing effect and cracking of rocks experiment with clay balls 1480:107

Freezing water causes rock movement demonstration 1023:108-109

Freezing water causes rock movement experiment 1405:77

Freezing water effect on rocks experiment 1046:32-34

Gemstones—making 400:52

Geological time line walk, how to do 1063:231

Geologist search for magnetic rocks experiment 1027:13

Granite; testing granite for hardness experiment 1438:100-102

Granite; testing granite with an acid experiment 1438:103-104

Hardness of minerals identification test experiment; hardness scale given 1046:12-14

Hardness test chart 364:74

Hardness test for minerals 234:90

Hardness test for rocks 900:136-137

Hardness; how hard is rock experiment 852:17-18

Hardness; measuring hardness of rocks experiment 1342:48-49

Heat capacity of rocks experiment 1342:49

Heat expansion in rocks—demonstrate 197:64-65

How porous are sand, clay and rock experiment 1027:11

How to collect rock specimens 1438:110-113

Hydration in rocks (water combines with other materials)—demonstrate 197:59

Ice splits rocks experiment 1479:69

Identify and record details of 300:24-25

Identify by acid tests 300:30

Identify by flame tests 300:31

Identify by hardness test 300:28-29

Identify rocks in a vacant lot 233:12-14

Identifying a particular rock experiment, how to do 1480:82-83

In what order do materials settle in water experiment 900:134

Layers of rock demonstrated with sandwich 1063:229

Limestone—vinegar test for limestone 317:52-53

Limestone; test for chalk or limestone in rocks experiment 1277:31

Magnetic properties of rocks experiment 1342:53-54

Make a permanent shell imprint experiment 900:152-153

Make stone, how to do 868:30

Marble; testing marble for hardness experiment 1438:105-107

Marble; testing marble with an acid experiment 1438:108-109

Mass—volume and density of rocks experiment 748:166

Match continents by age of rocks 400:51

Measure the density of a rock experiment 900:154

Measuring rock sections 400:52

Metamorphic rocks formation demonstration 1023:36-37

Meteorites; testing rocks for meteorite characteristics experiment 1062:84-88

Mineral identification chart 400:49

Mohs' hardness scale 689:45

Mohs' scale of hardness 1266:33

Mohs' hardness scale 1342:50

Moving water effect on rocks experiment 1046:29-31

Mosaic of owl from stones glued to cardboard, how to make 1292:28

Obstacles change direction of stream demonstration 1023:104-105

Oxidation of rocks—demonstrate 197:30-31

Oxygen causes rocks to crumble demonstration with steel wool and water 1479:74

340

Oxygen causes rocks to crumble demonstration 1023:90-91

Pebble hot plates, how to make 646:101-103

Pebble polisher, make with adult help; batteries, wood, electric motor 1480:90-91

Permeability of 197:50-51

Plants break rocks experiment using plaster of Paris and germinating bean seeds 1046:35-37

Plants break up rocks experiment using bean seeds planted in plaster 1438:14-17

Porosity of rocks—demonstrate 197:56-58

Properties of—experiment to show 128:61-62

Pumice volcanic rock model; make with can of aerosol insulating foam 1477:26-27

Reducing rocks by changes in temperature experiment 874:215

Reflectivity of rocks, how to measure experiment 1342:51-52

Ripple marks on rocks, how they were made demonstration 1480:86

Rock and mineral collection, making 689:44

Rock and mineral tests 400:48

Rock beds made from sand, food colors in tank experiment; how to make 1480:94-95

Rock board game shows how types of rocks are related to one another 1063:224

Rock chart with Mohs' scale for identification 748:172

Rock cycle chart 666:82

Rock erosion due to falling water demonstration 1023:100-101

Rock identification key 400:49

Rock test chart 400:47

Rock tumbler smoothes rocks faster if harder particles are used experiment 715:63-64

Rocks are broken down by plants experiment 1323:47-50

Rocks can be squeezed and folded demonstration using layers of clay 1438:4-7

Rocks change into sand and soil demonstration 1023:94-95

Rocks crack from freezing experiment with balls of clay 1277:39

Rocky games 400:48

Running water on incline board separates rocks from soil experiment 565:134-135

Sand; how rocks change into sand and thin soil demonstration 1479:74

Sandstone—scraping test for sand grains 317:42-43

Scale of hardness (Primary) 639:6

Scratch test for quartz 317:20-21

Sedimentary—demo angle of repose and cross bedding of sedimentary rocks 197:60-61

Sedimentary—demonstrate formation of 293:7

'Sedimentary' rock—make a 236:165

Sedimentary rock—how to make 666:83-84

Sedimentary rock formation demonstration 1023:38-39

Sedimentary rock formation demonstration 1405:72

Sedimentary rock layer sculpture in a jar, how to make 977:35

Sedimentary rock layers in a jar experiment 1266:21

Sedimentary rocks; demonstrate how sediments settle in water 854:90

Sedimentary rocks experiment to interpret geological history of rock in area 1004:1.012

Sedimentary rocks formation experiment 1364:8

Sedimentary rocks, how do sediments settle under water 253:124-125

Sedimentary rocks, how they are formed experiments 706:29-30

Sedimentary rocks, how to make from sand, plaster of Paris and food color 1480:85

Sedimentary rocks strata layers experiment using plaster of Paris, food colors 1277:29

Sedimentary rocks; grading grains of rocks experiment 1480:84

Shale—test for shale mud 317:48-49

Specific gravity of rocks and meteorites, how to measure experiment 1062:86-87

Specific gravity of rocks and minerals, how to measure experiment 1062:93-94

Stake out a watching rock—observe/record what happens around/under rock 452:44

Strata three flavor gelatin mold and crackers demonstrates 731:20-23

Streak test for minerals 1266:32

Streak test for rocks experiment 1480:77

Streak test for rocks, data sheet given 816:11

Streak test; demonstrate a mineral streak test 1479:70

Streak testing of rocks project 715:48-49

Structure—show content of more than two minerals 40:87

Structure—show inside of rocks and how rocks make soil 40:88

Sulfur heated turns to solid crystals 197:12-13

Superposition (layering of rocks)—demonstrate 197:52-53

Tension force effect in rocks demonstration 1023:68-69

Test for limestone in rocks experiment 827:54

Test local rocks for limestone experiment 715:65-66

Tests to examine rocks and minerals experiment; identification guide given 1063:396-399

Tests to identify minerals using vinegar (acid) experiment 1046:18-19

Thermal expansion, marble experiment 666:36

Tumbling and polishing rocks—how to 234:92-93

Vinegar test for limestone 666:85

Water and ice as transportation agents—demonstrate 197:36-37

Water speed and tilt of water moves rocks—demonstrate 197:38-39

Water wears away rock experiment using chalk sticks and jar of water 1202:12

Weathering—demonstrate chemical weathering of rocks 197:32-35

Weathering in a freezer experiment 738:11

Weathering of 382:103-107

Weathering of rocks—observe 175:26-27

Weathering; demonstrate how water wears away a solid experiment 1479:75

Weathering; effect of motion on weathering demonstration 1479:76

Weigh rock in air and in water to determine specific gravity experiment 940:62-63

What is conglomerate rock experiment 900:148

Which rocks are attracted by a magnet experiment 900:140

Which rocks can be dissolved in water experiment 900:143-144

Which rocks conduct electricity experiment 900:141-142

341

ROCKS—COLLECTION AND PRESERVATION
Classify, label and display collected rocks, how to do 1042:26-27
Collecting and classifying rocks project 1413:84
Collecting and displaying rocks, how to do 476:80-83; 1277:14-15
Collecting and identifying rocks, how to do 1441:33
Collecting and identifying rocks; rock key for identification given 1063:392-395
Collecting, organizing and storing rock collection, how to do 1480:80
Collector's items—collecting and identifying rocks 565:131-143
How to collect and display rocks 1342:37-44
How to collect and preserve rocks 824:67-76
How to start a rock collection 900:149-150
Make a rock collection [Primary] 880:28
Making and breaking a rock experiment 1441:37
Mineral hunting; collecting and classifying minerals project 1413:56
Minerals and your microscope—how to collect and study rocks 500:138-139
Show cases for rocks from small boxes, how to make 932:8-11

ROCKS—CRAFTS
Rocky the Hound Dog, Tommy Turtle and Bossy Bee—how to make 644:4-9

ROCKS—IDENTIFICATION
Chemical test for calcium carbonate content 565:139
How do rocks react to vinegar experiment 900:139
Scratch test—chart for rock identification 565:140
Scratch test for hardness of rocks and minerals (Mohs' Scale) 572:19
What classifications of rocks are there experiment 900:151
What color streak does a rock make 900:138

ROCKS—SEDIMENTARY
How sedimentary rocks are formed—experiment 565:136-137

ROCKS—WEATHERING
Force of freezing water experiment 706:22
Force of growing plants experiment 706:23-24

ROCKS AND MINERALS
Making a rock and mineral collection—how to 572:24-25

RODENTS. *See also* **MICE; RATS; SQUIRRELS**
Learning experiments for rodents 577:project #8

ROLLER COASTER
Roller coaster from marbles and cardboard tubes, making 1014:74
Roller coaster track and ball experiment 373:42-44
Experiments to demonstrate roller coaster science 1412:39-44

ROLLERS
Show ease of moving with rollers 125:28-31

ROLLING CAN
Mysterious rolling can—how to make 543:18-19

ROMAN HOUSE WAGON AND CHARIOT
Model—how to make 415:52-53

ROMAN NUMERALS
Roman numeral system explained—with activities 407:1-33

ROOFS. *See also* **DOMES**
Folded or corrugated paper makes strong roof experiment 802:25-26

Forces underneath roof support roof experiment 1386:20
Pneumatic roofs 328:142-147
Roof frames from trusses experiment, how to build 1518:34-35
Shapes in barrels, dishes, butterflies, bike wheels, eggs and saddle surfaces 328:122-137

ROOTS. *See also* **PLANTS—ROOTS**
Absorb water 382:41-42
Acid effect on roots 398:136-137
Adventure 44—inquire into structure of roots—roots under a microscope 403:160-167
Capillary action with roots and red dye experiment (Primary) 211:25-27
Check growth of seedling roots each day and chart growth project 854:50
Demonstrate value of root system experiment 860:147-149
Experiment about 128:41-42
Food—how plant uses food in a root 48:9-10
Force—demonstrate the binding force of roots 294:33
Geotropism—which direction roots grow—experiment (Primary) 540:16-17
Geotropism demonstrated with sprouting seeds between glass panes experiment 986:80
Geotropism, force of gravity affects way roots grow experiment 986:80
Geotropism; gravity affects the way roots grow experiment 1265:80
Geotropism; plant roots respond to gravity and grow downward experiment 1014:158
Gravity effect on plant roots; radish seeds experiment 784:96-97
Grow toward water 382:33-36
Growing a root system experiment 738:21
Growth—show direction of root growth 146:19
Growth—show downward growth—geotropism 94:26
Growth of seed roots in water; watch them grow (Primary) 211:21-24
Heliotropism roots grow toward water not light experiment 749:44-45
How do roots develop and grow experiment 901:25-26
Hydrotropism; roots of pea seeds grow toward water experiment 913:33
Onion root cells examined under microscope experiment 1060:44-47
Plant roots stop erosion experiment 1371:72-73
Power of growing roots demonstration using eggshells and marigold plants 1038:20-21
Report-plants grow from roots-sweet potatoes, carrots, beets, turnips, parsnip 270:7-11
Root growth viewing box, how to build 986:76
Root hair—how to make 264:21
Root hairs—see root hairs on seeds as they grow 211:8-11
Root hairs—show what root hairs look like 284:20-25
Root hairs and water experiment 959:57
Root of sweet potato grows vine (Primary) 540:38
Root strength demonstrated by beans planted in Plaster of Paris experiment 784:95-96
Root system collects and transports water in plants experiment 760:5-6
Root view box experiments; directions given for making the boxes 1078:30
Root viewing box—build to see how roots work 380:58-59

Root-view box to watch roots grow, how to make 1265:76

Rootarium—how to make 264:52

Roots hold the soil—experiment 585:149-150

Roots make their way around objects in soil experiment 1078:21

Roots protect soil from erosion experiment 722:77

Sprouting sweet potato plant—observe 352:49

Structure—show what inside of roots look like 284:26-32

Structure—show what roots look like 284:14-19

Structure—studying a typical root—a carrot 294:32

Types of roots 60:27-29

Water absorption—how carrots absorb water 48:7-8

What part of root grows in length 60:30-31

Where do roots go Experiment with direction of root growth 590:47

Why plants have roots experiment 1294:74-75

ROOTS—DIRECTION OF GROWTH. *See also* **PLANTS—TROPISMS**

Roots always grow downward experiment 819:46

What goes up, won't go down—experiment with bean seeds 574:27

ROOTS—STORAGE

Carrot hanging basket—making 465:116-118

Carrot, beet and other storage roots produce plants 465:115-116

Root division 465:110-111

Sweet potato vine 465:112-114

ROPE

Project 17:33-36

Rope machine for making rope—how to do 732:115-117

ROT. *See also* **DECAY; MOLDS**

Burial test for rotting; bury objects of different materials experiment 1414:20-21

Clay pot soaked in salt water deteriorates when buried in the ground experiment 1169:16

Do all buried things rot away experiment 1162:29

Life in a rotting log 268:23-27

Red pepper in plastic bag observed for days it takes to rot experiment 1414:20-21

ROTATIONAL MOTION

How rotational motion is changed; good and bad torque experiment 1164:39-40

Torque, force, axis of rotation experiment using bicycle wheel, spring scale 1164:40-43

ROTIFERS. *See also* **PROTOZOA**

Adventure 15—we meet with an optical illusion—rotifers under microscope 403:54-59

Feeding patterns—experiment 484:71

Make a microscopic algae jungle 279:34-36

Reviving rotifers—experiment 484:70-71

Rotifers, how to collect, care for and observe behaviors 771:201-206

RUBBER. *See also* **ELASTICITY; LATEX**

Artificially aging rubber 336:81-82

Compare reusability of different kinds of rubber 336:76-77

Contraction makes bucket fountain 291:26-27

Effect of temperature on vulcanized rubber experiment 1396:145

Elastic nature of rubber experiment 336:78-81

Get rubber from rubber cement 336:75-76

Heated rubber band moves mysterious arrow 202:118-119

Is rubber in rubber cement natural or vulcanized experiment 1396:145

Latex rubber ball—making 26:63-65

"Live" rubber—experiment 585:103-104

Make a ball do a delayed leap 228:28-29

Make a rubber molecule model 39:24-27

Making things from latex 26:65-66

Rubber gets hot 176:95-96

Shrinks when heated 95:31

Two experiments reveal which elements are in compound rubber 336:77-78

RUBBER—SYNTHETIC

Make a model Butadiene molecule 39:27-28

RUBBER BALL

Chemical magic too hot to hold 87:77-78

How to make 39:16-18

RUBBER BANDS

A rubber band trick 585:78-79

Aeolian harp—make 39:85

Air pollution effect on rubber bands experiment 1150:73-74

Amazing rolling can from rubber band energy 399:14-15

Bottle tractor experiment using rubber bands as energy 1318:24-25

Can stretching molecules make them give off heat 396:26-27

Carbon in a rubber band 39:20

Clockwork toy shows power in springy materials experiment 754:28

Come back can experiment 1063:306

Come-back can, making 685:28-29

Come-back drum demonstrates kinetic energy experiment 1136:38-39

Crawling experiment with rubber band and spool crawler 1389:17

Creeping crawler, making 909:120

Creepy crawler insect demonstrates stored energy in rubber band experiment 1024:18-19

Cross your silver with sulfur 39:20-22

Dashing darts 909:120-121

Do your own testing for modules, elongation and break strength 401:46-50

Does rubber band stretch evenly 381:149-150

Dragster from drink can demonstrates rubber band energy, how to make 1299:55

Effect of temperature on vulcanized rubber experiment 1396:145

Elastic balsa wood flyer demonstrates energy stored in rubber band 1179:74-75

Elastic car shows elastic force—experiment 682:15

Elastic motor driven bottle boat experiment 806:21-22

Elastic motor driven paddle boat experiment 806:20-21

Elastic motor driven toy experiments 806:19-22

Elastic motor fan and blow meter experiment 806:17-19

Elastic powered roller designed to make it go further experiment 806:15-17

Elastic powered roller experiment 806:14; 806:15

Elastic powered roller, making 806:12-15

Elasticity can be used in measurement; simple scale experiment 837:10-11

Energy is used to stretch a rubber band; shooting rubber bands exp. 837:8-9

Energy stored in twisted materials drives simple machines experiment 1073:16-17

First and second laws of thermodynamics experiment; data tables given 1004:3.015
Game—finding the loop 39:81-82
Heat affects movement of molecules in rubber band experiment 1403:64-67
Hot and cold band 39:22-23
How does a rubber band stretch 26:69
How far do rubber bands stretch experiment 754:8-9
How far will a rubber band stretch experiment 837:5-7
How to make 39:12-13
Hydrogen in a rubber band 39:18-19
Jumping experiment; frog jumps from twisted rubber band 1389:21
Jumping monsters, making 909:118
Killing the kinks 39:30
Law of stretch 39:36-43
Magic rolling can, making 909:119
Make a creeping toy 210:31
Make your own 401:13-15
Making rubber band music 401:68-70
Making rubber band things 39:86-92
Merry-go-round, making 909:121
Muscle 39:64-72
Musical rubber band—experiments 39:44-63
Mysteries 39:5-8
Paddleboat race; use twisted rubber band energy to push boats thru water 1497:8-9
Quicker than the eye 39:72-74
"Rattlesnake's teeth" trick 585:80-81
Returning can experiment with coffee can, rubber bands, and toothpicks 1436:93-96
Roadster uses twisted rubber band to turn propeller for power experiment 1446:36-37
Robert Hooke's science of stretching experiment 1133:4.008
Rocker can, making 882:9
Roll back can shows energy produced by unwinding rubber band experiment 1400:82-83
Roll back oatmeal box and rubber bands experiment 999:91-92
Roll back toy rolls back to you experiment 1030:16-17
Roly-poly can with rubber band demonstrates rubber band energy 1523:28
Rubber band changes from potential energy to kinetic energy experiment 1400:80-83
Rubber band energy moves tank made from thread spools experiment 1380:30-31
Rubber band magic—double jumping rubber bands 401:22-24
Rubber band magic—jumping rubber band 401:20-22
Rubber band molecules return to original position after stretching experiment 1091:39-40
Rubber band navy boat 401:73-76
Rubber band powered wooden airplane experiment, how to make 1446:38-39
Rubber band racer, how to make 1033:22-23
Rubber band scarf trick 401:25-27
Rubber band sound vibrations 401:67-68
Rubber band spring scales—how to make 631:58-59
Rubber band tractor 401:76-78
Rubber bands powered vehicle—making 756:28
Shrinking rubber experiment 909:119
Singing strings—making Aeolian sounds 39:82-84
Soda bottle roller uses energy in rubber bands experiment 1377:28-29

Sound waves 39:74-80
Spool tank demonstrates rubber band energy, how to make 1299:54
Spool tank powered by rubber bands experiment 1162:21
Stretch and twist—experiments 664:30-33
Temperature of rubber band rises when band is stretched 401:16
Toy demonstrates energy from twisted rubber band experiment 1496:16-17
Tractor model gets "energy" from rubber band—experiment 605:48-49
Tricks with mysterious heat production from 392:77-78
Tricks with puzzling expansion of rubber 392:79-81
Twisted rubber band energy demonstrated by model carousel, how to make 1073:17
Weighing machine from rubber band and cup, how to make 1380:29
Weighing machine from rubber bands—making 754:12-13
When rubber is heated it contracts 401:17-18
Why are rubber bands available in different widths experiment 837:7-8
Wonderful windup spool car, how to make 600:34-35
Wood roadster powered by rubber bands experiment 1162:21

RUBBINGS
Animal rubbings using cookie cutters 854:77
Bark rubbings, how to do 631:79; 913:36
Bark rubbings to identify different kinds of trees experiment 1184:11
Leaf rubbings, how to make 1071:95
Stump rubbings, how to do 879:210-211
Stump, bark and leaf rubbings, how to do 1063:255
Tree bark rubbings, how to do 932:22-23

RUBBINGS—BARK. See also **BARK RUBBINGS**
Bark rubbings, how to do 442:unpaged; 918:39

RUBE GOLDBERG MACHINES
How to make 373:68-73

RUBICS CUBE PAPER
Puzzler 399:44-45

RUDDERS
Rudder changes direction of paddleboat, how to make 1310:30-31

RUNNING
Crouched position gives sprinter an advantage experiment 1154:39-45
Running the bases speed experiment 1154:45-49

RUSHES
Rush mat—how to make 442:unpaged

RUSHLIGHTS
How to make 236:39

RUST. See also **IRON; OXIDATION**
Acid rain increases rate of rusting experiment 1396:162
Acidity affects rusting rate of iron experiment 1526:101
Adding oxygen experiment 735:29
Adventure 5—we inquire into the nature of rusting under a hand lens 29:27-30
Can iron combine with oxygen and water to form rust experiment 831:55-57
Coating solutions stop rust on iron materials above and below ground experiment 969:75-76
Combining two elements to form compound experiment 976:27

344

Corrosion of steel wool and nails 382:165-167
Demonstrate the nature of rust 291:209
How much oxygen is in the air experiment 1322:13-16
How to prevent rust—experiment 598:38-39
Investigate rusting of nails experiment 1286:13
Iron atoms and oxygen atoms combine to form iron oxide experiment 1396:162
Iron rusts faster in which liquid experiment 781:28-29
Iron rusts faster using vinegar as a catalyst experiment 1159:26-27
Iron rusts faster when wet experiment 1396:162
Make rust experiment 707:30-32
Measure the proportion of oxygen with rusting iron 186:22
Metals need moisture and oxygen to rust experiment using steel wool 1073:89
Nail rusts faster in dry jar experiment 1244:12-13
Oxygen combines with iron to make rust experiment 705:21
Oxygen content in the air experiment using steel wool 1003:47
Oxygen content of air measured by rusting steel wool experiment 1447:71-73
Prevention of rust experiment; coat steel wool with soap 905:88-89
Rust—experiment with water and salt water 585:96-97
Rust forms quickly on nails experiment using battery, wire and salty water 1435:110-112
Rust uses up oxygen 360:66
Rusting iron from steel wool in water produces oxygen gas experiment 1435:107-109
Rusting iron gives off heat experiment 735:30
Rusting metal uses oxygen experiment 860:51-52
Rusting metals—experiment 180:19
Rusting of iron—ways to prevent 26:19-21
Rusting of iron in steel wool pad experiment 1396:21-22
Rusting produces heat experiment 1405:63
Rusting steel wool—experiment 400:71; 1224:28
Rusting uses oxygen experiment 1212:13
Rusty nut knuckle unbuster—soda drink loosens stuck nut 404:140
Show rust is compound of iron, oxygen and water 146:24-25
Simple experiment to show only things made of iron will rust 1105:25
Staples in three solutions show rusting experiment 721:121
Steel wool and nails demonstrate 695:43
Steel wool and water—experiment 676:35
Steel wool experiment demonstrates rust formation 1014:42
Steel wool rusts faster when bleach is added to water and vinegar experiment 814:55-57
Timothy Lane's carbon dioxide and the formation of rust experiment 1133:2.004
To rust or not to rust—what makes things rust—experiment 589:48-49
Water and oxygen needed to cause rust—experiment 605:10-11
What happens when iron rusts experiment 834:78-79
What is rust; experiment with steel wool 902:23
What makes iron rust experiment 1162:28
What makes things rust—experiment 6:26
What substances make iron rust more quickly experiment 836:74-75
Why does metal rust experiment 1294:45-46

S

SACHETS
Recipe for 387:28-29
SAFETY
Safety rules near water game, making 869:28-29
SAFETY BELTS
Test importance of wearing safety belts experiment 1378:28
SAFETY LAMP
Sir Humphry Davy; who invented miner's safety lamp project 1525:98-100
SAILBOATS. *See also* **BOATS—SAILS**
Airfoil principle demonstrated with water and spoon 1165:13
Action and reaction of boat movement—experiment 95:12-13
Center of gravity—how a keel works 241:34-35
How to make (Primary) 523:38-39
Sail power experiment with plastic bottle sailboat 1332:14-15
Sailboat—making 660:33
Sailboat from plastic bottles and sail, how to make 1422:21
Sailing into the wind and against it experiment [Advanced] 762:95-97
Sails for boats; which works best experiment 1161:16
Wooden sailboat with fabric sail, how to make 1471:26-27
SAILBOATS—MODELS
Catamaran sailboat—how to make 54:57
Cork sailboat with variations—how to make 54:53-68
Model sailboat—how to make 267:19
SAILING YACHT
From ceiling tile, how to make 410:36-37
SAILOR'S SOAP
Sailor's soap—experiment 585:97-98
SAILS. *See also* **SAILBOATS; BOATS—SAILS**
Hand held sail—how to make 543:16-17
Skate sail—how to make 310:28-32
SALAMANDERS
Animal structure and environment 268:113-117
Collect and observe newts in terrarium, how to do 771:143-150
Collection and care of 279:18; 313:14-18; 390:43-45
Experiment to show where they go in winter 40:55-56
Exploration of pond, marsh or swamp for salamander egg masses 285:77
How do newts and salamanders hear without external ears experiment 1397:16-19
Observe behavior of salamanders 166:104-105
Raising 436:69
SALINITY
Temperature and salinity affect behavior of water experiment data tables given 1004:1.007
SALINITY—OCEAN. *See also* **OCEAN—SALINITY**
How salty is the sea 41:153-162
Ocean currents and salinity—experiment 93:37-38
Seawater salinity experiments 359:80-81
SALIVA. *See also* **HUMAN BODY**
Breaks starch into sugar 259:33
Test crackers with and without saliva for starch experiment 723:71-72
Test for enzymes in human saliva 482:32-34

SALT. *See also* **MINERALS**
Acid vinegar mixed with soluble salt and baking powder makes a salt experiment 1435:16-17
Can salt keep water from freezing 396:54-55
Can salt remove water from the air experiment 831:41-42
Crystals under microscope 82:67
Determine how salt beds are formed experiment 1023:24-25; 1405:70
Difference between salt and sugar experiments 1238:22-23
Different from sugar—experiments 676:22-23
Dissolving and recovering salt experiment 888:94-96
Does adding salt change boiling temperature of water experiment 715:41-42
Effect of salt on plant growth experiment 921:41
Egg floats in water experiment 1498:9
Electrolysis of salt 122:146-149
Experiments with salt 26:92-93
Getting salt out of the ocean—experiment 26:88-90
Grow large crystals of salt project 1296:1979
Grow salt crystals on a string (Primary) 468:3-9
How body keeps us from getting too much salt experiment 1238:14-15
How much salt in various foods project 1210:27
How much salt needed in water to get lowest temperature experiment 715:39-40
How salt crystals form experiment using soil sample and salt solution 1438:35-38
How salty is the ocean test 697:118
How to make a salt 84:68
Hygroscopic salt; salt absorbs water from air experiment 959:59
Ice and salt—does salt make ice melt faster 26:91-92
Ice and salt make things very cold; make ice cream experiment 1032:28-29
Ice; what happens when you put salt on ice experiment 1519:24
Investigation into the effect of table salt on plant life 420:133-134
Irrigation water leaves salts in soil experiment 1323:51-55
Make a solution of salt 598:18-19
Measuring salt in sea water 687:45
Ocean salt compared to table salt experiment 1290:7, 1.7
Pickled onions experiment, how to make 1498:15
Salt—making 666:64
Salt added to water lowers freezing point experiment 1396:82-84
Salt affects boiling water experiment 1238:18
Salt affects freezing temperature of water experiment 984:46-50,71-76
Salt affects temperature of water experiment 905:136-137
Salt and corrosion 382:167-168
Salt and ice 382:106-107; 382:133-134
Salt content of water measured experiment 1023:210-211
Salt crystals from salt water experiment 827:88-89
Salt crystals, how to grow 1509:14
Salt crystals, how to make 797:13-14; 1113:13-14; 1498:5
Salt dissolves more in water than in rubbing alcohol experiment 1250:43-45
Salt evaporator—how to make 507:1865-1866
Salt extracted from salty water by evaporation experiment 1081:23

Salt from ocean water experiment 706:83
Salt from roads and sidewalks and its effect on plant growth experiment 1061:76-78
Salt from seawater experiment 1498:17
Salt from solar evaporation 666:65
Salt in food; effect of salt on vegetable experiment 1238:13
Salt kills bacteria and prevents decay in food 26:87-88
Salt lowers freezing point of ice experiment 1435:10-12
Salt makes ice melts faster 26:91-92
Salt makes it harder for water to freeze experiment 905:128-129
Salt melts ice experiment 1498:11
Salt patterns from swinging pendulum experiment 999:100-102
Salt preserves meat—experiment 26:87-88
Salt put on icy sidewalks for a reason experiment 1020:148-150
Salt solution—lift that cube 16:58-61
Salt solutions—how to make 41:158
Salt travels on glass of water experiment 721:77
Salt's action on ice (Primary) 109:25
Secret of salt (Primary) 109:7
Separate salt and sand—experiment 563:163-164
Stalactite—growing a 532:11
Table salt is an electrolyte experiment 1396:91-96
Temperature of ice water is lowered by salt experiment 905:122-123
Using salt to conduct electricity 180:48
What happens when you mix salt and water experiment 1498:6-7
Why salt dissolves 366:218

SALT—POLLUTION
Does salt runoff from roads affect plant growth experiment 1527:67-68

SALT MEADOW GRASS
Scarecrow dolls—how to make from grass 359:63-65

SALT WATER SOAP
Sailor's soap—experiment 585:97-98

SALTMARSHES
Mapping a tidal creek, how to 772:72-74
Observation of salt marsh plants project 1225:118-130
Salt marsh word search 359:57-58
Salt marshes activities 236:106-107
Velocity of water in a salt marsh creek 236:106
Water temperature and salinity in a salt marsh 236:106-107

SALTWATER. *See also* **SEAWATER; WATER—SALT WATER**
Algae grown in saltwater environment experiment 1061:60-61
Compare salt water and fresh water for weight and freezing time experiment 1509:15
Concentration and density in solutions of saltwater experiment data tables 1004:4.005
Create your own salt water experiment 827:88
Does salt water have greater density than water experiment 831:31-32
Egg floats in salt water experiment 1244:16; 1393:25
Electricity in salt water produces solids experiment with steel nails/battery 1251:82-84
Fresh water from salt water experiment 947:22
Fresh water from salt water project, how to do 1296:1981
How does saltwater mix in an estuary experiment 997:67-69

Model solar device for distilling salt water experiment 762:126-128
Plants; salt water effect on growing plants experiment 1509:15
Purify water that is salty and polluted experiment 1441:65
Salt and water evaporation experiment [Primary] 873:51
Salt content of water measured experiment 1405:87
Salt from seawater experiment 1498:17
Salt water affects buoyancy experiment 1290 6
Salt water and its effect on growing plants experiment 888:97-101
Salt water is corrosive 687:45
Salty water doesn't make many soap bubbles experiment 1482:6-7
Saturated salt solution freezes at what temperature experiment 1526:41
Seawater denser than fresh water experiment with eggs in water 1488:19
Seawater salinity experiments 359:80-81
Simple salt water distiller—how to make 494:56
Water and salt can be separated from seawater by freezing experiment 1325:87-90
Water and salt separated from seawater by the Sun experiment 1325:91-94
What happens to metal in salty water—experiment 641:59
What happens to salt in water when water evaporates experiment 1441:63

SALVAGE
Air creates buoyancy needed to float salvage to the surface of sea experiment 1167:29
Currents and tides affect salvage of sunken ships from the sea experiment 1167:28
Visibility and salvage of sunken ships from the sea experiment 1167:28
Water pressure used to submerge and raise salvage at sea experiment 1167:29

SAND
Activities with beach sand 236:103-106
Beach sand observations, how to do 1225:168-180
Calcium carbonates in beach sand determined; adding vinegar to sand experiment 1225:174
Can molecules of water hold grains of sand together experiment 1250:46-47
Candle; sand candle, how to make 1335:85
Chemical magic—make grains of sand move like bugs 87:78
Collection box for different kinds of sand, how to make 1513:45
Color and composition chart for identifying sands 832:76
Colored sand—how to make for sand paintings and layered sand art 359:67-69
Colored sand experiment 906:84
Colored sand project 666:101
Does sand or soil hold more water experiment 1323:26-30
Grains of sand compared and classified experiment 1290:57, 4.4
How does sand feel and look (Primary) 378:6-9
How much does sand weigh 236:104
How porous are sand, clay and rock experiment 1027:11
How to color sand 494:38
How to tell sand from dirt (Primary) 378:10-15
Magic dancing beach sand with magnet 359:4-6

Making sand from shells, rocks and water experiment 1055:24
Pile driver and resistance of sand to it project 969:19-20
Portable sand slate—how to make 494:32
Ripple patterns on beach sand experiment 1266:20
Sand cast for candle 666:99-100
Sand casting—making 697:118-119; 772:59-62
Sand casting crafts 236:105
Sand clay—making 697:121
Sand clay is fun 236:105-106
Sand clumping—experiment 691:59
Sand coloring, sand painting, sand sculpture, making sandpaper 400:58
Sand combs to make textures in sand—making 732:80
Sand detective—examine for grain size and color, for magnetite and limestone 494:30-31
Sand from different beaches compared experiment 1290:56, 4.3
Sand has insulating properties determination experiment 1396:189-193
Sand jar art with colored sand 494:42
Sand lanterns—how to make 296:10-11
Sand magic 350:72-73
Sand paintings, how to make 646:104
Sand playdough, recipe, how to make 1055:21
Sand scoops, dolls and footprint casts—making (Primary) 535:48-50
Sand sculptures show adhesion between sand and water experiment 1396:156
Sand shake, jars of water and sand, demonstrate settling of sand 1014:82
Sand timers—how to make 494:36-37
Saturating sand with water makes it flow down slopes experiment 1480:111
Sculpture of sand, cornstarch and sand, how to make 1008:51
Separate salt and sand—experiment 563:163-164
Shifting sand experiment; pore pressure of sand demonstration 1480:109
Size of sand crystals experiment 1046:26-28
Size of sand particles in relation to their location on beach experiment 1225:173
Test different kinds of bricks for strength experiment 715:56-60
The absorbing sand—experiment with sand and soil 563:66
Wentworth Grain Size Scale for sand 1225:180
What are clay and sand and how do they differ experiment 1323:22-25
What can you do with sand (Primary) 378:28-29
What minerals are in sand 236:104
Wind; how wind keeps sand grains on the move experiment 1513:43

SAND CASTING
How to make sand casting 832:77; 854:97
Plaster casting in sand—how to do 733:9
Sand cast a footprint—how to do 494:33

SAND DUNES
Animals and insects adaptations to dune life experiment; recording chart given 1225:194-195
Demonstrate how sand dunes are formed 1479:75
How ocean water rises to create storm surge experiment 1465:97
Particle's size and weight determine how far wind will carry it experiment 1480:137

Plant life samples on dunes using quadrat for sampling experiment 1225:190-192
Plant survival strategies in Atlantic and Pacific Coast dune systems experiment 1225:189-192
Sand dune erosion caused by wind experiment 978:113-114
Sand dune observations, how to do 1225:182-196
Temperature variations above and below the sand experiment 1225:192-193
Weather conditions on foredune at hourly intervals experiment; recording chart 1225:192

SAND PAINTING
Color sand to make sand paintings, how to do 890:108
How to do 296:11-13
Recipe for sand painting 494:39
Sand painting, how to do 906:84-85

SAND PICTURES
Make using colored dyes from plants 436:70
Use colored dyes from plants to make 436:70

SAND SCULPTURE
How to do 494:28-29

SANDPAPER
How to make sandpaper 58:400; 400:400; 600:38-39; 666:99; 880:100; 1014:83 (activity)
Make your own (Primary) 378:30-31

SANDSTONE
Hardness test for sandstone experiment 1438:61-64
Scratch test to tell limestone from quartzite [sandstone] experiment 1438:78-79
Testing sandstone with water and acid experiment 1438:65-67

SANITARY LANDFILLS. *See* **LANDFILLS**
SATELLITES. *See also* **MODELS**
Build and experiment with a model satellite launcher model 12:16-19
Centripetal force and satellites in orbit demonstration 1434:103-106
Centripetal force keeps satellites in orbit experiment 1479:9
Communication satellites; how they work demonstration 1394:188-189
Demonstrate force on circling satellite 295:93
Explorer XVIII interplanetary monitoring platform (IMP)—making 315:60-72
Explorer XXIX geodetic explorer satellite—how to make 315:87-98
Foil covered egg carton and flashlight beams satellite activity 1014:139
Force that keeps satellites in orbit around the Earth demonstration 1405:8
How are satellites launched into orbit around the Earth experiment 1399:24-27
How communication satellites work experiment 1405:18
How to make (Primary) 113:10-11
How to make a model of 91:26-29
Make a simple satellite (Primary) 169:11
Model for communication satellites experiment 1502:61-63
OAO orbiting astronomical observatory—how to make 315:99-110
OGO orbiting geophysical observatory—how to make 315:138-153
ORS octahedral research satellite—how to make 315:81-86

OSO-1-satellite model—how to make 315:22-31
Relay communications satellite model—how to make 315:40-48
Satellite motion with an without an inward force experiment 1502:57-61
Satellite's position affects direction of its signal demonstration 1394:184-185
Satellites appear to be stationary demonstration 1394:72-73
Satellites stay in orbit demonstration 1394:68-69
Satellites stay in orbit due to centripetal force demonstration 1394:70-71
Scan can model satellite; axles turn by falling weight power, make 1190:16-20
Secor—how to make 315:73-80
Syncom—synchronous communications satellite—how to make 315:49-59
TRS tetrahedral research satellite—how to make 315:32-36
Why satellite stays in orbit demonstration 1405:7
Why satellites appear to be stationary experiment 1479:10

SATELLITES—COMMUNICATION
Unmanned Earth satellites—activities to demonstrate communication satellites 564:53

SATELLITES—EARTH RESOURCES SATELLITES
Unmanned Earth satellites—demonstrate Earth data collection 564:54-56

SATELLITES—GEODETIC
Unmanned Earth satellites—data on Earth's shape and gravitational field 564:54

SATELLITES—ORBIT
Demonstrate with string, ball-point pen and balls 419:18

SATELLITES—PHYSICS AND ASTRONOMY SATELLITES
Unmanned Earth satellites—collection of data about Earth, Sun, and space 564:56-58

SATELLITES—WEATHER
Unmanned Earth satellites—activities to demonstrate weather satellites 564:52-53

SATURN. *See also* **PLANETS**
Determine how Saturn can be seen through its rings experiment 1479:6
Making a model of Saturn project 833:243-245
Measurements of Saturn 292:94-95
Saturn seen through its rings demonstration 1394:44-45
Saturn's changing shape experiment with foamcore and orange 1478:74
Saturn's moons affect the planet's rings demonstration 1394:46-47
Saturn's rings and ringlets experiment with rotating cake stand 1478:75

SAVART'S WHEEL
Savart's Wheel demonstrates pitch depends on number of vibrations 2:20-23

SAVONIOUS ROTOR
How to make from wood 429:88-90

SAW MILL
Making from wood 429:104

SCALE INSECTS
Adventure 28—we view the scale insects under a hand lens 29:134-137

SCALES. *See* **FISH SCALES**

SCALES—MEASUREMENT
A letter scale—how to make 241:2-3
Balance scale used to measure mass (amount of matter present) experiment 1399:44-47
Balance scale, how to make 1446:7
Balance scale—construct 436:12-13
Balance scale—how to make 147:54-55; 293:42; 860:226
Balance scale, wooden, how to make 885:37-39
Compare mass of different materials using balance scale experiment 1521:22-23
Comparison of Celsius thermometer to Fahrenheit (Primary) 648:28-32
Elastic scale experiment 1112:27
Fahrenheit scale to measure temperature—how he made it (Primary) 648:18-27
Heavy spring scale—how to make 9:109
Height scale using pencil as unit of your scale—making (Primary) 648:8-11
Height scale using ruler and metric ruler as unit of scale (Primary) 648:12-17
Homemade from coat hanger (Primary) 535:67
How scale measures weight experiment 1293:129-130
Market balance scale, making 779:32-33
Measuring device—build your own scale 563:22-24
Model candy box scale—how to make 12:99-102
Rubber band scale for weighing small amounts of materials—making 9:108
Rubber band spring scales—how to make 631:58-59
Scale of 1-10, make chart of desserts, months, pets (Primary) 648:1-15
Scale, balancing, wooden, how to make 770:125
Simple scales, how to make 1248:8-9
Spring balance—making 664:6
Spring balance scale experiment 1521:20-21
Spring scale and pulley—experiment 605:44-47
Spring scale from wood, tape, rubber bands, clips; how to make and use 1462:3-7
Spring scale, how does it work experiment with paper cup, Slinky and string 1399:40-43
Spring scales—making 436:73

SCALLOPS
Scallop jet propulsion 236:120

SCANNERS
Coin recognizer reader, how to make 1249:26-30

SCARECROWS
Scare bottles to scare birds project; plastic soda bottles used 969:44-45

SCAVENGERS. *See* **BIODEGRADABILITY**

SCHEMAGRAPH
How to make 43:12-31

SCHLIEREN PATTERN
Experiment to demonstrate turbulence lines (atmospheric interference) 564:56

SCHWEIGGER, JOHANN
Using a movable—needle type galvanometer 63:62-65

SCIENCE EXPERIMENTS. *See also* **INVESTIGATIONS—SCIENCE EXPERIMENTS**
Designing a science experiment 829:62
Record keeping 11:58-63
Science experiments from A-Z—questions and answers (Primary) 353:entire book
Using good scientific method, how to do 829:1

SCIENCE FAIR PROJECTS. *See also* **SCIENCE FAIRS; SCIENCE PROJECTS**
Choosing a topic 785:4-14

Getting organized 785:15-16

Guide to Projects, getting started, conduct experiment, display and Fair 997:3-42

How to develop idea into a science project 906:153-162

How to plan research 777:3-4

Judging day, how to act 785:67-70

Organize results and conclusions of experiment, how to do 785:42-52

Presentation of project, how to do 785:53-66

Projects, sampling of 785:75-85

Questions to ask before beginning project 777:1-2

Research, scientific method, collecting data, displaying your project 1210:11-23

Researching, planning, selecting and presenting a project information 1438:119-125

Setting up your display, how to 785:67

The experiment; using the scientific method 785:26-41

The question and the hypothesis, how to write 785:24-25

Topic; choosing, how to do 1195:1-7

Writing the background research paper 785:17-23

SCIENCE FAIRS

How to organize a science fair—participation, organization 397:entire book

SCIENCE FICTION

Creating your own science fiction 400:113

SCIENCE KIT

Portable science kit for collecting animals, insects, plants, etc.—how to make 452:35

SCIENCE PROJECTS. *See also* **SCIENCE FAIR PROJECTS; SCIENCE PROJECTS**

Classification of properties, steps to follow for scientific method 769:16-19

Doing your project; safety, recording methods and data, and graphs 1297:29-37

Drawing conclusions and identifying variables, steps to follow 769:36-37

Formal report; steps to follow for scientific method 769:38-46

Gathering information on your project, how to do 1297:16-28

Guidelines to follow for science projects from start to finish 1062:1-6

How can a computer enhance your science project 584:11-15

How do you choose a science project 584:7-10

How to choose, design and complete a science project 954:9-96

How to do reports demonstrations and research 160:1-61

How to plan, research, build and present your project 531:1-56

How to use scientific methods to set up, do, evaluate and report 188:3-94

Hypothesis; steps to follow for scientific method 769:23-29

Ideas for displays, exhibits and projects 824:112-116

Ideas for project exhibits, demonstrations and investigations 1297:9-12

Ideas for projects to do 748:184-214

Ideas for science projects 762:9-144

Ideas for 51:entire book

Interpreting data, steps to follow for scientific method 769:32-35

Making an inference and prediction, steps to follow for scientific method 769:20-22

Observation as part of scientific method, steps to follow 769:4-15

Organize your project with project idea checklist, how to do 1195:95-107

Presenting your project, how to do 1297:39-44

Reporting your work—how to 398:141-148

Scientific method; answering questions by using 815:3-42

Skills to conduct and prepare for presentation of science projects 984:9-112

Step-by-step guide for preparing research type science fair project 746:1-43

Steps to follow using scientific method 1221:4-7; 1222:4-7; 1297:12-15

Suggestions for a better science fair project 190:1-62

Testing your hypothesis; steps to follow for scientific method 769:30-31

Tips for super science projects and how to follow scientific method 1482:61-62

What is a science project 371:13-28; 715:1-7

What is a science project (Advanced) 372:4-29

SCIENCE PROJECTS FAIR

How to organize, who participates, how to judge projects 397:entire book

SCINTILLATIONS. *See also* **STARS**

Experimenting with scintillations [twinkling] 958:26

SCORCH

Remove scorch—experiment 585:92

SCREEN PRINTING

How to screen print cloth experiment 1485:18

SCREWS. *See also* **SIMPLE MACHINES—SCREWS**

Demonstrating the principle of a screw 180:34

Experiment to get a feel for the mechanical advantage of a screw 17:60-63

Experiment to show function of 128:118

How they work 544:19-21

Screws and screw tops 281:52

What is a screw experiment 902:185-186

What kind of simple machine is the screwdriver experiment 902:187

'Wheel and axle' wrenches and screw drivers—experiment 17:63-65

SCUDS

Scuds, collect, care for and observe behaviors, how to do 771:185-187

SCULPTURE

Make a beach sculpture (with plaster of Paris) 32:76-77

SEA ANEMONE

Dividing anemones to test regeneration 484:104

How sea organisms attach themselves to rocks experiment 904:116-117; 1405:33

Sea anemone taste tests—experiment 484:103

Sea anemones and light—experiment 484:103

SEA ANIMALS

Effect of plastic garbage pollution on sea animals experiment 1479:34

SEA BREEZES. *See also* **OCEAN WINDS**

Movement of air during land and sea breezes experiment 1396:177

Sea breezes caused by warming difference of land and water experiment 1322:32

SEA LEVEL

How high above sea level are you 333:110-113

SEA LIFE
Aquarium and seaside activities 840:1-113
Life of the brine shrimp 93:54-56
Sea life along the shore 93:45-48
Studying plankton 93:49-51
SEA PLANTS AND ANIMALS
Activities with plankton 236:109
Make a simple water glass for viewing sea life 236:114
SEA STARS
Anatomy of sea star observations and recording experiment 1225:25-28
Feeding process of sea star observation 1225:29
How to dry and preserve sea stars 530:77
Movement of sea star over different objects experiment 1225:28-29
Somersault and turning over movements of sea star experiments 1225:29
SEA VEGETABLES
Recipes—bladder wrack tea, fried kelp chips, sea lettuce, Irish moss pudding 530:50
SEA WORMS
Straining for worms 236:117
SEASCOPE
How to make 41:56-59
SEASHELLS. *See also* **OCEAN SHORELINES; SHELLS**
How to collect, clean, mount and label 296:23-31
How to make wind chime, shell flowers and mobile 296:32-41
Making a collection of seashells and animals 294:61-62
Seashell picture frame, how to make 644:24-27
Seashell resonance 281:77
Shell display made of plywood or plaster of Paris 293:23
Test for limestone experiment 1405:71
Why seashells produce unusual sounds experiment 1432:32-33
SEASHORE
Action of water on coastlines experiment 1342:121-126
Activities with algae 646:108-110
Activities with beach materials for collages and sculptures 646:111-113
Activities with beach sand 236:103-104
Activities with driftwood 236:114; 646:94-99
Activities with pebbles and sand 646:100-104
Activities with waves 236:102
Bayside walk observation chart 772:32
Beach bingo—find and identify objects on the beach 359:36-37
Beach grass scarecrow dolls—how to make 359:63-65
Beach pebble mosaic—how to do 359:41-42
Clams in jar of sand and seawater—siphons used for breathing 193:22-23
Comparing and displaying shells 236:125
Effect of wave height and length on coastlines experiment 1342:124-126
Exploring a sandy beach 285:68-69
Exploring the micro community in a tide pool 285:68
Flat, round and segmented worms—collecting 436:88
Food chain game, making 772:86-91
Graph temperature of water, sand, and other areas at beach, graph given 772:97-102
Greenhouse effect as cause of rise in sea levels project 1342:126
Investigating marine animals associated with seaweeds 285:66-68
Investigation of the plants of beach and dune 285:71-72
Investigation of zonation in rocky shores 285:69-70
Make a simple water glass for viewing sea life 236:114
Make your own bottle of waves 236:102
Mapping shore life, how to 820:23
Marine animals—collect small marine life in rock crevices 285:82-83
Mask of seashore materials, how to make 1513:31
Measuring tide with sticks, graph given, experiment 772:54-56
Mini dune collage 359:7-10
Model sand beach, how to make 1342:121
Mud snail race, setting up, how to 772:26-27
Mural in 3D to show physical construction, life forms 359:28-33
Ocean walk observation chart 772:29-30
Rocky shore stone and pebble activities 236:102-103
Seaside animals—activities 236:114-124
Seining—how to construct and use a seine net 359:43-47
Shape and texture scavenger hunt 359:34-35
Shore sand—getting to the core of soil 93:76-77
Study of living barnacles 285:72-73
Swale observation walk chart 772:31
Temperatures at the beach 236:104
Transect—how to make to show zones of life 193:10-11
SEASHORE BIOLOGY. *See* **BARNACLES; LIMPETS; MUSSELS; PERIWINKLES; SEA STARS; SEAWEED**
SEASHORE PLANTS
Activities with seaside plants 236:111-114
SEASONS
Autumn activities 662:38-43
Cause of the seasons experiment with flashlight and globe 1516:53-54
Chart of seasons worldwide 246:1
Chart the seasonal changes for animals and plants 298:16-17
Demonstrate cause of seasons 128:74
Diagrams of four seasons on Earth 246:28-30
Different clothing for different seasons (Primary) 232:54
Dressing for the seasons 232:53
Earth's tilt; demonstrate effect of Earth's tilt on seasons experiment 1479:68
Experiment to explain the seasons 175:46-47
Fall—experiments to demonstrate 40:50-57
Fall activities 236:144-145
Game; how animals survive the winter game, how to make 1180:38-39
Game; how animals survive the winter game, how to make 1183:166-167
Globe and lamp demonstrate seasons 1063:296
How summer and winter happen; demonstrate with flashlight/tennis ball 1281:8-9
Ideas and things to make and do 231:1-121
In the fall—what to look for in a vacant lot 233:53-54
In the spring—what to look for in a vacant lot 233:49-53
In the winter—what to look for in a vacant lot 233:54-57
Keep scrapbook of changing seasons of a tree 275:26-27
Length of day and night changes with the seasons experiment with globe/lamp 1478:26-27
Model shows how seasons work experiment 1387:8-9
Posters to show why we have seasons 40:44-50
Reasons for changes—demo with orange, pencil and flashlight (Primary) 361:12-32

Seasons due to Earth's axis tilt demonstration 1441:10
Spring activities—make wind vane, kite, play hunters
     and hares game 493:42-43
Spring activities 236:157-158
Spring and fall—chart of Sun on equator 246:22-23
Sun's angle affects seasons demonstration 1434:6-8
Tilt of Earth causes changing seasons demonstration
     1434:3-5
Tilt of Earth's axis and sunshine make the seasons
     246:10-14
Tree sculptures show how trees change with the seasons,
     how to make 1044:20-21
Why are there seasons on Earth experiment 852:54-56
Why do we have seasons experiment 1003:34-36
Why is summer hotter than winter experiment 1003:19
Winter activities 236:147-156
Winter chart of North and South Poles 246:21
Winter tilt of Earth's axis—diagram 246:19
SEASONS—FALL. *See also* **FALL**
Harvest poster (Primary) 535:12
Signs of fall (Primary) 535:7
SEASONS—SPRING. *See also* **SPRING**
Signs of spring (Primary) 535:27
Smells and sounds of spring (Primary) 535:28
Spring activities—decorate eggs, make Easter cake,
     make charoset 493:40-41
Spring activities—sprouting seeds, study buds, field
     diary, collect frog egg 493:38-39
SEASONS—SUMMER. *See also* **SUMMER**
Activities using flowers—pressing, dried decorations,
     potpourri 552:40-41
Birdwatching—how to rough sketch birds you see 552:39
Look at nature—nature diary of plants, flowers, insects,
     moths at night 552:38
Summer recipes—rose petal drink (sharbatee gulab),
     milkshakes, fruit salad 552:42-43
SEASONS—WINTER. *See also* **WINTER**
Air is cooler in winter demonstration 1479:79
Signs and sounds of winter (Primary) 535:16
SEAT BELTS
Test importance of wearing safety belts experiment
     1378:28
Toy car and doll demonstrate seat belt safety experiment
     945:18
SEAWATER. *See also* **SALTWATER**
Activities with 236:99-100
Artificial sea water, making 860:164-166
Depth and light penetration 93:17-19
Determine minerals in seawater 93:3-5
Drop experiment shows sea water is heavier than fresh
     water 772:35-36
Effects of seawater on different materials 342:12-13
Finding the salinity of seawater 93:9-10
Freezing desalts seawater experiment 1020:43-48
Freezing point of seawater 93:6-8
Fresh water from seawater, how to make 909:42
How salty is seawater experiment 877:20-24
How to make 128:214
Make fresh water from seawater experiment 877:15-
     19
Making fresh water from seawater 93:11-13
Salinity experiments 359:80-81
Salt content of water measured experiment 1405:87
Salt water and its effect on plant growth experiment
     714:61-62

Salty water doesn't make many soap bubbles experiment
     1482:6-7
Seawater denser than fresh water experiment with eggs
     in water 1488:19
Seawater mixture used by marine aquariums, how to
     make 1294:76-77
Testing depth and water pressure 93:14-16
Testing depth and water temperature 93:20-21
Water and salt can be separated from seawater by freez-
     ing experiment 1325:87-90
Water and salt separated from seawater by the Sun experi-
     ment 1325:91-94
What is in seawater experiment 877:5-9; 900:25
When does seawater freeze experiment 877:10-14
Why is the ocean salty experiment 860:164-166;
     1294:76-77
SEAWATER SALINITY. *See* **OCEAN SALINITY**
SEAWEED. *See also* **ALGAE**
Annual growth rate of seaweeds experiment 1225:56-57
Collecting and studying seaweed 93:52-53
Comparisons between seaweeds project; charts given
     1225:54-56
Drying seaweeds 236:113
Growth patterns and growth rate in seaweeds experiment
     1225:56-57
How to collect, dry and mount 296:42-47
How to make pressed seaweed 193:12-13
Investigating marine animals associated with seaweeds
     285:66-68
Observations of world of seaweeds; how to do, charts
     given 1225:50-60
Pressing and collecting seaweed to start a herbarium,
     how to do 1118:36-37
Rate of drying for particular species of seaweed experi-
     ment; chart given 1225:57-59
Rate of water absorption by particular species of seaweed
     experiment 1225:58-59
Seaweed collection—how to make 236:113
Seaweed gelatin, how to make 1056:49
Seaweed mountings—how to make 359:21-23
Seaweed prints—how to make 236:111-112; 784:37
Test for antibacterial activity on different seaweed prepa-
     rations exp. 864:58-60
SECCHI DISC
Design a secchi disc to measure cloudiness of water
     175:28-29
How to make 285:27-28
To test clarity of water—how to make 363:72-73
SECRET CODES
Code cylinders, cardboard, making 999:58-59
Code wheels, cardboard, making 999:54-57
Make rolling pin secret code 203:58
Secret code machine—making 508:4-5
Secret code system, making 770:134
SECRET MESSAGES
Acid-base secret messages experiment; data tables given
     1004:4.001
Ammonia and phenolphthalein invisible ink experiment
     1159:25
Binary numeral code secret messages—how to do 536:1-
     33
Chemical changes caused by heat; secret writing demon-
     strates 1219:42
Colored filter transmits some colors and absorbs others
     experiment 1132:26-1-26-2

Create and reveal hidden messages with lemon juice 814:16-18

Creating secret messages 392:100-105

Hard boiled egg message, making 930:15

Invisible ink from lemon juice, how to make 1435:71-73

Lemon juice ink and salt make secret message experiment 1005:10-11

Lemon juice secret message experiment 1124:20-21

Lemon juice, milk or vinegar secret messages experiment 1063:172

Message magically appears experiment using iodine and lemon 1405:57

Milk ink to help you write invisible messages, how to do 1312:11

Secret messages made with lemon juice experiment 860:57-59

Secret messages written with laundry detergent experiment 1083:111

Secret messages, making 930:15

Stick scrambler message, ancient message sender, how to make 1236:10-11

SECRET WRITING. *See also* **CHEMISTRY—TRICKS; INVISIBLE INKS; PIGPEN CIPHER**

Experiment 563:36

How to do 122:97-98

Write using corn starch and iodine solution 538:81

SEDIMENTARY ROCKS. *See also* **ROCKS**

How do sediments settle under water 253:124-125

SEDIMENTATION. *See also* **EROSION**

Collecting sediments on the ocean floor 93:78-79

Filtering muddy water 368:36-40

Investigating coagulation and sedimentation in water 78:18-19

SEDIMENTS. *See* **EROSION; ROCKS**

SEEBACKASCOPE

How to make with mirrors to see behind you 350:134-135

SEEBECK, THOMAS J.

Discoverer of seeback effect and thermocouple 209:54-55

Electricity by thermocouples—experiment 627:35

Thermoelectricity, producing electricity from heat experiment 768:81-82

SEED SHRIMP. *See* **OSTRACODS**

SEED WHISTLE

How to make 364:58

SEEDS

Absorption of water by seeds 60:34

Activities with seed structure 236:43-44

Activities with seed uses 236:51

Adventure 3—give seeds more than a passing glance under a hand lens 29:18-23

Air ride—show how seeds get carried by the wind 483:24-26

Bean seed parts dissected and identified experiment 1395:9-14

Bean seed parts experiment 1060:56-57

Bean seeds absorb water experiment 1231:22-23

Bean seeds dissected to show parts experiment 904:42-43

Beans; parts of bean seed experiment 1479:26

Big seeds versus little seeds experiment 1375:71-76

Bird seed sprouts—experiment 277:56

Characteristics of seeds activities for classroom 1291:16-17

Chemicals—effects of colchicine on growth and development of 402:90-91

Collect and compare for shape, size, weight and color 380:38-39

Collect seeds and berries 662:39

Collect seeds and make clay casts of them, how to do 1115:28-29

Collect seeds and make display, how to do 917:26-27

Compare growth of seeds in variety of nutrients 86:80

Crack garden—good seeds for 376:20-21

Cress garden in a dish—how to do 376:5

Dissect lima bean seed and plant experiment 888:59-62

Do plants need water to grow—experiment 60:14-15

Do seeds need water to grow experiment 804:29

Do weed seeds last longer 268:80-81

Dried but alive 560:9

Embryo—observe parts of seed embryo 400:21

Examining seed pods—'dry' fruit 294:46-47

Examining seeds of 'fleshy' fruits 294:47

Experiment to show what happens when seeds are badly crowded 168:44

Experiment with seeds and seedlings 586:122-124

Experiments to show structure, germination and growth 128:48-49

Experiments to try 398:41-43

Flying monster plant—sponge and bird seed 376:10

Fruit is mature ovary of flower seed experiment 1060:55

Grass seed starters—making (Primary) 535:44

Grow a tree seed 275:18-19

Growing seeds without soil 293:14

Growth effected by gravitation 86:36-37

Household chemicals effect on germination and height of seedlings experiment 1004:2.012

How do grass and cress seeds grow experiment 799:28

How seeds grow—experiments 30:44-48

How seeds turn into plants 40:154-155

How to make a colored bean necklace 86:45

How to plant a seed and transplant a seedling 366:101-103

How to plant seeds and seedlings 400:9

Imbibition—effect when dry seeds are soaked in water 170:44-45

Inside of seed experiment with function of each part 1402:52-55

Inside of seed experiment 36:76-81; 1368:80

Investigate kinds of seeds found in a vacant lot 233:26-27

Investigations into variations in living things 420:59-61

Leaf responses to acid rain experiments 777:13

Look inside seed to find parts 380:39

Magic beans—see how seeds work 376:4

Magic flower 350:62-63

Make a bean bomb 146:40

Make a seed poster (Primary) 580:unpaged

Making a seed book (Primary) 232:64

Miracle of growth—seeds planted on blotting paper demonstrate growth 576:79-80

Model sycamore seed, how to make 1044:37

New plants from old—water absorption by seeds 560:10-11

Nuts have oil—experiment (Primary) 322:14-15

Observing root hairs 86:46, 59-60

Parts of flower that produce seeds 40:149-150

Peanuts and popcorn show how seeds sprout 560:20

Photocopies of different seeds experiment 1375:69-71

Picture—make a seed picture 400:24
Plant seed responses to acid rain experiments 777:11; 777:12
Plant your old sock after walking through lots of weeds and grass 452:55
Plants grow from seeds—lentil, grapefruit, orange, lemon 270:23-31
Popcorn push up experiment—dry corn swell from water; push in all directions 560:12-13
Power of plants as they absorb water 60:35
Pressure of growing plants 60:36
Project—to show seeds useful to man 309:61
Project—to test seeds for oil 309:51-52
Project—to test seeds for starch 309:52
Seed collage—making 480:104
Seed collection (Primary) 535:11
Seed craft activities 236:48-51
Seed dispersal—determine how plants disperse their seeds 586:119-120
Seed hunt—indoors and out of doors 465:29-31
Seed mosaics, how to make 646:67-68
Seed party—different plants have different seeds 232:59
Seed pictures and seed necklaces—how to make 473:55
Seeds and air—experiment 36:64-67
Seeds and light—experiment 36:70
Seeds and temperature—experiment 36:68-69
Seeds and water—experiment 36:60-64
Seeds and where they are found activities for classroom 1291:35-36
Seeds for gifts 376:27
Seeds in soil 231:25
Seeds under a microscope, observe 889:47
Seeds' needs—what do seed need to grow—experiment with peanuts 560:14-15
Seeing the plant in the seed experiment 60:9-10
Show that water starts some chemicals acting 309:26
Sizes—project to show the different sizes of seeds 309:16
Starch stored in seed parts tested with iodine experiment 1395:12-13
Starch test for starch in seeds experiment 1060:58
Start a seed collection—seeds in things you eat 32:6-7
Storehouses 280:58
Structure of seeds 294:47-48
Structure of seeds—what's inside a seed—experiment to show 352:13-15
Test for starch in seed leaves 270:37
Test seeds for oil 309:51
Test seeds for starch 309:52
Testing how seeds grow 473:57
Testing seeds for starch and oil 236:44
Tomato—enough tomatoes to cover the Earth—count seeds in 1/2 380:39
Viability of seeds of wild plants 289:92-93
Water in—popcorn, measuring water in seeds 74:101-103
What is inside a seed 236:44; 253:6-7; 560:7-8
What is inside seeds experiment 760:2; 834:40-41
Where do seeds come from 253:5
Where seeds may be found 40:150-151
Which fruits and seeds do birds like best experiment 799:28

SEEDS (AKENES)
Adventure 43—explore subject of variation—seeds (Akenes) under hand lens 29:194-197

SEEDS—ANATOMY
Bean and corn seed demonstrate dicotyledons and mono-cotyledons 465:33-35
SEEDS—AVOCADO
Seed grows in water—how to plant (Primary) 540:37
SEEDS—CRAFTS
Little Annie Acorn, how to make 644:16-17
Snooper critter, how to make from seeds 644:14-15
Treasure box from beans, how to make 644:32-35
Wooden seed plaque, how to make 644:38-41
SEEDS—DISPERSAL
Ailanthus seeds spread by wind experiment 1060:122-124
Clinging seeds and seed dispersal experiment 1061:128-129
Cone seed dispersal experiment 1061:122-123
Display of examples of seed and fruit dispersal project 1060:58
Do seeds bounce or roll—experiment with nuts 714:123-124
Does pH of streams affect dispersal distance of seeds experiment 714:133-135
Examine seeds on socks from sock walk [Primary] 897:47
Experiment to find how many burs hitchhike on dog in the fall 309:44
Experiment to see how much wings help seeds 309:41
Explosive seed dispersal experiments 806:30-31
Floating seeds—how long will they float experiment 714:130-132
Flying seeds game, how to make from paper, paint and glue 1184:25
Hooked seed dispersal experiments 806:31-32
How dandelion seeds are spread experiment 1060:125-127
How do seeds travel 236:46-47
How do seeds travel experiment 901:47
How far do seeds travel experiment 1368:81
How much heat is needed to release seeds from pine cones experiment 714:136-137
How seeds are carried 40:151-152
How seeds plant themselves 294:48-49
Masking tape on soles of your shoes and plant experiment 749:40-41
Mud from shoes planted to see what seeds will grow experiment 1181:8
Parachute to carry wheat seed experiment 806:26-28
Pine cone rain meter; observe dry and wet for seed dispersal mechanism 784:72
Planting seeds from mud on your shoes experiment 799:28
Propelled seeds from seed pods experiment 1061:130-131
Seed dispersal activities 236:46-47
Seed dispersal activities [Primary] 759:46
Seed dispersal by humans experiment 1134:4.001
Seed dispersal experiment 739:23
Seed shapes—measure wind speed and distance seeds travel project 714:125-127
Seeds are dispersed in many ways, data sheet given 817:5
Shape of seed determines length of flight experiment 1110:6
Shoes as seed carriers—experiment 574:21
Sock walk to collect seeds experiment 1063:402

Sock walk to collect seeds to plant experiment 1371: 23

Sycamore seed model and spinning experiment 806:23-26

Transport of seeds in water determined by how long seeds can float experiment 1061:64-65

Waterborne seed dispersal experiment 1061:126-127

When the weather's fine—collect fern seeds to grow—experiment 574:20

Which kinds of seeds travel the farthest experiment 1095:44-45

Wind helps seeds to travel 40:152-154

SEEDS—FRUIT. *See also* **FRUITS**

Avocado seed—how to grow 272:6-16; 376:12; 712:12-13; 770:98

Citrus fruit—how to grow 272:23-29

Demonstrate fruit seeds growing 119:79-90

Fruit and seeds move 271:56-63

Grow a little orchard indoors from orange, lemon or grape fruit seeds 416:8

Grow apple or orange plants from their seeds experiment 1490:23

Kiwi seed—how to grow 272:42-47

Mango seed—how to grow 272:30-35

Orange seed—how to plant and grow 712:9

Orange, grapefruit, tangerine and lemon seeds grow into trees 376:13

Papaya seed—how to grow 272:17-22

Pomegranate seed—how to grow 272:36-41

Seeds of fruits and plants that come from them (Primary) 232:66

SEEDS—GEOTROPISM

Does it matter which way a seed is planted (Primary) 481:9

Seed sense—does it matter which way you plant a seed 399:21

SEEDS—GERMINATION

Acid rain effect on germination of seeds experiment 1150:76-77

Acid rain effect on seed growth experiment 727:21

Acid rain effects on seeds and plants experiment 978: 177

Age of seed affects germination experiment 1060:62

Allelopathy experiment; chemicals from plants inhibit growth of seeds 1060:133

Angle of seed; seed germination depends on which side of seed is up experiment 1061:8-11

Apple seeds must have dormancy and be chilled (stratified) to grow experiment 1060:60-61

Apple seeds sprouting experiment 875:75-78

Are seeds useful to plants after they have sprouted experiment 852:1-2

Avocado pit grows into plant (Primary) 650:unpaged

Avocado seed—rooting and potting 465:47-51

Bean germination—experiment 507:1876-1877

Bean magic experiment 829:53-54

Bean or pea seed planting experiment with blotting paper in glass jar 1524:10

Bean seed in glass jar shows what happens during germination experiment 1486:9

Bean seed in jar with wet paper towels demonstrates growth of plant experiment 1038:8-9

Bean seed sprouts experiment 1063:404

Bean seed sprouts in tumbler garden 465:32-33

Bean seed strength experiment; seed grows and breaks hard plaster 1242:29

Bean seeds—planting (Primary) 479:1-33

Bean seeds germinating in glass jar for viewing experiment 1078:19

Bean seeds germination experiment 1063:403

Bean seeds in jar affected by wet paper, steel wool, dark/cold place experiment 1246:8-9

Bean seeds need soil, water, light, and air to sprout experiment 1491:14-16

Bean seeds sprout in clear plastic glass experiment 1406:24-25

Bean seeds sprout in glass jar or glass, how to do 1306:8-9

Bean seeds sprout on damp yarn in paper cup experiment 1406:30-33

Bean seeds, how to grow 1335:100-101

Bean seeds, how to plant and grow in eggshells 1204:9-13

Bean stalks, how to grow 684:8-9

Beans in a jar, how to grow 932:17

Beans spoiled rotten experiment 829:55-56

Beans sprout and grow in glass jar experiment 1078:20

Beans; grow bean in glass jar to observe roots experiment 1214:6-7

Beans; growing bean seed in glass jar lined with paper experiment 1145:22

Bird seed germination experiment 1375:118-121

Birdseed, sprouting experiment 918:12

Bury seeds at different levels to determine effect on germination experiment 714:8-10

Can seeds germinate and grow in different types of soil experiment 714:15-16

Carbon dioxide increase and reduced oxygen effect on seeds experiment 1375:94-96

Carbon dioxide release measured from germinating bean seeds experiment 1061:17-19

Carbon dioxide released by germinating seeds experiment 1395:103-104

Certain substances or solutions affect plant growth experiment 1527:93

Citrus fruit seeds for citrus gardens (Primary) 465:43-45

Color of light affects how seeds grow experiment 1181:17

Colored lights affect seed germination experiment 1060:62

Colors affect growth 680:24

Conditions that allow or prevent seeds from germinating project 1296:1985

Cooked bean seeds versus uncooked; which will grow experiment 784:78

Cress and bean seeds, how to grow 932:14-17

Cress portrait of yourself—how to grow 749:44

Cress seeds grow in name shape and in eggshells experiment 1183:13

Cress seeds grow into your initial experiment 1078:20

Crowded planting of seeds experiment 1368:82-83

Dandelion fuzz grows plants (Primary) 650:unpaged

Dandelion seeds; conditions necessary for seeds to germinate experiment 1060:127

Demonstrate osmosis with beans 291:200

Depth of planting affects germination of seeds experiment 1395:29

Depth of planting affects germination 86:70-71

Depth of planting experiment 867:9

355

Depth to plant seeds for best growth experiment 1078:20
Dill plants in a dish, how to grow 810:31
Do plants like light—experiment 693:12
Does crowding effect the growth of seeds (Primary) 481:7-8
Does direction of seed planting matter experiment 904:44-45
Does spinning turntable affect growth—experiment 693:13-14
Does temperature affect germination of seeds experiment 714:11-14
Dormancy period needed for seeds to germinate experiment 714:20-22
Effect of acid, alkaline and normal water on seedling growth—experiment 594:36-37
Effect of lack of minerals on plant growth 577:project 87
Effect of oxygen deficiency and excess oxygen on seed germination 577:project 86
Egg carton nursery (Primary) 535:42
Egg carton gardens (Primary) 465:37-39
Eggshell plant pots, how to plant with seeds 1011:45
Electromagnetic fields effect on seed germination experiment 1060:63-64
Environmental factors effect on dandelion seed germination experiment data table 1004:2.017
Ethylene gas promotes germination of some seeds experiment 1375:86-88
Exhaust fumes effect on germinating seeds experiment 933:43-45
Experiment to see what seeds need to germinate and grow 978:48
Experiment with germinating seeds 532:71
Experiments with germination inhibitors 577:project 90
Fast plants germinate and grow quickly experiment 1060:64-68
Feeding and growing seeds—what do plants need to grow—experiment 590:45
Force of growing seedlings experiment 878:12-13
Frozen seeds sprout experiment 1020:102-106
Fruit seeds grow (Primary) 650:unpaged
Fruit seeds, how to grow 868:15
Game; germination game, how to make from balloon and papier mache 1181:6
Geotropism in germinating bean seeds experiment; data tables given 1004:2.016
Germinating seeds experiment 117:75-79
Germinating seeds give off carbon dioxide experiment 722:70-71
Germination affected by moisture, light, dark, temperature experiment 1527:90
Germination and growth rates of different plants measured experiment 1069:52-53
Germination and stages of growth 86:11
Germination needs air 86:33
Germination of dandelion seeds experiment 913:23
Grapefruit seed "magic show"—experiment 612:6-9
Grass growing in a sponge garden (Primary) 465:39-40
Grass seed grows in potato and in eggshells experiment 1071:78-79
Grass seed on Big Foot sponge, how to do 918:14
Grass seed planted in containers grows experiment 835:24-26
Grass seeds in eggshells demonstrate 882:35
Grass seeds in eggshells, how to grow 868:15

Gravity and its effect on seed growth experiment 904:50-51
Grocery farm—grow plants from grocery vegetables and fruits 565:97-106
Grow—them—yourself birdseed plants 600:24-25
Grow grass seeds on a sponge 416:6-7
Grow seedlings indoors, how to do 1054:25
Grow tiny garden in bottle caps 416:38-39
Growing a plant from seed—experiment 60:11-13
Growing a root system experiment 738:21
Growing bird seed experiment 888:51-54
Growing dried peas or lentils 480:20
Growing plants from wild seeds—experiment 60:45-46
Growing seedlings and charting growth of each experiment 799:29
Growing seedlings in a sponge garden 294:51
Growing seeds using different liquids [tea, cola, etc.]—experiment graph given 924:73-74
Growing sprouts 219:3-6
Growth chambers for 398:21
Growth graph, making to show how fast does a seed grow experiment 899:178-179
Growth of seeds plotted on graph experiment 924:71-72
Hairy potato head from grass seeds—making 508:10
How deep should seeds be planted 577:project 91
How does a seed sprout and what does a seed need 380:40
How many seeds will sprout 333:106-107
How to sprout seeds 264:18
Is air needed for seeds to sprout 268:87
Jack's beanstalk—plants need air, water and sun to grow—experiment 576:82
Lentils in cotton, how to grow 810:31
Letters of your name from germinating seeds experiment, how to make 1181:5
Light affects rate of seed germination experiment 1060:62
Light and air tests 625:48
Light is factor in germination of seeds experiment 1395:29
Light needed by plants for growth experiment 1181:16
Light needed for seeds to sprout experiment 1078:20
Lima beans and wet blotting paper—experiment 612:13
Lima beans sprout in jar experiment 695:61
List of rapidly germinating small seeds 1375:142
Magnetism effect on seed germination experiment 1375:107-110
Make a graph of sprouting seeds 309:13
Make a jar germinator 203:33
Making seeds grow 693:11-12
Measuring seedlings and charting growth experiment 799:30
Mustard and cress seedlings bend toward the light 595:9
Mustard and watercress seeds—how to plant to get shoots to eat (Primary) 481:14-15
Needs of seeds experiment with lima beans 878:2-3
Nutrients speed up seed germination experiment 1395:15-17
Observe seed growth experiment [Primary] 822:4
Observe seeds sown in different types of soil 294:52
Observe seeds sprouting 40:155-158
Old sneaker and soil grow grass seed (Primary) 650:unpaged
Osmosis in potatoes and imbibition of water in lima bean seeds experiment 1004:2.014

Oxygen amount in soil affects seed germination experiment 1078:20
Oxygen needed for seed germination —jar and candle experiment 864:86
Pea Olympics—which pea will germinate and sprout first 712:18-19
Peas on wet paper grow experiment 766:unp.
Per cent of seeds germinating experiment 1375:118-121
Per cent of seeds that germinate experiment 1375:52-54
pH effect on germination of radish and bean seeds experiment 1526:98
Pine cone seeds—how to grow (Primary) 650:unpaged
Plant and record time and percentage of seeds to germinate 380:43
Planting depth of seeds for the best growth experiment 878:6-7
Planting seeds indoors experiment, how to do 1242:28-29
Plastic bottle strawberry jars for seeds (Primary) 465:40-42
Pollution effect on plant growth experiment using bleach and detergents 1073:88
Popcorn plant grows in plastic cup; observe growing parts 1189:42-43
Portable greenhouse for seeds 398:23-24
Potato head planted with quick growing seeds (Primary) 465:36-37
Pressure of swelling seeds breaks jar experiment 723:76-77
Primary experiments with germination 104:12-29
Project—to show that water starts some chemicals to act 309:26
Radish and tomato seeds project 612:36-39
Raising seedlings in a tumbler garden 294:50
Resting times; seeds have resting times during growth experiment 1061:14-16
Roots and the way they grow experiment 867:10
Roots of pea seeds grow toward water, how to demonstrate 1379:19
Scarlet runner beans—how to plant and grow 712:14-17
Seed germination 36:71-76
Seed germination—make a hot bed 86:20-23
Seed growth affected by magnets experiment 912:39
Seed needs for germination 398:20
Seed selection for projects 398:19-20
Seed viewer to observe plant growth, how to make 899:176-177
Seedlings start to grow 560:17
Seeds absorb water experiment 878:10-11
Seeds contain air experiment 867:10
Seeds germinate faster in dark or in light experiment 1063:410
Seeds germinate in cold or in warmth experiment 1038:13
Seeds germinate in darkness but need light to grow experiment 1038:12
Seeds grow on a sponge 86:28-29
Seeds grown under different amounts of water and light experiment 1073:88
Seeds in different soils experiment 854:95
Seeds need light to grow experiment 799:30
Seeds need light, water, warmth and air to grow experiments 1181:4-5
Seeds need moisture to grow experiment 782:44-47
Seeds need moisture, warmth and sunlight to sprout experiment 1440:46-48

Seeds need sunlight, water and warmth to grow experiment 1183:12-13
Seeds need to be soaked before germinating experiment 1060:61-62
Seeds need to breathe experiment with boiled water 722:82
Seeds need warmth, water and light to grow experiment 1176:18
Seeds need water to grow experiment 924:70
Seeds need water to sprout 86:34
Seeds need water to sprout (Primary) 154:18-19
Seeds need water, air and warmth experiment 819:61
Seeds need water, air and warmth to grow experiment 1028:59
Seeds need water, oxygen from air and warmth to grow experiment 1038:10-11
Seeds planted at different depths experiment; glass jars needed 1159:58-60
Seeds planted in sweet potato vine stem experiment 1375:62-66
Seeds sprout in glass jar in wet paper towels experiment 1054:9
Seeds sprout in potato and carrot experiment 1375:49-52
Shoots in the dark experiment 870:84-86
Show force of germinating seeds 309:23
Show germination of seeds from planting to plant 168:19-20
Show germination of seeds 86:54
Similarities and differences among seedlings, monocots and dicots 577:project 89
Size of cotyledon affects depth that seed can be planted experiment 1395:29-31
Soaking seeds reduces total germination time experiment 714:17-19
Soil collected from field will grow plants (Primary) 650:unpaged
Soil necessary for seeds to germinate experiment 1159:62
Soil needed by seeds experiment 878:4-5
Sowing seeds to compare germination and growth 146:41
Sponge garden grows seeds 203:56
Sponge garden grows seeds experiment 721:101
Sprout bean seeds to demonstrate germination 1227:13
Sprout grass seeds on sponge experiment 942:11
Sprout seeds on moist sponge experiment 1078:21
Sprout seeds without dirt or sunlight experiment 1231:44-45
Sprouting beans 480:18
Sprouting mung seeds 759:30
Sprouting of seeds experiments 867:8-9
Sprouting seed—how to do 384:7-11
Starch in germinating lima bean seed experiment 1060:57-58
Starter gardens with raw peanuts and popcorn 560:16-17
Starting mix for seeds 398:21
Starting seedlings in a plastic bag 294:54-55
Starting seeds indoors 376:28-29
Sterilized soil used for growing seeds experiment 1061:124-125
Strength of seed growth experiment; bean seed breaks plaster 1242:29
Strength of sprouting seeds experiment using cans of plaster 1491:58-59
Sun helps plants grow—miniature greenhouses—experiment 651:44-45

357

Sunflower seeds grow (Primary) 650:unpaged
Supermarket seeds, growing experiment 918:11
Tea bags used for sprouting seeds, how to do 1228:74-75
Temperature—moisture—and oxygen needed for germination experiment 760:4
Temperature affects growth of corn and pea seeds experiment 1159:60-61
Temperature effect on seed growth experiment 904:66-67
Temperature needed for seed germination experiment 878:8-9
Temperature needed for seeds to grow experiment temperature chart given 1078:19
Test for germination—how to do 398:22-23
Test seeds to see if they sprout in a seed doll experiment 1078:19
The great seed race; making and using a seed tester 600:10-11
Three musts for seeds to germinate—experiment 574:26
Tiny seeds, how to start 1440:93-94
Too much water shuts off oxygen supply of sprouting seeds experiment 1375:91-93
Tree seed, how to plant and grow 1142:33
Tree seeds, growing and charting growth experiment 799:31
"Vegetable factory"—miniature greenhouse from egg carton, dowels, plastic 483:21-23
Vine salad "trees" from vine seeds 465:45-47
Watch a seed grow experiment 733:26
Watch pea and bean seeds grow (Primary) 481:16
Watch roots grow in jar experiment 723:66
Watching seeds sprout experiment 819:60
Water affects seed germination experiment 1395:27-32
Water and light makes seeds grow experiment 1214:8-10
Water enters seed through microphyle experiment 760:3
Water helps seeds to germinate, how to demonstrate 1379:18
Water needed for seeds to grow, simple experiment 1101:27
Water; amount of water seeds need to germinate experiment 1509:28
Watering seeds at different times during the day affects growth experiment 1061:12-13
Waterlogged seeds and plants don't grow experiment 1063:411
Weed seeds, growing experiment 918:10
Wet brick helps seeds sprout experiment 722:76
What's inside a bean seed experiment 819:59
Wheat seeds experiment 739:33
Window salad germination 231:97-99
Winter sprouting of seeds—how to 629:137-138

SEEDS—GREENHOUSES
An indoor greenhouse—experiment 563:57

SEEDS—GROWTH
Crowding affects growth of plant seeds project 1296:1995
Crowding effect on growth of seedlings experiment 1134:4.003
Do cotyledons help baby bean plants 309:20
Growing plant embryos 36:81-83
Growth of bean seed demonstration 1440:41-45
How do plants begin to grow experiment 901:22
How do roots develop and grow experiment 901:25-26
How seeds grow 158:18-19
How seeds grow—lima beans and radishes 270:32-39

Observation of inside of bean or pea seed experiment 1440:37-40
Seed growth activities 236:44-46
Seedlings—show stages of growth 86:82-83
Seeds need food to grow—experiment 352:16-17
Seeds need food, water and air to grow—experiment 352:18-20
Seeds need food, water, air and warm temperature to grow—exp. 352:20-21
Seeds need food, water, air, warmth and light to grow—experiment 352:22-24
Seeds need warmth and air to grow 270:38-39
Show plant growth for one month 86:53
Showing the strength of growing seeds 148:24
Sprouting test—experiment 352:29-30
Temperature effect on seed growth experiment 904:66-67
Watch a seed start to grow 32:2-3
Watch seeds grow experiment 901:23
What do plants need in order to grow experiment 901:24
What happens if seeds are crowded 60:47
What makes seeds grow—experiment 352:16-24

SEEDS—POTTING SOIL
How to make and use 398:25-27

SEEDS—PROPAGATION
Bean seed grows in jar experiment 798:6-9
Seeds need water to grow experiment [Primary] 798:10-11

SEEDS—SPROUTS. *See also* **SPROUTS**
Chop suey—how beans sprout 74:98-101
Cress and mustard seed sprouts, how to grow 913:30
Grow and eat bean sprouts 32:4-5
Grow sprouts from seeds 722:66
Mung bean sprouts in a jar, how to grow 913:30
Sprouting seeds to eat 380:41
Sprouting with and without water 86:10
Sprouts in zip lock bags (Primary) 535:41

SEEDS—TREES. *See also* **TREES**
Miniforests—some tree seeds to collect and grow in a miniforest 465:74-84

SEINE NET
How to construct and use a seine net 359:43-47
Two handled seine for collecting minnows water insects and others 9:26-27

SEISMOGRAPH. *See also* **EARTHQUAKES**
Construct a simple seismograph 564:107
How does seismograph record magnitude of an earthquake experiment 1398:52-55
Human seismograph demonstration with paper, pencil, and toy car 1107:36
Lateral and vertical motion of earthquakes—build seismograph to measure 715:24-28
Seismic waves give clues to Earth's interior demonstration 1023:80-81
Seismic waves move slowly through sand demonstration 1023:76-77
Seismogram; demonstrate how seismogram is produced 1023:74-75
Seismograph model, making 666:11-13
Seismograph to detect and record shock waves experiment build with adult help 1476:145-149
Seismograph, how to make and use in demonstration 1134:1.002
Simple seismograph to record vibrations and tremors—how to make 9:103-107

358

Small seismograph—building 762:50-52

SEISMOMETER

How does seismometer record movements of magma beneath Earth's surface experiment 1477:56-59

How does seismometer record shaking of earthquakes experiment 1477:56-59

SENSATIONS

Hold friend on ground only by a thread 228:17

Hot stuff on your wrists 228:15

SENSES. *See also* **GERBILS**

Activities to identify and understand five senses [Primary] 758:77-84

Do we need five senses experiment 901:202-203

Ears and direction—experiment 507:1901

Eyes and distance—experiment 507:1900

Five experiments testing senses 762:56-57

Reaction time test; how fast do your senses work experiment 1037:23

Senses used to identify shapes activities for classroom 1291:21-22

Senses used when popping corn activities for classroom 1291:19-20

Simple activities that show how the senses work 907: entire book

What is warm and what is cold experiment 901:204

SENSES—HEARING. *See also* **HEARING**

Can you see with your ears experiment 901:187

Can your ears alone tell you what is happening experiment 901:190

Direction of sound activities for classroom 1291:31-32

Do you know your classmates' voices experiment 901:188

Ear model demonstrates how you hear sounds experiment 1037:8-9

Ear model from cardboard tube, and paper cone, how to make 1037:8-9

Effects of darkness on balance and hearing experiment 1159:56-57

How we hear experiment using spoons and cardboard tube 1433:113-115

Human ears made from funnels allow you to hear in all directions experiment 1330:62

Identifying and locating sounds 253:100-101

Listen to sounds around you (Primary) 239:16-19

Make different sounds with different objects (Primary) 239:20-23

Match things without seeing them experiment 901:189

Model ear demonstrates how ear works experiment, how to make 1028:67

Music everywhere—how sounds are produced (Primary) 232:73

Sensations from your ears experiment 993:14-15

Sounds around us (Primary) 232:72

Why we have two ears for hearing experiment 1037:10-11

SENSES—SENSE RECEPTORS

Hot or cold trick with hands 399:63

Hot spots and cold spots 399:66

SENSES—SIGHT. *See also* **VISION**

Cat and mouse game on paper demonstrates blind spot in each eye experiment 1037:18

Catch a ball using one or two eyes (Primary) 239:12

Eye model shows how light enters eye and forms images experiment 1037:16-17

Eye sees things for short time after they are out of sight experiment 1037:20-21

Eyes; make model eye to show how eyes work experiment 1517:36-37

How big does the moon look to you (Primary) 239:11

How do our eyes help us hear experiment 901:194

How much can you 'see' with your hands experiment 901:199

How well do you remember what you see experiment 901:192

In what ways do we depend on our eyes experiment 901:193

See and observe differences (Primary) 239:8-10

Seeing colors (Primary) 239:13-15

Seeing with one eye 253:103

Trick your sight—activities 590:49-50

Two eyes are better than one experiment; target practice game demonstrates 1037:19

Vertical distances and horizontal distances; which is longer experiment 1159:53-54

SENSES—SMELL

Check odors—pleasant and not so pleasant (Primary) 239:30-33

Different smells—experiment 400:42

Exploring odors (Primary) 232:77

How fast do odors travel experiment 901:177

How long can you retain a smell experiment 901:178

Identify smell of flowers 363:35

Identifying objects by their odor 253:104-105

Natural substances can be used as room deodorizers experiment 969:94-95

Play a smell game 32:22-23

Potpourri; create blend of different scents experiment 1037:28-29

Sense of smell activities [Primary] 759:62-63

Several simple experiments with smell (Primary) 131:22-32

Smell bottles—making (Primary) 535:63

Taste and smell are related senses 253:106

Teamwork with smell 280:61-62

"Triangle test" to see how well you smell perfumes 441:49-52

What foods can your nose identify experiment 901:176

What is that smell (Primary) 232:76

SENSES—TASTE. *See also* **SENSES—TASTE AND SMELL; TASTE**

Artichoke makes water taste sweeter experiment 1083:29

Blindfold taste test experiment 930:4

Blindfold test for tasting experiment 1315:17

Can you taste foods without smelling them experiment 792:25

Classify foods by taste experiment 901:184

Color and taste experiment 980:60

Determine your sensitivity to taste experiment 904:150-151

Experiment number 8—can ingredients of Coca Cola be detected 404:36

Fool your taste buds experiment 1287:23

Great taste test experiment; map your tongue 885:86-88

Green foods taste demonstration 759:20

How do you taste food—experiment to find the four taste buds on human tongue 482:44-47

How is taste affected by smell experiment 901:180

Identify tastes without seeing or smelling the food 622:28

Is taste affected by smell experiment 901:183
Location of taste receptors for sweet and salty experiment 871:2.016
Map of tongue experiment 980:59
Map taste areas of your tongue 266:30
Map your tongue experiment 1028:71
Map your tongue for taste buds experiment 1063:351; 1238:8-9; 1369:32
Mapping your tongue project 817:19
Plotting taste map of the tongue experiment 993:11
Salt makes sweet food taste sweeter experiment 1369:33
Smell cards and game—how to make 733:16
Sugar in frozen fruit juice experiment 1177:unp.
Sweet and sour taste—map of your tongue 590:50
Sweet and sour taste experiment 980:60
Sweet and sour taste spots on tongue experiment 1177:unp.
Taste and identify various foods while blindfolded experiment 978:104-105
Taste bud areas of your tongue 622:24-25
Taste buds location on your tongue experiment 1189:30-31
Taste buds locations—experiment 585:160-161
Taste buds on tongue detect four basic flavors experiment 1220:4-7
Taste buds on tongue, how to map using different tasting liquids 1433:116-119
Taste different foods, sweet, sour, salty, bitter 239:28-29
Taste foods with blindfold on 607:39
Taste illusions experiment 761:101-103
Taste reactions of other people—keep chart 630:55
Taste test for different types of taste experiment 822:8
Tasting (Primary) 232:75
Tasting tests experiments 685:14-15
Teamwork with taste 280:61-62
Temperature and taste experiment 980:61
Temperature of food affects taste experiment 1238:11-12
The four basic tastes map of tongue 625:40
The orange and grapefruit test 630:53
The wet and dry taste test 630:54
Tongue map of taste 366:215
Tongue; make gigantic styrofoam model tongue experiment 1517:39
Tongue; taste receptors on tongue experiment 1506:31-32
Tongue; wet or dry tongue affects tasting time experiment 1506:35
Tongue; where can you taste certain things test 792:25
What differences in taste do people have experiment 901:179
What skins (human) can taste 366:214
Which part of the tongue is most sensitive to taste experiment 901:181-182
You can't taste difference between apple, onion, and potato experiment 1083:20

SENSES—TASTE AND SMELL. *See also* **SENSES— TASTE; TASTE**
Are senses of taste and smell independent 402:59-60
Blindfold test to determine the four main flavors experiment 1517:38
Can you taste when you hold your nose (Primary) 514:16-25
How does smell affect taste project 1210:67-68
Odors affect our sense of taste experiment using dry, instant coffee 1433:120-122

Potato and apple experiment to test sense of taste and smell 1246:36-37
Relation of taste and smell senses experiment 871:2.017
Smell affects taste experiment with apple and vanilla extract 1479:36
Smell and taste needed to recognize flavors experiment 1037:24-25
Smell important to recognizing and tasting food experiment 1506:33-34
Smell influences how things taste experiment 1238:10
Smell versus taste experiment 1253:16-17
Smelling food helps you taste it experiment 817:20
Taste and smell are related senses 253:106
Taste and smell sometimes get mixed up with each other—(Primary) 239:34-37
Taste and smell test experiment 1063:352
Taste threshold for salt, how to test for experiment 1069:171
Tasteless coffee experiment 563:68
Tell foods apart without your sense of smell experiment 1369:30-31
Tongue taste test with good and bad tasting cookies experiment 1037:26-27

SENSES—TOUCH. *See also* **TOUCH**
A texture—matching game 253:107
A touch puzzle trick 585:82-83
Blindfold test to see how much you can tell from sense of touch experiment 1517:41
Braille alphabet; make to test touch receptors in fingers 1246:34-36
Can you observe with your sense of touch experiment 901:200
Chart the sensitive spots on the skin 335:17
Determine temperature by touch experiment 1433:126-128
Feel bag—making 759:7
Feeling different objects 239:24-27
"Feely box" to identify objects by feeling their shape and texture experiment 1280:28
Game to show what you can discover by touching (Primary) 512:9-33
Hot and cold water test experiment 930:5
Hot or cold—experiments 563:50-51
How accurate is sense of touch—experiment testing distance of touch receptor 482:87-88
How can you test your sense of touch—experiment 628:19-20
Investigations into the sense of touch 420:46-48
Map the sensors on the back of your hand 335:16
Mapping sense of touch on hand experiment using hot and cold paper clips 1069:170
Read by feeling things experiment 1037:14-15
Sense of touch experiment with two pencils on persons body 563:48
Sense of touch experiment 507:1901
Sense receptors in your skin, how to find experiment 1369:10-11
Skin sensitivity test with ruler and two pencils 1280:7
Skin; pain receptors in skin experiment 1506:26-28
Skin; temperature receptors in skin experiment 1506:28-30
Skin; test sensitivity of different parts of skin experiment 1479:42
Skin; touch receptors in skin experiment 1506:24-26

360

Skin; where is skin most sensitive experiment 1369:12-13

Soft feely box—how to make 356:62-63

Temperature by touch experiment 1515:8-10

Test skin 's reaction to heat and cold experiment 1517:40

Test touch receptors in human skin 266:27-28

Test your touch sensitivity 625:40

Texture eggs—making 759:24

Things can feel both hot and cold experiment 1037:11

Touch box—making [Primary] 744:29

Touch experiments with hairpin 993:12-13

Touch receptors experiments 1246:34-36

Touch test for nerves in skin of arm, fingers, and palm experiment 1037:12-13

Touch tests 684:4-5

Touch your fingers with your eyes closed (Primary) 551:unpaged

Touching (Primary) 232:78

Washing and feeling (Primary) 232:71

What are some kinds of touch sensitivity 402:60-61

What is hot and what is cold 625:40

Where is sense of touch most sensitive experiment 901:200

Where is touch most sensitive experiment 901:206

Where is your skin most 'touchy' 381:98-100

SENSITIVITY—LIVING THINGS

Are living things more sensitive than nonliving things 402:7-8

SENSORS

Analog sensor experiment 830:49

Intrusion detector, simple, how to make 830:51-52

Light sensor relay experiment 830:50-51

Moisture or water sensor, how to make 830:55-56

Sensors and thermistors—how to make 665:24-31

Tilt sensors, how to make 830:72-73

SENSORY PERCEPTION—HOW DO HERBS AND SPICES FLAVOR OUR FOOD

Celery logs with chives 537:45

Cheese Tom Ditty recipe 537:80

Identifying herbs worksheet 537:79

Sensory perception experiment—identifying herbs 537:42-44

Sensory perception experiment—making celery logs with chives 537:45

Sensory perception experiment—making cheese Tom Ditty 537:44

Sensory perception experiment—making spiced cabbage 537:45-46

Spiced cabbage recipe 537:82

SEPARATION. *See also* **MIXTURES**

Mayonnaise recipe 537:71

Meringue shells recipe 537:72

Separation experiment—how does beating affect ingredients—making mayonnaise 537:30-32

Separation experiment—making meringue shells 537:32-33

Separation experiment—making whipped cream 537:33-34

Whipped cream 537:73

SEPTIC TANK

Decomposition of foods by microorganisms 78:98-99

Do commercial septic tank products really contain bacteria experiment 864:33

SEQUENCE

Bottoms up 222:77

SEWAGE

Analysis of bacteria/heavy metals in sewage before/after treatment experiment 997:128-129

Effects of fertilizers and sewage in aquatic environments experiment 1450:121-127

Nutrient enriched waters and algae growth experiment 1450:135-142

Oxygen depletion of water by living organisms experiment 1134:6.010

SEWAGE SLUDGE

How to demonstrate 330:63-65

SEWAGE TREATMENT. *See also* **WASTE TREATMENT**

Effects of aerobic activity on sewage experiment 978:77

SEXTANT

Construct a sextant 167:143-148; 833:103-109

Make a model sextant 128:73

Make a simple sextant 564:42

Sextant to measure altitude of stars, how to make 862:82-93

SHADOW CLOCKS (SUNDIALS). *See also* **SUNDIALS**

How to make (sundials) 297:22-29

Make a model Egyptian shadow clock 137:7

Make a shadow clock 21:48-49; 588:50-51

SHADOWS

Activities with shadows [Primary] 759:10-11

Anatomy of a shadow experiment 1082:10-14

Cat and mouse shadows move around room demonstration 1103:12

Colored shadows experiment 1159:90

Dancing shadow machine from coffee can, magnets, batteries, wire, make 1442:55-60

Dark shadows experiment 400:75

Demonstrate ghostly shadows on wall with mirrors 176:33-34

Demonstrate with shadow theater 208:30-31

Device for tracking seasonal shadow changes—making 693:19-21

Do shadows change during the day experiment [Primary] 742:19

Double shadows experiment 1082:16

Earth 's shadow extends into space and as umbra increases so does penumbra 1062:45-47

Electric light bulbs demonstrate shadows 295:115-117

Finding north with shadows 21:54-57

Finding north with the Sun 's shadow—experiment 538:3

Flagpole shadow at different times on different days 538:2

Heated air shadow picture 95:22

Holes in shadow experiment 21:96-97

How a shadow is made 40:79-80

How a shadow moves 40:80-81

How do shadows change during the day 253:184-185

How is shadow like motion picture projector experiment 747:35-36

How shadows are formed 30:51-52; 72:62; 240:32-35; 684:14-15

How shadows work experiments 1163:20-21

How to make colored shadows 21:93-96

Length versus height of shadow experiment 1003:24

Light and shadow—experiment 659:4-7

Light rays obstructed by opaque object shown by shadow puppets experiment 1308:6-7

Make a shadow compass (Primary) 207:29

Make a shadow picture 32:42-43

Make a shadow theater 32:40-41
Make a shadow theater (Primary) 210:20-21
Make automatic shadow puppets 177:21-24
Make silhouettes 232:44
Making a Sun map with shadows 21:61-66
Making animal shadows (Primary) 206:unpaged
Making finger shadows (Primary) 321:9
Making shadows experiment 1092:10
Measure length of shadow from sun at each hour (difficult) 189:12-16
Measuring shadows, outside, how to do 770:122-123
Moving pictures experiment 1111:12-14
Multiple shadows experiment 1159:87
Play a shadow guessing game 32:38-39
Projects with light, shapes, cutouts and many objects (Primary) 534:1-33
Puppet shadow show, how to make 1213:11
Shadow box theater experiment 1417:27-31
Shadow clock—making 909:134; 928:9
Shadow clock—making (Primary) 535:26
Shadow demonstrations (Primary) 297:7-48
Shadow game (Primary) 551:unpaged
Shadow measures position of Sun in sky experiment 1003:22-23
Shadow pictures experiment 1111:11-12
Shadow portraits—how to make 76:34-35
Shadow portraits in morning and evening, how to make 890:108
Shadow puppet theater, make to demonstrate how shadows are cast 1073:73
Shadow puppets and theater, how to make 1016:18-19
Shadow puppets experiment 1066:88-89
Shadow record—making (Primary) 535:26
Shadow shapes—making (Primary) 696:28-29
Shadow shapes experiment 1159:89-90
Shadow size experiment 1159:87
Shadow sizes and changing shapes 366:199-202
Shadow sticks; measure summer and winter shadows 909:135
Shadow tricks 909:132-133
Shadows form when light is blocked experiment 1028:37
Shadows move as Sun moves experiment 956:8-9
Shadows under colored lights experiment 1158:140-142
Shadows with opaque and transparent objects (Primary) 329:24-25
Sharp and fuzzy shadows experiment 1159:88-89
Silhouettes, how to make 935:32-33
Simple shadow experiments 21:86-123
Sun clock from pencil and paper plate, how to make 1103:13
Sun shadows—how to measure through the day 569:39
Sundial, making 909:134
The umbra and penumbra—outline to show 595:17
Translucency of piece of paper changes experiment 1082:20-22
Upside down shadow 21:116
Use a shadow stick to measure time 137:5-6
Use flashlight to demonstrate kinds of shadows (Primary) 144:32-39
Water in cup; simple demonstrations 843:16-19
What causes a shadow 281:84-85
What makes shadows experiment 906:140
Which way does your shadow fall experiment 742:18
Why do shadows change in size experiment 902:67

SHADUF
Egyptian simple machine—how to make 323:14-15
SHAMPOOS
Effect of soap, shampoo and conditioners on hair—experiments 441:75-78
Recipe for 387:21-22
Difference in effectiveness of different brands of shampoos experiment 1403:72-75
Shampoo containing no chemicals, recipe, how to make 1228:88
SHAPES
3-D structures, cubes, tetrahedron, octahedron, isosahedron, how to make 1063:151
Curved strength of shapes—eggshells hold up heavy books 95:8-9
Curves—make a curved line by using straight lines 444:32-37
Designs from squares and curves 444:38-52
Disappearing magic square 27:25-29
Disappearing magic triangle and rectangle 27:29-30
Dodecahedron 3-D desk calendar, how to make 1299:86
Experiments with 107:60-73
Find diameter, radius and circumference of circle (Primary) 200:8-11
Fun with shapes 538:53-62
Illusions—bizarre shapes and sizes 229:52-69
Investigation into shapes of living things 420:64-67
Lines of different lengths produce different curves 444:53-61
Magic envelope and magic hexagon 27:30-32
Make a circle triangle and cone with paper cup (Primary) 201:5-7
Make cone from paper cup to show it rolls in circle 201:8-11
Making a hexagon 444:21-23
Making a pentagon 444:26-27
Making an octagon 444:24-26
Models of regular solids; cube, tetrahedron, octahedron, icosahedrone 1299:87
Nets or flat sheet fold into polyhedrons experiment, how to make 1518:40-41
Non-round rollers experiment 1132:71-1-71-5
Octahedron mobiles project, how to make 1353:49
Schlegel diagrams, a way of drawing solids 1353:57
Senses used to identify shapes activities for classroom 1291:21-22
Shape patterns, how to draw, measure and use in activities 1351:5-64
Shapes; how they can be drawn, measured and used in various activities 1352:1-64
Solid shapes; how to create, measure and use in activities and projects 1353:1-64
The importance of shape in buildings—experiment 589:52
Triangles; theory, problems and puzzles 1356:1-64
SHELLS. *See also* **SEASHELLS**
Calcium; testing shells for calcium carbonate experiment 1290:43, 3.2
Clam shell scrimshaw—how to make 359:1-3
Collecting and displaying shells—how to 476:39-41
Collecting, cleaning and saving shells, how to do 1118:16-17
Investigation of variations in one species of shell 285:70-71

Mold and cast fossils experiment to show how fossils are formed 1134:1.004

Univalves compared to bivalves demonstration 1290:44, 3.4

Whelk conch planter—how to make 359:19-20

Wooden box decorated with shells, how to make 1246:30

SHELLS—COLLECTION AND PRESERVATION

Collecting and labeling shells, how to 894:59

Collecting, cleaning and displaying shells, how to do 1085:16-17

Comparing and displaying shells 236:125

Identification and display 400:58

Shell collecting—how to gather, clean and mount 234:51-53

SHELTERS

Adobe house—how to make 415:42-43

Earth shelters to determine temperatures above and below ground experiment 1094:43

Grass hut model—how to make 415:44-45

Igloo model—how to make 415:45-46

Log cabin model—how to make 415:40

Plants—house of sticks—how to make 483:64-65

Roman house model—how to make 415:50

Teepee model—how to make 415:37-38

Tent model—how to make 415:38-39

SHIPS. *See also* **BOATS**

Air creates buoyancy needed to float salvage to surface of sea experiment 1167:29

Buoyancy of ships—experiment 368:53

Currents and tides affect salvage of sunken ships from the sea experiment 1167:28

Floating ships on the sea—demonstrate 93:66-67

Shape helps carry things (Primary) 324:11

Visibility and salvage of sunken ships from the sea experiment 1167:28

Water pressure used to submerge and raise salvage at sea experiment 1167:29

Watertight sections—how to make 321:27

Why do heavy metal ships float experiment 877:96-100

SHIPWRECKS

Raising wreck of ship experiment, how to do 1471:14-15

SHOCK WAVES

Candle flame extinguished by shock wave 291:84-85

SHOES

Which type of footwear grows the most bacteria experiment 997:132-134

SHORELINES. *See also* **OCEAN SHORELINES**

Dune windbreaker fences experiment to determine optimum spacing 715:89-91

Islands, peninsula and isthmuses—island in a tub—(Primary) 153:12-13

Model coastlines; make to demonstrate gradual erosion of coastline experiment 1080:27

Plant roots save shoreline soil experiment; grow radish plants 1492:24-25

Water velocity can be slowed down to prevent erosion experiment 715:94-95

SHORT CIRCUITS

The impossible circuit trick 392:71-76

What is a short circuit 278:41

SHREWS

Shrew skull 375:11

SHRIMP—BRINE. *See also* **BRINE SHRIMP**

Growing brine from fertilized eggs 400:19

How to raise shrimp 887:36-38

Life of the brine shrimp 93:54-56

Test shrimp for reactions to light, color, cold, heat experiment 887:36-38

SHUTTLES

Make a soda bottle shuttle (Primary) 113:28-29

SIDEREAL DAY. *See* **TIME**

SIEVES

Mud and sand sieve—how to make 359:52-53

SIGNALS. *See also* **CODES; MORSE CODE**

Flash signal system, making 779:23

Heliograph—how to build 507:1878-1879

How to make a railroad signal 278:59

Make a simple electric signaling system for two people 226:12

Model railway signals from electromagnet, how to make experiment 961:22-23

Old fashioned railroad signal experiment, how to make 1420:7

Secret sun messages and signals—how to do 494:21

Semaphore code 226:6

Solenoid controlled signal, how to make 910:40-41

Using mirrors 226:7

SILK

How much does silk weigh experiment 1485:7

How strong is silk experiment 1485:5

Silk of silkworm differs from silk of other insects experiment 1097:131-133

SILK SCREENING

Simple silk screening—how to do and how to make the screen 631:80-81

SILKWORMS

Examine fibers and cocoons 257:20-22

Raising your own silk 148:52

SILLY PUTTY

Recipe for Nutty Putty, how to make 1083:60-61

Silly Putty experiments 1091:47-48

SILVER

Case of the vanishing silver tarnish experiment 814:89-91

Chemical change in silver molecules—clean silver experiment 704:47-48

Chemical tests for with coins—match test and mustard test 548:39-41

Clean the silver 366:220

Color of silver chloride is changed by sunlight 122:160-161

How to find silver in a bottle of Argyrol 122:157-159

Removal of tarnish from silver demonstrates electron flow between metals 871:3.024

Show why silverware tarnishes and how to remove it 122:162-164

Silver tarnishes, what causes it experiment 976:50

What makes silver black 381:27-28

SILVER CLEANER

Clean silverware the easy way 291:224-225

Electrical silver polish (electrolyte and aluminum) 346:95-96

SILVERPLATING

How to silverplate a key 278:52

SIMPLE MACHINES

Acrobats whirl around on belt drive experiment, how to make 1446:16-17

Ball bearing reduces friction, how to demonstrate 1033:21

Belts make spools turn, build using wood, spools, belt 1033:14-15

Block and tackle to lift weight experiment 1411:17

Bobsleds; model bobsleds and run, make to demonstrate ball bearings 1446:14-15

Conveyor; gravity pulled conveyor machine experiment, how to make 1400:75

Demonstrate levers, gears and pulleys 210:32-33

Egyptian Shaduf—how to make 323:14-15

Experiments and tricks to demonstrate simple machines 1137:92-105

Experiments to show function of simple machines 128:115-121

Figure jumps up and down on machine that changes direction of motion experiment 1033:16-17

Float hammer demonstrates first-class lever 1462:16-17

Friction—wheels help us work 96:37-38

Gears; changing direction with gears experiment 909:111

Gravity screw spiral slide brings model planes toward ground experiment 1446:24-25

Inclined plane—inclined plane used to get stone blocks up sides of pyramids 448:7-10

Inclined plane experiments [Primary] 757:154-157

Lift a chair with a broom experiment 1523:21

Make your own mousetrap using ramps, levers and forces 554:28-29

Making a motor car 96:44-46

Making a paddle wheel boat 96:42-43

Mechanical arm, making 779:34

Mechanical extender experiment, how to make 1420:10

Mousetrap working model demonstrates complex machines experiment 1334:30-31

Observe and list simple machines in your home—pliers, chisels, drills, etc. 575:30-31

Pulleys—experiment with pulleys—how to build 507:1884-1885

Pulleys rope and pulley—experiment 656:26

Ruler seesaw experiments [Primary] 757:153

Seesaw can be balanced experiment 1405:98-99

Shaft and crane; advantage of demonstration 1436:88-89

Turtle racing game demonstrates how simple machines transmit forces experiment 1523:16

Windlass (wheel and axle)—making 436:86

SIMPLE MACHINES—BALLBEARINGS. *See also* **BALLBEARINGS**

Model ballbearing using cans and marbles experiment 1523:22

SIMPLE MACHINES—BELTS

Tests with model drive belts and pulleys experiment 1523:17

SIMPLE MACHINES—BLOCK AND TACKLE. *See also* **BLOCK AND TACKLE**

Block and tackle experiment 281:50

Strongman's secret 399:9

SIMPLE MACHINES—CAMS

Model camshaft experiment, how to make 1446:22-23

SIMPLE MACHINES—COMPOUND MACHINES

Circle drawing machine, how to make 1400:78

Compound machine using gears, wheel and axle to lift a load experiment 1400:68-71

Compound machine, what is it experiment 1400:68-71

Gravity used to power a compound machine experiment 1400:72-75

Pantograph is compound machine made up of levers; how does it work experiment 1400:76-79

Soap bubble machine; combining simple machines makes compound machines 1400:71

SIMPLE MACHINES—GEARS. *See also* **GEARS**

Bicycles gear shift patterns experiment; data tables given 1004:5.005

Bottle top gears 281:48

Cog gears from jam jar lids demonstrate machinery gears experiment 1024:14-15

Disco dancers on box demonstrate how cogs change direction of movement 1024:12-13

Fan model works to demonstrate gears, how to make 1028:114-115

Fan uses gears to show machines work at different speeds experiment 1033:18-20

Gear drawings experiments 1446:20-21

Gear model experiments 1446:18-19

Gear wheel to demonstrate how gears turn wheels, how to make 1380:18-19

Gears and how they work demonstrated by working gear model 1334:24-25

Gears from wooden spools, how to make 1028:112

Gears; model of gears to demonstrate gears change speed of moving parts 1400:50-51

Gears used to change movement from one direction to another experiment 1400:48-51

How do gears help us experiment 834:61

How gears change movement from one direction to another demonstration 1479:100

Making a set of gears, operating your model, experiments to try 606:36-49

Pedal power of bicycles demonstrated with working model cyclist on bike 1334:22-23

What gears do demonstration with bottle caps nailed on board 1436:86-87

Wheels with strong teeth 280:48

SIMPLE MACHINES—INCLINED PLANE. *See also* **INCLINED PLANE**

A board that does work 96:41-42

Cracking nuts project, how to build 1462:106-109

Force needed to move truck up inclined plane experiment 1462:101-103

Gravity and friction affect how far something will roll experiment 1014:66

How ramp overcomes force experiment with yardstick, books, blocks, rubber bands 1436:57-60

Inclined plane activities for classroom 1291:14-15

Inclined plane changes force needed to do simple job experiment 1157:104-106

Inclined plane makes lifting an object easy experiment 1400:24-27

Inclined plane makes work easier demonstration 1404:114-115

Inclined planes use a small force to lift a greater weight 253:177-178

Less force is needed to move object on inclined plane experiment 760:22-23

Measuring the effect of an inclined plane 180:31

Model slope or ramp demonstrates effort needed to get car up slope experiment 1334:6-7

Moving objects on inclined plane experiment; data tables given 871:4.006

Objects moving on inclined plane experiment 998:198-199

Screw is like an inclined plane experiment 1400:32-35

Screw; how it works like inclined plane demonstration 1404:109

What is an inclined plane experiment 902:179-182

Winding mountain road is an inclined plane demonstration 1404:105

Winding mountain road is an inclined plane demonstration 1479:102

SIMPLE MACHINES—LEVERS. *See also* **LEVERS**

Archimedes' principle of levers experiment 1133:4.002

Archimedes, who invented the lever and the screw experiment 1525:24-26

Balance; build to demonstrate lever used to weigh things experiment 1157:109-116

Calculating mechanical advantage of levers 180:37

Can a level help lift something experiment [Primary] 743:11

Cantilevers experiment; chart given for results 1462:52-54

Catapult is example of third-class lever experiment 1462:59-61

Catapult powered by rubber band, how to make 1446:8-9

Classifying lever action 180:36

Crank; experimenting with a wire crank 1523:14

Demonstrate the principle of a lever 293:42-43

Experiment—with weighted match box 596:8

Experiments with second and third class levers 902:155-164

First-class lever experiment with graph given for results 1462:18-24

First-class lever; what is it and what is advantage to using it experiment 1400:4-7

First-class, second-class, and third-class lever, how to construct 1400:22-23

Forearm cardboard model to demonstrate third-class lever experiment 1400:19

Forearm is like third-class lever experiment 1400:16-19

Hand can't be lifted off top of your head demonstration 1083:45

How can we lift objects with levers 253:172-174

How do levers help us do our work experiment 834:63-64

Jaw cardboard model to demonstrate third-class lever experiment 1400:15

Jumping coin shows where lever gives best lift experiment 909:114

Lever—a stick that does work 96:40

Lever demonstrates lifting heavy things; make from wood plank and block 1380:6

Lever from wood, tape, and paper clips, how to make 1462:8-9

Lever from wooden block and ruler experiment 1318:11

Lever model shows cat pouncing on bird, patterns given 1495:30-31

Lever's fulcrum position affects the lever demonstration 1404:122-123

Levers and lifting—experiments 664:26-27

Levers help move heavy objects experiment 898:36

Levers reduce force you apply to them experiment 1400:20-23

Lift glass bottle with straw experiment 1007:80-81

Lifting a giant 280:46-47

Load applied to lever affects performance deflection experiment graph given 1462:55-58

Machine mobiles demonstrate balance and first-class lever balance 1462:29-32

Mechanical advantage of first, second and third class levers experiment 1179:68-69

Model grabbing hand machine demonstrates levers experiment 1334:28-29

Model machine that hammers in nail demonstrates use of levers experiment 1334:26-27

Move object easily with lever experiment using book, ruler and pencil 1198:7

Pantograph drawing machine with linked levers, how to make 1446:10-11

Predict effort required to lift load with first class lever experiment 902:149-151

Pulley from spools, wire coat hanger and tape, how to make 1462:10-13

Second-class lever demonstration with toothpicks on fingers 1404:12

Second-class lever demonstration 1405:99

Second-class lever; what is it and what is advantage of using it experiment 1400:8-11

Second-class levers experiment; graph given for results 1462:35-41

Seesaw machine separates marbles, how to make from cardboard 1033:12-13

Seesaw model demonstrates levers, how to make 1523:8

Seesaws and scales are levers 281:46-47

Simple ruler balance experiment 1507:20

Third-class lever; what is it and what is advantage of using it experiment 1400:12-15

Third-class levers experiment; graph given for results 1462:44-51

Uses of levers demonstrated with cardboard strips and paper fasteners 1495:9-16

Using a lever 180:35

What is advantage of first class lever experiment 902:145-146

Wheelbarrow model demonstrates use of lever experiment 1028:109

Wheelbarrow moves things with less effort experiment; how to make 1033:8-9

Wheelbarrow-lever model demonstrates levers, how to make 1523:9

SIMPLE MACHINES—LEVERS AND PULLEYS

Experiment to show how to move a heavy load 168:33-34

SIMPLE MACHINES—PULLEY. *See also* **PULLEYS**

String tied to shaft of pencil sharpener lifts books experiment 940:76-78

Changing the direction of work 96:38-39

Construct pulleys to transport things 1014:72

Demonstrate increase in work efficiency 293:43-44

Different pulley setups to investigate how a pulley works experiment 1157:117-119

Experiments with fixed and movable pulleys 902:169-171

Fixed pulley, what is it and how does it make work easier experiment 1400:36-39

Fixed-pulleys demonstration; build moveable clothes line experiment 1400:39

Flagpole model demonstrates pulleys, how to make 1523:5

How a pulley works 281:49

How do pulleys lift weight experiment 802:29; 1293:131-132

How do wheels help to lift things experiment 834:58-59

How much can a crane lift experiment 802:30

Make your own pulleys 909:113

Making pulley arrangements, making weights, set up experiments to try 606:14-26

Match box moves under its own power; magic trick demonstrates pulleys 966:25-29

Milk carton pulley, how to make 945:44-45

Model crane with pulleys lifts weights easily experiment 1334:20-21

Moveable pulley demonstration; use paper clip, string and spoon 1400:42-43

Moveable pulley, what is it and how does it help you lift objects experiment 1400:40-43

Pulley can be used to lift a load experiment 836:36-39

Pulley demonstration with broom handle and rope 1318:13

Pulley from spools and string, how to make 1001:10

Pulley lifting power experiment using string, spools and book 1079:48-50

Pulley lifts heavy load experiment; make from wood, spools, string and box 1033:26-27

Pulley lifts weight experiment; how to make from wire, wooden spool and string 1436:82-85

Pulley power—experiments 664:24-25

Pulley system demonstration model, how to make 1523:10

Pulley system helps you lift things experiment, how to make 1024:10-11

Pulley system helps you lift things experiment 1024:10-11

Pulley using pulley to lift heavy object experiment 1420:16-17

Pulleys and mechanical advantage—how can we use pulleys to move objects 253:175-176

Pulleys can reduce friction experiment with spool, pencil, string, cups 1400:61-62

Pulleys help us do work experiment 898:35-36

Ship-to-shore pulley, making 779:52

Simple pulley made from spool, wire, hook and string 1380:17

Simple pulley, how to make 1243:32-33

Single pulley versus double pulley experiment; ease of lifting weight 1198:21

Single, double and quadruple pulley experiments 1446:12-13

Tests with model drive belts and pulleys experiment 1523:17

Tug of war demonstrates how easy it is to move things with pulley 1405:100

Use two pulleys to lift a load experiment 1378:24

Working with fixed and movable pulleys 180:32-33

SIMPLE MACHINES—RAMPS. *See also* RAMPS

How ramp overcomes force experiment with yardstick, books, blocks, rubber bands 1436:57-60

Ramp magic with rock and rubber band—experiment 399:55

Ramps make it easier to lift things experiment 898:34-35

Roll-on ramps for toy cars or balls, making 779:49

Screw is actually an inclined plane experiment with wood, screw and paper 1436:61-63

Something about ramps 281:51

Testing forces on a ramp with toy model car experiment 1523:12

Thread of screw is like a ramp experiment using pencil and paper 1198:28

SIMPLE MACHINES—SCREWS. *See also* SCREWS

Archimedean screw model lifts popcorn or cereal experiment 1446:26-27

Archimedes screw model moves water up plastic tube experiment 1523:28

Archimedes; who invented the lever and the screw experiment 1525:24-26

Auger lifting machine demonstrates power of auger, how to make 1033:10-11

Clothespin moving down wire to pop balloon demonstrates Archimedes screw 1523:29

Demonstrating the principle of a screw 180:34

How a screw jack works experiment 1523:13

Screw is actually an inclined plane experiment with wood, screw and paper 1436:61-63

Screws and screw tops 281:52

What is a screw experiment 902:185-186

What kind of simple machine is the screwdriver experiment 902:187

SIMPLE MACHINES—WEDGES. *See also* WEDGES

Demonstrate how a wedge works using pencil 1479:101

Wedge, what is it and how does it help to do work experiment 1400:28-31

Wedges—nails and knives 281:52

What is a wedge experiment 902:183-184

Working with wedges 180:33

SIMPLE MACHINES—WHEEL AND AXLE

Block and tackle experiment; make with spring scales, clips, tape 1462:82-86

Fixed pulleys experiment; how to make from spring scales, tape, clips 1462:73-77

Machines make work easier demonstration 1404:124-125

Mousetrap cars experiment 1462:96-99

Moveable pulleys experiment, how to make from spring scales, clips, tape 1462:78-81

Pencil sharpener used as wheel and axle machine experiment 1400:47

Pulley geoboards experiment with wood, spools, thread, rubber bands 1462:92-96

Setup to investigate properties of wheel and axle experiment 1157:120-122

String tied to shaft of pencil sharpener lifts books experiment:940

Testing a wheel and axle 180:30

Toy trucks experiment with force needed to move trucks 1462:65-67

What is wheel and axle experiment 902:165-166

What type of machine is the pencil sharpener experiment 902:167-168

Wheel and axle similar to a lever experiment 1400:56-59

Windlass, how to make from straws, paper cups, and clips experiment 1462:68-70

Windmill is a wheel and axle machine and helps do work experiment 1400:44-47

Wheel and axle machine 1400:46-47

366

SIMPLE MACHINES—WHEELS. *See also* **WHEELS**
   Can wheels help move something heavy experiment [Primary] 743:12
   Flywheel in automobiles experiment using spinning tops 1334:16-17
   Model of belt connected wheels, how to make 1400:55
   Roll on big wheels 232:97
   Rolling is easier than dragging experiment 898:35
   Spool roller, making 1001:9
   Steerable wheels demonstrated with model car made from cardboard experiment 1334:12-13
   Wheel and axle 281:47
   Wheels and gears—experiment 664:22-23
   Wheels can be made to rotate faster experiment 1400:60-63
   Wheels connected with belt experiment 1400:52-55
   Why are belts and chains used to turn wheels experiment 834:59-60
   Wind power and winch lifts bucket in model well experiment 1334:18-19

SIMPLE MACHINES—WINDLASS (WHEEL AND AXLE)
   Making a windlass and experiments to try 606:27-35

SIMPLE MACHINES—WORK
   Primary experiments with work 100:14-27

SIMPLESSE. *See also* **MICROPARTICULATION**
   Ice cream taste and texture compared with Simplesse fat substitute experiment 1484:132-133

SINGING
   How do notes rise and fall when singing experiment 1279:12
   How loudly can you sing experiment 1279:15
   How vibrations make sounds experiment with balloon 1279:7
   Making high and low sounds experiment 1279:25

SIPHONS
   Energy saving aquarium drainer 399:56
   Experiment—using siphon 597:20-21
   Flow of liquids in a group of siphons 604:12-15
   Gravity affects siphoning process experiment 1399:68-71
   How does the siphon operate—what part does air pressure play 55:131-135
   How to make siphon using plastic tubing 1331:93
   How to siphon demonstration 1211:23
   Liquids seek their own level demonstration 837:19-20
   Make a fountain siphon 385:15-17
   Make a simple siphon 360:45
   Make a siphon 161:66-67
   Make a siphon experiment 926:61-64; 965:23
   Make and demonstrate how siphon works 919:11
   Make self-starting siphon from straws 202:112
   Make siphon bottle—a multi purpose device 217:14-19
   Make siphon from glass bottles and plastic tubing experiment 1179:136-137
   Making a simple siphon (Primary) 210:15
   Making a siphon fountain 507:1902
   Measuring air pressure in siphons 217:38-43
   Move water back and forth between two glasses 611:47-49
   Operation of a siphon; three observations experiment 871:3.015
   Pressure fountain moves water upwards experiment 1179:136
   Pushing water up—fire extinguishers—balloon, siphon bottle 217:21-27

   Show how siphons use air pressure 128:84
   Simple siphon demonstration using cloth siphon experiment 1230:76-77
   Siphon clock, how to make with experiments 951:41-45
   Siphon experiments; how to do and how to have siphon race 1157:68-70
   Siphon fountain in plastic bottle with straws and cork experiment 1243:26-27
   Siphoning system produces continuous running water experiment 884:77-78
   Siphoning water, how to 884:73-76
   Siphons—action of—make water run uphill 385:14-15
   The siphon experiment 281:14
   Transfer water by siphon experiment 940:18-20
   Using a siphon 53:36-37
   Water siphon machine using two jars and tubing—how to make 558:58-59
   Water travels uphill experiment 884:68-71
   Water your plants through siphoning experiment 1243:20

SIREN DISK
   Siren disk demonstrates pitch depends on speed of rotation 2:24-27

SIZE
   Determine size and distance of object experiment 1132:87-1-87-2

SIZE—RELATIVITY
   Concepts of big and bigger, of small and smaller (Primary) 455:1-33

SKATE SAIL
   Country skate sail—how to make 310:28-32

SKATERS
   Skater model speeds up spin at end, how to make 1190:21-24

SKELETONS
   Animal skeletons—how to prepare 117:27-31
   Chicken skeleton—making 749:28-29
   Flesh out a cardboard dinosaur skeleton with paper strips, paste experiment 1169:28-29
   How to make small animal skeleton 400:30
   How to turn a carcass into a skeleton 375:47
   Model of giraffe demonstrates need for skeleton 1168:11
   Mounting—how to 436:71
   Necklace from bones, how to make 1168:82
   Skeleton from heavy paper and paper fasteners, how to make 1168:76-77
   Skeleton of bat 375:36
   Skeleton of bird 375:3, 38
   Skeleton of cat 375:31
   Skeleton of cow 375:25
   Skeleton of dog 375:30
   Skeleton of fish 375:44
   Skeleton of frog 375:43
   Skeleton of horse 375:27
   Skeleton of human joints made with toothpicks, how to do 898:67
   Skeleton of man 375:2, 21, 22
   Skeleton of mole 375:37
   Skeleton of mouse 375:35
   Skeleton of pig 375:29
   Skeleton of rabbit 375:33
   Skeleton of sheep 375:28
   Skeleton of snake 375:42
   Skeleton of squirrel 375:34
   Skeleton of tortoise 375:41

SKIER

Skier model toy—how to make 466:20-21

SKIING

Losing weight on skis experiment 1154:49-51

SKIMMY

How to make a skimmy 310:14-16

SKIN. *See also* **HUMAN BODY—SKIN**

A skin illusion—hot and cold hand test 366:172

Charting nerve endings in the skin 148:78

Checking the temperature receptors in the skin 148:79

Demonstrate built in thermostat of skin 294:90-91

Discovering some functions of the skin 148:61

How does our skin protect us project 901:159

How skin protects you 133:23-24

How the skin keeps cool and warm 133:26-27

How the skin throws off body wastes 294:89-90

Measure how much skin you have 133:22

Skin receptors project, data sheet given 817:18

Skin sensors—test with nail 549:17-19

Test how creams and lotions act as a barrier to water evaporation 441:33-36

Where is your skin most 'touchy' 381:98-100

SKIN—ANIMAL

Skinning and drying an animal skin—how to do 530:346

SKIN—SENSE RECEPTORS

Hot spots and cold spots 399:66

SKIN—SENSORS

Messages from the surface—locating sensors 366:168-172

SKIN CREAM

Recipe for 387:14-15

SKINKS

How to care for 279:11-13

SKULLS

Stripping skulls of matter and debris, how to do 1069:157

SKULLS—BIRDS

Black bird 375:12

Duck 375:13

Owl 375:12

Sparrow 375:13

SKULLS—MAMMALS

Cow 375:10

Dog 375:10

Mouse 375:11

Shrew 375:11

SKUNKS

Collection and care of 390:66-67

SKY

Blue color of Earth's sky demonstration with flashlight and milk 1394:28-29

Blue sky and red sunset experiment; demonstrate with flashlight and milk 1132:11-1-11-2

Building a star plotter—making 710:62-63

Charting the constellations—how to do 710:64

Clock in the sky—how to use 710:74

Color of sky 382:145

Colors in the sky experiment with glass of milk, flashlight 1480:165

Colors of night 292:123-124

Colors of sunset experiment 1126:13

Constellation projector, how to make 1293:57

Counting stars—how to do 710:71-72

Demonstrating how the colors of the sky are made project 833:141-142

Determine why Earth is called the blue planet experiment 1405:3

Eudoxus; who was first to draw a map of the sky project 1525:53-55

Halos in the sky, how to measure experiment 958:48-50

Handy way to make sky measurements 710:66-67

How planetariums produce images of the night sky experiment 1405:14-15

Light pollution survey of your local area project, how to do 1478:31

Make a sky map 231:117

Making a model of the celestial sphere project 833:77-78

Making a tennis sky dome 833:3-4

Mapping the sky by astrolabe—how to make 710:67-69

Measuring the blueness of the sky experiment 958:31

Measuring the Sun's altitude 710:69-70

Measuring the Sun's size 710:70-71

Model of sky—making [Primary] 742:61

Observing the motion of the sky 710:72

Observing the night sky 833:1

Photomap of the sky—making 710:64-66

Show color of sky and why it is that color 40:242-243

Sky clock to tell time on clear nights—how to make 763:33-38

Sky in a fishbowl experiment; how to make 958:33

Sky in a glass—experiment 670:53

Sky is blue and sunset is red; why—experiment 1322:80-83

Sky mapping—how to do 710:62-76

Sky mobile; what you might see in the sky, how to make 1373:18-19

Sky observations linked to holiday activities on Earth project 1062:116-117

Streetlight pollution experiment; design better light pollution streetlights 1478:30-31

Streetlight pollution of night sky viewing experiment; which pollutes most 1478:30-31

Sunset and blue sky—how to make experiment 761:84-85

Sunset; make using flashlight, milk and water experiment 1018:10-11

Sunset; why is sky colored experiment 1126:13

Surveying with triangles project 833:254-257

Telling time by the stars—how to do 710:75

Tyndall effect or why the sky is blue 102:127-129

What is your horizon 292:42-43

Why is the sky blue 176:38

Why is the sky blue and sunsets red experiment with gallon jug, water, flashlight 1478:28-29

Why is the sky blue flashlight—milk and water experiment [Primary] 742:22

Why is the sky blue; activities to demonstrate 1511:43-46

Why is the sky blue: because of colloids 382:143-145

Why is the sky red at sunset sometimes experiment 852:53-54

Why the sky is blue 705:12

Why the sky is blue, coffee creamer and water in glass experiment 893:24-25

Why the sky is blue experiment with soap in water 1482:52-53

Why the sky is not dark as soon as Sun goes down experiment 1405:7

SKY—NIGHT

Planetarium—making to project night sky 436:63

SKYSCRAPERS

Build a skyscraper from paper cups (Primary) 551:unpaged

Design of cantilevers supports load of skyscrapers demonstration 1094:34

Frame for skyscraper, how to make from straws 1122:10

How do skyscrapers keep from falling experiment 1293:47-48

Make your own skyscraper—building the core 496:24-26

Make your own skyscraper model—completed model illustration 496:55

Make your own skyscraper model—how to make the curtain walls (cladding) 496:36-37

Make your own skyscraper model—how to make the floors and roof 496:36-37

Make your own skyscraper model—start with the foundation 496:16

Making a movable elevator 496:32-33

Model city; how does design affect wind currents and shadows experiment 1094:38-39

Model skyscraper, how to build and test design in a wind experiment 1094:35-36

Newspaper tower, make and test for strength 1122:16

Raft foundation for skyscrapers, how it works experiment 1122:12

Skyscrapers in wind with balls on straw stands experiment 1332:16-17

Super structures for the future, how to make from clay and swizzle sticks 1094:40

Swaying in the wind experiment using tower of building blocks 1386:29

Foundation strength demonstration with sand and coin 987:26

Structure strength demonstration of curves, triangles, ribs and beams 987:26-27

Swaying in the wind dangerous to buildings; demonstrate 987:27

Wind funnels created by skyscrapers demonstration 987:27

SLEDGES

Make your own sledge 492:40

SLEEP

Dream time chart (Primary) 674:22

Practice relaxing your body (Primary) 674:16

Practice snoring (Primary) 674:24

Simple activities and demonstrations of sleep (Primary) 674:6-28

Sleep habits and sleep cycles of humans and animals experiment 1506:98-99

Sleep journal to survey sleeping habits of people 1272:28

To sleep perchance to dream—experiment 586:111-112

SLEIGH

Sleigh model—how to make (Primary) 466:24-25

SLIDE PROJECTORS. *See also* **PROJECTORS**

Flashlight slide projector, how to make 1053:15-16

Simple—how to make 472:2241

Slides for flashlight slide projector, how to make 1053:17-18

SLIDE RULE

Simple—how to make 406:34-35

SLIDES

Lantern slides for projecting 436:50

Microscopic slides—making 436:58

Mounting a slide, how to 889:20-22

Permanent slide mounts, making 889:22-24

Wet mount with bubbles, making 889:28

SLIDES—MICROSCOPE. *See also* **MICROSCOPE**

Slide box—how to make 713:32

Slides—making—how to do 713:28-31

Slide storage box—how to make 9:58-59

SLIDES—WATER

How to make water slides and give water slide show 236:137

SLIME

Gooey slime from cornstarch experiment 1231:34-35

Slimy goo 259:18-22

SLIME MOLDS. *See also* **MICROSCOPE; MOLDS**

Adventure 53—appearances can be deceptive—slime molds under microscope 403:205-209

How to grow and observe 500:141-142

SLOPES

Altering the sliding mass—demo with string and metal washer 247:8

Clinometer, make to measure angle of elevation and depression experiment 978:19-20

Determine slope of land and land use experiment 978:17-19

Different materials give different angles of rest on slopes experiment 1480:108

Experiments with slopes—use force measurer—how much pull to lift toy truck 419:12

Friction and gravity effect on slopes experiment with angle of failure 1480:108

Measure traveling speed and distance from different heights 274:30

Measuring a slope of land experiment 1424:47

Model hill or slope to compare slopes experiment 1480:112-113

Model slope or ramp demonstrates effort needed to get car up slope experiment 1334:6-7

Raindrops or rain impact shifts material on slope at an angle experiment 1480:119

Rock structure of slopes experiment, make from sand, and food colors in tank 1480:94-95

Sand saturated with water flows like liquid down slopes experiment 1480:111

Sand slopes experiment; shifting sand and pore pressure demonstration 1480:109

Shapes of slopes shown with model hillside experiment 1480:112

Size and weight of object affect speed when sliding down slopes experiment 1380:26

Ski jump game 247:7

Sliding a paper clip 247:6

Sliding different objects down slopes and time it takes experiment 1378:29

Slippery slopes experiment; show slipping slopes with soils in glass tank 1480:113

Slope affects soil erosion experiment 1046:52-54

Slope patterns, how to plot on map 1437:36-37

Slopes and gravity—overcoming gravity with toy car and rubber band 274:31

Slopes and rollers—experiments 664:20-21

Slopes hold together from cements in materials experiment with two sand castles 1480:110

Slopes of different materials—weight experiment 247:12

Slopes of same gradient—speeds of weight the same? 247:11

The gradient of a slope—how to calculate gradient of your slopes 247:10

The length of the slope—how long and how fast to move a weight 247:9

What's underneath surface of slopes can affect slipping of slope experiment 1480:111

SLOPES—NATURAL. *See also* HILLS

Temperature differences on a hill 253:95-96

SLUGS. *See also* SNAILS

Collecting snails and slugs, how to do 775:10-11

Effect of chemicals on slug's foot and movement experiment 864:93

Effect of cold temperature on slugs experiment 864:92-93

Effect of crowding on slugs experiment 864:93

Feeding slugs, how to 775:14-17

Food test experiment; what slugs and snails like to eat; shoe box, various food 1187:17

House for snails and slugs, how to make 1014:166

How to cage and care for 279:33

Jar home for snails and slugs, how to make 800:14-15

Raise slugs and snails in terrarium experiment 1472:24-29

Slugs' and snails' liquid armor—experiment 484:90

Tank for slugs, setting up, how to 775:12-13

Tongue prints from snails and slugs, how to collect experiment 1472:28

What leaves do snails and slugs like to eat best experiment 800:12-13

SMOG. *See also* AIR POLLUTION; POLLUTION—AIR

Create smog in a jar experiment 1063:361

Hydrocarbons in air pollution damage clothing experiment 1322:60-64

Make a particle trap 264:98

Make your own smog 112:21; 236:183-184

Make your own smog experiment 906:30-31

Making clouds, fog and smog experiment 947:36-37

Nylon stockings sensitive to acid pollutants experiment 1322:64

Pollution can harm clothing experiment 1322:60-64

Smog formation demonstration 1020:57-59

Smog formation; demonstrate how smog is formed experiment 978:171-172

Smog in a jar experiment, making 1017:57

Smog, making artificial smog experiment 933:40

Thermal inversion effect on air pollution experiment 1322:55-59

What causes smog experiment with match and jar 1003:81

SMOKE. *See also* FIRE; FIRE ALARMS

Chimneys, box and candle demonstrate how chimneys work 939:137-139

Make smoke obey 360:10-11

Smoke from the fingertips—chemical reaction experiment 563:33

Smoke has tiny solid particles experiment 1322:84-88

Smoke magic—make smoke appear 87:83

Smoke rises (Primary) 324:9

SMOKE RING CANNON

How to make 543:40-41

SMOKE RING MACHINE

How to make 487:16-17

SMOKING. *See also* CIGARETTES

Cigarette smoke pollutes your internal environment experiment 1427:56-58

Cigarette smoking machine experiment 933:41-42

Display to illustrate dangers of smoking 334:82

Does passive smoke harm mosquito larvae experiment 1096:58-63

Experiment to show effect of cigarette smoke on flies 174:48-49

How to make smoking machine 112:22-23

Is cigarette smoking really harmful—experiment 628:62-63

Material deposited by smoke from one cigarette experiment 1134:6.001

Second-hand smoke reduces lung capacity in children experiment 1195:69-77

Smoke from cigarettes remains inside smoker project 969:93

Smoking and the heart 334:32-33

Why do some people smoke—survey 400:40

SNAILS. *See also* SLUGS

Adventure 4—we become better acquainted with the snail under a hand lens 29:23-26

Adventure 41—do a bit of surgery on a snail's teeth under a microscope 403:151-153

Characteristics of snail observation 1290:73, 5.6

Collect and observe water snails for left and right handed shells 771:111-118

Collect eggs, hatch and observe 796:26

Collecting snails and slugs, how to do 775:10-11

Compare movement of with other small pond animals 173:18

Do pond animals prefer dim light or bright light experiment 796:28-29

Effect of chemicals on snail's foot and movement experiment 864:93

Effect of cold temperature on snails experiment 864:92-93

Effect of crowding on snails experiment 864:93

Estimate the snail population experiment 1070:26-27

Estimating and calculating a snail population 507:1903-1904

Experiment—snail maze 151:66-68

Experiments—view muscle, test sight, follow their trail over sharp surfaces 480:62

Feeding, how to 775:14-17

Felt snail pattern, making 894:57

Finding out how snails behave 148:51

Food test experiment; what slugs and snails like to eat; shoe box, various foods 1187:17

Hatch garden snail eggs experiment 1085:29

Have a snail race 264:38

Homing behavior in snails in the field and in the laboratory 266:49-52

House for snails and slugs, how to make 1014:166

How far a snail moves experiment 1298:7

How fast is a garden snail experiment 1524:25

How much food does a snail eat in a day experiment 792:28-29

How much food does water snail eat in a day experiment 796:29-30

How snail moves along experiment 1085:41

How snails grow experiment 1183:36

How to find and observe 264:37-39

Jar home for snails and slugs, how to make 800:14-15

Keeping a snail, how to 820:9

Keeping snails, how to do 975:28-29

Land snails—enjoy watching land snails 236:59-60

Land snails, how to keep and feed 1117:28-29
Limpets return to same spot after feeding on rocks experiment 1085:35
Magnetic snail toy—how to make (Primary) 466:14-15
Moist soil preferred by snails demonstration 1358:22
Mud snail race, setting up, how to 772:26-27
Mud snails, how to collect and observe feeding behavior 1117:31
Observe and record behavior of pond snails 166:105-106
Observe snails' behavior in aquariums experiment 1492:72-73
Pond snails—observe 62:59-60
Raise slugs and snails in terrarium experiment 1472:24-29
Snail eggs experiments 500:123-124
Snail race, how to set up for races 800:20
Snail race, how to set up for racing 1524:24
Snail races, how to set up 897:42
Snail shell dissolves in vinegar mixture experiment 1392:15
Snail watching experiment 1183:84
Snail watching, how to do 1182:36
Snail's pace affected by temperature 266:72
Snails give off or take up carbon dioxide experiment 1427:38-39
Snails like wet and dark places, simple experiment to test 1098:12
Tank, setting up to keep snails, how to 775:12-13
Test snails for sense of smell and sight experiment 762:66-68
Tongue prints from snails and slugs, how to collect experiment 1472:28
Tracking snails by marking their shells experiment 1069:116-117
Water snails, how to keep 894:53
What leaves do snails and slugs like to eat best experiment 800:12-13
Why is the snail so unusual experiment 901:98-99

SNAILS—COLLECTION AND PRESERVATION
Collecting snails 62:53-54
How to care for a snail (Primary) 254:entire book
How to catch and preserve 117:39-40
Make a snail house 119:106
Snails and slugs—how to cage and care for 279:33

SNAILS—WATER
How to set up aquarium and observations to make of water snails 163:18-21

SNAKES
How snakes shed their skin experiment 1405:35
Outdoor investigations for experiments 166:47-50
Outdoor projects with 118:57-63
Snake house, how to make 436:9

SNAKES—CHEMICAL
How to make 87:44-45

SNAKES—COLLECTION AND PRESERVATION
Collection and care of 390:51-54
How to cage and care for 134:36-37; 279:8-10
Snake cage—how to make 9:46-47; 128:59-60; 234:36-37

SNELL, WILLEBRORD
Law of refraction of light experiment 1133:6.004

SNOW
Activities with snow 236:148-151
Amount of air in snow experiment 1180:6; 1183:134

Black cloth and aluminum foil on snow melting experiment 1003:15
Blowing snow experiments 563:88-89
Convert snowfall into rain measurement experiment 860:196
Difference between snow and sleet experiment 1003:83-84
Do colors affect melting of snow 236:150
Does salt change temperature of snow 277:12
Does same amount of snow fall everywhere outdoor activity [Primary] 744:26
Experiments with snow 693:25-29
Filter variety of water samples and snow experiment 1063:371
How clean is snow 236:150
How is snow compacted into ice to form glaciers experiment 900:133
How is snowfall measured experiment 1293:91-92
How much snow to make one (1) cup of water 277:9
How much water comes from melted snow experiment 920:19
How much water in snow—experiment 694:36-37
How much water is formed when snow melts experiment 804:15
How much water is in snow experiment 921:40; 1086:24
How to measure snowfall as precipitation experiment 1439:92-94
Insulation properties of snow, measure with thermometers experiment 921:40
Is it warm under the snow 333:70-71
Keep snow from melting experiment 920:17
Liquid water content of snow, how to measure 1465:18-20
Make snow sherbet 236:150
Measuring snow and icicles experiment 885:46
Measuring snowfall—how to 629:64
Measuring snowfall experiment 978:137-138; 1063:448
Measuring the amount of water in snow experiment 1149:30
Melt snow faster with dark paper experiment 920:18
Melting snow—experiments with 75:83-84
Melting snow takes up less space (Primary) 541:32
Mini-experiments to study snow 1063:284
pH of acid rain and snow experiment 1526:98
Record and chart snow depths in various places 277:10
Silence of snow experiment 1066:100
Simulate snowfall in model forest, how to do 1063:220
Snow as insulator—check temperature in snow bank and air (Primary) 583:10-19
Snow candles—how to make 277:129-130
Snow equals how much rain experiment 762:43-44
Snow fall—experiment to measure snow fall 175:63
Snow games 277:127-129
Snow gauge—how to make 75:84-85; 236:149; 277:7-9; 494:84; 921:42
Snow gauge—making (Primary) 535:24
Snow gauge to measure snowfall, how to make 1070:24
Snow goggles—Eskimo snow goggles—how to make 494:89
Snow goggles, how to make 920:21; 921:7
Snow has air in it—experiment (Primary) 327:35
Snow igloo—how to make 277:130
Snow is good insulator, a temperature test for 629:69
Snow is made of water and air—experiment 40:61-64
Snow keep things warm—experiment 694:39

Snow lights—how to make 75:93
Snow lights from colored snowballs, how to make 920:23
Snow melts faster with certain colors 277:11-12
Snow painting in frame, how to make outdoors 921:49-50
Snow pollution tester and chart, how to make 850:23
Snow sculptures—how to make 277:130
Snow shadows 277:130
Snow snake—how to make 442:unpaged
Snow storm in a jar, making 905:156-157
Snow storm in jar experiment with boric acid crystals and water 1479:60
Snow taffy—how to make 277:130
Snow thermometer, how to make 850:24
Snowman—in a jar snowstorm 146:29
Snowstorm—make a snowstorm jar with a scene 410:12
Snowstorm—making a 146:28-29
Temperature of snow—how cold is snow 75:87-88
Temperatures—taking snow temperatures with thermometer and yard stick 494:85
Test for visible pollutants—how to 629:68-69
Tracks in snow—how to make permanent casts of them 75:92
Water content of snow, how to measure experiment 1516:104
Wet and dry snow—experiment with 75:86
What is snow made of experiment 834:18

SNOW SNAKES
How to make 629:121-122

SNOWFLAKES
Catching snowflakes—how to 694:38
Collect and study snowflakes, how to do 1063:285
Collect snowflakes, make slides and observe under microscope 921:37-39
Collect, examine and classify snowflakes experiment 1372:76-77
Collecting and recording shapes 277:6-8
Collecting crystals, how to do 909:16
Collecting snowflakes 62:17-18
Examine snowflakes with magnifying glass (Primary) 583:9
How to preserve and classify snowflakes as to shapes 75:90-91
Identifying (Primary) 535:25
Making permanent casts 436:71
Paper snowflakes, how to make 1227:51
Paper snowflakes, making 793:25
Patterns—shapes and sizes—evaluation experiment 715:134-135
Patterns to cut from paper, how to do 913:47
Preserve snow flakes with plastic spray 629:61
Preserve snowflakes on slides, how to do 1017:40
Preserve snowflakes to study their structure experiment 978:139-140
Preserving snowflakes 657:70-71
Preserving snowflakes experiment 959:94-96
Prove snowflakes are frozen water and snow is snowflakes with air between them 494:88
Save a snowflake—how to do 586:19-20
Six-sided paper flakes, how to make 1372:74-75
Snowflake catcher—how to make to observe single snowflakes 494:96
Snowflakes are crystals of water 44:74-75
Snowflakes under microscope—compare and draw 713:45-47

Wax "snowflakes"—making 585:144
What is the best way to catch snowflakes 381:72
Why snowflakes float demonstration 1479:84
Why snowflakes float experiment 1023:174-175

SNOWMOBILES
Snowmobile model—how to make (Primary) 466:26-27

SNOWSHOES
How to make 442:unpaged
Making snowshoes from conifer branches, wood frame and plywood 277:122-127

SOAP. *See also* **DETERGENTS**
Absorption effects from soap solutions 88:56-57
An emulsion of oil and water 122:164-168
As a colloid 88:28-29
As an emulsifying agent 88:26-27
Battery from soap solution, aluminum, and penny makes electric currents 1482:54-55
Biochemicals eat boiled egg experiment with regular and "biological" detergent 1271:32
Blowing bubbles experiment 909:31
Boat; soap boat races across water experiment 1482:60
Boiling of water affected by soap 88:36-37
Break it up—soap breaks big drops of oil into small ones—experiment 26:108-110
Breaks the skin (surface tension) of water 96:31
Capillarity of soap solutions 88:32-33
Characteristics of a base 88:20-21
Cohesion effects from soap in water 88:52-53
Colloids in soap 382:144-146
Copy picture from newspaper with soap, water, mineral spirits experiment 1482:56-57
Density—effects of melting and beating on a bar of soap 88:16-17
Deodorant soap is more able to kill bacteria than pure soap experiment 1395:123-124
Deodorant soap kills bacteria or retards bacterial growth—experiment 441:21-24
Detergents keep oil and water from separating experiment 1482:4-5
Does soap really help clean things—experiment 26:106-108
Doming or pouring of soap 88:30-31
Drops of soap needed to make suds in different water samples experiment 1396:131
Effect of soap, shampoo and conditioners on hair—experiments 441:75-78
Effects of different chemicals on solubility of soap in water 88:12-13
Effects on surface tension of water 88:10-11
Electrical conductivity of soap 88:22-23
Enzymes improve dirt removing power of soap—experiment to test 26:120
Evaporation of water effected by soap 88:40-41
Expansion and contraction of soap from heating and freezing 88:54-55
Freezing point of water effected by liquid soap 88:38-39
How does soap help clean things—experiment 26:108-110
How much soap is needed to soften water experiment 1396:132-133
How soap works 85:50-51
How soap works experiment using laundry detergent and grease or shortening 1435:49-52
How to make soap 83:43; 84:89-90
How to make soap and discover how it cleans 319:91-93

Indicator, making to see if soap is acid or base experiment 781:40-41
Lubricant—effect of soap as 88:18-19
Magic matches experiment 909:30
Magnification effects from soap in water 88:48-49
Make a bar of soap experiment 1482:18-19
Make salad oil soap 203:31
Make soap on a rope 364:110
Makes clothes cleaner (Primary) 322:12-13
Making soap experiment 1259:39-44
Marshmallow soap, how to make 859:19
Oil chaser—experiment 585:25-26
Oxidation effects from layer of soap 88:46-47
Painting pictures with detergent bubbles 150:134-135
Recipe for soap balls or soap tablets 387:16-17
Refraction effects from soap in water 88:50-51
Saltwater soap—sailors soap—experiment 585:97-98
Salty water doesn't make many soap bubbles experiment 1482:6-7
Saponification—effects of 88:58-59
Soap action—make an emulsion 585:93
Soap and hard water—effect of hard water on soap—experiment 441:12-14
Soap boats, making 909:30
Soap cleans skin and breaks surface tension of milk experiment 1482:10-11
Soap crayons—how to make 732:162
Soap curds—how to make 364:109
Soap defogger—demonstrate action on surface tension 203:49
Soap doesn't dissolve easily in cold water but detergents do experiment 1482:14-15
Soap floats—how to make from soap and plastic 732:77-78
Soap in hard water 85:52-53
Soap makes water wetter 122:168-173
Soap, making 860:49-50
Soap molecules spread more slowly on surface of water or oil experiment 1251:52-54
Soap on the job—soap helps get oil out of cotton materials—experiment 26:106-108
Soap or detergent acts as emulsifier experiment with oil/water/food colors 1476:128
Soap powder that works "biologically" and traditional powder experiment 1179:41
Soap power boats 663:22
Soap that has no chemical additives, how to make 1228:80-82
Soap versus detergent—test different soaps and detergents 441:14-16
Soap weakens surface tension 44:64-65
Soapless soap—how detergent works in hard water—experiment 26:117-118
Soaps and deodorants kill underarm bacteria experiment 1221:21-22, 36-37
Soaps and detergents as wetting agents or surfactants 17:8-10
Soaps and detergents hard surface cleaners—experiment 17:6-7
Spectrum of colors seen 88:44-45
Stains; which laundry detergent or soap removes clothing stains project 1210:57-60
Sudsing—effect of different waters on 88:14-15
Test soaps and detergents to see if they are acidic or basic 441:19-21

Testing hard water with soap solution 78:46-47
Testing suds making ability of soaps experiment 1259:45-47
Testing water for hardness with soap solution 78:42-43
Tricky soap 350:66-67
Tyndall effect using dry soap 88:34-35
Tyndall effect using powdered soap 88:34-35
Viscosity of soap 88:24-25
Wetting effect of soap and detergent experiment 905:54-55
What hard water does to soap—experiment 26:115-117
What's inside bars of soap that float experiment 1482:16-17
Where do bathtub rings come from experiment with hard water and soap 1482:58-59
Which solution washes cleanest, soap or detergent experiment 804:28
Why does soap get us clean: because of colloids? 382:145-146
Why does soap make suds experiment 860:49-50
Why sky is blue experiment with soap in water 1482:52-53
Why soap hurts your eyes experiment with cabbage juice acid/base indicator 1482:50-51
Why soap makes suds experiment 1294:42-44
SOAP BOAT
How to make 364:113
SOAP BUBBLES. *See also* **BUBBLES**
3-D bubble shapes experiment 1108:9
3-D bubbles, how to make 924:53
Air escaping from bubble moves paper experiment 827:125
Are soap bubbles attracted by a negative charge 396:56-58
Backyard and bathtub bubbles, how to make 838:38-40
Basic bubble blowing techniques with wire loops experiments 1412:230-231
Beginning bubbles, how to make 838:18-23
Best soap bubble solution with soap and glycerin experiment; recipe given 1482:20-21
Bigger the container; bigger the bubbles experiment 782:48-53
Blow bubbles inside other bubble experiment 1230:74-75
Blow many kinds of bubbles—how to 733:32
Blowing bubbles and catching in different ways (Primary) 339:34-39
Blowing bubbles experiment 1063:147-149; 1161:26
Blowing bubbles experiment; recipe for bubbles given and how to make frame 1331:26-27
Blowing bubbles inside other bubbles, how to do 924:56
Blowing bubbles, how to make solution [Primary] 897:39
Blowing bubbles, recipe for 827:113
Blowing soap bubbles (Primary) 339:7-21
Blowing soap bubbles, recipe, and how to do 1415:39
Bouncing a bubble, how to do 838:24-27
Bubble art experiment 1108:7-8
Bubble art works and sculpture, making 914:46-47
Bubble blower, how to make 827:116-117; 861:250-255
Bubble brew, making, different experiments to try 870:24-26
Bubble city, how to make from soap bubbles, recipe given 1289:6-7
Bubble cube, how to make 838:45-52
Bubble dome experiment 1108:8

Bubble films and boat races experiment; data tables given 871:3.013

Bubble images demonstration 722:31

Bubble jet motors experiment 914:32-33

Bubble juice, recipe, making 838:38

Bubble making machine—how to make 487:42-43

Bubble mix recipes 827:114

Bubble pipe and soap bubble mixture, how to make 1256:22-23

Bubble pipes, making 914:19

Bubble power station experiment 914:31

Bubble prints to show bubble cluster patterns, how to make 935:90-91

Bubble solution, make and blow bubbles 905:60-61

Bubble stand for your bubbles, how to make 827:122

Bubble tips for better bubbles 827:115

Bubbles dance with static electricity experiment 827:126

Bubbles from frame experiment, making 914:22

Bubbles inside bubbles, how to make 838:35-37

Bubbles that bounce and fly experiment 914:34-35

Carbon dioxide gas from baking soda and vinegar blows up soap bubble experiment 1482:38-39

Carousel bubbles, how to make 838:53-57

Caterpillar bubble, how to make 838:68-71

Circus of bubbles tricks, how to do 914:36-41

Colored soap bubbles from baking soda, vinegar, and food coloring experiment 919:31

Colored soap bubbles, how to make 1179:94-95

Colors and patterns in soap bubble film experiment with flashlight 1482:48-49

Colors and shapes of bubbles activities for classroom 1291:3-4

Crystal soap bubbles freeze into balls experiment 909:31

Cubic bubbles experiment, making 914:23

Detergents; which detergents make the best bubbles project 1210:44-45

Double and triple bubbles, how to make 924:49

Double bubble experiment 808:86-88

Elastic soap bubbles—experiment 563:121

Electricity and soap bubbles experiment; balloon attracts soap bubble 1482:36-37

Experiments with soap bubbles (Primary) 339:7-48

Flexible bubble frame by Bernie Zubrowski makes big bubbles experiment 1482:34-35

Frozen soap bubbles experiment, how to do 1482:53

Galactica bubble, how to make 838:65-67

Geometric art with soap films experiment 1132:88-1-88-2

Giant bubbles, how to make 924:50-51

Giant soap bubbles experiments; recipe for solution and big bubble device 1132:16-1-16-2

Giant soap sheet with frame and trough experiment, how to make 1476:46-48

Helium bubbles from helium balloon experiment 1482:46-47

Hoop produces giant soap bubbles experiment 1482:32-33

Hot bubbles fly up quickly experiment, recipe given 1014:106

How do two bubbles affect one another experiment 827:120-121

How thick is a soap bubble 586:27

Inside out bubble, how to make 838:31-34

Jewel bubble, how to make 838:58-63

Look for reflections in soap bubbles (Primary) 149:59-61

Love bubble, how to make 838:72-75

Lungs; measure how much air comes out of your lungs experiment with soap bubble 1482:42-43

Make bubble building blocks (Primary) 149:40-48

Make domes and other bubble houses (Primary) 149:34-39

Make geometric shapes (Primary) 149:29-33

Make giant bubbles 203:48

Make long lasting bubbles (Primary) 149:54-57

Make shapes that move and change (Primary) 149:26-28

Make shrinking bubbles (Primary) 149:50-53

Make soap film curves (Primary) 149:22-25

Make solution and blow big bubbles 804:28

Make solution and blow bubbles experiment 1405:50-51

Making big bubbles (Primary) 149:16-19

Making bubble sculpture (Primary) 149:21

Making soap bubbles to test wind direction experiment 935:55

Measure bubbles (Primary) 149:49

Minimal surfaces experiment with bubbles 914:20

Mixture for making bubbles 914:17

Monster and dome bubbles, making 914:42-43

Monster bubbles—how to make 487:40-41

Physics at work in soap bubbles 670:32

Put a bubble in your bubbles's bubble experiment 827:124

Putting things inside bubbles experiment 914:37

Racing soap bubbles, how to make 924:57

Rainbow in a bubble experiment 827:123

Recipe and bubble machines—making 697:46

Recipe for and ways to make bubble blowers 494:70

Recipe for bubble mix 924:48; 1124:14-15

Recipe for bubble solution and how to make bubble blower 1228:84

Recipes for long-lasting bubbles 762:42-43

Salty water doesn't make many soap bubbles experiment 1482:6-7

Shape of soap bubbles affected by gravity experiment 1399:72-75

Shimmering soap bubbles from bubble holder experiment, how to make 1476:44-45

Soap bubble blowers, the loop and the tube, how to make experiment 1482:22-23

Soap bubble blows back in funnel and puts out candle flames experiment 1482:24-25

Soap bubble carries passenger man experiment, pattern given 1007:20-21

Soap bubble expands in hot water and contracts in cold water experiment 1482:40-41

Soap bubble film on plastic spiral experiment 1482:30-31

Soap bubble machine; combining simple machines makes compound machine 1400:71

Soap bubble mix, making 859:7

Soap bubbles—experiment 538:22-25

Soap bubbles—making 732:136-137

Soap bubbles and their shapes 88:42-43

Soap bubbles dance experiment, how to do 1007:42-43

Soap bubbles float on cushion of carbon dioxide gas experiment 1132:15-1-15-2

Soap circles, how to make 808:83-85

Soap film highways experiment to figure shortest route 808:93-96

Soap film painting creates array of colors experiment 1132:89-1-89-2

Soap films on frames, how to do 808:89-92

Soap films on three-dimensional frames experiment 1482:28-29

Space; shape of soap bubble where gravity force greater than on Earth 1399:74

Square bubbles—can you blow one 722:34

Square soap bubble experiment 1066:64-65

Stick finger through bubble without popping it experiment 1083:74-75

Sticky bubbles, recipe, how to make 1175:83-84

Substances increase bubble life under varying atmospheric conditions 997:70-72

Suds that stretch for bubbles 676:44-47

Sugar molecules make soap bubbles last longer experiment 1251:49-51

Super bubble solution, making 983:11-12

Super bubbles with coat hanger, making 914:18

Super bubbles, making 827:118-119; 914:24

Surface tension—demonstrate water skin with bubbles 339:22-29

Surface tension—experiment to show 126:73-79

Three bubble exp.—monster bubbles, slow breakers and soap film 399:84-85

Two wand bubbles, how to make 838:28-30

Warmth sustains surface tension experiment with soap bubbles 1476:95-96

Whale size bubbles, how to make 838:39-40

Which detergent produces the biggest bubbles experiment 882:13

Why ordinary bubble is shaped like a sphere experiment 914:21

Wiggly worm bubbles, how to make 838:42-44

SOCCER

Home field playing gives winning advantage in sports experiment 1195:79-93

Soccer board game with magnets, how to make 1043:28-29

SOCIAL ORGANIZATION—ANIMALS

Do animals benefit from living in groups rather than alone 402:43-44

SOCIAL ORGANIZATION—ANTS

Do ants living in groups have organization 402:45-46

SOCIAL ORGANIZATION—BIRDS

Do groups of birds have an organization 402:44-45

SOCIAL SCIENCE

Advertising—evaluate effectiveness of advertising campaigns 542:20-21

Aging population—growing old in your town or city project 506:16

Animal behavior—study of farm animal behavior 542:116-117

Automobile advertising claims unsubstantiated research project 506:45-46

Automobiles—develop an automobile history project 506:90-91

Average American—research statistics to determine if you are Average America 506:65

Beauty—project to determine if people agree or disagree on what is beautiful 506:49-50

Blue laws—project to determine blue laws at each level—local and state 506:106

Borrowing and lending—project to compare attitudes and practices of people 506:17-18

Busing—ways transportation costs might be reduced 506:66-67

Catalogs—compare prices of 1930s and wages with today 506:96-97

Catalogs—compare prices of 1930s with today 506:94-96

Change in a lifetime—time line of changes in history of your family 542:114-115

Community survey—is there a generation gap 542:136-137

Conformity or individuality—see how long it takes to introduce a new word 542:140-141

Container survey—investigate the litter situation in your town 542:65-66

Dialect study—vocabulary use is influenced by many things 542:107-108

Discrimination effects 542:25-26

Dynamic language—dictionary of terms used by particular age, interest groups 542:128-129

Economics and you—find where survey materials/products in home were made 542:138-139

Facts—what are they—use photographs/paintings of historical people 506:37

Family mobility study 542:35-36

Fences—project to consider types of fences and why we have them 506:92-93

Future shock—how much of the future do we really control—project 506:103-105

Garbage—Part I—find weight and classify family garbage created each week 542:84-85

Garbage—Part II—does analyzing garbage provide information about people 542:86-88

Goals—study goals of different school age groups 506:21-22

Government—Parts 1, 2, 3—administrative, law making, legal procedures 542:73-79

Government expenses—how much governments spend on you—project 506:64

Grammar—project lists some beliefs about teaching grammar and usage 506:88-89

Gun control—research/evaluate pros and cons and legislation effectiveness 542:49-51

Habits—explore unconscious habits 542:89-90

Hair—survey people in various occupations and age ranges as to hair style 542:101-103

Have a nice day project—keep track of activities—is it a nice day 506:73-74

Headlines—test knowledge of people by asking for interpretation of headlines 506:98-99

Heroes and culture—research to identify America's culture heroes 542:70-72

History through street names—research 542:124-125

Holidays—analyzing a society's special days 506:27-28

Horsepower—survey of horse population 542:96-98

Housewives—how do women feel about their jobs as housewives 506:51-52

Housewives—how much is a woman's work worth—survey 506:53-54

Income tax forms—compare results from several people doing same form 542:45-46

Inflation survey—consumer price index for your family 542:130-131

Information retrieval system—making 542:22-24

Inventions—patent information project 506:72

Inventions—study gap between invention and adoption of products 506:55-57

Language and society—analyze common phrases, meanings, use and origin 542:52-53

Living—city versus country research 506:29

Locks and keys—how often do people use them—how many kinds are there 506:47-48

Mass production—set up simple mass production operation 542:104-106

Metric system change—project—determine effect on people and business 506:43-44

Modern day Rip Van Winkle—project—your town 28 years ago and in future 542:56-57

Movies as culture clues—project 506:58

Names—investigate the names people use 506:23

Names—what's in a name project 542:58-59

Nature and society—evaluate impact of nature on several businesses 542:43-44

Nature and society—impact of nature on people in industrialized economy 542:39-40

Nature and society—impact of one upon the other 542:41-42

News reports—comparing 542:63-64

"On hold" in modern life—determine time spent "on hold" in modern life 542:132-133

Organizing your study 506:12-14

Populations—on the move—develop rate of mobility table and map findings 542:67-69

Power—examine power and way it is used in personal relationships 506:60-61

Pressure—what causes it—how you and others react to it 542:94-95

Prices—find out which prices are fixed and which are flexible 506:59

Problems—projects to examine aspects of community life and human behavior 506:1-106

Problems—projects to examine aspects of community life and human behavior 542:1-141

Products replacement study 542:27-34

Propaganda—identify kinds found in newspaper articles 542:112-113

Propaganda—identify kinds used in advertising 542:109-111

Recall of manufacturers products—study 542:47-48

Reporting the news—research of coverage given to different stories 542:122-123

Rhythms—recognize patterns of rhythms in you 542:91-93

Road traffic survey of traffic speeds at various times project 1070:34-35

Rules—and other—directed society project, examine how other directed we are 506:85-87

Science projects—reporting your study 542:12-16

Services—analyze the requirements of providing a service 506:62

Services—research services to homes most people are not aware of 506:70-71

Sex roles and jobs—research 506:32

Sex roles and magazines—research 506:33-34

Sex roles and media—how are differences in men and women presented 506:30-34

Sex roles and schools—research 506:32-33

Shoplifting—project from several angles 506:68-69

Sign language in road signs—project 506:35-36

Signs—thou shalt not—group signs into categories—project 506:100-102

Signs of the times—highway billboards, impact of Beautification Act—survey 542:54-55

Small talk—analyze this talk to see what it means 506:20

Somebody knows you project—who has information on you 506:63

Songs—trace some developments of hit songs 506:25-26

Swearing index to rate people 542:37-38

Take a can of corn—research product from its beginning to its consumption 542:134-135

The cemetery—project studying town's history through local cemetery study 542:82-83

The numbers game—numbers used on manufactured products 542:120-121

The numbers game—numbers used to identify people 542:118-119

Time—effect of lack of uniform time in this country 506:75-76

Town or city growth—research settled area, growth/change have taken place 542:126-127

Traffic survey, how to do 802:24

Transportation—choose a company and find out why it is located where it is 506:77-84

Transportation—cutting pollution through public transportation—research 506:82-84

Transportation—getting from suburbs to work without polluting atmosphere 506:80-82

Transportation—investigate mass transportation in your town 506:19

TV commercials—"happiness is"—study effects on variety of people 542:60-62

Weights and measures—a day with the inspector of weights and measures 542:80-81

Women's lib—image of women presented in children's books—project 506:41-42

Women's lib—research project on women's rights movement 506:40-41

Women's lib—research wage discrimination between men and women 506:38-39

Words—research use of superlatives 506:24

Year round school survey of information from concerned people 542:99-100

SOCIAL SCIENCE—CONSUMER USE OF SOFT DRINKS. *See* **SOFT DRINKS**

SODIUM BICARBONATE. *See* **BAKING SODA**

SODIUM CHLORIDE. *See* **SALT**

SODIUM FLAME

Making a sodium flame 1:93

SOFT DRINKS

As temperature of soda increases amount of carbon dioxide increases experiment 984:41-44

Bone in the pop—experiment 630:50

Brew it and bottle it yourself—how to do 404:124-128

Carbon dioxide amount in popular soda pop drinks experiment 1208:89

Carbon dioxide bubbles cause clay balls to float and sink experiment 1405:93

Coke Classic sinks and Diet Coke floats experiment 1063:144

Diet drink more dense or less dense than non diet drink experiment 1251:19-22

Experiment number 2—how do 'health clubs' advertise use of water 404:4

Experiment number 3—list different brands of bottled water from supermarket 404:5

Experiment number 4—create carbon dioxide—two ways with baking soda/yeast 404:9

Experiment number 5—carbon dioxide gas produced by Alka-Seltzer—match test 404:10

Experiment number 6—write about feeling of satisfaction from a soft drink 404:13

Experiment number 7—question soft drink bottler on manufacture/consumption 404:30

Experiment number 8—can ingredients be detected from Coca Cola—taste test 404:36

Experiment number 9—collect Coke and Pepsi ads for comparison 404:39

Experiment number 10—what does 'moxie' mean to different generations 404:43

Experiment number 11—learn history and popularity of soft drink companies 404:56

Experiment number 12—investigate soda pop collectibles 404:63

Experiment number 13—soft drink celebrity endorsement quiz 404:68

Experiment number 14—do you buy a soda pop because of slogans or songs 404:72

Experiment number 15—test the immortality of the Pepsi jingle 404:73

Experiment number 16—have people your age heard rumors on cocaine and Coke 404:75

Experiment number 17—do preference taste test—determine Pepsi challenge 404:87

Experiment number 18—determine psychological/motivational appeal in ads 404:91

Experiment number 19—do some comparison pricing of soft drinks 404:99

Experiment number 20—results of asking for Coke or Pepsi at restaurants 404:100

Experiment number 21—list hidden sources of sugar consumed in processed f 404:104

Experiment number 22—how many teaspoons of sugar are in average soft drink 404:105

Experiment number 23—determine amount of additives consumed from soft drink 404:115

Gas bubbles pushed out of soda by salt experiment 1405:51

Gas pressure in a carbonated drink experiment 1250:14-17

Ginger ale drink from yeast, recipe, how to make 1214:26-27

Ginger ale, how to make using yeast 835:12-14

Home soda fountain—recipes for different flavored syrups 404:135-136

Home soda fountain—recipes for sugar syrup, soda fountain pop—how to do 404:133-134

Make your own ginger ale 607:90

Making 350:73-74

Mist forms above liquid of carbonated drink when it is opened experiment 1250:18-20

Pepsi or Coke preferences, as to age group/male/female computer project 1021:39-40

Pick can of regular cola from can of diet soda blindfolded experiment 1083:76-77

Priestley, Joseph; who invented carbonated water project 1525:65-66

Recipes for root beer, ginger ale, herbal tea pops, fruit juice soda—make 404:130-132

Regular soft drink can sinks; diet soft drink can floats experiment 924:40

Removal of gas from a solution inflates balloon experiment 1405:60

Salt added to carbonated drink causes gas to be released experiment 1251:23-24

Soda pop, make with juice and baking soda experiment 807:149

Soft drink recipes—ice cream soda, ginger, juice, baked apples, etc. 404:137-140

Soft drink record of use and advertisements 404:XI

Test for carbon dioxide in soda pop 676:42

Test soft drinks and fruit "drinks" for vitamin C content experiment 1267:42-43

Tooth soaked in Cola has decay experiment 1069:163

Why bubbles form in glass of soda experiment 1479:52

SOIL CONSERVATION. See EROSION; SOILS—EROSION

SOIL POLLUTION

Some substances in landfills are toxic to living things experiment 1427:85-87

What is a landfill; miniature landfill shows pollution problems 1427:82-83

SOILS. See also COMPOST

Absorption and drainage in different materials experiment [Primary] 880:22

Acid and alkaline soils experiment 738:19

Acid rain effect on pH of water and soil experiment; chart given 1171:54-55

Acid rain effect on soils around your home experiment 1228:18-19

Acid rain effect on water plants and land plants experiment 1171:56-58

Acid soil or alkaline soil; cabbage indicator experiment 784:121

Acidity of soil experiment 1259:69-73

Acidity of soil test using red cabbage indicator experiment 1480:100

Acidity or alkalinity of soil material experiment using red cabbage indicator 1323:31-35

Activities with rocks and soil 236:164-167

Air; how much air is there in soil experiment 1134:1.007

Air; measuring air space in soils experiment 1480:98-99

Animal life in soil and leaf litter experiment 1134:1.012

Animals in area of soil, how to count and graph experiment 924:79-80

Animals in soil collected in funnel using strong light and funnel experiment 1069:121

Animals in soil sample, measure and examine 820:15

Animals in soil water collected using strong light and funnel experiment 1069:122

Animals that are recyclers 264:31

Animals that live in soil experiment 1336:65

Baking mud pies—experiment 633:28-29

Berlese funnel captures small insects that are in soil, how to make 1096:85-88

Bog soil compared to forest soil experiment 1061:58-59

Buffering capacity of soils to buffer acid rain experiment 978:174-175

Capillary action of water through soil particles experiment 978:14-15

Characteristics of different soil types experiment 1063:238-239

Clay nest with and without straw—experiment 633:32-33

Clinometer, make to measure angle of elevation and depression experiment 978:19-20

Collect different types of soil and analyze 380:24

Collect garden, farmland and woodland soil experiment to compare soil layers 1414:20-22

Collection of living organisms in soil experiment; set up collection station 1173:26-27

Colors in dirt—examine with a magnifying glass 633:12

Colors of soil layers experiment 1042:30

Compaction of soil; two simple tests for experiment 1063:240

Compare different kinds of dirt (Primary) 535:46-47

Comparison of soils by growing plants in them experiment 978:10-11

Composition of soil; what makes up soil experiment 1134:1.005

Composition of soil 37:49-52; 382:51-53

Composition of soils experiment 1259:67-68

Contour plowing and straight plowing effect on soil erosion experiment 1008:46-47

Contours, making to demonstrate erosion 874:214-215

Core sampling demonstration 1023:42-43

Core sampling; demonstrate core sampling of soils experiment 1479:70

Dams to save soil from erosion—experiment 633:46

Deltas form when river's soil load sinks faster in salty water experiment 1384:18

Demonstrate effect of erosion on soils experiment 760:49

Demonstrate how to conserve topsoil 175:13

Determine factors necessary for humus breakdown 175:15

Determine slope of land and land use experiment 978:17-19

Determine water retention of soils 175:14

Different kinds of soil have different amounts of clay/sand/silt project 1296:2000

Different sizes of soil particles can be separated experiment 1323:17-20

Discover factors related to evaporation of water from soil 175:76

Diversity and number of insects affected by amount of topsoil humus experiment 1096:83-89

Does popcorn seed grow better in subsoil, topsoil, or drained soil exp. 835:36-38

Does sand or soil hold more water experiment 1323:26-30

Earthworms important to soil building experiment 978:86

Effect of acid rain on soils—experiment 594:31-44

Effect of contour plowing on soil erosion experiment 978:31-32

Effect of different soils on plant growth experiment 797:31

Effect of grass on soil to protect against erosion experiment 978:29-30

Effect of mulch in preventing soil loss experiment 978:30-31

Effect of rain water on soil structure experiment 934:46

Effect of soil pH on plant growth experiment; data table given 871:2.009

Effect of soils on water retention experiment 762:45-47

Effects of acids on soil minerals—plant grows in soda water 86:30

Erosion; some soils erode faster than other soils project 1195:10-17

Examine soil for insects, worms, bones, roots, stems, etc. (Primary) 471:18-20

Examining soil life experiment 738:23

Experimenting with types of soil and effect on plant growth 898:52

Experiments to show kinds of soil 175:10-12

Experiments to show structure and properties of soil 128:63-66

Experiments with soil 382:51-55

Factors that aid in soil formation experiment 1424:33

Fertilizer and soil experiment 738:31

Finding animals in soil experiment 797:27

Forest soils—exploration of 268:11-15

Formation of soil from freezing rocks 253:46

Frost line where is it in your area project 715:18-19

Hard and compact soil affects ability of soil to absorb water experiment 1063:240

Household chemicals effect on germination and height of seedlings experiment 1004:2.012

How dense is dirt experiment 1527:40-41

How do plant roots respond to different soils experiment 1527:42

How is soil made experiment 900:156-157

How many animals in a shovelful of dirt 633:18-19

How many living things can you find in soil 381:121-122

How much water can soil hold experiment 918:43

How sediment layers are formed experiment 760:48

How soil is formed experiment 978:5

How soil is made by nature experiments 1341:64-65

How water passes through different kinds of soil experiment 760:46

Humus and its effect on amount of water soil retains experiment data table 1004:1.008

Humus; how much humus is there in soil experiment 1134:1.006

Hydraulic mining demonstration 1023:46-47

Importance of soil to the biosphere—experiment 371:84-88

Insects in soil; observe insects caught with funnel/bottle under light 1188:38-39

Insects in three different kinds of soil experiment using Berlese funnel 1097:51-53

Investigate soil in a vacant lot 233:9-11

Investigating soils—experiment 666:52-56

Investigation into the water holding capacity of soil 420:110-113

Investigation of forest floor—what animal life is present exp. 166:52-57

Irrigation water leaves salts in soil experiment 1323:51-55

Is all soil the same experiment; soil samples and water in jars demonstrates 1189:34-35

Kinds of dirt—collect and examine 633:13-14

Landfill containment area with little biodegradation occurring experiment 1295:51-52

Layers of soil experiment 1042:30-31

Life existing in soils experiment 1424:35

Life in the soil 268:89-93

Living organisms in soil; set up collection station experiment 1173:26-27

Make from small stones—how to 607:59

Make soil from natural materials experiment 1336:65

Make up of soil experiment 1180:31

Making miniature soil profiles 400:53

Making soil 874:212-213

Materials in soil; examine with magnifying glass experiment 1438:12-13

378

Measure pH of soils 285:21-23
Measure some properties of soils 285:21-26
Measure the porosity of soils 175:18
Measuring a slope of land experiment 1424:47
Measuring moisture holding capacity of soil experiment
 934:52-53
Microbes make things biodegradable experiment 1221:22
Microscopic life in soil experiment 1134:1.009
Mineral salts in the soil, how to filter out 790:23-24
Minerals; collecting dissolved minerals in soil experi-
 ment 1060:70
Miniature landfills experiment; biodegradability of mate-
 rials in dry/wet soils 1295:51-52
Models of methods to prevent soil erosion experiment;
 data tables given 1004:1.009
Moisture retention of soils experiment 1259:68-69
Mud pie science—puddle tests for dirt that makes mud
 633:24-27
Mulch, making in plastic bag using leaves, how to do
 879:66
Nematodes and other soil animals; collect with Berlese
 funnel experiment 1063:416
Nitrates and phosphates in different soils experiment
 1395:25
Nitrogen content of soils; compare different types pro-
 ject 969:11
Nutrient differences in soils experiment 1395:21-25
Nutrients in soil experiment 1259:73-75
Nutrients in topsoil affected by rain experiment 1405:77
Nutrients leached from soil are sufficient for plant
 growth experiment 1395:21-25
Observe the colonization of a small section of bare soil
 285:48-50
Observe what soil is made of 760:47
Observing the beginning of soil formation 285:81-82
Organic content of soils experiment, how to measure
 1480:101
Organisms and bacteria in soils not completely destroyed
 by heating experiment 1061:51-53
Particles; what kinds of particles make up soil experiment 1402:76-79
Parts and particles in soil—experiment 633:9-11
pH of soil affects color of hydrangea flowers experiment
 1060:114
pH of soil affects growth of different plants experiment
 1060:113
pH of soil experiment 1046:71-73
pH of soil experiment 1134:1.008
pH of soil, how to measure 1233:69
pH test for soils experiment 1042:31
pH test of soil, how to do 1054:20-21
pH; measure soil pH experiment 1527:39
Pile driver and resistance of sand to it project 969:19-20
Placer ore deposits demonstration 1023:44-45
Plant decay experiment 738:15
Plant growth in different soils experiment 1424:16
Plant growth; effect of soil composition on plant growth
 experiment 1134:1.011
Planting experiment in different kinds of soil 633:15
Plants affect erosion experiment 1046:55-57
Plants break down rocks into soil experiment 1323:47-50
Plants grow better in ant hill mound soil project 969:64-
 65
Plants grown in different soils experiment with compost,
 sandy and clay soil 1292:29
Plants keep soil from being washed away (Primary)
 262:unpaged
Plants prevent erosion of soil—experiment 633:45
Plants; do all soils provide necessary nutrients for plant
 growth experiment 1395:19
Potting soils, how to make 832:40
Prairie—what does a prairie horizon look like, how is it
 formed 371:84-88
Profile of soil layers 380:27
Profile of soil layers experiment 1046:38-40
Profile of soil, how to make 797:27
Profiles from different soil sites project 1063:237
Properties of soil experiment; observe what is in soil sam-
 ple 1046:41-43
Put earth sample in pie tin or box—with magnifying
 glass record what is found 452:46
Rain affects topsoil demonstration 1023:98-99
Raindrops cause erosion experiment 1046:61-62
Relationship between earthworms and humus in the soil
 experiment 1450:60-65
Relationship between humus and diversity and numbers
 of insects experiment 1096:83-89
River's soil load sinks faster in salty water than in fresh
 water experiment 1384:18
Rocks break down into soil 262:unpaged
Roots hold soil together experiment 1368:31
Runaway soil experiment demonstrates erosion 1424:80-
 81
Sample of soil, how to sort into types 689:46
Sediment in soil from beach, stream or river experiment
 1413:10-21
Sediment in water, measuring 874:213-214
Sedimentation of soil samples experiment 1527:34-36
Sediments—how do sediments settle underwater
 253:124-125
See how fast water soaks into different kinds of soil—
 (Primary) 262:unpaged
Separate out soil particles (Primary) 262:unpaged
Separating different soils in jar of water, how to do
 1379:27
Set up Berlese funnel to check number of living organ-
 isms in soil 175:30
Set up Berlese funnel to collect soil critters 864:95-96
Slope affects soil erosion experiment 1046:52-54
Soil absorption and water holding capacity experiment
 978:15-17
Soil and water experiment with plants 398:43-44
Soil and water in jar demonstrates layers of soil
 1437:110-113
Soil bacteria necessary to plant growth experiment
 1221:20
Soil bricks, making 867:13
Soil compaction and permeability and its effect on plant
 growth experiment 978:11-14
Soil composition sample, make a graph 689:46
Soil contains air and water experiment 867:12-13
Soil filtration demonstration 363:76-77
Soil from life—compost, keep journal of decomposition
 time 380:28-30
Soil from rock—sand, silt or clay—separate from soil
 samples 380:25-27
Soil gives off carbon dioxide limewater experiment
 722:71
Soil heats and cools more quickly than water experiment
 767:112

Soil is made of different sized particles experiment 882:29

Soil layers examined experiment 1424:36-37

Soil made of one layer or several layers experiment 1323:12-16

Soil movement by water and wind experiment 867:13-14

Soil particle size experiment 978:6-7

Soil particles separation experiment 829:49-50

Soil pH—how to adjust 398:34

Soil profile—what kind of soil is underground 253:126-127

Soil profiles in habitats project 1313:83-87

Soil properties activities [Primary] 759:29

Soil recyclers—make a fungus garden 264:31-33

Soil samples have plant seeds and animals (Primary) 262:unpaged

Soil soup shows different size particles 236:167

Soil structure of layers 285:25-26

Soil survey; samples of soils compared in jars of water experiment 1277:53

Soil treated—how soil treated in various ways affects animals 402:88-89

Soil types experiment 978:7-10

Soil under a hand lens 29:15-16

Soil with least reflectivity has highest temperature due to absorption ex 1062:62-63

Soil-animal survey to see what animals live underground experiment 1117:13

Soils and drainage experiment 738:13

Soils and their ability to buffer acid rain experiment 727:15

Soils contain molds and do these molds have antibiotic capabilities experiment 1267:71-75

Solids in the soil experiment 738:17

Specific heat of water compared to soil and air experiment 1172:20-22

Speed of running water affects erosion demonstration 1023:102-103

Sterilized soil used for growing seeds experiment 1061:124-125

Structure of soil experiment with soil samples in jar of water 1069:123

Temperature of soil at bottom of lake when top is frozen project 969:17-18

Temperatures of different soils and how fast they heat up experiment 924:91

Test acidic basic nature of soil experiment 1396:71

Test fertility of topsoil and subsoil 86:81

Test soil for acidity and alkalinity 236:165

Test soil for compactness 236:165-166

Test soil for humus experiment 1292:29

Test soil for moisture 236:166

Test soil samples for soil type, how to do 1326:19

Testing acidity or alkalinity of soil experiment 1069:120-121

Testing soil for acid 122:116-117

Testing soil for acidity and alkalinity 116:180

Testing soil for pH experiment 1042:31

Testing soils to find what makes up soil experiment 1362:18

Testing the soil for nutrients experiment 1424:62-63

Topsoil and humus—simple understanding (Primary) 471:1-33

Topsoil is good for growing plants; spoiled soil is not good experiment 1476:196

Topsoil protected by plants—experiment 633:44

Topsoil, examine for dominant species project 969:9-10

Topsoil, homemade, how to make science project 969:8

Water absorbing sand—experiment with sand and soil 563:66

Water absorbing capacity of different soils experiment 784:119-120

Water and layers of soil sediments in water experiment 1046:49-51

Water drainage through soil experiment 984:66-67

Water drains away through different soils at different rate experiment 1480:121

Water erosion on soil experiment 738:29

Water holding capacity of different soils experiment 1492:20-21

Water holding capacity of soil affects growth of crops experiment 1189:36-37

Water—holding capacity of soil 285:23-25

Water holding capacity of soils experiment 1424:108

Water holding capacity of soil experiment with soil and soda bottles 1527:37-39

Water in soils—how much water can different kinds of soil hold 253:128-129

Water in the soil experiment 741:9

Water moves in soil—percolation 253:130-131

Water moving through different kinds of soil experiment 797:29-30

Water retention of different soils test experiment 1061:54-55

Water retention of soils experiment, how to test and graph results 1476:195-196

Water separates materials in soil into layers demonstration 1438:18-19

Water travels faster thru soil in lake with bottom vegetation project 969:12-14

Water; how fast does water go through soil experiment 1046:47-48

Water; how much water can soil hold experiment 1046:44-46

Water; how much water do different soils absorb experiment 1159:116-117

Weathering; effect of motion on weathering demonstration 1479:76

What are clay and sand and how do they differ experiment 1323:22-25

What can you learn from a square meter of soil experiment 900:155

What dirt is made of—experiment 633:7-8

What is our soil like 253:121

What is soil; examine particles and layers experiment 917:34-36

What is soil made of experiment 852:19-20

What soil is made up of experiment 1183:159; 1336:65

What's in the soil experiment using soil sample 1480:98-99

Which soils contain most humus project 969:15-16

Which soils hold the most moisture experiment 959:193; 852:20-21

Wind causes soil erosion experiment 1046:58-60

SOILS—ECOLOGY. *See* **EARTHWORMS**

SOILS—EROSION. *See also* **EROSION**

Can temperature changes cause erosion experiment 852:23-25

Create or prevent erosion by trying to flush away mini mountain experiment 1328:77

Does rain erode the soil experiment 852:22-23

Effects of soil erosion and ways to reduce soil erosion experiment 1176:34-35

Environment needs mosses; observe mosses in jar moss garden experiment 1472:54-59

Erosion difference in bare soil and in grass covered soil experiment 1379:29

Erosion of grassy soil compared to plain soil experiment 1468:28

Erosion of soil—experiments 563:73-74

Experiment to show soil erosion 128:65-66; 330:79

Moss magic experiment; mosses dry up but don't die 1472:57

Moss works to protect soil from rain and prevent erosion experiment 1472:58

Moving air causes erosion of uncovered soil experiment 1323:37-41

Moving water causes erosion of uncovered soil experiment 1323:42-46

Plant roots save shoreline soil experiment; grow radish plants 1492:24-25

Plants help prevent erosion experiment 1341:66

Project to demonstrate erosion of soil 864:123-124

Rain effect on hills with and without ground cover experiment 1405:75-78

Rain runoff and erosion effect on different mountain soils experiment 1465:93

Rain splash erosion experiment; show rock layers protect soil beneath 1480:119

Running water on inclined board demonstrates erosion of soil 565:134-135

Soil aquarium demonstrate 293:4

Soil transportation by water—experiment to show 363:59-61

Why does soil erosion occur experiment 1294:20-21

SOILS—POTTING FOR PLANTS

Sterilization, fertilizer, pH—how to prepare soil 398:25-27

SOLAR CELLS

Constructing a solar cell experiment 1476:36-37

Light energy changed to heat energy—experiment 564:40

Photovoltaic cell produces electrical energy experiment 1502:69-70

Solar cell experiment 289:55

Solar cells as source of electric power experiment 902:256-257

Using solar cells—experiment 608:54-55

SOLAR CLOCKS

Solar clock, how to make from stones 1115:112-113

SOLAR COLLECTORS

Build to grow greenhouse effect 289:38-39

Construct a simple solar collector 253:91-92

How to make instant solar collector 347:14-16

Make a solar collector 231:16; 693:28-29

Model solar collectors; which absorbs the most heat experiment 1134:7.001

Project 47—model flat plate collector 654:94-97

Solar collectors, jar and box model, make and compare; data tables given 1004:1.005

Solar energy collecting experiments 1164:59-61

Solar greenhouse collector, how to make 870:16-18

Solar heat box, how to make from box, paper and black paint 1175:180-181

Solar power collectors—make your own 681:25

Solar water collector, making 772:75-76

Solar water warmer, simple, how to make 1175:180-181

Testing an alternative energy source [solar collector] project 833:128-129

SOLAR COOKERS

Bake a potato in a solar cooker, how to make 909:165

Cardboard—silver-coated mylar—making 697:24

Cardboard and foil cooker, how to make 1412:91

Dessert of chocolate and marshmallows made using solar cooker experiment 1014:107

Heat hot dog in solar cooker experiment, how to make 1519:13

How to make 634:38

Reflecting solar cooker—how to make (Advanced) 347:49-54

Show how Sun's reflections cook food 140:11

Simple solar oven, how to make from boxes and aluminum foil 1115:115-118

Solar cardboard cooker—how to make 38:31-47

Solar cooker—how to make 140:12; 289:40-41; 399:28-29; 1175:181; 1303:28-29

Solar cooker—how to make with Fresnel lens 386:56-57

Solar cooker—make a sun dog cooker 171:24-25

Solar cooker cooks marshmallows experiment 1063:369

Solar cooker from cardboard and aluminum foil, how to make 1372:10-13

Solar cooker from cardboard boxes, foil, tape and wire experiment, make 1453:39-42

Solar cooker, cardboard boxes and foil, how to build 979:45-47

Solar cooker, how to build from cardboard, aluminum foil and wire 1269:74-75

Solar cooker, how to make from car headlamp 624:33

Solar furnace cooker—how to make 289:43-45

Solar oven—how to make 38:48-56

Solar oven and cooker—how to make 218:57-65

Solar toaster, make from oatmeal box and aluminum foil 1335:24

Sun's light and heat can be focused—experiment 489:27-29

Supper by sunlight experiment—make solar cooker with aluminum foil and bowl 575:24

Three solar cookers, how to make 887:60-62

Using the Sun to cook your food 189:62-68

SOLAR DISTILLATION. *See* **SOLAR STILL**

SOLAR ECLIPSES. *See* **ECLIPSES—SOLAR**

SOLAR ENERGY. *See also* **SUN**

Absorption of radiant heat by water and soil experiment 1516:47 48

Angle of slopes or surfaces affects heat it receives from Sun experiment 1480:154

Black box traps Sun's energy—experiment 489:30-31

Black can absorbs more heat experiment 723:154-155

Black cloth and aluminum foil on snow melting experiment 1003:15

Black hotter than white 289:33-34

Collect and use solar energy efficiently experiments 978:123-124

Color affects energy absorbed from light experiment 902:71-72

Constructing a solar furnace (Advanced) 189:45-59

Converging lenses focus Sun's ray to focal point 289:36-37

Cups of ice covered with colored cloths demonstrates (Primary) 695:30

Different colors and surfaces affect heat from Sun experiment 1003:14

Do colors absorb solar heat differently 236:184-185

Drying clothes calculate drying time in shade—sunlight—dryer experiment 715:108-109

Effect of solar energy on making fresh water from salt water experiment 978:124-125

Electricity directly from the Sun; silicon solar cell experiment 895:95-96

Electricity from sunlight experiment 1152:52-53

Food dryer using solar energy, how to build 986:89

Food dryer; solar food dryer, how to make 1265:89

Get the most energy from sun experiment 902:47

Greenhouse effect solar water heater; wooden frame, tubing, bottle, experiment 1249:11-16

Heat energy from sun warms—water (Primary) 626:5

Heat from Sun burns hole in paper experiment 1519:12

Heat from the Sun—experiment 659:36-37

Heat from the Sun, colored fabrics on snow experiment 898:18

Heat trap takes heat from sun and warms water experiment 1032:8-9

Heat water with solar energy experiment using pie pans, and black paint 1427:112-115

Heating with colored solar energy 586:93

How a solar house works diagram 634:27

Make a solar cell 140:29

Make a solar water heater (Primary) 155:22-23

Making sun tea 289:35

Maximizing the efficiency of solar cells experiment 1450:86-91

Measure how much solar energy is reaching your location on Earth experiment. 763:15-16

Photovoltaic cell experiments 762:124-125

Plants make sugars from sunlight energy; measure that stored energy experiment 1134:7.004

Project 43—solar air heating 654:90-92

Project 44—solar water heating 654:92

Project 45—color and solar energy 654:92-93

Project 46—greenhouse effect 654:93-94

Project 48—which way is south 654:97-98

Project 49—mapping the Sun 654:98-100

Project 50—storing solar energy 654:100-102

Project 51—salt or water storage (Advanced) 654:102-103

Project 52—tracking the Sun (Advanced) 654:103

Project 53—build model solar home 654:103-105

Project 56—solar to mechanical energy 654:106-107

Project 57—solar constant (Advanced) 654:107

Reradiation—measuring the Sun's energy 289:31-32

Salt from seawater experiment 1498:17

Show greenhouse effect with solar collectors 289:38-39

Simple expansion solar engine—how to make (Advanced) 289:48-54

Snow and ice reflect sunlight; dirt and dark ground absorb it experiment 1322:40-43

Solar baked apple slices 236:184

Solar battery, how to wire and set up 830:25-26

Solar building model; build to demonstrate heat from solar energy 1152:119-121

Solar cell current increases when reflector concentrates Sun's rays experiment 1243:28

Solar cell experiment 289:55

Solar cell, current increases from Sun's rays 472:2234

Solar cells; how we get energy from the Sun experiment 1293:35-37

Solar collectors, jar and box model, make and compare; data tables given 1004:1.005

Solar distillation of water experiment using coffee can, plastic wrap, cup 1427:108-111

Solar drying—make a solar powered fruit dryer 140:21

Solar drying—show evaporating of salt water 140:24

Solar drying—show how sun dries up water 140:22

Solar electric system, how to make 1426:112-114

Solar energy affects ocean salinity demonstration 1023:212-213

Solar energy collecting experiment 494:10

Solar energy machine experiment 762:128-129

Solar food dryer, how to make from cardboard box, aluminum foil and tape 1115:120-121

Solar heat box, how to make from box, paper, and black paint 1175:180-181

Solar heated dog house—how to build 347:59-61

Solar heated model house—how to make 218:37-48

Solar heater—how to make 49:142-144

Solar heating—demonstrate greenhouse effect on water and plants 140:10

Solar heating—demonstrate how things are warmer in sunlight 140:9

Solar heating—show difference in big and small collectors 140:14

Solar heating—show if house gets hotter with windows on N or S 140:27

Solar heating—show which color best absorbs heat from the Sun 140:15

Solar heating—show which material stores solar heat best 140:16-17

Solar heating—use the Sun's rays to burn paper 140:13

Solar heating—what happens when you slowly heat water 140:19

Solar hot water heater—making 38:57-70; 218:17-36; 698:6-7; 1175:181

Solar hot water heater, model, making 895:94-95

Solar mint tea, how to make 986:87

Solar mittens warm your face—how to make 651:38-39

Solar panels and cells 386:118-120

Solar panels; how they work experiment 1371:84-85

Solar powered airplane—how to make 39:109-124

Solar powered motor, how to build 860:116-120

Solar powered radio—how to make 39:91-108

Solar reflector—make from salad bowl 203:79

Solar still—how to make 218:49-55; 289:46-47

Storing heat with pebbles—experiment 489:32-33

Storing solar energy; which materials store heat best experiment 1152:121-122

Sun's energy when focused is very powerful—experiment 624:4

Sun's heat makes solar pinwheel turn—experiment 651:36-37

Sun's light and heat can be focused—experiment 489:27-28

Sunbeam alarm clock—how to make 543:2-3

Sunlight used to heat water experiment 1152:52

Temperatures in sun and shade experiment 1152:50-51

Test light dark rule of solar heating 355:22-23, 26

Test materials that best reflect Sun's rays experiment 715:110-111

Transform sunlight into electricity experiment 698:6-7
Use Sun's heat to make fresh water out of salt water—experiment 634:12
Use sunlight to make heat 634:35
Use sunlight to signal 634:34
Water heater; heating water with solar energy experiment 959:166-167
What is solar energy experiment using magnifier and sheets of paper 1427:106-107
Which gets hotter, land or water experiment 1003:16
Why is Summer hotter than Winter experiment 1003:19

SOLAR ENERGY—FURNACE
How to build 38:13-30
How to make with Fresnel lens 386:55-56

SOLAR ENGINE
Solar powered motor, how to build 860:116-120
Working model of a solar engine—how to make 577: project 64

SOLAR GREENHOUSE
How to build a passive system solar greenhouse (Advanced) 347:22-31

SOLAR HEAT
Concentrator solar panels—how to make 386:116-117
Is more heat produced by direct rays or slanted rays of sun experiment 834:68-69
Materials best to store heat from sun experiment 715:106-107
Solar heat experiment with soil in cups 770:130
Solar heating—experiments 657:84-85
Test light—dark rule of solar heating 355:22-23, 26
Which material stores solar heat the longest 236:185
Window box heater—how to make 762:122-124

SOLAR HEATERS
Greenhouse effect solar water heater, wooden frame, tubing, bottle experiment 1249:11-16
Solar hand warmer to carry, how to make 850:26-27

SOLAR HEATING
Solar energy collecting experiment 1164:59-61

SOLAR STILL
Fresh water from salt water 577:project #24
How to make 38:71-90; 289:46-47; 347:57-58; 941:25-26
Make a solar-powered clean water 'still' 140:23
Produce clean water make solar distiller—how to do 715:103-105
Simple still—how to make in ground 538:45
Solar still—how to make 585:63-64
Solar still purifies muddy water experiment 1063:370
Survival still—how to make 585:55-56
Use Sun's heat to make fresh water out of salt water—experiment 634:12
Water and salt separated from seawater by the Sun experiment 1325:91-94

SOLAR STONE
A solar stone and how to use it 292:22-23
Make your own solar stone 292:27
Solar stone to find North, how to make from cardboard, cork, dowel 1115:132-133

SOLAR SYSTEM. *See also* **METEORS; MOON; PLANETS; STARS; SUN**
Aristarchus; who first tried to determine size of heavenly bodies project 1525:50-52
Astronomers compare photographs to find comets computer simulation project 1062:51-53
Build an integrated system 347:140-141

Centrifugal force keeps the Sun, Earth and moon in place 274:16
Chart of planets' place in space 231:100-101
Comparing the distance and size of planets 898:17
Comparing the distances between planets 898:15-16
Comparing the sizes of the planets 898:16-17
Copernicus; who first suggested that Earth revolves around Sun experiment 1525:43-46
Demonstrate the distances between the planets (Primary) 169:22
Demonstrate the seasons with a flashlight (Primary) 169:19
Distance scale solar system in your school, making 900:255-256
Earth's shadow extends into space and as umbra increases so does penumbra 1062:45-47
Elliptical orbit of planets around Sun experiment 1478:64
Estimate the size of the Solar System project 1525:56-58
Gravitational pull of Moon affects the tides on Earth experiment 1062:43-44
Gravity holds planets in orbit—experiment 682:8-9
Group game to know the planets, how to do 1063:290
Know day and night by watching shadows of balls 292:37
Make a model of an eclipse of the Sun (Primary) 169:20-21
Make a planet mobile 293:39
Making models of the solar system 130:24-29
Map out on football field or track 292:99-101
Milky Way galaxy clustering of stars aids in observing them experiment 1062:81
Mobile of Solar System with sizes of planets done to scale experiment 1478:60-61
Model—make a working model of the solar systems 381:41-42
Model of Solar System—making 128:71-72; 748:148; 760:40-41; 882:30
Model of Solar System to scale, how to make 1441:5-6
Model shows how planets move in their orbits around the Sun—how to make 502:28-29
Motion and speed of planets as they travel around the Sun experiment 1478:62-63
Motion of stars and moon; observe and record experiment 871:1.014
Orrery demonstrates movement of Earth, Moon and Sun, how to make 1480:14-15
Outdoor model to scale project to show size of Solar System 967:12-13
Planet size and distance experiment using two scale models 1062:58-60
Planets and distances from the Sun 748:150-151
Project solar system—study of planets 400:106-107
Record and make a graph of sunrise and sunset for many days 169:18
Scale model of our solar system, making 871:1.013
Scale model of solar system shows relative sizes of Sun and planets experiment 1170:6
Size of planets and their distances from each other model, how to make 1441:5-6
Sky clock to tell time on clear nights—how to make 763:33-38
Solar constant and amount of solar power in your part of Earth project 762:21
Solar system model (Advanced) 658:59
Solar system models—how to make 292:102-103

Solar mobile model—making 748:147

Sun does not come up or set in East or West exactly each day experiment 1062:48-50

Sun's position at sunrise versus latitude and longitude experiment 1062:48-50

Sunrise not exactly in the East each day experiment 1062:48-50

Sunset not exactly in the West each day experiment 1062:48-50

Unmanned exploration of solar system—activities/experiments to demonstrate 564:60-72

What is a Solar System, demonstrate with diagram 900:251-252

SOLAR WATER CLEANER

Distillation of water experiment—how to do 399:25

SOLAR WATER HEATER

Heating water with solar energy experiment 959:166-167

How it works 386:106-115

How to build a thermosiphoning water heater—(Advanced) 347:39-46

How to make an instant solar water heater 347:36-38

Solar water heater, make from plastic tubing, wood, paint 1461:24-25

SOLDER

How to 665:29

SOLDERING

Experiment 544:44-45

How to solder 391:156-157

SOLENOID. *See also* **ELECTROMAGNETS**

Checking the magnetic polarity of a solenoid experiment 768:91-92

Construction of solenoid type of electromagnet 23:51-52

Electric chime 577:project #53

Electric flag—making 391:140-145

Let's make a bar electromagnet 63:52-53

Loudspeaker; construct to demonstrate sound reproduction experiment data table 1004:5.013

Magtron the Magnetic Marvel electromagnetic device—how to make 487:34-35

Make solenoid and watch mouse hide in the cheese experiment 1309:22-23

Making a magnet out of a coil of wire 63:48-49

Pole test of solenoid coil 567:39

Simple electromagnetic lock 23:51-52

Solenoid and electric meter, how to make 1020:25-30

Solenoid controlled signal, how to make 910:40-41

SOLID WASTES. *See also* **GARBAGE**

Effects of waste on environment and ways to reduce it experiment 978:163-165

How much waste do you generate experiment 1150:59-60

Separating trash experiment using magnets and static electricity 1150:37-38

Solid waste generated by people project 1173:22-24

SOLID WASTES—RECYCLING

Artificial jade jewelry from waste glass 363:121-122

Bottle or can xylophone—make and play 363:135-136

Can hand bells—make and play 363:129-131

Can lid cymbals—make and play 363:136-137

Christmas tree decorations from waste glass 363:119-121

Coffee can bongos—make and play 363:132-134

Free form art from waste glass pieces 363:115-116

Ham-cam rubber band-jo—how to make 363:131-132

Hand shaped waste glass 363:116-117

Making a lamp from waste glass 363:109-113

Paper recycling 363:123-124

Papier mache maracas (rattles)—how to make 363:134-135

Plastic bottle recycling 363:125-129

Polyethylene bag composting 363:107-108

Turkey—table decoration from waste glass 363:118-119

Waste glass candle holders 363:113-114

Which solids decompose easily project 900:192

SOLIDS

Can sound travel thru a solid 281:68

Change of state activities for classroom 1291:45-47

Changing a gas to a solid—experiment 180:12

Changing a liquid to a solid—experiment 180:13

Changing a solid to a gas 180:14

Changing solids to liquids 280:20

Demonstrate expansion and contraction 253:71-72

Density of liquids and solids, floating of substances that don't mix experiment 1004:3.003

Density; measuring density of different solids experiment 1179:19

Detecting unknown solids experiment using water, vinegar, iodine and heat 1526:57-60

Do solids expand when heated experiment 851:25-26

Expansion and contraction from temperature changes experiments 1164:66-71

How heat changes solid to liquid 281:57

Melting point of different substances experiment 1179:20

Octahedron mobiles project, how to make 1353:49

Relative densities of liquids and solids 577:project #22

Schlegel diagrams, a way of drawing solids 1353:57

Separating a dissolved solid from its solvent experiment 1526:54-56

Separating solids experiment using sand, iron filings and magnet 1179:32

Separating things that sink and float experiment 1526:52-53

Simple observations to make (Primary) 198:15-31

Solid shapes; how to create, measure and use in activities and projects 1353:1-64

Solids dissolve in liquids experiment 1162:9

Solids expand when heated experiment 902:51

Solids take up less space than liquids experiment 1179:21

Soluble and insoluble solids experiment with different substances 1526:44

Strength of materials affected by molecule arrangement experiment 1403:77

Temperature's effect on liquids, solids and gases experiment 1435:21-23

Weighing solids in liquids 295:39

SOLSTICE

Building a stone wheel observing circle project 833:18-19

Make your own medicine wheel 292:70-71

Day length, soltices and equinoxes experiment 1062:35-36

Length of sunlight shortens or lengthens equal amount each day experiment 1062:35-36

SOLUBILITY

Does temperature affect solubility experiment 902:30

Investigating the solubility of compounds 180:28

Sugar and salt dissolve at different rates as temperature increases experiment 722:121

SOLUTIONS

About solutions 346:22-25

Acids and bases—red cabbage indicator 74:25-27

384

Boiling point of water affected by added solutes experiment 1396:82

Boiling point of water determined experiment 1396:79-84

Change Coca Cola into water 176:23

Colloidal micelles can be separated from liquid by filtration experiment 1396:87-88

Colloidal particles can be made to coagulate experiment 1396:88-89

Colored liquid layers experiment 959:148-149

Colored liquids that sink or float experiment 959:146-147

Compare strength of tea solutions experiment 1479:61

Compare the strength of teas experiment 905:160-161

Concentration and density in solutions of saltwater experiment data tables 1004:4.004

Demonstrate evaporation of copper sulfate solution 197:22-23

Demonstrate nature of solutions in water 126:137-147

Demonstrate super saturation 197:20-21

Density of—the eggs that read 350:59-60

Disappearing salt in solution experiment 1066:56

Disappearing sugar into solution experiment 1066:58-59

Does 1 plus 1 always equal 2 experiment with solids and liquids 1526:36-38

Effect of heat on solutions—experiment 319:47-48

Experiment to show nature of dissolved and evaporated solutions 197:18-19

Filtering solids 147:29

Fruit drinks and dissolving rates of solutions 74:23-24

Gases dissolved in gases experiment 1526:48-49

Gases dissolved in liquids experiment 1526:48

How does temperature affect dissolving rate—make a solution—worksheet 537:5-8

How does temperature affect dissolving rate—make honey lemonade—worksheet 537:56

How full is full (Primary) 288:10-11

How to make solutions 157:6-7

How to tell if solution is an electrolyte 319:50-51

Ice pops and the freezing point of solutions 74:20-22

Insoluble gel forms from alum and ammonia experiment 905:98-99

Iodine is more soluble in mineral oil than in water experiment 1435:13-15

Kool-Aid in water experiment 782:26-29

Light used to distinguish colloidal suspension from pure solution experiment 1396:85-90

Liquids mix together or don't mix experiment 1162:9

Liquids other than water as solvents experiment 1526:45

Liquids that dissolve in other liquids experiment 1526:46-47

Magic potions using red cabbage 16:62-65

Magnesium milk from Epsom salt and ammonia experiment 905:100-101

Make a snowman with indicator arms in jar of water and mothballs 146:29

Make a snowstorm with boric acid 146:28-29

Make a solution of salt 598:18-19

Make a super saturated solution 147:68-69

Make supersaturated solution of sugar 598:21

Making solutions 98:28-29

Nonordinary solutions tested for acid with grape juice indicator experiment 1476:126-127

Observe color change as solution becomes more dilute experiment 905:170-171

Observe dissolving of a solute in a solvent experiment 905:148-149

Observe how solute dissolves in solvent experiment with powdered fruit drink 1479:59

Reaction that makes solutions thicken demonstrated with pudding 1289:12-13

Removal of gas from a solution inflates balloon experiment 1405:6

Rock candy—recovering solute crystals 74:16-19

Salt added to water lowers freezing point experiment 1396:82-84

Saturated salt solution freezes at what temperature experiment 1526:41

Saturated solution of sugar and water affected by water temperature experiment 1403:39

Saturated solution of sugar experiment 1263:14

Saturated solutions with salt, Epsom Salt and sugar experiment 1526:39-41

Separate solutes from solvents 319:48-50

Separating a dissolved solid from its solvent experiment 1526:54-56

Separating sand from salt—experiment 589:46

Separating the colors in inks 589:47

Show strength of solutions varies 122:33-34

Snow storm in a jar, making 905:156-157

Snow storm in jar experiment with boric acid crystals and water 1479:60

Solids dissolve in liquids experiment 1162:9

Solubility of salt and sugar in hot and cold water experiment 1091:18

Soluble and insoluble solids experiment with different substances 1526:44

Solutions and precipitates—experiments to show 116:77-85

Solutions and solubilities—simple experiments to show 84:17-23

Solutions and specific gravity 84:25-27

Solutions made with water 122:26-28

Solutions with color changes 84:23-25

Solutions; disappearing solids in water experiment 959:37-38

Solutions; hot water solution experiment 959:38

Solutions; salt in water solution experiment 959:38

Some substances will dissolve and others will not experiment 1159:10-11

Sour ball candy drink—effect of surface area on rate of dissolving 74:24-25

Substance divided into colloidal size particles increases surface area 1396:89-90

Substances that dissolve in hot or cold water or are suspended in it experiment 1331:20-21

Substances that will or will not dissolve in water experiment; graph given 960:23

Sugar added to warm and cold water experiment; which holds more sugar 1175:81

Sugar added to water forms homogenous mixture experiment 1403:40-43

Sugar dissolves in water faster with heat demonstration 780:26-27

Temperature affects how long it takes material to dissolve experiment 1479:60

Temperature affects solubility experiment 1526:42-43

Temperature of water affects amount of sugar that will dissolve experiment 1403:42

Testing solutions for solubility experiment 976:46

385

What are mixtures and solutions demonstrations 902:21

What happens when something dissolves 281:25

What happens when you mix a solid and a liquid 319:44-45

What happens when you mix different kinds of liquids 319:45-47

Will liquids mix together experiment; chart given 960:20-21

SOLUTIONS—SUPERSATURATED. *See* **CRYSTALS**

SOLVENTS

De-inker solvent lifts ink off magazine or newspaper experiment 1064:68

Hot or cold water; which dissolves the best experiment 1271:11

Investigating the solubility of compounds 180:28

Is hot or cold water best as solvent 122:34-36

Liquids other than water as solvents experiment 1526:45

Make your own secret printing press 146:56

Observe dissolving of a solute in a solvent experiment 905:148-149

Picture lifting liquid solvent 162:60-61

Potato removes food stains from clothing experiment 1065:14

Solvents—dissolve substances which water does not 122:28-33

Spots; will they come off clothing experiment; chart given 960:24-25

Sugar dissolves faster in cold or warm water experiment 1509:13

Universal solvent property of water experiment 1441:60

Universal solvent; which chemicals will dissolve in water experiment 1271:11

Water as solvent experiment 741:13

Water as universal solvent experiment 1172:22-23

Which things dissolve in water experiment 1509:12

SONIC BOOM

Small scale sound, make—experiment to show sonic boom 379:19

Vibrations from sonic booms demonstration 1201:26

SONOMETER

Sonometer—how to make 2:54-55

SOOT. *See also* **CARBON; COMBUSTION**

Carbon in flame deposited as soot if temperature of burning not high experiment 1435:115-117

Smoke has tiny solid particles experiment 1322:84-88

SOROBAN ANALOG COMPUTER

Directions for making (Advanced) 449:113-117

SOUND. *See also* **ACOUSTICS; HEARING; MUSICAL INSTRUMENTS; TELEPHONE**

A gun for sound rings 161:47-49

A jar of noise (Primary) 143:50-52

A lion's roar out of a box 186:51

A sonic boomer—how to make 94:10-11

Absorbing sound experiment; what materials are best 1209:84-85

Absorption of sound—show effect of different materials 90:37-44

Acoustics—musical bottle demonstrates 350:94

Acoustics—musical glass demonstrates 350:94-96

Acoustics—visible sound vibrations 350:92-94

Air banger, how to make 669:24-25

Alarm clock on cord swinging around you demonstrates 721:9

Banger from paper experiment 1028:79

Battery attached to head phones makes sound experiment 1030:18-19

Binaural hearing experiment; locating objects with sound 1155:77-78

Blind people use sound to get around experiment 1209:46-47

Bounce a sound experiment 1028:78

Bouncing sounds around corners experiment 957:41

Brain can measure difference in speed of sound experiment 1432:130-132

Can musical instrument be made with rubber bands project 834:15

Can sound travel through liquid demonstration 780:14-15

Can sound travel through solid materials experiment 834:48-49

Can you make a goblet sing experiment 902:128

Can you see your voice experiment 902:118

Chladni plate interference patterns experiment 1155:70-71

Cigar box violin demonstrates loud and soft and pitch 411:45-48

Concordant and discordant sounds from vibrating strings experiment 1155:90-91

Conduction of sound experiment with watch—funnel and wooden table 722:53

Conductors of sound energy—demonstrate 90:16-18

Demonstrations with a sound mirror (parabolic reflector) 577:project 98

Differences in and cause of sound activities [Primary] 759:63-64

Direction of sound activities for classroom 1291:31-32

Direction sounds are coming from experiment 1163:17

Does sound travel faster than light experiment 1284:14

Does sound travel through air experiment; simple stethoscope demonstrate 834:47-48

Doppler's motion of sound source affects pitch of sound experiment 1133:6.012

Doppler's principle—experiment 577:project 101

Ear detects sound experiment using vibrating rice on plastic drum 1036:10-11

Effect of sound and music on plants 398:124-127

Emotional sound responses—identify emotion 363:30-31

Experiment in acoustics 577:project 100

Experiment to demonstrate sound 186:48-60

Game; sound charades game, how to do 1209:38-39

Gro-o-ovy sounds, make your own amplifier 600:44-45

Harmonious and discordant motes experiment 1155:94-96

Hearing sensitivity and frequency of sound experiment 1155:75-76

How a sound starts 686:10-11

How can sound be controlled experiment 902:124-125

How can sounds be heard more clearly experiment 902:126

How can sounds be produced experiments 902:113-116

How do we get high and low sounds from musical instruments—exp. 587:43

How do we get sound from a phonograph record experiment 834:87-88

How does sound travel experiments 902:119-122

How far away is thunder 186:54

How fast does sound travel experiment 902:123

How good is your hearing experiment 734:9

How sound is heard experiment 904:172-173

How sound is produced and transmitted—experiment 128:131-134

How sounds are made 186:49

How to get chime sound from a spoon 179:73-74

How to measure distance with sound 101:32-33

How well does sound travel through solids experiment 902:14

Identify objects by the sound they make 253:100

Insulating against loud sounds experiment 1155:81

Insulation of sound experiment with clock and styrofoam ice container 722:50

Intensity of sound; how to measure experiment 1155:75

Locating source of sound experiment 1132:94-1-94-2

Locating the direction of sound 180:61

Loud or soft sound demonstration 1479:90

Loudspeaker; construct to demonstrate sound reproduction experiment data table 1004:5.013

Magical humming glass 350:98-99

Make a ruler sing (Primary) 143:42-43

Make yourself a 'rommel pot' 186:51-52

Making sound with hot air 293:46

Making sound with straws 12:20-23

Match sounds experiment [Primary] 902:107

Megaphone from paper, how to make (Primary) 1319:9

Megaphone, mighty megaphone, making 779:35

Megaphones and trumpets; do sounds get louder experiment 957:37

Mental picture from marble in box experiment 904:168-169

Moves things tuning fork and water demonstrate 695:9

Muffling sounds experiment 957:39

Music everywhere—how sounds are produced (Primary) 232:73

Musical instruments and their different sounds project 1296:2001

Name the bells—making a sound (Primary) 535:23

Noisemaker from paper, how to make 1036:14-15

Oscillograph—how to make 356:60-61; 558:86-87

Oscilloscope—how to make 90:81-89

Pin in roll of paper on turntable experiment 898:28

Pitch and vibration of sound are related experiment; data sheet given 818:11

Pitch increases as water level in jars increases experiment 984:67-69

Porous materials absorb sound 65:94-95

Principles of sound shown with balloon and tissue scraps on speaker 1073:33

Projects with sounds 1164:83-88

Radio waves demonstrated with homemade radio experiment 1045:24-25

Recognition; sounds people recognize experiment 1284:10

Record and reproduce sound—experiment 128:136-140

Recorded sounds people recognize experiment 1284:11

Recording sound using umbrella as amplifier experiment 1045:18-19

Resonance and non resonance in pendulums experiment; pendulum pushing pendulum 1155:44-46

Resonance; air columns, resonance and standing waves experiments 1155:48-52

Resonance; piano resonates to notes experiment 1155:46

Resonance; resonating air columns experiments 1155:46-47

Resonance; tuning fork starts next identical tuning fork vibrating experiment 1155:46

Reverberation time; time it takes sound to become inaudible in room experiment 1155:78-81

Robert Boyle's sound does not travel through a vacuum experiment 1133:6.006

Send secret signal through table top (Primary) 551:unpaged

Soda straws make high sounds and low sounds (Primary) 422:14-19

Solid things let sound pass through easily experiment 1284:18-19

Some sounds cannot be heard 65:98-99

Sound and architecture of concert halls experiment 1155:81-85

Sound bottles, taping sounds, sound travels—experiment (Primary) 535:63-65

Sound created by motion experiment with spinning disc 1035:26-27

Sound effects board, making 779:54

Sound experiments using straws (Primary) 24:22-25

Sound from a record without a needle, amplifier and speakers 400:83

Sound goes through air, the ground, wood or teeth—experiment 143:46-49

Sound goes through solid things 324:20-21

Sound makes sound with tuning fork and bottle—demonstrate 187:23

Sound memory experiment; identify things from their sound 957:9

Sound proofing projects 691:81-86

Sound travels better through solid than through air experiment 1209:26-27

Sound travels experiments 685:26-27

Sounds around us—different things make different sounds (Primary) 232:72

Soundscope—to hear and see your own voice—how to make 335:89

Sources of sound experiments 1155:14-16

Speed of sound experiment to measure your echo 1245:28-29

Speed of sound in open area experiment 1093:43

Standing waves from a bell or buzzer—experiment 577:project 99

Stethoscope—how to make 142:42; 179:79

Stethoscope—how to make and test (Primary) 215:16-17

Stethoscope—simple—how to make 187:15

String telephone carries sound—making 411:18-19

String telephone demonstrates sound traveling through objects experiment 036:16-17

Stringed instruments have sounding board experiment; make string guitar, piano 1155:98-104

The bulldog (roaring ruler) experiment 563:15-16

The match box monte trick 350:100-102

To show how sounds are produced on records with old record and pin 134:31

Transmission of sound thru various materials with tuning fork 187:13

Transmit sound with a flashlight beam experiment 1132:67-1-67-4

Transmitters of sound, which are best experiment 1209:24-25

Traveling sound—experiment 587:43

Tube keeps sound from spreading out—experiment 635:37-38

Two bottles in harmony—match sounds from two bottles 291:148-149

Ultrasound experiment; construct bat ultrasound game 1045:20-23

Underwater sound experiment; balloon filled with water and ticking watch 1385:7

Vibrating strings experiment with rubber band banjo, how to make 1155:87-90

Volume—measuring sound volume—how to make apparatus for 363:26-28

Wails from a ruler 186:57

Ways to use sound experiment 902:130-131

What causes sound 281:64

What causes sound experiment 902:109-110

What is sound—experiment 179:66-67

What is the best medium for sound to travel through 101:27-28

What sound is experiment; hacksaw blade, yardstick and rubber bands demonstrate 1432:3-5

Why do things make sounds 210:26

Why we hear unusual sounds in seashells and milk bottles 179:74-75

Wind instruments experiment with reed made from straw 1155:104-107

Woodwind (panpipe) from plastic tubing experiment 1155:107-109

You can feel sound (Primary) 143:44-45

SOUND—AMPLIFIERS

A funnel for sound amplification—how to make 45:48-49

Amplification experiment with cone, pin and record (Primary) 215:14-15

Amplify record with paper funnel 94:13

Amplify sound with paper cone and needle on old record experiment 1369:62-63

Amplify sound with paper cup (Primary) 201:20-21

Baking pan amplifier demonstrates amplifiers experiment 1432:70-74

Balloons increase volume of sound experiment 1079:58-59

Boards and boxes amplify sound 45:51-52

Can you make sounds louder 134:27

Deadening sound experiment 1432:89-91

Do ear trumpets work experiment 1284:16

Drinking glass amplifier experiment 1432:75-76

Ear trumpet—paper—making 734:6

Ear trumpet or megaphone amplifies sound experiment 1045:15

Frying pan amplifier 45:53

Funnel—tube and watch demonstrate 734:11

Gramophone from paper cone and needle, how to make 1333:30-31

Harp from rubber band and metal pan demonstrates amplification experiment 1432:97

Harp from tissue box and rubber bands demonstrates amplification 1209:56-57

How do speakers work experiment 1293:133-134

How do speaking tubes work experiment 1284:17

Loudspeaker from a paper cup—making 150:102-103

Make a speaking tube 134:26

Make large ears from cones to catch sounds (Primary) 215:19-20

Make megaphones (Primary) 215:15-16

Make sound louder with primitive phonograph 187:14

Megaphone and ear trumpet—how to make 134:28

Megaphone makes sounds louder, how to make 1036:19

Megaphone, how to make 1432:109-113

Mellow sound experiment 1432:86-88

Paper or plastic cup amplifies sound experiment 836:77-78

Recorded sound needs motion and amplification to be heard experiment 837:49

Sound amplifier experiment with rubber band 1163:9

Sound boards amplify sound—experiments 2:48-51

Sound can be reinforced and increased—experiments 385:86-88

Sound magnification—hear a fly walking in a cup—(Primary) 64:unpaged

Sound magnification—make a sound magnifier 350:97

Speaking tube, how to make 1432:107-108

Spoon and string amplify sound experiment 1079:60-61

Stethoscope—tubing and funnel—making 734:12

Stethoscope amplifies body sounds experiment 1045:14-15

Stethoscope from funnel and hose, how to make 1432:105-106

Telephone from funnels and tube—making 734:11

Telephone from yogurt cup and string—making 734:13

SOUND—ANIMALS

Capturing animals on tape recording; recorder, microphone, large umbrella 1093:50-51

SOUND—DIFFRACTION

Bending of sound waves—experiment 2:40-43

SOUND—DIRECTION

Difficulty using one ear—experiment 381:130-132

Ears can tell direction of sound—demonstrate (Primary) 215:17-19

How can we locate the direction of sounds we hear 253:101-102

SOUND—DISTANCE

How far the storm 563:5

SOUND—DOPPLER EFFECT

Doppler effect—how to show 90:45-51

Doppler effect—police car diagram explanation 501:14

Doppler effect—what causes the Doppler effect 161:46-47

Hear the Doppler effect 585:12-13

Repeat Doppler's motion sound and pitch experiment 448:48-50

Whistle and rubber tube demo rises and falls in pitch as object moves 2:28-31

SOUND—ECHOES. *See also* ECHOES

Bet you can make an echo in a dish 228:50

Echo—how to measure distance to reflecting surface 45:63-64

Echoes experiment 134:30

Echoes measure distance 281:70

Measure speed of sound using echoes experiment 1155:39-40

Reflected sound—what is echo 101:30-32

Show echoes are sound reflections 142:43

Show that sound travels thru water—experiment 385:84-85

Sound doubles back from sides of pail 45:61-62

Timing an echo experiment 1141:55-56

SOUND—EFFECTS. *See* SOUND EFFECTS

SOUND—FREQUENCY

Bells from copper pipe, how to make 1333:21

Frequency of vibrations of two glasses match experiment 1216:49-51

From 'zoop' to 'zeep'—experiments with comb 45:79

Long wave, short wave—frequency demonstration with a rope 45:75-76

Mellow the radio 585:12

String thickness and other materials—demonstrate 569:44

Thickness of strings in musical instrument affects sound experiment 1209:62-63

Xylophone from bottles and water, how to make 1333:20-21

SOUND—HUSHERS

Hushing sound—sound swallowers—piano dampers demonstration 45:72

Hushing sound dampers—demonstration 45:71

Hushing sound hushers—demonstration 45:67-68

Hushing sound mutes—demonstration 45:69-70

Muffling sound 134:29

Sound can be muzzled 65:92-93

SOUND—INSULATORS

Soundproof a box experiment 1333:16-17

SOUND—MUSICAL INSTRUMENTS. *See also* **MUSICAL INSTRUMENTS**

Aeolian harp—how to make 350:97-98

Drum—make a coffee can drum (Primary) 181:30-31

Guitar—make a cake pan guitar (Primary) 181:27

Harmonica—make a harmonica from wine glass 186:58

Kazoo—make a kazoo 32:28-29

Make a musical instrument from cardboard tubes 186:59

Make a stringed thing 32:30-31

Make musical instruments to show, straw whistle, xylophone pipes 90:60-67

Make musical straws 94:12

Make stretched strings, reed pipe, bottle organ, toy timpani 187:24-28

Making a musical instrument with cigar box and rubber bands 65:100-101

Musical glasses—demonstrate Franklin's harmonica 202:122

Musical glasses and xylophone—how to make 385:93-94

Organ—make an organ from empty bottles 186:56-57

Percussion instruments produce sounds 101:35

Piano—make a nail piano 186:55

Piano patter—check 88 different pitches of piano 45:82-83

Playing the ruler 734:22

Rattle—make a rattle 32:26-27

Sound experiments using homemade instruments 128:134-136

Stringed instruments produce sound 101:33-34

Water trombone—how to make 186:55

Xylophone—make an 8-note xylophone with water glasses (Primary) 181:28-29

Zither—make a zither with elastic bands 186:54-55

SOUND—PITCH

Banjo from wood, string and plastic tub, how to make 1045:42

Bass from wooden box and broom handle, how to make 1045:40

Bass viol from string, box and broom demonstrates sound vibrations/pitch 1432:66-69

Bells; tubular bells experiment 1045:29

Big sings low—demonstration with bottles 45:90

Bottle organ demonstrates musical notes of octave scale, how to make 1045:26-27

Bottle whistles—demonstrate pitch of large and small bottle 45:95

Box and rubber bands demonstrate pitch experiment 851:30-31

Change pitch of sound by changing speed of sound experiment 1209:28-29

Changing pitch of sound with water in glasses 179:69-71

Changing pitch with paper drinking straws 179:72-73

Demonstrate higher or lower pitch 187:16

Doppler effect experiment using water waves in tank of water 1155:62-65

Double bass instrument from cardboard box and broom handle, how to make 1333:22-23

Drum; bongo drum from tin can, how to make 1045:34

Drum; tunable drums from cardboard tubes, how to make 1045:35

Elastic band guitar demonstrates pitch 734:27

Experimenting with pitch 180:62-63

Faster the vibration, higher the pitch experiment with rubber bands and tin can 1432:62-65

Frequency affects pitch of sound demonstration with glasses of water 1479:91

Glass xylophone—making 734:25

Glasses and water produce sounds of different pitch 215:exp. #8

Grass whistle, how to make 1432:94-96

Guitar from cigar box experiment to demonstrate pitch 1066:98-99

Guitar from shoe box and rubber bands, how to make 1045:43

Guitar; how does it work experiment 898:26-27

Hear octaves 45:84-85

High and low notes experiment with water in bottles 1284:24

High pitch and low pitch of sounds experiment with recording sheet 747:37-38

High sounds and low sounds—experiment (Primary) 210:27

How frequency causes pitch—experiment 385:92-93

Length affects pitch of vibrating material demonstration 1479:91

Length of flute affects pitch of sound experiment 1405:108-109

Length of vibrating column determines pitch experiment 837:17

Length of vibrating object determines its pitch; pin harp demonstrates 837:48

Low tone, high tone—demonstration with long blade or ruler 45:77-78

Make simple xylophone to demonstrate 215:exp. #7

Model to demonstrate how human vocal cords change pitch of sound experiment 904:174-175

Music from glasses—demonstration 45:92-93

Musical bottles demonstrate sound vibrations and pitch experiment 1432:48-51

Musical glass demonstrates sound vibrations and pitch experiment 1432:52-53

Musical straw demonstrates sound vibrations and pitch 1432:38-39

Octaves on a rubber band 45:88-89

Packing case bass demonstrates pitch—making 734:26

Panpipes experiment, how to make 1045:28

Piano—bottle listens to piano—find key note or pitch of air in bottle 45:104-105

Pitch changes demonstrated on instruments made from fishing line, wood 1093:19-20

Pitch demonstrated with cake pan, dowel and rubber band 1141:73-75

Pitch experiment with eight bottles filled with water 1063:146

Pitch from bicycle wheel experiment 1432:92-93

Pitch from size and shape shown by balloons 92:38-39

Pitch of sound changes in large stainless bowl experiment 1209:30-31

Rattle from stick and bottle caps, how to make 1045:33

Rattle; whirling rattle from wood, how to make 1045:36-37

Recorder from thick cardboard tube, how to make 1045:30-31

Rubber band on box demonstrates 708:30-32—34-35

Sandpaper or wooden rasp, how to make 1045:33

Savart's wheel demonstrates pitch depends on number of vibrations 2:20-23

Shakers from cups or plastic bottles, how to make 1045:32-33

Singing glasses demonstrate pitch 1476:60-61

Singing wine glass—making 734:25

Siren disk—demonstrates pitch depends on speed of rotation 2:24-27

Soda straw demonstrates 411:53

Soda straw music—experiment 563:13-14

Sound differences—pitch 281:72

Sound of moving object demonstrates Doppler effect 1432:30-31

Sounds can be arranged according to pitch experiment; data sheet given 818:13

Sounds differ in pitch experiment; data sheet given 818:12

Spinner from poster board hums, how to make 1045:39

Straw whistles demonstrate sound vibrations and pitch 1432:40-42

Straws give low and high sounds (Primary) 215:exp. #6

Stretched strings demonstrate pitch 734:26-27

String pitch; what changes the sound made by string experiment 1284:26

Test sound and pitch with a plastic ruler (Primary) 165:9-12

Thickness of strings in musical instruments affects sound experiment 1209:62-63

Trombone bottle—demonstration with straw and bottle 45:96

Underwater recorder demonstrates pitch 734:24

Vary pitch of instrument with bass fiddle made from juice can and string 1209:60-61

Voice of a bottle 45:94

Water and pitch of glasses experiment 1432:45-47

Water in bottles—experiment 538:70

Wave machine demonstrates why moving vehicle changes pitch as it passes you 472:2221

Whirrer from poster board hums, how to make 1045:39

Whistle; slide whistle from copper pipe, how to make 1045:31

Why are some sounds higher than others experiment 851:28-29

Xylophone from glass bottles demonstrates pitch 411:55-56

Xylophone; how does it work experiment 898:27

Zither from strings and bottles, how to make 1045:41

SOUND—REFLECTION

Bouncing sound to produce echo, how to do using cardboard tubes 1036:20-21

Bouncing sound waves experiment 1045:12-13

Curved mirror and ticking watch demonstrate 2:32-35

Demonstrate sound reflection 187:18

Directed echo using clock and cardboard tube experiment 722:49

How to reflect sound 360:38

Reflection of sound experiment; alarm clock, styrofoam box, newspapers 1155:54-57

Reflection of sound 90:97-101; 161:42-43

Rubber band on box demonstrates 708:37

Test different materials for best reflection of sound experiment 1163:15

SOUND—REFRACTION

Balloons with air and carbon dioxide demonstrate 2:36-39

Carbon dioxide filled balloon demonstrates refraction sound waves experiment 1155:57

Does temperature affect refraction of sound 2:36-39

SOUND—RESONANCE

A tricky hummer—experiment 563:5-6

Demonstrate resonance mechanically—experiment 385:88-89

Paper clip moves on top of water glass experiment 1141:82-83

Piano—piano listens to you and vibrates your sound or note back to you 45:101-103

Pipes of Pan experiment demonstrates resonance 1132:77-1-77-2

Play the piano without touching the keys experiment 1209:36-37

Resonance—experiment to show 179:76-77

Resonance—seashell resonance 281:77

Resonance—two bottles in harmony 291:148-149

Show the wonder of resonance 186:58-59

The open and shut pipe—experiment 563:9-10

What is resonance 281:76

SOUND—SPEED

Balloon filled with flour experiment 1333:24-25

Demonstrate speed of sound 90:21-27

Finding speed of sound from wavelength and frequency experiment 762:88-90

Measuring speed of sound experiments 1155:37-41

Measuring speed of sound using electronics experiment [Advanced] 762:89-92

Measuring the speed of sound with stopwatch experiment 734:19

Solids effect on speed of sound demonstration 1405:108

Sound has speed limits—kind of material sets the speed for sound 45:40-41

Speed of sound—experiment 134:32; 281:69; 1158:82-84

Speed of sound—how far away lightning is 187:21

SOUND—TELEGRAPH

Sounds and electricity—telegraph set—how to make 90:68-72

SOUND—TELEPHONE

Make a hose telephone 32:32-33

Make a tin can telephone 291:147

Make private telephone 94:10-11

Make telephone from old tins 186:53

Make tin can telephone (Primary) 181:34
Make tin can telephone to show sound moves 187:12
Making a telephone 73:40-43
Sounds and electricity—telephone transmitter model—how to make 90:73-76
String telephone—how to make 333:41-43

SOUND—TONE

Match the tones of different tones 45:91
The larger the lower—thick band gives lower tone than thin band 45:86-87
Tone quality experiments 2:52-55

SOUND—TOYS

Clucking hen, hanger clanger, roaring ruler, singing bottle—how to make 410:9
Make a Aeolian harp 172:57-62
Make a bull-roarer 172:56-57
Make a cardboard telephone 172:52-53
Make a clucking hen 172:53-54
Make a speaking tube 172:54-56
Make a string rider or musical figures 172:48-50
Make toys to demo sounds—tin can phone, bull roarer, barking dog, whistle 90:52-59
Twirling tweeter toy, wailing whirler toy—how to make 410:8

SOUND—TRAVELS

African 'water telegraph' experiment 22:2-3
Can sound travel through a liquid 281:67
Can sound travel through a solid 281:68
Can sound travel through nothing 281:66
Does sound travel in a vacuum—experiment 179:67-69
Drum and flame—demonstrates sound travels 45:25-26
Ear to the ground—demonstrates sound travels 45:27-28
Ear to the table experiment 400:45
Hello, who's there—how sound travels (Primary) 232:74
How does sound travel 101:26-27
How sound travels—experiment 385:80-82; 399:51
Sound travels better thru wood than air 65:80-81
Sound travels through string 65:82-83
Sound travels through water—rocks and water experiment 215:13-14
The ringing spoon and string demonstrate 576:77-78
Tin can telephone—demonstrates sound travels 45:30-31

SOUND—VIBRATIONS. *See also* **MUSICAL INSTRUMENTS**

A musical rubber band—experiment 563:10
A mystery sound experiment 563:11-12
A singing pan 280:42
A song and dance act—sympathetic vibrations 205:98-102
A weird sound 280:41
Air vibrates; salt dances on stretched rubber sheet experiment 1155:16-17
And the bottle said 'boo' 161:37-39
Animal sounds produced by vibration from milk containers and string experiment 1020:72-74
Barking dog made from box and string 382:5-7
Baseball bat has sweet spot; how to find it experiment 1209:50-51
Bass viol from string, box and broom demonstrates sound vibrations/pitch 1432:66-69
Bottle band—demonstrates 670:35
Bottle band; play simple tunes experiment 1155:53
Bottle organ demonstrates sound vibrations experiment (Primary) 1319:23
Bowl bell—demonstrates sound travel 45:33

Bull roarer—how to make 734:23
Can you see sound experiment 902:117
Candle flame between speakers demonstrates vibrations 1330:68-69
Catching sounds out of the air with bottles and shells 45:47
Chimes from spoons and flatwear experiments 1432:98-104
Chladni figures—experiment 585:13-15
Cigar box violin demonstrates making a sound 411:5-6
Clock sounds heard through yardstick experiment 1079:62-63
Clucking chicken sound from vibrating string in cup experiment 1404:226-227
Comb and tissue paper make music experiment 1066:93-94
Cotton cord in oatmeal box produces growling sounds experiment 722:62
Crazy wire—demonstrates sound travel 45:21
Dancing lights show demonstrates sound vibrations, how to make 1476:58-59
Dancing salt experiment 836:75-77
Demonstrate 'seeing sound' 176:86-87
Demonstrate saw blade vibrations on index card 215:exp. #5
Demonstrate sound vibration 187:6-7
Doctor's ear—funnel and hose stethoscope—demonstrates sound travels 45:24
Drum and sand—demonstration 670:35
Drum demonstrates sound vibrations, how to make (Primary) 1319:25
Drum from metal pail demonstrates vibrations 1333:6-7
Drum from plastic bowl and plastic sheet, how to make 1036:22
Drum with rubber sheet or balloon demonstrates—making 754:26-27
Eardrum model demonstrates how we hear 1333:10-11
Edison's reproducer experiment 1476:67-68
Experiment to show how strings vibrate 385:94-95
Experiment to show sound vibrations 106:35-40
Faster the vibration, higher the pitch experiment with rubber bands and tin can 1432:62-65
Faster the vibrations the higher the sound 186:49-50
Feeling sound experiment; balloon full of air held against loudspeakers 1385:8
Find the keynote 45:108-109
Flower pot chimes demonstrate 722:58
Foil ball jumps away from tap on glass experiment 1253:21
Frequency—number of vibrations per second is called frequency 65:84-85
Frequency and length of things affects rate of vibrations 165:33-35
Frequency and thickness of things affects rate of vibrations 165:38-39
Frequency demonstrated by water in bottles 635:26
Frequency depends on length, weight and tightness of string—experiment 635:19-22
Friction causes glass to vibrate and hum demonstration 1479:90
Friction causes glass to vibrate demonstration 1404:218-219
Fry pan chimes experiment 722:43

Glass of water makes music when rubbed experiment 1229:6-7

Glasses filled with water are tuned to play musical scale experiment 1079:66-67

Gong experiments 686:21-22

Hear sound vibrations in your head with spoons and string experiment 734:21

Hear spoon ring from pieces of string experiment 1007:56-57

Hear through the teeth—experiment 563:11

Height of air column in bottles of water affects pitch of sound experiment 1404:216-217

How are sounds made experiment 902:108

How can we see sound vibrations—experiment to demonstrate 381:127-130

How do sound vibrations travel 291:131

How phonograph record makes sounds experiment 1432:133-135

How vibrations make sounds experiment with balloon 1279:7

How whistles work 686:30-33

Humming stick demonstrates irregular pattern of vibrations in sirens 1432:27-29

Increasing the intensity of vibrations 180:59

Inky feather attached to pendulum bob makes traces of vibrations 2:12-15

Irregular vibrations—experiment 563:9

Is it a bell 280:39-40

Jerky vibrations from glass, string and pencil experiment 1432:54-55

Jingle bells—why do they jingle 686:23

Knife and fork chimes experiments 563:7-9

Law of vibrating strings—experiments 2:56-59

Length and tension of strings affects pitch in stringed instruments experiment 1404:22

Length of flute affects sound produced experiment with straw 1404:224-225

Length of object affects sound from vibrating object experiment 1404:222-223

Light reflections demonstrate; can, balloon and flashlight experiment 937:118-119

Loudness experiment 281:75

Major diatonic scale—experiment 2:72-75

Make a clucking hen to show vibrations 172:53-54

Make bouncing woodpecker 94:8-9

Make music from water glasses 291:150-151

Make soda straw horns 95:38-39

Make string rider or musical figures to show vibrations 172:48-50

Making musical notes with bottles filled with different amounts of water 501:10

Making vibrations you can see and touch 180:60

Matter and particles—why sounds are louder thru solids than air 45:36-39

Measure vibrations to determine frequency of sound 2:8-11

Melde's experiment—how to do 2:60-63

Molecules as sound from ruler 366:173-174

Music box—demonstrates 670:34

Music from bottles filled with water to different levels experiment 1209:64-65

Music vision sets 386:17-19

Musical balloon—experiment 563:13

Musical bottles (Primary) 288:16-17

Musical bottles demonstrate sound vibrations and pitch experiment 1432:48-51

Musical chimes from glass bottles—making 696:40-41

Musical comb demonstrates sound vibrations experiment 1432:34-35

Musical fork trick to demonstrate 'sympathetic vibration' 202:123

Musical glass demonstrates sound vibrations and pitch experiment 1432:52-53

Musical glasses experiment 686:25-28

Musical intervals—experiments 2:68-71

Musical straw demonstrates sound vibrations and pitch 1432:38-39

Nail chimes experiment 686:24-25

Natural vibrations and resonance experiment 2:44-47

Nodes and anti nodes 585:16

Noisy balloon demonstrates sound vibrations experiment 1432:36-37

Object vibrating at high speed produces higher pitched sound experiment 760:31-32

Old record—paper cone and pin let you hear music vibrations experiment 723:9-10

Paper cone and pin make speaker for record player 538:70

Paper cup becomes loudspeaker or megaphone experiment 1229:8-9

Paper cup on string makes loud noises experiment 1014:58

Phonograph speaker experiment with paper cones to get best volume 1404:228-229

Pin piano—straight pins of different lengths demonstrate sound vibrations 576:76-77

Pipes cut at different lengths play scales and tunes 436:72

Pipes from plastic straws, how to make 1163:12

Pitch—blowing sounds 281:74

Pitch—striking sounds 281:73

Pitch—variations with strings 281:72-73

Pitch of sound can be changed demonstration with spoon on string 1404:23

Play water glasses like a musical instrument experiment 1231:24-25

Producing sympathetic vibrations 180:59

Quivering blade—see, hear and feel vibrations 45:14-15

Rate of vibrations determines pitch of a sound 65:86-87

Reducing the intensity of vibrations 180:61

Resonance and harmony in bottles experiment 1432:82

Resonance and sympathetic vibrations experiment 1432:80-81

Resonance of sound demonstrated by swinging pendulums 1179:109

Resonant frequency experiment with sand on oatmeal box 722:51

Rice dances on top of oatmeal box experiment 1066:102

Rice grains on drum demonstrate vibrations 957:27

Rubber bands around book demonstrate sound vibrations experiment (Primary) 1319:21

Rubber bands on box demonstrates—making 754:26-27

Rubber sheet over can and mirror pattern on wall experiment 723:11-12

Ruler on table demonstrates vibrations 226:8

Ruler on table demonstrates 501:8; 635:16-18

Seeing sound—experiment 399:64-65

Seeing sound experiment; see picture of your voice 1385:9

Seeing sound vibrations 150:100-101
Seeing sound vibrations experiment using plastic, cookie tin and sugar 1179:105
Seeing sound vibrations experiment 532:27; 656:30-31
Send sound thru a tube 45:22-23
Shakers, simple, how to make to demonstrate sound vibrations 1036:23
Simple experiments 105:44-47
Simple things to demonstrate vibrations 215:exp. #1,2,
Singing vibrators—rubber band fork 45:17
Singing wire—transformer and magnet experiment 722:38
Singing; making high and low sounds experiment 1279:25
Slinky toy over broom handle demonstrates sound waves in the air 1093:11
Soda bottles and homemade flute demonstrate 887:20-22
Solids favor sound—clock ticking sounds louder through wood 45:29
Sound and tension experiment 957:23
Sound gun; sound through cardboard tube gun puts out candle flame experiment 1093:10
Sound is caused by vibrations 65:78-79
Sound travels along string to cup experiment 1030:23
Sound travels through water and wood experiment 1432:56-57
Sound vibrations demonstrated with rice grains on drum experiment 1028:75
Sound vibrations demonstration with sugar on top of drum experiment 1253:20
Sound vibrations move puffed cereal experiment 1066:104-105
Sound viewer to view sound vibrations, how to make 1115:50-51
Sounds from vibrating bowl experiment 1079:63-64
Soundscope lets you see sound vibrations on wall, how to make 1369:70-71
Spinning discs—compare sound of coin and disc as they spin 45:16
Spoon bell—string makes sound louder 45:32
Spoons and string demonstrate sound vibrations (Primary) 422:18-25
Straw whistles demonstrate sound vibrations and pitch 1432:40-42
String and can telephone—making 635:13-15
String bass from large box and wooden pole, how to make 1163:11
String lengths demonstration 569:44
String telephone demonstrates—making 696:38-39
String telephone experiment; which materials work best to transmit sound 1284:20-21
String telephone, how to make 1007:57-59
String telephone, tuning forks, musical glasses experiments 1004:5.011
Strings on clothes hanger bring sound to your ears experiment 1330:72-73
Sympathetic and forced vibrations—experiment 90:28-36
Sympathetic vibrations demonstration with two glasses 937:120-121
Sympathetic vibrations in water glasses experiment 1432:83-85
Sympathetic vibrations with water glasses 360:51
Teeth; sound vibrations through our teeth experiment 1432:58-59

Telephone from cup and string demonstrates sound vibrations 1093:14
Telephone from yogurt containers lets you hear sound vibrations experiment 1255:24
The bigger the vibrations, the louder the note 186:50-51
The grass whistle 585:15
The musical comb 291:152
The noisy can experiment 563:14-15
The roaring ruler 360:86
The sounding board—experiment 585:11
Timbre experiment 585:10-11
Tone tests 686:13-14
Transverse vibrations with xylophone 2:80-83
Trumpet from hose and funnel, how to make 1163:11
Tune guitar without using your ears 350:96
Tuning fork and ping pong balls demonstrate vibration 837:33-34
Tuning fork experiment 957:29
Tuning fork in glass of water demonstrates 734:6-7
Tuning fork in water demonstrates 882:8
Tuning fork makes wave pattern in powder on glass experiment 1141:24
Tuning fork moves water around in glass experiment 1141:26
Tuning fork vibrations experiment 1284:9
Twanger to demonstrate vibrations—making 734:23
Vibrating comb against wooden door experiment 1432:60-61
Vibrating string produces a sound experiment 1405:109
Vibrating whirly-birds, how to make 600:16-17
Vibration detector—how to build 563:17-18
Vibration motor—vibrations in wood stick spin propeller 45:34-35
Vibration transmitter using a balloon—how to make 92:56-57
Vibrations—experiment 585:13
Vibrations from homemade drum going thru tunnel put out flame experiment 723:13-14
Vibrations in paper on comb produce sound 291:152
Vibrations in resonance in empty bottles experiment 1066:101
Vibrations of bell shaped objects—experiment 2:84-87
Vibrations of rods and wires—experiments 2:76-79
Visible sound vibrations 350:92-94
Voice vibrations demonstration with paper tube and tissue paper 1141:27-28
Voice vibrations experiment 957:27
Water pipe sound travel experiment 1432:77-79
What can carry sound—experiments 563:12
What is sound; coffee can and rubber cover experiment 851:27-28
Why a horn honks 686:36-40
Why does a bell ring 686:17-21
Why seashells produce unusual sounds experiment 1432:32-33
Wine glasses and water idiophone make music experiment 1209:66-67
Wire dances on rim of glass experiment 1007:62-63
Xylophones use columns of air to amplify the musical sounds experiment 1209:68-69
Yogurt cup record player demonstrates sound vibrations 1073:35
You see it before you hear it, measure when sound reaches you 45:42-43

SOUND—WAVELENGTH

Pan pipes demonstrate sound wavelengths experiment 1333:26-27

SOUND—WAVES

Air shock wave puts out candle flame experiment 1432:21-23

Blow out candle with sound waves sound cannon experiment 734:7

Books falling demonstrate 635:29-31

Boom-box tube experiment 1476:65-66

Bouncing sound from smooth surface demonstrates sound reflection experiment 1179:111

Bouncing sound to produce echo, how to do using cardboard tubes 1036:20-21

Bouncing sound waves experiment 1045:12-13

Bouncing sounds experiment using two long cardboard tubes and ticking watch 1093:17

Bouncing waves 95:36

Broomstick and watch demonstration (Primary) 215:exp. #10

Can thread carry your voice experiment 902:13

Cannon fires sound waves at foil curtain experiment 1333:8-9

Cannon from cardboard tubes blows out candles experiment 1045:6-7

Carbon dioxide filled balloon acts as lens to focus sound experiment 1132:29-1-29-2

Chicken sound from string in styrofoam cup experiment 1141:34-35

Constructive and destructive interference of sound waves experiment 1155:65-70

Controlling the direction of sound—make speaking tube and stethoscope 281:71

Crova's disk demo—what happens to air when sound waves pass thru air 2:24-27

Demonstrate complex sound waves 90:90-96

Demonstrate how sound travels to your ears 187:8-9

Demonstrate moving sounds 187:17

Demonstrate radio waves 90:76-77

Demonstrate sound waves 101:29-30

Demonstrate with coat hanger chimes 202:120-121

Demonstrating the speed of sound waves 180:62

Diffraction of sound waves experiment 1155:58-61

Doppler Effect demonstration with alarm clock tied to strong string 1209:48-49

Doppler Effect experiment using tennis ball with battery and buzzer 1132:41-1-41-2

Ears as sound wave collectors—diagram 366:174-175

Echo produced with paper tubes experiment 1066:92-93

Echoes; bouncing sound waves experiment with pan of water, pencil, carton 1209:34-35

Energy from sound causes something to move experiment 902:55

Ernst Chladni's vibration of metal plates experiment 1133:6.010

Exp. Shows sound waves need substance to put into wave motion 385:83-84

Experiment to show sound travels thru air, water and solids 165:23-29

Experiment to show sound waves travel in all directions 165:20-21

Experiment to show sound waves travel thru air 165:17

Experiment to show the effect of sound 'beats' 385:91-92

Experiments to show the interference of sound waves 385:89-90

Goose horn noisemaker demonstrates 999:16-17

Guitar from plywood and cardboard demonstrates sound waves 1333:14-15

Hearing aid—bet you can hear watch ticking across room with ears covered 228:51

High pitched sounds and sound shadow experiment high pitched sounds don't bend 1432:24-26

How can sounds be heard more clearly experiment 902:129

How compressional waves work—experiment 385:82-83

How far can the ground carry sound 333:43-44

How sound travels experiment 1155:22-23

How sound waves are reflected experiment using rope 1432:11-13

Magic trick; tuning fork sound projected where you want it 1010:28-31

Make a model of sound waves 161:41

Make Chladni's figures 172:65-66

Making a telephone 96:55-56

Making water waves experiment; mark frequency and wavelength 957:14

Marbles demonstrate sound waves experiment 734:6

Megaphone—make paper cone to demonstrate sound waves experiment 723:15-16

Megaphone from plastic jug demonstrates sound waves 1066:106-107

Milk bottle instrument—milk bottles with water make musical sounds 569:44

Moving air affects sound waves experiment 1432:127-129

Paper cup and string telephone demonstrate sound waves 1141:32-34

Parabolic sound collecting dish collects sound waves experiment 1476:71-75

Projects on sound waves 691:86-88

Reflecting sound waves experiment with watch, cardboard tubes, table 1432:17-18

Ripple water tank demonstrates sound waves, how to do 1179:111

See sound waves being made in tub of water experiment 1141:36

See sound waves experiment with yard stick, felt pen, cardboard, rubber bands 1209:32-33

Seeing sound waves 281:65

Seeing sound waves experiment with can covered with stretched rubber and mirror 1079:68-69

Sending sound waves through liquids and solids 180:58

Singing piano sends back your voice 95:37

Slinky demonstrates 723:18-19

Slinky on table—demonstrates 635:31-32

Slinky spring demonstrates sound waves experiment 1284:13

Slinky toy demonstrates sound waves 957:17

Sound + sound = silence 161:43-44

Sound bounces—steering sounds around a corner—experiment 45:57

Sound can be reflected 65:96-97

Sound conduction—experiment 585:8

Sound makes waves 96:48-49

Sound moving in different materials experiments 1155:35-37

Sound wave fired at target experiment 1028:76

Sound wave makes candle flicker experiment 1163:7

Sound wave patterns in a room experiment with pattern of ripples in water 1432:14-16
Sound wave transfer tube and cone experiment to hear and see sound waves 999:10-12
Sound waves—experiment 350:93-94
Sound waves can be directed 65:90-91
Sound waves demonstrated by pebbles in tub of water 45:58-60
Sound waves from a rubber band experiment 1432:8-10
Sound waves travel—make paper cup telephone (Primary) 215:exp. #11
Sound waves travel—spoon and string—experiment 215:12-13
Sound waves travel better through carbon dioxide than through air experiment 1476:69-70
Sound waves travel through air 96:49-50
Sound waves travel through cardboard tube experiment 1036:12-13
Sound waves travel through metal 96:52-53
Sound waves travel through strings and fingers 96:53-54
Sound waves travel through wood 96:51-52
Soundscope makes sound waves visible—how to make 366:180
Speed of sound in air; measure experiment 871:4.009
Standing waves in string—experiment 691:61-66
Standing waves projects 691:67-68
Straw horn demonstrates 999:7-8
Stringed instrument to demonstrate waves, making 870:44-46
Sugar on cake tin drum demonstrates sound waves 1045:6
Telephone from oatmeal carton demonstrates sound waves experiment 999:13-15
Telephone from paper cups and wire experiment 1045:16-17
Transverse and longitudinal waves on a Slinky experiment 1155:30-32
Travel—table top Indian experiment with watch 360:89
Travel—use fork, spoon, cans and thread to demonstrate 360:39-41
Tube kazoo demonstrates 999:17-18
Tuning fork vibrations over cylinder experiment 1132:72-1-72-2
Two-tone straw experiment demonstrates 999:9
Vibrating flames and mirrors—experiment to demonstrate 2:64-67
Vibrating speakers experiment; show waves of air produce waves of sound 1432:19-20
Water glass xylophone demonstrates 576:75-76
Wavelength of sound measured in a vibrating column of air experiment 1155:50-52
Waves in clear dish of water demonstrate wave motion and sound motion 1155:23-24
Waves on a rope experiment 1155:25-27
Waves on a Slinky experiment 1155:28-32
Wire spring demonstrate longitudinal waves and transverse waves 2:16-19

SOUND EFFECTS
Create nine different sound effects experiment 1209:72-73
How to do several sound effects 229:35-38

SOUNDING
Sounding a puddle, lake or pond—how to 636:109-110

SOW BUGS. *See also* **PILL BUGS**
Animal behavior and environment experiment 268:107-111

Are sow bugs afraid of the dark 264:37
Collect and observe sow bugs, how to do 913:12-13
Do sow bugs prefer dry or damp places—experiment 629:128
Effect of humidity on sowbugs; build sowbug hygrometer 864:103
Find a home for sow bugs 236:60
Glass jar filled with soil to observe sow bugs or wood lice experiment 1472:20-23
Hold a pillbug derby—how to 629:129
Home for sowbugs, how to make 1289:32-33
Isopod race, how to set up and do 1189:14-15
Keep sow bugs for observation 236:60
Observing wood lice experiment 1183:38
Reflex behavior; response to temperature changes experiment 936:18-19
Reflex behavior; response to touch experiment 936:20-21
Responses of terrestrial crustaceans 577:project #10
Sow bugs prefer dark and moist places experiment 1158:137-138
Sow bugs prefer dark, damp spots experiment 1363:29
Watching woodlice or sow bugs experiment 1181:30
What conditions of temperature, light and moisture do sow bugs like—exp. 586:135-137
Where do pill bugs like to live; observe and record; data table given 871:2.005
Wood lice prefer dry or wet places, light or dark places experiment 1183:55
Woodlice and insects prefer dry or damp, light or dark places experiment 1182:7
Which habitat is best; dark or light experiment 820:11

SPACE
Distance in space—how far away is it—ways to measure 253:196-198
Distances in, measure (Advanced) 668:62-64
How gravity affects inertia experiment 1405:20
Life on planets, detect (Advanced) 668:67-69
Life on planets; detect; repeat Gulliver Experiment 887:72-74
Magnetic fields, detect (Advanced) 668:70-72
Making a model of warped space-time project 833:259-260
Moon's surface, testing (Advanced) 668:65-66
Nebula; simulate an absorption nebula experiment 1479:19
Plotting a world line project 833:257-258
Space language, devise (Advanced) 668:73-75
Why space is dark demonstration 1394:202-203
Why space is dark experiment 1405:19

SPACE—MAN IN SPACE
Activities and experiments to demonstrate 564:86-100

SPACE BOX
How to make 358:56-57

SPACE CITY MODEL
How to make 365:49-51

SPACE COLONY
Model to build 362:10-11

SPACE COMPUTERS
Lunar colony computer—how to make 632:27-31

SPACE CREATURES
Aliens survive on planet you invent experiment 871:1.010
Bleep and peep—how to make 632:46-47
Cosmic centipede—how to make 632:32-35
Orbital be-bops—how to make 632:43-45

Saucerettes—how to make 632:41-42
Triangle transistors—how to make 632:22-26
SPACE CREATURES—TOYS
Bionic beasties—how to make 365:38
Downhill racer—how to make 365:39
Make a life size bionic buddy out of a friend 365:40-43
SPACE CRUISER
Model to make for space cruiser(solar panels, nose cones, radar dishes, and jet 362:16-21
Model to make 362:22-23
SPACE EQUIPMENT
Orbital ray detector—how to make 632:52-55
SPACE EXPLORATION
Activities/experiments to demonstrate new and possible systems and programs 564:101-110
SPACE FACTORY
Model for walking factory 1 and 2 362:12-15
SPACE METEORS
Meteors—how to make 632:68-71
SPACE MONSTER COSTUME
How to make 365:45
SPACE MONSTERS—TOYS
Make your own monster 365:36-37
SPACE ORBIT MOBILE
How to make 356:40-41
SPACE PEOPLE
Meteor man—how to make 632:16-22
Models to make 362:24-25
SPACE PEOPLE—TOYS
Little green people from outer space—how to make 365:28-29
Nut heads—how to make 365:30-31
Stringlies—how to make 365:32
SPACE PLANTS
Planetary plants—how to make 632:64-67
SPACE PROBES
Make a cardboard launcher 91:21-25
Unmanned exploration of solar system—demo activities on space probe data 564:60-72
SPACE PUPPETS
Directions for making a variety of space puppets 252:4-32
SPACE ROBOTS—TOYS
Robots—how to make 365:34-35
SPACE SCIENCE
Air pressure; potential force exerted by air pressure experiment (Advanced) 592:36-38
Alloy formation—experiment (Advanced) 592:67-68
Apparatus to demo. Why satellites and spaceship remain in orbit (Advanced) 592:24-26
Are earthworms sensitive to touch—experiment (Advanced) 593:45-46
Artificial gravity model experiment 1502:75-76
Bathroom in space—how does it work experiment 763:100
Buoyancy and sedimentation—experiment (Advanced) 592:58-59
Buoyancy effect—experiment (Advanced) 592:58-59
Chemical energy from solar energy and electrical energy—exp. (Advanced) 592:32-36
Circadian rhythm—determine circadian rhythm of an organism-exp. (Advanced) 592:78-79
Combustion—investigate the nature of burning (Advanced) 592:74-77

Convection currents-determine characteristics and causes of in gravity (adv.) 592:56
Convection in space experiment 763:95-96
Coordination and orientation-experiencing changes in gravity-exp. (Advanced) 592:95-96
Determine persons reaction to vibrational stress (Advanced) 592:98-100
Diluting gravity reduces acceleration of falling object experiment 1502:40-42
Eating in space experiment 1502:74-75
Egg in packing box dropped from height experiment 748:160-161
Electrical energy converted to chemical energy—experiment (Advanced) 592:32
Electrophoresis—studying ion migration to learn electrophoresis (Advanced) 592:71-73
Energy absorption—how various sources absorb energy—exp. (Advanced) 592:51-53
Falling object accelerates experiment 1502:40-42
Falling objects—experiments (Advanced) 592:16-19
Finding your weight in space experiment 763:101-103
Fluids in weightless environment—experiment (Advanced) 592:60
Food for space—experiment (Advanced) 592:100-105
Force of gravity and acceleration experiment 1502:40-42
Force of gravity is proportional to mass of object experiment 1502:43-45
Forces in space affect shape of drops of liquid demonstration 1394:206-207
Fractional distillation at low temperatures (Advanced) 592:42-43
Gas diffusion-rate of gas diffusion from spacecraft exp. (Advanced) 592:38-41
Gravity affects inertia demonstration 1394:208-209
Gravity; effect of gravity on height of Astronauts demonstration 1394:218-219
Grow crystals to find effects of gravity on crystals-formation (Advanced) 592:66-67
Growing plants in space experiments 763:98-99
How mass can be measured in space experiment 1405:16
Hydrostatic pressure on a spaceship experiment 763:93-94
Inertia balance—construct and calibrate an inertia balance (Advanced) 592:26-30
Insect flight observations (Advanced) 592:80-81
Making up your own experiments—guide for designing and recording (adv.) 593:49
Mars on Earth—simulate the conditions on Mars—experiment (Advanced) 592:88-93
Mass can be measured in space demonstration 1394:170-171
Materials separate because of gravity experiment 1502:67-68
Pendulum experiment; moving object moves unless force changes its direction 1502:26-28
Photovoltaic cell produces electrical energy experiment 1502:69-70
Plant fluids-determine speed at which fluids move thru stems (Advanced) 592:86-88
Satellite motion—investigate with ball and string—experiment (Advanced) 592:22-24
Sedimentation effects—experiment (Advanced) 592:59
Solar energy—converting solar energy to chemical energy (Advanced) 592:32
Solar energy in space experiment 763:102-105

Space module for living in space, how to build from thick cardboard 1518:44-45

Sun spots—observing solar activity (Advanced) 592:46-47,50

Surface tension—observe effects of surface tension—experiment (Advanced) 592:61-63

Weight of various masses when weighed on Moon's surface experiment 1502:44-45

Weightless burning candle experiment 763:96-97

Weightlessness; demonstrate apparent weightlessness in space 1394:210-211

Weightlessness in space experiment with plastic space capsule 1478:34

SPACE SHUTTLE

Lift off force makes cup rocket fly upward experiment 1035:8-9

Orbiter paper model—making and flying 314:77-82

Super space shuttle—how to make from sheet of paper 494:68

Rockets thrust demonstrated with balloon and thread 1478:33

SPACE STATION

Buildings—models to make 362:26-27

Clipper model collects and deposits paper clips from space station, make 1190:39-47

Control center model—how to make 415:70-71

Demonstrating how a space station rotates project 833:294-295

Fuel tanks models—how to make 415:68-69

How to make (Primary) 113:18-19

Launching pad model—how to make 415:67-68

Make a model space station 419:19

Plants; how would plants grow in a rotating space station experiment 1399:50-51

Space helmet model—how to make 415:76-78

Space men models—how to make 415:72-73

Space module for living in space, how to build from thick cardboard 1518:44-45

Space ships and moon base model—how to build 415:61-78

Space station from cutting board, making 779:55

Space station model, how to make from cardboard tubes, foil, paints 1449:22-23

Space wagons models—how to make 415:74-75

SPACE SUITS

How space suits affect an astronaut's blood demonstration 1394:214-215

Space suit materials help regulate temperature demonstration 1394:212-213

Water inside space suit; what happens to it in space demonstration 1394:216-217

What happens to perspiration inside a space suit experiment 1405:20

SPACE TOYS CONTAINER

How to make 365:46-48

SPACE TRAVEL. *See also* **ROCKETS**

A matter of gravity 68:30-31

Air pressure—empty space 68:46-48

Crystal light might benefit space travel demonstration using Life Savers 1394:200-201

Danger—meteoroids ahead 68:44-45

Design information space capsule for aliens to receive 1449:26-27

Designing interplanetary travel brochures project 833:252

Eating and drinking in space demonstration 1434:94-96

G-Forces, how to experience demonstration 1434:97-99

Gyroscope from old phonograph record shows gyroscope use in space travel 1434:116-119

How do gravity and inertia affect space travel experiment 900:225

How fast is your spaceship 68:38-40

How to lose weight in space 68:32-34

Is anything listening 68:61-63

Magnetic fields in space 68:58-60

Make a balloon rocket (Primary) 169:5

Plants in space 68:55-57

Plants; space weightlessness effect on growth of plants experiment 1434:124-127

Problem of carbon dioxide 68:52-54

Radiant heat from Sun makes energy in space experiment with cans of water 1434:120-123

Radio signals—Saturn calling 68:41-43

Star temperature—star light, star bright 68:64-65

Star tracks—color spectrums 68:66-68

The problem of water 68:49-51

Who was the first man in space project 1525:18-23

SPACE TRAVELER—TOYS

How to make 365:33

SPACE VEHICLES

Escape velocity of space rockets demonstration 1394:204-205

How rockets move in space demonstration 1394:194-195

Space probe model, how to make using cardboard tubes, foil, paints 1449:10-11

Space shuttle model, how to make from plastic bottle, paper, paints 1449:18-19

SPACE WEAPONS—TOYS

Laser cannon—how to make 365:44

SPACECRAFT

Altitude and mass ratio, compute (Advanced) 668:14-16

Apparatus to see how mass—radius and period relate to centripetal force 763:85-87

Artificial gravity—making (Advanced) 668:37-39

Astro shuttle—how to make 632:12-15

Atmosphere—experiments to demonstrate atmosphere control in spacecraft 564:74-75

Balloon rocket and multistage balloon rocket experiment 1502:55-57

Carbon dioxide, removal (Advanced) 668:53-54

Chemical batteries—activities and experiments to demonstrate 564:39-40

Closed life support system (Advanced) 668:55-57

Cosmic ray bombarder—how to make 632:56-59

Creeping moon bug—how to make 410:4-5

Data collection—activities and experiments to demonstrate 564:44-46

Data collection—computers—activities and experiments to demonstrate 564:47-48

Data collection—instruments—activities and experiments to demonstrate 564:45-46

Demonstrate roll, pitch and yaw motions of a spacecraft experiment 1405:21

Effects of low air pressure (Advanced) 668:46-47

Escape velocity—experiment (Advanced) 668:19-21

Food—experiments to demonstrate food supply on a spacecraft 564:75-76

Food—recipe for algae cookies—how to make 564:105

G-forces—experiment (Advanced) 668:30-32

Guidance—activities and experiments to demonstrate 564:44

Heat problems in return to Earth (Advanced) 668:24-26

Heat shield, design (Advanced) 668:27-29

Hot rod transporter—how to make 632:8-11

How do space rockets work experiment 1293:13-15

How to gain weight in space 68:35-37

Interplanetary rover—how to make 632:48-51

Life support systems—activities and experiments to demonstrate 564:73-80

Life support systems—hydroponics—plants without soil to provide food 564:104

Lunar Orbiter V—how to make 315:124-137

Make a lunar buggy 94:14-15

Mariner 5 Venus Spacecraft—how to make 315:111-123

Meteoroid shield for—making (Advanced) 668:44-45

Model for communication satellites experiment 1502:61-63

Model to build 362:8-9

Navigation and guidance—activities/experiments to demonstrate 564:39-40

Navigation and guidance—orbit—activities/experiments to demonstrate 564:42-43

Orbital workshop—construct model of orbital workshop 564:96-97

Paper match rocket—experiment (Advanced) 668:9-11

Personal hygiene—experiments demonstrate personal hygiene on spacecraft 564:77

Projectile launcher—experiments (Advanced) 668:3-8

Protection of payload—demo activities on protection from temperature extreme 564:48-50

Psychological aspects of space travel (Advanced) 668:58-60

Push-push back experiment with toy trucks 1502:46-49

Radio beacons in space (Advanced) 668:42-43

Reentry—activities/experiments to demonstrate reentry into Earth's atmosphere 564:79-80

Reentry and landing; balloon experiments to demonstrate 908:88-89

Replacing oxygen in (Advanced) 668:50-52

Rocket's thrust, measure (Advanced) 668:12-13

Satellite motion with and without an inward force experiment 1502:57-61

Simulate aiming a spacecraft for the Moon demonstration 1394:106-107

Solar cells—activities and experiments to demonstrate 564:40

Solar saucer—how to make 632:36-40

Space shuttle, how to make and launch experiment 1126:20-21

Space suit—activities/experiments to demonstrate space suit needed 564:78

Spacecraft into orbit experiment 908:84-86

Spaceship—how to make 652:24-25

Spaceships that fly from paper plates, straws, styrofoam cups and other materials 311:9-40

Speed changes on, measure (Advanced) 668:40-41

Stabilizing a space craft (Advanced) 668:22-23

Supersonic space patroller—how to make 632:60-63

Temperature—experiments to demonstrate temperature control on spacecraft 564:76-77

Testing for pure fuels (Advanced) 668:17-18

Waste—experiment to demonstrate waste facilities on a spacecraft 564:77

Waste products—waste water can be purified by distillation—how to 564:105

Water supply—experiments to demonstrate water supply on a spacecraft 564:75

Weightlessness experiment with doll in jar 908:86-87

What causes feeling of weightlessness experiment 1399:52-55

SPACECRAFT—FUTURISTIC MODELS

Alley-n-ship—making 581:38

Astronaut—making 581:29

Cupnik 2—making 581:31

Cupniks—making 581:30

Flat brat—making 581:40

Hoop-la—making 581:45-46

Hoopship—making 581:43-44

How to make and fly 581:7-18

Hula hoop—making 581:47

Mach mite—making 581:19

Nip ship—making 581:22

Petal ship—making 581:21

Plain old platter ship—making 581:35

Rim spinner—making 581:36

Rim spinners (eat your own space ship)—making 581:37

Ring racer and sprinter—making 581:24-25

Rope-a-lope—making 581:39

Spinnerator—making 581:26

Spinnerator 2—making 581:27

Super flatship—making 581:41-42

Tri-fly—making 581:23

Tri-mite—making 581:20

Trimaran—making 581:32-33

Water and water vapor in (Advanced) 668:48-49

Weightlessness aboard—experiment (Advanced) 668:34-36

Wobbler—making 581:34

X-plorer—making 581:28

SPACECRAFT—TOYS

All-terrain cola cargo carrier—how to make 365:14-17

Cola creeper—how to make 365:18-20

Ketchup craft surface speeder—how to make 365:12-13

Runabout—how to make 365:21

Shampoo speedster—how to make 365:9-11

Surface personnel transporter—how to make 365:22

SPARKLERS

Bright sparks from rosin powder 146:50-51

SPARKS

Flint and steel sparks—explanation of 322:20-21

SPATTER PRINT BOX

How to make 9:122-123

SPEAKERS. See SOUND—AMPLIFIERS

SPEAKING TUBE

How to make 172:54-56

SPECIES DIVERSITY

Ancient forest structure layers, how to draw project 1336:64

Biodiversity or species model of plants and animals experiment 1340:69-70

Conifers in your neighborhood or park, how to identify project 1336:63

Food web in ancient forests project, how to do 1336:64

Ideas to help save the ancient forests 1336:62-63

Log investigation; identify insects, animals and soil project 1336:64

SPECIES SURVIVAL

Biodiversity concept demonstrated project 1338:66-67

SPECIFIC GRAVITY. *See also* **HYDROMETER**

Archimedes; who discovered principles of specific gravity project 1525:89-91

Balance and weight used to measure specific gravity 577:project #31

Calculating specific gravity of rocks experiment 1342:44-46

Calculating the specific gravity of materials 180:24

Demonstration hydrometer—how to make 577:project #14

Density of rock measured by specific gravity experiment 1480:79

Estimating the specific gravity of certain floating solids 604:72-75

Liquid layers demonstrate specific gravity experiment 723:95-96

Make hydrometer to determine 436:44-45

Potato with high starch has higher specific gravity than low starch one 1065:41

Specific gravity—experiment 585:35-37

Specific gravity of rocks and meteorites, how to measure experiment 1062:86-87

Specific gravity of rocks and minerals, how to measure experiment 1062:86-87

Specific gravity of wood, how to measure 1075:58

Weigh rock in air and in water to determine specific gravity experiment 940:62-63

SPECIFIC HEAT

Calculate specific heat of materials experiment 1396:177-178

Compare specific heat of metals experiment 1515:72-75

How to measure 128:152-153

More heat has to be gained or lost to change temperature of water experiment 1396:176-177

Movement of air during land and sea breezes experiment 1396:177

Specific heat of water compared to soil and air experiment 1172:20-22

SPECIMENS

How to handle and mount specimen slides for your microscope 11:38-43

Specimen animals—specimen jars—how to do 293:22

Specimen replicas—plaster replicas of your plants flower seeds 9:124-125

SPECIMENS—MARINE ANIMALS

How to preserve specimens 530:76

SPECTOGRAPH

Mass spectograph model—how to make 577:project 68

SPECTROSCOPE

Chlorophyll spectrum as seen through a spectroscope experiment 1060:27-28

Colored filters absorptions measured by spectroscope experiment 860:215-216

Composition of stars determined using record spectroscope 1394:178-179

Constructing and using a spectroscope 400:107

Fraunhofer's dark lines in spectrum experiment; how to make simple spectroscope 1478:97

How to make and assemble 175:52

How to make prism type spectroscope 208:148-154

How to make spectroscope from shoe box 1434:20-24

Make a spectroscope 8:49-53; 564:57

Make a student spectroscope 386:64-66

Making a spectrum analyzing instrument project 833:189-192

Shoe box spectroscope—making 748:155; 763:49-52

Spectroscope—making (Advanced) 658:24-27

Spectroscope separates light into colors of rainbow experiment, how to make 1516:19-20

SPECTRUM. *See also* **COLORS; PRISMS; RAINBOWS**

"After-image" color of colors of spectrum experiment 1369:55

Chlorophyll spectrum as seen through a spectroscope experiment 1060:27-28

Color disc experiment 928:19

Color disk, making 941:48-51

Color filters change color of light experiment 860:214-216

Color from spinning black and white lines experiment 761:46-47

Color on color background effects experiment 761:37-38

Color wheel demonstrates how colors mix experiment with spinning color wheel 1213:26-27

Colored light on colors changes color experiment 928:23

Colored shadows experiment 761:35-36

Colored spinning discs appear to be white experiment 1073:80-81

Colors in colored light experiment 761:34

Colors in different shades differ in effects on photosynthesis experiment 1060:27-28

Colors of spectrum experiment 696:16-17

Colors of the rainbow experiment using mirror, water, and oaktag 1308:22-23

Demonstrate with colored disc and blue cellophane viewing box 595:35

Different ways of making rainbows experiment 1163:30-31

Diffraction grating spreads light into its component colors experiment 1132:90-1-90-2

Experiment with different colored cellophane papers 911:27

Filtering light with colored plastic experiment 935:16-17

Filters change the color of light experiment 941:56

Focal length and color experiment 761:44-45

Fraunhofer's dark lines in spectrum experiment; how to make simple spectroscope 1478:97

How to experiment with spectrum 128:201-202

Illusions using color to see if eye or brain is doing it experiment 761:57-58

Invisible colors of spectrum can be located experiment 715:112-114

Light box—building to experiment with mixing colors 761:32-34

Make a pure light spectrum 625:36

Make white light by spinning wheel of different colors 555:16

Making a spectrum analyzing instrument project 833:189-192

Making colors of the spectrum experiment 956:12-13

Making prism 436:64

Making rainbows 281:85

Meyer's experiment with colored shadows 761:37

Mirror and bowl of water create spectrum from sunlight project 967:14-15

Mixing colors with light experiment 928:18

Newton's white light through a prism experiment 1156:73-76

399

Newton's white light's constituent colors experiment 1133:6.007

Photosynthesis affected by colors of the spectrum experiment 1060:27-28

Prism, how to make experiment 941:54-55

Prism, slide projector and screen used to mix colored light experiment 1153:40-43

Seeing the spectrum—experiment 570:8-9

Separate light into colors experiment 1405:105-118

Shoe box spectroscope—making 748:155

Spectra and splitting light—experiment with prisms 569:39

Spectrum made from flashlight, water and mirror experiment 1478:96

Spectrum on paper, how to make using glass of water 1179:95

Spectrum; make using mirror, cardboard and container of water 1073:81

Spinning colors disc, making 935:18-19

Spinning disc with black and white colors shows other colors experiment 1369:56-57

Spinning disc with colors of spectrum experiment 1369:51-53

Splitting sunlight into the full spectrum of colors experiment 1092:43

Use prism to break light into mini-rainbow experiment 1063:177

Water and mirror makes spectrum 472:2216

Which colors of spectrum are hottest experiment 715:115

White light breaks into different colors 428:30

White light can be split into seven colors using glass prism experiment 1073:80-81

Why is light white; experiment with colored filters 860:217

Why light is white experiment 941:45-47

William Herschel's discovery of infrared rays experiment 1133:6.009

SPEED

Activities explain how time, distance and speed can be measured 1355:5-64

Find speed you travel over a distance experiment 1389:7

How fast is your toy car; calculating speed experiment; data table 1004:5.003

Measure speed of toy car experiment 1521:18-19

Measuring—how fast can people run 357:18-19

Measuring speed—how fast can you go 304:16-17

Muscle velocity—falling at constant speed 49:90-91

Terminal velocity—falling at constant speed 295:67-69

Time, distance, speed experiment with toy cars; data table given 871:4.001

Walking speed—how fast are you walking 333:123-127

SPEED BOAT

Make an electric powered swamp boat 223:26-27

SPICES

Adventure 30—perform a spicy experiment—mustard/pepper under microscope 403:107-109

SPIDER WEBS. See SPIDERS—WEBS

SPIDERS

Adventure 19—we look a spider in the eye under a hand lens 29:93-99

Adventure 43—inspect a spinning machine—spiders under microscope 403:156-160

Care of as pets 354:43-51

Collecting and keeping spiders, how to do 1117:49

Construct cage of wire mesh to house and observe 436:12

Daddy longlegs—how to examine with magnifying glass (Primary) 474:9-15

Do house spiders like light or dark best experiment 801:18-19

Do spiders produce an economically useful community 402:83-84

Experiments with jumping spiders 118:119-122

Hatching cage for spiders, making 801:17

How spider evaluates size of intruder in web experiment 1479:30

How to distinguish from other animals 40:212

Keeping live spiders 286:20-21

Net frame for collecting spiders, how to make 864:101

Orb weaver spiders and effect of coffee and aspirin on their webs exp. 864:102

Shoe box home for spider, how to make 801:9

Silk from spiders, how strong is it experiment 864:100

Spider house—how to make 234:66

Spider model toy—how to make (Primary) 466:28-29

Spiders live and reproduce in captivity (Primary) 232:34

Tarantulas—how to cage and care for 279:30-31

SPIDERS—COLLECTION AND PRESERVATION

Collecting and housing spiders, how to 776:14-17

Food for spiders 776:20-21

Catch spiders by beating bushes 286:19

Collecting spiders and webs 234:66-67

Daddy longlegs spider—how to catch and care for (Primary) 474:24-31

Finding spiders 286:17-18

Garden spiders—how to cage and care for 279:30-31

How to catch and cage 364:41

Making a spider collection 286:21-22

Making a sweep net 286:18-19

Orbweaver—how to cage and care for 279:30-31

SPIDERS—WEBS

Build a spider web, how to do 860:137-141

Building a frame for an orb web 286:40-42

Catching an orb spider web 236:64

Collect and mount spider web experiment, how to do 1464:88-89

Collect and mount spider webs, how to do 1071:84

Collect and preserve spider webs, how to do 1183:70

Collect and spray 436:72-73

Collect, display and study—how to 381:114-117

Collecting and observing webs, how to do 1094:47

Collecting and photographing spider webs 234:67

Collecting and preserving spider webs experiment 1476:109-110

Collecting spider webs, how to do 62:54-55; 854:83; 586:137-138; 723:82

Collecting webs and preserving with clear spray lacquer, how to do 1188:91

Constructing a web, how to do 1063:274

Determine how spider evaluates size of intruder in his web experiment 904:102-103

Do all spider webs have the same geometric pattern experiment 904:100-101

Embroidered spider web, how to make 1115:35-37

Find and preserve a spider web, how to do 1182:22

Finding webs 286:35-36

Game; web game, making web and how to play 1183:69

Glue on black cardboard catches web for you, how to do 801:10

How do spiders spin webs experiment 1293:43-45
How to observe and collect webs 119:123-132
How to observe how the spider spins a web 294:68-69
Model web and model spider, how to make 1445:24-25
Observe spider building web 40:212
Observe spider spinning web experiment 1158:132-135
Orb web, spray and put on cardboard, how to do 913:7
Outdoor projects with spiders and webs 118:123-137
Painting and collecting spider webs, how to do 879:206-207
Preserve a spider web, how to 832:66
Preserving spider web experiment 1158:135-136
Preserving webs 286:37-39; 1063:274
Record daily web catches for type and amount of insects project 969:48-49
Spider in container spins web on twig, how to set up 1188:90
Spider web collection 532:60
Spider web pictures, how to paint and collect 810:48
Spider web printing, how to 646:30-32
Spider webs are all different (Primary) 232:35
Spraying spider webs 236:64
Taking photos 286:37
Testing webs 286:36-37
Watching a dragline 286:39
Watching and collecting—how to 480:88-89
Web game, how to make and play 1182:21
Wood frame for spider to spin on experiment, how to make 1464:90-91

SPIES
Read message without opening envelope experiment 1083:104
Spy maps, how to make 812:22-23
Spy trap game, how to make 812:24-25
Traps to catch intruders, how to make 812:37

SPINNERS
Cardboard disc spinners, designs and patterns given, how to make 1299:62-63
Cardboard spinner on string demonstrates stored energy experiment 1496:18-19
Make a spinner experiment 1507:23
Paper spinners, how to make 1299:47
Straight lines appear to be circles on spinner—how to make 721:4

SPINNING
Amazing spin-dry experiment 231:121
Black and white on spinning disc produces colors experiment 736:41-44
Colors on spinning disc produces white experiment 736:45-46
Experiments with tops and speed 952:90-94
Speed measuring device for tops, how to make 952:87-90
Spinning disc—making 736:25-27
Spinning object can curve as it goes thru air 95:18-19
Top experiments with spinning doll 952:82-86
Top launching, how to do with experiments 952:15-21
Top with spinning doll, how to make 952:72-81
Top, how to make and do experiments 952:10-14
Top, metal ring top, how to make 952:26-29
Tops, comparing tops experiment 952:22-26
Tops, stroboscope and spinning tops experiment 952:50-53
Tops, testing different designs experiments 952:29-34
Tops, visual effects experiments with designs, making 952:34-44

SPINNING YARN
Make threads by teasing and spinning 257:25-29
SPIRALS
Drawing a spiral, how to do 1112:13-14
Flowering spiral 356:7-9
Merry-go-round mobile 356:42-43
Moving spirals experiment 1112:29
Soap bubble film on plastic spiral experiment 1482:30-31
Spiral flyer demonstrates spiral motion 1112:14-15
Spiral pattern of nautilus shell; overlay pattern with yarn, how to do 1299:35
Spiral patterns experiment; draw a spiral 1391:29
SPIRIT LEVEL
Spirit level, how to make to check exact horizontal line 1247:19
SPIROGYRA
Does acid rain affect the cell structure of Spirogyra experiment 997:99-101
Make a microscopic algae jungle 279:34-36
SPIROMETER
How to make 335:64
Spirometer measures amount of air in lungs experiment 1220:18
Spirometer measures lung capacity—how to make 577:project #3
SPIROSTOMA
New growth of spirostomum—experiment 484:41
Shrinking stentors or spirostoma—experiment 484:42
Spirostomum's digestion—experiment 484:42
SPONGES
Adventure 26—we learn something about sponges under a microscope 403:91-94
Comparing natural and synthetic sponges experiment 1290:75, 5.7
Damaged sponges grow through reaggregation experiment 1117:23
Freshwater sponge, collect and observe growth and water passage 771:152-157
How do sponges eat 236:116
Isolating sponge spicules experiment 1117:22
What happens to latex sponge in water experiment 1402:60-63
SPONTANEOUS GENERATION
Can life arise from lifeless material 402:94-95
Does life arise by spontaneous generation experiment 1156:50-51
Louis Pasteur's do microbes arise spontaneously experiment 1133:3.009
Redi's famous experiment that decaying food doesn't produce living organisms 1397:6-7
SPOOL PEOPLE
How to make a spool man pirate 545:28-31
SPOOLS
Toys from 364:122-123
SPORE PRINTS
Fern cycle observed 436:35
Grow your own ferns from spores using brick, moss and water 483:42-44
Moist bread in closed jar produces mold—collect spores from it (Primary) 452:65
Moss garden terrarium—how to make 483:68-70
Mushroom spore prints on paper, how to make 1038:27
Mushroom spore prints, how to make 784:39-40; 1044:36; 1071:86

Spore patterns from mushroom caps, how to make 1214:22; 1379:13

Spore prints from toadstool caps, how to make 1069:69

Spore prints from wetland mushrooms experiment 1492:50-51

Spore prints, how to do 442:unpaged; 749:42; 1063:256; 1114:62-63; 1145:29; 1298:53; 1313:126-127; 1440:68-70; 1457:35; 1490:43

SPORES. *See also* **FUNGI; MOSSES; MUSHROOMS; SLIME MOLDS**

Bread mold produces spores 294:23-24

Collecting mushrooms to see growth patterns 459:28-32

Cycles of a fern; how to grow ferns from spores experiment 1440:73-76

Demonstrate how plants grow from spores 119:91-99

Fern spores, how to grow plants from 879:180

Ferns grown from spores experiment 1069:63

Grow new plants from spores project 1313:59-63, 96

Growing one-celled microscopic organisms—bacteria of decay 294:20

Growing spores—experiment 352:39-40

Growing spores—the life cycle of a moss 148:12

How to see a spore 264:33

Making spore prints 148:13; 400:7; 585:156-157

Mushroom spores grow into mushrooms to eat, how to plant experiment 1306:18-19

Reproduction of spores experiment; make spore prints, how to do 978:54

Spore lore 231:73-74

Spore prints from mushrooms and ferns, how to make 646:78-80

Spores identify different types of fungi experiment 1134:4.002

Spores under a microscope, observe 889:47-48

Where do spores come from experiment 852:3-5

Why a puffball smokes demonstration 1440:71-72

Why bread molds experiment 1440:64-67

SPORTS

Aluminum versus wooden bats experiment 1154:114-115

Anaerobic workout test 881:22

Applied science and athletics—experiment 382:97-99

Balance tests 881:34-35

Ball bounce affected by surface experiment 881:72

Ball bounce affected by temperature experiment 881:73

Baseball bat has sweet spot; how to find it experiment 1209:50-51

Baseball; left handed players have advantage in baseball experiment 1154:20-22

Baseballs; why do curved balls curve experiment 881:28-29

Basketball "insurance" project 1070:32-33

Body position affects motion through air experiment 1154:51-53

Body type, shape and size chart project, how to make 881:6-7

Center of gravity and sports experiment 1154:72-76

Center of gravity test for human body, how to do 881:16-17

Clothes make a difference when you're sweating experiment 881:20-21

Crouched position gives sprinter an advantage experiment 1154:39-45

Discus throwers; effect of wind on their results experiment 1154:24-25

Draft importance in bicycle racing experiment 881:86-87

Drag and its effects experiment 881:78-79

Fat in food; fat finding experiment 881:49

Flexibility test comparing boys and girls, how to do 881:12-13

Flexibility tests; how good is your flexibility 881:14-15

Frozen sneakers give less friction experiment 881:62-63

Gravity affects playing paddle ball experiment 1399:76-79

Hang gliding, why it works demonstration 881:80-81

Heart beats; hear, see and calculate heartbeats, how to do 881:10-11

Helmets for eggs experiments 881:56-57

Hockey puck and Newton's Laws of Motion experiment 1154:30-37

Home field playing gives winning advantage in sports experiment 1195:79-93

Ice skates or roller skates demonstrate Third Law of Motion 1154:37-39

Landing from a jump experiment 881:40-41

Leg, arm rhythm keeps you in balance, how to test 881:44-45

Levers in sports equipment experiment 1154:25-28

Losing weight on skis experiment 1154:49-51

Lung capacity test 881:36-37

Muscle fibers, which are fast—twitch fibers 881:18-19

Patterns in sports play; test to demonstrate 881:24-25

Pitchers throw different kinds of balls experiment 1154:93-100

Reaction time; how fast is your reaction time test 881:42-43

Rotating or spinning balls in sports experiments 1154:80-93

Runners and walkers footprint tracks, how to tell the difference 881:46-47

Running experiment; how to measure your stride 1389:19

Running the bases speed experiment 1154:45-49

Running; what happens to average speed as distance of run increases experiment 1154:16-18

Shape of trajectory depends on how object is thrown experiment 1389:9

Shoes; friction and athletic footwear experiment 1154:22-23

Soccer board game with magnets, how to make 1043:28-29

Spin on ball is important demonstration 881:68-69

Sports team analysis of players spread sheet program computer project 1021:72-74

Sweet spot on baseball bat, how to find it 881:64-65

Sweet spot on tennis racket or baseball bat experiment 1154:115-121

Track surfaces; runner's speed affected by track surface experiment 1154:23-24

Use of helmets important in sports experiment 1154:69-72

SPRAY BOTTLES

Water flows uphill experiment using plastic bottle, tubing and balloon 1208:46-47

SPRAYERS

Demonstrate principle of sprayers; when air goes faster, pressure falls 1211:22

SPRING. *See also* **SEASONS—SPRING**

Spring activities—decorate eggs, make Easter cake, make charoset 493:40-41

Spring activities—make wind vane, kite, play hunters and hares game 493:42-43

Spring activities—study seed sprouts, buds, field diary, collect frog eggs 493:38-39

Why is Spring sometimes late experiment with soils and light bulb 1003:13

SPRING PEEPERS. *See also* **FROGS**

Collection and care of 313:38-42

SPRING SCALES. *See also* **SCALES—MEASUREMENT**

Making 436:73

SPRINGS

Creeping toy demonstrates (Primary) 210:31

Elastic scale experiment 1112:27

How do springs help with work experiment [Primary] 743:14

Metal spring experiment 1112:26

Paper spring experiment 1112:25-26

Spring board—spring board action—demonstrate with ruler (Primary) 324:7

Spring engines—rubber band model boat 267:29-30

Springy toy—how to make 754:11

Teeter-totter toy, how to make 948:6-7

SPRINGTAILS

Adventure 37—view the most primitive insects under the microscope 403:133-136

Springtails and water film experiment 484:93

SPRINKLERS

Compressed air makes water sprinkler and pop-gun work experiment 1211:25

How sprinklers work demonstration 1230:12-13

Why a water sprinkler turns experiment 1436:51-53

SPROUTS. *See also* **SEEDS—SPROUTS**

Alfalfa seeds or mung beans, how to make sprouts to eat 1406:75

Alfalfa sprouts—growing 733:27; 759:19-20; 880:116

Alfalfa sprouts in a jar, how to grow 899:187

Bean sprout sandwiches 236:46

Bean sprouts, how to grow 770:99; 1264:13; 1486:8

Chia seed sprouts on sculpture, how to grow 899:186-187

Cress and mustard seed sprouts, how to grow 913:30

Cress seed sprouts, growing, how to 879:137-138

Cress sprouts, how to grow 1486:4-5

Cress sprouts on a sponge, how to grow 899:186

Dried bean sprouts, how to do and experiments with 898:46

Eggshell containers with mustard or cress sprouts, how to do 1306:4-5

Grow and harvest sprouts experiment 888:56-58

Grow edible sprouts without soil experiment 904:70-71

Grow mung bean sprouts 376:4; 624:27

Grow seeds on a sponge 780:32-33

Grow sprouts from seeds 264:18; 722:66

Grow sprouts from seeds experiment 1335:114

Growing sprouts, how to 219:3-6; 231:98-99; 629:139; 832:53; 854:51; 866:152

Growing your own sprouts experiment 1194:27

How to grow sprouts experiment 980:74

Mung bean sprouts in a jar, making 868:15

Mung bean sprouts, how to grow 784:75-77; 879:140-141

Mustard and watercress seeds grow quickly into shoots (Primary) 481:14-15

Mustard or cress seeds, how to make sprouts to eat 1406:83

Mustard seed sprouts grow on potato, how to do 913:30

New sprouts from old vegetables experiment, how to grow 1486:12-13

Sprout garden bags—making in zip lock bags (Primary) 535:41

Sprout seeds without dirt or sunlight experiment 1231:44-45

Sprouting alfalfa seeds, how to do 1491:54-55

Sprouting beans experiment 748:86; 1238:62-63

Sprouting seeds (germination)—how to 384:7-11

Sprouting seeds to eat 380:41

Sprouts as storehouses 280:58

Sprouts from beans, how to grow 1178:24

Sprouts from lentils, how to grow 1178:27-28

Sprouts from sunflower seeds, how to grow 1178:30

Sprouts give energy for life, how to grow 1030:8-9

Starch; test sprouts for starch experiment 784:77

Test seeds to see if they sprout in a seed doll experiment 1078:19

Wheat sprouts, how to grow 1486:32

Winter garden—how to 442:unpaged

SQUARES

Tricks with 27:13-19; 27:25-29

SQUASH

Squash seeds, how to plant and grow indoors 1178:23

SQUEEZE BOTTLE

The squeeze bottle experiment 563:188-189

SQUID

Dissecting—how to 692:31-37

Squid anatomy experiment 1117:37

Demonstrate squirt of squid in water with balloon 977:55

SQUIRRELS

Collection and care of 390:59-61

Flying squirrels—care of 390:84-86

Flying squirrels jump by gliding demonstration 1186:27

Make a nest box for squirrels 264:92

STABILITY. *See also* **BALANCE**

Shape of bottles effects stability 274:24

STAGE PERFORMING BOX

How to make 358:68-69

STAGECOACH

Model—how to make 415:13-14

STAIN REMOVERS. *See also* **STAINS**

Duplicate advertising claims experiment using stained fabrics and cleaners 1295:123

Potato removes food stains from clothing experiment 1065:14

What kind of stain removers work best experiment 1063:317

STAINED GLASS

Colored paper filtering white light stained glass window experiment 1308:8-9

Stained glass window, how to make 1357:29

STAINING. *See also* **MICROSCOPE**

Staining bacteria for microscope slides—how to do 11:128-135

STAINS. *See also* **STAIN REMOVERS**

Laundry detergents effect on clothing stains experiment 1396:28

Which laundry detergent or soap removes clothing stains project 1210:57-60

STALACTITES

Crystal pillars experiment 883:42-43

Gravity affects formation of stalactites experiment 1399:64-67

Grow a stalactite 532:11
Make stalactites, how to do 663:33; 666:43; 909:41
Stalactites formed in caves experiment with small jars/string/Epsom salts 1399:66-67
Stalactites from Epsom Salts solution experiment 1020:49-52

STALACTITES AND STALAGMITES. *See also* **CRYSTALS**
Baking soda stalactite, how to grow experiment 1277:41
Crystal pillars that meet in the middle experiment 1136:14-15
Demonstrate formation of 176:22; 293:5; 715:45-47
Form these structures using baby food jars and Epsom Salt experiment 1396:121
Formation of stalactites and stalagmites demonstration 1023:30-31
Grow magnesium sulfate crystals to demonstrate 346:37-38
How do stalactites form in caves experiment 852:27-28
How stalactites and stalagmites form experiment using jars of Epsom salts 1435:42-44
Make stalactites and stalagmites 175:31
Make stalagmites from gelatin 203:21
Make your own stalactites and stalagmites experiment 1384:9; 1428:11
Make your own stalactites experiment 1286:17
Model of how stalactites and stalagmites form in caves experiment 1046:88-90
Stalactite, how to grow 1028:23
Stalactites and stalagmites, how to make experiment 1042:28-29
Washing soda stalactite experiment; how to grow 1480:121

STAMENS. *See also* **FLOWERS**
Flower stamens react to touch—barberries, cornflowers 271:52-55

STAR MAPS
The night sky—make star maps to use with flashlight 588:52

STAR WORLD
Create your own star world 632:1-71

STARCH. *See also* **COMPOUNDS; IODINE**
A formula for paste 336:57-58
A test for starch 30:33
Adventure 17—take a lesson in food analysis—starch grains under microscope 403:61-65
Body converts starch to sugar with saliva experiment 1238:94
Chemical test for starch 335:79-80
Chemical trick starch on finger in iodine water—how to do 723:47
Chemist's test for starch 122:92-95
Chlorophyll extracted from plant leaves demonstrates starch in plants 978:41-42
Cornstarch will thicken a sauce experiment 1484:114
Creamed celery recipe 537:70
Do plants produce starch 97:32-33; 273:32-33
Does popcorn dissolve in water experiment 1250:41-42
Enzyme effect on starch in digestive tract experiment 1395:171-176
Experiments in finding starch in plants 784:78-79
Experiments to show presence of starch 97:32-33
Food tests for starch 253:115-116

Gottlieb Kirchhof's starch is made up of sugar units experiment 1133:2.009
Heat breaks starch into smaller molecules experiment using cornstarch 1251:77-79
How does acid pH affect enzymatic activity on starch experiment 1395:174
How does heat affect starch—thickening experiment—making creamed celery 537:29
How does heat affect starch—thickening experiment—making popcorn 537:26-27
How does heat affect starch—thickening experiment—making potential 537:28-29
How to find starch 261:36-37
In what foods is starch present and how can it be detected 402:77
Iodine on rice identifies starch experiment 814:41-44
Iodine test for starch in foods experiment 1214:13
Iodine test for starch in foods 283:27-38
Iodine test to show starch in potato 876:72-74
Iodine tests for starch experiments 980:52-53
Iodine tests on paper experiment 980:53
Iodine to ink—a test for starch 147:81-82
Leaf starch test proves chlorophyll in leaves makes food 366:220
Making popcorn recipe 537:68
Photos from photosynthesis experiment show starch produced in plant leaf 1476:105-106
Photosynthesis; starch is produced when leaves photosynthesize experiment 1308:11
Plants make starch experiment 737:13
Potato starch grains under microscope using iodine stain experiment 713:54
Potatoes have starch experiment 1238:40-41
Potatoes; test for starch in potatoes experiment 1065:41
Potential recipe 537:69
Saliva effect on a starch experiment 1395:168-169
Specific gravity higher in high starch potatoes than in low starch ones 1065:41
Starch and heat—experiment 585:84-85
Starch digestion by enzymes in plants 273:42-43
Starch from potatoes 85:30-31
Starch in germinating lima bean seed experiment 1060:57-58
Starch in plants demonstration 978:40
Starch iodine test for vitamin C in foods experiment 1259:33-34
Starch is produced in plant leaves during photosynthesis experiment 1479:25
Starch is produced in plant leaves experiment 904:28-29
Starch molecules larger than sugar molecules experiment 1251:75-76
Starch solution for experiments, how to make 1395:198-199
Starch stored in seed parts tested with iodine experiment 1395:12-13
Starch test—experiment 598:46
Starch test for leaves of plant kept in sunlight and in darkness experiment 1069:43
Starch test for starch in plant leaves experiment 1028:63
Starch test for starch in seeds experiment 1060:58
Starch test on leaves 146:52-53
Test crackers with and without saliva for starch experiment 723:71-72
Test food for starch experiment; chart given 792:29

Test for enzymes in human saliva that break down starch molecules 482:32-34

Test for presence of starch in different materials experiment 1479:55

Test for starch 72:54-55; 346:131

Test for starch—we can't make it but plants can 280:54

Test for starch in apples using iodine experiment 971:47

Test for starch in certain foods experiment using iodine as indicator 1435:27-29

Test for starch in chewed and unchewed food experiment 1396:64-65

Test for starch in different materials experiment 905:106-107

Test for starch in flour 157:25

Test for starch in food 807:92; 146:38-39

Test for starch in paper experiment using iodine as indicator 1435:33-34

Test for starch in plants 86:39-40

Test for starch in potatoes 83:33-34

Test for starch in seed leaves 270:37

Test for starch in toast experiment using iodine as indicator 1435:30-32

Test for starch in toasted bread experiment 723:199

Test for starches in various foods experiment 1259:26-27

Test materials for presence of starch experiment 1405:56

Test sprouts for starch experiment 784:77

Testing foods for starch 116:180-181

Testing foods for starch experiment 739:13

Testing for starch—prove that starch is produced in a leaf 574:35

Testing for starch in a leaf 294:39

Testing for starch in foods with iodine experiment 924:36

Testing for starch in potatoes—experiment 628:71

Testing for starch, fat and protein in food using chemicals experiment 1069:19

Testing solution for starch, how to make 1396:206

Testing your food for starch with iodine 571:35

The blue test game 146:38-39

What foods contain starch experiment recording sheet given 747:39-40

Which foods contain starch experiment 901:215

White paper turns blue; test for starch experiment 781:44-45

STARFISH

Adventure 49—starfish under a hand lens 29:212-216

How do starfish open shells of mussels experiment 1397:64 67

Spy on a starfish walking and eating 236:122

Starfish model toy—how to make (Primary) 467:6-7

Studying a starfish 294:62-63

STARS

Absorption nebulae, how to demonstrate 1394:152-153

Alphabetical list of the bright stars 386:144-145

Altitude of a star, how to estimate 1434:58-60

Astrolabe to show altitude of star, make from poster board, straw, string 1434:42-44

Black hole formation demonstration 1394:132-133

Brightness of star's light, how to measure demonstration 1394:180-181

Brightness of stars due to distance or to stars giving off more light experiment 1062:8-9

Brightness of stars, how to measure experiment 1063:460

Brightness of stars, how to measure with star magnitude gauge, how to do 1115:138-139

Brightness; how distance affects stars brightness experiment 1479:17

Building a star plotter—how to do 710:62-63

Calculating the changing brightness of a cepheid variable project 833:269

Cepheids; why variable stars pulsate experiment 1479:18

Classification; how stars are classified 1293:61-62

Clock; star clock to tell time, patterns given, make from cardboard 1299:79

Color of experiment (Advanced) 668:79-80

Compare distances between stars using astrolabe experiment 1405:17

Composition of (Advanced) 668:81-82

Composition of stars determined using record spectroscope 1394:178-179

Constellation finder, how to make 1063:461-464

Constellation viewers, how to make from tin cans, paper, glue 1114:133

Counting stars—how to do 710:71-72

Counting stars 586:39-40

Cross staff used to measure altitude of stars, how to make 1115:140-142

Daytime stars; demonstrate stars are always shining 1394:140-141

Daytime; why we cannot see stars during day experiment with lamp/posterboard 1478:29

Demonstrate star brightness and distance (Primary) 169:29

Diffusion of Sun's light keeps us from seeing stars in daytime experiment 1062:78

Distance affects star's brightness demonstration 1394:136-137

Distances between stars measured using astrolabe, how to make 1394:176-177

Double star; who was first to detect a double star project 1525:59-60

Drawing star trails 833:2-3

Faint stars, how to see 1434:70

Finding out the brightness of stars project 833:60-61

Finding Polaris—how to do 491:40-41

Five and ten pointed stars, how to make 1352:55-56

Five pointed stars—making 444:28-31

Four and eight pointed stars, how to make 1352:56

Guided tour to see stars and constellations 1063:465-469

How far is a star 292:111-119

How to make a star map 175:48

How to measure altitude by stars 292:43

Keeping time by stars—make device for 381:33-37

Light box and slides with constellations experiment, how to build 1476:166-167

Light pollution survey of your local area project, how to do 1478:31

Locating stars methods experiment, how to do 1063:455

Locating stars; soda straw star finder, how to make 837:12-13

Magnitude (relative brightness of stars) experiment; how to categorize 1062:28

Magnitude—how to measure 231:115

Make a five pointed star with one snip 392:106 108

Make a sky map 231:117

Make a star chart 169:28

Make believe stars—show why stars twinkle 291:194

Making a brightness measuring tool project 833:61-63

Mapping stars project 833:83-85

Measure altitude of stars and planets with instrument you build 834:124-125

Measure altitude of stars and Sun, how to make astrolabe 1115:134-137

Measuring brightness and distance project 833:63-65

Measuring degrees between the stars project 833:79-82

Metal and its effect on energy waves from stars demonstration 1394:182-183

Milky Way appears to be a hazy cloud demonstration 1394:146-147

Mobile of stars with blue stars, red giants, white dwarfs experiment 1478:120

Model star—making (Advanced) 658:34-36

Nearest stars, model shows three-dimensional positions of nearest stars 1478:117

Night sky, how to observe 1063:456-458

Nocturnal star clock, patterns, how to make 1063:298-299

Parallax effect using homemade stars experiment 1478:116

Path of stars near North Star seems longer than stars farther away experiment 1062:71-73

Photographing stars and planets project 833:181-182

Planisphere to observe stars in sky at certain time and date, how to do 1521:8-9

Planisphere, map of sky, how to make working model 1478:112-113

Plotting the life cycles of stars project 833:267-268

Polaris—altitude measured by astrolabe you build 763:5-6

Polaris—how to find in sky 763:3-4

Position of Big Dipper and Polaris, how to record 1394:156-157

Pulsar; flashing model of pulsar, make with batteries, wires, bulbs 1478:127

Quadrant to determine stars altitude, how to make 862:45-56

Radio wave receivers are curved demonstration 1394:186-187

Scintillations; experimenting with scintillations [twinkling] 958:26

Setting up an astrolabe 175:56-57

Shooting stars and their cause demonstration 1394:150-151

Shooting stars; cause of shooting stars experiment 1479:19

Show Milky Way and other galaxies with tea leaves 169:31

Sidereal time and synodic time 292:78-80

Six and twelve pointed stars, how to make 1352:53-54

Size affects star's brightness demonstration 1394:138-139

Sky—spy gadget to view stars—how to make 649:26-27

Spectroscope measures light from stars—how to make 763:49-52

Spiral galaxy movement demonstration 1394:154-155

Star closest to the Earth demonstration 1394:134-135

Star clusters; explore stars around certain constellations experiment 1217:32-33

Star dial instrument experiment; make, adjust to correct date, point at Polaris 1478:25

Star directions (Primary) 303:22

Star finder, how to make from cardboard 1329:35-37

Star map pattern, how to make 862:64

Star maps and charts—how to make 234:102-103

Star patterns can be seen only from our particular position in space experiment 1062:74-75

Star theater planetarium experiment made from battery, wires, bulb, posterboard 1478:108-109

Star tracks, how to photograph 1434:90-93

Star trails—take a good picture of star trails 381:44-45

Star watching 231:114-115

Star wheel to show motion of stars using batteries 102:144-145

Star-trail photographs experiment, how to make 958:82-85

Stargazing, how to do 1063:454

Starlight; how starlight travels experiment 1479:17

Stars—latitude from 382:110-111

Stars appear to rotate demonstration 1394:142-143

Stars are always shining demonstration 1405:13

Stars seem to move in circles in the night sky demonstration 1394:130-131

Star scope—making (Primary) 535:62

Stellar pancakes, recipe given, help you see constellations 887:12-13

Streetlight pollution experiment; design better light pollution streetlights 1478:30-31

Streetlight pollution of night sky viewing experiment; which pollutes most 1478:30-31

Taking pictures of star trails 175:50-51

Technique to count stars 657:96-97

Tell time by the stars, nocturne night dial, pattern given, how to make 1114:128-131

Telling time by the stars—how to do 710:75

Theodolite to find altitude and azimuth of star, how to make 1434:45-49

Theodolite, how to make from wooden post, straw, compass, protractor 1217:10-11

Tin can planetarium—how to make 292:18

Twinkling, cause of (Advanced) 668:76-78

Twinkling; why does a star twinkle 577:project #35; 1217:42

Twinkling; why stars twinkle and planets do not experiment 1478:114-115

Twinkling; why stars twinkle demonstration 1394:158-159

Twinkling; why stars twinkle experiment 941:17-19; 1434:79-81

Use a balloon to show our expanding universe (Primary) 169:32

Variable stars (cepheids) pulsate demonstration 1394:148-149

Variable stars, observation (Advanced) 658:89-93

Why can't we see stars in the daytime—experiment to see stars 381:30-33

Why do stars twinkle 40:246-247; 102:146-147; 291:194

Why stars appear to rotate experiment 1405:14

Why stars disappear during the day 40:246

Why stars seem to move in circles across the night sky experiment 1405:13

STARS—CONSTELLATIONS. *See also* **CONSTELLATIONS**

Demonstrate do the constellations move (Primary) 169:27

Make a oatmeal box planetarium 202:16

Make a star box to show the constellations 119:179-187

Make a star map to show constellations 169:26

Make star patterns and models of constellations 169:25

Make star shiner with can and flashlight 288:28-29

Patterns in the sky 253:186-187
What is a constellation 40:247-250

STATIC ELECTRICITY. *See also* **ELECTRICITY—STATIC ELECTRICITY; ELECTROSCOPE; ELECTROSTATICS; LEYDEN JAR**

Aluminum leaf electroscope—making 5:34-37
Are you attractive balloon experiment 906:103
Attracting/repelling forces between objects due to electrical charges 1404:26-27
Attraction between charged particles demonstration 1479:107
Balloon—this dog rolls over (Primary) 64:unpaged
Balloon demonstrates 695:48
Balloon experiment 445:65-66
Balloon experiments with static electricity 1063:161
Balloon trick solution experiment 829:45-46
Balloons and static electricity experiments 1200:31
Balloons charged with static electricity experiment 1066:122-123
Balloons demonstrate static electricity 682:23; 760:34-35; 1016:6-7
Balloons repel one another experiment 955:5
Bending water experiment; balloon attracts water demonstration 1029:8
Bending water with static electricity and balloon experiment 1073:53
Bet you can fill a stocking with an invisible leg 228:57
Can static electricity do work experiment 851:13-15
Cereal acrobats 280:30
Cereal sticks to rubbed comb experiment 722:14
Charge a balloon experiment 768:3-4
Charge an object with static electricity experiment data table 1405:87-88
Charge detector—how to make 1028:100-101
Charge detector shows static electricity can travel experiment 1029:16-18
Charge electroscope negatively—how to 5:42-45
Charge newspaper and get a spark 827:33
Charge object with static electricity using comb experiment 1404:16-17
Charge piece of paper experiment 768:4-5
Charge two or three balloons to demonstrate same charge repels experiment 768:9
Charge yourself and light fluorescent bulb experiment 768:3
Charged balloons attract cereal; jumping cereal event experiment 1208:72-73
Charged balloons repel one another and attract water experiment 926:100-102
Charged comb experiment 906:101
Charged grains experiment 768:21-22
Charged objects affect other objects experiment 1426:23-24
Charged objects react; charges travel and effect experiment 1012:47-48
Charges make static detector go round experiment 723:122-123
Charging electroscope by induction 5:46-49
Charging object (pithball) by contact 5:30-33
Charging the ends of a conductor by induction 5:38-41
Comb makes stream of water bend experiment 1005:6
Comb picks up paper experiment 1005:6
Dancing dolls—demonstrate 651:42-43
Dancing papers experiment 906:100
Dancing snow experiment 885:77-78
Dancing tissue paper dolls demonstrate 938:7-8
Defy gravity balloon experiment 906:98
Demonstrate with balloon 780:34-35
Demonstrate with invisible leg from nylon stocking 202:90
Demonstrate with plastic bags 780:18-19
Detector—how to make 436:74
Do electrically charged objects attract nonmetal objects experiment 851:11-13
Do like charges attract or repel experiment 831:11-14
Effect of static electricity on cellophane tape demonstration 1404:28-29
Effect of static electricity on foil pieces demonstration 1479:109
Effect of static electricity on pieces of foil experiment 1404:220-221
Electric capacitor—using homemade capacitor to store electrical charges 5:78-81
Electric charge stored produces sparks experiment using electrophorus you make 1132:20-1-20-3
Electric horses, how to make 669:10-11
Electric induction experiment with glass tube and puffed cereal 1426:22-23
Electric pendulum from static electricity—cans and balloon experiment 723:128-129
Electric storm of tissue paper magic trick 1216:8-10
Electric wand comb 366:226
Electrical charges—experiments 693:29-33
Electrical charges demonstrated with balloons hanging on strings 1330:20-21
Electrified dice experiment, how to make 1007:41-42
Electrify objects and test for static electricity experiment; data table 1004:5.017
Electrophorus—learning how to use—charging an electrophorus 5:58-61
Electrophorus—understanding how an electrophorus works 5:62-65
Electrophorus, building, how to 768:16-17
Electrophorus, using, how to 768:17-18
Electroscope detects static charge experiment, how to build 1476:8-9
Electroscope detects static charges experiment 1063:163
Electroscope detects static charges experiment, how to make 1426:20-22
Electroscope from paper detects static charges experiment 972:13
Electroscope measures strength of static charge, how to make 1179:149
Electroscope shows materials can be charged without touching, how to make 1501:24-27
Electroscope, making from metal foil leaves 768:11-14
Electrostatic action experiment 885:76-77
Electrostatic airplane from aluminum foil demonstrates 938:9-10
Electrostatic attraction—attracting other large objects to 5:18-21
Electrostatic attraction—will elec. bodies attract all or only some light 5:14-17
Electrostatic field—shielding a charged conductor 5:66-69
Electrostatic palm tree spreads out experiment 768:25-26
Experiment 15:4-5
Experiment to demonstrate 382:11-17
Experiment to demonstrate sparks 40:74-76
Experiment to explore static electricity 400:88

Experiment to show 366:224-227
Experiment with comb, balloon and water (Primary) 434:13-15
Experiments with comb, and balloons 1072:4-5
Experiments with static electricity 902:215-223; 1514:33-35
Faraday's ice pail experiment 5:74-77
Fill nylon stocking experiment 768:7
Fingertip thunderstorm 366:225
Five tests for static electricity experiment with recording sheet 747:41-42
Fleas from styrofoam bits jump up and down from static electricity experiment 1132:46-1-46-2
Fluorescent bulb gives off light experiment 1250:63-64
Fluorescent tube glows from static electricity experiment 1501:20-23
Fluorescent tube glows when rubbed demonstration 938:11-12
Fluorescent tube lights up from static electricity on balloon experiment 1208:78-79
Fluttering butterfly experiment 906:102
Frogs and birds of tissue paper jump from static electricity experiment 1307:6-7
From friction 40:70-73
Hair—raising experiment with balloon 360:26
Hard candy sparks in your mouth 366:227
Hindu thread trick 16:68-70; 202:88
How is static electricity produced experiment 1501:12-15
How to charge a balloon experiment 906:97
How to get electricity by rubbing 278:27-28
How to make an electrophorus 278:31
Humidity levels indicated by static electricity experiment 1405:83
Is it alive 142:52
Is it charged 280:31
Jumping paper people on balloon demonstrates static electricity 1029:12-13
Life Savers make static electricity in your mouth experiment 1411:64
Light a fluorescent lamp in your hands 381:62
Lightning flashes from static electricity experiment 1307:8-9
Lightning made in a dark room with charged balloons experiment 1208:74-75
Like charges repel opposite charges attract 40:73-74
Like electric charges repel each other experiment use ruler/paper/wool scrap 1218:9
Magic balloon—demonstration 651:32-33
Magic comb 27:90-92
Magic wand tricks 399:10-11
Magnetic charge of balloon moves tin can experiment 1208:76-77
Make newspaper stay on wall experiment [Primary] 743:25
Make paper and cork dance under glass 360:7-8
Make static electricity with balloon [Primary] 743:24
Making electrophorus or simple electric generator 5:54-57
Making static electricity experiment 955:4
Making static electricity from plastic objects and balloons experiment 1073:52
Making water wiggle experiment 768:8
Marionettes walk and dance from static electricity experiment 1208:80-81

Materials can be charged without being touched experiment with aluminum strips 1501:24-27
Materials that can be picked up using static electricity experiment 1200:30-31
Merry-go-round turns from static electricity on balloon experiment 1208:82-83
Metal leaf electroscope 5:34-35
Metal protects objects from outside static charges experiment 1501:27
Negative electrical charge—the magic motor 16:71-76
Neon light bulb glows from static charge experiment 1426:16-19
Newspaper sticks to table demonstration 722:10
Newspaper strips demonstrate like charges repel experiment 768:10-11
Obedient ping pong ball experiment 768:8
Objects rubbed with wool demonstrate static electricity 972:7
Paper dances on table experiment 1139:46
Paper people jump up and down from static electricity experiment 1028:98
Paper snake reacts to charged plastic pen experiment 1179:148
Paper spider moves around experiment 768:24-25
Pepper pick-up using back of charged spoon 1229:2-3
Pitch ball electroscope—making and using 5:2-9
Pitch ball electroscope—more tests with 5:12-13
Plastic comb experiments with static electricity 1063:162
Positive and negative charges attract or repel experiment 1029:10-11
Positive and negative charges experiments with balloons 972:11
Power of static electricity makes silver balls dance on vinyl record experiment 1029:14-15
Primary experiments 105:10-13
Produce electric charge by rubbing lots of different things 17:67-68
Proving that there are two kinds of electricity 5:22-25
Puffed cereal static indicator 203:13
Pushing and pulling plastic toy duck with static electricity experiment 1497:25
Repel or push away balloons using static electricity experiment 1029:9
Rods with charge attract and repel one another experiment 1139:49-50
Rolling tricks with pen and straws demonstrate static electricity 955:6
Rubbed balloon makes your hair stand up experiment 1005:6
Separate salt from pepper experiment 1072:7
Separate salt from pepper trick 955:7
Silver balls dance on plastic record experiment 1028:99
Simple experiments demonstrate 867:31-32
Simple experiments to show 825:16-17
Soap bubbles and electricity experiment; balloon attracts soap bubble 1482:36-37
Soap bubbles dance experiment, how to do 827:126; 1007:42-43
Sparks from dry newspaper experiment 768:6-7
Sparks from foil on record demonstration 722:13
Sparks from static electricity experiment with baking pan, plastic bag/clay 1136:22
Spraying water balloon experiment 906:99
Static cereal box with dancing cereal, making 887:45

Static charges experiments with a balloon 972:9
Static charges produce sound experiment 1404:24-25;
  1405:90
'Static cling'—wash day experiment 366:226-227
Static electricity can cause motion demonstration 837:
  32
Static electricity experiments 1247:12-13
Static electricity from cork and string, making 1014:70
Static electricity keeps charged balloons apart experi-
  ment 1208:70-71
Static electricity pendulum, how to make 768:24
Static electricity tester experiment 834:91-92
Static surprises experiments 685:16-17
Test power of static electricity 364:129
Test weak static charges by making a simple electro-
  scope 605:56-57
Testing for like and unlike static charges experiment
  1072:6-7
Testing static charges with polystyrene bead experiment
  955:6-7
The law of electrostatics 341:6
The magic motor 16:71-76
Tricks with a comb experiment 768:5-6
Understanding why objects acquire an electric charge
  5:26-29
Unpepper the salt 202:89
Use a charged electroscope to identify the charges 5:50-
  53
Using a needle point to discharge an electrified body
  5:70-73
Versorium, how to make to detect static electricity
  1007:40
What happens when static electricity is discharged experi-
  ment 1501:16-19
William Gilbert's substances that conduct static electric-
  ity experiment 1133:5.001

STATISTICS
Averages; mean, median and mode, how to use 1354:43-
  51
Bar charts represent information gathered, how to use
  1354:24-28
Line graphs, how to use 1354:57-59
Pictogram tally charts to record results of survey, how to
  use 1354:20-22
Pie charts to record results of survey, how to use
  1354:29-39
Range; difference between values in the data, how to use
  1354:54-55
Statistic gathering projects for home and school 528:1-33
Statistical data compiled and studied in tally and bar
  charts and others 1354:7-64
Surveys, how to use 1354:40-42
Take a poll project, how to do 1070:18-19
Tally charts to record results of survey, how to use
  1354:7-14

STATUES. See also ACID RAIN; MONUMENTS
Acid rain; effect of acid rain on building materials experiment 1233:85
Chemical erosion of statues experiment using coins, salt
  and vinegar 1228:40-41

STEADINESS TESTER
Bell rings in test for steady hand, how to make 938:27-28
Detector lights up if your hand trembles, how to make
  1029:26-27

Hand steadiness machine, how to make to test two eyes
  working together 1069:166
Hand steadiness test with wire loop and electric circuit
  experiment 1160:21
How steady are you electric testers, how to make
  768:115-116
How to make to test fine motion hand control 487:32-
  33
Steadiness of hands tester, how to make 1218:16-17
Steadiness tester game experiment using batteries, wire
  and bulb 1043:18-19
Steadiness tester, how to make 910:14
Steady hand game experiment using battery, bulb and
  wire 1072:20
Steady hand game, how to make 955:20
Steady hand game, how to make using battery, bulb, and
  wire 1016:44-45
Steady hand game, make from balsa wood, dowel, wire,
  bulbs and tape 1179:153
Steady hand tester experiment; simple circuit with bat-
  tery, bulb and wire 1307:10-11
Steady hand tester, how to make 1418:14-17
Wobble detector demonstrates need for two eyes to judge
  distances experiment 1028:70

STEAM
Make a model steam engine 267:40-41
Make a simple steam engine 227:8
Siphon bottle—demonstrate principle of 217:60-63
Steam on mirror in bathroom; how long it takes to disap-
  pear project 1210:38-41
Steam powered boat 342:16-17
Steamboat—making 664:39
Water expands upon turning to steam experiment
  752:100

STEAM ENGINES
Building a steam motor project 833:283
De Witt Clinton steam engine model—how to make
  415:20-22
Geothermal steam engine model, making 895:106-107
How to make 436:75
Model—how to make 415:15-17
Model wooden steam boats powered by steam from can-
  dles experiment, how to make 1446:40-41
Nonreciprocating steam engine 577:project #55
Paper cup steam engine, how to make 837:30-31
Watt, James; who invented the steam engine project
  1525:27-31

STEAM LOCOMOTIVES
How to make an old-fashioned steam locomotive 545:20-
  23

STEAM POWERED BOAT
Model metal cigar tube boat—demonstrate power of
  steam 573:23

STEAM TURBINE ENGINE. See also TURBINES
Candle powered steam engine—how to build 487:24-
  25
Construct a steam turbine 167:96-98
How to make 12:33-36; 176:90-91; 293:41-42
Making a steam turbine—experiment 575:25
Model geothermal steam engine—making 698:26-28
Steam turbine boats—how to demonstrate 342:21
Steam turbine experiment; make working model of steam
  turbine 1301:28-29

Working model of—making 532:102

Model steam turbine experiment, how to make 1269:69

Model steam turbine to show how steam does work experiment 834:65-66

Nuclear power plant steam turbine model, making 895:120-121

STEAMBOAT

Candle powered steamboat—how to build 487:22-23

Heat energy changes to movement experiment balsa wood steamboat, how to make 1179:48-49

Heat used to produce steam experiment with metal cigar tube 1219:39

Model wooden steam boats powered by steam from candles experiment, how to make 1446:40-41

Steamboat, how to make 909:127

STEAMROLLER

Model—how to make 431:12-13

STEEL

Compass, simple one to make from steel needle and cork 1224:29

How to burn steel 360:6

Rusting steel wool experiment 1224:28

STEEL WOOL. *See also* **RUST**

Rusting 382:165-167

STEMS. *See also* **PLANTS—STEMS**

Adventure 45—examine extraordinary pipe line—stems under microscope 403:167-173

Do stems bend to all colors of light 60:39-40

Does water move in stems and leaves 60:32-33

Effect of light on stems transport liquids 128:42-43

How light affects stems and leaves 60:37-38

How they carry water—carnation and colored water—experiment (Primary) 540:19

Plants grow from stems—potatoes, onions, narcissus, pussy willows, flowers 270:12-18

Potato stem sprout—experiment 352:50-51

Staining asparagus veins 48:14-16

Staining broccoli veins to observe xylem and phloem 48:13-14

Stem from geranium plant grows in water (Primary) 540:39

Stem vein scars on a kohlrabi—observe 48:12

Stems grow straight up 270:60-63

Strawberry veins—examining 48:16-17

What part of a stem grows in length 60:26

STENTORS. *See* **INFUSORIA; SPIROSTOMA**

STEP DOWN TRANSFORMER

How to make 382:29-32

STEREOSCOPE

Construct a mirror stereoscope 167:89-95

How to make 172:31-36

Stereoscope from wood, cardboard, mirrors, patterns, how to make 1088:36-38

Stereoscope to view 3-D photographs, how to build 1253:36-37

Stereoscope, how to make, pattern given 863:79-85

Three-dimensional photographs experiment 1253:36-37

Stereoscope stimulates depth perception using homemade drawings experiment 1476:219-221

STETHOSCOPE. *See also* **LAENNEC, RENE**

Funnel and hose stethoscope, how to make 1432:105-106

Funnels, balloon and tubing stethoscope, how to make 1209:44-45

Heart beats heard through stethoscope, how to make 1036:18

How to make 436:75; 128:209-210; 142:42; 179:79; 187:15; 281:71; 293:28; 335:51; 382:1-4

How to make (Primary) 215:16-17

How to make from tubing and funnel 734:12

Make a funnel stethoscope 203:59

Make and listen to beat of your heart 161:37

Model from funnel and tubing, making 794:16

Plastic funnels and rubber tubing stethoscope, how to make 1385:14

Plastic tubing and paper cup stethoscope, how to make 1441:95

Rubber tube and funnel, making [Primary] 803:21

Simple stethoscope to hear heart sounds, how to make 1370:54-55

Stethoscope amplifies body sounds experiment 1045:14-15

Stethoscope from tubing and funnel lets you hear heart beats, how to make 1433:105-107

Stethoscope made from plastic funnel and plastic tube, how to do 1073:35

What is a stethoscope demonstration 901:12

What is it and how to use 402:58-59

STICK—MAGNETIZED

Magnetized stick rises from your hand 350:23-24

STICKLEBACK FISH

Courtship and nesting 266:128-129

Keep in aquarium, observe nest building and hatching eggs 771:76-83

Stickleback fish in aquarium, how to keep 913:39

STILTS

Juice can stilts, how to make 811:26

Stilt puddle jumpers, how to make 948:19-20

STIMULANTS

Stimulants effect on euglena microorganisms experiment 1267:93-97

STOKES, GEORGE

Effect of viscous drag on small spheres falling thru liquids experiment 1133:4.010

STOKES' LAW

Spherical objects falling in viscous fluid obey Stokes' Law experiment 997:156-158

STOMATA. *See also* **LEAVES**

Do plants need air 236:36

Experiment with stomata under the microscope 11:51-57

Gas exchange regulators in plant leaves experiment 1395:95-99

Getting raw material into a plant—importance of stoma—experiment 148:26-27

How leaves pull water through plants experiment 784:85-86

How many stomata on leaf surfaces experiment 1134:4.005

How plants breathe—experiment 585:155-156

Microscope studies of stomates on different leaves, how to do 864:86-87

Number of stomates on leaves experiment 1158:125-127

Observe under surface of a leaf—stomates 294:39-40

Plant leaves have openings through which gases can enter experiment 1395:95-99

Plants breathe through leaves experiment 1368:55

Plants contain less chlorophyll if leaf stomata are blocked experiment 714:33-35

Stomata allow gases to move in and out of leaves experiment 1405:26

Stomata holes in leaves give off water from tree experiment 1184:18

Stomata impressions, make using Duco cement and observe under microscope 1295:76-81

Stomata in leaf structure and transpiration of water and plant gases experiment 1004:2.013

Stomata of leaves 382:38-40

Stomata on bottom surface of plant leaves allow plant to breathe experiment 1440:12-14

Stomata on leaves let out water and take in carbon dioxide experiment 1075:48

Stomata under a microscope, how to do 886:28-29

Stomate density (number per area) on leaves experiment 762:78-79

Stomates of leaves affected by moisture experiment 1060:35

Stomates of leaves close or open during day and night experiment 1060:35

Stomates of leaves give off water vapor into the air experiment 1060:35

Stomates of leaves observed under microscope experiments 1060:33-36

Stomates of leaves when blocked affect the leaves experiment 1060:35

Transpiration, loss of water from leaves experiment 1405:26

Trees lose water through stomata on bottom of leaves experiment 1183:106

Water moves in plant through stomata holes and xylem tubes experiment 1405:25

Where does water enter plants experiment 852:7-8

Which side of plant leaf takes in gases experiment 904:30-31

STONE AGE
Lattice dome; Stone Age tent experiment, how to build 1518:36-37

STONE CIRCLES
Building a stone wheel observing circle project 833:18-19

Make your own medicine wheels 292:70-71

STORAGE BATTERY. *See also* BATTERIES
Making 436:76

STORAGE CELL. *See also* BATTERIES
How to make 381:60-61

STORMS
Measuring distance to a storm, how to do 1439:105-109

Tracking storms of the season; ideas for projects 1447:107-110

STOVES
Buddy burner, from tuna can, how to make 807:155

How to build a saw dust stove 347:128-130

Vagabond stove from tin can, how to make 807:154-155

STRAWS
Atomizer from straw, making 827:12-13

How a straw works demonstration 1479:103

How does a straw work 827:10-11

How straws work experiment 909:64

Lifting a bottle with 350:122-123

Medicine dropper from straw, making 827:12

Medicine dropper from straw, making 827:12

Paper straw, making 827:10

Potato trick—stick thru potato 291:126-127

Soda straw clarinet—how to make 576:77

Test structural strength of straws experiment 887:64-66

STREAM TABLE. *See also* STREAMS
Stream table—how to make 748:170

Stream table record sheet 748:171

A model for studying water flow and erosion—experiment 586:27-28

STREAMLINING
Air slows things down 281:16

Candle flame and piece of cardboard demonstrate streamlining 1179:129

Demonstrate with paper glider 561:35-36

Drag test with toy cars, making 981:12-13

Making paper darts 660:22-23

Projects on force and motion 691:58-60

Streamlined shape in autos increases speed experiment with toy car 1166:29

Streamlined shapes move smoothly through air experiment 1332:20-21

Super paper model demonstrates streamlining 561:46-48

Test movement of shapes through air and water 237:13-27

Test some boat shapes for speed 342:8-9

Wind tunnel shows airstreams over different shapes experiment 1332:24-25

STREAMS. *See also* FRESHWATER; PONDS; LAKES
Activities with water 236:127-130

Aquarium—set up to show stream creatures 194:20-21

Artificial stream, making 934:47

Bed load of stream experiment; how to set up and measure 1480:125

Calculate the flow speed of streams and rivers 175:26

Comparing pond and stream microhabitats experiment 1134:5.014

Demonstrate capacity of a stream 197:42-43

Demonstrate carrying capacity of stream due to its pitch experiment 715:96-97

Demonstrate particle density—why we pan for gold 197:44-45

Demonstrate water volume and flooding 197:40-41

Diorama represents a fast moving stream 371:70-71

Diorama represents a slow moving stream 371:72-73

Erosion by streams demonstration 934:43-45

Flow in streams is not smooth but turbulent demonstration 1480:126

Keeping temperature records of a stream experiment 934:54-57

Meandering of streams and how meanders develop experiment 1480:128-129

Measure and draw a stream profile to show shape of stream bed 194:19

Measure how fast a stream is flowing 194:18

Measuring flow velocity of a stream experiment 934:48-51

Measuring the depth of a stream 173:27

Obstacles change direction of stream demonstration 1023:104-105

Plant growth in stream beds affected by water flow experiment 1061:92-93

Pollution; outreaching effect of pollution on stream and wildlife experiment 1479:34

Running water on inclined board demonstrates deposit of materials in streams 565:134-135

Speed of flow or how fast stream flows demonstration 1480:127

Stream investigation for evidences of pollution experiment 1012:94-96

Stream profile; stones, vegetation, banks (topography) of stream map experiment 1134:5.006

Stream table activities 400:56-57

Stream table, how to build 400:56

Stream tray shows how streams form and change over time experiment 1480:122-123

Stream velocity measurement—how to do 363:96-99

Study a stream—flow rate, what's in the water, what's at bottom of stream 452:47

The living community of a small brook or stream 285:76

Volcanic explosion effect on streams and rivers experiment 1477:72-75

STREET LIGHTS

Design better streetlights for least amount of light pollution experiment 1478:30-31

Light pollution survey of your local area project, how to do 1478:31

Making in a parallel circuit 436:77

Streetlight pollution of night sky viewing experiment; which pollutes most 1478:30-31

STRENGTH. *See also* **FORCE**

Arch test of strength 566:43

Breaking either one of two strings 150:88-89

Bridge loads—test of stress—dead load and live loads 566:39

Compression and tension test with knitting needles 566:39

Cutting a potato with paper 150:82-83

Demonstrate 'sticky' water 156:7

Paper or potato—which is stronger 156:6

Ping pong lift demonstrates 566:41

Squares and triangles—strength experiment 566:43

Strength test trick 585:75-76

Suction—adapting suction—empty container of water 566:40

Triangular strength—experiment 566:43

STRENGTH—CYLINDER

Sheet of paper holds up book 291:116

Strength of hollow tubes experiment 837:31-32

STRESS

Time limits on tests help or hinder performance experiment 1267:58-59

STRING

Swing time string experiment 827:100-101

Very simple experiments with a string (Primary) 199:5-32

STRING INSTRUMENTS. *See also* **MUSICAL INSTRUMENTS**

Make a stringed thing 32:30-31

STROBOSCOPE

Be your own stroboscope 229:100-101

Discs for stroboscope, how to make 1020:12

Experiment to understand a stroboscope 385:113-115

Experiments with hand strobe and spinning top 952:50-53

Hand strobe, how to make 952:45-49

How to make using cardboard, and large nail 1153:57-60

How to make 8:130-132; 76:30-31

Make a stroboscope and use to stop motion experiment 761:73-75

Paper stroboscope, how to make 999:39-41

Persistence of vision whirling watcher experiment 1132:107-1-107-3

Phantascope, how to make, pattern given 1007:30-32

Simple stroboscope, how to make 1020:9-10

Stroboscope or strobe light, how to make 835:20-22

Stroboscope, how to build experiment 941:125-129

Stroboscope, making 898:32-33

Stroboscopic top—making 176:55-56

Stroboscopic vision—experiments 229:97-98

TV as a stroboscope 585:114

TV turned into stroboscope, how to do 1289:40-41

STROBOSCOPIC EFFECTS

With fan, pendulum and wheel in front of TV—experiment 532:14-15

STRUCTURAL STRENGTH. *See also* **COMPRESSIONAL STRENGTH; PAPER ENGINEERING**

Arch increases structural strength of cardboard bridge experiment 1436:101-102

Arches; why arches don't fall down experiment 1294:22-24

Balance a newspaper on its edge 228:30

Beam, cantilever and arch bridges, how to make from books experiment 1386:25

Books piled on eggshells demonstrate dome strength experiment 960:42

Bricks; amount of straw, sand and clay needed to make the strongest brick 1094:24-25

Bridge built with beams and arches; which is strongest experiment 1094:15-16

Bridges; strength test for cardboard bridge experiment 1507:18

Buttresses add support to buildings experiment 1386:29

Cantilever experiments 806:58-59

Cement mixtures; which is strongest experiment 1094:27

Cofferdam, how to make one from clay, plastic cup, building blocks 1094:30

Demonstrate supporting strength of a tube experiment 836:90

Demonstrate with crushing egg 203:40

Demonstrating the strength of an eggshell 150:86-87

Design of cantilevers supports load of skyscraper demonstration 1094:34

Dollar bill holds up eight quarters experiment 1083:39

Domes and arches strength test 1011:43

Egg box dome experiments 806:56-58

Eggshell strength experiment with books and egg 1011:42

Eggshell strength test to demonstrate strength of domes experiment 1386:28

Eggshells support a lot of weight experiment 827:73

Eggshells support books without breaking experiment 1229:18-19

Eggshells support weight experiment 937:20-23

Floating pontoon bridge; how much weight will it support experiment 1386:29

Forces underneath roof support roof experiment 1386:20

Foundations of structures need support experiment 1094:11-12

Foundations support buildings experiment 1386:23

House built from rolled paper has strength experiment 1024:20-21

House of cards from playing cards, how to make 1299:71

I-Beam strength demonstration 1436:107-109

Knocking down walls you build to test them for strength experiment 1386:28

Laminated beam strength demonstration with yardsticks and clamps 1436:110-112

Make a bridge of paper 161:13
Make a tough tube, a zigzag bridge, an arch and strong eggs 156:10-13
Model city; how does design affect wind currents and shadows experiment 1094:38-39
Model skyscraper, how to build and test design in a wind experiment 1094:35-36
Paper bridge experiment demonstrates 829:29-30
Paper folded into different shapes supports books experiment 1064:38
Paper is stronger than you think 161:12
Paper rolled into tube holds book up experiment 1009:18
Paper tube has strength to hold up a book experiment 1436:113-116
Potato trick with a straw 291:126-127
Shape affects strength of object experiment 1405:94
Show secret strength of paper structure 142:17
Soda cans hold your weight until dent causes can to collapse experiment 1330:42-43
Spear a potato to show hollow tubes have great strength experiment 836:30
Straw penetrates potato and demonstrates tube shape strength 1436:117-118
Straw through potato tricks demonstrate 723:44-45
Strength of different shapes experiment 802:31
Strength of different shapes of paper experiment 1288:16-17
Strength of domes with books on eggshells experiment 1436:119-122
Strength of hollow tubes experiment 837:31-32
Strength test of different kinds of paper experiment 1508:8
Strong bridge shape, how to design it experiment 1162:26
Strong paper holds your weight experiment 721:78
Structural strength of corrugated cardboard bridge demonstration 1436:97-100
Super structures for the future, how to make from clay and swizzle sticks 1094:40
Support book with piece of paper experiment 937:18-19
Swaying in the wind experiment using tower of building blocks 1386:29
Test strength of different hollow objects 623:28
Test structural strength of straws experiments 887:64-66
Tissue paper strength test experiment 1508:9
Tower of cards from playing cards, how to make 1299:71
Tower that can withstand strong winds experiment 1159:43-46
Tower, paper, making 806:55-56
Tower, straw, experiments with 806:59-60
Triangles are stronger than squares experiment toothpicks, peas, plasticine 1168:35
Truss, how to build from wire hanger and straw experiment 1436:103-106
Tube or rod has the most strength experiment 1392:19
Tubes; strength test for paper tubes experiment 1507:19
Tunnel walls are curved for strength experiment 1198:32
Which framework is strongest; box shaped or triangular experiment 1094:21

STRUCTURES. *See also* **ARCHITECTURE; BUILDING**
3-D structures, cubes, tetrahedron, octahedron, isosahedron, how to make 1063:151
Arch bridge from wooden crates or cardboard experiment, how to build 1518:26-27
Bricks and absorption of water experiment 1386:15

Building boxes for strength experiment, how to build 1518:38-39
Demonstrate elasticity needed in materials 328:30-34
Foundations of structures need support experiment 1094:11-12
How to make a stick tower from toothpicks 545:8-10
How to make dowel towers 545:10-11
Loads, live and dead—demonstrate 328:35-39
Make structure stronger by changing its shapes; paper experiment 827:24-25
Newspaper dowels—how to make 631:67
Paper logs—how to make 631:66
Peas, marshmallows and toothpicks—how to make 631:68
Resonant rings experiment; objects vibrate at different frequencies 1132:83-1-83-2
Resonator experiment; vibrate something at right frequency and get big reaction 1132:84-1-84-2
Roofs—different shapes demonstrate strength 328:122-137
Rope and cables—use of 328:76-85
Shape and strength thru curvature and creasing 328:112-121
Straw and paper chips—how to make 631:69
Test strength of two different brick walls experiment 802:12
Test structural strength of straws experiments 887:64-66
Triangle power experiment; build 3 legged stool, how to do 1518:20-21
Trusses—how to build 328:100-111

STURGEON, WILLIAM
Bar shaped electromagnet 63:50-53

SUBLIMATION
Blowing snow experiments 563:88-89

SUBMARINES. *See also* **DIVING—SUBMARINES**
Air used to lift submarines demonstration 1405:84
Balloons filled with water move in water experiment 994:43-45
Bottle submarine, jar and tubing demonstrate 558:56-57
Buoyancy of submarines 368:54-55; 660:7
Construct two model diving submarines 167:58-62
Deep water diver experiment 996:18-19
Demonstrate up and down in water 295:69
Diving submarine model experiment 1476:81-82
Experiment to learn how a submarine works 385:38-39
Experiment to show how a submarine is raised and lowered 128:111-112
How a submarine dives 342:27
How a submarine works 343:14-24
How do submarines go up and down experiment 877:101-105
How to make a submarine (Primary) 109:26-27
Identifying submarines and parts of submarines 343:25-28
Jellyfish dives and floats in water filled soda bottle experiment 1310:20-21
Make a working model submarine 142:14
Making a submarine 342:25-27; 909:55
Model submarine demonstrates how sinking machines dive and then surface 1165:33
Model submarine from plastic bottle, how to make 1422:25
Models—how to make 343:34-44
Object floats or sinks as air increases or decreases density experiment 1004:3.001

413

Prepare to submerge—model submarine. Shows why sub dives and returns 12:31-32

Raise plastic bottle submarine with air experiment 868:57

Shape design—test movement of flat shape, round shape 237:13-24

Sink a submarine experiment with balloons 1208:50-51

Submarine floats and sinks experiment 937:44-47

Submarine from plastic bottle rises and sinks experiment 1316:21

Submarine model dives and surfaces in water filled bottle experiment 1256:13

Submarine model, wooden, making 922:38-47

Submarines under the sea 93:68-69

Water affects submarine's ability to dive experiment 1290:33, 2.2

What makes a submarine rise and sink 126:45-49

Why do submarines use periscopes experiment 1294:106-107

SUBMARINES—MODELS

Deutschland model—how to make 343:83-87

Fulton's Nautilus model—how to make 343:51-56

George Washington model—how to make 343:115-120

Holland model—how to make 343:67-72

Hunley model—how to make 343:57-61

Lake's Argonaut model—how to make 343:62-66

Nautilus model—how to make 343:98-103

Skipjack model—how to build 343:73-77; 343:104-109

Triton model—how to build 343:110-114

Turtle model—how to make 343:45-50

U-boat of World War 1 model—how to make 343:78-82

U.S. submarine of World War 1 model—how to make 343:88-92

U.S. submarine of World War II model—how to make 343:93-97

SUBMERSIBLES. *See also* **DIVING—SUBMARINES**

How diving bells work 687:46

Pressure of water increases with depth demonstration 1165:35

SUCCESSION

How does succession occur in a lake—experiment 371:58-65

Turn pond into forest experiment with one habitat replacing another habitat 1472:60-63

SUCTION

Adapting suction—empty container of water 566:40

Magdeburg Sphere principle experiment with glasses and candle 1007:14-16

Ping pong lift demonstrates 566:41

Using straws (Primary) 24:26-29

SUGAR

Body converts starch to sugar with saliva experiment 1238:94

Burning sugar—experiment 382:131-132

Burning sugar to show elements of 85:20-21

Can light be made by breaking sugar crystals 396:69-71

Can sugar be changed to carbon 396:76-77

Can sugar molecules rotate light experiment 831:91-94

Changing sugar into alcohol 85:42-43

Chemical change in sugar when it is heated experiment 1435:18-20

Compare sugar and fructose for sweetness experiment 1177:unp.

Cooking up cookies (using different kinds of sweeteners) 219:11-13

Difference between salt and sugar experiments 1238:22-23

Different from salt—experiments 676:22-23

Dissolution of sugar by heating activities for classroom 1291:9-10

Experiment with colloids 382:144-146

Fermentation of sugar and yeast produces carbon dioxide experiment 1396:168

Function of digestive enzymes experiment 1395:165-170

Gottlieb Kirchhof's starch is made up of sugar units experiment 1133:2.009

Grow sugar crystals experiment 1484:137-138

How are sugar crystals shaped experiment 1293:73-74

How much sugar is in honey experiment 1096:144-148

Is there space between sugar crystals 396:12-13

Make tricky sugar that won't dissolve 87:91

Making sugar crystals 399:69

Muscle strength affected by sugar—experiment 630:43

Optical activity and chirality; polarimeter identifies substance experiment 1004:4.014

Piezoelectricity glow from sugar cubes rubbed together experiment 1083:87

Reducing sugars 84:85-86

Saturated solution of sugar experiment 1263:14

Show sugar crystal formation 293:8

Starch molecules larger than sugar molecules experiment 1251:75-76

Sticky goo 259:13-14

Sugar (carbohydrate) product of photosynthesis found in plant parts experiment 1061:26-27

Sugar added to warm and cold water experiment; which holds more sugar 1175:81

Sugar content of chewing gum experiment; data tables given 1004:4.011

Sugar dissolves faster in cold or warm water experiment 1509:13

Sugar gem crystal jewelry—making 676:19

Sugar heated turns to caramel experiment 1271:34

Sugar in honey experiment; how much sugar is there in honey 1097:141-143

Sugar molecules make soap bubbles last longer experiment 1251:49-51

Sugar power to make a boat go (Primary) 109:9

Sugar used as preservative for fruit experiment 1395:130

Sugar water attracts what animals and insects in daytime and night experiment 969:35

Taste and feel of different sugars in cookies experiment 1238:26-27

Test for presence of monosaccharides (single sugar) in foods experiment 1396:61-66

Test for sugar 346:128-131

Test for sugar in foods experiment 1259:24-26

Test for sugar in plants 86:41

Testing for glucose in different foods experiment; data table given 871:2.019

Testing for simple sugar in milk—experiment 628:69-70

Tooth soaked in Cola has decay experiment 1069:163

Which foods contain sugar experiment 901:214

SULFUR. *See also* **CARBON**

Sulfur crystals experiment, how to do 1342:58-61

SULFUR DIOXIDE. *See also* **ACID RAIN**

Erupting volcanoes produce sulfur dioxide experiment 1174:43-45

Plants exposed to too much sulfur dioxide gas will be harmed experiment 1453:30-31

Sulfur dioxide gas, how to produce experiment 1171:35-37

Sulfur dioxide harms plants experiment 1324:65-68

Sulfur dioxide gas effect on growth of seedlings experiment 1134:6.003

SUMMER. *See also* SEASONS—SUMMER

Bird watching—how to rough sketch birds you see 552:39

Summer activities—nature diary of plants, flowers, insects; attract moths 552:38

Summer activities—recipes—rose petal drink, milkshakes, fruit salad 552:42-43

Summer things to do—using flowers—pressing, dried decorations, potpourri 552:40-41

SUN

Altitude of Sun, how to find 1434:33-35

Analemma, recording (Advanced) 658:14-15

Atmosphere affects viewed shape of Sun demonstration 1394:96-97

Black colors absorb Sun's heat experiment with cans of water and thermometers 1213:30

Building a stone wheel observing circle project 833:18-19

Calculating the period of the sunspot cycle project 833:203-204

Chart of night and day 246:8-9

Chart of seasons worldwide 246:1

Color of clothes best for a hot climate experiment 1219:18

Colors of sunset experiment 1126:13

Colors that make up white light from Sun experiment 1405:10-11

Comparing density of Sun from different angles project 833:17-18

Convection heat currents of Sun experiment with glitter in water 1478:99

Converging lenses focus Sun's rays to focal point 289:36-37

Copernicus; who first suggested that Earth revolves around Sun experiment 1525:43-46

Creating images with a computer project 833:185

Day length, soltices and equinoxes experiment 1062:35-36

Define and observe radiation, convection and conduction with popcorn ex 1447:12-17

Demonstrate light bending effect of Earth's atmosphere 231:18

Demonstrate rays for summer and winter 231:17

Demonstrate Sun's heat with black and white color objects 189:42-45

Demonstrate the Sun's ray and temperature during the day 189:19-21

Demonstrate where winter, summer Sun is due to Earth's tilted axis 189:27-34

Diagrams of four seasons on Earth 246:28-30

Diameter of Sun and Moon, how to measure experiment 1158:43-46

Diameter of the Sun—how to measure experiment 763:12-14

Diameter of the Sun experiment, how to measure approximate diameter 1447:2-6

Diameter of the Sun, how to measure 1434:29-32

Displaying the path of the analemma project 833:22

Distance from Sun affects atmospheric temperature experiment 1405:24

Does slant of light rays affect amount of light energy delivered on a spot 489:16-17

Does Sun follow same path everyday experiment 834:27

Does Sun rise in the morning experiment 1003:26-27

Dough model of Sun—recipe given—making 742:52

Earth is protected from solar winds demonstration 1394:98-99

Earth's shadow extends into space and as umbra increases so does penumbra 1062:45-47

Elevation of Sun studied experiment 1410:61

Evaporation makes water from salt water (Primary) 171:26-27

Evaporation of salt water makes sun crystals (Primary) 171:20-21

Examining sunspots project 833:201-203

Experiment and act. With light, rainbows, shadows, movement, plants(Primary) 307:unpaged

Finding directions from a shadow stick project 833:7

Finding North by the Sun using stick in the ground, how to do 1434:61-63

Follow the Sun's path 400:106

Greenhouse effect 289:38-39

Heat from sun—effect on sand—soil air and water experiment 760:52

Heat from Sun travels through space demonstration 1394:76-77

Heat from the Sun experiment 909:164

Heat in the atmosphere experiment 1447:18-22

Heat of Sun effect on soil, sand and water experiment; chart given 1012:10-11

Height of Sun relationship to latitude experiment 1480:18-19

How atmosphere affects viewed shape of Sun experiment 1479:14

How bright is the Sun compared to 60 watt bulb experiment 1478:93

How do different colors absorb the Sun's rays experiment 793:29

How energy from the Sun travels through space demonstration 1479:11

How to see and measure sunspots 101:45-46

Image of Sun seen before sunrise and after sunset demonstration 1394:90-91

Isotherms in the classroom experiment 1447:7-11

Keeping track of the Sun during the day project 833:5-7

Length versus height of shadow experiment 1003:24

Lunar eclipse effect on studying Sun's corona demonstration 1394:82-83

Lunar eclipse effect on studying Sun's corona demonstration 1405:8

Magnetic force field around Earth protects it from solar winds experiment 1405:8

Make a model of an eclipse of the Sun 169:20-21

Make a sun compass 120:9

Make a sun tattoo (Primary) 171:10-11

Make dried fruit sun treats (Primary) 171:14-15

Make model to show path of Sun among stars 128:71

Make sun signs on construction paper 171:16-17

Making a Sun map 21:61-66

Making a sundial project 833:25-27

Mapping Sun's path across the sky experiment 1158:47-49

Mapping the Sun's path 657:91-93

Mapping the Sun 586:33-35

Marking sunrise and sunset project 833:4-5

Measure and map Sun's path across the sky—how to do 763:6-9

Measure length of shadow from sun at each hour 189:12-16

Measuring Sun's altitude from length of a shadow experiment 1159:98-102

Measuring the Sun—experiment (Advanced) 565:19-29

Measuring the Sun project 833:198-199

Measuring the Sun's altitude—how to do 710:69-70

Measuring the Sun's size—how to do 710:70-71

Mercury; brightness of Sun from Mercury experiment 1478:64

Mercury; why Mercury's day is longer than its year experiment 1478:65

Model of Sun and its rays—making [Primary] 742:49

Movement measured by shadows experiment 760:43-44

Movement of planets around the Sun demonstration with cardboard spinner 1394:56-57

Movement of Sun shown by marking shadows on cardboard wheel 1390:5

Observation of projects (Advanced) 658:37-43

Observe image of Sun safely experiment 1405:9

Path of Sun across the sky demonstration 1394:100-101

Path; demonstrate apparent path of Sun across the sky experiment 1479:15

Pinhole images of the Sun 657:81-83

Planets; determine why planets move smoothly around the Sun experiment 1479:6

Reradiation—measuring the Sun's energy 289:31-32

Role of Sun in evaporation of water in air experiment 1003:73

Shadow measures position of Sun in sky experiment 1003:22-23

Shadows—make a model Egyptian shadow clock 137:7

Shadows—make a shadow stick 140:25

Shadows—use a shadow stick to measure time 137:5-6

Shadows, device to track seasonal changes—making 693:19-21

Size of Sun, how to determine experiment 1394:94-95

Solar cells; how we get energy from the Sun experiment 1293:35-37

Solar eclipse demonstration using a sundial 1394:80-81

Solar eclipse demonstration 1394:78-79

Solar magnetic field demonstration 1479:10

Spectrum made from flashlight, water and mirror experiment 1478:96

Sun can be seen before rising above the horizon experiment 1405:9

Sun does not come up or set in the East or West exactly same each day experiment 1062:48-50

Sun energy can burn paper (more difficult) 189:39-40

Sun energy can melt ice 189:35-36

Sun energy can separate salt water into fresh water and salt 189:36-38

Sun gives light and heat (Primary) 232:51

Sun in your room experiment to prove Earth changes position 1003:33

Sun is more powerful at the equator than at the poles experiment 1311:20

Sun moves thru Zodiac as Earth moves experiment; working model demonstrates 1478:26-27

Sun pictures, printing, how to do 898:18

Sun power—sun dried fruit leather 494:11

Sun prints, sun cooking, hot rocks (Primary), sun reflectors 121:1-32

Sun projector—making to see picture of the Sun [Primary] 716:27-29

Sun scope—make a safe sun scope 649:10-11

Sun shines on Earth's equator during fall and spring—diagram 246:22-23

Sun spots—make a pinhole camera to observe sun spots 231:19

Sun spots—see sun spots 161:99-101

Sun viewing box, how to make from cardboard boxes, black paper, foil 1169:40-41

Sun warms different substances by different amounts experiment 1281:7

Sun's angle affects seasons demonstration 1434:6-8

Sun's center has greater density than the outside experiment 1405:10

Sun's heat 243:16-17

Sun's light and heat can be focused—experiment 489:27-28

Sun's position at sunrise versus latitude and longitude experiment 1062:48-50

Sun-viewer box, how to make 1062:19-21

Sunlight reflected—experiment 693:21-24

Sunrise and sunset 253:182-183

Sunrise not exactly in the East each day experiment 1062:48-50

Sunrise position versus latitude and longitude experiment 1062:48-50

Sunrise, sunset—observe and record changes in Sun's position 381:37-41

Sunset from flashlight and milky water, how to do 1028:50

Sunset not exactly in the West each day experiment 1062:48-50

Sunspots; how to observe and draw on paper 1170:30

Suntan oil—how to make 697:26-27

Test Sun's reflective heat melting ice on light and dark paper 171:12-13

Tilt of Earth causes changing seasons demonstration 1434:3-5

Tilt of Earth's axis and sunlight affects the seasons experiment 763:10-11

Tilt of Earth's axis and sunshine make the seasons 246:10-14

Use Sun's heat to make sun tea 171:18-19

Using Sun to find direction and tell time 189:60-62

View Sun and sunspots safely; construct Sun viewing box 1062:19-21

When does Sun really set experiment 761:85-86

Why different parts of Sun rotate at different rates experiment 1479:11

Why do we see the Sun after it sets experiment 1003:30-31

Why is Equator hotter than North Pole experiment 1003:20-21

Why is Summer hotter than Winter experiment 1003:19

Why Sun's image is seen before sunrise and after sunset demonstration 1479:13

Winter chart of the North and South Pole 246:21

Winter, summer, where is the Sun (more difficult) 189:16-18

Working Sun model to find true directions 532:68-69

SUN—ECLIPSES. *See also* **ECLIPSES**
Flashlight, coin and white card demonstrate how eclipses occur 569:39

SUN ANIMALCULE
Adventure 55—we look at the Sun animalcule under a microscope 403:212-215

SUN CLOCK
How to make 312:11-14
How to make 494:25

SUN COMPASS
How to do 494:24

SUN PRINTS
How to make 359:24-27; 494:22-23; 697:29-30; 863:48-51; 899:166-167; 1114:50-51
Pictures from bleaching power of the Sun experiment 1335:27-28
Sun pictures of weeds, how to make 646:8-10
Sun prints of natural materials, how to make 1071:94

SUN SCORCHER TRICKS
Paper scorcher, sun brands, sunburst of balloons, balloon bursting race 494:12-13

SUN SCREENS
How effective are products in protecting against ultraviolet radiation 997:111-112

SUN SPOTS
Cycle of sunspots over 11 year period experiment; make model to demonstrate 1478:101
How to observe sunspots and draw on paper 1170:30
Observe sunspots project using binocular projection 967:26-27
Project image of Sun to examine sunspots, how to do 1329:32-33
Sun spots experiment 1062:19-21
Sunspot projector experiment, make from poster board and binoculars 1478:94-95
Tracing and set up for drawing sunspots experiment, how to make 1476:180-181
View Sun and sunspots safely; construct Sun viewing box experiment 1062:19-21
Viewer for looking for sunspots, prominence and movement, how to make 1330:90-91

SUN TEA
How to make 697:37
Making sun tea 289:35

SUN VIEWER
Use this Sun viewer to softly watch the Sun—how to make 494:14

SUNBEAM ALARM CLOCK
How to make 543:2-3

SUNBURN CREAM
Recipe for 387:22-23

SUNDEW PLANTS
Insectivorous plants 279:37-38
Leaves catch insects 271:30-36
Sundews, how to grow 1260:36

SUNDIALS
An anywhere sundial—how to do 292:64
Beach sundial, making 772:43-45
Build a simple sundial 400:106
Can Sun's shadow help us to tell time experiment 834:29
Cardboard and pencil sundial, how to make 1387:11
Cardboard and wooden dowel sundial, how to make 1335:28
Cardboard box sundial—making 697:21

Cardboard sundial, how to make 1421:12; 860:33-34; 999:69-72
Construct a pocket sundial 167:120-123
Corrugated cardboard sundial, how to make 887:16-18
Demonstrate shadows and sundials (Primary) 169:8
Flowerpot sundial, how to make 1179:81
Garden sundial made from board and cardboard 1281:8
Hand as sundial, how to use 1434:54-55
Hand held sundial from wood and nail, how to make 1421:11
Hand sundial—how to make 192:50-55
Hand sundial—how to use 710:73
Horizontal sundial, how to make 1063:297
How to make—disc pattern given 747:43-44
How to make a sundial 21:49-53; 94:28-29; 120:8; 128:73-74; 161:101; 175:43; 218:11-15; 832:81; 192:36-49; 208:34-37; 399:22-23
How to make a sundial experiment 941:20-22
How to make and set up a sundial 178:12
Large pole sundial, how to make 1421:11
Make a sunny sundial (Primary) 171:22-23
Make sundial from cardboard, thread spool and pencil 1073:72
Make sundial from paper plate 200:24-25; 207:32
Making a sundial project 833:25-27
Pocket sundial to tell time, patterns given, make from cardboard 1299:78
Pocket sundial, how to make; pattern for sundial graph given 1114:54-55
Shadow and equatorial sundials, how to make to determine time experiment 978:125-127
Shadow sticks sundial to tell time, how to make 956:9
Simple pencil and cardboard sundial, how to make 920:12-13
Simple sundial—making 555:10; 640:30-31
Small pocket sundial, cardboard, making 999:75-78
Stick sundial project 967:24-25
Sun clock for your pocket, how to make from cardboard 1329:27-29
Sun clock from pencil and paper plate, how to make 1103:13
Sun clock from wood and paint, how to make 1114:52-53
Sun clock—how to make 312:11-14; 823:14-15
Sundial—making (Advanced) 658:10-15
Sundial—how to make 605:66-67; 657:75-79; 659:6; 732:55-56; 909:134; 947:8-9
Sundial adjusted to altitude of where you live, how to make 862:25-37
Sundial from glass jar and knitting needle, how to make 1247:34
Sundial from large plant pot, how to make 1213:9
Sundial from wood, cardboard and protractor, how to make 1480:18
Sundial from wooden board and coat hanger wire, how to make 1086:9
Sundial observation experiments; how to make 951:10-15
Sundial to measure Sun's path—making 763:6-9
Sundial's shadow doesn't fall exactly on same mark all year long experiment 1062:30-32
Sundial, accurate—how to make 640:32-33
Sundial, make from jar, paper and knitting needle 1478:22-23

Telling time by the Sun; stick in ground experiment 898:18-19

Watch compass sundial, cardboard and watch, making 999:72-74

What time is it?—making sundial 748:154

Why did ancient people make sundials experiment 1294:28-31

Wood and cardboard sundial, how to make 1434:50-53

Wooden board and pencil sundial, how to make 885:42-43

Wooden sundial on pedestal, how to make 1236:14-15

SUNFLOWERS

Giant sunflower race with friends 376:16-17

Grow a giant plant outdoors 416:9

Growing sunflowers and sunflower seed harvest 494:16

How to plant and grow sunflowers 919:33

How to plant and grow sunflowers 988:28-29

Sprouts from sunflower seeds, how to grow 1178:30

Sunflower seeds grow (Primary) 650:unpaged

SUNGLASSES

Far out sunglasses from egg cartons, making 1017:17

How polarized sunglasses reduce glare experiment 941:11-12

How sunglasses reduce glare experiment 1293:127-128

Polarized sunglasses experiment 1132:79-1-79-2

Polarized sunglasses stop time on LCD wristwatch experiment 1082:162-164

Show how Polaroid sunglasses cut glare experiment 860:216

Sun blinders made from corrugated cardboard 558:42-43

Sunglasses—paper—making 697:27

SUNLIGHT

Black hotter than white 289:33-34

Can it shine through water and through an ice cube (Primary) 432:10-11

Color composition of sunlight demonstration 1394:84-85

Color composition of sunlight experiment 1479:12

Color wheel demonstrates how colors mix experiment with spinning color wheel 1213:26-27

Colors of sunlight experiment 1391:7

Does sunlight change the color of things experiment [Primary] 742:20

Grass covered with board loses color experiment 919:38

Length of sunlight per day shortens or lengthens equal amount each day ex 1062:35-36

Light from sun ignites paper experiment 902:48

Light mill spins in sunlight experiment, how to make 1213:30-31

Measuring the amount of sunlight in an area 236:162

Miracle with light: chemical reaction—experiment 585:120-121

Painted cardboard circle whizzer turns white as it spins experiment [Primary] 788:14-15

Plants—effect on plants growth 432:22-23

Skin protection needed from rays of Sun experiment using newspapers/cellophane 1228:22-23

Snow and ice reflect sunlight; dirt and dark ground absorb it experiment 1322:40-43

Splitting sunlight into the full spectrum of colors experiment 1092:43

Sunlight fades colors activities [Primary] 759:45

Sunlight intensity sensor, how to make 830:63-64

Sunlight makes spectrum or rainbow experiment 1213:27

SUNLIGHT—REFLECTED

Reflectors change path of light in room experiment 697:28

Catch sunlight with mirror in water—reflect to piece of paper (Primary) 432:20

Making a heliograph 507:1878-1879

Reflect sunlight into a room with a mirror (Primary) 432:16-17

SUNSCREENS

Sunscreen molecules block sunlight that causes colors to fade experiment 1251:62-64

Test effectiveness of suntan lotions experiment 1395:159-164

SUNSETS

Blue sky and red sunset experiment; demonstrate with flashlight and milk 1132:11-1-11-2

Colors of sunset experiment 1126:13

See sunset in a glass of water experiment 1083:107

Sunset—color of 382:145

Sunset from flashlight and milky water, how to do 1028:50

Sunset in glass of water experiment 1082:103-107

The sunset experiment to show colors of sunsets 577: project #34

Why are hot days followed by gorgeous sunsets—colloids 382:143-146

Why is sky blue and sunsets red experiment with gallon jug, water, flashlight 1478:28-29

Why is sky colored experiment 1126:13

SUNSHINE RECORDER

Automatic sunshine recorder—how to make 12:44-49

SUNTAN LOTIONS. See SUNSCREENS

SUPER STRUCTURES

How to make 399:71

SUPERSTITIONS

Superstitions versus science project 1062:114-115

SURFACE AREA

Small things have more surface area for their size experiment 1411:27

SURFACE TENSION. See also LIQUIDS; WATER—SURFACE TENSION

Breaking the surface tension of water experiments 1091:27-28

Bubble films and boat races experiment; data tables given 871:3.013

Demonstrate effect of gravity on weak surface tension experiment 905:42-43

Food color and alcohol on water demonstrate 721:14

Gauze over water bottle experiment 747:45-46

Glass with wet cloth over it demonstrates 721:16

How strong is a liquid's skin experiment 1091:23-24

Jar lids with holes demonstrate 721:17

Milk explosion of color demonstrates surface tension 1312:17

Pepper on water demonstrates 721:23

Plastic basket—waxed paper—paper towel demonstrate 721:15

Sink or float with boxes 114:44

Soap bubble puts out candle experiment 1007:4-5

Soap film tricks demonstrate surface tension 1243:17

Soap film tricks demonstrate 472:2227

Strength and effect of surface tension experiments 1164:71-73

Sudsy water and thread demonstrate 721:13

418

Surface tension—experiment to show 128:112-114
Surface tension—water magic harbor 27:98
Surface tension experiments 507:1905-1906
Tricks from surface tension of liquids project 1296:2002
Warmth sustains surface tension experiment with soap bubbles 1476:95-96
Water, soap and toothpick demonstrate 882:18

SURFACTANTS. *See* **DETERGENTS; SOAP; WATER SOFTENERS**

SURFBOARD AND RIDER
Model toy—how to make (Primary) 467:16-17

SURVEYING
Bearing board to measure an angle, how to make 1381:20-21

SURVEYING THEODOLITE. *See also* **THEODOLITE**
Construct a theodolite to survey 167:137-142

SURVIVAL
Game; how animals survive the winter game, how to make 1180:38-39; 1183:166-167
Game; hungry owls survival game, how to make 1180:11; 1183:139
Game; people play role of animals trying to survive 1063:208-209
Keeping warm in winter experiment with four jars of water 1181:35
Keeping warm; how animals survive experiment 1183:43
Predator competition experiment with normal color/monochromatic vision; tables 1004:2.008
Technology used by you in one day for your survival 1337:65

SUSPENSIONS. *See also* **EMULSIONS**
Borscht cocktail—separating suspended particles 74:29-31
Capillary filtering of suspensions 360:87
Cornstarch purple goo experiment 1066:78-79
Decanting a liquid suspension experiment with salt and water 1476:127-128
Float spheres of colored water between layers of water and oil experiment 905:158-159
Floating drop of oil demonstrates 203:30
Flour and water suspension experiment 905:166-167
Gooey slime from cornstarch experiment 1231:34-35
How a filter works 360:79
Iron sulfate solution—how to prepare 346:17-22
Magic mud, making 669:8-9
Observe layering of undissolved materials experiment 1479:61
Observe layering of undissolved materials experiment 905:164-165
Salad dressing—a liquid suspended in a liquid 74:33-35
Separate floating parts of a suspension by spinning experiment 905:162-163
Separate suspended parts of a suspension by spinning experiment 1479:62
Stunts with matches 350:121-124
Substances that dissolve in hot or cold water or are suspended in it experiment 1331:20-21
Use of colloidal gel in absorbent diaper experiment, data table given 1004:4.012

SUSPENSIONS—EMULSIONS
Mayonnaise—a stabilized suspension 74:35-38
Strawberry bomb—a frozen emulsion 74:38-39

SWAMP BUGGY
Make an electric powered swamp buggy 223:26-27

SWAMPS
Activities with water 236:127-130
Bog soil compared to forest soil experiment 1061:58-59
Exploring swamp life 118:215-219
Insect-eating plants from bogs or swamps, how to grow experiment 1074:24-25
Soil from dried up marsh area contains life experiment 1074:66
Swamp terrarium—making (Primary) 650:unpaged

SWAN
Swan model toy—how to make (Primary) 467:14-15

SWEET POTATOES. *See also* **PLANTS—SWEET POTATOES; POTATOES—SWEET**
Grow pretty plant [Primary] 757:31
Grow yam vine in water, how to do 1178:36-37
Jelly glass farm grows vine (Primary) 650:unpaged
Phototropism; vine from sweet potato experiment 1375:60-62
Seeds planted in sweet potato vine stem experiment 1375:62-66
Sprout and get a vine 629:139
Sweet potato plant, how to grow 1078:22
Sweet potato vine plants, how to grow 1368:14
Sweet potato, how to grow 980:80; 1006:27
Vine from sweet potato, how to grow 810:30; 879:169-170; 1406:34; 1440:83-84
Vine grows from sweet potato rooted in water experiment 722:72; 1065:19
Will sweet potato change seed's genes experiment 1375:58-60

SWEETENERS
Cooking up cookies (using different kinds of sweeteners) 219:11-13

SWEETNESS (TASTE)
Compare sugar and fructose for sweetness experiment 1177:unp.

SWIMMING POOL PHYSICS
Experiments 41:15-54

SWINGS
How swings work activity 1230:10-11
Moving the center of gravity from side to side 241:38-39
Swing's period time, measuring 657:101

SWITCHES. *See also* **ELECTRIC; ELECTRICITY—SWITCHES**
Add lights and switches to doll house, how to do 955:18
Automatic switch machine experiment, how to make 1420:26-27
Dim the lamps experiments 563:100-101
Dimmer switch, how to make 1043:21; 1382:20-21
Dollhouse lights and switches, how to make 1072:18
Double-throw switches, how to make 1476:20
Electric switch from block of wood and wires, how to make 1200:27
How do switches work 278:37
How to control a light with two switches 278:38
Lead pencil demonstrates dimmer switch 287:21
Make shaky hand detector switch 287:18
Make two way switch circuit 287:19
Make your own electric switch experiment 1072:17
One way and two way switch—how to make 366:233

Paper clip switch completes electric circuit experiment 955:17

Pressure switch, how to make 1043:21

See-saw switch experiment, how to make 1420:25

Several types of switches to build 23:34

Simple and double switch, how to make 1073:62

Simple switch controls current 287:17

Simple switch on electric circuit experiment 1282:28-29

Simple switch to control circuit experiment 1160:17

Simple switch, how to make 1043:20

Switch in electrical circuit in a shoe box room, how to make 1099:13

Switch turns electric current on and off experiment 1029:22

Switch, electric, how to make 768:105

Switches, how to make from paper clip, clothes pin and cardboard experiment 1382:18

Switches, several types to build, how to do 830:36

Tapper switch, how to make 1043:21

Tricky switches—experiment 563:99-100

Two way switch, how it works experiment 895:2-3

Two-way switch, how to make 1382:20-21

SYMBIOSIS

Do dissimilar organisms benefit from each other 402:92-93

Nitrogen-fixing bacteria help clover plants to grow experiment 1060:111-112

Nitrogen-fixing bacteria on clover plant nodules experiment 1060:110

Nitrogen-fixing bacteria on roots of legume plants experiment 1060:110

Nitrogen-fixing bacteria replace nitrogen compounds in hydroponic solution 1060:112

Symbiotic relationship between some species of plants experiment 978:95

SYMBOLIC HIERONYMOUS MACHINE

Experiment to demonstrate (Advanced) 393:81-94

SYMBOLIC MACHINES

Experiment to demonstrate (Advanced) 393:72-80

SYMMETRY

Bilateral symmetry experiment 956:22-23

Completing reflections activity 1351:43

Finding lines of symmetry investigation 1351:46

Lines of symmetry investigations 1351:28-36

Look alike designs 241:10-15

Make a mirror maze 162:97

Make a symmetry tester 162:92-93

Making mutants 162:95

Mirror codes investigations with symmetrical letters of the alphabet 1351:42

Mirror codes 162:98-99

Reflections without drawing activities; paint and scissors patterns 1351:44-45

Rotational symmetry investigations 1351:37-38

Symmetry and color investigations 1351:39-41

Symmetry designs and experiments 521:8-15

Test for line and point symmetry (Primary) 521:1-33

SYNODIC TIME. *See* **TIME**

SYRUP

Investigating formulas and pancake syrup experiment 888:91-93

Make syrup 322:18-19

Clover syrup, recipe, how to make 1464:73

T

TADPOLES. *See also* **FROGS**
  Adventure 22—we trace a tadpole's development under a hand lens 29:107-115
  Collect eggs and hatch, how to keep and feed 796:25-26
  Collection and care of 313:24-28
  Computer population model for population changes in tadpoles 864:119-120
  Do temperature and light effect skin color of tadpoles experiment 864:118
  Does temperature effect egg development of tadpoles experiment 864:118
  Frog eggs hatch into tadpoles experiment, how to do 1488:25
  Hatching tadpoles in aquarium experiment 1492:66-67
  How do tadpoles turn into frogs experiment 1293:109-111
  How frogs grow experiment with frog spawn 1181:29
  How to care for 279:16
  How to collect and care for 530:127
  How to collect eggs, hatch and observe 771:49-56
  How to identify tadpoles of different frogs and toads experiment 771:191-193
  How to keep and observe tadpoles 901:111-115
  How to raise 236:70
  Indoor puddles for and how to feed 264:106
  Iodine or thyroid experiments to increase growth of tadpoles 771:193-195
  Life cycle of frogs experiment; hatch frog eggs 1504:31
  Metamorphosis or change of tadpoles into frogs experiment 978:90-91
  Observe growth changes in 759:31
  Population control experiment 864:117
  Raise toad tadpoles experiment; observe how tiny swimmers live on land 1472:36-41
  Tadpole growth, observation experiment 860:176-180
  Tadpoles in aquarium turn into frogs, how to do 1433:34-36

TALBOT, WILLIAM HENRY
  Who is ancestor of today's photography project 1525:101-106

TALC
  The talc trick 291:36-37

TALEIDOSCOPE. *See also* **KALEIDOSCOPES**
  Making your own, how to do 861:45-51

TALKING
  How you talk—simple experiments to demonstrate (Primary) 513:1-36

TANGRAMS
  Easter tangram makes a decorated egg 1352:37
  How to play tangram 1352:36
  Magic egg tangram, patterns given, how to make 1299:85
  Project 399:44-45
  Tangram puzzle, patterns given, how to make 1299:84
  Tangram set, how to make 1352:33-35

TANK
  Cotton spool tank model—how to make 431:22-23

TANKER
  Tanker cab—how to make 431:14-15
  Tanker trailer—how to make 431:16-17

TAP DANCER
  Ball bearing steel balls dance 356:44-47

TAP ROOT. *See also* **ROOTS**
  Studying a typical tap root—a carrot 294:32

TARANTULAS
  How to cage and care for 279:30-31

TARNISH
  Case of the vanishing silver tarnish experiment 814:89-91
  Dirty penny tarnish remover, how to make 859:5
  Electrical silver polish 346:95-96
  Removal of tarnish from silver demonstrates electron flow between metals 871:3.024
  What makes silver black 381:27-28

TASTE. *See also* **SENSES—TASTE**
  Blindfold taste test and survey 400:42
  Demonstrate taste areas of the tongue 294:82-83
  Fool your taste buds 228:23
  How do you taste food—experiment—find four taste bud areas on human tongue 482:44-47
  Identify foods by taste alone 294:81-82
  Illusion—food that is almost the real thing 229:48-51
  Location of taste receptors for sweet and salty experiment 871:2.016
  Mapping the tongue 152:118-126
  No clues! Coke versus 7-up 152:110-112
  Play a taste game 32:20-21
  Several simple experiments with tongue and taste (Primary) 131:4-21
  Smell without taste—artificial strawberry 'flavoring' 152:105-106
  Sweetening melons 152:113-114
  Taste and smell are related senses 253:106
  Taste and smell experiments 366:210-216
  Taste liquids, solids and test taste threshold 363:31-34
  Taste test experiment 399:62
  Taste without smell! Apple versus potato versus onion 152:106-109
  Test for taste on parts of tongue 174:24-25
  Test to see if butterfly can tell the difference. Between sugar and salt 174:32-33
  Testing for taste discrimination 148:60
  The artichoke phenomenon 152:114-118

TASTE AND SMELL. *See also* **SENSES—TASTE AND SMELL**
  Can you taste foods without smelling them experiment 792:25
  Taste and smell test experiment 1063:352

TAXIS BEHAVIOR
  Experiment to show reaction of daphnias to strong light 174:50-51

TEA
  Brewing solar mint tea, how to do 1265:87
  Can tea be served in different ways 402:75-76
  Compare strengths of tea solutions experiment 1479:61
  Compare the strength of teas experiment 905:160-161
  Into water trick 27:38
  Making sun tea 289:35
  Solar mint tea, how to make 986:87
  Tea bags used for sprouting seeds, how to do 1228:74-75

TECTONIC PLATES
  Buildings on fault lines fall down during earthquake experiment 1383:11
  World map tectonic jigsaw puzzle, how to make 1042:25

TEEPEE
  Model—how to make 415:37-38

TEETH. *See also* **HUMAN BODY—TEETH**
  Make cast of your teeth 366:117-119

Memory metal used by orthodontists for braces experiment 1083:62-63

Plaque dye demonstrates food on teeth experiment 882:38

Teeth activities for classroom 1291:37-38

Toothpaste test—does brushing with toothpaste remove bacteria—experiment 441:27-29

Which toothpaste is most effective for cleaning teeth experiment 997:104-105

Who has the most teeth (Primary) 551:unpaged

TELEGRAPH. *See also* **MORSE CODE**

A simple telegraph—making 179:159-162

Basic telegraph sounder—how to make 22:12-13

Build a telegraph set 278:45-47

Build a telegraph set, how to do, Morse Code given 1012:66-68

Build a telegraph set with a bulb 278:47

Can electricity help us to communicate experiment 902:258-259

Cigar box telegraph and key—how to make 128:178

Code set telegraph, making 895:56-59

Complete telegraph system—base construction 22:15

Complete telegraph system—electromagnet construction 22:15-16

Complete telegraph system—final wiring 22:20

Complete telegraph system—key construction 22:17-18

Complete telegraph system—send/receive and contact strip construction 22:18-19

Complete telegraph system—sounder construction 22:16-17

Complete telegraph system—tester 22:20-21

Connect a two-way telegraph system 128:179

Dr. Zed's terrific tap-tap-tap telegraph set, making 890:24-25

Homemade telegraph—making 291:237

Hookup for two simple telegraph stations 22:13

How to make and send messages 382:23-28

How to make 22:11-21; 90:68-72; 655:26-27898:41

Morse code oscillator, how to make 860:101-105

Morse code sender, how to make 1073:63

Morse code sender, how to make using batteries, bulb, paper clips, wire 1073:63

Morse code signaling set, how to make 910:21

Morse code transmitter, how to make 955:21

Open circuit controlled by switch experiment; can use as telegraph 1307:12-13

Relay in action on telegraph experiment 895:35-36

Relay telegraph system, how to make 1426:103-106

Signaling by sound and light 127:88-92

Simple telegraph—how to make 677:29; 828:34; 938:113-116

Talking on a light beam—light beam transmitter system—how to build 22:36-49

Telegraph—speaking or telespecan Edison's experiment 230:41-44

Telegraph code—Morse 382:27

Telegraph code practice set—how to make 191:9-18

Telegraph from wood, battery and bulb, how to make 1043:22-23

Telegraph from wood, wire, tacks and battery, how to make 1209:90-93

Telegraph key—making 34:91-95

Telegraph key and sounder—how to make 123:81-86; 128:177

Telegraph oscillator, how to build 1226:60-61

Telegraph set—how to make 391:95-100; 445:62-64; 1426:91-93

Telegraph set—making; Morse code given 436:78-79

Telegraph set sender and receiver, how to make 1001:24-25

Telegraph sounder and telegraph system, how to make 768:110-112

Telegraph system—making 226:14-15

Telegraph to communicate over wires, how to make 825:28

Telegraph using Morse code, how to make 1072:22

Telegraph with Morse code experiment 1160:20

Tin-can telegraph, making 870:80-82

'Water telegraph'—experiment 22:2-3

TELEKINESIS

Mind over matter sensitive motion detector experiment 1249:58-59

TELEPATHY

Thought message sending experiment with playing cards 1369:82-83

TELEPHONE

Carbon microphone—how to build 22:24-29

Cardboard telephone—making 172:52-53

Cardboard tube and string telephone, how to make 1028:77

Complete two station telephone hookup—how to build 22:24-29

Cup and string telephone, how to make 1102:24

Dial phone from cardboard box, how to make 1175:177

Duplicate Bell's telephone easily (diagram given) 22:22-25

Homemade telephone—how to make 563:20-21

Hose telephone—making 32:32-33

How telephone works experiment 1432:136-141

How to make a telephone 22:22-35; 102:118-120

Make a telephone from old tins 186:53

Make a telephone using cans or paper boxes 179:77-78

Make your own cardboard and string telephone 501:28-29

Mini-mobile telephone from box, cellophane and dowel 1175:179

Oatmeal carton telephone, making 999:13-15

Old-fashioned upright telephone, how to make from cardboard tubes 1175:176-177

Paper cup and string telephone demonstrate sound waves 1141:32-34

Paper cup telephone—make (Primary) 215:exp. #11

Paper cup telephone, making 837:27-28; 860:230-231

Party line telephone from paper cups, making 837:28-29

Plastic glass phone—making 203:72

Simple telephone—how to make 226:9

Simple telephone line—how to make 128:180

Simple telephone transmitter—how to make 128:180-181

Speaking tubes demonstration using paper towel tubes, how to do 1209:76-77

String and can telephone—making 635:13-15

String and can telephone, how to make 1209:88-89; 1369:76-77

String and garden hose telephone—making 733:23

String and paper cup telephone—making 411:18-19

String party line telephone, making 1020:79

String telephone—best way to make 333:41-43

String telephone—how to make 134:21; 178:13; 625:16-17; 696:38-39; 888:145-148;1007:57-59; 1333:12-13

String telephone demonstrates sound traveling through objects experiment 1036:16-17

String telephone experiment; which materials work best to transmit sound 1284:20-21

String telephone experiment 1004:5.011

String telephone, make from tin cans and string 1245:30-31

Telephone booths—how to make 363:28-29

Telephone carbon microphone 391:109-114

Telephone from cup and string demonstrates sound vibrations 1093:14

Telephone from paper cups and wire experiment 1045:16-17

Telephone from paper cups, wire and paper, how to make 1179:168-169

Telephone receiver 391:115-120

Telephone transmitter model, making 895:17

Telephones—speaking tube—how to make 341:53

Tin can and string telephone, how to make 45:30-31; 90:53-54; 94:10-11; 96:55-56; 187:12; 291:147; 427:entire book; unpaged; 436:79; 508:14; 576:78; 759:17-18; 811:26-27; 867:34-35; 898:28; 1001:22-23; 1298:15; 1432:114-118

Tin can telephone—making (Primary) 181:34; 535:65

Touch-tone telephone from cardboard box, how to make 1175:178

Transmitter model—how to make 90:73-76

Tube and funnel telephone—making 734:11

Tube telephone—making 732:71-72

Walkie-talkie, how to make 643:24-25

Wire telephone—how to make 341:54

Yogurt container and string telephone, how to make 1163:13

Yogurt cup and string telephone—making 734:13

Yogurt cup and string telephone, how to make 1073:34

TELESCOPE

3 inch reflecting telescope—how to use 386:122-130

4 power (4x) Galilean telescope—how to make 208:122-129

Astronomical and land telescopes—simple, how to make 472:2214

Astronomical telescope—how to make 507:1906; 161:96-97; 1053:38-39; 1257:38-39

Astronomical telescope, 8x—how to make 208:136-147

Build a simple refracting telescope 564:57

Build a simple telescope 168:25-27

Build a telescope, how to do 860:200-202

Cardboard tube telescope, how to make 885:26-27

Construct an astronomical telescope 167:33-40

Galilean telescope—how to make 507:1906

Galileo type telescope—making 400:105

Heavy duty mount for larger telescopes 386:135-136

How light travels through lens of refractive telescope demonstration 1394:162-163

How light travels through the lens of refractive telescope experiment 1405:150-151

How reflective telescope works demonstration 1394:166-167; 1394:168-169

Learning how lenses in telescope work experiment 1170:19

Make a simple reflecting telescope 595:42-43

Make a telescope 625:23; 928:15

Make telescope from two lenses, thick black paper, sticky tape experiment 1500:27

Making a reflecting telescope project 833:170-171; 833:175

Model refracting telescope—making 128:199

Optical telescope—making (Advanced) 658:16-20

Precision reflecting telescope—making 128:67-68

Radio telescope—making (Advanced) 658:21

Reflecting telescope to look at the Moon, how to make 1308:16-17

Reflecting telescope, how it works experiment 942:121-122; 1434:82-84

Reflecting telescope, how to make 862:134-161

Reflecting telescopes use concave mirror to collect and focus light experiment 1073:79

Refracting telescope with wooden tripod, how to build 1476:175-179

Refracting telescope, how to build experiment 941:123-124

Refracting telescope, how to make 436:80; 862:117-126; 1434:85-89

Refracting telescope, simple, make from cardboard tubes/cork/clay 1217:37

Resolution of a lens demonstration 1394:190-191

Simple cardboard tube telescope, how to make 1308:20-21

Simple reflecting telescope—making 128:67

Simple refracting telescope—making 128:67

Simple telescope, how to make 967:18-19; 1417:24-25

Size of cone affects telescope images demonstration 1394:164-165

Telescope—making 659:17; 909:145

Telescope, how to make and mount (Advanced) 688:44-46

Telescope, how to make from cardboard and lenses 1213:25

Telescope, make from cardboard tubes, black paper, and lens 1478:12-13

Why does a telescope magnify objects experiment 1294:100-102

TELEVISION

A close-up of a color TV picture—experiment 591:64

Bending light experiment; TV picture shows on cardboard screen 1257:10-11

Control TV from another room experiment 1083:102

HDTV (high definition television) model set, how to make 1175:186-188

How does color television work experiment 1283:26

How many hours a day is TV set and electrical items on in home experiment 1020:143-146

Make big screen TV with a shaving mirror experiment 1083:101

Milk carton television viewer—making 631:110

Speed of TV waves how to measure experiment (Advanced) 762:93-94

The scan lines in a TV picture—observation experiment 591:63-64

TV picture tube—lines black and white dots 12:76-79

TV shows for children have more commercials per hour computer project 1021:84-85

Watch TV upside down on piece of paper experiment 1083:100

Wheels seem to go backward in front of television screen experiment 1283:27

TEMPERATURE. See also COLD; HEAT; THERMOMETERS; THERMOSTAT

Activities with temperature—chart given 748:138-139

Air temperature warmer over asphalt road than over grassy lawn experiment 969:98-99

Air thermometer measures temperature 293:41

Alarm 391:81-86

Being wet makes you cooler experiment 829:41-42

Black hotter than white 289:33

Can cricket chirp give us the temperature 333:66-67

Charting temperature (Primary) 232:48

Coldest temperature of air experiment 1515:35-36

Colors to wear on hot day, light or dark experiment using paper/water in sun 1017:15

Cooling curves of ice and water experiment 1515:88-91

Creating heat by shaking experiment 1515:110-115

Cricket chirps give temperature experiment 721:50

Cricket chirps used as gauge of air temperature, how to do 1209:59

Demonstrate what it does to buildings 328:64-65

Difference between heat and temperature experiment 1158:85-92

Fahrenheit scale to measure temperature—how he made it (Primary) 648:18-27

Fat or lard or blubber insulates against cold project 969:30-31

Finding the kindling temperature of materials 180:74-75

Freezing points—experiments 182:16-17

Fruit flies response to cold temperature experiment 936:15-16

Galileo's how hot is hot experiment 1133:7.001

Graph temperature in three different places; data sheet given 816:4

Graph temperature of water, sand, and other areas at beach, graph given 772:97-102

Hand test for hot and cold water experiment 793:26-27

Hands in water—experiment 629:25-26

Heat convection in liquids experiment 1515:102-104

Heat of vaporization experiment 1158:94-96

Heat or temperature?—experiment 585:135-136

Hidden heat of melting ice experiment 1515:81-84

Hidden heat; melting, boiling, freezing and condensation experiment 1515:76-84

Hot and cold experiment with thermo., ice cubes, wax, water, coins, pencil 383:entire book

Hot and cold water—which is heavier 280:22

Hot places and cold places—insulation experiment 153:22-23

How accurate are hands for recording temperature 179:59-60

How do different temperatures affect animal life 402:89-90

How does sudden change in temperature affect us experiment 901:10

How does temperature of lake change 381:74

Human—using a thermometer—natural body heat 294:88-89

Human body—what is temperature of human body 402:55-56

Human thermometer using hands 617:9

Is it cooler in the shade experiment 834:17

Is it warm under the snow 333:70-71

Is the temperature the same all over your home 333:134-136

Keeping cool, insulation experiment 587:41

Land (soil) and sea (water) absorb heat at different rates experiment 1086:11

Latent heat of melting ice experiment 1515:81-84

Latent heat of vaporization of water experiment 1515:85-88

Mass and temperature change are involved in measuring heat experiment 1515:56-62

Measurement of car interior and reradiation of heat 289:31-32

Measuring—how cold is it 304:24-25

Model of matter to demonstrate heat processes experiment 1515:116-123

Newton's Law of Cooling experiment 1090:20-21

Record winter temperature differences outside in different. Places 277:11

Reflective versus absorptive surfaces experiment 969:98-99

Rules of temperature change experiment with fluid level changes 1515:45-55

Rules of temperature change experiment, how to graph 1515:38-44

Sensor—computer experiments 665:24-31

Show with thermometers—experiment 128:143-145

Simple experiments describing changes of hot and cold (Primary) 417:1-33

Specific heat; compare specific heat of metals experiment 1515:72-75

Sun warms different substances by different amounts experiment 1281:7

Temperature affects solubility experiment 1526:42-43

Temperature by touch experiment 1515:8-10

Temperature changes in water and cooking oil experiment 1515:65-69

Temperature differences on a hill 253:93-94

Temperature effect on the length of wires experiment 1515:12-14

Temperature illusions experiment 761:100

Temperature of the air experiments 1086:10

Temperature regulation in animals using elephant ear models experiment 1134:3.004

Temperature scale model—making 748:42

Temperature scales to convert Celsius, Fahrenheit and Kelvin 1396:221

Test for hot or cold with fingers 249:15

Test for insulation with thermometer in refrigerator experiment 1086:11

Thermal conductivities of steel, glass and insulation experiment 1515:95-101

Volume of air of a gas affected by temperature experiment 1515:17-19

Warm and cool colors experiment 1086:11

Warmest time of day temperature experiment 1516:46

Water and paper—a paper percolator 114:45

Which coffee cools faster—experiment 585:143-144

Wind caused by temperature differences experiment 1322:28-32

World chart showing places hotter than body temperature experiment 1275:28

You can't measure temperature of water with your fingers 238:50-52

TEMPERATURE—SPACECRAFT

Experiments to demonstrate temperature control on a spacecraft 564:76-77

TEMPERATURE INVERSION. *See also* **AIR POLLUTION; SMOG**

Temperature inversion experiment; demonstrate what happens 978:173

Temperature inversion experiment; observe how warm air traps smoke particles 1447:68-70
Temperature inversion experiment 1174:23-26
Temperature inversion prevents convection of air and makes air stagnant 1174:23-26

TENDONS

Action of tendons demonstrated with chicken foot 577:project #5
What are tendons and how do they work experiment 901:167

TENNIS

"Sweet spot" on tennis racket or baseball bat experiment 1154:115-121

TENSILE STRENGTH. *See also* **STRUCTURAL STRENGTH**

Of paper 105:18-23
Paper pipe holds up books (Primary) 109:22-23
Tensile strength of paper measured experiment 1157:76-78

TENTS

Hooped tent experiment, how to erect 1518:12-13
Model—how to make 328:13-14; 415:38-39
Ridge tent experiment, how to erect 1518:10-11

TERMITES

Studying a social insect in field and lab 266:142-146

TERRARIUMS. *See also* **ECOSYSTEMS**

A bog community terrarium 268:57-62
A desert community terrarium 268:29-33
A grassy field community terrarium 268:41-44
A woodland community terrarium 268:17-21
Aquaterrarium to raise frogs experiment, how to make 1492:68-69
Aquavivarium for turtles—making 720:56
Beach—how to make 296:63-65
Bog terrarium—making 465:155-158; 748:79
Build a terrarium 291:198
Building a terrarium case 465:139-143
Containers for 234:70-71
Cultivated garden terrarium—making 465:152-155
Desert—how to make 400:14
Desert community terrarium—setting up and observing 285:89
Desert or woodland terrarium project, how to make 1296:1982
Desert terrarium—making 465:145-146; 748:77
Desert terrarium—materials and animals for; how to set up and maintain 475:32-34
Desert woodland and soil—making 234:72-73
Explore link between land and water in terraqua column experiment 1527:61-63
For winter insects—how to make 277:84-88
Forest floor community terrarium—setting up and observing 285:88
Forest floor terrarium, how to make 1075:32-33
Forest plants—build glass enclosed terrarium 294:25-26
Forest terrarium in large soda bottle, how to make 1071:76-77
From a rotting log 268:26-27
Garden in a glass, making 887:40-42
Garden toad and lizard need different habitats and different food (Primary) 559:1-31
Grow a garden in a glass bowl 416:42-43
How to make a terrarium 86:23-25; 264:36; 644:42-45; 879:199-202; 991:23-29

How to set up and maintain a terrarium 475:5-13
How to set up different kinds of terrariums—fishbowl, mirror, large plant 497:100-112
Indoor garden in a plastic jar, how to make 1038:24-25
Insect terrarium for observing and keeping insects, how to make 1320:38
Jar garden, how to make using jar, soil, and plants 1054:32-33
Jar terrarium—making 203:35
Jungle in a jar terrarium, how to make 913:31
Jungle terrarium—materials and animals for; how to set up and maintain 475:20-26
Lichens grow in terrariums 436:53
Making 62:31-32
Making woodland, desert, bog and semiaquatic 436:80-82
Marshland terrarium—materials and animals for; how to set up and maintain 475:36-46
Meadow terrarium—materials and animals for; how to set up and maintain 475:14-20
Milk carton terrarium—making 631:112
Miniature bead garden—directions for making 449:95-99
Moss garden—making 739:19
Moss garden terrarium—how to make 483:68-70
Mosses—growing mosses in glass enclosed terrarium 294:25-27
Plant growth in 236:35
Plants use same air and water over and over again 232:39
Plastic bottle terrarium, making 854:114
Plastic cup terrarium—making (Primary) 535:43
Pond terrarium—making 748:78
Pond water terrariums—materials and animals for; how to set up and maintain 475:35-38
Put together a simple terrarium with plants 476:58-60
Reflector lamp for terrariums—making 279:7
Rotting log community terrarium—setting up and observing 285:87-88
Setting up a terrarium 253:20-22
Setting up and caring for a grassy terrarium 108:44-47
Setting up life in a jar project 833:125-127
Soda bottle terrarium, how to make 1527:110
Soil for terrariums, how to prepare 784:123-124
Swamp terrarium—making (Primary) 650:unpaged
Terrarium, how to set up 901:92-94
Terrarium, making 901:45-46; 918:16
Terrarium, set up to demonstrate water cycle 884:12-13
To set up a terrarium 62:31-32
Vivarium—how to make 720:54-55
Wildlife—how to make 390:12-13
Woodland—how to make 400:14
Woodland garden terrarium, how to make 832:59
Woodland habitat terrarium, how to make 1188:22-23
Woodland terrarium—making 465:146-151; 646:75-77; 748:76; 899:160-161
Woodland terrariums—materials and animals for; how to set up and maintain 475:14-20

TERRESTRIAL SUCCESSION

Woodland terrestrial succession experiment; data tables given 1004:2.011

TERRITORIALITY

Animals defense of a territory in the field and in the laboratory 266:153-156

TESLA, NIKOLA

AC induction motor, making 627:61
His experiments 42:140-159

TESLA COILS
How to make 43:93-108

TESSELLATION
Tessellation activities 1351:49-59

TEST TUBE
Holder and rack—how to make 85:2-5; 319:15-16
Holder 9:72-73; 9:82-83
Rack 9:74-75

TESTS. *See also* **INDICATORS**
Electric questioner for matching tests—how to make
    532:88-89
Paper towel tester on different brands of paper towels
    487:58-59

TEXTILES. *See also* **CLOTH; FABRICS; FIBERS**
Absorption and shrinkage of natural and synthetic fibers
    experiment 1259:80-81
Acids, bases and bleach effect on fibers experiment
    1259:81-82
Adventure 38—examine textile fibers—cotton, wool, silk
    under microscope 403:136-141
Appearance and strength of natural and synthetic fibers
    compared experiment 1259:77-80
Bacteria attacks fibers in fabrics and wears out clothing
    experiment 1259:83-84
Combustibility of fibers; which will burn experiment
    1259:82-83
Does wool or cotton cloth hold more water project
    1210:46-47
Dyeing fabric fibers by direct dyeing and by vat dyeing
    experiment 1259:86-88
Dyeing of cloth and indirect dyeing of cloth experiment
    1396:107-108
Dyes from plants and their effect on different fabrics ex-
    periment 871:2.021
Factors that affect how well different textiles absorb dyes
    project 1296:2003
Fading effect of sunlight on fabric samples experiment
    1396:108-109
Fibers—cotton fuzz makes cotton cloth 257:14
Fibers—make threads by teasing and spinning 257:25-29
Fibers—pineapple fibers make fine cloth pina and nets
    for fishing 257:15-18
Fibers—silk worm fibers and cocoons 257:20-22
Fibers under microscope—compare cotton—silk—poly-
    ester and others 713:41-45
Flame test to show different kinds 83:27-28
Flame test to show kinds of textiles 176:18
Heat retention of fibers in clothing experiment 1259:84-
    85
Identify by burning 116:182-183
Natural or synthetic fibers absorbency experiment
    1294:40-41
Rayon—how to make from chemicals 97:40-41
Some fabrics are more absorbent than others experiment
    860:47-48
What fabric is most durable; brick test experiment 795:29

TEXTURE
Texture box (Primary) 535:70
Texture races demonstrate friction (Primary) 535:71

THALES
His "magnetizing" amber experiment with static electric-
    ity 627:2

THAUMATROPE
Cardboard and pencil thaumatrope, how to make 1369:45

How to make 172:36-38; 558:118-119
Making from wood and cardboard 429:51
Making your own thaumatrope, how to do, patterns
    given 861:13-17
Optical toy thaumatrope, how to make with pictures
    given 1299:16-17
Simple thaumatrope, how to make 935:78
'Thaumatrope' 350:128-129
Thaumatrope, how to make, patterns given 1007:28-30
Thaumatrope, make to show how movies work experi-
    ment 1216:40-42

THEODOLITE
Building a theodolite (Advanced) 658:5-9
Construct a theodolite to survey 167:137-142
Measure altitude of stars and planets with instrument you
    build 834:124-125
Theodolite measures altitude and horizontal distance
    from North Star experiment 1476:173-174
Theodolite measures height of objects experiment, how
    to make 1521:28-29
Theodolite to find altitude and azimuth of star, how to
    make 1434:45-49
Theodolite, how to make from wooden post, straw, com-
    pass, protractor 1217:10-11

THEODORIC OF FREIBOURG
How rainbows are formed experiment 1133:6.003

THERMAL INVERSION
Thermal inversion effect on air pollution experiment
    1322:55-59

THERMAL POLLUTION. *See also* **WATER—POLLU-
TION; WATER POLLUTION**
Air is a gas that can dissolve in water experiment
    1250:11-13
Increased temperature of water effect on insect growth
    experiment 1097:48-50
More molecules in air will dissolve in cold water than in
    hot water experiment 1250:11-13
Temperature changes density of water experiment
    1325:18-21
Thermal pollution in lakes/rivers caused by warm water
    from industries 1250:11-13
Water animals and plants killed by heat pollution from in-
    dustry experiment 1074:84-85
Water used for cooling by industry causes thermal pollu-
    tion experiment 1250:11-13
What is thermal water pollution experiment 1325:65-69

THERMISTORS
Sensors and thermistors—how to make 665:24-31

THERMOCLINE
Making 741:23

THERMOCOUPLES
Demonstrate heat energy and current electricity relation-
    ships 209:54-55
Electricity by thermocouples—experiment 627:35
How to make 577:project #17; 608:55-56
Thermoelectricity, producing electricity from heat experi-
    ment 768:81-82

THERMODYNAMICS
Determine direction of energy transfer of two materials
    experiment 1396:173-179
First and second laws of thermodynamics experiment;
    data tables given 1004:3.015
First Law of Thermodynamics experiment; light energy
    transferred/transformed 1453:14-15
Laws of—demonstrate 642:142-144

Movement of air during land and sea breezes experiment 1396:177

Second Law of Thermodynamics experiment; some transferred energy is useless 1453:15-18

THERMOMETERS. *See also* **HEAT; TEMPERATURE**

A cricket thermometer—experiment 563:57-58

Accuracy of 381:72-73

Air and spirit thermometer—making 128:143-145

Air expansion thermometer, how to build 1515:26-27

Air thermometer—demonstrate principle of 217:32-37

Air thermometer—experiment to make 385:120-123

Air thermometer—how to make 472:2216; 1243:29

Ball-point pen thermometer 71:46-49

Bottle and glass tube thermometer, making 867:21-22

Bottle and straw thermometer, how to make 885:63-64

Calibration—experiment to show 182:24-25

Check temperatures at different points 91:58-61

Coldest temperature of air experiment 1515:35-36

Color change for dry and wet—experiment to demonstrate 87:59-60

Colored water thermometer, how to make 1042:42-43

Comparison of Celsius thermometer to Fahrenheit thermometer (Primary) 648:28-32

Construct model of Galileo's gas thermometer experiment 1396:181-187

Cricket thermometer experiment 1158:129-130

Cricket thermometer, how to count chirps and determine temperature 1439:81-82

Cricket thermometer, how to count chirps and figure out temperature experiment 959:112

Demonstration thermometer with activities, making 891:38-43

Determine temperature from a cricket's chirp experiment 904:104-105

Draw diagrams comparing Fahrenheit/Celsius/Kelvin thermometer scales experiment 1396:186-187

Drinking straw thermometer, how to make 1219:30

Experiments with 107:11-16

Fahrenheit measurements versus Celsius measurements experiment 1439:72-74

Fahrenheit scale to measure temperature—how he made it (Primary) 648:18-27

Galileo thermometer—experiment to make 385:118-120

Galileo's 'thermoscope'—demonstrate 217:57-59

Gas expansion bottle thermometer, making 906:22-23

Glass bottle and colored ink thermometer, how to make 1430:21

Glass bottle thermometer, how to make 1179:125

Gum wrapper thermometer—making 697:23-25

How a thermometer works 281:56-57

How a thermometer works demonstration 834:121; 1405:81

How does a thermometer work [Primary] 744:8

How thermometer works demonstration 1023:140-141

How to make a thermometer 161:75; 293:41; 681:17; 900:79-80; 900:81-82; 939:12-17

Laboratory thermometer measurement of several objects experiment 1515:32-34

Liquid expansion thermometer, how to build 1515:23-25

Make thermometer from soda bottle and colored water experiment 1063:435

Make thermometer using glass bottle, cork, straw, food colors 1439:77-80

Make your own from glass bottle, food coloring experiment 1519:6

Measuring temperature of air experiment 939:8-18

Plastic bottle, straw and colored water thermometer, how to make 1387:13

Rey's liquid thermometer; construct model of experiment 1396:184-187

Rubber stoppered bottle and colored water thermometer, how to make 837:55-56

Simple thermometer—how to make 14:5-10; 179:62; 249:14; 360:77

Simple thermometer—make a (Primary) 70:38-39

Simple thermometer from colored water in plastic bottle experiment 1028:29

Snow thermometer, how to make 850:24

Straw and plastic container thermometer—making 767:19

Straw thermometers, making to show how thermometers work 1003:96-97

Temperature conversion chart, Fahrenheit and Centigrade 1003:98

Temperature scales to convert Celsius, Fahrenheit and Kelvin 1396:221

Temperatures in outdoor environments—experiment 175:74

Temperatures—maximum to minimum 9:102

Thermometer from straw, glass bottle, and food colors, how to make 1465:15-16

Thermometer measures temperature experiment using glass bottle, colored water 1032:16-17

Thermometer reading on play thermometer (Primary) 535:31

Thermometer strips register fever from flashlight or TV clicker experiment 1083:93

Up and down 280:34

Use of 40:134-135

Use wet and dry bulb thermometer to determine relative humidity 291:40-41

Water thermometer—how to make 253:57-58

Wet and dry bulb thermometers measure humidity in air experiment 1359:14

Wet bulb thermometer, how to make 865:86

THERMOSCOPE

Construct model of Galileo's gas thermometer experiment 1396:181-187

Make a simple one 128:149

THERMOSTAT

Air expansion—how to make 43:7-11

Bimetallic—how to make 43:1-6

Bimetallic strip—experiment 585:60-61

Bimetallic strip—making 762:119-120

Constructing a thermostat, how to 830:53-55

Make thermostat and demonstrate use of bimetallic strip 183:20-23

THIGMOTROPISM. *See also* **PLANTS—TROPISMS**

Leaf triggering mechanism on mimosa leaves experiment 1061:85-86

Water, wind and touch stimuli affect plant growth experiment 1450:77-84

THOMPSON, BENJAMIN

Caloric theory experiment; there is no mass change when ice freezes 1156:94

THREAD

How to make rayon thread 319:85-87

How are cotton threads made experiment 1508:10

THUMB. *See* **HUMAN BODY**

THUNDER AND LIGHTNING
Boomer paper demonstrates thunder, making 983:98-99
Calculate how far away storm is, how to do 1149:19
Demonstrate production of thunder 1023:182-183
Determine how far away thunderstorm is experiment 959:111-112
Homemade thunder—making 670:55
How far away is lightning flash experiment, how to measure 1372:86; 1141:48-49
How far away is the storm experiment 1163:4; 1516:82
How far away is thunder, how to determine 1209:79
How positive and negative charges separate using balloon/pepper experiment 1465:91-92
How thunder is produced demonstration with paper bag 1479:85
Lightning made in a dark room with charged balloons experiment 1208:74-75
Lightning produces radio waves demonstration 1023:180-181
Make lightning experiment 1480:177
Measure distance to thunderstorm experiment 1432:6-7
Measure how far away is the storm 295:51-52
Paper bags demonstrate [Primary] 759:41
Paper banger sounds like thunder, how to make 1209:78-79
Photographing lightning, how to do 959:111
Simulate down draft or cold front reaching ground in thunderstorm experiment 1465:87-88
Sparks from static electricity experiment with baking pan, plastic bag/clay 1136:22
Thunder stick musical instrument, how to make from plastic pipe 1115:76
Thunder time—how to measure how far away is storm 366:180
Why do you hear thunder experiment 1294:60-61
Why does it thunder—paper bag experiment (Primary) 452:54

THUNDERCLOUDS
Make imitation thunder clouds and lightning 172:155-158

THUNDERSTORMS
Thunder from cardboard and paper, how to make 890:94

TIDE POOLS
Exploring the micro community in a tide pool 285:68
Measure depth, water density, temperature of tide pools experiment 871:2.006
Observing life in 118:187-201

TIDES. *See also* **OCEAN TIDES**
Activities with tides 236:100-102
Centrifugal force effect on tides demonstration 1023:220-221
Check high and low tide project 869:14
Falling/rising tides at ocean measured and compared to tide tables experiment 1225:203-207
Find out times of low and high tides (Primary) 601:unpaged
Gravitational pull of Moon affects the tides on Earth experiment 1062:43-44
Illustrate spring and neap tide 299:8-9
Investigating tides 41:109-123
Measuring tide with sticks, graph given, experiment 772:54-56
Mobile to demonstrate tides, making 840:22
Shape of shorelines affects height of tides demonstration 1023:218-219; 1405:87

Showing how the tides occur project 833:212-213
Tidal height calculator, making (Advanced) 687:44
Tide dial gives tide progression as Moon orbits Earth experiment 1478:53
Tide observations, how to do 1225:198-207
Tides and gravity 274:15
Time and tides; connection between moon and ocean experiment 877:67-72
Time and tides 93:41-43
What time is the tide due experiment, make tide dial to demonstrate 1478:53

TIGHTROPE WALKERS
Demonstrate principle with cardboard gravity fighter 288:32-33

TILTMETER
Tiltmeter measures tilting of ground on sides of volcano experiment 1477:48-51

TIME. *See also* **CLOCKS; NIGHT AND DAY; SHADOWS; SUNDIALS**
Activities explain how time, distance and speed can be measured 1355:5-64
Big time line of Earth 231:92-93
Body clocks—I got rhythm 231:52
Calendar—history chart 137:28
Calibrated candle, how to make 1355:13
Can you split seconds accurately 333:119-121
Candle alarm clock from candle, metal nut and metal tray, how to make 1421:26
Candle alarm clock with electric light, how to make 1421:27
Candle clock—how to make 137:12; 192:65-68; 803:14-16
Candle clock from large candle, how to make 1421:19
Candle timer, making 887:24
Chart of night and day on Earth 246:8-9
Chart position of moon 137:29
Check and show star time 137:27
Chinese water clock—making a model 137:10
Custom sun clock—make 231:47
Digital twenty-four hour time chart, how to make 1421:25
Displaying the path of the analemma project 833:22
Egyptian time stick—making 192:23-25
Egyptian water clock—making 192:27-34
Flowers that bloom on time—make a flower clock 640:90
Graph units of time 137:25
Hour bottles—how to make 231:48
Hourglass or 3-minute timer, making 887:26
Hours by flowers; time—keeping flower garden 231:53
How time flies—experiment with people 586:108-109
Making a night clock nocturnal project 833:29-31
Making a sundial project 833:25-27
Making water clocks project 833:27-29
Marble clock using marbles on ramp experiment, how to make 1521:16-17
Mean astronomical time, how to find experiment 1476:158-159
Measure time with your fingers, how to do 1434:56-57
Measuring (metric) seconds pendulum 357:9
Measuring—how can we measure time 253:192-193
Measuring time—a sand clock timer 304:18-19
Measuring time—an anytime calendar 304:20-21

Metric clock makes working with time easier experiment 1062:40

Nocturnal clock—how to make to tell time at night 192:56-64

Paper cup makes water clock (Primary) 201:22-23

Pattern for a night clock 292:65-66

Shape of shorelines affects height of tides demonstration 1023:218-219; 1405:87

Pendulum clock experiment 806:39-41

Pendulum clock experiment, how to make 1521:14-15

Rolling marble timed experiments 806:33-35

Salt timer experiment, how to make 1521:12-13

Sand clock measures time experiment; how to make from plastic bottles 1062:37-39

Sand clock, making 137:11; 803:8-9

Sand timer, how to make 1355:14

Sandglass that runs for three (3) minutes experiment, how to make 1521:13

Sense-human time clocks in the field and in the laboratory 266:43-46

Sidereal time and synodic time 292:78-80

String timer, making 887:24

Sun noon and clock noon—check with shadow 640:21

Sundial—an anywhere sundial—how to do 292:64

Sundial—how to make 101:40-44; 137:8; 192:36-49; 192:50-55

Tell time by the stars, nocturne night dial, pattern given, how to make 1114:128-131

Tell time of day by flower blossoms opening and closing 271:41-48

Telling time on your fingers 772:46-47

Three different sundials, how to make 1421:11-12

Time and dates around the Earth 577:project #39

Time zones 137:26

Timer—ball-point timer 71:50-52

Tin can clock—how to make 231:41

Twister alarm clock experiments 806:42-43

Water clock—make a 137:9; 231:48; 803:10-13; 1355:14

Water clock experiment 1521:17

Water timer, making 887:24-25

Water-soak clock experiment 806:36-39

Your lifeline—how to make 640:118; 640:121-122

TIME LINES

Geological time lines, how to make 1342:76-80

TIME TABLES

Computer travel time program 665:14-19

TIME ZONES

Demonstrate time zones 169:9

Explanation of time zones and lines of longitude 1434:15-17

Telling time around the world 175:51

What time is it where you live (Primary) 303:26-27

TIMERS

Bottle timer from soda bottle, how to make 1527:116

Digital timer, how to make 860:113-116

Marble timer from cardboard box and marbles, how to make 1421:21

Sand or salt timer to measure one, two or three minutes—making 508:20

Sand timer—how to make 494:36-37

Sand timer—how to make (Primary) 535:79

Sand timer from plastic bottle and jar, how to make 1421:20

Sand timer, how to make from soda bottle, wood, jar lids and cardboard 1512:16-17

TIRES

Smooth tires on toy auto won't climb hill experiment 1073:13

TOADS

Collection and care of 313:29-32

Collection and care of 390:41-42

Exploration of a pond, marsh or swamp for toad egg masses 285:77

Food—what is proper food for toads 402:49-50

Horned toads—how to care for in a terrarium 475:33-34

How far can toad's tongue reach for food experiment 1069:79

How to care for 279:17

How to care for in a terrarium 475:15-17

How to catch and care for 234:40-41

Raise toad tadpoles experiment; observe how tiny swimmers live on land 1472:36-41

Record toad choruses 236:70

Toad house for the garden, how to make 986:82

Toad house, how to make from flowerpot 1115:24-25

TOASTER

How to make an electric toaster 128:186

TOBACCO

Effects of nicotine on daphnia experiment 1267:97-101

Tobacco under a hand lens 29:15

TOBACCO HABIT. *See* SMOKING

TOILET PAPER

How fast do different brands of toilet paper break up in water experiment 1371:64

Toilet paper survey to determine which brand is best for the environment 1013:41

TOMATOES

How to grow indoors 231:35

How to ripen a tomato 366:221

Plant and grow tomatoes indoors, how to do 1178:32

TONGUE—HUMAN

Demonstrate taste areas of the tongue 294:82-83

Four basic tastes map of tongue 625:40

Map taste areas of your tongue 266:30

Taste areas on tongue chart 402:60

Taste buds locations—experiment 585:160-161

Tasty tongue—taste buds—experiment 607:38-39

Tongue map 366:215

Tongue, mapping taste areas of your tongue, how to do 835:44-46

Which part of the tongue is most sensitive to taste experiment 901:181-182

TOOTHPASTE

How to make 319:87-88

Tooth powder and toothpaste, how to make experiment 1259:58-60

Toothpaste dispenser—how to make 487:44-45

Toothpaste is both plastic liquid and visco elastic experiment 1091:33-34

Toothpaste test experiment—does brushing with toothpaste remove bacteria 441:27-29

Which tooth cleaner is most effective for cleaning teeth experiment 997:104-105

TOOTHPASTE AND POWDER

Formulate your own toothpaste and powder 381:22-25

TOOTHPICKS

Abstract art with toothpicks 418:12-14

Build a space frame structure from toothpicks 557:61-63

How to make a stick tower from toothpicks 545:8-10

How to shape and glue for projects 418:6-11

Make a toothpick log cabin (Primary) 155:14-15
Pea and toothpick building—how to make 732:112-113
Toothpick bridges, ideas for projects 858:1-28
Toothpick bridges 66:78-92
Toothpick giraffe—how to make 418:20-23
Toothpick house—how to make 418:27-31
Toothpick sailboat—how to make 418:24-26
Toothpick structures—pea joints hold a toothpick in
place 203:15
Toothpick tree—how to make 418:15-19

TOPOGRAPHY
Basic explanation of graph theory and networks 477:1-33
Curses, coiled again—the inside curve fix 222:70-71
Cut paper in half and still get one piece experiment
937:16-17
Famous Mobius strip 550:111-115
Ideas for science projects 460:1-33
Konigsberg bridge problem experiment 808:60
Magic trick with paper belts 1010:77-80
Make a rubber band jump from one finger to another
228:107
Mathematical hieroglyphics experiment 808:61-63
Mobius strip—the will that wouldn't 222:78-79
No loophole here 222:72-74
Out of order 222:69
Pass a quarter thru a hole the size of dime 228:105
Slip your body through an index card experiment
1007:72-73
Topographic models—making 532:72-73
Tricks with paper loops experiment 842:18-31
Twenty-one-sided polygon, how to make 808:56-58

TOPS
Spinning top, designs and patterns for circles given, how
to make 1299:60-61

TORNADOES
Air pressure crush the can or jug experiment 700:55-56
Demonstrate appearance of a tornado 1023:178-179
Demonstrate what they do to buildings 328:58-63
Demonstrate what they do to buildings 328:66-73
Dust devils—making 700:57
Force of tornado demonstration with potato and straw
1020:66-67
Formation and effect of low pressure demonstration
1023:176-177
Large tornado in a box experiment—how to make 700:58
Liquid tornado—making 700:56
Make a liquid tornado experiment 1516:86-87
Plastic bottle demonstrates pressure in center of tornado
experiment 1003:62-63
Simulate tornado lifting action in bottle of water experi-
ment 1465:89-90
Swirling water in bottles demonstrates action of tornado
1229:66-67
Tornado in a box 577:project #43
Tornado in a jar experiment using food coloring and de-
tergent 1127:38
Tornado low air pressure experiment 1003:64-65
Vortex bottle experiment to demonstrate how vortex
works 1480:178-179
Water in two plastic soda bottles demonstrates tornado
1014:114-115
Wind velocity experiment with potato and straw 700:54

TORQUE
Demonstrate torque 291:139
Experiment with box rolling up hill 291:141
How rotational motion is changed; good and bad torque
experiment 1164:39-40
Mini-boomerangs, making 669:6-7

TORRICELLI, EVANGELISTA
Velocity of jets of liquid escaping from a receptacle ex-
periment 1133:4.006
Water barometer experiment 1156:54-55

TORTOISES
Care of and how to keep 279:14-15; 720:58-59
Keeping a pet tortoise 507:1907-1908

TOTEM POLES
How to make a totem pole 545:25-27; 644:18-19

TOUCH. *See also* **SENSES—TOUCH**
Demonstrate different kinds of touch 133:4-14
Demonstrate sensitivity of touch 133:15-21
Make a touch tester 107:92-93
Mystery touch box 32:18-19
Play a touch game 32:16-17
Texture matching game 253:107
Touch illusions experiment 761:101

TOURNIQUET
To demonstrate blood flow 335:54

TOWERS
Cable car; model cable car runs between towers experi-
ment, how to build 1518:18-19
Design and build a tower 755:16
Framework for towers building project 755:14-15
How to make (Primary) 220:22-26
How to make a stick tower from toothpicks 545:8-10
How to make towers from dowels 545:10-11
Straw towers, how to build 1408:16-17
Suspension bridge model, how to make from bricks,
wood strips, string 1518:32-33
Suspension bridge on towers experiment 1024:22-23
Tower crane with swinging boom experiment, how to
build 1518:22-23
Tower that can withstand strong winds experiment
1159:43-46
Trembling wooden tower, how to build experiment
1518:9
Who can build the tallest tower project [Primary] 755:6-9

TOWERS AND BRIDGES
Experiments with 107:45-51

TOXIC CHEMICALS
Farmers alternatives to using toxic chemicals experiment
using ladybugs/aphids 1427:88-89
Household cleaners compared for hazards and disposal
problems experiment 1361:50-51
Household items tested for acid using red cabbage indica-
tor experiment 1328:62
Labels on cleaning products experiment 1361:56
Parts per million (ppm); discover how small it is in
chemicals experiment 1361:45
Toxic chemicals hurt plants experiment using two plants,
one watered with salt 1427:85-87

TOYS
Aeolian top, making 861:205-211
Balance toys—high wire walker—how to make 410:24
Balance toys—trick cyclist—how to make 410:25
Balancing Bill and balancing Jill plastic bottle, patterns
given, make 1299:72-73
Balancing boat from tennis ball and knitting needles,
how to make 1299:75
Balancing boys from cardboard, balsa wood and wire,
how to make 1299:75

430

Cup and ball toy, how to make 861:193-198
Dandy the Dashing Dragon toy—how to make 410:16-17
Fearsome Fred balancing face from thick cardboard, patterns given, make 1299:74
Floppy hounddog—how to make 410:7
Gallery shoot out toy—how to make 410:44-45
Investigate scientific principles behind toys experiments 1412:8
Jumping bean roller—how to make 410:6
Jumping jack toy, how to make 1299:58
Mouse on the move toy, how to make 1299:59
Mr. Twitch—his arms go around—how to make 410:38-39
Noddy clown—make a 94:30-31
Paper wrestlers, how to make 861:176-180
Rocking egghead toy—how to make 410:6
'Roly-poly' toy from potato and straw—making 203:91
Rubber band tractor 401:76-78
Ruler and string noise roarer 364:136
Sound toys—clucking hen, roaring ruler, singing bottle, etc.—how to make 410:8-9
Spinning top—make with paper plate and pencil 200:18-19
Spinning top, designs and patterns given for circles, how to make 1299:60-61
Spool top—how to make 364:123
Spoolie toss up—how to make 364:122
Spoolman from outer space—how to make 364:123
Thank-you money bank—how to make 410:20-21
Tightrope walker—make 94:32-33
Train—how to make 415:18-19
Wind up toy—make a 91:117-119

TRACING PAPER
Make tracing paper 563:159-160

TRACKS. *See* **TRACKS AND TRACKING**

TRACKS—BALL GAMES
Acceleration of ball to moving target 373:24-27
Assembling the track 373:8-9
Ball release mechanism—how to make 373:12-16
Billiards 373:62-67
Circles and curves tracks 373:38-53
Circular raceway 373:49-53
Collisions 373:65-67
Connecting moldings 373:10-11
Experiments to try with slanted tracks 373:21-37
Flying and colliding balls 373:54-67
Jump the gap 373:54-58
Loop the loop 373:45-48
Musical tracks—how to make 373:32-37
Racing balls—how to 373:18-20
Roller coaster track 373:42-44
Rube Goldberg machines 373:68-80
Ski jump 373:59-61
Spiral ball return 373:74-80
Straight tracks—how to make 373:17
Zigzag game track 373:28-31

TRACKS AND TRAILING
Animal footprints cast in plaster, how to do 1363:17
Animal track cast—make in field and preserve 436:10
Animal tracks—how to cast 62:63-64; 234:34-35; 236:139-140; 293:7; 890:107
Animal tracks—how to collect 236:95; 629:120
Animal tracks, how to preserve 586:140-141
Animal tracks made of plaster casts, how to do 921:33; 1371:16-17; 1427:18-20

Animal tracks; paraffin casts, how to make 921:33-34
Be a snow snoop for animal tracks 494:83
Become a track detective 277:30-34
Casts of animal prints using plaster of Paris, how to make 1183:141
Casts of animal tracks, how to prepare using plaster of Paris 918:24-25; 1313:115-120; 1425:74-77
Discovering tracks of winter active animals 277:26-30
Guide to patterns in snow 277:27-30
Observing and collecting 480:92
Outdoor projects with 118:141-150
Plaster casts and molds of footprints, how to make 977:13
Plaster casts of animal tracks—how to make 476:12-15; 726:58-59; 731:40; 824:48-49; 832:50; 854:71; 860:169-170; 932:44-45; 1063:270; 1069:181; 1071:61
Plaster casts of snow tracks—making 661:38
Preservation of—make paraffin negative, plaster positive casts 277:36-37
Preservation of—make plaster casts 277:34-36
Preservation of—make smoked paper prints 277:37-38
Preserving animal tracks 657:16-19

TRACTION ENGINE
Titan traction engine machine model—how to build 410:10-11

TRAFFIC
Effects of road pollution on populations of insects and arthropods experiment 1096:69-74
Road traffic survey of traffic speeds at various times project 1070:34-35

TRAFFIC LIGHTS
Electric traffic light, how to make from box, battery, bulbs, and wire 1382:26-27
Make traffic lights 224:30-31
Rotary switch traffic light, how to make from coffee can 1442:31-40
Working model of a traffic light—how to make 577: project 59

TRAFFIC SAFETY
Warning colors experiment; test which colors reflect light best at night 1283:29
Warning colors experiment; test which colors work best on sign 1283:28

TRAFFIC SIGNS
Design traffic signs project 1470:10-11

TRAILBLAZING
Make an outdoor trail for someone to follow (Primary) 580:unpaged

TRAINS
Bogie wheels and train model project, how to build 1470:22-23
Electric train working model, how to make 1043:42-43
Electromagnetic train model experiment 1249:50-52
How magnetic trains move above their tracks demonstration 1479:106
Maglev train floats and moves experiment using bar magnets 1034:22-23
Maglev train, how it works experiment 961:13
Matchbox train model—how to make 431:24-25
Meaning of train whistle sounds chart 1209:83
Steam engine model—how to make 415:15-17
Train whistle, how to make 1209:83

TRANSECT
Measuring elevation using a transect, how to do 1117:41

431

Set up transect for observing an area, how to do 1117:40-41

TRANSFORMER

Demonstrate electrical repulsion and the transformer principle 291:248

Electric—how to make 382:29-32

Experiments with a bell transformer 532:97

Make your own simple transformer 291:165

Transformer from a C Clamp—making 532:96

Transformer, how to make 768:99-101; 938:43-49

Transformer, how to make experiment 973:45

What is a transformer 278:62

TRANSISTORS

Construction packaging and basic operating circuit of the transistor 22:31-35

Experiment to see how transistor works 830:45-47

What are transistors 278:69-70

TRANSPIRATION

Experiment 146:60-61

Green plants give off water from their leaves 294:41-42

How does water leave a plant experiment 852:10-11

How to demonstrate 117:61-64

In plants 146:47

Plant leaves give off water into the air 233:30

Plants release water experiment 959:58-59

Show plants lose water 282:34-41

Transpiration of trees 264:41

Water from a plant test 617:11

Watery plants 112:19

TRANSPORTATION. *See also* **AUTOMOBILES; AIRPLANES; BOATS; CANOES; RAFTS; RAILROADS**

By water-demonstrate canoes, sailing ships, propeller ships 363:63-69

How far does your family travel everyday project 1067:53

Make tape road networks (Primary) 153:24-25

Raft—model—how to make 415:8

TRAPS

Animal box trap—making 657:28-29

Animal tin can trap—making 657:30-31

Animal trap—making 291:246-247

Insect pitfall trap—how to make 590:44

Make your own mousetrap using ramps, levers and forces 554:28-29

Mud and sand sieve—how to make 359:52-53

Pitfall trap captures night animals experiment 1180:27

Pitfall trap captures night animals experiment 1183:155

Pitfall trap for collecting small animals or invertebrates, how to make 864:97

Pitfall trap in ground to collect insects, how to make 1274:51

Pitfall trap to catch insects, how to make 915:12-13

Pitfall trap, how to make 1182:4; 1183:52

Pitfall trap; make to trap, identify and count small animals experiment 1134:5.003

Pitfall traps for collecting small animals from forest floor 285:83-84

Pooter for catching minibeasts, how to make 1182:4

Pooter trap; making and using a pooter to sample small animals experiment 1134:5.002

Potato trap; make to trap, identify and count small animals experiment 1134:5.004

Trap box—animals 9:20-23

TRAPS—INSECTS. *See also* **INSECTS—TRAPS**

Beetle trap—how to make 332:22

How to make 331:16-17

Make a pooter for collecting small insects 285:51

Pit trap for insects, making 932:26-27

Screen trap—how to make 332:36-37

TRASH. *See also* **GARBAGE; SOLID WASTES**

Separating trash experiment using magnets and static electricity 1150:37-38

TRAVEL

Distances—milepost you can make showing distances to any place on Earth 532:92-93

How far does your family travel everyday project 1067:53

TRAVOIS (INDIAN)

Makes pulling easy (Primary) 324:14-15

TREASURE

Treasure map, how to make 1235:17

TREES

A rootarium—how to make 264:52

A tree study 590:43

Absorb water 382:41-42

Activities to learn about trees 236:15-16

Activities with leaves 236:17-20

Activities with tree bark 236:20-22

Adopt a tree and study it 253:16-17

Age—calculate age of tree by counting rings or by measuring trees' girth 574:33

Age of branches and buds experiment 1063:248

Age of tree determined by measuring circumference 1490:31

Age of tree, how to measure to determine age 1184:5

Age of tree; simple way to measure 1069:56

Age; determining tree age experiment 1134:4.004

Air conditioning by trees experiment with thermometer and plastic bag 1240:18-19

Alianthus seeds spread by wind experiment 1060:122-124

All about trees (Primary) 535:8-9

Annual tree growth for pounds of wood to make paper 363:124-125

Are only the north sides of trees green—experiment 381:108-110

Bark and leaf rubbings 146:9

Bark is important to tree's life, cambrium layer experiment 1184:11

Bark pattern from clay mold filled with plaster of Paris experiment 1483:10

Bark rubbings—how to do 62:25-26; 264:46; 275:23; 913:36; 932:22-23

Bark rubbings to identify different kinds of trees experiment 1184:11

Bark weavings from twig bark, how to make 1184:11

Black walnut trees release chemicals that prevent plant growth project 969:50-51

Bonsai tree, how to make and grow 1148:21

Bracket or shelf fungi grow on trees at the same height experiment 1061:114-115

Broom from tree wood and twigs, how to make 1184:36

Buds—show buds while dormant and after partial opening 168:24

Buds and twigs—adventure 33—buds under a hand lens 29:152-158

Buds and twigs—how to identify 275:10-11

Buds; where do tree buds grow best experiment 1184:13

Carbon dioxide amount absorbed by trees and concrete building site experiment 1057:108
Characteristics and uses—poster to show type, leaves and wood uses 293:17
Collect different tree fruits 275:21
Collecting tree twigs 62:23-24
Collection of wood specimens, bark, seeds, twigs and buds—how to 234:82-83
Color in leaves—experiment 30:49-50
Color of leaves in fall explanation 1227:43
Comparing trees; observe and record; data table given 871:2.002
Conifers in your neighborhood or park, how to identify project 1336:63
Decomposition rates of tree leaves—design experiment 586:119
Determine if limestone can protect pine trees from acid rain experiment 997:93-94
Dirt on evergreen trees affects photosynthesis experiment 1134:6.004
Do roots always grow down 264:51
Dormant seeds kept in refrigerator may germinate 413:51-52
Estimating height and age 236:22-23
Estimating the age of a living tree experiment 1524:22-23
Estimating the height of a tree, how to do 784:103-104
Evergreen leaves don't lose water or dehydrate like deciduous leaves experiment 1184:19
Evergreen needles have more chlorophyll than deciduous tree leaves experiment 1061:35-36
Flower buds and leaf buds—find the differences 413:59-60
Fruit seed collection—plaster casts, making 413:52-53
Fruit trees grow from pits or seeds, how to do 590:52
Galls collected and examined for larva inside experiment 117:82-84
Game; seeds game; flying tree seeds game, how to make 1183:113
Game; tree game shows problems tree has in growing, how to make 1183:116-117
Game; tree game shows problems trees encounter as they grow, how to make 1184:28-29
Germinating seeds from pine cones 117:75-79
Girdling tree stops flow of water and food to tree branches experiment 1061:107-108
Give off water 382:37-41
Grow a chemical tree 87:85-86
Grow a tree seed 275:18-19
Grow evergreens for miniature forest experiment 1075:26
Grow forest trees from seeds experiment 1176:16
Grow trees from twigs, how to do 1379:31
Growing trees from seed, how to do 662:39; 931:8-9
Growth rates of buds on small twigs brought indoors experiment 1183:101
Habitats in trees, observe animal life 820:19
Height—how tall is your tree—how to figure out 574:39
Height of tree measured by using Sun's shadows experiment 1294:31
Height of tree, how to estimate experiment 1183:93
Height of tree, how to measure 1069:57; 1184:5; 1379:31
Height, diameter, circumference of tree measured with simple instruments 978:50-51
Height; measure height of tree experiment 1148:22

Height; measure height of tree, how to do 1142:9; 1145:31
Hoppers—adventure 6—meet insect brownies—tree hoppers under hand lens 29:30-34
How high is a tree 585:106-107
How tall is a tree experiment 1368:90-91
How tall is that tree—measure using shadows 1073:72
How tall is tree—measure tree by stick and thumb method 748:72
How to collect tree flowers and fruits 62:27-28
How trees take in carbon dioxide experiment 1057:104
Identify parts of tree using tree cross section experiment 978:49-50
Identify shapes of broad leaves and conifers 275:12-13
Identifying—how to 234:76-77
Identify trees; tree identification key given 1063:250-251
Identifying trees using twig keys 117:69-72
Investigate trees found in a vacant lot 233:31-36
Investigation into the history of a tree 420:74-78
Keep a tree diary 480:81
Keep scrapbook of changing seasons of a tree 275:26-27
Leaf collection to identify different trees—make 275:14
Leaf fungi as indicator organisms for air pollution experiment 1134:6.005
Leaf rubbings—how to 275:15
Leaf scars—adventure 30—leaf scars under a hand lens 29:137-139
Leaves—how much do leaves on a tree weigh 236:20
Life in a tree; who lives there project 1184:32-33
Litter from trees dried and compressed for fuel use project 969:79-80
Magic forest of trees—how to make 312:29-33
Make a polished tree slab 538:97
Make a tree from newspapers and cardboard 1184:9
Making a collection of tree leaves 294:35-37
Measure age, girth and height 275:24-25
Measuring growth from rings 436:82
Measuring tree height and diameter 413:17-20
Metric measurement—find height of a tree 357:16-17
Model tree from newspaper strips, how to make 1183:97
Observe and record yearly changes in a tree 760:10-11
Organisms of many types decompose trees project 969:62-63
Parts of a stem or twig 60:24-25
Planting trees—how to 234:84-85
Pollinate flowers on fruit trees, how to do 1184:26
Poster board forest of trees, how to make 1044:22-23
Ring pattern on stump—make a paper record 413:16-17
Root willow twigs to plant for trees experiment 1524:11
Sampling of life in tree ecosystem experiment 1134:5.007
Sap from trees—collecting to determine which trees produce most sugar 714:106-107
Seeds—collect and display tree seeds—how to do 476:69-72
Seeds—miniforest—some tree seeds to collect and grow in a miniforest 465:74-84
Seeds of trees, how far do they fly experiment 1419:17
Seeds of trees; collect and display project 1184:22
Seeds; flying seeds game, how to make from paper, paint and glue 1184:25
Seeds; grow chestnut tree from chestnut, how to do 1486:28

Seeds; grow your own tree from seeds experiment 1148:17

Seeds; helicopter seeds model from cardboard, how to make 1184:25

Seeds; helicopter seeds model, how to make 1183:113

Seeds; number of seeds that survive to adulthood project 1313:63-65

Seeds; planting tree seeds, how to do 1414:31

Seeds; tree seed, how to plant and grow 1142:33

Seeds; water that tree seedling drinks and what happens to it experiment 1414:36-39

Simple measuring device to measure height of tall things, how to make 834:137-138

Solar panel effect of tree leaves; determine how big experiment 1184:17

Sounds of a tree, how to record on cardboard "tape" experiment 1184:8

Starting a tree from cuttings, how to do 1321:45

Study an individual oak or maple or other mature hardwood tree 285:57-61

Study of different kinds of trees near your home project 1049:22

Stump detective—how to observe stumps 476:76-78

Stump rubbing tells tree's life story, how to do 1368:92-93

Transpiration in 264:41

Transplant tree seedling 413:30

Tree force—observation of force of growing roots 563:54-55

Tree is home for animals and plants 275:28-29

Tree plaques, how to make 646:81-82

Tree sculptures show how trees change with the seasons, how to make 1044:20-21

Trees are our friends 236:14

Trees as directional compasses using organism growth experiment 1134:5.008

Trees lose water through stomata on bottom of leaves experiment 1183:106

Twig belt—how to make 442:unpaged

Twigs—collect and mount twigs—how to do 476:65-68

Twigs—forcing to grow in winter 413:60

Twigs grow in water experiment 1180:17; 1183:145

Twigs in winter 413:55-59

Water loss from tree leaves experiment 1184:18

Water; how trees take up water experiment 1148:11

Where do buds grow best experiment 1183:101

Why leaves fall observation 1440:24-27

Wild trees from seeds, how to grow 1183:111

Wild trees; growing wild trees from seeds project 1184:23

Winter tree identification 277:62-69

Winter twig collection 236:151-152

Winter twig collection—making 629:129-133

Winter's effect on tree leaves; how to imitate experiment 1184:19

Wood lying on ground decomposes faster than dead standing wood project 969:26-27

TRIANGLES

Experiments—examine basic triangle concepts—paper folding (Primary) 503:1-33

Triangles; theory, problems and puzzles 1356:1-64

TRIBOLUMINESCENCE. *See also* STATIC ELECTRICITY

Crystal light might benefit space travel demonstration using Life Savers 1394:200-201

Life Saver crystals broken by pressure give off light experiment 1405:19

Life Savers make static electricity in your mouth experiment 1411:48

TRIPOD BURNER

Make 9:86-87

TROLLEY

Make to ride or carry things 358:70-71

Trolley ride—how to make 585:58

Trolley with electric motor moves things experiment 1299:57

TROPICAL FISH

Care of 390:79-89

Cichlids and anabantids—fishes that make nests 266:121-129

Investigate schooling behavior 266:148-149

Territoriality in a fish tank 266:154-156

TROPISMS. *See also* CHEMOTROPISM; GEOTROPISM; GRAVITROPISM; HELIOTROPISM; HYDROTROPISM; PHOTOTROPISM; PLANTS—TROPISMS; THIGMOTROPISM

Bean seeds grown upside down in jar show effect of gravity on growth 1038:16

Geotropism; bean plant in jar demonstrates geotropism experiment 1457:19

Geotropism; roots always point down experiment 1368:39

Graviotropism; gravity affects bean seed roots experiment 1047:15

Hydrotropism; roots grow toward water experiment 1368:40

Hydrotropism; roots react to source of moisture experiment 1060:75-76

Phototropism; do plants always grow toward the light experiment 852:12-14

Phototropism; geranium plant project 1060:75

Phototropism; maze demonstrates plants grow toward light experiment 1038:14-15

Phototropism; plant maze with bean plant growing toward light experiment 1368:41

Phototropism; plants grow toward light experiment 1047:17

TRUCKS

Dump truck model, how to make 1420:20-21

Dump truck, making 779:18-19

Oatmeal-box tank truck—how to make 652:12-15

TRUSSES

Build a truss from wire hanger and straw experiment 1436:103-106

Build a truss of rigid frames 557:65

How to build 328:100-101; 557:61

Roof frames from trusses experiment, how to build 1518:34-35

Takenaka space truss—how to build 328:108-111

TSUNAMIS

Tsunami waves caused by ocean earthquake experiment 1441:45

TUBERS. *See* PLANTS; ROOTS

TUBIFEX WORMS

Adventure 31—we dig for worms—tubifex under a microscope 403:109-111

TUGBOAT

Tugboat model toy—how to make (Primary) 467:30-31

TUNDRA ECOLOGY

Arctic mammal; invent one that might survive in the Arctic project 1337:68-69

Calendar of Arctic wildlife activity through months of year 1337:69-71

Food web to show interdependence of Arctic animals 1337:71-72

Hours of sunshine in one day using sundial experiment 1337:67-68

Oil spills effect on birds experiment 1337:72-73

Projects to understand why and how tundra ecology must be saved 1337:64-75

Technology used by you in one day for your survival 1337:65

Time line showing history of people on Earth 1337:64

TUNING FORKS

Experiment with 400:83

TUNNELS

Laying tunnels under a city, how to demonstrate 1327:35

Make a tunnel for a canal 223:16-17

Piston relief tunnel demonstration 968:28

Strongest shape for tunnels experiment 1123:9

Sunken tube tunnel, how to make 1327:33

Testing the ground for tunnel construction experiment 1123:8

Tissue box tunnel models—how to make 431:29

Tunnel boring machine demonstration 968:29

Tunnel boring machine model, use to make tunnel in wet sand experiment 1123:13

Tunnel shapes, compare strength of flat and curved shape experiment 968:28

Tunnel walls are curved for strength experiment 1198:32

Tunnel-boring machine (TBM) model, how to build 1459:22-23

Underwater tunnel model, how to build 1459:26-27

Ventilation in a tunnel experiment 1327:39

Water pressure changes with depth experiment 1123:14

Which tunnel is the strongest, square-shaped or tube-shaped experiment 1327:19

TURBINES. *See also* **STEAM TURBINES; WATER WHEELS**

Building a model jet turbine project 833:291-292

Can water be made to do work; water turbine, making to demonstrate work 851:51-52

How to make model turbines 128:153-154

Make a model steam turbine 267:40-41

Make a turbine 641:43

Make a turbine and paddle wheel 142:50

Make an air driven turbine using heat of your hand 176:99

Make simple turbine 436:83

Make simple water wheels 227:6

Making a turbine 382:78-82

Model steam turbine experiment, how to make 1269:69

Model water turbine from plastic bottle experiment 1126:15

Model wind turbine experiment 1134:7.003

Simple turbine—how to make 585:56

Steam turbine—how to make 293:41-42; 575:25

Steam turbine experiment; make working model of turbine 1301:28-29

Steam turbine, working model of—making 532:102

Turbine from cardboard blades and straws, how to make 1026:33

Turbine wheel—making 655:21

Water turbine—make your own water turbine 419:23

Water turbine from detergent bottle top, making experiment 965:29

Water turbine, simple, how to make from knitting needle, cork, container 1212:17

Wind turbine project, how to build 1305:28-29

Wind turbine working model, how to make 1476:38-39

TURBOJET ENGINE

Make a model turbojet engine 564:21

TURBOPROP ENGINE

Make a model turboprop engine 564:21

TURNER, C. J.

Repeat his experiment with cockroaches 264:70-72

TURTLES

Aquavivarium for turtles—making 720:56

Collect, care for and observe behaviors, how to 771:209-214

Collection and care of 390:49-51

Experiment to show where they go in winter 40:55-56

Floating turtle trap—how to make 234:38

How to care for 279:14-15

How to care for in a terrarium 475:18-19

How to keep and study 163:29-31

Keeping a pet tortoise 507:1907-1908

Keeping turtles in a terrarium, how to do 1433:46-48

Land—collection and care of 313:9-13

Mazes to test intelligence—how to build 510:104-105

Observe and record turtle behavior 166:117-119

Outdoor projects with 118:73-78

Raising pet turtles 294:74-75

Turtle model toy—how to make (Primary) 466:10-11

Turtle shell paper bags—how to make 236:71

Turtle terrarium and a turtle pen—how to make 234:39

Walnut shell turtle—how to make 236:51

Water—collection and care of 313:9-13

TWEEZERS

Laboratory 9:88-89

TWIGS. *See also* **TREES**

Collect and classify winter twigs project 1060:37-38

Collect and mount twigs—how to do 476:65-68

Root willow twigs to plant for trees experiment 1524:11

Test for starch in autumn twigs experiment 1060:38

Twig weaving, how to make using twigs, grasses and yarn 1114:136-137

TWINING. *See* **PLANTS—VINES; VINES**

TYNDALL EFFECT. *See also* **COLLOIDS; SKY**

Flour and water suspension experiment; show reflection with flashlight 905:166-167

Light used to distinguish colloidal suspension from pure solution experiment 1396:85-90

Test to show colloidal mixture of milk and water experiment with flashlight 1476:128

Tyndall Effect demonstrated with light, coffee cans and milk 563:147-148

Tyndall Effect experiments with bacteria 864:32-33

U

UFO. *See also* **FLYING SAUCERS**
Unidentified flying objects 356:16-17

ULTRASONICS
Effect on plants 398:126-127

ULTRAVIOLET RADIATION
How effective are products in protecting against ultraviolet radiation 997:111-112
Johann Ritter's discovery of ultraviolet rays experiment 1133:6.011
Using computer modeling software to analyze UV exposure experiment 1450:49-57

UNDERGROUND HOMES. *See* **HOUSES**

UNDERGROUND WATER
Model in aquarium shows destruction and shrinking of water table experiment 1476:193-194

UNDERWATER BINOCULARS
Making from milk cartons 494:62

UNDERWATER DIVER
How to make (Primary) 109:30-31

UNDERWATER FLASHLIGHT (TORCH)
How to make with jar and flashlight 430:54

UNDERWATER OBSERVATION
Glass—how to make 9:66-67
How to make a seascope 41:56-59
Underwater viewer from plastic pipe and plastic wrap, how to make 1085:55

UNDERWATER VIEWER
How to make 530:74-75
Underwater viewer, how to make from plastic jug 1115:92
Underwater viewer for ponds, how to make 1146:31
Underwater viewer from plastic pipe experiment 1134:3.006
Wood and plexiglas viewer, how to make 1505:52-53

UNIVERSE
Big Bang to Big Crunch theory models experiment, how to make 1478:144-145
Make a model of the expanding universe 161:93
Making a model of the expanding universe project 833:122-123
Making a moveable plan of the Earth-centered universe project 833:72-75

URANUS. *See also* **PLANETS**
Discovery of Uranus's rings experiment with foamcore, black paint, flashlight 1478:77
Making a model of the orbits of Uranus, Neptune, and Pluto project 833:249-251
Measurements of Uranus 292:95-96
Uranus model revolves around Sun to show its topsy turvy traveling experiment 1478:76

URCHINS
Pickled urchins—how to preserve specimens 530:76

URINALYSIS
Using urinalysis techniques 148:81

V

VACUUM
Balloon holds cups in air experiment 924:32
Egg sucked into narrow necked bottle experiment 1011:55
Galileo's drop in a vacuum experiment 1132:50-1-50-2
Magdeburg Sphere principle experiment with glasses and candle 1007:14-16
Otto Von Guericke's creating a vacuum demonstrates atmospheric pressure 1133:4.005
Partial vacuum in cooled can experiment 709:53-54
Radish vacuum demonstrates air pressure 360:32-33
Robert Boyle's objects of different masses fall thru vacuum at same rate 1133:4.007

VACUUM PUMP
Another bet for suckers—bet you can't suck water from a jar 222:47
Make a sucker of sucker 222:46

VALLEYS AND HILLS
Making contour maps 303:24-25

VALSALVA'S EXPERIMENT
Influence of respiration on blood circulation 334:38-39

VAN GUERICKE, OTTO. *See* **GUERICKE, OTTO VON**

VAN MUSSCHENBROEK, PETER
Constructing a Leyden jar—experiment 627:19
Inventor of Leyden jar 209:20-21

VAPOR. *See also* **WATER—VAPOR**
Evaporation and vapor pressure experiment; data tables given 1004:3.014
In air 382:128-130
Latent heat of vaporization of water experiment 1515:85-88
To show pressure changing vapor to fog and fog to vapor 385:77-78

VAPORIZATION. *See* **SOLAR STILL**

VARIATION
Investigations into variations in living things 420:59-61

VEGETABLES. *See also* **GARDENING;** *individual names of vegetables, plants*
Baking soda makes cooked vegetables look good experiment 1238:51
Beans cooked with acid and sugar experiment 1238:59-60
Beans soaked in water are less gassy to eat experiment 1238:57-58
Best way to store carrots experiment 1238:33-34
Boiled potato cooks faster than baked potato experiment 1238:42-43
Carrot and potato plant grow from roots experiment 1063:405
Carrot as miniature hanging plant, how to grow 1406:10-11
Carrot hanging basket, how to grow 1078:22
Carrot or beet top garden, how to make 899:180
Carrot plant from carrot top, how to plant and grow 1176:12; 1406:109-111; 1054:64
Carrot top grows into plant experiment 904:60-61; 1440:52-54
Carrots do not lose color when cooked experiment 1238:55
Carrots; grow plant from carrot experiment 1368:15
Cucumber in a bottle, how to grow 899:75
Dried sweet potatoes 231:45

Green vegetables cooked in cold and boiling water experiment 1238:52
Green vegetables cooked with and without pot lid experiment 1238:53
Green vegetables lose color in cooking experiment 1238:50
Grow plants from carrot tops experiment 1405:28
Grow plants from tops and eyes of vegetables 835:52-54
Grow plants from vegetable and fruit tops; carrots, beets, potato 1071:74-75
Investigate who eats what vegetables 630:111-112
Is wax applied to produce purchased from supermarkets experiment 1450:26-33
Mystery of the evaporating vegetables-exp. How to build a mini-scale 600:60-61
Plants from vegetable tops, how to grow 1306:6-7
Root vegetables grow on pebbles indoors, how to do 1178:34
Root vegetables, how to plant and grow indoors 1178:35
Stamp printing with vegetables 646:65-66
Sweet potato plant, how to grow 1078:22
Taming an onion experiment 1238:37-38
Tops grow into garden; carrots, beets, parsnips; how to do 913:31
Tops grow into a garden, carrots, turnips, beets, parsnips 376:13
Tops of root vegetables grow into indoor garden experiment 1524:11
Tops of vegetables grow into hanging garden experiment 1440:49-51
Torn lettuce turns limp experiment 1238:35-36
Vitamin C; detect Vitamin C in fruits and vegetables experiment 1476:136-137
Water quantity in vegetables and fruits experiment 1189:46-47
Water; how much water in vegetables experiment 1509:26
Why do some vegetables smell bad when cooking experiment 1238:48-49

VEGETATIVE PROPAGATION. *See* **PLANTS—VEGETATIVE PROPAGATION**

VEHICLES
Vehicle for extreme climates; polar regions, jungles, deserts; design 1470:18-19

VELOCITY. *See also* **SPEED**
Egg in packing box dropped from height experiment 748:160-161
Relation of centrifugal force to velocity 577:project #37
Time, distance, speed experiment with toy cars; data table given 871:4.001
Velocity of water "bullet" experiment 1158:72-79

VENN DIAGRAMS
Diagrams, tools of logic used to sort objects or ideas into categories 461:1-33

VENTRAL SEGMENTS OF VIBRATION
Demonstrate 350:96

VENTURI
Venturi effect demonstrated with sand erosion project—how to do 715:12-13
Venturi's experiment to make water run up hill 385:29-30

VENTURI THROAT
Experiment-prove that the Venturi throat may be used to remove air from a flask 385:43-45

437

VENTURI TUBE
How to make 363:154-155
VENUS. *See also* **PLANETS**
Finding Venus morning, noon and night project 833:224-226
How to find Venus in the sky 1434:75-76
Mapping Venus 762:17-18
Measurements 292:84-85
Phases of Venus experiment with foamcore, battery, and wires 1478:67
Plumb line experiment demonstrates radar mapping of Venus 1478:66
Sun's heat is trapped by gases in Venus's atmosphere experiment 1478:67
Venus' atmosphere hard to see through demonstration 1394:20-21
Venus' atmosphere traps infrared waves making it very hot demonstration 1394:22-23
Why Venus is so hot experiment 1479:4
Why Venus' atmosphere is so hard to see through experiment 1479:3
VENUS FLYTRAP
How to care for 475:42-45
Insectivorous plant 279:37-38
Leaves catch insects 271:36-39
Venus flytraps, how to grow 1260:19-20
VERSORIUM
Gilbert's versorium experiment 627:9
Versorium, how to make to detect static electricity 1007:40
VERTEBRATES
Collection and preservation of, how to do 824:36-50
Game to get to know animals with backbones 1063:260-261
Setting up a food chain 148:55
Skeletons—mounting—how to 436:71
VIBRATIONS
Experiments to investigate vibrations 1164:81-83
Seismograph 9:103-107
Ventral segments of 350:96
Visible sound 350:93-94
VIEWERS
How to make 3-D viewer 887:32-34
Spinning viewer—making 736:99-102
Underwater viewer from plastic pipe, how to make 1134:3.006
VIEWERS—3-D
How to make 3-D viewer 360:75; 659:21
VIKING HELMET
How to make 415:27-29
VIKING LONG SHIP MODEL
How to make 431:20-21
VIKING SHIELDS
How to make 415:29-30
VIKING SHIP
Model—how to make 415:24-27
VIKING SOLAR STONE
Make your own solar stone 292:27
Solar stone and how to use it 292:22-23
Solar stone to find North, how to make from cardboard, cork, dowel 1115:132-133
VINCI, LEONARDO DA
His experiments 42:16-23
Leonardo da Vinci's experiment with turbine 382:79
Leonardo's paddle boat—how to make 429:68

VINEGAR. *See also* **ACIDS**
Make vinegar experiment 1238:81
VINES
Do all vines turn in same direction 333:100-101
Grow a "vine house" indoors 416:14
VINES—LEAF CLIMBERS
Rub petioles to make leaves bend 271:91-96
VINES—ROOT CLIMBERS AND WEAVERS
Observe 271:120-127
VINES—TENDRIL CLIMBERS
Observe and record circling action 271:97-119
VINES—TWINING
Determine direction of winding plants experiment 904:46-47
Observe and record circling action 271:74-90
VIRUS
Chart of virus invasion of cells 231:77
Dirt from fingernails grows molds on potato mush mixture experiment 1482:8-9
The bug 231:75-78
Why we wash our hands experiment with molds growing on potato mush mixture 1482:8-9
Virus transmission experiment 1267:68-69
VISCOMETER
How to make to test viscosity of liquids experiment 1477:64-67
Viscometer measures flow rate of fluid experiment, how to make 1477:64-67
Viscometer measures flow rate of liquids experiment 1396:111-116
VISCOSITY. *See also* **LIQUIDS**
Glob, creezy ooze, how to make to show "non-Newtonian" fluid 1396:139-140
Higher weights of motor oil indicate more viscosity experiment 1396:114
Temperature affects viscosity of liquids experiment test with marble in liquid 1477:19
Temperature affects viscosity of oil experiment 1396:114
Temperature of liquid affects its viscosity experiment with viscometer, make 1477:64-67
Temperature of liquid affects its viscosity experiment 1396:112
Viscometer measures flow rate of fluid experiment, how to make 1477:64-67
Viscometer measures flow rate of liquids experiment 1396:111-116
Viscosity of body lubricants compared experiment 1396:114-115
Viscosity of liquids compared by dropping marble in liquid samples experiment 1396:114
Viscosity of liquids experiment 1091:31
Viscosity of other liquids compared to viscosity of water experiment 1396:112-113
Viscosity of other liquids compared to water experiment with viscometer, make 1477:64-67
VISIBILITY
Visibility chart—how to make 381:63-66
VISION. *See also* **EYE; OPTICAL ILLUSIONS; PERCEPTION; SENSES—SIGHT**
"After-image" color of colors of spectrum experiment 1369:55
Afterimage experiment; flash of light leaves image in your eye 1132:1-1-1-2
Afterimages experiments 1111:28-29

Afterimages experiments with colored lightbulbs 1506:66-67

Afterimages using colors experiment 1158:142-143

Ames window, make to show much of what we see happens in our mind experiment 1088:48-49

Angle of peripheral vision in different people test, how to do 1397:23

Anti-gravity mirrors make you appear to be flying experiment 1132:2-1-2-2

Apparent size of objects (accommodation) 4:42-43

Astigmatism in a curved mirror experiment 1082:72-76

Background color affects the colors you see experiment 1109:10

Bad aim—hole in card—experiment 585:158-159

Benham's Top; black and white design as it spins appears to be colored 1088:81

Binocular vision produces three-dimensional view experiment 1397:22-23

Bird in the cage; stare at color and see it change experiment 1132:8-1-8-2

Blind spot—locate the 'blind spot' in your eye 291:204

Blind spot in eye and how to find it experiment 1390:7

Blind spot in human eyes experiment 1132:10-1–10-2; 1506:51-52

Blind spot test 1253:14; 1276:10

Blind spot; testing your blind spot experiment 1088:27

Blind spot,-what is the blind spot and how can size be mapped 402:65-66

Boxes seen and moving where there are none experiment with black box and light 1132:51-1-51-2

Brain has special cells that detect motion experiment using spinning spiral 1088:58-59

Brain judges how large something is according to how far away object is 1088:46

Brain needs different amount of time to record color waves presence experiment 1405:38

Brain sometimes makes you see things that aren't there experiment 1037:22

Brand your eyeball 162:63-64

Can you judge depth with one eye experiment 901:197

Can you see through a solid object experiment 901:11

Cat and mouse game on paper demonstrates blind spot in each eye experiment 1037:18

Cats eyes glow in the dark experiment using coffee can and flashlight 1397:24-27

Cats; does size of pupil affect glow of cat's eye experiment 1397:26-27

Choroid layer on back surface of human eye reflects light 1397:27

Color changes 162:67-68

Color fatigue—experiment 585:154-155

Color; do people see the same color at the same time project 1210:64-66

Colored light bulbs on different colored sheets of paper experiment 1253:30-31

Contrast and brightness and their effect on vision experiments 1088:64-71

Crooked finger vision 585:123

Cylindrical mirror lets you see yourself as others see you experiment 1132:35-1-35-3

Demonstrate persistence of vision 208:20-23

Depth perception—two eyes are better than one 399:61

Depth perception experiment; wide eyes device makes catching ball difficult 1330:34-35

Different lengths of time needed for brain to record color waves experiment 904:162-163

Distance; judging distance with one eye and both eyes experiment 1506:56-57

Dominant eye test 622:28

Dominant eye experiment 1506:55-56

Dot fades from your view experiment 1132:49

Effect on perception—seeing with one eye 253:103

Experiment to demonstrate seeing colors 135:16-23

Experiments with vision and the eye 1425:138-147

Eye and vision demonstration (Primary) 673:6-28

Eye model demonstrates how eyes work experiment 1028:68

Eye; effect of light on size of eye pupil experiment 904:156-157

Eye; effect of tiring the rods and cones in the eye experiment 904:158-159

Eye; monocle makes words clearer experiment 904:154-155

Eyes as cameras experiment 1506:59-60

Eyes receive different images experiment; friend disappears but smile remains 1132:21-1-21-2

Field of vision decreases as lens magnification increases experiment 1062:24-25

Finding your blind spot 400:44

Floaters in your eyes—test for 736:37-38

Focusing lines of light and the inverted image experiment 941:96-100

Focusing near and far experiment 1506:52-54

Fool-your-eyes flipper 162:66

Ghost light—experiment demonstrates "persistence of vision" 563:47

Grate vision experiment; moving grate lets you read material under it 1216:11-13

Gray ring of paper on black and white paper illusion 1159:54-55

Hand steadiness tester, how to make to test two eyes working together 1069:166

Hole in your hand and finger sausage illusions 1369:40-41

Hole in your hand experiment 904:212-213

How can eyes appear to make colors change experiment 901:9

How do images of large objects fit on retina of eye experiment 1402:28-31

How effective is your side vision experiment 901:191

How far around can you see—test (Primary) 673:13

How to make 3-D glasses 162:75

How we see demonstrated with pencil, how to do 1433:108-110

How your eyes work experiments 1088:22-31

Illusion of depth from motion experiment using lamp, clay, pipe cleaner 1088:61

Images from pinhole in box—demonstrates 605:28-29

Images like those on the retina experiment 1506:49-51

Irradiation or spillover effect on vision experiment 1476:217-218

Jerky motion of your eyes experiment 1088:30

Light and color and their effect on vision experiments 1088:72-82

Light and sight—experiments 659:18-23

Light rays on retina—make a pinhole camera to demonstrate 281:80

Make one-eyed theater to look double but see single 162:74-75

Make simple cartoon movie with metal tin, stick and cardboard 570:13

Make twirlers to change a design 162:69-70

Making sense of what you see experiments 1088:42-51

Mini movies 162:65-66

Motion picture experiment; persistence of vision effect 895:40-41

Movement; how you see movement experiments 1088:52-63

Night vision experiment; demonstrate ability to see contrasting colors at night 1479:39

Optic nerve and its effect on vision experiment 904:164-165

Optic nerve effect on vision demonstration with dots on paper 1479:38

Pencil pick up with one eye (Primary) 551:unpaged

Perception experiments; hole in hand, overlapping images; data tables 1004:2.006

Peripheral—side vision experiment 400:42

Peripheral vision and color experiment 762:55-56

Peripheral vision is worse in people who wear glasses experiment 1195:63-69

Peripheral vision test for how much peripheral vision people have 1506:64-65

Peripheral vision; test limits of your peripheral vision experiment 1132:74-1-74-2

Persistence of vision—bird in a cage pictures 563:141-142

Persistence of vision—how to demonstrate 577:project 80

Persistence of vision—moving mouse machine, making 669:42-43

Persistence of vision—test for using coins 548:23-26

Persistence of vision experiment using phenakistoscope, how to make 1405:42

Persistence of vision experiment with cards 1506:61-63

Persistence of vision experiment with horse and rider pictures 1138:36-38

Persistence of vision experiment with moving illusion 904:160-161

Persistence of vision experiment; Chinese ring trick 1138:41-42

Persistence of vision experiment; chromatrope, how to make 861:69-76

Persistence of vision experiment; ghost tube trick 1138:42-44

Persistence of vision experiment; how to make thaumatrope 1216:40-42

Persistence of vision experiment; see pictures in thin air 1132:62-1-62-2

Persistence of vision experiment; square circle trick 1138:44-46

Persistence of vision experiment 911:42-43; 941:41; 669:28-29; 1132:75-1-75-2

Persistence of vision whirling watcher experiment 1132:107-1-107-3

Persistence of vision with illusions experiment 761:71-73

Persistence of vision; thaumatrope, how to build, patterns given 861:13-17

Perspective changes size 601:unpaged

Predator competition experiment with normal color/monochromatic vision; tables 1004:2.008

Pupil of eye controls how much light enters eye experiment 1132:80-1-80-2

Pupil's reaction to bright and dim light experiment 1506:48-49

Read message through slit in paper experiment 1083:28

Reflected light—dust helps us to see 281:81

Retinal afterimages, blind spot, dominant eye, depth perception, experiments. 1004:2.007

Right- or left-eyed test 1253:15

Rod cells and cone cells experiment 1506:58-59

Rods and cones color test 1253:15

Rotating spiral makes things seem to move toward or away from you experiment 1132:36-1-36-2

See two pictures as one experiment 1028:69

Seeing better in the dark—experiment 571:9

Simple experiment to show how we see 135:4-15

Size—recognition of with coins 548:10-13

Some colors easier to see from a distance than others experiment 1088:82

Spinning disc with black and white colors shows other colors experiment 1369:56-57

Spinning disc with colors of spectrum experiment 1369:51-53

Stereo vision experiments 1088:32-41

Stereo vision; seeing depth with your eyes experiment 1088:34

Stereoscope simulates depth perception using homemade drawings experiment 1476:219-221

Stereoscope to see in stereo vision, how to make 1088:36-38

Structure of your eyes 135:14

Test shifty-eyed sight at night and peripheral vision 335:94-95

The blind spot 350:129-130

Things to do to check one or both eyes vision 872:52-53

Trick of the eyes trick 585:78-80

Tricks with your eyes 538:114-115

Two eyes are better than one experiment; target practice game demonstrates 1037:19

Two eyes are better than one for 3-D vision experiments 1088:40

Two eyes working together let you judge distance experiment 1069:166

Type of vision in animals whose eyes face forward experiment 1397:20-23

Using two eyes tricks 909:148-149

Vertical distances and horizontal distances; which is longer experiment 1159:53-54

Visions on the wall paper toy, making 999:37-38

Visual cues to your eyes determine what you see 1132:17-1-17-3

Water drop simulates an eye lens experiment 904:166-167

What happens to the iris as light changes experiment 901:195

Which is your dominant eye experiment 901:198

White light experiment; make white light from 3 filter lights, red, green, blue 1088:75

Why it is hard to see when you walk into a dark theater experiment 1088:70

Wobble detector demonstrates need for two eyes to judge distances experiment 1028:70

X-ray vision; fact or fiction experiment 1411:13

VITAMIN C. *See also* **VITAMINS**

A test for vitamin C 585:100-101

Amount of vitamin C in various foods and vitamin tablets experiment 1396:43-48

Analyzing foods for their vitamin C content experiment 1267:41-43

Boiling juice destroys vitamin C experiment 723:182-183

Compare vitamin C content of fruit juices experiment; data table given 871:2.020

Cooking and preparation methods affect vitamin C content of foods experiment 1267:42-43

Detect vitamin C in fruits and vegetables experiment 1476:136-137

Does heat effect vitamin C content of fruit juice experiment 871:2.020

Effects of cooking and chemicals on vitamin C in foods experiment 1259:34-35

Enzymatic browning of apples experiment 1396:47

Fruit juices are a good source of vitamin C experiment 1267:42-43

Heat destroys vitamin C in fruit juices experiment 1476:137

Indicators plus vitamin C pill in water identifies acids and bases experiment 1526:93-94

Investigating into the breaking down of vitamin C 420:136-139

Iodine test for vitamin C experiment 980:54

Starch iodine test for vitamin C in foods experiment 1259:33-34

Test for vitamin C 148:64; 346:131-135

Test for vitamin C in food 807:92-93; 83:36; 1259:31-33

Test for vitamin C in juice experiment 723:79

Test soft drinks and fruit "drinks" for vitamin C content experiment 1267:42-43

Vitamin C content in food, how to calculate 1396:207

Vitamin C content of fruit juices and other drinks experiment 1370:70-71

Vitamins in food 261:50-53

Which methods of food storage preserve vitamin C over time experiment 1267:42-43

VITAMINS. *See also* **VITAMIN C**

Chart of vitamins found in common foods experiment 1264:11

VIVARIUMS

Aquavivariums for turtles—making 720:56

Building a vivarium 625:58

Lizard vivarium, how to make 810:78-79

Raise small animals, frogs, toads, lizards, in vivarium, how to make 1176:28-29

Vivarium—how to make 720:54-55

VOICE. *See also* **LARYNX**

Breathe helium to change voice 291:68

How do notes rise and fall when singing experiment 1279:12

How loudly can you sing experiment 1279:15

Make a voice distinguisher 231:89

Voice vibrations demonstration with paper tube and tissue paper 1141:27-28

Why your voice doesn't sound like you on a tape recording experiment 1209:16-17

VOLCANIC POLLUTION

Of the air—experiment 371:32-36

VOLCANOES

A volcanic spray—experiment 87:45-47

Bottle volcano; jar, water and food coloring experiment 1016:8-9

Bubbling lava volcano from papier mache over chicken wire model experiment 1487:28-29

Build to show action of and lava flow 293:5-6

Carbon dioxide flows down mountain because it is heavier than air experiment 1477:47

Carbon dioxide presence experiment; test for to predict volcanic eruption 1477:44-47

Chemical volcano, how to make 814:84-87

Clay model of Earth's interior experiment, how to make 1477:7

Crater or caldera formation experiment; how volcanic caldera is formed 1477:80-83

Crust; how does volcanic movement change shape of Earth's crust experiment 1477:60-63

Demonstrate an erupting volcano 175:37

Earth's crust and volcanoes, how to demonstrate 1437:80-83

Erupting volcano experiment 1028:11

Erupting volcano experiment using sand model, food coloring, soda, vinegar 1179:31

Erupting volcano experiment, how to make 1405:52; 1441:47

Erupting volcano model experiment with baking soda, vinegar, red food coloring 1526:66-67

Erupting volcano model using vinegar, baking soda for eruption project 1296:2004

Erupting volcano model, how to make 1042:23

Erupting volcano, how to build; foaming recipe given 905:76-77

Erupting volcano, how to make 882:26; 1063:225; 1342:97-99; 811:12-13

Erupting volcano, make from baking soda, vinegar and food coloring 1383:23

Erupting volcano model with plaster of Paris over screen wire, make 1477:22-23

Erupting volcano model with plastic bottle, baking soda, vinegar, 1477:20-23

Erupting volcanoes produce sulfur dioxide experiment 1174:43-45

Extensiometer measures change in size of volcano experiment; how to make model 1477:52-55

Fiery model volcano; using vinegar and baking soda experiment 960:19

Friction between rocks causes heat experiment 1477:34-35

How does seismometer record movements of magma beneath Earth's surface ex 1477:56-59

How does seismometer record shaking of earthquakes experiment 1477:56-59

How magma is like soda pop—experiment 641:15

How minerals expand and force their way up experiment 706:60-61

How to make a model volcano 128:63

How to make a volcano 40:111-115; 400:50; 666:25-26

Interior of Earth experiment; model shows sections/temperature at each level 1477:4-7

Intrusive volcanism changes shape of Earth's crust experiment 1477:60-63

Lava flow demonstration 1266:17

Lava rocks; what type of rock is formed when lava cools experiment 1477:68-71

Lava; different types of lava and how they flow experiment 1480:59

Lava; what happens to lava flow rate when it contains solid particles experiment 1477:67-68

Magma on the move demonstration with tank and bottle of colored oil 1480:61

Magma rise and sinking of crust at mid-ocean ridges experiment 1477:10-11

Magma; gases in magma shown with antacid tablets in soda bottle experiment 1477:24-27

Magma; how does density affect movement of magma experiment 1477:12-15

Magma; how does pressure affect the gases dissolved in magma experiment 1477:24-27

Magma; how does temperature affect the movement of magma experiment 1477:16-19

Magma; what happens when magma hardens inside volcano experiment 1477:28-31

Make a volcano replica project 900:131-132

Make a water volcano 142:15

Make an underwater volcano 142:27; 176:89

Mantle; how does pressure affect rock in asthenosphere experiment 1477:8-11

Mantle; putty rock shows how rock in mantle behaves like liquid/solid ex 1477:8-11

Measure strength of magnetic field to predict volcanic eruption experiment 1477:40-43

Model volcano from papier mache over chicken wire, how to make 1487:28

Model volcano from play dough experiment using baking soda/vinegar/food color 1271:15

Models compare largest volcanoes on Mars and on Earth experiment 1478:68

Optical pyrometer measures temperature of hot lava flow from volcano experiment 1477:42-43

Plaster of Paris model, making 797:14

Pumice volcanic rock model; make with can of aerosol insulating foam experiment 1477:26-27

Red food coloring and baking soda volcano experiment 1286:21

Red food coloring in plastic bottle of fizzy water volcano experiment 1277:21

Rilles or valleys on Moon surface from lava flow demonstration 1477:83

Shield volcano action demonstration 1023:86-87

Simple volcano, how to build, recipe for eruption 854:88

Streams and rivers affected by volcanic explosion experiment 1477:72-75

Tiltmeter measures tilting of ground on sides of volcano experiment 1477:48-51

Types; model shows how composite volcanoes are formed experiment 1477:36-39

Underwater erupting volcano experiment 1028:20

Using dry ice—make a chemical volcano 87:71

Vinegar—soda—detergent volcano—making 759:38

Viscosity of lava affects its flow rate experiment 1477:64-67

Volcanic clouds lower atmospheric temperature and reduce sunlight experiment 1477:76-79

Volcanic explosion effect on rivers and streams experiment 1477:72-75

Volcano from vinegar, detergent, baking soda and food coloring 1175:140-141

Volcano made from two jars of water and food coloring 1431:17

Warm water rises experiment with bottle volcano 1136:24-25

Water volcano, using colored ink experiment 996:14-15

Why are volcanoes found in areas of great crustal movement experiment 1477:32-35

VOLTA, COUNT ALESSANDRO

About the voltaic pile 63:66-69

Chemical reaction battery gives electricity Volta's way experiment 1063:164

Duplicate Volta's discovery experiment 830:3-5

First electric battery, similar to Volta's, experiment 895:7-9

His experiments 42:81-92

Invented the electrophorus 209:33

Make a model of Volta's pile 30:61-63

Repeat Volta's experiment with electric current 72:47-49

Voltaic cell experiment 1156:110-113

Voltaic pile produces electric current experiment 1133:5.003

Voltaic pile, make your own 768:77-78

Volta's discovery—how to build a simple detector 23:3-5

VOLTAGE

Batteries connected in reverse give no voltage 287:24

Batteries connected in series or in parallel give different voltage 287:23

Bulbs connected in series or in parallel get different voltage 287:22

Demonstrate voltage drop 287:20

Demonstrate voltage with eggs and tennis balls experiment 1501:28-31

Dimmer switch changes the voltage 287:21

Several batteries connected in series give high voltage 287:26

VOLTAIC CELL

Lemon battery—how to make 507:1854-1855

Wet battery experiment, how to construct 1476:13-14

VOLTAIC PILE

Alessandro Volta's Voltaic pile produces electric current experiment 1133:5.003

Decomposition of water into hydrogen and oxygen using electricity experiment 1133:2.008

How to make 1133:2.008

VOLTMETER

Voltage/current indicator—how to build 23:25-30

What does a voltmeter measure experiment 1158:102-106

What does a voltmeter measure 586:105-106

VOLUME. *See also* **MEASUREMENTS**

Air pressure affects volume of marshmallow demonstration 1479:92

Alcohol and water take up less space than just water experiment 1435:6-9

Area and volume introduced through problems and activities 1346:5-64

Change in volume when water freezes experiment 1526:32-34

Cooking experiments demonstrate volume 885:86

Demonstrate with glass of water puzzle 203:81

Effect of popping process on volume and density of corn experiment data tables 1004:3.004

Egg floats in salt water experiment 1216:28-30

How to make a calibrated measuring jar 55:162

Measure volume and weight of stones using cup of water experiment 1256:15

Measuring volume of ordinary containers experiment 1230:8-9

Salt added to glass of water experiment in volume 1435:3-5

Simple concepts of volume (Primary) 527:1-33

442

Surfaces and spaces in a room reconstructed in model room, how to do 1521:24-25
Volume of liquids affected by temperature experiment 1515:15-16
Volume of rock measured by amount of water displaced experiment 1507:24
Water—volume measurement of lake—how to do 363:91-92

VOLVOX. *See* **EUGLENA**
VON GUERICKE, OTTO. *See* **GUERICKE, OTTO VON**
VORTEX RINGS
Make vortex rings—try to put out candle flame— experiment 532:12-13

W

WAGONS
Rubber band buggy, made from plastic bottle 1423:20
Wagon, made from wood with passenger seat project 1423:19

WALKIE TALKIE. *See also* TELEPHONES
Can and string—making 508:14

WALL COVERINGS
Is plastic or paper best for wall covering experiment 1508:13

WASPS
Biocontrol of insect pests by parasitoid wasps experiment 1097:134-136
Parasitoid wasps lay eggs in other insects experiment 1097:13-15
Wasp model, how to make 1445:36-37
Wasp nest model, how to make 1445:44-45

WASTE. *See also* GARBAGE; ORGANIC WASTE
Biodegradable and non biodegradable garbage experiment 978:162-163
Household trash can be recycled experiment 1323:57-61
How much and what kind of waste does family throw away in one week project 1455:49
Product container size and relation to waste products and consumer use 969:81-82

WASTE—SPACECRAFT
Experiments to demonstrate waste facilities on a spacecraft 564:77

WASTE TREATMENT. *See also* RECYCLING; SEWAGE TREATMENT
Air pollution, ideas for projects 841:64
Garbage pollution, ideas for projects 841:67-69
Land pollution, ideas for projects 841:64
Lobster shell chitin effect in filtering wastewater metallic ions experiment 997:64-66
Pesticides pollution, ideas for projects 841:66
Toxic substances, ideas for projects 841:66-67
Trickling filter waste treatment—how to make 363:87-88
Water pollution, ideas for projects 841:63-64

WASTEWATER TREATMENT
Settling tank for wastewater experiment 1234:92
Wastewater cleaned and reused experiment use dirty water/coloring/bleach 1240:53-54

WATCHES
Tricks using 228:50-51

WATER. *See also* FLUIDS; ICE; RAIN; SIPHONS
A hot water mystery—experiment 585:141-142
A water "smokestack"—experiment 585:28
Absorption—experiment 170:56-57
Absorption—paper worm wiggles and moves 288:22-23
Absorption of paper towels experiment 829:43-44
Acidity of water experiment using red cabbage indicator 1325:12-17
Activities and experiments with water 804:12-15
Adhesion—it sticks 170:30-31
Adhesion and capillary action—experiment 126:81-89
Adhesion and capillary attraction experiment 940:16-17
Adhesion at work 670:18
Adhesion demonstration 719:28
Adhesion keeps water in glass experiment 940:8-10
Air in water experiment 741:19
Air is dissolved in most water experiment 706:83-84
Air pressure—raising water 98:8-9

Air thermometer—moving water up another way 217:32-37
Air transport of water 363:153
And fire—protection by water 146:21
Are there empty spaces in water 381:88-89
Atmosphere—water is in the air—experiment (Primary) 327:20-35
Attraction—bet you can pour water sideways 228:73
Bending water—demonstrate 147:40-41
Bernoulli effect on a water surface 585:19
Boil water—heat needed to boil water 147:63-65
Boil water by cooling it—experiment 175:61
Boil water in a paper cup experiment 900:18; 900:62
Boil water in paper cup experiment 1229:40-41
Boil water with ice experiment 585:138; 906:51-53
Boil water without heat experiment 937:54-55; 1066:42-43
Boiling point—demonstrated 291:57
Boiling point—how hot 170:22-23
Boiling point and effect of pressure—experiment 183:60-63
Boiling point and freezing point of water experiment 1219:31
Boiling point of salt water cooks egg faster experiment 960:39
Boiling point of water affected by added solutes experiment 1396:82
Boiling point of water determined experiment 1396:79-84
Boiling water by cooling it 577:project #21
Boiling water in a paper cup 44:100; 179:52-53; 291:52-53
Boiling water in paper pan experiment 1002:17
Bricks soak up water 253:48-49
Bucket—water bucket for well—how to make 363:99-100
Bucket—water bucket fountain—making 291:26-27
Buoyancy experiments 719:39-41
Can bend light rays 240:39-41
Can water act like glue experiment 831:26-27
Capillarity (adhesion vs. Cohesion)—experiments 56:56-59
Capillarity—demonstrated 146:10-11
Capillary action experiment 719:29-30
Carbon dioxide—bubbles make objects more buoyant 44:50-51
Carbon dioxide—moth balls dance a ballet for you 186:68
Carbon dioxide is held in water experiment 1322:48-52
Causes rust 382:166-167
Caves formed by power of water 132:27
Changing communities in a drop of water 268:95-99
Chemical magic—how to make dry water 87:80
Chemical magic—make water turn solid and get hard 87:84
Chemical magic—water changes into rainbow colors 87:83
Chinese water carrier—how to make 363:83-84
Climbing water—experiment 538:50
Climbing water: a way to defy gravity—experiment 586:25-27
Coanda effect spoon appears glued to stream of water experiment 722:21
Cohesion—surface film—demonstrate 56:52-55
Cohesion—watertight—experiment 222:61

Cohesion action of water experiment 1066:68-69

Cohesion action of water in water drop painting experiment 1066:72-73

Cohesion, adhesion and capillary action—demonstrate 291:23

Cold water is heavier than hot water—experiment 651:16-17

Cold water is heavier than warm water experiment with colored water 1281:11

Cold water is heavy (Primary) 143:22-24

Cold water sinks experiment 1066:77

Collecting—solar still—how to make 289:46-47

Collecting water—how to collect from ponds lakes and streams 41:72-75

Colors—water in many colors—experiment (Primary) 103:11-18

Compare salt water and fresh water for weight and freezing time experiment 1509:15

Composition—hydrogen—how to prepare 128:102-103

Composition—hydrogen bubbles—blowing soap bubbles with hydrogen 128:103

Composition of water—experiment (Primary) 346:61-62, 65-6

Composition of water—what's it made of 170:10-11; 368:5-8

Compress water—show it is difficult 44:41

Condensation—air condenses into water—simple experiment 14:22-25

Condensation—experiment 368:14-15

Condensation—get water from air 146:60

Condensation—how are dew and frost made 291:35

Condensation—tin cup, water and ice—demonstrate (Primary) 327:26

Condensation—water coming out of the air 281:20

Condensation of water vapor forms clouds 44:72-73

Conductivity—experiment 170:54-55

Containers; just how full can you fill a container with water project 1210:48-49

Contraction—cool water takes up less room 96:26

Contraction of water: an ice puzzle—experiment 585:141

Convection current experiment with hot and cold water and food coloring 1079:99-100

Convection currents—experiments 243:22-23

Convection currents in hot water experiment 871:3.008

Convection in liquids—demonstrate 291:42

Cooling curves of ice and water experiment 1515:88-91

Cooling water experiment—which size container cools the fastest 538:51

Currents—experiment 132:30

Decomposed—how water can be decomposed 128:102

Dehydration and water—dry beans—experiment 585:29-30

Density—afloat in a boat 98:14-15

Density—differing densities 98:16-17

Density—drop test to compare densities of liquids 295:33-34

Density—experiments 56:9-13

Density—how heavy 170:14-15

Density—liquid layers make water float, sink or mix 98:18-19

Density—make water denser 360:64

Density of salt and fresh water experiment using eggs 1207:26

Density; floating egg experiment 829:47-48

Detergent action—make water wetter with soap 122:168-173

Detergent action—make water wetter 150:118-119; 381:85

Detergent action—making water wetter 364:112

Dew point—finding the dew point 44:68-69

Dew point—measure dew point 101:18-19

Displacement—pushed away—where do bubbles go 170:8-9

Displacement—weighty mystery experiment 399:33

Displacement of—Archimedes buoyancy experiment 368:51-55

Displacement of water—experiment 346:11-16

Displacement-wise king decides which apple is bigger 288:24-25

Dissolves things experiment 719:17-20

Dissolving materials in water experiment 829:31-32

Dissolving; which things dissolve in water experiment 1509:12

Distortion—demonstrate 170:46-47

Does adding salt change boiling temperature of water experiment 715:41-42

Does salt affect boiling point of water experiment 748:116

Drop—racing 350:104-105

Drop lens—making 11:12-15

Drops—on waxed paper to show absorbency spreading and evaporation 12:41-43

Drops—why drops are round (Primary) 143:6-7

Drying—race (Primary) 70:35-36

Effect of water on different objects experiment 760:50

Effect on minerals 37:46-48

Effects on soil 119:54-57

Evaporation and condensation experiment 737:17

Expands when it freezes experiment 719:21-22

Experiments with water 116:129-139; 186:68-76; 232:88; 693:36-43

Fish breathe in water 232:91

Flocculation and settling—demonstration 363:75-76

Flow from a gurgling jug 585:33

Flow from a jug—experiments number 1 and 2 585:31-32

Flow measurement of water 363:92-93

Flow of water experiment; make a water clock 909:24

Flow of water from a hose; measuring rate of disc. and range of stream of water 604:64-67

Flow of water; why water can flow at an angle experiment 1403:160-161

Flows downward (Primary) 326:14-15

Food coloring flow through hot and cold water experiment 905:176-177

Force of water works against force of gravity experiment 1031:26-27

Friction of water—experiments 563:191

From hydrogen and oxygen 382:162-163

Generates electricity 101:23-24

Getting water out of the air 30:28-29

Glaciers; melting mini-glaciers to get water experiment 959:166-167

Glasses of whirling without spilling 350:107-108

Ground—water in the ground—experiment 368:16-22

Ground water and sand experiment [Primary] 873:53

Groundwater system model to demonstrate contamination of groundwater 1342:127-130

Groundwater system model to demonstrate groundwater movement 1342:127-130

Heat absorbed by water; boil water in paper cup experiment 882:5

Heat retention—it's still hot 170:32-33

Heat water in paper cup experiment 837:29-30

Heated water expands and rises, two jars experiment 814:58-60

Holes in water experiment 1028:23

Hot and cold water in bottles—do they lose heat at the same rate 532:33

Hot water is lighter than cold water patterns experiment 696:12-13

Hot water is lighter than cold water; colored water explosion experiment 1136:20

Hot water is lighter than cold water; ink bottle in bowl of water experiment 937:98-99

Hot water rises in cold water experiment 959:75-76

Hot water rises 360:43

Hot water tap always leaks experiment 1079:98-99

How a percolator works with water experiment 939:94-96

How fast do different volumes of water lose heat experiment graph given 731:71-73

How pure is the water—experiment 563:79

How water goes into the air 30:27-28

Imbibition—effect when dry seeds are soaked in water 170:44-45

Interpreting patterns of movement in water project 833:138

Invisible water 98:26-27

Is water important to life experiment with apples 1324:28-31

Level of water in containers is same level experiment 1161:19

Lift pump to demonstrate air pressure—making 142:20

Lift water in a glass experiment 909:22

Lifting power of water—pour water down tube to water bottle, it lifts books 419:26

Light is affected by the depth of water experiment 877:30-34

Liquids have different densities experiment 884:48-50

Living place—water as a living place for air breathers 363:47-49

Living things contain water experiment; chart given for recording results 1172:40-41

Living things; how much water do living things contain experiment 1509:26

Lubrication—it's slippery 170:38-39

Magnification—it looks different 170:28-29

Magnifies in curved containers 719:35-36

Magnifying glass—making, primary 64:unpaged

Materials that absorb and repel water experiment 1124:6-7

Matter; two forms of matter can't occupy the same space experiment 1066:45

Measure attractiveness (stickiness) between water molecules experiment 1396:153-158

Measure volume and temp. In lakes, ponds, streams 41:76-80

Measurement—measuring water—ways of doing—experiment (Primary) 103:26-40

Mixing liquids 170:40-41

Molecular motion—experiment 585:17-18

Molecules—diffusion—do hot molecules move faster than cold molecules 396:10-11

Molecules move faster when heated—boiled egg pot experiment 399:58

Molecules of cold water and warm water experiment with food colors 1479:63

Molecules of water contract when cold experiment 1066:61

Molecules of water pull together experiment 1405:49-50

Molecules of water take up less space as a liquid or a gas experiment 1251:33-35

Molecules; are water molecules in constant motion experiment 1403:21

Molecules; do water molecules in liquid water fit tightly together experiment 1403:16-19

Molecules; how close do molecules of water have to be to attract experiment 1403:19

Molecules; space between molecules in liquids experiment with sugar and water 1179:22

Molecules; water molecules are in constant motion experiment 1396:137-138

Motor and alternator for water wheel—how to make 43:32-43

Movement of water molecules in waves demonstration 1405:85

Moving water—demonstrate 142:15

Music from bottles filled with water experiment 1207:26

Nutrients (minerals) in—demonstrate 56:22-25

Observe movement of hot colored water through cooler water experiment 905:178-179

Organisms exist in various water sources experiment 884:16-18

Osmosis in salt water experiment 741:33

Oxygen 56:26-30

Oxygen in water shown by indicator experiment 882:10

Particle reflection 170:48-49

Percolator action—demonstrate 291:56

pH of water; how to determine experiment 978:75-76

Plastic bag experiments (Primary) 99:5-15

Plastic sheet over hole in ground shows evaporation and condensation 1135:39

Poster representing all water on Earth; salt, fresh, and frozen, make 1441:57

Precipitation experiment 368:15

Primary experiments with water and air 982:1-69

Properties of air and water experiment 1161:5

Properties of water experiment; data table given 1004:1.006

Pulling water upward using heat 217:57-59

Pushes up with a buoyant force 44:46-47

Rainbows—experiment 350:75-77

Rainbows come from scattering of light—experiment 126:111-117

Refraction—it looks different 170:26-27

Refraction of light—experiment 56:60-63

Regelation—it's still one 170:34-35

Rivers and streams-where does water come from in rivers and streams 290:4

Rotating water forms curve called a parabola experiment 1132:106-1-106-2

Salt absorbs water from air experiment 959:59

Salt affects boiling water experiment 1238:18

Salt affects temperature of water experiment 905:136-137

Salt dissolves more in water than in rubbing alcohol experiment 1250:43-45

Salt solution—lift that cube 16:58-61

Salt water and fresh water and their differences experiment 760:51

Sand sculptures show adhesion between sand and water experiment 1396:156

Science in the bathtub—experiment 32:70-71

Sediment in water, measuring 874:213-214

Seeks it own level—experiments 663:12-13

Seeks its own level experiment using soda bottle and plastic tubing 1212:15

Separate salt and sand from water 97:12-13

Shape—water takes the shape of its container 44:38-39

Shape of water—demonstrate (Primary) 103:4-10

Shape-simple experiment to test the shape and molecular action of water-liquid solution. 308:entire book

Show molecular motion 585:21-22

Simple activities and experiments with water [Primary] 854:30-31

Simple water experiments [Primary] 757:135-140

Sink or float—experiment (Primary) 535:76

Siphon—raising water with air pressure 98:8-9

Siphon—simple siphon—making (Primary) 210:15

Siphon experiment 538:49

Siphoning system produces continuous running water experiment 884:77-78

Siphoning water, how to 884:73-76

Size-the strange story of water's size-expanding and contraction with heat and cold 281:22-23

Skin—soap breaks the skin of water 96:31

Skin—soap weakens water skin (Primary) 339:30-33

Skin—water and its skin—experiment (Primary) 70:33-34

Skin—water has skin—test the strength of water surface 98:22-23

Smoke rings in water 585:31

Snowflakes are crystals of water 44:74-75

Soil heats and cools more quickly than water experiment 767:112

Soils; which soils hold the most moisture experiment 959:193

Solar water cleaner—making (Primary) 154:28-29

Solubility of gas in water 55:41-47

Solubility of gases in liquids—demonstrate 126:149-157

Solutes affect the cohesiveness of water experiment 1396:156

Solutions—making 98:28-29; 122:26-28

Solutions—making, and making salt 98:28-29

Solutions—nature of solutions in water—demonstrate 126:137-147

Solutions—what happens when something dissolves 281:25

Solvent—experiments to show dissolving ability 330:30-31

Solvent; hot or cold water; which dissolves the best experiment 1271:11

Solvent; water as universal solvent experiment 1172:22-23

Sound travels through water and wood experiment 1432:56-57

Spaces between water molecules experiment 905:26-27

Specific gravity—suspend an egg in water—experiment 186:74

Specific heat of water compared to soil and air experiment 1172:20-22

States of—demonstrate water as solid, liquid, gas 253:41-42

Steam exerts pressure—experiment 44:66-67

Steam turbine—making 161:84-85

Steam; what is steam experiment 909:14

Substances that dissolve in hot or cold water or are suspended in it experiment 1331:20-21

Substances that will or will not dissolve in water experiment; graph given 960:23

Sugar dissolves faster in cold or warm water experiment 1509:13

Surface tension experiments 719:23-27

Teaching activities with water; art, music and science 1056:8-35

Temperature—water temperatures—experiment (Primary) 103:41-48

Temperature affects molecular motion of water molecules experiment 1396:138

Temperature experiment 719:31-32

Temperature of water affects its density experiment 884:51-53

Temperature—is there a difference between temperature of water, heat of water-experiment 126:129-136

Test electrical conductivity of liquids experiment 959:149-150

Testing water for minerals experiment 1438:23-25

Thermocline for ponds—making 741:23

Transparency of water 236:129

Transpiration—water given of by plants—experiments 382:37-41

Two-straw magic experiment; blow in straw and water comes out of other straw 1230:56-57

Types of water and their effect on plant growth experiment, tap, distilled, etc. 1061:56-57

Underwater binoculars—making from milk carton 494:62

Underwater volcano; hot water rises experiment 909:22

Universal solvent property of water experiment 1441:60

Universal solvent; which chemicals will dissolve in water experiment 1271:11

Used to bring about chemical reaction 122:52-53

Velocity—stream velocity measurement—experiment 363:96-99

Viscosity—how gooey 170:16-17

Viscosity of fluids—experiment 585:20-21

Volume change it gets bigger 170:18-19

Volume measurement of lake—how to do 363:91-92

Volume of liquids affected by temperature experiment 1515:15-16

Warm water holds more sugar 676:17

Warm water is lighter than cold water 44:58-59

Warm water rises experiment 741:11

Warm water rises experiment with bottle volcano 1136:24-25

Water—holding capacity of the soil 285:23-25

Water appears to boil at touch of finger experiment 905:34-35

Water appears to boil experiment 1405:49

Water as solvent experiment 741:13

Water can push 98:10-11

Water changes its state from liquid to ice to steam demonstration 707:26-27

Water currents and effect of temperature and salinity on water density 871:1.003
Water cycle experiment 719:14-16
Water dissolves in air—experiment 693:42
Water dissolves in air; measure humidity experiment 959:191-193
Water drainage through soil experiment 984:66-67
Water exists in three states experiment 884:6-7
Water expands and contracts 56:14-21
Water expands upon turning to steam experiment 752:100
Water expands when heated experiment with colored water in glass jars 1212:30
Water experiments (Primary) 100:33-45
Water experiments 538:43-52
Water flows up—tree mystery experiment 399:35
Water flows uphill experiment with tubing 996:16-17
Water from the desert—experiment 663:37
Water gets into the air through evaporation experiment 1439:62-64
Water goes from liquid to a gas when popcorn is heated experiment 1250:35-37
Water goes thru some materials faster (Primary) 327:27-28
Water has dissolving power 132:26
Water has more cohesiveness than other liquids do experiment 1396:153-156
Water has weight experiment [Primary] 744:15
Water has weight experiment 902:25-26
Water has weight; simple experiments to demonstrate [Primary] 854:35
Water in soil 236:128
Water in the air 236:128
Water is wet—things float/sink; soap bubbles, water evaporates/freezes, more 433:entire book:unpaged
Water isn't pure 281:23
Water movement and temperature 170:42-43
Water on the level, demonstrate 589:41
Water overcomes gravity—experiments 663:12-15
Water pipe from wool or cotton threads 161:64-65
Water reduces weight of object experiment 1230:44-45
Water spurts—demonstrate how 360:9
Water stores heat 56:38-41
Water table demonstration experiment 1234:30
Water takes the shape of its container 44:38
Water temperature changes with depth experiment 877:35-39
Water-to-wine trick 346:140-141
Water travels uphill experiment 884:68-71
Water trick (Primary) 232:86
Water volcano, using colored ink experiment 996:14-15
Water wheel—make and watch water flow make it spin (Primary) 70:44-45
Weight; which weighs more?; Hot or cold water experiment 1516:63-64
Well and aquifer experiment, how to do 1234:101
"Wet water" making water wetter 604:80-83
Wetting ability of water increased by adding liquid laundry detergents 1403:33-34
Wetting action of water; why do some materials get wetter than others ex 1403:32-35
Wetting the water—experiment 585:25
What dissolves in water; simple experiments demonstrate [Primary] 854:39
What does or doesn't dissolve in water experiment (Primary) 695:22-26
What floats and what sinks in water experiment 867:14-15
What materials will dissolve in water experiment 885:89-90
What substances dissolve in water experiment 884:88-91
What things dissolve in water experiment [Primary] 744:19
Why does a toy-dunking bird drink 586:29
Why does oil float 126:51-54
Will the glasses overflow 532:34
Wood pieces float and gather together 146:20
You can get water from air (Primary) 143:20-21
You see it; then you don't—salt dissolves in water; evaporation brings back 573:9

WATER—ABSORPTION
Water race with two pieces of cloth—experiment 563:154

WATER—ADHESION
Cohesion and adhesion forces in operation experiment 1004:3.007
Stuck sticks—experiments 563:82-83

WATER—AQUIFER. *See also* **AQUIFERS**
Model aquifer, making 959:77

WATER—BENDING
Bending water with electricity 586:95-96

WATER—BUOYANCY. *See also* **ARCHIMEDES; BUOYANCY; FLOATING AND SINKING; WATER—FLOATING AND SINKING**
Archimedes' principle of buoyancy experiment with vinegar, baking soda, pasta 1290:9, 1.9
Bottle submarine 281:33
Buoyancy—experiment 368:49-55
Buoyancy—experiment 56:47-51
Carbon dioxide bubbles make objects more buoyant 44:50-51
Cartesian diver or what makes a submarine rise and sink 126:45-49
Experiments to show 330:18-21
Float an egg 281:34; 585:20
Floating and sinking—experiment 34:31-37
How does a steel ship float 126:29-35
It floats 170:36-37
Lump of clay on spring balance demonstrates 804:29
Salt water affects buoyancy experiment 1290:6, 1.6
Salt water is more buoyant than fresh water 44:48-49
Sink float game 32:72-73
Water pushes up with a buoyant force 44:46-47
You 'weigh' less in water 281:31

WATER—CAPILLARY ACTION
Capillary action—experiments 170:58-59
Capillary action demonstrated with colored water and strips of paper 1331:29
Capillary action of water demonstration with filter paper and markers 1441:60
Capillary filter—experiment 585:23-24
Capillary tricks and tests to show capillary action 142:28-29
Carnation flower in two glasses of colored water turns two colors experiment 1331:28
Celery and food coloring in water demonstrates capillary action 1004:1.006
Celery stalk in jar of red colored water demonstrates capillary action 1393:22
Climbing water—experiment 44:54-55

Climbing water and capillary action experiments 959:35-37

Demonstrate capillary action with colored water and fabric strip 1056:26

Different kinds of paper products affect water's capillary action experiment 1403:23

Experiments to show 330:26-29

How does water rise to tops of trees 101:24-25

How water rises in plants—demonstrate 293:19

Nodding water bird demonstrates capillary action 1393:5

Paper towel transports water experiment 1079:80-81

Salt garden—experiment 585:22-23

Water moves upward on paper towel experiment 1230:78-79

Which colors from felt tip pens spread out the farthest experiment 1509:9

Why does water rise in paper towel experiment 1403:25

WATER—CLOCKS. *See* WATER CLOCKS

WATER—COHESION

Cohesion and adhesion forces in operation experiment 1004:3.007

Cohesive attractive forces among molecules of different liquids experiment 1004:3.008

Merging streams—experiment 563:77

Size of water drops affected by cohesion and gravity experiment data tables 1004:3.009

WATER—CONDENSATION

Bowl of water experiment to show condensation or dew 492:43

Cans with water, ice and salt, demonstrate 782:40-43

Drinking amount—experiment 665:39

Get moisture out of air; plastic in jar experiment 900:61

Get water out of air; ice cubes in glass experiment 900:52, 60

How water gets out of air experiment 1003:75-76

Making water appear experiment 909:14

Moisture trap for water in the desert experiment 1281:17

Removing water from air, ice cube in glass experiment 888:66-68

Solar still—simple still made in ground 538:45

Water from the desert experiment 909:45

Water on the wall—experiment 563:81

Water vapor condenses at what temperature experiment 852:42-43

Water vapor condenses when cooled experiments 767:25-26

What is condensation; glass over boiling water experiment 900:58

WATER—CONVECTION

Convection currents; temperature affects movement of water experiment 1479:86

Hot water rises and cold water falls experiment with colored water 1519:11

Warm water rises experiment 741:11

WATER—DENSITY

Can water float on top of water experiment 836:28-30

Colored liquid layers experiment 959:148-149

Colored liquids that sink or float experiment 959:146-147

Dancing mothballs experiment with mothballs, vinegar and baking soda 1212:31

Density affects water movement demonstration 1405:86

Density differences cause water to move experiment 1405:83-95

Density of common household objects and liquids compared to water experiment 1004:4.004

Does salt water have greater density than water experiment 831:31-32

Egg floats in salt water experiment 1006:46

Float an egg in salt solution experiment 1479:51

Floating water on water—experiments 538:47

Fresh water is lighter or less dense than salt water experiment 1331:32

Heat affects water density experiment 1290:10, 1.10

Hydrometer measures density of water and oil experiment, how to make 1521:26-27

Is cold water more dense than hot water experiment 831:28-30

Make hydrometer to determine density of water 436:44-45

Measuring the density of water, oil and clay experiment 1159:11-13

Object floats or sinks as air increases or decreases density experiment 1004:3.001

Penny dropping into water (Primary) 551:unpaged

Potato slice floats in salt water but sinks in fresh water experiment 1310:10-11

Temperature and salinity affect behavior of water experiment data tables given 1004:1.007

Temperature changes density of water experiment 1325:18-21

Warm water is lighter or less dense than cold water experiment 1331:31

Water currents and effect of temperature and salinity on water density 871:1.003

What floats in water (Primary) 529:26-33

WATER—DESALINIZATION. *See also* DESALINIZATION

Get fresh water from salty water—experiment 320:7

How to demonstrate 330:66-69

Purify water that is salty and polluted experiment 1441:65

WATER—DETECTOR RODS

Experiment to demonstrate 393:10-19

WATER—DISPLACEMENT

Add weight to water by touching it experiment 937:24-25

Archimedes discovery; weight and volume measured by water displaced experiment 1156:18-19

Archimedes Principle proved experiment using spring scale, water, wooden block 1243:30-31

Boat with balloon rig demonstrates water displacement 561:12-13

Boats float; measuring displaced water experiment 871:3.014

Bowl of water used as weighing scale experiment 1079:79

Clay boats and weights in dish of water demonstration 1310:14-15

Deep dive using medicine dropper in bottle of water experiment 748:109

Density of object related to water displacement experiment data tables given 1004:3.002

Displaced water weighs same as the floating object experiment 1028:18

Displacement of water experiment 998:195

Do objects in water have weight experiment 851:50

Eye dropper in bottle of water demonstrates 780:42-43

Floating object displaces equal volume or weight of liquid experiment 1179:139

Floating of objects determined by weight of water displaced experiment 760:25

Glass floats in glass experiment 1066:55

Hull shape of boat and its effect on buoyancy demonstration 1165:9

Measure amount of water objects displace experiment 760:23-24

Object immersed in liquid loses weight experiment 1456:32

Objects in water have different weight than in air experiment 1405:92-93

Operation octopus—mini octopus dives up/down in bottle of water—experiment 573:35

Repeat Archimedes experiment—weight and volume cause water to be displaced 448:16-18

Swimmer using survival bobbing experiment with cigar tube, clothespins, clay 1136:10

The fisherman's puzzle—experiment 563:84-86

Things weigh less in water experiment 898:7

Volume of rock measured by amount of water displaced experiment 1507:24

Water and weight mystery—experiments 563:79-80

WATER—DISTILLATION. *See also* **DISTILLATION; SOLAR STILL**

Clean dirty water by heating and cooling it experiment 1032:18-19

Collect and purify water by distillation experiment 1372:44-45

Collect water from ground with plastic sheet over hole in ground experiment 1374:30

Distill water—experiment 170:52-53; 319:39-40

Distilling water 293:35

Distilling water; fast and slow methods experiment 959:145-146

Fresh water from salt water experiment 947:22

Fresh water from salt water project, how to do 577:project #24; 1296:1981

Fresh water from seawater, how to make 909:42

Model solar device for distilling salt water experiment 762:126-128

Salt evaporator—how to make 507:1865-1866

Separate salt from water experiment 1179:33

Separating substances from solutions by distillation 604:44-47

Simple distillation 157:8

Solar water cleaner—how to make 399:25

Water and salt separated from seawater by the Sun experiment 1325:91-94

WATER—DRINKING. *See also* **FILTERS; WATER—FILTERS AND FILTERING; WATER TREATMENT PLANTS**

Activated charcoal in water experiment 959:133-134

Bacteria in drinking water experiment using potato slices 1331:83

Cleaning dirty water experiment 1134:6.008

Coagulation of muddy water experiment 959:133

Community water problem—how to solve 363:93-96

Drinking water free from pollutants experiment 1427:66-71

Effects of acid rain on drinking water 594:45-53

How pure is the water from your faucet—simple test for 611:18-19

How water can be purified 128:103-104

How water is made fit to drink 319:36-38

pH of solution experiment using lemon, grape juice, milk, baking soda, water 1427:66-67

pH of tap water experiment using pH test paper 1427:70-71

Water from aquifer fills well if surrounding sand is kept wet experiment 1331:60

Well that draws water from a small aquifer experiment 1331:60

WATER—ELECTROLYSIS. *See also* **ELECTROLYSIS; HYDROGEN; OXYGEN**

Analyzing water by electrolysis 625:24

Breaking compound water into its elements experiment 976:26

Breaking up water into hydrogen and oxygen experiment 1514:114-119

Change water to gases with electricity 147:111-114

Decompose water by electrolysis 319:34-36

Decompose water using electricity experiment 752:106-107

Decomposition of water by electrolysis experiment 978:79-80

Electric current passed through water makes hydrogen and oxygen gas experiment 1172:17-20

Electric current splits water into hydrogen and oxygen gases experiment 1244:14-15

Electricity passing thru water splits water into hydrogen and oxygen experiment 1473:32-33

Electrolysis experiment 126:159-169

Electrolysis of—demonstrate 209:32-33

Electrolysis of salt water 102:114-115

Electrolysis of water experiment 768:83-84; 1396:94

Nails for electrodes—experiment 532:17

Separate water into hydrogen and oxygen experiment using battery, wires, water 1435:101-103

Separate water into oxygen and hydrogen 97:16-17; 122:53-64

Split water—electric gas 146:34-35

Split water into oxygen and hydrogen 176:25-26

Splitting water, how to 346:60-67

Splitting water using battery and wire in salt water experiment 1271:29

Splitting water with electrolysis experiment 910:44-45

Use electrolysis to separate water into hydrogen and oxygen—experiment 642:122-124

Water splits into hydrogen and oxygen when current passes thru water experiment 1179:157

WATER—EROSION. *See also* **EROSION**

How does water erode 236:141-142

Make your own canyon (Primary) 153:16-17

Model of water erosion on a mountain experiment 1063:226-227

Moving water causes erosion of uncovered soil experiment 1323:42-46

Slopes of sand eroded by water demonstration 1080:24

Soil transportation—experiment 363:59-61

What factors affect water erosion experiment 900:128-129

WATER—EUTROPHICATION. *See* **EUTROPHICATION**

WATER—EVAPORATION. *See also* **EVAPORATION**

Activities to demonstrate water evaporation 1230:32-35

Air blowing over water lowers temperature of water experiment 1439:35-37

An evaporation trick—experiment 563:87-88

Can water evaporation be reduced 532:32
Can you cool drinking water with a wet towel 333:132-134
Case of the vanishing water 330:12-15
Causes and effects 55:137-143
Cloth and foil evaporation experiment 867:15
Come back sugar come back (Primary) 288:12-13
Cool your feet 399:27
Cooling and evaporation experiments 959:59-61
Cooling effect of evaporation 56:35-37
Cooling effect of evaporation experiment using two thermometers and fan 1397:43
Demonstrate with sugar water 780:22-23
Effect of wind on water in the air experiment 1003:72
Evaporating water keeps milk cool experiment 1519:18
Evaporation—condensation 56:31-34
Evaporation—condensation process in nature to purify water—demonstrate 363:80-81
Evaporation—experiments 663:4-5
Evaporation and heat experiment [Primary] 873:54
Evaporation and temperature—experiment 657:98-99
Evaporation causes a liquid to cool down experiment 1090:30-31
Evaporation cools air experiment 1003:74
Evaporation demonstrates 295:45-47
Evaporation experiment 34:38-41; 170:50-51; 368:9-10, 12-14; 1281:16
Evaporation experiment (Primary) 232:89
Evaporation keeps things cool experiment 909:13
Evaporation of liquid dependent on surface exposed to air experiment 1090:28
Evaporation of water activities for classroom 1291:11-12
Evaporation of water from containers experiment 1003:71
Evaporation of water molecules causes cooling experiment 1250:29-31
Evaporation races experiments with different liquids 538:44
Evaporation rates of specific amounts of water from heat source experiment 1447:24-26
Evaporation rates of water; how to measure experiment 978:139
Evaporation takes away heat experiment 1405:58
Gravity and pressure siphon experiment 867:16-17
Heat energy from Sun affects water evaporation experiment 1325:33-36
Heated water evaporates faster—experiment 672:14
How cold can you make it (Primary) 551:unpaged
How fast water evaporates from different containers experiment 1516:28-29
Investigate evaporation 909:12
Investigate how quickly water evaporates 1161:27
Invisible water 98:26-27
Jars of water show evaporation experiment [Primary] 873:52
Keeps things cool 323:18-19
Making a crystal 281:26
Measure effect of oil film on the evaporation rate of water 333:75-77
Moisture trap for water in desert experiment 1281:17
Nodding water bird demonstrates evaporation of water 1393:5
Record water evaporation from three different containers experiment 780:8-9

Role of Sun in evaporation of water in air experiment 1003:73
Salt water evaporates in the sun and leaves salt behind experiment 1344:9
Simple activities to show water evaporation [Primary] 880:19
Simple demonstration of evaporation using two jars of water 1359:7
Simple experiments to show evaporation (Primary) 103:19-25
Simple outdoor experiment (Primary) 678:15
Sugar water evaporates slower than pure water experiment 1250:26-28
Surface evaporation—experiment 672:15
Temperature and evaporation of water experiment 1447:24-26
The popcorn test 607:86-87
Vanishing water (Primary) 210:10-11
Water and food coloring in jar lids demonstrates 721:42
Water bullets—experiments 563:87
Water disappears 96:28
Water evaporates into air—experiment (Primary) 541:22
Water evaporates into air—simple experiment 14:17-21
Water evaporates more in warm weather than in cold weather experiment 1180:14; 1183:142
Water evaporates more quickly on flat surface experiment 1372:43
Water evaporation cools things experiment using clay pot/bottles of juice 1228:66-67
Water going into the air 281:21
Water in cups in sun and shade demonstrate rate of evaporation 919:24
Water in pans in shade and sun 327:23-25
Water in saucer and in covered glass of water experiment 996:22-23
Water level in jars—one open and one covered demonstrates (Primary) 518:34-37
Water you cannot see 143:18-19
What happens to salt in water when water evaporates experiment 1441:63
Which container has the least water—experiment 601: unpaged

WATER—EXPANSION
Expansion—demonstrate 170:24-25
Expansion and contraction—the stuck glasses 291:24
Expansion shown with balloons 92:28-29
Freezing water expands—experiment 183:40-43
Peculiar expansion of water—experiment 385:123-124
Warm water takes up more room 96:25
Water expands and rises when heated—hot sips of cocoa exp. 399:42
Water expands when it freezes 360:44
Water has air in it 96:33
WATER—FILTERS AND FILTERING
Activated charcoal in water experiment 959:133-134
Best filter for cleaning dirty water experiment 1509:16
Can organic chemicals be removed from water experiment 1325:82-86
Can we clean dirty water; make filter experiment 804:30
Clean dirty water with activated charcoal experiment 1046:91-93
Clean dirty water with sand and coffee filter experiment 1344:21
Clean water by removing the mud experiment 909:43
Cleaning dirty water experiment 1134:6.008

451

Cleaning muddy water with rocks and sand, how to do 1014:95

Coagulation of muddy water experiment 959:133

Device for filtering water through soil experiment 998:134

Filter to filter water, make from plastic bottle, gravel, sand and cotton 1427:72-75

Filter variety of water samples and snow experiment 1063:371

Filtering—observe coagulation 319:39

Filtering—sand and gravel useful in filtering—demonstrate 319:39

Filtering—simple experiment 132:32

Filtering muddy water—model filtering plant—how to make 368:38-40

Filtering water experiment using flower pots 1362:17

Filtering water experiment 1234:81

Filters—evaluation of paper and cloth filters 363:77-78

How to filter water experiment 909:43

Is water that looks clean always pure experiment 867:17

Lobster shell chitin effect in filtering wastewater metallic ions experiment 997:64-66

Make clean water with flower pot filter 868:59

Materials that filter faster will not clean water experiment 969:105-107

Milk carton and soil filter—making [Primary] 759:45

Muddy water filtered through paper filter, sand and charcoal experiment 1371:38-39

Paper filter that filters best experiment 1509:17

Purifying water experiment [Primary] 873:55

Simple way to clean water with funnel filled with gravel 1105:14

Soil filtration demonstration 363:76-77

Water filter—making 741:27; 934:30-31

Water filter for muddy water experiment 1161:31

Water filter to clean dirty water, how to make 1384:30

WATER—FILTERS AND FILTRATION

Clean water from dirty water experiment in water filtration 1240:4

Funnel filters water through gravel and sand experiment 1243:18-19

Water filter from funnel, paper filter, gravel and sand, how to make 1331:77

Water filter using sand, gravel and charcoal in flowerpot, how to make 1179:132-133

Water filter, how to make to filter dirty water 1414:18-19

WATER—FLOATING AND SINKING. *See also* **WATER—BUOYANCY**

A floating object displaces its own weight 281:32

Floating—what floats 281:31

Floating and sinking—experiment 98:12-13; 128:108-112

Floating egg trick 98:17

Floating science in the bath tub 32:70-71

Sinking ice—floating ice—experiment 147:53-56

WATER—FOODS

Food is mostly water 281:19

How much of the food you eat is water 295:35

Water in foods—can it be water 280:19

WATER—FREEZING. *See also* **FREEZING; ICE; WATER—ICE**

Boiled water freezes faster experiment 939:97-98

Can salt keep water from freezing 396:54-55

Can water be purified by freezing experiment 831:33-34

Can you freeze water with ice experiment 1250:38-40

Change in volume when water freezes experiment 1526:32-34

Cool hat for hot day; frozen wet cotton squares, how to make 1014:103

Does freezing of salt water differ from freezing tap water—experiment 168:42

Does hot water freeze faster than cold water experiment 793:31

Does orange juice freeze like water experiment 905:126-127

Expanding ice saves water organisms demonstration 1023:214-215

Expansion and contraction of water and ice experiment 939:92-93

Experiment—substances added to water lower its freezing point 563:131-132

Faucets dripping on cold winter nights experiment 1066:57

Finding the fractional increase in volume when water freezes 604:32-35

Freezing expands water—more than you started with 280:17

Freezing point—demonstrate with ice cube lift 203:24

Freezing point—how cold 170:20-21

Freezing point—lift ice cube out of glass of water with string 399:4

Freezing point and boiling point of water experiment 1219:31

Freezing point experiment with string, ice cube and salt 1004:1.006

Freezing point of water changes when you add salt experiment 1004:3.006

Freezing point of water experiment 748:117; 1032:25

Freezing point; do ocean and fresh water freeze at same temperature exp. 852:34-35

Freezing rate of water changes when salt and alcohol are added experiment 781:48-49

Freezing water experiment 1180:6; 1183:134

Frozen water expands to make a column of ice 150:36-37

Frozen water takes up more space (Primary) 288:14-15

Heat energy to melt ice experiment 1441:71

How much salt needed in water to get lowest temperature experiment 715:39-40

Ice cube experiments 884:64-66

Ice expands and floats experiment 867:17-18

Ice takes up more room 96:27

Ice takes up more space than water experiment 1073:93

Iceberg floats and melts in soda bottle experiment 1310:8-9

Lower the temperature of icy water experiment with salt in ice water 1479:57

Make it yourself icicles 236:148

Making frost (Primary) 232:90

Oddball water expands as it freezes—experiment 629:41-42

Orange icebergs—making 280:18

Plain water freezes faster than fruit juice experiment 1231:14-15

Removing water from a solution by fractional freezing 604:40-43

Rock movement caused by freezing water experiment 1405:78

Rocks; power of frozen water to weather and shatter rocks experiment 1480:106

Salt added to water lowers freezing point experiment
1396:82-84
Salt affects freezing action of water experiment 882:7
Salt affects freezing temperature of water experiment
984:46-50,71-76
Salt affects the grouping of water molecules into ice crystals experiment 1403:52-55
Salt does it—lift an ice cube with a string 291:46-47
Salt lowers freezing point of ice experiment 1435:10-12
Salt lowers freezing point of water; magic trick demonstrates 966:62-63
Salt lowers the melting point of ice experiment 867:22
Salt makes it harder for water to freeze experiment
905:128-129
Salt melts ice experiment 884:56-59
Saturated salt solution freezes at what temperature experiment 1526:41
Simple freezing and thawing experiments [Primary]
854:40-41
Strength of freezing water experiment 1126:14
Supercooled water freezes instantly when it touches ice
experiment 767:46
Temperatures of ice, ice water and ice brine vary experiment 884:60-63
Thermometer in tin can with ice cubes, water, salt experiment shows dew point 1439:52-55
Time needed to freeze water 277:12
Unfreezable water made from salt solution experiment
1271:24
Water expands and takes up more space when frozen experiment 1331:18
Water expands during freezing experiment 752:99;
1484:121
Water expands when frozen experiment with water, straw
and food coloring 1479:57
Water expands when frozen experiment 905:124-125;
1084:15; 1230:38-39; 1231:12-13; 1441:61
Water expands when it freezes experiment; water filled
test tube in freezer 1212:29
Water freezes fastest when it is warm or cold experiment
1403:54-55
What can ice do to glass experiment 766:unp.
What happens when water freezes 253:43-44
What happens when water freezes experiment 804:14;
851:48-49
What happens when water turns to a solid experiment
900:75
What happens when you put salt on ice experiment
1519:24
Why an iceberg floats 399:46
Why lakes don't freeze solid experiment 1439:42-43

WATER—FREEZING POINT
Svante Arrhenius's separation of substances into charged particles or ion 1133:2.010

WATER—HARD AND SOFT. See also **WATER—SOFTENERS**
Compare hardness of different water samples experiment
1396:131
Detergent in hard and soft water experiment 959:133
Does hard water clean as well as soft water 396:51-53
Drops of soap needed to make suds in different water
samples experiment 1396:131
Experiment to see hard water in action 611:19-21
Faucet water tested for hardness, how to do 1179:39
Hard and soft water—experiment 368:41-44

Hard water—experiment 585:94
Hard water made soft experiment using tap water and
washing soda 1435:39-41
Hard water makes soap curds 364:109
Hard water that wastes soap 85:52-53
Hard water to soft water experiment 947:23
Hardness test for 364:108
How much soap is needed to soften water experiment
1396:132-133
How soft is rain water experiment 1396:131
How to make and demonstrate hard and soft water
128:104-105
How to test 84:91-93
Investigating permanent hardness in water 78:46-47
Investigating temporary hardness in water 78:42-43
Lather test experiment 678:19-20
Permanent hard water and temporary hard water, how to
make experiment 1259:47-48
Show hard and soft water 122:64-69
Softening hard water experiment 1259:49-51
Test for hardness of water experiment 762:40-41;
1259:47-49; 1266:43; 1396:129-133
Testing for hard water experiment using tap water, distilled water, and soap 1435:35-38
Testing tap water and rain water for hardness experiment
1438:26-29
Water from faucets; hard or soft experiment 1028:25
Water-softening chemicals added to hard water make
more suds experiment 1396:131
What is hard water 281:24
What makes water hard experiment with Epsom salts and
detergent in water 1479:56
Where do bathtub rings come from experiment with hard
water and soap 1482:58-59

WATER—ICE. See also **WATER—FREEZING**
Demonstrate ways of preserving ice 147:58-59
How much heat to melt ice 147:59-61
Ice cubes—demonstrate expansion of water (Primary)
144:44-45
Ice cubes—demonstrate how shapes affect melting (Primary) 144:46-47
Ice cubes—demonstrate insulation 144:40-43
Ice is lighter than water 236:129
Ice melting experiment (Primary) 154:24-25
Melting ice experiments 147:45-53
Power of ice—experiments 132:25
Temperature of ice water is lowered by salt experiment
905:122-123
Water and ice experiment (Primary) 232:85
Why don't fish freeze in winter ice 101:16-17
Why is ice lighter than water 101:17-18

WATER—INSECTS. See also **INSECTS—WATER**
Aquarium for pond insects—set up and observe insect
life 414:119-120
Back swimmer, collect and observe 771:132-134
Caddis case; camouflaged case protects caddis larvae,
how to make 1182:23
Caddis fly—collecting and keeping caddis larvae
414:134-138
Collect and observe circle swimming pattern under different conditions 771:124-128
Collecting and observing water insects experiment
1183:64-65
Collecting water insects—how to make collecting net
and underwater torch 430:54-55

453

Creatures from a pond, how to collect and observe 810:54-56

Dragonflies—investigation of dragonfly's territory 414:122-126

Dragonfly model, how to make 1183:66

Dragonfly nymph—food color shows breathing system used for movement 414:126-127

Dragonfly nymph behavior studied in aquarium—how to 414:126-130

Dying insects—adding oxygen to water—experiment 484:91-92

Equipment needed 414:111-112

How to collect and keep water insects 821:54-55

Increased temperature of water effect on insect growth experiment 1097:48-50

Mayflies, collect and observe, how to 771:87-91

Mayfly nymphs—collection and observation of 414:117-119

Midges, collect and observe 771:141-143

Mosquito wrigglers—collection and observation of 414:114-116

Motor boats trail of oil on water surfaces; effect on aquatic insects experiment 1097:45-47

Net for pond dipping to collect water insects, how to make 1182:16

Respiration in water insects experiment 1097:98-100

Skimmer net, how to make from wire and pantyhose 1115:98-99

Springtails—springtails and water film—experiment 484:93

The big freeze—experiment to test survival in winter 484:93

Water bears—adventure 19—go bear hunting—water bears under microscope 403:68-70

Water boatmen—tests for reactions to position and to land—experiment 484:92

Water fleas (daphnia)—life cycle—observe/record changes in development 500:144-145

Water fleas (daphnia) collected and observed experiment 1402:68-71

Water fleas—adventure 3—one-eyed monster—water fleas under microscope 403:7-12

Water fleas—heartbeat and effect of chemicals—experiment 484:78

Water fleas—heartbeat and effect of electricity—experiment 484:79

Water fleas—investigation into the heartbeat of 420:48-49

Water fleas—investigation into the life span of the water flea 420:123-129

Water fleas—water film wall—experiment 484:79

Water fleas—water flea's heartbeat—experiment 484:78

Water fleas—water fleas' attraction to light—experiment 484:79-80

Water insect net, making 821:54

Water insects made of foil and paper clips float on water surface experiment 1310:16-17

Water strider model, how to make 1445:28-29

Water striders—collection and care of 414:113-114

Water striders, collect and observe, how to 771:83-86

Water top insects affected by oil and soap reducing surface tension experiment 1097:61-62

Why is water strider able to walk on water experiment 796:30

WATER—LEVEL

Finding out about water levels (Primary) 210:14

Fluid level changes in connected containers experiment 1515:45-50

Guess the water level experiment 909:20

Impossible straw that water stays in 909:21

Make water flow upward experiment 909:21

Measuring water levels with plants 146:60-61

Rules of fluid level change experiment 1515:51-55

Rules of temperature change experiment with fluid level changes 1515:45-55

Water level experiments 98:6-7; 132:4-6

Water seeks its own level 44:52-53; 281:28; 368:23-26

WATER—LIGHT

Flashlight in jar for underwater observation 476:37-38

WATER—LIGHT REFRACTION

Candle floats separate from its flame 538:52

WATER—PLANTS

Circulation of water from roots to leaves—demonstrate 294:34

How water is used by plants and animals 402:14-15

Soil and water experiment with plants 398:43-44

WATER—POLLUTION. *See also* **PHOSPHATES; POLLUTION—WATER**

Absorption—absorption experiment to clean water 363:79-80

Acid lake; how to make mini acid lake and buffer it experiment 1328:63

Acid rain effect on pH of water and soil experiment; chart given 1171:54-55

Acid rain effect on water plants and land plants experiment 1171:56-58

Acid rain effects on micro-organisms experiments 777:14

Aquatic ecosystems; measure factors necessary to sustain life experiment 978:70-72

Bacteria in drinking water experiment using potato slices 1331:83

Bacteria test for groundwater pollution experiment; how to do 1173:41-42

Beachcombing for litter experiment 1150:56-57

Biodegradability of a soap and of a detergent—experiment 78:73-75

Can we clean dirty water; make filter experiment 804:30

Checking water pollution—how to do 725:56-57

Chemical and thermal sterilization—demonstrate 363:81-82

Chemically polluted water detected by allium test using onions experiment 1060:118-119

Chromosome changes from water pollutants using onions experiment 1060:119-121

Clean water from dirty water experiment in water filtration 1240:4

Cleaning up an oil spill experiment 950:114-115

Decomposition of foods by microorganisms in septic tanks 78:98-99

Destroying the bacteria in water with chlorine experiment 934:29

Detergents, phosphates and pond life—effect on living things experiment 10:60-64

Determine chloride content of water experiment 934:19

Determine dissolved oxygen content of water experiment 934:20

Determine effect that polluting detergents can have on birds experiment 904:138-139

454

Determine effects of simulated oil spill on flora in aquatic environment 997:91-92

Determine the hardness of water experiment 934:18

Detrimental effect of phosphates in detergents on pond plants/animals experiment 1476:192

Dirty water test for pollutants getting into plants experiment, how to do 1414:14-15

Dispersing oil experiment 741:31

Dissolved oxygen content of body of water; how to measure experiment 978:69-70

Drinking water free from pollutants experiment 1427:66-71

Duckweed growth affected by water pollution experiment 1492:48-49

Effect of chlorination on microorganisms (yeast cells) 78:30-31

Effect of detergent on aquatic life experiment 934:38-39

Effect of fertilizer on algae growth experiment 950:36

Effect of industrial pollutants on behavior of convict Cichlid fish experiment 997:89-90

Effect of pollution on aquatic ecosystem experiment 978:73

Effects of fertilizers and sewage in aquatic environments experiment 1450:121-127

Effects of municipalities and industry on water—experiment 371:72-77

Effects of phosphate detergents on fish breathing rates experiment 950:58-60

Eutrophication or oxygen depletion of water in lakes and ponds experiment 978:75

Fertilizers in lake water cause overgrowth of plants experiment 1328:66-67

Filter to clean dirty water, how to make 1384:30

Filtering out some water pollution 400:10

Fresh water added to polluted water does not purify experiment 1441:67

Groundwater system model to demonstrate contamination of groundwater 1342:127-130

Heavy metal contamination in aquatic ecosystems experiment 1450:114-120

Household chemicals effect on germination and height of seedlings experiment 1004:2.012

How clean is the water experiment using coffee filters 1013:93

How does municipal pollution reduce dissolved O_2 content 371:75-77

How pollution affects wetland wildlife experiment 1492:88 89

Investigating coagulation and sedimentation 78:18-20

Investigating dissolved air in water 78:62-63

Landfills and leachates experiment 1234:68

Landfills cause water pollution experiment fish tank with pond/landfill area 1173:36-42

Lead in household water; how to test for project 969:92

Materials that filter faster will not clean water experiment 969:105-109

Measuring amount of dissolved solids and suspended solids in water experiment 934:17

Measuring relative turbidity of water experiment 934:15

Measuring the amount of air in water experiment 934:16

Measuring water pollution by observing organisms 507:1895

Measuring water pollution by recording plants and animals experiment 934:40-41

Measuring water pollution using indicator animals experiment 1134:6.007

Motor boats trail of oil on water surfaces; effect on aquatic insects experiment 1097:45-47

Natural cleaners replace chemical cleaners experiment 1063:374

Neutralizing capacities of body of water experiment 1233:55

Nutrient enriched waters and algae growth experiment 1450:135-142

Nutrients added to lakes and ponds cause water pollution experiment 1325:55-59

Oil slick, how to make and clean up experiment 1328:64-65

Oil spills are difficult to clean up experiment 1063:375

Oil spills are harmful to aquatic environments experiment 1453:32-34

Oil spills effect on plant growth experiment 714:69-70

Oil spills, effect of oil spills on aquatic ecosystems experiment 978:76-77

Organic matter pollution in soil and water experiment 950:75-76

Outreaching effect of small amount of pollution on stream and wildlife 904:140-141

Oxygen depletion of water by living organisms experiment 1134:6.010

Parts per million measurement experiment 1234:56

Permanent hardness in water 78:46-47

Pesticides and pollution of our water 371:77-80

pH test for groundwater pollution, how to do 1173:40

Phosphate amount in detergents; how phosphates affect sudsing experiment 1012:89-91

Phosphate detergents overfeed algae and harm pond life experiment 1331:81

Phosphate pollutant can be removed from water experiment 1325:60-64

Phosphates and fertilizers effect on water quality for animals experiment 978:73-74

Phosphates in detergents and their relationship to sudsing experiment 1013:88-89

Plant adaptation—how different types of plants adapt 371:53-58

Plant growth affected by pollution experiment using bleach and detergents 1073:88

Plant growth stunted by air and water pollution experiment 1362:11

Plants drink contaminated water; celery stalk and colored water experiment 1127:37

Plastics; effect of plastic garbage pollution on sea animals experiment 1479:34

Pleasure boating activities contribute to water pollution experiment 969:110

Pollution of the seas—oil and pollution; water affects living things in jars of water 10:70-74

Polluted water can get into food experiment using celery, water, food coloring 1228:28-29

Polluting detergents effect on bird feathers experiment 1479:33

Polluting the duck pond demonstration 827:112

Pollution experiments 330:85-97

Pollution in water carried into plants experiment 1067:60

Potato pollution detector—how to make 494:57

Purify water that is salty and polluted experiment 1441:65

Purifying sewage contaminated water experiment 934:27

455

Remove the mud—experiment 663:35

Removing oil from water experiment 1290:4-5, 1.4

Sampling—how to collect and check water 358:102-103

Sedimentation and effluent demonstration 363:73-75

Sewage and pollution—experiment with bird manure 10:50-54

Sewage, effects of aerobic activity on sewage experiment 978:77

Slipper limpets growth rate effected by particulate pollution in water 1225:36-37

Softening of water with polyphosphates 78:50-51

Speeding up the settling process experiment 934:32-33

Stream investigation for evidences of pollution experiment 1012:94-96

Streams; outreaching effect of pollution on stream and its wildlife experiment 1479:34

"Suspended particulate" in wild water experiment; how to test for 1328:56-57

Temporary hardness in water 78:42-43

Test water for chemical pollution 10:48-49

Tests for dissolved solids and detergents experiment 934:14

Thermal pollution and water life—effect of temperature change on goldfish and daphnia—experiment 10:65-69

Toxic metals in water—investigating 78:88-89

Toxicity of substances and toxic level of pollutants, how to determine 978:78

Toxicity test on invertebrates for effect of lawn fertilizers experiment 1267:81-83

Toxicology test for pesticides on water fleas experiment 950:88-89

Visibility, filtration and foam test of dirty water experiment 1134:6.009

Waste treatment-trickling filter waste treatment—how to make 363:87-88

Water animals and plants killed by heat pollution from industry experiment 1074:84-85

Water filter, making 934:30-31

Water pollution around your neighborhood—project 10:45-49

Water sample, describe and measure the pH experiment 934:12-1

Water top insects affected by oil and soap reducing surface tension experiment 1097:61-62

Water, how to filter 663:35

What is thermal water pollution experiment 1325:65-69

What lives in polluted water—experiment 10:55-59

WATER—PRESSURE. *See also* **CARTESIAN DIVER; PASCAL'S LAW**

A hot water bag lifts books 281:30

Aqua jet working model, how to build, patterns given 1022:19-24

Aqua pod car, working model, how to build, patterns given 1022:38-43

Balancing air pressure and water pressures in inverted containers 604:16-19

Bubblediver goes up and down experiment 1161:21

Can with holes experiment 719:37-38

Can with three holes demonstrates water pressure experiment 926:45-46

Cartesian driver—making 142:22

Cherry picker working model, how to build, patterns given 1022:58-62

Chicken working model pecks up water, how to build, patterns given 1022:13-18

Dams have to be thicker at the bottom than at the top experiment 1374:29

Depth changes water pressure; measure with manometer experiment 1020:41-42

Depth increases water pressure experiment with milk containers 1020:42-43

Depth of water in towers determines how fast water flows out experiment 1066:48-49

Detergent bottle and water experiment demonstrate pressure [Primary] 880:21

Diving project to explain the great pressure beneath the sea 877:25-29

Does deep water push harder than shallow water 589:42

Does water exert pressure experiment 851:45-46

Experiment with depth and water pressure power 132:15-17

Flowing fountain experiment 1066:46-47

Fountain demonstrates water pressure increases with depth experiment 1310:24-25

Fountain from plastic bottle and tube demonstrates water pressure 804:13

Fountain in a jar experiment with jars, straws and modeling clay 1436:46-48

Fountain in miniature shows water and air pressure—making 142:21

Fountain inside a bottle—making 150:38-39

Fountain working model, how to build, patterns given 1022:25-30

Funnels and rubber tubing demonstrate water levels experiment 804:13

Gypsy's brew 16:48-52

Height where water pressure is greatest experiment 1509:18

Holes in bottle of water demonstrate water pressure 965:27

How does water multiply pressure 126:19-26

In dams—depth of water and pressure on it—experiment 382:92-96

Increases with depth—experiment 150:32-33

Increases with depth—experiment 44:44-45

Leaky can experiment demonstrates 829:33-34

Lifting action of—demonstrate 385:19-20

Making a bottle rise and fall in water 150:10-11

Manometer; making to measure air and water pressure experiment 1020:37-40

Measure water pressure experiment using bucket, colored water and tubing 1436:43-45

Measuring water pressure 281:29

Ping-pong ball—mysterious 585:18-19

Plastic bottle with holes demonstrates 804:15

Popcorn kernels pop from water (steam) expansion 560:36-37

Pouring air into water 16:42-44

Power of water demonstrated with holes in can of water 1066:52-53

Pressure and depth experiment 741:35

Pressure increases with depth experiment 802:26

Pressure of water increases with depth demonstration 1165:35

Pressure of water increases with depth experiment using bottle with holes 1179:134

Pushing paper underwater without getting it wet 150:4-5

See water pressure; cans with holes experiment 900:63

Siphon clock working model, how to build, patterns given 1022:51-57

Siphons—demonstrate 142:19

Table tennis ball, strange antics 161:72-73

Twin tilter machine, working model, how to build, patterns given 1022:44-50

Underwater volcano—making 142:27

Upside down water glass trick 494:60

Water and candle in cup demonstrate water pressure 1063:340

Water depth affects water pressure; can with holes experiment 1290:3, 1.2

Water exerts pushing pressure in dams experiment 1120:12

Water flow—experiments 663:16-17

Water flows uphill—make the 'impossible fountain' 291:32

Water in plastic drink container with holes demonstrates water pressure 1243:21

Water level, how to make from garden hose 1436:40-42

Water power experiment with holes in can 909:25

Water powered rocket—making 132:18

Water pressure—demonstrate 291:33

Water pressure—experiments 56:42-46; 98:20-21; 106:19-21; 128:105-108; 281:26; 368:27-31; 693:51-52

Water pressure acts in all directions 44:42-43

Water pressure affected by volume experiment 1023:202-203

Water pressure changes with depth experiment 1123:14

Water pressure depends on depth of water experiment 1436:34-36

Water pressure depends on depth of water not container size or shape experiment 1436:37-39

Water pressure increases in deeper water experiment using plastic bottle 1256:11

Water pressure increases with depth 687:46

Water pressure increases with depth experiment; use bottle with holes 1212:16

Water pressure puzzles 1 and 2 399:38-39

Water pressure, shape and size experiment 281:28

Water pushes more when it is deeper 96:34-35

Water rises in an inverted bottle—demonstrate 291:78

Water rises in narrow tube 323:20-21

Water squirts from holes in can experiment to demonstrate water pressure 1331:30

Water stays in bottle under water demonstration 1230:18-19

Well—"wacky well" working model, how to build, patterns given 1022:31-37

What is water pressure; holes in cans experiment 900:29

Where is pressure greatest in bottle 678:24

Which hole will win 161:67

Which way does water run 281:27

WATER—PURIFICATION. *See also* **DISTILLATION; FILTERS; FILTERS AND FILTRATION; WATER—FILTERS AND FILTERING**

Can charcoal remove molecules from water experiment 831:38-40

Can organic chemicals be removed from water experiment 1325:82-86

Can water be purified by freezing experiment 831:33-34

Clean dirty water with activated charcoal experiment 1046:91-93

How is drinking water purified experiment 1325:76-81

Investigating effect of chlorination on microorganisms 78:62-63

Model of steps in purification plant 436:85

Purify water with aluminum hydroxide 122:128

Purify water with soil filter—how to 330:60-61

Purifying water—experiment 98:29

Solar still purifies muddy water experiment 1063:370

WATER—SALINITY

Seawater salinity experiments 359:80-81

WATER—SALTWATER. *See also* **SALTWATER**

Drop experiment shows sea water heavier than fresh water 772:35-36

Measure amount of salt in seawater 333:78-79

Salt water is more buoyant than fresh water 44:48-49

Salt water weighs more than fresh water 44:60-61

Seawater effect on different materials 342:12-13

Which is heavier, fresh or salt water experiment 852:30-31

WATER—SAMPLING

Water sampling below the surface 363:101

WATER—SECCHI DISC

Make one to measure clearness of water in ponds, lakes, streams 41:59-61

WATER—SOFTENERS. *See also* **WATER—HARD AND SOFT**

Change hard water to soft water 319:40-42

Investigating the softening of water with polyphosphates 78:50-51

Make hard water soft 26:120-121

WATER—SOLUTIONS

Solutions; disappearing solids in water experiment 959:37-38

Solutions; hot water solution experiment 959:38

Solutions; salt in water solution experiment 959:38

WATER—SPECIFIC GRAVITY

Balance and weight used to measure specific gravity 577:project #31

WATER—STEAM

Full steam ahead—metal cigar tube boat demonstrates power of steam 573:23

WATER—STREAMS

Stream table—how to build 400:56

Stream table activities 400:56-57

WATER—SURFACE TENSION. *See also* **SURFACE TENSION**

A brush of fresh air—experiment 162:47

Acting like Moses—breaking surface tension 205:67-69

Alcohol and oil on water surface experiment 722:19

Alcohol has less surface tension than water experiment 722:17

An oil drop engine—experiment 563:75-76

Anti-gravity trick—water on a string 669:30-31

Attract and repel experiments with sugar and soap 884:28-31

Attracting a matchstick with a lump of sugar 150:60-61

Beads of water and detergent glide over water surface experiment 1393:21

Bet you can hold water in a sieve 228:70-71

Bet you can make a dry spot in two liquids 228:69

Bet you can part a pepper sea 228:72

Blowing bubbles 77:30; 142:25

Blowing bubbles (Primary) 210:17

Blowing bubbles experiment 909:31

Blowing bubbles experiment; recipe for bubbles given and how to make frame 1331:26-27

457

Boat—camphor boat demonstrates 77:30-31; 146:13
Boat—propelling toy boat with detergent 360:52
Boat—soap boat experiment 281:35
Boat moves on water with soap behind it experiment 996:20-21
Boat moves with piece of soap demonstration 937:80-81
Boat of holes—experiments 563:83
Boat propelled by soap—making 186:69
Boats move with camphor, soap, or mothballs 291:30
Boats to test surface tension—how to make 167:106-108
Break the tension experiment 909:29
Bubbles—making them last longer 150:66-67
Can surface tension be disturbed; pepper and detergent experiment 900:65
Carton boat and detergent demonstrate 780:28-29
Castor oil test 291:25
Center the cork trick 202:117
Chase the pepper—experiment (Primary) 143:10-11
Circle of toothpicks come and go experiment 827:111
Coin test 291:22
Coins in glass of water and in alcohol experiment; compare results, data tables 1004:1.006
Compare surface tension of different liquids; balance to make for experiment, 914:9
Cork drifts to center of water in glass demonstration of surface tension 1079:74
Cork floats to highest possible point experiment 1230:60-61
Curving water experiment 909:26
Dancers dance on water experiment with mothballs 1007:7-9
Demonstrate difference in pulling power of water and alcohol experiment 905:40-41
Demonstrate why soap makes washing easier experiment 827:109
Detergent breaks surface tension of water experiment 1179:143
Detergent drop makes circular shape loop demonstration 722:18
Detergent weakens water's skin experiment with water, cornstarch and detergent 1331:24
Detergent; how it works experiment 914:14
Detergents keep oil and water from separating experiment 1482:4-5
Does water have skin 210:16-17
Does water stretch demonstration 884:20-23
Drop quarters into glass of water without overflowing it experiment 1007:2
Drop racing 162:48
Duco cement experiment to demonstrate 748:98-99
Elastic soap bubbles—experiment 563:121
Fill a cup beyond its rim experiment 836:20
Fishing game with paper clips experiment 1066:70-71
Fit ten pennies in a glass filled with water 548:5-7
Float a needle experiment 589:43; 909:27; 965:19
Float a paper clip on water experiment 836:21-22
Float metal on water to demonstrate surface tension 937:78-79
Floating basket—experiment 95:32-33
Floating odds 222:62-63
Food color and alcohol on water demonstrate 721:14
Fuller than full 16:49
Gauze over water bottle experiment 747:45-46
Glass filled with water to overflowing without spilling a drop experiment 1079:72

Glass with wet cloth over it demonstrates 721:16
Heaping and water's "skin" experiment 1159:13-16
Holding water in a strainer 281:35
Holes in the water—experiment 563:69-70
How can surface tension be disturbed; pepper and detergent experiment 900:15
How many dimes will it hold 281:36
How many drops of water on a coin experiment 748:100-101
How many quarters will glassful of water hold experiment 1007:1
Hula skirt paint brush and water experiment 906:132
Instant shipwreck experiment with metal sieve and paper figures 914:11
Investigating the motions of bits of camphor on water 604:60-63
Iron floats on water 186:69
Jar and cheesecloth—demonstrate 203:34
Jar lids with holes demonstrate 721:17
Keep the water out experiment 909:27
Leakproof sieve—a study of surface tension 205:62-66
Leaping lizards paper experiment 906:131
Looking at the surface skin of liquids 573:39
Looking at water drops 132:28
Loop of thread in bowl of water expands around soap experiment 1079:73
Magic matches experiment 909:30
Magic on water with sticks 95:35
Making perfect ink circles without a compass 150:70-71
Making water wetter 532:35
Marriage of the water drops—experiment 563:75
Metal paper clip floats on water experiment 1231:52-53
Molecules of water cling tightly together experiment 1331:25
Motorized paper fish moves on water experiment 1007:5-7
Moving match sticks 77:31
Moving pepper with a bar of soap 150:64-65
Moving water with a handkerchief 150:72-73
Needle floats on water experiment [Primary] 1002:14
Needle floating on water—experiment 35:29; 101:22-23; 126:57-60; 291:28-29; 722:16; 924:64; 940:3-4; 980:34; 1007:2-3; 1161:25; 1331:95
Needle on tissue on water surface floats experiment 709:33-34
No spills; water and bottle experiment 906:135
Observe skin of water in glass experiment 804:27-28
Observing the surface tension of water 173:10
Oil chaser—experiment 585:25-26
Oil spot moves when soap is added to water experiment 940:11-13
Oily smear—experiment 563:72
On the move—force in a water surface is strong 98:24-25
On the move—paper speed boats 98:24-25
Overfill glass with no spills experiment 937:76-77
Paper boat and detergent in water demonstrate 814:75-77
Paper circles on water demonstrates surface tension experiment 905:48-49
Paper clip floats on water experiment 926:109-111
Paper clip floats on water to demonstrate surface tension 1179:142
Paper clips—demonstrate 670:21
Pepper on water demonstrates 721:23
Pepper pot—pepper, water, detergent and sugar demonstrate 558:53

Pepper runs across bowl of water when detergent is added demonstration 1479:95

Pepper walks on water experiment 1271:25

Pepper trick 563:32-33

Pepper, toothpick and detergent demonstrate surface tension 924:63

Piece of cardboard and detergent demonstrate surface tension of water 1330:86-87

Plastic basket—waxed paper—paper towel demonstrate 721:15

Pond skater insect model, making to test surface tension experiment 914:13

Pour water down a string experiment 909:28

Race with a drop of water (Primary) 551:unpaged

Razor blade, paper clip—demonstrate 364:110-111

Screen floats on water—experiment 538:46

See and feel water's skin experiment 1509:6

Seeing is believing—needle and cork float on water 573:40

Several simple experiments demonstrate surface tension 898:8-9

Sewing pins in glass of water demonstrate surface tension 1256:20

Shape of the poured water—experiments 563:92

Silver skier—experiment 77:29

Simple experiment 670:33

Simple experiments to demonstrate surface tension 1288:18-19

Skin of a water drop experiment 935:50

Skin of water—experiment 96:30

Skin of water holds things together 96:32

Skin on water experiments; talcum powder, toothpicks, boat and soap 804:31

Skin-testing the skin of water—experiment 360:20

Soap as defogger—demonstrate 203:49

Soap boat experiment 906:134

Soap boats, making 909:30

Soap breaks surface tension experiment 935:51

Soap breaks tension on water surface and things sink experiment 1014:40

Soap cleans skin and breaks surface tension of milk experiment 1482:10-11

Soap engine balsa wood boat demonstrates surface tension experiment 1476:79-80

Soap lowers surface tension of water experiment with cardboard boat 1212:27

Soap molecules spread out on the surface of water—experiment 396:43-44

Soap motorboat experiment 900:16; 900:66

Soap tricks demonstrate surface tension 203:46

Soap weakens surface tension 44:64-65

Soapy smear—experiment 563:71

Soapy straw surprises experiments 685:12-13

Speed boat from a match—making 150:62-63

Spiral whirl experiment 906:133

Splitting up water—experiment 573:10

Stack water on a penny experiment 926:112

Strainer coated with oil holds water experiment 1079:75-76

Strainer mesh holds water in bottle experiment [Primary] 1002:15

Strength of surface tension experiment with bobbing frame and cork 914:8

Strength of surface tension experiment with glass of water 1441:61

Stretch a water surface—experiment 563:70-71

Stretching the skin of water experiment 909:29

Stretchy "skin"—experiments 663:18-23

Stubborn paper experiments 563:81-82

Styrofoam floats in center of glass of water 611:42-44

Sudsy water and thread demonstrate 721:13

Sugar attracts water—soap repels water 360:58

Sugar pulls toothpicks and soap pushes them apart demonstration 937:82-83

Surface tension—examples and explanations 577:project #18

Surface tension—experiment—numbers 1 and 2 585:28-29

Surface tension—experiments 281:34-35; 330:22-26; 368:56-60

Surface tension allows water to expand experiment—with paper clips 884:35-37

Surface tension and capillary action—experiment 291:21

Surface tension can support certain objects 44:62-63

Surface tension demonstrated with soap, talcum powder and plate of water 1079:78

Surface tension measurement 585:26-27

Surface tension motor boats experiment 914:7

Surface tension of water drops 236:130

Surface tension of water experiment 236:129-130

Surface tension power experiment 132:29

Surface tension tricks 600:50-51

Testing for surface tension—experiment 625:26

The floating and sinking pin trick 494:60

The lively soap—experiment 563:77-78

The loop test 291:31

The mysterious needle—experiment 563:73

The rising raisins—buoyancy and surface tension—experiment 205:74-76

The screen that holds water tension trick 600:54-55

The toothpick trick 288:8-9

Things can rest on water surface skin experiment 1509:7

Tie water in knots experiment 909:28

Toothpicks and detergent demonstrate surface tension 905:38-39

Triangle test for surface tension with straws and detergent experiment 914:6

Trick is a corker (glass of water and cork demonstration) 392:60

Various substances lower the surface tension of water—exp. 126:63-70

Water and alcohol with food coloring experiment 1066:62-63

Water balls—how to make 77:29

Water clings to string experiment 884:32-33

Water doesn't spill out of upside down bottle experiment 1079:76-77

Water drops; what happens to water drops on different surfaces experiment 1509:5

Water flows along string—experiment 95:34

Water has skin—curving water and floating needles—exp. 98:22-23

Water has skin—experiment 96:29

Water insects made of foil and paper clips float on water surfaces experiment 1310:16-17

Water molecules—demonstrate 162:50-52

Water pours along a string experiment 914:10

Water rises above edge of cup without spilling experiment 905:46-47

459

Water stream from a faucet—experiment 563:84
Water waltzers—soap and disc with cardboard dancers moves on surface of water 573:41
Water wonder with full glass of water 399:43
Water's invisible skin 106:25-28
Water's invisible skin 142:24
Water's skin 147:25
Water's skin experiments 959:33
Water's weird skin—a tall drop of water 162:46
Water, detergent and food coloring demonstrate 814:78-79
Waterproof bandage—making 161:70-71
Watertight sieve—making 142:26
Waxed wire floats on water—experiment 146:21
Weaken and strengthen surface tension experiments 884:24-27
Weakening surface tension experiment with talcum powder and detergent 914:6
Wetter water experiment 914:15
Wetter water experiments—detergent breaks surface film of water 563:71-72
Why does water form drops experiment 851:46-47
Why is water strider able to walk on water experiment 796:30
Why round drops of water—experiments 563:76-77
Wine glasses and water demonstrate 150:68-69

WATER—TESTING
Clarity testing 363:72-73
Clean water test (Primary) 154:26-27
Design a Secchi disk to measure cloudiness in a body of water 175:28-29
Test for chemical pollution in water 10:48-49
Test water, bogs, lakes, rivers, oceans—how to in ponds 175:33
Testing water for acidity or alkalinity 236:129

WATER—TOYS
Soap circle—making 366:167
Waterspout—making 366:165

WATER—TREATED
How does water treated in various ways affect animal life 402:87-88
Make a water treatment plant experiment 900:193-194

WATER—UNDERWATER OBSERVATION
Glass—making 9:66-67

WATER—USES
Community—discover water use in home, school, community, farm, industry and nature 363:39-47
Temperature control—demonstrate 363:70-72
Transportation by boats and ships—demonstrate 363:63-69

WATER—VAPOR. See also HUMIDITY
Air turns into water experiment using tin can filled with ice cubes 1415:25
Can of water, food coloring and thermometer demonstrate water vapor 1012:22
Change water into vapor—onions cooking demonstration 146:61
Clouds—making 295:48-49
Clouds—making (Primary) 232:84
Clouds and snowstorm—make your own 161:80-81
Condensation—make fog experiment 291:34
Condensation of water vapor—demonstrate 293:10-11
Condense water from air—experiment 146:60
Dew-point temperature experiments 767:26-27
Dispersing fog with heat 577:project #38

Evaporation of water experiment 1281:16
Fog in a bottle—making 95:26-27
Fun with fog 291:34
Gas to liquid 676:33
How does water get into air 400:65
How fog forms 44:70-71
How water becomes fog 295:41-42
Ice—making 112:18
Ice cubes in glass demonstrate vapor and dew experiment 996:24-25
Latent heat of vaporization of water experiment 1515:85-88
Make a cloud 507:1909
Make water vapor from drops (Primary) 541:26
Moisture in the air 400:65
Plants produce water vapor—simple experiment to show 597:36-37
Rain—make your own 360:67
Rain cycle—how water vapor behaves in air 319:33
Relative humidity; calculate the relative humidity experiment 1070:23
Steam—making (Primary) 232:83
Sweating jars experiments 563:72
Tin can and ice cubes demonstrate 804:14
Vapor in air 382:128-130
Warm air holds more water than cool air experiment 767:24
Water from air (Primary) 210:12-13
Water from air experiments 663:6-7
Water is always in the air—experiment 671:19
Water vapor condenses when cooled experiments 767:25-26
Water vapor cooling—experiment 672:17
Water vapor from air changes to solid ice experiment 1325:29-32
Water vapor in air measured by psychrometer experiment, how to make 1281:17

WATER—VIEWER
Coffee can viewer, how to make 1505:52
Snorkel viewer from plastic container, how to make 918:19
Underwater viewer—making (Primary) 535:57
Underwater viewer from plastic pipe and plastic wrap, how to make 1085:55
Wood and plexiglas viewer, how to make 1505:52-53

WATER—WASTE
Measure water waste from leaking faucet 333:74-75

WATER—WATER SPRAY
How it works 44:56-57

WATER—WEIGHT
Experiment to show if hot water weighs the same as cold water 126:119-128
Investigating the range of an emerging stream of water 604:76-79
Is water really heavy 126:13-16
Water can push 98:10-11
Weighing water in water 295:38
Weight and evaporation—experiment (Primary) 73:36-39
Weight of water—demonstrate 142:15
Which is heavier—experiment 280:22

WATER—WET AND DRY
Simple investigations into wet and dry (Primary) 518:5-39

WATER AND LIGHT
Light transmission—light goes through water 170:12-13

Show reflection and refraction—experiment 126:97-108

WATER ANIMALS

Amoeba—threatening an amoeba to show contraction—experiment 484:39

Amoeba's reactions to food, touch, chemicals, and light under microscope 771:17-20

Blackfly larva under hand lens, observe 771:73-76

Brine shrimp—stimulating weak brine fish—experiment 484:89-90

Bryozoa, observe food canal and growth under hand lens 771:67-72

Caddis fly for your aquarium, how to collect and observe 913:40

Caddis worms, collect and observe, how to 771:158-164

Comb-jellies—comb-jelly flashes—experiment 484:104

Crayfish, collect and observe behavioral responses in aquarium 771:164-169

Cyclops, collect, care for and observe behaviors, how to do 771:195-198

Daphnia, how to keep and feed 771:174-175

Daphnia; observe heart beat under microscope experiment 913:40

Do pond animals prefer dim light or bright light experiment 796:28-29

Dragonfly nymph; collect and observe change to dragonfly experiment 913:41

Expanding ice saves water organisms demonstration 1023:214-215

Freshwater sponge, collect and observe growth and water passage 771:152-157

Hand dip net for collecting water animals, how to make 1331:66

How to collect 41:65-72

Hydras—encouraging sexual reproduction—experiment 484:52-53

Hydras—how well can a hydra stick (stay attached)—experiment 484:52

Hydras—hydras and light—experiment 484:53

Hydras—nema to cyst explosion—experiment 484:53

Hydras—self repair of hydras—experiment 484:52

Insect populations are different in running and standing bodies of water 1096:96-101

King crabs—king crabs' water—reaction to change from salt to fresh water 484:102-103

Leeches—a leech's grip—experiment 484:65

Leeches—leech senses—experiment 484:65

Leeches, how to collect, care for and observe behaviors 771:178-183

Mussels, collect and observe young mussels under hand lens 771:60-64

Oil spills effect on shrimp experiment 1058:94-95

Ostracods, the seed shrimp, collect and observe 771:198-201

Paramecia—attracting paramecia to weak acid—experiment 484:41

Paramecia—hot/cold—show temperature they are comfortable with—experiment 484:40-41

Paramecia response to light, touch, chemicals under microscope experiment 771:24-26

Planarians, collect and observe feeding, response to light, regeneration 771:99-108

Planarias—contraction in planarias 484:64-65

Planarias—planarias and light—experiment 484:63

Planarias—planarias and water currents—experiment 484:63-64

Planarias—regenerating planarias 484:64

Pond skater insect model, making to test water surface tension experiment 914:13

Protozoa—making culture to test which one protozoas like 484:43

Protozoa—staining protozoa—how to 484:43

Rotifers, how to collect, care for and observe behaviors 771:201-206

Rotifiers—feeding patterns—experiment 484:71

Rotifiers—reviving rotifiers—experiment 484:70-71

Scuds, collect, care for and observe behaviors, how to do 771:185-187

Sea anemone—dividing anemones to test regeneration 484:104

Sea anemone—sea anemone taste tests—experiment 484:103

Sea anemone—sea anemones and light—experiment 484:103

Snails; how much food does water snail eat in a day experiment 796:29-30

Spirostoma—new growth of spirostomun—experiment 484:41

Spirostoma—shrinking stentors or spirostoma—experiment 484:42

Spirostoma—spirostomum's digestion—experiment 484:42

Sticklebacks, frogs and newts in aquarium, how to keep 913:39

Tools, methods and cultures for examining water animals under microscope 484:5-20

Toxicity of substances and toxic level of pollutants, how to determine 978:78

Trap for underwater night animals, how to make and use with light 1069:75

Water fleas, collect and observe behavior 771:169-175

Water measurer, how to collect, care for and observe behaviors 771:214-217

Water scavenger beetles, collect, care for and observe behaviors 771:206-209

Water tigers, how to collect, care for and observe behaviors 771:187-190

WATER BEDS

Which substance most effective to prevent bacteria in water beds experiment 997:121-123

WATER CLOCKS. *See also* **CLOCKS**

Chinese water clock, how to make with experiments 951:30-33

Chinese water clock—making 132:14

Circular water clock, how to make with experiments 951:63-71

Egyptian water clock, how to make with experiments 951:33-37

How to make 487:46-48; 543:58-60; 631:52-53; 640:34-36

How to make from plastic bottle 410:42-43

Making water clocks project 833:27-29

Simple to make with experiments 951:22-29

Sinking water clocks, how to make with experiments 951:37-40

Water clock shows that gravity causes water to fall at regular rate experiment 1031:16-17

Water powered clock—making 132:13

Water-wheel clock, how to make with experiments 951:53-63

461

WATER CONSERVATION
Bath or shower; which uses the most water experiment 1150:86-88

Can taking a shower help save electricity experiment 1012:71

Faucet test for leaks and dripping water experiment 1063:373

Faucets that leak waste water; how to measure leaking water project 1013:87

Flush toilets; amount of toilet water flushed per day experiment 1150:85-86

Flush toilets; how much water per flush experiment 1150:82-85

Flush toilets; reducing water used for toilet flushes experiment 1150:86-87

How much water do you use in your home project 1210:42-43

Leaks; checking for water leaks in home experiment 1150:80-81

Leaky faucets experiment to determine water loss in one day in home 1150:82

Leaky toilets experiment to see if toilet is leaking 1150:82

Minutes spent showering by family members project 1013:85

Record the amount of water used in your home experiment 1041:29

Recycled water used to water plants experiment 1323:72-76

Saving water resources ideas; what you can do 1234:117-122

Shower heads; how much water is used by shower heads experiment 1150:88-89

Shower versus bath and amounts of water used in each experiment 1328:53

Toilet check for leaking water experiment 1063:372

Toilet flushes charted for one week project 1013:86

Water use in the home project 1234:40-41

WATER CYCLE. *See also* **RAIN**
Demonstrate principles of water cycle experiment 978:63-65

Demonstrate 128:99-100; 236:128-129; 253:47-48

Demonstrate water cycle with bowl of water, cup and plastic wrap 1013:71

Demonstrate water cycle, how to do 1325:24-28

Evaporation in jars demonstrates 760:42-43

Experiment shows evaporation and condensation (Primary) 535:18

Experiment to demonstrate 368:9-15

Heat makes water evaporate 40:140-141

How fast water evaporates from different containers experiment 1516:28-29

How water goes into air—demonstrate 40:139-140

Make Wardian case to demonstrate water cycle in a miniature environment 172:128-131

Making a model of the water cycle project 833:146-147

Mini-water cycle experiment 1041:28

Miniature water cycle experiment with plastic bag over plant 1328:23

Natural water cycle using soil and plants in terrarium experiment 1336:66

Picture of with Navajo Indian rain dance sign 380:62-63

Plant in jar demonstrates 712:30-31

Simple demonstration of water cycle experiment 1362:13

Simple experiment demonstrates 132:31

Stomata on leaves let out water and take in carbon dioxide experiment 1075:48

Terrarium as miniature water cycle, making 898:10-11

Terrarium demonstrates water cycle in action experiment 1234:17

Terrarium, set up to demonstrate water cycle 884:12-13

Transpiration—demonstrate 146:47

Water cycle—evaporation, condensation—demonstrate 363:54-58

Water cycle column experiment using soda bottles 1527:70

Water cycle demonstration with plants in plastic bottle experiment 1384:7

Water cycle experiment with potted plant 950:11

Water cycle in a cup demonstration 998:152

Water, soil and plants added to water cycle column experiment 1527:70-71

Wind makes water evaporate 40:141-142

WATER DIVINING
Dowsing for water with tree branch, how to do 879:40

How to do 358:108-109

WATER DROP MAGNIFIER. *See also* **MAGNIFIERS**
Droplet lenses experiment 1257:43-44

How to make 494:58

Ice lens magnifier, how to make 941:111-114

Water drop microscope, making 890:108

Water lens, how to make 827:80-81

Waterdrop microscope, making 914:5

Simple microscope, how to make with water drop 1417:23

Water drop lens, how to make 1053:43-44; 1073:78; 1402:4-7; 1415:20-21

Water-drop lens, how to make from plastic tray and wrap 1331:91

Water drop magnifier from paper clip, how to make 1079:96-97

Water drop magnifiers, simple experiment 1163:26

Water drop magnifies print experiment 1285:16

Water drop simulates eye lens experiment 1405:38-39

Water magnifying lens, how to make 941:109-110

WATER DROPS
Breaking the surface tension of water experiments 1091:27-28

Do all liquids mix experiment with water drops 1124:8-9

Drop racing game on waxed paper, how to do 1063:154

How big are raindrops 586:16-18

Investigation into how droplets form 420:55-58

Leidenfrost's lifetime of droplets on very hot surfaces experiment 1133:7.003

Liquid molecules are attracted to one another experiment 1091:25-26

Making drops and experiment with drops 538:19-22

Shape drops make when they hit water experiment 1393:27

Size of water drops affected by cohesion and gravity experiment data tables 1004:3.009

Three ways of making water drops 1509:4

Viscosity of liquids experiment 1091:31

Water drop race, on board and waxed paper, how to do 1014:71

Water drops attracted to electrical charge demonstration 1230:30-31

Water drops attraction to liquids and solids experiment 1091:25-26

Water drops cling tightly to each other demonstrations 1230:26-29

Water drops like to stick together demonstration 1230:24-25

What happens to water drops on different surfaces experiment 1509:5

WATER DROPS—LENS

Lens from drop of water, making 902:78

Water drop makes things larger experiment 900:68

Water drop simulates an eye lens experiment 904:166-167

Water drop used to simulate eye lens experiment 1479:38

Water lens from nail and wire, how to make 1295:13

World through a drop of water—make a water drop lens 565:107-108

WATER FLEAS. *See* **MICROSCOPE; DAPHNIA**

WATER FOUNTAINS

How do fountains work experiment 1509:19

WATER JET ENGINES

Water-jet boat; demonstrate water jet power experiment 1165:19

WATER LENS

Water lens from plastic wrap and oatmeal box, how to make 1115:103

WATER LILY

Water lily model toy—how to make (Primary) 467:10-11

WATER MAGNIFIER

Can water act as a lens experiment 836:54-57

Handmade—plastic container (Primary) 535:58

Plastic wrap over cup of water magnifier, making 1019:22-23

Water magnifier from jar of water, how to make 1330:16-17

WATER OF HYDRATION. *See also* **CRYSTALS**

Change hydrate into anhydrous compound 122:46-48

The meaning of "anhydrous"—experiment 585:101-102

WATER POLLUTION. *See* **WATER—POLLUTION**

WATER POWER. *See also* **TURBINES; WATER-WHEELS**

Experiments 368:32-35

Hydraulic marble machine—making 347:64-65

Model grist mill works, how to make 1115:93-96

Pelton wheel—how to make an experimental Pelton wheel 347:79-81

Power of rain, streams, waves and moving waters—experiment 132:19-24

Waterwheel—how to make 330:56 57

Waterwheel lifts weight, make from plastic bottle, and knitting needle 1073:27

WATER PRESSURE. *See* **WATER—PRESSURE**

WATER PURIFICATION. *See also* **WATER—PURIFICATION**

Different methods of purifying water, how to demonstrate 978:80-81

WATER SCALE

Water scale—making 161:68

WATER SCOPE

Bucket and plastic scope 558:80-81

Build water scope for underwater observation 1313:107, 109-111

Can covered with plastic wrap scope, making 796:24-25

How to make 234:44-45; 285:37-39; 312:7-10

Milk carton water viewer, making 832:64

Plastic carton scope, how to make 943:14

Quart size detergent bottle scope—how to make 476:35-37

Underwater viewer for ponds, how to make 1146:31

Underwater viewer from plastic pipe, how to make 1134:3.006

Water scope from juice can and plastic, how to make 1188:9

Water scope from plastic bucket, making 885:23-24

Water scope from plastic pail and plastic wrap, how to make 1331:66

Water scope, making 732:58-59; 772:48-50

Water viewer from plastic pipe, how to make 1069:92

Water viewer from tin cans, how to make 947:24-25

WATER SOFTENERS. *See also* **WATER—SOFTENERS**

Water softener experiment with bath salts made from washing soda/perfume 1179:38

WATER SUPPLY—HOUSES

Standpipe—need for demonstration 610:44

Water supply in houses—experiment to demonstrate 610:42-43

WATER SUPPLY—ON SPACECRAFT

Experiments to demonstrate water supply on a spacecraft 564:75

WATER TABLE

Model in aquarium to show destruction and shrinking of water table experiment 1476:193-194

Water table—demonstrate 173:30

Water table—experiments 368:20-22

Working model of a water table 532:58-59

WATER TREATMENT PLANTS

Can organic chemicals be removed from water experiment 1325:82-86

How is drinking water purified experiment 1325:76-81

Wastewater cleaned and reused experiment use dirty water/coloring/bleach 1240:53-54

WATER TRICK

Gypsy mystery—experiment 563:34

WATER TURBINES

How to make a water turbine motor and alternator 43:32-43

Make a water turbine 419:23; 573:17

WATER VAPOR. *See* **WATER—VAPOR**

WATER WHEELS

Cardboard paddle wheel shows that moving water moves things 322:8-9

Make your own 678:23

Model water wheel—making 267:9-11

Simple water wheels—making 227:6

Water-powered wheel—making 132:7; 223:8-9

Water-wheel clock, how to make with experiments 951:53-63

Water wheel from paper plates—making (Primary) 200:28-29

Water wheel—making 128:108; 280:50-51; 330:56-57; 363:89-91; 368:33-35; 385:41-42; 664:37; 909:125

Water wheel—making (Primary) 70:44-45

Water wheel motor and alternator—how to make 43:32-43

Water wheel rock rumbler—how to build (Advanced) 347:70-77

WATER WRITING

Writing on water 71:55-58

WATERCLOCKS. *See* **WATER CLOCKS**

WATERFALL ILLUSION

Experiment 229:90

WATERMARKS

Do watermark writing 202:74

Watermarks on stamps and make your own watermark 550:31-33

WATERMELONS

Plant and grow watermelon seeds, how to do 1178:41

WATERPROOFING

Cloth—how to 321:29

Commercial fabric waterproofing agents tested for effect/durability experiment 1295:122-123

Making cloth waterproof experiment 1162:23

Simple waterproofing experiment with five different materials 1106:9

Waterproof tests on different materials demonstration 1113:21

What makes a duck waterproof—experiment with feathers or brown bags (primary 488:unpaged

WATERSPOUT

Waterspout demonstrated with plastic bottles, how to make 1115:82-83

WATERWAYS

Waterway for boats model, how to build from cardboard boxes, paints 1460:6-7

WATERWHEELS

Aluminum pie plate waterwheel experiment 1063:305

Construct waterwheel to demonstrate work they do experiment 834:66-67

How to make from wood 429:94-98

Hydroelectric generator with paddle wheel experiment 1126:28-29

Make from yogurt carton and knitting needle 804:26-27

Make miniature waterwheel from thread spool, clay and pencil experiment 1509:20

Make your own waterwheel from cardboard, thread spool and straw, make 1256:28-29

Making a horizontal waterwheel, set up waterwheel experiments 606:68-79

Making a vertical waterwheel, setting up waterwheel, and experiments to try 606:50-67

Making waterwheel contraptions-mechanical music maker, bubble blowing device 606:80-91

Mass of falling water affects energy it produces as it falls experiment 1399:56-59

Miniature paddle steamer from cork and plastic blades demonstration 1509:21

Model grist mill works, how to make 1115:93-96

Model waterwheel from pencil and plastic plate experiment 1066:75

Motorized water wheel experiment; how to build water wheel 1304:28-29

Oatmeal box water wheel, how to make 1056:24

Pinwheel and running water demonstrates 780:50-51

Plastic bottle working model of water wheel, making 1024:8-9

Plastic lid waterwheel—making 756:27

Sand wheel—how to make 699:15

Simple water wheel, how to make from wood 1423:25

Simple water wheel experiment, how to make 1446:35

Water lifts things experiment; make cardboard wheel 1230:50-51

Water powered wheel produces energy experiment 1269:56

Water wheel—making 741:39

Water wheel from cork and plastic spoons, how to make 1161:29

Water wheel from plastic bottle, clay, tubing, blades, how to make 1030:13-15

Water wheel from plastic lid and straw, how to make 1393:17

Water wheel model moves by water power experiment 1028:116-117

Water wheel model, construct as an example of wheel and axle machine 1400:46-47

Water wheel that will lift a load project 1423:26-27

Water wheel demonstrates kinetic energy experiment, how to make 1377:25

Water wheel from cardboard, knitting needle and clay 1318:15

Water wheel from plastic bottle, knitting needles and corks, how to make 1380:38-39

Water wheel from yogurt cup and cork—making 587:47

Water wheel lifts weight, make from plastic bottle and knitting needle 1073:27

Water wheel made from plastic bottles, straws raises bucket of water experiment 1310:26-27

WATT, JAMES

Who invented the steam engine project 1525:27-31

WAVES. *See also* **OCEAN WAVES**

Action of waves—demonstration 299:6-7

Action of waves breaking changes the coastline demonstration 840:20

Action of waves on the beach—demonstrate 299:4-5

Activities with waves 236:102

Bottle of waves—making 236:102

Can ocean waves be used to generate electricity experiment 997:76-77

Conservation of momentum, wave transmission—experiment 585:38-39

Density affects water movement demonstration 1023:196-197

Depth of waves 93:32-33

Diffraction of water waves experiment using ripple tank 1153:81-85

Diffraction of waves experiment 1082:133-135

Effect of wave height and length on coastlines experiment 1342:124-126

Erosion of beach sand by waves experiment 1290:54, 4.1

Forward movement of wave energy demonstration 1405:85

Interference bands or fringes in waves experiment 1082:135-138

Interference patterns of water waves in ripple tank experiment 1153:86-97

Make waves in a jar 580:unpaged

Making waves 93:26-28

Making waves in the bathtub experiment 877:40-43

Making waves in your room experiment 877:44-47

Model shows how waves can be used to produce electricity experiment 1134:7.002

Motion of a wave—demonstrate 93:23-24

Motion of water waves demonstration 1023:188-189

Movement of water molecules in waves demonstration 1405:84-85

Movement of waves—observe and illustrate 299:12-13

Observing waves in an aquarium experiment 877:48-52

Periodic waves experiments using ripple tank 1153:76-79

Reflection of water waves similar to reflection of light experiment 1153:73-74

Refraction waves experiment using ripple tank 1153:74-76

Ripple tank demonstrates motion of waves in two dimensions, how to build 1153:70-73

Ripple tank to generate straight line waves experiment, how to do 1082:130-133

Shape of a wave, drawing 687:44

Soda bottle, oil, water and small ship demonstrate stormy seas 887:45-46

Temperature affects motion of water experiment 1023:194-195

Toy wave machine experiment 960:22

Transverse and longitudinal waves on a Slinky experiment 1155:30-32

Transverse wave motion experiments 563:187-188

Tsunami waves caused by ocean earthquake experiment 1441:45

Water molecules movement in waves demonstration 1023:190-191

Water waves—project with 691:104-107

Wave bottle to demonstrate waves, making 832:73

Wave energy forward movement demonstration 1023:192-193

Wave generator, making 647:122

Wave machine—making 723:23

Wave machine—making (Primary) 535:77

Wave machine to study wave motion, how to make 1247:30-31

Wave machine to study wave motion 472:2221

Wave maker—jar, oil, water and blue coloring—how to do 558:55

Wave shapes demonstration 1290:4, 1.3

Wave tank—making 691:101-104

Wave tank demonstrates diffraction—how to do 642:70-71

Wave tank demonstrates interference—how to do 642:73-75

Waves at the shore—demonstrate 93:29-31

Waves in clear dish of water demonstrate wave motion and sound motion 1155:23-24

Waves on a rope experiment 1155:25-27

Waves on a Slinky experiment 1155:28-32

Wind and wave action—experiment 363:158-159

Wind and waves—experiment 243:58-59

Wind produces water waves at sea demonstration 1023:186-187

Winds cause surface currents demonstration 1023:198-199

WAXES

Warm goo—experiment 259:24-29

Wax sculptures—how to make 77:20

Waxes—experiments 17:17-20

WEATHER. See also AIR; RAIN; SNOW; WINDS

Activities with weather and climate 236:162-164

Air—evaporation experiment 72:31

Air and weather experiment (Primary) 541:8-9

Air has weight and exerts pressure experiment 1311:10-11

Air masses and fronts demonstration 1003:56-57

Air pressure—how to make a barometer 91:66-69

Air pressure and weather predictions experiment 1003:58-59

Air pressure changes in Earth's sea of air experiment 1516:12-13

Air vaporization—experiment 72:31-32

Anemometer, wind speed gauge, how to make 1311:28

Aneroid barometer—making 9:98-99

Calculate the speed of sound and lightning 175:77

Cloud formation—build a cloud chamber 293:12

Cloud formation—experiment 12:86-90

Cloud formation—making clouds 293:13

Clouds, direction and speed experiment—nephoscope making 9:96-97

Cold front experiment; observe collision of cold and warm air 1447:61-64

Cold front movement demonstrated with window pane box 532:70

Convection cycle currents in air experiment, make spiral air current detector 1311:21

Convection cycle of heated and cooled air experiment 1447:27-30

Cookies and the effect of weather on them experiment 1238:109-110

Coriolis Effect and weather experiment 748:141

Daily weather record chart—making 748:136

Define and observe radiation, convection and conduction with popcorn ex 1447:12-17

Dew and frost formation—experiment 175:61

Dew point experiment 182:28-29

Difference between snow and sleet experiment 1003:83-84

Eclipse of Sun—demonstration 12:53-56

Effect of weather on plant and animal life experiment 978:138

Effects of cube shaped Earth on climate/weather patterns/flora/fauna experiment 997:159-162

Elements and signs of weather 234:94-95

Environment and ecology ideas for science projects 1447:123-127

Factors of weather and effect on our weather experiment 978:141-143

Fog—problems caused by 298:14-15

Getting water out of the air 30:28-29

Heat absorption of white and black colors in the sun (Primary) 327:18-19

Heat and weather—measure temperature difference in air, land, water (primary 541:10-12

Hill's effect on climate—observe and record 301:23-26

Homemade rainstorm 30:30

Hot humid days are more uncomfortable than hot dry days experiment 852:40-41

How accurate is the weather bureau 333:64-66

How hot do you feel, air temperature and relative humidity heat index 1003:114

How water goes into the air 30:27-28; 72:30

How winds are made 30:24-25; 72:26-29

Humidity—absolute humidity—demonstrate 295:43-44

Humidity—hygrometer to measure—making 91:62-65

Humidity—relative humidity—making a hygrometer to test 253:59-61

Humidity—water dissolves in air 295:42-43

Humidity indicator experiment with cobalt chloride, paper and paint 1244:34

Humidity; measure with Stevenson screen and wet and dry bulb thermometers 1311:43

Indicators—simple indicators of weather—making 119:164-173

Interaction of warm and cold air masses—demonstrate 253:49-50

Isotherms in the classroom experiment 1447:7-11

Land (soil) and sea (water) absorb heat at different rates experiment 1086:11

Lightning and imitation thunder clouds—making 172:155-158

Lightning demonstration—experiment 12:50-52

Make water vapor from drops (Primary) 541:26

Maximum/minimum thermometer—making 9:102

Metric wind chill chart and customary unit wind chill chart 748:44

Motion booklet shows meeting of cold front and warm front produces rain 1063:280-283

Occluded front experiment; observe sandwiches of cold and warm air 1447:65-67

Oxygen; what fraction of air is oxygen experiment with rusting steel wool 1516:22-25

Precipitation records of Earth 1003:69

Predicting weather with air pressure experiment 767:72

Protection against weather—12 ways 298:8-9

Psychrometer—making 9:92-93

Rain gauge—making 9:94-95; 293:9

Rainfall—how to measure 40:135-137

Rainfall—making a rain gauge to measure 253:62-63

Rainstorm, homemade—making 72:33

Recording and predicting the weather 175:78

Recording weather—how to keep a daily chart of weather 175:77-78

Relative humidity computation computer project 1021:158-160

Relative humidity table 1003:113

Snow and ice experiment 30:31; 72:34

Spectroscope separates light into colors of rainbow experiment, how to make 1516:19-20

Storm in a cake pan—making 694:93

Sun is more powerful at the equator than at the poles experiment 1311:20

Sunshine recorder—making 12:44-49

Temperature chart of daily weather (Primary) 327:10-11

Temperature humidity index 1003:115-116

Temperature inversion experiment; observe how warm air traps smoke particles 1447:68-70

Temperature of the air experiments 1086:10

Temperature scale conversions computer project 1021:156-157

Temperature; measuring temperature using a Stevenson screen experiment 1311:42

Thunder and lightning—measure how far away 295:51-52

Tracking a storm experiment 1136:26

Tracking storms of the season; ideas for projects 1447:107-110

Visibility chart—how to make 381:63-66

Warmest time of day temperature experiment 1516:46

Warmth of air, ground and water—temperature readings 327:10-17

Water evaporation into air (Primary) 541:22

Water is in the air—experiments (Primary) 327:20-35

Water temperature experiment 719:31-32

Weather analysis chart 978:130

Weather chart—keeping a 400:63

Weather chart—making 298:12-13

Weather chart patterns 767:131

Weather charts, making 874:220

Weather clue chart—making 234:98

Weather forecasts—how to chart 298:18-19

Weather graphs, making 874:221

Weather house predicts weather experiment; make from cardboard, wood, hair 1480:161

Weather instruments and a weather station—making 128:92-96

Weather maps—using 253:66-67

Weather prediction chart to list weather data 860:184-186

Weather recording and reporting more efficient on a computer project 1021:161-164

Weather related heat and wind-chill warnings computer project 1021:99-101

Weather signs and sayings—how to demonstrate if true 298:20

Weather vane—making 9:68-69; 41:146; 234:99

Weather watch prediction activity [Primary] 758:26

Weathering of rocks 382:103-107

What is a cold front 900:111-113

Wind chill factor experiment with thermometers and fan 1012:19

Wind chill factor when wind blows across body of water experiment 1447:50-55

Wind chill table 1003:110

Wind direction—experiment 40:130-132

Wind direction—making a wind vane 253:64-65

Wind direction—recording by graph 298:11

Wind direction shown by wind vane—how to make (Primary) 541:15

Wind gauge—making 9:100-101

Wind speed—measure by anemometer 40:132-134

Wind speed measured by anemometer—how to make (Primary) 541:16-17

Wind station, how to make from plywood, dowel, tubing and fasteners 1179:126-127

Wind vane—making 9:68-69; 298:10

Wind-chill factor computer project 1021:142-145

WEATHER BALLOONS

The pressure of air—experiment 243:14-15

WEATHER FORECASTING. *See also* **WEATHER INSTRUMENTS**

Chemical weather glass—making 172:124-127

Clouds used to predict weather computer project 1021:146-148

Collecting weather data, how to do 865:93-99

Doll weather forecaster—making 291:226

Factors of weather as related to weather forecasting 978:143-145

Forecasting weather by clouds and winds chart 694:66-67

Instrument shelter—simple—how to make 767:144

Long-term weather observations and graph project 1447:94-98

Operate a weather station, how to do 900:98-99

Satellite pictures from newspaper show cloud/weather patterns experiment 1447:99-101

Seaweed and pinecone forecasters 588:44

Unusual ways to predict and explain weather 900:102-103

Use National Weather Service data to make your own forecast project 1447:102-104

Weather almanac—computer project 584:91-93

Weather data station for long term weather observations, how to make 1447:105-106

Weather forecasting by cloud type table project 715:119-120

Weather forecasting equipment—how to make 234:98-99

Weather history used to predict weather computer project 1021:152-155

Weather house—how to make 172:117-122; 186:22-23

Weather house to depict weather—making 128:95

Weather man who changes colors—making 146:30-31

Weather picture—making 186:23

Weather picture—using chemicals to show wet and dry—making 87:85

Weather station—how to build barometers—hygrometers—anemometers 767:137-144

Weather station and weather instruments; how to make and set up experiment 978:145-152

Weather station in the yard-barometer, rain gauge, anemometer, how to make 588:46-49

Weather station, how to make 749:10-11; 830:58-65

Wet bulb thermometer, how to make 865:86

What is best source for predicting weather 900:100-101

Wind direction and pressure used to predict weather computer project 1021:149-151

Wind sock, making 865:80

WEATHER INSTRUMENTS. *See also* **ANEMOMETER; BAROMETERS; WIND VANES**

Anemometer, wind speed detector, how to make 830:61-62

Make an anemometer 564:3

Rain gauge, how to make 830:62-63

Sunlight intensity sensor, how to make 830:63-64

Wind direction indicator, how to make 830:58-61

Windsock—making 749:10

WEATHER PREDICTIONS

Aching corns and bad weather explanation 1439:116-117

Forecasters of bad weather; ants, pinecones, sheep wool, frogs 1439:118-120

Why birds roost before a storm explanation 1439:114-115

WEATHER STATION

Barometer, rain gauge, thermometer, wind sock, how to make 1430:19-21

Barometer, thermometer, wind vane, anemometer, hygrometer, making 1003:94-119

Barometer, wind gauge, dry and wet bulb thermometer, how to make 898:5-6

Box with slotted sides; Stevenson Screen Weather Station box, how to make 1086:30-31

How to set up with homemade equipment 1063:434-452

Setting up a weather station project, how to do 1296:2005

Stevenson screen for shade temperature readings, how to make from wood 1480:155

Weather station, how to make 1237:8-10

Wind vane, rain gauge and barometer, making 1016:14-17

Wooden weather station, how to make 1042:44-45

WEATHER VANES. *See also* **WIND VANES**

Balsa wood weather vane, how to make 1149:31

Cardboard weather vane, how to make 1136:8-9

Drinking straw weather vane, making 1003:104-105

Fish vanes from cardboard, how to make 854:21

How to make 543:42-43; 779:62

How to make from bottle, knitting needle and cork 1388:28

How to make from broom handle, wood strips, metal dish 1237:86-89

How to make from cardboard 770:117

How to make from clothes hanger and cardboard experiment 947:38

How to make (Primary) 523:20-21

Pencil, straw, and paper vane—making [Primary] 508:11; 751:28-29

Weather vane shows direction of wind experiment, how to make 1211:13

WEATHERING. *See* **EROSION**

WEAVING

Belt of knotted cord—how to make 325:unpaged

Cardboard weaving—how to do 732:156-157

Eager weaver machine—how to make 410:34-35

Straw weaving, how to do 854:113

Twig weaving, make from twigs, grasses and yarn 1114:136-137

Weave 'thread'—make a piece of cloth (Primary) 326:22-23

Weave a piece of woolen cloth—making loom, stringing yarn weaving 26:79-82

Weaving a place mat 545:14-17

WEAVING—PLANTS

Grass weaving—how to do 749:82-83

Weed weaving—how to do 483:66-67

WEBS. *See also* **SPIDERS—WEBS**

Spider web collection 532:60

WEDGES. *See also* **INCLINED PLANE**

Glamorizing the wedge—comment 563:186-187

Nails and knives—experiment 281:52

What is a wedge experiment 902:183-184

Working with wedges 180:33

WEEDS

A weed's way—experiment 268:77-81

Casts of weeds, how to make using plaster of Paris 1071:100

Characteristics of dandelions experiment 1063:252

Dandelions—demonstrate why so hardy and undesirable in lawns 381:110-113

Dandelions; projects with dandelions, how to do 1524:18-19

Field studies: dandelion distributions computer project 584:59-50

Good plants in wrong places—make weed collection cookbook 380:70-71

How to plant a weed 264:85

Investigate kinds of weeds in a vacant lot 233:23-24

Natural weed control for lawns project 969:46-47

Size, depth and width of fibrous root system of common weeds experiment 1060:40

Sun pictures of, how to make 646:8-10

Weeds affect growth of plants experiment 1254:29

WEEDS—GERMINATION

Soil collected from different places will grow plants from weed seeds (primary 481:29

Weed seeds, growing experiment 918:10

WEEDS—WEED KILLERS

Effect of herbicides on plants experiment 950:101-102

Over growth induced by chemicals 577:project 92

WEIGHING MACHINES

Weighing machine made from wood, cardboard, wire and paper, how to do 1512:8-9

WEIGHT. *See also* **MEASUREMENT**
  Balance scale—simple—making 759:15
  Chart of the weight of 100 pound person on the Moon
    and the planets 1157:36
  Do things weigh the same when they are wet experiment
    [Primary] 744:17
  Experiment—balance from wooden rod, string, cup
    hooks, paper plates (primary 529:18-33
  Investigation into sensing weight 420:69-70
  Make a weighing machine from wood, cardboard, wire,
    and paper 1512:8-9
  Make and calibrate a weighing machine 178:56
  Measure heights and weights of kids in your class; graph
    results experiment 794:27-28
  Measure volume and weight of stones using cup of water
    experiment 1256:15
  Measuring weight—a weight guessing game 304:12-13
  Measuring with coat hanger balance (metric) 357:6
  Objects in water have different weight than in air experi-
    ment 1405:93
  Paper cup used to weigh things in water—experiment
    201:24-25
  Sensitive balance detects weight of the lightest objects ex-
    periment 1031:24-25
  Simple scales, how to make 1248:8-9
  Spring balance scale experiment 1521:20-21
  Spring scale—making 210:28
  Spring scale from paper plate—making 200:22-23
  Spring scales—making simple to measure weight (metric)
    357:7-8
  Very quick way to lose weight 392:22-23
  Water reduces weight of object experiment 1230:44-45
  Ways to measure weight-by angle of string pitch of
    sound 12:95-98
  Weighing and balancing—experiment 71:14-16
  Weighing machine from rubber band and cup, how to
    make 1380:29
  Weighing machine from rubber bands—making 754:12-13
  Weight and mass—computer project 584:101-102
  Weight of various masses when weighed on Moon's sur-
    face experiment 1502:44-45
  Weightlessness—how to see 585:34
  Weightlessness in space demonstration 1394:210-211
  Weighty mystery—weight of displaced water—experi-
    ment 399:33
  What are the weights of X, Y and Z—how to make
    mobile to demonstrate 577:project 71
  What is proper weight for a grown person 402:71-72
  Which nails are heavier in water—iron or aluminum ex-
    periment 721:19
WEIGHT LIFTING
  Weight lifting experiment 563:185-186
WEIGHTLESSNESS
  Weightlessness in space experiment with plastic bottle
    space capsule 1478:34
  What causes feeling of weightlessness experiment
    1399:52-55
WEIGHTS AND BALANCES
  Density of different materials—demonstrate 295:32
  How much does air weigh 295:37
  How much of the food you eat is water 295:35
  How sticky are different liquids 295:29-30
  Paper towel soak up—experiment 295:31
  Simple scales, how to make 1248:8-9

  Some density investigations 295:35-37
  Weighing solids in liquids 295:39
  Weighing water in water 295:38
  Weights and balances—make your own 748:41
WEIGHTS AND MEASURES—VOLUME
  Simple concepts of volume (Primary) 527:1-33
WELDING
  Electric welding and cutting—experiment 127:32-34
  Welding it together 544:42-43
WELLS
  Artesian well model demonstrates how it works experi-
    ment 965:21
  Gas pressure can pump a liquid experiment 1081:15
  Water bucket for well—how to make 363:99-100
  Water from aquifer fills well if surrounding sand is kept
    wet experiment 1331:60
  Well and aquifer experiment, how to do 1234:101
  Well that draws water from a small aquifer experiment
    1331:60
  Wind power and winch lifts bucket in model well experi-
    ment 1334:18-19
WET BULB. *See* **HYGROMETER**
WET CELL BATTERY. *See also* **BATTERIES**
  Experiment 391:50-54
  Making a lemon wet cell 608:45-46
WETLANDS
  Animal tracks around wetlands; make plaster casts experi-
    ment 1492:32-33
  Aquarium to study small wetland animals experiment,
    how to do 1492:58-59
  Delta formation experiment 1074:32
  Game; endangered wetlands game, how to make
    1492:90-91
  Grow some plankton experiment 1492:28
  Insect-eating plants from bogs or swamps, how to grow
    experiment 1074:24-25
  Marsh plants investigations project 1074:78
  Observe leeches behavior in jar of water with plants ex-
    periment 1492:70-71
  Observe snails' behavior in aquarium experiment
    1492:72-73
  Projects to do to protect wetlands 1074:115-121
  Raise damselfly nymph experiment, how to do 1492:80-
    81
  Salt run off from highways destroys plants in wetlands
    experiment 1074:83
  Sediment trap shows how wetlands filter water in streams
    and rivers experiment 1492:22-23
  Soil from dried up marsh area contains life experiment
    1074:66
  Spore prints from wetland mushrooms experiment
    1492:50-51
  Testing water for oxygen, carbon dioxide and pH in
    marshes experiment 1074:22
  Water animals and plants killed by heat pollution from in-
    dustry experiment 1074:84-85
  Water holding capacity of different soils experiment
    1492:20-21
WETLANDS—POLLUTION
  Duckweed growth affected by water pollution experi-
    ment 1492:48-49
  How pollution affects wetland wildlife experiment
    1492:88-89

WETTING AGENTS. *See* **DETERGENTS; SOAP; SURFACTANTS**

WHALES
What is in a whale's spout experiment 1397:80-83

WHEAT. *See also* **FLOUR**
Frumenty—how to make 662:42
Gluten from flour experiment 1238:90-91
Gluten in action in popovers experiment 1238:93
Grow some wheat seeds experiment 739:33
Growing problems—the wheat game—making 607:55-57
Growing wheat plant 26:99-100
Wheat seed experiment to show white flour and brown flour 26:96-98
Why not eat flour raw experiment 1238:87

WHEAT BERRIES
How to plant and grow indoors 1178:28-29

WHEATSTONE, CHARLES
His kaleidophone—how to make 2:76-79

WHEEL AND AXLE. *See also* **SIMPLE MACHINES— WHEELS AND AXLES**
What is wheel and axle experiment 902:165-166
What type of machine is the pencil sharpener experiment 902:167-168

WHEELS. *See also* **SIMPLE MACHINES—WHEELS; WATERWHEELS; WINDMILLS**
Belt drive wheels experiment 756:22-23
Book spins on marbles to demonstrate wheel function 909:110
Buggy model, making to demonstrate wheels 806:46-49
Capstan wheel experiment 756:19
Cart from cardboard with wheels project 1423:8-9
Cog wheels made from popsicle sticks and cardboard 1423:23
Dragging and rolling motion of—experiment 125:32-37
Gear wheels experiment 756:20-21
Inventing a wheel experiment 806:44-46
Inventing a wheel to turn a corner experiment 806:45-46
Make wheels turn other wheels experiment 836:34-35
Oil on road effect on wheels experiment 756:14
Paddle wheel boats—making a paddle wheel boat and experiment to try 606:106-111
Path of a rolling spool effected by the surface it rolls on experiment 836:31-33
Pulley wheel experiment 756:18
Return of hoop—demonstrate 291:128
Roll big wheels (Primary) 232:97
Rollers overcome friction experiment 1423:5
Rolling wheels reduce friction experiment 1159:40-41
Rubber band powered wheels—making 756:28
Sliding wheels; toy car with its "brakes" on experiment 1159:41-42
Steering wheels—making 756:11
Test how wheels move on different surfaces experiment 756:13
Testing a wheel and axle 180:30
Three models of cars to make that move freely 631:98-101
Toy insect with wheels, how to make 1423:17
Turbine and paddle wheel—making 142:50
Up and down wheels model to show how they work—making 756:24-25
Using straws—experiment (Primary) 24:14-17
Wacky wheel model; machine driven by its own weight goes uphill, make 1190:11-15

Wagon from wood with wooden wheels project, how to make 1423:14
Wagon with axles, simple project, how to make 1423:12-13
Waterwheel—making 756:27
Wheel experiment 563:193-194
Wheels—making 756:8-10
Wheels make work easier—demonstrate 321:31
Wheels make work easier (Primary) 539:38-39
Wheels make work easier; books on straws roll experiment 827:18
Wheels move heavy loads faster demonstrate 759:47
Wheels reduce friction experiment with toy cars 1166:6
Wheels with axles project, how to make 1423:11
Windmill wheel—making 756:27
Wobbly wheels experiment 806:52-54

WHEELS—AXLE
Demonstrate with paper plates (Primary) 200:20-21
Function of experiments 128:115-118
Wheel and axle experiment 281:47

WHEELS—MEDICINE
Make your own medicine wheels 292:70-71

WHIRLIGIGS INSECTS
Collect and observe circle swimming pattern under different conditions 771:124-128
Collection, care and observation of whirligigs 331:21-30

WHIRLPOOLS
Bottle whirlpool, how to make using plastic bottles and colored water 1331:96

WHIRLWINDS
Paper wad in bottle demonstrates 999:118-119

WHISTLES
Grass whistle, how to make 1432:94-96
Straw whistles demonstrate sound vibrations and pitch 1432:40-42
Willow whistle—how to make 90:59; 442:unpaged

WHITE BLOOD CELLS
Diagram and explanation of (Primary) 245:20-21

WHIZZ BANG
How to make 178:44

WILD FLOWERS. *See also* **FLOWERS—WILD**
Blooming wildflowers exp.-does height in bloom change-with seasons 586:120
Daisies in the field; experiment examining structures of daisies 1060:129
Measuring growth—experiment 693:10-11
Outdoor projects with wildflowers and plants 118:223-232
Survey of wildflowers in patch of garden using quadrat 1145:18
Wild plants and their growth experiment 749:52-53

WILDFLOWERS—COLLECTION
How to do 382:64-67

WILDLIFE MAP
How to make 264:118

WILDLIFE OBSERVATION
Equipment to use-binoculars, small mammal trap, tape recorder and parabolic ref 115:49
How to camouflage yourself 115:7-14
How to know where you are and not get lost 115:23-28
How to record your findings 115:57-65
How to walk silently 115:15-22

Observation posts—how to make 115:29-40
Observing plants and animals 590:41-42
Photograph wildlife—how to 115:41-48
Prepare a skull—how to 115:61
Preserve footprints—how to 115:62-63

WILDLIFE ORPHANS
Formula for and how to feed 442:unpaged

WILLIAM, THOMSON
Lord Kelvin—his experiments 42:126-134

WILSON CLOUD CHAMBER
How to make 43:164-177

WIND. *See also* **ANEMOMETER; WEATHER**
Air convection experiment 243:24-25
Air currents and wind demonstration with talc powder and lamp 1003:46
Anemometer tells how fast the wind is blowing, how to make 1281:15
Anemometer to measure wind speed—making 624:31
Anemometer, how to make experiment 947:39
Anemometer, make to record wind speed project 1070:22
Anemometer, wind speed detector, how to make 830:61-62
As a brake—demonstrate effects of streamlining 139:14
As a brake—make a spinner 139:13
As a brake—make an air brake 139:9
As a brake—make parachutes 139:10
As a brake—make paper darts 139:12
Beaufort scale 139:6
Beaufort wind scale (Hussey) 62:6-7
Beaufort wind scale—how to use 175:67
Beaufort wind scale 494:75; 617:40
Breezes; cause of land and sea breezes demonstration 1023:132-133
Can you blow the ball out of a funnel (Primary) 551:unpaged
Centrifugal force 243:36-37
Centripetal force 243:34-35
Charting the wind chart 770:116
Chimes, making 983:96-97
Coastal offshore and onshore breezes—chart of 299:28-29
Convection currents 243:22-23
Convection currents demonstrated with candles and chimneys on box experiment 767:58
Convection cycle of wind experiment 1447:58-60
Cooling and drying of wind—demonstrate 139:28-31
Cooling effect of wind experiment using jar of water and thermometer 1275:27
Coriolis Effect experiment with paper on record player turntable 1012:13
Coriolis Effect experiment; winds are deflected by effect of Earth's rotation 1480:158-159
Coriolis force—experiment 243:38-39
Coriolis Force; demonstrate Coriolis Force on spinning globe using chalk 1439:11-14
Coriolis strength—experiment 243:40-41
Current of air in atmosphere returning from warm to cold experiment 1480:158
Direction—can shape of tree indicate direction of wind 381:119-121
Direction—experiment—heat and weather at the seashore 585:131
Direction—setting up wind directional devices 175:72
Direction—wind direction—demonstrate 139:4
Direction—wind direction—recording by graph 298:11

Direction of wind determined by use of nephoscope experiment, how to make 1405:81-87
Direction of wind determined by wind vane experiment, how to make 1063:438
Direction of wind determined with wind vane experiment 837:17-18
Direction of wind measured with wind vane experiment 1028:14-15
Direction-what is wind dir. In upper air-make nephoscope to observe. Cloud dir. 381:69-71
Dust devil model—making 767:59
Earth's rotation effect on wind and water currents demonstration 1023:200-201
Earth's rotation effect on wind and water currents demonstration 1405:86
Earth's wind records 1003:41
Eddy currents motion experiment 243:48-49
Effect of friction on wind 243:42-43
Effect of wind on water in the air experiment 1003:72
Effects of wind erosion experiment 978:140-141
Equal volumes—different weights—experiment 243:12-13
Erosion; moving air causes erosion of uncovered soil experiment 1323:37-41
Flow of air across Earth's surface as it rotates experiment 1516:71-75
Force of wind experiment 737:21
Force of wind machine, how to make 1416:13
Force of wind, how to measure experiment 1416:8-9
Force scale to measure wind force, how to make 1360:9
Gauge; make wind gauge using styrofoam ball, straw, and cardboard 1439:83-85
Gravity and wind experiment 243:26-27
Heat absorption—experiment 243:18-19
How does the wind blow experiment 1293:87-88
How fast does the wind blow experiment 837:14-15; 909:79
How strong is the wind 236:162
How winds are made 30:24-25; 72:26-28
How winds are formed experiment 805:16-17
Instruments to track the wind, how to make 1086:18-19
Inversion model using aquarium and blue ink experiment 767:59
Land racer with sails experiment 1108:25-27
Lift of winds—experiment 243:46-47
Make an anemometer 564:3
Making a wind vane and an anemometer 597:30-31
Measure wind speed experiment 805:20
Measure wind speed and direction experiment; how to make wind vane/anemometer 1134:2.003
Measuring the wind—a butterfly kite 304:26-27
Measuring way the wind blows experiment with wind vane, how to make 1281:10
Meter to measure wind, making 981:11
Micro wind detector 577:project #20
Moving air pushes things experiments 854:18-20
Pinwheel—how to make to test wind (Primary) 523:36-37
Pinwheel shows air movement over candle (Primary) 363:149-151
Pinwheel to demonstrate wind—making 733:31
Pinwheel, making to test wind's strength experiment 983:89-91
Pinwheels from different patterns and different papers test breezes experiment 1373:26-27

470

Power of wind demonstrated with pinwheel, how to make 1017:48

Pressure differences in air—experiment 243:30-31

Pressure gradients—imbalance reactions 243:28-29

Prevailing winds experiment using anemometer and wind vane 1012:16-17

Prevailing winds experiment 1003:51-52

Sailboat, making 909:81

Sail power experiment with plastic bottle sailboat 1332:14-15

Sand; how wind keeps sand grains on the move experiment 1513:43

Sea and land breezes caused by land or water heating up experiment 1020:53-57

Sea breeze convection currents experiment 767:59

Sea breezes caused by warming difference of land and water experiment 1322:32

Show speed of wind experiment 834:20-21

Simple pinwheel to test the wind experiment 1106:26

Skate sail, how to make 947:34-35

Skyscrapers in wind with balls on straw stands experiment 1332:16-17

Smoky air—experiment 243:20-21

Soil heats and cools more quickly than water experiment 767:112

Speed—wind speed indicator—making 694:100-102

Speed of wind, measure with anemometer, how to make 834:142-143

Streamers of paper and straw demonstrate work of wind 1014:127

Temperature differences cause wind experiment 1322:28-32

Turbulence, how to test—experiment 694:25-26

Using the wind—flying kites 139:17

Using the wind—mobile making 139:15

Using the wind—sail boat making 139:18

Using the wind—windmill making 139:16

Warm air expands and rises experiments 767:57

Weather vane shows direction of wind experiment, how to make 1211:13

Weather vane tells direction of wind experiment 1108:19-20

What is wind 281:10

What is wind experiment 834:21; 852:38-39

What makes the wind blow experiment 1012:12

What things will wind carry the farthest experiment 834:21-22

Where does the wind come from 399:40-41

Where the wind blows balloon and post card experiment 759:48-49

Which objects move easily on the water with the wind exp. [Primary] 880:20

Whirling winds above and below equator experiment 1003:53

Why does the wind blow experiment with soap bubbles and candle 860:194-195

Why the wind blows 55:83-89; 382:124-127

Wind activities—evaporation, noises, direction, strength (Primary) 490:entire book; unpaged

Wind and air pollution 243:54-55

Wind and clouds 243:52-53

Wind and erosion of land 243:54-55

Wind and pressure systems 243:44-45

Wind and waves 243:58-59

Wind anemometer, how to make from cardboard, paper cups and dowel 1175:87-88

Wind can produce energy, spinner demonstrates 898:6

Wind changes things; dunes and sandy beaches 139:7

Wind chart 234:99

Wind chill factor experiment with thermometers and fan 1012:19

Wind chill factor when wind blows across body of water experiment 1447:50-55

Wind chimes, how to make 947:32-33

Wind circulation 243:32-33

Wind currents over mountains shown with pile of books, tissue paper, fan 1439:86-88

Wind direction experiment; make wind vane 900:91-92

Wind direction indicator—making 694:98-99

Wind direction indicator, how to make 830:58-61

Wind dragon—making 356:36-39

Wind eddies experiments 767:60

Wind effects on evaporation 243:50-51

Wind erosion demonstration 577:project #40

Wind erosion of land affected by moisture experiment 1405:77

Wind force—experiment 139:19

Wind force scale 236:163

Wind gauge—calibrated wind gauge—making 347:90-92

Wind gauge—making 9:100-101

Wind generator—building 608:38-40

Wind generator model makes electricity experiment 698:12-13

Wind is forceful activities [Primary] 759:49-50

Wind making activities [Primary] 880:24

Wind machine—making (Primary) 155:24-25

Wind meter, making 779:63

Wind plant generator—how to build a bicycle-wheel wind plant generator 347:98-103

Wind power land yacht, making 685:8-9

Wind produces water waves at sea demonstration 1023:186-187

Wind rose record chart, how to make 1086:19

Wind scale chart 277:136; 694:103

Wind sock from old shirt sleeve measures wind direction experiment 1372:34-35

Wind sock, how to make 112:35; 865:80; 1108:16

Wind sock, make from cloth, wire coat hanger and broom handle 1430:20

Wind speed—measure speed of wind 139:5

Wind speed—wind speed with paper plate—experiment 200:26-27

Wind speed anemometer—making 40:132-134; 176:83-84; 277:15-17; 293:10

Wind speed anemometer—making (Primary) 327:40

Wind speed anemometer to measure speed of wind—making 14:54-58; 264:97

Wind speed box to measure wind speed, how to make 1388:28

Wind speed gauge, making 783:35-36

Wind speed indicator—making 41:147; 128:93-94

Wind speed measurement demonstration 1023:134-135

Wind speed meter—making 657:62; 767:64

Wind speed meter—making (Primary) 70:14-16

Wind spinner—making, primary 64:unpaged

Wind station to measure wind direction and speed experiment; how to build 1480:168-169

Wind station, how to make from plywood, dowel, tubing and fasteners 1179:126-127

Wind vane, make to find wind direction 1017:45
Wind vane, making 909:78
Wind wagons—how to make 54:45-52
Wind wave action experiment 363:158-159
Wind wheel demonstrates wind power 669:22-23
Wind wheel experiment, how to make 1416:7
Windchill factor—experiment 277:13-14
Windchill factor—make anemometer and wind vane to
    determine 277:15-19
Windchill factor chart 629:30
Windmill, making 909:80
Winds around the world chart 694:97
Windsock from fabric, how to make 1115:66-67
Windsock to measure speed of wind—making 767:142
Windsock, how to make 805:1849; 1281:13
Windy day—experiment with balloons and other objects
    (Primary) 535:51-54
World wind patterns model to demonstrate wind patterns;
    adult help needed 1480:172-173

WIND CAR
Ice boat—how to make from wood 429:72-74

WIND CHIMES
Chimes from various materials, how to make 1335:25
Clay pot wind chimes, how to make 1115:46-47
How to make 543:10-11
How to make from buttons, bells, bottle tops and ribbon
    1373:18
How to make from milk carton (Primary) 523:20
How to make three kinds 494:76

WIND DARTS
Wind darts game—how to make 364:135

WIND DETECTOR
Yardstick and cloth flag used to make wind detector (Pri-
    mary) 523:12-13

WIND ENERGY. *See also* **WINDMILLS**
Converting wind energy into electricity; build wind gen-
    erator experiment 895:98-99
Double paper windmill experiment 1108:22
Model wind turbine experiment 1134:7.003
Paper windmill demonstrates wind energy experiment,
    how to make 1497:13
Pinwheel windmill demonstrates wind power 1161:17
Sails for boats; which works best experiment 1161:16
Straw mill demonstrates wind energy 1523:26
Wind energy raises toy or model windmill 1523:27
Wind energy to power toys with sails experiment
    1255:21
Wind power experiment using fabrics and mini-windmill
    1063:367
Wind sails windmill experiment 1108:23-24
Wind turbine makes electricity experiment 1426:114-
    118
Windmill made from paper demonstrates wind energy ex-
    periment 1108:21
Windmill model turns acrobat figure attached to crank on
    blades experiment 1073:98-99
Windmill runs generator and lights bulbs experiment
    1249:4-10
Windmill, wooden, patterns of parts given, how to make
    1249:4-5
Windmills turn coils in generators experiment 1501:82-
    83
Working model windmill, how to make from box and
    straw 1073:26

WIND POWER
Savonious rotor—how to make from wood 429:88-90
Sidewalk sail car—how to make 494:65
Which combination of blades and wind speed produces
    the most energy experiment 1450:92-99
Windmill to demonstrate power from wind experiment
    1281:12

WIND RESISTANCE
Body position affects motion through air experiment
    1154:51-53
Falling twirler demonstrates wind resistance 999:107-109
Free fall spinner demonstrates wind resistance, making
    999:105-106

WIND SPEED
Anemometer measures wind speed—experiment 1211:13
Anemometer measures wind speed—how to make
    541:16-17; 1042:36-37; 1311:28
Anemometer measures wind speed experiment, how to
    make 1063:436-437
Can wind speed be measured; making anemometer ex-
    periment 900:94-95
How does anemometer work experiment 900:96
How wind speed is measured experiment with protractor
    and string anemometer 1479:79
Speed of wind measured by anemometer experiment
    1108:18
Wind speed meter from cardboard box, how to make
    1115:72-73
Wind streamer to test wind speed and direction—how to
    make 494:66

WIND TUNNELS
Aerodynamics in a wind tunnel experiment 1476:88-
    90
How to make 293:40-41; 436:86; 691:38-41; 779:64;
    908:63-65; 1476:88-90
How to make wind tunnel using milk cartons and tape
    1095:15; 1436:23-24
Make a wind tunnel for testing model aircraft 564:17
Test objects for 691:43
What is a wind tunnel demonstration 900:201
Which angle of attack generates the most lift experiment
    997:151-155
Wind tunnel shows airstreams over different shapes ex-
    periment 1332:24-25
Wing shapes tested in wind tunnel experiment 860:27-30

WIND TURBINES
Which combination of blades and wind speed produces
    the most energy experiment 1450:92-99
Wind turbine project, how to build 1305:28-29
Wind turbine working model, how to make 1476:38-
    39

WIND VANES
Cardboard wind vane, making 999:112-114
Cat or dog pattern wind vane, how to make from ply-
    wood 1114:20-21
Direction of wind determined by wind vane experiment,
    how to make 1063:438
Direction of wind measured with wind vane experiment
    1028:14-15
Direction of wind; determine with wind vane experiment
    837:17-18
Make from cardboard 493:42

Make from cardboard, broom handle, nail and compass 1311:29
Make from cardboard, plastic straw and dowel 1073:31
Make from cardboard, wood and straw 1373:30
Make from drinking straw, cardboard and pencil 1360:16
Make from plastic pot, cork and straw 1104:11
Make from plywood and wooden posts 1516:97-98
Make from posterboard, pencils and straw 1465:13
Make from wood 852:47-48; 918:30; 978:147; 1086:18
Make from wood and nail 767:141
Make wind vane and record wind direction for several days 834:19-20
Measure wind speed and direction experiment; make wind vane and anemometer 1134:2.003
Measuring way the wind blows experiment with wind vane, how to make 1281:10
Record the way wind blows (Primary) 232:43
Simple vane from yogurt cup and straw, how to make 832:38
Tell wind direction; make wind vane experiment 900:91-92
Use a weather vane experiment 900:93-94
Weather vane tells direction of wind experiment 1108:19-20
Weathervane, how to make from drinking straw and block of wood 1175:86-87
Whirling wind vane—how to make 494:67
Wind direction indicator—making 694:98-99
Wind vane—making 9:68-69; 14:50-53; 253:64-65; 128:93; 264:99; 277:17-19; 298:10; 358:54-55; 588:49; 657:61-62; 660:30; 705:75-76; 783:37; 891:60-64; 981:7; 1387:18-19
Wind vane—making (Primary) 327:38-39; 541:15
Wind vane and gauge, making from tin, wood and post 1476:155-157
Wind vane measures wind and its direction experiment, how to build 1453:43-49
Wind vane measures wind direction experiment 1042:38-39
Wooden block and arrow vane, making 1012:15
Yogurt container and pencil vane, making 1016:15

WINDLASS
Making 436:86

WINDMILLS
Cork and toothpick windmill—making 756:26
Double paper windmill experiment 1108:22
Generator coils turned by windmills experiment 1501:82-83
Make from dowel, cork and cardboard 1388:29
Make from paper to demonstrate wind energy experiment 1497:13
Make from wood 948:42-45
Make from wood, patterns for parts given 1249:4-5
Make simple windmill 227:7; 377:28-29
Making a horizontal windmill, setting up model and experiments to try 606:92-99
Making a vertical windmill, setting up model and experiments to try 606:100-105
Mini-windmill, make with pinwheel from stiff paper 1335:25
Model water windmill from cardboard, clay, toothpicks, how to make 1175:89-92
Model windmill, how to make 1416:27
Model windmill to generate electricity—how to build 762:130-134
Outdoor windmill toy—making 173:131-134
Paper windmill experiment demonstrates wind energy 1108:21
Pinwheel demonstrates windmill 832:38
Pinwheel windmill—making 705:82-83; 868:71
Pinwheel windmill demonstrates energy from wind, how to make 1380:37
Pinwheel windmill demonstrates wind power 1161:17
Pinwheels, paper, making to demonstrate 770:119
Savonious rotor fish pond agitator—making 347:105-107
Which combination of blades and wind speed produces the most energy experiment 1450:92-99
Wind energy raises toy or model windmill 1523:27
Wind power and winch lifts bucket in model well experiment 1334:18-19
Wind sails windmill experiment 1108:23-24
Windmill—making 66:94-104; 112:36; 660:32-33; 737:37; 909:80
Windmill—making (Primary) 539:35
Windmill and hammer model, making 981:9
Windmill experiment; make from straws, clips, shoe box, wire hanger 1462:87-91
Windmill in shape of pinwheel, how to make from paper 1299:49
Windmill is a wheel and axle machine and helps do work experiment 1400:44-47
Windmill lifts weights experiment using pinwheel and paper towel roll 1228:50-53
Windmill model—making 267:20-21
Windmill model turns acrobat figure attached to crank on blades experiment 1073:98-99
Windmill runs generator and lights bulbs experiment 1249:4-10
Windmill to demonstrate power from wind experiment 1281:12
Working model windmill, how to make from box and straw 1073:26
Working windmill experiment, how to make 1446:34-35
Working windmill model experiment 1332:28-29

WINE
Make wine and cider 625:46-47

WINE AND WATER TRICKS
Is it wine or water 350:56-57

WINTER. *See also* **SEASONS—WINTER**
Sun's rays carry less energy due to slant—demonstration 629:8-9

WINTER ACTIVITIES
Activities with temperature 236:147-148
Detecting animals in winter 277:20-43
Exploring water communities in winter 277:115-121
Plants—discovering plants in winter 277:59-72
Record temperature differences outside in different places 277:11
Searching for small creatures—insects and galls 277:73-114
Snow, ice and temperature experiments 277:6-19
Winter activities 661:38-42

WINTER ANIMALS
How to trap 117:21-23
Observe feeders, animals, nest and droppings—how to 117:14-21

WINTER INSECTS
Observation and collection 277:77-90
WIRELESS SIGNALS
Send signals using mirror 176:50-51
'Wireless' telephone—making 22:36-49
WIRES
Temperature effect on the length of wires experiment 1515:12-14
Wire length and resistance to electric charge flow experiment 1514:60-65
WISHING MACHINE
Experiment to demonstrate (Advanced) 393:95-103
WOOD
Are composites of wood stronger than solid wood experiment 997:148-150
Broom from tree wood and twigs, how to make 1184:36
Burning wood produces carbon dioxide experiment 1269:46
Collect and display wood samples 476:73-75
Flammability of wood experiment 969:102-104
Floating wood experiment; which kind of wood floats best experiment 1508:5
Flooring; testing kind of wood best to use for flooring experiment 1508:5
Log cabin from sticks of wood, how to make 1125:29
Make particleboard experiment 1508:4
Measure content of woods; softwood and hardwood experiment 969:102-104
Mount samples of wood, tree shape, leaf shape and fruit for display 436:87
Poster to show different trees and use of their products 293:17
Properties of wood—hardness and density 236:25
Some types of wood rot faster than others do experiment 1221:5-7, 28
Sound travels through water and wood experiment 1432:56-57
Specific gravity of wood, how to measure experiment 1075:58
Wood (sawdust) can soak up water (Primary) 320:31
Wood ash; make and test a basic solution experiment 905:212-213
Wooden boat from oval piece of wood, how to make 1125:28
WOOD—PRESERVATIVES
Which solution preserves wood the best project 969:77-78
WOOD BURNING STOVES
Measure particulate matter sent into air from chimneys experiment 969:108-109
WOOD GAS
Demonstrate production of gas from wood burning 472:2233
Production of gas and other substances from burning wood experiment 1244:20
WOOD LICE. *See also* **SOW BUGS**
Sow bugs like dry or moist, light or dark experiment using wooden test box 1069:117
WOOD LOUSE. *See* **SOW BUGS**
WOODLAND TERRARIUMS
Community terrarium—making 268:17-21
Desert or woodland terrarium project, how to make 1296:1982
Making 465:146-151

Materials and animals for—how to set up and maintain 475:14-20
Woodland terrarium—how to make 400:14
WOODS. *See* **FOREST**
WOODWORKING
Archimedes screw—how to make from wood 429:84-87
Bench—making from wood 429:115-116
Block boats and paddles—how to make 429:64
Boat sails—how to make 429:65-66
Catamaran from wood and coffee cans—how to make 429:70
Doll house furnishings—how to make 429:61-62
Dymaxion tent—how to make a wooden model 429:81-83
Flag pole—how to make from wood 429:78-80
Glider—easy glider from wood and roller skate wheels and sail—how to make 429:56-59
Hammer mill to grind grains—how to make from wood 429:91-93
How to make a giraffe 545:34-37
Ice boat—wind car, how to make from wood 429:72-74
Ice cream stick art projects—how to make 418:36-63
Leonardo's paddle boat—how to make 429:68
Letter and pencil holders—how to make 543:24-25
Millworks—crane making from wood 429:107
Millworks—grist mill—making from wood 429:103
Millworks—how to make from wood 429:98-102
Millworks—pump—making from wood 429:106
Millworks—sawmill—making from wood 429:104
Millworks bellows and trip hammer—making from wood 429:105
Mousetrap tractor—how to build from wood 429:75-77
Naval cannon that shoots—how to make from wood 545:54-57
Newton's steamboat—how to make 429:69
Pinball machine—how to make 429:52-55
Rotating message sign for your door—how to make 543:4-5
Savonious's rotor—how to make from wood 429:88-90
Spool people—how to make a spool man pirate 545:28-31
Thaumatrope—how to make 429:51
Totem poles—how to make a totem pole 545:25-27
Waterwheels—how to make from wood 429:94-98
Wooden relatives—how to make 429:60
WOOL
Do woolens keep us warmer—heat preserver experiment 26:72-73
Does wool keep heat out 26:83
Does wool or cotton cloth hold more water project 1210:46-47
How strong is wool 26:84
Is wool better than other materials to keep us warm-trapped air experiment 26:73-74
Weave a piece of woolen cloth—make loom string yarn 26:79-82
Wool balls and toys, making 795:15
Wool keeps sheep warm 257:8-9
WORK. *See* **FORCE; ENERGY**
WORLD
Around the world poster of weather, plants and animals 153:8-9
Globe of world made from beach ball and paper 1340:68-69

Map of (grapefruit) 382:114-120

WORMS. *See also* **EARTHWORMS**
Bristleworms, collect and observe 771:134-138
Earthworms—collecting 436:88
Flat, round and segmented from ocean shores—collecting 436:88
How to care for a worm (Primary) 255:unpaged
Planaria—collecting 436:88
Show burrowing worms 94:22-23
Test worms reaction to stimuli 293:24
Worm box—making 9:44-45
Worm castings—how to use 276:70-76
Worm farm—how to make 358:94-95

WOUND—MAGIC
Experiment 350:68-69

WRITING—INVISIBLE. *See also* **INVISIBLE INKS; SECRET WRITING**
Invisible writing—invisible writing on wet paper and with salt 558:54

WRITING INSTRUMENTS. *See also* **PENCILS; PENS**
Ball-point pen, how to make one experiment 1063:319
Ball-point pens—experiment to see how it works 336:41-43
Chalk—make your own chalk 336:46-48
Chalk acid test shows white and anti-dust are different 336:45-46
Crayons—test light fastness of crayons—experiment 336:52-54
Show capillarity between ink and paper—experiment 336:37-39
Test different writing devices—experiment 336:36-37

X

XYLOPHONE
Making 436:89
Sound vibrations—transverse vibrations—experiment, with xylophone 2:80-83

Y

YAMS. *See also* SWEET POTATOES
Grow yam vine in water, how to do 1178:36-37

YEAST
Adventure 28—we inquire into the nature of yeast under a microscope 403:97-100
Anerobic respiration experiment with yeast 1395:104
Baking yeast bread 219:15-18
Balloon inflates on bottle filled with water, yeast, and sugar experiment 1229:20-21
Blow up balloon on soda bottle with yeast, sugar, water and flour experiment 1208:90-91
Blow up balloon using sugar and yeast experiment 781:12-13
Blowing up balloons with yeast—chemicals harmful to yeast growth—experiment 565:151-154
Blowing up balloons with yeast—experiment 565:145-156
Blowing up balloons with yeast—grow different colonies of yeast—experiment 565:145-151
Can molecules in yeast make a gas from hydrogen peroxide experiment 831:88-90
Carbon dioxide by fermentation—experiment 563:170
Carbon dioxide gas made more rapidly when ginger added to sugar/yeast 1251:68-70
Carbon dioxide gas makes pizza dough swell (recipe for pizza) 472:2234
Carbon dioxide makes dough swell experiment; make pizza to demonstrate, recipe 1244:36
Catching and growing yeast 400:1
Compare growth of yeast in hot, warm and cold water experiment 1484:64
Determine why there are holes in bread slices experiment 1405:54
Effect of yeast on a sugar solution experiment 904:82-83
Effect of yeast on food decomposition experiment 904:92-93
Experiment with yeast and making bread, recipe given 887:80-82
Experiments to show growth of yeast 128:52
Feast for yeast experiment 735:28
Fermentation—making wind—experiment 6:31
Fermentation and its products experiment using yeast and sugar 1069:67
Fermentation of sugar and yeast produces carbon dioxide experiment 1396:168
Fermentation of yeast produces carbon dioxide experiment 1395:104
Fermentation of yeast produces carbon dioxide gas experiment 1221:18-19
Foods best for yeast to grow experiment using balloons 1063:414
Gas from fruit 77:39
Gas increases from yeast as amount of sugar is increased experiment 984:62-65
Ginger ale drink from yeast, recipe, how to make 1214:26-27
Ginger ale, how to make using yeast 835:12-14

Grow yeast cells to look at under microscope 82:35-37
Grow yeast in bottles—test for carbon dioxide and effect of sugar 507:1911-1912
Growing bacterial cultures 148:10-11
Growing yeast—experiment 585:91-92
Growing yeast in bottle with cork experiment 790:12
Growing yeast plants 294:22-23
Growth of yeast experiment 1014:150
Growth of yeast experiment 978:53-54
Growth, respiration and reproduction of yeast cells experiment; data tables 1004:2.019
How does bread dough rise experiment 1484:61-63
How does temperature effect action of yeast in raising dough 26:104-105
How temperature affects the production of carbon dioxide by yeast 586:126-130
Life and death of yeast culture experiment 762:84-85
Limewater test for carbon dioxide produced by yeast experiment 905:74-75
Make carbon dioxide—experiment using yeast 563:169-170
Make ginger beer 231:60
Make pretzels from yeast—breath experiment 231:59
Mix yeast with sugar and water—watch it grow 366:75-76
Observing yeast eat and reproduce 148:10
Overgrowth of population effect on yeast colony experiment 1476:201
Population growth of yeast cells computer project 584:79-80
Populations change the food supply experiment using yeast 1324:85-89
Presence of carbon dioxide in yeast bubbles experiment 998:207
Rising and baking (recipe given) 452:66-67
Seeing the effect of yeast on dough 148:9
Show magic power of yeast 146:26-27
Sugar and yeast blow up balloons—experiment 589:50-51
Sugar and yeast produce carbon dioxide experiment 1176:38-39
What do yeast plants look like 26:105
Which foods does yeast like best—experiment 586:126-130
Why bread is full of holes—make bread with yeast and bread without yeast 26:101-102
Why bread is full of holes—make bread with yeast and without yeast 11:95-100
Yeast—sugar and water experiment 722:89
Yeast and limewater produce carbon dioxide experiment 723:80
Yeast and sugar—experiment with bottles and balloons 598:40-41
Yeast and sugar mix makes carbon dioxide gas that inflates balloon experiment 1038:26
Yeast and sugar produce carbon dioxide gas and blows cork off bottle experiment 1479:53
Yeast and sugar produce carbon dioxide gas experiment 1405:30-31
Yeast and sugar to make carbon dioxide 84:45-46
Yeast breathes—experiment 231:58
Yeast cells in fermenting cider experiment 917:23
Yeast cells under microscope—observe 713:90-92
Yeast cells under microscope, observe 889:50-51
Yeast enzymes 77:36-37

Yeast gives off carbon dioxide experiment 1214:24-25
Yeast makes carbon dioxide gas from sugar 396:28-30
Yeast mixture doubles in size experiment 1238:97
Yeast mixture in jar blows up balloon experiment 980:
    46
Yeast multiply be dividing 231:58
Yeast needs food to grow experiment 829:5-6
Yeast needs right temperature to grow experiment
    1238:98-101
Yeast produces carbon dioxide experiment 1441:99
Yeast puffs up plastic bag experiment 1189:12-13
Yeast puts air into breads and cakes experiment 1238:95-
    96
Yeast starter experiment; make sourdough bread, recipe
    980:48-50
Yeast works better with cold, warm or hot water project
    1210:50-53
Yeast, sugar and warm water in bottle blow up balloon
    experiment 1101:8

YO-YO

Diablo Yo-Yo, how to make 952:95-96
Experiments with a Yo-Yo 952:60-62
Horizontal Yo-Yo, making 779:26
Inuit Yo-Yo demonstrates centripetal force experiment
    871:4.002
Investigate scientific principles behind toys experiments
    1412:81-87
Macrame ring Yo-Yo, how to make experiment 952:62-64
Make a mini Yo-Yo 94:18-19
Making a Yo-Yo experiment 952:56-59

Weight affects spin of Yo-Yo experiment 952:65-69
What makes the Yo-Yo Yo-Yo 291:134
Yo-Yo experiments—change the axle to see what hap-
    pens 54:28-30
Yo-Yo experiments—change the material to see what
    happens 54:36-37
Yo-Yo experiments—change the shape to see what
    happens 54:20-25
Yo-Yo experiments—change the size to see what hap-
    pens 54:38
Yo-Yo experiments—change the string to test action
    54:16-19
Yo-Yo experiments—change the weight to see what hap-
    pens 54:31-34
Yo-Yo experiments—change to a Diablo-type Yo-Yo
    54:41-43

YOGURT

Determine optimal temperature for making yogurt exp.;
    Data table given 871:2.012
How to make 77:27
How to make yogurt 579:45-46; 820:37; 980:96-97
How to make yogurt experiment 563:158
Insulated warming box for making yogurt, how to do
    887:84-85
Make yogurt and experiment with bacteria growth
    887:84-86

YOUNG, THOMAS

Measuring the strength and elasticity of materials experi-
    ment 1133:4.009

Z

ZEHNDER BALANCE

Make and do several experiments with this instrument 176:80-83

ZERO GRAVITY

What causes feeling of weightlessness experiment 1399:52-55

ZODIAC

Making a moveable star chart [planesphere] project 833:48-49

Model of—making 532:54-55

Showing how Sun and Moon move in the zodiac project 833:47-48

Sketching the daily movement of the zodiac project 833:45-47

Sun moves thru Zodiac as Earth moves experiment; working model demonstrates 1478:26-27

Zodiac ring game 292:59

Zodiac signs 292:55-59

ZODIACAL LIGHT

And counter glow 292:110

ZOETROPE

Basic zoetrope strips, how to make 1215:30-32

Creating different zoetrope strips, how to do 1215:33-65

Creating zoetrope strips, how to do 1215:25-29

How to make 172:41-44

How to make from plastic cake cover and wooden ball bearing turntable 1476:213-214

Light table for tracing pictures, how to make 1215:110-111

Making a zoetrope, how to do 1215:15-17

Motorized zoetropes, how to make 1215:101-111

Preparing strips, how to do 1215:18-20

Sample projects, how to do 1215:72-91

Sample strips, how to make 1215:119-133

Viewer to see figures in action—how to make 558:122-123

Viewing strips, how to do 1215:21-22

Zoetrope toy to see moving pictures, patterns given, how to make 1299:24-27

Zoetrope, how to make 861:121-127; 911:44

Zoetrope, how to make from cardboard and dowel 1179:92-93

ZONATION

Investigation of zonation in rocky shores 285:69-70

ZOO ANIMALS—BEHAVIOR

Do more complex animals show almost human behavior 402:48-49

BOOKS INDEXED BY NUMBER

1. Beeler, Nelson F., and Franklyn M. Branley. *Experiments in Optical Illusion.* New York: Thomas Y. Crowell Company, 1951.
2. Sootin, Harry. *Science Experiments with Sound.* New York: W. W. Norton & Company, 1964.
3. Zubrowski, Bernie. *Messing Around with Drinking Straw Construction.* Boston: Little, Brown & Company, 1981.
4. Sootin, Harry. *Light Experiments for Home Workshop and School Laboratory.* New York: W. W. Norton & Company, 1963.
5. Sootin, Harry. *Experiments with Static Electricity.* New York: W. W. Norton & Company, 1969.
6. Chisholm, Jane, and Mary Johnson. *Introduction to Chemistry.* London: Usborne Publishing Ltd., 1983.
7. Rahn, Joan Elma. *Watch It Grow, Watch It Change.* New York: Atheneum Publishers, 1978.
8. Beeler, Nelson. *Experiments with Light.* New York: Thomas Y. Crowell Company, 1964.
9. Moore, William. *Here Is Your Hobby, Science Equipment.* New York: G. P. Putnam's Sons, 1962.
10. Simon, Seymour. *Science Projects in Pollution.* New York: Holiday House, 1972.
11. Beeler, Nelson F. *Experiments with a Microscope.* New York: Thomas Y. Crowell Company, 1957.
12. Milgrom, Harry. *Explorations in Science, a Book of Basic Experiments.* New York: E. P. Dutton & Company, Inc., 1961.
13. Bender, Alfred. *Science Projects with Electrons and Computers.* New York: Arco Publishing Company, Inc., 1977.
14. Feravolo, Rocco. *Junior Science Book of Weather Experiments.* Champaign, Ill.: Garrard Publishing Company, 1963.
15. Amery, Heather. *The Know How Book of Experiments with Batteries & Magnets.* New York: Sterling Publishing Company, Inc., 1976.
16. Arnold, Ned, and Lois Arnold. *The Great Science Magic Show.* New York: Franklin Watts, Inc., 1979.
17. Cobb, Vicki. *The Secret Life of HardwAre.* New York: J. B. Lippincott Company, 1982.
18. Cummings, Richard. *Make Your Own Robots.* New York: David McKay Company, Inc., 1981.
19. Freeman, Mae. *Fun & Experiments with Light.* New York: Random House, 1963.
20. Rahn, Joan Elma. *Grocery Store Zoology.* New York: Atheneum Publishers, 1977.
21. Gardner, Robert and David Webster. *Shadow Science.* New York: Doubleday & Company, Inc., 1976.
22. Math, Irwin. *Morse, Marconi and You.* New York: Charles Scribner's Sons, 1979.
23. Math, Irwin. *Wires and Watts, Understanding and Using Electricity.* New York: Charles Scribner's Sons, 1981.
24. Milgrom, Harry. *Adventures with a Straw.* New York: E. P. Dutton & Company, Inc., 1967.
25. Roberts, Howard R. *Fun with Sun Prints and Box Cameras.* New York: David McKay Company, Inc., 1981.
26. Schwartz, Julius. *It's Fun to Know Why, Experiments with Things Around Us,* 2d ed. New York: McGraw-Hill Book Company, 1973.
27. Shalit, Nathan. *Science Magic Tricks, Over 50 Fun Tricks That Mystify and Dazzle.* New York: Holt, Rinehart and Winston, 1981.
28. Sootin, Harry. *Experiments with Magnetism.* New York: W. W. Norton & Company, 1968.
29. Headstrom, Richard. *Adventures with a Hand Lens.* New York: J. B. Lippincott Company, 1962.
30. Wyler, Rose. *The First Book of Science Experiments.* New York: Franklin Watts, Inc., 1971.
31. Smith, Norman F. *How Fast Do Your Oysters Grow?* New York: Julian Messner, 1982.
32. Stetten, Mary. *Let's Play Science.* New York: Harper & Row, 1979.
33. Williams, D. I., and D. Anglesea. *Experiments on Land Pollution.* Hove, England: Wayland Publishers, Ltd., 1978.
34. Fisher, S. H. *Table Top Science, Physics Experiments for Everyone.* New York: Natural History Press, 1972.
35. Windley, Charles. *Teaching and Learning with Magic.* Washington, D.C.: Acropolis Books, Ltd., 1976.
36. Selsam, Millicent E. *Play with Seeds.* New York: William Morrow & Company, 1957.
37. Sootin, Harry, and Laura Sootin. *The Young Experimenters' Workbook, Treasures of the Earth.* New York: W. W. Norton & Company, 1965.
38. Halacy, D. S., Jr. *Experiments with Solar Energy.* New York: W. W. Norton & Company, 1969.
39. White, Laurence B., Jr. *Investigating Science with Rubber Bands.* Reading, Mass.: Addison-Wesley Publishing Company, Inc., 1969.
40. Blackwelder, Sheila Keyser. *Science for All Seasons.* Englewood Cliffs, N.J.: Prentice Hall, Inc., 1980.
41. Anderson, Norman D. *Investigating Science in the Swimming Pool and Ocean.* New York: McGraw-Hill Book Company, 1978.
42. Brown, Bob. *Science Treasures: Let's Repeat the Great Experiments.* New York: Fleet Press Corp., 1968.
43. Bulman, Alan Davidson. *Models for Experiments in Physics.* New York: Thomas Y. Crowell Company, 1966.
44. Feravolo, Rocco. *Easy Physics Projects! Air, Water, Heat.* Englewood Cliffs, N.J.: Prentice Hall, Inc., 1966.
45. Baer, Marian E. *Sound, an Experiment Book.* New York: Holiday House, 1952.
46. Milgrom, Harry. *First Experiments with Gravity.* New York: E. P. Dutton & Company, Inc., 1966.
47. Cyr, Don. *Teaching Your Children Photography.* New York: American Photographic Book Publishing Company, 1977.
48. Rahn, Joan Elma. *Grocery Store Botany.* New York: Atheneum Publishers, 1974.
49. Gardner, Robert, and David Webster. *Moving Right Along, a Book of Science Experiments and Puzzlers About Motion.* New York: Doubleday & Company, Inc., 1978.
50. Zubrowski, Bernie. *Messing Around with Baking Chemistry.* Boston: Little, Brown & Company, 1981.
51. Beller, Joel. *So You Want to Do a Science Project.* New York: Arco Publishing Company, Inc., 1982.
52. Carona, Philip B. *Chemistry and Cooking.* Englewood Cliffs, N.J.: Prentice Hall, Inc., 1975.

53. Simon, Seymour. *Projects with Air*. New York: Franklin Watts, Inc., 1975.

54. Renner, Al G. *Experimental Fun with the Yo-Yo and Other Science Projects*. New York: Dodd, Mead & Company, 1979.

55. Rosenfeld, Sam. *Science Experiments with Air*. New York: Harvey House, Inc., 1969.

56. Arnov, Boris. *Water, Experiments to Understand It*. New York: Lothrop, Lee & Shepard Books, 1980.

57. Harbeck, Richard. *Exploring Science in Your Home Laboratory*. New York: Four Winds Press, 1963.

58. Stone, A. Harris, and Robert J. Stein. *Biology Project Puzzlers*. Englewood Cliffs, N.J.: Prentice Hall, Inc., 1973.

59. Rahn, Joan Elma. *Seven Ways to Collect Plants*. New York: Atheneum Publishers, 1978.

60. Rahn, Joan Elma. *Seeing What Plants Do*. New York: Atheneum Publishers, 1972.

61. Johnson, Gaylord, and Maurice Bleifeld. *Hunting with the Microscope*. New York: Arco Publishing Company, Inc., 1980.

62. Hussey, Lois J. *Collecting for the City Naturalist*. New York: Thomas Y. Crowell Company, 1975.

63. Sootin, Harry. *Experiments with Electric Currents*. New York: W. W. Norton & Company, 1969.

64. White, Laurence B., Jr. *Science Toys & Tricks*. Reading, Mass.: Addison-Wesley Publishing Company, Inc., 1980.

65. Feravolo, Rocco. *More Easy Physics Projects, Magnetism, Electricity, Sound*. Englewood Cliffs, N.J.: Prentice Hall, Inc., 1968.

66. Renner, Al G. *How to Build a Better Mouse Trap Car*. New York: Dodd, Mead & Company, 1977.

67. Pettigrew, Mark. *Radiation*. New York: Gloucester Press, 1986.

68. Simon, Seymour. *How to Be a Space Scientist in Your Own Home*. New York: J. B. Lippincott Company, 1982.

69. Milgrom, Harry. *Paper Science*. New York: Walker & Company, 1978.

70. Schneider, Herman. *Science Fun for You in a Minute or Two, Quick Science Experiments You Can Do*. New York: McGraw-Hill Book Company, 1975.

71. Zubrowski, Bernie. *A Children's Museum Activity Book: Ball Point Pens*. Boston: Little, Brown & Company, 1979.

72. Wyler, Rose. *First Book of Science Experiments*. New York: Franklin Watts, Inc., 1952.

73. Podendorf, Illa. *The True Book of Science Experiments*. Chicago: Children's Press, 1954.

74. Cobb, Vicki. *Science Experiments You Can Eat*. New York: J. B. Lippincott Company, 1972.

75. Webster, David. *Snow Stumpers*. New York: Natural History Press, 1968.

76. Watson, Philip. *Light Fantastic*. New York: Lothrop, Lee & Shepard Books, 1982.

77. Watson, Philip. *Liquid Magic*. New York: Lothrop, Lee & Shepard Books, 1982.

78. Sootin, Harry. *Easy Experiments with Water Pollution*. New York: Four Winds Press, 1974.

79. Cosgrove, Margaret. *Wonders Under a Microscope*. New York: Dodd, Mead & Company, 1959.

80. Lewis, Lucia Z. *The First Book of Microbes*. New York: Franklin Watts, Inc., 1972.

81. Selsam, Millicent E. *Microbes at Work*. New York: William Morrow & Company, 1953.

82. Simon, Seymour. *Exploring with a Microscope*. New York: Random House, 1969.

83. Simon, Seymour. *Chemistry in the Kitchen*. New York: Viking Press, 1971.

84. Shalit, Nathan. *Cup & Saucer Chemistry*. New York: Grosset & Dunlap, Inc., 1972.

85. Freeman, Mae, and Ira Freeman. *Fun with Chemistry*. New York: Random House, 1962.

86. Budlong, Ware. *Experimenting with Seeds & Plants*. New York: G. P. Putnam's Sons, 1970.

87. Palder, Edward L. *Magic with Chemistry; Mystery Experiments and Demonstrations for Science Clubs*. New York: Grosset & Dunlap, Inc., 1966.

88. Stone, A. Harris. *Chemistry of Soap*. Englewood Cliffs, N.J.: Prentice Hall, Inc., 1968.

89. Stone, A. Harris. *Chemistry of a Lemon*. Englewood Cliffs, N.J.: Prentice Hall, Inc., 1966.

90. Beeler, Nelson F. *Experiments in Sound*. New York: Thomas Y. Crowell Company, 1961.

91. Milgrom, Harry. *Further Explorations in Science: A Second Book of Basic Experiments*. New York: E. P. Dutton & Company, Inc., 1963.

92. Stone, A. Harris. *Take a Balloon*. Englewood Cliffs, N.J.: Prentice Hall, Inc., 1967.

93. Simon, Seymour. *Science at Work, Projects in Oceanography*. New York: Franklin Watts, Inc., 1972.

94. Watson, Philip. *Super Motion*. New York: Lothrop, Lee & Shepard Books, 1982.

95. Freeman, Mae, and Ira Freeman. *Fun with Scientific Experiments*. New York: Random House, 1960.

96. Stockard, Jimmy J. *Experiments for Young Scientists*. Boston: Little, Brown & Company, 1964.

97. Roberson, Paul. *Chemistry by Experiment*. New York: The John Day Company, 1965.

98. Ardley, Neil. *Working with Water*. New York: Franklin Watts, Inc., 1983.

99. Milgrom, Harry. *Adventures with a Plastic Bag*. New York: E. P. Dutton & Company, Inc., 1967.

100. Podendorf, Illa. *The True Book of More Science Experiments*. Chicago: Children's Press, 1956.

101. Keen, Martin L. *The How & Why Wonder Book of Science Experiments*. New York: Grosset & Dunlap, Inc., 1962.

102. Rosenfeld, Sam. *The Magic of Electricity, One Hundred Experiments with Batteries*. New York: Lothrop, Lee & Shepard Books, 1963.

103. Podendorf, Illa. *Things to Do with Water*. Chicago: Children's Press, 1971.

104. Podendorf, Illa. *The True Book of Plant Experiments*. Chicago: Children's Press, 1960.

105. Stone, A. Harris. *Puttering with Paper*. Englewood Cliffs, N.J.: Prentice Hall, Inc., 1968.

106. Freeman, Mae, and Ira Freeman. *Fun with Science*. New York: Random House, 1956.

107. Webster, David. *Brain Boosters*. New York: Natural History Press, 1965.

108. Simon, Seymour. *Exploring Fields & Lots, Easy Science Projects*. Champaign, Ill.: Garrard Publishing Company, 1978.

109. Lehane, M. S. *Science Tricks*. New York: Franklin Watts, Inc., 1980.

110. Gelman, Rita Golden, and Susan Kovacs Buxbaum. *Boats That Float*. New York: Franklin Watts, Inc., 1981.

111. Nicklaus, Carol. *Flying, Gliding & Whirling, Making Things That Fly*. New York: Franklin Watts, Inc., 1981.

112. Smith, Henry. *Amazing Air*. New York: Lothrop, Lee & Shepard Books, 1982.

113. Pitcher, Caroline. *Planes and Space*. New York: Franklin Watts, Inc., 1983.

114. Gardner, Robert. *Magic Through Science*. New York: Doubleday & Company, Inc., 1978.

115. Burness, Gordon. *How to Watch Wildlife*. New York: Van Nostrand Reinhold Company, 1972.

116. Cooper, Elizabeth K. *Discovering Chemistry*. New York: Harcourt, Brace & World, Inc., 1959.

117. Youngpeter, John M. *Winter Science Activities: Experiments and Projects*. New York: Holiday House, 1966.

118. Brown, Vinson. *Investigating Nature Through Outdoor Projects*. Harrisburg, Pa.: Stackpole Books, 1983.

119. Cooper, Elizabeth K. *Science in Your Own Backyard*. New York: Harcourt, Brace & World, Inc., 1958.

120. Ardley, Neil. *Sun and Light*. New York: Franklin Watts, Inc., 1983.

121. Arnold, Caroline. *Sun Fun*. New York: Franklin Watts, Inc., 1981.

122. Morgan, Alfred. *First Chemistry Book for Boys & Girls*. New York: Charles Scribner's Sons, 1962.

123. Morgan, Alfred. *A First Electrical Book for Boys*. New York: Charles Scribner's Sons, 1951.

124. Milgrom, Harry. *Adventures with a Cardboard Tube*. New York: E. P. Dutton & Company, Inc., 1972.

125. Schneider, Herman, and Nina Schneider. *Now Try This to Move a Heavy Load - Push, Pull, Lift*. New York: Young Scott Books, 1947.

126. Rosenfeld, Sam. *Science Experiments with Water*. New York: Harvey House, Inc., 1965.

127. Beeler, Nelson F. *Experiments with Electricity*. New York: Thomas Y. Crowell Company, 1949.

128. United Nations Educational, Scientific and Cultural Organization; *700 Science Experiments for Everyone*. New York: Doubleday & Company, Inc., 1958.

129. Davis, Barbara. *Learning Science and Metric Through Cooking*. New York: Sterling Publishing Company, Inc., 1977.

130. Branley, Franklyn M. *The Planets in Our Solar System*. New York: Thomas Y. Crowell Company, 1981.

131. Catherall, Ed. *Taste and Smell*. Morristown, N.J.: Silver Burdett Company, 1982.

132. Catherall, Ed. *Water Power*. Morristown, N.J.: Silver Burdett Company, 1981.

133. Catherall, Ed. *Touch*. Morristown, N.J.: Silver Burdett Company, 1982.

134. Catherall, Ed. *Hearing*. Morristown, N.J.: Silver Burdett Company, 1981.

135. Catherall, Ed. *Sight*. Morristown, N.J.: Silver Burdett Company, 1981.

136. Catherall, Ed. *Magnets*. Morristown, N.J.: Silver Burdett Company, 1982.

137. Catherall, Ed. *Clocks & Time*. Morristown, N.J.: Silver Burdett Company, 1982.

138. Catherall, Ed. *Electric Power*. Morristown, N.J.: Silver Burdett Company, 1982.

139. Catherall, Ed. *Wind Power*. Morristown, N.J.: Silver Burdett Company, 1981.

140. Catherall, Ed. *Solar Power*. Morristown, N.J.: Silver Burdett Company, 1981.

141. Bendick, Jeanne. *Measuring*. New York: Franklin Watts, Inc., 1971.

142. Richards, Kay. *Science Magic with Physics*. New York: Arco Publishing Company, Inc., 1975.

143. Wyler, Rose, and Gerald Ames. *Prove It*. New York: Harper & Row, 1963.

144. Wyler, Rose. *What Happens If? Science Experiments You Can Do by Yourself*. New York: Walker & Company, 1974.

145. Ardley, Neil. *Exploring Magnetism*. New York: Franklin Watts, Inc., 1983.

146. Johnson, Ted. *Science Magic with Chemistry & Biology*. New York: Arco Publishing Company, Inc., 1975.

147. Gardner, Robert. *Kitchen Chemistry Science Experiments to Do at Home*. New York: Julian Messner, 1982.

148. Challand, Helen J. *Activities in the Life Sciences*. Chicago: Children's Press, 1982.

149. Zubrowski, Bernie. *A Children's Museum Activity Book: Bubbles*. Boston: Little, Brown & Company, 1979.

150. Goldstein-Jackson, Kevin. *Experiments with Everyday Objects*. Englewood Cliffs, N.J.: Prentice Hall, Inc., 1978.

151. Ford, Barbara. *Can Invertebrates Learn?* New York: Julian Messner, 1972.

152. Cobb, Vicki. *More Science Experiments You Can Eat*. New York: J. B. Lippincott Company, 1979.

153. Arnold, Caroline. *Land Masses, Fun, Facts and Activities*. New York: Franklin Watts, Inc., 1985.

154. Arnold, Caroline. *Bodies of Water, Fun, Facts and Activities*. New York: Franklin Watts, Inc., 1985.

155. Arnold, Caroline. *Natural Resources, Fun, Facts and Activities*. New York: Franklin Watts, Inc., 1985.

156. Ardley, Neil. *Force and Strength*. New York: Franklin Watts, Inc., 1984.

157. Ardley, Neil. *Simple Chemistry*. New York: Franklin Watts, Inc., 1984.

158. Leutscher, Alfred. *Flowering Plants*. New York: Franklin Watts, Inc., 1984.

159. Pope, Joyce. *Insects*. New York: Franklin Watts, Inc., 1984.

160. Webster, David. *How to Do a Science Project*. New York: Franklin Watts, Inc., 1974.

161. De Vries, Leonard. *The Second Book of Experiments*. New York: The Macmillan Company, 1964.

162. Allison, Linda, and David Katz. *Gee Wiz! How to Mix Art and Science or the Art of Thinking Scientifically*. Boston: Little, Brown & Company, 1983.

163. Pringle, Laurence P. *Discovering Nature Indoors - A Natural and Science Guide to Investigations*. New York: Doubleday & Company, Inc., 1970

164. Michel, John D. *Small Motors You Can Make*. New York: Van Nostrand Reinhold Company, 1963.

165. Broekel, Ray. *Sound Experiments, a New True Book*. Chicago: Children's Press, 1983.

166. Pringle, Laurence P. *Discovering the Outdoors*. New York: Doubleday & Company, 1969

167. Hopwood, Robert R. *Science Model Making*. New York: The Macmillan Company, 1963.

168. Boy Scouts of America. *General Science*. Irving, Tex.: Boy Scouts of America, 1972.

169. Catherall, Ed. *Astronomy*. Hove, England: Wayland Publishers, Ltd., 1984.

170. Stone, A. Harris, and Dale Ingmanson. *Drop by Drop: A Look at Water*. Englewood Cliffs, N.J.: Prentice Hall, Inc., 1969.

171. Hillerman, Anne. *Done in the Sun, Solar Projects for Children*. Santa Fe, N. Mex.: Sunstone Press, 1983.

172. Ritchie, Carson I. A. *Making Scientific Toys*. New York: Thomas Nelson, Inc., 1975.

173. Catherall, Ed. *Life in Fresh Water*. Hove, England: Wayland Publishers, Ltd., 1984.

174. Leskowitz, Irving and A. Harris Stone. *Animals Are Like This*. New York: Prentice Hall, Inc., 1968.

175. Challand, Helen J. *Activities in the Earth Sciences*. Chicago: Children's Press, 1982.

176. De Vries, Leonard. *The Third Book of Experiments*. New York: The Macmillan Company, 1965.

177. Mueller, Robert E. *Inventor's Notebook*. New York: The John Day Company, 1963.

178. Berry, Roland. *Easy to Make Contraptions*. New York: Harvey House, Inc., 1978.

179. Mark, Steven J. *A Physics Lab of Your Own*. Boston: Houghton Mifflin Company, 1964.

180. Challand, Helen J. *Activities in the Physical Sciences*. Chicago: Children's Press, 1984.

181. Ridiman, Bob. *Simple Science Fun, Experiences with Light, Sound, Air & Water*. New York: Parents Magazine Press, 1972.

182. Stone, A. Harris. *The Heat's On*. Englewood Cliffs, N.J.: Prentice Hall, Inc., 1970.

183. Sootin, Harry. *Experiments with Heat*. New York: W. W. Norton & Company, 1964.

184. Sootin, Harry. *Experiments in Magnetism & Electricity*. New York: Franklin Watts, Inc., 1962.

185. Feravolo, Rocco V. *Junior Science Book of Electricity*. Champaign, Ill.: Garrard Publishing Company, 1960.

186. De Vries, Leonard. *The Book of Experiments*. New York: The Macmillan Company, 1959.

187. Ardley, Neil. *Sound and Music*. New York: Franklin Watts, Inc., 1984.

188. Moorman, Thomas. *How to Make Your Science Project Scientific*. New York: Atheneum Publishers, 1974.

189. Adams, Florence. *Catch a Sunbeam, a Book of Solar Study and Experiments*. New York: Harcourt Brace Jovanovich, Inc., 1978.

190. Van Deman, Barry, and Ed McDonald. *Nuts & Bolts, a Matter of Fact Guide to Science Fair Projects*. Harwood Heights, Ill.: The Science Man Press, 1980.

191. Stanley, Leon S. *Easy to Make Electric Gadgets*. New York: Harvey House, Inc., 1980.

192. Humphrey, Henry. *When Is Now? Experiments with Time and Timekeeping Devices*. New York: Doubleday & Company, Inc., 1980.

193. Pope, Joyce. *The Seashore*. New York: Franklin Watts, Inc., 1985.

194. Court, Judith. *Ponds and Streams*. New York: Franklin Watts, Inc., 1985.

195. Vogt, Gregory. *Electricity and Magnetism*. New York: Franklin Watts, Inc., 1985.

196. Webster, David. *Science Projects with Eggs*. New York: Franklin Watts, Inc., 1976.

197. Stone, A. Harris, and Dale Ingmanson. *Rocks & Rills: A Look at Geology*. Englewood Cliffs, N.J.: Prentice Hall, Inc., 1967.

198. Bendick, Jeanne. *Solids, Liquids & Gases*. New York: Franklin Watts, Inc., 1974.

199. Milgrom, Harry. *Adventures with a String*. New York: E. P. Dutton & Company, Inc., 1965.

200. Milgrom, Harry. *Adventures with a Party Plate*. New York: E. P. Dutton & Company, Inc., 1968.

201. Milgrom, Harry. *Adventures with a Paper Cup*. New York: E. P. Dutton & Company, Inc., 1968.

202. Gardner, Martin. *Science Puzzlers*. New York: Viking Press, 1960.

203. Herbert, Don. *Mr. Wizard's Supermarket Science*. New York: Random House, 1980.

204. Hellman, Hal. *The Lever and the Pulley*. New York: J.B. Lippincott Company, 1971.

205 Cobb, Vicki. *Magic ... Naturally! Science Entertainments and Amusements*. New York: J. B. Lippincott Company, 1976.

206. Schneider, Herman, and Nina Schneider. *Science Fun with a Flashlight*. New York: McGraw-Hill Book Company, 1975.

207. Ridiman, Bob. *What Is a Shadow? A Second Book of Simple Science Fun!* New York: Parents Magazine Press, 1973.

208. Neal, Charles D. *Exploring Light & Color*. New York: Grosset & Dunlap, Inc., 1964.

209. Stone, A. Harris, and Bertram M. Siegel. *Turned On! a Look at Electricity*. Englewood Cliffs, N.J.: Prentice Hall, Inc., 1970.

210. Wilkes, Angela. *Simple Science*. London: Usborne Publishing Ltd., 1983.

211. Branley, Franklyn M. *Roots Are Food Finders*. New York: Thomas Y. Crowell Company, 1975.

212. Haines, Gail Kay. *What Makes a Lemon Sour?* New York: William Morrow & Company, 1977.

213. Milgrom, Harry. *Egg-Ventures, First Science Experiments*. New York: E. P. Dutton & Company, Inc., 1974.

214. Milgrom, Harry. *Adventures with a Ball, First Science Experiments*. New York: E. P. Dutton & Company, Inc., 1965.

215. Alexenberg, Melvin L. *Sound Science*. Englewood Cliffs, N.J.: Prentice Hall, Inc., 1968.

216. Cobb, Vicki. *Lots of Rot*. New York: J. B. Lippincott Company, 1981.

217. Zubrowski, Bernie. *Messing Around with Water Pumps and Siphons*. Boston: Little, Brown & Company, 1982.

218. Spooner, Maggie. *Sunpower Experiments: Solar Energy Explained. rev.ed.* New York: Sterling Publishing Company, Inc., 1981.

219. Noad, Susan Strand. *Recipes for Science Fun*. New York: Franklin Watts, Inc., 1979.

220. Zubrowski, Bernie. *A Children's Museum Activity Book: Milk Carton Blocks*. Boston: Little, Brown & Company, 1979.

221. MacGregor, Anne, and Scott MacGregor. *Domes, a Project Book*. New York: Lothrop, Lee & Shepard Books, 1981.

222. Cobb, Vicki, and Kathy Darling. *Bet You Can't, Science Impossibilities to Fool You*. New York: Lothrop, Lee & Shepard Books, 1980.

223. Dixon, Malcolm. *Young Engineer on the Waterway*. New York: The Bookwright Press, 1984.

224. Dixon, Malcolm. *Young Engineer on the Road*. New York: The Bookwright Press, 1983.

225. Weston, Graham. *Young Engineer in the Air*. New York: The Bookwright Press, 1983.

226. Dixon, Malcolm. *Young Engineer in Communication*. New York: The Bookwright Press, 1983.

227. Dixon, Malcolm. *Young Engineer in the Factory*. New York: The Bookwright Press, 1983.

228. Cobb, Vicki. *Bet You Can, Science Possibilities to Fool You*. New York: Avon Books, 1983.

229. Cobb, Vicki. *How to Really Fool Yourself, Illusions for All Your Senses*. New York: J. B. Lippincott Company, 1981.

230. Van de Water, Marjorie. *Edison Experiments You Can Do*. New York: Harper & Row, 1960.

231. Allison, Linda. *The Reasons for Seasons, the Great Mega-galactic Trip Without Moving*. Boston: Little, Brown & Company, 1975.

232. Brown, Sam, ed. *Bubbles, Rainbows & Worms, Science Experiments for Pre-School Children*. Mount Ranier, Md.: Gryphon House, Inc., 1981.

233. Simon, Seymour. *Science in a Vacant Lot*. New York: Viking Press, 1970.

234. Hillcourt, William. *Outdoor Things to Do*. New York: Golden Press, 1975.

235. Simon, Seymour. *Discovering What Goldfish Do*. New York: McGraw-Hill Book Company, 1970.

236. Sisson, Edith A. *Nature with Children of All Ages, Activities & Adventures for Exploring*. Englewood Cliffs, N.J.: Prentice Hall, Inc., 1982.

237. Kaufman, John. *Streamlined, Let's Read and Find Out Science Book*. New York: Thomas Y. Crowell Company, 1974.

238. Feravolo, Rocco V. *Junior Science Book of Heat*. Champaign, Ill.: Garrard Publishing Company, 1964.

239. Simon, Seymour. *Finding Out with Your Senses*. New York: McGraw-Hill Book Company, 1971.

240. Feravolo, Rocco V. *Junior Science Book of Light*. Champaign, Ill.: Garrard Publishing Company, 1961.

241. Smith, Howard E., Jr. *Balance It*. New York: Four Winds Press, 1982.

242. Bendick, Jeanne. *How to Make a Cloud*. New York: Parents Magazine Press, 1971.

243. Stone, A. Harris, and Herbert Spiegel. *The Winds of Weather*. Englewood Cliffs, N.J.: Prentice Hall, Inc., 1969.

244. Fletcher, Helen Jill. *Secret Codes*. New York: Franklin Watts, Inc., 1980.

245. Showers, Paul. *A Drop of Blood, Let's Read and Find Out*. New York: Thomas Y. Crowell Company, 1967.

246. Branley, Franklyn. *Sunshine Makes the Seasons*. New York: Thomas Y. Crowell Company, 1974.

247. Catherall, Ed. *Friction*. Hove, England: Wayland Publishers, Ltd., 1983.

248. Bolwell, Laurie, and Clifford Lines. *Where Plants Grow*. Hove, England: Wayland Publishers, Ltd., 1983.

249. Ardley, Neil. *Hot and Cold*. New York: Franklin Watts, Inc., 1983.

250. Ross, Dave. *Making Robots*. New York: Franklin Watts, Inc., 1980.

251. Hayes, Phyllis. *Musical Instruments You Can Make*. New York: Franklin Watts, Inc., 1981.

252. Ross, Dave. *Making Space Puppets*. New York: Franklin Watts, Inc., 1980.

253. Jacobson, Willard J., and Abby B. Bergman. *Science Activities for Children*. Englewood Cliffs, N.J.: Prentice Hall, Inc., 1983.

254. O'Hagan, Caroline. *It's Easy to Have a Snail Visit You*. New York: Lothrop, Lee & Shepard Books, 1980.

255. O'Hagan, Caroline. *It's Easy to Have a Worm Visit You*. New York: Lothrop, Lee & Shepard Books, 1980.

256. O'Hagan, Caroline. *It's Easy to Have a Caterpillar Visit You*. New York: Lothrop, Lee & Shepard Books, 1980.

257. Cobb, Vicki. *Fuzz Does It*. New York: J. B. Lippincott Company, 1982.

258. Simon, Seymour. *The Optical Illusion Book*. New York: Four Winds Press, 1976.

259. Cobb, Vicki. *Gobs of Goo*. New York: J. B. Lippincott Company, 1983.

260. Ardley, Neil. *Making Things Move*. New York: Franklin Watts, Inc., 1984.

261. Newson, Lesley. *Meatballs and Molecules, the Science Behind Food*. London: Adam and Charles Black, 1984.

262. Simon, Seymour. *Beneath Your Feet*. New York: Walker & Company, 1977.

263. Stone, A. Harris, and Stephen Collins. *Populations, Experiments in Ecology*. New York: Franklin Watts, Inc., 1973.

264. Rights, Mollie. *Beastly Neighbors, All About Wild Things in the City or Why Earthwigs Make....* Boston: Little, Brown & Company, 1981.

265. Simon, Seymour. *Mirror Magic*. New York: Lothrop, Lee & Shepard Books, 1980.

266. Simon, Seymour. *Animals in the Field and Laboratory, Science Projects in Animal Behavior*. New York: McGraw-Hill Book Company, 1968.

267. Weiss, Harvey. *Motors & Engines and How They Work*. New York: Thomas Y. Crowell Company, 1969.

268 Simon, Seymour. *Science Projects in Ecology*. New York: Holiday House, 1972.

269. Dixon, Malcolm. *Young Engineer on the Railway*. New York: The Bookwright Press, 1984.

270. Selsam, Millicent E. *Play with Plants*. New York: William Morrow & Company, 1949.

271. Selsam, Millicent E. *Plants That Move*. New York: William Morrow & Company, 1962.

272. Selsam, Millicent E. *Eat the Fruit, Plant the Seed*. New York: William Morrow & Company, 1980.

273. Stone, A. Harris, and Irving Leskowitz. *Plants Are Like That*. Englewood Cliffs, N.J.: Prentice Hall, Inc., 1968.

274. Catherall, Ed. *Gravity*. Hove, England: Wayland Publishers, Ltd., 1983.

275. Boulton, Carolyn. *Trees*. New York: Franklin Watts, Inc., 1984.

276. Appelhof, Mary. *Worms Eat My Garbage*. Kalamazoo, Mich.: Flower Press, 1982.

277. Nestor, William P. *Into Winter, Discovering a Season*. Boston: Houghton Mifflin Company, 1982.

278. Reuben, Gabriel. *Electricity Experiments for Children*. New York: Dover Publications, Inc., 1968.

279. Kipping, John. *Nature's Pets*. San Francisco: Troubador Press, 1975.

280. Fox, Sally. *Tasty Adventures in Science*. New York: Lantern Press, 1963.

281. Mandell, Muriel. *Physics Experiments for Children*. New York: Dover Publications, Inc., 1968.

282. Gutnik, Martin J. *How Plants Make Food*. Chicago: Children's Press, 1976.

283. Gutnik, Martin J. *What Plants Produce*. Chicago: Children's Press, 1976.

284. Gutnik, Martin J. *How Plants Are Made*. Chicago: Children's Press, 1975.

285. Schwartz, George I., and Bernice S. Schwartz. *Food Chains and Ecosystems*. New York: Doubleday & Company, Inc., 1974.

286. Webster, David. *Spider Watching*. New York: Julian Messner, 1984.

287. Ardley, Neil. *Discovering Electricity*. New York: Franklin Watts, Inc., 1984.

288. Supraner, Robyn. *Science Secrets*. Mahwah, N.J.: Troll Associates, 1981.

289. Metos, Thomas H., and Gary G. Bitter. *Exploring with Solar Energy*. New York: Julian Messner, 1978.

290. Sleep, Mark C. W. *Rivers and Streams*. Hove, England: Wayland Publishers, Ltd., 1983.

291. Brown, Bob. *Science Circus*. New York: Fleet Publishing Corp., 1960.

292. Jobb, Jamie. *The Night Sky Book, an Everyday Guide to Every Night*. Boston: Little, Brown & Company, 1977.

293. Schneider, Maxine Springer. *Science Projects for the Intermediate Grades*. Belmont, Calif.: Fearon Publishers, 1971.

294. Hanauer, Ethel. *Biology Experiments for Children*. New York: Dover Publications, Inc., 1962.

295. Gardner, Robert. *Science Around the House*. New York: Julian Messner, 1985.

296. Kohn, Bernice. *The Beachcomber's Book*. New York: Viking Press, 1970.

297. Simon, Seymour. *Shadow Magic*. New York: Lothrop, Lee & Shepard Books, 1984.

298. Bolwell, Laurie, and Clifford Lines. *Climate and Weather*. Hove, England: Wayland Publishers, Ltd., 1984.

299. Sleep, Mark C. W. *Around the Coast*. Hove, England: Wayland Publishers, Ltd., 1983.

300. Sleep, Mark C. W. *Rocks, Minerals and Fossils*. Hove, England: Wayland Publishers, Ltd., 1984.

301. Sleep, Mark C. W. *Hills and Mountains*. Hove, England: Wayland Publishers, Ltd., 1983.

302. Hogan, Paula Z. *Inventions That Changed Our Lives - the Compass*. New York: Walker & Company, 1982.

303. Arnold, Caroline. *Maps and Globes, Fun, Facts and Activities*. New York: Franklin Watts, Inc., 1984.

304. Arnold, Caroline. *Measurements, Fun, Facts and Activities*. New York: Franklin Watts, Inc., 1984.

305. Boulton, Carolyn. *Birds*. New York: Franklin Watts, Inc., 1984.

306. Simon, Seymour. *Everything Moves*. New York: Walker & Company, 1976.

307. Smith, Howard E. *Play with the Sun*. New York: McGraw-Hill Book Company, 1975.

308. Goldin, Augusta. *The Shapes of Water*. New York: Doubleday & Company, Inc., 1979.

309. Hammond, Winifred G. *The Riddle of Seeds*. New York: Coward McCann, Inc., 1965.

310. Linsley, Leslie, and Jon Avon. *Air Crafts, Playthings to Make and Fly*. New York: E. P. Dutton & Company, Inc., 1982.

311. Blocksma, Mary, and Dewey Blocksma. *Easy-to-Make Spaceships That Really Fly*. Englewood Cliffs, N.J.: Prentice Hall, Inc., 1983.

312. Condit, Martha Olson. *Something to Make, Something to Think About*. New York: Four Winds Press, 1975.

313. Piecewicz, Ann Thomas. *See What I Caught*. Englewood Cliffs, N.J.: Prentice Hall, Inc., 1974.

314. Ross, Frank, Jr. *The Space Shuttle, Its Story & How to Make a Flying Paper Model*. New York: Lothrop, Lee & Shepard Books, 1979.

315. Ross, Frank, Jr. *Model Satellites and Spacecraft, Their Stories & How to Make Them*. New York: Lothrop, Lee & Shepard Books, 1969.

316. Grummer, Arnold E. *Paper by Kids*. Minneapolis, Minn.: Dillon Press, Inc., 1980.

317. Wyler, Rose, and Gerald Ames. *Secrets in Stones*. New York: Four Winds Press, 1972.

318. Freeman, Mae. *The Book of Magnets*. New York: Four Winds Press, 1969.

319. Mullin, Virginia L. *Chemistry Experiments for Children*. New York: Dover Publications, Inc., 1962.

320. Pine, Tillie S., and Joseph Levine. *The Eskimos Knew*. New York: McGraw-Hill Book Company, 1962.

321. Pine, Tillie S., and Joseph Levine. *The Chinese Knew*. New York: McGraw-Hill Book Company, 1958.

322. Pine, Tillie S., and Joseph Levine. *The Pilgrims Knew*. New York: McGraw-Hill Book Company, 1957.

323. Pine, Tillie S., and Joseph Levine. *The Egyptians Knew*. New York: McGraw-Hill Book Company, 1964.

324. Pine, Tillie S., and Joseph Levine. *The Indians Knew*. New York: McGraw-Hill Book Company, 1957.

325. Pine, Tillie S., and Joseph Levine. *The Polynesians Knew*. New York: McGraw-Hill Book Company, 1974.

326. Pine, Tillie S., and Joseph Levine. *The Incas Knew*. New York: McGraw-Hill Book Company, 1968.

327. Podendorf, Illa. *The True Book of Weather Experiments*. Chicago: Children's Press, 1961.

328. Salvadori, Mario. *Building, the Fight Against Gravity*. New York: Atheneum Publishers, 1979.

329. Simon, Seymour. *Let's Try It Out: Light and Dark*. New York: McGraw-Hill Book Company, 1970.

330. Berger, Melvin. *The New Water Book*. New York: Thomas Y. Crowell Company, 1973.

331. Stevens, Carla. *Insect Pets: Catching & Caring for Them*. New York: Greenwillow Books, 1978.

332. Ewbank, Constance. *Insect Zoo! How to Collect & Care for Insects*. New York: Walker & Company, 1973.

333. Barr, George. *Research Ideas for Young Scientists*. New York: McGraw-Hill Book Company, 1958.

334. Dunbar, Robert E. *The Heart & Circulatory System*. New York: Franklin Watts, Inc., 1984.

335. Allison, Linda. *Blood & Guts, a Working Guide to Your Own Insides*. Boston: Little, Brown & Company, 1976.

336. Cobb, Vicki. *The Secret Life of School Supplies*. New York: J. B. Lippincott Company, 1981.

337. Weston, Graham. *Young Engineer in the Home*. Hove, England: Wayland Publishers, Ltd., 1982.

338. Vogt, Gregory. *Model Rockets*. New York: Franklin Watts, Inc., 1982.

339. Simon, Seymour. *Soap Bubble Magic*. New York: Lothrop, Lee & Shepard Books, 1985.

340. Whyman, Kathryn. *Electricity and Magnetism*. New York: Gloucester Press, 1986.

341. Gutnik, Martin J. *Simple Electrical Devices*. New York: Franklin Watts, Inc., 1986.

342. Dixon, Malcolm. *Young Engineer at Sea*. Hove, England: Wayland Publishers, Ltd., 1983.

343. Gilmore, H. H. *Model Submarines for Beginners*. New York: Harper & Row, 1959.

344. Gilmore, H. H. *Model Boats for Beginners*. New York: Harper & Row, 1959.

345. Fitzpatrick, Julie. *Mirrors*. Morristown, N.J.: Silver Burdett Company, 1984.

346. Cobb, Vicki. *Chemically Active Experiments You Can Do at Home*. New York: J. B. Lippincott Company, 1985.

484

347. Cummings, Richard. *Make Your Own Alternative Energy.* New York: David McKay Company, Inc., 1979.

348. MacGregor, Anne, and Scott MacGregor. *Bridges, a Project Book.* New York: Lothrop, Lee & Shepard Books, 1980.

349. Simon, Seymour. *Let's Try It Out, About Your Heart.* New York: McGraw-Hill Book Company, 1974.

350. McGill, Ormond. *Science Magic, 101 Experiments You Can Do.* New York: Arco Publishing Company, Inc., 1984.

351. Stwertka, Eve, and Albert Stwertka. *Make It Graphic, Drawing Graphs for Science and Social Studies Projects.* New York: Julian Messner, 1985.

352. Webber, Irma E. *Bits That Grow Big, Where Plants Come From.* Chippewa Falls, Wisc.: E.M. Hale & Company, 1949.

353. Milgrom, Harry. *ABC Science Experiments.* New York: Crowell-Collier Press, 1970.

354. Olney, Ross, and Pat Olney. *Keeping Insects as Pets.* New York: Franklin Watts, Inc., 1978.

355. Petersen, David. *Solar Energy at Work, a New True Book.* Chicago: Children's Press, 1985.

356. Wickers, David, and Sharon Finmark. *How to Make Your Own Kinetics.* New York: Van Nostrand Reinhold Company, 1972,

357. Ardley, Neil. *Making Metric Measurements.* New York: Franklin Watts, Inc., 1983.

358. *Do It Yourself Book.* New York: Penguin Books, 1984.

359. Heinz, Brian J. *Beachcraft Bonanza.* New York: Ballyhoo Books, 1985.

360. Vivian, Charles. *Science Experiments and Amusements for Children.* New York: Dover Publications, Inc., 1963.

361. Branley, Franklyn M. *Sunshine Makes the Seasons.* New York: Thomas Y. Crowell Company, 1985.

362. Pitcher, Caroline. *Build Your Own Space Station.* New York: Franklin Watts, Inc., 1985.

363. Hamilton, Charles E. *ECO: Suggested Activities to Motivate the Teaching of Elementary Ecology.* Stevensville, Mich.: Educational Service, Inc., 1974.

364. Allison, Linda. *The Wild Inside: Sierra Club's Guide to the Great Indoors.* New York: Sierra Club Books, Charles Scribner's Sons, 1979.

365. Williams, J. Alan. *The Interplanetary Toy Book, Space People, Vehicles, Creatures and More.* New York: The Macmillan Company, 1985.

366. Stein, Sara. *The Science Book.* New York: Workman Publishing, 1979.

367. Feravolo, Rocco V. *Junior Science Book of Magnets.* Champaign, Ill.: Garrard Press, 1960.

368. Feravolo, Rocco V. *Junior Science Book of Water Experiments.* Champaign, Ill.: Garrard Press, 1965.

369. David, Eugene. *Crystal Magic.* Englewood Cliffs, N.J.: Prentice Hall, Inc., 1965.

370. Simon, Seymour. *Discovering What Gerbils Do.* New York: McGraw-Hill Book Company, 1971.

371. Gutnik, Martin J. *Ecology Projects for Young Scientists.* New York: Franklin Watts, Inc., 1984.

372. Gutnik, Martin J. *Genetics Projects for Young Scientists.* New York: Franklin Watts, Inc., 1985.

373. Zubrowski, Bernie. *Raceways: Having Fun with Balls & Tracks.* New York: William Morris, 1985.

374. Sander, Lenore. *The Curious World of Crystals.* Englewood Cliffs: N.J.: Prentice Hall, Inc., 1964.

375. Allen, Gwen. *Bones.* New York: Franklin Watts, Inc., 1970.

376. Brown, Marc. *Your First Garden Book.* Boston: Little, Brown & Company, 1981.

377. Whyman, Kathryn. *Heat & Energy.* New York: Gloucester Press, 1986.

378. Cartwright, Sally. *Sand.* New York: Coward, McCann & Geoghegan, Inc., 1975.

379. Hewish, Mark. *The Young Scientist's Book of Jets.* London: Usborne Publishing Ltd., 1976.

380. Sommerville Public Schools, Project Inside/Outside. *Ladybugs and Lettuce Leaves.* Washington, D.C.: Pub. of Center for Science in the Public Interest, 1982.

381. Barr, George. *More Research Ideas for Young Scientists.* New York: McGraw-Hill Book Company, 1961.

382. Beeler, Nelson. *More Experiments in Science.* New York: Thomas Y. Crowell Company, 1950.

383. Simon, Seymour. *Let's Try It Out, Hot and Cold.* New York: McGraw-Hill Book Company, 1972.

384. Johnsen, Jan. *Gardening Without Soil.* New York: J. B. Lippincott Company, 1979.

385. Bradley, Duane, and Eugene Lord. *Here's How It Works.* New York: J. B. Lippincott Company, 1962.

386. Wels, Byron G. *Science Fair Projects, Invent, Devise, Create & Win.* New York: Drake Publishers, Inc., 1976.

387. Lewis, Anne Gillespie. *Lotions, Soaps and Scents.* Minneapolis, Minn.: Lerner Publications Company, 1975.

388. Pitcher, Caroline. *Build Your Own Airport.* New York: Franklin Watts, Inc., 1985.

389. Goeller, Lee. *How to Make an Adding Machine That Even Adds Roman Numerals.* New York: Harcourt Brace Jovanovich, Inc., 1979.

390. Case, Marshall T. *Look What I Found.* Old Greenwich, Conn.: Chatham Press, Inc., 1971.

391. Neal, Charles D. *Safe & Simple Projects with Electricity.* Chicago: Children's Press, 1965.

392. Barr, George. *Fun & Tricks for Young Scientists.* New York: McGraw-Hill Book Company, 1968.

393. Stine, G. Harry. *On the Frontiers of Science, Strange Machines You Can Build.* New York: Atheneum Publishers, 1985.

394. Showers, Paul. *What Happens to a Hamburger.* New York: Thomas Y. Crowell Company, 1970.

395. Roberts, Hortense Roberta. *You Can Make an Insect Zoo.* Chicago: Children's Press, 1974.

396. Mebane, Robert C. *Adventures with Atoms and Molecules, Chemistry Experiments for Young People.* Hillside, N.J.: Enslow Publishers, Inc., 1985.

397. *Science Fairs and Projects.* Washington, D.C.: National Science Teachers Association, 1984.

398. Beller, Joel. *Experimenting with Plants, Projects for Home, Garden and Classroom.* New York: Arco Publishing Company, Inc., 1985.

399. Ontario Science Centre. *Science Works. 65 Experiments That Introduce the Wonder of Science.* Reading, Mass.: Addison-Wesley Publishing Company, Inc., 1984.

400. Abruscato, Joe, and Jack Hassard. *The Whole Cosmos Catalog of Science Activities.* Glenview, Ill.: Scott, Foresman & Company, 1977.

401. Graham, Ada, and Frank Graham. *The Big Stretch.* New York: Alfred A. Knopf, 1985.

402. Goran, Morris. *Experimental Biology for Boys.* New York: John F. Rider Publisher, Inc., 1961.

403. Headstrom, Richard. *Adventures with a Microscope.* New York: J. B. Lippincott Company, 1941.

404. Tchudi, Stephen N. *Soda Poppery, the History of Soft Drinks in America with Recipes* New York: Charles Scribner's Sons, 1986.

405. Adler, David A. *Base Five.* New York: Thomas Y. Crowell Company, 1975.

406. Adler, Irving. *Integers, Positive and Negative.* New York: The John Day Company, 1972.

407. Adler, David A. *Roman Numerals.* New York: Thomas Y. Crowell Company, 1977.

408. Adler, David A. *3D, 2D, 1D.* New York: Thomas Y. Crowell Company, 1975.

409. Alexenberg, Melvin L. *Light and Sight.* Englewood Cliffs, N.J.: Prentice Hall, Inc., 1969.

410. Amery, Heather. *The Know How Book of Action Toys.* New York: Sterling Publishing Company, Inc., 1976.

411. Anderson, Dorothy S. *Junior Science Book of Sound.* Champaign, Ill.: Garrard Press, 1962.

412. Anderson, Lucia. *The Smallest Life Around Us.* New York: Crown Publishers, Inc., 1978.

413. Anderson, Margaret J. *Exploring City Trees and the Need for Urban Forests.* New York: McGraw-Hill Book Company, 1976.

414. Anderson, Margaret J. *Exploring the Insect World.* New York: McGraw-Hill Book Company, 1974.

415. Arnold, Wesley F., and Wayne C. Cardy. *Fun with Next to Nothing, Handicraft Projects for Boys and Girls.* New York: Harper & Row, 1962.

416. Baker, Samm Sinclair. *The Indoor Outdoor Grow It Book.* New York: Random House, 1966.

417. Balestrino, Philip. *Hot as an Ice Cube.* New York: Thomas Y. Crowell Company, 1971.

418. Bowman, Bruce. *Toothpick Sculpture and Ice-Cream Stick Art.* New York: Sterling Publishing Company, Inc., 1976.

419. Bramwell, Martyn, and David Mostyn. *How Things Work.* London: Usborne Publishing Ltd., 1984.

420. Brandwein, Paul F., and Hy Ruchlis. *Invitations to Investigate, an Introduction to Scientific Exploration.* New York: Harcourt Brace Jovanovich, Inc., 1970.

421. Branley, Franklyn M. *Eclipse, Darkness in Daytime.* New York: Thomas Y. Crowell Company, 1973.

422. Branley, Franklyn M. *High Sounds, Low Sounds.* New York: Thomas Y. Crowell Company, 1967.

423. Branley, Franklyn M. *Measure with Metric.* New York: Thomas Y. Crowell Company, 1975.

424. Branley, Franklyn M., and Eleanor K. Vaughan. *Mickey's Magnet.* New York: Thomas Y. Crowell Company, 1965.

425. Branley, Franklyn M., and Eleanor K. Vaughan. *Rusty Rings a Bell.* New York: Thomas Y. Crowell Company, 1957.

426. Branley, Franklyn M. *The Sky Is Full of Stars.* New York: Thomas Y. Crowell Company, 1981.

427. Branley, Franklyn M. *Timmy and the Tin Can Telephone.* New York: Thomas Y. Crowell Company, 1959.

428. Broekel, Ray. *Experiments with Light, a New True Book.* Chicago: Children's Press, 1986.

429. Brown, William F. *Wood Works, Experiments with Common Wood and Tools.* New York: Atheneum Publishers, 1984.

430. Burton, Maurice. *The Life of Insects.* New York: Golden Press, 1972.

431. Pitcher, Caroline. *Cars and Boats.* New York: Franklin Watts, Inc., 1983.

432. Cartwright, Sally. *Sunlight.* New York: Coward, McCann & Geoghegan, Inc., 1974.

433. Cartwright, Sally. *Water Is Wet.* New York: Coward, McCann & Geoghegan, Inc., 1973.

434. Challand, Helen J. *Experiments with Electricity, a New True Book.* Chicago: Children's Press, 1986.

435. Challand, Helen J. *Experiments with Magnets, a New True Book.* Chicago: Children's Press, 1986.

436. Challand, Helen J. *Science Projects and Activities.* Chicago: Children's Press, 1985.

437. Charosh, Mannis. *The Ellipse.* New York: Thomas Y. Crowell Company, 1971.

438. Charosh, Mannis. *Mathematical Games for One or Two.* New York: Thomas Y. Crowell Company, 1972.

439. Charosh, Mannis. *Number Ideas Through Pictures.* New York: Thomas Y. Crowell Company, 1974.

440. Charosh, Mannis. *Straight Lines, Parallel Lines, Perpendicular Lines.* New York: Thomas Y. Crowell Company, 1970.

441. Cobb, Vicki. *The Secret Life of Cosmetics, a Science Experiment Book.* New York: J. B. Lippincott Company, 1985.

442. Mitchell, John, and the Massachusetts Audubon Society. *The Curious Naturalist, a Handbook of Crafts, Games, Activities and Ideas.* Englewood Cliffs, N.J.: Prentice Hall, Inc., 1980.

443. Dennis, J. Richard. *Fractions Are Parts of Things.* New York: Thomas Y. Crowell Company, 1971.

444. Ellison, Elsie E. *Fun with Lines and Curves.* New York: Lothrop, Lee & Shepard Books, 1972.

445. Epstein, Sam, and Beryl Epstein. *Electricity.* New York: Franklin Watts, Inc., 1966.

446. Feravolo, Rocco V. *Junior Science Book of Flying.* Champaign, Ill.: Garrard Publishing Company, 1960.

447. Fey, James T. *Long, Short, High, Low, Thin, Wide.* New York: Thomas Y. Crowell Company, 1971.

448. Filson, Brent. *Famous Experiments and How to Repeat Them.* New York: Julian Messner, 1986.

449. Filstrup, Chris, and Janie Filstrup. *Beadazzled, the Story of Beads.* New York: Frederick Warne, 1982.

450. Fitzpatrick, Julie. *In the Air (Science Spirals).* Morristown, N.J.: Silver Burdett Company, 1984.

451. Fitzpatrick, Julie. *Magnets.* Morristown, N.J.: Silver Burdett Company, 1984.

452. Forte, Imogene. *Science Fun, Discovering the World Around Us.* Nashville, Tenn.: Incentive Publications, 1985.

453. Frederique and Papy. *Graph Games.* New York: Thomas Y. Crowell Company, 1971.

454. Froman, Robert. *Angles Are as Easy as Pie.* New York: Thomas Y. Crowell Company, 1975.

455. Froman, Robert. *Bigger and Smaller.* New York: Thomas Y. Crowell Company, 1971.

456. Froman, Robert. *A Game of Functions.* New York: Thomas Y. Crowell Company, 1974.

457. Froman, Robert. *The Greatest Guessing Game, a Book About Dividing.* New York: Thomas Y. Crowell Company, 1978.

458. Froman, Robert. *Less Than Nothing Is Really Something.* New York: Thomas Y. Crowell Company, 1973.

459. Froman, Robert. *Mushrooms and Molds.* New York: Thomas Y. Crowell Company, 1972.

460. Froman, Robert. *Rubber Bands, Baseballs and Dough-nuts, a Book About Topology*. New York: Thomas Y. Crowell Company, 1972.

461. Froman, Robert. *Venn Diagrams*. New York: Thomas Y. Crowell Company, 1972.

462. Gans, Roma. *Birds Eat and Eat and Eat*. New York: Thomas Y. Crowell Company, 1963.

463. Gans, Roma. *Hummingbirds in the Garden*. New York: Thomas Y. Crowell Company, 1969.

464. Gersting, Judith L. *Yes-No; Stop-Go, Some Patterns in Mathematical Logic*. New York: Thomas Y. Crowell Company, 1977.

465. Gesmer, Anna B., and Elisabeth Gitter. *The Complete Book of Flowerpot Ecology*. New York: Coward, McCann & Geoghegan, Inc., 1975.

466. Gilbreath, Alice. *Making Toys That Crawl and Slide*. Chicago: Follett Publishing Company, 1978.

467. Gilbreath, Alice. *Making Toys That Swim and Float*. Chicago: Follett Publishing Company, 1978.

468. Goldin, Augusta. *Salt*. New York: Thomas Y. Crowell Company, 1965.

469. Goldin, Augusta. *Straight Hair, Curly Hair*. New York: Thomas Y. Crowell Company, 1966.

470. Goldin, Augusta. *The Sunlit Sea*. New York: Thomas Y. Crowell Company, 1968.

471. Goldin, Augusta. *Where Does Your Garden Grow*. New York: Thomas Y. Crowell Company, 1967.

472. *Growing Up with Science, the Illustrated Encyclopedia of Inventions, V.25*. Westport, Conn.: H. S. Stuttman, Inc., 1984.

473. Gunthrop, Dale. *The Life of Plants*. London: MacDonald Educational, 1976.

474. Hawes, Judy. *My Daddy Longlegs*. New York: Thomas Y. Crowell Company, 1972.

475. Hess, Lilo. *Small Habitats*. New York: Charles Scribner's Sons, 1976.

476. Hillcourt, William H. *Fun with Nature Hobbies*. New York: G. P. Putnam's Sons, 1970.

477. Holt, Michael. *Maps, Tracks and the Bridges of Konigsberg, a Book About Networks*. New York: Thomas Y. Crowell Company, 1975.

478. Hussey, Lois J., and Catherine Pessino. *Collecting Cocoons*. New York: Thomas Y. Crowell Company, 1953.

479. Jordan, Helele J. *How a Seed Grows*. New York: Thomas Y. Crowell Company, 1960.

480. Katz, Adrienne. *Naturewatch, Exploring Nature with Your Children*. Reading, Mass.: Addison-Wesley Publishing Company, Inc., 1986.

481. Kirkpatrick, Rena K. *Look at Seeds and Weeds*. Milwaukee, Wisc.: Raintree Children's Books, 1978.

482. Klein, Aaron E. *You and Your Body, a Book of Experiments to Perform on Yourself*. New York: Doubleday & Company, Inc., 1977.

483. Kramer, Jack. *Plant Hobbies, a Beginner's Book of Gardening Projects....* New York: Collins World, 1978.

484. Lindemann, Edward. *Water Animals for Your Microscope*. New York: Crowell-Collier Press, 1967.

485. Linn, Charles F. *Estimation*. New York: Thomas Y. Crowell Company, 1970.

486. Linn, Charles F. *Probability*. New York: Thomas Y. Crowell Company, 1972.

487. McCormack, Alan J. *Inventor's Workshop*. Belmont, Calif.: Fearon Teacher Aids, Pitman Learning, 1981.

488. Goldin, Augusta. *Ducks Don't Get Wet*. New York: Thomas Y. Crowell Company, 1965.

489. Blackwood, Paul. *Push and Pull, the Story of Energy*. New York: McGraw-Hill Book Company, 1966.

490. Hatch, Shirley Cook. *Wind Is to Feel*. New York: Coward, McCann & Geoghegan, Inc., 1973.

491. Kentzer, Michael. *Space: Collins Young Scientist's Book of Space*. Morristown, N.J.: Silver Burdett Company, 1979.

492. Kentzer, Michael. *Cold, Collins Young Scientist's Book of Cold*. Morristown, N.J.: Silver Burdett Company, 1976.

493. Lambert, David. *Spring*. New York: The Bookwright Press, 1987.

494. McCoy, Elin. *The Incredible Year-Round Playbook, Fun with Sun, Sand, Water, Wind & Snow*. New York: Random House, 1979.

495. McGill, Ormond. *Balancing Magic*. New York: Franklin Watts, Inc., 1986.

496. MacGregor, Anne, and Scott MacGregor. *Skyscrapers, a Project Book*. New York: Lothrop, Lee & Shepard Books, 1980.

497. Millard, Adele. *Plants for Kids to Grow Indoors*. New York: Sterling Publishing Company, Inc., 1975.

498. O'Brien, Thomas C. *Odds and Evens*. New York: Thomas Y. Crowell Company, 1971.

499. Olesky, Walter. *Experiments with Heat, a New True Book*. Chicago: Children's Press, 1986.

500. Patent, Dorothy Hinshaw. *Microscopic Animals and Plants*. New York: Holiday House, 1974.

501. Pettigrew, Mark. *Music and Sound*. New York: Gloucester Press, 1987.

502. Pettigrew, Mark. *Planet Earth*. New York: Gloucester Press, 1987.

503. Phillips, Jo. *Exploring Triangles, Paper Folding Geometry*. New York: Thomas Y. Crowell Company, 1975.

504. Phillips, Jo. *Right Angles, Paper Folding Geometry*. New York: Thomas Y. Crowell Company, 1972.

505. Prescott, Gerald W. *The Diatoms*. New York: Coward, McCann & Geoghegan, Inc., 1977.

506. Protheroe, Donald W., and Thomas P. Weinland. *More Social Science Projects You Can Do*. Englewood Cliffs, N.J.: Prentice Hall, Inc., 1974.

507. *Raintree Illustrated Science Encyclopedia, Volume 20*. Milwaukee, Wisc.: Raintree Publishers, 1984.

508. Ris, Thomas F. *The Neat Stuff Something-to-Do Book*. New York: Julian Messner, 1979.

509. St. John, Glory. *How to Count Like a Martian*. New York: Henry Z. Walck., Inc, 1975.

510. Sattler, Helen Roney. *Fish Facts and Bird Brains, Animal Intelligence*. New York: Lodestar Books, E. P. Dutton, 1984.

511. Speitel, Tom, et al. *Science Computer Programs for Kids and Other People - Apple Version*. Reston, Va.: Reston Publishing Company, 1984.

512. Showers, Paul. *Find Out by Touching*. New York: Thomas Y. Crowell Company, 1961.

513. Showers, Paul. *How You Talk*. New York: Thomas Y. Crowell Company, 1966.

514. Showers, Paul. *Follow Your Nose*. New York: Thomas Y. Crowell Company, 1963.

515. Simon, Seymour. *Discovering What Crickets Do*. New York: McGraw-Hill Book Company, 1973.

516. Simon, Seymour. *Discovering What Earthworms Do*. New York: McGraw-Hill Book Company, 1969.

517. Simon, Seymour. *Discovering What Frogs Do*. New York: McGraw-Hill Book Company, 1969.

518. Simon, Seymour. *Let's Try It Out, Wet and Dry*. New York: McGraw-Hill Book Company, 1969.

519. Sitomer, Mindel, and Harry Sitomer. *Circles*. New York: Thomas Y. Crowell Company, 1971.

520. Sitomer, Mindel, and Harry Sitomer. *How Did Numbers Begin*. New York: Thomas Y. Crowell Company, 1976.

521. Sitomer, Mindel, and Harry Sitomer. *What Is Symmetry?* New York: Thomas Y. Crowell Company, 1970.

522. Sitomer, Mindel, and Harry Sitomer. *Zero Is Not Nothing*. New York: Thomas Y. Crowell Company, 1978.

523. Smith, Howard E., Jr. *Play with the Wind*. New York: McGraw-Hill Book Company, 1972.

524. Srivastava, Jane Jonas. *Area*. New York: Thomas Y. Crowell Company, 1974.

525. Srivastava, Jane Jonas. *Averages*. New York: Thomas Y. Crowell Company, 1975.

526. Srivastava, Jane Jonas. *Number Families*. New York: Thomas Y. Crowell Company, 1979.

527. Srivastava, Jane Jonas. *Spaces, Shapes and Sizes*. New York: Thomas Y. Crowell Company, 1980.

528. Srivastava, Jane Jonas. *Statistics*. New York: Thomas Y. Crowell Company, 1973.

529. Srivastava, Jane Jonas. *Weighing and Balancing*. New York: Thomas Y. Crowell Company, 1970.

530. Stein, Sara. *The Evolution Book*. New York: Workman Publishing, 1986.

531. Stepp, Ann. *Setting Up a Science Project*. Englewood Cliffs, N.J.: Prentice Hall, Inc., 1966.

532. Stone, George K. *More Science Projects You Can Do*. Englewood Cliffs: N.J.: Prentice Hall, Inc., 1970.

533. Trivett, John V. *Building Tables on Tables, a Book About Multiplication*. New York: Thomas Y. Crowell Company, 1975.

534. Trivett, Daphne Harwood. *Shadow Geometry*. New York: Thomas Y. Crowell Company, 1974.

535. Warren, Jean. *Science Time; Early Learning Activities for Parents and Teachers of Young....* Palo Alto, Calif.: Monday Morning Books, 1984.

536. Watson, Clyde. *Binary Numbers*. New York: Thomas Y. Crowell Company, 1977.

537. Waxter, Julia B. *The Science Cookbook, Experiment-Recipes That Teach Science and Nutrition*. Belmont, Calif.: Fearon Teacher Aids, Pitman Learning, 1981.

538. Webster, David. *More Brain Boosters*. New York: Doubleday & Company, Inc., 1975.

539. Webster, Vera R. *Science Experiments, a New True Book*. Chicago: Children's Press, 1982.

540. Webster, Vera R. *Plant Experiments, a New True Book*. Chicago: Children's Press, 1982.

541. Webster, Vera R. *Weather Experiments, a New True Book*. Chicago: Children's Press, 1982.

542. Weinland, Thomas P., and Donald W. Protheroe. *Social Science Projects You Can Do*. Englewood Cliffs, N.J.: Prentice Hall, Inc., 1973.

543. Weiss, Harvey. *The Gadget Book*. New York: Thomas Y. Crowell Company, 1971.

544. Weiss, Harvey. *What Holds It Together*. Boston: Little, Brown & Company, 1977.

545. Weiss, Harvey. *Sticks, Spools and Feathers*. New York: Young Scott Books, 1962.

546. Weiss, Malcolm E. *666 Jellybeans! All That? an Introduction to Algebra*. New York: Thomas Y. Crowell Company, 1976.

547. Weiss, Malcolm E. *Solomon Grundy, Born on Monday, a Finite Arithmetic Puzzle*. New York: Thomas Y. Crowell Company, 1977.

548. White, Laurence B., Jr. *Investigating Science with Coins*. Reading, Mass.: Addison-Wesley Publishing Company, Inc., 1969.

549. White, Laurence B., Jr. *Investigating Science with Nails*. Reading, Mass.: Addison-Wesley Publishing Company, Inc., 1970.

550. White, Laurence B., Jr. *Investigating Science with Paper*. Reading, Mass.: Addison-Wesley Publishing Company, Inc., 1970.

551. White, Laurence B., Jr. *Science Games*. Reading, Mass.: Addison-Wesley Publishing Company, Inc., 1975.

552. Whitlock, Ralph. *Summer*. New York: The Bookwright Press, 1987.

553. Whyman, Kathryn. *Chemical Changes*. New York: Gloucester Press, 1986.

554. Whyman, Kathryn. *Forces in Action*. New York: Gloucester Press, 1986.

555. Whyman, Kathryn. *Light and Lasers*. New York: Gloucester Press, 1986.

556. Whyman, Kathryn. *Living Things*. New York: Gloucester Press, 1987.

557. Wilson, Forrest. *Architecture: A Book of Projects for Young Adults*. New York: Reinhold Book Corp., 1968.

558. Wilt, Joy, and Terre Watson. *Look! 70 Visual Experiments for Children, Including 35 Toys and Projects*. Cincinnati, Ohio: Creative Resources, 1978.

559. Wong, Herbert H., and Matthew F. Vessel. *Our Terrariums*. Reading, Mass.: Addison-Wesley Publishing Company, Inc., 1969.

560. Wyler, Rose. *Science Fun with Peanuts and Popcorn*. New York: Julian Messner, 1986.

561. Wyler, Rose. *Science Fun with Toy Boats and Planes*. New York: Julian Messner, 1986.

562. Branley, Franklyn M. *Air Is All Around You*. New York: Thomas Y. Crowell Company, 1986.

563. Brown, Robert J. *333 Science Tricks and Experiments*. Blue Ridge Summit, Pa.: Tab Books, Inc., 1984.

564. *Elementary School Aerospace Activities, a Resource for Teachers*. Washington, D.C.: National Aeronautics and Space Administration, 1977.

565. Herbert, Don. *Mr. Wizard's Experiments for Young Scientists*. New York: Doubleday & Company, Inc., 1959.

566. Kentzer, Michael. *Strength: Collins Young Scientist's Book of Strength*. Morristown, N.J.: Silver Burdett Company, 1979.

567. Kentzer, Michael. *Power, Collins Young Scientist's Book of Power*. Morristown, N.J.: Silver Burdett Company, 1979.

568. Kentzer, Michael. *Heat, Collins Young Scientist's Book of Heat*. Morristown, N.J.: Silver Burdett Company, 1976.

569. Kentzer, Michael. *Waves, Collins Young Scientist's Book of Waves*. Morristown, N.J.: Silver Burdett Company, 1977.

570. Parker, Steve. *Light, the Marshall Cavendish Science Project Book of Light*. New York: Marshall Cavendish Corp., 1986.

571. Parker, Steve. *The Human Body, the Marshall Cavendish Science Project Book of the Human Body.* New York: Marshall Cavendish Corp., 1986.

572. Parker, Steve. *The Earth, the Marshall Cavendish Science Project Book of the Earth.* New York: Marshall Cavendish Corp., 1986.

573. Parker, Steve. *Water, the Marshall Cavendish Science Project Book of Water.* New York: Marshall Cavendish Corp., 1986.

574. Parker, Steve. *Plants, the Marshall Cavendish Science Project Book of Plants.* New York: Marshall Cavendish Corp., 1986.

575. Parker, Steve. *Mechanics, the Marshall Cavendish Science Project Book of Mechanics.* New York: Marshall Cavendish Corp., 1986.

576. Cassell, Sylvia. *Indoor Games and Activities.* New York: Harper & Row, 1960.

577. Stone, George K. *Science Projects You Can Do.* Englewood Cliffs, N.J.: Prentice Hall, Inc., 1963.

578. Fitzpatrick, Julie. *On the Water.* Morristown, N.J.: Silver Burdett Company, 1985.

579. Anderson, Lucia. *Mammals and Their Milk.* New York: Dodd, Mead & Company, 1985.

580. Forte, Imogene, and Joy MacKenzie. *For the Love of a Ladybug.* Nashville, Tenn.: Incentive Publications, 1978.

581. Blocksma, Mary, and Dewey Blocksma. *Space-Crafting, Invent Your Own Flying Spaceship.* New York: Prentice Hall, Inc., 1986.

582. Criswell, Susie Gwen. *Nature with Art, Classroom and Outdoor Art Activities with Natural History.* Englewood Cliffs, N.J.: Prentice Hall, Inc., 1986.

583. Branley, Franklyn M. *Snow Is Falling,* rev.ed. New York: Harper & Row, 1986.

584. Schulman, Elayne. *Science Projects with Computers.* New York: Arco Publishing Company, Inc., 1985.

585. Brown, Robert J. *200 Illustrated Science Experiments for Children.* Blue Ridge Summit, Pa.: Tab Books, Inc., 1987.

586. Gardner, Robert. *Ideas for Science Projects.* New York: Franklin Watts, Inc., 1986.

587. Kerrod, Robin. *Moving Things.* Morristown, N.J.: Silver Burdett Press, 1987.

588. Kerrod, Robin. *All Around.* Morristown, N.J.: Silver Burdett Press, 1987.

589. Kerrod, Robin. *Changing Things.* Morristown, N.J.: Silver Burdett Press, 1987.

590. Kerrod, Robin. *Living Things.* Morristown, N.J.: Silver Burdett Press, 1987.

591. Leblanc, Wayne J., and Alden R. Carter. *Modern Electronics.* New York: Franklin Watts, Inc., 1986.

592. McKay, David W., and Bruce G. Smith. *Space Science Projects for Young Scientists.* New York: Franklin Watts, Inc., 1986.

593. McLaughlin, Molly. *Earthworms, Dirt, and Rotten Leaves, an Exploration in Ecology.* New York: Atheneum Publishers, 1986.

594. Miller, Christina G., and Louise A. Berry. *Acid Rain, a Source Book for Young People.* New York: Julian Messner, 1986.

595. Paull, John, and Dorothy Paull. *Light.* Loughborough, England: Ladybird Books, 1982.

596. Paull, John, and Dorothy Paull. *Simple Mechanics.* Loughborough, England: Ladybird Books, 1982.

597. Paull, John, and Dorothy Paull. *Air.* Loughborough, England: Ladybird Books, 1982.

598. Paull, John, and Dorothy Paull. *Simple Chemistry.* Loughborough, England: Ladybird Books, 1982.

599. Paull, John, and Dorothy Paull. *Magnets and Electricity.* Loughborough, England: Ladybird Books, 1982.

600. Penrose, Gordon. *It's Dr. Zed's Brilliant Book of Science Experiments.* Woodbury, N.J.: Barron's Educational Series, Inc., 1977.

601. Pine, Tillie S., and Joseph Levine. *The Arabs Knew.* New York: McGraw-Hill Book Company, 1976.

602. Pine, Tillie S., and Joseph Levine. *Scientists and Their Discoveries.* New York: McGraw-Hill Book Company, 1978.

603. Rahn, Joan Elma. *More About What Plants Do.* New York: Atheneum Publishers, 1975.

604. Sootin, Harry. *Experiments with Water.* New York: Grosset & Dunlap, Inc., 1971.

605. Tuey, John, and David Wickers. *How to Be a Scientist at Home.* New York: Van Nostrand Reinhold Company, 1972.

606. Zubrowski, Bernie. *Wheels at Work: Building and Experimenting with Models of Machines.* New York: William Morrow & Company, Inc., 1986.

607. Ontario Science Centre. *Foodworks, Over 100 Science Activities and Fascinating Facts That Explore.* Reading, Mass.: Addison-Wesley Publishing Company, Inc., 1987.

608. Vogt, Gregory. *Generating Electricity.* New York: Franklin Watts, Inc., 1986.

609. Simon, Seymour. *About the Foods You Eat.* New York: McGraw-Hill Book Company, 1979.

610. Dugan, William. *All About Houses.* New York: Western Publishing Company, 1975.

611. Cobb, Vicki. *The Trip of a Drip.* Boston: Little, Brown & Company, 1986.

612. Shuttlesworth, Dorothy E. *The Hidden Magic of Seeds.* Emmaus, Pa.: Rodale Press, Inc., 1976.

613. Dean, Anabel. *Submerge, the Story of Divers and Their Crafts.* Philadelphia: Westminster Press, 1976.

614. Branley, Franklyn M. *What Makes Day and Night,* rev.ed. New York: Thomas Y. Crowell Company, 1986.

615. De Paola, Tomie. *The Quicksand Book.* New York: Holiday House, 1977.

616. Dorros, Arthur. *Ant Cities.* New York: Thomas Y. Crowell Company, 1987.

617. Ford, Adam. *Weather Watch.* New York: Lothrop, Lee & Shepard Books, 1981.

618. Gaskin, John. *Breathing.* New York: Franklin Watts, Inc., 1984.

619. Gaskin, John. *Teeth.* New York: Franklin Watts, Inc., 1984.

620. Gaskin, John. *The Heart.* New York: Franklin Watts, Inc., 1985.

621. Gaskin, John. *Eating.* New York: Franklin Watts, Inc., 1984.

622. Gaskin, John. *The Senses.* New York: Franklin Watts, Inc., 1985.

623. Gaskin, John. *Movement.* New York: Franklin Watts, Inc., 1984.

624. Satchwell, John. *Energy at Work.* New York: Lothrop, Lee & Shepard Books, 1981.

625. Taylor, Ron. *Projects.* New York: Facts on File, Inc., 1986.

626. Berger, Melvin. *Energy from the Sun*. New York: Thomas Y. Crowell Company, 1976.

627. Leon, George de Lucenay. *The Electricity Story, 2500 Years of Experiments and Discoveries*. New York: Arco Publishing Company, Inc., 1983.

628. Wong, Ovid K. *Your Body and How It Works*. Chicago: Children's Press, 1986.

629. Markle, Sandra. *Exploring Winter*. New York: Atheneum Publishers, 1984.

630. Burns, Marilyn. *Good For Me! All About Food in 32 Bites*. Boston: Little, Brown & Company, 1978.

631. Simons, Robin. *Recyclopedia, Games, Science Equipment and Crafts from Recycled Materials*. Boston: Houghton Mifflin Company, 1976.

632. West, Robin. *Far Out, How to Create Your Own Star World*. Minneapolis, Minn.: Carolrhoda Books, Inc., 1987.

633. Wyler, Rose. *Science Fun with Mud and Dirt*. New York: Julian Messner, 1986.

634. Bendick, Jeanne. *Putting the Sun to Work*. Champaign, Ill.: Garrard Publishing Company, 1979.

635. Scott, John M. *What Is Sound?* New York: Parents Magazine Press, 1973.

636. Bell, Neill. *The Book of Where or How to Be Naturally Geographic*. Boston: Little, Brown & Company, 1982.

637. Simon, Seymour. *Let's Try It Out, About Your Lungs*. New York: McGraw-Hill Book Company, 1978.

638. Lefkowitz, R. J. *Forces in the Earth, a Book About Gravity and Magnetism*. New York: Parents Magazine Press, 1976.

639. Gans, Roma. *Rock Collecting*. New York: Thomas Y. Crowell Company, 1984.

640. Burns, Marilyn. *This Book Is About Time*. Boston: Little, Brown & Company, 1978.

641. Lauber, Patricia. *Tapping Earth's Heat*. Champaign, Ill.: Garrard Publishing Company, 1978.

642. Fleisher, Paul. *Secrets of the Universe, Discovering the Universal Laws of Science*. New York: Atheneum Publishers, 1987.

643. Conaway, Judith. *Detective Tricks You Can Do*. Mahwah, N.J.: Troll Associates, 1986.

644. Supraner, Robyn. *Fun-to-Make Nature Crafts*. Mahwah, N.J.: Troll Associates, 1981.

645. Showers, Paul. *You Can't Make a Move Without Your Muscles*. New York: Thomas Y. Crowell Company, 1982.

646. Graham, Ada. *Foxtails, Ferns and Fish Scales: Handbook of Art and Nature Projects*. New York: Four Winds Press, 1976.

647. Renner, Al G. *How to Make and Use Electric Motors*. New York: G. P. Putnam's Sons, 1974.

648. Branley, Franklyn M. *How Little and How Much, a Book About Scales*. New York: Thomas Y. Crowell Company, 1976.

649. Maynard, Christopher. *The Young Scientist Book of Stars and Planets*. St. Paul, Minn.: EMC Corp., 1978.

650. Mandry, Kathy, and Joe Toto. *How to Grow a Jelly Glass Farm*. New York: Pantheon Books, 1974.

651. Conaway, Judith. *More Science Secrets*. Mahwah, N.J.: Troll Associates, 1987.

652. Conaway, Judith. *Things That Go! How to Make Toy Boats, Cars, and Planes*. Mahwah, N.J.: Troll Associates, 1987.

653. Supraner, Robyn. *Stop and Look! Illusions*. Mahwah, N.J.: Troll Associates, 1981.

654. Gardner, Robert. *Energy Projects for Young Scientists*. New York: Franklin Watts, Inc., 1987.

655. Chapman, Philip. *The Young Scientist Book of Electricity*. London: Usborne Publishing Ltd., 1976.

656. Vowles, Andrew. *Amazing Experiments You Can Do at Home*. Tulsa, Okla.: EDC Publishing Company, 1985.

657. Gardner, Robert, and David Webster. *Science in Your Backyard*. New York: Julian Messner, 1987.

658. Apfel, Necia. H. *Astronomy Projects for Young Scientists*. New York: Arco Publishing Company, Inc., 1984.

659. Walpole, Brenda. *Light*. New York: Warwick Press, 1987.

660. Walpole, Brenda. *Air*. New York: Warwick Press, 1987.

661. Whitlock, Ralph. *Winter*. New York: The Bookwright Press, 1987.

662. Whitlock, Ralph. *Autumn*. New York: The Bookwright Press, 1987.

663. Walpole, Brenda. *Water*. New York: Warwick Press, 1987.

664. Walpole, Brenda. *Movement*. New York: Warwick Press, 1987.

665. Davies, Helen. *Experiments with Your Computer*. London: Usborne Publishing Ltd., 1985.

666. Markle, Sandra. *Digging Deeper, Investigations into Rocks, Shocks, Quakes and Other Earthy....* New York: Lothrop, Lee & Shepard Books, 1987.

667. Potter, Tony. *How to Make Computer Model Controllers*. London: Usborne Publishing Ltd., 1984.

668. Simon, Seymour. *Science at Work, Projects in Space Science*. New York: Franklin Watts, Inc., 1971.

669. Penrose, Gordon. *Magic Mud and Other Great Experiments*. Canada: Greey de Pencier Books, 1987.

670. McGrath, Susan. *Fun with Physics*. Washington, D.C.: National Geographic Society, 1986.

671. Jeffries, Lawrence. *Air Air Air*. Mahwah, N.J.: Troll Associates, 1983.

672. Dickinson, Jane. *Wonders of Water*. Mahwah, N.J.: Troll Associates, 1983.

673. Richardson, Joy. *What Happens When You Look?* Milwaukee, Wisc.: Gareth Stevens Publishing, 1986.

674. Richardson, Joy. *What Happens When You Sleep?* Milwaukee, Wisc.: Gareth Stevens Publishing, 1986.

675. Richardson, Joy. *What Happens When You Grow?* Milwaukee, Wisc.: Gareth Stevens Publishing, 1986.

676. Wyler, Rose. *Science Fun with a Homemade Chemistry Set*. New York: Julian Messner, 1987.

677. Johnston, Tom. *Electricity Turns the World On*. Milwaukee, Wisc.: Gareth Stevens Publishing, 1988.

678. Johnston, Tom. *Water, Water*. Milwaukee, Wisc.: Gareth Stevens Publishing, 1988.

679. Johnston, Tom. *Air, Air Everywhere*. Milwaukee, Wisc.: Gareth Stevens Publishing, 1988.

680. Johnston, Tom. *Light! Color! Action!* Milwaukee, Wisc.: Gareth Stevens Publishing, 1988.

681. Johnston, Tom. *Energy: Making It Work*. Milwaukee, Wisc.: Gareth Stevens Publishing, 1988.

682. Johnston, Tom. *The Forces with You*. Milwaukee, Wisc.: Gareth Stevens Publishing, 1988.

683. Hvass, Ulrik. *How Do I Breathe?* New York: Viking Kestrel, Viking Penguin, Inc., 1986.

684. Waters, Gaby. *Science Tricks and Magic*. London: Usborne Publishing Ltd., 1986.

685. Waters, Gaby. *Science Surprises*. London: Usborne Publishing Ltd., 1986.

686. Wyler, Rose. *Science Fun with Drums, Bells and Whistles*. New York: Julian Messner, 1987.

687. Andrews, Keith. *Beneath the Oceans*. New York: Grosset & Dunlap, Inc., 1972.

688. Gatland, Kenneth W. *Exploring Space*. New York: Grosset & Dunlap, Inc., 1972.

689. Davis, Alan. *Inside the Earth*. New York: Grosset & Dunlap, Inc., 1972.

690. Bucknall, Rixon. *Trains*. New York: Grosset & Dunlap, Inc., 1971.

691. Goodwin, Peter H. *Engineering Projects for Young Scientists*. New York: Franklin Watts, Inc., 1987.

692. Webster, David. *Dissection Projects*. New York: Franklin Watts, Inc., 1988.

693. Gardner, Robert. *Science Experiments*. New York: Franklin Watts, Inc., 1988.

694. Branley, Franklyn M. *It's Raining Cats and Dogs, All Kinds of Weather and Why We Have It*. Boston: Houghton Mifflin Company, 1987.

695. *Activities for the Young Scientist*. Florissant, Mo.: Ferguson-Florissant School District, 1984.

696. Alexander, Alison. *Science Magic*. New York: Simon and Schuster, Inc., 1986.

697. Allison, Linda. *The Sierra Club Summer Book*. San Francisco, Calif.: Sierra Club Books, 1977.

698. *Alternative Energy Sources*. Southfield, Mich.: Thomas Alva Edison Foundation, 1981.

699. Ardley, Neil, *Muscles to Machines*. New York: Gloucester Press, 1990.

700. Armbruster, Ann. *Tornadoes*. New York: Franklin Watts, 1989.

701. Arnosky, Jim. *I Was Born in a Tree and Raised by Bees*. New York: G. P. Putnam's Sons, 1977.

702. Barta, Ginevera. *Metric Cooking for Beginners*. Short Hills, N.J.: Enslow Publishers, 1978.

703. Bender, Lionel. *Atoms and Cells*. New York: Gloucester Press, 1990.

704. Berger, Melvin. *Atoms, Molecules and Quarks*. New York: G. P. Putnam's Sons, 1986.

705. Berger, Melvin. *The New Air Book*. New York: Thomas Y. Crowell Co., 1974.

706. Berger, Melvin. *The New Earth Book*. New York: Thomas Y. Crowell Co., 1980.

707. Berger, Melvin. *Our Atomic World*. New York: Franklin Watts, 1989.

708. Berger, Melvin. *The Science of Music*. New York: Thomas Y. Crowell Co., 1989.

709. Berger, Melvin. *Solids, Liquids, and Gases*. New York: G. P. Putnam's Sons, 1989.

710. Berger, Melvin. *Star Gazing, Comet Tracking, and Sky Mapping*. New York: G. P. Putnam's Sons, 1985.

711. Berger, Melvin. *Switch On, Switch Off*. New York: Thomas Y. Crowell Co., 1989.

712. Bjork, Christina, *Linnea's Windowsill Garden*. New York: R and S Books, 1988.

713. Bleifeld, Maurice. *Experimenting with a Microscope*. New York: Franklin Watts, 1988.

714. Bonnet, Robert L. *Botany: 49 Science Fair Projects*. Blue Ridge Summit, Pa.: Tab Books, Inc., 1989.

715. Bonnet, Robert L. *Earth Science, 49 Science Fair Projects*. Blue Ridge Summit, Pa.: Tab Books, Inc., 1990.

716. Branley, Franklyn. *Eclipse, Darkness in Daytime*. New York: Thomas Y. Crowell Co., 1988.

717. Branley, Franklyn M. *The Sun, Our Nearest Star*. New York: Thomas Y. Crowell Co., 1988.

718. Broekel, Ray. *Experiments with Air*. Chicago: Children's Press, 1988.

719. Broekel, Ray. *Experiments with Water*. Chicago: Children's Press, 1988.

720. Bromley, James. *Life of Reptiles and Amphibians*. Morristown, N.J.: Silver Burdett Co., 1978.

721. Brown, Bob. *More Science for You, 112 Illustrated Experiments*. Blue Ridge Summit, Pa.: Tab Books, Inc., 1988.

722. Brown, Bob. *Science for You, 112 Illustrated Experiments*. Blue Ridge Summit, Pa.: Tab Books, Inc., 1988.

723. Brown, Robert J. *333 More Science Tricks and Experiments*. Blue Ridge Summit, Pa.: Tab Books, Inc., 1984.

724. Burton, Maurice. *The Life of Birds*. New York: Golden Press, 1972.

725. Burton, Maurice. *The Life of Fishes*. New York: Golden Press, 1972.

726. Burton, Maurice. *Life of Meat Eaters*. Morristown, N.J.: Silver Burdett, 1975.

727. Baines, John. *Acid Rain*. Austin, Tex.: Steck-Vaughn Co., 1990.

728. Banks, Martin. *Conserving Rain Forests*. Austin, Tex.: Steck-Vaughn Co., 1990.

729. Bender, Lionel. *The Body*. New York: Gloucester Press, 1989.

730. Bender, Lionel. *Life on a Coral Reef*. New York: Gloucester Press, 1989.

731. Booth, Jerry. *The Big Beast Book*. Boston: Little, Brown and Co., 1988.

732. Caney, Steven. *Steven Caney's Toy Book*. New York: Workman Publishing Co., 1972.

733. Carson, Mary Stetten. *The Scientific Kid*. New York: Harper and Row Publishers, Inc., 1989.

734. Cash, Terry. *Fun with Science, Sound*. New York: Warwick Press, 1989.

735. Challand, Helen J. *Experiments with Chemistry*. Chicago: Children's Press, 1988.

736. Churchill, E. Richard. *Optical Illusion Tricks and Toys*. New York: Sterling Publishing, Co., 1989.

737. Cochrane, Jennifer. *Air Ecology*. New York: The Bookwright Press, 1987.

738. Cochrane, Jennifer. *Land Ecology*. New York: The Bookwright Press, 1987.

739. Cochrane, Jennifer. *Plant Ecology*. New York: The Bookwright Press, 1987.

740. Cochrane, Jennifer. *Urban Ecology*. New York: The Bookwright Press, 1988.

741. Cochrane, Jennifer. *Water Ecology*. New York: The Bookwright Press, 1987.

742. Cohen, Lynn. *Air and Space*. Palo Alto, Calif.: Monday Morning Books, Inc., 1988.

743. Cohen, Lynn. *Energy and Machines*. Palo Alto, Calif.: Monday Morning Books, Inc., 1988.

744. Cohen, Lynn. *Weather and Seasons*. Palo Alto, Calif.: Monday Morning Books, Inc., 1988.

745. Cusack, Anne E. *Plant Mysteries*. New York: Julian Messner, 1978.

746. Daab, Marcia J. *Science Fair Workshop*. Carthage, Ill.: Fearon Teacher Aids, 1990.

747. Daniel, Becky. *I Wonder*. Carthage, Ill.: Good Apple, Inc., 1980.

748. DeBruin, Jerry. *Creative Hands-On Science Experiences*. Carthage, Ill.: Good Apple, Inc., 1986.

749. Dekkers, Midas. *The Nature Book*. New York: Macmillan Publishing Co., 1988.

750. Disney Productions. *Disney's World of Adventure Presents Cars! Cars! Cars!* New York: Random House, 1977.
751. Dorros, Arthur. *Feel the Wind.* New York: Thomas Y. Crowell Co., 1989.
752. Faraday, Michael. *Faraday's Chemical History of a Candle.* Chicago: Chicago Review Press, 1988.
753. Fitzpatrick, Julie. *Balancing.* Englewood Cliffs, N.J.: Silver Burdett Press, 1988.
754. Fitzpatrick, Julie. *Bounce, Stretch and Spring.* Englewood Cliffs, N.J.: Silver Burdett Press, 1988.
755. Fitzpatrick, Julie. *Towers and Bridges.* Englewood Cliffs, N.J.: Silver Burdett Press, 1988.
756. Fitzpatrick, Julie. *Wheels.* Englewood Cliffs, N.J.: Silver Burdett Press, 1988.
757. Forte, Imogene. *Creative Science Experiences.* Nashville, Tenn.: Incentive Publications, Inc., 1983.
758. Forte, Imogene. *Exploring Science.* Nashville, Tenn.: Incentive Publications, Inc., 1988.
759. Foster, Betty. *Creative Science for Young Children.* Elgin, Ill.: Child's World, 1988.
760. Fredericks, Anthony D. *The Science Discovery Book.* Glenview, Ill.: Scott, Foresman and Co., 1987.
761. Gardner, Robert. *Experimenting with Illusions.* New York: Franklin Watts, 1990.
762. Gardner, Robert. *More Ideas for Science Projects.* New York: Franklin Watts, 1989.
763. Gardner, Robert. *Projects in Space Science.* New York: Julian Messner, 1988.
764. Gibbons, Gail. *Catch the Wind.* Boston: Little, Brown and Co., 1989.
765. Gibbons, Gail. *Monarch Butterfly.* New York: Holiday House, 1989.
766. Gould, Toni S. *Science Fun with Water and Ice.* New York: Walker and Co., 1983.
767. Graf, Mike. *Weather Report.* Belmont, Calif.: Fearon Teacher Aids, 1989.
768. Graf, Rudolph F. *Safe and Simple Electrical Experiments.* New York: Dover Publications, Inc., 1973.
769. Gutnik, Martin J. *How to Do a Science Project and Report.* New York: Franklin Watts, 1980.
770. Haas, Carolyn. *Big Book of Fun.* Chicago: Chicago Review Press, 1987.
771. Headstrom, Richard. *Adventures with Freshwater Animals.* New York: Dover Publications, 1964.
772. Heinz, Brian J. *Beachcrafts Too.* Shoreham, N.Y.: Ballyhoo Books, 1986.
773. Henwood, Chris. *Keeping Minibeasts, Earthworms.* New York: Franklin Watts, 1988.
774. Henwood, Chris. *Keeping Minibeasts, Frogs.* New York: Franklin Watts. 1988.
775. Henwood, Chris. *Keeping Minibeasts, Snails and Slugs.* New York: Franklin Watts, 1988.
776. Henwood, Chris. *Keeping Minibeasts, Spiders.* New York: Franklin Watts, 1988.
777. Hessler, Edward W. *Acid Rain.* St. Paul, Minn.: Acid Rain Foundation, Inc., 1987.
778. Hickman, Pamela M. *Birdwise.* Reading, Mass.: Addison-Wesley Publishing Co., 1989.
779. Hodgson, Harriet. *Contraptions.* Palo Alto, Calif.: Monday Morning Books, Inc., 1987.
780. Hoffman, Jane. *Backyard Scientist.* Irvine, Calif.: Backyard Scientist, 1987.
781. Hoffman, Jane. *Backyard Scientist, Series Two.* Irvine, Calif.: Backyard Scientist, 1989.
782. Hoffman, Jane. *The Original Backyard Scientist.* Irvine, Calif.: Backyard Scientist, 1987.
783. Hosking, Wayne. *Flights of Imagination.* Washington, D.C.: National Science Teachers Association, 1987.
784. Hunken, Jorie. *Discovering Nature Through Activities Using Plants.* Chester, Conn.: Globe Pequot Press, 1989.
785. Iritz, Maxine Haren. *Science Fair.* Blue Ridge Summit, Pa.: Tab Books, 1987.
786. Jennings, Terry. *Balancing.* New York: Gloucester Press, 1989.
787. Jennings, Terry. *Bouncing and Rolling.* New York: Gloucester Press, 1988.
788. Jennings, Terry. *Color.* New York: Gloucester Press, 1989.
789. Jennings, Terry. *Earthworms.* New York: Gloucester Press, 1988.
790. Jennings, Terry. *Everyday Chemicals.* Chicago: Children's Press, 1988.
791. Jennings, Terry. *Floating and Sinking.* New York: Gloucester Press, 1988.
792. Jennings, Terry. *Food.* Chicago: Children's Press, 1988.
793. Jennings, Terry. *Heat.* Chicago: Children's Press, 1988.
794. Jennings, Terry. *The Human Body.* Chicago: Children's Press, 1988.
795. Jennings, Terry. *Materials.* Chicago: Children's Press, 1988.
796. Jennings, Terry. *Pond Life.* Chicago: Children's Press, 1985.
797. Jennings, Terry. *Rocks and Soil.* Chicago: Children's Press, 1989.
798. Jennings, Terry. *Seeds.* New York: Gloucester Press, 1988.
799. Jennings, Terry. *Seeds and Seedlings.* Chicago: Children's Press, 1988.
800. Jennings, Terry. *Slugs and Snails.* New York: Gloucester Press, 1989.
801. Jennings, Terry. *Spiders.* New York: Gloucester Press, 1989.
802. Jennings, Terry. *Structures.* Chicago: Children's Press, 1984.
803. Jennings, Terry. *Time.* New York: Gloucester Press, 1988.
804. Jennings, Terry. *Water.* Chicago: Children's Press, 1988.
805. Jennings, Terry. *Weather.* New York: Gloucester Press, 1988.
806. Johnsey, Robert. *Problem Solving in School Science.* London, England: Macdonald Educational Co., 1986.
807. *Junior Girl Scout Handbook.* New York: Girl Scouts of the U.S.A., 1986.
808. Kadesch, Robert R. *Math Menagerie.* New York: Harper and Row Publishers, 1970.
809. Kerby, Mona. *Cockroaches.* New York: Franklin Watts, 1989
810. Kirkman, Will. *Nature Crafts Workshop.* Belmont, Calif.: Fearon Teacher Aids, 1981.
811. Editors of Owl Magazine. *Kitchen Fun.* Boston: Little, Brown and Co., 1988.
812. *Know How Book of Codes, Secret Agents and Spies.* New York: Sterling Publishing Co., 1976.
813. Koral, April. *Our Global Greenhouse.* New York: Franklin Watts, 1989.

814. Kramer, Alan. *How to Make a Chemical Volcano*. New York: Franklin Watts, 1989.

815. Kramer, Stephen P. *How to Think Like a Scientist*. New York: Thomas Y. Crowell Co., 1987.

816. Kuntz, Margy. *Adventures in Earth Science*. Belmont, Calif.: David S. Lake Publishers, 1987.

817. Kuntz, Margy. *Adventures in Life Science*. Belmont, Calif.: David S. Lake Publishers, 1987.

818. Kuntz, Margy. *Adventures in Physical Science*. Belmont, Calif.: David S. Lake Publishers, 1987.

819. Ladyman, Phyllis. *Learning About Flowering Plants*. New York: Young Scott Books, 1970.

820. Lambert, Mark. *Animal Ecology*. New York: The Bookwright Press, 1988.

821. Littler, Angela. *The Life of Insects*. Morristown N.J.: Silver Burdett Co., 1979.

822. Lowery, Lawrence. *Explorations in Life Science*. Belmont, Calif.: David S. Lake Publishers, 1987.

823. Macfarlan, Alan A. *The Boy's Book of Outdoor Discovery*. New York: Galahad Books, 1974.

824. MacFarlane, Ruth B. *Making Your Own Nature Museum*. New York: Franklin Watts, 1989.

825. Mackie, Dan. *Electricity*. Ontario, Canada: Hayes Publishing Ltd., 1986.

826. McVey, Vicki. *The Sierra Wayfinding Book*. Boston: Little, Brown and Co., 1989.

827. Mandell, Muriel. *Simple Science Experiments with Everyday Materials*. New York: Sterling Publishing Co. Inc., 1989.

828. Markle, Sandra. *Power Up*. New York: Atheneum, 1989.

829. Markle, Sandra. *Science Mini-Mysteries*. New York: Atheneum, 1988.

830. Math, Irwin. *More Wires and Watts*. New York: Charles Scribner's Sons, 1988.

831. Mebane, Robert C. *Adventures with Atoms and Molecules, Book II*. Hillside, N.J.: Enslow Publishers, Inc., 1987.

832. Milord, Susan. *The Kids Nature Book*. Charlotte, Vt.: Williamson Publishing Co., 1989.

833. Moeschl, Richard. *Exploring the Sky: 100 Projects for Beginning Astronomers*. Chicago: Chicago Review Press, Inc., 1989.

834. Moore, William. *Your Science Fair Project*. New York: G. P. Putnam's Sons, 1964.

835. *More Science Activities*. New York: Smithsonian Institution, Galison Books, 1988.

836. Munson, Howard R. *Science Experiences with Everyday Things*. Belmont, Calif.: David S. Lake Publishers, 1988.

837. Munson, Howard R. *Science Activities with Simple Things*. Belmont, Calif.: David S. Lake Publishers, 1972.

838. Noddy, Tom. *Tom Noddy's Bubble Magic*. Philadelphia: Running Press, 1988.

839. Norsgaard, E. Jaediker. *How to Raise Butterflies*. New York: Dodd, Mead and Co., 1988.

840. *Ocean Book: Aquarium and Seaside Activities*. New York: John Wiley and Sons, Inc., 1989.

841. O'Connor, Karen. *Garbage*. San Diego, Calif.: Lucent Books, Inc., 1989.

842. Orii, Eiji. *Simple Science Experiments with Circles*. Milwaukee, Wisc.: Gareth Stevens Children's Books, 1989.

843. Orii, Eiji. *Simple Science Experiments with Light*. Milwaukee, Wisc.: Gareth Stevens Children's Books, 1989.

844. Orii, Eiji. *Simple Science Experiments with Marbles*. Milwaukee, Wisc.: Gareth Stevens Children's Books, 1989.

845. Orii, Eiji. *Simple Science Experiments with Optical Illusions*. Milwaukee, Wisc.: Gareth Stevens Children's Books, 1989.

846. Orii, Eiji. *Simple Science Experiments with Ping-Pong Balls*. Milwaukee, Wisc.: Gareth Stevens Children's Books, 1989.

847. Orii, Eiji. *Simple Science Experiments with Starting and Stopping*. Milwaukee, Wisc.: Gareth Stevens Children's Books, 1989.

848. Orii, Eiji. *Simple Science Experiments with Straws*. Milwaukee, Wisc.: Gareth Stevens Children's Books, 1989.

849. Orii, Eiji. *Simple Science Experiments with Water*. Milwaukee, Wisc.: Gareth Stevens Children's Books, 1989.

850. *Owl's Winter Fun*. Owl Magazine/Golden Press Book. Toronto, Canada: Greey de Pencier, 1983.

851. Pearce, Q. L. *Amazing Energy Experiments*. New York: Tom Doherty Associates, Inc., 1989.

852. Pearce, Q. L. *Wondrous Plant and Earth Experiments*. New York: Tom Doherty Associates, Inc., 1989.

853. Pellino, John. *Discovering Science on Your Apple II, IIt, II3, IIc, and IIGS*. Blue Ridge Summit, Pa.: Tab Books, Inc., 1987.

854. Perez, Jeannine. *Explore and Experiment*. Bridgeport, Conn.: First Teacher Press, Inc., 1988.

855. Petty, Kate. *Birds of Prey*. New York: Gloucester Press, 1987.

856. Philpott, Violet. *The Know How Book of Flying Models*. New York: Sterling Publishing Co., Inc., 1976.

857. Pluckrose, Henry. *Look at Fur and Feathers*. New York: Franklin Watts, 1989.

858. Pollard, Jeanne. *Building Toothpick Bridges*. Palo Alto, Calif.: Dale Seymour Publications, 1985.

859. Price, Lowi. *Concoctions*. New York: E. P. Dutton Co., 1976.

860. Prochnow, Dave. *101 Experiments for the Young Scientist*. Blue Ridge Summit. PA: Tab Books Inc., 1988.

861. Provenzo, Eugene F. Jr. *The Historian's Toybook*. Englewood Cliffs, N.J.: Prentice-Hall, Inc., 1979.

862. Provenzo, Eugene F. *Rediscovering Astronomy*. La Jolla, Calif.: Oak Tree Publications, Inc., 1980.

863. Provenzo, Eugene F., Jr. *Rediscovering Photography*. La Jolla, Calif.: Oak Tree Publications, Inc., 1980.

864. Rainis, Kenneth G. *Nature Projects for Young Scientists*. New York: Franklin Watts, 1989.

865. Ramsey, Dan. *Weather Forecasting*. Blue Ridge Summit, Pa.: Tab Books, Inc., 1990.

866. *Ready to Use Activities for Before and After School Programs*. West Nyack, N.Y.: The Center for Applied Research in Education, 1989.

867. Reid, Robert W. *Science Experiments for the Primary Grades*. Belmont, Calif.: David S. Lake Publishers, 1962.

868. Richards, Roy. *An Early Start to Science*. London, England: Macdonald Educational, 1987.

869. Sanders, Pete. *Near Water, Safety Guide*. New York; Gloucester Press, 1989.

870. *Science Activity Book. Smithsonian Family Learning Project*. New York: Galison Books, GMG Publishing Corp., 1987.

871. *Science Experiments on File*. New York: Facts on File, 1989.

872. Seddon, Tony. *Animal Vision*. New York: Facts on File Publications, 1988.

873. Seixas, Judith S. *Water, What It Is, What It Does*. New York: Greenwillow Books, 1987.

874. Silver, James F. *Geography Skills Activities Kit*. West Nyack, N.Y.: The Center for Applied Research in Education, 1988.

875. Silverstein, Alvin. *Apples, All About Them*. Englewood Cliffs, N.J.: Prentice-Hall, Inc., 1976

876. Silverstein, Alvin. *Potatoes, All About Them*. Englewood Cliffs, N.J.: Prentice-Hall, Inc., 1976

877. Simon, Seymour. *How to Be an Ocean Scientist in Your Own Home*. New York: J. B. Lippincott, 1988.

878. Simon, Seymour. *Projects with Plants*. New York: Franklin Watts 1973.

879. Skelsey, Alice. *Growing Up Green*. New York: Workman Publishing Co., 1973.

880. Snowball, Marilyn. *Preschool Packrat*. Santa Barbara, Calif.: The Learning Works, Inc., 1982.

881. *Sportsworks: More Than 50 Fun Games and Activities*. Ontario Science Centre. Reading, Mass.: Addison-Wesley Publishing Co., Inc., 1989.

882. Stacy, Dennis. *Nifty (and Thrifty) Science Activities*. Belmont, Calif.: David S. Lake Publishers, 1988.

883. Stangl, Jean. *Crystals and Crystal Garden You Can Grow*. New York: Franklin Watts, 1990.

884. Stangl, Jean. *H_2O Science*. Carthage, Ill.: Fearon Teacher Aids, 1990.

885. Stangl, Jean. *The Tools of Science*. New York: Dodd, Mead and Co., 1987.

886. Stidworthy, John. *Plants and Seeds*. New York: Gloucester Press, 1990.

887. *Still More Science Activities*. The Smithsonian Institution. New York: Galison Books, GMG Publishing Corp., 1989.

888. Strongin, Herb. *Science on a Shoestring*. Reading, Mass.: Addison-Wesley Publishing Co., 1976.

889. Stwertka, Eve. *Microscope, How to Use It and Enjoy It*. Englewood Cliffs, N.J.: Julian Messner, 1988.

890. *Summer Fun*. Editors of Owl Magazine. Toronto, Canada: Greey de Pencier Books, 1984.

891. Tannenbaum, Beulah. *Making and Using Your Own Weather Station*. New York: Franklin Watts, 1989.

892. Taylor, Barbara. *Bouncing and Bending Light*. New York: Franklin Watts, 1990.

893. Taylor, Barbara. *Color and Light*. New York: Franklin Watts, 1990.

894. Taylor, Ron B. *Life of Animals with Shells*. Morristown, N.J.: Silver Burdett Co., 1979.

895. The Thomas Alva Edison Foundation. *Thomas Edison Book of Easy and Incredible Experiments*. New York: John Wiley and Sons, Inc., 1988.

896. *Through the Microscope, Insects*. New York: Gloucester Press, 1989.

897. Thurman-Veith, Jan. *Natural Wonders*. Palo Alto, Calif.: Monday Morning Books, 1986.

898. Ticotsky, Alan. *Who Says You Can't Teach Science?* Glenview, Ill.: Scott, Foresman and Co., 1985.

899. Tilgner, Linda. *Let's Grow: 72 Gardening Adventures*. Pownal, Vt.: Storey Communications, Inc., 1988.

900. Tolman, Marvin N. *Earth Science Activities for Grades 2-8*. West Nyack, N.Y.: Parker Publishing Co., Inc., 1986.

901. Tolman, Marvin N. *Life Science Activities for Grades 2-8*. West Nyack, N.Y.: Parker Publishing Co., Inc., 1986.

902. Tolman, Marvin N. *Physical Science Activities for Grades 2-8*. West Nyack, N.Y.: Parker Publishing Co., Inc., 1986.

903. Turner, Barrie Carson. *I Like Music, Make and Play Your Own Instruments*. New York: Warwick Press, 1989.

904. VanCleave, Janice Pratt. *Biology for Every Kid*. New York: John Wiley and Sons, Inc., 1990.

905. VanCleave, Janice Pratt. *Chemistry for Every Kid*. New York: John Wiley and Sons, Inc., 1988.

906. VanCleave, Janice Pratt. *Teaching the Fun of Physics*. New York: Prentice-Hall Press, 1985.

907. Van der Meer, Ron. *Your Amazing Senses*. New York: Aladdin Books, Macmillan Publishing Co., 1987.

908. Walker, Ormiston, H. *Experimenting with Air and Flight*. New York: Franklin Watts, 1989.

909. Walpole, Brenda. *175 Science Experiments to Amuse and Amaze Your Friends*. New York: Random House, 1988.

910. Ward, Alan. *Experimenting with Batteries, Bulbs and Wires*. London, England: Dryad Press Limited, 1986.

911. Ward, Alan. *Experimenting with Light and Illusions*. London, England: Dryad Press Limited, 1985.

912. Ward, Alan. *Experimenting with Magnetism*. London, England: Dryad Press Limited, 1987.

913. Ward, Alan. *Experimenting with Nature Study*. London, England: Dryad Press Limited, 1986.

914. Ward, Alan. *Experimenting with Surface Tension*. London, England: Dryad Press Limited, 1986.

915. Watts, Barrie. *Keeping Minibeasts, Beetles*. New York: Franklin Watts, 1985.

916. Watts, Barrie. *Keeping Minibeasts, Caterpillars*. New York: Franklin Watts, 1989.

917. Webster, David. *Exploring Nature Around the Year: Fall*. Englewood Cliffs, N.J.: Julian Messner, 1989.

918. Webster, David. *Exploring Nature Around the Year: Spring*. Englewood Cliffs, N.J.: Julian Messner, 1990.

919. Webster, David. *Exploring Nature Around the Year: Summer*. Englewood Cliffs, N.J.: Julian Messner, 1990.

920. Webster, David. *Exploring Nature Around the Year: Winter*. Englewood Cliffs, N.J.: Julian Messner, 1989.

921. Webster, Harriet. *Winter Book*. New York: Charles Scribner's Sons, 1988.

922. Weiss, Harvey. *Ship Models and How to Build Them*. New York: Thomas Y. Crowell Co., 1973.

923. Weitzman, David. *Windmills, Bridges, & Old Machines*. New York: Charles Scribner's Sons, 1982.

924. Wellnitz, William R. *Science Magic for Kids*. Blue Ridge Summit, Pa.: Tab Books, 1990.

925. West, Robin. *Dinosaur Discoveries*. Minneapolis, Minn.: Carolrhoda Books, Inc., 1989.

926. White, Jack R. *The Hidden World of Forces*. New York: Dodd, Mead and Co., 1987.

927. White, Laurence B. *Optical Illusions*. New York: Franklin Watts, 1986.

928. Whyman, Kathryn. *Rainbows to Lasers*. New York: Gloucester Press, 1989.

929. Whyman, Kathryn. *Sparks to Power Stations*. New York: Gloucester Press, 1989.

930. Wicks, Keith. *Science Can Be Fun*. Minneapolis, Minn.: Lerner Publications Co., 1988.

931. Wilkes, Angela. *Growing Things*. England: Usborne Publication Ltd., 1984.
932. Wilkes, Angela. *My First Nature Book*. New York: Alfred A. Knopf, 1990.
933. Williams, David Ivor. *Experiments on Air Pollution*. Hove, England: Wayland Publishers Limited, 1978.
934. Williams, David Ivor. *Experiments on Water Pollution*. Hove, England: Wayland Publishers Limited, 1978.
935. Willow, Diane. *Science Sensations*. Reading, Mass.: Addison-Wesley Publishing Co. Inc., 1989.
936. Wong, Ovid K. *Experiments with Animal Behavior*. Chicago: Children's Press, 1989.
937. Wong, Ovid K. *Is Science Magic?* Chicago: Children's Press, 1988.
938. Wood, Robert W. *Physics for Kids; 49 Easy Experiments with Electricity and Magnetism*. Blue Ridge Summit, Pa.: Tab Books, 1990.
939. Wood, Robert W. *Physics for Kids; 49 Easy Experiments with Heat*. Blue Ridge Summit, Pa.: Tab Books, 1990.
940. Wood, Robert W. *Physics for Kids; 49 Easy Experiments with Mechanics*. Blue Ridge Summit, Pa.: Tab Books, 1989.
941. Wood, Robert W. *Physics for Kids; 49 Easy Experiments with Optics*. Blue Ridge Summit, Pa.: Tab Books, 1990.
942. Wyler, Rose. *Grass and Grasshoppers*. Englewood Cliffs, N.J.: Julian Messner, 1990.
943. Wyler, Rose. *Puddles and Ponds*. Englewood Cliffs, N.J.: Julian Messner, 1990.
944. Wyler, Rose. *Raindrops and Rainbows*. Englewood Cliffs, N.J.: Julian Messner, 1989.
945. Wyler, Rose. *Science Fun with Toy Cars and Trucks*. Englewood Cliffs, N.J.: Julian Messner, 1988.
946. Wyler, Rose. *The Starry Sky*. Englewood Cliffs, N.J.: Julian Messner, 1989.
947. Yerian, Cameron. *Fun Time Projects, Earth and Sky*. Chicago: Children's Press, 1974.
948. Yerian, Cameron. *Fun Time, Working with Wood*. Chicago: Children's Press, 1975.
949. Zaslavsky, Claudia. *Zero, Is It Something? Is It Nothing?* New York: Franklin Watts, 1989.
950. Zipko, Stephen J. *Toxic Threat*. Englewood Cliffs, N.J.: Julian Messner, 1986.
951. Zubrowski, Bernie. *Clocks, Building and Experimenting with Model Timepieces*. New York: Morrow Junior Books, 1988.
952. Zubrowski, Bernie. *TOPS, Building and Experimenting with Spinning Toys*. New York: Morrow Junior Books, 1989.
953. Bjork, Christina. *Linnea's Almanac*. New York: R & S Books, Farrar, Straus and Giroux, 1989.
954. Bombaugh, Ruth. *Science Fair Success*. Hillside, N.J.: Enslow Publishers, Inc., 1990.
955. Cash, Terry. *Electricity and Magnets*. New York: Warwick Press, 1989.
956. Catherall, Ed. *Exploring Light*. Austin, Tex.: Steck-Vaughn Co., 1989.
957. Catherall, Ed. *Exploring Sound*. Austin, Tex.: Steck-Vaughn Co., 1989.
958. Gallant, Roy A. *Rainbows, Mirages and Sundogs*. New York: Macmillan Publishing Co., 1987.
959. Gardner, Robert. *Water, the Life Sustaining Resource*. Englewood Cliffs, N.J.: Julian Messner, 1982.
960. Hoyt, Marie Agnes. *Kitchen Chemistry and Front Porch Physics*. New York: Educational Services Press, 1983.
961. Lafferty, Peter. *Magnets to Generators*. New York: Gloucester Press, 1989.
962. McGavin, George. *Discovering Bugs*. New York: The Bookwright Press, 1989.
963. Mulleneux, Jane. *Discovering Bats*. New York: The Bookwright Press, 1989.
964. Parker, Phillip. *The Life Cycle of a Stickleback*. New York: The Bookwright Press, 1988.
965. Twist, Clint. *Rain to Dams*. New York: Gloucester Press, 1990.
966. Friedhoffer, Robert. *Magic Tricks, Science Facts*. New York: Franklin Watts, 1990.
967. Asimov, Isaac. *Projects in Astronomy*. Milwaukee, Wisc.: Gareth Stevens Publishing, 1990.
968. Bender, Lionel. *Eurotunnel*. New York: Gloucester Press, 1990.
969. Bonnet, Robert L. *Environmental Science; 49 Science Fair Projects*. Blue Ridge Summit, Pa.: Tab Books, 1990.
970. Bornstein, Sandy. *What Makes You What You Are*. Englewood Cliffs, N.J.: Julian Messner, 1989.
971. Bourgeois, Paulette. *The Amazing Apple*. Reading, Mass.: Addison-Wesley Publishing, 1987.
972. Catherall, Ed. *Exploring Electricity*. Austin, Tex.: Steck-Vaughn Company, 1990.
973. Catherall, Ed. *Exploring Magnets*. Austin, Tex.: Steck-Vaughn Company, 1990.
974. Cawthorne, Nigel. *Airliner*. New York: Gloucester Press, 1987.
975. Coldrey, Jennifer. *The Life Cycle of a Snail*. New York: The Bookwright Press, 1989.
976. Conway, Lorraine. *Chemistry Concepts*. Carthage, Ill. Good Apple, Inc., 1983.
977. Eldredge, Niles. *The Fossil Factory*. Reading, Mass.: Addison-Wesley Publishing Co., Inc., 1989.
978. Gates, Julie M. *Consider the Earth*. Englewood, Colo.: Libraries Unlimited, 1989.
979. Kaplan, Sheila. *Solar Energy*. Milwaukee, Wisc.: Raintree Publishers, Inc., 1983.
980. Kenda, Margaret. *Cooking Wizardry for Kids*. Hauppauge, N.Y.: Barron's Educational Series, Inc., 1990.
981. Lafferty, Peter. *Wind to Flight*. New York: Gloucester Press, 1989.
982. Lewis, James. *Rub a Dub-Dub, Science in the Tub*. Deephaven, Minn.: Meadowbrook Press, 1989.
983. Markle, Sandra. *Exploring Spring*. New York: Atheneum, 1990.
984. Markle, Sandra. *The Young Scientist's Guide to Successful Science Projects*. New York: Lothrop, Lee and Shepard Books, 1990.
985. Moncure, Jane Belk. *What Was It Before It Was Orange Juice?* Elgin, Ill.: The Child's World, 1985.
986. Ocone, Lynn. *National Gardening Association Guide to Kids Gardening*. New York: John W. Wiley & Sons, Inc., 1990.
987. Ostler, Tim. *Skyscraper*. New York: Gloucester Press, 1987.
988. Parker, Philip. *The Life Cycle of a Sunflower*. New York: The Bookwright Press, 1988.
989. Pollard, Michael. *Air, Water and Weather*. New York: Facts on File Publications, 1987.

990. Stidworthy, John. *Insects*. New York: Gloucester Press, 1989.

991. Sweningson, Sally. *Indoor Gardening*. Minneapolis, Minn.: Lerner Publications Company, 1975.

992. Terry, Trevor. *The Life Cycle of a Butterfly*. New York: The Bookwright Press, 1988.

993. Ward, Alan. *Experimenting with Science About Yourself*. London, England: Dryad Press Limited, 1988.

994. Zubrowski, Bernie. *Balloons, Building and Experimenting with Inflatable Toys*. New York: Morrow Junior Books, 1990.

995. Ardley, Neil. *The Science Book of Air*. New York: Harcourt Brace Jovanovich Publishers, 1991.

996. Ardley, Neil. *The Science Book of Water*. New York: Harcourt Brace Jovanovich Publishers, 1991.

997. Bochinski, Julianne Blair. *The Complete Handbook of Science Fair Projects*. New York: John Wiley & Sons, Inc., 1991.

998. Butzow, Carol M. *Science Through Children's Literature*. Englewood, Colo.: Libraries Unlimited, 1989.

999. Churchill, E. Richard. *Paper Science Toys*. New York: Sterling Publishing Company, Inc., 1990.

1000. Francis, Dorothy B. *Drift Bottles in History and Folklore*. Shoreham, N.Y.: Ballyhoo Books, 1990.

1001. Kerrod, Robin. *How Things Work*. New York: Marshall Cavendish, 1989.

1002. Kerrod, Robin. *Is It Magic?* New York: Marshall Cavendish, 1989.

1003. Mandell, Muriel. *Simple Weather Experiments with Everyday Materials*. New York: Sterling Publishing Company, Inc., 1990.

1004. *More Science Experiments on File*. New York: Facts on File, Inc., 1990.

1005. Penrose, Gordon. *Dr. Zed's Science Surprises*. New York: Simon & Schuster Inc., 1989.

1006. *Please Touch Cookbook*. Englewood Cliffs, N.J.: Silver Press, 1990.

1007. Provenzo, Eugene F., Jr. *47 Easy-to-Do Classic Science Experiments*. New York: Dover Publications, Inc., 1989.

1008. Bourgeois, Paulette. *The Amazing Dirt Book*. Reading, Mass.: Addison-Wesley Publishing Co., Inc., 1990.

1009. Broekel, Ray. *Experiments with Straws and Paper*. Chicago: Children's Press, 1990.

1010. Freidhoffer, Robert. *More Magic Tricks, Science Facts*. New York: Franklin Watts, Inc., 1990.

1011. Griffin, Margaret. *The Amazing Egg Book*. Reading, Mass.: Addison-Wesley Publishing Co., Inc., 1990.

1012. Markle, Sandra. *Weather, Electricity, Environmental Investigations*. Santa Barbara, Calif.: The Learning Works, Inc., 1982.

1013. Schwartz, Linda. *Earth Book for Kids: Activities to Help Heal the Environment*. Santa Barbara, Calif.: The Learning Works, Inc., 1990.

1014. Sherwood, Elizabeth A. *More Mudpies to Magnets*. Mt. Rainier, Md.: Gryphon House, Inc., 1990.

1015. Turner, Dorothy. *Eggs*. Minneapolis, Minn.: Carolrhoda Books, Inc., 1989.

1016. Wilkes, Angela. *My First Science Book*. New York: Alfred A. Knopf, Inc., 1990.

1017. Wyatt, Valerie. *Weatherwatch*. Reading, Mass.: Addison-Wesley Publishing Co., Inc., 1990.

1018. Ardley, Neil. *The Science Book of Color*. New York: Harcourt Brace Jovanovich Publishers, 1991.

1019. Ardley, Neil. *The Science Book of Light*. New York: Harcourt Brace Jovanovich Publishers, 1991.

1020. Barr, George. *Science Projects for Young People*. New York: Dover Publications, Inc., 1986. Originally published: *Research Adventures for Young Scientists*.

1021. Bonnet, Robert L. *Computers: 49 Science Fair Projects*. Blue Ridge Summit, Pa.: Tab Books, Inc., 1990.

1022. Holland, Peter. *Amazing Models! Water Power*. Blue Ridge Summit, Pa.: Tab Books, Inc., 1990.

1023. VanCleave, Janice. *Janice VanCleave's Earth Science for Every Kid*. New York: John Wiley & Sons, Inc., 1991.

1024. Alexander, Alison. *Power Magic: Science Activities for Children*. New York: Simon & Schuster, 1991.

1025. Ardley, Neil. *Bridges*. Ada, Okla.: Garrett Educational Corp., 1989.

1026. Ardley, Neil. *Dams*. Ada, Okla.: Garrett Educational Corp., 1990.

1027. Ardley, Neil. *Oil Rigs*. Ada, Okla.: Garrett Educational Corp., 1990.

1028. Ardley, Neil. *101 Great Science Experiments*. New York: Dorling Kindersley, 1993.

1029. Ardley, Neil. *The Science Book of Electricity*. New York: Harcourt Brace Jovanovich Publishers, 1991.

1030. Ardley, Neil. *The Science Book of Energy*. New York: Harcourt Brace Jovanovich Publishers, 1992.

1031. Ardley, Neil. *The Science Book of Gravity*. New York: Harcourt Brace Jovanovich Publishers, 1992.

1032. Ardley, Neil. *The Science Book of Hot & Cold*. New York: Harcourt Brace Jovanovich Publishers, 1992.

1033. Ardley, Neil. *The Science Book of Machines*. New York: Harcourt Brace Jovanovich Publishers, 1992.

1034. Ardley, Neil. *The Science Book of Magnets*. New York: Harcourt Brace Jovanovich Publishers, 1991.

1035. Ardley, Neil. *The Science Book of Motion*. New York: Harcourt Brace Jovanovich Publishers, 1992.

1036. Ardley, Neil. *The Science Book of Sound*. New York: Harcourt Brace Jovanovich Publishers, 1991.

1037. Ardley, Neil. *The Science Book of the Senses*. New York: Harcourt Brace Jovanovich Publishers, 1992.

1038. Ardley, Neil. *The Science Book of Things That Grow*. New York: Harcourt Brace Jovanovich Publishers, 1991.

1039. Aust, Siegfried. *Lenses, Take a Closer Look*. Minneapolis, Minn.: Lerner Publishing Co., 1991.

1040. Bailey, Jill. *Birds*. New York: Dorling Kindersley, 1992.

1041. Baines, John D. *Water*. New York: Thomson Learning, 1993.

1042. Baker, Wendy. *Earth: A Creative, Hands-on Approach to Science*. New York: Macmillan Publishing Co., 1993.

1043. Baker, Wendy. *Electricity: A Creative Hands-on Approach to Science*. New York: Macmillan Publishing Co., 1992.

1044. Baker, Wendy. *Plants: A Creative Hands-on Approach to Science*. New York: Macmillan Publishing Co., 1993.

1045. Baker, Wendy. *Sound: A Creative Hands-on Approach to Science*. New York: Macmillan Publishing Co., 1993.

1046. Barrow, Lloyd H. *Adventures with Rocks and Minerals, Geology Experiments for Young People*. Hillside, N.J.: Enslow Publishers, 1991.

1047. Bates, Jeffrey. *Seeds to Plants: Projects with Biology.* New York: Gloucester Press, 1991.
1048. Behm, Barbara J. *Investigating the Color Blue.* Milwaukee, Wisc.: Gareth Stevens Publishing, 1993.
1049. Behm, Barbara J. *Investigating the Color Green.* Milwaukee, Wisc.: Gareth Stevens Publishing, 1993.
1050. Behm, Barbara J. *Investigating the Color Red.* Milwaukee, Wisc.: Gareth Stevens Publishing, 1993.
1051. Behm, Barbara J. *Investigating the Color Yellow.* Milwaukee, Wisc.: Gareth Stevens Publishing, 1993.
1052. Bender, Lionel. *Forensic Detection.* New York: Gloucester Press, 1990.
1053. *Bending Light: An Exploratorium Toolbook.* N.Y. Little, Brown & Co., 1993.
1054. *Best Kids Garden Book.* Menlo Park, Calif.: Sunset Publishing Corp., 1992.
1055. Bittinger, Gayle. *Exploring Sand and the Desert.* Everett, Wash.: Warren Publishing House, 1993.
1056. Bittinger, Gayle. *Exploring Water and the Ocean.* Everett, Wash.: Warren Publishing House, 1993.
1057. Blashfield, Jean F. *Global Warming.* Chicago: Childrens Press, 1991.
1058. Blashfield, Jean F. *Oil Spills.* Chicago: Childrens Press, 1991.
1059. Blashfield, Jean F. *Too Many People?* Chicago: Childrens Press, 1992.
1060. Bleifeld, Maurice. *Botany Projects for Young Scientists.* New York: Franklin Watts, 1992.
1061. Bonnet, Robert L. *Botany: 49 More Science Fair Projects.* Blue Ridge Summit, Pa.: Tab Books, 1991.
1062. Bonnet, Robert L. *Space & Astronomy: 49 Science Fair Projects.* Blue Ridge Summit, Pa.: Tab Books, 1991.
1063. Bosak, Susan V. *Science Is.* Ontario, Canada: Scholastic Canada Ltd., 1991.
1064. Bourgeois, Paulette. *The Amazing Paper Book.* Reading, Mass.: Addison-Wesley Publishing Co., 1989.
1065. Bourgeois, Paulette. *The Amazing Potato Book.* Reading, Mass.: Addison-Wesley Publishing Co., 1991.
1066. Breckenridge, Judy. *Simple Physics Experiments with Everyday Materials.* New York: Sterling Publishing Co., 1993.
1067. Bruning, Nancy. *Cities Against Nature.* Chicago: Childrens Press, 1992.
1068. Burnie, David. *Flowers.* New York: Dorling Kindersley, 1992.
1069. Burnie, David. *How Nature Works.* Pleasantville, N.Y.: Reader's Digest Association, 1991.
1070. *Calculation and Chance.* Freeport, N.Y.: Marshall Cavendish Corp., 1990.
1071. Carlson, Laurie. *EcoArt!* Charlotte, Vt.: Williamson Publishing Co., 1992.
1072. Cash, Terry. *Electricity and Magnets.* New York: Warwick Press, 1989.
1073. Cash, Terry. *101 Physics Tricks: Fun Experiments with Everyday Materials.* New York: Sterling Publishing Co., 1992.
1074. Challand, Helen J. *Disappearing Wetlands.* Chicago: Childrens Press, 1992.
1075. Challand, Helen J. *Vanishing Forests.* Chicago: Childrens Press, 1991.
1076. Challoner, Jack. *My First Batteries & Magnets Book.* New York: Dorling Kindersley, 1992.
1077. Charman, Andrew. *Materials.* New York: Franklin Watts, 1992.
1078. *Child's Garden.* San Francisco: Chevron Chemical Co., Ortho Division, 1984.
1079. Churchill, E. Richard. *Amazing Science Experiments with Everyday Materials.* New York: Sterling Publishing Co., 1991.
1080. Clark, John. *Earthquakes to Volcanoes.* New York: Gloucester Press, 1992.
1081. Clark, John. *Mining to Minerals.* New York: Gloucester Press, 1992.
1082. Cobb, Vicki. *Light Action! Amazing Experiments with Optics.* New York: Harper Collins Publishers, 1993.
1083. Cobb, Vicki. *Wanna Bet? Science Challenges to Fool You.* New York: Lothrop, Lee & Shepard Books, 1992.
1084. Cobb, Vicki. *Why Can't You Unscramble an Egg?* New York: Lodestar Books, 1990.
1085. Coldrey, Jennifer. *Shells.* New York: Dorling Kindersley, 1993.
1086. Cork, Barbara Taylor. *Be an Expert Weather Forecaster.* New York: Gloucester Press, 1992.
1087. Cox, Shirley. *Chemistry.* Vero Beach, Fla.: Rourke Publications, 1993.
1088. Crystal, Nancy. *You Won't Believe Your Eyes.* Toronto: Annick Press Ltd., 1992.
1089. Daeschler, Ted. *Start Collecting Fossils.* Philadelphia, Pa.: Running Press, 1988.
1090. Darling, David J., Dr. *Between Fire and Ice: The Science of Heat.* New York: Dillon Press, 1992.
1091. Darling, David J., Dr. *From Glasses to Gases: The Science of Matter.* New York: Dillon Press, 1992.
1092. Darling, David J., Dr. *Making Light Work: The Science of Optics.* New York: Dillon Press, 1991.
1093. Darling, David J., Dr. *Sounds Interesting: The Science of Acoustics.* New York: Dillon Press, 1991.
1094. Darling, David J., Dr. *Spiderwebs to Sky-scrapers: The Science of Structures.* New York: Dillon Press, 1991.
1095. Darling, David J., Dr. *Up, Up, and Away: The Science of Flight.* New York: Dillon Press, 1991.
1096. Dashefsky, H. Steven. *Entomology: High-School Science Fair Projects.* Blue Ridge Summit, Pa.: Tab Books, 1994.
1097. Dashefsky, H. Steven. *Insect Biology: 49 Science Fair Projects.* Blue Ridge Summit, Pa.: Tab Books, 1992.
1098. Davies, Kay. *Animals.* Austin, Tex.: Steck-Vaughn Co., 1992.
1099. Davies, Kay. *Electricity and Magnetism.* Austin, Tex.: Steck-Vaughn Co., 1992.
1100. Davies, Kay. *Floating and Sinking.* Austin, Tex.: Steck-Vaughn Co., 1992.
1101. Davies, Kay. *Food.* Austin, Tex.: Steck-Vaughn Co., 1992.
1102. Davies, Kay. *Sound and Music.* Austin, Tex.: Steck-Vaughn Co., 1992.
1103. Davies, Kay. *The Super Science Book of Time.* New York: Thomson Learning, 1992.
1104. Davies, Kay. *The Super Science Book of Weather.* New York: Thomson Learning, 1993.
1105. Davies, Kay. *Waste.* Austin, Tex.: Steck-Vaughn Co., 1992.
1106. Davies, Kay. *Weather.* Austin, Tex.: Steck-Vaughn Co., 1992.
1107. Deery, Ruth. *Earthquakes & Volcanoes.* Carthage, Ill.: Good Apple, Inc., 1985.
1108. Devonshire, Hilary. *Air.* New York: Franklin Watts, 1992.

1109. Devonshire, Hilary. *Color*. New York: Franklin Watts, 1992.

1110. Devonshire, Hilary. *Flight*. New York: Franklin Watts, 1992.

1111. Devonshire, Hilary. *Light*. New York: Franklin Watts, 1991.

1112. Devonshire, Hilary. *Movement*. New York: Franklin Watts, 1992.

1113. Devonshire, Hilary. *Water*. New York: Franklin Watts, 1991.

1114. Diehn, Gwen. *Nature Crafts for Kids*. New York: Sterling Publishing Co., 1992.

1115. Diehn, Gwen. *Science Crafts for Kids*. New York: Sterling Publishing Co., 1994.

1116. Doris, Ellen. *Entomology*. New York: Thames and Hudson Inc., 1993.

1117. Doris, Ellen. *Invertebrate Zoology*. New York: Thames and Hudson Inc., 1993.

1118. Doris, Ellen. *Marine Biology*. New York: Thames and Hudson Inc., 1993.

1119. Dunn, Andrew. *Bridges*. New York: Thomson Learning, 1993.

1120. Dunn, Andrew. *Dams*. New York: Thomson Learning, 1993.

1121. Dunn, Andrew. *The Power of Pressure*. New York: Thomson Learning, 1993.

1122. Dunn, Andrew. *Skyscrapers*. New York: Thomson Learning, 1993.

1123. Dunn, Andrew. *Tunnels*. New York: Thomson Learning, 1993.

1124. Durant, Penny Raife. *Make a Splash: Science Activities with Liquids*. New York: Franklin Watts, 1991.

1125. Dyson, Sue. *Wood*. New York: Thomson Learning, 1993.

1126. *Earth and Space*. Freeport, N.Y.: Marshall Cavendish Corp., 1990.

1127. Erickson, Donna. *More Prime Time Activities with Kids*. Minneapolis, Minn.: Augsburg Fortress, 1992.

1128. Evans, David. *Make It Balance*. New York: Dorling Kindersley, 1992.

1129. Evans, David. *Make It Change*. New York: Dorling Kindersley, 1992.

1130. Evans, David. *Make It Go*. New York: Dorling Kindersley, 1992.

1131. Evans, David. *Me and My Body*. New York: Dorling Kindersley, 1992.

1132. *Exploratorium Science Snackbook*. San Francisco: Exploratorium Teacher Institute: 1991.

1133. Facts on File, Inc. *Historical Science Experiments on File*. New York: Facts on File, Inc., 1993.

1134. Facts on File, Inc. *Nature Projects on File*. New York: Facts on File, Inc., 1992.

1135. Farndon, John. *Weather*. New York: Dorling Kindersley, 1992.

1136. *Forces of Nature*. Freeport, N.Y.: Marshall Cavendish Corp.: 1990.

1137. Friedhoffer, Robert. *Forces, Motion, and Energy*. New York: Franklin Watts, 1992.

1138. Friedhoffer, Robert. *Light*. New York: Franklin Watts, 1992.

1139. Friedhoffer, Robert. *Magnetism and Electricity*. New York: Franklin Watts, 1992.

1140. Friedhoffer, Robert. *Matter and Energy*. New York: Franklin Watts, 1992.

1141. Friedhoffer, Robert. *Sound, Book 4*. New York: Franklin Watts, 1992.

1142. Gamlin, Linda. *Trees*. New York: Dorling Kindersley, 1993.

1143. Ganeri, Anita. *Birds*. New York: Gloucester Press, 1992.

1144. Ganeri, Anita. *Insects*. New York: Franklin Watts, 1992.

1145. Ganeri, Anita. *Plants*. New York: Franklin Watts, 1992.

1146. Ganeri, Anita. *Ponds and Pond Life*. New York: Franklin Watts, 1993.

1147. Ganeri, Anita. *Small Mammals*. New York: Franklin Watts, 1993.

1148. Ganeri, Anita. *Trees*. New York: Gloucester Press, 1992.

1149. Ganeri, Anita. *Weather*. New York: Franklin Watts, 1993.

1150. Gardner, Robert. *Celebrating Earth Day: A Sourcebook of Activities and Experiments*. Brookfield, Conn.: The Millbrook Press, 1992.

1151. Gardner, Robert. *Crime Lab 101: Experimenting with Crime Detection*. New York: Walker and Company, 1992.

1152. Gardner, Robert. *Experimenting with Energy Conservation*. New York: Franklin Watts, 1992.

1153. Gardner, Robert. *Experimenting with Light*. New York: Franklin Watts, 1991.

1154. Gardner, Robert. *Experimenting with Science in Sports*. New York: Franklin Watts, 1993.

1155. Gardner, Robert. *Experimenting with Sound*. New York: Franklin Watts, 1991.

1156. Gardner, Robert. *Famous Experiments You Can Do*. New York: Franklin Watts, 1990.

1157. Gardner, Robert. *Forces and Machines*. Englewood Cliffs, N.J.: Julian Messner, 1991.

1158. Gardner, Robert. *Robert Gardner's Challenging Science Experiments*. New York: Franklin Watts, 1993.

1159. Gardner, Robert. *Robert Gardner's Favorite Science Experiments*. New York: Franklin Watts, 1992.

1160. Glover, David. *Batteries, Bulbs, and Wires*. New York: Kingfisher Books, 1993.

1161. Glover, David. *Flying and Floating*. New York: Kingfisher Books, 1993.

1162. Glover, David. *Solids and Liquids*. New York: Kingfisher Books, 1993.

1163. Glover, David. *Sound and Light*. New York: Kingfisher Books, 1993.

1164. Goodwin, Peter H. *Physics Projects for Young Scientists*. New York: Franklin Watts, 1991.

1165. Graham, Ian. *Boats, Ships, Submarines and Other Floating Machines*. New York: Kingfisher Books, 1993.

1166. Graham, Ian. *Cars, Bikes, Trains, and Other Land Machines*. New York: Kingfisher Books, 1993.

1167. Graham, Ian. *Salvage at Sea*. New York: Gloucester Press, 1990.

1168. Grant, Lesley. *Discover Bones: Explore the Science of Skeletons*. Reading, Mass.: Addison-Wesley Publishing Co., 1992.

1169. Grier, Katherine. *Discover: Investigating the Mysteries of History*. Reading, Mass.: Addison-Wesley Publishing Co., 1989.

1170. Gustafson, John. *Planets, Moons and Meteors: The Young Stargazer's Guide to the Galaxy*. New York: Julian Messner, 1992.

1171. Gutnik, Martin J. *Experiments That Explore Acid Rain.* Brookfield, Conn.: The Millbrook Press, 1992.

1172. Gutnik, Martin J. *Experiments That Explore Oil Spills.* Brookfield, Conn.: The Millbrook Press, 1991.

1173. Gutnik, Martin J. *Experiments That Explore Recycling.* Brookfield, Conn.: The Millbrook Press, 1992.

1174. Gutnik, Martin J. *Experiments That Explore the Greenhouse Effect.* Brookfield, Conn.: The Millbrook Press, 1991.

1175. Haas, Carolyn. *My Own Fun.* Chicago: Chicago Review Press, 1990.

1176. *Habitats and Environments.* Freeport, N.Y.: Marshall Cavendish Corp.: 1990.

1177. Haines, Gail Kay. *Sugar Is Sweet.* New York: Atheneum, 1992.

1178. Handelsman, Judith F. *Gardens from Garbage.* Brookfield, Conn.: The Millbrook Press, 1993.

1179. Hann, Judith. *How Science Works.* Pleasantville, N.Y.: Reader's Digest Association, 1991.

1180. Harlow, Rosie. *Cycles and Seasons.* New York: Warwick Press, 1991.

1181. Harlow, Rosie. *Energy and Growth.* New York: Warwick Press, 1991.

1182. Harlow, Rosie. *Observing Minibeasts.* New York: Warwick Press, 1991.

1183. Harlow, Rosie. *175 Amazing Nature Experiments.* New York: Random House, 1992.

1184. Harlow, Rosie. *Trees and Leaves.* New York: Warwick Press, 1991.

1185. Hemsley, William. *Feeding to Digestion.* New York: Gloucester Press, 1992.

1186. Hemsley, William. *Fins to Wings.* New York: Gloucester Press, 1992.

1187. Hemsley, William. *Jellyfish to Insects.* New York: Gloucester Press, 1991.

1188. Hickman, Pamela M. *Bugwise.* Reading, Mass.: Addison-Wesley Publishing Co., 1991.

1189. Hoffman, Jane. *Backyard Scientist, Series Three.* Irvine, Calif.: Backyard Scientist, 1990.

1190. Holland, Peter. *Amazing Models: Gravity Power.* Blue Ridge Summit, Pa.: Tab Books, 1990.

1191. Houghton, Graham. *Bioenergy.* Milwaukee, Wisc.: Gareth Stevens Publishing, 1991.

1192. Hume, Rob. *Birdwatching.* New York: Random House, 1992.

1193. Inglis, Jane. *Fiber.* Minneapolis, Minn.: Carolrhoda Books, 1992.

1194. Inglis, Jane. *Proteins.* Minneapolis, Minn.: Carolrhoda Books, 1992.

1195. Iritz, Maxine Haren. *Blue-Ribbon Science Fair Projects.* Blue Ridge Summit, Pa.: Tab Books, 1991.

1196. Jackman, Wayne. *Gas.* New York: Thomson Learning, 1993.

1197. Jackman, Wayne. *Plastics.* New York: Thomson Learning, 1993.

1198. Jennings, Terry J. *Cranes, Dump Trucks, Bulldozers & Other Building Machines.* New York: Kingfisher Books, 1993.

1199. Jennings, Terry J. *Electricity.* New York: Gloucester Press, 1990.

1200. Jennings, Terry J. *Electricity and Magnetism.* Chicago: Childrens Press, 1989.

1201. Jennings, Terry J. *Planes, Gliders, Helicopters, and Other Flying Machines.* New York: Kingfisher Books, 1993.

1202. Jennings, Terry J. *Rocks.* Ada, Okla.: Garrett Educational Corp., 1991.

1203. Johnson, Sylvia A. *Roses Red, Violets Blue.* Minneapolis, Minn.: Lerner Publications Co., 1991.

1204. Jordan, Helene J. *How a Seed Grows.* New York: Harper Collins Publishers, 1992 rev. ed.

1205. Kalman, Bobbie. *I Am a Part of Nature.* New York: Crabtree Publishing Co., 1992.

1206. Kalman, Bobbie. *Squirmy Wormy Composters.* New York: Crabtree Publishing Co., 1992.

1207. Kalman, Bobbie. *Wonderful Water.* New York: Crabtree Publishing Co., 1992.

1208. Kaner, Etta. *Balloon Science.* Reading, Mass.: Addison-Wesley Publishing Co., 1989.

1209. Kaner, Etta. *Sound Science.* Reading, Mass.: Addison-Wesley Publishing Co., 1991.

1210. Katz, Phyllis. *Great Science Fair Projects.* New York: Franklin Watts, 1992.

1211. Kerrod, Robin. *Air in Action.* Freeport, N.Y.: Marshall Cavendish Corp., 1989.

1212. Kerrod, Robin. *Fire and Water.* Freeport, N.Y.: Marshall Cavendish Corp., 1989.

1213. Kerrod, Robin. *Light Fantastic.* Freeport, N.Y.: Marshall Cavendish Corp., 1989.

1214. Kerrod, Robin. *Plants in Action.* Freeport, N.Y.: Marshall Cavendish Corp., 1989.

1215. Kukes, Roger. *The Zoetrope Book.* Portland, Oreg.: Klassroom Kinetics, 1985.

1216. Ladizinsky, Eric. *Magical Science: Magic Tricks for Young Scientists.* Los Angeles, Calif.: Lowell House Juvenile, 1992.

1217. Lafferty, Peter. *Marshall Cavendish More Science Projects, Astronomy.* Freeport, N.Y.: Marshall Cavendish Corp., 1989.

1218. Lafferty, Peter. *Marshall Cavendish More Science Projects, Electricity and Magnetism.* Freeport, N.Y.: Marshall Cavendish Corp., 1989.

1219. Lafferty, Peter. *Marshall Cavendish More Science Projects, Heat.* Freeport, N.Y.: Marshall Cavendish Corp., 1989.

1220. Lammert, John M. *Human Body.* Vero Beach, Fla.: Rourke Publications, 1993.

1221. Lammert, John M. *Microbes.* Vero Beach, Fla.: Rourke Publications, 1992.

1222. Lammert, John M. *Plants.* Vero Beach, Fla.: Rourke Publications, 1992.

1223. Langley, Andrew. *Paper.* New York: Thomson Learning, 1993.

1224. Langley, Andrew. *Steel.* New York: Thomson Learning, 1993.

1225. Lawlor, Elizabeth P. *Discover Nature at the Seashore: Things to Know and Things to Do.* Harrisburg, Pa.: Stackpole Books, 1992.

1226. Leon, George deLucenay. *Electronic Projects for Young Scientists.* New York: Franklin Watts, 1991.

1227. Leslie, Clare Walker. *Nature All Year Long.* New York: Greenwillow Books, 1991.

1228. Levine, Shar. *Projects for a Healthy Planet.* New York: John Wiley & Sons, 1992.

1229. Lewis, James. *Hocus Pocus Stir & Cook.* Deephaven, Minn.: Meadowbrook Press, 1991.

1230. Lewis, James. *Learn While You Scrub: Science in the Tub.* Deephaven, Minn.: Meadowbrook Press, 1989.

1231. Lewis, James. *Measure, Pour & Mix Kitchen Science Tricks.* Deephaven, Minn.: Meadowbrook Press, 1990.

1232. Love, Ann. *Take Action: An Environmental Book for Kids*. New York: Tambourine Books, 1993.

1233. Lucas, Eileen. *Acid Rain*. Chicago: Childrens Press, 1991.

1234. Lucas, Eileen. *Water: A Resource in Crisis*. Chicago: Childrens Press, 1991.

1235. Lye, Keith. *Measuring and Maps*. New York: Gloucester Press, 1991.

1236. McInnes, Celia. *Projects for Summer & Holiday Activities*. Ada, Okla.: Garrett Educational Corp., 1989.

1237. McVey, Vicki. *The Sierra Club Book of Weatherwisdom*. Boston, Mass.: Little, Brown and Co., 1991.

1238. Mandell, Muriel. *Simple Kitchen Experiments*. New York: Sterling Publishing Co., 1993.

1239. Markle, Sandra. *Exploring Autumn*. New York: Atheneum, 1991.

1240. Markle, Sandra. *The Kids' Earth Handbook*. New York: Atheneum, 1991.

1241. Markle, Sandra. *Pioneering Space*. New York: Atheneum, 1992.

1242. Markmann, Erika. *Grow It! An Indoor/Outdoor Gardening Guide for Kids*. New York: Random House, 1991.

1243. *Marshall Cavendish Science in Action, Experiments in Physics*. Freeport, N.Y.: Marshall Cavendish Corp., 1988.

1244. *Marshall Cavendish Science in Action, Fun with Chemistry*. Freeport, N.Y.: Marshall Cavendish Corp., 1988.

1245. *Marshall Cavendish Science in Action, Light and Sound*. Freeport, N.Y.: Marshall Cavendish Corp., 1988.

1246. *Marshall Cavendish Science in Action, the Living World*. Freeport, N.Y.: Marshall Cavendish Corp., 1988.

1247. *Marshall Cavendish Science in Action, Projects in Physics*. Freeport, N.Y.: Marshall Cavendish Corp., 1988.

1248. *Marshall Cavendish Science in Action, the World of Numbers*. Freeport, N.Y.: Marshall Cavendish Corp., 1988.

1249. Math, Irwin. *Tomorrow's Technology: Experimenting with the Science of the Future*. New York: Charles Scribner's Sons, 1992.

1250. Mebane, Robert C. *Adventures with Atoms and Molecules, Book IV*. Hillside, N.J.: Enslow Publishers, 1992.

1251. Mebane, Robert C. *Adventures with Atoms and Molecules, Book III*. Hillside, N.J.: Enslow Publishers, 1991.

1252. Millspaugh, Ben, Dr. *Aviation and Space Science Projects*. Blue Ridge Summit, Pa.: Tab Books, 1991.

1253. *Mind and Perception*. Freeport, N.Y.: Marshall Cavendish Corp.: 1990.

1254. Morgan, Nina. *The Plant Cycle*. New York: Thomson Learning, 1993.

1255. Murphy, Bryan. *Experiment with Air*. Minneapolis, Minn.: Lerner Publications Co., 1991.

1256. Murphy, Bryan. *Experiment with Water*. Minneapolis, Minn.: Lerner Publications Co., 1991.

1257. Murphy, Pat. *Bending Light*. Boston, Mass.: Little, Brown and Company, 1993.

1258. Murray, Peter. *Silly Science Tricks*. Plymouth, Minnesota: The Child's World, 1993.

1259. Newton, David E. *Consumer Chemistry Projects for Young Scientists*. New York: Franklin Watts, 1991.

1260. Nielsen, Nancy J. *Carnivorous Plants*. New York: Franklin Watts, 1992.

1261. Nottridge, Rhoda. *Additives*. Minneapolis, Minn.: Carolrhoda Books, 1992.

1262. Nottridge, Rhoda. *Fats*. Minneapolis, Minn.: Carolrhoda Books, 1992.

1263. Nottridge, Rhoda. *Sugars*. Minneapolis, Minn.: Carolrhoda Books, 1992.

1264. Nottridge, Rhoda. *Vitamins*. Minneapolis, Minn.: Carolrhoda Books, 1992.

1265. Ocone, Lynn. *The Youth Gardening Book*. Burlington, Vt.: National Gardening Association, 1987 rev. ed.

1266. Oliver, Ray. *Rocks & Fossils*. New York: Random House, 1993.

1267. O'Neil, Karen E. *Health and Medicine Projects for Young Scientists*. New York: Franklin Watts, 1993.

1268. O'Reilly, Susie. *Papermaking*. New York: Thomson Learning, 1993.

1269. Pack, Janet. *Fueling the Future*. Chicago: Childrens Press, 1992.

1270. Parker, Steve. *Catching a Cold*. New York: Franklin Watts, 1992.

1271. Parker, Steve. *Chemistry*. New York: Warwick Press, 1990.

1272. Parker, Steve. *Dreaming in the Night*. New York: Franklin Watts, 1991.

1273. Parker, Steve. *Eating a Meal*. New York: Franklin Watts, 1991.

1274. Parker, Steve. *Insects*. New York: Dorling Kindersley, 1992.

1275. Parker, Steve. *Keeping Cool*. New York: Franklin Watts, 1992.

1276. Parker, Steve. *Learning a Lesson*. New York: Franklin Watts, 1991.

1277. Parker, Steve. *Rocks and Minerals*. New York: Dorling Kindersley, 1993.

1278. Parker, Steve. *Running a Race*. New York: Franklin Watts, 1991.

1279. Parker, Steve. *Singing a Song*. New York: Franklin Watts, 1992.

1280. Parker, Steve. *Touching a Nerve*. New York: Franklin Watts, 1992.

1281. Parker, Steve. *Weather*. New York: Warwick Press, 1990.

1282. Peacock, Graham. *Electricity*. New York: Thomson Learning, 1993.

1283. Peacock, Graham. *Light*. New York: Thomson Learning, 1993.

1284. Peacock, Graham. *Sound*. New York: Thomson Learning, 1993.

1285. Peacock, Graham. *The Super Science Book of Light*. New York: Thomson Learning, 1993.

1286. Peacock, Graham. *The Super Science Book of Materials*. New York: Thomson Learning, 1993.

1287. Peacock, Graham. *The Super Science Book of Our Bodies*. New York: Thomson Learning, 1993.

1288. Penrose, Gordon. *More Science Surprises from Dr. Zed*. New York: Simon & Schuster, 1992.

1289. Penrose, Gordon. *Sensational Science Activities with Dr. Zed*. New York: Simon & Schuster, 1990.

1290. Perdue, Peggy K. *Diving into Science*. Glenview, Ill.: Scott, Foresman and Co., 1990.

1291. Perdue, Peggy K. *Small Wonders, Hands-On Science Activities for Young Children*. Glenview, Ill.: Scott, Foresman and Co., 1989.

1292. Petty, Kate. *Earth*. New York: Franklin Watts, 1991.

1293. Prochnow, Dave. *How? More Experiments for the Young Scientist.* Blue Ridge Summit, Pa.: Tab Books, 1993.

1294. Prochnow, Dave. *Why? Experiments for the Young Scientist.* Blue Ridge Summit, Pa.: Tab Books, 1993.

1295. Rainis, Kenneth G. *Exploring with a Magnifying Glass.* New York: Franklin Watts, 1991.

1296. *Raintree Illustrated Science Encyclopedia, Vol. 18.* Milwaukee, Wisc.: Raintree Publishers: 1991.

1297. Reed, Catherine. *Environment.* Vero Beach, Fla.: Rourke Publications, 1993.

1298. Richards, Roy. *101 Science Surprises.* New York: Sterling Publishing Co., 1992.

1299. Richards, Roy. *101 Science Tricks: Fun Experiments with Everyday Materials.* New York: Sterling Publishing Co., 1991.

1300. Rickard, Graham. *Bricks.* New York: Thomson Learning, 1993.

1301. Rickard, Graham. *Geothermal Energy.* Milwaukee, Wisc.: Gareth Stevens Publishing, 1991.

1302. Rickard, Graham. *Oil.* New York: Thomson Learning, 1993.

1303. Rickard, Graham. *Solar Energy.* Milwaukee, Wisc.: Gareth Stevens Publishing, 1991.

1304. Rickard, Graham. *Water Energy.* Milwaukee, Wisc.: Gareth Stevens Publishing, 1991.

1305. Rickard, Graham. *Wind Energy.* Milwaukee, Wisc.: Gareth Stevens Publishing, 1991.

1306. Robson, Denny. *Grow It for Fun.* New York: Gloucester Press, 1991.

1307. Robson, Pam. *Electricity.* New York: Gloucester Press, 1993.

1308. Robson, Pam. *Light, Color and Lenses.* New York: Franklin Watts, 1993.

1309. Robson, Pam. *Magnetism.* New York: Gloucester Press, 1993.

1310. Robson, Pam. *Water, Paddles & Boats.* New York: Gloucester Press, 1992.

1311. Rogers, Daniel K. *Marshall Cavendish More Science Projects Weather.* Freeport, N.Y.: Marshall Cavendish Corp., 1989.

1312. Ross, Catherine. *The Amazing Milk Book.* Reading, Mass.: Addison-Wesley Publishing Co., 1991.

1313. Roth, Charles E. *The Amateur Naturalist: Explorations and Investigations.* New York: Franklin Watts, 1993.

1314. Rowe, Julian. *Colorful Light.* Chicago: Childrens Press, 1993.

1315. Rowe, Julian. *Feel and Touch.* Chicago: Childrens Press, 1993.

1316. Rowe, Julian. *Keep It Afloat.* Chicago: Childrens Press, 1993.

1317. Rowe, Julian. *Keeping Your Balance.* Chicago: Childrens Press, 1993.

1318. Rowe, Julian. *Make It Move.* Chicago: Childrens Press, 1993.

1319. Rowe, Julian. *Making Sounds.* Chicago: Childrens Press, 1993.

1320. Russo, Monica. *The Insect Almanac: A Year-Round Activity Guide.* New York: Sterling Publishing Co., 1991.

1321. Russo, Monica. *Tree Almanac: A Year-Round Activity Guide.* New York: Sterling Publishing Co., 1993.

1322. Rybolt, Thomas R. *Environmental Experiments About Air.* Hillside, N.J.: Enslow Publishers, 1993.

1323. Rybolt, Thomas R. *Environmental Experiments About Land.* Hillside, N.J.: Enslow Publishers, 1993.

1324. Rybolt, Thomas R. *Environmental Experiments About Life.* Hillside, N.J.: Enslow Publishers, 1993.

1325. Rybolt, Thomas R. *Environmental Experiments About Water.* Hillside, N.J.: Enslow Publishers, 1993.

1326. Sauvain, Philip. *Roads.* Ada, Okla.: Garrett Educational Corp., 1990.

1327. Sauvain, Philip. *Tunnels.* Ada, Okla.: Garrett Educational Corp., 1990.

1328. Savan, Beth. *Earthwatch: Earthcycles and Ecosystems.* Reading, Mass.: Addison-Wesley Publishing Co., 1992.

1329. Schatz, Dennis. *Astronomy Activity Book.* New York: Simon & Schuster, 1991.

1330. *Science Express: 50 Scientific Stunts from the Ontario Science Centre.* Reading, Mass.: Addison-Wesley Publishing Co.: 1991.

1331. Seed, Deborah. *Water Science.* Reading, Mass.: Addison-Wesley Publishing Co., 1992.

1332. Seller, Mick. *Air, Wind and Flight.* New York: Gloucester Press, 1992.

1333. Seller, Mick. *Sound, Noise & Music.* New York: Gloucester Press, 1992.

1334. Seller, Mick. *Wheels, Pulleys & Levers.* New York: Gloucester Press, 1993.

1335. Sheehan, Kathryn. *Earth Child.* Tulsa, Okla.: Council Oak Books, 1991.

1336. Siy, Alexandra. *Ancient Forests.* New York: Dillon Press, 1991.

1337. Siy, Alexandra. *Arctic National Wildlife Refuge.* New York: Dillon Press, 1991.

1338. Siy, Alexandra. *The Brazilian Rain Forest.* New York: Dillon Press, 1992.

1339. Siy, Alexandra. *The Great Astrolabe Reef.* New York: Dillon Press, 1992.

1340. Siy, Alexandra. *Hawaiian Islands.* New York: Dillon Press, 1991.

1341. Siy, Alexandra. *Native Grasslands.* New York: Dillon Press, 1991.

1342. Smith, Bruce. *Geology Projects for Young Scientists.* New York: Franklin Watts, 1992.

1343. Smith, David. *The Food Cycle.* New York: Thomson Learning, 1993.

1344. Smith, David. *The Water Cycle.* New York: Thomson Learning, 1993.

1345. Smoothey, Marion. *Angles.* North Bellmore, N.Y.: Marshall Cavendish Corp., 1993.

1346. Smoothey, Marion. *Area and Volume.* North Bellmore, N.Y.: Marshall Cavendish Corp., 1993.

1347. Smoothey, Marion. *Let's Investigate Circles.* North Bellmore, N.Y.: Marshall Cavendish Corp., 1992.

1348. Smoothey, Marion. *Number Patterns.* North Bellmore, N.Y.: Marshall Cavendish Corp., 1993.

1349. Smoothey, Marion. *Let's Investigate Numbers.* North Bellmore, N.Y.: Marshall Cavendish Corp., 1992.

1350. Smoothey, Marion. *Let's Investigate Quadrilaterals.* North Bellmore, N.Y.: Marshal Cavendish Corp., 1992.

1351. Smoothey, Marion. *Shape Patterns.* North Bellmore, N.Y.: Marshal Cavendish Corp., 1993.

1352. Smoothey, Marion. *Let's Investigate Shapes.* North Bellmore, N.Y.: Marshall Cavendish Corp., 1993.

1353. Smoothey, Marion. *Let's Investigate Solids.* North Bellmore, N.Y.: Marshall Cavendish Corp., 1993.

1354. Smoothey, Marion. *Let's Investigate Statistics.* North Bellmore, N.Y.: Marshall Cavendish Corp., 1993.

1355. Smoothey, Marion. *Time, Distance and Speed.* North Bellmore, N.Y.: Marshall Cavendish Corp., 1993.

1356. Smoothey, Marion. *Let's Investigate Triangles*. North Bellmore, N.Y.: Marshall Cavendish Corp., 1992.

1357. Songhurst, Hazel. *Glass*. New York: Thomson Learning, 1993.

1358. Steele, Philip. *Heatwave, Causes and Effects*. New York: Franklin Watts, 1991.

1359. Steele, Philip. *Rain, Causes and Effects*. New York: Franklin Watts, 1991.

1360. Steele, Philip. *Wind, Causes and Effects*. New York: Franklin Watts, 1991.

1361. Stenstrup, Allen. *Hazardous Waste*. Chicago: Childrens Press, 1991.

1362. Stidworthy, John. *Be an Expert Environmentalist*. New York: Gloucester Press, 1992.

1363. Stidworthy, John. *Be an Expert Naturalist*. New York: Gloucester Press, 1991.

1364. Stidworthy, John. *Fossils*. Freeport, N.Y.: Marshall Cavendish Corp., 1989.

1365. Stott, Carole. *Night Sky*. New York: Dorling Kindersley, 1993.

1366. Stwertka, Eve. *Cleaning Up*. New York: Julian Messner, 1993.

1367. Stwertka, Eve. *Tuning In: The Sounds of Radio*. New York: Julian Messner, 1992.

1368. Suzuki, David T. *Looking at Plants*. New York: John Wiley & Sons, 1992.

1369. Suzuki, David T. *Looking at Senses*. New York: John Wiley & Sons, 1991.

1370. Suzuki, David T. *Looking at the Body*. New York: John Wiley & Sons, 1991.

1371. Suzuki, David T. *Looking at the Environment*. New York: John Wiley & Sons, 1991.

1372. Suzuki, David T. *Looking at Weather*. New York: John Wiley & Sons, 1991.

1373. Swallow, Su. *Air*. New York: Franklin Watts, 1991.

1374. Swallow, Su. *Water*. New York: Franklin Watts, 1990.

1375. Tant, Carl. *Seeds, etc....* Angleton, Tex.: Biotech Publishing, Plant Something Different, Inc., 1992.

1376. Taylor, Barbara. *Air and Flying*. New York: Franklin Watts, 1991.

1377. Taylor, Barbara. *Energy and Power*. New York: Franklin Watts, 1990.

1378. Taylor, Barbara. *Force and Movement*. New York: Franklin Watts, 1990.

1379. Taylor, Barbara. *Green Thumbs Up! The Science of Growing Plants*. New York: Random House, 1992.

1380. Taylor, Barbara. *Machines and Movement*. New York: Warwick Press, 1990.

1381. Taylor, Barbara. *Maps and Mapping*. New York: Kingfisher Books, 1993.

1382. Taylor, Barbara. *More Power to You! The Science of Batteries and Magnets*. New York: Random House, 1992.

1383. Taylor, Barbara. *Mountains and Volcanoes*. New York: Kingfisher Books, 1993.

1384. Taylor, Barbara. *Rivers and Oceans*. New York: Kingfisher Books, 1993.

1385. Taylor, Barbara. *Sound and Music*. New York: Warwick Press, 1990.

1386. Taylor, Barbara. *Structures and Materials*. New York: Franklin Watts, 1991.

1387. Taylor, Barbara. *Weather and Climate*. New York: Kingfisher Books, 1993.

1388. Taylor, Barbara. *Wind and Weather*. New York: Franklin Watts, 1991.

1389. Taylor, Kim. *Action*. New York: John Wiley & Sons, 1992.

1390. Taylor, Kim. *Light*. New York: John Wiley & Sons, 1992.

1391. Taylor, Kim. *Pattern*. New York: John Wiley & Sons, 1992.

1392. Taylor, Kim. *Structure*. New York: John Wiley & Sons, 1992.

1393. Taylor, Kim. *Water*. New York: John Wiley & Sons, 1992.

1394. VanCleave, Janice. *Astronomy for Every Kid*. New York: John Wiley & Sons, 1991.

1395. VanCleave, Janice. *Janice VanCleave's A+ Projects in Biology*. New York: John Wiley & Sons, 1993.

1396. VanCleave, Janice. *Janice VanCleave's A+ Projects in Chemistry*. New York: John Wiley & Sons, 1993.

1397. VanCleave, Janice. *Janice VanCleave's Animals*. New York: John Wiley & Sons, 1993.

1398. VanCleave, Janice. *Janice VanCleave's Earthquakes*. New York: John Wiley & Sons, 1993.

1399. VanCleave, Janice. *Janice VanCleave's Gravity*. New York: John Wiley & Sons, 1993.

1400. VanCleave, Janice. *Janice VanCleave's Machines*. New York: John Wiley & Sons, 1993.

1401. VanCleave, Janice. *Janice VanCleave's Magnets*. New York: John Wiley & Sons, 1993.

1402. VanCleave, Janice. *Janice VanCleave's Microscopes and Magnifying Lenses*. New York: John Wiley & Sons, 1993.

1403. VanCleave, Janice. *Janice VanCleave's Molecules*. New York: John Wiley & Sons, 1993.

1404. VanCleave, Janice. *Janice VanCleave's Physics for Every Kid*. New York: John Wiley & Sons, 1991.

1405. VanCleave, Janice. *Janice VanCleave's 200 Gooey, Slippery, Slimy, Weird & Fun Experiments*. New York: John Wiley & Sons, 1993.

1406. Walker, Lois. *Get Growing! Exciting Indoor Plant Projects for Kids*. New York: John Wiley & Sons, 1991.

1407. Watts, Barrie. *Keeping Minibeasts, Butterflies and Moths*. New York: Franklin Watts, 1991.

1408. Webster, David. *Towers*. Garden City, N.Y.: The Natural History Press, 1971.

1409. Weiss, Harvey. *Maps, Getting from Here to There*. Boston, Mass.: Houghton Mifflin Co., 1991.

1410. Wellington, Jerry. *The Super Science Book of Space*. New York: Thomson Learning, 1993.

1411. Weyland, Jack. *Megapowers: Can Science Fact Defeat Science Fiction*. Reading, Mass.: Addison-Wesley Publishing Co., 1992.

1412. Wiese, Jim. *Roller Coaster Science*. New York: John Wiley & Sons, 1994.

1413. Wiggers, Raymond. *The Amateur Geologist*. New York: Franklin Watts, 1993.

1414. Wilkes, Angela. *My First Green Book*. New York: Alfred A. Knopf, 1991.

1415. Wilkins, Mary-Jane. *Air, Light & Water*. New York: Random House, 1991.

1416. Williams, John. *Projects with Air*. Milwaukee, Wisc.: Gareth Stevens Publishing, 1992.

1417. Williams, John. *Projects with Color and Light*. Milwaukee, Wisc.: Gareth Stevens Publishing, 1992.

1418. Williams, John. *Projects with Electricity*. Milwaukee, Wisc.: Gareth Stevens Publishing, 1992.

1419. Williams, John. *Projects with Flight*. Milwaukee, Wisc.: Gareth Stevens Publishing, 1992.

1420. Williams, John. *Projects with Machines*. Milwaukee, Wisc.: Garcth Stcvens Publishing, 1992.

1421. Williams, John. *Projects with Time*. Milwaukee, Wisc.: Gareth Stevens Publishing, 1992.

1422. Williams, John. *Projects with Water*. Milwaukee, Wisc.: Gareth Stevens Publishing, 1992.

1423. Williams, John. *Projects with Wheels*. Milwaukee, Wisc.: Gareth Stevens Publishing, 1991.

1424. Willis, Terri. *Land Use and Abuse*. Chicago: Childrens Press, 1992.

1425. Witherspoon, James D. *From Field to Lab: 200 Life Science Experiments for Amateur Biologist*. Blue Ridge Summit, Pa.: Tab Books, 1993.

1426. Wong, Ovid K. *Experimenting with Electricity and Magnetism*. New York: Franklin Watts, 1993.

1427. Wong, Ovid K. *Hands-on Ecology*. Chicago: Childrens Press, 1991.

1428. Wood, Jenny. *Caves: An Underground Wonderland*. Milwaukee, Wisc.: Gareth Stevens Publishing, 1991.

1429. Wood, Jenny. *Icebergs: Titans of the Oceans*. Milwaukee, Wisc.: Gareth Stevens Publishing, 1991.

1430. Wood, Jenny. *Storms: Nature's Fury*. Milwaukee, Wisc.: Gareth Stevens Publishing, 1991.

1431. Wood, Jenny. *Volcanoes*. Milwaukee, Wisc.: Gareth Stevens Publishing, 1990.

1432. Wood, Robert W. *Physics for Kids: 49 Easy Experiments with Acoustics*. Blue Ridge Summit, Pa.: Tab Books, 1990.

1433. Wood, Robert W. *Science for Kids: 39 Easy Animal Biology Experiments*. Blue Ridge Summit, Pa.: Tab Books, 1991.

1434. Wood, Robert W. *Science for Kids: 39 Easy Astronomy Experiments*. Blue Ridge Summit, Pa.: Tab Books, 1991.

1435. Wood, Robert W. *Science for Kids: 39 Easy Chemistry Experiments*. Blue Ridge Summit, Pa.: Tab Books, 1991.

1436. Wood, Robert W. *Science for Kids: 39 Easy Engineering Experiments*. Blue Ridge Summit, Pa.: Tab Books, 1992.

1437. Wood, Robert W. *Science for Kids: 39 Easy Geography Activities*. Blue Ridge Summit, Pa.: Tab Books, 1992.

1438. Wood, Robert W. *Science for Kids: 39 Easy Geology Experiments*. Blue Ridge Summit, Pa.: Tab Books, 1991.

1439. Wood, Robert W. *Science for Kids: 39 Easy Meteorology Experiments*. Blue Ridge Summit, Pa.: Tab Books, 1991.

1440. Wood, Robert W. *Science for Kids: 39 Easy Plant Biology Experiments*. Blue Ridge Summit, Pa.: Tab Books, 1991.

1441. Zike, Dinah. *The Earth Science Book: Activities for Kids*. New York: John Wiley & Sons, 1993.

1442. Zubrowski, Bernie. *Blinkers and Buzzers: Building and Experimenting with Electricity*. New York: Morrow Junior Books, 1991.

1443. Zubrowski, Bernie. *Mirrors: Finding Out About the Properties of Light*. New York: Beech Tree Books, 1992.

1444. Zubrowski, Bernie. *Mobiles: Building and Experimenting with Balancing Toys*. New York: William Morrow and Co., 1993.

1445. Baker, Wendy. *Insects*. New York: Thomson Learning, 1993.

1446. Baker, Wendy. *Machines*. New York: Thomson Learning, 1993.

1447. Baker, Thomas Richard. *Weather in the Lab*. Blue Ridge Summit, Pa.: Tab Books, 1993.

1448. Blackman, Steve. *Planes and Flight*. New York: Franklin Watts, 1993.

1449. Blackman, Steve. *Space*. New York: Franklin Watts, 1993.

1450. Dashefsky, H. Steven. *Environmental Science: High School Science Fair Experiments*. Blue Ridge Summit, Pa.: Tab Books, 1994.

1451. Davies, Kay. *Light*. Austin, Tex.: Steck-Vaughn Co., 1992.

1452. Dudman, John. *Earthquake*. New York: Thomson Learning, 1993.

1453. Gutnik, Martin J. *Projects That Explore Energy*. Brookfield, Conn.: The Millbrook Press, 1994.

1454. Kerrod, Robin. *Communications*. North Bellmore, N.Y.: Marshall Cavendish Corp., 1994.

1455. Kerrod, Robin. *The Environment*. North Bellmore, N.Y.: Marshall Cavendish Corp., 1994.

1456. Kerrod, Robin. *Force and Motion*. North Bellmore, N.Y.: Marshall Cavendish Corp., 1994.

1457. Kerrod, Robin. *Plant Life*. North Bellmore, N.Y.: Marshall Cavendish Corp., 1994.

1458. Markle, Sandra. *Science to the Rescue*. New York: Atheneum, 1994.

1459. Oxlade, Chris. *Bridges and Tunnels*. New York: Franklin Watts, 1994.

1460. Oxlade, Chris. *Canals and Waterways*. New York: Franklin Watts, 1994.

1461. Oxlade, Chris. *Houses and Homes*. New York: Franklin Watts, 1994.

1462. St. Andre, Ralph E. *Simple Machines Made Simple*. Englewood, Colo.: Teacher Ideas Press, 1993.

1463. Waterlow, Julia. *Flood*. New York: Thomson Learning, 1993.

1464. Suzuki, David T. *Looking at Insects*. New York: John Wiley & Sons, 1991.

1465. Mogil, H. Michael. *The Amateur Meteorologist*. New York: Franklin Watts, 1993.

1466. Hogan, Paula. *Dying Oceans*. Milwaukee, Wisc.: Gareth Stevens Publishing, 1991.

1467. Hogan, Paula. *Expanding Deserts*. Milwaukee, Wisc.: Gareth Stevens Publishing, 1991.

1468. Hogan, Paula. *Fragile Mountains*. Milwaukee, Wisc.: Gareth Stevens Publishing, 1991.

1469. Hogan, Paula. *Vanishing Rain Forests*. Milwaukee, Wisc.: Gareth Stevens Publishing, 1991.

1470. Blackman, Steve. *Land Transportation*. New York: Franklin Watts, 1993.

1471. Blackman, Steve. *Ships and Shipwrecks*. New York: Franklin Watts, 1993.

1472. Hickman, Pamela M. *Habitats: Making Homes for Animals and Plants*. Reading, Mass.: Addison-Wesley Publishing Co., 1993.

1473. Kerrod, Robin. *Electricity and Magnetism*. North Bellmore, N.Y.: Marshall Cavendish Corp., 1994.

1474. Kerrod, Robin. *The Weather*. North Bellmore, N.Y.: Marshall Cavendish Corp., 1994.

1475. Ray, Robert D. *Integrating Aerospace Science into the Curriculum: K-12*. Englewood, Colo.: Teacher Ideas Press, 1992.

1476. Vecchione, Glen. *100 Amazing Make-It-Yourself Science Fair Projects*. New York: Sterling Publishing Co., 1994.

1477. VanCleave, Janice. *Janice VanCleave's Volcanoes*. New York: John Wiley & Sons, 1994.

1478. Couper, Heather. *How the Universe Works*. Pleasantville, N.Y.: Reader's Digest Association, 1994.

1479. VanCleave, Janice. *Janice VanCleave's 201 Awesome, Magical, Bizarre & Incredible Experiments*. New York: John Wiley & Sons, 1994.

1480. Farndon, John. *How the Earth Works*. Pleasantville, N.Y.: Reader's Digest Association, 1992.

1481. VanCleave, Janice. *Janice VanCleave's Dinosaurs for Every Kid*. New York: John Wiley & Sons, 1994.

1482. Bell, J. L. *Soap Science*. Reading, Mass.: Addison-Wesley Publishing Co., 1993.

1483. Cash, Terry. *Plastics*. Ada, Okla.: Garrett Educational Corp., 1990.

1484. D'Amico, Joan. *The Science Chef*. New York: John Wiley & Sons, 1995.

1485. Deshpande, Chris. *Silk*. Ada, Okla.: Garrett Educational Corp., 1994.

1486. Dietl, Ulla. *The Plant-and-Grow Project Book*. New York: Sterling Publishing Co., 1993.

1487. Dudman, John. *Volcano*. New York: Thomson Learning, 1993.

1488. Ganeri, Anita. *Animal Science*. New York: Dillon Press, 1993.

1489. Ganeri, Anita. *Body Science*. New York: Dillon Press, 1993.

1490. Ganeri, Anita. *Plant Science*. New York: Dillon Press, 1993.

1491. Henry, Peggy. *The Great Seed Mystery for Kids*. Corte Madera, Calif.: NK Lawn and Garden Co., 1993.

1492. Hickman, Pamela. *Wetlands*. Toronto, Canada: Kids Can Press, 1993.

1493. Ollerenshaw, Chris. *Electricity*. Milwaukee, Wisc.: Gareth Stevens Publishing, 1994.

1494. Ollerenshaw, Chris. *Gears*. Milwaukee, Wisc.: Gareth Stevens Publishing, 1994.

1495. Ollerenshaw, Chris. *Levers*. Milwaukee, Wisc.: Gareth Stevens Publishing, 1994.

1496. Ollerenshaw, Chris. *Wind-ups*. Milwaukee, Wisc.: Gareth Stevens Publishing, 1994.

1497. Rowe, Julian. *Using Energy*. Chicago: Childrens Press, 1994.

1498. Walpole, Brenda. *Salt*. Ada, Okla.: Garrett Educational Corp., 1994.

1499. Woodbridge, Renu Nagrath. *Cotton*. Ada, Okla.: Garrett Educational Corp., 1994.

1500. Kerrod, Robin. *Stars and Planets*. North Bellmore, N.Y.: Marshall Cavendish Corp., 1991.

1501. VanCleave, Janice. *Janice VanCleave's Electricity*. New York: John Wiley & Sons, 1994.

1502. Gardner, Robert. *Space*. New York: Twenty-First Century Books, 1994.

1503. Bennett, Paul. *Catching a Meal*. New York: Thomson Learning, 1994.

1504. Bennett, Paul. *Changing Shape*. New York: Thomson Learning, 1994.

1505. Doris, Ellen. *Woods, Ponds & Fields*. New York: Thames and Hudson, 1994.

1506. Gardner, Robert. *Science Projects About the Human Body*. Hillside, N.J.: Enslow Publishers, 1993.

1507. Peacock, Graham. *Forces*. New York: Thomson Learning, 1994.

1508. Peacock, Graham. *Materials*. New York: Thomson Learning, 1994.

1509. Peacock, Graham. *Water*. New York: Thomson Learning, 1994.

1510. Rood, Ronald. *Wetlands*. New York: HarperCollins Publishers, 1994.

1511. Tomecek, Steve. *Bouncing and Bending Light*. New York: W.H. Freeman and Co., 1995.

1512. Oxlade, Chris. *Everyday Things*. New York: Franklin Watts, 1994.

1513. Burnie, David. *Seashore*. New York: Dorling Kindersley, 1994.

1514. Gardner, Robert. *Science Projects About Electricity and Magnets*. Springfield, N.J.: Enslow Publishers, 1994.

1515. Gardner, Robert. *Science Projects About Temperature and Heat*. Hillside, N.J.: Enslow Publishers, 1994.

1516. Gardner, Robert. *Science Projects About Weather*. Hillside, N.J.: Enslow Publishers, 1994.

1517. Haslam, Andrew. *Body*. New York: Thomson Learning, 1994.

1518. Haslam, Andrew. *Building*. New York: Thomson Learning, 1994.

1519. Peacock, Graham. *Heat*. New York: Thomson Learning, 1993.

1520. Quinn, John R. *The Fascinating Freshwater Fish Book*. New York: John Wiley & Sons, 1994.

1521. Robson, Pam. *Clocks, Scales & Measurements*. New York: Gloucester Press, 1993.

1522. Wellington, Jerry. *The Super Science Book of Forces*. New York: Thomson Learning, 1994.

1523. Ward, Alan. *Machines at Work*. New York: Franklin Watts, 1993.

1524. Ward, Alan. *Plants and Animals*. New York: Franklin Watts, 1993.

1525. Wood, Robert W. *Who? Famous Experiments for the Young Scientists*. New York: Tab Books, 1994.

1526. Gardner, Robert. *Science Projects About Chemistry*. Springfield, N.J.: Enslow Publishers, 1994.

1527. *Bottle Biology* Dubuque: Iowa: Kendall/Hunt Publishing Co., 1993.